RANDOM HOUSE WEBSTER'S

STUDENT notebook SPANISH DICTIONARY

2nd Ed.

ENGLISH ABBREVIATIONS/ABREVIATURAS INGLESAS

a.	adjective		*interrog.*	interrogative
abbr.	abbreviation		*Leg.*	legal
adv.	adverb		*m.*	masculine
Aero.	aeronautics		*Mech.*	mechanics
Agr.	agriculture		*Mex.*	Mexico
Anat.	anatomy		*Mil.*	military
art.	article		*Mus.*	music
Auto.	automotive		*n.*	noun
Biol.	biology		*Naut.*	nautical
Bot.	botany		*Phot.*	photography
Carib.	Caribbean		*pl.*	plural
Chem.	chemistry		*Pol.*	politics
Colloq.	colloquial		*prep.*	preposition
Com.	commerce		*pron.*	pronoun
conj.	conjunction		*Punct.*	punctuation
dem.	demonstrative		*rel.*	relative
Econ.	economics		*Relig.*	religion
Elec.	electrical		*S.A.*	Spanish America
esp.	especially		*Theat.*	theater
f.	feminine		*v.*	verb
Fig.	figurative			
Fin.	finance			
Geog.	geography			
Govt.	government			
Gram.	grammar			
interj.	interjection			

Note: If a main entry term is repeated in a boldface subentry in exactly the same form, it is abbreviated. Example: **comedor** *n.m.* dining room. **coche c.,** dining car.

SPANISH STRESS

In a number of words, spoken stress is marked by an accent (´): *nación, país, médico, día.*

Words which are not so marked are, generally speaking, stressed on the next-to-the-last syllable if they end in a vowel, *n,* or *s;* and on the last syllable if they end in a consonant other than *n* or *s.*

Note: An accent is placed over some words to distinguish them from others having the same spelling and pronunciation but differing in meaning.

SPANISH ALPHABETIZATION

In Spanish, *ch* and *ll* are no longer considered to be separate letters of the alphabet. They are now alphabetized as they would be in English. However, words with *ñ* are alphabetized after *n.*

PRONUNCIATION KEY FOR SPANISH

IPA Symbols	Key Words	Approximate Equivalents
a	alba, banco, cera	father, depart
e	esto, del, parte, mesa	bet; like rain when e ends syllable and is not followed by r, rr, or t
i	ir, fino, adiós, muy	like beet, but shorter
o	oler, flor, grano	like vote, but shorter
u	un, luna, cuento, vergüenza, guarda	fool, group
b	bajo, ambiguo, vaca	by, abet
β	hablar, escribir, lavar	like vehicle, but with lips almost touching
d	dar, desde, andamio, dueña	deal, adept
ð	pedir, edredón, verdad	that, gather
f	fecha, afectar, golf	fan, after
g	gato, grave, gusto, largo, guerra	garden, ugly
h	gemelo, giro, junta, bajo	horse
k	cacao, claro, cura, cuenta, que, quinto	kind, actor
l	lado, lente, habla, papel	lot, altar
ʎ	(in Spain) llama, calle, olla	like million, but with tongue behind teeth
m	mal, amor	more, commit
n	nada, nuevo, mano, bien	not, enter
ɲ	ñapa, año	canyon, companion
ŋ	angosto, aunque	ring, anchor
p	peso, guapo	pill, applaud
r	real, faro, deber	like rice, but with single flap of tongue on roof of mouth
rr	perro, sierra	like rice, but with trill, or vibration of tongue, against upper teeth
s	sala, espejo, mas;	say, clasp
	(in Latin America) cena, hacer, vez	
θ	(in Spain) cena, hacer, cierto, cine, zarzuela, lazo, vez	thin, myth
t	tocar, estado, cenit	table, attract
y	ya, ayer; (in Latin America) llama, calle	you, voyage
tʃ	chica, mucho	chill, batch

Diphthongs

ai, ay	baile, hay	high, rye
au	audacia, laudable	out, round
ei, ey	veinte, seis, rey	ray
ie	miel, también	fiesta
oi, oy	estoico, hoy	coin, loyal
ua	cuanto	quantity
ue	buena, suerte	sway, quaint

GUÍA DE PRONUNCIACIÓN DEL INGLÉS

Símbolos del AFI

Ejemplos

/æ/ *ingl.* h**a**t; como la **a** de *esp.* p**a**ro, pero más cerrada

/ei/ *ingl.* st**ay**; *esp.* r**ei**na

/ɛə/ [followed by /r/] *ingl.* h**air**; *esp.* v**e**r

/ɑ/ *ingl.* f**a**ther; similar a las **a**s de *esp.* c**a**sa, pero más larga

/ɛ/ *ingl.* b**e**t; *esp.* **e**ntre

/i/ *ingl.* b**ee**; como la **i** de *esp.* v**i**da, pero más larga

/ɪə/ [followed by /r/] *ingl.* h**ear**; como la **i** de *esp.* ven**i**r, pero menos cerrada

/ɪ/ *ingl.* s**i**t; como la **i** de *esp.* Ch**i**le, pero menos cerrada

/ai/ *ingl.* tr**y**; *esp.* h**ay**

/ɒ/ *ingl.* h**o**t; *esp.* p**o**ner

/o/ *ingl.* b**oa**t; similar a la **o** de *esp.* sac**o**, pero más cerrada

/ɔ/ *ingl.* s**aw**; similar a la **o** de *esp.* c**o**rte, pero más cerrada

/ɔi/ *ingl.* t**oy**; *esp.* h**oy**

/ʊ/ *ingl.* b**oo**k; como la **u** de *esp.* ins**u**lto, pero menos cerrada

/u/ *ingl.* t**oo**; como la **u** de *esp.* l**u**na, pero más larga

/au/ *ingl.* c**ow**; *esp.* p**au**sa

/ʌ/ *ingl.* **u**p; entre la **o** de *esp.* b**o**rde y la **a** de *esp.* b**a**rro

/ɜ/ [followed by /r/] *ingl.* b**ur**n; *fr.* fl**eu**r

/ə/ *ingl.* **a**lone; *fr.* d**e**main

/ɵ/ *ingl.* f**ire** (fi**ɵ**r); *fr.* b**a**stille

/b/ *ingl.* **b**oy; como la **b** de *esp.* **b**oca, pero más aspirada

/tʃ/ *ingl.* **ch**ild; *esp.* mu**ch**o

/d/ *ingl.* **d**ad; *esp.* **d**ar

/f/ *ingl.* **f**or; *esp.* **f**echa

/g/ *ingl.* **g**ive; *esp.* **g**ato

/h/ *ingl.* **h**appy; como la **j** de *esp.* **j**abón, pero más aspirada y menos aspera

/dʒ/ *ingl.* **j**ust; *it.* **gi**orno

/k/ *ingl.* **k**ick; similar a la **k** de *esp.* **k**ilogramo, pero más aspirada

/l/ *ingl.* **l**ove; *esp.* **l**ibro

/m/ *ingl.* **m**other; *esp.* li**m**bo

/n/ *ingl.* **n**ow; *esp.* **n**oche

/ŋ/ *ingl.* si**ng**; *esp.* bla**n**co

/p/ *ingl.* **p**ot; como las **p**s de *esp.* **p**a**p**a, pero más aspirada

/r/ *ingl.* **r**ead; como la **r** de *esp.* pa**r**a, pero con la lengua elevada hacia el paladar, sin tocarlo

/s/ *ingl.* **s**ee; *esp.* ha**s**ta

/ʃ/ *ingl.* **sh**op; *fr.* **ch**er**ch**er

/t/ *ingl.* **t**en; similar a la **t** de *esp.* **t**omar, pero más aspirada

/θ/ *ingl.* **th**ing; *esp.* (en España) **c**erdo, **z**apato

/ð/ *ingl.* fa**th**er; *esp.* co**d**o

/v/ *ingl.* **v**ictory; como la **b** de *esp.* ha**b**a, pero es labiodental en vez de bilabial

/w/ *ingl.* **w**itch; como la **u** de *esp.* p**u**esto, pero con labios más cerrados

/y/ *ingl.* **y**es; *esp.* **y**acer

/z/ *ingl.* **z**ipper; *fr.* **z**éro

/ʒ/ *ingl.* plea**s**ure; *fr.* **j**eune

Las consonantes /ļ/, /ṃ/, y /ṇ/ son similares a las **l**, **m**, y **n** del español, pero alargadas y resonantes

Spanish–English

español–inglés

A

a /a/ *prep.* to; at.

abacería /aβaθe'ria; aβase'ria/ *n. f.* grocery store.

abacero /aβa'θero; aβa'sero/ *n. m.* grocer.

ábaco /'aβako/ *n. m.* abacus.

abad /a'βað/ *n. m.* abbot.

abadía /aβa'ðia/ *n. f.* abbey.

abajar /aβa'har/ *v.* lower; go down.

abajo /a'βaho/ *adv.* down; downstairs.

abandonar /aβando'nar/ *v.* abandon.

abandono /aβan'dono/ *n. m.* abandonment.

abanico /aβa'niko/ *n. m.* fan. —**abanicar,** *v.*

abaratar /aβara'tar/ *v.* cheapen.

abarcar /aβar'kar/ *v.* comprise; clasp.

abastecer /aβaste'θer; aβaste'ser/ *v.* supply, provide.

abatido /aβa'tiðo/ *a.* dejected, despondent.

abatir /aβa'tir/ *v.* knock down; dismantle; depress, dishearten.

abdicación /aβðika'θion; aβðika'sion/ *n. f.* abdication.

abdicar /aβði'kar/ *v.* abdicate.

abdomen /aβ'ðomen/ *n. m.* abdomen.

abdominal /aβðomi'nal/ *a.* 1. abdominal. —*n.* 2. *m.* sit-up.

abecé /aβe'θe; aβe'se/ *n. m.* ABCs, rudiments.

abecedario /aβeθe'ðario; aβese'ðario/ *n. m.* alphabet; reading book.

abeja /a'βeha/ *n. f.* bee.

abejarrón /aβeha'rron/ *n. m.* bumblebee.

aberración /aβerra'θion; aβerra'sion/ *n. f.* aberration.

abertura /aβer'tura/ *n. f.* opening, aperture, slit.

abeto /a'βeto/ *n. m.* fir.

abierto /a'βierto/ *a.* open; overt.

abismal /aβis'mal/ *a.* abysmal.

abismo /a'βismo/ *n. m.* abyss, chasm.

ablandar /aβlan'dar/ *v.* soften.

abnegación /aβnega'θion; aβnega'sion/ *n. f.* abnegation.

abochornar /aβotʃor'nar/ *v.* overheat; embarrass.

abogado /aβo'gaðo/ **-da** *n.* lawyer, attorney.

abolengo /aβo'lengo/ *n. m.* ancestry.

abolición /aβoli'θion; aβoli'sion/ *n. f.* abolition.

abolladura /aβoʎa'ðura; aβoya'ðura/ *n. f.* dent. —**abollar,** *v.*

abominable /aβomi'naβle/ *a.* abominable.

abominar /aβomi'nar/ *v.* abhor.

abonado /aβo'naðo/ **-da** *n. m. & f.* subscriber.

abonar /aβo'nar/ *v.* pay; fertilize.

abonarse /aβo'narse/ *v.* subscribe.

abono /a'βono/ *n. m.* fertilizer; subscription; season ticket.

aborigen /aβor'ihen/ *a. & n.* aboriginal.

aborrecer /aβorre'θer; aβorre'ser/ *v.* hate, loathe, abhor.

abortar /aβor'tar/ *v.* abort, miscarry.

aborto /a'βorto/ *n. m.* abortion.

abovedar /aβoβe'ðar/ *v.* vault.

abrasar /aβra'sar/ *v.* burn.

abrazar /aβra'θar; aβra'sar/ *v.* embrace; clasp.

abrazo /a'βraθo; a'βraso/ *n. m.* embrace.

abrelatas /aβre'latas/ *n. m.* can opener.

abreviar /aβre'βiar/ *v.* abbreviate, abridge, shorten.

abreviatura /aβreβia'tura/ *n. f.* abbreviation.

abrigar /aβri'gar/ *v.* harbor, shelter.

abrigarse /aβri'garse/ *v.* bundle up.

abrigo /a'βrigo/ *n. m.* overcoat; shelter; (*pl.*) wraps.

abril /a'βril/ *n. m.* April.

abrir /a'βrir/ *v.* open; *Med.* lance.

abrochar /aβro'tʃar/ *v.* clasp.

abrogación /aβroga'θion; aβroga'sion/ *n. f.* abrogation, repeal.

abrogar /aβro'gar/ *v.* abrogate.

abrojo /a'βroho/ *n. m.* thorn.

abrumar /aβru'mar/ *v.* overwhelm, crush, swamp.

absceso /aβs'θeso; aβ'sseso/ *n. m.* abscess.

absolución /aβsolu'θion; aβsolu'sion/ *n. f.* absolution; acquittal.

absoluto /aβso'luto/ *a.* absolute; downright.

absolver /aβsol'βer/ *v.* absolve, pardon.

absorbente /aβsor'βente/ *a.* absorbent.

absorber /aβsor'βer/ *v.* absorb.

absorción /aβsor'θion; aβsor'sion/ *n. f.* absorption.

abstemio /aβs'temio/ *a.* abstemious.

abstenerse /aβste'nerse/ *v.* abstain; refrain.

abstinencia /aβsti'nenθia; aβsti'nensia/ *n. f.* abstinence.

abstracción /aβstrak'θion; aβstrak'sion/ *n. f.* abstraction.

abstracto /aβs'trakto/ *a.* abstract.

abstraer /aβstra'er/ *v.* abstract.

absurdo /aβ'surðo/ *a.* 1. absurd. —*n.* 2. *m.* absurdity.

abuchear /aβutʃe'ar/ *v.* boo.

abuela /a'βuela/ *n. f.* grandmother.

abuelo /a'βuelo/ *n. m.* grandfather; (*pl.*) grandparents.

abultado /aβul'taðo/ *a.* bulky.

abultamiento /aβulta'miento/ *n. m.* bulge. —**abultar,** *v.*

abundancia /aβun'danθia; aβun'dansia/ *n. f.* abundance, plenty.

abundante /aβun'dante/ *a.* abundant, plentiful.

abundar /aβun'dar/ *v.* abound.

aburrido /aβu'rriðo/ *a.* boring, tedious.

aburrimiento /aβurri'miento/ *n. m.* boredom.

aburrir /aβu'rrir/ *v.* bore.

abusar /aβu'sar/ *v.* abuse, misuse.

abusivo /aβu'siβo/ *a.* abusive.

abuso /a'βuso/ *n. m.* abuse.

abyecto /aβ'yekto/ *a.* abject, low.

a.C., *abbr.* (**antes de Cristo**) BC.

acá /a'ka/ *adv.* here.

acabar /aka'βar/ *v.* finish. **a. de...,** to have just....

acacia /a'kaθia; a'kasia/ *n. f.* acacia.

academia /aka'ðemia/ *n. f.* academy.

académico /aka'ðemiko/ *a.* academic.

acaecer /akae'θer; akae'ser/ *v.* happen.

acanalar /akana'lar/ *v.* groove.

acaparar /akapa'rar/ *v.* hoard; monopolize.

acariciar /akari'θiar; akari'siar/ *v.* caress, stroke.

acarrear /akarre'ar/ *v.* cart, transport; occasion, entail.

acaso /a'kaso/ *n. m.* chance. **por si a.,** just in case.

acceder /akθe'ðer; akse'ðer/ *v.* accede.

accesible /akθe'siβle; akse'siβle/ *a.* accessible.

acceso /ak'θeso; ak'seso/ *n. m.* access, approach.

accesorio /akθe'sorio; akse'sorio/ *a.* accessory.

accidentado /akθiðen'taðo; aksiðen'taðo/ *a.* hilly.

accidental /akθiðen'tal; aksiðen'tal/ *a.* accidental.

accidente /akθi'ðente; aksi'ðente/ *n. m.* accident, wreck.

acción /ak'θion; ak'sion/ *n. f.* action, act; *Com.* share of stock.

accionista /akθio'nista; aksio'nista/ *n. m. & f.* shareholder.

acechar /aθe'tʃar; ase'tʃar/ *v.* ambush, spy on.

acedia /a'θeðia; a'seðia/ *n. f.* heartburn.

aceite /a'θeite; a'seite/ *n. m.* oil.

aceite de hígado de bacalao /a'θeite de i'gaðo de baka'lao; a'seite/ cod-liver oil.

aceitoso /aθei'toso; asei'toso/ *a.* oily.

aceituna /aθei'tuna; asei'tuna/ *n. f.* olive.

aceleración /aθelera'θion; aselera'sion/ *n. f.* acceleration.

acelerar /aθele'rar; asele'rar/ *v.* accelerate, speed up.

acento /a'θento; a'sento/ *n. m.* accent.

acentuar /aθen'tuar; asen'tuar/ *v.* accent, accentuate, stress.

acepillar /aθepi'ʎar; asepi'yar/ *v.* brush; plane (wood).

aceptable /aθep'taβle; asep'taβle/ *a.* acceptable.

aceptación /aθepta'θion; asepta'sion/ *n. f.* acceptance.

aceptar /aθep'tar; asep'tar/ *v.* accept.

acequia /a'θekia; a'sekia/ *n. f.* ditch.

acera /a'θera; a'sera/ *n. f.* sidewalk.

acerca de /a'θerka de; a'serka de/ *prep.* about, concerning.

acercar /aθer'kar; aser'kar/ *v.* bring near.

acercarse /aθer'karse; aser'karse/ *v.* approach, come near, go near.

acero /a'θero; a'sero/ *n. m.* steel.

acero inoxidable /a'θero inoksi'ðaβle; a'sero inoksi'ðaβle/ stainless steel.

acertar /aθer'tar; aser'tar/ *v.* guess right. **a. en,** hit (a mark).

acertijo /aθer'tiho; aser'tiho/ *n. m.* puzzle, riddle.

achicar /atʃi'kar/ *v.* diminish, dwarf; humble.

acidez /aθi'ðeθ; asi'ðes/ *n. f.* acidity.

ácido /'aθiðo; 'asiðo/ *a.* 1. sour. —*n.* 2. *m.* acid.

aclamación /aklama'θion; aklama'sion/ *n. f.* acclamation.

aclamar /akla'mar/ *v.* acclaim.

aclarar /akla'rar/ *v.* brighten; clarify, clear up.

acoger /ako'her/ *v.* welcome, receive.

acogida /ako'hiða/ *n. f.* welcome, reception.

acometer /akome'ter/ *v.* attack.

acomodador /akomoða'ðor/ *n. m.* usher.

acomodar /akomo'ðar/ *v.* accommodate, fix up.

acompañamiento /akompaɲa'miento/ *n. m.* accompaniment; following.

acompañar /akompa'ɲar/ *v.* accompany.

acondicionar /akondiθio'nar; akondisio'nar/ *v.* condition.

aconsejable /akonse'haβle/ *a.* advisable.

aconsejar /akonse'har/ *v.* advise.

acontecer /akonte'θer; akonte'ser/ *v.* happen.

acontecimiento /akonteθi'miento; akontesi'miento/ *n. m.* event, happening.

acorazado /akora'θaðo; akora'saðo/ *n.* 1. *m.* battleship. —*a.* 2. armor-plated, ironclad.

acordarse /akor'ðarse/ *v.* remember, recollect.

acordeón /akorðe'on/ *n. m.* accordion.

acordonar /akorðo'nar/ *v.* cordon off.

acortar /akor'tar/ *v.* shorten.

acosar /ako'sar/ *v.* beset, harry.

acostar /ako'star/ *v.* lay down; put to bed.

acostarse /akos'tarse/ *v.* lie down; go to bed.

acostumbrado /akostum'braðo/ *a.* accustomed; customary.

acostumbrar /akostum'brar/ *v.* accustom.

acrecentar /akreθen'tar; akresen'tar/ *v.* increase.

acreditar /akreði'tar/ *v.* accredit.

acreedor /akree'ðor/ **-ra** *n.* creditor.

acróbata /a'kroβata/ *n. m. & f.* acrobat.

acrobático /akro'βatiko/ *a.* acrobatic.

actitud /akti'tuð/ *n. f.* attitude.

actividad /aktiβi'ðað/ *n. f.* activity.

activista /akti'βista/ *a. & n.* activist.

activo /ak'tiβo/ *a.* active.

acto /'akto/ *n. m.* act.

actor /ak'tor/ *n. m.* actor.

actriz /ak'triθ; ak'tris/ *n. f.* actress.

actual /ak'tual/ *a.* present; present day.

actualidades /aktuali'ðaðes/ *n. f.pl.* current events.

actualmente /aktual'mente/ *adv.* at present; nowadays.

actuar /ak'tuar/ *v.* act.

acuarela /akua'rela/ *n. f.* watercolor.

acuario /a'kuario/ *n. m.* aquarium.

acuático /a'kuatiko/ *a.* aquatic.

acuchillar /akutʃi'ʎar; akutʃi'yar/ *v.* slash, knife.

acudir /aku'ðir/ *v.* rally; hasten; be present.

acuerdo /a'kuerðo/ *n. m.* accord, agreement; settlement. **de a.,** in agreement, agreed.

acumulación /akumula'θion; akumula'sion/ *n. f.* accumulation.

acumular /akumu'lar/ *v.* accumulate.

acuñar /aku'ɲar/ *v.* coin, mint.

acupuntura /akupun'tura/ *n. f.* acupuncture.

acusación /akusa'θion; akusa'sion/ *n. f.* accusation, charge.

acusado /aku'saðo/ **-da** *a. & n.* accused; defendant.

acusador /akusa'ðor/ **-ra** *n.* accuser.

acusar /aku'sar/ *v.* accuse; acknowledge.

acústica /a'kustika/ *n. f.* acoustics.

adaptación /aðapta'θion; aðapta'sion/ *n. f.* adaptation.

adaptador /aðapta'ðor/ *n. m.* adapter.

adaptar /aðap'tar/ *v.* adapt.

adecuado /aðe'kuaðo/ *a.* adequate.

adelantado /aðelan'taðo/ *a.* advanced; fast (clock).

adelantamiento /aðelanta'miento/ *n. m.* advancement, promotion.

adelantar /aðelan'tar/ *v.* advance.

adelante /aðe'lante/ *adv.* ahead, forward, onward, on.

adelanto /aðe'lanto/ *n. m.* advancement, progress, improvement.

adelgazar /aðelga'θar; aðelga'sar/ *v.* make thin.

ademán /aðe'man/ *n. m.* attitude; gesture.

además /aðe'mas/ *adv.* in addition, besides, also.

adentro /a'ðentro/ *adv.* in, inside.

adepto /a'ðepto/ *a.* adept.

aderezar /aðere'θar; aðere'sar/ *v.* prepare; trim.

adherirse /aðe'rirse/ *v.* adhere, stick.

adhesivo /aðe'siβo/ *a.* adhesive.

adicción /aðik'θion; aðik'sion/ *n. f.* addiction.

adición /aði'θion; aði'sion/ *n. f.* addition.

adicional /aðiθio'nal; aðisio'nal/ *a.* additional, extra.

adicto /a'ðikto/ **-ta** *a. & n.* addicted; addict.

adinerado /aðine'raðo/ **-a** *a.* wealthy.

adiós /a'ðios/ *n. m. & interj.* good-bye, farewell.

adivinar /aðiβi'nar/ *v.* guess.

adjetivo /aðhe'tiβo/ *n. m.* adjective.

adjunto /að'hunto/ *a.* enclosed.

administración /aðministra'θion; aðministra'sion/ *n. f.* administration.

administrador /aðministra'ðor/ **-ra** *n.* administrator.

administrar /aðminis'trar/ *v.* administer; manage.

administrativo /aðministra'tiβo/ *a.* administrative.

admirable /aðmi'raβle/ *a.* admirable.

admiración. /aðmira'θion; aðmirai'a-prim;sion/ *n. f.* admiration; wonder.

admirar /aðmiˈrar/ *v.* admire.

admisión /aðmiˈsion/ *n. f.* admission.

admitir /aðmiˈtir/ *v.* admit, acknowledge.

ADN, *abbr.* **(ácido desoxirribonucleico)** DNA (deoxyribonucleic acid).

adobar /adoˈβar/ *v.* marinate.

adolescencia /aðolesˈθenθia; aðolesˈsensia/ *n. f.* adolescence, youth.

adolescente /aðolesˈθente; aðolesˈsente/ *a. & n.* adolescent.

adónde /aˈðonde/ *adv.* where.

adondequiera /a͵ðondeˈkiera/ *conj.* wherever.

adopción /aðopˈθion; aðopˈsion/ *n. f.* adoption.

adoptar /aðopˈtar/ *v.* adopt.

adoración /aðoraˈθion; aðoraˈsion/ *n. f.* worship, love, adoration. **—adorar,** *v.*

adormecer /aðormeˈθer; aðormeˈser/ *v.* drowse.

adornar /aðorˈnar/ *v.* adorn; decorate.

adorno /aˈðorno/ *n. m.* adornment, trimming.

adquirir /aðkiˈrir/ *v.* acquire, obtain.

adquisición /aðkisiˈθion; aðkisiˈsion/ *n. f.* acquisition, attainment.

aduana /aˈðuana/ *n. f.* custom house, customs.

adujada /aðuˈhaða/ *n. f. Naut.* coil of rope.

adulación /aðulaˈθion; aðulaˈsion/ *n. f.* flattery.

adular /aðuˈlar/ *v.* flatter.

adulterar /aðulteˈrar/ *v.* adulterate.

adulterio /aðulˈterio/ *n. m.* adultery.

adulto /aˈðulto/ **-ta** *a. & n.* adult.

adusto /aˈðusto/ *a.* gloomy; austere.

adverbio /aðˈβerβio/ *n. m.* adverb.

adversario /aðβerˈsario/ *n. m.* adversary.

adversidad /aðβersiˈðað/ *n. f.* adversity.

adverso /aðˈβerso/ *a.* adverse.

advertencia /aðβerˈtenθia; aðβerˈtensia/ *n. f.* warning.

advertir /aðβerˈtir/ *v.* warn; notice.

adyacente /aðyaˈθente; aðyaˈsente/ *a.* adjacent.

aéreo /aˈereo/ *a.* aerial; air.

aerodeslizador /aeroðesliˈðaˈðor; aeroðeslisaˈðor/ *n. m.* hovercraft.

aeromoza /aeroˈmoθa; aeroˈmosa/ *n. f.* stewardess, flight attendant.

aeroplano /aeroˈplano/ *n. m.* light plane.

aeropuerto /aeroˈpuerto/ *n. m.* airport.

aerosol /aeroˈsol/ *n. m.* aerosol, spray.

afable /aˈfaβle/ *a.* affable, pleasant.

afanarse /afaˈnarse/ *v.* toil.

afear /afeˈar/ *v.* deface, mar, deform.

afectación /afektaˈθion; afektaˈsion/ *n. f.* affectation.

afectar /afekˈtar/ *v.* affect.

afecto /aˈfekto/ *n. m.* affection, attachment.

afeitada /afeiˈtaða/ *n. f.* shave. **—afeitarse,** *v.*

afeminado /afemiˈnaðo/ *a.* effeminate.

afición /afiˈθion; afiˈsion/ *n. f.* fondness, liking; hobby.

aficionado -da *n.* fan, devotee; amateur.

aficionarse a /afiθioˈnarse a; afisioˈnarse a/ *v.* become fond of.

afilado /afiˈlaðo/ *a.* sharp.

afilar /afiˈlar/ *v.* sharpen.

afiliación /afiliaˈθion; afiliaˈsion/ *n. f.* affiliation.

afiliado /afiˈliaðo/ **-da** *n.* affiliate. **—afiliar,** *v.*

afinar /afiˈnar/ *v.* polish; tune up.

afinidad /afiniˈðað/ *n. f.* relationship, affinity.

afirmación /afirmaˈθion; afirmaˈsion/ *n. f.* affirmation, statement.

afirmar /afirˈmar/ *v.* affirm, assert.

afirmativa /afirmaˈtiβa/ *n. f.* affirmative. **—afirmativo,** *a.*

aflicción /aflikˈθion; aflikˈsion/ *n. f.* affliction; sorrow, grief.

afligido /afliˈhiðo/ *a.* sorrowful, grieved.

afligir /afliˈhir/ *v.* grieve, distress.

aflojar /afloˈhar/ *v.* loosen.

afluencia /aˈfluenθia; aˈfluensia/ *n. f.* influx.

afortunado /afortuˈnaðo/ *a.* fortunate, successful, lucky.

afrenta /aˈfrenta/ *n. f.* insult, outrage, affront. **—afrentar,** *v.*

afrentoso /afrenˈtoso/ *a.* shameful.

africano /afriˈkano/ **-na** *a. & n.* African.

afuera /aˈfuera/ *adv.* out, outside.

afueras /aˈfueras/ *n. f.pl.* suburbs.

agacharse /agaˈtʃarse/ *v.* squat, crouch; cower.

agarrar /agaˈrrar/ *v.* seize, grasp, clutch.

agarro /aˈgarro/ *n. m.* clutch, grasp.

agencia /aˈhenθia; aˈhensia/ *n. f.* agency.

agencia de colocaciones /aˈhenθia de kolokaˈθiones; aˈhensia de kolokaˈsiones/ employment agency.

agencia de viajes /aˈhenθia de ˈbiahes; aˈhensia de ˈbiahes/ travel agency.

agente /aˈhente/ *n. m. & f.* agent, representative.

agente de aduana /aˈhente de aˈðuana/ *mf.* customs officer.

agente inmobiliario /aˈhente imoβiˈliario/ **-ria** *n.* real-estate agent.

ágil /ˈahil/ *a.* agile, spry.

agitación /ahitaˈθion; ahitaˈsion/ *n. f.* agitation, ferment.

agitado /ahiˈtaðo/ *a.* agitated; excited.

agitador /ahitaˈðor/ *n. m.* agitator.

agitar /ahiˈtar/ *v.* shake, agitate, excite.

agobiar /agoˈβiar/ *v.* oppress, burden.

agosto /aˈgosto/ *n. m.* August.

agotamiento /a͵gotaˈmiento/ *n. m.* exhaustion.

agotar /agoˈtar/ *v.* exhaust, use up, sap.

agradable /agraˈðaβle/ *a.* agreeable, pleasant.

agradar /agraˈðar/ *v.* please.

agradecer /agraðeˈθer; agraðeˈser/ *v.* thank; appreciate, be grateful for.

agradecido /agraðeˈθiðo; agraðeˈsiðo/ *a.* grateful, thankful.

agradecimiento /agraðeθiˈmiento; agraðesiˈmiento/ *n. m.* gratitude, thanks.

agravar /agraˈβar/ *v.* aggravate, make worse.

agravio /aˈgraβio/ *n. m.* wrong. **—agraviar,** *v.*

agregado /agreˈgaðo/ *a. & n.* aggregate; *Pol.* attaché.

agregar /agreˈgar/ *v.* add; gather.

agresión /agreˈsion/ *n. f.* aggression; *Leg.* battery.

agresivo /agreˈsiβo/ *a.* aggressive.

agresor /agreˈsor/ **-ra** *n.* aggressor.

agrícola /aˈgrikola/ *a.* agricultural.

agricultor /agrikulˈtor/ *n. m.* farmer.

agricultura /agrikulˈtura/ *n. f.* agriculture, farming.

agrio /ˈagrio/ *a.* sour.

agrupar /agruˈpar/ *v.* group.

agua /ˈagua/ *n. f.* water. **—aguar,** *v.*

aguacate /aguaˈkate/ *n. m.* avocado, alligator pear.

aguafuerte /͵aguaˈfuerte/ *n. f.* etching.

agua mineral /ˈagua mineˈral/ mineral water.

aguantar /aguanˈtar/ *v.* endure, stand, put up with.

aguardar /aguarˈðar/ *v.* await; expect.

aguardiente /aguarˈðiente/ *n. m.* brandy.

aguas abajo /ˈaguas aˈβaho/ *adv.* downriver, downstream.

aguas arriba /ˈaguas aˈrriβa/ *adv.* upriver, upstream.

agudo /aˈguðo/ *a.* sharp, keen, shrill, acute.

agüero /aˈguero/ *n. m.* omen.

águila /ˈagila/ *n. f.* eagle.

aguja /aˈguha/ *n. f.* needle.

agujero /aguˈhero/ *n. m.* hole.

aguzar /aguˈθar; aguˈsar/ *v.* sharpen.

ahí /aˈi/ *adv.* there.

ahogar /aoˈgar/ *v.* drown; choke; suffocate.

ahondar /aonˈdar/ *v.* deepen.

ahora /aˈora/ *adv.* now.

ahorcar /aorˈkar/ *v.* hang (execute).

ahorrar /aoˈrrar/ *v.* save, save up; spare.

ahorros /aˈorros/ *n. m.pl.* savings.

ahumar /auˈmar/ *v.* smoke.

airado /aiˈraðo/ *a.* angry, indignant.

aire /ˈaire/ *n. m.* air. **—airear,** *v.*

aire acondicionado /ˈaire akondiˈθioˈnaðo; ˈaire akondisioˈnaðo/ air conditioning.

aislamiento /aislaˈmiento/ *n. m.* isolation.

aislar /aisˈlar/ *v.* isolate.

ajedrez /aheˈðreθ; aheˈðres/ *n. m.* chess.

ajeno /aˈheno/ *a.* alien; someone else's.

ajetreo /aheˈtreo/ *n. m.* hustle and bustle.

ají /aˈhi/ *n. m.* chili.

ajo /ˈaho/ *n. m.* garlic.

ajustado /ahusˈtaðo/ *a.* adjusted; trim; exact.

ajustar /ahusˈtar/ *v.* adjust.

ajuste /aˈhuste/ *n. m.* adjustment, settlement.

al /al/ *contr.* of a + el.

ala /ˈala/ *n. f.* wing; brim (of hat).

alabanza /alaˈβanθa; alaˈβansa/ *n. f.* praise. **—alabar,** *v.*

alabear /alaβeˈar/ *v.* warp.

ala delta /ˈala ˈðelta/ hang glider.

alambique /alamˈbike/ *n. m.* still.

alambre /aˈlambre/ *n. m.* wire. **a. de púas,** barbed wire.

alarde /aˈlarðe/ *n. m.* boasting, ostentation.

alargar /alarˈgar/ *v.* lengthen; stretch out.

alarma /aˈlarma/ *n. f.* alarm. **—alarmar,** *v.*

alba /ˈalβa/ *n. f.* daybreak, dawn.

albanega /alβaˈnega/ *n. f.* hair net.

albañil /alβaˈɲil/ *n. m.* bricklayer; mason.

albaricoque /alβariˈkoke/ *n. m.* apricot.

alberca /alˈβerka/ *n. f.* swimming pool.

albergue /alˈβerge/ *n. m.* shelter. **—albergar,** *v.*

alborotar /alβoroˈtar/ *v.* disturb, make noise, brawl, riot.

alboroto /alβoˈroto/ *n. m.* brawl, disturbance, din, tumult.

álbum /ˈalβum/ *n. m.* album.

álbum de recortes /ˈalβum de reˈkortes/ scrapbook.

alcachofa /alkaˈtʃofa/ *n. f.* artichoke.

alcalde /alˈkalde/ *n. m.* mayor.

alcance /alˈkanθe; alˈkanse/ *n. m.* reach; range, scope.

alcanfor /alkanˈfor/ *n. m.* camphor.

alcanzar /alkanˈθar; alkanˈsar/ *v.* reach, overtake, catch.

alcayata /alkaˈyata/ *n. f.* spike.

alce /ˈalθe; ˈalse/ *n. m.* elk.

alcoba /alˈkoβa/ *n. f.* bedroom; alcove.

alcoba de huéspedes /alˈkoβa de ˈuespeðes/ guest room.

alcoba de respeto /alˈkoβa de rresˈpeto/ guest room.

alcohol /alˈkool/ *n. m.* alcohol.

alcohólico /alkoˈoliko/ **-ca** *a. & n.* alcoholic.

aldaba /alˈdaβa/ *n. f.* latch.

aldea /alˈdea/ *n. f.* village.

alegación /alegaˈθion; alegaˈsion/ *n. f.* allegation.

alegar /aleˈgar/ *v.* allege.

alegrar /aleˈgrar/ *v.* make happy, brighten.

alegrarse /aleˈgrarse/ *v.* be glad.

alegre /aˈlegre/ *a.* glad, cheerful, merry.

alegría /aleˈgria/ *n. f.* gaiety, cheer.

alejarse /aleˈharse/ *v.* move away, off.

alemán /aleˈman/ **-ana** *a. & n.* German.

Alemania /aleˈmania/ *n. f.* Germany.

alentar /alenˈtar/ *v.* cheer up, encourage.

alergia /alerˈhia/ *n. f.* allergy.

alerta /aˈlerta/ *adv.* on the alert.

aleve /aˈleβe/ **alevoso** *a.* treacherous.

alfabeto /alfaˈβeto/ *n. m.* alphabet.

alfalfa /alˈfalfa/ *n. f.* alfalfa.

alfarería /alfareˈria/ *n. f.* pottery.

alférez /alˈfereθ; alˈferes/ *n. m.* (naval) ensign.

alfil /alˈfil/ *n. m.* (chess) bishop.

alfiler /alfiˈler/ *n. m.* pin.

alfombra /alˈfombra/ *n. f.* carpet, rug.

alforja /alˈforha/ *n. f.* knapsack; saddlebag.

alga /ˈalga/ *n. f.* seaweed.

alga marina /ˈalga maˈrina/ seaweed.

algarabía /algaraˈβia/ *n. f.* jargon; din.

álgebra /ˈalheβra/ *n. f.* algebra.

algo /ˈalgo/ *pron. & adv.* something, somewhat; anything.

algodón /algoˈðon/ *n. m.* cotton.

algodón hidrófilo /algoˈðon iˈðrofilo/ absorbent cotton.

alguien /ˈalgien/ *pron.* somebody, someone; anybody, anyone.

algún /alˈgun/ **-no -na** *a. & pron.* some; any.

alhaja /aˈlaha/ *n. f.* jewel.

aliado /aˈliaðo/ **-da** *a. & n.* allied; ally. **—aliar,** *v.*

alianza /aˈlianθa; aˈliansa/ *n. f.* alliance.

alicates /aliˈkates/ *n. m.pl.* pliers.

aliento /aˈliento/ *n. m.* breath. **dar a.,** encourage.

aligerar /aliheˈrar/ *v.* lighten.

alimentar /alimenˈtar/ *v.* feed, nourish.

alimento /aliˈmento/ *n. m.* nourishment, food.

alinear /alineˈar/ *v.* line up; *Pol.* align.

aliñar /aliˈɲar/ *v.* dress (a salad).

aliño /aˈliɲo/ *n. m.* salad dressing.

alisar /aliˈsar/ *v.* smooth.

alistamiento /alistaˈmiento/ *n. m.* enlistment.

alistar /alisˈtar/ *v.* make ready, prime.

alistarse /alisˈtarse/ *v.* get ready; *Mil.* enlist.

aliviar /aliˈβiar/ *v.* alleviate, relieve, ease.

alivio /aˈliβio/ *n. m.* relief.

allá /aˈʎa; aˈya/ *adv.* there. **más a.,** beyond, farther on.

allanar /aʎaˈnar; ayaˈnar/ *v.* flatten, smooth, plane.

allí /aˈʎi; aˈyi/ *adv.* there. **por a.,** that way.

alma /ˈalma/ *n. f.* soul.

almacén /almaˈθen; almaˈsen/ *n. m.* department store; storehouse, warehouse.

almacenaje /almaθeˈnahe; almaseˈnahe/ *n. m.* storage.

almacenar /almaθeˈnar; almaseˈnar/ *v.* store.

almanaque /almaˈnake/ *n. m.* almanac.

almeja /alˈmeha/ *n. f.* clam.

almendra /alˈmendra/ *n. f.* almond.

almíbar /alˈmiβar/ *n. m.* syrup.

almidón /almiˈðon/ *n. m.* starch. **—almidonar,** *v.*

almirante /almiˈrante/ *n. m.* admiral.

almohada /almoˈaða/ *n. f.* pillow.

almuerzo /al'muerθo; al'muerso/ *n. m.* lunch. —**almorzar,** *v.*

alojamiento /aloha'miento/ *n. m.* lodging, accommodations.

alojar /alo'har/ *v.* lodge, house.

alojarse /alo'harse/ *v.* stay, room.

alquiler /alki'ler/ *n. m.* rent. —**alquilar,** *v.*

alrededor /alreðe'ðor/ *adv.* around.

alrededores /alreðe'ðores/ *n. m.pl.* environs.

altanero /alta'nero/ *a.* haughty.

altar /al'tar/ *n. m.* altar.

altavoz /ˌalta'βoθ; ˌalta'βos/ *n. m.* loudspeaker.

alteración /altera'θion; altera'sion/ *n. f.* alteration.

alterar /alte'rar/ *v.* alter.

alternativa /alterna'tiβa/ *n. f.* alternative. —**alternativo,** *a.*

alterno /al'terno/ *a.* alternate. —**alternar,** *v.*

alteza /al'teθa; al'tesa/ *n. f.* highness.

altivo /al'tiβo/ *a.* proud, haughty; lofty.

alto /'alto/ *a.* **1.** high, tall; loud. —*n.* **2.** *m.* height, story (house).

altura /al'tura/ *n. f.* height, altitude.

alud /a'luð/ *n. m.* avalanche.

aludir /alu'ðir/ *v.* allude.

alumbrado /alum'braðo/ *n. m.* lighting.

alumbrar /alum'brar/ *v.* light.

aluminio /alu'minio/ *n. m.* aluminum.

alumno /a'lumno/ -**na** *n.* student, pupil.

alusión /alu'sion/ *n. f.* allusion.

alza /'alθa; 'alsa/ *n. f.* rise; boost.

alzar /al'θar; al'sar/ *v.* raise, lift.

ama /'ama/ *n. f.* housewife, mistress (of house). **a. de llaves,** housekeeper.

amable /a'maβle/ *a.* kind; pleasant, sweet.

amalgamar /amalga'mar/ *v.* amalgamate.

amamantar /amaman'tar/ *v.* suckle, nurse.

amanecer /amane'θer; amane'ser/ *n.* **1.** *m.* dawn, daybreak. —*v.* **2.** dawn; awaken.

amante /a'mante/ *n. m. & f.* lover.

amapola /ama'pola/ *n. f.* poppy.

amar /a'mar/ *v.* love.

amargo /a'margo/ *a.* bitter.

amargón /amar'gon/ *n. m.* dandelion.

amargura /amar'gura/ *n. f.* bitterness.

amarillo /ama'riʎo; ama'riyo/ *a.* yellow.

amarradero /amarra'ðero/ *n. m.* mooring.

amarrar /ama'rrar/ *v.* hitch, moor, tie up.

amartillar /amarti'ʎar; amarti'yar/ *v.* hammer; cock (a gun).

amasar /ama'sar/ *v.* knead, mold.

ámbar /'ambar/ *n. m.* amber.

ambarino /amba'rino/ *a.* amber.

ambición /ambi'θion; ambi'sion/ *n. f.* ambition.

ambicionar /ambiθio'nar; ambisio'nar/ *v.* aspire to.

ambicioso /ambi'θioso; ambi'sioso/ *a.* ambitious.

ambientalista /ambienta'lista/ *n. m. & f.* environmentalist.

ambiente /am'biente/ *n. m.* environment, atmosphere.

ambigüedad /ambigue'ðað/ *n. f.* ambiguity.

ambiguo /am'biguo/ *a.* ambiguous.

ambos /'ambos/ *a. & pron.* both.

ambulancia /ambu'lanθia; ambu'lansia/ *n. f.* ambulance.

amenaza /ame'naθa; ame'nasa/ *n. f.* threat, menace.

amenazar /amena'θar; amena'sar/ *v.* threaten, menace.

ameno /a'meno/ *a.* pleasant.

americana /ameri'kana/ *n. f.* suit coat.

americano /ameri'kano/ -**na** *a. & n.* American.

ametralladora /ametraʎa'ðora; ametraya'ðora/ *n. f.* machine gun.

amigable /ami'gaβle/ *a.* amicable, friendly.

amígdala /a'migðala/ *n. f.* tonsil.

amigo /a'migo/ -**ga** *n.* friend.

aminorar /amino'rar/ *v.* lessen, reduce.

amistad /amis'tað/ *n. f.* friendship.

amistoso /amis'toso/ *a.* friendly.

amniocéntesis /amnioθen'tesis; amniosen'tesis/ *n. m.* amniocentesis.

amo /'amo/ *n. m.* master.

amonestaciones /amonesta'θiones; amonesta'siones/ *n. f.pl.* banns.

amonestar /amones'tar/ *v.* admonish.

amoníaco /amo'niako/ *n. m.* ammonia.

amontonar /amonto'nar/ *v.* amass, pile up.

amor /a'mor/ *n. m.* love. **a. propio,** self-esteem.

amorío /amo'rio/ *n. m.* romance, love affair.

amoroso /amo'roso/ *a.* amorous, loving.

amortecer /amorte'θer; amorte'ser/ *v.* deaden.

amparar /ampa'rar/ *v.* aid, befriend; protect, shield.

amparo /am'paro/ *n. m.* protection.

ampliar /amp'liar/ *v.* enlarge; elaborate.

amplificar /amplifi'kar/ *v.* amplify.

amplio /'amplio/ *a.* ample, roomy.

ampolla /am'poʎa; am'poya/ *n. f.* bubble; bulb; blister.

amputar /ampu'tar/ *v.* amputate.

amueblar /amue'βlar/ *v.* furnish.

analfabeto /analfa'βeto/ -**ta** *a. & n.* illiterate.

analgésico /anal'hesiko/ *n. m.* pain killer.

análisis /a'nalisis/ *n. m.* analysis.

analizar /anali'θar; anali'sar/ *v.* analyze.

analogía /analo'hia/ *n. f.* analogy.

análogo /a'nalogo/ *a.* similar, analogous.

anarquía /anar'kia/ *n. f.* anarchy.

anatomía /anato'mia/ *n. f.* anatomy.

ancho /'antʃo/ *a.* wide, broad.

anchoa /an'tʃoa/ *n. f.* anchovy.

anchura /an'tʃura/ *n. f.* width, breadth.

anciano /an'θiano; an'siano/ -**na** *a. & n.* old, aged (person).

ancla /'ankla/ *n. f.* anchor. —**anclar,** *v.*

anclaje /an'klahe/ *n. m.* anchorage.

andamio /an'damio/ *n. m.* scaffold.

andar /an'dar/ *v.* walk; move, go.

andén /an'den/ *n. m.* (railroad) platform.

andrajoso /andra'hoso/ *a.* ragged, uneven.

anécdota /a'nekðota/ *n. f.* anecdote.

anegar /ane'gar/ *v.* flood, drown.

anestesia /anes'tesia/ *n. f.* anesthetic.

anexar /anek'sar/ *v.* annex.

anexión /anek'sion/ *n. f.* annexation.

anfitrión /anfitri'on/ -**na** *n.* host.

ángel /'anhel/ *n. m.* angel.

angosto /aŋ'gosto/ *a.* narrow.

anguila /aŋ'gila/ *n. f.* eel.

angular /aŋgu'lar/ *a.* angular.

ángulo /'aŋgulo/ *n. m.* angle.

angustia /aŋ'gustia/ *n. f.* anguish, agony.

angustiar /aŋgus'tiar/ *v.* distress.

anhelar /ane'lar/ *v.* long for.

anidar /ani'ðar/ *v.* nest, nestle.

anillo /a'niʎo; a'niyo/ *n. m.* ring; circle.

animación /anima'θion; anima'sion/ *n. f.* animation; bustle.

animado /ani'maðo/ *a.* animated, lively; animate.

animal /ani'mal/ *a. & n.* animal.

ánimo /'animo/ *n. m.* state of mind, spirits; courage.

aniquilar /aniki'lar/ *v.* annihilate, destroy.

aniversario /aniβer'sario/ *n. m.* anniversary.

anoche /a'notʃe/ *adv.* last night.

anochecer /anotʃe'θer; anotʃe'ser/ *n.* **1.** *m.* twilight, nightfall. —*v.* **2.** get dark.

anónimo /a'nonimo/ *a.* anonymous.

anorexia /ano'reksia/ *n. f.* anorexia.

anormal /anor'mal/ *a.* abnormal.

anotación /anota'θion; anota'sion/ *n. f.* annotation.

anotar /ano'tar/ *v.* annotate.

ansia /'ansia/ **ansiedad** *n. f.* anxiety.

ansioso /an'sioso/ *a.* anxious.

antagonismo /antago'nismo/ *n. m.* antagonism.

antagonista /antago'nista/ *n. m. & f.* antagonist, opponent.

anteayer /antea'yer/ *adv.* day before yesterday.

antebrazo /ante'βraθo; ante'βraso/ *n. m.* forearm.

antecedente /anteθe'ðente; antese'ðente/ *a. & m.* antecedent.

anteceder /anteθe'ðer; antese'ðer/ *v.* precede.

antecesor /anteθe'sor; antese'sor/ *n. m.* ancestor.

antemano /ante'mano/ *de a.,* in advance.

antena /an'tena/ *n. f.* antenna.

antena parabólica /an'tena para'βolika/ satellite dish.

anteojos /ante'ohos/ *n. m.pl.* eyeglasses.

antepasado /antepa'saðo/ *n. m.* ancestor.

antepenúltimo /antepe'nultimo/ *a.* antepenultimate.

anterior /ante'rior/ *a.* previous, former.

antes /'antes/ *adv.* before; formerly.

antibala /anti'bala/ *a.* bulletproof.

anticipación /antiθipa'θion; antisipa'sion/ *n. f.* anticipation.

anticipar /antiθi'par; antisi'par/ *v.* anticipate; advance.

anticonceptivo /antikonθep'tiβo; antikonsep'tiβo/ *a.* contraceptive.

anticongelante /antikoŋge'lante/ *n. m.* antifreeze.

anticuado /anti'kuaðo/ *a.* antiquated, obsolete.

antídoto /an'tiðoto/ *n. m.* antidote.

antigüedad /antigue'ðað/ *n. f.* antiquity; antique.

antiguo /an'tiguo/ *a.* former; old; antique.

antihistamínico /antiista'miniko/ *n. m.* antihistamine.

antílope /an'tilope/ *n. m.* antelope.

antinuclear /antinukle'ar/ *a.* antinuclear.

antipatía /antipa'tia/ *n. f.* antipathy.

antipático /anti'patiko/ *a.* disagreeable, nasty.

antiséptico /anti'septiko/ *a. & m.* antiseptic.

antojarse /anto'harse/ *v.* **se me antoja...** etc., I desire..., take a fancy to..., etc.

antojo /an'toho/ *n. m.* whim, fancy.

antorcha /an'tortʃa/ *n. f.* torch.

antracita /antra'θita; antra'sita/ *n. f.* anthracite.

anual /a'nual/ *a.* annual, yearly.

anudar /anu'ðar/ *v.* knot; tie.

anular /anu'lar/ *v.* annul, void.

anunciar /anun'θiar; anun'siar/ *v.* announce; proclaim, advertise.

anuncio /a'nunθio; a'nunsio/ *n. m.* announcement; advertisement.

añadir /aɲa'ðir/ *v.* add.

añil /a'ɲil/ *n. m.* bluing; indigo.

año /'aɲo/ *n. m.* year.

apacible /apa'θiβle; apa'siβle/ *a.* peaceful, peaceable.

apaciguamiento /aˌpaθigua'miento; aˌpasigua'miento/ *n. m.* appeasement.

apaciguar /apaθi'guar; apasi'guar/ *v.* appease; placate.

apagado /apa'gaðo/ *a.* dull.

apagar /apa'gar/ *v.* extinguish, quench, put out.

apagón /apa'gn/ *n. m.* blackout.

aparador /apara'ðor/ *n. m.* buffet, cupboard.

aparato /apa'rato/ *n. m.* apparatus; machine; appliance, set.

aparcamiento /aparka'miento/ *n. m.* parking lot; parking space.

aparecer /apare'θer; apare'ser/ *v.* appear, show up.

aparejo /apa'reho/ *n. m.* rig. —**aparejar,** *v.*

aparentar /aparen'tar/ *v.* pretend; profess.

aparente /apa'rente/ *a.* apparent.

apariencia /apa'rienθia; apa'riensia/ **aparición** *n. f.* appearance.

apartado /apar'taðo/ *a.* **1.** aloof; separate. —*n.* **2.** *m.* post-office box.

apartamento /aparta'mento/ *n. m.* apartment. **a. en propiedad,** condominium.

apartar /apar'tar/ *v.* separate; remove.

aparte /a'parte/ *adv.* apart; aside.

apartheid /apar'teið/ *n. m.* apartheid.

apasionado /apasio'naðo/ *a.* passionate.

apatía /apa'tia/ *n. f.* apathy.

apearse /ape'arse/ *v.* get off, alight.

apedrear /apeðre'ar/ *v.* stone.

apelación /apela'θion; apela'sion/ *n. f.* appeal. —**apelar,** *v.*

apellido /ape'ʎiðo; ape'yiðo/ *n. m.* family name.

apellido materno /ape'ʎiðo ma'terno; ape'yiðo ma'terno/ mother's family name.

apellido paterno /ape'ʎiðo pa'terno; ape'yiðo pa'terno/ father's family name.

apenas /a'penas/ *adv.* scarcely, hardly.

apéndice /a'pendiθe; a'pendise/ *n. m.* appendix.

apercibir /aperθi'βir; apersi'βir/ *v.* prepare, warn.

aperitivo /aperi'tiβo/ *n. m.* appetizer.

aperos /a'peros/ *n. m.pl.* implements.

apestar /apes'tar/ *v.* infect; stink.

apetecer /apete'θer; apete'ser/ *v.* desire, have appetite for.

apetito /ape'tito/ *n. m.* appetite.

ápice /'apiθe; 'apise/ *n. m.* apex.

apilar /api'lar/ *v.* stack.

apio /'apio/ *n. m.* celery.

aplacar /apla'kar/ *v.* appease; placate.

aplastar /aplas'tar/ *v.* crush, flatten.

aplaudir /aplau'ðir/ *v.* applaud, cheer.

aplauso /a'plauso/ *n. m.* applause.

aplazar /apla'θar; apla'sar/ *v.* postpone, put off.

aplicable /apli'kaβle/ *a.* applicable.

aplicado /apli'kaðo/ *a.* industrious, diligent.

aplicar /apli'kar/ *v.* apply.

aplomo /a'plomo/ *n. m.* aplomb, poise.

apoderado /apoðe'raðo/ -**da** *n.* attorney.

apoderarse de /apoðe'rarse de/ *v.* get hold of, seize.

apodo /a'poðo/ *n. m.* nickname. —**apodar,** *v.*

apologético /apolo'hetiko/ *a.* apologetic.

apoplejía /aople'hia/ *n. f.* apoplexy.

aposento /apo'sento/ *n. m.* room, flat.

apostar /apos'tar/ *v.* bet, wager.

apóstol /a'postol/ *n. m.* apostle.

apoyar /apo'yar/ *v.* support, prop; lean.

apoyo /a'poyo/ *n. m.* support; prop; aid; approval.

apreciable /apreθia'βle; apresia'βle/ *a.* appreciable.

apreciar /apre'θiar; apre'siar/ *v.* appreciate, prize.

aprecio /a'preθio; a'presio/ *n. m.* appreciation, regard.

apremio /a'premio/ *n. m.* pressure, compulsion.

aprender /apren'der/ *v.* learn.

aprendiz /apren'diθ; apren'dis/ *n. m.* apprentice.

aprendizaje /aprendi'θahe; aprendi'sahe/ *n. m.* apprenticeship.

aprensión /apren'sion/ *n. f.* apprehension.

aprensivo /apren'siβo/ *a.* apprehensive.

apresurado /apresu'raðo/ *a.* hasty, fast.

apresurar /apresu'rar/ *v.* hurry, speed up.

apretado /apre'taðo/ *a.* tight.

apretar /apre'tar/ *v.* squeeze, press; tighten.

apretón /apre'ton/ *n. m.* squeeze.

aprieto /a'prieto/ *n. m.* plight, predicament.

aprobación /aproβa'θion; aproβa'sion/ *n. f.* approbation, approval.

aprobar /apro'βar/ *v.* approve.

apropiación /apropia'θion; apropia'sion/ *n. f.* appropriation.

apropiado /apro'piaðo/ *a.* appropriate. **—apropiar,** *v.*

aprovechar /aproβe't∫ar/ *v.* profit by.

aprovecharse /aproβe't∫arse/ *v.* take advantage.

aproximado /aproksi'maðo/ *a.* approximate.

aproximarse a /aproksi'marse a/ *v.* approach.

aptitud /apti'tuð/ *n. f.* aptitude.

apto /'apto/ *a.* apt.

apuesta /a'puesta/ *n. f.* bet, wager, stake.

apuntar /apun'tar/ *v.* point, aim; prompt; write down.

apunte /a'punte/ *n. m.* annotation, note; promptings, cue.

apuñalar /apuɲa'lar/ *v.* stab.

apurar /apu'rar/ *v.* hurry, worry.

apuro /a'puro/ *n. m.* predicament, scrape, trouble.

aquel /a'kel/ **aquella** *dem. a.* that.

aquél /a'kel/ **aquélla** *dem. pron.* that (one); the former.

aquello /a'keʎo; a'keyo/ *dem. pron.* that.

aquí /a'ki/ *adv.* here. **por a.,** this way.

aquietar /akie'tar/ *v.* allay; lull, pacify.

ara /'ara/ *n. f.* altar.

árabe /'araβe/ *a.* & *n.* Arab, Arabic.

arado /a'raðo/ *n. m.* plow. **—arar,** *v.*

arándano /a'randano/ *n. m.* cranberry.

araña /a'raɲa/ *n. f.* spider. **a. de luces,** chandelier.

arbitración /arβitra'θion; arβitra'sion/ *n. f.* arbitration.

arbitrador /arβitra'ðor/ **-ra** *n.* arbitrator.

arbitraje /arβi'trahe/ *n. m.* arbitration.

arbitrar /arβi'trar/ *v.* arbitrate.

arbitrario /arβi'trario/ *a.* arbitrary.

árbitro /'arβitro/ *n. m.* arbiter, umpire, referee.

árbol /'arβol/ *n. m.* tree; mast.

árbol genealógico /'arβol henea'lohiko/ family tree.

arbusto /ar'βusto/ *n. m.* bush, shrub.

arca /'arka/ *n. f.* chest; ark.

arcada /ar'kaða/ *n. f.* arcade.

arcaico /ar'kaiko/ *a.* archaic.

arce /'arθe; 'arse/ *n. m.* maple.

archipiélago /art∫i'pielago/ *n. m.* archipelago.

archivador /art∫iβa'ðor/ *n. m.* file cabinet.

archivo /ar't∫iβo/ *n. m.* archive; file. **—archivar,** *v.*

arcilla /ar'θiʎa; ar'siya/ *n. f.* clay.

arco /'arko/ *n. m.* arc; arch; (archer's) bow. **a. iris,** rainbow.

arder /ar'ðer/ *v.* burn.

ardid /ar'ðið/ *n. m.* stratagem, cunning.

ardiente /ar'ðiente/ *a.* ardent, burning, fiery.

ardilla /ar'ðiʎa; ar'ðiya/ *n. f.* squirrel.

ardor /ar'ðor/ *n. m.* ardor, fervor.

ardor de estómago /ar'ðor de es'tomago/ heartburn.

arduo /'arðuo/ *a.* arduous.

área /'area/ *n. f.* area.

arena /a'rena/ *n. f.* sand; arena.

arenoso /are'noso/ *a.* sandy.

arenque /a'renke/ *n. m.* herring.

arete /a'rete/ *n.* earring.

argentino /arhen'tino/ **-na** *a.* & *n.* Argentine.

argüir /ar'guir/ *v.* dispute, argue.

árido /'ariðo/ *a.* arid.

aristocracia /aristo'kraθia; aristo'krasia/ *n. f.* aristocracy.

aristócrata /aris'tokrata/ *n. f.* aristocrat.

aristocrático /aristo'kratiko/ *a.* aristocratic.

aritmética /arit'metika/ *n. f.* arithmetic.

arma /'arma/ *n. f.* weapon, arm.

armadura /arma'ðura/ *n. f.* armor; reinforcement; framework.

armamento /arma'mento/ *n. m.* armament.

armar /ar'mar/ *v.* arm.

armario /ar'mario/ *n. m.* cabinet, bureau, wardrobe.

armazón /arma'θon; arma'son/ *n. m.* framework, frame.

armería /arme'ria/ *n. f.* armory.

armisticio /armis'tiθio; armis'tisio/ *n. m.* armistice.

armonía /armo'nia/ *n. f.* harmony.

armonioso /armo'nioso/ *a.* harmonious.

armonizar /armoni'θar; armoni'sar/ *v.* harmonize.

arnés /ar'nes/ *n. m.* harness.

aroma /a'roma/ *n. f.* aroma, fragrance.

aromático /aro'matiko/ *a.* aromatic.

arpa /'arpa/ *n. f.* harp.

arquear /arke'ar/ *v.* arch.

arquitecto /arki'tekto/ *n. m.* architect.

arquitectura /arkitek'tura/ *n. f.* architecture.

arquitectural /arkitektu'ral/ *a.* architectural.

arrabal /arra'βal/ *n. m.* suburb.

arraigar /arrai'gar/ *v.* take root, settle.

arrancar /arran'kar/ *v.* pull out, tear out; start up.

arranque /a'rranke/ *n. m.* dash, sudden start; fit of anger.

arrastrar /arras'trar/ *v.* drag.

arrebatar /arreβa'tar/ *v.* snatch, grab.

arrebato /arre'βato/ *n. m.* sudden attack, fit of anger.

arrecife /arre'θife; arre'sife/ *n. m.* reef.

arreglar /arre'glar/ *v.* arrange; repair, fix; adjust, settle.

arreglárselas /arre'glarselas/ *v.* manage, shift for oneself.

arreglo /a'rreglo/ *n. m.* arrangement, settlement.

arremangarse /arremaŋ'garse/ *v.* roll up one's sleeves; roll up one's pants.

arremeter /arreme'ter/ *v.* attack.

arrendar /arren'dar/ *v.* rent.

arrepentimiento /arrepenti'miento/ *n. m.* repentance.

arrepentirse /arrepen'tirse/ *v.* repent.

arrestar /arres'tar/ *v.* arrest.

arriba /a'rriβa/ *adv.* up; upstairs.

arriendo /a'rriendo/ *n. m.* lease.

arriero /a'rriero/ *n. m.* muleteer.

arriesgar /arries'gar/ *v.* risk.

arrimarse /arri'marse/ *v.* lean.

arrodillarse /arroði'ʎarse; arroði'yarse/ *v.* kneel.

arrogancia /arro'ganθia; arro'gansia/ *n. f.* arrogance.

arrogante /arro'gante/ *a.* arrogant.

arrojar /arro'har/ *v.* throw, hurl; shed.

arrollar /arro'ʎar; arro'yar/ *v.* roll, coil.

arroyo /a'rroyo/ *n. m.* brook; gully; gutter.

arroz /a'rroθ; a'rros/ *n. m.* rice.

arruga /a'rruga/ *n. f.* ridge; wrinkle.

arrugar /arru'gar/ *v.* wrinkle, crumple.

arruinar /arrui'nar/ *v.* ruin, destroy, wreck.

arsenal /arse'nal/ *n. m.* arsenal; armory.

arsénico /ar'seniko/ *n. m.* arsenic.

arte /'arte/ *n. m.* (*f.* in *pl.*) art, craft; wiliness.

arteria /ar'teria/ *n. f.* artery.

artesa /ar'tesa/ *n. f.* trough.

artesano /arte'sano/ **-na** *n.* artisan, craftsman.

ártico /'artiko/ *a.* arctic.

articulación /artikula'θion; artikula'sion/ *n. f.* articulation; joint.

articular /artiku'lar/ *v.* articulate.

artículo /ar'tikulo/ *n. m.* article.

artífice /ar'tifiθe; ar'tifise/ *n. m.* & *f.* artisan.

artificial /artifi'θial; artifi'sial/ *a.* artificial.

artificio /arti'fiθio; arti'fisio/ *n. m.* artifice, device.

artificioso /artifi'θioso; artifi'sioso/ *a.* affected.

artillería /artiʎe'ria; artiye'ria/ *n. f.* artillery.

artista /ar'tista/ *n. m.* & *f.* artist.

artístico /ar'tistiko/ *a.* artistic.

artritis /ar'tritis/ *n. f.* arthritis.

arzobispo /arθo'βispo; arso'βispo/ *n. m.* archbishop.

as /as/ *n. m.* ace.

asado /a'saðo/ *a.* & *n.* roast.

asaltador /asalta'ðor/ **-ra** *n.* assailant.

asaltante /asal'tante/ *n. m.* & *f.* mugger.

asaltar /asal'tar/ *v.* assail, attack.

asalto /a'salto/ *n. m.* assault. **—asaltar,** *v.*

asamblea /asam'βlea/ *n. f.* assembly.

asar /a'sar/ *v.* roast; broil, cook (meat).

asaz /a'saθ; a'sas/ *adv.* enough; quite.

ascender /asθen'der; assen'der/ *v.* ascend, go up; amount.

ascenso /as'θenso; as'senso/ *n. m.* ascent.

ascensor /asθen'sor; assen'sor/ *n. m.* elevator.

ascensorista /asθenso'rista; assenso'rista/ *n. m.* & *f.* (elevator) operator.

asco /'asko/ *n. m.* nausea; disgusting thing. **qué a.,** how disgusting.

aseado /ase'aðo/ *a.* tidy. **—asear,** *v.*

asediar /ase'ðiar/ *v.* besiege.

asedio /a'seðio/ *n. m.* siege.

asegurar /asegu'rar/ *v.* assure; secure.

asegurarse /asegu'rarse/ *v.* make sure.

asemejarse a /aseme'harse a/ *v.* resemble.

asentar /asen'tar/ *v.* settle; seat.

asentimiento /asenti'miento/ *n. m.* assent. **—asentir,** *v.*

aseo /a'seo/ *n. m.* neatness, tidiness.

aseos /a'seos/ *n. m.pl.* restroom.

asequible /ase'kiβle/ *a.* attainable; affordable.

aserción /aser'θion; aser'sion/ *n. f.* assertion.

aserrar /ase'rrar/ *v.* saw.

asesinar /asesi'nar/ *v.* assassinate; murder, slay.

asesinato /asesi'nato/ *n. m.* assassination, murder.

asesino /ase'sino/ **-na** *n.* murderer, assassin.

aseveración /aseβera'θion; aseβera'sion/ *n. f.* assertion.

aseverar /aseβe'rar/ *v.* assert.

asfalto /as'falto/ *n. m.* asphalt.

así /a'si/ *adv.* so, thus, this way, that way. **a. como,** as well as. **a. que,** as soon as.

asiático /a'siatiko/ **-ca** *a.* & *n.* Asiatic.

asiduo /a'siðuo/ *a.* assiduous.

asiento /a'siento/ *n. m.* seat; chair; site.

asiento delantero /a'siento delan'tero/ front seat.

asiento trasero /a'siento tra'sero/ back seat.

asignar /asig'nar/ *v.* assign; allot.

asilo /a'silo/ *n. m.* asylum, sanctuary.

asimilar /asimi'lar/ *v.* assimilate.

asir /a'sir/ *v.* grasp.

asistencia /asis'tenθia; asistensia/ *n. f.* attendance, presence.

asistir /asis'tir/ *v.* be present, attend.

asno /'asno/ *n. m.* donkey.

asociación /asoθia'θion; asosia'sion/ *n. f.* association.

asociado /aso'θiaðo; aso'siaðo/ *n. m.* associate, partner.

asociar /aso'θiar; aso'siar/ *v.* associate.

asolar /aso'lar/ *v.* desolate; burn, parch.

asoleado /asole'aðo/ *a.* sunny.

asomar /aso'mar/ *v.* appear, loom up, show up.

asombrar /asom'βrar/ *v.* astonish, amaze.

asombro /a'sombro/ *n. m.* amazement, astonishment.

aspa /'aspa/ *n. f.* reel. **—aspar,** *v.*

aspecto /as'pekto/ *n. m.* aspect.

aspereza /aspe'reθa; aspe'resa/ *n. f.* harshness.

áspero /'aspero/ *a.* rough, harsh.

aspiración /aspira'θion; aspira'sion/ *n. f.* aspiration.

aspirador /aspira'ðor/ *n. m.* vacuum cleaner.

aspirar /aspi'rar/ *v.* aspire.

aspirina /aspi'rina/ *n. f.* aspirin.

asqueroso /aske'roso/ *a.* dirty, nasty, filthy.

asta /'asta/ *n. f.* shaft.

asterisco /aste'risko/ *n. m.* asterisk.

astilla /as'tiʎa; as'tiya/ *n. f.* splinter, chip. **—astillar,** *v.*

astillero /asti'ʎero; asti'yero/ *n. m.* dry dock.

astro /'astro/ *n. m.* star.

astronauta /astro'nauta/ *n. m.* & *f.* astronaut.

astronave /astro'naβe/ *n. f.* spaceship.

astronomía /astrono'mia/ *n. f.* astronomy.

astucia /as'tuθia; as'tusia/ *n. f.* cunning.

astuto /as'tuto/ *a.* astute, sly, shrewd.

asumir /asu'mir/ *v.* assume.

asunto /a'sunto/ *n. m.* matter, affair, business; subject.

asustar /asus'tar/ *v.* frighten, scare, startle.

atacar /ata'kar/ *v.* attack, charge.

atajo /a'taho/ *n. m.* shortcut.

ataque /a'take/ *n. m.* attack, charge; spell, stroke.

ataque cardíaco /a'take kar'ðiako/ heart attack.

atar /a'tar/ *v.* tie, bind, fasten.

atareado /atare'aðo/ *a.* busy.

atascar /atas'kar/ *v.* stall, stop, obstruct.

atasco /a'tasko/ *n. m.* traffic jam.

ataúd /ata'uð/ *n. m.* casket, coffin.

atavío /ata'βio/ *n. m.* dress; gear, equipment.

atemorizar /atemori'θar; atemori'sar/ *v.* frighten.

atención /aten'θion; aten'sion/ *n. f.* attention.

atender /aten'der/ *v.* heed; attend to, wait on.

atenerse a /ate'nerse a/ *v.* count on, depend on.

atentado /aten'taðo/ *n. m.* crime, offense.

atento /a'tento/ *a.* attentive, courteous.

ateo /a'teo/ *n. m.* atheist.

aterrizaje /aterri'θahe; aterri'sahe/ *n. m.* landing (of aircraft).

aterrizaje forzoso /aterri'θahe for'θoso; aterri'sahe for'soso/ emergency landing, forced landing.

aterrizar /aterri'θar; aterri'sar/ *v.* land.

atesorar /ateso'rar/ *v.* hoard.

atestar /ates'tar/ *v.* witness.

atestiguar /atesti'guar/ *v.* attest, testify.

atinar /ati'nar/ *v.* hit upon.

atisbar /atis'βar/ *v.* scrutinize, pry.

Atlántico /at'lantiko/ *n. m.* Atlantic.

atlántico *a.* Atlantic.

atlas /'atlas/ *n. m.* atlas.

atleta /at'leta/ *n. m. & f.* athlete.

atlético /at'letiko/ *a.* athletic.

atletismo /atle'tismo/ *n. m.* athletics.

atmósfera /at'mosfera/ *n. f.* atmosphere.

atmosférico /atmos'feriko/ *a.* atmospheric.

atolladero /atoʎa'ðero; atoya'ðero/ *n. m.* dead end, impasse.

atómico /a'tomiko/ *a.* atomic.

átomo /'atomo/ *n. m.* atom.

atormentar /atormen'tar/ *v.* torment, plague.

atornillar /atorni'ʎar; atorni'yar/ *v.* screw.

atracción /atrak'θion; atrak'sion/ *n. f.* attraction.

atractivo /atrak'tiβo/ *a.* **1.** attractive. —*n.* **2.** *m.* attraction.

atraer /atra'er/ *v.* attract; lure.

atrapar /atra'par/ *v.* trap, catch.

atrás /a'tras/ *adv.* back; behind.

atrasado /atra'saðo/ *a.* belated; backward; slow (clock).

atrasar /atra'sar/ *v.* delay, retard; be slow.

atraso /a'traso/ *n. m.* delay; backwardness; (*pl.*) arrears.

atravesar /atraβe'sar/ *v.* cross.

atreverse /atre'βerse/ *v.* dare.

atrevido /atre'βiðo/ *a.* daring, bold.

atrevimiento /atreβi'miento/ *n. m.* boldness.

atribuir /atri'βuir/ *v.* attribute, ascribe.

atributo /atri'βuto/ *n. m.* attribute.

atrincherar /atrintʃe'rar/ *v.* entrench.

atrocidad /atroθi'ðað; atrosi'ðað/ *n. f.* atrocity, outrage.

atronar /atro'nar/ *v.* deafen.

atropellar /atrope'ʎar; atrope'yar/ *v.* trample; fell.

atroz /a'troθ; a'ntros/ *a.* atrocious.

atún /a'tun/ *n. m.* tuna.

aturdir /atur'ðir/ *v.* daze, stun, bewilder.

audacia /au'ðaθia; au'ðasia/ *n. f.* audacity.

audaz /au'ðaθ; au'ðas/ *a.* audacious, bold.

audible /au'ðiβle/ *a.* audible.

audífono /au'ðifono/ *n. m.* hearing aid.

audiovisual /auðioβi'sual/ *a.* audiovisual.

auditorio /auði'torio/ *n. m.* audience.

aula /'aula/ *n. f.* classroom, hall.

aullar /au'ʎar; au'ðas/ *v.* howl, bay.

aullido /au'ʎiðo; au'yiðo/ *n. m.* howl.

aumentar /aumen'tar/ *v.* augment; increase, swell.

aun /a'un/ **aún** *adv.* still; even. **a. cuando,** even though, even if.

aunque /'aunke/ *conj.* although, though.

áureo /'aureo/ *a.* golden.

aureola /aure'ola/ *n. f.* halo.

auriculares /auriku'lares/ *n. m.pl.* headphones.

aurora /au'rora/ *n. f.* dawn.

ausencia /au'senθia; au'sensia/ *n. f.* absence.

ausentarse /ausen'tarse/ *v.* stay away.

ausente /au'sente/ *a.* absent.

auspicio /aus'piθio; aus'pisio/ *n. m.* auspice.

austeridad /austeri'ðað/ *n. f.* austerity.

austero /aus'tero/ *a.* austere.

austriaco /aus'triako/ **-ca** *a. & n.* Austrian.

auténtico /au'tentiko/ *a.* authentic.

auto /'auto/ **automóvil** *n. m.* auto, automobile.

autobús /auto'βus/ *n. m.* bus.

autocine /auto'θine; auto'sine/ **autocinema** *n. m.* drive-in (movie theater).

automático /auto'matiko/ *a.* automatic.

autonomía /autono'mia/ *n. f.* autonomy.

autopista /auto'pista/ *n. f.* expressway.

autor /au'tor/ *n. m.* author.

autoridad /autori'ðað/ *n. f.* authority.

autoritario /autori'tario/ *a.* authoritarian; authoritative.

autorizar /autori'θar; autori'sar/ *v.* authorize.

autostop /auto'stop/ *n. m.* hitchhiking. **hacer a.,** to hitchhike.

auxiliar /auksi'liar/ *a.* **1.** auxiliary. —*v.* **2.** assist, aid.

auxilio /auk'silio/ *n. m.* aid, assistance.

avaluar /aβa'luar/ *v.* evaluate, appraise.

avance /a'βanθe; a'βanse/ *n. m.* advance. —**avanzar,** *v.*

avaricia /aβa'riθia; aβa'risia/ *n. f.* avarice.

avariento /aβa'riento/ *a.* miserly, greedy.

avaro /a'βaro/ **-ra** *a. & m.* miser; miserly.

ave /'aβe/ *n. f.* bird.

avellana /aβe'ʎana; aβe'yana/ *n. f.* hazelnut.

avena /a'βena/ *n. f.* oat.

avenida /aβe'niða/ *n. f.* avenue; flood.

avenirse /aβe'nirse/ *v.* compromise; agree.

aventajar /aβenta'har/ *v.* surpass, get ahead of.

aventar /aβen'tar/ *v.* fan; scatter.

aventura /aβen'tura/ *n. f.* adventure.

aventurar /aβentu'rar/ *v.* venture, risk, gamble.

aventurero /aβentu'rero/ **-ra** *a. & n.* adventurous; adventurer.

avergonzado /aβergon'θaðo; aβergon'saðo/ *a.* ashamed, abashed.

avergonzar /aβergon'θar; aβergon'sar/ *v.* shame, abash.

avería /aβe'ria/ *n. f.* damage. —**averiar,** *v.*

averiguar /aβeri'guar/ *v.* ascertain, find out.

aversión /aβer'sion/ *n. f.* aversion.

avestruz /aβes'truθ; aβes'trus/ *n. m.* ostrich.

aviación /aβia'θion; aβia'sion/ *n. f.* aviation.

aviador /aβia'ðor/ **-ra** *n.* aviator.

ávido /'aβiðo/ *a.* avid; eager.

avión /a'βion/ *n. m.* airplane.

avisar /aβi'sar/ *v.* notify, let know; warn, advise.

aviso /a'βiso/ *n. m.* notice, announcement; advertisement; warning.

avispa /a'βispa/ *n. f.* wasp.

avivar /aβi'βar/ *v.* enliven, revive.

axila /ak'sila/ *n. f.* armpit.

aya /'aya/ *n. f.* governess.

ayatolá /aya'tola/ *n. m.* ayatollah.

ayer /a'yer/ *adv.* yesterday.

ayuda /a'yuða/ *n. f.* help, aid. —**ayudar,** *v.*

ayudante /ayu'ðante/ *a.* assistant, helper; adjutant.

ayuno /a'yuno/ *n. m.* fast. —**ayunar,** *v.*

ayuntamiento /ayunta'miento/ *n. m.* city hall.

azada /a'θaða; a'saða/ *n. f.,* **azadón,** *m.* hoe.

azafata /aθa'fata; asa'fata/ *n. f.* stewardess, flight attendant.

azar /a'θar; a'sar/ *n. m.* hazard, chance. **al a.,** at random.

azotar /aθo'tar; aso'tar/ *v.* whip, flog; belabor.

azote /a'θote; a'sote/ *n. m.* scourge, lash.

azúcar /a'θukar; a'sukar/ *n. m.* sugar.

azucarero /aθuka'rero; asuka'rero/ *n. m.* sugar bowl.

azúcar moreno /a'θukar mo'reno; a'sukar mo'reno/ brown sugar.

azul /a'θul/ *a.* blue.

azulado /aθu'laðo; asu'laðo/ *a.* blue, bluish.

azulejo /aθu'leho; asu'leho/ *n. m.* tile; bluebird.

azul marino /a'θul ma'rino; a'sul ma'rino/ navy blue.

B

baba /'baβa/ *n. f.* drivel. —**babear,** *v.*

babador /baβa'ðor, ba'βero/ *n. m.* bib.

babucha /ba'βutʃa/ *n. f.* slipper.

bacalao /baka'lao/ *n. m.* codfish.

bachiller /batʃi'ʎer; batʃi'yer/ **-ra** *n.* bachelor (degree).

bacía /ba'θia; ba'sia/ *n. f.* washbasin.

bacterias /bak'terias/ *n. f.pl.* bacteria.

bacteriología /bakteriolo'hia/ *n. f.* bacteriology.

bahía /ba'ia/ *n. f.* bay.

bailador /baila'ðor/ **-ra** *n.* dancer.

bailar /bai'lar/ *v.* dance.

bailarín /baila'rin/ **-ina** *n.* dancer.

baile /'baile/ *n. m.* dance.

baja /'baha/ *n. f.* fall (in price); *Mil.* casualty.

bajar /ba'har/ *v.* lower; descend.

bajeza /ba'heθa; ba'hesa/ *n. f.* baseness.

bajo /'baho/ *prep.* **1.** under, below. —*a.* **2.** low; short; base.

bala /'bala/ *n. f.* bullet; ball; bale.

balada /ba'laða/ *n. f.* ballad.

balancear /balanθe'ar; balanse'ar/ *v.* balance; roll, swing, sway.

balanza /ba'lanθa; ba'lansa/ *n. f.* balance; scales.

balbuceo /balβu'θeo; balβu'seo/ *n. m.* stammer; babble. —**balbucear,** *v.*

Balcanes /bal'kanes/ *n. m.pl.* Balkans.

balcón /bal'kon/ *n. m.* balcony.

balde /'balde/ *n. m.* bucket, pail. **de b.,** gratis. **en b.,** in vain.

balística /ba'listika/ *n. f.* ballistics.

ballena /ba'ʎena; ba'yena/ *n. f.* whale.

balneario /balne'ario/ *n. m.* bathing resort; spa.

balompié /balom'pie/ *n. m.* football.

balón /ba'lon/ *n. m.* football; *Auto.* balloon tire.

baloncesto /balon'θesto; balon'sesto/ *n. m.* basketball.

balota /ba'lota/ *n. f.* ballot, vote. —**balotar,** *v.*

balsa /'balsa/ *n. f.* raft.

bálsamo /'balsamo/ *n. m.* balm.

baluarte /ba'luarte/ *n. m.* bulwark.

bambolearse /bambole'arse/ *v.* sway.

bambú /bam'βu/ *n. m.* bamboo.

banal /ba'nal/ *a.* banal, trite.

banana /ba'nana/ *n. f.* banana.

banano /ba'nano/ *n. m.* banana tree.

bancarrota /banka'rrota/ *n. f.* bankruptcy.

banco /'banko/ *n. m.* bank; bench; school of fish.

banco cooperativo /'banko koopera'tiβo/ credit union.

banda /'banda/ *n. f.* band.

bandada /ban'daða/ *n. f.* covey; flock.

banda sonora /'banda so'nora/ *n. f.* soundtrack.

bandeja /ban'deha/ *n. f.* tray.

bandera /ban'dera/ *n. f.* flag; banner; ensign.

bandido /ban'diðo/ **-da** *n.* bandit.

bando /'bando/ *n. m.* faction.

bandolero /bando'lero/ **-ra** *n.* bandit, robber.

banquero /ban'kero/ **-ra** *n.* banker.

banqueta /ban'keta/ *n. f.* stool; (Mex.) sidewalk.

banquete /ban'kete/ *n. m.* feast, banquet.

banquillo /ban'kiʎo; ban'kiyo/ *n. m.* stool.

bañar /ba'nar/ *v.* bathe.

bañera /ba'nera/ *n. f.* bathtub.

baño /'bano/ *n. m.* bath; bathroom.

bar /bar/ *n. m.* bar, pub.

baraja /ba'raha/ *n. f.* pack of cards; game of cards.

baranda /ba'randa/ *n. f.* railing, banister.

barato /ba'rato/ *a.* cheap.

barba /'barβa/ *n. f.* beard; chin.

barbacoa /barβa'koa/ *n. f.* barbecue; stretcher.

barbaridad /barβari'ðað/ *n. f.* barbarity; *Colloq.* excess (in anything).

bárbaro /'barβaro/ *a.* barbarous; crude.

barbería /barβe'ria/ *n. f.* barbershop.

barbero /bar'βero/ *n. m.* barber.

barca /'barka/ *n. f.* (small) boat.

barcaza /bar'kaθa; bar'kasa/ *n. f.* barge.

barco /'barko/ *n. m.* ship, boat.

barniz /bar'niθ; bar'nis/ *n. m.* varnish. —**barnizar,** *v.*

barómetro /ba'rometro/ *n. m.* barometer.

barón /ba'ron/ *n. m.* baron.

barquilla /bar'kiʎa; bar'kiya/ *n. f.* *Naut.* log.

barra /'barra/ *n. f.* bar.

barraca /ba'rraka/ *n. f.* hut, shed.

barrear /barre'ar/ *v.* bar, barricade.

barreno /ba'rreno/ *n. m.* blast, blasting. —**barrenar,** *v.*

barrer /ba'rrer/ *v.* sweep.

barrera /ba'rrera/ *n. f.* barrier.

barricada /barri'kaða/ *n. f.* barricade.

barriga /ba'rriga/ *n. f.* belly.

barril /ba'rril/ *n. m.* barrel; cask.

barrio /'barrio/ *n. m.* district, ward, quarter.

barro /'barro/ *n. m.* clay, mud.

base /'base/ *n. f.* base; basis. —**basar,** *v.*

base de datos /'base de 'datos/ database.

bastante /bas'tante/ *a.* **1.** enough, plenty of. —*adv.* **2.** enough; rather, quite.

bastar /bas'tar/ *v.* suffice, be enough.

bastardo /bas'tarðo/ **-a** *a. & n.* bastard.

bastear /baste'ar/ *v.* baste.

bastidor /basti'ðor/ *n. m.* wing (in theater).

bastón /bas'ton/ *n. m.* (walking) cane.

bastos /'bastos/ *n. m.pl.* clubs (cards).

basura /ba'sura/ *n. f.* refuse, dirt; garbage; junk.

basurero /basu'rero/ **-ra** *n.* scavenger.

batalla /ba'taʎa; ba'taya/ *n. f.* battle. —**batallar,** *v.*

batallón /bata'ʎon; bata'yon/ *n. m.* battalion.

batata /ba'tata/ *n. f.* sweet potato.

bate /'bate/ *n. m.* bat. —**batear,** *v.*

batería /bate'ria/ *n. f.* battery.

batido /ba'tiðo/ *n. m.* (cooking) batter; milkshake.

batidora /bati'ðora/ *n. f.* mixer (for food).

batir /ba'tir/ v. beat; demolish; conquer.

baúl /ba'ul/ n. m. trunk.

bautismo /bau'tismo/ n. m. baptism.

bautista /bau'tista/ n. m. & f. Baptist.

bautizar /bauti'θar; bauti'sar/ v. christen, baptize.

bautizo /bau'tiθo; bau'tiso/ n. m. baptism.

baya /'baia/ n. f. berry.

bayoneta /bayo'neta/ n. f. bayonet.

beato /be'ato/ a. blessed.

bebé /be'βe/ n. m. baby.

beber /be'βer/ v. drink.

bebible /be'βiβle/ a. drinkable.

bebida /be'βiδa/ n. f. drink, beverage.

beca /'beka/ n. f. grant, scholarship.

becado /be'kaδo/ **-da** n. scholar.

becerro /be'θerro; be'serro/ n. m. calf; calfskin.

beldad /bel'daδ/ n. f. beauty.

belga /'belɣa/ a. & n. Belgian.

Bélgica /'belhika/ n. f. Belgium.

belicoso /beli'koso/ a. warlike.

beligerante /belihe'rante/ a. & n. belligerent.

bellaco /be'ʎako; be'yako/ a. **1.** sly, roguish. —n. **2.** m. rogue.

bellas artes /'beʎas 'artes; 'beyas 'artes/ n. f.pl. fine arts.

belleza /be'ʎeθa; be'yesa/ n. f. beauty.

bello /'beʎo; 'beyo/ a. beautiful.

bellota /be'ʎota; be'yota/ n. f. acorn.

bendecir /bende'θir; bende'sir/ v. bless.

bendición /bendi'θion; bendi'sion/ n. f. blessing, benediction.

bendito /ben'dito/ a. blessed.

beneficio /bene'fiθio; bene'fisio/ n. m. benefit. —**beneficiar,** v.

beneficioso /benefi'θioso; benefi'sioso/ a. beneficial.

benevolencia /beneβo'lenθia; beneβo'lensia/ n. f. benevolence.

benévolo /be'neβolo/ a. benevolent.

benigno /be'nigno/ a. benign.

beodo /be'oδo/ **-da** a. & n. drunk.

berenjena /beren'hena/ n. f. eggplant.

beso /'beso/ n. m. kiss. —**besar,** v.

bestia /'bestia/ n. f. beast, brute.

betabel /beta'βel/ n. m. beet.

Biblia /'biβlia/ n. f. Bible.

bíblico /'biβliko/ a. Biblical.

biblioteca /biβlio'teka/ n. f. library.

bicarbonato /bikarβo'nato/ n. m. bicarbonate.

bicicleta /biθi'kleta; bisi'kleta/ n. f. bicycle.

bien /bien/ adv. **1.** well. —n. **2.** good; (pl.) possessions.

bienes inmuebles /'bienes i'mueβles/ n. m.pl. real estate.

bienestar /bienes'tar/ n. m. wellbeing, welfare.

bienhechor /biene'tʃor/ **-ra** n. benefactor.

bienvenida /biembe'niδa/ n. f. welcome.

bienvenido /biembe'niδo/ a. welcome.

biftec /bif'tek/ n. m. steak.

bifurcación /bifurka'θion; bifurka'sion/ n. f. fork. —**bifurcar,** v.

bigamia /bi'gamia/ n. f. bigamy.

bígamo /'bigamo/ **-a** n. bigamist.

bigotes /bi'gotes/ n. m.pl. mustache.

bikini /bi'kini/ n. m. bikini.

bilingüe /bi'liŋgue/ a. bilingual.

bilingüismo /biliŋ'guismo/ n. m. bilingualism.

bilis /'bilis/ n. f. bile.

billar /bi'ʎar; bi'yar/ n. m. billiards.

billete /bi'ʎete; bi'yete/ n. m. ticket; bank note, bill.

billete de banco /bi'ʎete de 'banko; bi'yete de 'banko/ bank note.

billón /bi'ʎon; bi'yon/ n. m. billion.

bingo /'biŋgo/ n. m. bingo.

biodegradable /bioδeɣra'δaβle/ a. biodegradable.

biografía /biogra'fia/ n. f. biography.

biología /biolo'hia/ n. f. biology.

biombo /'biombo/ n. m. folding screen.

bisabuela /bisa'βuela/ n. f. greatgrandmother.

bisabuelo /bisa'βuelo/ n. m. greatgrandfather.

bisel /bi'sel/ n. m. bevel. —**biselar,** v.

bisonte /bi'sonte/ n. m. bison.

bisté /bis'te/ **bistec** n. m. steak.

bisutería /bisute'ria/ n. f. costume jewelry.

bizarro /bi'θarro; bi'sarro/ a. brave; generous; smart.

bizco /'biθko/ **-ca** n. **1.** cross-eyed person. —a. **2.** cross-eyed, squinting.

bizcocho /biθ'kotʃo; bis'kotʃo/ n. m. biscuit, cake.

blanco /'blanko/ a. **1.** white; blank. —n. **2.** m. white; target.

blandir /blan'dir/ v. brandish, flourish.

blando /'blando/ a. soft.

blanquear /blanke'ar/ v. whiten; bleach.

blasfemar /blasfe'mar/ v. blaspheme, curse.

blasfemia /blas'femia/ n. f. blasphemy.

blindado /blin'daδo/ a. armored.

blindaje /blin'dahe/ n. m. armor.

bloque /'bloke/ n. m. block. —**bloquear,** v.

bloqueo /blo'keo/ n. m. blockade. —**bloquear,** v.

blusa /'blusa/ n. f. blouse.

bobada /bo'βaδa/ n. f. stupid, silly thing.

bobo /'boβo/ **-ba** a. & n. fool; foolish.

boca /'boka/ n. f. mouth.

bocado /bo'kaδo/ n. m. bit; bite, mouthful.

bocanada /boka'naδa/ n. f. puff (of smoke); mouthful (of liquor).

bocazas /bo'kaθas/ n. m. & f. Colloq. bigmouth.

bochorno /bo'tʃorno/ n. m. sultry weather; embarrassment.

bocina /bo'θina; bo'sina/ n. f. horn.

boda /'boδa/ n. f. wedding.

bodega /bo'δeɣa/ n. f. wine cellar; Naut. hold; (Carib.) grocery store.

bofetada /bofe'taδa/ n. f. **bofetón,** m. slap.

boga /'boɣa/ n. f. vogue; fad.

bogar /bo'ɣar/ v. row (a boat).

bohemio /bo'emio/ **-a** a. & n. Bohemian.

boicoteo /boiko'teo/ n. m. boycott. —**boicotear,** v.

boina /'boina/ n. f. beret.

bola /'bola/ n. f. ball.

bola de nieve /'bola de 'nieβe/ snowball.

bolas de billar /'bolas de bi'ʎar; 'bolas de bi'yar/ billiard balls.

bolera /bo'lera/ n. f. bowling alley.

boletín /bole'tin/ n. m. bulletin.

boletín informativo /bole'tin informa'tiβo/ news bulletin.

boleto /bo'leto/ n. m. ticket. **b. de embarque,** boarding pass.

boliche /bo'litʃe/ n. m. bowling alley.

bolígrafo /bo'liɣrafo/ n. m. ballpoint pen.

boliviano /boli'βiano/ **-a** a. & n. Bolivian.

bollo /'boʎo; 'boyo/ n. m. bun, loaf.

bolos /'bolos/ n. m.pl. bowling.

bolsa /'bolsa/ n. f. purse; stock exchange.

bolsa de agua caliente /'bolsa de 'agua ka'liente/ hot-water bottle.

bolsillo /bol'siʎo; bol'siyo/ n. m. pocket.

bomba /'bomba/ n. f. pump; bomb; gas station.

bombardear /bombarδe'ar/ v. bomb; bombard, shell.

bombear /bombe'ar/ v. pump.

bombero /bom'βero/ n. m. fireman.

bombilla /bom'βiʎa; bom'βiya/ n. f. (light) bulb.

bonanza /bo'nanθa; bo'nansa/ n. f. prosperity; fair weather.

bondad /bon'daδ/ n. f. kindness; goodness.

bondadoso /bonda'δoso/ a. kind, kindly.

bongó /boŋ'go/ n. m. bongo drum.

bonito /bo'nito/ a. pretty.

bono /'bono/ n. m. bonus; Fin. bond.

boqueada /boke'aδa/ n. f. gasp; gape. —**boquear,** v.

boquilla /bo'kiʎa; bo'kiya/ n. f. cigarette holder.

bordado /bor'δaδo/ n. m., **bordadura,** f. embroidery.

bordar /bor'δar/ v. embroider.

borde /'borδe/ n. m. border, rim, edge, brink, ledge.

borde de la carretera /'borδe de la karre'tera/ roadside.

borla /'borla/ n. f. tassel.

borracho /bo'rratʃo/ **-a** a. & n. drunk.

borrachón /borra'tʃon/ **-na** n. drunkard.

borrador /borra'δor/ n. m. eraser.

borradura /borra'δura/ n. f. erasure.

borrar /bo'rrar/ v. erase, rub out.

borrasca /bo'rraska/ n. f. squall, storm.

borrico /bo'rriko/ n. m. donkey.

bosque /'boske/ n. m. forest, wood.

bosquejo /bos'keho/ n. m. sketch, draft. —**bosquejar,** v.

bostezo /bos'teθo; bos'teso/ n. m. yawn. —**bostezar,** v.

bota /'bota/ n. f. boot.

botalón /bota'lon/ n. m. Naut. boom.

botánica /bo'tanika/ n. f. botany.

botar /bo'tar/ v. throw out, throw away.

bote /'bote/ n. m. boat; can, box.

bote salvavidas /'bote salβa'βiδas/ lifeboat.

botica /bo'tika/ n. f. pharmacy, drugstore.

boticario /boti'kario/ n. m. pharmacist, druggist.

botín /bo'tin/ n. m. booty, plunder, spoils.

boto /'boto/ a. dull, stupid.

botón /bo'ton/ n. m. button.

botones /bo'tones/ n. m. bellboy (in a hotel).

bóveda /'boβeδa/ n. f. vault.

boxeador /boksea'δor/ n. m. boxer.

boxeo /bok'seo/ n. m. boxing. —**boxear,** v.

boya /'boya/ n. f. buoy.

boyante /bo'yante/ a. buoyant.

bozal /bo'θal; bo'sal/ n. m. muzzle.

bragas /'braɣas/ n. f.pl. panties.

bramido /bra'miδo/ n. m. roar, bellow. —**bramar,** v.

brasa /'brasa/ n. f. embers, grill. —**brasear,** v.

brasileño /brasi'leɲo/ **-ña** a. & n. Brazilian.

bravata /bra'βata/ n. f. bravado.

bravear /braβe'ar/ v. bully.

braza /'braθa; 'brasa/ n. f. fathom.

brazada /bra'θaδa; bra'saδa/ n. f. (swimming) stroke.

brazalete /braθa'lete; brasa'lete/ n. m. bracelet.

brazo /'braθo; 'braso/ n. m. arm.

brea /'brea/ n. f. tar, pitch.

brecha /'bretʃa/ n. f. gap, breach.

brécol /'brekol/ n. m. broccoli.

bregar /bre'ɣar/ v. scramble.

breña /'breɲa/ n. f. rough country with brambly shrubs.

Bretaña /bre'taɲa/ n. f. Britain.

breve /'breβe/ a. brief, short. **en b.,** shortly, soon.

brevedad /breβe'δaδ/ n. f. brevity.

bribón /bri'βon/ **-na** n. rogue, rascal.

brida /'briδa/ n. f. bridle.

brigada /bri'ɣaδa/ n. f. brigade.

brillante /bri'ʎante; bri'yante/ a. **1.** brilliant, shiny. —n. **2.** m. diamond.

brillo /'briʎo; 'briyo/ n. m. shine, glitter. —**brillar,** v.

brinco /'brinko/ n. m. jump; bounce, skip. —**brincar,** v.

brindis /'brindis/ n. m. toast. —**brindar,** v.

brío /'brio/ n. m. vigor.

brioso /'brioso/ a. vigorous, spirited.

brisa /'brisa/ n. f. breeze.

brisa marina /'brisa ma'rina/ sea breeze.

británico /bri'taniko/ a. British.

brocado /bro'kaδo/ **-da** a. & n. brocade.

brocha /'brotʃa/ n. f. brush.

broche /'brotʃe/ n. m. brooch, clasp, pin.

broma /'broma/ n. f. joke. —**bromear,** v.

bronca /'bronka/ n. f. Colloq. quarrel, row, fight.

bronce /'bronθe; 'bronse/ n. m. bronze; brass.

bronceador /bronθea'δor; bronsea'δor/ n. m. suntan lotion, suntan oil.

bronquitis /bron'kitis/ n. f. bronchitis.

brotar /bro'tar/ v. gush; sprout; bud.

brote /'brote/ n. m. bud, shoot.

bruja /'bruha/ n. f. witch.

brújula /'bruhula/ n. f. compass.

bruma /'bruma/ n. f. mist.

brumoso /bru'moso/ a. misty.

brusco /'brusko/ a. brusque; abrupt, curt.

brutal /bru'tal/ a. savage, brutal.

brutalidad /brutali'δaδ/ n. f. brutality.

bruto /'bruto/ **-ta** a. **1.** brutish; ignorant. —n. **2.** blockhead.

bucear /buθe'ar; buse'ar/ v. dive.

bueno /'bueno/ a. good, fair; well (in health).

buey /buei/ n. m. ox, steer.

búfalo /'bufalo/ n. m. buffalo.

bufanda /bu'fanda/ n. f. scarf.

bufón /bu'fon/ **-ona** a. & n. fool, buffoon, clown.

búho /'buo/ n. m. owl.

buhonero /buo'nero/ n. m. peddler, vendor.

bujía /bu'hia/ n. f. spark plug.

bulevar /bule'βar/ n. m. boulevard.

bulimia /bu'limia/ n. f. bulimia.

bullicio /bu'ʎiθio; bu'yisio/ n. m. bustle, noise.

bullicioso /buʎi'θioso; buyi'sioso/ a. boisterous, noisy.

bulto /'bulto/ n. m. bundle; lump.

buñuelo /bu'ɲuelo/ n. m. bun.

buque /'buke/ n. m. ship.

buque de guerra /'buke de 'gerra/ warship.

buque de pasajeros /'buke de pasa'heros/ passenger ship.

burdo /'burδo/ a. coarse.

burgués /bur'ges/ **-esa** a. & n. bourgeois.

burla /'burla/ n. f. mockery; fun.

burlador /burla'δor/ **-ra** n. trickster, jokester.

burlar /bur'lar/ v. mock, deride.

burlarse de /bur'larse de/ v. scoff at; make fun of.

burro /'burro/ n. m. donkey.

busca /'buska/ n. f. search, pursuit, quest.

buscar /bus'kar/ v. seek, look for; look up.

busto /'busto/ n. m. bust.

butaca /bu'taka/ n. f. armchair; Theat. orchestra seat.

buzo /'buθo; 'buso/ n. m. diver.

buzón /bu'θon; bu'son/ n. m. mailbox.

C

cabal /ka'βal/ a. exact; thorough.

cabalgar /kaβal'gar/ v. ride horseback.

caballeresco /kaβaʎe'resko; kaβaye'resko/ *a.* gentlemanly, chivalrous.

caballería /kaβaʎe'ria; kaβaye'ria/ *n. f.* cavalry; chivalry.

caballeriza /kaβaʎe'riθa; kaβaye'risa/ *n. f.* stable.

caballero /kaβa'ʎero; kaβa'yero/ *n. m.* gentleman; knight.

caballete /kaβa'ʎete; kaβa'yete/ *m.* sawhorse; easel; ridge (of roof).

caballo /ka'βaʎo; ka'βayo/ *n. m.* horse.

cabaña /ka'βaɲa/ *n. f.* cabin; booth.

cabaré /kaβa're/ *n. m.* nightclub.

cabaretero /kaβare'tero/ **-a** *n. m. & f.* nightclub owner.

cabecear /kaβeθe'ar; kaβese'ar/ *v.* pitch (as a ship).

cabecera /kaβe'θera; kaβe'sera/ *n. f.* head (of bed, table).

cabello /ka'βeʎo; ka'βeyo/ *n. m.* hair.

caber /ka'βer/ *v.* fit into, be contained in. **no cabe duda**, there is no doubt.

cabeza /ka'βeθa; ka'βesa/ *n. f.* head; warhead.

cabildo /ka'βildo/ *n. m.* city hall.

cabildo abierto /ka'βildo a'βierto/ town meeting.

cabizbajo /kaβiθ'βaho; kaβis'βaho/ *a.* downcast.

cablegrama /kaβle'grama/ *n. m.* cablegram.

cabo /'kaβo/ *n. m.* end; *Geog.* cape; *Mil.* corporal. **llevar a c.**, carry out, accomplish.

cabra /'kaβra/ *n. f.* goat.

cacahuete /kaka'uete/ *n. m.* peanut.

cacao /ka'kao/ *n. m.* cocoa; chocolate.

cacerola /kaθe'rola; kase'rola/ *n. f.* pan, casserole.

cachondeo /katʃon'deo/ *n. m.* fun, hilarity.

cachondo /ka'tʃondo/ *a.* funny; *Colloq.* horny.

cachorro /ka'tʃorro/ *n. m.* cub; puppy.

cada /'kaða/ *a.* each, every.

cadáver /ka'ðaβer/ *n. m.* corpse.

cadena /ka'ðena/ *n. f.* chain.

cadera /ka'ðera/ *n. f.* hip.

cadete /ka'ðete/ *n. m.* cadet.

caer /ka'er/ *v.* fall.

café /ka'fe/ *n. m.* coffee; café.

café exprés /ka'fe eks'pres/ espresso.

café soluble /ka'fe so'luβle/ instant coffee.

cafetal /kafe'tal/ *n. m.* coffee plantation.

cafetera /kafe'tera/ *n. f.* coffee pot.

caída /ka'iða/ *n. f.* fall, drop; collapse.

caimán /kai'man/ *n. m.* alligator.

caja /'kaha/ *n. f.* box, case; checkout counter.

caja de ahorros /'kaha de a'orros/ savings bank.

caja de cerillos /'kaha de θe'riʎos; 'kaha de se'riyos/ matchbox.

caja de fósforos /'kaha de 'fosforos/ matchbox.

caja torácica /'kaha to'raθika; 'kaha to'rasika/ rib cage.

cajero /ka'hero/ **-ra** *n.* cashier.

cajón /ka'hon/ *n. m.* drawer.

cal /kal/ *n. f.* lime.

calabaza /kala'βaθa; kala'βasa/ *n. f.* calabash, pumpkin.

calabozo /kala'βoθo; kala'βoso/ *n. m.* jail, cell.

calambre /ka'lambre/ *n. m.* cramp.

calamidad /kalami'ðað/ *n. f.* calamity, disaster.

calcetín /kalθe'tin; kalse'tin/ *n. m.* sock.

calcio /'kalθio; 'kalsio/ *n. m.* calcium.

calcular /kalku'lar/ *v.* calculate, figure.

cálculo /'kalkulo/ *n. m.* calculation, estimate.

caldera /kal'dera/ *n. f.* kettle, caldron; boiler.

caldo /'kaldo/ *n. m.* broth.

calefacción /kalefak'θion; kalefak'sion/ *n. f.* heat, heating.

calendario /kalen'dario/ *n. m.* calendar.

calentar /kalen'tar/ *v.* heat, warm.

calidad /kali'ðað/ *n. f.* quality, grade.

caliente /ka'liente/ *a.* hot, warm.

calificar /kalifi'kar/ *v.* qualify.

callado /ka'ʎaðo; ka'yaðo/ *a.* silent, quiet.

callarse /ka'ʎarse; ka'yarse/ *v.* quiet down; keep still; stop talking.

calle /'kaʎe; 'kaye/ *n. f.* street.

callejón /kaʎe'hon; kaye'hon/ *n. m.* alley.

calle sin salida /'kaʎe sin sa'liða; 'kaye sin sa'liða/ dead end.

callo /'kaʎo; 'kayo/ *n. m.* callus, corn.

calma /'kalma/ *n. f.* calm, quiet.

calmado /kal'maðo/ *a.* calm.

calmante /kal'mante/ *a.* soothing, calming.

calmar /kal'mar/ *v.* calm, quiet, lull, soothe.

calor /ka'lor/ *n.* heat, warmth. **tener c.**, to be hot, warm; feel hot, warm. **hacer c.**, to be hot, warm (weather).

calorífero /kalo'rifero/ *a.* **1.** heat-producing. —*n.* **2.** *m.* radiator.

calumnia /ka'lumnia/ *n. f.* slander. —**calumniar**, *v.*

caluroso /kalu'roso/ *a.* warm, hot.

calvario /kal'βario/ *n. m.* Calvary.

calvo /'kalβo/ *a.* bald.

calzado /kal'θaðo; kal'saðo/ *n. m.* footwear.

calzar /kal'θar; kal'sar/ *v.* wear (as shoes).

calzoncillos /kalθon'θiʎos; kalson'siyos/ *n. m.pl.* shorts.

calzones /kal'θones; kal'sones/ *n. m.pl.* trousers.

cama /'kama/ *n. f.* bed.

cámara /'kamara/ *n. f.* chamber; camera.

camarada /kama'raða/ *n. m. & f.* comrade.

camarera /kama'rera/ *n. f.* chambermaid; waitress.

camarero /kama'rero/ *n. m.* steward; waiter.

camarón /kama'ron/ *n. m.* shrimp.

camarote /kama'rote/ *n. m.* stateroom, berth.

cambiar /kam'βiar/ *v.* exchange, change, trade; cash.

cambio /'kambio/ *n. m.* change, exchange. **en c.**, on the other hand.

cambista /kam'βista/ *n. m. & f.* money changer; banker, broker.

cambur /kam'βur/ *n. m.* banana.

camello /ka'meʎo; ka'meyo/ *n. m.* camel.

camilla /ka'miʎa; ka'miya/ *n. f.* stretcher.

caminar /kami'nar/ *v.* walk.

caminata /kami'nata/ *n. f.* tramp, hike.

camino /ka'mino/ *n. m.* road; way.

camión /ka'mion/ *n. m.* truck.

camisa /ka'misa/ *n. f.* shirt.

camisería /kamise'ria/ *n. f.* haberdashery.

camiseta /kami'seta/ *n. f.* undershirt; T-shirt.

campamento /kampa'mento/ *n. m.* camp.

campana /kam'pana/ *n. f.* bell.

campanario /kampa'nario/ *n. m.* bell tower, steeple.

campaneo /kampa'neo/ *n. m.* chime.

campaña /kam'paɲa/ *n. f.* campaign.

campeón /kampe'on/ **-na** *n.* champion.

campeonato /kampeo'nato/ *n. m.* championship.

campesino /kampe'sino/ **-na** *n.* peasant.

campestre /kam'pestre/ *a.* country, rural.

campo /'kampo/ *n. m.* field; (the) country.

campo de concentración /'kampo de konθentra'θion; 'kampo de konsentra'sion/ concentration camp.

campo de golf /'kampo de 'golf/ golf course.

Canadá /kana'ða/ *n. m.* Canada.

canadiense /kana'ðiense/ *a. & n.* Canadian.

canal /ka'nal/ *n. m.* canal; channel.

Canal de la Mancha /ka'nal de la 'mantʃa/ *n. m.* English Channel.

canalla /ka'naʎa; ka'naya/ *n. f.* rabble.

canario /ka'nario/ *n. m.* canary.

canasta /ka'nasta/ *n. f.* basket.

cáncer /'kanθer; 'kanser/ *n. m.* cancer.

cancha de tenis /'kantʃa de 'tenis/ *n. f.* tennis court.

canciller /kanθi'ʎer; kansi'yer/ *n. m.* chancellor.

canción /kan'θion; kan'sion/ *n. f.* song.

candado /kan'daðo/ *n. m.* padlock.

candela /kan'dela/ *n. f.* fire; light; candle.

candelero /kande'lero/ *n. m.* candlestick.

candidato /kandi'ðato/ **-ta** *n.* candidate; applicant.

candidatura /kandiða'tura/ *n. f.* candidacy.

canela /ka'nela/ *n. f.* cinnamon.

cangrejo /kaŋ'greho/ *n. m.* crab.

caníbal /ka'niβal/ *n. m.* cannibal.

caniche /ka'nitʃe/ *n. m.* poodle.

canje /'kanhe/ *n. m.* exchange, trade. —**canjear**, *v.*

cano /'kano/ *a.* gray.

canoa /ka'noa/ *n. f.* canoe.

cansado /kan'saðo/ *a.* tired, weary.

cansancio /kan'sanθio; kan'sansio/ *m.* fatigue.

cansar /kan'sar/ *v.* tire, fatigue, wear out.

cantante /kan'tante/ *n. m. & f.* singer.

cantar /kan'tar/ *n.* **1.** *m.* song. —*v.* **2.** sing.

cántaro /'kantaro/ *n. m.* pitcher.

cantera /kan'tera/ *n. f.* (stone) quarry.

cantidad /kanti'ðað/ *n. f.* quantity, amount.

cantina /kan'tina/ *n. f.* bar, tavern; restaurant.

canto /'kanto/ *n. m.* chant, song, singing; edge.

caña /'kaɲa/ *n. f.* cane, reed; sugar cane; small glass of beer.

cañón /ka'ɲon/ *n. m.* canyon; cannon; gun barrel.

caoba /ka'oβa/ *n. f.* mahogany.

caos /'kaos/ *n. m.* chaos.

caótico /ka'otiko/ *a.* chaotic.

capa /'kapa/ *n. f.* cape, cloak; coat (of paint).

capacidad /kapaθi'ðað; kapasi'ðað/ *n. f.* capacity; capability.

capacitar /kapaθi'tar; kapasi'tar/ *v.* enable.

capataz /kapa'taθ; kapa'tas/ *n. m.* foreman.

capaz /ka'paθ; ka'pas/ *a.* capable, able.

capellán /kape'ʎan; kape'yan/ *n. m.* chaplain.

caperuza /kape'ruθa; kape'rusa/ *n. f.* hood.

capilla /ka'piʎa; ka'piya/ *n. f.* chapel.

capital /kapi'tal/ *n.* **1.** *m.* capital. **2.** *f.* capital (city).

capitalista /kapita'lista/ *a. & n.* capitalist.

capitán /kapi'tan/ *n. m.* captain.

capitular /kapitu'lar/ *v.* yield.

capítulo /ka'pitulo/ *n. m.* chapter.

capota /ka'pota/ *n. f.* hood.

capricho /ka'pritʃo/ *n. m.* caprice; fancy, whim.

caprichoso /kapri'tʃoso/ *a.* capricious.

cápsula /'kapsula/ *n. f.* capsule.

capturar /kaptu'rar/ *v.* capture.

capucha /ka'putʃa/ *n. f.* hood.

capullo /ka'puʎo; ka'puyo/ *n. m.* cocoon.

cara /'kara/ *n. f.* face.

caracol /kara'kol/ *n. m.* snail.

carácter /ka'rakter/ *n. m.* character.

característica /karakte'ristika/ *n. f.* characteristic.

característico /karakte'ristiko/ *a.* characteristic.

caramba /ka'ramba/ mild exclamation.

caramelo /kara'melo/ *n. m.* caramel; candy.

carátula /ka'ratula/ *n. f.* dial.

caravana /kara'βana/ *n. f.* caravan.

carbón /kar'βon/ *n. m.* carbon; coal.

carbonizar /karβoni'θar; karβoni'sar/ *v.* char.

carburador /karβura'ðor/ *n. m.* carburetor.

carcajada /karka'haða/ *n. f.* burst of laughter.

cárcel /'karθel; 'karsel/ *n. f.* prison, jail.

carcelero /karθe'lero; karse'lero/ *n. m.* jailer.

carcinogénico /karθino'heniko; karsino'heniko/ *a.* carcinogenic.

cardenal /karðe'nal/ *n. m.* cardinal.

cardiólogo /kar'ðiologo/ **-a** *m & f.* cardiologist.

carecer /kare'θer; kare'ser/ *v.* lack.

carestía /kares'tia/ *n. f.* scarcity; famine.

carga /'karga/ *n. f.* cargo; load, burden; freight.

cargar /kar'gar/ *v.* carry; load; charge.

cargo /'kargo/ *n. m.* load, charge, office.

caricatura /karika'tura/ *n. f.* caricature; cartoon.

caricaturista /karikatu'rista/ *n. m. & f.* caricaturist; cartoonist.

caricia /ka'riθia; ka'risia/ *n. f.* caress.

caridad /kari'ðað/ *n. f.* charity.

cariño /ka'riɲo/ *n. m.* affection, fondness.

cariñoso /kari'ɲoso/ *a.* affectionate, fond.

carisma /ka'risma/ *n. m.* charisma.

caritativo /karita'tiβo/ *a.* charitable.

carmesí /karme'si/ *a. & m.* crimson.

carnaval /karna'βal/ *n. m.* carnival.

carne /'karne/ *n. f.* meat, flesh; pulp.

carne acecinada /'karne aθeθi'naða; 'karne asesi'naða/ *n.* corned beef.

carnero /kar'nero/ *n. m.* ram; mutton.

carnicería /karniθe'ria; karnise'ria/ *n. f.* meat market; massacre.

carnicero /karni'θero; karni'sero/ **-ra** *n.* butcher.

carnívoro /kar'niβoro/ *a.* carnivorous.

caro /'karo/ *a.* dear, costly, expensive.

carpa /'karpa/ *n. f.* tent.

carpeta /kar'peta/ *n. f.* folder; briefcase.

carpintero /karpin'tero/ *n. m.* carpenter.

carrera /ka'rrera/ *n. f.* race; career.

carrera de caballos /ka'rrera de ka'βaʎos; ka'rrera de ka'βayos/ horse race.

carreta /ka'rreta/ *n. f.* wagon, cart.

carrete /ka'rrete/ *n. m.* reel, spool.

carretera /karre'tera/ *n. f.* road, highway.

carril /ka'rril/ *n. m.* rail.

carrillo /ka'rriʎo; ka'rriyo/ *n. m.* cart (for baggage or shopping).

carro /'karro/ *n. m.* car, automobile; cart.

carroza /ka'rroθa; ka'rrosa/ *n. f.* chariot.

carruaje /ka'rruahe/ *n. m.* carriage.

carta /'karta/ *n. f.* letter; (*pl.*) cards.

cartel /kar'tel/ *n. m.* placard, poster; cartel.

cartelera /karte'lera/ *n. f.* billboard.

cartera /kar'tera/ *n. f.* pocketbook, handbag, wallet; portfolio.

cartero /kar'tero/ **(-ra)** *n.* mail carrier.

cartón /kar'ton/ n. m. cardboard.

cartón piedra /kar'ton 'piedra/ n. m. papier-mâché.

cartucho /kar'tutʃo/ n. m. cartridge; cassette.

casa /'kasa/ n. f. house, dwelling; home.

casaca /ka'saka/ n. f. dress coat.

casa de pisos /'kasa de 'pisos/ apartment house.

casado /ka'saðo/ a. married.

casamiento /kasa'miento/ n. m. marriage.

casar /ka'sar/ v. marry, marry off.

casarse /ka'sarse/ v. get married. **c. con**, marry.

cascabel /kaska'βel/ n. m. jingle bell.

cascada /kas'kaða/ n. f. waterfall, cascade.

cascajo /kas'kaho/ n. m. gravel.

cascanueces /kaska'nueθes; kaska-'nueses/ n. m. nutcracker.

cascar /kas'kar/ v. crack, break, burst.

cáscara /'kaskara/ n. f. shell, rind, husk.

casco /'kasko/ n. m. helmet; hull.

casera /ka'sera/ n. f. landlady; housekeeper.

caserío /kase'rio/ n. m. settlement.

casero /ka'sero/ a. **1.** homemade. —n. **2.** m. landlord, superintendent.

caseta /ka'seta/ n. f. cottage, hut.

casi /'kasi/ adv. almost, nearly.

casilla /ka'siʎa; ka'siya/ n. f. booth; ticket office; pigeonhole.

casimir /kasi'mir/ n. m. cashmere.

casino /ka'sino/ n. m. club; clubhouse.

caso /'kaso/ n. m. case. **hacer c. a**, pay attention to.

casorio /ka'sorio/ n. m. informal wedding.

caspa /'kaspa/ n. f. dandruff.

casta /'kasta/ n. f. caste.

castaña /kas'taɲa/ n. f. chestnut.

castaño /kas'taɲo/ a. **1.** brown. —n. **2.** m. chestnut tree.

castañuela /kasta'ɲuela/ n. f. castanet.

castellano /kaste'ʎano; kaste'yano/ **-na** a. & n. Castilian.

castidad /kasti'ðað/ n. f. chastity.

castigar /kasti'gar/ v. punish, castigate.

castigo /kas'tigo/ n. m. punishment.

castillo /kas'tiʎo; kas'tiyo/ n. m. castle.

castizo /kas'tiθo; kas'tiso/ a. pure, genuine; noble.

casto /'kasto/ a. chaste.

castor /kas'tor/ n. m. beaver.

casual /ka'sual/ adj. accidental, coincidental.

casualidad /kasuali'ðað/ n. f. coincidence. **por c.**, by chance.

casuca /ka'suka/ n. f. hut, shanty, hovel.

cataclismo /kata'klismo/ n. m. cataclysm.

catacumba /kata'kumba/ n. f. catacomb.

catadura /kata'ðura/ n. f. act of tasting; appearance.

catalán /kata'lan/ **-na** a. & n. Catalonian.

catálogo /ka'talogo/ n. m. catalogue. —**catalogar**, v.

catapulta /kata'pulta/ n. f. catapult.

catar /ka'tar/ v. taste; examine, try; bear in mind.

catarata /kata'rata/ n. f. cataract, waterfall.

catarro /ka'tarro/ n. m. head cold, catarrh.

catástrofe /ka'tastrofe/ n. f. catastrophe.

catecismo /kate'θismo; kate'sismo/ n. m. catechism.

cátedra /'kateðra/ n. f. professorship.

catedral /kate'ðral/ n. f. cathedral.

catedrático /kate'ðratiko/ **-ca** n. professor.

categoría /katego'ria/ n. f. category.

categórico /kate'goriko/ a. categorical.

catequismo /kate'kismo/ n. m. catechism.

catequizar /kateki'θar; kateki'sar/ v. catechize.

cátodo /'katoðo/ n. m. cathode.

catolicismo /katoli'θismo; katoli-'sismo/ n. m. Catholicism.

católico /ka'toliko/ **-ca** a. & n. Catholic.

catorce /ka'torθe; ka'torse/ a. & pron. fourteen.

catre /'katre/ n. m. cot.

cauce /'kauθe; 'kause/ n. m. riverbed; ditch.

cauchal /kau'tʃal/ n. m. rubber plantation.

caucho /'kautʃo/ n. m. rubber.

caución /kau'θion; kau'sion/ n. f. precaution; security, guarantee.

caudal /kau'ðal/ n. m. means, fortune; (pl.) holdings.

caudaloso /kauða'loso/ a. prosperous, rich.

caudillaje /kauði'ʎahe; kauði'yahe/ n. m. leadership; tyranny.

caudillo /kau'ðiʎo; kau'ðiyo/ n. m. leader, chief.

causa /'kausa/ n. f. cause. —**causar**, v.

cautela /kau'tela/ n. f. caution.

cauteloso /kaute'loso/ n. m. cautious.

cautivar /kauti'βar/ v. captivate.

cautiverio /kauti'βerio/ n. m. captivity.

cautividad /kautiβi'ðað/ n. f. captivity.

cautivo /kau'tiβo/ **-va** a. & n. captive.

cauto /'kauto/ a. cautious.

cavar /ka'βar/ v. dig.

caverna /ka'βerna/ n. f. cavern, cave.

cavernoso /kaβer'noso/ a. cavernous.

cavidad /kaβi'ðað/ n. f. cavity, hollow.

cavilar /kaβi'lar/ v. criticize, cavil.

cayado /ka'yaðo/ n. m. shepherd's staff.

cayo /'kayo/ n. m. small rocky islet, key.

caza /'kaθa; 'kasa/ n. f. hunting, pursuit, game.

cazador /kaθa'ðor; kasa'ðor/ n. m. hunter.

cazar /ka'θar; ka'sar/ v. hunt.

cazatorpedero /kaθatorpe'ðero; kasatorpe'ðero/ n. m. torpedo-boat, destroyer.

cazo /'kaθo; 'kaso/ n. m. ladle, dipper; pot.

cazuela /ka'θuela; ka'suela/ n. f. crock.

cebada /θe'βaða; se'βaða/ n. f. barley.

cebiche /θe'bitʃe/ n. m. dish of marinated raw fish.

cebo /'θeβo; 'seβo/ n. m. bait. —**cebar**, v.

cebolla /θe'βoʎa; se'βoya/ n. f. onion.

cebolleta /θeβo'ʎeta; seβo'yeta/ n. f. spring onion.

ceceo /θe'θeo; se'seo/ n. m. lisp. —**cecear**, v.

cecina /θe'θina; se'sina/ n. f. dried beef.

cedazo /θe'ðaθo; se'ðaso/ n. m. sieve, sifter.

ceder /θe'ðer; se'ðer/ v. cede; transfer; yield.

cedro /'θeðro; 'seðro/ n. m. cedar.

cédula /'θeðula; 'seðula/ n. f. decree. **c. personal**, identification card.

céfiro /'θefiro; 'sefiro/ n. m. zephyr.

cegar /θe'gar; se'gar/ v. blind.

ceguedad /θege'ðað, θe'gera; sege-'ðað, se'gera/ **ceguera** n. f. blindness.

ceja /'θeha; 'seha/ n. f. eyebrow.

cejar /θe'har; se'har/ v. go backwards; yield, retreat.

celada /θe'laða; se'laða/ n. f. trap; ambush.

celaje /θe'lahe; se'lahe/ n. m. appearance of the sky.

celar /θe'lar; se'lar/ v. watch carefully, guard.

celda /'θelda; 'selda/ n. f. cell.

celebración /θeleβra'θion; seleβra-'sion/ n. f. celebration.

celebrante /θele'βrante; sele'βrante/ n. m. officiating priest.

celebrar /θele'βrar; sele'βrar/ v. celebrate, observe.

célebre /'θeleβre; 'seleβre/ a. celebrated, noted, famous.

celebridad /θeleβri'ðað; seleβri'ðað/ n. f. fame; celebrity; pageant.

celeridad /θeleri'ðað; seleri'ðað/ n. f. speed, rapidity.

celeste /θe'leste; se'leste/ a. celestial.

celestial /θeles'tial; seles'tial/ a. heavenly.

celibato /θeli'βato; seli'βato/ n. m. celibacy.

célibe /'θeliβe; 'seliβe/ a. **1.** unmarried. —n. **2.** m. & f. unmarried person.

celista /θe'lista; se'lista/ n. m. & f. cellist.

cellisca /θe'ʎiska; se'yiska/ n. f. sleet. —**cellisquear**, v.

celo /'θelo; 'selo/ n. m. zeal; (pl.) jealousy.

celofán /θelo'fan; selo'fan/ n. m. cellophane.

celosía /θelo'sia; selo'sia/ n. f. Venetian blind.

celoso /θe'loso; se'loso/ a. jealous; zealous.

céltico /'θeltiko; 'seltiko/ a. Celtic.

célula /'θelula; 'selula/ n. f. Biol. cell.

celuloide /θelu'loiðe; selu'loiðe/ n. m. celluloid.

cementar /θemen'tar; semen'tar/ v. cement.

cementerio /θemen'terio; semen-'terio/ n. m. cemetery.

cemento /θe'mento; se'mento/ n. m. cement.

cena /'θena; 'sena/ n. f. supper.

cenagal /θena'gal; sena'gal/ n. m. swamp, marsh.

cenagoso /θena'goso; sena'goso/ a. swampy, marshy, muddy.

cenar /θe'nar; se'nar/ v. dine, eat.

cencerro /θen'θerro; sen'serro/ n. m. cowbell.

cendal /θen'dal; sen'dal/ n. m. thin, light cloth; gauze.

cenicero /θeni'θero; seni'sero/ n. m. ashtray.

ceniciento /θeni'θiento; seni'siento/ a. ashen.

cenit /'θenit; 'senit/ n. m. zenith.

ceniza /θe'niθa; se'nisa/ n. f. ash, ashes.

censo /'θenso; 'senso/ n. m. census.

censor /θen'sor; sen'sor/ n. m. censor.

censura /θen'sura; sen'sura/ n. f. reproof, censure; censorship.

censurable /θensu'raβle; sensu'raβle/ a. objectionable.

censurar /θensu'rar; sensu'rar/ v. censure, criticize.

centavo /θen'taβo; sen'taβo/ n. m. cent.

centella /θen'teʎa; sen'teya/ n. f. thunderbolt, lightning.

centellear /θenteʎe'ar; senteye'ar/ v. twinkle, sparkle.

centelleo /θente'ʎeo; sente'yeo/ n. m. sparkle.

centenar /θente'nar; sente'nar/ n. m. (a) hundred.

centenario /θente'nario; sente'nario/ n. m. centennial, centenary.

centeno /θen'teno; sen'teno/ n. m. rye.

centígrado /θen'tigraðo; sen'tigraðo/ a. centigrade.

centímetro /θen'timetro; senti'metro/ n. m. centimeter.

céntimo /'θentimo; 'sentimo/ n. m. cent.

centinela /θenti'nela; senti'nela/ n. m. sentry, guard.

central /θen'tral; sen'tral/ a. central.

centralita /θentra'lita; sentra'lita/ n. f. switchboard.

centralizar /θentrali'θar; sentrali'sar/ v. centralize.

centrar /θen'trar; sen'trar/ v. center.

céntrico /'θentriko; 'sentriko/ a. central.

centro /'θentro; 'sentro/ n. m. center.

centroamericano /θentroameri'kano; sentroameri'kano/ **-na** a. & n. Central American.

centro de mesa /'θentro de 'mesa; 'sentro de 'mesa/ centerpiece.

ceñidor /θeɲi'ðor; seɲi'ðor/ n. m. belt, sash; girdle.

ceñir /θe'ɲir; se'ɲir/ v. gird.

ceño /'θeɲo; 'seɲo/ n. m. frown.

ceñudo /θe'ɲuðo; se'ɲuðo/ a. frowning, grim.

cepa /'θepa; 'sepa/ n. f. stump.

cepillo /θe'piʎo; se'piyo/ n. m. brush; plane. —**cepillar**, v.

cera /'θera; 'sera/ n. f. wax.

cerámica /θe'ramika; se'ramika/ n. f. ceramics.

cerámico /θe'ramiko; se'ramiko/ a. ceramic.

cerca /'θerka; 'serka/ adv. **1.** near. —n. **2.** f. fence, hedge.

cercado /θer'kaðo; ser'kaðo/ n. m. enclosure; garden.

cercamiento /θerka'miento; serka-'miento/ n. m. enclosure.

cercanía /θerka'nia; serka'nia/ n. f. proximity.

cercano /θer'kano; ser'kano/ a. near, nearby.

cercar /θer'kar; ser'kar/ v. surround.

cercenar /θerθe'nar; serse'nar/ v. clip; lessen, reduce.

cerciorar /θerθio'rar; sersio'rar/ v. make sure; affirm.

cerco /'θerko; 'serko/ n. m. hoop; siege.

cerda /'θerða; 'serða/ n. f. bristle.

cerdo /'θerðo; 'serðo/ **-da** n. m. hog.

cerdoso /θer'ðoso; ser'ðoso/ a. bristly.

cereal /θere'al; sere'al/ a. & m. cereal.

cerebro /θe'reβro; se'reβro/ n. m. brain.

ceremonia /θere'monia; sere'monia/ n. f. ceremony.

ceremonial /θeremo'nial; seremo-'nial/ a. & m. ceremonial, ritual.

ceremonioso /θeremo'nioso; seremo'nioso/ a. ceremonious.

cereza /θe'reθa; se'resa/ n. f. cherry.

cerilla /θe'riʎa; se'riya/ n. f., **cerillo**, m. match.

cerner /θer'ner; ser'ner/ v. sift.

cero /'θero; 'sero/ n. m. zero.

cerrado /θe'rraðo; se'rraðo/ a. closed; cloudy; obscure; taciturn.

cerradura /θerra'ðura; serra'ðura/ n. f. lock.

cerrajero /θerra'hero; serra'hero/ n. m. locksmith.

cerrar /θe'rrar; se'rrar/ v. close, shut.

cerro /'θerro; 'serro/ n. m. hill.

cerrojo /θe'rroho; se'rroho/ n. m. latch, bolt.

certamen /θer'tamen; ser'tamen/ n. m. contest; competition.

certero /θer'tero; ser'tero/ a. accurate, exact; certain, sure.

certeza /θer'teθa; ser'tesa/ n. f. certainty.

certidumbre /θerti'ðumbre; serti-'ðumβre/ n. f. certainty.

certificado /θertifi'kaðo; serti-fi'kaðo/ n. m. certificate.

certificado de compra /θertifi'kaðo de 'kompra; sertifi'kaðo de 'kompra/ proof of purchase.

certificar /θertifi'kar; sertifi'kar/ v. certify; register (a letter).

cerúleo /θe'ruleo; se'ruleo/ *a.* cerulean, sky-blue.
cervecería /θerβeθe'ria; serβese'ria/ *n. f.* brewery; beer saloon.
cervecero /θerβe'θero; serβe'sero/ *n. m.* brewer.
cerveza /θer'βeθa; ser'βesa/ *n. f.* beer.
cesante /θe'sante; se'sante/ *a.* unemployed.
cesar /θe'sar; se'sar/ *v.* cease.
césped /'θespeð; 'sespeð/ *n. m.* sod, lawn.
cesta /'θesta; 'sesta/ *n. f.*, **cesto,** *m.* basket.
cetrino /θe'trino; se'trino/ *a.* yellow, lemon-colored.
cetro /'θetro; 'setro/ *n. m.* scepter.
chabacano /tʃaβa'kano/ *a.* vulgar.
chacal /tʃa'kal/ *n. m.* jackal.
chacó /'tʃako/ *n. m.* shako.
chacona /tʃa'kona/ *n. f.* chaconne.
chacota /tʃa'kota/ *n. f.* fun, mirth.
chacotear /tʃakote'ar/ *v.* joke.
chacra /'tʃakra/ *n. f.* small farm.
chafallar /tʃafa'ʎar; tʃafa'yar/ *v.* mend badly.
chagra /'tʃagra/ *n. m.* rustic; rural person.
chal /tʃal/ *n. m.* shawl.
chalán /tʃa'lan/ *n. m.* horse trader.
chaleco /tʃa'leko/ *n. m.* vest.
chaleco salvavidas /tʃa'leko salβa'βiðas/ life jacket.
chalet /tʃa'le; tʃa'let/ *n. m.* chalet.
challí /tʃa'ʎi; tʃa'yi/ *n. m.* challis.
chamada /tʃa'maða/ *n. f.* brushwood.
chamarillero /tʃamari'ʎero; tʃamari'yero/ *n. m.* gambler.
chamarra /tʃa'marra/ *n. f.* coarse linen jacket.
chambelán /tʃambe'lan/ *n. m.* chamberlain.
champaña /tʃam'paɲa/ *n. m.* champagne.
champú /tʃam'pu/ *n. m.* shampoo.
chamuscar /tʃamus'kar/ *v.* scorch.
chancaco /tʃan'kako/ *a.* brown.
chance /'tʃanθe/ *n. m. & f.* opportunity, break.
chancear /tʃanθe'ar; tʃanse'ar/ *v.* jest, joke.
chanciller /tʃanθi'ʎer; tʃansi'yer/ *n. m.* chancellor.
chancillería /tʃanθiʎe'ria; tʃansiye'ria/ *n. f.* chancery.
chancla /'tʃankla/ *n. f.* old shoe.
chancleta /tʃan'kleta/ *n. f.* slipper.
chanclos /'tʃanklos/ *n. m.pl.* galoshes.
chancro /'tʃankro/ *n. m.* chancre.
changador /tʃaŋga'ðor/ *n. m.* porter; handyman.
chantaje /tʃan'tahe/ *n. m.* blackmail.
chantajista /tʃanta'hista/ *n. m. & f.* blackmailer.
chantejear /tʃantehe'ar/ *v.* blackmail.
chanto /'tʃanto/ *n. m.* flagstone.
chantre /'tʃantre/ *n. m.* precentor.
chanza /'tʃanθa; 'tʃansa/ *n. f.* joke, jest. **—chancear,** *v.*
chanzoneta /tʃanθo'neta; tʃanso'neta/ *n. f.* chansonette.
chapa /'tʃapa/ *n. f.* (metal) sheet, plate; lock.
chapado en oro /tʃa'paðo en 'oro/ *a.* gold-plated.
chapado en plata /tʃa'paðo en 'plata/ *a.* silver-plated.
chaparrada /tʃapa'rraða/ *n. f.* downpour.
chaparral /tʃapa'rral/ *n. m.* chaparral.
chaparreras /tʃapa'rreras/ *n. f.pl.* chaps.
chaparrón /tʃapa'rron/ *n. m.* downpour.
chapear /tʃape'ar/ *v.* veneer.
chapeo /tʃa'peo/ *n. m.* hat.
chapero /tʃa'pero/ *n. m. Colloq.* male homosexual prostitute.
chapitel /tʃapi'tel/ *n. m.* spire, steeple; (architecture) capital.
chapodar /tʃapo'ðar/ *v.* lop.
chapón /tʃa'pon/ *n. m.* inkblot.
chapotear /tʃapote'ar/ *v.* paddle or splash in the water.
chapoteo /tʃapo'teo/ *n. m.* splash.
chapucear /tʃapuθe'ar; tʃapuse'ar/ *v.* fumble, bungle.
chapucero /tʃapu'θero; tʃapu'sero/ *a.* sloppy, bungling.
chapurrear /tʃapurre'ar/ *v.* speak (a language) brokenly.
chapuz /tʃa'puθ; tʃa'pus/ *n. m.* dive; ducking.
chapuzar /tʃapu'θar; tʃapu'sar/ *v.* dive; duck.
chaqueta /tʃa'keta/ *n. f.* jacket, coat.
chaqueta deportiva /tʃa'keta depor'tiβa/ sport jacket.
charada /tʃa'raða/ *n. f.* charade.
charamusca /tʃara'muska/ *n. f.* twisted candy stick.
charanga /tʃa'raŋga/ *n. f.* military band.
charanguero /tʃaraŋ'guero/ *n. m.* peddler.
charca /'tʃarka/ *n. f.* pool, pond.
charco /'tʃarko/ *n. m.* pool, puddle.
charla /'tʃarla/ *n. f.* chat; chatter, prattle. **—charlar,** *v.*
charladuría /tʃarlaðu'ria/ *n. f.* chatter.
charlatán /tʃarla'tan/ **-ana** *n.* charlatan.
charlatanismo /tʃarlata'nismo/ *n. m.* charlatanism.
charol /tʃa'rol/ *n. m.* varnish.
charolar /tʃaro'lar/ *v.* varnish; polish.
charquear /tʃarke'ar/ *v.* jerk (beef).
charquí /tʃar'ki/ *n. m.* jerked beef.
charrán /tʃa'rran/ *a.* roguish.
chascarillo /tʃaska'riʎo; tʃaska'riyo/ *n. m.* risqué story.
chasco /'tʃasko/ *n. m.* disappointment, blow; practical joke.
chasis /'tʃasis/ *n. m.* chassis.
chasquear /tʃaske'ar/ *v.* fool, trick; disappoint; crack (a whip).
chasquido /tʃas'kiðo/ *n. m.* crack (sound).
chata /'tʃata/ *n. f.* bedpan.
chatear /tʃate'ar/ *v.* chat (on the Internet).
chato /'tʃato/ *a.* flat-nosed, pugnosed.
chauvinismo /tʃauβi'nismo/ *n. m.* chauvinism.
chauvinista /tʃauβi'nista/ *n. & a.* chauvinist.
chelín /tʃe'lin/ *n. m.* shilling.
cheque /'tʃeke/ *n. m.* (bank) check.
chica /'tʃika/ *n. f.* girl.
chicana /tʃi'kana/ *n. f.* chicanery.
chicha /'tʃitʃa/ *n. f.* an alcoholic drink.
chícharo /'tʃitʃaro/ *n. f.* pea.
chicharra /tʃi'tʃarra/ *n. f.* cicada; talkative person.
chicharrón /tʃitʃa'rron/ *n. m.* crisp fried scrap of meat.
chichear /tʃitʃe'ar/ *v.* hiss in disapproval.
chichón /tʃi'tʃon/ *n. m.* bump, bruise, lump.
chicle /'tʃikle/ *n. m.* chewing gum.
chico /'tʃiko/ *a.* **1.** little. **—***n.* **2.** *m.* boy.
chicote /tʃi'kote/ *n. m.* cigar; cigar butt.
chicotear /tʃikote'ar/ *v.* whip, flog.
chifladura /tʃifla'ðura/ *n. f.* mania; whim; jest.
chiflar /tʃi'flar/ *v.* whistle; become insane.
chiflido /tʃi'fliðo/ *n. m.* shrill whistle.
chile /'tʃile/ *n. m.* chili.
chileno /tʃi'leno/ **-na** *a. & n.* Chilean.
chillido /tʃi'ʎiðo; tʃi'yiðo/ *n. m.* shriek, scream, screech. **—chillar,** *v.*
chillón /tʃi'ʎon; tʃi'yon/ *a.* shrill.
chimenea /tʃime'nea/ *n. f.* chimney, smokestack; fireplace.
china /'tʃina/ *n. f.* pebble; maid; Chinese woman.
chinarro /tʃi'narro/ *n. m.* large pebble, stone.
chinche /'tʃintʃe/ *n. f.* bedbug; thumbtack.
chincheta /tʃin'tʃeta/ *n. f.* thumbtack.
chinchilla /tʃin'tʃiʎa; tʃin'tʃiya/ *n. f.* chinchilla.
chinchorro /tʃin'tʃorro/ *n. m.* fishing net.
chinela /tʃi'nela/ *n. f.* slipper.
chinero /tʃi'nero/ *n. m.* china closet.
chino /'tʃino/ **-na** *a. & n.* Chinese.
chipirón /tʃipi'ron/ *n. m.* baby squid.
chiquero /tʃi'kero/ *n. m.* pen for pigs, goats, etc.
chiquito /tʃi'kito/ **-ta** *a.* **1.** small, tiny. **—***n.* **2.** *m. & f.* small child.
chiribitil /tʃiriβi'til/ *n. m.* small room, den.
chirimía /tʃiri'mia/ *n. f.* flageolet.
chiripa /tʃi'ripa/ *n. f.* stroke of good luck.
chirla /'tʃirla/ *n. f.* mussel.
chirle /'tʃirle/ *a.* insipid.
chirona /tʃi'rona/ *n. f.* prison, jail.
chirrido /tʃi'rriðo/ *n. m.* squeak, chirp. **—chirriar,** *v.*
chis /tʃis/ *interj.* hush!
chisgarabís /tʃisgara'βis/ *n.* meddler; unimportant person.
chisguete /tʃis'gete/ *n. m.* squirt, splash.
chisme /'tʃisme/ *n. m.* gossip. **—chismear,** *v.*
chismero /tʃis'mero/ **-ra** *n.* gossiper.
chismoso /tʃis'moso/ *adj.* gossiping.
chispa /'tʃispa/ *n. f.* spark.
chispeante /tʃispe'ante/ *a.* sparkling.
chispear /tʃispe'ar/ *v.* sparkle.
chisporrotear /tʃisporrote'ar/ *v.* emit sparks.
chistar /tʃis'tar/ *v.* speak.
chiste /'tʃiste/ *n. m.* joke, gag; witty saying.
chistera /tʃis'tera/ *n. f.* fish basket; top hat.
chistoso /tʃis'toso/ *a.* funny, comic, amusing.
chito /'tʃito/ *interj.* hush!
chiva /'tʃiβa/ *n. f.* female goat.
chivato /tʃi'βato/ *n. m.* kid, young goat.
chivo /'tʃiβo/ *n. m.* male goat.
chocante /tʃo'kante/ *a.* striking; shocking; unpleasant.
chocar /tʃo'kar/ *v.* collide, clash, crash; shock.
chocarrear /tʃokarre'ar/ *v.* joke, jest.
chochear /tʃotʃe'ar/ *v.* be in one's dotage.
chochera /tʃo'tʃera/ *n. f.* dotage, senility.
choclo /'tʃoklo/ *n. m.* clog; overshoe; ear of corn.
chocolate /tʃoko'late/ *n. m.* chocolate.
chocolate con leche /tʃoko'late kon 'letʃe/ milk chocolate.
chocolatería /tʃokolate'ria/ *n. f.* chocolate shop.
chofer /'tʃofer/ **chófer** *n. m.* chauffeur, driver.
chofeta /tʃo'feta/ *n. f.* chafing dish.
cholo /'tʃolo/ *n. m.* half-breed.
chopo /'tʃopo/ *n. m.* black poplar.
choque /'tʃoke/ *n. m.* collision, clash, crash; shock.
chorizo /tʃo'riθo; tʃo'riso/ *n. m.* sausage.
chorrear /tʃorre'ar/ *v.* spout; drip.
chorro /'tʃorro/ *n. m.* spout; spurt, jet. **llover a chorros,** to pour (rain).
choto /'tʃoto/ *n. m.* calf, kid.
choza /'tʃoθa; 'tʃosa/ *n. f.* hut, cabin.
chozno /'tʃoθno; 'tʃosno/ **-na** *n.* great-great-great-grandchild.
chubasco /tʃu'βasko/ *n. m.* shower, squall.
chubascoso /tʃuβas'koso/ *a.* squally.
chuchería /tʃutʃe'ria/ *n. f.* trinket, knickknack.
chucho /'tʃutʃo/ *n. m. Colloq.* mutt.
chulería /tʃule'ria/ *n. f.* pleasant manner.
chuleta /tʃu'leta/ *n. f.* chop, cutlet.
chulo /'tʃulo/ *n. m.* rascal, rogue; joker.
chupa /'tʃupa/ *n. f.* jacket.
chupada /tʃu'paða/ *n. f.* suck, sip.
chupado /tʃu'paðo/ *a.* very thin.
chupaflor /tʃupa'flor/ *n. m.* hummingbird.
chupar /tʃu'par/ *v.* suck.
churrasco /tʃu'rrasko/ *n. m.* roasted meat.
churros /'tʃuros/ *n. m.pl.* long, slender fritters.
chuscada /tʃus'kaða/ *n. f.* joke, jest.
chusco /'tʃusko/ *a.* funny, humorous.
chusma /'tʃusma/ *n. f.* mob, rabble.
chuzo /'tʃuθo; 'tʃuso/ *n. m.* pike.
CI, *abbr.* **(coeficiente intelectual)** IQ (intelligence quotient).
ciberespacio /θiβeres'paθio/ *n. m.* cyberspace.
cibernauta /θiβer'nauta/ *n. m. & f.* cybernaut.
cicatero /θika'tero; sika'tero/ *a.* stingy.
cicatriz /θika'triθ; sika'tris/ *n. f.* scar.
cicatrizar /θikatri'θar; sikatri'sar/ *v.* heal.
ciclamato /θi'klamato; si'klamato/ *n. m.* cyclamate.
ciclista /θi'klista; si'klista/ *m & f.* cyclist.
ciclo /'θiklo; 'siklo/ *n. m.* cycle.
ciclón /θi'klon; si'klon/ *n. m.* cyclone.
ciego /'θiego; 'siego/ **-ga** *a.* **1.** blind. **—***n.* **2.** blind person.
cielo /'θielo; 'sielo/ *n. m.* heaven; sky, heavens; ceiling.
ciempiés /θiem'pies; siem'pies/ *n. m.* centipede.
cien /θien; sien/ **ciento** *a. & pron.* hundred. **por c.,** per cent.
ciénaga /'θienaga; 'sienaga/ *n. f.* swamp, marsh.
ciencia /'θienθia; 'siensia/ *n. f.* science.
cieno /'θieno; 'sieno/ *n. m.* mud.
científico /θien'tifiko; sien'tifiko/ **-ca** *a.* **1.** scientific. **—***n.* **2.** scientist.
cierre /'θierre; 'sierre/ *n. m.* fastener, snap, clasp.
cierto /'θierto; 'sierto/ *a.* certain, sure, true.
ciervo /'θierβo; 'sierβo/ *n. m.* deer.
cierzo /'θierθo; 'sierso/ *n. m.* northerly wind.
cifra /'θifra; 'sifra/ *n. f.* cipher, number. **—cifrar,** *v.*
cigarra /θi'garra; si'garra/ *n. f.* locust.
cigarrera /θiga'rrera; siga'rrera/ **cigarrillera** *f.* cigarette case.
cigarrillo /θiga'rriʎo; siga'rriyo/ *n. m.* cigarette.
cigarro /θi'garro; si'garro/ *n. m.* cigar; cigarette.
cigüeña /θi'gueɲa; si'gueɲa/ *n. f.* stork.
cilíndrico /θi'lindriko; si'lindriko/ *a.* cylindrical.
cilindro /θi'lindro; si'lindro/ *n. m.* cylinder.
cima /'θima; 'sima/ *n. f.* summit, peak.
cimarrón /θima'rron; sima'rron/ *a.* **1.** wild, untamed. **—***n.* **2.** *m.* runaway slave.
címbalo /'θimbalo; 'simbalo/ *n. m.* cymbal.
cimbrar /θim'βrar, θimbre'ar; sim'βrar, simbre'ar/ *v.* shake, brandish.
cimientos /θi'mientos; si'mientos/ *n. m.pl.* foundation.
cinc /θink; sink/ *n. m.* zinc.
cincel /θin'θel; sin'sel/ *n. m.* chisel. **—cincelar,** *v.*
cincha /'θintʃa; 'sintʃa/ *n. f.* (harness) cinch. **—cinchar,** *v.*
cinco /'θinko; 'sinko/ *a. & pron.* five.
cincuenta /θin'kuenta; sin'kuenta/ *a. & pron.* fifty.

cine /'θine; 'sine/ *n. m.* movies; movie theater.
cíngulo /'θiŋgulo; 'siŋgulo/ *n. m.* cingulum.
cínico /'θiniko; 'siniko/ **-ca** *a. & n.* cynical; cynic.
cinismo /θi'nismo; si'nismo/ *n. m.* cynicism.
cinta /'θinta; 'sinta/ *n. f.* ribbon, tape; (movie) film.
cintilar /θinti'lar; sinti'lar/ *v.* glitter, sparkle.
cinto /'θinto; 'sinto/ *n. m.* belt; girdle.
cintura /θin'tura; sin'tura/ *n. f.* waist.
cinturón /θintu'ron; sintu'ron/ *n. m.* belt.
cinturón de seguridad /θintu'ron de seguri'ðað; sintu'ron de seguri'ðað/ safety belt.
ciprés /θi'pres; si'pres/ *n. m.* cypress.
circo /'θirko; 'sirko/ *n. m.* circus.
circuito /θir'kuito; sir'kuito/ *n. m.* circuit.
circulación /θirkula'θion; sirkula'sion/ *n. f.* circulation.
circular /θirku'lar; sirku'lar/ *a. & m.* **1.** circular. **—***v.* **2.** circulate.
círculo /'θirkulo; 'sirkulo/ *n. m.* circle, club.
circundante /θirkun'dante; sirkun'dante/ *a.* surrounding.
circundar /θirkun'dar; sirkun'dar/ *v.* encircle, surround.
circunferencia /θirkunfe'renθia; sirkunfe'rensia/ *n. f.* circumference.
circunlocución /θirkunloku'θion; sirkunloku'sion/ *n.* circumlocution.
circunscribir /θirkunskri'βir; sirkunskri'βir/ *v.* circumscribe.
circunspección /θirkunspek'θion; sirkunspek'sion/ *n.* decorum, propriety.
circunspecto /θirkuns'pekto; sirkuns'pekto/ *a.* circumspect.
circunstancia /θirkuns'tanθia; sirkuns'tansia/ *n. f.* circumstance.
circunstante /θirkuns'tante; sirkuns'tante/ *n. m.* bystander.
circunvecino /θirkumbe'θino; sirkumbe'sino/ *a.* neighboring, adjacent.
cirio /'θirio; 'sirio/ *n. m.* candle.
cirrosis /θi'rrosis; si'rrosis/ *n. f.* cirrhosis.
ciruela /θi'ruela; si'ruela/ *n. f.* plum; prune.
cirugía /θiru'hia; siru'hia/ *n. f.* surgery.
cirujano /θiru'hano; siru'hano/ *n. m.* surgeon.
cisne /'θisne; 'sisne/ *n. m.* swan.
cisterna /θis'terna; sis'terna/ *n. f.* cistern.
cita /'θita; 'sita/ *n. f.* citation; appointment, date.
citación /θita'θion; sita'sion/ *n. f.* citation; (legal) summons.
citar /θi'tar; si'tar/ *v.* cite, quote; summon; make an appointment with.
cítrico /'θitriko; 'sitriko/ *a.* citric.
ciudad /θiu'ðað; siu'ðað/ *n. f.* city.
ciudadanía /θiuðaða'nia; siuðaða'nia/ *n. f.* citizenship.
ciudadano /θiuða'ðano; siuða'ðano/ **-na** *n.* citizen.
ciudadela /θiuða'ðela; siuða'ðela/ *n. f.* fortress, citadel.
cívico /'θiβiko; 'siβiko/ *a.* civic.
civil /θi'βil; si'βil/ *a. & n.* civil; civilian.
civilidad /θiβili'ðað; siβili'ðað/ *n. f.* politeness, civility.
civilización /θiβiliθa'θion; siβilisa'sion/ *n. f.* civilization.
civilizador /θiβiliθa'ðor; siβilisa'ðor/ *a.* civilizing.
civilizar /θiβili'θar; siβili'sar/ *v.* civilize.
cizallas /θi'θaʎas; si'sayas/ *n. f.pl.* shears. **—cizallar,** *v.*
cizaña /θi'θaɲa; si'saɲa/ *n. f.* weed; vice.
clamar /kla'mar/ *v.* clamor.
clamor /kla'mor/ *n. m.* clamor.
clamoreo /klamo'reo/ *n. m.* persistent clamor.
clamoroso /klamo'roso/ *a.* clamorous.
clandestino /klandes'tino/ *a.* secret, clandestine.
clara /'klara/ *n. f.* white (of egg).
claraboya /klara'βoya/ *n. m.* skylight; bull's-eye.
clara de huevo /'klara de 'ueβo/ egg white.
clarear /klare'ar/ *v.* clarify; become light, dawn.
clarete /kla'rete/ *n. m.* claret.
claridad /klari'ðað/ *n. f.* clarity.
clarificar /klarifi'kar/ *v.* clarify.
clarín /kla'rin/ *n. m.* bugle, trumpet.
clarinete /klari'nete/ *n. m.* clarinet.
clarividencia /klariβi'ðenθia; klariβi'ðensia/ *n. f.* clairvoyance.
clarividente /klariβi'ðente/ *a.* clairvoyant.
claro /'klaro/ *a.* clear; bright; light (in color); of course.
clase /'klase/ *n. f.* class; classroom; kind, sort.
clase nocturna /'klase nok'turna/ evening class.
clásico /'klasiko/ *a.* classic, classical.
clasificar /klasifi'kar/ *v.* classify, rank.
claustro /'klaustro/ *n. m.* cloister.
claustrofobia /klaustro'foβia/ *n. f.* claustrophobia.
cláusula /'klausula/ *n. f.* clause.
clausura /klau'sura/ *n. f.* cloister; inner sanctum; closing.
clavado /kla'βaðo/ *a.* **1.** nailed. **—***n.* **2.** *m. & f.* dive.
clavar /kla'βar/ *v.* nail, peg, pin.
clave /'klaβe/ *n. f.* code; *Mus.* key.
clavel /kla'βel/ *n. m.* carnation.
clavetear /klaβete'ar/ *v.* nail.
clavícula /kla'βikula/ *n. f.* collarbone.
clavija /kla'βiha/ *n. f.* pin, peg.
clavo /'klaβo/ *n. m.* nail, spike; clove.
clemencia /kle'menθia; kle'mensia/ *n. f.* clemency.
clemente /kle'mente/ *a.* merciful.
clementina /klemen'tina/ *n. f.* tangerine.
clerecía /klere'θia; klere'sia/ *n. f.* clergy.
clerical /kleri'kal/ *a.* clerical.
clérigo /'klerigo/ *n. m.* clergyman.
clero /'klero/ *n. m.* clergy.
cliente /'kliente/ *n. m. & f.* customer, client.
clientela /klien'tela/ *n. f.* clientele, practice.
clima /'klima/ *n. m.* climate.
clímax /'klimaks/ *n. m.* climax.
clínca de reposo /'klinka de rre'poso/ convalescent home.
clínica /'klinika/ *n. f.* clinic.
clínico /'kliniko/ *a.* clinical.
clíper /'kliper/ *n. m.* clipper ship.
cloaca /klo'aka/ *n. f.* sewer.
cloquear /kloke'ar/ *v.* cluck, cackle.
cloqueo /klo'keo/ *n. m.* cluck.
cloro /'kloro/ *n. m.* chlorine.
cloroformo /kloro'formo/ *n. m.* chloroform.
club /kluβ/ *n. m.* club, association.
club juvenil /kluβ huβe'nil/ youth club.
clueca /'klueka/ *n. f.* brooding hen.
coacción /koak'θion; koak'sion/ *n.* compulsion.
coagular /koagu'lar/ *v.* coagulate, clot.
coágulo /ko'agulo/ *n. m.* clot.
coalición /koali'θion; koali'sion/ *n. f.* coalition.
coartada /koar'taða/ *n. f.* alibi.
coartar /koar'tar/ *v.* limit.
cobarde /ko'βarðe/ *a. & n.* cowardly; coward.
cobardía /koβar'ðia/ *n. f.* cowardice.
cobayo /ko'βayo/ *n. m.* guinea pig.
cobertizo /koβer'tiθo; koβer'tiso/ *n. m.* shed.
cobertor /koβer'tor/ *n. m.*, **cobija,** *f.* blanket.
cobertura /koβer'tura/ *n. f.* cover, wrapping.
cobijar /koβi'har/ *v.* cover; protect.
cobrador /koβra'ðor/ *n. m.* collector.
cobranza /ko'βranθa; ko'βransa/ *n. f.* collection or recovery of money.
cobrar /ko'βrar/ *v.* collect; charge; cash.
cobre /'koβre/ *n. m.* copper.
cobrizo /ko'βriθo; ko'βriso/ *a.* coppery.
cobro /'koβro/ *n. m.* collection or recovery of money.
coca /'koka/ *n. f.* coca leaves.
cocaína /koka'ina/ *n. f.* cocaine.
cocal /ko'kal/ *n. m.* coconut plantation.
cocear /koθe'ar; kose'ar/ *v.* kick; resist.
cocer /ko'θer; ko'ser/ *v.* cook, boil, bake.
coche /'kotʃe/ *n. m.* coach; car, automobile.
cochecito de niño /kotʃe'θito de 'niɲo; kotʃe'sito de 'niɲo/ baby carriage.
coche de choque /'kotʃe de 'tʃoke/ dodgem.
cochera /ko'tʃera/ *n. f.* garage.
cochero /ko'tʃero/ *n. m.* coachman; cab driver.
cochinada /kotʃi'naða/ *n. f.* filth; herd of swine.
cochino /ko'tʃino/ *n. m.* pig, swine.
cocido /ko'θiðo; ko'siðo/ *n. m.* stew.
cociente /ko'θiente; ko'siente/ *n. m.* quotient.
cocimiento /koθi'miento; kosi'miento/ *n. m.* cooking.
cocina /ko'θina; ko'sina/ *n. f.* kitchen.
cocinar /koθi'nar; kosi'nar/ *v.* cook.
cocinero /koθi'nero; kosi'nero/ **-ra** *n.* cook.
coco /'koko/ *n. m.* coconut; coconut tree.
cocodrilo /koko'ðrilo/ *n. m.* crocodile.
cóctel /kok'tel/ *n. m.* cocktail.
codazo /ko'ðaθo; ko'ðaso/ *n. m.* nudge with the elbow.
codicia /ko'ðiθia; ko'ðisia/ *n. f.* avarice, greed; lust.
codiciar /koðiθi'ar; koðisi'ar/ *v.* covet.
codicioso /koðiθi'oso; koðisi'oso/ *a.* covetous; greedy.
código /'koðigo/ *n. m.* (law) code.
codo /'koðo/ *n. m.* elbow.
codorniz /koðor'niθ; koðor'nis/ *n. f.* quail.
coeficiente /koefi'θiente; koefi'siente/ *n. m.* quotient.
coeficiente intelectual /koefi'θiente intelek'tual; koefi'siente intelek'tual/ intelligence quotient.
coetáneo /koe'taneo/ *a.* contemporary.
coexistir /koeksis'tir/ *v.* coexist.
cofrade /ko'fraðe/ *n. m.* fellow member of a club, etc.
cofre /'kofre/ *n. m.* coffer; chest; trunk.
coger /ko'her/ *v.* catch; pick; take.
cogote /ko'gote/ *n. m.* nape.
cohecho /ko'etʃo/ *n. m.* bribe. **—cohechar,** *v.*
coheredero /koere'ðero/ **-ra** *n.* coheir.
coherente /koe'rente/ *a.* coherent.
cohesión /koe'sion/ *n. f.* cohesion.
cohete /ko'ete/ *n. m.* firecracker; rocket.
cohibición /koiβi'θion; koiβi'sion/ *n.* restraint; repression.
cohibir /koi'βir/ *v.* restrain; repress.
coincidencia /koinθi'ðenθia; koinsi'ðensia/ *n. f.* coincidence.
coincidir /koinθi'ðir; koinsi'ðir/ *v.* coincide.
cojear /kohe'ar/ *v.* limp.
cojera /ko'hera/ *n. m.* limp.
cojín /ko'hin/ *n. m.* cushion.
cojinete /kohi'nete/ *n. m.* small cushion, pad.
cojo /'koho/ **-a** *a.* **1.** lame. **—***n.* **2.** lame person.
col /kol/ *n. f.* cabbage.
cola /'kola/ *n. f.* tail; glue; line, queue. **hacer c.,** stand in line.
colaboración /kolaβora'θion; kolaβora'sion/ *n. f.* collaboration.
colaborar /kolaβo'rar/ *v.* collaborate.
cola de caballo /'kola de ka'βaʎo; 'kola de ka'βayo/ ponytail.
coladera /kola'ðera/ *n. f.* strainer.
colador /kola'ðor/ *n. m.* colander, strainer.
colapso /ko'lapso/ *n. m.* collapse, prostration.
colar /ko'lar/ *v.* strain; drain.
colateral /kolate'ral/ *a.* collateral.
colcha /'koltʃa/ *n. f.* bedspread, quilt.
colchón /kol'tʃon/ *n. m.* mattress.
colear /kole'ar/ *v.* wag the tail.
colección /kolek'θion; kolek'sion/ *n. f.* collection, set.
coleccionar /kolekθio'nar; koleksio'nar/ *v.* collect.
colecta /ko'lekta/ *n. f.* collection; collect (a prayer).
colectivo /kolek'tiβo/ *a.* collective.
colector /kolek'tor/ *n. m.* collector.
colega /ko'lega/ *n. m. & f.* colleague.
colegial /kole'hial/ *n. m.* college student.
colegiatura /kolehia'tura/ *n. f.* scholarship; tuition.
colegio /ko'lehio/ *n. m.* (private) school, college.
colegir /kole'hir/ *v.* infer, deduce.
cólera /'kolera/ *n.* **1.** *f.* rage, wrath. **2.** *m.* cholera.
colérico /ko'leriko/ *adj.* angry, irritated.
colesterol /koleste'rol/ *n. m.* cholesterol.
coleta /ko'leta/ *n. f.* pigtail; postscript.
coleto /ko'leto/ *n. m.* leather jacket.
colgado /kol'gaðo/ **-da** *n.* **1.** crazy person. **—***a.* **2.** hanging, pending.
colgador /kolga'ðor/ *n. m.* rack, hanger.
colgaduras /kolga'ðuras/ *n. f.pl.* drapery.
colgante /kol'gante/ *a.* hanging.
colgar /kol'gar/ *v.* hang up, suspend.
colibrí /koli'βri/ *n. m.* hummingbird.
coliflor /koli'flor/ *n. f.* cauliflower.
coligarse /koli'garse/ *v.* band together, unite.
colilla /ko'liʎa; ko'liya/ *n. f.* butt of a cigar or cigarette.
colina /ko'lina/ *n. f.* hill, hillock.
colinabo /koli'naβo/ *n. m.* turnip.
colindante /kolin'dante/ *a.* neighboring, adjacent.
colindar /kolin'dar/ *v.* neighbor, abut.
coliseo /koli'seo/ *n. m.* theater; coliseum.
colisión /koli'sion/ *n. f.* collision.
collado /ko'ʎaðo; ko'yaðo/ *n. m.* hillock.
collar /ko'ʎar; ko'yar/ *n. m.* necklace; collar.
colmar /kol'mar/ *v.* heap up, fill liberally.
colmena /kol'mena/ *n. f.* hive.
colmillo /kol'miʎo; kol'miyo/ *n. m.* eyetooth; tusk; fang.
colmo /'kolmo/ *n. m.* height, peak, extreme.
colocación /koloka'θion; koloka'sion/ *n. f.* place, position; employment, job; arrangement.
colocar /kolo'kar/ *v.* place, locate, put, set.
colombiano /kolom'biano/ **-na** *a. & n.* Colombian.
colon /'kolon/ *n. m.* colon (of intestines).
colonia /ko'lonia/ *n.* **1.** *f.* colony; eau de Cologne.
Colonia *n.* **2.** *f.* Cologne.
colonial /kolo'nial/ *a.* colonial.
colonización /koloniθa'θion; kolonisa'sion/ *n. f.* colonization.

colonizador /koloniθa'ðor; koloni-sa'ðor/ **-ra** n. colonizer.

colonizar /koloni'θar; koloni'sar/ v. colonize.

colono /ko'lono/ n. m. colonist; tenant farmer.

coloquio /ko'lokio/ n. m. conversation, talk.

color /ko'lor/ n. m. color. —**colorar,** v.

coloración /kolora'θion; kolora'sion/ n. f. coloring.

colorado /kolo'raðo/ a. red, ruddy.

colorar /kolo'rar/ v. color, paint; dye.

colorete /kolo'rete/ n. m. rouge.

colorido /kolo'riðo/ n. m. color, coloring. —**colorir,** v.

colosal /kolo'sal/ a. colossal.

columbrar /kolum'brar/ v. discern.

columna /ko'lumna/ n. f. column, pillar, shaft.

columpiar /kolum'piar/ v. swing.

columpio /ko'lumpio/ n. m. swing.

coma /'koma/ n. f. coma; comma.

comadre /ko'maðre/ n. f. midwife; gossip; close friend.

comadreja /koma'ðreha/ n. f. weasel.

comadrona /koma'ðrona/ n. f. midwife.

comandancia /koman'danθia; koman'dansia/ n. m. command; command post.

comandante /koman'dante/ n. m. commandant; commander; major.

comandar /koman'dar/ v. command.

comandita /koman'dita/ n. f. silent partnership.

comanditario /komandi'tario/ **-ra** n. silent partner.

comando /ko'mando/ n. m. command.

comarca /ko'marka/ n. f. region; border, boundary.

comba /'komba/ n. f. bulge.

combar /kom'bar/ v. bend; bulge.

combate /kom'bate/ n. m. combat. —**combatir,** v.

combatiente /komba'tiente/ a. & n. combatant.

combinación /kombina'θion; kombina'sion/ n. f. combination; slip (garment).

combinar /kombi'nar/ v. combine.

combustible /kombus'tiβle/ a. **1.** combustible. —n. **2.** m. fuel.

combustión /kombus'tion/ n. f. combustion.

comedero /kome'ðero/ n. m. trough.

comedia /ko'meðia/ n. f. comedy; play.

comediante /kome'ðiante/ n. m. actor; comedian.

comedido /kome'ðiðo/ a. polite, courteous; obliging.

comedirse /kome'ðirse/ v. to be polite or obliging.

comedor /kome'ðor/ n. m. dining room. **coche c.,** dining car.

comendador /komenda'ðor/ n. m. commander.

comensal /komen'sal/ n. m. table companion.

comentador /komenta'ðor/ **-ra** n. commentator.

comentario /komen'tario/ n. m. commentary.

comento /ko'mento/ n. m. comment. —**comentar,** v.

comenzar /komen'θar; komen'sar/ v. begin, start, commence.

comer /ko'mer/ v. eat, dine.

comercial /komer'θial; komer'sial/ a. commercial.

comercializar /komerθiali'θar; komersiali'sar/ v. market.

comerciante /komer'θiante; komer'siante/ **-ta** n. merchant, trader, businessperson.

comerciar /komer'θiar; komer'siar/ v. trade, deal, do business.

comercio /ko'merθio; ko'mersio/ n. m. commerce, trade, business; store.

comestible /komes'tiβle/ a. **1.** edible. —n. **2.** m. (pl.) groceries, provisions.

cometa /ko'meta/ n. **1.** m. comet. **2.** f. kite.

cometer /kome'ter/ v. commit.

cometido /kome'tiðo/ n. m. commission; duty; task.

comezón /kome'θon; kome'son/ n. f. itch.

comicios /ko'miθios; ko'misios/ n. m.pl. primary elections.

cómico /'komiko/ **-ca** a. & n. comic, comical; comedian.

comida /ko'miða/ n. f. food; dinner; meal.

comidilla /komi'ðiʎa; komi'ðiya/ n. f. light meal; gossip.

comienzo /ko'mienθo; ko'mienso/ n. m. beginning.

comilitona /komili'tona/ n. f. spread, feast.

comillas /ko'miʎas; ko'miyas/ n. f.pl. quotation marks.

comilón /komi'lon/ **-na** n. glutton; heavy eater.

comisario /komi'sario/ n. m. commissary.

comisión /komi'sion/ n. f. commission. —**comisionar,** v.

comisionado /komisio'naðo/ **-da** n. agent, commissioner.

comisionar /komisio'nar/ v. commission.

comiso /ko'miso/ n. m. (law) confiscation of illegal goods.

comistrajo /komis'traho/ n. m. mess, hodgepodge.

comité /komi'te/ n. m. committee.

comitiva /komi'tiβa/ n. f. retinue.

como /'komo/ conj. & adv. like, as.

cómo adv. how.

cómoda /'komoða/ n. f. bureau, chest (of drawers).

cómodamente /komoða'mente/ adv. conveniently.

comodidad /komoði'ðað/ n. f. convenience, comfort; commodity.

comodín /komo'ðin/ n. m. joker (playing card).

cómodo /'komoðo/ a. comfortable; convenient.

comodoro /komo'ðoro/ n. m. commodore.

compacto /kom'pakto/ a. compact.

compadecer /kompaðe'θer; kompaðe'ser/ v. be sorry for, pity.

compadraje /kompa'ðrahe/ n. m. clique.

compadre /kom'paðre/ n. m. close friend.

compaginar /kompahi'nar/ v. put in order; arrange.

compañerismo /kompaɲe'rismo/ n. m. companionship.

compañero /kompa'ɲero/ **-ra** n. companion, partner.

compañía /kompa'ɲia/ n. f. company.

comparable /kompa'raβle/ a. comparable.

comparación /kompara'θion; kompara'sion/ n. f. comparison.

comparar /kompa'rar/ v. compare.

comparativamente /komparatiβa'mente/ adv. comparatively.

comparativo /kompara'tiβo/ a. comparative.

comparecer /kompare'θer; kompare'ser/ v. appear.

comparendo /kompa'rendo/ n. m. summons.

comparsa /kom'parsa/ n. f. carnival masquerade; retinue.

compartimiento /komparti'miento/ n. m. compartment.

compartir /kompar'tir/ v. share.

compás /kom'pas/ n. m. compass; beat, rhythm.

compasar /kompa'sar/ v. measure exactly.

compasión /kompa'sion/ n. f. compassion.

compasivo /kompa'siβo/ a. compassionate.

compatibilidad /kompatiβili'ðað/ n. f. compatibility.

compatible /kompa'tiβle/ a. compatible.

compatriota /kompa'triota/ n. m. & f. compatriot.

compeler /kompe'ler/ v. compel.

compendiar /kompen'diar/ v. summarize; abridge.

compendiariamente /kompendiaria'mente/ adv. briefly.

compendio /kom'pendio/ n. m. summary; abridgment.

compendiosamente /kompendiosa'mente/ adv. briefly.

compensación /kompensa'θion; kompensa'sion/ n. f. compensation.

compensar /kompen'sar/ v. compensate.

competencia /kompe'tenθia; kompe'tensia/ n. f. competence; competition.

competente /kompe'tente/ a. competent.

competentemente /kompetente'mente/ adv. competently.

competición /kompeti'θion; kompeti'sion/ n. f. competition.

competidor /kompeti'ðor/ **-ra** a. & n. competitive; competitor.

competir /kompe'tir/ v. compete.

compilación /kompila'θion; kompila'sion/ n. f. compilation.

compilar /kompi'lar/ v. compile.

compinche /kom'pintʃe/ n. m. pal.

complacencia /kompla'θenθia; kompla'sensia/ n. f. complacency.

complacer /kompla'θer; kompla'ser/ v. please, oblige, humor.

complaciente /kompla'θiente; kompla'siente/ a. pleasing, obliging.

complejidad /komplehi'ðað/ n. f. complexity.

complejo /kom'pleho/ **-ja** a. & n. complex.

complemento /komple'mento/ n. m. complement; Gram. object.

completamente /kompleta'mente/ adv. completely.

completamiento /kompleta'miento/ n. m. completion, finish.

completar /komple'tar/ v. complete.

completo /kom'pleto/ a. complete, full, perfect.

complexión /komplek'sion/ n. f. nature, temperament.

complicación /komplika'θion; komplika'sion/ n. f. complication.

complicado /kompli'kaðo/ a. complicated.

complicar /kompli'kar/ v. complicate.

cómplice /'kompliθe; 'komplise/ n. m. & f. accomplice, accessory.

complicidad /kompliθi'ðað; komplisi'ðað/ n. f. complicity.

complot /kom'plot/ n. m. conspiracy.

componedor /kompone'ðor/ **-ra** n. typesetter.

componenda /kompo'nenda/ n. f. compromise; settlement.

componente /kompo'nente/ a. & m. component.

componer /kompo'ner/ v. compose; fix, repair.

componible /kompo'niβle/ a. reparable.

comportable /kompor'taβle/ a. endurable.

comportamiento /komporta'miento/ n. m. behavior.

comportarse /kompor'tarse/ v. behave.

comporte /kom'porte/ n. m. behavior.

composición /komposi'θion; komposi'sion/ n. f. composition.

compositivo /komposi'tiβo/ a. synthetic; composite.

compositor /komposi'tor/ **-ra** n. composer.

compost /kom'post/ n. m. compost.

compostura /kompos'tura/ n. f. composure; repair; neatness.

compota /kom'pota/ n. f. (fruit) sauce.

compra /'kompra/ n. f. purchase. **ir de compras,** to go shopping.

comprador /kompra'ðor/ **-ra** n. buyer, purchaser.

comprar /kom'prar/ v. buy, purchase.

comprender /kompren'der/ v. comprehend, understand; include, comprise.

comprensibilidad /komprensiβili'ðað/ n. f. comprehensibility.

comprensible /kompren'siβle/ a. understandable.

comprensión /kompren'sion/ n. f. comprehension, understanding.

comprensivo /kompren'siβo/ a. comprehensive.

compresa /kom'presa/ n. f. medical compress.

compresión /kompre'sion/ n. f. compression.

comprimir /kompri'mir/ v. compress; restrain, control.

comprobación /komproβa'θion; komproβa'sion/ n. f. proof.

comprobante /kompro'βante/ a. **1.** proving. —n. **2.** m. proof.

comprobar /kompro'βar/ v. prove; verify, check.

comprometer /komprome'ter/ v. compromise.

comprometerse /komprome'terse/ v. become engaged.

compromiso /kompro'miso/ n. m. compromise; engagement.

compuerta /kom'puerta/ n. f. floodgate.

compuesto /kom'puesto/ n. m. composition; compound.

compulsión /kompul'sion/ n. f. compulsion.

compulsivo /kompul'siβo/ a. compulsive.

compunción /kompun'θion; kompun'sion/ n. f. compunction.

compungirse /kompuɲ'girse/ v. regret, feel remorse.

computación /komputa'θion; komputa'sion/ n. f. computation.

computador /komputa'ðor/ n. m. computer.

computadora de sobremesa /komputa'ðora de soβre'mesa/ n. f. desktop computer.

computadora doméstica /komputa'ðora do'mestika/ n. f. home computer.

computar /kompu'tar/ v. compute.

cómputo /'komputo/ n. m. computation.

comulgar /komul'gar/ v. take communion.

comulgatorio /komulga'torio/ n. m. communion altar.

común /ko'mun/ a. common, usual.

comunal /komu'nal/ a. communal.

comunero /komu'nero/ n. m. commoner.

comunicable /komuni'kaβle/ a. communicable.

comunicación /komunika'θion; komunika'sion/ n. f. communication.

comunicante /komuni'kante/ n. m. & f. communicant.

comunicar /komuni'kar/ v. communicate; convey.

comunicativo /komunika'tiβo/ a. communicative.

comunidad /komuni'ðað/ n. f. community.

comunión /komu'nion/ n. f. communion.

comunismo /komu'nismo/ n. m. communism.

comunista /komu'nista/ a. & n. communistic; communist.

comúnmente /komu'mente/ adv. commonly; usually; often.

con /kon/ prep. with.

concavidad /konkaβi'ðað/ n. f. concavity.

cóncavo /'konkaβo/ a. **1.** concave. —n. **2.** m. concavity.

concebible /konθe'βiβle; konse'βiβle/ *a.* conceivable.

concebir /konθe'βir; konse'βir/ *v.* conceive.

conceder /konθe'ðer; konse'ðer/ *v.* concede.

concejal /konθe'hal; konse'hal/ *n. m.* councilman.

concejo /kon'θeho; kon'seho/ *n. m.* city council.

concento /kon'θento; kon'sento/ *n. m.* harmony (of singing voices).

concentración /konθentra'θion; konsentra'sion/ *n. f.* concentration.

concentrar /konθen'trar; konsen'trar/ *v.* concentrate.

concepción /konθep'θion; konsep'sion/ *n. f.* conception.

conceptible /konθep'tiβle; konsep'tiβle/ *a.* conceivable.

concepto /kon'θepto; kon'septo/ *n. m.* concept; opinion.

concerniente /konθer'niente; konser'niente/ *a.* concerning.

concernir /konθer'nir; konser'nir/ *v.* concern.

concertar /konθer'tar; konser'tar/ *v.* arrange.

concertina /konθer'tina; konser'tina/ *n. f.* concertina.

concesión /konθe'sion; konse'sion/ *n. f.* concession.

concha /'kontʃa/ *n. f. S.A.* shell.

conciencia /konθien'θia; konsiensia/ *n. f.* conscience; consciousness; conscientiousness.

concienzudo /konθien'θuðo; konsien'suðo/ *a.* conscientious.

concierto /kon'θierto; kon'sierto/ *n. m.* concert.

conciliación /konθilia'θion; konsilia'sion/ *n. f.* conciliation.

conciliador /konθilia'ðor; konsilia'ðor/ *-ra n.* conciliator.

conciliar /konθi'liar; konsi'liar/ *v.* conciliate.

concilio /kon'θilio; kon'silio/ *n. m.* council.

concisión /konθi'sion; konsi'sion/ *n. f.* conciseness.

conciso /kon'θiso; kon'siso/ *a.* concise.

concitar /konθi'tar; konsi'tar/ *v.* instigate, stir up.

conciudadano /konθiuða'ðano; konsiuða'ðano/ *-na n.* fellow citizen.

concluir /kon'kluir/ *v.* conclude.

conclusión /konklu'sion/ *n. f.* conclusion.

conclusivo /konklu'siβo/ *a.* conclusive.

concluso /kon'kluso/ *a.* concluded; closed.

concluyentemente /konkluyente'mente/ *adv.* conclusively.

concomitante /konkomi'tante/ *a.* concomitant, attendant.

concordador /konkorða'ðor/ *-ra n.* moderator; conciliator.

concordancia /konkor'ðanθia; konkor'ðansia/ *n. f.* agreement, concord.

concordar /konkor'ðar/ *v.* agree; put or be in accord.

concordia /kon'korðia/ *n. f.* concord, agreement.

concretamente /konkreta'mente/ *adv.* concretely.

concretar /konkre'tar/ *v.* summarize; make concrete.

concretarse /konkre'tarse/ *v.* limit oneself to.

concreto /kon'kreto/ *a. & m.* concrete.

concubina /konku'βina/ *n. f.* concubine, mistress.

concupiscente /konkupis'θente; konkupis'sente/ *a.* lustful.

concurrencia /konku'rrenθia; konku'rrensia/ *n. f.* assembly; attendance; competition.

concurrente /konku'rrente/ *a.* concurrent.

concurrido /konku'rriðo/ *a.* heavily attended or patronized.

concurrir /konku'rrir/ *v.* concur; attend.

concurso /kon'kurso/ *n. m.* contest, competition; meeting.

conde /'konde/ *n. m.* (title) count.

condecente /konde'θente; konde'sente/ *a.* appropriate, proper.

condecoración /kondekora'θion; kondekora'sion/ *n. f.* decoration; medal; badge.

condecorar /kondeko'rar/ *v.* decorate with a medal.

condena /kon'dena/ *n. f.* prison sentence.

condenación /kondena'θion; kondena'sion/ *n. f.* condemnation.

condenar /konde'nar/ *v.* condemn; damn; sentence.

condensación /kondensa'θion; kondensa'sion/ *n. f.* condensation.

condensar /konden'sar/ *v.* condense.

condesa /kon'desa/ *n. f.* countess.

condescendencia /kondesθen'denθia; kondessen'densia/ *n. f.* condescension.

condescender /kondesθen'der; kondessen'der/ *v.* condescend, deign.

condescendiente /kondesθen'diente; kondessen'diente/ *a.* condescending.

condición /kondi'θion; kondi'sion/ *n. f.* condition.

condicional /kondiθio'nal; kondisio'nal/ *a.* conditional.

condicionalmente /kondiθional'mente; kondisional'mente/ *adv.* conditionally.

condimentar /kondimen'tar/ *v.* season, flavor.

condimento /kondi'mento/ *n. m.* condiment, seasoning, dressing.

condiscípulo /kondis'θipulo; kondis'sipulo/ *-la n.* schoolmate.

condolencia /kondo'lenθia; kondo'lensia/ *n. f.* condolence, sympathy.

condolerse de /kondo'lerse de/ *v.* sympathize with.

condominio /kondo'minio/ *n. m.* condominium.

condómino /kon'domino/ *n. m.* co-owner.

condonar /kondo'nar/ *v.* condone.

cóndor /'kondor/ *n. m.* condor (bird).

conducción /konduk'θion; konduk'sion/ *n. f.* conveyance.

conducente /kondu'θente; kondu'sente/ *a.* conducive.

conducir /kondu'θir; kondu'sir/ *v.* conduct, escort, lead; drive.

conducta /kon'dukta/ *n. f.* conduct, behavior.

conducto /kon'dukto/ *n. m.* pipe, conduit; sewer.

conductor /konduk'tor/ *-ra n.* driver; conductor.

conectar /konek'tar/ *v.* connect.

conejera /kone'hera/ *n. f.* rabbit warren; place of ill repute.

conejillo de Indias /kone'hiʎo de 'indias; kone'hiyo de 'indias/ guinea pig.

conejo /ko'neho/ *-ja n.* rabbit.

conexión /konek'sion/ *n. f.* connection; coupling.

conexivo /konek'siβo/ *a.* connective.

conexo /ko'nekso/ *a.* connected, united.

confalón /konfa'lon/ *n. m.* ensign, standard.

confección /konfek'θion; konfek'sion/ *n. f.* workmanship; ready-made article; concoction.

confeccionar /konfekθio'nar; konfeksio'nar/ *v.* concoct.

confederación /konfeðera'θion; konfeðera'sion/ *n. f.* confederation.

confederado /konfeðe'raðo/ *-da n. & m.* confederate.

confederar /konfeðe'rar/ *v.* confederate, unite, ally.

conferencia /konfe'renθia; konfe'rensia/ *n. f.* lecture; conference. **c. interurbana,** long-distance call.

conferenciante /konferen'θiante;

konferen'siante/ *n. m. & f.* lecturer, speaker.

conferenciar /konferen'θiar; konferen'siar/ *v.* confer.

conferencista /konferen'θista; konferen'sista/ *n. m. & f.* lecturer, speaker.

conferir /konfe'rir/ *v.* confer.

confesar /konfe'sar/ *v.* confess.

confesión /konfe'sion/ *n. f.* confession.

confesionario /konfesio'nario; konfeso'nario/ *n. m.* confessional.

confesor /konfe'sor/ *-ra n.* confessor.

confeti /kon'feti/ *n. m. pl.* confetti.

confiable /kon'fiaβle/ *a.* dependable.

confiado /kon'fiaðo/ *a.* confident; trusting.

confianza /kon'fianθa; kon'fiansa/ *n. f.* confidence, trust, faith.

confiar /kon'fiar/ *v.* entrust; trust, rely.

confidencia /konfi'ðenθia; konfi'ðensia/ *n. f.* confidence, secret.

confidencial /konfiðen'θial; konfiðen'sial/ *a.* confidential.

confidente /konfi'ðente/ *n. m. & f.* confidant.

confidentemente /konfiðente'mente/ *adv.* confidently.

confín /kon'fin/ *n. m.* confine.

confinamiento /konfina'miento/ *n. m.* confinement.

confinar /konfi'nar/ *v.* confine, imprison; border on.

confirmación /konfirma'θion; konfirma'sion/ *n. f.* confirmation.

confirmar /konfir'mar/ *v.* confirm.

confiscación /konfiska'θion; konfiska'sion/ *n. f.* confiscation.

confiscar /konfis'kar/ *v.* confiscate.

confitar /konfi'tar/ *v.* sweeten; make into candy or jam.

confite /kon'fite/ *n. m.* candy.

confitería /konfite'ria/ *n. f.* confectionery; candy store.

confitura /konfi'tura/ *n. f.* confection.

conflagración /konflagra'θion; konflagra'sion/ *n. f.* conflagration.

conflicto /kon'flikto/ *n. m.* conflict.

confluencia /kon'fluenθia; kon'fluensia/ *n. f.* confluence, junction.

confluir /kon'fluir/ *v.* flow into each other.

conformación /konforma'θion; konforma'sion/ *n. f.* conformation.

conformar /konfor'mar/ *v.* conform.

conforme /kon'forme/ *a.* **1.** acceptable, right, as agreed; in accordance, in agreement. —*conj.* **2.** according, as.

conformidad /konformi'ðað/ *n. f.* conformity; agreement.

conformismo /konfor'mismo/ *n. m.* conformism.

conformista /konfor'mista/ *n. m. & f.* conformist.

confortar /konfor'tar/ *v.* comfort.

confraternidad /konfraterni'ðað/ *n. f.* brotherhood, fraternity.

confricar /konfri'kar/ *v.* rub vigorously.

confrontación /konfronta'θion; konfronta'sion/ *n. f.* confrontation.

confrontar /konfron'tar/ *v.* confront.

confucianismo /konfuθia'nismo; konfusia'nismo/ *n. m.* Confucianism.

confundir /konfun'dir/ *v.* confuse; puzzle, mix up.

confusamente /konfusa'mente/ *adv.* confusedly.

confusión /konfu'sion/ *n. f.* confusion, mix-up; clutter.

confuso /kon'fuso/ *a.* confused; confusing.

confutación /konfuta'θion; konfuta'sion/ *n. f.* disproof.

confutar /konfu'tar/ *v.* refute, disprove.

congelable /konʒe'laβle/ *a.* congealable.

congelación /konhela'θion; kon-

hela'sion/ *n. f.* congealment; deep freeze.

congelado /konʒe'laðo/ *a.* frozen, congealed.

congelar /konhe'lar/ *v.* congeal, freeze.

congenial /konʒe'nial/ *a.* congenial; analogous.

congeniar /konhe'niar/ *v.* be congenial.

congestión /konhes'tion/ *n. f.* congestion.

conglomeración /konglomera'θion; konglomera'sion/ *n. f.* conglomeration.

congoja /kon'goha/ *n. f.* grief, anguish.

congraciamiento /kongraθia'miento; kongrasia'miento/ *n. m.* flattery; ingratiation.

congraciar /kongra'θiar; kongra'siar/ *v.* flatter; ingratiate oneself.

congratulación /kongratula'θion; kongratula'sion/ *n. f.* congratulation.

congratular /kongratu'lar/ *v.* congratulate.

congregación /kongrega'θion; kongrega'sion/ *n. f.* congregation.

congregar /kongre'gar/ *v.* congregate.

congresista /kongre'sista/ *n. m. & f.* congressional representative.

congreso /kon'greso/ *n. m.* congress; conference.

conjetura /konhe'tura/ *n. f.* conjecture. —**conjeturar,** *v.*

conjetural /konhetu'ral/ *a.* conjectural.

conjugación /konhuga'θion; konhuga'sion/ *n. f.* conjugation.

conjugar /konhu'gar/ *v.* conjugate.

conjunción /konhun'θion; konhun'sion/ *n. f.* union; conjunction.

conjuntamente /konhunta'mente/ *adv.* together, jointly.

conjunto. /kon'hunto/ *a.* **1.** joint, unified. —*n.* **2.** *m.* whole.

conjuración /konhura'θion; konhura'sion/ *n. f.* conspiracy, plot.

conjurado /konhu'raðo/ *-da n.* conspirator, plotter.

conjurar /konhu'rar/ *v.* conjure.

conjuro /kon'huro/ *n. m.* exorcism; spell; plea.

conllevador /konʎeβa'ðor; konyeβa'ðor/ *n. m.* helper, aide.

conmemoración /konmemora'θion; konmemora'sion/ *n. f.* commemoration; remembrance.

conmemorar /konmemo'rar/ *v.* commemorate.

conmemorativo /konmemora'tiβo/ *a.* commemorative, memorial.

conmensal /konmen'sal/ *n. m.* messmate.

conmigo /kon'migo/ *adv.* with me.

conmilitón /konmili'ton/ *n. m.* fellow soldier.

conminación /konmina'θion; konmina'sion/ *n. f.* threat, warning.

conminar /konmi'nar/ *v.* threaten.

conminatorio /konmina'torio/ *a.* threatening, warning.

conmiseración /konmisera'θion; konmisera'sion/ *n. f.* sympathy.

conmoción /konmo'θion; konmo'sion/ *n. f.* commotion, stir.

conmovedor /konmoβe'ðor/ *a.* moving, touching.

conmover /konmo'βer/ *v.* move, affect, touch.

conmutación /konmuta'θion; konmuta'sion/ *n. f.* commutation.

conmutador /konmuta'ðor/ *n. m.* electric switch.

conmutar /konmu'tar/ *v.* exchange.

connatural /konnatu'ral/ *a.* innate, inherent.

connotación /konnota'θion; konnota'sion/ *n. f.* connotation.

connotar /konno'tar/ *v.* connote.

connubial /konnu'βial/ *a.* connubial.

connubio /ko'nnuβio/ *n. m.* matrimony.

cono /'kono/ *n. m.* cone.

conocedor /konoθe'ðor; konose'ðor/ **-ra** *n.* expert, connoisseur.

conocer /kono'θer; kono'ser/ *v.* know, be acquainted with; meet, make the acquaintance of.

conocible /kono'θiβle; kono'siβle/ *a.* knowable.

conocido /kono'θiðo; kono'siðo/ **-da** *a.* 1. familiar, well-known. —*n.* 2. acquaintance, person known.

conocimiento /konoθi'miento; konosi'miento/ *n. m.* knowledge, acquaintance; consciousness.

conque /'konke/ *conj.* so then; and so.

conquista /kon'kista/ *n. f.* conquest.

conquistador /konkista'ðor/ **-ra** *n.* conqueror.

conquistar /konkis'tar/ *v.* conquer.

consabido /konsa'βiðo/ *a.* aforesaid.

consagración /konsagra'θion; konsagra'sion/ *n. f.* consecration.

consagrado /konsa'graðo/ *a.* consecrated.

consagrar /konsa'grar/ *v.* consecrate, dedicate, devote.

consanguinidad /konsaŋguini'ðað/ *n. f.* consanguinity.

consciente /kons'θiente; kons'siente/ *a.* conscious, aware.

conscientemente /konsθiente'mente; konssiente'mente/ *adv.* consciously.

conscripción /konskrip'θion; konskrip'sion/ *n. f.* conscription for military service.

consecución /konseku'θion; konseku'sion/ *n. f.* attainment.

consecuencia /konse'kuenθia; konse'kuensia/ *n. f.* consequence.

consecuente /konse'kuente/ *a.* consequent; consistent.

consecuentemente /konsekuente'mente/ *adv.* consequently.

consecutivamente /konsekutiβa'mente/ *adv.* consecutively.

consecutivo /konseku'tiβo/ *a.* consecutive.

conseguir /konse'gir/ *v.* obtain, get, secure; succeed in, manage to.

conseja /kon'seha/ *n. f.* fable.

consejero /konse'hero/ **-ra** *n.* adviser, counselor.

consejo /kon'seho/ *n. m.* council; counsel; (piece of) advice. **c. de redacción,** editorial board.

consenso /kon'senso/ *n. m.* consensus.

consentido /konsen'tiðo/ *a.* spoiled, bratty.

consentimiento /konsenti'miento/ *n. m.* consent.

consentir /konsen'tir/ *v.* allow, permit.

conserje /kon'serhe/ *n. m.* superintendent, keeper.

conserva /kon'serβa/ *n. f.* conserve, preserve.

conservación /konserβa'θion; konserβa'sion/ *n. f.* conservation.

conservador /konserβa'ðor/ **-ra** *a. & n.* conservative.

conservar /konser'βar/ *v.* conserve.

conservativo /konserβa'tiβo/ *a.* conservative, preservative.

conservatorio /konserβa'torio/ *n. m.* conservatory.

considerable /konsiðe'raβle/ *a.* considerable, substantial.

considerablemente /konsiðeraβle'mente/ *adv.* considerably.

consideración /konsiðera'θion; konsiðera'sion/ *n. f.* consideration.

consideradamente /konsiðeraða'mente/ *adv.* considerably.

considerado /konsiðe'raðo/ *a.* considerate; considered.

considerando /konsiðe'rando/ *conj.* whereas.

considerar /konsiðe'rar/ *v.* consider.

consigna /kon'signa/ *n. f.* watchword.

consignación /konsigna'θion; konsigna'sion/ *n. f.* consignment.

consignar /konsig'nar/ *v.* consign.

consignatorio /konsigna'torio/ **-ria** *n.* consignee; trustee.

consigo /kon'sigo/ *adv.* with herself, with himself, with oneself, with themselves, with yourself, with yourselves.

consiguiente /konsi'giente/ *a.* 1. consequent. —*n.* 2. *m.* consequence.

consiguientemente /konsigiente'mente/ *adv.* consequently.

consistencia /konsis'tenθia; konsis'tensia/ *n. f.* consistency.

consistente /konsis'tente/ *a.* consistent.

consistir /konsis'tir/ *v.* consist.

consistorio /konsis'torio/ *n. m.* consistory.

consocio /kon'soθio; kon'sosio/ *n. m.* associate; partner; comrade.

consola /kon'sola/ *n. f.* console.

consolación /konsola'θion; konsola'sion/ *n. f.* consolation.

consolar /konso'lar/ *v.* console.

consolativo /konsola'tiβo/ *a.* consolatory.

consolidación /konsoliða'θion; konsoliða'sion/ *n.* consolidation.

consolidado /konsoli'ðaðo/ *a.* consolidated.

consolidar /konsoli'ðar/ *v.* consolidate.

consonancia /konso'nanθianb; konso'nansia/ *n. f.* agreement, accord, harmony.

consonante /konso'nante/ *a. & f.* consonant.

consonar /konso'nar/ *v.* rhyme.

consorte /kon'sorte/ *n. m. & f.* consort, mate.

conspicuo /kons'pikuo/ *a.* conspicuous.

conspiración /konspira'θion; konspira'sion/ *n. f.* conspiracy, plot.

conspirador /konspira'ðor/ **-ra** *n.* conspirator.

conspirar /konspi'rar/ *v.* conspire, plot.

constancia /kons'tanθia; kons'tansia/ *n. f.* perseverance; record.

constante /kons'tante/ *a.* constant.

constantemente /konstante'mente/ *adv.* constantly.

constar /kons'tar/ *v.* consist; be clear, be on record.

constelación /konstela'θion; konstela'sion/ *n. f.* constellation.

consternación /konsterna'θion; konsterna'sion/ *n. f.* consternation.

consternar /konster'nar/ *v.* dismay.

constipación /konstipa'θion; konstipa'sion/ *n. f.* head cold.

constipado /konsti'paðo/ *a.* 1. having a head cold. —*n.* 2. *m.* head cold.

constitución /konstitu'θion; konstitu'sion/ *n. f.* constitution.

constitucional /konstituθio'nal; konstitusio'nal/ *a.* constitutional.

constitucionalidad /konstituθionali'ðað; konstitusionali'ðað/ *n. f.* constitutionality.

constituir /konsti'tuir/ *v.* constitute.

constitutivo /konstitu'tiβo/ *n. m.* constituent.

constituyente /konstitu'yente, konstitu'tiβo/ *a.* constituent.

constreñidamente /konstreɲiða'mente/ *adv.* compulsively; with constraint.

constreñimiento /konstreɲi'miento/ *n. m.* compulsion; constraint.

constreñir /konstre'ɲir/ *v.* constrain.

constricción /konstrik'θion; konstrik'sion/ *n. f.* constriction.

construcción /konstruk'θion; konstruk'sion/ *n. f.* construction.

constructivo /konstruk'tiβo/ *a.* constructive.

constructor /konstruk'tor/ **-ra** *n.* builder.

construir /kons'truir/ *v.* construct, build.

consuelo /kon'suelo/ *n. m.* consolation.

cónsul /'konsul/ *n. m.* consul.

consulado /konsu'laðo/ *n. m.* consulate.

consular /konsu'lar/ *a.* consular.

consulta /kon'sulta/ *n. f.* consultation.

consultación /konsulta'θion; konsulta'sion/ *n. f.* consultation.

consultante /konsul'tante/ *n. m. & f.* consultant.

consultar /konsul'tar/ *v.* consult.

consultivo /konsul'tiβo/ *a.* consultative.

consultor /konsul'tor/ **-ra** *n.* adviser.

consumación /konsuma'θion; konsuma'sion/ *n. f.* consummation; end.

consumado /konsu'maðo/ *a.* consummate, downright.

consumar /konsu'mar/ *v.* consummate.

consumidor /konsumi'ðor/ **-ra** *n.* consumer.

consumir /konsu'mir/ *v.* consume.

consumo /kon'sumo/ *n. m.* consumption.

consunción /konsun'θion; konsun'sion/ *n. m.* consumption, tuberculosis.

contabilidad /kontaβili'ðað/ *n. f.* accounting, bookkeeping.

contabilista /kontaβi'lista/ **contable** *n. m. & f.* accountant.

contacto /kon'takto/ *n. m.* contact.

contado /kon'taðo/ *n. m.* **al c.,** (for) cash.

contador /konta'ðor/ **-ra** *n.* accountant, bookkeeper; meter.

contagiar /konta'hiar/ *v.* infect.

contagio /kon'tahio/ *n. m.* contagion.

contagioso /konta'hioso/ *a.* contagious.

contaminación /kontamina'θion; kontamina'sion/ *n. f.* contamination, pollution. **c. del aire, c. atmosférica,** air pollution.

contaminar /kontami'nar/ *v.* contaminate, pollute.

contar /kon'tar/ *v.* count; relate, recount, tell. **c. con,** count on.

contemperar /kontempe'rar/ *v.* moderate.

contemplación /kontempla'θion; kontempla'sion/ *n. f.* contemplation.

contemplador /kontempla'ðor/ **-ra** *n.* thinker.

contemplar /kontem'plar/ *v.* contemplate.

contemplativamente /kontemplatiβa'mente/ *adv.* thoughtfully.

contemplativo /kontempla'tiβo/ *a.* contemplative.

contemporáneo /kontempo'raneo/ **-nea** *a. & n.* contemporary.

contención /konten'θion; konten'sion/ *n. f.* contention.

contencioso /konten'θioso; konten'sioso/ *a.* quarrelsome; argumentative.

contender /konten'der/ *v.* cope, contend; conflict.

contendiente /konten'diente/ *n. m. & f.* contender.

contenedor /kontene'ðor/ *n. m.* container.

contener /konte'ner/ *v.* contain; curb, control.

contenido /konte'niðo/ *n. m.* contents.

contenta /kon'tenta/ *n. f.* endorsement.

contentamiento /kontenta'miento/ *n. m.* contentment.

contentar /konten'tar/ *v.* content, satisfy.

contentible /konten'tiβle/ *a.* contemptible.

contento /kon'tento/ *a.* 1. contented, happy. —*n.* 2. *m.* contentment, satisfaction, pleasure.

contérmino /kon'termino/ *a.* adjacent, abutting.

contestable /kontes'taβle/ *a.* disputable.

contestación /kontesta'θion; kontesta'sion/ *n. f.* answer. —**contestar,** *v.*

contestador automático /kontesta'ðor auto'matiko/ *n. m.* answering machine.

contextura /konteks'tura/ *n. f.* texture.

contienda /kon'tienda/ *n. f.* combat; match; strife.

contigo /kon'tigo/ *adv.* with you.

contiguamente /kontigua'mente/ *adv.* contiguously.

contiguo /kon'tiguo/ *a.* adjoining, next.

continencia /konti'nenθia; konti'nensia/ *n. f.* continence, moderation.

continental /konti'nental/ *a.* continental.

continente /konti'nente/ *n. m.* continent; mainland.

continentemente /kontinente'mente/ *adv.* in moderation.

contingencia /kontin'henθia; kontin'hensia/ *n. f.* contingency.

contingente /kontin'hente/ *a.* contingent; incidental.

continuación /kontinua'θion; kontinua'sion/ *n. f.* continuation. **a c.,** thereupon, hereupon.

continuamente /kontinua'mente/ *adv.* continuously.

continuar /konti'nuar/ *v.* continue, keep on.

continuidad /kontinui'ðað/ *n. f.* continuity.

continuo /kon'tinuo/ *a.* continual; continuous.

contorcerse /kontor'θerse; kontor'serse/ *v.* writhe, twist.

contorción /kontor'θion; kontor'sion/ *n. f.* contortion.

contorno /kon'torno/ *n. m.* contour; profile, outline; neighborhood.

contra /'kontra/ *prep.* against.

contraalmirante /kontraalmi'rante/ *n. m.* rear admiral.

contraataque /kontraa'take/ *n. m.* counterattack.

contrabajo /kontra'βaho/ *n. m.* double bass.

contrabalancear /kontraβalanθe'ar; kontraβalanse'ar/ *v.* counterbalance.

contrabandear /kontraβande'ar/ *v.* smuggle.

contrabandista /kontraβan'dista/ *n. m. & f.* smuggler.

contrabando /kontra'βando/ *n. m.* contraband, smuggling.

contracción /kontrak'θion; kontrak'sion/ *n. f.* contraction.

contracepción /kontraθep'θion; kontrasep'sion/ *n. f.* contraception, birth control.

contractual /kontrak'tual/ *a.* contractual.

contradecir /kontraðe'θir; kontraðe'sir/ *v.* contradict.

contradicción /kontraðik'θion; kontraðik'sion/ *n. f.* contradiction.

contradictorio /kontraðik'torio/ *adj.* contradictory.

contraer /kontra'er/ *v.* contract; shrink.

contrahacedor /kontraaθe'ðor; kontraase'ðor/ **-ra** *n.* imitator.

contrahacer /kontraa'θer; kontraa'ser/ *v.* forge.

contralor /kontra'lor/ *n. m.* comptroller.

contramandar /kontraman'dar/ *v.* countermand.

contraorden /kontra'orðen/ *n. f.* countermand.

contraparte /kontra'parte/ *n. f.* counterpart.

contrapesar /kontrape'sar/ *v.* counterbalance; offset.

contrapeso /kontra'peso/ *n. m.* counterweight.

contraproducente /kontraproðu'θente; kontraproðu'sente/ *a.* counterproductive.

contrapunto /kontra'punto/ *n. m.* counterpoint.

contrariamente /kontraria'mente/ *adv.* contrarily.

contrariar /kontra'riar/ *v.* contradict; vex; antagonize; counteract.

contrariedad /kontrarie'ðað/ *n. f.* contrariness; opposition; contradiction; disappointment; trouble.

contrario /kon'trario/ *a. & m.* contrary, opposite.

contrarrestar /kontrarres'tar/ *v.* resist; counteract.

contrasol /kontra'sol/ *n. m.* sunshade.

contraste /kon'traste/ *n. m.* contrast. —**contrastar,** *v.*

contratar /kontra'tar/ *v.* engage, contract.

contratiempo /kontra'tiempo/ *n. m.* accident; misfortune.

contratista /kontra'tista/ *n. m. & f.* contractor.

contrato /kon'trato/ *n. m.* contract.

contribución /kontriβu'θion; kontriβu'sion/ *n. f.* contribution; tax.

contribuir /kontri'βuir/ *v.* contribute.

contribuyente /kontriβu'yente/ *n. m. & f.* contributor; taxpayer.

contrición /kontri'θion; kontri'sion/ *n. f.* contrition.

contristar /kontris'tar/ *v.* afflict.

contrito /kon'trito/ *a.* contrite, remorseful.

control /kon'trol/ *n. m.* control. —**controlar,** *v.*

controlador aéreo /kontrola'ðor a'ereo/ *n. m.* air traffic controller.

controversia /kontro'βersia/ *n. f.* controversy.

controversista /kontroβer'sista/ *n. m. & f.* controversialist.

controvertir /kontroβer'tir/ *v.* dispute.

contumacia /kontu'maθia; kontu'masia/ *n. f.* stubbornness.

contumaz /kontu'maθ; kontu'mas/ *adj.* stubborn.

contumelia /kontu'melia/ *n. f.* contumely; abuse.

conturbar /kontur'βar/ *v.* trouble, disturb.

contusión /kontu'sion/ *n. f.* contusion; bruise.

convalecencia /kombale'θenθia; kombale'sensia/ *n. f.* convalescence.

convalecer /kombale'θer; kombale'ser/ *v.* convalesce.

convaleciente /kombale'θiente; kombale'siente/ *a.* convalescent.

convecino /kombe'θino; kombe'sino/ -na *a.* 1. near, close. —*n.* 2. neighbor.

convencedor /kombenθe'ðor; kombense'ðor/ *adj.* convincing.

convencer /komben'θer; komben'ser/ *v.* convince.

convencimiento /kombenθi'miento; kombensi'miento/ *n. m.* conviction; firm belief.

convención /komben'θion; komben'sion/ *n. f.* convention.

convencional /kombenθio'nal; kombensio'nal/ *a.* conventional.

conveniencia /kombe'nienθia; kombe'niensia/ *n. f.* suitability; advantage; interest.

conveniente /kombe'niente/ *a.* suitable; advantageous, opportune.

convenio /kom'benio/ *n. m.* pact, treaty; agreement.

convenir /kombe'nir/ *v.* assent, agree, concur; be suitable, fitting, convenient.

convento /kom'bento/ *n. m.* convent.

convergencia /komber'henθia; komber'hensia/ *n. f.* convergence.

convergir /komber'hir/ *v.* converge.

conversación /kombersa'θion; kombersa'sion/ *n. f.* conversation.

conversar /komber'sar/ *v.* converse.

conversión /komber'sion/ *n. f.* conversion.

convertible /komber'tiβle/ *a.* convertible.

convertir /komber'tir/ *v.* convert.

convexidad /kombeksi'ðað/ *n. f.* convexity.

convexo /kom'bekso/ *a.* convex.

convicción /kombik'θion; kombik'sion/ *n. f.* conviction.

convicto /kom'bikto/ *a.* found guilty.

convidado /kombi'ðaðo/ -da *n.* guest.

convidar /kombi'ðar/ *v.* invite.

convincente /kombin'θente; kombin'sente/ *a.* convincing.

convite /kom'bite/ *n. m.* invitation; treat.

convocación /komboka'θion; komboka'sion/ *n. f.* convocation.

convocar /kombo'kar/ *v.* convoke, assemble.

convoy /kom'boi/ *n. m.* convoy, escort.

convoyar /kombo'yar/ *v.* convey; escort.

convulsión /kombul'sion/ *n. f.* convulsion.

convulsivo /kombul'siβo/ *a.* convulsive.

conyugal /konyu'gal/ *a.* conjugal.

cónyuge /'konyuhe/ *n. m. & f.* spouse, mate.

coñac /ko'ɲak/ *n. m.* cognac, brandy.

cooperación /koopera'θion; koopera'sion/ *n. f.* cooperation.

cooperador /koopera'ðor/ *a.* cooperative.

cooperar /koope'rar/ *v.* cooperate.

cooperativa /koopera'tiβa/ *n. f.* (food, etc.) cooperative, co-op.

cooperativo /koopera'tiβo/ *a.* cooperative.

coordinación /koorðina'θion; koorðina'sion/ *n. f.* coordination.

coordinar /koorði'nar/ *v.* coordinate.

copa /'kopa/ *n. f.* goblet.

copartícipe /kopar'tiθipe; kopar'tisipe/ *n & f* partner.

copete /ko'pete/ *n. m.* tuft; toupee.

copia /'kopia/ *n. f.* copy. —**copiar,** *v.*

copiadora /kopia'ðora/ *n. f.* copier.

copioso /ko'pioso/ *a.* copious.

copista /ko'pista/ *n. m. & f.* copyist.

copla /'kopla/ *n. f.* popular song.

coplero /ko'plero/ *n. m.* poetaster.

cópula /'kopula/ *n. f.* connection.

coqueta /ko'keta/ *n. f.* flirt. —**coquetear,** *v.*

coraje /ko'rahe/ *n. m.* courage, bravery; anger.

coral /ko'ral/ *a.* 1. choral. —*n.* 2. *m.* coral.

coralino /kora'lino/ *a.* coral.

Corán /ko'ran/ *n. m.* Koran.

corazón /kora'θon; kora'son/ *n. m.* heart.

corazonada /koraθo'naða; koraso'naða/ *n. f.* foreboding.

corbata /kor'βata/ *n. f.* necktie.

corbeta /kor'βeta/ *n. f.* corvette.

corcho /'kortʃo/ *n. m.* cork.

corcova /kor'koβa/ *n. f.* hump, hunchback.

corcovado /korko'βaðo/ -da *a. & n.* hunchback.

cordaje /kor'ðahe/ *n. m.* rigging.

cordel /kor'ðel/ *n. m.* string, cord.

cordero /kor'ðero/ *n. m.* lamb.

cordial /kor'ðial/ *a.* cordial; hearty.

cordialidad /korðiali'ðað/ *n. f.* cordiality.

cordillera /korði'ʎera; korði'yera/ *n. f.* mountain range.

cordón /kor'ðon/ *n. m.* cord; (shoe) lace.

cordura /kor'ðura/ *n. f.* sanity.

Corea /ko'rea/ *n. f.* Korea.

coreano /kore'ano/ -a *a. & n.* Korean.

coreografía /koreogra'fia/ *n. f.* choreography.

corista /ko'rista/ *n. f.* chorus girl.

corneja /kor'neha/ *n. f.* crow.

córneo /'korneo/ *a.* horny.

corneta /kor'neta/ *n. f.* bugle, horn; cornet.

corniforme /korni'forme/ *a.* horn-shaped.

cornisa /kor'nisa/ *n. f.* cornice.

cornucopia /kornu'kopia/ *n. f.* cornucopia.

coro /'koro/ *n. m.* chorus; choir.

corola /ko'rola/ *n. f.* corolla.

corolario /koro'lario/ *n. m.* corollary.

corona /ko'rona/ *n. f.* crown; halo; wreath.

coronación /korona'θion; korona'sion/ *n. f.* coronation.

coronamiento /korona'miento/ *n. m.* completion of a task.

coronar /koro'nar/ *v.* crown.

coronel /koro'nel/ *n. m.* colonel.

coronilla /koro'niʎa; koro'niya/ *n. f.* crown, top of the head.

corporación /korpora'θion; korpora'sion/ *n. f.* corporation.

corporal /korpo'ral/ *adj.* corporeal, bodily.

corpóreo /kor'poreo/ *a.* corporeal.

corpulencia /korpu'lenθia; korpu'lensia/ *n. f.* corpulence.

corpulento /korpu'lento/ *a.* corpulent, stout.

corpuscular /korpusku'lar/ *a.* corpuscular.

corpúsculo /kor'puskulo/ *n. m.* corpuscle.

corral /ko'rral/ *n. m.* corral, pen, yard.

correa /ko'rrea/ *n. f.* belt, strap.

correa transportadora /ko'rrea transporta'ðora/ conveyor belt.

corrección /korrek'θion; korrek'sion/ *n. f.* correction.

correcto /ko'rrekto/ *a.* correct, proper, right.

corrector /korrek'tor/ -ra *n.* corrector, proofreader.

corredera /korre'ðera/ *n. f.* race course.

corredizo /korre'ðiθo; korre'ðiso/ *a.* easily untied.

corredor /korre'ðor/ *n. m.* corridor; runner.

corregible /korre'hiβle/ *a.* corrigible.

corregidor /korrehi'ðor/ *n. m.* corrector; magistrate, mayor.

corregir /korre'hir/ *v.* correct.

correlación /korrela'θion; korrela'sion/ *n. f.* correlation.

correlacionar /korrelaθio'nar; korrelasio'nar/ *v.* correlate.

correlativo /korrela'tiβo/ *a.* correlative.

correo /ko'rreo/ *n. m.* mail.

correoso /korre'oso/ *a.* leathery.

correr /ko'rrer/ *v.* run.

correría /korre'ria/ *n. f.* raid; escapade.

correspondencia /korrespon'denθia; korrespon'densia/ *n. f.* correspondence.

corresponder /korrespon'der/ *v.* correspond.

correspondiente /korrespon'diente/ *a. & m.* corresponding; correspondent.

corresponsal /korrespon'sal/ *n. m.* correspondent.

corretaje /korre'tahe/ *n. m.* brokerage.

correvedile /korreβe'ðile/ *n. m.* tale bearer; gossip.

corrida /ko'rriða/ *n. f.* race. **c. (de toros),** bullfight.

corrido /ko'rriðo/ *a.* abashed; expert.

corriente /ko'rriente/ *a.* 1. current, standard. —*n.* 2. *f.* current, stream. 3. *m.* **al c.,** informed, up to date. **contra la c.,** against the current; upriver, upstream.

corroboración /korroβora'θion; korroβora'sion/ *n. f.* corroboration.

corroborar /korroβo'rar/ *v.* corroborate.

corroer /korro'er/ *v.* corrode.

corromper /korrom'per/ *v.* corrupt.

corrompido /korrom'piðo/ *a.* corrupt.

corrupción /korrup'θion; korrup'sion/ *n. f.* corruption.

corruptela /korrup'tela/ *n. f.* corruption; vice.

corruptibilidad /korruptiβili'ðað/ *n. f.* corruptibility.

corruptor /korrup'tor/ -ra *n.* corrupter.

corsario /kor'sario/ *n. m.* corsair.

corsé /kor'se/ *n. m.* corset.

corso /'korso/ *n. m.* piracy.

cortacésped /korta'θespeð; korta'sespeð/ *n. m.* lawnmower.

cortadillo /korta'ðiʎo; korta'ðiyo/ *n. m.* small glass.

cortado /kor'taðo/ *a.* cut.

cortadura /korta'ðura/ *n. f.* cut.

cortante /kor'tante/ *a.* cutting, sharp, keen.

cortapisa /korta'pisa/ *n. f.* obstacle.

cortaplumas /korta'plumas/ *n. m.* penknife.

cortar /kor'tar/ *v.* cut, cut off, cut out.

corte /'korte/ *n. f.* court, *m.* cut.

cortedad /korte'ðað/ *n. f.* smallness; shyness.

cortejar /korte'har/ *v.* pay court to, woo.

cortejo /kor'teho/ *n. m.* court; courtship; sweetheart.

cortés /kor'tes/ *a.* civil, courteous, polite.

cortesana /korte'sana/ *n. f.* courtesan.

cortesano. 1. /korte'sano/ *a.* 1. courtly, courteous. —*n.* 2. *m.* courtier.

cortesía /korte'sia/ *n. f.* courtesy.

corteza /kor'teθa; kor'tesa/ *n. f.* bark; rind; crust.

cortijo /kor'tiho/ *n. m.* farmhouse.

cortina /kor'tina/ *n. f.* curtain.

corto /'korto/ *a.* short.

corva /'korβa/ *n. f.* back of the knee.

cosa /'kosa/ *n. f.* thing. **c. de,** a matter of, roughly.

cosecha /ko'setʃa/ *n. f.* crop, harvest. —**cosechar,** *v.*

coser /ko'ser/ *v.* sew, stitch.

cosmético /kos'metiko/ *a. & m.* cosmetic.

cósmico /'kosmiko/ *a.* cosmic.

cosmonauta /kosmo'nauta/ *n. m. & f.* cosmonaut.

cosmopolita /kosmopo'lita/ *a. & n.* cosmopolitan.

cosmos /'kosmos/ *n. m.* cosmos.

coso /'koso/ *n. m.* arena for bull fights.

cosquilla /kos'kiʎa; kos'kiya/ *n. f.* tickle. —**cosquillar,** *v.*

cosquilloso /koski'ʎoso; koski'yoso/ *a.* ticklish.

costa /'kosta/ *n. f.* coast; cost, expense.

costado /kos'taðo/ *n. m.* side.

costal /kos'tal/ *n. m.* sack, bag.

costanero /kosta'nero/ *a.* coastal.

costar /kos'tar/ *v.* cost.

costarricense /kostarri'θense; kostarri'sense/ *a. & n.* Costa Rican.

coste /'koste/ *n. m.* cost, price.

costear /koste'ar/ *v.* defray, sponsor; sail along the coast of.

costilla /kos'tiʎa; kos'tiya/ *n. f.* rib; chop.

costo /'kosto/ *n. m.* cost, price.

costoso /kos'toso/ *a.* costly.

costra /'kostra/ *n. f.* crust.

costumbre /kos'tumbre/ *n. f.* custom, practice, habit.

costura /kos'tura/ *n. f.* sewing; seam.

costurera /kostu'rera/ *n. f.* seamstress, dressmaker.

costurero /kostu'rero/ *n. m.* sewing basket.

cota de malla /'kota de 'maʎa; 'kota de 'maya/ coat of mail.

cotejar /kote'har/ *v.* compare.

cotidiano /koti'ðiano/ a. daily; everyday.

cotillón /koti'ʎon; koti'yon/ n. m. cotillion.

cotización /kotiθa'θion; kotisa'sion/ n. f. quotation.

cotizar /koti'θar; koti'sar/ v. quote (a price).

coto /'koto/ n. m. enclosure; boundary.

cotón /ko'ton/ n. m. printed cotton cloth.

cotufa /ko'tufa/ n. f. Jerusalem artichoke.

coturno /ko'turno/ n. m. buskin.

covacha /ko'βatʃa/ n. f. small cave.

coxal /kok'sal/ a. of the hip.

coy /koi/ n. m. hammock.

coyote /ko'yote/ n. m. coyote.

coyuntura /koyun'tura/ n. f. joint; juncture.

coz /koθ; kos/ n. f. kick.

crac /krak/ n. m. failure.

cráneo /'kraneo/ n. m. skull.

craniano /kra'niano/ a. cranial.

crapuloso /krapu'loso/ a. drunken.

crasiento /kra'siento/ a. greasy, oily.

craso /'kraso/ a. fat; gross.

cráter /'krater/ n. m. crater.

craza /'kraθa; 'krasa/ n. f. crucible.

creación /krea'θion; krea'sion/ n. f. creation.

creador /krea'ðor/ **-ra** a. & n. creative; creator.

crear /kre'ar/ v. create.

creativo /krea'tiβo/ a. creative.

crébol /'kreβol/ n. m. holly tree.

crecer /kre'θer; kre'ser/ v. grow, grow up; increase.

creces /'kreθes; 'kreses/ n. f.pl. increase, addition.

crecidamente /kreθiða'mente; kresiða'mente/ adv. abundantly.

crecido /kre'θiðo; kre'siðo/ a. increased, enlarged; swollen.

creciente /kre'θiente; kre'siente/ a. **1.** growing. —n. **2.** m. crescent.

crecimiento /kreθi'miento; kresi'miento/ n. m. growth.

credenciales /kreðen'θiales; kreðen'siales/ f.pl. credentials.

credibilidad /kreðiβili'ðað/ n. f. credibility.

crédito /'kreðito/ n. m. credit.

credo /'kreðo/ n. m. creed, belief.

crédulamente /kreðula'mente/ adv. credulously, gullibly.

credulidad /kreðuli'ðað/ n. f. credulity.

crédulo /'kreðulo/ a. credulous.

creedero /kree'ðero/ a. credible.

creedor /kree'ðor/ a. credulous, believing.

creencia /kre'enθia; kre'ensia/ n. f. belief.

creer /kre'er/ v. believe; think.

creíble /kre'iβle/ a. credible, believable.

crema /'krema/ n. f. cream.

cremación /krema'θion; krema'sion/ n. f. cremation.

crema dentífrica /'krema den'tifrika/ toothpaste.

cremallera /krema'ʎera; krema'yera/ n. f. zipper.

crémor tártaro /'kremor 'tartaro/ m. cream of tartar.

cremoso /kre'moso/ a. creamy.

creosota /kreo'sota/ n. f. creosote.

crepitar /krepi'tar/ v. crackle.

crepuscular /krepusku'lar/ a. of or like the dawn or dusk; crepuscular.

crepúsculo /kre'puskulo/ n. m. dusk, twilight.

crescendo /kres'θendo; kres'sendo/ n. m. crescendo.

crespo /'krespo/ a. curly.

crespón /kres'pon/ n. m. crepe.

cresta /'kresta/ n. f. crest; heraldic crest.

crestado /kres'taðo/ a. crested.

creta /'kreta/ n. f. chalk.

cretáceo /kre'taθeo; kre'taseo/ a. chalky.

cretinismo /kreti'nismo/ n. m. cretinism.

cretino /kre'tino/ **-na** n. & a. cretin.

cretona /kre'tona/ n. f. cretonne.

creyente /kre'yente/ a. **1.** believing. —n. **2.** believer.

creyón /kre'yon/ n. m. crayon.

cría /'kria/ n. f. (stock) breeding; young (of an animal), litter.

criada /kri'aða/ n. f. maid.

criadero /kria'ðero/ n. m. Agr. nursery.

criado /kri'aðo/ **-da** n. servant.

criador /kria'ðor/ a. fruitful, prolific.

crianza /kri'anθa; kri'ansa/ n. f. breeding; upbringing.

criar /kri'ar/ v. raise, rear; breed.

criatura /kria'tura/ n. f. creature; infant.

criba /'kriβa/ n. f. sieve.

cribado /kri'βaðo/ a. sifted.

cribar /kri'βar/ v. sift.

crimen /'krimen/ n. m. crime.

criminal /krimi'nal/ a. & n. criminal.

criminalidad /kriminali'ðað/ n. f. criminality.

criminalmente /kriminal'mente/ adv. criminally.

criminología /kriminolo'hia/ n. f. criminology.

criminoso /krimi'noso/ a. criminal.

crines /'krines/ n. f.pl. mane of a horse.

crinolina /krino'lina/ n. f. crinoline.

criocirugía /krioθiru'hia; kriosiru'hia/ n. f. cryosurgery.

criollo /kri'oʎo; 'krioyo/ **-lla** a. & n. native; Creole.

cripta /'kripta/ n. f. crypt.

criptografía /kriptogra'fia/ n. f. cryptography.

crisantemo /krisan'temo/ n. m. chrysanthemum.

crisis /'krisis/ n. f. crisis.

crisis nerviosa /'krisis ner'βiosa/ nervous breakdown.

crisma /'krisma/ n. m. chrism.

crisol /kri'sol/ n. m. crucible.

crispamiento /krispa'miento/ n. m. twitch, contraction.

crispar /kris'par/ v. contract (the muscles); twitch.

cristal /kris'tal/ n. m. glass; crystal; lens.

cristalería /kristale'ria/ n. f. glassware.

cristalino /krista'lino/ a. crystalline.

cristalización /kristaliθa'θion; kristalisa'sion/ n. f. crystallization.

cristalizar /kristali'θar; kristali'sar/ v. crystallize.

cristianar /kristia'nar/ v. baptize.

cristiandad /kristian'dað/ n. f. Christendom.

cristianismo /kristia'nismo/ n. m. Christianity.

cristiano /kris'tiano/ **-na** a. & n. Christian.

Cristo /'kristo/ n. m. Christ.

criterio /kri'terio/ n. m. criterion; judgment.

crítica /'kritika/ n. f. criticism; critique.

criticable /kriti'kaβle/ a. blameworthy.

criticador /kritika'ðor/ a. critical.

criticar /kriti'kar/ v. criticize.

crítico /'kritiko/ **-ca** a. & n. critical; critic.

croar /kro'ar/ v. croak.

crocante /kro'kante/ n. m. almond brittle.

crocitar /kroθi'tar; krosi'tar/ v. crow.

cromático /kro'matiko/ a. chromatic.

cromo /'kromo/ n. m. chromium.

cromosoma /kromo'soma/ n. m. chromosome.

cromotipia /kromo'tipia/ n. f. color printing.

crónica /'kronika/ n. f. chronicle.

crónico /'kroniko/ a. chronic.

cronicón /kroni'kon/ n. m. concise chronicle.

cronista /kro'nista/ n. m. & f. chronicler.

cronología /kronolo'hia/ n. f. chronology.

cronológicamente /kronolohika'mente/ adv. chronologically.

cronológico /krono'lohiko/ a. chronologic.

cronometrar /kronome'trar/ v. time.

cronómetro /kro'nometro/ n. m. stopwatch; chronometer.

croqueta /kro'keta/ n. f. croquette.

croquis /'krokis/ n. m. sketch; rough outline.

crótalo /'krotalo/ n. m. rattlesnake; castanet.

cruce /'kruθe; 'kruse/ n. m. crossing, crossroads, junction.

crucero /kru'θero; kru'sero/ n. m. cruiser.

crucífero /kru'θifero; kru'sifero/ a. cross-shaped.

crucificado /kruθifi'kaðo; krusifi'kaðo/ a. crucified.

crucificar /kruθifi'kar; krusifi'kar/ v. crucify.

crucifijo /kruθi'fiho; krusi'fiho/ n. m. crucifix.

crucifixión /kruθifik'sion; krusifik'sion/ n. f. crucifixion.

crucigrama /kruθi'grama; krusi'grama/ n. m. crossword puzzle.

crudamente /kruða'mente/ adv. crudely.

crudeza /kru'ðeθa; kru'ðesa/ n. f. crudeness.

crudo /'kruðo/ a. crude, raw.

cruel /kruel/ a. cruel.

crueldad /kruel'dað/ n. f. cruelty.

cruelmente /kruel'mente/ adv. cruelly.

cruentamente /kruenta'mente/ adv. bloodily.

cruento /'kruento/ a. bloody.

crujía /kru'hia/ n. f. corridor.

crujido /kru'hiðo/ n. m. creak.

crujir /kru'hir/ v. crackle; creak; rustle.

cruórico /'kruoriko/ a. bloody.

crup /krup/ n. m. croup.

crupié /kru'pie/ n. m. & f. croupier.

crustáceo /krus'taθeo; krus'taseo/ n. & a. crustacean.

cruz /kruθ; krus/ n. f. cross.

cruzada /kru'θaða; kru'saða/ n. f. crusade.

cruzado /kru'θaðo; kru'saðo/ **-da** n. crusader.

cruzamiento /kruθa'miento; krusa'miento/ n. m. crossing.

cruzar /kru'θar; kru'sar/ v. cross.

cruzarse con /kru'θarse kon; kru'sarse kon/ v. to (meet and) pass.

cuaderno /kua'ðerno/ n. m. notebook.

cuadra /'kuaðra/ n. f. block; (hospital) ward.

cuadradamente /kuaðraða'mente/ adv. exactly, precisely; completely, in full.

cuadradillo /kuaðra'ðiʎo; kuaðra'ðiyo/ n. m. lump of sugar.

cuadrado /kua'ðraðo/ **-da** a. & n. square.

cuadrafónico /kuaðra'foniko/ a. quadraphonic.

Cuadragésima /kuaðra'hesima/ n. f. Lent.

cuadragesimal /kuaðrahesi'mal/ a. Lenten.

cuadrángulo /kua'ðraŋgulo/ n. m. quadrangle.

cuadrante /kua'ðrante/ n. m. quadrant; dial.

cuadrar /kua'ðrar/ v. square; suit.

cuadricular /kuaðriku'lar/ a. in squares.

cuadrilátero /kuaðri'latero/ a. quadrilateral.

cuadrilla /kua'ðriʎa; kua'ðriya/ n. f. band, troop, gang.

cuadro /'kuaðro/ n. m. picture; painting; frame. **a cuadros,** checked, plaid.

cuadro de servicio /'kuaðro de ser'βiθio; 'kuaðro de ser'βisio/ timetable.

cuadrupedal /kuaðrupe'ðal/ a. quadruped.

cuádruplo /'kuaðruplo/ a. fourfold.

cuajada /kua'haða/ n. f. curd.

cuajamiento /kuaha'miento/ n. m. coagulation.

cuajar /kua'har/ v. coagulate; overdecorate.

cuajo /'kuaho/ n. m. rennet; coagulation.

cual /kual/ rel. pron. which.

cuál a. & pron. what, which.

cualidad /kuali'ðað/ n. f. quality.

cualitativo /kualita'tiβo/ a. qualitative.

cualquiera /kual'kiera/ a. & pron. whatever, any; anyone.

cuando /'kuando/ conj. when.

cuando adv. when. **de cuando en cuando,** from time to time.

cuantía /kuan'tia/ n. f. quantity; amount.

cuantiar /kuan'tiar/ v. estimate.

cuantiosamente /kuantiosa'mente/ adv. abundantly.

cuantioso /kuan'tioso/ a. abundant.

cuantitativo /kuantita'tiβo/ a. quantitative.

cuanto /'kuanto/ a., adv. & pron. as much as, as many as; all that which. **en c.,** as soon as. **en c. a,** as for. **c. antes,** as soon as possible. **c. más... tanto más,** the more... the more. **unos cuantos,** a few.

cuánto a. & adv. how much, how many.

cuaquerismo /kuake'rismo/ n. m. Quakerism.

cuáquero /'kuakero/ **-ra** n. & a. Quaker.

cuarenta /kua'renta/ a. & pron. forty.

cuarentena /kuaren'tena/ n. f. quarantine.

cuaresma /kua'resma/ n. f. Lent.

cuaresmal /kuares'mal/ a. Lenten.

cuarta /'kuarta/ n. f. quarter; quadrant; quart.

cuartear /kuarte'ar/ v. divide into quarters.

cuartel /kuar'tel/ n. m. Mil. quarters; barracks; Naut. hatch. **c. general,** headquarters. **sin c.,** giving no quarter.

cuartelada /kuarte'laða/ n. f. military uprising.

cuarterón /kuarte'ron/ n. & a. quadroon.

cuarteto /kuar'teto/ n. m. quartet.

cuartillo /kuar'tiʎo; kuar'tiyo/ n. m. pint.

cuarto /'kuarto/ a. **1.** fourth. —n. **2.** m. quarter; room.

cuarto de baño /'kuarto de 'baɲo/ bathroom.

cuarto de dormir /'kuarto de dor'mir/ bedroom.

cuarto para invitados /'kuarto para imbi'taðos/ guest room.

cuarzo /'kuarθo; 'kuarso/ n. m. quartz.

cuasi /'kuasi/ adv. almost, nearly.

cuate /'kuate/ a. & n. twin.

cuatrero /kua'trero/ n. m. cattle rustler.

cuatrillón /kuatri'ʎon; kuatri'yon/ n. m. quadrillion.

cuatro /'kuatro/ a. & pron. four.

cuatrocientos /kuatro'θientos; kuatro'sientos/ a. & pron. four hundred.

cuba /'kuβa/ n. f. cask, tub, vat.

cubano /ku'βano/ **-na** a. & n. Cuban.

cubero /ku'βero/ n. m. cooper.

cubeta /ku'βeta/ n. f. small barrel, keg.

cúbico /'kuβiko/ a. cubic.

cubículo /ku'βikulo/ n. m. cubicle.

cubierta /ku'βierta/ *n. f.* cover; envelope; wrapping; tread (of a tire); deck.

cubiertamente /kuβierta'mente/ *adv.* secretly, stealthily.

cubierto /ku'βierto/ *n. m.* place (at table).

cubil /ku'βil/ *n. m.* lair.

cubismo /ku'βismo/ *n. m.* cubism.

cubito de hielo /ku'βito de 'ielo/ *n. m.* ice cube.

cubo /'kuβo/ *n. m.* cube; bucket.

cubo de la basura /'kuβo de la ba'sura/ trash can.

cubrecama /kuβre'kama/ *n. f.* bedspread.

cubrir /ku'βrir/ *v.* cover.

cubrirse /ku'βrirse/ *v.* put on one's hat.

cucaracha /kuka'ratʃa/ *n. f.* cockroach.

cuchara /ku'tʃara/ *n. f.* spoon, tablespoon.

cucharada /kutʃa'raða/ *n. f.* spoonful.

cucharita /kutʃa'rita/ **cucharilla** *n. f.* teaspoon.

cucharón /kutʃa'ron/ *n. m.* dipper, ladle.

cuchicheo /kutʃi'tʃeo/ *n. m.* whisper. —**cuchichear**, *v.*

cuchilla /ku'tʃiʎa; ku'tʃiya/ *n. f.* cleaver.

cuchillada /kutʃi'ʎaða; kutʃi'yaða/ *n. f.* slash.

cuchillería /kutʃiʎe'ria, kutʃiye'ria/ *n. f.* cutlery.

cuchillo /ku'tʃiʎo; ku'tʃiyo/ *n. m.* knife.

cucho /'kutʃo/ *n. m.* fertilizer.

cuchufleta /kutʃu'fleta/ *n. f.* jest.

cuclillo /ku'kliʎo; ku'kliyo/ *n. m.* cuckoo.

cuco /'kuko/ *a.* sly.

cuculla /ku'kuʎa; ku'kuya/ *n. f.* hood, cowl.

cuelga /'kuelga/ *n. f.* cluster, bunch.

cuelgacapas /kuelga'kapas/ *n. m.* coat rack.

cuello /'kueʎo; 'kueyo/ *n. m.* neck; collar.

cuenca /'kuenka/ *n. f.* socket; (river) basin; wooden bowl.

cuenco /'kuenko/ *n. m.* earthen bowl.

cuenta /'kuenta/ *n. f.* account; bill. **darse c.,** to realize. **tener en c.,** to keep in mind.

cuenta bancaria /'kuenta ban'karia/ bank account.

cuenta de ahorros /'kuenta de a'orros/ savings account.

cuentagotas /kuenta'gotas/ *n. m.* dropper (for medicine).

cuentista /kuen'tista/ *n. m. & f.* storyteller; informer.

cuento /'kuento/ *n. m.* story, tale.

cuerda /'kuerða/ *n. f.* cord; chord; rope; string; spring (of clock). **dar c. a,** to wind (clock).

cuerdamente /kuerða'mente/ *adv.* sanely; prudently.

cuerdo /'kuerðo/ *a.* sane; prudent.

cuerno /'kuerno/ *n. m.* horn.

cuero /'kuero/ *n. m.* leather; hide.

cuerpo /'kuerpo/ *n. m.* body; corps.

cuervo /'kuerβo/ *n. m.* crow, raven.

cuesco /'kuesko/ *n. m.* pit, stone (of fruit).

cuesta /'kuesta/ *n. f.* hill, slope. **llevar a cuestas,** to carry on one's back.

cuestación /kuesta'θion; kuesta'sion/ *n. f.* solicitation for charity.

cuestión /kues'tion/ *n. f.* question; affair; argument.

cuestionable /kuestio'naβle/ *a.* questionable.

cuestionar /kuestio'nar/ *v.* question; discuss; argue.

cuestionario /kuestio'nario/ *n. m.* questionnaire.

cuete /'kuete/ *n. m.* firecracker.

cueva /'kueβa/ *n. f.* cave; cellar.

cuguar /ku'guar/ *n. m.* cougar.

cugujada /kugu'haða/ *n. f.* lark.

cuidado /kui'ðaðo/ *n. m.* care, caution, worry. **tener c.,** to be careful.

cuidadosamente /kuiðaðosa'mente/ *adv.* carefully.

cuidadoso /kuiða'ðoso/ *a.* careful, painstaking.

cuidante /kui'ðante/ *n.* caretaker, custodian.

cuidar /kui'ðar/ *v.* take care of.

cuita /'kuita/ *n. f.* trouble, care; grief.

cuitado /kui'taðo/ *a.* unfortunate; shy, timid.

cuitamiento /kuita'miento/ *n. m.* timidity.

culata /ku'lata/ *n. f.* haunch, buttock; butt of a gun.

culatada /kula'taða/ *n. f.* recoil.

culatazo /kula'taθo/ *n. m.* blow with the butt of a gun; recoil.

culebra /ku'leβra/ *n. f.* snake.

culero /ku'lero/ *a.* lazy, indolent.

culinario /kuli'nario/ *a.* culinary.

culminación /kulmina'θion; kulmina'sion/ *n. f.* culmination.

culminar /kulmi'nar/ *v.* culminate.

culpa /'kulpa/ *n. f.* fault, guilt, blame. **tener la c.,** to be at fault. **echar la culpa a,** to blame.

culpabilidad /kulpaβili'ðað/ *n. f.* guilt, fault, blame.

culpable /kul'paβle/ *a.* at fault, guilty, to blame, culpable.

culpar /kul'par/ *v.* blame, accuse.

cultamente /kulta'mente/ *adv.* politely, elegantly.

cultivable /kulti'βaβle/ *a.* arable.

cultivación /kultiβa'θion; kultiβa'sion/ *n. f.* cultivation.

cultivador /kultiβa'ðor/ **-ra** *n.* cultivator.

cultivar /kulti'βar/ *v.* cultivate.

cultivo /kul'tiβo/ *n. m.* cultivation; (growing) crop.

culto /'kulto/ *a.* **1.** cultured, cultivated. —*n.* **2.** *m.* cult; worship.

cultura /kul'tura/ *n. f.* culture; refinement.

cultural /kultu'ral/ *a.* cultural.

culturar /kultu'rar/ *v.* cultivate.

culturismo /kultu'rismo/ *n. m.* body building.

culturista /kultu'rista/ *n. m. & f.* body builder.

cumbre /'kumbre/ *n. m.* summit, peak.

cumpleaños /kumple'aɲos/ *n. m.pl.* birthday.

cumplidamente /kumpliða'mente/ *adv.* courteously, correctly.

cumplido /kum'pliðo/ *a.* polite, polished.

cumplimentar /kumplimen'tar/ *v.* compliment.

cumplimiento /kumpli'miento/ *n. m.* fulfillment; compliment.

cumplir /kum'plir/ *v.* comply; carry out, fulfill; reach (years of age).

cumulativo /kumula'tiβo/ *a.* cumulative.

cúmulo /'kumulo/ *n. m.* heap, pile.

cuna /'kuna/ *n. f.* cradle.

cundir /kun'dir/ *v.* spread; expand; propagate.

cuneiforme /kunei'forme/ *a.* cuneiform, wedge-shaped.

cuneo /ku'neo/ *n. m.* rocking.

cuña /'kuɲa/ *n. f.* wedge.

cuñada /ku'ɲaða/ *n. f.* sister-in-law.

cuñado /ku'ɲaðo/ *n. m.* brother-in-law.

cuñete /ku'ɲete/ *n. m.* keg.

cuota /'kuota/ *n. f.* quota; dues.

cuotidiano /kuoti'ðiano/ *a.* daily.

cupé /ku'pe/ *n. m.* coupé.

cupo /'kupo/ *n. m.* share; assigned quota.

cupón /ku'pon/ *n. m.* coupon.

cúpula /'kupula/ *n. f.* dome.

cura /'kura/ *n. m.* priest; *f.* treatment, (medical) care. **c. de urgencia,** first aid.

curable /ku'raβle/ *a.* curable.

curación /kura'θion; kura'sion/ *n. f.* healing; cure; (surgical) dressing.

curado /ku'raðo/ *a.* cured, healed.

curador /kura'ðor/ **-ra** *n.* healer.

curandero /kuran'dero/ **-ra** *n.* healer, medicine man.

curar /ku'rar/ *v.* cure, heal, treat.

curativo /kura'tiβo/ *a.* curative, healing.

curia /'kuria/ *n. f.* ecclesiastical court.

curiosear /kuriose'ar/ *v.* snoop, pry, meddle.

curiosidad /kuriosi'ðað/ *n. f.* curiosity.

curioso /ku'rioso/ *a.* curious.

curro /'kurro/ *a.* showy, loud, flashy.

cursante /kur'sante/ *n.* student.

cursar /kur'sar/ *v.* frequent; attend.

cursi /'kursi/ *a.* vulgar, shoddy, in bad taste.

curso /'kurso/ *n. m.* course.

curso por correspondencia /'kurso por korrespon'denθia; 'kurso por korrespon'densia/ *n. m.* correspondence course.

cursor /kur'sor/ *n. m.* cursor.

curtidor /kurti'ðor/ *n. m.* tanner.

curtir /kur'tir/ *v.* tan.

curva /'kurβa/ *n. f.* curve; bend.

curvatura /kurβa'tura, kurβi'ðað/ *n. f.* curvature.

cúspide /'kuspiðe/ *n. f.* top, peak.

custodia /kus'toðia/ *n. f.* custody.

custodiar /kusto'ðiar/ *v.* guard, watch.

custodio /kus'toðio/ *n. m.* custodian.

cutáneo /ku'taneo/ *a.* cutaneous.

cutícula /ku'tikula/ *n. f.* cuticle.

cutis /'kutis/ *n. m. or f.* skin, complexion.

cutre /'kutre/ *a.* shoddy.

cuyo /'kuyo/ *a.* whose.

D

dable /'daβle/ *a.* possible.

dactilógrafo /dakti'lografo/ **-fa** *n.* typist.

dádiva /'daðiβa/ *n. f.* gift.

dadivosamente /daðiβosa'mente/ *adv.* generously.

dadivoso /daði'βoso/ *a.* generous, bountiful.

dado /'daðo/ *n. m.* die.

dador /da'ðor/ **-ra** *n.* giver.

dados /'daðos/ *n. m.pl.* dice.

daga /'daga/ *n. f.* dagger.

dalia /'dalia/ *n. f.* dahlia.

dallador /daʎa'ðor; daya'ðor/ *n. m.* lawn mower.

dallar /da'ʎar; da'yar/ *v.* mow.

daltonismo /dalto'nismo/ *n. m.* color blindness.

dama /'dama/ *n. f.* lady.

damasco /da'masko/ *n. m.* apricot; damask.

damisela /dami'sela/ *n. f.* young lady, girl.

danés /da'nes/ **-esa** *a. & n.* Danish, Dane.

danza /'danθa; 'dansa/ *n. f.* (the) dance. —**danzar,** *v.*

danzante /dan'θante; dan'sante/ **-ta** *n.* dancer.

dañable /da'ɲaβle/ *a.* condemnable.

dañar /da'ɲar/ *v.* hurt, harm; damage.

dañino /da'ɲino/ *a.* harmful.

daño /'daɲo/ *n. m.* damage; harm.

dañoso /da'ɲoso/ *a.* harmful.

dar /dar/ *v.* give; strike (clock). **d. a,** face, open on. **d. con,** find, locate. **¡Dalo por hecho!** Consider it done!

dardo /'darðo/ *n. m.* dart.

dársena /'darsena/ *n. f.* dock.

datar /da'tar/ *v.* date.

dátil /'datil/ *n. m.* date (fruit).

dativo /da'tiβo/ *n. m.* & *a.* dative.

datos /'datos/ *n. m.pl.* data.

de /de/ *prep.* of; from; than.

debajo /de'βaho/ *adv.* underneath. **d. de,** under.

debate /de'βate/ *n. m.* debate.

debatir /deβa'tir/ *v.* debate, argue.

debe /'deβe/ *n. m.* debit.

debelación /deβela'θion; deβela'sion/ *n. f.* conquest.

debelar /deβe'lar/ *v.* conquer.

deber /de'βer/ *v.* **1.** owe; must; be to, be supposed to. —*n.* **2.** *m.* obligation.

deberes /de'βeres/ *n. m.pl.* homework.

debido /de'βiðo/ *a.* due.

débil /'deβil/ *a.* weak, faint.

debilidad /deβili'ðað/ *n. f.* weakness.

debilitación /deβilita'θion; deβilita'sion/ *n. f.* weakness.

debilitar /deβili'tar/ *v.* weaken.

débito /'deβito/ *n. m.* debit.

debutar /deβu'tar/ *v.* make a debut.

década /'dekaða/ *n. f.* decade.

decadencia /deka'ðenθia; dekaðen'sia/ *n. f.* decadence, decline, decay.

decadente /deka'ðente/ *a.* decadent, declining, decaying.

decaer /deka'er/ *v.* decay, decline.

decalitro /deka'litro/ *n. m.* decaliter.

decálogo /de'kalogo/ *n. m.* decalogue.

decámetro /de'kametro/ *n. m.* decameter.

decano /de'kano/ *n. m.* dean.

decantado /dekan'taðo/ *a.* much discussed; overexalted.

decapitación /dekapita'θion; dekapitasion/ *n. f.* beheading.

decapitar /dekapi'tar/ *v.* behead.

decencia /de'θenθia; de'sensia/ *n. f.* decency.

decenio /de'θenio; de'senio/ *n. m.* decade.

decente /de'θente; de'sente/ *a.* decent.

decentemente /deθente'mente; desente'mente/ *adv.* decently.

decepción /deθep'θion; desep'sion/ *n. f.* disappointment, letdown; delusion.

decepcionar /deθepθio'nar; desepsio'nar/ *v.* disappoint, disillusion.

dechado /de'tʃaðo/ *n. m.* model; sample; pattern; example.

decibelio /deθi'βelio; desi'βelio/ *n. m.* decibel.

decididamente /deθiðiða'mente; desiðiða'mente/ *adv.* decidedly.

decidir /deθi'ðir; desi'ðir/ *v.* decide.

decigramo /deθi'gramo; desi'gramo/ *n. m.* decigram.

decilitro /deθi'litro; desi'litro/ *n. m.* deciliter.

décima /'deθima; 'desima/ *n. f.* ten-line stanza.

decimal /deθi'mal; desi'mal/ *a.* decimal.

décimo /'deθimo; 'desimo/ *a.* tenth.

decir /de'θir; de'sir/ *v.* tell, say. **es d.,** that is (to say).

decisión /deθi'sion; desi'sion/ *n. f.* decision.

decisivamente /deθisiβa'mente; desisiβa'mente/ *adv.* decisively.

decisivo /deθi'siβo; desi'siβo/ *a.* decisive.

declamación /deklama'θion; deklama'sion/ *n. f.* declamation, speech.

declamar /dekla'mar/ *v.* declaim.

declaración /deklara'θion; deklara'sion/ *n. f.* declaration; statement; plea.

declaración de la renta /deklara'θion de la 'rrenta; deklara'sion de la 'rrenta/ tax return.

declarar /dekla'rar/ *v.* declare, state.

declarativo /deklara'tiβo, deklara'torio/ *a.* declarative.

declinación /deklina'θion; deklina'sion/ *n. f.* descent; decay; decline; declension.

declinar /dekli'nar/ *v.* decline.

declive /de'kliβe,/ *n. m.* declivity, slope.

decocción /dekok'θion; dekok'sion/ *n. f.* decoction.

decomiso /deko'miso/ *n. m.* seizure, confiscation.

decoración /dekora'θion; dekora'sion/ *n. f.* decoration, trimming.

decorado /deko'raðo/ *n. m. Theat.* scenery, set.

decorar /deko'rar/ *v.* decorate, trim.

decorativo /dekora'tiβo/ *a.* decorative, ornamental.

decoro /de'koro/ *n. m.* decorum; decency.

decoroso /deko'roso/ *a.* decorous.

decrecer /dekre'θer; dekre'ser/ *v.* decrease.

decrépito /de'krepito/ *a.* decrepit.

decreto /de'kreto/ *n. m.* decree. —**decretar**, *v.*

dedal /de'ðal/ *n. m.* thimble.

dédalo /'deðalo/ *n. m.* labyrinth.

dedicación /deðika'θion; deðika'sion/ *n. f.* dedication.

dedicar /deði'kar/ *v.* devote; dedicate.

dedicatoria /deðika'toria/ *n. f.* dedication, inscription.

dedo /'deðo/ *n. m.* finger, toe.

dedo anular /'deðo anu'lar/ ring finger.

dedo corazón /'deðo kora'θon; 'deðo kora'son/ middle finger.

dedo índice /'deðo 'indiθe; 'deðo 'indise/ index finger.

dedo meñique /'deðo me'ɲike/ little finger, pinky.

dedo pulgar /'deðo pul'gar/ thumb.

deducción /deðuk'θion; deðuk'sion/ *n. f.* deduction.

deducir /deðu'θir; deðu'sir/ *v.* deduce; subtract.

defectivo /defek'tiβo/ *a.* defective.

defecto /de'fekto/ *n. m.* defect, flaw.

defectuoso /defek'tuoso/ *a.* defective, faulty.

defender /defen'der/ *v.* defend.

defensa /de'fensa/ *n. f.* defense.

defensivo /defen'siβo/ *a.* defensive.

defensor /defen'sor/ **-ra** *n.* defender.

deferencia /defe'renθia; deferensia/ *n. f.* deference.

deferir /defe'rir/ *v.* defer.

deficiente /defi'θiente; defi'siente/ *a.* deficient.

déficit /'defiθit; 'defisit/ *n. m.* deficit.

definición /defini'θion; defini'sion/ *n. f.* definition.

definido /defi'niðo/ *a.* definite.

definir /defi'nir/ *v.* define; establish.

definitivamente /definitiβa'mente/ *adv.* definitely.

definitivo /defini'tiβo/ *a.* definitive.

deformación /deforma'θion; deforma'sion/ *n. f.* deformation.

deformar /defor'mar/ *v.* deform.

deforme /de'forme/ *a.* deformed; ugly.

deformidad /deformi'ðað/ *n. f.* deformity.

defraudar /defrau'ðar/ *v.* defraud.

defunción /defun'θion; defun'sion/ *n. f.* death.

degeneración /dehenera'θion; henera'sion/ *n. f.* degeneration.

degenerado /dehene'raðo/ *a.* degenerate. —**degenerar**, *v.*

deglutir /deglu'tir/ *v.* swallow.

degollar /dego'ʎar; dego'yar/ *v.* behead.

degradación /degraða'θion; degraða'sion/ *n. f.* degradation.

degradar /degra'ðar/ *v.* degrade, debase.

deidad /dei'ðað/ *n. f.* deity.

deificación /deifika'θion; deifika'sion/ *n. f.* deification.

deificar /deifi'kar/ *v.* deify.

deífico /de'ifiko/ *a.* divine, deific.

deísmo /de'ismo/ *n. m.* deism.

dejadez /deha'ðeθ; deha'ðes/ *n. f.* neglect, untidiness; laziness.

dejado /de'haðo/ *a.* untidy; lazy.

dejar /de'har/ *v.* let, allow; leave. **d. de,** stop, leave off. **no d. de,** not fail to.

dejo /'deho/ *n. m.* abandonment; negligence; aftertaste; accent.

del /del/ *contr. of* **de** + **el**.

delantal /delan'tal/ *n. m.* apron; pinafore. **delantal de niña,** pinafore.

delante /de'lante/ *adv.* ahead, forward; in front.

delantero /delan'tero/ *a.* forward, front, first.

delator /dela'tor/ *n. m.* informer; accuser.

delegación /delega'θion; delega'sion/ *n. f.* delegation.

delegado /dele'gaðo/ **-da** *n.* delegate. —**delegar**, *v.*

deleite /de'leite/ *n. m.* delight. —**deleitar**, *v.*

deleitoso /delei'toso/ *a.* delightful.

deletrear /deletre'ar/ *v.* spell; decipher.

delfín /del'fin/ *n. m.* dolphin; dauphin.

delgadez /delga'ðeθ; delgaðes/ *n. f.* thinness, slenderness.

delgado /del'gaðo/ *a.* thin, slender, slim, slight.

deliberación /deliβera'θion; deliβera'sion/ *n. f.* deliberation.

deliberadamente /deliβeraða'mente/ *adv.* deliberately.

deliberar /deliβe'rar/ *v.* deliberate.

deliberativo /deliβera'tiβo/ *a.* deliberative.

delicadamente /delikaða'mente/ *adv.* delicately.

delicadeza /delika'ðeθa; delika'ðesa/ *n. f.* delicacy.

delicado /deli'kaðo/ *a.* delicate, dainty.

delicia /deli'θia; deli'sia/ *n. f.* delight; deliciousness.

delicioso /deli'θioso; deli'sioso/ *a.* delicious.

delincuencia /delin'kuenθia; delin'kuensia/ *n. f.* delinquency.

delincuencia de menores /delin'kuenθia de me'nores; delin'kuensia de me'nores/ **delincuencia juvenil** juvenile delinquency.

delincuente /delin'kuente/ *a. & n.* delinquent; culprit, offender.

delineación /delinea'θion; delinea'sion/ *n. f.* delineation, sketch.

delinear /deline'ar/ *v.* delineate, sketch.

delirante /deli'rante/ *a.* delirious.

delirar /deli'rar/ *v.* rave, be delirious.

delirio /de'lirio/ *n. m.* delirium; rapture, bliss.

delito /de'lito/ *n. m.* crime, offense.

delta /'delta/ *n. m.* delta (of river); hang glider.

demacrado /dema'kraðo/ *a.* emaciated.

demagogia /dema'gohia/ *n. f.* demagogy.

demagogo /dema'gogo/ *n. m.* demagogue.

demanda /de'manda/ *n. f.* demand, claim.

demandador /demanda'ðor/ **-ra** *n.* plaintiff.

demandar /deman'dar/ *v.* sue; demand.

demarcación /demarka'θion; demarka'sion/ *n. f.* demarcation.

demarcar /demar'kar/ *v.* demarcate, limit.

demás /de'mas/ *a. & n.* other; (the) rest (of). **por d.,** too much.

demasía /dema'sia/ *n. f.* excess; audacity; iniquity.

demasiado /dema'siaðo/ *a. & adv.* too; too much; too many.

demencia /de'menθia; de'mensia/ *n. f.* dementia; insanity.

demente /de'mente/ *a.* demented.

democracia /demo'kraθia; demo'krasia/ *n. f.* democracy.

demócrata /de'mokrata/ *n. m. & f.* democrat.

democrático /demo'kratiko/ *a.* democratic.

demoler /demo'ler/ *v.* demolish, tear down.

demolición /demoli'θion; demoli'sion/ *n. f.* demolition.

demonio /de'monio/ *n. m.* demon, devil.

demontre /de'montre/ *n. m.* devil.

demora /de'mora/ *n. f.* delay. —**demorar**, *v.*

demostración /demostra'θion; demostra'sion/ *n. f.* demonstration.

demostrador /demostra'ðor/ **-ra** *n.* demonstrator.

demostrar /demos'trar/ *v.* demonstrate, show.

demostrativo /demostra'tiβo/ *a.* demonstrative.

demudar /demu'ðar/ *v.* change; disguise, conceal.

denegación /denega'θion; denega'sion/ *n. f.* denial; refusal.

denegar /dene'gar/ *v.* deny; refuse.

dengue /'dengue/ *n. m.* prudishness; dengue.

denigración /denigra'θion; denigra'sion/ *n. f.* defamation, disgrace.

denigrar /deni'grar/ *v.* defame, disgrace.

denodado /deno'ðaðo/ *a.* brave, dauntless.

denominación /denomina'θion; denomina'sion/ *n. f.* denomination.

denominar /denomi'nar/ *v.* name, call.

denotación /denota'θion; denota'sion/ *n. f.* denotation.

denotar /deno'tar/ *v.* denote, betoken, express.

densidad /densi'ðað/ *n. f.* density.

denso /'denso/ *a.* dense.

dentado /den'taðo/ *a.* toothed; serrated; cogged.

dentadura /denta'ðura/ *n. f.* set of teeth.

dentadura postiza /denta'ðura pos'tiθa; denta'ðura pos'tisa/ false teeth, dentures.

dental /den'tal/ *a.* dental.

dentífrico /den'tifriko/ *n. m.* dentifrice, toothpaste.

dentista /den'tista/ *n. m. & f.* dentist.

dentistería /dentiste'ria/ *n. f.* dentistry.

dentro /'dentro/ *adv.* within, inside. **d. de poco,** in a short while.

dentudo /den'tuðo/ *a.* toothy (person).

denuedo /de'nueðo/ *n. m.* bravery, courage.

denuesto /de'nuesto/ *n. m.* insult, offense.

denuncia /de'nunθia; de'nunsia/ *n. f.* denunciation; declaration; complaint.

denunciación /denunθia'θion; denunsia'sion/ *n. f.* denunciation.

denunciar /denun'θiar; denun'siar/ *v.* denounce.

deparar /depa'rar/ *v.* offer; grant.

departamento /departa'mento/ *n. m.* department, section.

departir /depar'tir/ *v.* talk, chat.

dependencia /depen'denθia; depen'densia/ *n. f.* dependence; branch office.

depender /depen'der/ *v.* depend.

dependiente /depen'diente/ *a. & m.* dependent; clerk.

depilar /depi'lar/ *v.* depilate, pluck.

depilatorio /depila'torio/ *a. & n.* depilatory.

depistar *v.* mislead, put off the track.

deplorable /deplo'raβle/ *a.* deplorable, wretched.

deplorablemente /deploraβle'mente/ *adv.* deplorably.

deplorar /deplo'rar/ *v.* deplore.

deponer /depo'ner/ *v.* depose.

deportación /deporta'θion; deporta'sion/ *n. f.* deportation; exile.

deportar /depor'tar/ *v.* deport.

deporte /de'porte/ *n. m.* sport. —**deportivo**, *a.*

deposición /deposi'θion; deposi'sion/ *n. f.* assertion, deposition; removal; movement.

depositante /deposi'tante/ *n. m. & f.* depositor.

depósito /de'posito/ *n. m.* deposit. —**depositar**, *v.*

depravación /depraβa'θion; depraβa'sion/ *n. f.* depravation; depravity.

depravado /depra'βaðo/ *a.* depraved, wicked.

depravar /depra'βar/ *v.* deprave, corrupt, pervert.

depreciación /depreθia'θion; depresia'sion/ *n. f.* depreciation.

depreciar /depre'θiar; depre'siar/ *v.* depreciate.

depredación /depreða'θion; depreða'sion/ *n. f.* depredation.

depredar /depre'ðar/ *v.* pillage, depredate.

depresión /depre'sion/ *n. f.* depression.

depresivo /depre'siβo/ *a.* depressive.

deprimir /depri'mir/ *v.* depress.

depurar /depu'rar/ *v.* purify.

derecha /de'retʃa/ *n. f.* right (hand, side).

derechera /de'retʃera/ *n. f.* shortcut.

derecho /de'retʃo/ *a.* **1.** right; straight. —*n.* **2.** *m.* right; (the) law. **derechos, Com.** duty.

derechos civiles /de'retʃos θi'βiles; de'retʃos si'βiles/ *n. m.pl.* civil rights.

derechos de aduana /de'retʃos de a'ðuana/ *n. m.pl.* customs duty.

derechura /dere'tʃura/ *n. f.* straightness.

derelicto /dere'likto/ *a.* abandoned, derelict.

deriva /de'riβa/ *n. f. Naut.* drift.

derivación /deriβa'θion; deriβa'sion/ *n. f.* derivation.

derivar /deri'βar/ *v.* derive.

dermatólogo /derma'tologo/ **-a** *n.* dermatologist, skin doctor.

derogar /dero'gar/ *v.* derogate; repeal, abrogate.

derramamiento /derrama'miento/ *n. m.* overflow.

derramar /derra'mar/ *v.* spill, pour, scatter.

derrame /de'rrame/ *n. m.* overflow; discharge.

derretir /derre'tir/ *v.* melt, dissolve.

derribar /derri'βar/ *v.* demolish, knock down; bowl over, floor, fell.

derrocamiento /derroka'miento/ *n. m.* overthrow.

derrocar /derro'kar/ *v.* overthrow; oust; demolish.

derrochar /derro'tʃar/ *v.* waste.

derroche /de'rrotʃe/ *n. m.* waste.

derrota /de'rrota/ *n. f.* rout, defeat. —**derrotar**, *v.*

derrotismo /derro'tismo/ *n. m.* defeatism.

derruir /de'rruir/ *v.* destroy, devastate.

derrumbamiento /derrumba'miento/ **derrumbe** *m.* collapse; landslide.

derrumbarse /derrum'βarse/ *v.* collapse, tumble.

derviche /der'βitʃe/ *n. m.* dervish.

desabotonar /desaβoto'nar/ *v.* unbutton.

desabrido /desa'βriðo/ *a.* insipid, tasteless.

desabrigar /desaβri'gar/ *v.* uncover.

desabrochar /desaβro'tʃar/ *v.* unbutton, unclasp.

desacato /desa'kato/ *n. m.* disrespect, lack of respect.

desacierto /desa'θierto; desa'sierto/ *n. m.* error.

desacobardar /desakoβar'ðar/ *v.* remove fear; embolden.

desacomodadamente /desakomoðaða'mente/ *adv.* inconveniently.

desacomodado /desakomo'ðaðo/ *a.* unemployed.

desacomodar /desakomo'ðar/ *v.* molest; inconvenience; dismiss.

desacomodo /desako'moðo/ *n. m.* loss of employment.

desaconsejar /desakonse'har/ v. dissuade (someone); advise against (something).

desacordadamente /desakorða ða'mente/ adv. unadvisedly.

desacordar /desakor'ðar/ v. differ, disagree; be forgetful.

desacorde /desa'korðe/ a. discordant.

desacostumbradamente /desakostumbraða'mente/ adv. unusually.

desacostumbrado /desakostum 'braðo/ a. unusual, unaccustomed.

desacostumbrar /desakostum'brar/ v. give up a habit or custom.

desacreditar /desakreði'tar/ v. discredit.

desacuerdo /desa'kuerðo/ n. m. disagreement.

desadeudar /desaðeu'ðar/ v. pay one's debts.

desadormecer /desaðorme'θer; desaðorme'ser/ v. waken, rouse.

desadornar /desaðor'nar/ v. divest of ornament.

desadvertidamente /desaðβertiða'mente/ adv. inadvertently.

desadvertido /desaðβer'tiðo/ a. imprudent.

desadvertimiento /desaðβerti 'miento/ n. m. imprudence, rashness.

desadvertir /desaðβer'tir/ v. act imprudently.

desafección /desafek'θion; desafek 'sion/ n. f. disaffection.

desafecto /desa'fekto/ a. disaffected.

desafiar /desa'fiar/ v. defy; challenge.

desafinar /desafi'nar/ v. be out of tune.

desafío /desa'fio/ n. m. defiance; challenge.

desaforar /desafo'rar/ v. infringe one's rights; be outrageous.

desafortunado /desafortu'naðo/ a. unfortunate.

desafuero /desa'fuero/ n. m. violation of the law; outrage.

desagraciado /desagra'θiaðo; desagra'siaðo/ a. graceless.

desagradable /desagra'ðaβle/ a. disagreeable, unpleasant.

desagradablemente /desagra ðaβle'mente/ adv. disagreeably.

desagradecido /desagraðe'θiðo; desagraðe'siðo/ a. ungrateful.

desagradecimiento /desagraðe θi'miento; desagraðesimiento/ n. m. ingratitude.

desagrado /desa'graðo/ n. m. displeasure.

desagraviar /desagra'βiar/ v. make amends.

desagregar /desagre'gar/ v. separate, disintegrate.

desagriar /desa'griar/ v. mollify, appease.

desaguadero /desagua'ðero/ n. m. drain, outlet; cesspool; sink.

desaguador /desagua'ðor/ n. m. water pipe.

desaguar /desa'guar/ v. drain.

desaguisado /desagi'saðo/ n. m. offense; injury.

desahogadamente /desaogaða 'mente/ adv. impudently; brazenly.

desahogado /desao'gaðo/ a. impudent, brazen; cheeky.

desahogar /desao'gar/ v. relieve.

desahogo /desa'ogo/ n. m. relief; nerve, cheek.

desahuciar /desau'θiar; desau'siar/ v. give up hope for; despair of.

desairado /desai'raðo/ a. graceless.

desaire /des'aire/ n. m. slight; scorn. —desairar, v.

desajustar /desahus'tar/ v. mismatch, misfit; make unfit.

desalar /desa'lar/ v. hurry, hasten.

desalentar /desalen'tar/ v. make out of breath; discourage.

desaliento /desa'liento/ n. m. discouragement.

desaliñar /desali'nar/ v. disarrange; make untidy.

desaliño /desa'lino/ n. m. slovenliness, untidiness.

desalivar /desali'βar/ v. remove saliva from.

desalmadamente /desalmaða 'mente/ adv. mercilessly.

desalmado /desal'maðo/ a. merciless.

desalojamiento /desaloha'miento/ n. m. displacement; dislodging.

desalojar /desalo'har/ v. dislodge.

desalquilado /desalki'laðo/ a. vacant, unrented.

desamar /desa'mar/ v. cease loving.

desamasado /desama'saðo/ a. dissolved, disunited, undone.

desamistarse /desamis'tarse/ v. quarrel, disagree.

desamor /desa'mor/ n. m. disaffection, dislike; hatred.

desamorado /desamo'raðo/ a. cruel; harsh; rude.

desamparador /desampara'ðor/ n. m. deserter.

desamparar /desampa'rar/ v. desert, abandon.

desamparo /desam'paro/ n. m. desertion, abandonment.

desamueblado /desamue'βlaðo/ a. unfurnished.

desamueblar /desamue'βlar/ v. remove furniture from.

desandrajado /desandra'haðo/ a. shabby, ragged.

desanimadamente /desanimaða 'mente/ adv. in a discouraged manner; spiritlessly.

desanimar /desani'mar/ v. dishearten, discourage.

desánimo /des'animo/ n. m. discouragement.

desanudar /desanu'ðar/ v. untie; loosen; disentangle.

desapacible /desapa'θiβle; desapa'siβle/ a. rough, harsh; unpleasant.

desaparecer /desapare'θer; desapare'ser/ v. disappear.

desaparición /desapari'θion; desapari'sion/ n. f. disappearance.

desapasionadamente /desapa sionaða'mente/ adv. dispassionately.

desapasionado /desapasio'naðo/ a. dispassionate.

desapego /desa'pego/ n. m. impartiality.

desapercibido /desaperθi'βiðo; desapersi'βiðo/ a. unnoticed; unprepared.

desapiadado /desapia'ðaðo/ a. merciless, cruel.

desaplicación /desaplika'θion; desaplika'sion/ n. f. indolence, laziness; negligence.

desaplicado /desapli'kaðo/ a. indolent, lazy; negligent.

desaposesionar /desaposesio'nar/ v. dispossess.

desapreciar /desapre'θiar; desapre'siar/ v. depreciate.

desapretador /desapreta'ðor/ n. m. screwdriver.

desapretar /desapre'tar/ v. loosen; relieve, ease.

desaprisionar /desaprisio'nar/ v. set free, release.

desaprobación /desaproβa'θion; desaproβa'sion/ n. f. disapproval.

desaprobar /desapro'βar/ v. disapprove.

desaprovechado /desaproβe't ʃaðo/ a. useless, profitless; backward.

desaprovechar /desaproβe't ʃar/ v. waste; be backward.

desarbolar /desarβo'lar/ v. unmast.

desarmado /desar'maðo/ a. disarmed, defenseless.

desarmar /desar'mar/ v. disarm.

desarme /de'sarme/ n. m. disarmament.

desarraigado /desarrai'gaðo/ a. rootless.

desarraigar /desarrai'gar/ v. uproot; eradicate; expel.

desarreglar /desarre'glar/ v. disarrange, mess up.

desarrollar /desarro'ʎar; desarro'yar/ v. develop.

desarrollo /desa'rroʎo; des'arroyo/ n. m. development.

desarropar /desarro'par/ v. undress; uncover.

desarrugar /desarru'gar/ v. remove wrinkles from.

desaseado /desase'aðo/ a. dirty; disorderly.

desasear /desase'ar/ v. make dirty or disorderly.

desaseo /desa'seo/ n. m. dirtiness; disorder.

desasir /desa'sir/ v. loosen; disengage.

desasociable /desaso'θiaβle; desaso'siaβle/ a. unsociable.

desasosegar /desasose'gar/ v. disturb.

desasosiego /desaso'siego/ n. m. uneasiness.

desastrado /desas'traðo/ a. ragged, wretched.

desastre /de'sastre/ n. m. disaster.

desastroso /desas'troso/ a. disastrous.

desatar /desa'tar/ v. untie, undo.

desatención /desaten'θion; desaten'sion/ n. f. inattention; disrespect; rudeness.

desatender /desaten'der/ v. ignore; disregard.

desatentado /desaten'taðo/ a. inconsiderate; imprudent.

desatinado /desati'naðo/ a. foolish; insane, wild.

desatino /desa'tino/ n. m. blunder. —desatinar, v.

desatornillar /desatorni'ʎar; desatorni'yar/ v. unscrew.

desautorizado /desautori'θaðo; desautori'saðo/ a. unauthorized.

desautorizar /desautori'θar; desautori'sar/ v. deprive of authority.

desavenencia /desaβe'nenθia; desaβe'nensia/ n. f. disagreement, discord.

desaventajado /desaβenta'haðo/ a. disadvantageous.

desayuno /desa'yuno/ n. m. breakfast. —desayunar, v.

desazón /desa'θon; desa'son/ n. f. insipidity; uneasiness.

desazonado /desaθo'naðo; desaso'naðo/ a. insipid; uneasy.

desbandada /desβan'daða/ n. f. disbanding.

desbandarse /desβan'darse/ v. disband.

desbarajuste /desβara'huste/ n. m. disorder, confusion.

desbaratar /desβara'tar/ v. destroy.

desbastar /desβas'tar/ v. plane, smoothen.

desbocado /desβo'kaðo/ a. foulspoken, indecent.

desbocarse /desβo'karse/ v. use obscene language.

desbordamiento /desβorða'miento/ n. m. overflow; flood.

desbordar /desβor'ðar/ v. overflow.

desbrozar /desβro'θar; desβro'sar/ v. clear away rubbish.

descabal /deska'βal/ a. incomplete.

descabalar /deskaβa'lar/ v. render incomplete; impair.

descabellado /deskaβe'ʎaðo; deskaβe'yaðo/ a. absurd, preposterous.

descabezar /deskaβe'θar; deskaβe'sar/ v. behead.

descaecimiento /deskaeθi'miento; deskaesi'miento/ n. m. weakness; dejection.

descafeinado /deskafei'naðo/ a. decaffeinated.

descalabrar /deskala'βrar/ v. injure, wound (esp. the head).

descalabro /deska'laβro/ n. m. accident, misfortune.

descalzarse /deskal'θarse; deskal'sarse/ v. take off one's shoes.

descalzo /des'kalθo; des'kalso/ a. shoeless; barefoot.

descaminado /deskami'naðo/ a. wrong, misguided.

descaminar /deskami'nar/ v. mislead; lead into error.

descamisado /deskami'saðo/ a. shirtless; shabby.

descansillo /deskan'siʎo; deskan'siyo/ n. m. landing (of stairs).

descanso /des'kanso/ n. m. rest. —descansar, v.

descarado /deska'raðo/ a. saucy, fresh.

descarga /des'karga/ n. f. discharge.

descargar /deskar'gar/ v. discharge, unload, dump.

descargo /des'kargo/ n. m. unloading; acquittal.

descarnar /deskar'nar/ v. skin.

descaro /des'karo/ n. m. gall, effrontery.

descarriar /deska'rriar/ v. lead or go astray.

descarrilamiento /deskarrila 'miento/ n. m. derailment.

descarrilar /deskarri'lar/ v. derail.

descartar /deskar'tar/ v. discard.

descascarar /deskaska'rar/ v. peel; boast, brag.

descendencia /desθen'denθia; dessen'densia/ n. f. descent, origin; progeny.

descender /desθen'der; dessen'der/ v. descend.

descendiente /desθen'diente; dessen'diente/ n. m. & f. descendant.

descendimiento /desθendi'miento; dessendi'miento/ n. m. descent.

descenso /des'θenso; des'senso/ n. m. descent.

descentralización /desθentrali liθa'θion; dessentralisa'sion/ n. f. decentralization.

descifrar /desθi'frar; dessi'frar/ v. decipher, puzzle out.

descoco /des'koko/ n. m. boldness, brazenness.

descolgar /deskol'gar/ v. take down.

descollar /desko'ʎar; desko'yar/ v. stand out; excel.

descolorar /deskolo'rar/ v. discolor.

descolorido /deskolo'riðo/ a. pale, faded.

descomedido /deskome'ðiðo/ a. disproportionate; rude.

descomedirse /deskome'ðirse/ v. be rude.

descomponer /deskompo'ner/ v. decompose; break down, get out of order.

descomposición /deskomposi'θion; deskomposi'sion/ n. f. discomposure; disorder, confusion.

descompuesto /deskom'puesto/ a. impudent, rude.

descomulgar /deskomul'gar/ v. excommunicate.

descomunal /deskomu'nal/ a. extraordinary, huge.

desconcertar /deskonθer'tar; deskonser'tar/ v. disconcert, baffle.

desconcierto /deskon'θierto; deskon'sierto/ n. m. confusion, disarray.

desconectar /deskonek'tar/ v. disconnect.

desconfiado /deskon'fiaðo/ a. distrustful.

desconfianza /deskon'fianθa; deskon'fiansa/ n. f. distrust.

desconfiar /deskon'fiar/ v. distrust, mistrust; suspect.

descongelar /deskonge'lar/ v. defrost.

descongestionante /deskongestio 'nante/ n. m. decongestant.

desconocer /deskono'θer; deskono'ser/ v. ignore, fail to recognize.

desconocido /deskono'θiðo; deskono'siðo/ -da n. stranger.

desconocimiento /deskonoθi'mien to; deskonosi'miento/ n. m. ingratitude; ignorance.

desconsejado /deskonse'haðo/ a. imprudent, ill advised, rash.

desconsolado /deskonso'laðo/ a. disconsolate, wretched.

desconsuelo /deskon'suelo/ n. m. grief.

descontar /deskon'tar/ v. discount, subtract.

descontentar /deskonten'tar/ v. dissatisfy.

descontento /deskon'tento/ n. m. discontent.

descontinuar /deskonti'nuar/ v. discontinue.

desconvenir /deskombe'nir/ v. disagree.

descorazonar /deskoraθo'nar/; deskoraso'nar/ v. dishearten.

descorchar /deskor'tʃar/ v. uncork.

descortés /deskor'tes/ a. discourteous, impolite, rude.

descortesía /deskorte'sia/ n. f. discourtesy, rudeness.

descortezar /deskorte'θar; deskor;te'sar/ v. peel.

descoyuntar /deskoyun'tar/ v. dislocate.

descrédito /des'kreðito/ n. m. discredit.

describir /deskri'βir/ v. describe.

descripción /deskrip'θion; deskrip'sion/ n. f. description.

descriptivo /deskrip'tiβo/ a. descriptive.

descuartizar /deskuarti'θar; deskuarti'sar/ v. dismember, disjoint.

descubridor /deskuβri'ðor/ **-ra** n. discoverer.

descubrimiento /deskuβri'miento/ n. m. discovery.

descubrir /desku'βrir/ v. discover; uncover; disclose.

descubrirse /desku'βrirse/ v. take off one's hat.

descuento /des'kuento/ n. m. discount.

descuidado /deskui'ðaðo/ a. reckless, careless; slack.

descuido /des'kuiðo/ n. m. neglect. —**descuidar,** v.

desde /'desðe/ prep. since; from. **d. luego,** of course.

desdén /des'ðen/ n. m. disdain. —**desdeñar,** v.

desdeñoso /desðe'ɲoso/ a. contemptuous, disdainful, scornful.

desdicha /des'ðitʃa/ n. f. misfortune.

deseable /dese'aβle/ a. desirable.

desear /dese'ar/ v. desire, wish.

desecar /dese'kar/ v. dry, desiccate.

desechable /dese'tʃaβle/ a. disposable.

desechar /dese'tʃar/ v. scrap, reject.

desecho /de'setʃo/ n. m. remainder, residue; (pl.) waste.

desembalar /desemba'lar/ v. unpack.

desembarazado /desembara'θaðo; desembara'saðo/ a. free; unrestrained.

desembarazar /desembara'θar; desembara'sar/ v. free; extricate; unburden.

desembarcar /desembar'kar/ v. disembark, go ashore.

desembocar /desembo'kar/ v. flow into.

desembolsar /desembol'sar/ v. disburse; expend.

desembolso /desem'bolso/ n. m. disbursement.

desemejante /deseme'hante/ a. unlike, dissimilar.

desempacar /desempa'kar/ v. unpack.

desempeñar /desempe'ɲar/ v. carry out; redeem.

desempeño /desempe'ɲo/ n. m. fulfillment.

desencajar /desenka'har/ v. disjoint; disturb.

desencantar /desenkan'tar/ v. disillusion.

desencanto /desen'kanto/ n. m. disillusion.

desencarcelar /desenkarθe'lar; desenkarse'lar/ v. set free; release.

desenchufar /desentʃu'far/ v. unplug.

desenfadado /desenfa'ðaðo/ a. free; unembarrassed; spacious.

desenfado /desen'faðo/ n. m. freedom; ease; calmness.

desenfocado /desenfo'kaðo/ a. out of focus.

desengaño /deseŋ'gaɲo/ m. disillusion. —**desengañar** v.

desenlace /desen'laθe; desen'lase/ n. m. outcome, conclusion.

desenredar /desenre'ðar/ v. disentangle.

desensartar /desensar'tar/ v. unthread (pearls).

desentenderse /desenten'derse/ v. overlook; avoid noticing.

desenterrar /desente'rrar/ v. disinter, exhume.

desenvainar /desembai'nar/ v. unsheath.

desenvoltura /desembol'tura/ n. f. confidence; impudence, boldness.

desenvolver /desembol'βer/ v. evolve, unfold.

deseo /de'seo/ n. m. wish, desire, urge.

deseoso /dese'oso/ a. desirous.

deserción /deser'θion; deser'sion/ n. f. desertion.

desertar /deser'tar/ v. desert.

desertor /deser'tor/ **-ra** n. deserter.

desesperación /desespera'θion; desespera'sion/ n. f. despair, desperation.

desesperado /desespe'raðo/ a. desperate; hopeless.

desesperar /desespe'rar/ v. despair.

desfachatez /desfatʃa'teθ; desfatʃa'tes/ n. f. cheek (gall).

desfalcar /desfal'kar/ v. embezzle.

desfase horario /des'fase o'rario/ n. m. jet lag.

desfavorable /desfaβo'raβle/ a. unfavorable.

desfigurar /desfigu'rar/ v. disfigure, mar.

desfiladero /desfila'ðero/ n. m. defile.

desfile /des'file/ n. m. parade. —**desfilar,** v.

desfile de modas /des'file de 'moðas/ fashion show.

desgaire /des'gaire/ n. m. slovenliness.

desgana /des'gana/ n. f. lack of appetite; unwillingness; repugnance.

desgarrar /desga'rrar/ v. tear, lacerate.

desgastar /desgas'tar/ v. wear away; waste; erode.

desgaste /des'gaste/ n. m. wear; erosion.

desgracia /des'graθia; des'grasia/ n. f. misfortune.

desgraciado /desgra'θiaðo; desgra'siaðo/ a. unfortunate.

desgranar /desgra'nar/ v. shell.

desgreñar /desgre'ɲar/ v. dishevel.

deshacer /desa'θer; desa'ser/ v. undo, take apart, destroy.

deshacerse de /desa'θerse de; desa'serse de/ v. get rid of, dispose of.

deshecho /des'etʃo/ a. undone; wasted.

deshelar /dese'lar/ v. thaw; melt.

desheredamiento /desereða'miento/ n. m. disinheriting.

desheredar /desere'ðar/ v. disinherit.

deshielo /des'ielo/ n. m. thaw, melting.

deshinchar /desin'tʃar/ v. reduce a swelling.

deshojarse /deso'harse/ v. shed (leaves).

deshonestidad /desonesti'ðað/ n. f. dishonesty.

deshonesto /deso'nesto/ a. dishonest.

deshonra /de'sonra/ n. f. dishonor.

deshonrar /deson'rar/ v. disgrace; dishonor.

deshonroso /deson'roso/ a. dishonorable.

desierto /de'sierto/ n. m. desert, wilderness.

designar /desig'nar/ v. appoint, name.

designio /de'signio/ n. m. purpose, intent.

desigual /desi'gual/ a. uneven, unequal.

desigualdad /desigual'dað/ n. f. inequality.

desilusión /desilu'sion/ n. f. disappointment.

desinfección /desinfek'θion; desinfek'sion/ n. f. disinfection.

desinfectar /desinfek'tar/ v. disinfect.

desintegrar /desinte'grar/ v. disintegrate, zap.

desinterés /desinte'res/ n. m. indifference.

desinteresado /desintere'saðo/ a. disinterested, unselfish.

desistir /desis'tir/ v. desist, stop.

desleal /desle'al/ a. disloyal.

deslealtad /desleal'tað/ n. f. disloyalty.

desleir /desle'ir/ v. dilute, dissolve.

desligar /desli'gar/ v. untie, loosen; free, release.

deslindar /deslin'dar/ v. make the boundaries of.

deslinde /des'linde/ n. m. demarcation.

desliz /des'liθ; des'lis/ n. m. slip; false step; weakness.

deslizarse /desli'θarse; desli'sarse/ v. slide; slip; glide; coast.

deslumbramiento /deslumbra'miento/ n. m. dazzling glare; confusion.

deslumbrar /deslumb'rar/ v. dazzle; glare.

deslustre /des'lustre/ n. m. tarnish. —**deslustrar,** v.

desmán /des'man/ n. m. mishap; misbehavior; excess.

desmantelar /desmante'lar/ v. dismantle.

desmañado /desma'ɲaðo/ a. awkward, clumsy.

desmaquillarse /desmaki'ʎarse; desmaki'yarse/ v. remove one's makeup.

desmayar /desma'yar/ v. depress, dishearten.

desmayo /des'mayo/ n. m. faint. —**desmayarse,** v.

desmejorar /desmeho'rar/ v. make worse; decline.

desmembrar /desmem'brar/ v. dismember.

desmemoria /desme'moria/ n. f. forgetfulness.

desmemoriado /desmemo'riaðo/ a. forgetful.

desmentir /desmen'tir/ v. contradict, disprove.

desmenuzable /desmenu'θaβle; desmenu'saβle/ a. crisp, crumbly.

desmenuzar /desmenu'θar; desmenu'sar/ v. crumble, break into bits.

desmesurado /desmesu'raðo/ a. excessive.

desmobilizar /desmoβili'θar; desmoβili'sar/ v. demobilize.

desmonetización /desmonetiθa'θion; desmonetisa'sion/ n. f. demonetization.

desmonetizar /desmoneti'θar; desmoneti'sar/ v. demonetize.

desmontado /desmon'taðo/ a. dismounted.

desmontar /desmon'tar/ v. dismantle.

desmontarse /desmon'tarse/ v. dismount.

desmoralización /desmoraliθa'θion; desmoralisa'sion/ n. f. demoralization.

desmoralizar /desmorali'θar; desmorali'sar/ v. demoralize.

desmoronar /desmoro'nar/ v. crumble, decay.

desmovilizar /desmoβili'θar; desmoβili'sar/ v. demobilize.

desnatar /desna'tar/ v. skim.

desnaturalización /desnaturaliθa'θion; desnaturalisa'sion/ n. f. denaturalization.

desnaturalizar /desnaturali'θar; desnaturali'sar/ v. denaturalize.

desnegamiento /desnega'miento/ n. m. denial, contradiction.

desnervar /desner'βar/ v. enervate.

desnivel /desni'βel/ n. m. unevenness or difference in elevation.

desnudamente /desnuða'mente/ adv. nakedly.

desnudar /desnu'ðar/ v. undress.

desnudez /desnu'ðeθ; desnu'ðes/ n. f. bareness, nudity.

desnudo /des'nuðo/ a. bare, naked.

desnutrición /desnutri'θion; desnutri'sion/ n. f. malnutrition.

desobedecer /desoβeðe'θer; desoβeðe'ser/ v. disobey.

desobediencia /desoβeðien'θia; desoβeðien'sia/ n. f. disobedience.

desobediente /desoβe'ðiente/ a. disobedient.

desobedientemente /desoβeðiente'mente/ adv. disobediently.

desobligar /desoβli'gar/ v. release from obligation; offend.

desocupado /desoku'paðo/ a. idle, not busy; vacant.

desocupar /desoku'par/ v. vacate.

desolación /desola'θion; desola'sion/ n. f. desolation; ruin.

desolado /deso'laðo/ a. desolate. —**desolar,** v.

desollar /deso'ʎar; deso'yar/ v. skin.

desorden /de'sorðen/ n. m. disorder.

desordenar /desorðe'nar/ v. disarrange.

desorganización /desorganiθa'θion; desorganisa'sion/ n. f. disorganization.

desorganizar /desorgani'θar; desorgani'sar/ v. disorganize.

despabilado /despaβi'laðo/ a. vigilant, watchful; lively.

despachar /despa'tʃar/ v. dispatch, ship, send.

despacho /despa'tʃo/ n. m. shipment; dispatch, promptness; office.

despacio /des'paθio; des'pasio/ adv. slowly.

desparpajo /despar'paho/ n. m. glibness; fluency of speech.

desparramar /desparra'mar/ v. scatter.

despavorido /despaβo'riðo/ a. terrified.

despecho /des'petʃo/ n. m. spite.

despedazar /despeða'θar; despeða'sar/ v. tear up.

despedida /despe'ðiða/ n. f. farewell; leave-taking; discharge.

despedir /despe'ðir/ v. dismiss, discharge; see off.

despedirse de /despe'ðirse de/ v. say good-bye to, take leave of.

despegar /despe'gar/ v. unglue; separate; Aero. take off.

despego /des'pego/ n. m. indifference; disinterest.

despejar /despe'har/ v. clear, clear up.

despejo /des'peho/ n. m. sprightliness; clarity; without obstruction.

despensa /des'pensa/ n. f. pantry.

despensero /despen'sero/ n. m. butler.

despeñar /despe'ɲar/ v. throw down.

desperdicio /desper'ðiθio; desper'ðisio/ n. m. waste. —**desperdiciar,** v.

despertador /desperta'ðor/ n. m. alarm clock.

despertar /desper'tar/ v. wake, wake up.

despesar /despe'sar/ n. m. dislike.

despicar /despi'kar/ v. satisfy.

despidida /despi'ðiða/ n. f. gutter.

despierto /des'pierto/ a. awake; alert, wide-awake.

despilfarrado /despilfa'rraðo/ *a.* wasteful, extravagant.
despilfarrar /despilfa'rrar/ *v.* waste, squander.
despilfarro /despil'farro/ *n. m.* waste, extravagance.
despique /des'pike/ *n. m.* revenge.
despistar /despis'tar/ *v.* mislead, put off the track.
desplazamiento /desplaθa'miento; desplasa'miento/ *n. m.* displacement.
desplegar /desple'gar/ *v.* display; unfold.
desplome /des'plome/ *n. m.* collapse. **—desplomarse,** *v.*
desplumar /desplu'mar/ *v.* defeather, pluck.
despoblar /despo'βlar/ *v.* depopulate.
despojar /despo'har/ *v.* strip; despoil, plunder.
despojo /des'poho/ *n. m.* plunder, spoils; (*pl.*) remains, debris.
desposado /despo'saðo/ *a.* newly married.
desposar /despo'sar/ *v.* marry.
desposeer /despose'er/ *v.* dispossess.
déspota /'despota/ *n. m. & f.* despot.
despótico /des'potiko/ *a.* despotic.
despotismo /despo'tismo/ *n. m.* despotism, tyranny.
despreciable /despre'θiaβle; despre-'siaβle/ *a.* contemptible.
despreciar /despre'θiar; despre'siar/ *v.* spurn, despise, scorn.
desprecio /des'preθio; des'presio/ *n. m.* scorn, contempt.
desprender /despren'der/ *v.* detach, unfasten.
desprenderse /despren'derse/ *v.* loosen, come apart. **d. de,** part with.
desprendido /despren'diðo/ *a.* disinterested.
despreocupado /despreoku'paðo/ *a.* unconcerned; unprejudiced.
desprevenido /despreβe'niðo/ *a.* unprepared, unready.
desproporción /despropor'θion; despropor'sion/ *n. f.* disproportion.
despropósito /despro'posito/ *n. m.* nonsense.
desprovisto /despro'βisto/ *a.* devoid.
después /des'pues/ *adv.* afterwards, later; then, next. **d. de, d. que,** after.
despuntar /despun'tar/ *v.* blunt; remove the point of.
desquiciar /deski'θiar; deski'siar/ *v.* unhinge; disturb, unsettle.
desquitar /deski'tar/ *v.* get revenge, retaliate.
desquite /des'kite/ *n. m.* revenge, retaliation.
desrazonable /desraθo'naβle; desraso'naβle/ *a.* unreasonable.
destacamento /destaka'mento/ *n. m. Mil.* detachment.
destacarse /desta'karse/ *v.* stand out, be prominent.
destajero /desta'hero/ **-a** *n.* **destajista,** *m. & f.* pieceworker.
destapar /desta'par/ *v.* uncover.
destello /des'teʎo; deste'yo/ *n. m.* sparkle, gleam.
destemplar /destem'plar/ *v. Mus.* untune; disturb, upset.
desteñir /deste'ɲir/ *v.* fade, discolor.
desterrado /deste'rraðo/ **-da** *n.* exile.
desterrar /deste'rrar/ *v.* banish, exile.
destetar /deste'tar/ *v.* wean.
destierro /des'tierro/ *n. m.* banishment, exile.
destilación /destila'θion; destila-'sion/ *n. f.* distillation.
destilar /desti'lar/ *v.* distill.
destilería /destile'ria/ *n. f.* distillery.
destilería de petróleo /destile'ria de pe'troleo/ oil refinery.
destinación /destina'θion; destina-'sion/ *n. f.* destination.
destinar /desti'nar/ *v.* destine, intend.
destinatario /destina'tario/ **-ria** *n.* addressee (mail); payee (money).
destino /des'tino/ *n. m.* destiny, fate; destination.
destitución /destitu'θion; destitu'sion/ *n. f.* dismissal; abandonment.
destituido /desti'tuiðo/ *a.* destitute.
destorcer /destor'θer; destor'ser/ *v.* undo, straighten out.
destornillado /destorni'ʎaðo; destorni'yaðo/ *a.* reckless, careless.
destornillador /destorni'ʎaðor; destorni'yaðor/ *n. m.* screwdriver.
destraillar /destrai'ʎar; destrai'yar/ *v.* unleash; set loose.
destral /des'tral/ *n. m.* hatchet.
destreza /des'treθa; des'tresa/ *n. f.* cleverness; dexterity, skill.
destripar /destri'par/ *v.* eviscerate, disembowel.
destrísimo /des'trisimo/ *a.* extremely dexterous.
destronamiento /destrona'miento/ *n. m.* dethronement.
destronar /destro'nar/ *v.* dethrone.
destrozador /destroθa'ðor; destrosa'ðor/ *n. m.* destroyer, wrecker.
destrozar /destro'θar; destro'sar/ *v.* destroy, wreck.
destrozo /des'troθo; des'troso/ *n. m.* destruction, ruin.
destrucción /destruk'θion; destruk-'sion/ *n. f.* destruction.
destructibilidad /destruktiβili'ðað/ *n. f.* destructibility.
destructible /destruk'tiβle/ *a.* destructible.
destructivamente /destruktiβa-'mente/ *adv.* destructively.
destructivo /destruk'tiβo/ *a.* destructive.
destruir /destruir/ *v.* destroy; wipe out.
desuello /desue'ʎo; desue'yo/ *n. m.* impudence.
desunión /desu'nion/ *n. f.* disunion; discord; separation.
desunir /desu'nir/ *v.* disconnect, sever.
desusadamente /desusaða'mente/ *adv.* unusually.
desusado /desu'saðo/ *a.* archaic; obsolete.
desuso /de'suso/ *n. m.* disuse.
desvalido /des'βaliðo/ *a.* helpless; destitute.
desvalijador /desβaliha'ðor/ *n. m.* highwayman.
desván /des'βan/ *n. m.* attic.
desvanecerse /desβane'θerse; desβane'serse/ *v.* vanish; faint.
desvariado /desβa'riaðo/ *a.* delirious; disorderly.
desvarío /desβa'rio/ *n. m.* raving. **—desvariar,** *v.*
desvedado /desβe'ðaðo/ *a.* free; unrestrained.
desveladamente /desβelaða'mente/ *adv.* watchfully, alertly.
desvelado /desβe'laðo/ *a.* watchful; alert.
desvelar /desβe'lar/ *v.* be watchful; keep awake.
desvelo /des'βelo/ *n. m.* vigilance; uneasiness; insomnia.
desventaja /desβen'taha/ *n. f.* disadvantage.
desventar /desβen'tar/ *v.* let air out of.
desventura /desβen'tura/ *n. f.* misfortune.
desventurado /desβentu'raðo/ *a.* unhappy; unlucky.
desvergonzado /desβergon'θaðo; desβergonsaðo/ *a.* shameless, brazen.
desvergüenza /desβer'guenθa; desβer'guensa/ *n. f.* shamelessness.
desvestir /desβes'tir/ *v.* undress.
desviación /desβia'θion; desβia'sion/ *n. f.* deviation.
desviado /des'βiaðo/ *a.* deviant; remote.
desviar /des'βiar/ *v.* divert; deviate, detour.
desvío /des'βio/ *n. m.* detour; side track; indifference.
desvirtuar /desβir'tuar/ *v.* decrease the value of.
deszumar /desθu'mar; dessu'mar/ *v.* remove the juice from.
detalle /de'taʎe; de'taye/ *n. m.* detail. **—detallar,** *v.*
detective /de'tektiβe/ *n. m. & f.* detective.
detención /deten'θion; deten'sion/ *n. f.* detention, arrest.
detenedor /detene'ðor/ **-ra** *n.* stopper; catch.
detener /dete'ner/ *v.* detain, stop; arrest.
detenidamente /deteniða'mente/ *adv.* carefully, slowly.
detenido /dete'niðo/ *adv.* stingy; thorough.
detergente /deter'hente/ *a.* detergent.
deterioración /deteriora'θion; deteriora'sion/ *n. f.* deterioration.
deteriorar /deterio'rar/ *v.* deteriorate.
determinable /determi'naβle/ *a.* determinable.
determinación /determina'θion; determina'sion/ *n. f.* determination.
determinar /determi'nar/ *v.* determine, settle, decide.
determinismo /determi'nismo/ *n. m.* determinism.
determinista /determi'nista/ *n. & a.* determinist.
detestable /detes'taβle/ *a.* detestable, hateful.
detestablemente /detestaβle-'mente/ *adv.* detestably, hatefully, abhorrently.
detestación /detesta'θion; detesta-'sion/ *n. f.* detestation, hatefulness.
detestar /detes'tar/ *v.* detest.
detonación /detona'θion; detona-'sion/ *n. f.* detonation.
detonar /deto'nar/ *v.* detonate, explode.
detracción /detrak'θion; detrak'sion/ *n. f.* detraction, defamation.
detractar /detrak'tar/ *v.* detract, defame, vilify.
detraer /detra'er/ *v.* detract.
detrás /de'tras/ *adv.* behind; in back.
detrimento /detri'mento/ *n. m.* detriment, damage.
deuda /'deuða/ *n. f.* debt.
deudo /'deuðo/ **-da** *n.* relative, kin.
deudor /deu'ðor/ **-ra** *n.* debtor.
Deuteronomio /deutero'nomio/ *n. m.* Deuteronomy.
devalar /deβa'lar/ *v.* drift off course.
devanar /deβa'nar/ *v.* to wind, as on a spool.
devanear /deβane'ar/ *v.* talk deliriously, rave.
devaneo /deβa'neo/ *n. m.* frivolity; idle pursuit; delirium.
devastación /deβasta'θion; deβasta-'sion/ *n. f.* devastation, ruin, havoc.
devastador /deβasta'ðor/ *a.* devastating.
devastar /deβas'tar/ *v.* devastate.
devenir /deβe'nir/ *v.* happen, occur; become.
devoción /deβo'θion; deβo'sion/ *n. f.* devotion.
devocionario /deβoθio'nario; deβosio'nario/ *n. m.* prayer book.
devocionero /deβoθio'nero; deβosio-'nero/ *a.* devotional.
devolver /deβol'βer/ *v.* return, give back.
devorar /deβo'rar/ *v.* devour.
devotamente /deβota'mente/ *adv.* devotedly, devoutly, piously.
devoto /de'βoto/ *a.* devout; devoted.
deyección /deiek'θion; deiek'sion/ *n. f.* depression, dejection.
día /dia/ *n. m.* day. **buenos días,** good morning.
diabetes /dia'βetes/ *n. f.* diabetes.
diabético /dia'βetiko/ *a.* diabetic.
diablear /diaβle'ar/ *v.* play pranks.
diablo /'diaβlo/ *n. m.* devil.
diablura /dia'βlura/ *n. f.* mischief.
diabólicamente /diaβolika'mente/ *adv.* diabolically.
diabólico /dia'βoliko/ *a.* diabolic, devilish.
diaconato /diako'nato/ *n. m.* deaconship.
diaconía /diako'nia/ *n. f.* deaconry.
diácono /'diakono/ *n. m.* deacon.
diacrítico /dia'kritiko/ *a.* diacritic.
diadema /dia'ðema/ *n. f.* diadem; crown.
diáfano /'diafano/ *a.* transparent.
diafragma /dia'fragma/ *n. m.* diaphragm.
diagnosticar /diagnosti'kar/ *v.* diagnose.
diagonal /diago'nal/ *n. f.* diagonal.
diagonalmente /diagonal'mente/ *adv.* diagonally.
diagrama /dia'grama/ *n. m.* diagram.
dialectal /dialek'tal/ *a.* dialectal.
dialéctico /dia'lektiko/ *a.* dialectic.
dialecto /dia'lekto/ *n. m.* dialect.
diálogo /'dialogo/ *n. m.* dialogue.
diamante /dia'mante/ *n. m.* diamond.
diamantista /diaman'tista/ *n. m. & f.* diamond cutter; jeweler.
diametral /diame'tral/ *a.* diametric.
diametralmente /diametral'mente/ *adv.* diametrically.
diámetro /'diametro/ *n. m.* diameter.
diana /'diana/ *n. f.* reveille; dartboard.
diapasón /diapa'son/ *n. m.* standard pitch; tuning fork.
diaplejía /diaple'hia/ *n. f.* paralysis.
diariamente /diaria'mente/ *adv.* daily.
diario /'diario/ *a. & m.* daily; daily paper; diary; journal.
diarrea /dia'rrea/ *n. f.* diarrhea.
diatriba /dia'triβa/ *n. f.* diatribe, harangue.
dibujo /di'βuho/ *n. m.* drawing, sketch. **—dibujar,** *v.*
dicción /dik'θion; dik'sion/ *n. f.* diction.
diccionario /dikθio'nario; diksio'nario/ *n. m.* dictionary.
diccionarista /dikθiona'rista; diksiona'rista/ *n. m. & f.* lexicographer.
dicha /'ditʃa/ *n. f.* happiness.
dicho /'ditʃo/ *n. m.* saying.
dichoso /di'tʃoso/ *a.* happy; fortunate.
diciembre /di'θiembre; di'siembre/ *n. m.* December.
dicotomía /dikoto'mia/ *n. f.* dichotomy.
dictado /dik'taðo/ *n. m.* dictation.
dictador /dikta'ðor/ **-ra** *n.* dictator.
dictadura /dikta'ðura/ *n. f.* dictatorship.
dictamen /dik'tamen/ *n. m.* dictate.
dictar /dik'tar/ *v.* dictate; direct.
dictatorial /diktato'rial/ **dictatorio** *a.* dictatorial.
didáctico /di'ðaktiko/ *a.* didactic.
diecinueve /dieθi'nueβe; diesi'nueβe/ *a. & pron.* nineteen.
dieciocho /die'θiotʃo; die'siotʃo/ *a. & pron.* eighteen.
dieciseis /dieθi'seis; diesi'seis/ *a. & pron.* sixteen.
diecisiete /dieθi'siete; diesi'siete/ *a. & pron.* seventeen.
diente /diente/ *n. m.* tooth.
diestramente /diestra'mente/ *adv.* skillfully, ably; ingeniously.
diestro /'diestro/ *a.* dexterous, skillful; clever.
dieta /'dieta/ *n. f.* diet; allowance.
dietética /die'tetika/ *n. f.* dietetics.
dietético /die'tetiko/ *a.* **1.** dietetic; dietary. *—n.* **2. -ca.** dietician.
diez /dieθ; dies/ *a. & pron.* ten.
diezmal /dieθ'mal; dies'mal/ *a.* decimal.
diezmar /dieθ'mar; dies'mar/ *v.* decimate.
difamación /difama'θion; difama'sion/ *n. f.* defamation, smear.
difamar /difa'mar/ *v.* defame, smear, libel.

difamatorio /difama'torio/ *a.* defamatory.

diferencia /dife'renθia; dife'rensia/ *n. f.* difference.

diferencial /diferen'θial; diferen'sial/ *a. & f.* differential.

diferenciar /diferen'θiar; diferen'siar/ *v.* differentiate, distinguish.

diferente /dife'rente/ *a.* different.

diferentemente /diferente'mente/ *adv.* differently.

diferir /dife'rir/ *v.* differ; defer, put off.

difícil /di'fiθil; di'fisil/ *a.* difficult, hard.

difícilmente /difiθil'mente; difisil'mente/ *adv.* with difficulty or hardship.

dificultad /difikul'taδ/ *n. f.* difficulty.

dificultar /difikul'tar/ *v.* make difficult.

dificultoso /difikul'toso/ *a.* difficult, hard.

difidencia /difi'δenθia; difi'δensia/ *n. f.* diffidence.

difidente /difi'δente/ *a.* diffident.

difteria /dif'teria/ *n. f.* diphtheria.

difundir /difun'dir/ *v.* diffuse, spread.

difunto /di'funto/ *a.* **1.** deceased, dead, late. —*n.* **2. -ta,** deceased person.

difusamente /difusa'mente/ *adv.* diffusely.

difusión /difu'sion/ *n. f.* diffusion, spread.

digerible /dihe'riβle/ *a.* digestible.

digerir /dihe'rir/ *v.* digest.

digestible /dihes'tiβle/ *a.* digestible.

digestión /dihes'tion/ *n. f.* digestion.

digestivo /dihes'tiβo/ *a.* digestive.

digesto /di'hesto/ *n. m.* digest or code of laws.

digitado /dihi'taδo/ *a.* digitate.

digital /dihi'tal/ *a.* **1.** digital. —*n.* **2.** *f.* foxglove, digitalis.

dignación /digna'θion; digna'sion/ *f.* condescension; deigning.

dignamente /digna'mente/ *adv.* with dignity.

dignarse /dig'narse/ *v.* condescend, deign.

dignatario /digna'tario/ **-ra** *n.* dignitary.

dignidad /digni'δaδ/ *n. f.* dignity.

dignificar /dignifi'kar/ *v.* dignify.

digno /'digno/ *a.* worthy; dignified.

digresión /digre'sion/ *n. f.* digression.

digresivo /digre'siβo/ *a.* digressive.

dij, dije /dih; 'dihe/ *n. m.* trinket, piece of jewelry.

dilación /dila'θion; dila'sion/ *n. f.* delay.

dilapidación /dilapiδa'θion; dilapi'δasion/ *n. f.* dilapidation.

dilapidado /dilapi'δaδo/ *a.* dilapidated.

dilatación /dilata'θion; dilata'sion/ *n. f.* dilatation, enlargement.

dilatar /dila'tar/ *v.* dilate; delay; expand.

dilatoria /dila'toria/ *n. f.* delay.

dilatorio /dila'torio/ *a.* dilatory.

dilecto /di'lekto/ *a.* loved.

dilema /di'lema/ *n. m.* dilemma.

diligencia /dili'henθia; dili'hensia/ *f.* diligence, industriousness.

diligente /dili'hente/ *a.* diligent, industrious.

diligentemente /dilihente'mente/ *adv.* diligently.

dilogía /dilo'hia/ *n. f.* ambiguous meaning.

dilución /dilu'θion; dilu'sion/ *n. f.* dilution.

diluir /dili'uir/ *v.* dilute.

diluvial /dilu'βial/ *a.* diluvial.

diluvio /di'luβio/ *n. m.* flood, deluge.

dimensión /dimen'sion/ *n. f.* dimension; measurement.

diminución /diminu'θion; diminu'sion/ *n. f.* diminution.

diminuto /dimi'nuto/ **diminutivo** *a.* diminutive, little.

dimisión /dimi'sion/ *n. f.* resignation.

dimitir /dimi'tir/ *v.* resign.

Dinamarca /dina'marka/ *n. f.* Denmark.

dinamarqués /dinamar'kes/ **-esa** *a. & n.* Danish, Dane.

dinámico /di'namiko/ *a.* dynamic.

dinamita /dina'mita/ *n. f.* dynamite.

dinamitero /dinami'tero/ **-ra** dynamiter.

dínamo /'dinamo/ *n. m.* dynamo.

dinasta /di'nasta/ *n. m.* dynast, king, monarch.

dinastía /dinas'tia/ *n. f.* dynasty.

dinástico /di'nastiko/ *a.* dynastic.

dinero /di'nero/ *n. m.* money, currency.

dinosauro /dino'sauro/ *n. m.* dinosaur.

diócesis /'dioθesis; 'diosesis/ *n. f.* diocese.

Dios /dios/ *n.* **1.** *m.* God.

dios -sa *n.* **2.** god, goddess.

diploma /di'ploma/ *n. m.* diploma.

diplomacia /diplo'maθia; diplo'masia/ *n. f.* diplomacy.

diplomado /diplo'maδo/ **-da** *n.* graduate.

diplomarse /diplo'marse/ *v.* graduate (from a school).

diplomática /diplo'matika/ *n. f.* diplomacy.

diplomático /diplo'matiko/ **-ca** *a. & n.* diplomat; diplomatic.

dipsomanía /dipsoma'nia/ *n. f.* dipsomania.

diptongo /dip'toŋgo/ *n. m.* diphthong.

diputación /diputa'θion; diputa'sion/ *n. f.* deputation, delegation.

diputado /dipu'taδo/ **-da** *n.* deputy; delegate.

diputar /dipu'tar/ *v.* depute, delegate; empower.

dique /'dike/ *n. m.* dike; dam.

dirección /direk'θion; direk'sion/ *n. f.* direction; address; guidance; *Com.* management.

directamente /direkta'mente/ *adv.* directly.

directo /di'rekto/ *a.* direct.

director /direk'tor/ **-ra** *n.* director; manager.

directorio /direk'torio/ *n. m.* directory.

dirigente /diri'hente/ *a.* directing, controlling, managing.

dirigible /diri'hiβle/ *n. m.* dirigible.

dirigir /diri'hir/ *v.* direct; lead; manage.

dirigirse a /diri'hirse a/ *v.* address; approach, turn to; head for.

disanto /di'santo/ *n. m.* holy day.

discantar /diskan'tar/ *v.* sing (esp. in counterpoint); discuss.

disceptación /disθepta'θion; dissepta'sion/ *n. f.* argument, quarrel.

disceptar /disθep'tar/ *v.* argue, quarrel.

discernimiento /disθerni'miento; disserni'miento/ *n. m.* discernment.

discernir /disθer'nir; disser'nir/ *v.* discern.

disciplina /disθi'plina; dissi'plina/ *n. f.* discipline.

disciplinable /disθipli'naβle; dissipli'naβle/ *a.* disciplinable.

disciplinar /disθipli'nar; dissipli'nar/ *v.* discipline, train, teach.

discípulo /dis'θipulo; dis'sipulo/ **-la** *n.* disciple, follower; pupil.

disco /'disko/ *n. m.* disk; (phonograph) record.

disco compacto /'disko kom'pakto/ compact disk.

disco duro /'disko 'duro/ hard disk.

disco flexible /'disko flek'siβle/ floppy disk.

discontinuación /diskontinua'θion;

diskontinua'sion/ *n. f.* discontinuation.

discontinuar /diskonti'nuar/ *v.* discontinue, break off, cease.

discordancia /diskor'δanθia; diskor'δansia/ *n. f.* discordance.

discordar /diskor'δar/ *v.* disagree, conflict.

discordia /dis'korδia/ *n. f.* discord.

discoteca /disko'teka/ *n. f.* disco, discotheque.

discreción /diskre'θion; diskre'sion/ *n. f.* discretion.

discrecional /diskreθio'nal; diskresio'nal/ *a.* optional.

discrecionalmente /diskreθional'mente; diskresional'mente/ *adv.* optionally.

discrepancia /diskre'panθia; diskre'pansia/ *n. f.* discrepancy.

discretamente /diskreta'mente/ *adv.* discreetly.

discreto /dis'kreto/ *a.* discreet.

discrimen /dis'krimen/ *n. m.* risk, hazard.

discriminación /diskrimina'θion; diskrimina'sion/ *n. f.* discrimination.

discriminar /diskrimi'nar/ *v.* discriminate.

disculpa /dis'kulpa/ *n. f.* excuse; apology.

disculpar /diskul'par/ *v.* excuse; exonerate.

disculparse /diskul'parse/ *v.* apologize.

discurrir /disku'rrir/ *v.* roam; flow; think; plan.

discursante /diskur'sante/ *n.* lecturer, speaker.

discursivo /diskur'siβo/ *a.* discursive.

discurso /dis'kurso/ *n. m.* speech, talk.

discusión /disku'sion/ *n. f.* discussion.

discutible /disku'tiβle/ *a.* debatable.

discutir /disku'tir/ *v.* discuss; debate; contest.

disecación /diseka'θion; diseka'sion/ *n. f.* dissection.

disecar /dise'kar/ *v.* dissect.

disección /disek'θion; disek'sion/ *n. f.* dissection.

diseminación /disemina'θion; disemina'sion/ *n. f.* dissemination.

diseminar /disemi'nar/ *v.* disseminate, spread.

disensión /disen'sion/ *n. f.* dissension; dissent.

disenso /di'senso/ *n. m.* dissent.

disentería /disente'ria/ *n. f.* dysentery.

disentir /disen'tir/ *v.* disagree, dissent.

diseñador /diseɲa'δor/ **-ra** *n.* designer.

diseño /di'seɲo/ *n. m.* design. —**diseñar,** *v.*

disertación /diserta'θion; diserta'sion/ *n. f.* dissertation.

disforme /dis'forme/ *a.* deformed, monstrous, ugly.

disformidad /disformi'δaδ/ *n. f.* deformity.

disfraz /dis'fraθ; dis'fras/ *n. m.* disguise. —**disfrazar,** *v.*

disfrutar /disfru'tar/ *v.* enjoy.

disfrute /dis'frute/ *n. m.* enjoyment.

disgustar /disgus'tar/ *v.* displease; disappoint.

disgusto /dis'gusto/ *n. m.* displeasure; disappointment.

disidencia /disi'δenθia; disi'δensia/ *n. f.* dissidence.

disidente /disi'δente/ *a. & n.* dissident.

disímil /di'simil/ *a.* unlike.

disimilitud /disimili'tuδ/ *n. f.* dissimilarity.

disimulación /disimula'θion; disimula'sion/ *n. f.* dissimulation.

disimulado /disimu'laδo/ *a.* dissembling, feigning; sly.

disimular /disimu'lar/ *v.* hide; dissemble.

disimulo /di'simulo/ *n. m.* pretense.

disipación /disipa'θion; disipa'sion/ *n. f.* dissipation.

disipado /disi'paδo/ *a.* dissipated; wasted; scattered.

disipar /disi'par/ *v.* waste; scatter.

dislexia /dis'leksia/ *n. f.* dyslexia.

disléxico /dis'leksiko/ *a.* dyslexic.

dislocación /disloka'θion; disloka'sion/ *n. f.* dislocation.

dislocar /dislo'kar/ *v.* dislocate; displace.

disminuir /dismi'nuir/ *v.* diminish, lessen, reduce.

disociación /disoθia'θion; disosia'sion/ *n. f.* dissociation.

disociar /diso'θiar; diso'siar/ *v.* dissociate.

disolubilidad /disoluβili'δaδ/ *n. f.* dissolubility.

disoluble /diso'luβle/ *a.* dissoluble.

disolución /disolu'θion; disolu'sion/ *n. f.* dissolution.

disolutamente /disoluta'mente/ *adv.* dissolutely.

disoluto /diso'luto/ *a.* dissolute.

disolver /disol'βer/ *v.* dissolve.

disonancia /diso'nanθia; diso'nansia/ *n. f.* dissonance; discord.

disonante /diso'nante/ *a.* dissonant; discordant.

disonar /diso'nar/ *v.* be discordant; clash in sound.

dísono /di'sono/ *a.* dissonant.

dispar /dis'par/ *a.* unlike.

disparadamente /disparaδa'mente/ *adv.* hastily, hurriedly.

disparar /dispa'rar/ *v.* shoot, fire (a weapon).

disparatado /dispara'taδo/ *a.* nonsensical.

disparatar /dispara'tar/ *v.* talk nonsense.

disparate /dispa'rate/ *n. m.* nonsense, tall tale.

disparejo /dispa'reho/ *a.* uneven, unequal.

disparidad /dispari'δaδ/ *n. f.* disparity.

disparo /dis'paro/ *n. m.* shot.

dispendio /dis'pendio/ *n. m.* extravagance.

dispendioso /dispen'dioso/ *a.* expensive; extravagant.

dispensa /dis'pensa/ **dispensación** *n. f.* dispensation.

dispensable /dispen'saβle/ *a.* dispensable; excusable.

dispensar /dispen'sar/ *v.* dispense, excuse; grant.

dispensario /dispen'sario/ *n. m.* dispensary.

dispepsia /dis'pepsia/ *n. f.* dyspepsia.

dispéptico /dis'peptiko/ *a.* dyspeptic.

dispersar /disper'sar/ *v.* scatter; dispel; disband.

dispersión /disper'sion/ *n. f.* dispersion, dispersal.

disperso /dis'perso/ *a.* dispersed.

displicente /displi'θente; displi'sente/ *a.* unpleasant.

disponer /dispo'ner/ *v.* dispose. **d. de,** have at one's disposal.

disponible /dispo'niβle/ *a.* available.

disposición /disposi'θion; disposi'sion/ *n. f.* disposition; disposal.

dispuesto /dis'puesto/ *a.* disposed, inclined; attractive.

disputa /dis'puta/ *n. f.* dispute, argument.

disputable /dispu'taβle/ *a.* disputable.

disputador /disputa'δor/ **-ra** *n.* disputant.

disputar /dispu'tar/ *v.* argue; dispute.

disquete /dis'kete/ *n. m.* diskette.

disquetera /diske'tera/ *n. f.* disk drive.

disquisición /diskisi'θion; diskisi'sion/ *n. f.* disquisition.

distancia /dis'tanθia; dis'tansia/ *n. f.* distance.

distante /dis'tante/ *a.* distant.

distantemente /distante'mente/ adv. distantly.

distar /dis'tar/ v. be distant, be far.

distender /disten'der/ v. distend, swell, enlarge.

distensión /disten'sion/ n. f. distension, swelling.

dístico /'distiko/ n. m. couplet.

distinción /distin'θion; distin'sion/ n. f. distinction, difference.

distingo /dis'tiŋgo/ n. m. restriction.

distinguible /distiŋ'guiβle/ a. distinguishable.

distinguido /distiŋ'guiðo/ a. distinguished, prominent.

distinguir /distiŋ'guir/ v. distinguish; make out, spot.

distintamente /distinta'mente/ adv. distinctly, clearly; differently.

distintivo /distin'tiβo/ a. distinctive.

distintivo del país /distin'tiβo del pa'is/ country code.

distinto /dis'tinto/ a. distinct, different.

distracción /distrak'θion; distrak'sion/ n. f. distraction, pastime; absent-mindedness.

distraer /distra'er/ v. distract.

distraídamente /distraiða'mente/ adv. absent-mindedly, distractedly.

distraído /distra'iðo/ a. absent-minded; distracted.

distribución /distriβu'θion; distriβu'sion/ n. f. distribution.

distribuidor /distriβui'ðor/ -ra n. distributor.

distribuir /distri'βuir/ v. distribute.

distributivo /distriβu'tiβo/ a. distributive.

distributor /distriβu'tor/ n. m. distributor.

distrito /dis'trito/ n. m. district.

disturbar /distur'βar/ v. disturb, trouble.

disturbio /dis'turβio/ n. m. disturbance, outbreak; turmoil.

disuadir /disua'ðir/ v. dissuade.

disuasión /disua'sion/ n. f. dissuasion; deterrence.

disuasivo /disua'siβo/ a. dissuasive.

disyunción /disyun'θion; disyun'sion/ n. f. disjunction.

ditirambo /diti'rambo/ n. m. dithyramb.

diurno /'diurno/ a. diurnal.

diva /'diβa/ n. f. diva, prima donna.

divagación /diβaga'θion; diβaga'sion/ n. f. digression.

divagar /diβa'gar/ v. digress, ramble.

diván /di'βan/ n. m. couch.

divergencia /diβer'henθia; diβer'hensia/ n. f. divergence.

divergente /diβer'hente/ a. divergent, differing.

divergir /diβer'hir/ v. diverge.

diversamente /diβersa'mente/ adv. diversely.

diversidad /diβersi'ðað/ n. f. diversity.

diversificar /diβersifi'kar/ v. diversify, vary.

diversión /diβer'sion/ n. f. diversion, pastime.

diverso /di'βerso/ a. diverse, different; (pl.) various, several.

divertido /diβer'tiðo/ a. humorous, amusing.

divertimiento /diβerti'miento/ n. m. diversion; amusement.

divertir /diβer'tir/ v. entertain, amuse.

divertirse /diβer'tirse/ v. enjoy oneself, have a good time.

dividendo /diβi'ðendo/ n. m. dividend.

divididero /diβiði'ðero/ a. to be divided.

dividido /diβi'ðiðo/ a. divided.

dividir /diβi'ðir/ v. divide; separate.

divieso /di'βieso/ n. m. Med. boil.

divinamente /diβina'mente/ adv. divinely.

divinidad /diβini'ðað/ n. f. divinity.

divinizar /diβini'θar; diβini'sar/ v. deify.

divino /di'βino/ a. divine; heavenly.

divisa /di'βisa/ n. f. badge, emblem.

divisar /diβi'sar/ v. sight, make out.

divisibilidad /diβisiβili'ðað/ n. f. divisibility.

divisible /diβi'siβle/ a. divisible.

división /diβi'sion/ n. f. division.

divisivo /diβi'siβo/ a. divisive.

divo /'diβo/ n. m. movie star.

divorcio /di'βorθio; di'βorsio/ n. m. divorce. —**divorciar**, v.

divulgable /diβul'gaβle/ a. divulgable.

divulgación /diβulga'θion; diβulga'sion/ n. f. divulgation.

divulgar /diβul'gar/ v. divulge, reveal.

dobladamente /doβlaða'mente/ adv. doubly.

dobladillo /doβla'ðiʎo; doβla'ðiyo/ n. m. hem of a skirt or dress.

dobladura /doβla'ðura/ n. f. fold; bend.

doblar /do'βlar/ v. fold; bend.

doble /'doβle/ a. double.

doblegable /doβle'gaβle/ a. flexible, foldable.

doblegar /doβle'gar/ v. fold, bend; yield.

doblez /do'βleθ; do'βles/ n. m. fold; duplicity.

doblón /do'βlon/ n. m. doubloon.

doce /'doθe; 'dose/ a. & pron. twelve.

docena /do'θena; do'sena/ n. f. dozen.

docente /do'θente; do'sente/ a. educational.

dócil /'doθil; 'dosil/ a. docile.

docilidad /doθili'ðað; dosili'ðað/ n. f. docility, tractableness.

dócilmente /doθil'mente; dosil'mente/ adv. docilely, meekly.

doctamente /dokta'mente/ adv. learnedly, profoundly.

docto /'dokto/ a. learned, expert.

doctor /dok'tor/ -ra n. doctor.

doctorado /dokto'raðo/ n. m. doctorate.

doctoral /dokto'ral/ a. doctoral.

doctrina /dok'trina/ n. f. doctrine.

doctrinador /doktrina'ðor/ -ra n. teacher.

doctrinal /doktri'nal/ n. m. doctrinal.

doctrinar /doktri'nar/ v. teach.

documentación /dokumenta'θion; dokumenta'sion/ n. f. documentation.

documental /dokumen'tal/ a. documentary.

documento /doku'mento/ n. m. document.

dogal /do'gal/ n. m. noose.

dogma /'dogma/ n. m. dogma.

dogmáticamente /dogmatika'mente/ adv. dogmatically.

dogmático /dog'matiko/ n. m. dogmatic.

dogmatismo /dogma'tismo/ n. m. dogmatism.

dogmatista /dogma'tista/ n. m. & f. dogmatist.

dogo /'dogo/ n. m. bulldog.

dolar /'dolar/ v. cut, chop, hew.

dólar /'dolar/ n. m. dollar.

dolencia /do'lenθia; do'lensia/ n. f. pain; disease.

doler /do'ler/ v. ache, hurt, be sore.

doliente /do'liente/ a. ill; aching.

dolor /do'lor/ n. m. pain; grief, sorrow, woe.

dolor de cabeza /do'lor de ka'βeθa; do'lor de ka'βesa/ headache.

dolor de espalda /do'lor de es'palda/ backache.

dolor de estómago /do'lor de es'tomago/ stomachache.

dolorido /dolo'riðo/ a. painful, sorrowful.

dolorosamente /dolorosa'mente/ adv. painfully, sorrowfully.

doloroso /dolo'roso/ a. painful, sorrowful.

dolosamente /dolosa'mente/ adv. deceitfully.

doloso /do'loso/ a. deceitful.

domable /do'maβle/ a. that can be tamed or managed.

domar /do'mar/ v. tame; subdue.

dombo /'dombo/ n. m. dome.

domesticable /domesti'kaβle/ a. that can be domesticated.

domesticación /domestika'θion; domestika'sion/ n. f. domestication.

domésticamente /domestika'mente/ adv. domestically.

domesticar /domesti'kar/ v. tame, domesticate.

domesticidad /domestiθi'ðað; domestisi'ðað/ n. f. domesticity.

doméstico /do'mestiko/ a. domestic.

domicilio /domi'θilio; domi'silio/ n. m. dwelling, home, residence, domicile.

dominación /domina'θion; domina'sion/ n. f. domination.

dominador /domina'ðor/ a. dominating.

dominante /domi'nante/ a. dominant.

dominar /domi'nar/ v. rule, dominate; master.

dómine /'domine/ n. m. teacher.

domingo /do'miŋgo/ n. m. Sunday.

dominio /do'minio/ n. m. domain; rule; power.

dominó /domi'no/ n. m. domino.

domo /'domo/ n. m. dome.

don /don/ title used before a man's first name.

don /don/ n. m. gift.

donación /dona'θion; dona'sion/ n. f. donation.

donador /dona'ðor/ -ra n. giver, donor.

donaire /do'naire/ n. m. grace.

donairosamente /donairosa'mente/ adv. gracefully.

donairoso /donai'roso/ a. graceful.

donante /do'nante/ n. giver, donor.

donar /do'nar/ v. donate.

donativo /dona'tiβo/ n. m. donation, contribution; gift.

doncella /don'θeʎa; don'seya/ n. f. lass; maid.

donde /'donde/ **dónde** conj. & adv. where.

dondequiera /donde'kiera/ adv. wherever, anywhere.

donosamente /donosa'mente/ adv. gracefully; wittily.

donoso /do'noso/ a. graceful; witty.

donosura /dono'sura/ n. f. gracefulness; wittiness.

doña /'doɲa/ title used before a lady's first name.

dopar /do'par/ v. drug, dope.

dorado /do'raðo/ a. gilded.

dorador /dora'ðor/ -ra n. gilder.

dorar /do'rar/ v. gild.

dórico /'doriko/ a. Doric.

dormidero /dormi'ðero/ a. sleep-inducing; soporific.

dormido /dor'miðo/ a. asleep.

dormir /dor'mir/ v. sleep.

dormirse /dor'mirse/ v. fall asleep, go to sleep.

dormitar /dormi'tar/ v. doze.

dormitorio /dormi'torio/ n. m. dormitory; bedroom.

dorsal /dor'sal/ a. dorsal.

dorso /'dorso/ n. m. spine.

dos /dos/ a. & pron. two. **los d.**, both.

dosañal /dosa'ɲal/ a. biennial.

doscientos /dos'θientos; dos'sientos/ a. & pron. two hundred.

dosel /do'sel/ n. m. canopy; platform, dais.

dosificación /dosifika'θion; dosifika'sion/ n. f. dosage.

dosis /'dosis/ n. f. dose.

dotación /dota'θion; dota'sion/ n. f. endowment; Naut. crew.

dotador /dota'ðor/ -ra n. donor.

dotar /do'tar/ v. endow; give a dowry to.

dote /'dote/ n. f. dowry; (pl.) talents.

dragaminas /draga'minas/ n. m. mine sweeper.

dragar /dra'gar/ v. dredge; sweep.

dragón /dra'gon/ n. m. dragon; dragoon.

dragonear /dragone'ar/ v. pretend to be.

drama /'drama/ n. m. drama; play.

dramática /dra'matika/ n. f. drama, dramatic art.

dramáticamente /dramatika'mente/ adv. dramatically.

dramático /dra'matiko/ a. dramatic.

dramatizar /dramati'θar; dramati'sar/ v. dramatize.

dramaturgo /drama'turgo/ -ga n. playwright, dramatist.

drástico /'drastiko/ a. drastic.

drenaje /dre'nahe/ n. m. drainage.

dríade /'driaðe/ n. f. dryad.

dril /dril/ n. m. denim.

driza /'driθa; 'drisa/ n. f. halyard.

droga /'droga/ n. f. drug.

drogadicto /droga'ðikto/ -ta n. drug addict.

droguería /droge'ria/ n. f. drugstore.

droguero /dro'gero/ n. m. druggist.

dromedario /drome'ðario/ n. m. dromedary.

druida /'druiða/ n. m. & f. Druid.

dualidad /duali'ðað/ n. f. duality.

dubitable /duβi'taβle/ a. doubtful.

dubitación /duβita'θion; duβita'sion/ n. f. doubt.

ducado /du'kaðo/ n. m. duchy.

ducal /du'kal/ a. ducal.

ducha /'dutʃa/ n. f. shower (bath).

ducharse /du'tʃarse/ v. take a shower.

dúctil /'duktil/ a. ductile.

ductilidad /duktili'ðað/ n. f. ductility.

duda /'duða/ n. f. doubt.

dudable /du'ðaβle/ a. doubtful.

dudar /du'ðar/ v. doubt; hesitate; question.

dudosamente /duðosa'mente/ adv. doubtfully.

dudoso /du'ðoso/ a. dubious; doubtful.

duela /'duela/ n. f. stave.

duelista /due'lista/ n. m. & f. duelist.

duelo /'duelo/ n. m. duel; grief; mourning.

duende /'duende/ n. m. elf, hobgoblin.

dueño /'dueɲo/ -ña n. owner; landlord -lady; master, mistress.

dulce /'dulθe; dulse/ a. **1.** sweet. **agua d.**, fresh water. —n. **2.** m. piece of candy; (pl.) candy.

dulcedumbre /dulθe'ðumbre; dulse'ðumbre/ n. f. sweetness.

dulcemente /dulθe'mente; dulse'mente/ adv. sweetly.

dulcería /dulθe'ria; dulse'ria/ n. f. confectionery; candy shop.

dulcificar /dulθifi'kar; dulsifi'kar/ v. sweeten.

dulzura /dul'θura; dul'sura/ n. f. sweetness; mildness.

duna /'duna/ n. f. dune.

dúo /'duo/ n. m. duo, duet.

duodenal /duoðe'nal/ a. duodenal.

duplicación /duplika'θion; duplika'sion/ n. f. duplication; doubling.

duplicadamente /duplikaða'mente/ adv. doubly.

duplicado /dupli'kaðo/ a. & m. duplicate.

duplicar /dupli'kar/ v. double, duplicate, repeat.

duplicidad /dupliθi'ðað; duplisi'ðað/ n. f. duplicity.

duplo /'duplo/ a. double.

duque /'duke/ n. m. duke.

duquesa /du'kesa/ n. f. duchess.

durabilidad /duraβili'ðað/ n. f. durability.

durable /du'raβle/ a. durable.

duración /dura'θion; dura'sion/ n. f. duration.

duradero /dura'ðero/ a. lasting, durable.

duramente /dura'mente/ adv. harshly, roughly.

durante /du'rante/ prep. during.

durar /du'rar/ v. last.

durazno /du'raθno; du'rasno/ n. m. peach; peach tree.

dureza /du'reθa; du'resa/ n. f. hardness.

durmiente /dur'miente/ a. sleeping.

duro /'duro/ a. hard; stiff; stern; stale.

dux /duks/ n. m. doge.

E

e /e/ conj. and.

ebanista /eβa'nista/ n. m. & f. cabinetmaker.

ebanizar /eβani'θar; eβani'sar/ v. give an ebony finish to.

ébano /'eβano/ n. m. ebony.

ebonita /eβo'nita/ n. f. ebonite.

ebrio /'eβrio/ a. drunken, inebriated.

ebullición /eβuλi'θion; eβuyi'sion/ n. f. boiling.

echada /e'tʃaða/ n. f. throw.

echadillo /etʃa'ðiλo; etʃa'ðiyo/ n. m. foundling; orphan.

echar /e'tʃar/ v. throw, toss; pour. **e. a,** start to. **e. a perder,** spoil, ruin. **e. de menos,** miss.

echarse /e'tʃarse/ v. lie down.

eclecticismo /eklekti'θismo; eklekti'sismo/ n. m. eclecticism.

ecléctico /e'klektiko/ n. a. eclectic.

eclesiástico /ekle'siastiko/ a. & m. ecclesiastic.

eclipse /e'klipse/ n. m. eclipse. —**eclipsar,** v.

écloga /'ekloga/ n. f. eclogue.

eco /'eko/ n. m. echo.

ecología /ekolo'hia/ n. f. ecology.

ecológico /eko'lohiko/ n. f. ecological.

ecologista /ekolo'hista/ n. m. & f. ecologist.

economía /ekono'mia/ n. f. economy; thrift; economics. **e. política,** political economy.

económicamente /ekonomika'mente/ adv. economically.

económico /eko'nomiko/ a. economic; economical, thrifty; inexpensive.

economista /ekono'mista/ n. m. & f. economist.

economizar /ekonomi'θar; ekonomi'sar/ v. save, economize.

ecuación /ekua'θion; ekua'sion/ n. f. equation.

ecuador /ekua'ðor/ n. m. equator.

ecuanimidad /ekuanimi'ðað/ n. f. equanimity.

ecuatorial /ekuato'rial/ a. equatorial.

ecuatoriano /ekuato'riano/ -na a. & n. Ecuadorian.

ecuestre /e'kuestre/ a. equestrian.

ecuménico. /eku'meniko/ a. ecumenical.

edad /e'ðað/ n. f. age.

edecán /eðe'kan/ n. m. aide-de-camp.

Edén /e'ðen/ n. m. Eden.

edición /eði'θion; eði'sion/ n. f. edition; issue.

edicto /e'ðikto/ n. m. edict, decree.

edificación /eðifika'θion; eðifika'sion/ n. f. construction; edification.

edificador /eðifika'ðor/ n. constructor; builder.

edificar /eðifi'kar/ v. build.

edificio /eði'fiθio; eði'fisio/ n. m. edifice, building.

editar /eði'tar/ v. publish, issue; edit.

editor /eði'tor/ n. m. publisher; editor.

editorial /eðito'rial/ n. m. editorial; publishing house.

edredón /eðre'ðon/ n. m. quilt.

educación /eðuka'θion; eðuka'sion/ n. f. upbringing, breeding; education.

educado /eðu'kaðo/ a. well-mannered; educated.

educador /eðuka'ðor/ -ra n. educator.

educar /eðu'kar/ v. educate; bring up; train.

educativo /eðuka'tiβo/ a. educational.

educción /eðuk'θion; eðuk'sion/ n. f. deduction.

educir /eðu'θir; eðu'sir/ v. educe.

efectivamente /efektiβa'mente/ adv. actually, really.

efectivo /efek'tiβo/ a. effective; actual, real. **en e.,** Com. in cash.

efecto /e'fekto/ n. m. effect.

efecto invernáculo /e'fekto imber'nakulo/ greenhouse effect.

efectuar /efek'tuar/ v. effect; cash.

eferente /efe'rente/ a. efferent.

efervescencia /eferβes'θenθia; eferβes'sensia/ n. f. effervescence; zeal.

eficacia /efi'kaθia; efi'kasia/ n. f. efficacy.

eficaz /efi'kaθ; efi'kas/ a. efficient, effective.

eficazmente /efikaθ'mente; efikas'mente/ adv. efficaciously.

eficiencia /efi'θienθia; efi'siensia/ n. f. efficiency.

eficiente /efi'θiente; efi'siente/ a. efficient.

efigie /e'fihie/ n. f. effigy.

efímera /efi'mera/ n. f. mayfly.

efímero /e'fimero/ a. ephemeral, passing.

efluvio /e'fluβio/ n. m. effluvium.

efundir /efun'dir/ v. effuse; pour out.

efusión /efu'sion/ n. f. effusion.

egipcio /e'hipθio; e'hipsio/ -cia a. & n. Egyptian.

Egipto /e'hipto/ n. m. Egypt.

egoísmo /ego'ismo/ n. m. egoism, egotism, selfishness.

egoísta /ego'ista/ a. & n. selfish, egoistic; egoist.

egotismo /ego'tismo/ n. m. egotism.

egotista /ego'tista/ n. m. & f. egotist.

egreso /e'greso/ n. m. expense, outlay.

eje /'ehe/ n. m. axis; axle.

ejecución /eheku'θion; eheku'sion/ n. f. execution; performance; enforcement.

ejecutar /eheku'tar/ v. execute; enforce; carry out.

ejecutivo /eheku''tiβo/ -va a. & n. executive.

ejecutor /eheku'tor/ -ra n. executor.

ejemplar /ehem'plar/ a. **1.** exemplary. —n. **2.** m. copy.

ejemplificación /ehemplifika'θion; ehemplifika'sion/ n. f. exemplification.

ejemplificar /ehemplifi'kar/ v. illustrate.

ejemplo /e'hemplo/ n. m. example.

ejercer /eher'θer; eher'ser/ v. exert; practice.

ejercicio /eher'θiθio; eher'sisio/ n. m. exercise, drill. —**ejercitar,** v.

ejercitación /eherθita'θion; ehersita'sion/ n. f. exercise, training, drill.

ejercitar /eherθi'tar; ehersi'tar/ v. exercise, train, drill.

ejército /e'herθito; e'hersito/ n. m. army.

ejotes /e'hotes/ n. m.pl. string beans.

el /el/ art. & pron. the; the one.

él pron. he, him; it.

elaboración /elaβora'θion; elaβora'sion/ n. f. elaboration; working up.

elaborado /elaβo'raðo/ a. elaborate.

elaborador /elaβora'ðor/ n. m. manufacturer, maker.

elaborar /elaβo'rar/ v. elaborate; manufacture; brew.

elación /ela'θion; ela'sion/ n. f. elation; magnanimity; turgid style.

elasticidad /elastiθi'ðað; elastisi'ðað/ n. f. elasticity.

elástico /e'lastiko/ a. elastic.

elección /elek'θion; elek'sion/ n. f. election; option, choice.

electivo /elek'tiβo/ a. elective.

electo /e'lekto/ a. elected, chosen, appointed.

electorado /elekto'raðo/ n. m. electorate.

electoral /elekto'ral/ a. electoral.

electricidad /elektriθi'ðað; elektrisi'ðað/ n. f. electricity.

electricista /elektri'θista; elektri'sista/ n. m. & f. electrician.

eléctrico /e'lektriko/ a. electric.

electrización /elektriθa'θion; elektrisa'sion/ n. f. electrification.

electrocardiograma /e,lektrokar'ðio'grama/ n. m. electrocardiogram.

electrocución /elektroku'θion; elektroku'sion/ n. f. electrocution.

electrocutar /elektroku'tar/ v. electrocute.

electrodo /elek'troðo/ n. m. electrode.

electrodoméstico /e,lektroðo'mestiko/ n. m. electrical appliance, home appliance.

electroimán /elektroi'man/ n. m. electromagnet.

electrólisis /elek'trolisis/ n. f. electrolysis.

electrólito /elek'trolito/ n. m. electrolyte.

electrón /elek'tron/ n. m. electron.

electrónico /elek'troniko/ a. electronic.

elefante /ele'fante/ n. m. elephant.

elegancia /ele'ganθia; ele'gansia/ n. f. elegance.

elegante /ele'gante/ a. elegant, smart, stylish, fine.

elegantemente /elegante'mente/ adv. elegantly.

elegía /ele'hia/ n. f. elegy.

elegibilidad /elehiβili'ðað/ n. f. eligibility.

elegible /ele'hiβle/ a. eligible.

elegir /ele'hir/ v. select, choose; elect.

elemental /elemen'tal/ a. elementary.

elementalmente /elemental'mente/ adv. elementally; fundamentally.

elemento /ele'mento/ n. m. element.

elepé /ele'pe/ n. m. long-playing (record), LP.

elevación /eleβa'θion; eleβa'sion/ n. f. elevation; height.

elevador /eleβa'ðor/ n. m. elevator.

elevamiento /eleβa'miento/ n. m. elevation.

elevar /ele'βar/ v. elevate; erect, raise.

elidir /eli'ðir/ v. elide.

eliminación /elimina'θion; elimina'sion/ n. f. elimination.

eliminar /elimi'nar/ v. eliminate.

elipse /e'lipse/ n. f. ellipse.

elipsis /e'lipsis/ n. f. ellipsis.

elíptico /e'liptiko/ a. elliptic.

ella /'eλa; 'eya/ pron. she, her; it.

ello /'eλo; 'eyo/ pron. it.

ellos /'eλos; 'eyos/ -as pron. pl. they, them.

elocuencia /elo'kuenθia; elo'kuensia/ n. f. eloquence.

elocuente /elo'kuente/ a. eloquent.

elocuentemente /elokuente'mente/ adv. eloquently.

elogio /e'lohio/ n. m. praise, compliment. —**elogiar,** v.

elucidación /eluθiða'θion; elusiða'sion/ n. f. elucidation.

elucidar /eluθi'ðar; elusi'ðar/ v. elucidate.

eludir /elu'ðir/ v. elude.

emanar /ema'nar/ v. emanate, stem.

emancipación /emanθipa'θion; emansipa'sion/ n. f. emancipation; freeing.

emancipador /emanθipa'ðor; emansipa'ðor/ -ra n. emancipator.

emancipar /emanθi'par; emansi'par/ v. emancipate; free.

embajada /emba'haða/ n. f. embassy; legation; Colloq. errand.

embajador /embaha'ðor/ -ra n. ambassador.

embalar /emba'lar/ v. pack, bale.

embaldosado /embaldo'saðo/ n. m. tile floor.

embalsamador /embalsama'ðor/ n. m. embalmer.

embalsamar /embalsa'mar/ v. embalm.

embarazada /embara'θaða; embara'saða/ a. pregnant.

embarazadamente /embaraθaða'mente; embarasaða'mente/ adv. embarrassedly.

embarazar /embara'θar; embara'sar/ v. make pregnant; embarrass.

embarazo /emba'raθo; emba'raso/ n. m. embarrassment; pregnancy.

embarbascado /embarβas'kaðo/ a. difficult; complicated.

embarcación /embarka'θion; embarka'sion/ n. f. boat, ship; embarkation.

embarcadero /embarka'ðero/ n. m. wharf, pier, dock.

embarcador /embarka'ðor/ n. m. shipper, loader, stevedore.

embarcar /embar'kar/ v. embark, board ship.

embarcarse /embar'karse/ v. embark; sail.

embargador /embarga'ðor/ n. m. one who impedes; one who orders an embargo.

embargante /embar'gante/ a. impeding, hindering.

embargar /embar'gar/ v. impede, restrain; Leg. seize, embargo.

embargo /em'bargo/ n. m. seizure, embargo. **sin e.,** however, nevertheless.

embarnizar /embarni'θar; embarni'sar/ v. varnish.

embarque /em'barke/ n. m. shipment.

embarrador /embarra'ðor/ -ra n. plasterer.

embarrancar /embarran'kar/ v. get stuck in mud; Naut. run aground.

embarrar /emba'rrar/ v. plaster; besmear with mud.

embasamiento /embasa'miento/ n. m. foundation of a building.

embastecer /embaste'θer; embaste'ser/ v. get fat.

embaucador /embauka'ðor/ -ra n. impostor.

embaucar /embau'kar/ v. deceive, trick, hoax.

embaular /embau'lar/ v. pack in a trunk.

embausamiento /embausa'miento/ n. m. amazement.

embebecer /embeβe'θer; embeβe'ser/ v. amaze, astonish; entertain.

embeber /embe'βer/ v. absorb; incorporate; saturate.

embelecador /embeleka'ðor/ -ra n. impostor.

embeleco /embe'leko/ n. m. fraud, perpetration.

embeleñar /embele'ɲar/ v. fascinate, charm.

embelesamiento /embelesa'miento/ n. m. rapture.

embelesar /embele'sar/ v. fascinate, charm.

embeleso /embe'leso/ n. m. rapture, bliss.

embellecer /embeλe'θer; embeye'ser/ v. beautify, embellish.

embestida /embes'tiða/ n. f. violent assault; attack.

emblandecer /emblande'θer; emblande'ser/ v. soften; moisten; move to pity.

emblema /em'blema/ n. m. emblem.

emblemático /emble'matiko/ a. emblematic.

embocadura /emboka'ðura/ n. f. narrow entrance; mouth of a river.

embocar /embo'kar/ v. eat hastily; gorge.

embolia /em'bolia/ n. f. embolism.

émbolo /'embolo/ n. m. piston.

embolsar /embol'sar/ v. pocket.

embonar /embo'nar/ v. improve, fix, repair.

emborrachador /emborratʃa'ðor/ a. intoxicating.

emborrachar /emborra'tʃar/ v. get drunk. —**emborrar**, v.

emboscada /embos'kaða/ n. f. ambush.

emboscar /embos'kar/ v. put or lie in ambush.

embotado /embo'taðo/ a. blunt, dull (edged). —**embotar**, v.

embotadura /embota'ðura/ n. f. bluntness; dullness.

embotellamiento /emboteʎa'mien-to; emboteya'miento/ n. m. bottling (liquids); traffic jam.

embotellar /embote'ʎar; embote-'yar/ v. put in bottles.

embozado /embo'θaðo; embo'saðo/ v. muzzled; muffled.

embozar /embo'θar; embo'sar/ v. muzzle; muffle.

embozo /em'boθo; em'boso/ n. m. muffler.

embrague /em'braɣe/ n. m. Auto. clutch.

embravecer /embraβe'θer; embraβe-'ser/ v. be or make angry.

embriagado /embria'ɣaðo/ a. drunken, intoxicated.

embriagar /embria'ɣar/ v. intoxicate.

embriaguez /embria'ɣeθ; em-bria'ɣes/ n. f. drunkenness.

embrión /em'brion/ n. m. embryo.

embrionario /embrio'nario/ a. embryonic.

embrochado /embro'tʃaðo/ a. embroidered.

embrollo /em'broʎo; em'broyo/ n. m. muddle. —**embrollar**, v.

embromar /embro'mar/ v. tease; joke.

embuchado /embu'tʃaðo/ n. m. pork sausage.

embudo /em'buðo/ n. m. funnel.

embuste /em'buste/ n. m. lie, fib.

embustear /embuste'ar/ v. lie, fib.

embustero /embus'tero/ **-ra** a. liar.

embutir /embu'tir/ v. stuff, cram.

emergencia /emer'henθia; emer'hen-sia/ n. f. emergency.

emérito /e'merito/ a. emeritus.

emético /e'metiko/ n. m. & a. emetic.

emigración /emiɣra'θion; emi-ɣra'sion/ n. f. emigration.

emigrante /emi'ɣrante/ a. & n. emigrant.

emigrar /emi'ɣrar/ v. emigrate.

eminencia /emi'nenθia; emi'nensia/ n. f. eminence, height.

eminente /emi'nente/ a. eminent.

emisario /emi'sario/ **-ria** n. emissary, spy; outlet.

emisión /emi'sion/ n. f. issue; emission.

emisor /emi'sor/ n. m. radio transmitter.

emitir /emi'tir/ v. emit.

emoción /emo'θion; emo'sion/ n. f. feeling, emotion, thrill.

emocional /emo'θional; emo'sional/ a. emotional.

emocionante /emoθio'nante; emosio'nante/ a. exciting.

emocionar /emoθio'nar; emosio'nar/ v. touch, move, excite.

emolumento /emolu'mento/ n. m. emolument; perquisite.

empacar /empa'kar/ v. pack.

empacho /em'patʃo/ n. m. shyness, timidity; embarrassment.

empadronamiento /empaðrona-'miento/ n. m. census; list of taxpayers.

empalizada /empali'θaða; empali'sa-ða/ n. f. palisade, stockade.

empanada /empa'naða/ n. f. meat pie.

empañar /empa'ɲar/ v. blur; soil, sully.

empapar /empa'par/ v. soak.

empapelado /empape'laðo/ n. m. wallpaper.

empapelar /empape'lar/ v. wallpaper.

empaque /em'pake/ n. m. packing; appearance, mien.

empaquetar /empake'tar/ v. pack, package.

emparedado /empare'ðaðo/ n. m. sandwich.

emparejarse /empare'harse/ v. match, pair off; level, even off.

emparentado /emparen'taðo/ a. related by marriage.

emparrado /empa'rraðo/ n. m. arbor.

empastadura /empasta'ðura/ n. f. (dental) filling.

empastar /empas'tar/ v. fill (a tooth); paste.

empate /em'pate/ n. m. tie, draw. —**empatarse**, v.

empecer /empe'θer; empe'ser/ v. hurt, harm, injure; prevent.

empedernir /empeðer'nir/ v. harden.

empeine /em'peine/ n. m. groin; instep; hoof.

empellar /empe'ʎar; empe'yar/ v. shove, jostle.

empellón /empe'ʎon; empe'yon/ n. m. hard push, shove.

empeñar /empe'ɲar/ v. pledge; pawn.

empeñarse en /empe'ɲarse en/ v. persist in, be bent on.

empeño /em'peɲo/ n. m. persistence; pledge; pawning.

empeoramiento /empeora'miento/ n. m. deterioration.

empeorar /empeo'rar/ v. get worse.

emperador /empera'ðor/ n. m. emperor.

emperatriz /empera'triθ; empera'tris/ n. f. empress.

empernar /emper'nar/ v. bolt.

empero /em'pero/ conj. however; but.

emperramiento /emperra'miento/ n. m. stubbornness.

empezar /empe'θar; empe'sar/ v. begin, start.

empinado /empi'naðo/ a. steep.

empinar /empi'nar/ v. raise; exalt.

empíreo /em'pireo/ a. celestial, heavenly; divine.

empíricamente /empirika'mente/ adv. empirically.

empírico /em'piriko/ a. empirical.

empirismo /empi'rismo/ n. m. empiricism.

emplastarse /emplas'tarse/ v. get smeared.

emplasto /em'plasto/ n. m. salve.

emplazamiento /emplaθa'miento; emplasa'miento/ n. m. court summons.

emplazar /empla'θar; empla'sar/ v. summon to court.

empleado /emple'aðo/ **-da** n. employee.

emplear /em'plear/ v. employ; use.

empleo /em'pleo/ n. m. employment, job; use.

empobrecer /empoβre'θer; empoβre-'ser/ v. impoverish.

empobrecimiento /empoβreθi'mien-to; empoβresi'miento/ n. m. impoverishment.

empollador /empoʎa'ðor; empoya-'ðor/ n. m. incubator.

empollar /empo'ʎar; empo'yar/ v. hatch.

empolvado /empol'βaðo/ a. dusty.

empolvar /empol'βar/ v. powder.

emporcar /empor'kar/ v. soil, make dirty.

emporio /em'porio/ n. m. emporium.

emprendedor /emprende'ðor/ a. enterprising.

emprender /empren'der/ v. undertake.

empreñar /empre'ɲar/ v. make pregnant; beget.

empresa /em'presa/ n. f. enterprise, undertaking; company.

empresario /empre'sario/ **-ria** n. businessperson; impresario.

empréstito /em'prestito/ n. m. loan.

empujón /empu'hon/ n. m. push; shove. —**empujar**, v.

empuñar /empu'ɲar/ v. grasp, seize; wield.

emulación /emula'θion; emula'sion/ n. f. emulation; envy; rivalry.

emulador /emula'ðor/ n. m. emulator; rival.

émulo /'emulo/ a. rival. —**emular**, v.

emulsión /emul'sion/ n. f. emulsion.

emulsionar /emulsio'nar/ v. emulsify.

en /en/ prep. in, on, at.

enaguas /e'naɣuas/ n. f.pl. petticoat; skirt.

enajenable /enahe'naβle/ a. alienable.

enajenación /enahena'θion; enahena'sion/ n. f. alienation; derangement, insanity.

enajenar /enahe'nar/ v. alienate.

enamoradamente /enamoraða'men-te/ adv. lovingly.

enamorado /enamo'raðo/ a. in love.

enamorador /enamora'ðor/ n. m. wooer; suitor; lover.

enamorarse /enamo'rarse/ v. fall in love.

enano /e'nano/ **-na** n. midget; dwarf.

enardecer /enarðe'θer; enarðe'ser/ v. inflame.

enastado /enas'taðo/ a. horned.

encabestrar /enkaβe'strar/ v. halter.

encabezado /enkaβe'θaðo; enkaβe-'saðo/ n. m. headline.

encabezamiento /enkaβeθa'miento; enkaβesa'miento/ n. m. title; census; tax roll.

encabezar /enkaβe'θar; enkaβe'sar/ v. head.

encachar /enka'tʃar/ v. hide.

encadenamiento /enkaðena'miento/ n. m. connection, linkage.

encadenar /enkaðe'nar/ v. chain; link, connect.

encajar /enka'har/ v. fit in, insert.

encaje /en'kahe/ n. m. lace.

encalar /enka'lar/ v. whitewash.

encallarse /enka'ʎarse; enka'yarse/ v. be stranded.

encallecido /enkaʎe'θiðo; enkaye'si-ðo/ a. hardened; calloused.

encalvecer /enkalβe'θer; enkalβe'ser/ v. lose one's hair.

encaminar /enkami'nar/ v. guide; direct; be on the way to.

encandilar /enkandi'lar/ v. dazzle; daze.

encantación /enkanta'θion; enkanta-'sion/ n. f. incantation.

encantado /enkan'taðo/ a. charmed, fascinated, enchanted.

encantador /enkanta'ðor/ a. charming, delightful.

encante /en'kante/ n. m. public auction.

encanto /en'kanto/ n. m. charm, delight. —**encantar**, v.

encapillado /enkapi'ʎaðo; enkapi'ya-ðo/ n. m. clothes one is wearing.

encapotar /enkapo'tar/ v. cover, cloak; muffle.

encaprichamiento /enkapritʃa-'miento/ n. m. infatuation.

encaramarse /enkara'marse/ v. perch; climb.

encararse con /enka'rarse kon/ v. face.

encarcelación /enkarθela'θion; en-karsela'sion/ n. f. imprisonment.

encarcelar /enkarθe'lar; enkarse'lar/ v. jail, imprison.

encarecer /enkare'θer; enkare'ser/ v. recommend; extol.

encarecidamente /enkareθiða'men-te; enkaresiða'mente/ adv. extremely; ardently.

encargado /enkar'ɣaðo/ **-da** n. agent; attorney; representative.

encargar /enkar'ɣar/ v. entrust; order.

encargarse /enkar'ɣarse/ v. take charge, be in charge.

encargo /en'karɣo/ n. m. errand; assignment; Com. order.

encarnación /enkarna'θion; enkarna-'sion/ n. f. incarnation.

encarnado /enkar'naðo/ a. red.

encarnar /enkar'nar/ v. embody.

encarnecer /enkarne'θer; enkarne-'ser/ v. grow fat or heavy.

encarnizado /enkarni'θaðo; enkarni-'saðo/ a. bloody, fierce.

encarrilar /enkarri'lar/ v. set right; put on the track.

encartar /enkar'tar/ v. ban, outlaw; summon.

encastar /enkas'tar/ v. improve by crossbreeding.

encastillar /enkasti'ʎar; enkasti'yar/ v. be obstinate or unyielding.

encatarrado /enkata'rraðo/ a. suffering from a cold.

encausar /enkau'sar/ v. prosecute; take legal action against.

encauzar /enkau'θar; enkau'sar/ v. channel; direct.

encefalitis /enθefa'litis; ensefa'litis/ n. f. encephalitis.

encelamiento /enθela'miento; ense-la'miento/ n. m. envy, jealousy.

encelar /enθe'lar; ense'lar/ v. make jealous.

encenagar /enθena'ɣar; ensena'ɣar/ v. wallow in mud.

encendedor /enθende'ðor; ensende-'ðor/ n. m. lighter.

encender /enθen'der; ensen'der/ v. light; set fire to, kindle; turn on.

encendido /enθen'diðo; ensen'diðo/ n. m. ignition.

encerado /enθe'raðo; ense'raðo/ n. m. oilcloth; tarpaulin.

encerar /enθe'rar; ense'rar/ v. wax.

encerrar /enθe'rrar; ense'rrar/ v. enclose; confine, shut in.

enchapado /entʃa'paðo/ n. m. veneer.

enchufe /en'tʃufe/ n. m. Elec. plug, socket.

encía /en'θia; en'sia/ n. f. gum.

encíclico /en'θikliko; en'sikliko/ a. **1.** encyclic. —n. **2.** f. encyclical.

enciclopedia /enθiklo'peðia; ensiklo-'peðia/ n. f. encyclopedia.

enciclopédico /enθiklo'peðiko; en-siklo'peðiko/ a. encyclopedic.

encierro /en'θierro; en'sierro/ n. m. confinement; enclosure.

encima /en'θima; en'sima/ adv. on top. **e. de**, on. **por e. de**, above.

encina /en'θina; en'sina/ n. f. oak.

encinta /en'θinta; en'sinta/ a. pregnant.

enclavar /enkla'βar/ v. nail.

enclenque /en'klenke/ a. frail, weak, sickly.

encogerse /enko'herse/ v. shrink. **e. de hombros**, shrug the shoulders.

encogido /enko'hiðo/ a. shy, bashful, timid.

encojar /enko'har/ v. make or become lame; cripple.

encolar /enko'lar/ v. glue, paste, stick.

encolerizar /enkoleri'θar; enkoleri-'sar/ v. make or become angry.

encomendar /enkomen'dar/ v. commend; recommend.

encomiar /enko'miar/ v. praise, laud, extol.

encomienda /enko'mienda/ n. f. commission, charge; (postal) package.

encomio /en'komio/ n. m. encomium, eulogy.

enconar /enko'nar/ v. irritate, annoy, anger.

encono /en'kono/ n. m. rancor, resentment.

enconoso /enko'noso/ a. rancorous, resentful.

encontrado /enkon'traðo/ a. opposite.

encontrar /enkon'trar/ v. find; meet.

encorajar /enkora'har/ v. encourage; incite.

encornar /enkor'nar/ v. gore.

encorralar /enkorra'lar/ v. corral.

encorvadura /enkorβa'ðura/ n. f. bend, curvature.

encorvar /enkor'βar/ v. arch, bend.
encorvarse /enkor'βarse/ v. stoop.
encrucijada /enkruθi'haða; enkrusi-'haða/ n. f. crossroads.
encuadrar /enkuað'rar/ v. frame.
encubierta /enku'βierta/ a. **1.** secret, fraudulent. —n. **2.** f. fraud.
encubrir /enkuβ'rir/ v. hide, conceal.
encuentro /en'kuentro/ n. m. encounter; match, bout.
encurtido /enkur'tiðo/ n. m. pickle.
endeble /en'deβle/ a. rail, weak, sickly.
enderezar /endere'θar; endere'sar/ v. straighten; redress.
endeudarse /endeu'ðarse/ v. get into debt.
endiablado /endia'βlaðo/ a. devilish.
endibia /en'diβia/ n. f. endive.
endiosar /endio'sar/ v. deify.
endorso /en'dorso/ **endoso** n. m. endorsement.
endosador /endosa'ðor/ **-ra** n. endorser.
endosar /endo'sar/ v. endorse.
endosatario /endosa'tario/ **-ria** n. endorsee.
endulzar /endul'θar; endul'sar/ v. sweeten; soothe.
endurar /endu'rar/ v. harden.
endurecer /endure'θer; endure'ser/ v. harden.
enemigo /ene'migo/ **-ga** n. foe, enemy.
enemistad /enemis'tað/ n. f. enmity.
éneo /'eneo/ a. brass.
energía /ener'hia/ n. f. energy.
energía nuclear /ener'hia nukle'ar/ atomic energy, nuclear energy.
energía vital /ener'hia bi'tal/ élan vital, vitality.
enérgicamente /e'nerhikamente/ adv. energetically.
enérgico /e'nerhiko/ a. forceful; energetic.
enero /e'nero/ n. m. January.
enervación /enerβa'θion; enerβa-'sion/ n. f. enervation.
enfadado /enfa'ðaðo/ a. angry.
enfadar /enfa'ðar/ v. anger, vex.
enfado /en'faðo/ n. m. anger, vexation.
énfasis /'enfasis/ n. m. or f. emphasis, stress.
enfáticamente /en'fatikamente/ adv. emphatically.
enfático /en'fatiko/ a. emphatic.
enfermar /enfer'mar/ v. make ill; fall ill.
enfermedad /enferme'ðað/ n. f. illness, sickness, disease.
enfermera /enfer'mera/ n. f. nurse.
enfermería /enferme'ria/ n. f. sanatorium.
enfermo /en'fermo/ **-ma** a. & n. ill, sick; sickly; patient.
enfilar /enfi'lar/ v. line up; put in a row.
enflaquecer /enflake'θer; enflake-'ser/ v. make thin; grow thin.
enfoque /en'foke/ n. m. focus. —**enfocar,** v.
enfrascamiento /enfraska'miento/ n. m. entanglement.
enfrascar /enfras'kar/ v. bottle; entangle oneself.
enfrenar /enfre'nar/ v. bridle, curb; restrain.
enfrentamiento /enfrenta'miento/ n. m. clash, confrontation.
enfrente /en'frente/ adv. across, opposite; in front.
enfriadera /enfria'ðera/ n. f. icebox; cooler.
enfriar /enf'riar/ v. chill, cool.
enfurecer /enfure'θer; enfure'ser/ v. infuriate, enrage.
engalanar /engala'nar/ v. adorn, trim.
enganchar /engan'tʃar/ v. hook, hitch, attach.
engañar /enga'ɲar/ v. deceive, cheat.

engaño /en'gaɲo/ n. m. deceit; delusion.
engañoso /enga'ɲoso/ a. deceitful.
engarce /en'garθe; engarse/ n. m. connection, link.
engastar /engas'tar/ v. to put (gems) in a setting.
engaste /en'gaste/ n. m. setting.
engatusar /engatu'sar/ v. deceive, trick.
engendrar /enhen'drar/ v. engender, beget, produce.
engendro /en'hendro/ n. m. fetus, embryo.
englobar /englo'βar/ v. include.
engolfar /engol'far/ v. be deeply absorbed.
engolosinar /engolosi'nar/ v. allure, charm, entice.
engomar /engo'mar/ v. gum.
engordador /engor'ðaðor/ a. fattening.
engordar /engor'ðar/ v. fatten; grow fat.
engranaje /engra'nahe/ n. m. Mech. gear.
engranar /engra'nar/ v. gear; mesh together.
engrandecer /engrande'θer; engrande'ser/ v. increase, enlarge; exalt; exaggerate.
engrasación /engrasa'θion; engrasa-'sion/ n. f. lubrication.
engrasar /engra'sar/ v. grease, lubricate.
engreído /engre'iðo/ a. conceited.
engreimiento /engrei'miento/ n. m. conceit.
engullidor /enguʎi'ðor; enguyi'ðor/ **-ra** n. devourer.
engullir /engu'ʎir; engu'yir/ v. devour.
enhebrar /ene'βrar/ v. thread.
enhestadura /enesta'ðura/ n. f. raising.
enhestar /enes'tar/ v. raise, erect, set up.
enhiesto /en'iesto/ a. erect, upright.
enhorabuena /enora'βuena/ n. f. congratulations.
enigma /e'nigma/ n. m. enigma, puzzle.
enigmáticamente /enigmatika'mente/ adv. enigmatically.
enigmático /enig'matiko/ a. enigmatic.
enjabonar /enhaβo'nar/ v. soap, lather.
enjalbegar /enhalβe'gar/ v. whitewash.
enjambradera /enhambra'ðera/ n. f. queen bee.
enjambre /en'hambre/ n. m. swarm. —**enjambrar,** v.
enjaular /enhau'lar/ v. cage, coop up.
enjebe /en'heβe/ n. m. lye.
enjuagar /enhua'gar/ v. rinse.
enjuague bucal /en'huage bu'kal/ n. m. mouthwash.
enjugar /enhu'gar/ v. wipe, dry off.
enjutez /enhu'teθ; enhu'tes/ n. f. dryness.
enjuto /en'huto/ a. dried; lean, thin.
enlace /en'laθe; en'lase/ n. m. attachment; involvement; connection.
enladrillador /enlaðriʎa'ðor; enlaðri-ya'ðor/ **-ra** n. bricklayer.
enlardar /enlar'ðar/ v. baste.
enlatado /enla'taðo/ **-da** a. canned (food).
enlatar /enla'tar/ v. can (food).
enlazar /enla'θar; enla'sar/ v. lace; join, connect; wed.
enlodar /enlo'ðar/ v. cover with mud.
enloquecer /enloke'θer; enloke'ser/ v. go insane; drive crazy.
enloquecimiento /enlokeθi'miento; enlokesi'miento/ n. m. insanity.
enlustrecer /enlustre'θer; enlustre-'ser/ v. polish, brighten.
enmarañar /emara'ɲar/ v. entangle.
enmendación /emenda'θion; emen-da'sion/ n. f. emendation.

enmendador /emenda'ðor/ **-ra** n. emender, reviser.
enmendar /emen'dar/ v. amend, correct.
enmienda /e'mienda/ n. f. amendment; correction.
enmohecer /emoe'θer; emoe'ser/ v. rust; mold.
enmohecido /emoe'θiðo; emoe'siðo/ a. rusty; moldy.
enmudecer /emuðe'θer; emuðe'ser/ v. silence; become silent.
ennegrecer /ennegre'θer; ennegre-'ser/ v. blacken.
ennoblecer /ennoβle'θer; ennoβle-'ser/ v. ennoble.
enodio /e'noðio/ n. m. young deer.
enojado /eno'haðo/ a. angry, cross.
enojarse /eno'harse/ v. get angry.
enojo /e'noho/ n. m. anger. —**enojar,** v.
enojosamente /enohosa'mente/ adv. angrily.
enorme /e'norme/ a. enormous, huge.
enormemente /enorme'mente/ adv. enormously; hugely.
enormidad /enormi'ðað/ n. f. enormity; hugeness.
enraizar /enrai'θar; enrai'sar/ v. take root, sprout.
enramada /enra'maða/ n. f. bower.
enredadera /enreða'ðera/ n. f. climbing plant.
enredado /enre'ðaðo/ a. entangled, snarled.
enredar /enre'ðar/ v. entangle, snarl; mess up.
enredo /en'reðo/ n. m. tangle, entanglement.
enriquecer /enrike'θer; enrike'ser/ v. enrich.
enrojecerse /enrohe'θerse; enrohe-'serse/ v. color; blush.
enrollar /enro'ʎar; enro'yar/ v. wind, coil, roll up.
enromar /enro'mar/ v. make dull, blunt.
enronquecimiento /enronkeθi-'miento; enronkesi'miento/ n. m. hoarseness.
enroscar /enros'kar/ v. twist, curl, wind.
ensacar /ensa'kar/ v. put in a bag.
ensalada /ensa'laða/ n. f. salad.
ensaladera /ensala'ðera/ n. f. salad bowl.
ensalmo /en'salmo/ n. m. charm, enchantment.
ensalzamiento /ensalθa'miento; ensalsa'miento/ n. m. praise.
ensalzar /ensal'θar; ensal'sar/ v. praise, laud, extol.
ensamblar /ensam'blar/ v. join; unite; connect.
ensanchamiento /ensantʃa'miento/ n. m. widening, expansion, extension.
ensanchar /ensan'tʃar/ v. widen, expand, extend.
ensangrentado /ensangren'taðo/ a. bloody; bloodshot.
ensañar /ensa'ɲar/ v. enrage, infuriate; rage.
ensayar /ensa'yar/ v. try out; rehearse.
ensayista /ensa'yista/ n. m. & f. essayist.
ensayo /ensa'yo/ n. m. attempt; trial; rehearsal.
ensenada /ense'naða/ n. f. cove.
enseña /en'seɲa/ n. f. ensign, standard.
enseñador /enseɲa'ðor/ **-ra** n. teacher.
enseñanza /ense'ɲanθa; ense'ɲansa/ n. f. education; teaching.
enseñar /ense'ɲar/ v. teach, train; show.
enseres /en'seres/ n. m.pl. household goods.
ensilaje /ensi'lahe/ n. m. ensilage.
ensillar /ensi'ʎar; ensi'yar/ v. saddle.
ensordecedor /ensorðeθe'ðor; ensor-ðese'ðor/ a. deafening.

ensordecer /ensorðe'θer; ensorðe-'ser/ v. deafen.
ensordecimiento /ensorðeθi'miento; ensorðesi'miento/ n. m. deafness.
ensuciar /ensu'θiar; ensu'siar/ v. dirty, muddy, soil.
ensueño /en'sueɲo/ n. m. illusion, dream.
entablar /enta'βlar/ v. board up; initiate, begin.
entallador /entaʎa'ðor; entaya'ðor/ n. m. sculptor, carver.
entapizar /entapi'θar; entapi'sar/ v. upholster.
ente /'ente/ n. m. being.
entenada /ente'naða/ n. f. stepdaughter.
entenado /ente'naðo/ n. m. stepson.
entender /enten'der/ v. understand.
entendimiento /entendi'miento/ n. m. understanding.
entenebrecer /enteneβre'θer; enteneβre'ser/ v. darken.
enterado /ente'raðo/ a. aware, informed.
enteramente /entera'mente/ adv. entirely, completely.
enterar /ente'rar/ v. inform.
enterarse /ente'rarse/ v. find out.
entereza /ente'reθa; ente'resa/ n. f. entirety; integrity; firmness.
entero /en'tero/ a. entire, whole, total.
enterramiento /enterra'miento/ n. m. burial, interment.
enterrar /ente'rrar/ v. bury.
entestado /entes'taðo/ a. stubborn, willful.
entibiar /enti'βiar/ v. to cool; moderate.
entidad /enti'ðað/ n. f. entity.
entierro /en'tierro/ n. m. interment, burial.
entonación /entona'θion; en-tona'sion/ n. f. intonation.
entonamiento /entona'miento/ n. m. intonation.
entonar /ento'nar/ v. chant; harmonize.
entonces /en'tonθes; entonses/ adv. then.
entono /en'tono/ n. m. intonation; arrogance; affectation.
entortadura /entorta'ðura/ n. f. crookedness.
entortar /entor'tar/ v. make crooked; bend.
entrada /en'traða/ n. f. entrance; admission, admittance.
entrambos /en'trambos/ a. & pron. both.
entrante /en'trante/ a. coming, next.
entrañable /entra'ɲaβle/ a. affectionate.
entrañas /en'traɲas/ n. f.pl. entrails, bowels; womb.
entrar /en'trar/ v. enter, go in, come in.
entre /'entre/ prep. among; between.
entreabierto /entrea'βierto/ a. ajar, half-open.
entreabrir /entrea'βrir/ v. set ajar.
entreacto /entre'akto/ n. m. intermission.
entrecejo /entre'θeho; entre'seho/ n. m. frown; space between the eyebrows.
entrecuesto /entre'kuesto/ n. m. spine, backbone.
entredicho /entre'ðitʃo/ n. m. prohibition.
entrega /en'trega/ n. f. delivery.
entregar /entre'gar/ v. deliver, hand; hand over.
entrelazar /entrela'θar; entrela'sar/ v. intertwine, entwine.
entremedias /entre'meðias/ adv. meanwhile; halfway.
entremés /entre'mes/ n. m. side dish.
entremeterse /entreme'terse/ v. meddle, intrude.
entremetido /entreme'tiðo/ **-da** n. meddler.

entrenador /entrena'ðor/ **-ra** n. coach. —**entrenar,** v.

entrenarse /entre'narse/ v. train.

entrepalado /entrepa'laðo/ a. variegated; spotted.

entrerenglonar /entrerenglo'nar/ v. interline.

entresacar /entresa'kar/ v. select, choose; sift.

entresuelo /entre'swelo/ n. m. mezzanine.

entretanto /entre'tanto/ adv. meanwhile.

entretenedor /entretene'ðor/ **-ra** n. entertainer.

entretener /entrete'ner/ v. entertain, amuse; delay.

entretenimiento /entreteni'miento/ n. m. entertainment, amusement.

entrevista /entre'βista/ n. f. interview. —**entrevistar,** v.

entrevistador /entreβista'ðor/ **-ra** n. interviewer.

entristecedor /entristeθe'ðor; entristese'ðor/ a. sad.

entristecer /entriste'θer; entriste'ser/ v. sadden.

entronar /entro'nar/ v. enthrone.

entroncar /entron'kar/ v. be related or connected.

entronización /entroniθa'θion; entronisa'sion/ n. f. enthronement.

entronque /entron'ke/ n. m. relationship; connection.

entumecer /entume'θer; entume'ser/ v. become or be numb; swell.

entusiasmado /entusias'maðo/ a. enthusiastic.

entusiasmo /entu'siasmo/ n. m. enthusiasm.

entusiasta /entu'siasta/ n. m. & f. enthusiast.

entusiástico /entu'siastiko/ a. enthusiastic.

enumeración /enumera'θion; enumera'sion/ n. f. enumeration.

enumerar /enume'rar/ v. enumerate.

enunciación /enunθia'θion; enunsia'sion/ n. f. enunciation; statement.

enunciar /enun'θiar; enun'siar/ v. enunciate.

envainar /embai'nar/ v. sheathe.

envalentonar /embalento'nar/ v. encourage, embolden.

envanecimiento /embaneθi'miento; embanesi'miento/ n. m. conceit, vanity.

envasar /emba'sar/ v. put in a container; bottle.

envase /em'base/ n. m. container.

envejecer /embehe'θer; embehe'ser/ v. age, grow old.

envejecimiento /embeheθi'miento; embehesi'miento/ n. m. oldness, aging.

envenenar /embene'nar/ v. poison.

envés /em'bes/ n. m. wrong side; back.

envestir /embes'tir/ v. put in office; invest.

enviada /em'biaða/ n. f. shipment.

enviado /em'biaðo/ **-da** n. envoy.

enviar /em'biar/ v. send; ship.

envidia /em'biðia/ n. f. envy. —**envidiar,** v.

envidiable /embi'ðiaβle/ a. enviable.

envidioso /embi'ðioso/ a. envious.

envilecer /embile'θer; embile'ser/ v. vilify, debase, disgrace.

envío /em'bio/ n. m. shipment.

envión /em'bion/ n. m. shove.

envoltura /embol'tura/ n. f. wrapping.

envolver /embol'βer/ v. wrap, wrap up.

enyesar /enye'sar/ v. plaster.

enyugar /enyu'gar/ v. yoke.

eperlano /eper'lano/ n. m. smelt (fish).

épica /'epika/ n. f. epic.

épico /'epiko/ a. epic.

epicureísmo /epikure'ismo/ n. m. epicureanism.

epicúreo /epi'kureo/ n. & a. epicurean.

epidemia /epi'ðemia/ n. f. epidemic.

epidémico /epi'ðemiko/ a. epidemic.

epidermis /epi'ðermis/ n. f. epidermis.

epigrama /epi'grama/ n. m. epigram.

epigramático /epigra'matiko/ **-ca** a. epigrammatic.

epilepsia /epi'lepsia/ n. f. epilepsy.

epiléptico /epi'leptiko/ **-ca** n. & a. epileptic.

epílogo /e'pilogo/ n. m. epilogue.

episcopado /episko'paðo/ n. m. bishopric; episcopate.

episcopal /episko'pal/ a. episcopal.

episódico /epi'soðiko/ a. episodic.

episodio /epi'soðio/ n. m. episode.

epístola /e'pistola/ n. f. epistle, letter.

epitafio /epi'tafio/ n. m. epitaph.

epitomadamente /epitomaða'mente/ adv. concisely.

epitomar /epito'mar/ v. epitomize, summarize.

época /'epoka/ n. f. epoch, age.

epopeya /epo'peya/ n. f. epic.

epsomita /epso'mita/ n. f. Epsom salts.

equidad /eki'ðað/ n. f. equity.

equilibrado /ekili'βraðo/ a. stable.

equilibrio /eki'liβrio/ n. m. equilibrium, balance.

equinoccio /eki'nokθio; ekinoksio/ n. m. equinox.

equipaje /eki'pahe/ n. m. luggage, baggage. **e. de mano,** luggage.

equipar /eki'par/ v. equip.

equiparar /ekipa'rar/ v. compare.

equipo /e'kipo/ n. m. equipment; team.

equitación /ekita'θion; ekita'sion/ f. horsemanship; horseback riding, riding.

equitativo /ekita'tiβo/ a. fair, equitable.

equivalencia /ekiβa'lenθia; ekiβa'lensia/ n. f. equivalence.

equivalente /ekiβa'lente/ a. equivalent.

equivaler /ekiβa'ler/ v. equal, be equivalent.

equivocación /ekiβoka'θion; ekiβoka'sion/ n. f. mistake.

equivocado /ekiβo'kaðo/ a. wrong, mistaken.

equivocarse /ekiβo'karse/ v. make a mistake, be wrong.

equívoco /e'kiβoko/ a. equivocal, ambiguous.

era /'era/ n. f. era, age.

erario /e'rario/ n. m. exchequer.

erección /erek'θion; erek'sion/ n. f. erection; elevation.

eremita /ere'mita/ n. m. hermit.

erguir /er'gir/ v. erect; straighten up.

erigir /eri'hir/ v. erect, build.

erisipela /erisi'pela/ n. f. erysipelas.

erizado /eri'θaðo; eri'saðo/ a. bristly.

erizarse /eri'θarse; eri'sarse/ v. bristle.

erizo /e'riθo; e'riso/ n. m. hedgehog; sea urchin.

ermita /er'mita/ n. f. hermitage.

ermitaño /ermi'taɲo/ n. m. hermit.

erogación /eroga'θion; eroga'sion/ n. f. expenditure. —**erogar,** v.

erosión /ero'sion/ n. f. erosion.

erótico /e'rotiko/ a. erotic.

erradicación /erraðika'θion; erraðika'sion/ n. f. eradication.

erradicar /erraði'kar/ v. eradicate.

errado /e'rraðo/ a. mistaken, erroneous.

errante /e'rrante/ a. wandering, roving.

errar /e'rrar/ v. be mistaken.

errata /e'rrata/ n. f. erratum.

errático /e'rratiko/ a. erratic.

erróneamente /errones'mente/ adv. erroneously.

erróneo /e'rroneo/ a. erroneous.

error /e'rror/ n. m. error, mistake.

eructo /e'rukto/ n. m. belch. —**eructar,** v.

erudición /eruði'θion; eruði'sion/ f. scholarship, learning.

eruditamente /eruðita'mente/ adv. learnedly.

erudito /eru'ðito/ **-ta** n. 1. scholar. —a. 2. scholarly.

erupción /erup'θion; erup'sion/ n. f. eruption; rash.

eruptivo /erup'tiβo/ a. eruptive.

esbozo /es'βoθo; es'βoso/ n. m. outline, sketch. —**esbozar,** v.

escabechar /eskaβe'tʃar/ v. pickle; preserve.

escabeche /eska'βetʃe/ n. m. brine.

escabel /eska'βel/ n. m. small stool or bench.

escabroso /eska'βroso/ a. rough, irregular; craggy; rude.

escabullirse /eskaβu'ʎirse; eskaβu'yirse/ v. steal away, sneak away.

escala /es'kala/ n. f. scale; ladder. **hacer e.,** to make a stop.

escalada /eska'laða/ n. f. escalation.

escalador /eskala'ðor/ **-ra** n. climber.

escalar /eska'lar/ v. climb; scale.

escaldar /eskal'dar/ v. scald.

escalera /eska'lera/ n. f. stairs, staircase; ladder.

escalfado /eskal'faðo/ a. poached.

escalofriado /eskalo'friaðo/ a. chilled.

escalofrío /eskalo'frio/ n. m. chill.

escalón /eska'lon/ n. m. step.

escalonar /eskalo'nar/ v. space out, stagger.

escaloña /eska'loɲa/ n. f. scallion.

escalpar /eskal'par/ v. scalp.

escalpelo /eskal'pelo/ n. m. scalpel.

escama /es'kama/ n. f. (fish) scale. —**escamar,** v.

escamondar /eskamon'dar/ v. trim, cut; prune.

escampada /eskam'paða/ n. f. break in the rain, clear spell.

escandalizar /eskandali'θar; eskandali'sar/ v. shock, scandalize.

escandalizativo /eskandaliθa'tiβo; eskandalisa'tiβo/ a. scandalous.

escándalo /es'kandalo/ n. m. scandal.

escandaloso /eskanda'loso/ a. scandalous; disgraceful.

escandinavo /eskandi'naβo/ **-va** n. & a. Scandinavian.

escandir /eskan'dir/ v. scan.

escanear /eskane'ar/ v. scan (on a computer).

escáner /es'kaner/ v. scanner (of a computer).

escanilla /eska'niʎa; eska'niya/ n. f. cradle.

escañuelo /eska'ɲuelo/ n. m. small footstool.

escapada /eska'paða/ n. f. escapade.

escapar /eska'par/ v. escape.

escaparate /eskapa'rate/ n. m. shop window, store window.

escape /es'kape/ n. m. escape; Auto. exhaust.

escápula /es'kapula/ n. f. scapula.

escarabajo /eskara'βaho/ n. m. black beetle; scarab.

escaramucear /eskaramuθe'ar; eskaramuse'ar/ v. skirmish; dispute.

escarbadientes /eskarβa'ðientes/ n. m. toothpick.

escarbar /eskar'βar/ v. scratch; poke.

escarcha /es'kartʃa/ n. f. frost.

escardar /eskar'ðar/ v. weed.

escarlata /eskar'lata/ n. f. scarlet.

escarlatina /eskarla'tina/ n. f. scarlet fever.

escarmentar /eskarmen'tar/ v. correct severely.

escarnecedor /eskarneθe'ðor; eskarneseðor/ **-ra** n. scoffer; mocker.

escarnecer /eskarne'θer; eskarne'ser/ v. mock, make fun of.

escarola /eska'rola/ n. f. endive.

escarpa /es'karpa/ n. m. escarpment.

escarpado /eskar'paðo/ a. 1. steep. —n. 2. m. bluff.

escasamente /eskasa'mente/ adv. scarcely; sparingly; barely.

escasear /eskase'ar/ v. be scarce.

escasez /eska'seθ; eska'ses/ n. f. shortage, scarcity.

escaso /es'kaso/ a. scant; scarce.

escatimar /eskati'mar/ v. be stingy, skimp, save.

escatimoso /eskati'moso/ a. malicious; sly, cunning.

escena /es'θena; es'sena/ n. f. scene; stage.

escenario /esθe'nario; esse'nario/ n. m. stage (of theater); scenario.

escénico /es'θeniko; es'seniko/ a. scenic.

escépticamente /esθeptika'mente; esseptika'mente/ adv. skeptically.

escepticismo /esθepti'θismo; essepti'sismo/ n. m. skepticism.

escéptico /es'θeptiko; es'septiko/ **-ca** a. & n. skeptic; skeptical.

esclarecer /esklare'θer; esklare'ser/ v. clear up.

esclavitud /esklaβi'tuð/ n. f. slavery; bondage.

esclavizar /esklaβi'θar; esklaβi'sar/ v. enslave.

esclavo /es'klaβo/ **-va** n. slave.

escoba /es'koβa/ n. f. broom.

escocés /esko'θes; esko'ses/ **-esa** a. & n. Scotch, Scottish; Scot.

Escocia /es'koθia; eskosia/ n. f. Scotland.

escofinar /eskofi'nar/ v. rasp.

escoger /esko'her/ v. choose, select.

escogido /esko'hiðo/ a. chosen, selected.

escogimiento /eskohi'miento/ n. m. choice.

escolar /esko'lar/ a. 1. scholastic, (of) school. —n. 2. m.& f. student.

escolasticismo /eskolasti'θismo; eskolasti'sismo/ n. m. scholasticism.

escollo /es'koʎo; es'koyo/ n. m. reef.

escolta /es'kolta/ n. f. escort. —**escoltar,** v.

escombro /es'kombro/ n. m. mackerel.

escombros /es'kombros/ n. m.pl. debris, rubbish.

esconce /es'konθe; es'konse/ n. m. corner.

escondedero /eskonde'ðero/ n. m. hiding place.

esconder /eskon'der/ v. hide, conceal.

escondidamente /eskondiða'mente/ adv. secretly.

escondimiento /eskondi'miento/ n. m. concealment.

escondrijo /eskon'driho/ n. m. hiding place.

escopeta /esko'peta/ n. f. shotgun.

escopetazo /eskope'taθo; eskope'taso/ n. m. gunshot.

escoplo /es'koplo/ n. m. chisel.

escorbuto /eskor'βuto/ n. m. scurvy.

escorpena /eskor'pena/ n. f. grouper.

escorpión /eskor'pion/ n. m. scorpion.

escorzón /eskor'θon; eskor'son/ n. m. toad.

escotado /esko'taðo/ a. low-cut, with a low neckline.

escote /es'kote/ n. m. low neckline.

escribiente /eskri'βiente/ n. m. & f. clerk.

escribir /eskri'βir/ v. write.

escritor /eskri'tor/ **-ra** n. writer, author.

escritorio /eskri'torio/ n. m. desk.

escritura /eskri'tura/ n. f. writing, handwriting.

escrófula /es'krofula/ n. f. scrofula.

escroto /es'kroto/ n. m. scrotum.

escrúpulo /es'krupulo/ n. m. scruple.

escrupuloso /eskrupu'loso/ a. scrupulous.

escrutinio /eskru'tinio/ n. m. scrutiny; examination.

escuadra /es'kuaðra/ *n. f.* squad; fleet.

escuadrón /eskuað'ron/ *n. m.* squadron.

escualidez /eskuali'ðeθ; eskuali'ðes/ *n. f.* squalor; poverty; emaciation.

escuálido /es'kualiðo/ *a.* squalid.

escualo /es'kualo/ *n. m.* shark.

escuchar /esku'tʃar/ *v.* listen; listen to.

escudero /esku'ðero/ *n. m.* squire.

escudo /es'kuðo/ *n. m.* shield; protection; coin of certain countries.

escuela /es'kuela/ *n. f.* school.

escuela nocturna /es'kuela nok-'turna/ night school.

escuela por correspondencia /es-'kuela por korrespon'denθia; es'kuela por korrespon'densia/ correspondence school.

escuerzo /es'kuerθo; es'kuerso/ *n. m.* toad.

esculpir /eskul'pir/ *v.* carve, sculpture.

escultor /eskul'tor/ **-ra** *n.* sculptor.

escultura /eskul'tura/ *n. f.* sculpture.

escupidera /eskupi'ðera/ *n. f.* cuspidor.

escupir /esku'pir/ *v.* spit.

escurridero /eskurri'ðero/ *n. m.* drain board.

escurridor /eskurri'ðor/ *n. m.* colander, strainer.

escurrir /esku'rrir/ *v.* drain off; wring out.

escurrirse /esku'rrirse/ *v.* slip; sneak away.

ese /'ese/ **esa** *dem. a.* that.

ése, ésa *dem. pron.* that (one).

esencia /e'senθia; e'sensia/ *n. f.* essence; perfume.

esencial /esen'θial; esen'sial/ *a.* essential.

esencialmente /esenθial'mente; esensial'mente/ *adv.* essentially.

esfera /es'fera/ *n. f.* sphere.

esfinge /es'finhe/ *n. f.* sphinx.

esforzar /esfor'θar; esfor'sar/ *v.* strengthen.

esforzarse /esfor'θarse; esfor'sarse/ *v.* strive, exert oneself.

esfuerzo /es'fuerθo; es'fuerso/ *n. m.* effort, attempt; vigor.

esgrima /es'grima/ *n. f.* fencing.

esguince /es'ginθe; es'ginse/ *n. m.* sprain.

eslabón /esla'βon/ *n. m.* link (of a chain).

eslabonar /eslaβo'nar/ *v.* link, join, connect.

eslavo /es'laβo/ **-va** *a. & n.* Slavic; Slav.

esmalte /es'malte/ *n. m.* enamel, polish. **—esmaltar,** *v.*

esmerado /esme'raðo/ *a.* careful, thorough.

esmeralda /esme'ralda/ *n. f.* emerald.

esmerarse /esme'rarse/ *v.* take pains, do one's best.

esmeril /es'meril/ *n. m.* emery.

eso /'eso/ *dem. pron.* that.

esófago /e'sofago/ *n. m.* esophagus.

esotérico /eso'teriko/ *a.* esoteric.

espacial /espa'θial; espa'sial/ *a.* spatial.

espacio /es'paθio; es'pasio/ *n. m.* space. **—espaciar,** *v.*

espaciosidad /espaθiosi'ðað; espasiosi'ðað/ *n. f.* spaciousness.

espacioso /espa'θioso; espa'sioso/ *a.* spacious.

espada /es'paða/ *n. f.* sword; spade (in cards).

espadarte /espa'ðarte/ *n. m.* swordfish.

espaguetis /espa'getis/ *n. m.pl.* spaghetti.

espalda /es'palda/ *n. f.* back.

espaldera /espal'dera/ *n. f.* espalier.

espantar /espan'tar/ *v.* frighten, scare; scare away.

espanto /es'panto/ *n. m.* fright.

espantoso /espan'toso/ *a.* frightening, frightful.

España /es'paɲa/ *n. f.* Spain.

español /espa'ɲol/ **-ola** *a. & n.* Spanish; Spaniard.

esparcir /espar'θir; espar'sir/ *v.* scatter, disperse.

espárrago /es'parrago/ *n. m.* asparagus.

espartano /espar'tano/ **-na** *n. & a.* Spartan.

espasmo /es'pasmo/ *n. m.* spasm.

espasmódico /espas'moðiko/ *a.* spasmodic.

espata /es'pata/ *n. f.* spathe.

espato /es'pato/ *n. m.* spar (mineral).

espátula /es'patula/ *n. f.* spatula.

especia /es'peθia; es'pesia/ *n. f.* spice. **—especiar,** *v.*

especial /espe'θial; espe'sial/ *a.* special, especial.

especialidad /espeθiali'ðað; espesiali'ðað/ *n. f.* specialty.

especialista /espeθia'lista; espesia-'lista/ *n. m. & f.* specialist.

especialización /espeθialiθa'θion; espesialisa'sion/ *n. f.* specialization.

especialmente /espeθial'mente; espesial'mente/ *adv.* especially.

especie /es'peθie; es'pesie/ *n. f.* species; sort.

especiería /espeθie'ria; espesie'ria/ *n. f.* grocery store; spice store.

especiero /espe'θiero; espe'siero/ **-ra** *n.* spice dealer; spice box.

especificar /espeθifi'kar; espesifi'kar/ *v.* specify.

específico /espe'θifiko; espe'sifiko/ *a.* specific.

espécimen /es'peθimen; es'pesimen/ *n. m.* specimen.

especioso /espe'θioso; espe'sioso/ *a.* neat; polished; specious.

espectacular /espektaku'lar/ *a.* spectacular.

espectáculo /espek'takulo/ *n. m.* spectacle, show.

espectador /espekta'ðor/ **-ra** *n.* spectator.

espectro /es'pektro/ *n. m.* specter, ghost.

especulación /espekula'θion; espekula'sion/ *n. f.* speculation.

especulador /espekula'ðor/ **-ra** *n.* speculator.

especular /espeku'lar/ *v.* speculate.

especulativo /espekula'tiβo/ *a.* speculative.

espejo /es'peho/ *n. m.* mirror.

espelunca /espe'lunka/ *n. f.* dark cave, cavern.

espera /es'pera/ *n. f.* wait.

esperanza /espe'ranθa; espe'ransa/ *n. f.* hope, expectation.

esperar /espe'rar/ *v.* hope; expect; wait, wait for, watch for.

espesar /espe'sar/ *v.* thicken.

espeso /es'peso/ *a.* thick, dense, bushy.

espesor /espe'sor/ *n. m.* thickness, density.

espía /es'pia/ *n. m. & f.* spy. **—espiar,** *v.*

espigón /espi'gon/ *n. m.* bee sting.

espina /es'pina/ *n. f.* thorn.

espinaca /espi'naka/ *n. f.* spinach.

espina dorsal /es'pina dor'sal/ spine.

espinal /espi'nal/ *a.* spinal.

espinazo /espi'naθo; espi'naso/ *n. m.* backbone.

espineta /espi'neta/ *n. f.* spinet.

espino /es'pino/ *n. m.* briar.

espinoso /espi'noso/ *a.* spiny, thorny.

espión /es'pion/ *n. m.* spy.

espionaje /espio'nahe/ *n. m.* espionage.

espiral /espi'ral/ *a. & m.* spiral.

espirar /espi'rar/ *v.* expire; breathe, exhale.

espíritu /es'piritu/ *n. m.* spirit.

espiritual /espi'ritual/ *a.* spiritual.

espiritualidad /espirituali'ðað/ *n. f.* spirituality.

espiritualmente /espiritual'mente/ *adv.* spiritually.

espita /es'pita/ *n. f.* faucet, spigot.

espléndido /es'plendiðo/ *a.* splendid.

esplendor /esplen'dor/ *n. m.* splendor.

espolear /espole'ar/ *v.* incite, urge on.

espoleta /espo'leta/ *n. f.* wishbone.

esponja /es'ponha/ *n. f.* sponge.

esponjoso /espon'hoso/ *a.* spongy.

esponsales /espon'sales/ *n. m.pl.* engagement, betrothal.

esponsalicio /esponsa'liθio; esponsa'lisio/ *a.* nuptial.

espontaneidad /espontanei'ðað/ *n. f.* spontaneity.

espontáneamente /espontanea-'mente/ *adv.* spontaneously.

espontáneo /espon'taneo/ *a.* spontaneous.

espora /es'pora/ *n. f.* spore.

esporádico /espo'raðiko/ *a.* sporadic.

esposa /es'posa/ *n. f.* wife.

esposar /espo'sar/ *v.* shackle; handcuff.

esposo /es'poso/ *n. m.* husband.

espuela /es'puela/ *n. f.* spur. **—espolear,** *v.*

espuma /es'puma/ *n. f.* foam. **—espumar,** *v.*

espumadera /espuma'ðera/ *n. f.* whisk; skimmer.

espumajear /espumahe'ar/ *v.* foam at the mouth.

espumajo /espu'maho/ *n. m.* foam.

espumar /espu'mar/ *v.* foam, froth; skim.

espumoso /espu'moso/ *a.* foamy; sparkling (wine).

espurio /es'purio/ *a.* spurious.

esputar /espu'tar/ *v.* spit, expectorate.

esputo /es'puto/ *n. m.* spit, saliva.

esquela /es'kela/ *n. f.* note.

esqueleto /eske'leto/ *n. m.* skeleton.

esquema /es'kema/ *n. m.* scheme; diagram.

esquero /es'kero/ *n. m.* leather sack, leather pouch.

esquiar /es'kiar/ *v.* ski.

esquiciar /eski'θiar; eski'siar/ *v.* outline, sketch.

esquicio /es'kiθio; es'kisio/ *n. m.* rough sketch, rough outline.

esquife /es'kife/ *n. m.* skiff.

esquilar /eski'lar/ *v.* fleece, shear.

esquilmo /es'kilmo/ *n. m.* harvest.

esquimal /eski'mal/ *n. & a.* Eskimo.

esquina /es'kina/ *n. f.* corner.

esquivar /eski'βar/ *v.* evade, shun.

estabilidad /estaβili'ðað/ *n. f.* stability.

estable /es'taβle/ *a.* stable.

establecedor /estaβleθe'ðor; estaβlese'ðor/ *n. m.* founder, originator.

establecer /estaβle'θer; estaβle'ser/ *v.* establish, set up.

establecimiento /estaβleθi'miento; estaβlesi'miento/ *n. m.* establishment.

establero /estaβ'lero/ *n. m.* groom.

establo /es'taβlo/ *n. m.* stable.

estaca /es'taka/ *n. f.* stake.

estación /esta'θion; esta'sion/ *n. f.* station; season.

estacionamiento /estaθiona'miento; estasiona'miento/ *n. m.* parking; parking lot; parking space.

estacionar /estaθio'nar; estasio'nar/ *v.* station; park (a vehicle).

estacionario /estaθio'nario; estasio-'nario/ *a.* stationary.

estación de servicio /esta'θion de ser'βiθio; esta'sion de ser'βisio/ service station.

estación de trabajo /esta'θion de tra'βaho; esta'sion de tra'βaho/ work station.

estadista /esta'ðista/ *n. m. & a.* statesman.

estadística /esta'ðistika/ *n. f.* statistics.

estadístico /esta'ðistiko/ *a.* statistical.

estado /es'taðo/ *n. m.* state; condition; status.

Estados Unidos /es'taðos u'niðos/ *n. m.pl.* United States.

estafa /es'tafa/ *n. f.* swindle, fake. **—estafar,** *v.*

estafeta /esta'feta/ *n. f.* post office.

estagnación /estagna'θion; estagna-'sion/ *n. f.* stagnation.

estallar /esta'ʎar; esta'yar/ *v.* explode; burst; break out.

estallido /esta'ʎiðo; esta'yiðo/ *n. m.* crash; crack; explosion.

estampa /es'tampa/ *n. f.* stamp. **—estampar,** *v.*

estampado /estam'paðo/ *n. m.* printed cotton cloth.

estampida /estam'piða/ *n. f.* stampede.

estampilla /estam'piʎa; estam'piya/ *n. f.* (postage) stamp.

estancado /estan'kaðo/ *a.* stagnant.

estancar /estan'kar/ *v.* stanch, stop, check.

estancia /es'tanθia; es'tansia/ *n. f.* stay; (S.A.) small farm.

estanciero /estan'θiero; estan'siero/ **-ra** *n.* small farmer.

estandarte /estan'darte/ *n. m.* banner.

estanque /es'tanke/ *n. m.* pool; pond.

estante /es'tante/ *n. m.* shelf.

estaño /es'taɲo/ *n. m.* tin. **—estañar,** *v.*

estar /es'tar/ *v.* be; stand; look.

estática /es'tatika/ *n. f.* static.

estático /es'tatiko/ *a.* static.

estatua /es'tatua/ *n. f.* statue.

estatura /esta'tura/ *n. f.* stature.

estatuto /esta'tuto/ *n. m.* statute, law.

este /'este/ *n. m.* east.

este, esta *dem. a.* this.

éste, ésta *dem. pron.* this (one); the latter.

estelar /este'lar/ *a.* stellar.

estenografía /estenogra'fia/ *n. f.* stenography.

estenógrafo /este'nografo/ **-fa** *n.* stenographer.

estera /es'tera/ *n. f.* mat, matting.

estereofónico /estereo'foniko/ *a.* stereophonic.

estéril /es'teril/ *a.* barren; sterile.

esterilidad /esterili'ðað/ *n. f.* sterility, fruitlessness.

esterilizar /esterili'θar; esterili'sar/ *v.* sterilize.

esternón /ester'non/ *n. m.* breastbone.

estética /es'tetika/ *n. f.* esthetics.

estético /es'tetiko/ *a.* esthetic.

estetoscopio /esteto'skopio/ *n. m.* stethoscope.

estibador /estiβa'ðor/ *n. m.* stevedore.

estiércol /es'tierkol/ *n. m.* dung, manure.

estigma /es'tigma/ *n. m.* stigma; disgrace.

estilarse /esti'larse/ *v.* be in fashion, be in vogue.

estilo /es'tilo/ *n. m.* style; sort.

estilográfica /estilo'grafika/ *n. f.* (fountain) pen.

estima /es'tima/ *n. f.* esteem.

estimable /esti'maβle/ *a.* estimable, worthy.

estimación /estima'θion; estima'sion/ *n. f.* estimation.

estimar /esti'mar/ *v.* esteem; value; estimate; gauge.

estimular /estimu'lar/ *v.* stimulate.

estímulo /es'timulo/ *n. m.* stimulus.

estío /es'tio/ *n. m.* summer.

estipulación /estipula'θion; estipula-'sion/ *n. f.* stipulation.

estipular /estipu'lar/ *v.* stipulate.

estirar /esti'rar/ *v.* stretch.

estirpe /es'tirpe/ *n. m.* stock, lineage.

esto /'esto/ *dem. pron.* this.

estocada /esto'kaða/ *n. f.* stab, thrust.

estofado /esto'faðo/ *n. m.* stew. —**estofar,** *v.*

estoicismo /estoi'θismo; estoi'sismo/ *n. m.* stoicism.

estoico /es'toiko/ *n. & a.* stoic.

estómago /es'tomago/ *n. m.* stomach.

estorbar /estor'βar/ *v.* bother, hinder, interfere with.

estorbo /es'torβo/ *n. m.* hindrance.

estornudo /estor'nuðo/ *n. m.* sneeze. —**estornudar,** *v.*

estrabismo /estra'βismo/ *n. m.* strabismus.

estrago /es'trago/ *n. m.* devastation, havoc.

estrangulación /estraŋgula'θion; estraŋgula'sion/ *n. f.* strangulation.

estrangular /estraŋgu'lar/ *v.* strangle.

estraperlista /estraper'lista/ *n. m. & f.* black marketeer.

estraperlo /estra'perlo/ *n. m.* black market.

estratagema /estrata'hema/ *n. f.* stratagem.

estrategia /estra'tehia/ *n. f.* strategy.

estratégico /estra'tehiko/ *a.* strategic.

estrato /es'trato/ *n. m.* stratum.

estrechar /estre't∫ar/ *v.* tighten; narrow.

estrechez /estre't∫eθ; estre't∫es/ *n. f.* narrowness; tightness.

estrecho /es'tret∫o/ *a.* **1.** narrow, tight. —*n.* **2.** strait.

estregar /estre'gar/ *v.* scour, scrub.

estrella /es'treʎa; es'treya/ *n. f.* star.

estrellamar /estreʎa'mar; estreya'mar/ *n. f.* starfish.

estrellar /estre'ʎar; estre'yar/ *v.* shatter, smash.

estremecimiento /estremeθi'miento; estremesi'miento/ *n. m.* shudder. —**estremecerse,** *v.*

estrenar /estre'nar/ *v.* wear for the first time; open (a play).

estreno /es'treno/ *n. m.* debut, first performance.

estrenuo /es'trenuo/ *a.* strenuous.

estreñido /estre'ɲiðo/ **-da** *a.* constipated.

estreñimiento /estreɲi'miento/ *n. m.* constipation.

estreñir /estre'ɲir/ *v.* constipate.

estrépito /es'trepito/ *n. m.* din.

estreptococo /estrepto'koko/ *n. m.* streptococcus.

estría /es'tria/ *n. f.* groove.

estribillo /estri'βiʎo; estri'βiyo/ *n. m.* refrain.

estribo /es'triβo/ *n. m.* stirrup.

estribor /estri'βor/ *n. m.* starboard.

estrictamente /estrikta'mente/ *adv.* strictly.

estrictez /estrik'teθ; estrik'tes/ *n. f.* strictness.

estricto /es'trikto/ *a.* strict.

estrofa /es'trofa/ *n. f.* stanza.

estropajo /estro'paho/ *n. m.* mop.

estropear /estrope'ar/ *v.* cripple, damage, spoil.

estructura /estruk'tura/ *n. f.* structure.

estructural /estruktu'ral/ *a.* structural.

estruendo /es'truendo/ *n. m.* din, clatter.

estuario /es'tuario/ *n. m.* estuary.

estuco /es'tuko/ *n. m.* stucco.

estudiante /estu'ðiante/ **-ta** *n.* student.

estudiar /estu'ðiar/ *v.* study.

estudio /es'tuðio/ *n. m.* study; studio.

estudioso /estu'ðioso/ *a.* studious.

estufa /es'tufa/ *n. f.* stove.

estufa de aire /es'tufa ðe 'aire/ fan heater.

estulto /es'tulto/ *a.* foolish.

estupendo /estu'pendo/ *a.* wonderful, grand, fine.

estupidez /estupi'ðeθ; estupi'ðes/ *n. f.* stupidity.

estúpido /es'tupiðo/ *a.* stupid.

estupor /estu'por/ *n. m.* stupor.

estuque /es'tuke/ *n. m.* stucco.

esturión /estu'rion/ *n. m.* sturgeon.

etapa /e'tapa/ *n. f.* stage.

éter /'eter/ *n. m.* ether.

etéreo /e'tereo/ *a.* ethereal.

eternal /eter'nal/ *a.* eternal.

eternidad /eterni'ðað/ *n. f.* eternity.

eterno /e'terno/ *a.* eternal.

ética /'etika/ *n. f.* ethics.

ético /'etiko/ *a.* ethical.

etimología /etimolo'hia/ *n. f.* etymology.

etiqueta /eti'keta/ *n. f.* etiquette; tag, label.

étnico /'etniko/ *a.* ethnic.

etrusco /e'trusko/ **-ca** *n. & a.* Etruscan.

eucaristía /eukaris'tia/ *n. f.* Eucharist.

eufemismo /eufe'mismo/ *n. m.* euphemism.

eufonía /eufo'nia/ *n. f.* euphony.

Europa /eu'ropa/ *n. f.* Europe.

europeo /euro'peo/ **-pea** *a. & n.* European.

eutanasia /euta'nasia/ *n. f.* euthanasia.

evacuación /eβakua'θion; eβakua'sion/ *n. f.* evacuation.

evacuar /eβa'kuar/ *v.* evacuate.

evadir /eβa'ðir/ *v.* evade.

evangélico /eβaŋ'heliko/ *a.* evangelical.

evangelio /eβaŋ'helio/ *n. m.* gospel.

evangelista /eβaŋhe'lista/ *n. m.* evangelist.

evaporación /eβapora'θion; eβapora'sion/ *n. f.* evaporation.

evaporarse /eβapo'rarse/ *v.* evaporate.

evasión /eβa'sion, eβa'siβa/ *n. f.* evasion.

evasivamente /eβasiβa'mente/ *adv.* evasively.

evasivo /eβa'siβo/ *a.* evasive.

evento /e'βento/ *n. m.* event, occurrence.

eventual /eβen'tual/ *a.* eventual.

eventualidad /eβentuali'ðað/ *n. f.* eventuality.

evicción /eβik'θion; eβik'sion/ *n. f.* eviction.

evidencia /eβi'ðenθia; eβiðensia/ *n. f.* evidence.

evidenciar /eβiðen'θiar; eβiðen'siar/ *v.* prove, show.

evidente /eβi'ðente/ *a.* evident.

evitación /eβita'θion; eβita'sion/ *n. f.* avoidance.

evitar /eβi'tar/ *v.* avoid, shun.

evocación /eβoka'θion; eβoka'sion/ *n. f.* evocation.

evocar /eβo'kar/ *v.* evoke.

evolución /eβolu'θion; eβolu'sion/ *n. f.* evolution.

exacerbar /eksaθer'βar; eksaser'βar/ *v.* irritate deeply; exacerbate.

exactamente /eksakta'mente/ *adv.* exactly.

exactitud /eksakti'tuð/ *n. f.* precision, accuracy.

exacto /ek'sakto/ *a.* exact, accurate.

exageración /eksahera'θion; eksahera'sion/ *n. f.* exaggeration.

exagerar /eksahe'rar/ *v.* exaggerate.

exaltación /eksalta'θion; eksalta'sion/ *n. f.* exaltation.

exaltamiento /eksalta'miento/ *n. m.* exaltation.

exaltar /eksal'tar/ *v.* exalt.

examen /ek'samen/ *n. m.* test, examination.

examen de ingreso /ek'samen de iŋ'greso/ entrance examination.

examinar /eksami'nar/ *v.* test, examine.

exánime /eksa'nime/ *a.* spiritless, weak.

exasperación /eksaspera'θion; eksaspera'sion/ *n. f.* exasperation.

exasperar /eksaspe'rar/ *v.* exasperate.

excavación /ekskaβa'θion; ekskaβa'sion/ *n. f.* excavation.

excavar /ekska'βar/ *v.* excavate.

exceder /eksθe'ðer; eksse'ðer/ *v.* exceed, surpass; outrun.

excelencia /eksθe'lenθia; eksse'lensia/ *n. f.* excellence.

excelente /eksθe'lente; eksse'lente/ *a.* excellent.

excéntrico /ek'θentriko; eks'sentriko/ *a.* eccentric.

excepción /eksθep'θion; ekssep'sion/ *n. f.* exception.

excepcional /eksθepθio'nal; ekssepsio'nal/ *a.* exceptional.

excepto /eks'θepto; eks'septo/ *prep.* except, except for.

exceptuar /eksθep'tuar; ekssep'tuar/ *v.* except.

excesivamente /eksθesiβa'mente; ekssesiβa'mente/ *adv.* excessively.

excesivo /eksθe'siβo; eksse'siβo/ *a.* excessive.

exceso /eks'θeso; eks'seso/ *n. m.* excess.

excitabilidad /eksθitaβili'ðað; ekssitaβili'ðað/ *n. f.* excitability.

excitación /eksθita'θion; ekssita'sion/ *n. f.* excitement.

excitar /eksθi'tar; ekssi'tar/ *v.* excite.

exclamación /eksklama'θion; eksklama'sion/ *n. f.* exclamation.

exclamar /ekskla'mar/ *v.* exclaim.

excluir /eksk'luir/ *v.* exclude, bar, shut out.

exclusión /eksklu'sion/ *n. f.* exclusion.

exclusivamente /eksklusiβa'mente/ *adv.* exclusively.

exclusivo /eksklu'siβo/ *a.* exclusive.

excomulgar /ekskomul'gar/ *v.* excommunicate.

excomunión /ekskomu'nion/ *n. f.* excommunication.

excreción /ekskre'θion; ekskre'sion/ *n. f.* excretion.

excremento /ekskre'mento/ *n. m.* excrement.

excretar /ekskre'tar/ *v.* excrete.

exculpar /ekskul'par/ *v.* exonerate.

excursión /ekskur'sion/ *n. f.* excursion.

excursionista /ekskursio'nista/ *n. m. & f.* excursionist; tourist.

excusa /eks'kusa/ *n. f.* excuse. —**excusar,** *v.*

excusado /eksku'saðo/ *n. m.* toilet.

excusarse /eksku'sarse/ *v.* apologize.

exención /eksen'θion; eksen'sion/ *n. f.* exemption.

exento /ek'sento/ *a.* exempt. —**exentar,** *v.*

exhalación /eksala'θion; eksala'sion/ *n. f.* exhalation.

exhalar /eksa'lar/ *v.* exhale, breathe out.

exhausto /ek'sausto/ *a.* exhausted.

exhibición /eksiβi'θion; eksiβi'sion/ *n. f.* exhibit, exhibition.

exhibir /eksi'βir/ *v.* exhibit, display.

exhortación /eksorta'θion; eksorta'sion/ *n. f.* exhortation.

exhortar /eksor'tar/ *v.* exhort, admonish.

exhumación /eksuma'θion; eksuma'sion/ *n. f.* exhumation.

exhumar /eksu'mar/ *v.* exhume.

exigencia /eksi'henθia; eksi'hensia/ *n. f.* requirement, demand.

exigente /eksi'hente/ *a.* exacting, demanding.

exigir /eksi'hir/ *v.* require, exact, demand.

eximir /eksi'mir/ *v.* exempt.

existencia /eksis'tenθia; eksis'tensia/ *n. f.* existence; *Econ.* supply.

existente /eksis'tente/ *a.* existent.

existir /eksis'tir/ *v.* exist.

éxito /'eksito/ *n. m.* success.

éxodo /'eksoðo/ *n. m.* exodus.

exoneración /eksonera'θion; eksonera'sion/ *n. f.* exoneration.

exonerar /eksone'rar/ *v.* exonerate, acquit.

exorar /ekso'rar/ *v.* beg, implore.

exorbitancia /eksorβi'tanθia; eksorβi'tansia/ *n. f.* exorbitance.

exorbitante /eksorβi'tante/ *a.* exorbitant.

exorcismo /eksor'θismo; eksor'sismo/ *n. m.* exorcism.

exornar /eksor'nar/ *v.* adorn, decorate.

exótico /ek'sotiko/ *a.* exotic.

expansibilidad /ekspansiβili'ðað/ *n. f.* expansibility.

expansión /ekspan'sion/ *n. f.* expansion.

expansivo /ekspan'siβo/ *a.* expansive; effusive.

expatriación /ekspatria'θion; ekspatria'sion/ *n. f.* expatriation.

expatriar /ekspa'triar/ *v.* expatriate.

expectación /ekspekta'θion; ekspekta'sion/ *n. f.* expectation.

expectorar /ekspekto'rar/ *v.* expectorate.

expedición /ekspeði'θion; ekspeði'sion/ *n. f.* expedition.

expediente /ekspe'ðiente/ *n. m.* expedient; means.

expedir /ekspe'ðir/ *v.* send off, ship; expedite.

expeditivo /ekspeði'tiβo/ *a.* speedy, prompt.

expedito /ekspe'ðito/ *a.* speedy, prompt.

expeler /ekspe'ler/ *v.* expel, eject.

expendedor /ekspende'ðor/ **-ra** *n.* dealer.

expender /ekspen'der/ *v.* expend.

expensas /eks'pensas/ *n. f.pl.* expenses, costs.

experiencia /ekspe'rienθia; ekspe'riensia/ *n. f.* experience.

experimentado /eksperimen'taðo/ *a.* experienced.

experimental /eksperimen'tal/ *a.* experimental.

experimentar /eksperimen'tar/ *v.* experience.

experimento /eksperi'mento/ *n. m.* experiment.

expertamente /eksperta'mente/ *adv.* expertly.

experto /ek'sperto/ **-ta** *a. & n.* expert.

expiación /ekspia'θion; ekspia'sion/ *n. f.* atonement.

expiar /eks'piar/ *v.* atone for.

expiración /ekspira'θion; ekspira'sion/ *n. f.* expiration.

expirar /ekspi'rar/ *v.* expire.

explanación /eksplana'θion; eksplana'sion/ *n. f.* explanation.

explanar /ekspla'nar/ *v.* make level.

expletivo /eksple'tiβo/ *n. & a.* expletive.

explicable /ekspli'kaβle/ *a.* explicable.

explicación /eksplika'θion; eksplika'sion/ *n. f.* explanation.

explicar /ekspli'kar/ *v.* explain.

explicativo /eksplika'tiβo/ *a.* explanatory.

explícitamente /ekspliθita'mente; eksplisita'mente/ *adv.* explicitly.

explícito /eks'pliθito; eksplisito/ *adj.* explicit.

exploración /eksplora'θion; eksplorasion/ *n. f.* exploration.

explorador /eksplora'ðor/ **-ra** *n.* explorer; scout.

explorar /eksplo'rar/ *v.* explore, scout.

exploratorio /eksplora'torio/ *a.* exploratory.

explosión /eksplo'sion/ *n. f.* explosion; outburst.

explosivo /eksplo'siβo/ *a. & m.* explosive.

explotación /eksplota'θion; eksplota'sion/ *n. f.* exploitation.

explotar /eksplo'tar/ *v.* exploit.

exponer /ekspo'ner/ *v.* expose; set forth.

exportación /eksporta'θion; eksporta'sion/ *n. f.* exportation; export.

exportador /eksporta'ðor/ **-ra** *n.* exporter.

exportar /ekspor'tar/ *v.* export.

exposición /eksposi'θion; eksposi'sion/ *n. f.* exhibit; exposition; exposure.

expósito /eks'posito/ **-ta** *n.* foundling; orphan.

expresado /ekspre'saðo/ *a.* aforesaid.

expresamente /ekspresa'mente/ *adv.* clearly, explicitly.

expresar /ekspre'sar/ *v.* express.

expresión /ekspre'sion/ *n. f.* expression.

expresivo /ekspre'siβo/ *a.* expressive; affectionate.

expreso /eks'preso/ *a. & m.* express.

exprimidera de naranjas /eksprimi'ðera de na'ranhas/ *n. f.* orange squeezer.

exprimir /ekspri'mir/ *v.* squeeze.

expropiación /ekspropia'θion; ekspropia'sion/ *n. f.* expropriation.

expropiar /ekspro'piar/ *v.* expropriate.

expulsar /ekspul'sar/ *v.* expel, eject; evict.

expulsión /ekspul'sion/ *n. f.* expulsion.

expurgación /ekspurga'θion; ekspurga'sion/ *n. f.* expurgation.

expurgar /ekspur'gar/ *v.* expurgate.

exquisitamente /ekskisita'mente/ *adv.* exquisitely.

exquisito /eks'kisito/ *a.* exquisite.

éxtasis /'ekstasis/ *n. m.* ecstasy.

extemporáneo /ekstempo'raneo/ *a.* extemporaneous, impromptu.

extender /eksten'der/ *v.* extend; spread; widen; stretch.

extensamente /ekstensa'mente/ *adv.* extensively.

extensión /eksten'sion/ *n. f.* extension, spread, expanse.

extenso /eks'tenso/ *a.* extensive, widespread.

extenuación /ekstenua'θion; ekstenua'sion/ *n. f.* weakening; emaciation.

extenuar /ekste'nuar/ *v.* extenuate.

exterior /ekste'rior/ *a. & m.* exterior, foreign.

exterminar /ekstermi'nar/ *v.* exterminate.

exterminio /ekster'minio/ *n. m.* extermination, ruin.

extinción /ekstin'θion; ekstin'sion/ *n. f.* extinction.

extinguir /ekstiŋ'guir/ *v.* extinguish.

extinto /eks'tinto/ *a.* extinct.

extintor /ekstin'tor/ *n. m.* fire extinguisher.

extirpar /ekstir'par/ *v.* eradicate.

extorsión /ekstor'sion/ *n. f.* extortion.

extra /'ekstra/ *n.* extra.

extracción /ekstrak'θion; ekstrak'sion/ *n. f.* extraction.

extractar /ekstrak'tar/ *v.* summarize.

extracto /eks'trakto/ *n. m.* extract; summary.

extradición /ekstraði'θion; ekstraði'sion/ *n. f.* extradition.

extraer /ekstra'er/ *v.* extract.

extranjero /ekstran'hero/ **-ra** *n.* **1.** foreign. —*n.* **2.** foreigner; stranger.

extrañar /ekstra'ɲar/ *v.* surprise; miss.

extraño /eks'traɲo/ *a.* strange, queer.

extraordinariamente /ekstraorðinaria'mente/ *adv.* extraordinarily.

extraordinario /ekstraorði'nario/ *a.* extraordinary.

extravagancia /ekstraβa'ganθia; ekstraβa'gansia/ *n. f.* extravagance.

extravagante /ekstraβa'gante/ *a.* extravagant.

extraviado /ekstra'βiaðo/ *a.* lost, misplaced.

extraviarse /ekstra'βiarse/ *v.* stray, get lost.

extravío /ekstra'βio/ *n. m.* misplacement; aberration, deviation.

extremadamente /ekstremaða'mente/ *adv.* extremely.

extremado /ekstre'maðo/ *a.* extreme.

extremaunción /ekstremaun'θion; ekstremaun'sion/ *n. f.* extreme unction.

extremidad /ekstremi'ðað/ *n. f.* extremity.

extremista /ekstre'mista/ *n. & a.* extremist.

extremo /eks'tremo/ *a. & m.* extreme, end.

extrínseco /ekstrin'seko/ *a.* extrinsic.

exuberancia /eksuβe'ranθia; eksuβeransia/ *n. f.* exuberance.

exuberante /eksuβe'rante/ *a.* exuberant.

exudación /eksuða'θion; eksuða'sion/ *n. f.* exudation.

exudar /eksu'ðar/ *v.* exude, ooze.

exultación /eksulta'θion; eksulta'sion/ *n. f.* exultation.

eyaculación /eyakula'θion; eyakula'sion/ *n. f.* ejaculation.

eyacular /eyaku'lar/ *v.* ejaculate.

eyección /eyek'θion; eyek'sion/ *n. f.* ejection.

eyectar /eyek'tar/ *v.* eject.

F

fábrica /'faβrika/ *n. f.* factory.

fabricación /faβrika'θion; faβrika'sion/ *n. f.* manufacture, manufacturing.

fabricante /faβri'kante/ *n. m. & f.* manufacturer, maker.

fabricar /faβri'kar/ *v.* manufacture, make.

fabril /fa'βril/ *a.* manufacturing, industrial.

fábula /'faβula/ *n. f.* fable, myth.

fabuloso /faβu'loso/ *a.* fabulous.

facción /fak'θion; fak'sion/ *n. f.* faction, party; (*pl.*) features.

faccioso /fak'θioso; fak'sioso/ *a.* factious.

fachada /fa'tʃaða/ *n. f.* façade, front.

fácil /'faθil; 'fasil/ *a.* easy.

facilidad /faθili'ðað; fasili'ðað/ *n. f.* facility, ease.

facilitar /faθili'tar; fasili'tar/ *v.* facilitate, make easy.

fácilmente /,faθil'mente; ,fasil'mente/ *adv.* easily.

facsímile /fak'simile/ *n. m.* facsimile.

factible /fak'tiβle/ *a.* feasible.

factor /fak'tor/ *n. m.* factor.

factótum /fak'totum/ *n. m.* factotum; jack of all trades.

factura /fak'tura/ *n. f.* invoice, bill.

facturar /faktu'rar/ *v.* bill; check (baggage).

facultad /fakulta'ð/ *n. f.* faculty; ability.

facultativo /fakulta'tiβo/ *a.* optional.

faena /fa'ena/ *n. f.* task; work.

faisán /fai'san/ *n. m.* pheasant.

faja /'faha/ *n. f.* band; sash; zone.

falacia /fa'laθia; fa'lasia/ *n. f.* fallacy; deceitfulness.

falda /'falda/ *n. f.* skirt; lap.

falibilidad /faliβili'ðað/ *n. f.* fallibility.

falla /'faʎa; faya/ *n. f.* failure; fault.

fallar /fa'ʎar; fa'yar/ *v.* fail.

fallecer /faʎe'θer; faye'ser/ *v.* pass away, die.

fallo /'faʎo; 'fayo/ *n. m.* verdict; shortcoming.

falsear /false'ar/ *v.* falsify, counterfeit; forge.

falsedad /false'ðað/ *n. f.* falsehood; lie; falseness.

falsificación /falsifika'θion; falsifika'sion/ *n. f.* falsification; forgery.

falsificar /falsifi'kar/ *v.* falsify, counterfeit, forge.

falso /'falso/ *a.* false; wrong.

falta /'falta/ *n. f.* error, mistake; fault; lack. **hacer f.,** to be lacking, to be necessary. **sin f.,** without fail.

faltar /fal'tar/ *v.* be lacking, be missing; be absent.

faltriquera /faltri'kera/ *n. f.* pocket.

fama /'fama/ *n. f.* fame; reputation; glory.

familia /fa'milia/ *n. f.* family; household.

familiar /fami'liar/ *a.* familiar; domestic; (of) family.

familiaridad /familiari'ðað/ *n. f.* familiarity, intimacy.

familiarizar /familiari'θar; familiari'sar/ *v.* familiarize, acquaint.

famoso /fa'moso/ *a.* famous.

fanal /fa'nal/ *n. m.* lighthouse; lantern, lamp.

fanático /fa'natiko/ **-ca** *a. & n.* fanatic.

fanatismo /fana'tismo/ *n. m.* fanaticism.

fanfarria /fan'farria/ *n. f.* bluster. —**fanfarrear,** *v.*

fango /'faŋgo/ *n. m.* mud.

fantasía /fanta'sia/ *n. f.* fantasy; fancy, whim.

fantasma /fan'tasma/ *n. m.* phantom; ghost.

fantástico /fan'tastiko/ *a.* fantastic.

faquín /fa'kin/ *n. m.* porter.

faquir /fa'kir/ *n. m.* fakir.

farallón /fara'ʎon; fara'yon/ *n. m.* cliff.

Faraón /fara'on/ *n. m.* Pharaoh.

fardel /far'ðel/ *n. m.* bag; package.

fardo /far'ðo/ *n. m.* bundle.

farináceo /fari'naθeo; fari'naseo/ *a.* farinaceous.

faringe /fa'rinhe/ *n. f.* pharynx.

fariseo /fari'seo/ *n. m.* pharisee, hypocrite.

farmacéutico /farma'θeutiko; farma'seutiko/ **-ca** *a.* **1.** pharmaceutical. —*n.* **2.** pharmacist.

farmacia /far'maθia; far'masia/ *n. f.* pharmacy.

faro /'faro/ *n. m.* beacon; lighthouse; headlight.

farol /fa'rol/ *n. m.* lantern; (street) light, street lamp.

farra /'farra/ *n. f.* spree.

fárrago /'farrago/ *n. m.* medley; hodgepodge.

farsa /'farsa/ *n. f.* farce.

fascinación /fasθina'θion; fassina'sion/ *n. f.* fascination.

fascinar /fasθi'nar; fassi'nar/ *v.* fascinate, bewitch.

fase /'fase/ *n. f.* phase.

fastidiar /fasti'ðiar/ *v.* disgust, irk, annoy.

fastidio /fasti'ðio/ *n. m.* disgust; annoyance.

fastidioso /fasti'ðioso/ *a.* annoying; tedious.

fasto /'fasto/ *a.* happy, fortunate.

fatal /fa'tal/ *a.* fatal.

fatalidad /fatali'ðað/ *n. f.* fate; calamity, bad luck.

fatalismo /fata'lismo/ *n. m.* fatalism.

fatalista /fata'lista/ *n. & a.* fatalist.

fatiga /fa'tiga/ *n. f.* fatigue. —**fatigar,** *v.*

fauna /'fauna/ *n. f.* fauna.

fauno /'fauno/ *n. m.* faun.

favor /fa'βor/ *n. m.* favor; behalf. **por f.,** please.

¡Favor! Puh-lease!

favorable /faβo'raβle/ *a.* favorable.

favorablemente /faβoraβle'mente/ *adv.* favorably.

favorecer /faβore'θer; faβore'ser/ *v.* favor; flatter.

favoritismo /faβori'tismo/ *n. m.* favoritism.

favorito /faβo'rito/ **-ta** *a. & n.* favorite.

fax /faks/ *n. m.* fax.

faz /faθ; fas/ *n. f.* face.

fe /fe/ *n. f.* faith.

fealdad /feal'dað/ *n. f.* ugliness, homeliness.

febrero /fe'βrero/ *n. m.* February.

febril /fe'βril/ *a.* feverish.

fecha /'fetʃa/ *n. f.* date. —**fechar,** *v.*

fecha de caducidad /'fetʃa de kaðuθi'ðað; 'fetʃa de kaðusi'ðað/ expiration date.

fécula /'fekula/ *n. f.* starch.

fecundar /fekun'dar/ *v.* fertilize.

fecundidad /fekundi'ðað/ *n. f.* fecundity, fertility.

fecundo /fe'kundo/ *a.* fecund, fertile.

federación /feðera'θion; feðera'sion/ *n. f.* federation.

federal /feðe'ral/ *a.* federal.

felicidad /feliθi'ðað; felisi'ðað/ *n. f.* happiness; bliss.

felicitación /feliθita'θion; felisita'sion/ *n. f.* congratulation.

felicitar /feliθi'tar; felisi'tar/ *v.* congratulate.

feligrés /feli'gres/ **-esa** *n.* parishioner.

feliz /fe'liθ; fe'lis/ *a.* happy; fortunate.

felón /fe'lon/ *n. m.* felon.

felonía /felo'nia/ *n. f.* felony.

felpa /'felpa/ *n. f.* plush.

felpudo /fel'puðo/ *n. m.* doormat.

femenino /feme'nino/ *a.* feminine.

feminismo /femi'nismo/ *n. m.* feminism.

feminista /femi'nista/ *n. m. & f.* feminist.

fenecer /fene'θer; fene'ser/ *v.* conclude; die.

fénix /'feniks/ *n. m.* phoenix; model.

fenomenal /fenome'nal/ *a.* phenomenal.

fenómeno /fe'nomeno/ *n. m.* phenomenon.

feo /'feo/ *a.* ugly, homely.

feracidad /feraθi'ðað; ferasi'ðað/ *n. f.* feracity, fertility.

feraz /'feraθ; 'feras/ *a.* fertile, fruitful; copious.

feria /'feria/ *n. f.* fair; market.

feriado /fe'riaðo/ *a.* **día f.,** holiday.

fermentación /fermenta'θion; fermenta'sion/ *n. f.* fermentation.

fermento /fer'mento/ *n. m.* ferment. —**fermentar,** *v.*

ferocidad /feroθi'ðað; ferosi'ðað/ *n. f.* ferocity, fierceness.

feroz /fe'roθ; fe'ros/ *a.* ferocious, fierce.

férreo /'ferreo/ *a.* of iron.

ferrería /ferre'ria/ *n. f.* ironworks.

ferretería /ferrete'ria/ *n. f.* hardware; hardware store.

ferrocarril /ferroka'rril/ *n. m.* railroad.

fértil /'fertil/ *a.* fertile.

fertilidad /fertili'ðað/ *n. f.* fertility.

fertilizar /fertili'θar; fertili'sar/ *v.* fertilize.

férvido /'ferβiðo/ *a.* fervid, ardent.

ferviente /fer'βiente/ *a.* fervent.

fervor /fer'βor/ *n. m.* fervor, zeal.

fervoroso /ferβo'roso/ *a.* zealous, eager.

festejar /feste'har/ *v.* entertain, fete.

festejo /fes'teho/ *n. m.* feast.

festín /fes'tin/ *n. m.* feast.

festividad /festiβi'ðað/ *n. f.* festivity.

festivo /fes'tiβo/ *a.* festive.

fétido /'fetiðo/ *adj.* fetid.

feudal /feu'ðal/ *a.* feudal.

feudo /'feuðo/ *n. m.* fief; manor.

fiado /'fiaðo, al/ *adj.* on trust, on credit.

fiambrera /fiam'brera/ *n. f.* lunch box.

fianza /'fianθa; 'fiansa/ *n. f.* bail.

fiar /fi'ar/ *v.* trust, sell on credit; give credit.

fiarse de /'fiarse de/ *v.* trust (in), rely on.

fiasco /'fiasko/ *n. m.* fiasco.
fibra /'fiβra/ *n. f.* fiber; vigor.
fibroso /fi'βroso/ *a.* fibrous.
ficción /fik'θion; fik'sion/ *n. f.* fiction.
ficha /'fitʃa/ *n. f.* slip, index card; chip.
fichero /fi'tʃero/ *n. m.* computer file, filing cabinet, card catalog.
ficticio /fik'tiθio; fik'tisio/ *a.* fictitious.
fidedigno /fiðe'ðigno/ *a.* trustworthy.
fideicomisario /fiðeikomi'sario/ **-ria** *n.* trustee.
fideicomiso /fiðeiko'miso/ *n. m.* trust.
fidelidad /fiðeli'ðað/ *n. f.* fidelity.
fideo /fi'ðeo/ *n. m.* noodle.
fiebre /'fieβre/ *n. f.* fever.
fiebre del heno /'fieβre del 'eno/ hayfever.
fiel /fiel/ *a.* faithful.
fieltro /'fieltro/ *n. m.* felt.
fiera /'fiera/ *n. f.* wild animal.
fiereza /fie'reθa; fie'resa/ *n. f.* fierceness, wildness.
fiero /'fiero/ *a.* fierce; wild.
fiesta /'fiesta/ *n. f.* festival, feast; party.
figura /fi'gura/ *n. f.* figure. —**figurar,** *v.*
figurarse /figu'rarse/ *v.* imagine.
figurón /figu'ron/ *n. m.* dummy.
fijar /fi'har/ *v.* fix; set, establish; post.
fijarse en /fi'harse en/ *v.* notice.
fijeza /fi'heθa; fi'hesa/ *n. f.* firmness.
fijo /'fiho/ *a.* fixed, stationary, permanent, set.
fila /'fila/ *n. f.* row, rank, file, line.
filantropía /filantro'pia/ *n. f.* philanthropy.
filatelia /fila'telia/ *n. f.* philately, stamp collecting.
filete /fi'lete/ *n. m.* fillet; steak.
film /film/ *n. m.* film. —**filmar,** *v.*
filo /'filo/ *n. m.* (cutting) edge.
filón /fi'lon/ *n. m.* vein (of ore).
filosofía /filoso'fia/ *n. f.* philosophy.
filosófico /filo'sofiko/ *a.* philosophical.
filósofo /fi'losofo/ **-fa** *n.* philosopher.
filtro /'filtro/ *n. m.* filter. —**filtrar,** *v.*
fin /fin/ *n. m.* end, purpose, goal. **a f. de que,** in order that. **en f.,** in short. **por f.,** finally, at last.
final /fi'nal/ *a.* **1.** final. —*n.* **2.** *m.* end.
finalidad /finali'ðað/ *n. f.* finality.
finalmente /final'mente/ *adv.* at last.
financiero /finan'θiero; finan'siero/ **-ra** *a.* **1.** financial. —*n.* **2.** financier.
finca /'finka/ *n. f.* real estate; estate; farm.
finés /fi'nes/ **-esa** *a.* & *n.* Finnish; Finn.
fineza /fi'neθa; fi'nesa/ *n. f.* courtesy, politeness; fineness.
fingimiento /finhi'miento/ *n. m.* pretense.
fingir /fin'hir/ *v.* feign, pretend.
fino /'fino/ *a.* fine; polite, courteous.
firma /'firma/ *n. f.* signature; *Com.* firm.
firmamento /firma'mento/ *n. m.* firmament, heavens.
firmar /fir'mar/ *v.* sign.
firme /'firme/ *a.* firm, fast, steady, sound.
firmemente /firme'mente/ *adv.* firmly.
firmeza /fir'meθa; fir'mesa/ *n. f.* firmness.
fisco /'fisko/ *n. m.* exchequer, treasury.
física /'fisika/ *n. f.* physics.
físico /'fisiko/ **-ca** *a.* & *n.* physical; physicist.
fisiología /fisiolo'hia/ *n. f.* physiology.
fláccido /'flakθiðo; 'flaksiðo/ *a.* flaccid, soft.
flaco /'flako/ *a.* thin, gaunt.
flagelación /flahela'θion; flahela'sion/ *n. f.* flagellation.
flagelar /flahe'lar/ *v.* flagellate, whip.
flagrancia /fla'granθia; fla'gransia/ *n. f.* flagrancy.
flagrante /fla'grante/ *a.* flagrant.
flama /'flama/ *n. f.* flame; ardor, zeal.
flamante /fla'mante/ *a.* flaming.
flamenco /fla'menko/ *n. m.* flamingo.
flan /flan/ *n. m.* custard.
flanco /'flanko/ *n. m.* side; *Mil.* flank.
flanquear /flanke'ar/ *v.* flank.
flaqueza /fla'keθa; fla'kesa/ *n. f.* thinness; weakness.
flauta /'flauta/ *n. f.* flute.
flautín /flau'tin/ *n. m.* piccolo.
flautista /flau'tista/ *n. m.* & *f.* flutist, piper.
flecha /'fletʃa/ *n. f.* arrow.
flechazo /fle'tʃaθo; fle'tʃaso/ *n. m.* love at first sight.
flechero /fle'tʃero/ **-ra** *n.* archer.
fleco /'fleko/ *n. m.* fringe; flounce.
flema /'flema/ *n. f.* phlegm.
flemático /fle'matiko/ *a.* phlegmatic.
flequillo /fle'kiʎo; fle'kiyo/ *n. m.* fringe; bangs (of hair).
flete /'flete/ *n. m.* freight. —**fletar,** *v.*
flexibilidad /fleksiβili'ðað/ *n. f.* flexibility.
flexible /fle'ksiβle/ *a.* flexible, pliable.
flirtear /flirte'ar/ *v.* flirt.
flojo /'floho/ *a.* limp; loose, flabby, slack.
flor /flor/ *n. f.* flower; compliment.
flora /'flora/ *n. f.* flora.
floral /flo'ral/ *a.* floral.
florecer /flore'θer; flore'ser/ *v.* flower, bloom; flourish.
floreo /flo'reo/ *n. m.* flourish.
florero /flo'rero/ *n. m.* flower pot; vase.
floresta /flo'resta/ *n. f.* forest.
florido /flo'riðo/ *a.* flowery; flowering.
florista /flo'rista/ *n. m.* & *f.* florist.
flota /'flota/ *n. f.* fleet.
flotante /flo'tante/ *a.* floating.
flotar /flo'tar/ *v.* float.
flotilla /flo'tiʎa; flo'tiya/ *n. f.* flotilla, fleet.
fluctuación /fluktua'θion; fluktua'sion/ *n. f.* fluctuation.
fluctuar /fluktu'ar/ *v.* fluctuate.
fluente /'fluente/ *a.* fluent; flowing.
fluidez /flui'ðeθ; flui'ðes/ *n. f.* fluency.
fluido /'fluiðo/ *a.* & *m.* fluid, liquid.
fluir /flu'ir/ *v.* flow.
flujo /'fluho/ *n. m.* flow, flux.
fluor /fluor/ *n. m.* fluorine.
fluorescencia /fluores'θenθia; fluores'sensia/ *n. f.* fluorescence.
fluorescente /fluores'θente; fluores'sente/ *a.* fluorescent.
fobia /'foβia/ *n. f.* phobia.
foca /'foka/ *n. f.* seal.
foco /'foko/ *n. m.* focus, center; floodlight.
fogata /fo'gata/ *n. f.* bonfire.
fogón /fo'gon/ *n. m.* hearth, fireplace.
fogosidad /fogosi'ðað/ *n. f.* vehemence, ardor.
fogoso /fo'goso/ *a.* vehement, ardent.
folclore /fol'klore/ *n. m.* folklore.
follaje /fo'ʎahe; fo'yahe/ *n. m.* foliage.
folleto /fo'ʎeto; fo'yeto/ *n. m.* pamphlet, booklet.
follón /fo'ʎon; fo'yon/ *n. m.*mess, chaos.
fomentar /fomen'tar/ *v.* develop, promote, further, foster.
fomento /fo'mento/ *n. m.* fomentation.
fonda /'fonda/ *n. f.* eating house, inn.
fondo /'fondo/ *n. m.* bottom; back (part); background; (*pl.*) funds; finances. **a f.,** thoroughly.
fonética /fo'netika/ *n. f.* phonetics.
fonético /fo'netiko/ *a.* phonetic.
fonógrafo /fo'nografo/ *n. m.* phonograph.
fontanero /fonta'nero/ **-era** *n.* plumber.
forastero /foras'tero/ **-ra** *a.* **1.** foreign, exotic. —*n.* **2.** stranger.
forjar /for'har/ *v.* forge.
forma /'forma/ *n. f.* form, shape. —**formar,** *v.*
formación /forma'θion; forma'sion/ *n. f.* formation.
formal /for'mal/ *a.* formal.
formaldehido /formalde'iðo/ *n. m.* formaldehyde.
formalidad /formali'ðað/ *n. f.* formality.
formalizar /formali'θar; formali'sar/ *v.* finalize; formulate.
formidable /formi'ðaβle/ *a.* formidable.
formidablemente /formiðaβle'mente/ *adv.* formidably.
formón /for'mon/ *n. m.* chisel.
fórmula /'formula/ *n. f.* formula.
formular /formu'lar/ *v.* formulate, draw up.
formulario /formu'lario/ *n. m.* form.
foro /'foro/ *n. m.* forum.
forrado /fo'rraðo/ *a.* stuffed; *Colloq.* filthy rich.
forraje /fo'rrahe/ *n. m.* forage, fodder.
forrar /fo'rrar/ *v.* line.
forro /'forro/ *n. m.* lining; condom.
fortalecer /fortale'θer; fortale'ser/ *v.* fortify.
fortaleza /forta'leθa; forta'lesa/ *n. f.* fort, fortress; fortitude.
fortificación /fortifika'θion; fortifika'sion/ *n. f.* fortification.
fortitud /forti'tuð/ *n. f.* fortitude.
fortuitamente /fortuita'mente/ *adv.* fortuitously.
fortuito /for'tuito/ *a.* fortuitous.
fortuna /for'tuna/ *n. f.* fortune; luck.
forúnculo /fo'runkulo/ *n. m.* boil.
forzar /for'θar; for'sar/ *v.* force, compel, coerce.
forzosamente /forθosa'mente; forsosa'mente/ *adv.* compulsorily; forcibly.
forzoso /for'θoso; for'soso/ *a.* compulsory; necessary. **paro f.,** unemployment.
forzudo /for'θuðo; for'suðo/ *a.* powerful, vigorous.
fosa /'fosa/ *n. f.* grave; pit.
fósforo /'fosforo/ *n. m.* match; phosphorus.
fósil /'fosil/ *n. m.* fossil.
foso /'foso/ *n. m.* ditch, trench; moat.
fotocopia /foto'kopia/ *n. f.* photocopy.
fotocopiadora /fotokopia'ðora/ *n. f.* photocopier.
fotografía /fotogra'fia/ *n. f.* photograph; photography. —**fotografiar,** *v.*
frac /frak/ *n. m.* dress coat.
fracasar /fraka'sar/ *v.* fail.
fracaso /fra'kaso/ *n. m.* failure.
fracción /frak'θion; frak'sion/ *n. f.* fraction.
fractura /frak'tura/ *n. f.* fracture, break.
fragancia /fra'ganθia; fra'gansia/ *n. f.* fragrance; perfume; aroma.
fragante /fra'gante/ *a.* fragrant.
frágil /'frahil/ *a.* fragile, breakable.
fragilidad /frahili'ðað/ *n. f.* fragility.
fragmentario /fragmen'tario/ *a.* fragmentary.
fragmento /frag'mento/ *n. m.* fragment, bit.
fragor /fra'gor/ *n. m.* noise, clamor.
fragoso /fra'goso/ *a.* noisy.
fragua /'fragua/ *n. f.* forge. —**fraguar,** *v.*
fraile /'fraile/ *n. m.* monk.
frambuesa /fram'buesa/ *n. f.* raspberry.
francamente /franka'mente/ *adv.* frankly, candidly.
francés /fran'θes; fran'ses/ **-esa** *a.* & *n.* French; Frenchman, Frenchwoman.
Francia /'franθia; 'fransia/ *n. f.* France.
franco /'franko/ *a.* frank.
franela /fra'nela/ *n. f.* flannel.
frangible /fraŋ'giβle/ *a.* breakable.
franqueo /fran'keo/ *n. m.* postage.
franqueza /fran'keθa; fran'kesa/ *n. f.* frankness.
franquicia /fran'kiθia; fran'kisia/ *n. f.* franchise.
frasco /'frasko/ *n. m.* flask, bottle.
frase /'frase/ *n. f.* phrase; sentence.
fraseología /fraseolo'hia/ *n. f.* phraseology; style.
fraternal /frater'nal/ *a.* fraternal, brotherly.
fraternidad /fraterni'ðað/ *n. f.* fraternity, brotherhood.
fraude /'frauðe/ *n. m.* fraud.
fraudulento /frauðu'lento/ *a.* fraudulent.
frazada /fra'θaða; fra'saða/ *n. f.* blanket.
frecuencia /fre'kuenθia; fre'kuensia/ *n. f.* frequency.
frecuente /fre'kuente/ *a.* frequent.
frecuentemente /frekuente'mente/ *adv.* frequently, often.
fregadero /frega'ðero/ *n. m.* sink.
fregadura /frega'ðura/ *n. f.* scouring, scrubbing.
fregar /fre'gar/ *v.* scour, scrub, mop.
fregona /fre'gona/ *n. f.* mop.
freír /fre'ir/ *v.* fry.
fréjol /'frehol/ *n. m.* kidney bean.
frenazo /fre'naθo; fre'naso/ *n. m.* sudden braking, slamming on the brakes.
frenesí /frene'si/ *n. m.* frenzy.
frenéticamente /fre'netikamente/ *adv.* frantically.
frenético /fre'netiko/ *a.* frantic, frenzied.
freno /'freno/ *n. m.* brake. —**frenar,** *v.*
freno de auxilio /'freno de auk'silio/ emergency brake.
freno de mano /'freno de 'mano/ hand brake.
frente /'frente/ *n.* **1.** *f.* forehead. **2.** *m.* front. **en f., al f.,** opposite, across. **f. a,** in front of.
fresa /'fresa/ *n. f.* strawberry.
fresca /'freska/ *n. f.* fresh, cool air.
fresco /'fresko/ *a.* fresh; cool; crisp.
frescura /fres'kura/ *n. f.* coolness, freshness.
fresno /'fresno/ *n. m.* ash tree.
fresquería /freske'ria/ *n. f.* soda fountain.
friabilidad /friaβili'ðað/ *n. f.* brittleness.
friable /'friaβle/ *a.* brittle.
frialdad /frial'dað/ *n. f.* coldness.
fríamente /fria'mente/ *adv.* coldly; coolly.
fricandó /'frikando/ *n. m.* fricandeau.
fricar /fri'kar/ *v.* rub together.
fricción /frik'θion; frik'sion/ *n. f.* friction.
friccionar /frikθio'nar; friksio'nar/ *v.* rub.
friega /'friega/ *n. f.* friction; massage.
frigidez /frihi'ðeθ; frihi'ðes/ *n. f.* frigidity.
frígido /'frihiðo/ *a.* frigid.
frijol /fri'hol/ *n. m.* bean.
frío /'frio/ *a.* & *n.* cold. **tener f.,** to be cold, feel cold. **hacer f.,** to be cold (weather).
friolento /frio'lento/ **friolero** *a.* chilly; sensitive to cold.
friolera /frio'lera/ *n. f.* trifle, trinket.
friso /'friso/ *n. m.* frieze.
fritillas /fri'tiʎas; fri'tiyas/ *n. f.pl.* fritters.
frito /'frito/ *a.* fried.
fritura /fri'tura/ *n. f.* fritter.
frívolamente /'friβolamente/ *adv.* frivolously.
frivolidad /friβoli'ðað/ *n. f.* frivolity.
frívolo /'friβolo/ *a.* frivolous.
frondoso /fron'doso/ *a.* leafy.
frontera /fron'tera/ *n. f.* frontier; border.
frotar /fro'tar/ *v.* rub.

fructífero /fruk'tifero/ a. fruitful.
fructificar /fruktifi'kar/ v. bear fruit.
fructuosamente /fruktuosa'mente/ adv. fruitfully.
fructuoso /fruk'tuoso/ a. fruitful.
frugal /fru'gal/ a. frugal; thrifty.
frugalidad /frugali'ðað/ n. f. frugality; thrift.
frugalmente /frugal'mente/ adv. frugally, thriftily.
fruncir /frun'θir; frun'sir/ v. gather, contract. **f. el entrecejo,** frown.
fruslería /frusle'ria/ n. f. trinket.
frustrar /frus'trar/ v. frustrate, thwart.
fruta /'fruta/ n. f. fruit.
frutería /frute'ria/ n. f. fruit store.
fruto /'fruto/ n. m. fruit; product; profit.
fucsia /'fuksia/ n. f. fuchsia.
fuego /'fuego/ n. m. fire.
fuelle /'fueʎe; 'fueye/ n. m. bellows.
fuente /'fuente/ n. f. fountain; source; platter.
fuera /'fuera/ adv. without, outside.
fuero /'fuero/ n. m. statute.
fuerte /'fuerte/ a. **1.** strong; loud. —n. **2.** m. fort.
fuertemente /fuerte'mente/ adv. strongly; loudly.
fuerza /'fuerθa; 'fuersa/ n. f. force, strength.
fuga /'fuga/ n. f. flight, escape.
fugarse /fu'garse/ v. flee, escape.
fugaz /fu'gaθ; fu'gas/ a. fugitive, passing.
fugitivo /fuhi'tiβo/ **-va** a. & n. fugitive.
fulano /fu'lano/ **-na** n. Mr., Mrs. so-and-so.
fulcro /'fulkro/ n. m. fulcrum.
fulgor /ful'gor/ n. m. gleam, glow. —**fulgurar,** v.
fulminante /fulmi'nante/ a. explosive.
fumador /fuma'ðor/ **-ra** n. smoker.
fumar /fu'mar/ v. smoke.
fumigación /fumiga'θion; fumiga'sion/ n. f. fumigation.
fumigador /fumiga'ðor/ **-ra** n. fumigator.
fumigar /fumi'gar/ v. fumigate.
fumoso /fu'moso/ a. smoky.
función /fun'θion; fun'sion/ n. f. function; performance, show.
funcionar /funθio'nar; funsio'nar/ v. function; work, run.
funcionario /funθio'nario; funsio'nario/ **-ria** n. official, functionary.
funda /'funda/ n. f. case, sheath, slipcover.
fundación /funda'θion; funda'sion/ n. f. foundation.
fundador /funda'ðor/ **-ra** n. founder.
fundamental /funda'mental/ a. fundamental, basic.
fundamentalmente /fundamental'mente/ adv. fundamentally.
fundamento /funda'mento/ n. m. base, basis, foundation.
fundar /fun'dar/ v. found, establish.
fundición /fundi'θion; fundi'sion/ n. f. foundry; melting; meltdown.
fundir /fun'dir/ v. fuse; smelt.
fúnebre /'funeβre/ a. dismal.
funeral /fune'ral/ n. m. funeral.
funeraria /fune'raria/ n. f. funeral home, funeral parlor.
funestamente /funesta'mente/ adv. sadly.
fungo /'fuŋgo/ n. m. fungus.
furente /fu'rente/ a. furious, enraged.
furgoneta /furgo'neta/ n. f. van.
furia /'furia/ n. f. fury.
furiosamente /furiosa'mente/ adv. furiously.
furioso /fu'rioso/ a. furious.
furor /fu'ror/ n. m. furor; fury.
furtivamente /furtiβa'mente/ adv. furtively.
furtivo /fur'tiβo/ a. furtive, sly.
furúnculo /fu'runkulo/ n. m. boil.
fusibilidad /fusiβili'ðað/ n. f. fusibility.

fusible /fu'siβle/ n. m. fuse.
fusil /fu'sil/ n. m. rifle, gun.
fusilar /fusi'lar/ v. shoot, execute.
fusión /fu'sion/ n. f. fusion; merger.
fusionar /fusio'nar/ v. unite, fuse, merge.
fútbol /'futβol/ n. m. football, soccer.
fútil /'futil/ a. trivial.
futilidad /futili'ðað/ n. f. triviality.
futuro /fu'turo/ a. & m. future.
futurología /futurolo'hia/ n. f. futurology.

G

gabán /ga'βan/ n. m. overcoat.
gabardina /gaβar'ðina/ n. f. raincoat.
gabinete /gaβi'nete/ n. m. closet; cabinet; study.
gacela /ga'θela; ga'sela/ n. f. gazelle.
gaceta /ga'θeta; ga'seta/ n. f. gazette, newspaper.
gacetilla /gaθe'tiʎa; gase'tiya/ n. f. personal news section of a newspaper.
gaélico /ga'eliko/ a. Gaelic.
gafas /'gafas/ n. f.pl. eyeglasses.
gaguear /gage'ar/ v. stutter, stammer.
gaita /'gaita/ n. f. bagpipes.
gaje /'gahe/ n. m. salary; fee.
gala /'gala/ n. f. gala, ceremony; (pl.) regalia. **tener a g.,** be proud of.
galán /ga'lan/ n. m. gallant.
galano /ga'lano/ a. stylishly dressed; elegant.
galante /ga'lante/ a. gallant.
galantería /galante'ria/ n. f. gallantry, compliment.
galápago /ga'lapago/ n. m. freshwater turtle.
galardón /galar'ðon/ n. m. prize; reward.
gáleo /'galeo/ n. m. swordfish.
galera /ga'lera/ n. f. wagon; shed; galley.
galería /gale'ria/ n. f. gallery, Theat. balcony.
galés /'gales/ **-esa** a. & n. Welsh; Welshman, Welshwoman.
galgo /'galgo/ n. m. greyhound.
galillo /ga'liʎo; ga'liyo/ n. m. uvula.
galimatías /galima'tias/ n. m. gibberish.
gallardete /gaʎar'ðete; gayar'ðete/ n. m. pennant.
galleta /ga'ʎeta; ga'yeta/ n. f. cracker.
gallina /ga'ʎina; ga'yina/ n. f. hen.
gallinero /gaʎi'nero; gayi'nero/ n. m. chicken coop.
gallo /ga'ʎo; ga'yo/ n. m. rooster.
galocha /ga'lotʃa/ n. f. galosh.
galón /ga'lon/ n. m. gallon; Mil. stripe.
galope /ga'lope/ n. m. gallop. —**galopar,** v.
galopín /galo'pin/ n. m. ragamuffin, urchin (child).
gamba /'gamba/ n. f. prawn.
gamberro /gam'βerro/ **-ra** n. hooligan.
gambito /gam'bito/ n. m. gambit.
gamuza /ga'muθa; ga'musa/ n. f. chamois.
gana /'gana/ n. f. desire, wish, mind (to). **de buena g.,** willingly. **tener ganas de,** to feel like.
ganado /ga'naðo/ n. m. cattle.
ganador /gana'ðor/ **-ra** n. winner.
ganancia /ga'nanθia; ga'nansia/ n. f. gain, profit; (pl.) earnings.
ganapán /gana'pan/ n. m. drudge.
ganar /ga'nar/ v. earn; win; beat.
ganchillo /gan'tʃiʎo; gan'tʃiyo/ n. m. crochet work.
gancho /'gantʃo/ n. m. hook, hanger, clip, hairpin.
gandul /gan'dul/ **-la** n. idler, tramp, hobo.
ganga /'gaŋga/ n. f. bargain.
gangrena /gaŋ'grena/ n. f. gangrene.
gansarón /gansa'ron/ n. m. gosling.

ganso /'ganso/ n. m. goose.
garabato /gara'βato/ n. m. hook; scrawl, scribble.
garaje /ga'rahe/ n. m. garage.
garantía /garan'tia/ n. f. guarantee; collateral, security.
garantizar /garanti'θar; garanti'sar/ v. guarantee, secure, pledge.
garbanzo /gar'βanθo; gar'βanso/ n. m. chickpea.
garbo /'garβo/ n. m. grace.
garboso /gar'βoso/ a. graceful, sprightly.
gardenia /gar'ðenia/ n. f. gardenia.
garfa /'garfa/ n. f. claw, talon.
garganta /gar'ganta/ n. f. throat.
gárgara /'gargara/ n. f. gargle. —**gargarizar,** v.
garita /ga'rita/ n. f. sentry box.
garito /ga'rito/ n. m. gambling house.
garlopa /gar'lopa/ n. f. carpenter's plane.
garra /'garra/ n. f. claw.
garrafa /ga'rrafa/ n. f. decanter, carafe.
garrideza /garri'ðeθa; garri'ðesa/ n. f. elegance, handsomeness.
garrido /ga'rriðo/ a. elegant, handsome.
garrote /ga'rrote/ n. m. club, cudgel.
garrotillo /garro'tiʎo; garro'tiyo/ n. m. croup.
garrudo /ga'rruðo/ a. powerful, brawny.
garza /'garθa; 'garsa/ n. f. heron.
gas /gas/ n. m. gas.
gasa /'gasa/ n. f. gauze.
gaseosa /gase'osa/ n. f. carbonated water.
gaseoso /gase'oso/ a. gaseous.
gasolina /gaso'lina/ n. f. gasoline.
gasolinera /gasoli'nera/ n. f. gas station.
gastar /gas'tar/ v. spend; use up; wear out; waste.
gastritis /gas'tritis/ n. f. gastritis.
gastrómano /gas'tromano/ n. m. glutton.
gastrónomo /gas'tronomo/ **-ma** n. gourmet, epicure, gastronome.
gatear /gate'ar/ v. creep.
gatillo /ga'tiʎo; ga'tiyo/ n. m. trigger.
gato /'gato/ **-ta** n. cat.
gaucho /'gautʃo/ n. m. Argentine cowboy.
gaveta /ga'βeta/ n. f. drawer.
gavilla /ga'βiʎa; ga'βiya/ n. f. sheaf.
gaviota /ga'βiota/ n. f. seagull.
gayo /'gayo/ a. merry, gay.
gayola /ga'yola/ n. f. cage; Colloq. prison.
gazapera /gaθa'pera; gasa'pera/ n. f. rabbit warren.
gazapo /ga'θapo; ga'sapo/ n. m. rabbit.
gazmoñada /gaθmo'ɲaða; gasmo'ɲaða/ n. f. prudishness.
gazmoño /gaθ'moɲo; gas'moɲo/ n. m. prude.
gaznate /gaθ'nate; gas'nate/ n. m. windpipe.
gazpacho /gaθ'patʃo; gas'patʃo/ n. m. cold tomato soup; gazpacho.
gelatina /hela'tina/ n. f. gelatine.
gemelo /he'melo/ **-la** n. twin.
gemelos /he'melos/ n. m.pl. cuff links; opera glasses; **-as,** twins.
gemido /he'miðo/ n. m. moan, groan, wail. —**gemir,** v.
genciana /hen'θiana; hen'siana/ n. f. gentian.
genealogía /henealo'hia/ n. f. genealogy, pedigree.
generación /henera'θion; henera'sion/ n. f. generation.
generador /henera'ðor/ n. m. generator.
general /hene'ral/ a. & m. general.
generalidad /henerali'ðað/ n. f. generality.
generalización /heneraliθa'θion; heneralisa'sion/ n. f. generalization.

generalizar /henerali'θar; henerali'sar/ v. generalize.
generalmente /heneral'mente/ adv. generally.
género /'henero/ n. **1.** m. gender; kind. **2.** (pl.) goods, material.
generosidad /henerosi'ðað/ n. f. generosity.
generoso /hene'roso/ a. generous.
génesis /'henesis/ n. m. genesis.
genético /he'netiko/ a. genetic.
genial /he'nial/ a. genial; brilliant.
genio /'henio/ n. m. genius; temper; disposition.
genitivo /heni'tiβo/ n. m. genitive.
genocidio /heno'θiðio; heno'siðio/ n. m. genocide.
gente /'hente/ n. f. people, folk.
gentil /hen'til/ a. gracious; graceful.
gentileza /henti'leθa; henti'lesa/ n. f. grace, graciousness.
gentío /hen'tio/ n. m. mob, crowd.
genuino /he'nuino/ a. genuine.
geografía /heogra'fia/ n. f. geography.
geográfico /heo'grafiko/ a. geographical.
geométrico /heo'metriko/ a. geometric.
geranio /he'ranio/ n. m. geranium.
gerencia /he'renθia; he'rensia/ n. f. management.
gerente /he'rente/ n. m. & f. manager, director.
germen /'hermen/ n. m. germ.
germinar /hermi'nar/ v. germinate.
gerundio /he'rundio/ n. m. gerund.
gesticulación /hestikula'θion; hestikula'sion/ n. f. gesticulation.
gesticular /hestiku'lar/ v. gesticulate, gesture.
gestión /hes'tion/ n. f. conduct; effort; action.
gesto /'hesto/ n. m. gesture, facial expression.
gigante /hi'gante/ a. & n. gigantic, giant.
gigantesco /higan'tesko/ a. gigantic, huge.
gilipollas /gili'poʎas; gili'poyas/ n. m. & f. Colloq. fool, idiot.
gimnasio /him'nasio/ n. m. gymnasium.
gimnástica /him'nastika/ n. f. gymnastics.
gimotear /himote'ar/ v. whine.
ginebra /hi'neβra/ n. f. gin.
ginecólogo /hine'kologo/ **-ga** n. gynecologist.
gira /'hira/ n. f. tour, trip.
girado /hi'raðo/ **-da** n. Com. drawee.
girador /hira'ðor/ **-ra** n. Com. drawer.
girar /hi'rar/ v. revolve, turn, spin, whirl.
giratorio /hira'torio/ a. rotary, revolving.
giro /'hiro/ n. m. whirl, turn, spin; Com. draft. **g. postal,** money order.
gitano /hi'tano/ **-na** a. & n. Gypsy.
glacial /gla'θial; gla'sial/ a. glacial, icy.
glaciar /gla'θiar; gla'siar/ n. m. glacier.
gladiador /glaðia'ðor/ n. m. gladiator.
glándula /'glandula/ n. f. gland.
glándula endocrina /'glandula endo'krina/ endocrine gland.
glándula pituitaria /'glandula pitui'taria/ pituitary gland.
glándula prostática /'glandula pros'tatika/ prostate gland.
glasé /gla'se/ n. m. glacé.
glicerina /gliθe'rina; glise'rina/ n. f. glycerine.
globo /'gloβo/ n. m. globe; balloon.
gloria /'gloria/ n. f. glory.
glorieta /glo'rieta/ n. f. bower.
glorificación /glorifika'θion; glorifika'sion/ n. f. glorification.
glorificar /glorifi'kar/ v. glorify.
glorioso /glo'rioso/ a. glorious.

glosa /'glosa/ n. f. gloss. —**glosar,** v.

glosario /glo'sario/ n. m. glossary.

glotón /glo'ton/ **-ona** a. & n. gluttonous; glutton.

glucosa /glu'kosa/ n. f. glucose.

gluten /'gluten/ n. m. gluten; glue.

gobernación /goßerna'θion; goßerna'sion/ n. f. government.

gobernador /goßerna'ðor/ **-ra** n. governor.

gobernalle /goßer'naʎe; goßer'naye/ n. m. rudder, tiller, helm.

gobernante /goßer'nante/ n. m. & f. ruler.

gobernar /goßer'nar/ v. govern.

gobierno /go'ßierno/ n. m. government.

goce /'goθe; 'gose/ n. m. enjoyment.

gola /'gola/ n. f. throat.

golf /golf/ n. m. golf.

golfista /gol'fista/ n. m. & f. golfer.

golfo /'golfo/ n. m. gulf.

gollete /go'ʎete; go'yete/ n. m. upper portion of one's throat.

golondrina /golon'drina/ n. f. swallow.

golosina /golo'sina/ n. f. delicacy.

goloso /go'loso/ a. sweet-toothed.

golpe /'golpe/ n. m. blow, stroke. **de g.,** suddenly.

golpear /golpe'ar/ v. strike, beat, pound.

goma /'goma/ n. f. rubber; gum; glue; eraser.

góndola /'gondola/ n. f. gondola.

gordo /'gordo/ a. fat.

gordura /gor'ðura/ n. f. fatness.

gorila /go'rila/ n. m. gorilla.

gorja /'gorha/ n. f. gorge.

gorjeo /gor'heo/ n. m. warble, chirp. —**gorjear,** v.

gorrión /go'rrion/ n. m. sparrow.

gorro /'gorro/ n. m. cap.

gota /'gota/ n. f. drop (of liquid).

gotear /gote'ar/ v. drip, leak.

goteo /go'teo/ n. m. leak.

gotera /go'tera/ n. f. leak; gutter.

gótico /'gotiko/ a. Gothic.

gozar /go'θar; go'sar/ v. enjoy.

gozne /'goθne; 'gosne/ n. m. hinge.

gozo /'goθo; 'goso/ n. m. enjoyment, delight, joy.

gozoso /go'θoso; go'soso/ a. joyful, joyous.

grabado /gra'ßaðo/ n. **1.** m. engraving, cut, print. —a. **2.** recorded.

grabador /graßa'ðor/ n. m. engraver.

grabadora /graßa'ðora/ n. f. tape recorder.

grabar /gra'ßar/ v. engrave; record.

gracia /'graθia; 'grasia/ n. f. grace; wit, charm. **hacer g.,** to amuse, strike as funny. **tener g.,** to be funny, to be witty.

gracias /'graθias; 'grasias/ n. f.pl. thanks, thank you.

gracioso /gra'θioso; gra'sioso/ a. witty, funny.

grada /'graða/ n. f. step.

gradación /graða'θion; graða'sion/ n. f. gradation.

grado /'graðo/ n. m. grade; rank; degree.

graduado /gra'ðuaðo/ **-da** n. graduate.

gradual /gra'ðual/ a. gradual.

graduar /gra'ðuar/ v. grade; graduate.

gráfico /'grafiko/ a. graphic, vivid.

grafito /gra'fito/ n. m. graphite.

grajo /'graho/ n. m. jackdaw.

gramática /gra'matika/ n. f. grammar.

gramo /'gramo/ n. m. gram.

gran /gran/ **grande** a. big, large; great.

granada /gra'naða/ n. f. grenade; pomegranate.

granar /gra'nar/ v. seed.

grandes almacenes /'grandes alma'θenes; 'grandes alma'senes/ n. m.pl. department store.

grandeza /gran'deθa; gran'desa/ n. f. greatness.

grandiosidad /grandiosi'ðað/ n. f. grandeur.

grandioso /gran'dioso/ a. grand, magnificent.

grandor /gran'dor/ n. m. size.

granero /gra'nero/ n. m. barn; granary.

granito /gra'nito/ n. m. granite.

granizada /grani'θaða; grani'saða/ n. f. hailstorm.

granizo /gra'niθo; gra'niso/ n. m. hail. —**granizar,** v.

granja /'granha/ n. f. grange; farm; farmhouse.

granjear /granhe'ar/ v. earn, gain, get.

granjero /gran'hero/ **-era** n. farmer.

grano /'grano/ n. m. grain; kernel.

granuja /gra'nuha/ n. m. waif, urchin.

grapa /'grapa/ n. f. clamp, clip.

grapadora /grapa'ðora/ n. f. stapler.

grasa /'grasa/ n. f. grease, fat.

grasiento /gra'siento/ a. greasy.

gratificación /gratifika'θion; gratifika'sion/ n. f. gratification; reward; tip.

gratificar /gratifi'kar/ v. gratify; reward; tip.

gratis /'gratis/ adv. gratis, free.

gratitud /grati'tuð/ n. f. gratitude.

grato /'grato/ a. grateful; pleasant.

gratuito /gra'tuito/ a. gratuitous; free.

gravamen /gra'ßamen/ n. m. tax; burden; obligation.

grave /'graße/ a. grave, serious, severe.

gravedad /graße'ðað/ n. f. gravity, seriousness.

gravitación /graßita'θion; graßita'sion/ n. f. gravitation.

gravitar /graßi'tar/ v. gravitate.

gravoso /gra'ßoso/ a. burdensome.

graznido /graθ'niðo; gras'niðo/ n. m. croak. —**graznar,** v.

Grecia /'greθia; 'gresia/ n. f. Greece.

greco /'greko/ **-ca** a. & n. Greek.

greda /'greða/ n. f. clay.

gresca /'greska/ n. f. revelry; quarrel.

griego /'griego/ **-ga** a. & n. Greek.

grieta /'grieta/ n. f. opening; crevice; crack.

grifo /'grifo/ n. m. faucet.

grillo /'griʎo; 'griyo/ n. m. cricket.

grima /'grima/ n. f. fright.

gringo /'gringo/ **-ga** n. foreigner (usually North American).

gripa /'gripa/ **gripe** n. f. grippe.

gris /gris/ a. gray.

grito /'grito/ n. m. shout, scream, cry. —**gritar,** v.

grosella /gro'seʎa; gro'seya/ n. f. currant.

grosería /grose'ria/ n. f. grossness; coarseness.

grosero /gro'sero/ a. coarse, vulgar; discourteous.

grotesco /gro'tesko/ a. grotesque.

grúa /'grua/ n. f. crane; tow truck.

gruesa /'gruesa/ n. f. gross.

grueso /'grueso/ a. **1.** bulky; stout; coarse, thick. —n. **2.** m. bulk.

grulla /'gruʎa; 'gruya/ n. f. crane.

gruñido /gru'niðo/ n. m. growl, snarl, mutter. —**gruñir,** v.

grupo /'grupo/ n. m. group, party.

gruta /'gruta/ n. f. cavern.

guacamol /guaka'mol/ **guacamole** n. m. avocado sauce; guacamole.

guadaña /gua'ðaɲa/ n. f. scythe. —**guadañar,** v.

guagua /'guagua/ n. f. (S.A.) baby; (Carib.) bus.

gualdo /'gualdo/ a. yellow, golden.

guano /'guano/ n. m. guano (fertilizer).

guante /'guante/ n. m. glove.

guantera /guan'tera/ n. f. glove compartment.

guapo /'guapo/ a. handsome.

guarda /'guarða/ n. m. or f. guard.

guardabarros /guarða'ßarros/ n. m. fender.

guardacostas /guarða'kostas/ n. m. revenue ship.

guardaespaldas /,guarðaes'paldas/ n. m. & f. bodyguard.

guardameta /guarða'meta/ n. m. & f. goalkeeper.

guardar /guar'ðar/ v. keep, store, put away; guard.

guardarropa /guarða'rropa/ n. f. coat room.

guardarse de /guar'ðarse de/ v. beware of, avoid.

guardia /'guarðia/ n. **1.** f. guard; watch. —n. **2.** m. policeman.

guardián /guar'ðian/ **-na** n. guardian, keeper, watchman.

guardilla /guar'ðiʎa; guar'ðiya/ n. f. attic.

guarida /gua'riða/ n. f. den.

guarismo /gua'rismo/ n. m. number, figure.

guarnecer /guarne'θer; guarne'ser/ v. adorn.

guarnición /guarni'θion; guarni'sion/ n. f. garrison; trimming.

guasa /'guasa/ n. f. joke, jest.

guayaba /gua'yaßa/ n. f. guava.

gubernativo /gußerna'tißo/ a. governmental.

guerra /'gerra/ n. f. war.

guerrero /ge'rrero/ **-ra** n. warrior.

guía /'gia/ n. **1.** m. & f. guide. **2.** f. guidebook, directory.

guiar /giar/ v. guide; steer, drive.

guija /'giha/ n. f. pebble.

guillotina /giʎo'tina; giyo'tina/ n. f. guillotine.

guindar /gin'dar/ v. hang.

guinga /'ginga/ n. f. gingham.

guiñada /gi'naða/ n. f., **guiño,** m. wink. —**guiñar,** v.

guión /gi'on/ n. m. dash, hyphen; script.

guirnalda /gir'nalda/ n. f. garland, wreath.

guisa /'gisa/ n. f. guise, manner.

guisado /gi'saðo/ n. m. stew.

guisante /gi'sante/ n. m. pea.

guisar /gi'sar/ v. cook.

guiso /'giso/ n. m. stew.

guita /'gita/ n. f. twine.

guitarra /gi'tarra/ n. f. guitar.

guitarrista /gita'rrista/ n. m. & f. guitarist.

gula /'gula/ n. f. gluttony.

gurú /gu'ru/ n. m. guru.

gusano /gu'sano/ n. m. worm, caterpillar.

gustar /gus'tar/ v. please; taste.

gustillo /gus'tiʎo; gus'tiyo/ n. m. aftertaste, slight pleasure.

gusto /'gusto/ n. m. pleasure; taste; liking.

gustoso /gus'toso/ a. pleasant; tasteful.

gutural /gutu'ral/ a. guttural.

H

haba /'aßa/ n. f. bean.

habanera /aßa'nera/ n. f. Cuban dance melody.

haber /a'ßer/ v. have. **h. de,** be to, be supposed to.

haberes /a'ßeres/ n. m.pl. property; worldly goods.

habichuela /aßi'tʃuela/ n. f. bean.

hábil /'aßil/ a. skillful; capable; clever.

habilidad /aßili'ðað/ n. f. ability; skill; talent.

habilidoso /aßili'ðoso/ a. able, skillful, talented.

habilitar /aßili'tar/ v. qualify; supply, equip.

hábilmente /'aßilmente/ adv. ably.

habitación /aßita'θion; aßita'sion/ n. f. dwelling; room. **h. individual,** single room.

habitante /aßi'tante/ n. m. & f. inhabitant.

habitar /aßi'tar/ v. inhabit; dwell.

hábito /'aßito/ n. m. habit; custom.

habitual /aßi'tual/ a. habitual.

habituar /aßi'tuar/ v. accustom, habituate.

habla /'aßla/ n. f. speech.

hablador /aßla'ðor/ a. talkative.

hablar /a'ßlar/ v. talk, speak.

haca /'aka/ n. f. pony.

hacedor /aθe'ðor; ase'ðor/ n. m. maker.

hacendado /aθen'daðo; asen'daðo/ **-da** n. hacienda owner; farmer.

hacendoso /aθen'doso; asen'doso/ a. industrious.

hacer /a'θer; a'ser/ v. do; make. **hace dos años,** etc., two years ago, etc.

hacerse /a'θerse; a'serse/ v. become, get to be.

hacha /'atʃa/ n. f. ax, hatchet.

hacia /'aθia; 'asia/ prep. toward.

hacienda /a'θienda; a'sienda/ n. f. property; estate; ranch; farm; Govt. treasury.

hada /'aða/ n. f. fairy.

hado /'aðo/ n. m. fate.

halagar /ala'gar/ v. flatter.

halar /a'lar/ v. haul, pull.

halcón /al'kon/ n. m. hawk, falcon.

haleche /a'letʃe/ n. m. anchovy.

hallado /a'ʎaðo; a'yaðo/ a. found. **bien h.,** welcome. **mal h.,** uneasy.

hallar /a'ʎar; a'yar/ v. find, locate.

hallarse /a'ʎarse; a'yarse/ v. be located; happen to be.

hallazgo /a'ʎaθgo; a'yasgo/ n. m. find, thing found.

hamaca /a'maka/ n. f. hammock.

hambre /'ambre/ n. f. hunger. **tener h., estar con h.,** to be hungry.

hambrear /ambre'ar/ v. hunger; starve.

hambriento /am'briento/ a. starving, hungry.

hamburguesa /ambur'gesa/ n. f. beefburger, hamburger.

haragán /ara'gan/ **-na** n. idler, lazy person.

haraganear /aragane'ar/ v. loiter.

harapo /a'rapo/ n. m. rag, tatter.

haraposo /ara'poso/ a. ragged, shabby.

harén /a'ren/ n. m. harem.

harina /a'rina/ n. f. flour, meal.

harnero /ar'nero/ n. m. sieve.

hartar /ar'tar/ v. satiate.

harto /'arto/ a. stuffed; fed up.

hartura /ar'tura/ n. f. superabundance, glut.

hasta /'asta/ prep. **1.** until, till; as far as, up to. **h. luego,** good-bye, so long. —adv. **2.** even.

hastío /as'tio/ n. m. distaste, loathing.

hato /'ato/ n. m. herd.

hay /ai/ v. there is, there are. **h. que,** it is necessary to. **no h. de qué,** you're welcome, don't mention it.

haya /'aya/ n. f. beech tree.

haz /aθ; as/ n. f. bundle, sheaf; face.

hazaña /a'θaɲa; a'saɲa/ n. f. deed; exploit, feat.

hebdomadario /eßðoma'ðario/ a. weekly.

hebilla /e'ßiʎa; e'ßiya/ n. f. buckle.

hebra /'eßra/ n. f. thread, string.

hebreo /e'ßreo/ **-rea** a. & n. Hebrew.

hechicero /etʃi'θero; etʃi'sero/ **-ra** n. wizard, witch.

hechizar /etʃi'θar; etʃi'sar/ v. bewitch.

hechizo /e'tʃiθo; e'tʃiso/ n. m. spell.

hecho /'etʃo/ n. m. fact; act; deed.

hechura /e'tʃura/ n. f. workmanship, make.

hediondez /eðion'deθ; eðion'des/ n. f. stench.

hégira /'ehira/ n. f. hegira.

helada /e'laða/ n. f. frost.

heladería /elaðe'ria/ n. f. ice-cream parlor.

helado /e'laðo/ n. m. ice cream.

helar /e'lar/ v. freeze.
helecho /e'letʃo/ n. m. fern.
hélice /'eliθe; 'elise/ n. f. propeller; helix.
helicóptero /eli'koptero/ n. m. helicopter.
helio /'elio/ n. m. helium.
hembra /'embra/ n. f. female.
hemisferio /emis'ferio/ n. m. hemisphere.
hemoglobina /emoglo'βina/ n. f. hemoglobin.
hemorragia /emo'rrahia/ n. f. hemorrhage.
hemorragia nasal /emo'rrahia na'sal/ nosebleed.
henchir /en'tʃir/ v. stuff.
hendedura /ende'ðura/ n. f. crevice, crack.
hendido /en'diðo/ a. cloven, cleft (lip).
heno /'eno/ n. m. hay.
hepática /e'patika/ n. f. liverwort.
hepatitis /epa'titis/ n. f. hepatitis.
heraldo /e'raldo/ n. m. herald.
herbáceo /er'βaθeo; er'βaseo/ a. herbaceous.
herbívoro /er'βiβoro/ a. herbivorous.
heredar /ere'ðar/ v. inherit.
heredero /ere'ðero/ -ra n. heir; successor.
hereditario /ereði'tario/ a. hereditary.
hereje /e'rehe/ n. m. & f. heretic.
herejía /ere'hia/ n. f. heresy.
herencia /e'renθia; e'rensia/ n. f. inheritance; heritage.
herético /e'retiko/ a. heretical.
herida /e'riða/ n. f. wound, injury.
herir /e'rir/ v. wound, injure.
hermafrodita /ermafro'ðita/ a. & n. hermaphrodite.
hermana /er'mana/ n. f. sister.
hermano /er'mano/ n. m. brother.
hermético /er'metiko/ a. airtight.
hermoso /er'moso/ a. beautiful, handsome.
hermosura /ermo'sura/ n. f. beauty.
hernia /'ernia/ n. f. hernia, rupture.
héroe /'eroe/ n. m. hero.
heroico /e'roiko/ a. heroic.
heroína /ero'ina/ n. f. heroine.
heroísmo /ero'ismo/ n. m. heroism.
herradura /erra'ðura/ n. f. horseshoe.
herramienta /erra'mienta/ n. f. tool; implement.
herrería /erre'ria/ n. f. blacksmith's shop.
herrero /e'rrero/ n. m. blacksmith.
herrumbre /e'rrumbre/ n. f. rust.
hertzio /'ertθio; 'ertsio/ n. m. hertz.
hervir /er'βir/ v. boil.
hesitación /esita'θion; esita'sion/ n. f. hesitation.
heterogéneo /etero'heneo/ a. heterogeneous.
heterosexual /eterosek'sual/ a. heterosexual.
hexagonal /eksago'nal/ a. hexagonal.
hexágono /e'ksagono/ n. m. hexagon.
hez /eθ; es/ n. f. dregs, sediment.
híbrido /'iβriðo/ -da n. & a. hybrid.
hidalgo /i'ðalgo/ n. m. noble.
hidalguía /iðal'gia/ n. f. nobility; generosity.
hidráulico /i'ðrauliko/ a. hydraulic.
hidroavión /iðroa'βion/ n. m. seaplane, hydroplane.
hidrofobia /iðro'foβia/ n. f. rabies.
hidrógeno /i'ðroheno/ n. m. hydrogen.
hidropesía /iðrope'sia/ n. f. dropsy.
hiedra /'ieðra/ n. f. ivy.
hiel /iel/ n. f. gall.
hielo /'ielo/ n. m. ice.
hiena /'iena/ n. f. hyena.
hierba /'ierβa/ n. f. grass; herb; marijuana.
hierbabuena /ierβa'βuena/ n. f. mint.
hierro /'ierro/ n. m. iron.
hígado /'igaðo/ n. m. liver.

higiene /i'hiene/ n. f. hygiene.
higiénico /i'hieniko/ a. sanitary, hygienic.
higo /'igo/ n. m. fig.
higuera /i'gera/ n. f. fig tree.
hija /'iha/ n. f. daughter.
hija adoptiva /'iha aðop'tiβa/ adopted daughter.
hijastro /i'hastro/ -tra n. stepchild.
hijo /'iho/ n. m. son.
hijo adoptivo /'iho aðop'tiβo/ n. m. adopted child, adopted son.
hila /'ila/ n. f. line.
hilandero /ilan'dero/ -ra n. spinner.
hilar /i'lar/ v. spin.
hilera /i'lera/ n. f. row, line, tier.
hilo /'ilo/ n. m. thread; string; wire; linen.
himno /'imno/ n. m. hymn.
hincar /in'kar/ v. drive, thrust; sink into.
hincarse /in'karse/ v. kneel.
hinchar /in'tʃar/ v. swell.
hindú /in'du/ n. & a. Hindu.
hinojo /i'noho/ n. m. knee.
hiperenlace /iperen'laθe, iperen'lase/ n. m. hyperlink.
hipermercado /ipermer'kaðo/ n. m. hypermarket.
hipertexto /iper'teksto/ n. m. hypertext.
hipnótico /ip'notiko/ a. hypnotic.
hipnotismo /ipno'tismo/ n. m. hypnotism.
hipnotista /ipno'tista/ n. m. & f. hypnotist.
hipnotizar /ipnoti'θar; ipnoti'sar/ v. hypnotize.
hipo /'ipo/ n. m. hiccough.
hipocresía /ipokre'sia/ n. f. hypocrisy.
hipócrita /i'pokrita/ a. & n. hypocritical; hypocrite.
hipódromo /i'poðromo/ n. m. race track.
hipoteca /ipo'teka/ n. f. mortgage. —hipotecar, v.
hipótesis /i'potesis/ n. f. hypothesis.
hirsuto /ir'suto/ a. hairy, hirsute.
hispano /is'pano/ a. Hispanic, Spanish American.
Hispanoamérica /ispanoa'merika/ f. Spanish America.
hispanoamericano /ispanoameri'kano/ -na a. & n. Spanish American.
histerectomía /isterekto'mia/ n. f. hysterectomy.
histeria /is'teria/ n. f. hysteria.
histérico /is'teriko/ a. hysterical.
historia /is'toria/ n. f. history; story.
historiador /istoria'ðor/ -ra n. historian.
histórico /is'toriko/ a. historic, historical.
histrión /is'trion/ n. m. actor.
hocico /o'θiko; o'siko/ n. m. snout, muzzle.
hogar /o'gar/ n. m. hearth; home.
hoguera /o'gera/ n. f. bonfire, blaze.
hoja /'oha/ n. f. leaf; sheet (of paper); pane; blade.
hoja de cálculo /'oha de 'kalkulo/ spreadsheet.
hoja de inscripción /'oha de inskrip'θion; 'oha de inskrip'sion/ entry blank.
hoja de pedidos /'oha de pe'ðiðos/ order blank.
hoja informativa /'oha informa'tiβa/ newsletter.
hojalata /oha'lata/ n. f. tin.
hojalatero /ohala'tero/ -ra n. tinsmith.
hojear /ohe'ar/ v. scan, skim through.
hola /'ola/ interj. hello.
Holanda /o'landa/ n. f. Holland, Netherlands.
holandés /olan'des/ -esa a. & n. Dutch; Hollander.
holganza /ol'ganθa; ol'gansa/ n. f. leisure; diversion.
holgazán /olga'θan; olga'san/ -ana a.

1. idle, lazy. —n. 2. m. idler, loiterer, tramp.
holgazanear /olgaθane'ar; olgasane'ar/ v. idle, loiter.
hollín /o'ʎin; o'yin/ n. m. soot.
holografía /ologra'fia/ n. f. holography.
holograma /olo'grama/ n. m. hologram.
hombre /'ombre/ n. m. man.
hombría /om'βria/ n. f. manliness.
hombro /'ombro/ n. m. shoulder.
hombruno /om'bruno/ a. mannish, masculine (woman).
homenaje /ome'nahe/ n. m. homage.
homeópata /ome'opata/ n. m. homeopath.
homicidio /omi'θiðio; omi'siðio/ n. m. homicide.
homilía /omi'lia/ n. f. homily.
homosexual /omose'ksual/ a. homosexual, gay.
honda /'onda/ n. f. sling.
hondo /'ondo/ a. deep.
hondonada /ondo'naða/ n. f. ravine.
hondura /on'dura/ n. f. depth.
honestidad /onesti'ðað/ n. f. modesty, unpretentiousness.
honesto /o'nesto/ a. honest; pure; just.
hongo /'oŋgo/ n. m. fungus; mushroom.
honor /o'nor/ n. m. honor.
honorable /ono'raβle/ a. honorable.
honorario /ono'rario/ a. 1. honorary. —n. 2. m. honorarium, fee.
honorífico /ono'rifiko/ a. honorary.
honra /'onra/ n. f. honor. —honrar, v.
honradez /onra'ðeθ; onra'ðes/ n. f. honesty.
honrado /on'raðo/ a. honest, honorable.
hora /'ora/ n. f. hour; time (of day).
horadar /ora'ðar/ v. perforate.
hora punta /'ora 'punta/ rush hour.
horario /o'rario/ n. m. timetable, schedule.
horca /'orka/ n. f. gallows; pitchfork.
horda /'orða/ n. f. horde.
horizontal /oriθon'tal; orison'tal/ a. horizontal.
horizonte /ori'θonte; ori'sonte/ n. m. horizon.
hormiga /or'miga/ n. f. ant.
hormiguear /ormige'ar/ v. itch.
hormiguero /ormi'gero/ n. m. ant hill.
hornero /or'nero/ -ra n. baker.
hornillo /or'niʎo; or'nijo/ n. m. stove.
horno /'orno/ n. m. oven; kiln.
horóscopo /o'roskopo/ n. m. horoscope.
horrendo /o'rrendo/ a. dreadful, horrendous.
horrible /o'rriβle/ a. horrible, hideous, awful.
hórrido /'orriðo/ a. horrid.
horror /o'rror/ n. m. horror.
horrorizar /orrori'θar; orrori'sar/ v. horrify.
horroroso /orro'roso/ a. horrible, frightful.
hortelano /orte'lano/ n. m. horticulturist.
hospedaje /ospe'ðahe/ n. m. lodging.
hospedar /ospe'ðar/ v. give or take lodgings.
hospital /ospi'tal/ n. m. hospital.
hospitalario /ospita'lario/ a. hospitable.
hospitalidad /ospitali'ðað/ n. f. hospitality.
hospitalmente /ospital'mente/ adv. hospitably.
hostia /'ostia/ n. f. host; Colloq. hit, blow.
hostil /os'til/ a. hostile.
hostilidad /ostili'ðað/ n. f. hostility.
hotel /o'tel/ n. m. hotel.
hoy /oi/ adv. today. **h. día, h. en día,** nowadays.
hoya /'oya/ n. f. dale, valley.

hoyo /'oyo/ n. m. pit, hole.
hoyuelo /o'yuelo/ n. m. dimple.
hoz /oθ; os/ n. f. sickle.
hucha /'utʃa/ n. f. chest, money box; savings.
hueco /'ueko/ a. 1. hollow, empty. —n. 2. m. hole, hollow.
huelga /'uelga/ n. f. strike.
huelgista /uel'hista/ n. m. & f. striker.
huella /'ueʎa; 'ueya/ n. f. track, trace; footprint.
huérfano /'uerfano/ -na a. & n. orphan.
huero /'uero/ a. empty.
huerta /'uerta/ n. f. (vegetable) garden.
huerto /'uerto/ n. m. orchard.
hueso /'ueso/ n. m. bone; fruit pit.
huésped /'uespeð/ n. m. & f. guest.
huesudo /ue'suðo/ a. bony.
huevo /'ueβo/ n. m. egg.
huída /'uiða/ n. f. flight, escape.
huir /uir/ v. flee.
hule /'ule/ n. m. oilcloth.
humanidad /umani'ðað/ n. f. humanity, mankind; humaneness.
humanista /uma'nista/ n. m. & f. humanist.
humanitario /umani'tario/ a. humane.
humano /u'mano/ a. human; humane.
humareda /uma'reða/ n. f. dense cloud of smoke.
humear /ume'ar/ v. emit smoke or steam.
humedad /ume'ðað/ n. f. humidity, moisture, dampness.
humedecer /umeðe'θer; umeðe'ser/ v. moisten, dampen.
húmedo /'umeðo/ a. humid, moist, damp.
humildad /umil'dað/ n. f. humility, meekness.
humilde /u'milde/ a. humble, meek.
humillación /umiʎa'θion; umiya'sion/ n. f. humiliation.
humillar /umi'ʎar; umi'yar/ v. humiliate.
humo /'umo/ n. m. smoke; (pl.) airs, affectation.
humor /u'mor/ n. m. humor, mood.
humorista /umo'rista/ n. m. & f. humorist.
hundimiento /undi'miento/ n. m. collapse.
hundir /un'dir/ v. sink; collapse.
húngaro /'uŋgaro/ -ra a. & n. Hungarian.
Hungría /uŋ'gria/ n. f. Hungary.
huracán /ura'kan/ n. m. hurricane.
huraño /u'rapo/ a. shy, bashful.
hurgar /ur'gar/ v. stir.
hurón /u'ron/ n. m. ferret.
hurtadillas /urta'ðiʎas; urta'ðiyas/ n. f.pl. **a h.,** on the sly.
hurtador /urta'ðor/ -ra n. thief.
hurtar /ur'tar/ v. steal, rob of; hide.
hurtarse /ur'tarse/ v. hide; withdraw.
husmear /usme'ar/ v. scent, smell.
huso /'uso/ n. m. spindle; bobbin.
huso horario /'uso o'rario/ time zone.

I

ibérico /i'βeriko/ a. Iberian.
iberoamericano /iβeroameri'kano/ -na a. & n. Latin American.
ida /'iða/ n. f. departure; trip out. **i. y vuelta,** round trip.
idea /i'ðea/ n. f. idea.
ideal /i'ðeal/ a. & m. ideal.
idealismo /iðea'lismo/ n. m. idealism.
idealista /iðea'lista/ n. m. & f. idealist.
idear /iðe'ar/ v. plan, conceive.
idéntico /i'ðentiko/ a. identical.
identidad /iðenti'ðað/ n. f. identity; identification.

identificar /iðentifiˈkar/ v. identify.

idilio /iˈðilio/ n. m. idyll.

idioma /iˈðioma/ n. m. language.

idiota /iˈðiota/ a. & n. idiotic; idiot.

idiotismo /iðioˈtismo/ n. m. idiom; idiocy.

idolatrar /iðolaˈtrar/ v. idolize, adore.

ídolo /ˈiðolo/ n. m. idol.

idóneo /iˈðoneo/ a. suitable, fit, apt.

iglesia /iˈglesia/ n. f. church.

ignición /igniˈθion; igniˈsion/ n. f. ignition.

ignominia /ignoˈminia/ n. f. ignominy, shame.

ignominioso /ignomiˈnioso/ a. ignominious, shameful.

ignorancia /ignoˈranθia; ignoˈransia/ n. f. ignorance.

ignorante /ignoˈrante/ a. ignorant.

ignorar /ignoˈrar/ v. be ignorant of, not know.

ignoto /igˈnoto/ a. unknown.

igual /iˈgual/ a. equal; the same; (pl.) alike. m. equal.

igualar /igualˈar/ v. equal; equalize; match.

igualdad /igualˈdad/ n. f. equality; sameness.

ijada /iˈhaða/ n. f. flank (of an animal).

ilegal /ileˈgal/ a. illegal.

ilegítimo /ileˈhitimo/ a. illegitimate.

ileso /iˈleso/ a. unharmed.

ilícito /iˈliθito; iˈlisito/ a. illicit, unlawful.

iluminación /iluminaˈθion; iluminaˈsion/ n. f. illumination.

iluminar /ilumiˈnar/ v. illuminate.

ilusión /iluˈsion/ n. f. illusion.

ilusión de óptica /iluˈsion de ˈoptika/ optical illusion.

ilusorio /iluˈsorio/ a. illusive.

ilustración /ilustraˈθion; ilustraˈsion/ n. f. illustration; learning.

ilustrador /ilustraˈðor/ -ra n. illustrator.

ilustrar /ilusˈtrar/ v. illustrate.

ilustre /iˈlustre/ a. illustrious, honorable, distinguished.

imagen /iˈmahen/ n. f. image.

imaginación /imahinaˈθion; imahinaˈsion/ n. f. imagination.

imaginar /imahiˈnar/ v. imagine.

imaginario /imahiˈnario/ a. imaginary.

imaginativo /imahinaˈtiβo/ a. imaginative.

imán /iˈman/ n. m. magnet; imam.

imbécil /imˈbeθil; imˈbesil/ a. & n. imbecile; stupid, foolish; fool.

imbuir /imˈbuir/ v. imbue, instil.

imitación /imitaˈθion; imitaˈsion/ n. f. imitation.

imitador /imitaˈðor/ -ra n. imitator.

imitar /imiˈtar/ v. imitate.

impaciencia /impaˈθienθia; impaˈsiensia/ n. f. impatience.

impaciente /impaˈθiente; impaˈsiente/ a. impatient.

impar /imˈpar/ a. unequal, uneven, odd.

imparcial /imparˈθial; imparˈsial/ a. impartial.

impasible /impaˈsiβle/ a. impassive, unmoved.

impávido /imˈpaβiðo/ adj. fearless, intrepid.

impedimento /impeðiˈmento/ n. m. impediment, obstacle.

impedir /impeˈðir/ v. impede, hinder, stop, obstruct.

impeler /impeˈler/ v. impel; incite.

impensado /impenˈsaðo/ a. unexpected.

imperar /impeˈrar/ v. reign; prevail.

imperativo /imperaˈtiβo/ a. imperative.

imperceptible /imperθepˈtiβle; impersepˈtiβle/ a. imperceptible.

imperdible /imperˈðiβle/ n. m. safety pin.

imperecedero /impereθeˈðero; impereseˈðero/ a. imperishable.

imperfecto /imperˈfekto/ a. imperfect, faulty.

imperial /impeˈrial/ a. imperial.

imperialismo /imperiaˈlismo/ n. m. imperialism.

impericia /impeˈriθia; impeˈrisia/ n. f. inexperience.

imperio /imˈperio/ n. m. empire.

imperioso /impeˈrioso/ a. imperious, domineering.

impermeable /impermeˈaβle/ a. waterproof. m. raincoat.

impersonal /impersoˈnal/ a. impersonal.

impertinencia /impertinenˈθia; impertinenˈsia/ n. f. impertinence.

ímpetu /ˈimpetu/ n. m. impulse; impetus.

impetuoso /impeˈtuoso/ a. impetuous.

impiedad /impieˈðad/ n. f. impiety.

impío /imˈpio/ a. impious.

implacable /implaˈkaβle/ a. implacable, unrelenting.

implicar /impliˈkar/ v. implicate, involve.

implorar /imploˈrar/ v. implore.

imponente /impoˈnente/ a. impressive.

imponer /impoˈner/ v. impose.

impopular /impopuˈlar/ a. unpopular.

importación /importaˈθion; importaˈsion/ n. f. importation, importing.

importador /importaˈðor/ -ra n. importer.

importancia /imporˈtanθia; imporˈtansia/ n. f. importance.

importante /imporˈtante/ a. important.

importar /imporˈtar/ v. be important, matter; import.

importe /imˈporte/ n. m. value; amount.

importunar /importuˈnar/ v. beg, importune.

imposibilidad /imposiβiliˈðad/ n. f. impossibility.

imposibilitado /imposiβiliˈtaðo/ a. helpless.

imposible /impoˈsiβle/ a. impossible.

imposición /imposiˈθion; imposiˈsion/ n. f. imposition.

impostor /imposˈtor/ -ra n. imposter, faker.

impotencia /impoˈtenθia; impoˈtensia/ n. f. impotence.

impotente /impoˈtente/ a. impotent.

imprecar /impreˈkar/ v. curse.

impreciso /impreˈθiso; impreˈsiso/ adj. inexact.

impregnar /impregˈnar/ v. impregnate.

imprenta /imˈprenta/ n. f. press; printing house.

imprescindible /impresθinˈdiβle; impressinˈdiβle/ a. essential.

impresión /impreˈsion/ n. f. impression.

impresionable /impresioˈnaβle/ a. impressionable.

impresionar /impresioˈnar/ v. impress.

impresor /impreˈsor/ n. m. printer.

imprevisión /impreβiˈsion/ n. f. oversight; thoughtlessness.

imprevisto /impreˈβisto/ a. unexpected, unforeseen.

imprimir /impriˈmir/ v. print, imprint.

improbable /improˈβaβle/ a. improbable.

improbo /imˈproβo/ a. dishonest.

improductivo /improðukˈtiβo/ a. unproductive.

improperio /improˈperio/ n. m. insult.

impropio /imˈpropio/ a. improper.

improvisación /improβisaˈθion; improβisaˈsion/ n. f. improvisation.

improvisar /improβiˈsar/ v. improvise.

improviso /improˈβiso, improˈβisto/ a. unforeseen.

imprudencia /impruˈðenθia; impruˈðensia/ n. f. imprudence.

imprudente /impruˈðente/ a. imprudent, reckless.

impuesto /imˈpuesto/ n. m. tax.

impuesto sobre la renta /imˈpuesto soβre la ˈrrenta/ income tax.

impulsar /impulˈsar/ v. prompt, impel.

impulsivo /impulˈsiβo/ a. impulsive.

impulso /imˈpulso/ n. m. impulse.

impureza /impuˈreθa; impuˈresa/ n. f. impurity.

impuro /imˈpuro/ a. impure.

imputación /imputaˈθion; imputaˈsion/ n. f. imputation.

imputar /impuˈtar/ v. impute, attribute.

inaccesible /inakθeˈsiβle; inakseˈsiβle/ a. inaccessible.

inacción /inakˈθion; inakˈsion/ n. f. inaction; inactivity.

inaceptable /inaθepˈtaβle; inasepˈtaβle/ a. unacceptable.

inactivo /inakˈtiβo/ a. inactive; sluggish.

inadecuado /inaðeˈkuaðo/ a. inadequate.

inadvertencia /inaðβerˈtenθia; inaðβerˈtensia/ n. f. oversight.

inadvertido /inaðβerˈtiðo/ a. inadvertent, careless; unnoticed.

inagotable /inagoˈtaβle/ a. inexhaustible.

inalterado /inalteˈraðo/ a. unchanged.

inanición /inaniˈθion; inaniˈsion/ n. f. starvation.

inanimado /inaniˈmaðo/ adj. inanimate.

inapetencia /inapeˈtenθia; inapeˈtensia/ n. f. lack of appetite.

inaplicable /inapliˈkaβle/ a. inapplicable; unfit.

inaudito /inauˈðito/ a. unheard of.

inauguración /inauguraˈθion; inauguraˈsion/ n. f. inauguration.

inaugurar /inauguˈrar/ v. inaugurate, open.

incandescente /inkandesˈθente; inkandesˈsente/ a. incandescent.

incansable /inkanˈsaβle/ a. tireless.

incapacidad /inkapaθiˈðad; inkapasiˈðad/ n. f. incapacity.

incapacitar /inkapaθiˈtar; inkapasiˈtar/ v. incapacitate.

incapaz /inkaˈpaθ; inkaˈpas/ a. incapable.

incauto /inˈkauto/ a. unwary.

incendiar /inθenˈdiar; insenˈdiar/ v. set on fire.

incendio /inˈθendio; inˈsendio/ n. m. fire; conflagration.

incertidumbre /inθertiˈðumbre; insertiˈðumbre/ n. f. uncertainty, suspense.

incesante /inθeˈsante; inseˈsante/ a. continual, incessant.

incidente /inθiˈðente; insiˈðente/ m. incident, event.

incienso /inˈθienso; inˈsienso/ n. m. incense.

incierto /inˈθierto; inˈsierto/ a. uncertain, doubtful.

incinerar /inθineˈrar; insineˈrar/ v. incinerate; cremate.

incisión /inθiˈsion; insiˈsion/ n. f. incision, cut.

incitamiento /inθitaˈmiento; insitaˈmiento/ n. m. incitement, motivation.

incitar /inθiˈtar; insiˈtar/ v. incite, instigate.

incivil /inθiˈβil; insiˈβil/ a. impolite, rude.

inclemencia /inkleˈmenθia; inkleˈmensia/ n. f. inclemency.

inclemente /inkleˈmente/ a. inclement, merciless.

inclinación /inklinaˈθion; inklinaˈsion/ n. f. inclination, bent; slope.

inclinar /inkliˈnar/ v. incline; influence.

inclinarse /inkliˈnarse/ v. slope; lean, bend over; bow.

incluir /inˈkluir/ v. include; enclose.

inclusivo /inkluˈsiβo/ a. inclusive.

incluso /inˈkluso/ prep. including.

incógnito /inˈkognito/ a. unknown.

incoherente /inkoeˈrente/ a. incoherent.

incombustible /inkombusˈtiβle/ a. fireproof.

incomible /inkoˈmiβle/ a. inedible.

incomodar /inkomoˈðar/ v. disturb, bother, inconvenience.

incomodidad /inkomoðiˈðað/ n. f. inconvenience.

incómodo /inˈkomoðo/ n. m. uncomfortable; cumbersome; inconvenient.

incomparable /inkompaˈraβle/ a. incomparable.

incompatible /inkompaˈtiβle/ a. incompatible.

incompetencia /inkompeˈtenθia; inkompeˈtensia/ n. f. incompetence.

incompetente /inkompeˈtente/ a. incompetent.

incompleto /inkomˈpleto/ a. incomplete.

incondicional /inkondiθioˈnal; inkondisioˈnal/ a. unconditional.

inconexo /inkoneˈkso/ a. incoherent; unconnected.

incongruente /inkoŋgruˈente/ a. incongruous.

inconsciencia /inkonsˈθienθia; inkonsˈsiensia/ n. f. unconsciousness.

inconsciente /inkonsˈθiente; inkonsˈsiente/ a. unconscious.

inconsecuencia /inkonseˈkuenθia; inkonseˈkuensia/ n. f. inconsistency.

inconsecuente /inkonseˈkuente/ a. inconsistent.

inconsiderado /inkonsiðeˈraðo/ a. inconsiderate.

inconstancia /inkonsˈtanθia; inkonsˈtansia/ n. f. changeableness.

inconstante /inkonsˈtante/ a. changeable.

inconveniencia /inkombeˈnienθia; inkombeˈniensia/ n. f. inconvenience; unsuitability.

inconveniente /inkombeˈniente/ a. unsuitable. m. disadvantage; objection.

incorporar /inkorpoˈrar/ v. incorporate, embody.

incorporarse /inkorpoˈrarse/ v. sit up.

incorrecto /inkoˈrrekto/ a. incorrect, wrong.

incredulidad /inkreðuliˈðað/ n. f. incredulity.

incrédulo /inˈkreðulo/ a. incredulous.

increíble /inkreˈiβle/ a. incredible.

incremento /inkreˈmento/ n. m. increase.

incubadora /inkuβaˈðora/ n. f. incubator.

incubar /inkuˈβar/ v. hatch.

inculto /inˈkulto/ a. uncultivated.

incumplimiento de contrato /inkumpliˈmento de konˈtrato/ n. m. breach of contract.

incurable /inkuˈraβle/ a. incurable.

incurrir /inkuˈrrir/ v. incur.

indagación /indagaˈθion; indagaˈsion/ n. f. investigation, inquiry.

indagador /indagaˈðor/ -ra n. investigator.

indagar /indaˈgar/ v. investigate, inquire into.

indebido /indeˈβiðo/ a. undue.

indecencia /indeˈθenθia; indeˈsensia/ n. f. indecency.

indecente /indeˈθente; indeˈsente/ a. indecent.

indeciso /indeˈθiso; indeˈsiso/ a. undecided.

indefenso /indeˈfenso/ a. defenseless.

indefinido /indefiˈniðo/ a. indefinite; undefined.

indeleble /indeˈleβle/ a. indelible.

indemnización de despido /indem-

niθa'θion de des'piðo; indemnisa'sion de des'piðo/ *n. f.* severance pay.
indemnizar /indemni'θar; indemni'sar/ *v.* indemnify.
independencia /indepen'denθia; independ'densia/ *n. f.* independence.
independiente /indepen'diente/ *a.* independent.
indesmallable /indesma'ʎaβle; indesma'yaβle/ *a.* runproof.
India /'india/ *n. f.* India.
indicación /indika'θion; indika'sion/ *n. f.* indication.
indicar /indi'kar/ *v.* indicate, point out.
indicativo /indika'tiβo/ *a. & m.* indicative.
índice /'indiθe; 'indise/ *n. m.* index; forefinger.
índice de materias /'indiθe de ma'terias; 'indise de ma'terias/ table of contents.
indicio /in'diθio; in'disio/ *n. m.* hint, clue.
indiferencia /indife'renθia; indife'rensia/ *n. f.* indifference.
indiferente /indife'rente/ *a.* indifferent.
indígena /in'dihena/ *a. & n.* native.
indigente /indi'hente/ *a.* indigent, poor.
indignación /indigna'θion; indigna'sion/ *n. f.* indignation.
indignado /indig'naðo/ *a.* indignant, incensed.
indignar /indig'nar/ *v.* incense.
indigno /in'digno/ *a.* unworthy.
indio /'indio/ **-dia** *a. & n.* Indian.
indirecto /indi'rekto/ *a.* indirect.
indiscreción /indiskre'θion; indiskre'sion/ *n. f.* indiscretion.
indiscreto /indis'kreto/ *a.* indiscreet.
indiscutible /indisku'tiβle/ *a.* unquestionable.
indispensable /indispen'saβle/ *a.* indispensable.
indisposición /indisposi'θion; indisposi'sion/ *n. f.* indisposition, ailment; reluctance.
indistinto /indis'tinto/ *a.* indistinct, unclear.
individual /indiβi'ðual/ *a.* individual.
individualidad /indiβiðuali'ðað/ *n. f.* individuality.
individuo /indi'βiðuo/ *a. & m.* individual.
indócil /in'doθil; in'dosil/ *a.* headstrong, unruly.
índole /'indole/ *n. f.* nature, character, disposition.
indolencia /indo'lenθia; indo'lensia/ *n. f.* indolence.
indolente /indo'lente/ *a.* indolent.
indómito /in'domito/ *a.* untamed, wild; unruly.
inducir /indu'θir; indu'sir/ *v.* induce, persuade.
indudable /indu'ðaβle/ *a.* certain, indubitable.
indulgencia /indul'henθia; indul'hensia/ *n. f.* indulgence.
indulgente /indul'hente/ *a.* indulgent.
indultar /indul'tar/ *v.* free; pardon.
industria /in'dustria/ *n. f.* industry.
industrial /indus'trial/ *a.* industrial.
industrioso /indus'trioso/ *a.* industrious.
inédito /i'neðito/ *a.* unpublished.
ineficaz /inefi'kaθ; inefi'kas/ *a.* inefficient.
inepto /i'nepto/ *a.* incompetent.
inequívoco /ine'kiβoko/ *a.* unmistakable.
inercia /i'nerθia; i'nersia/ *n. f.* inertia.
inerte /i'nerte/ *a.* inert.
inesperado /inespe'raðo/ *a.* unexpected.
inestable /ines'taβle/ *a.* unstable.
inevitable /ineβi'taβle/ *a.* inevitable.
inexacto /ine'ksakto/ *a.* inexact.
inexperto /ineks'perto/ *a.* unskilled.
inexplicable /inekspli'kaβle/ *a.* inexplicable, unexplainable.
infalible /infa'liβle/ *a.* infallible.
infame /in'fame/ *a.* infamous, bad.
infamia /in'famia/ *n. f.* infamy.
infancia /in'fanθia; in'fansia/ *n. f.* infancy; childhood.
infante /in'fante/ **-ta** *n.* infant.
infantería /infante'ria/ *n. f.* infantry.
infantil /infan'til/ *a.* infantile, childish.
infarto (de miocardio) /in'farto de mio'karðio/ *n. m.* heart attack.
infatigable /infati'gaβle/ *a.* untiring.
infausto /in'fausto/ *a.* unlucky.
infección /infek'θion; infek'sion/ *n. f.* infection.
infeccioso /infek'θioso; infek'sioso/ *a.* infectious.
infectar /infek'tar/ *v.* infect.
infeliz /infe'liθ; infe'lis/ *a.* unhappy, miserable.
inferior /infe'rior/ *a.* inferior; lower.
inferir /infe'rir/ *v.* infer; inflict.
infernal /infer'nal/ *a.* infernal.
infestar /infes'tar/ *v.* infest.
infiel /in'fiel/ *a.* unfaithful.
infierno /in'fierno/ *n. m.* hell.
infiltrar /infil'trar/ *v.* infiltrate.
infinidad /infini'ðað/ *n. f.* infinity.
infinito /infi'nito/ *a.* infinite.
inflación /infla'θion; infla'sion/ *n. f.* inflation.
inflamable /infla'maβle/ *a.* flammable.
inflamación /inflama'θion; inflama'sion/ *n. f.* inflammation.
inflamar /infla'mar/ *v.* inflame, set on fire.
inflar /in'flar/ *v.* inflate, pump up, puff up.
inflexible /infle'ksiβle/ *a.* inflexible, rigid.
inflexión /infle'ksion/ *n. f.* inflection.
infligir /infli'hir/ *v.* inflict.
influencia /influ'enθia; influ'ensia/ *n. f.* influence.
influenza /in'fluenθa; in'fluensa/ *n. f.* influenza, flu.
influir /in'fluir/ *v.* influence, sway.
influyente /influ'yente/ *a.* influential.
información /informa'θion; informa'sion/ *n. f.* information.
informal /infor'mal/ *a.* informal.
informar /infor'mar/ *v.* inform; report.
informática /infor'matika/ *n. f.* computer science; information technology.
informe /in'forme/ *n. m.* report; (*pl.*) information, data.
infortunio /infor'tunio/ *n. m.* misfortune.
infracción /infrak'θion; infrak'sion/ *n. f.* violation.
infraestructura /infraeθtruk'tura; infraestruk'tura/ *n. f.* infrastructure.
infrascrito /infras'krito/ **-ta** *n.* signer, undersigned.
infringir /infrin'hir/ *v.* infringe, violate.
infructuoso /infruk'tuoso/ *a.* fruitless.
infundir /infun'dir/ *v.* instil, inspire with.
ingeniería /inhenie'ria/ *n. f.* engineering.
ingeniero /inhe'niero/ **-ra** *n.* engineer.
ingenio /in'henio/ *n. m.* wit; talent.
ingeniosidad /inheniosi'ðað/ *n. f.* ingenuity.
ingenioso /inhe'nioso/ *a.* witty; ingenious.
ingenuidad /inhenui'ðað/ *n. f.* candor; naïveté.
ingenuo /in'henuo/ *a.* ingenuous, naïve, candid.
Inglaterra /iŋgla'terra/ *n. f.* England.
ingle /'iŋgle/ *n. f.* groin.
inglés /iŋ'gles/ **-esa** *a. & n.* English; Englishman; Englishwoman.
ingratitud /iŋgrati'tuð/ *n. f.* ingratitude.
ingrato /iŋ'grato/ *a.* ungrateful.
ingravidez /iŋgraβi'ðeθ; iŋgraβi'ðes/ *n. f.* weightlessness.
ingrávido /iŋ'graβiðo/ *a.* weightless.
ingrediente /iŋgre'ðiente/ *n. m.* ingredient.
ingresar en /iŋgre'sar en/ *v.* enter; join.
ingreso /iŋ'greso/ *n. m.* entrance; (*pl.*) *earnings, income.*
inhábil /in'aβil/ *a.* unskilled; incapable.
inhabilitar /inaβili'tar/ *v.* disqualify.
inherente /ine'rente/ *a.* inherent.
inhibir /ini'βir/ *v.* inhibit.
inhumano /inu'mano/ *a.* cruel, inhuman.
iniciador /iniθia'ðor; inisia'ðor/ **-ra** *n.* initiator.
inicial /ini'θial; ini'sial/ *a.* initial.
iniciar /ini'θiar; ini'siar/ *v.* initiate, begin.
iniciativa /iniθia'tiβa; inisia'tiβa/ *n. f.* initiative.
inicuo /ini'kuo/ *a.* wicked.
iniquidad /iniki'ðað/ *n. f.* iniquity; sin.
injuria /in'huria/ *n. f.* insult. —**injuriar,** *v.*
injusticia /inhus'tiθia; inhus'tisia/ *n. f.* injustice.
injusto /in'husto/ *a.* unjust, unfair.
inmaculado /imaku'laðo/ *a.* immaculate; pure.
inmediato /ime'ðiato/ *a.* immediate.
inmensidad /imensi'ðað/ *n. f.* immensity.
inmenso /i'menso/ *a.* immense.
inmersión /imer'sion/ *n. f.* immersion.
inmigración /imigra'θion; imigra'sion/ *n. f.* immigration.
inmigrante /imi'grante/ *a. & n.* immigrant.
inmigrar /imi'grar/ *v.* immigrate.
inminente /imi'nente/ *a.* imminent.
inmoderado /imoðe'raðo/ *a.* immoderate.
inmodesto /imo'ðesto/ *a.* immodest.
inmoral /imo'ral/ *a.* immoral.
inmoralidad /imorali'ðað/ *n. f.* immorality.
inmortal /imor'tal/ *a.* immortal.
inmortalidad /imortali'ðað/ *n. f.* immortality.
inmóvil /i'moβil/ *a.* immobile, motionless.
inmundicia /imun'diθia; imun'disia/ *n. f.* dirt, filth.
inmune /i'mune/ *a.* immune; exempt.
inmunidad /imuni'ðað/ *n. f.* immunity.
innato /in'nato/ *a.* innate, inborn.
innecesario /inneθe'sario; innese'sario/ *a.* unnecessary, needless.
innegable /inne'gaβle/ *a.* undeniable.
innoble /in'noβle/ *a.* ignoble.
innocuo /inno'kuo/ *a.* innocuous.
innovación /innoβa'θion; innoβa'sion/ *n. f.* innovation.
innumerable /innume'raβle/ *a.* innumerable, countless.
inocencia /ino'θenθia; ino'sensia/ *n. f.* innocence.
inocentada /inoθen'taða; inosen'taða/ *n. f.* practical joke.
inocente /ino'θente; ino'sente/ *a.* innocent.
inocular /inoku'lar/ *v.* inoculate.
inodoro /ino'ðoro/ *n. m.* toilet.
inofensivo /inofen'siβo/ *a.* inoffensive, harmless.
inolvidable /inolβi'ðaβle/ *a.* unforgettable.
inoportuno /inopor'tuno/ *a.* inopportune.
inoxidable /inoksi'ðaβle/ *a.* stainless.
inquietante /inkie'tante/ *a.* disturbing, worrisome, worrying, upsetting.
inquietar /inkie'tar/ *v.* disturb, worry, trouble.
inquieto /in'kieto/ *a.* anxious, uneasy, worried; restless.
inquietud /inkie'tuð/ *n. f.* concern, anxiety, worry; restlessness.
inquilino /inki'lino/ **-na** *n.* occupant, tenant.
inquirir /inki'rir/ *v.* inquire into, investigate.
inquisición /inkisi'θion; inkisi'sion/ *n. f.* inquisition, investigation.
insaciable /insa'θiaβle; insa'siaβle/ *a.* insatiable.
insalubre /insa'luβre/ *a.* unhealthy.
insano /in'sano/ *a.* insane.
inscribir /inskri'βir/ *v.* inscribe; record.
inscribirse /inskri'βirse/ *v.* register, enroll.
inscripción /inskrip'θion; inskrip'sion/ *n. f.* inscription; registration.
insecticida /insekti'θiða; insekti'siða/ *n. m.* insecticide.
insecto /in'sekto/ *n. m.* insect.
inseguro /inse'guro/ *a.* unsure, uncertain; insecure, unsafe.
insensato /insen'sato/ *a.* stupid, senseless.
insensible /insen'siβle/ *a.* unfeeling, heartless.
inseparable /insepa'raβle/ *a.* inseparable.
inserción /inser'θion; inser'sion/ *n. f.* insertion.
insertar /inser'tar/ *v.* insert.
inservible /inser'βiβle/ *a.* useless.
insidioso /insi'ðioso/ *a.* insidious, crafty.
insigne /in'signe/ *a.* famous, noted.
insignia /in'signia/ *n. f.* insignia, badge.
insignificante /insignifi'kante/ *a.* insignificant, negligible.
insincero /insin'θero; insin'sero/ *a.* insincere.
insinuación /insinua'θion; insin;ua'sion/ *n. f.* insinuation; hint.
insinuar /insi'nuar/ *v.* insinuate, suggest, hint.
insipidez /insipi'ðeθ; insipi'ðes/ *n. f.* insipidity.
insípido /in'sipiðo/ *a.* insipid.
insistencia /insis'tenθia; insis'tensia/ *n. f.* insistence.
insistente /insis'tente/ *a.* insistent.
insistir /insis'tir/ *v.* insist.
insolación /insola'θion; insola'sion/ *n. f.* sunstroke.
insolencia /inso'lenθia; inso'lensia/ *n. f.* insolence.
insolente /inso'lente/ *a.* insolent.
insólito /in'solito/ *a.* unusual.
insolvente /insol'βente/ *a.* insolvent.
insomnio /in'somnio/ *n. m.* insomnia.
insonorizado /insonori'θaðo; insonori'saðo/ *a.* soundproof.
insonorizar /insonori'θar; insonori'sar/ *v.* soundproof.
insoportable /insopor'taβle/ *a.* unbearable.
inspección /inspek'θion; inspek'sion/ *n. f.* inspection.
inspeccionar /inspekθio'nar; inspeksio'nar/ *v.* inspect, examine.
inspector /inspek'tor/ **-ra** *n.* inspector.
inspiración /inspira'θion; inspira'sion/ *n. f.* inspiration.
inspirar /inspi'rar/ *v.* inspire.
instalación /instala'θion; instala'sion/ *n. f.* installation, fixture.
instalar /insta'lar/ *v.* install, set up.
instantánea /instan'tanea/ *n. f.* snapshot.
instantáneo /instan'taneo/ *a.* instantaneous.
instante /ins'tante/ *a. & m.* instant. **al i.,** at once.
instar /ins'tar/ *v.* coax, urge.
instigar /insti'gar/ *v.* instigate, urge.
instintivo /instin'tiβo/ *a.* instinctive.
instinto /ins'tinto/ *n. m.* instinct. **por i.,** by instinct, instinctively.
institución /institu'θion; institu'sion/ *n. f.* institution.

instituto /insti'tuto/ n. m. institute. **—instituir,** v.

institutriz /institu'triθ; institu'tris/ n. f. governess.

instrucción /instruk'θion; instruk'sion/ n. f. instruction; education.

instructivo /instruk'tiβo/ a. instructive.

instructor /instruk'tor/ **-ra** n. instructor.

instruir /ins'truir/ v. instruct, teach.

instrumento /instru'mento/ n. m. instrument.

insuficiente /insufi'θiente; insufi'siente/ a. insufficient.

insufrible /insu'friβle/ a. intolerable.

insular /insu'lar/ a. island, insular.

insulto /in'sulto/ n. m. insult. **—insultar,** v.

insuperable /insupe'raβle/ a. insuperable.

insurgente /insur'hente/ n. & a. insurgent, rebel.

insurrección /insurrek'θion; insurrek'sion/ n. f. insurrection, revolt.

insurrecto /insu'rrekto/ **-ta** a. & n. insurgent.

intacto /in'takto/ a. intact.

integral /inte'gral/ a. integral.

integridad /integri'ðað/ n. f. integrity; entirety.

íntegro /'integro/ a. entire; upright.

intelecto /inte'lekto/ n. m. intellect.

intelectual /intelek'tual/ a. & n. intellectual.

inteligencia /inteli'henθia; inteli'hensia/ n. f. intelligence.

inteligente /inteli'hente/ a. intelligent.

inteligible /inteli'hiβle/ a. intelligible.

intemperie /intem'perie/ n. f. bad weather.

intención /inten'θion; inten'sion/ n. f. intention.

intendente /inten'dente/ n. m. manager.

intensidad /intensi'ðað/ n. f. intensity.

intensificar /intensifi'kar/ v. intensify.

intensivo /inten'siβo/ a. intensive.

intenso /in'tenso/ a. intense.

intentar /inten'tar/ v. attempt, try.

intento /in'tento/ n. m. intent; attempt.

intercambiable /interkam'biaβle/ a. interchangeable.

intercambiar /interkam'βiar/ v. exchange, interchange.

interceptar /interθep'tar; intersep'tar/ v. intercept.

intercesión /interθe'sion; interse'sion/ n. f. intercession.

interés /inte'res/ n. m. interest; concern; appeal.

interesante /intere'sante/ a. interesting.

interesar /intere'sar/ v. interest, appeal to.

interfaz /inter'faθ; inter'fas/ n. f. interface.

interferencia /interfe'renθia; interfe'rensia/ n. f. interference.

interino /inte'rino/ a. temporary.

interior /inte'rior/ a. **1.** interior, inner. **—n. 2.** m. interior.

interjección /interhek'θion; interhek'sion/ n. f. interjection.

intermedio /inter'meðio/ a. **1.** intermediate. **—n. 2.** m. intermediary; intermission.

interminable /intermi'naβle/ a. interminable, endless.

intermisión /intermi'sion/ n. f. intermission.

intermitente /intermi'tente/ a. intermittent.

internacional /internaθio'nal; internasio'nal/ a. international.

internarse en /inter'narse en/ v. enter into, go into.

Internet, el /inter'net/ n. m. the Internet.

interno /in'terno/ a. internal.

interpelar /interpe'lar/ v. ask questions; implore.

interponer /interpo'ner/ v. interpose.

interpretación /interpreta'θion; interpreta'sion/ n. f. interpretation.

interpretar /interpre'tar/ v. interpret; construe.

intérprete /in'terprete/ n. m. & f. interpreter; performer.

interrogación /interroga'θion; interroga'sion/ n. f. interrogation.

interrogar /interro'gar/ v. question, interrogate.

interrogativo /interroga'tiβo/ a. interrogative.

interrumpir /interrum'pir/ v. interrupt.

interrupción /interrup'θion; interrup'sion/ n. f. interruption.

intersección /intersek'θion; intersek'sion/ n. f. intersection.

intervalo /inter'βalo/ n. m. interval.

intervención /interβen'θion; interβen'sion/ n. f. intervention.

intervenir /interβe'nir/ v. intervene, interfere.

intestino /intes'tino/ n. m. intestine.

intimación /intima'θion; intima'sion/ n. f. intimation, hint.

intimar /inti'mar/ v. suggest, hint.

intimidad /intimi'ðað/ n. f. intimacy.

intimidar /intimi'ðar/ v. intimidate.

íntimo /'intimo/ a. & n. intimate.

intolerable /intole'raβle/ a. intolerable.

intolerancia /intole'ranθia; intole'ransia/ n. f. intolerance, bigotry.

intolerante /intole'rante/ a. intolerant.

intoxicación alimenticia /intoksika'θion alimen'tiθia; intoksika'sion alimen'tisia/ n. f. food poisoning.

intranquilo /intran'kilo/ a. uneasy.

intravenoso /intraβe'noso/ a. intravenous.

intrepidez /intrepi'ðeθ; intrepi'ðes/ n. f. daring.

intrépido /in'trepiðo/ a. intrepid.

intriga /in'triga/ n. f. intrigue, plot, scheme. **—intrigar,** v.

intrincado /intrin'kaðo/ a. intricate, involved; impenetrable.

introducción /introðuk'θion; introðuk'sion/ n. f. introduction.

introducir /introðu'θir; introðu'sir/ v. introduce.

intruso /in'truso/ **-sa** n. intruder.

intuición /intui'θion; intui'sion/ n. f. intuition.

inundación /inunda'θion; inunda'sion/ n. f. flood. **—inundar,** v.

inútil /i'nutil/ a. useless.

invadir /imba'ðir/ v. invade.

inválido /im'baliðo/ **-da** a. & n. invalid.

invariable /imba'riaβle/ a. constant.

invasión /imba'sion/ n. f. invasion.

invasor /imba'sor/ **-ra** n. invader.

invencible /imben'θiβle; imben'siβle/ a. invincible.

invención /imben'θion; imben'sion/ n. f. invention.

inventar /imben'tar/ v. invent; devise.

inventario /imben'tario/ n. m. inventory.

inventivo /imben'tiβo/ a. inventive.

invento /im'bento/ n. m. invention.

inventor /imben'tor/ **-ra** n. inventor.

invernáculo /imber'nakulo/ n. m. greenhouse.

invernal /imber'nal/ a. wintry.

inverosímil /imbero'simil/ a. improbable, unlikely.

inversión /imber'sion/ n. f. inversion; Com. investment.

inverso /im'berso/ a. inverse, reverse.

inversor /imber'sor/ **-ra** n. investor.

invertir /imber'tir/ v. invert; reverse; Com. invest.

investigación /imbestiga'θion; imbestiga'sion/ n. f. investigation.

investigador /imbestiga'ðor/ **-ra** n. investigator; researcher.

investigar /imbesti'gar/ v. investigate.

invierno /im'bierno/ n. m. winter.

invisible /imbi'siβle/ a. invisible.

invitación /imbita'θion; imbita'sion/ n. f. invitation.

invitar /imbi'tar/ v. invite.

invocar /imbo'kar/ v. invoke.

involuntario /imbolun'tario/ a. involuntary.

inyección /inyek'θion; inyek'sion/ n. f. injection.

inyectar /inyek'tar/ v. inject.

ir /ir/ v. go. **irse,** go away, leave.

ira /'ira/ n. f. anger, ire.

iracundo /ira'kundo/ a. wrathful, irate.

iris /'iris/ n. m. iris. **arco i.,** rainbow.

Irlanda /ir'landa/ n. f. Ireland.

irlandés /irlan'des/ **-esa** a. & n. Irish; Irishman, Irishwoman.

ironía /iro'nia/ n. f. irony.

irónico /i'roniko/ a. ironical.

irracional /irraθio'nal; irrasio'nal/ a. irrational; insane.

irradiación /irraðia'θion; irraðia'sion/ n. f. irradiation.

irradiar /irra'ðiar/ v. radiate.

irrazonable /irraθo'naβle; irraso'naβle/ a. unreasonable.

irregular /irregu'lar/ a. irregular.

irreligioso /irreli'hioso/ a. irreligious.

irremediable /irreme'ðiaβle/ a. irremediable, hopeless.

irresistible /irresis'tiβle/ a. irresistible.

irresoluto /irreso'luto/ a. irresolute, wavering.

irrespetuoso /irrespe'tuoso/ a. disrespectful.

irreverencia /irreβe'renθia; irreβe'rensia/ n. f. irreverence.

irreverente /irreβe'rente/ adj. irreverent.

irrigación /irriga'θion; irriga'sion/ n. f. irrigation.

irrigar /irri'gar/ v. irrigate.

irritación /irrita'θion; irrita'sion/ n. f. irritation.

irritar /irri'tar/ v. irritate.

irrupción /irrup'θion; irrup'sion/ n. f. raid, attack.

isla /'isla/ n. f. island.

isleño /is'leɲo/ **-ña** n. islander.

israelita /israe'lita/ n. & a. Israelite.

Italia /i'talia/ n. f. Italy.

italiano /ita'liano/ **-na** a. & n. Italian.

itinerario /itine'rario/ n. m. itinerary; timetable.

IVA, abbrev. (**impuesto sobre el valor añadido**) VAT (value-added tax).

izar /i'θar; i'sar/ v. hoist.

izquierda /iθ'kierða; is'kierða/ n. f. left (hand, side).

izquierdista /iθ'kierðista; is'kierðista/ n. & a. leftist.

izquierdo /iθ'kierðo; is'kierðo/ a. left.

J

jabalí /haβa'li/ n. m. wild boar.

jabón /ha'βon/ n. m. soap. **j. en polvo,** soap powder.

jabonar /haβo'nar/ v. soap.

jaca /'haka/ n. f. nag.

jacinto /ha'θinto; ha'sinto/ n. m. hyacinth.

jactancia /hak'tanθia; hak'tansia/ n. f. boast. **—jactarse,** v.

jactancioso /haktan'θioso; haktan'sioso/ a. boastful.

jadear /haðe'ar/ v. pant, puff.

jaez /ha'eθ; ha'es/ n. m. harness; kind.

jalar /ha'lar/ v. haul, pull.

jalea /ha'lea/ n. f. jelly.

jaleo /ha'leo/ n. m. row, uproar; hassle.

jamás /ha'mas/ adv. never, ever.

jamón /ha'mon/ n. m. ham.

Japón /ha'pon/ n. m. Japan.

japonés /hapo'nes/ **-esa** a. & n. Japanese.

jaqueca /ha'keka/ n. f. headache.

jarabe /ha'raβe/ n. m. syrup.

jaranear /harane'ar/ v. jest; carouse.

jardín /har'ðin/ n. m. garden.

jardín de infancia /har'ðin de in'fanθia; har'ðin de in'fansia/ nursery school.

jardinero /harði'nero/ **-ra** n. gardener.

jarra /'harra/ n. f. jar; pitcher.

jarro /'harro/ n. m. jug, pitcher.

jaspe /'haspe/ n. m. jasper.

jaula /'haula/ n. f. cage; coop.

jauría /hau'ria/ n. f. pack of hounds.

jazmín /haθ'min; has'min/ n. m. jasmine.

jefatura /hefa'tura/ n. f. headquarters.

jefe /'hefe/ **-fa** n. chief, boss.

jefe de comedor /'hefe de kome'ðor/ headwaiter.

jefe de sala /'hefe de 'sala/ maître d'.

jefe de taller /'hefe de ta'ʎer; 'hefe de ta'yer/ foreman.

Jehová /heo'βa/ n. m. Jehovah.

jengibre /hen'hiβre/ n. m. ginger.

jerez /he'reθ; he'res/ n. m. sherry.

jerga /'herga/ n. f. slang.

jergón /her'gon/ n. m. straw mattress.

jerigonza /heri'gonθa; heri'gonsa/ n. f. jargon.

jeringa /he'ringa/ n. f. syringe.

jeringar /herin'gar/ v. inject; annoy.

jeroglífico /hero'glifiko/ n. m. hieroglyph.

jersey /her'sei/ n. m. pullover; **j. de cuello alto,** turtleneck sweater.

Jerusalén /herusa'len/ n. m. Jerusalem.

jesuita /he'suita/ n. m. Jesuit.

Jesús /he'sus/ n. m. Jesus.

jeta /'heta/ n. f. snout.

jícara /'hikara/ n. f. cup.

jinete /hi'nete/ **-ta** n. horseman.

jingoísmo /hingo'ismo/ n. m. jingoism.

jingoísta /hingo'ista/ n. & a. jingoist.

jira /'hira/ n. f. picnic; outing.

jirafa /hi'rafa/ n. f. giraffe.

jiu-jitsu /hiu'hitsu/ n. m. jujitsu.

jocundo /ho'kundo/ a. jovial.

jornada /hor'naða/ n. f. journey; day's work.

jornal /hor'nal/ n. m. day's wage.

jornalero /horna'lero/ n. m. day laborer, workman.

joroba /ho'roβa/ n. f. hump.

jorobado /horo'βaðo/ a. humpbacked.

joven /'hoβen/ a. **1.** young. **—n. 2.** m. & f. young person.

jovial /ho'βial/ a. jovial, jolly.

jovialidad /hoβiali'ðað/ n. f. joviality.

joya /'hoia/ n. f. jewel, gem.

joyas de fantasía /'hoias de fanta'sia/ n. f.pl. costume jewelry.

joyelero /hoie'lero/ n. m. jewel box.

joyería /hoie'ria/ n. f. jewelry; jewelry store.

joyero /ho'iero/ n. m. jeweler; jewel case.

juanete /hua'nete/ n. m. bunion.

jubilación /huβila'θion; huβila'sion/ n. f. retirement; pension.

jubilar /huβi'lar/ v. retire, pension.

jubileo /huβi'leo/ n. m. jubilee, public festivity.

júbilo /'huβilo/ n. m. glee, rejoicing.

jubiloso /huβi'loso/ a. joyful, gay.

judaico /hu'ðaiko/ a. Jewish.

judaísmo /huða'ismo/ n. m. Judaism.

judía /hu'ðia/ n. f. bean, string bean.

judicial /huði'θial; huði'sial/ a. judicial.

judío /hu'ðio/ **-día** a. & n. Jewish; Jew.

juego /'huego/ n. m. game; play;

gambling; set. **j. de damas,** checkers. **j. limpio,** fair play.
Juegos Olímpicos /huegos o'limpikos/ *n. m.pl.* Olympic Games.
juerga /'huerga/ *n. f.* spree.
jueves /'hueβes/ *n. m.* Thursday.
juez /hueθ; hues/ *n. m.* judge.
jugador /huga'ðor/ **-ra** *n.* player.
jugar /hu'gar/ *v.* play; gamble.
juglar /hug'lar/ *n. m.* minstrel.
jugo /'hugo/ *n. m.* juice. **j. de naranja,** orange juice.
jugoso /hu'goso/ *a.* juicy.
juguete /hu'gete/ *n. m.* toy, plaything.
juguetear /hugete'ar/ *v.* trifle.
juguetón /huge'ton/ *a.* playful.
juicio /'huiθio; 'huisio/ *n. m.* sense, wisdom, judgment; sanity; trial.
juicioso /hui'θioso; hui'sioso/ *a.* wise, judicious.
julio /'hulio/ *n. m.* July.
jumento /hu'mento/ *n. m.* donkey.
junco /'hunko/ *n. m.* reed, rush.
jungla /'huŋgla/ *n. f.* jungle.
junio /'hunio/ *n. m.* June.
junípero /hu'nipero/ *n. m.* juniper.
junquillo /hun'kiʎo; hun'kiyo/ *n. m.* jonquil.
junta /'hunta/ *n. f.* board, council; joint, coupling.
juntamente /hunta'mente/ *adv.* jointly.
juntar /hun'tar/ *v.* join; connect; assemble.
junto /'hunto/ *a.* together. **j. a,** next to.
juntura /hun'tura/ *n. f.* joint, juncture.
jurado /hu'raðo/ *n. m.* jury.
juramento /hura'mento/ *n. m.* oath.
jurar /hu'rar/ *v.* swear.
jurisconsulto /huriskon'sulto/ *n. m.* jurist.
jurisdicción /hurisðik'θion; hurisðik'sion/ *n. f.* jurisdiction; territory.
jurisprudencia /hurispru'ðenθia; hurispru'ðensia/ *n. f.* jurisprudence.
justa /'husta/ *n. f.* joust. **—justar,** *v.*
justicia /hus'tiθia; hus'tisia/ *n. f.* justice, equity.
justiciero /husti'θiero; husti'siero/ *a.* just.
justificación /hustifika'θion; hustifika'sion/ *n. f.* justification.
justificadamente /hustifikaða'mente/ *adv.* justifiably.
justificar /hustifi'kar/ *v.* justify, warrant.
justo /'husto/ *a.* right; exact; just; righteous.
juvenil /huβe'nil/ *a.* youthful.
juventud /huβen'tuð/ *n. f.* youth.
juzgado /huθ'gaðo; hus'gaðo/ *n. m.* court.
juzgar /huθ'gar; hus'gar/ *v.* judge, estimate.

K

káiser /'kaiser/ *n. m.* kaiser.
karate /ka'rate/ *n. m.* karate.
kepis /'kepis/ *n. m.* military cap.
kerosena /kero'sena/ *n. f.* kerosene.
kilo /'kilo/ **kilogramo** *n. m.* kilogram.
kilohercio /kilo'erθio; kilo'ersio/ *n. m.* kilohertz.
kilolitro /kilo'litro/ *n. m.* kiloliter.
kilometraje /kilome'trahe/ *n. m.* mileage.
kilómetro /ki'lometro/ *n. m.* kilometer.
kiosco /'kiosko/ *n. m.* newsstand; pavilion.

L

la /la/ *art. & pron.* **1.** the; the one. *—pron.* **2.** her, it, you; (*pl.*) them, you.
laberinto /laβe'rinto/ *n. m.* labyrinth, maze.
labia /'laβia/ *n. f.* eloquence, fluency.
labio /'laβio/ *n. m.* lip.
labor /la'βor/ *n. f.* labor, work.
laborar /laβo'rar/ *v.* work; till.
laboratorio /laβora'torio/ *n. m.* laboratory.
laborioso /laβo'rioso/ *a.* industrious.
labrador /laβra'ðor/ *n. m.* farmer.
labranza /la'βranθa; la'βransa/ *n. f.* farming; farmland.
labrar /la'βrar/ *v.* work, till.
labriego /la'βriego/ **-ga** *n.* peasant.
laca /'laka/ *n. f.* shellac.
lacio /'laθio; 'lasio/ *a.* withered; limp; straight.
lactar /lak'tar/ *v.* nurse, suckle.
lácteo /'lakteo/ *a.* milky.
ladear /laðe'ar/ *v.* tilt, tip; sway.
ladera /la'ðera/ *n. f.* slope.
ladino /la'ðino/ *a.* cunning, crafty.
lado /'laðo/ *n. m.* side. **al l. de,** beside. **de l.,** sideways.
ladra /'laðra/ *n. f.* barking. **—ladrar,** *v.*
ladrillo /la'ðriʎo; la'ðriyo/ *n. m.* brick.
ladrón /la'ðron/ **-ona** *n.* thief, robber.
lagarto /la'garto/ *n. m.* lizard; (Mex.) alligator.
lago /'lago/ *n. m.* lake.
lágrima /'lagrima/ *n. f.* tear.
lagrimear /lagrime'ar/ *v.* weep, cry.
laguna /la'guna/ *n. f.* lagoon; gap.
laico /'laiko/ *a.* lay.
laja /'laha/ *n. f.* stone slab.
lamentable /lamen'taβle/ *a.* lamentable.
lamentación /lamenta'θion; lamenta'sion/ *n. f.* lamentation.
lamentar /lamen'tar/ *v.* lament; wail; regret, be sorry.
lamento /la'mento/ *n. m.* lament, wail.
lamer /la'mer/ *v.* lick; lap.
lámina /'lamina/ *n. f.* print, illustration.
lámpara /'lampara/ *n. f.* lamp.
lampiño /lam'piɲo/ *a.* beardless.
lana /'lana/ *n. f.* wool.
lanar /la'nar/ *a.* woolen.
lance /'lanθe; 'lanse/ *n. m.* throw; episode; quarrel.
lancha /'lantʃa/ *n. f.* launch; small boat.
lanchón /lan'tʃon/ *n. m.* barge.
langosta /laŋ'gosta/ *n. f.* lobster; locust.
langostino /laŋgos'tino/ *n. m.* king prawn.
languidecer /laŋguiðe'θer; laŋguiðe'ser/ *v.* languish, pine.
languidez /laŋgui'ðeθ; laŋgui'ðes/ *n. f.* languidness.
lánguido /'laŋguiðo/ *a.* languid.
lanza /'lanθa; 'lansa/ *n. f.* lance, spear.
lanzada /lan'θaða; lan'saða/ *n. f.* thrust, throw.
lanzar /lan'θar; lan'sar/ *v.* hurl; launch.
lañar /la'ɲar/ *v.* cramp; clamp.
lapicero /lapi'θero; lapi'sero/ *n. m.* mechanical pencil.
lápida /'lapiða/ *n. f.* stone; tombstone.
lápiz /'lapiθ; 'lapis/ *n. m.* pencil; crayon.
lápiz de ojos /'lapiθ de 'ohos; 'lapis de 'ohos/ *n. m.* eyeliner.
lapso /'lapso/ *n. m.* lapse.
lardo /'larðo/ *n. m.* lard.
largar /lar'gar/ *v.* loosen; free.
largo /'largo/ *a.* **1.** long. **a lo l. de,** along. *—n.* **2.** *m.* length.
largometraje /largome'trahe/ *n. m.* feature film.
largor /lar'gor/ *n. m.* length.
largueza /lar'geθa; lar'gesa/ *n. f.* generosity; length.
largura /lar'gura/ *n. f.* length.
laringe /la'rinhe/ *n. f.* larynx.
larva /'larβa/ *n. f.* larva.
lascivia /las'θiβia; las'siβia/ *n. f.* lasciviousness.
lascivo /las'θiβo; las'siβo/ *a.* lascivious.
láser /'laser/ *n. m.* laser.
laso /'laso/ *a.* weary.
lástima /'lastima/ *n. f.* pity. **ser l.,** to be a pity, to be too bad.
lastimar /lasti'mar/ *v.* hurt, injure.
lastimoso /lasti'moso/ *a.* pitiful.
lastre /'lastre/ *n. m.* ballast. **—lastrar,** *v.*
lata /'lata/ *n. f.* tin can; tin (plate); *Colloq.* annoyance, bore.
latente /la'tente/ *a.* latent.
lateral /late'ral/ *a.* lateral, side.
latigazo /lati'gaθo; lati'gaso/ *n. m.* lash, whipping.
látigo /'latigo/ *n. m.* whip.
latín /la'tin/ *n. m.* Latin (language).
latino /la'tino/ *a.* Latin.
latir /la'tir/ *v.* beat, pulsate.
latitud /lati'tuð/ *n. f.* latitude.
latón /la'ton/ *n. m.* brass.
laúd /la'uð/ *n. m.* lute.
laudable /lau'ðaβle/ *a.* laudable.
láudano /'lauðano/ *n. m.* laudanum.
laurel /lau'rel/ *n. m.* laurel.
lava /'laβa/ *n. f.* lava.
lavabo /la'βaβo/ **lavamanos** *n. m.* washroom, lavatory.
lavadora /laβa'ðora/ *n. f.* washing machine.
lavandera /laβan'dera/ *n. f.* washerwoman, laundress.
lavandería /laβande'ria/ *f.* laundry; laundromat.
lavaplatos /laβa'platos/ *n.* **1.** *m.* dishwasher (machine). *—n.* **2.** *m. & f.* dishwasher (person).
lavar /la'βar/ *v.* wash.
lavatorio /laβa'torio/ *n. m.* lavatory.
laya /'laia/ *n. f.* spade. **—layar,** *v.*
lazar /la'θar; la'sar/ *v.* lasso.
lazareto /laθa'reto; lasa'reto/ *n. m.* isolation hospital; quarantine station.
lazo /'laθo; 'laso/ *n. m.* tie, knot; bow; loop.
le /le/ *pron.* him, her, you; (*pl.*) them, you.
leal /le'al/ *a.* loyal.
lealtad /leal'tað/ *n. f.* loyalty.
lebrel /le'βrel/ *n. m.* greyhound.
lección /lek'θion; lek'sion/ *n. f.* lesson.
leche /'letʃe/ *n. f.* milk.
lechería /letʃe'ria/ *n. f.* dairy.
lechero /le'tʃero/ *n. m.* milkman.
lecho /'letʃo/ *n. m.* bed; couch.
lechón /le'tʃon/ *n. m.* pig.
lechoso /le'tʃoso/ *a.* milky.
lechuga /le'tʃuga/ *n. f.* lettuce.
lechuza /le'tʃuθa; le'tʃusa/ *n. f.* owl.
lecito /le'θito; le'sito/ *n. m.* yolk.
lector /lek'tor/ **-ra** *n.* reader.
lectura /lek'tura/ *n. f.* reading.
leer /le'er/ *v.* read.
legación /lega'θion; lega'sion/ *n. f.* legation.
legado /le'gaðo/ *n. m.* bequest.
legal /le'gal/ *a.* legal, lawful.
legalizar /legali'θar; legali'sar/ *v.* legalize.
legar /le'gar/ *v.* bequeath, leave, will.
legible /le'hiβle/ *a.* legible.
legión /le'hion/ *n. f.* legion.
legislación /lehisla'θion; lehisla'sion/ *n. f.* legislation.
legislador /lehisla'ðor/ **-ra** *n.* legislator.
legislar /lehis'lar/ *v.* legislate.
legislativo /lehisla'tiβo/ *a.* legislative.
legislatura /lehisla'tura/ *n. f.* legislature.
legítimo /le'hitimo/ *a.* legitimate.
lego /'lego/ *n. m.* layman.
legua /'legua/ *n. f.* league (measure).
legumbre /le'gumbre/ *n. f.* vegetable.
lejano /le'hano/ *a.* distant, far-off.
lejía /le'hia/ *n. f.* lye.
lejos /'lehos/ *adv.* far. **a lo l.,** in the distance.
lelo /'lelo/ *a.* stupid, foolish.
lema /'lema/ *n. m.* theme; slogan.
lengua /'leŋgua/ *n. f.* tongue; language.
lenguado /leŋ'guaðo/ *n. m.* sole, flounder.
lenguaje /leŋ'guahe/ *n. m.* speech; language.
lenguaraz /leŋgua'raθ; leŋgua'ras/ *a.* talkative.
lente /'lente/ *n.* **1.** *m. or f.* lens. **2.** *m.pl.* eyeglasses.
lenteja /len'teha/ *n. f.* lentil.
lentilla /len'tiʎa; len'tiya/ *n. f.* contact lens.
lentitud /lenti'tuð/ *n. f.* slowness.
lento /'lento/ *a.* slow.
leña /'leɲa/ *n. f.* wood, firewood.
león /le'on/ *n. m.* lion.
leopardo /leo'parðo/ *n. m.* leopard.
lerdo /'lerðo/ *a.* dull-witted.
lesbiana /les'βiana/ *n. f.* lesbian.
lesión /le'sion/ *n. f.* wound; damage.
letanía /leta'nia/ *n. f.* litany.
letárgico /le'tarhiko/ *a.* lethargic.
letargo /le'targo/ *n. m.* lethargy.
letra /'letra/ *n. f.* letter (of alphabet); print; words (of a song).
letrado /le'traðo/ *a.* **1.** learned. *—n.* **2.** *m.* lawyer.
letrero /le'trero/ *n. m.* sign, poster.
leva /'leβa/ *n. f. Mil.* draft.
levadura /leβa'ðura/ *n. f.* yeast, leavening, baking powder.
levantador /leβanta'ðor/ *n. m.* lifter; rebel, mutineer.
levantar /leβan'tar/ *v.* raise, lift.
levantarse /leβan'tarse/ *v.* rise, get up; stand up.
levar /le'βar/ *v.* weigh (anchor).
leve /'leβe/ *a.* slight, light.
levita /le'βita/ *n. f.* frock coat.
léxico /'leksiko/ *n. m.* lexicon, dictionary.
ley /lei/ *n. f.* law, statute.
leyenda /le'ienda/ *n. f.* legend.
lezna /'leθna; 'lesna/ *n. f.* awl.
libación /liβa'θion; liβa'sion/ *n. f.* libation.
libelo /li'βelo/ *n. m.* libel.
libélula /li'βelula/ *n. f.* dragonfly.
liberación /liβera'θion; liβera'sion/ *n. f.* liberation, release.
liberal /liβe'ral/ *a.* liberal.
libertad /liβer'tað/ *n. f.* freedom.
libertador /liβerta'ðor/ **-ra** *n.* liberator.
libertar /liβer'tar/ *v.* free, liberate.
libertinaje /liβerti'nahe/ *n. m.* licentiousness.
libertino /liβer'tino/ **-na** *n.* libertine.
libídine /li'βiðine/ *n. f.* licentiousness; lust.
libidinoso /liβiði'noso/ *a.* lustful.
libra /'liβra/ *n. f.* pound.
libranza /li'βranθa; li'βransa/ *n. f.* draft, bill of exchange.
librar /li'βrar/ *v.* free, rid.
libre /'liβre/ *a.* free, unoccupied.
librería /liβre'ria/ *n. f.* bookstore.
librero /li'βrero/ **-ra** *n.* bookseller.
libreta /li'βreta/ *n. f.* notebook; booklet.
libreto /li'βreto/ *n. m.* libretto.
libro /'liβro/ *n. m.* book.
libro de texto /'liβro de 'teksto/ textbook.
licencia /li'θenθia; li'sensia/ *n. f.* permission, license, leave; furlough. **l. de armas,** gun permit.
licenciado /liθen'θiaðo; lisen'siaðo/ **-da** *n.* graduate.
licencioso /liθen'θioso; lisen'sioso/ *a.* licentious.
lícito /'liθito; 'lisito/ *a.* lawful.
licor /li'kor/ *n. m.* liquor.
licuadora /likua'ðora/ *n. f.* blender (for food).
lid /lið/ *n. f.* fight. **—lidiar,** *v.*
líder /'liðer/ *n. m. & f.* leader.
liebre /'lieβre/ *n. f.* hare.
lienzo /'lienθo; 'lienso/ *n. m.* linen.

liga /'liga/ n. f. league, confederacy; garter.

ligadura /liga'ðura/ n. f. ligature.

ligar /li'gar/ v. tie, bind, join.

ligero /li'hero/ a. light; fast, nimble.

ligustro /li'gustro/ n. m. privet.

lija /li'ha/ n. f. sandpaper.

lijar /li'har/ v. sandpaper.

lima /'lima/ n. f. file; lime.

limbo /'limbo/ n. m. limbo.

limitación /limita'θion; limita'sion/ n. f. limitation.

límite /'limite/ n. m. limit. —**limitar**, v.

limo /'limo/ n. m. slime.

limón /li'mon/ n. m. lemon.

limonada /limo'naða/ n. f. lemonade.

limonero /limo'nero/ n. m. lemon tree.

limosna /li'mosna/ n. f. alms.

limosnero /limos'nero/ **-ra** n. beggar.

limpiabotas /limpia'βotas/ n. m. bootblack.

limpiadientes /limpia'ðientes/ n. m. toothpick.

limpiar /lim'piar/ v. clean, wash, wipe.

límpido /'limpiðo/ a. limpid, clear.

limpieza /lim'pieθa; lim'piesa/ n. f. cleanliness.

limpio /'limpio/ n. m. clean.

limusina /limu'sina/ n. f. limousine.

linaje /li'nahe/ n. m. lineage, ancestry.

linaza /li'naθa; li'nasa/ n. f. linseed.

lince /'linθe; 'linse/ a. sharp-sighted, observing.

linchamiento /lintʃa'miento/ n. m. lynching.

linchar /lin'tʃar/ v. lynch.

lindar /lin'dar/ v. border, bound.

linde /'linde/ n. m. boundary; landmark.

lindero /lin'dero/ n. m. boundary.

lindo /'lindo/ a. pretty, lovely, nice.

línea /'linea/ n. f. line.

línea de puntos /'linea de 'puntos/ dotted line.

lineal /line'al/ a. lineal.

linfa /'linfa/ n. f. lymph.

lingüista /liŋ'guista/ n. m. & f. linguist.

lingüístico /liŋ'guistiko/ a. linguistic.

linimento /lini'mento/ n. m. liniment.

lino /'lino/ n. m. linen; flax.

linóleo /li'noleo/ n. m. linoleum.

linterna /lin'terna/ n. f. lantern; flashlight.

lío /'lio/ n. m. pack, bundle; mess, scrape; hassle.

liquidación /likiða'θion; likiða'sion/ n. f. liquidation.

liquidar /liki'ðar/ v. liquidate; settle up.

líquido /'likiðo/ a. & m. liquid.

lira /'lira/ n. f. lyre.

lírico /'liriko/ a. lyric.

lirio /'lirio/ n. m. lily.

lirismo /li'rismo/ n. m. lyricism.

lis /'lis/ n. f. lily.

lisiar /li'siar/ v. cripple, lame.

liso /'liso/ a. smooth, even.

lisonja /li'sonha/ n. f. flattery.

lisonjear /lisonhe'ar/ v. flatter.

lisonjero /lison'hero/ **-ra** n. flatterer.

lista /'lista/ n. f. list; stripe; menu.

lista negra /'lista 'negra/ blacklist.

listar /lis'tar/ v. list; put on a list.

listo /'listo/ a. ready; smart, clever.

listón /lis'ton/ n. m. ribbon.

litera /li'tera/ n. f. litter, bunk, berth.

literal /lite'ral/ a. literal.

literario /lite'rario/ a. literary.

literato /lite'rato/ n. m. literary person, writer.

literatura /litera'tura/ n. f. literature.

litigación /litiga'θion; litiga'sion/ n. f. litigation.

litigio /li'tihio/ n. m. litigation; lawsuit.

litoral /lito'ral/ n. m. coast.

litro /'litro/ n. m. liter.

liturgia /li'turhia/ n. f. liturgy.

liviano /li'βiano/ a. light (in weight).

lívido /'liβiðo/ a. livid.

llaga /'ʎaga; 'yaga/ n. f. sore.

llama /'ʎama; 'yama/ n. f. flame; llama.

llamada /ʎa'maða; ya'maða/ n. f. call; knock. —**llamar**, v.

llamarse /ʎa'marse; ya'marse/ v. be called, be named. **se llama...** etc., his name is... etc.

llamativo /ʎama'tiβo; yama'tiβo/ a. gaudy, showy.

llamear /ʎame'ar; yame'ar/ v. blaze.

llaneza /ʎa'neθa; ya'nesa/ n. f. simplicity.

llano /'ʎano; 'yano/ a. **1.** flat, level; plain. —n. **2.** m. plain.

llanta /'ʎanta; 'yanta/ n. f. tire.

llanto /'ʎanto; 'yanto/ n. m. crying, weeping.

llanura /ʎa'nura; ya'nura/ n. f. prairie, plain.

llave /'ʎaβe; 'yaβe/ n. f. key; wrench; faucet; *Elec.* switch. **ll. inglesa,** monkey wrench.

llegada /ʎe'gaða; ye'gaða/ n. f. arrival.

llegar /ʎe'gar; ye'gar/ v. arrive; reach. **ll. a ser**, become, come to be.

llenar /ʎe'nar; ye'nar/ v. fill.

lleno /'ʎeno; 'yeno/ a. full.

llenura /ʎe'nura; ye'nura/ n. f. abundance.

llevadero /ʎeβa'ðero; yeβa'ðero/ a. tolerable.

llevar /ʎe'βar; ye'βar/ v. take, carry, bear; wear (clothes). **ll. a cabo,** carry out.

llevarse /ʎe'βarse; ye'βarse/ v. take away, run away with. **ll. bien,** get along well.

llorar /ʎo'rar; yo'rar/ v. cry, weep.

lloroso /ʎo'roso; yo'roso/ a. sorrowful, tearful.

llover /ʎo'βer; yo'βer/ v. rain.

llovido /ʎo'βiðo; yo'βiðo/ n. m. stowaway.

llovizna /ʎo'βiθna; yo'βisna/ n. f. drizzle, sprinkle. —**lloviznar**, v.

lluvia /'ʎuβia; 'yuβia/ n. f. rain.

lluvia ácida /'ʎuβia 'aθiða; 'yuβia 'asiða/ acid rain.

lluvioso /ʎu'βioso; yu'βioso/ a. rainy.

lo /lo/ pron. the; him, it, you; (pl.) them, you.

loar /lo'ar/ v. praise, laud.

lobina /lo'βina/ n. f. striped bass.

lobo /'loβo/ n. m. wolf.

lóbrego /'loβrego/ a. murky; dismal.

local /lo'kal/ a. **1.** local. —n. **2.** m. site.

localidad /lokali'ðað/ n. f. locality, location; seat (in theater).

localizar /lokali'θar; lokali'sar/ v. localize.

loción /lo'θion; lo'sion/ n. f. lotion.

loco /'loko/ **-ca** a. **1.** crazy, insane, mad. —n. **2.** lunatic.

locomotora /lokomo'tora/ n. f. locomotive.

locuaz /lo'kuaθ; lo'kuas/ a. loquacious.

locución /loku'θion; loku'sion/ n. f. locution, expression.

locura /lo'kura/ n. f. folly; madness, insanity.

lodo /'loðo/ n. m. mud.

lodoso /lo'ðoso/ a. muddy.

lógica /'lohika/ n. f. logic.

lógico /'lohiko/ a. logical.

lograr /lo'grar/ v. achieve; succeed in.

logro /'logro/ n. m. accomplishment.

lombriz /lom'βriθ; lom'βris/ n. f. earthworm.

lomo /'lomo/ n. m. loin; back (of an animal).

lona /'lona/ n. f. canvas, tarpaulin.

longevidad /lonheβi'ðað/ n. f. longevity.

longitud /lonhi'tuð/ n. f. longitude; length.

lonja /'lonha/ n. f. shop; market.

lontananza /lonta'nanθa; lonta'nansa/ n. f. distance.

loro /'loro/ n. m. parrot.

losa /'losa/ n. f. slab.

lote /'lote/ n. m. lot, share.

lotería /lote'ria/ n. f. lottery.

loza /'loθa; 'losa/ n. f. china, crockery.

lozanía /loθa'nia; losa'nia/ n. f. freshness, vigor.

lozano /lo'θano; lo'sano/ a. fresh, spirited.

lubricación /luβrika'θion; luβrika'sion/ n. f. lubrication.

lubricar /luβri'kar/ v. lubricate.

lucero /lu'θero; lu'sero/ n. m. (bright) star.

lucha /'lutʃa/ n. f. fight, struggle; wrestling. —**luchar**, v.

luchador /lutʃa'ðor/ **-ra** n. fighter, wrestler.

lúcido /lu'θiðo; lu'siðo/ a. lucid, clear.

luciente /lu'θiente; lu'siente/ a. shining, bright.

luciérnaga /lu'θiernaga; lu'siernaga/ n. f. firefly.

lucimiento /luθi'miento; lusi'miento/ n. f. success; splendor.

lucir /lu'θir; lu'sir/ v. shine, sparkle; show off.

lucrativo /lukra'tiβo/ a. lucrative, profitable.

luego /'luego/ adv. right away; afterwards, next. **l. que**, as soon as. **desde l.,** of course. **hasta l.,** goodbye, so long.

lugar /lu'gar/ n. m. place, spot; space, room.

lúgubre /'luguβre/ a. gloomy; dismal.

lujo /'luho/ n. m. luxury. **de l.,** deluxe.

lujoso /lu'hoso/ a. luxurious.

lumbre /'lumbre/ n. f. fire; light.

luminoso /lumi'noso/ a. luminous.

luna /'luna/ n. f. moon.

lunar /lu'nar/ n. m. beauty mark, mole; polka dot.

lunático /lu'natiko/ **-ca** a. & n. lunatic.

lunes /'lunes/ n. m. Monday.

luneta /lu'neta/ n. f. *Theat.* orchestra seat.

lupa /'lupa/ n. f. magnifying glass.

lustre /'lustre/ n. m. polish, shine. —**lustrar**, v.

lustroso /lus'troso/ a. shiny.

luto /'luto/ n. m. mourning.

luz /luθ; lus/ n. f. light. **dar a l.,** give birth to.

M

maca /'maka/ n. f. blemish, flaw.

macaco /ma'kako/ a. ugly, horrid.

macareno /maka'reno/ a. boasting.

macarrones /maka'rrones/ n. m.pl. macaroni.

macear /maθe'ar; mase'ar/ v. molest, push around.

macedonia de frutas /maθe'ðonia de 'frutas; mase'ðonia de 'frutas/ n. f. fruit salad.

maceta /ma'θeta; ma'seta/ n. f. vase; mallet.

machacar /matʃa'kar/ v. pound; crush.

machina /ma'tʃina/ n. f. derrick.

machista /ma'tʃista/ a. macho.

macho /'matʃo/ n. m. male.

machucho /ma'tʃutʃo/ a. mature, wise.

macizo /ma'θiθo; ma'siso/ a. **1.** solid. —n. **2.** m. bulk; flower bed.

macular /maku'lar/ v. stain.

madera /ma'ðera/ n. f. lumber; wood.

madero /ma'ðero/ n. m. beam, timber.

madrastra /ma'ðrastra/ n. f. stepmother.

madre /'maðre/ n. f. mother. **m. política,** mother-in-law.

madreperla /maðre'perla/ n. f. mother-of-pearl.

madriguera /maðri'gera/ n. f. burrow; lair, den.

madrina /ma'ðrina/ n. f. godmother.

madroncillo /maðron'θiʎo; maðron'siyo/ n. m. strawberry.

madrugada /maðru'gaða/ n. f. daybreak.

madrugar /maðru'gar/ v. get up early.

madurar /maðu'rar/ v. ripen.

madurez /maðu'reθ; maðu'res/ n. f. maturity.

maduro /ma'ðuro/ a. ripe; mature.

maestría /maes'tria/ n. f. mastery; master's degree.

maestro /ma'estro/ n. m. master; teacher.

mafia /'mafia/ n. f. mafia.

maganto /ma'ganto/ a. lethargic, dull.

magia /'mahia/ n. f. magic.

mágico /'mahiko/ a. & m. magic; magician.

magistrado /mahis'traðo/ n. m. magistrate.

magnánimo /mag'nanimo/ a. magnanimous.

magnético /mag'netiko/ a. magnetic.

magnetismo /magne'tismo/ n. m. magnetism.

magnetófono /magne'tofono/ n. m. tape recorder.

magnificar /magnifi'kar/ v. magnify.

magnificencia /magnifi'θenθia; magnifi'sensia/ n. f. magnificence.

magnífico /mag'nifiko/ a. magnificent.

magnitud /magni'tuð/ n. f. magnitude.

magno /'magno/ a. great, grand.

magnolia /mag'nolia/ n. f. magnolia.

mago /'mago/ n. m. magician; wizard.

magosto /ma'gosto/ n. m. chestnut roast; picnic fire for roasting chestnuts.

magro /'magro/ a. meager; thin.

magullar /magu'ʎar; magu'yar/ v. bruise.

mahometano /maome'tano/ n. & a. Mohammedan.

mahometismo /maome'tismo/ n. m. Mohammedanism.

maíz /ma'iθ; ma'is/ n. m. corn.

majadero /maha'ðero/ **-ra** a. & n. foolish; fool.

majar /ma'har/ v. mash.

majestad /mahes'tað/ n. f. majesty.

majestuoso /mahes'tuoso/ a. majestic.

mal /mal/ adv. **1.** badly; wrong. —n. **2.** m. evil, ill; illness.

mala /'mala/ n. f. mail.

malacate /mala'kate/ n. m. hoist.

malandanza /malan'danθa; malan'dansa/ n. f. misfortune.

malaventura /malaβen'tura/ n. f. misfortune.

malcomido /malko'miðo/ a. underfed; malnourished.

malcontento /malkon'tento/ a. dissatisfied.

maldad /mal'dað/ n. f. badness; wickedness.

maldecir /malde'θir; malde'sir/ v. curse, damn.

maldición /maldi'θion; maldi'sion/ n. f. curse.

maldito /mal'dito/ a. accursed, damned.

malecón /male'kon/ n. m. embankment.

maledicencia /maleði'θenθia; maleði'sensia/ n. f. slander.

maleficio /male'fiθio; male'fisio/ n. m. spell, charm.

malestar /males'tar/ n. m. indisposition.

maleta /ma'leta/ n. f. suitcase, valise.

malévolo /ma'leβolo/ a. malevolent.

maleza /ma'leθa; ma'lesa/ n. f. weeds; underbrush.

malgastar /malgas'tar/ v. squander.

malhechor /male'tʃor/ **-ra** n. malefactor, evildoer.

malhumorado /malumo'raðo/ a. morose, ill-humored.

malicia /ma'liθia; ma'lisia/ *n. f.* malice.

maliciar /mali'θiar; mali'siar/ *v.* suspect.

malicioso /mali'θioso; mali'sioso/ *a.* malicious.

maligno /ma'ligno/ *a.* malignant, evil.

malla /'maʎa; 'maya/ *n. f.* mesh, net.

mallas /'maʎas; 'mayas/ *n. f.pl.* leotard.

mallete /ma'ʎete; ma'yete/ *n. m.* mallet.

malo /'malo/ *a.* bad; evil, wicked; naughty; ill.

malograr /malo'grar/ *v.* miss, lose.

malparto /mal'parto/ *n. m.* abortion, miscarriage.

malquerencia /malke'renθia; malke-'rensia/ *n. f.* hatred.

malquerer /malke'rer/ *v.* dislike; bear ill will.

malsano /mal'sano/ *a.* unhealthy; unwholesome.

malsín /mal'sin/ *n. m.* malicious gossip.

malta /'malta/ *n. f.* malt.

maltratar /maltra'tar/ *v.* mistreat.

malvado /mal'βaðo/ **-da** *a.* **1.** wicked. —*n.* **2.** villain.

malversar /malßer'sar/ *v.* embezzle.

malvís /mal'βis/ *n. m.* redwing.

mamá /'mama/ *n. f.* mama, mother.

mamar /ma'mar/ *v.* suckle; suck.

mamífero /ma'mifero/ *n. m.* mammal.

mampara /mam'para/ *n. f.* screen.

mampostería /mamposte'ria/ *n. f.* masonry.

mamut /ma'mut/ *n. m.* mammoth.

manada /ma'naða/ *n. f.* flock, herd, drove.

manantial /manan'tial/ *n. m.* spring (of water).

manar /ma'nar/ *v.* gush, flow out.

mancebo /man'θeβo; man'seβo/ *n. m.* young man.

mancha /'mantʃa/ *n. f.* stain, smear, ble spot. —**manchar,** *v.*

mancilla /man'θiʎa; man'siya/ *n. f.* stain; blemish.

manco /'manko/ *a.* armless; one-armed.

mandadero /manda'ðero/ *n. m.* messenger.

mandado /man'daðo/ *n. m.* order, command.

mandamiento /manda'miento/ *n. m.* commandment; command.

mandar /man'dar/ *v.* send; order, command.

mandatario /manda'tario/ *n. m.* attorney; representative.

mandato /man'dato/ *n. m.* mandate, command.

mandíbula /man'diβula/ *n. f.* jaw; jawbone.

mando /'mando/ *n. m.* command, order; leadership.

mando a distancia /'mando a dis'tanθia; 'mando a dis'tansia/ remote control.

mandón /man'don/ *a.* domineering.

mandril /man'dril/ *n. m.* baboon.

manejar /mane'har/ *v.* handle, manage; drive (a car).

manejo /ma'neho/ *n. m.* management; horsemanship.

manera /ma'nera/ *n. f.* way, manner, means. **de m. que,** so, as a result.

manga /'manga/ *n. f.* sleeve.

mangana /maŋ'gana/ *n. f.* lariat, lasso.

manganeso /maŋga'neso/ *n. m.* manganese.

mango /'mango/ *n. m.* handle; mango (fruit).

mangosta /maŋ'gosta/ *n. f.* mongoose.

manguera /maŋ'guera/ *n. f.* hose.

manguito /maŋ'guito/ *n. m.* muff.

maní /ma'ni/ *n. m.* peanut.

manía /ma'nia/ *n. f.* mania, madness; hobby.

maníaco /ma'niako/ **-ca, maniático -ca** *a. & n.* maniac.

manicomio /mani'komio/ *n. m.* insane asylum.

manicura /mani'kura/ *n. f.* manicure.

manifactura /manifak'tura/ *n. f.* manufacture.

manifestación /manifesta'θion; manifesta'sion/ *n. f.* manifestation.

manifestar /manifes'tar/ *v.* manifest, show.

manifiesto /mani'fiesto/ *a. & m.* manifest.

manija /ma'niha/ *n. f.* handle; crank.

maniobra /ma'nioβra/ *n. f.* maneuver. —**maniobrar,** *v.*

manipulación /manipula'θion; manipula'sion/ *n. f.* manipulation.

manipular /manipu'lar/ *v.* manipulate.

maniquí /mani'ki/ *n. m.* mannequin.

manivela /mani'βela/ *n. f. Mech.* crank.

manjar /man'har/ *n. m.* food, dish.

manlieve /man'lieβe/ *n. m.* swindle.

mano /'mano/ *n. f.* hand.

manojo /ma'noho/ *n. m.* handful; bunch.

manómetro /ma'nometro/ *n. m.* gauge.

manopla /ma'nopla/ *n. f.* gauntlet.

manosear /manose'ar/ *v.* handle, feel, touch.

manotada /mano'taða/ *n. f.* slap, smack. —**manotear,** *v.*

mansedumbre /manse'ðumbre/ *n. f.* meekness, tameness.

mansión /man'sion/ *n. f.* mansion; abode.

manso /'manso/ *a.* tame, gentle.

manta /'manta/ *n. f.* blanket.

manteca /man'teka/ *n. f.* fat, lard; butter.

mantecado /mante'kaðo/ *n. m.* ice cream.

mantecoso /mante'koso/ *a.* buttery.

mantel /man'tel/ *n. m.* tablecloth.

mantener /mante'ner/ *v.* maintain, keep; sustain; support.

mantenimiento /manteni'miento/ *n. m.* maintenance.

mantequera /mante'kera/ *n. f.* butter dish; churn.

mantequilla /mante'kiʎa; mante'kiya/ *n. f.* butter.

mantilla /man'tiʎa; man'tiya/ *n. f.* mantilla; baby clothes.

mantillo /man'tiʎo; man'tiyo/ *n. m.* humus; manure.

manto /'manto/ *n. m.* mantle, cloak.

manual /ma'nual/ *a. & m.* manual.

manubrio /ma'nuβrio/ *n. m.* handle; crank.

manufacturar /manufaktu'rar/ *v.* manufacture; make.

manuscrito /manus'krito/ *n. m.* manuscript.

manzana /man'θana; man'sana/ *n. f.* apple; block (of street).

manzanilla /manθa'niʎa; mansa'niya/ *n. f.* dry sherry.

manzano /man'θano; man'sano/ *n. m.* apple tree.

maña /'maɲa/ *n. f.* skill; cunning; trick.

mañana /ma'ɲana/ *adv.* **1.** tomorrow. —*n.* **2.** *f.* morning.

mañanear /maɲane'ar/ *v.* rise early in the morning.

mañero /ma'ɲero/ *a.* clever; skillful; lazy.

mapa /'mapa/ *n. m.* map, chart.

mapache /ma'patʃe/ *n. m.* raccoon.

mapurito /mapu'rito/ *n. m.* skunk.

máquina /'makina/ *n. f.* machine. **m. de coser,** sewing machine. **m. de lavar,** washing machine.

maquinación /makina'θion; makina-'sion/ *n. f.* machination; plot.

maquinador /makina'ðor/ **-ra** *n. m.* plotter, schemer.

maquinal /maki'nal/ *a.* mechanical.

maquinar /maki'nar/ *v.* scheme, plot.

maquinaria /maki'naria/ *n. f.* machinery.

maquinista /maki'nista/ *n. m.* machinist; engineer.

mar /mar/ *n. m. or f.* sea.

marabú /mara'βu/ *n. m.* marabou.

maraña /ma'raɲa/ *n. f.* tangle; maze; snarl; plot.

maravilla /mara'βiʎa; mara'βiya/ *n. f.* marvel, wonder. —**maravillarse,** *v.*

maravilloso /maraβi'ʎoso; maraβi-'yoso/ *a.* marvelous, wonderful.

marbete /mar'βete/ *n. m.* tag, label; check.

marca /'marka/ *n. f.* mark, sign; brand, make.

marcador /marka'ðor/ *n. m.* highlighter.

marcapáginas /marka'pahinas/ *n. m.* bookmark.

marcar /mar'kar/ *v.* mark; observe, note.

marcha /'martʃa/ *n. f.* march; progress. —**marchar,** *v.*

marchante /mar'tʃante/ *n. m.* merchant; customer.

marcharse /mar'tʃarse/ *v.* go away, depart.

marchitable /martʃi'taβle/ *a.* perishable.

marchitar /martʃi'tar/ *v.* fade, wilt, wither.

marchito /mar'tʃito/ *a.* faded, withered.

marcial /mar'θial; mar'sial/ *a.* martial.

marco /'marko/ *n. m.* frame.

marea /ma'rea/ *n. f.* tide.

mareado /mare'aðo/ *a.* seasick.

marearse /mare'arse/ *v.* get dizzy; be seasick.

mareo /ma'reo/ *n. m.* dizziness; seasickness.

marfil /mar'fil/ *n. m.* ivory.

margarita /marga'rita/ *n. f.* pearl; daisy.

margen /'marhen/ *n. m. or f.* margin, edge, rim.

marido /ma'riðo/ *n. m.* husband.

marijuana /mari'huana/ *n. f.* marijuana.

marimacha /mari'matʃa/ *n. f.* lesbian.

marimacho /mari'matʃo/ *n. m.* mannish woman.

marimba /ma'rimba/ *n. f.* marimba.

marina /ma'rina/ *n. f.* navy; seascape.

marinero /mari'nero/ *n. m.* sailor, seaman.

marino /ma'rino/ *a. & m.* marine, (of) sea; mariner, seaman.

marión /ma'rion/ *n. m.* sturgeon.

mariposa /mari'posa/ *n. f.* butterfly.

mariquita /mari'kita/ *n. f.* ladybird.

mariscal /maris'kal/ *n. m.* marshal.

marisco /ma'risko/ *n. m.* shellfish; mollusk.

marital /mari'tal/ *a.* marital.

marítimo /ma'ritimo/ *a.* maritime.

marmita /mar'mita/ *n. f.* pot, kettle.

mármol /'marmol/ *n. m.* marble.

marmóreo /mar'moreo/ *a.* marble.

maroma /ma'roma/ *n. f.* rope.

marqués /mar'kes/ *n. m.* marquis.

marquesa /mar'kesa/ *n. f.* marquise.

Marruecos /ma'rruekos/ *n. m.* Morocco.

Marte /'marte/ *n. m.* Mars.

martes /'martes/ *n. m.* Tuesday.

martillo /mar'tiʎo; mar'tiyo/ *n. m.* hammer. —**martillar,** *v.*

mártir /'martir/ *n. m. & f.* martyr.

martirio /mar'tirio/ *n. m.* martyrdom.

martirizar /martiri'θar; martiri'sar/ *v.* martyrize.

marzo /'marθo; 'marso/ *n. m.* March.

mas /mas/ *conj.* but.

más /mas/ *a. & adv.* more, most; plus. **no m.,** only; no more.

masa /'masa/ *n. f.* mass; dough.

masaje /ma'sahe/ *n. m.* massage.

mascar /mas'kar/ *v.* chew.

máscara /'maskara/ *n. f.* mask.

mascarada /maska'raða/ *n. f.* masquerade.

mascota /mas'kota/ *n. f.* mascot; good-luck charm.

masculino /masku'lino/ *a.* masculine.

mascullar /masku'ʎar; masku'yar/ *v.* mumble.

masón /ma'son/ *n. m.* Freemason.

masticar /masti'kar/ *v.* chew.

mástil /'mastil/ *n. m.* mast; post.

mastín /mas'tin/ *n. m.* mastiff.

mastín danés /mas'tin da'nes/ Great Dane.

mastuerzo /mas'tuerθo; mas'tuerso/ *n. m.* fool, ninny.

mata /'mata/ *n. f.* plant; bush.

matadero /mata'ðero/ *n. m.* slaughterhouse.

matador /mata'ðor/ **-ra** *n.* matador.

matafuego /mata'fuego/ *n. m.* fire extinguisher.

matanza /ma'tanθa; ma'tansa/ *n. f.* killing, bloodshed, slaughter.

matar /ma'tar/ *v.* kill, slay; slaughter.

matasanos /mata'sanos/ *n. m.* quack.

mate /'mate/ *n. m.* checkmate; Paraguayan tea.

matemáticas /mate'matikas/ *n. f.pl.* mathematics.

matemático /mate'matiko/ *a.* mathematical.

materia /ma'teria/ *n. f.* material; subject (matter).

material /mate'rial/ *a. & m.* material.

materialismo /materia'lismo/ *n. m.* materialism.

materializar /materiali'θar; materiali'sar/ *v.* materialize.

maternal /mater'nal/ **materno** *a.* maternal.

maternidad /materni'ðað/ *n. f.* maternity; maternity hospital.

matiné /mati'ne/ *n. f.* matinee.

matiz /ma'tiθ; ma'tis/ *n. m.* hue, shade.

matizar /mati'θar; mati'sar/ *v.* blend; tint.

matón /ma'ton/ *n. m.* bully.

matorral /mato'rral/ *n. m.* thicket.

matoso /ma'toso/ *a.* weedy.

matraca /ma'traka/ *n. f.* rattle. —**matraquear,** *v.*

matrícula /ma'trikula/ *n. f.* registration; tuition.

matricularse /matriku'larse/ *v.* enroll, register.

matrimonio /matri'monio/ *n. m.* matrimony, marriage; married couple.

matriz /ma'triθ; ma'tris/ *n. f.* womb; *Mech.* die, mold.

matrona /ma'trona/ *n. f.* matron.

maullar /mau'ʎar; mau'yar/ *v.* mew.

máxima /'maksima/ *n. f.* maxim.

máxime /'maksime/ *a.* principally.

máximo /'maksimo/ *a. & m.* maximum.

maya /'maya/ *n. f.* daisy.

mayo /'mayo/ *n. m.* May.

mayonesa /mayo'nesa/ *n. f.* mayonnaise.

mayor /ma'yor/ *a.* larger, largest; greater, greatest; elder, eldest, senior. **m. de edad,** major, of age. **al por m.,** at wholesale. *m.* major.

mayoral /mayo'ral/ *n. m.* head shepherd; boss; foreman.

mayordomo /mayor'ðomo/ *n. m.* manager; butler, steward.

mayoría /mayo'ria/ *n. f.* majority, bulk.

mayorista /mayo'rista/ *n. m. & f.* wholesaler.

mayúscula /ma'yuskula/ *n. f.* capital letter, upper-case letter.

mazmorra /maθ'morra; mas'morra/ *n. f.* dungeon.

mazorca /ma'θorka; ma'sorka/ *n. f.* ear of corn.

me /me/ *pron.* me; myself.

mecánico /me'kaniko/ **-ca** *a. & n.* mechanical; mechanic.

mecanismo /meka'nismo/ n. m. mechanism.

mecanizar /mekani'θar; mekani'sar/ v. mechanize.

mecanografía /mekanogra'fia/ n. f. typewriting.

mecanógrafo /meka'nografo/ **-fa** n. typist.

mecedor /meθe'ðor; mese'ðor/ n. m. swing.

mecedora /meθe'ðora; mese'ðora/ n. f. rocking chair.

mecer /me'θer; me'ser/ v. rock; swing, sway.

mecha /'metʃa/ n. f. wick; fuse.

mechón /me'tʃon/ n. m. lock (of hair).

medalla /me'ðaʎa; me'ðaya/ n. f. medal.

médano /'meðano/ n. m. sand dune.

media /'meðia/ n. f. stocking.

mediación /meðia'θion; meðia'sion/ n. f. mediation.

mediador /meðia'ðor/ **-ra** n. mediator.

mediados /me'ðiaðos/ n. m.pl. **a m. de,** about the middle of (a period of time).

medianero /meðia'nero/ n. m. mediator.

medianía /meðia'nia/ n. f. mediocrity.

mediano /me'ðiano/ a. medium; moderate; mediocre.

medianoche /meðia'notʃe/ n. f. midnight.

mediante /me'ðiante/ prep. by means of.

mediar /me'ðiar/ v. mediate.

medicamento /meðika'mento/ n. m. medicine, drug.

medicastro /meði'kastro/ n. m. quack.

medicina /meði'θina; meði'sina/ n. f. medicine.

medicinar /meðiθi'nar; meðisi'nar/ v. treat (as a doctor).

médico /'meðiko/ a. **1.** medical. —n. **2.** m. & f. doctor, physician.

medida /me'ðiða/ n. f. measure, step.

medidor /meði'ðor/ n. m. meter.

medieval /meðie'βal/ a. medieval.

medio /'meðio/ a. **1.** half; mid, middle of. —n. **2.** m. middle; means.

mediocre /me'ðiokre/ a. mediocre.

mediocridad /meðiokri'ðað/ n. f. mediocrity.

mediodía /meðio'ðia/ n. m. midday, noon.

medir /me'ðir/ v. measure, gauge.

meditación /meðita'θion; meðita'sion/ n. f. meditation.

meditar /meði'tar/ v. meditate.

mediterráneo /meðite'rraneo/ a. Mediterranean.

medrar /me'ðrar/ v. thrive; grow.

medroso /me'ðroso/ a. fearful, cowardly.

megáfono /me'gafono/ n. m. megaphone.

megahercio /mega'erθio; mega'ersio/ n. f. megahertz.

mejicano /mehi'kano/ **-na** a. & n. Mexican.

mejilla /me'hiʎa; me'hiya/ n. f. cheek.

mejillón /mehi'ʎon; mehi'yon/ n. m. mussel.

mejor /me'hor/ a. & adv. better; best. **a lo m.,** perhaps.

mejora /me'hora/ n. f., **mejoramiento,** m. improvement.

mejorar /meho'rar/ v. improve, better.

mejoría /meho'ria/ n. f. improvement; superiority.

melancolía /melanko'lia/ n. f. melancholy.

melancólico /melan'koliko/ a. melancholy.

melaza /me'laθa; me'lasa/ n. f. molasses.

melena /me'lena/ n. f. mane; long or loose hair.

melenudo /mele'nuðo/ **-da** a. long-haired.

melindroso /melin'droso/ a. fussy.

mella /'meʎa; 'meya/ n. f. notch; dent. —**mellar,** v.

mellizo /me'ʎiθo; me'yiso/ **-za** n. & a. twin.

melocotón /meloko'ton/ n. m. peach.

melodía /melo'ðia/ n. f. melody.

melodioso /melo'ðioso/ a. melodious.

melón /me'lon/ n. m. melon.

meloso /me'loso/ a. like honey.

membrana /mem'brana/ n. f. membrane.

membrete /mem'brete/ n. m. memorandum; letterhead.

membrillo /mem'briʎo; mem'briyo/ n. m. quince.

membrudo /mem'bruðo/ a. strong, muscular.

memorable /memo'raβle/ a. memorable.

memorándum /memo'randum/ n. m. memorandum; notebook.

memoria /me'moria/ n. f. memory; memoir; memorandum.

mención /men'θion; men'sion/ n. f. mention. —**mencionar,** v.

mendigar /mendi'gar/ v. beg (for alms).

mendigo /men'digo/ **-a** n. beggar.

mendrugo /men'drugo/ n. m. (hard) crust, chunk.

menear /mene'ar/ v. shake, wag; stir.

menester /menes'ter/ n. m. need, want; duty, task. **ser m.,** to be necessary.

menesteroso /meneste'roso/ a. needy.

mengua /'mengua/ n. f. decrease; lack; poverty.

menguar /men'guar/ v. abate, decrease.

meningitis /menin'xitis/ n. f. meningitis.

menopausia /meno'pausia/ n. f. menopause.

menor /me'nor/ a. smaller, smallest; lesser, least; younger, youngest, junior. **m. de edad,** minor, under age. **al por m.,** at retail.

menos /'menos/ a. & adv. less, least; minus. **a m. que,** unless. **echar de m.,** to miss.

menospreciar /menospre'θiar; menospre'siar/ v. cheapen; despise; slight.

mensaje /men'sahe/ n. m. message.

mensajero /mensa'hero/ **-ra** n. messenger.

menstruar /menstru'ar/ v. menstruate.

mensual /men'sual/ a. monthly.

mensualidad /mensuali'ðað/ n. f. monthly income or allowance; monthly payment.

menta /'menta/ n. f. mint, peppermint.

mentado /men'taðo/ a. famous.

mental /men'tal/ a. mental.

mentalidad /mentali'ðað/ n. f. mentality.

menta romana /'menta rro'mana/ spearmint.

mente /'mente/ n. f. mind.

mentecato /mente'kato/ a. foolish, stupid.

mentir /men'tir/ v. lie, tell a lie.

mentira /men'tira/ n. f. lie, falsehood. **parece m.,** it seems impossible.

mentiroso /menti'roso/ a. lying, untruthful.

mentol /men'tol/ n. m. menthol.

menú /me'nu/ n. m. menu.

menudeo /menu'ðeo/ n. m. retail.

menudo /menu'ðo/ a. small, minute. **a m.,** often.

meñique /me'ɲike/ a. tiny.

meple /'meple/ n. m. maple.

merca /'merka/ n. f. purchase.

mercader /merka'ðer/ n. m. merchant.

mercaderías /merkaðe'rias/ n. f.pl. merchandise, commodities.

mercado /mer'kaðo/ n. m. market.

Mercado Común /mer'kaðo ko'mun/ Common Market.

mercado negro /mer'kaðo 'negro/ black market.

mercancía /merkan'θia; merkan'sia/ n. f. merchandise; (pl.) wares.

mercante /mer'kante/ a. merchant.

mercantil /merkan'til/ a. mercantile.

merced /mer'θeð; mer'seð/ n. f. mercy, grace.

mercenario /merθe'nario; merse'nario/ **-ria** a. & n. mercenary.

mercurio /mer'kurio/ n. m. mercury.

merecedor /mereθe'ðor; merese'ðor/ a. worthy.

merecer /mere'θer; mere'ser/ v. merit, deserve.

merecimiento /mereθi'miento; meresi'miento/ n. m. merit.

merendar /meren'dar/ v. eat lunch; snack.

merendero /meren'dero/ n. m. lunchroom.

meridional /meriðio'nal/ a. southern.

merienda /me'rienda/ n. f. midday meal, lunch; afternoon snack.

mérito /'merito/ n. m. merit, worth.

meritorio /meri'torio/ a. meritorious.

merla /'merla/ n. f. blackbird.

merluza /mer'luθa; mer'lusa/ n. f. haddock.

mermelada /merme'laða/ n. f. marmalade.

mero /'mero/ a. mere.

merodeador /meroðea'ðor/ **-ra** n. prowler.

mes /'mes/ n. m. month.

mesa /'mesa/ n. f. table.

meseta /me'seta/ n. f. plateau.

mesón /me'son/ n. m. inn.

mesonero /meso'nero/ **-ra** n. innkeeper.

mestizo /mes'tiθo; mes'tiso/ **-za** a. & n. half-caste.

meta /'meta/ n. f. goal, objective.

metabolismo /metaβo'lismo/ n. m. metabolism.

metafísica /meta'fisika/ n. f. metaphysics.

metáfora /me'tafora/ n. f. metaphor.

metal /me'tal/ n. m. metal.

metálico /me'taliko/ a. metallic.

metalurgia /metalur'hia/ n. f. metallurgy.

meteoro /mete'oro/ n. m. meteor.

meteorología /meteorolo'hia/ n. f. meteorology.

meter /me'ter/ v. put (in).

meterse /me'terse/ v. interfere, meddle; go into.

metódico /me'toðiko/ a. methodic.

método /'metoðo/ n. m. method, approach.

metralla /me'traʎa; me'traya/ n. f. shrapnel.

métrico /'metriko/ a. metric.

metro /'metro/ n. m. meter (measure); subway.

metrópoli /me'tropoli/ n. f. metropolis.

mexicano /meksi'kano/ **-na** a. & n. Mexican.

mezcla /'meθkla; 'meskla/ n. f. mixture; blend.

mezclar /meθ'klar; mes'klar/ v. mix; blend.

mezcolanza /meθko'lanθa; mesko'lansa/ n. f. mixture; hodgepodge.

mezquino /meθ'kino; mes'kino/ a. stingy; petty.

mezquita /meθ'kita; mes'kita/ n. f. mosque.

mi /'mi/ a. my.

mí /'mi/ pron. me; myself.

microbio /mi'kroβio/ n. m. microbe, germ.

microbús /mikro'βus/ n. m. minibus.

microchip /mikro'tʃip/ n. m. microchip.

microficha /mikro'fitʃa/ n. f. microfiche.

micrófono /mi'krofono/ n. m. microphone.

microforma /mikro'forma/ n. f. microform.

microscópico /mikros'kopiko/ a. microscopic.

microscopio /mikros'kopio/ n. m. microscope.

microtaxi /mikro'taksi/ n. m. minicab.

miedo /'mieðo/ n. m. fear. **tener m.,** fear, be afraid.

miedoso /mie'ðoso/ a. fearful.

miel /miel/ n. f. honey.

miembro /mi'embro/ n. m. & f. member; limb.

mientras /'mientras/ conj. while. **m. tanto,** meanwhile. **m. más... más,** the more... the more.

miércoles /'mierkoles/ n. m. Wednesday.

miércoles de ceniza /'mierkoles de θe'niθa; 'mierkoles de se'nisa/ Ash Wednesday.

miga /'miga/ **migaja** n. f. scrap; crumb.

migración /migra'θion; migra'sion/ n. f. migration.

migratorio /migra'torio/ a. migratory.

mil /mil/ a. & pron. thousand.

milagro /mi'lagro/ n. m. miracle.

milagroso /mila'groso/ a. miraculous.

milicia /mi'liθia; mi'lisia/ n. f. militia.

militante /mili'tante/ a. militant.

militar /mili'tar/ a. **1.** military. —n. **2.** m. military man.

militarismo /milita'rismo/ n. m. militarism.

milla /'miʎa; 'miya/ n. f. mile.

millar /mi'ʎar; mi'yar/ n. m. (a) thousand.

millón /mi'ʎon; mi'yon/ n. m. million.

millonario /miʎo'nario; miyo'nario/ **-ria** n. millionaire.

mimar /mi'mar/ v. pamper, spoil (a child).

mimbre /'mimbre/ n. m. willow; wicker.

mímico /'mimiko/ a. mimic.

mimo /'mimo/ n. m. mime, mimic.

mina /'mina/ n. f. mine. —**minar,** v.

mineral /mine'ral/ a. & m. mineral.

minero /mi'nero/ **-ra** n. miner.

miniatura /minia'tura/ n. f. miniature.

miniaturizar /miniaturi'θar; miniaturi'sar/ v. miniaturize.

mínimo /'minimo/ a. & m. minimum.

ministerio /minis'terio/ n. m. ministry; cabinet.

ministro /mi'nistro/ **-a** n. Govt. minister, secretary.

minoría /mino'ria/ n. f. minority.

minoridad /minori'ðað/ n. f. minority (of age).

minucioso /minu'θioso; minu'sioso/ a. minute; thorough.

minué /mi'nue/ n. m. minuet.

minúscula /mi'nuskula/ n. f. lowercase letter, small letter.

minuta /mi'nuta/ n. f. draft.

mío /'mio/ a. mine.

miopía /mio'pia/ n. f. myopia.

mira /'mira/ n. f. gunsight.

mirada /mi'raða/ n. f. look; gaze, glance.

miramiento /mira'miento/ n. m. consideration; respect.

mirar /mi'rar/ v. look, look at; watch. **m. a,** face.

miríada /mi'riaða/ n. f. myriad.

mirlo /'mirlo/ n. m. blackbird.

mirón /mi'ron/ **-ona** n. bystander, observer.

mirra /'mirra/ n. f. myrrh.

mirto /'mirto/ n. m. myrtle.

misa /'misa/ *n. f.* mass, church service.

misceláneo /misθe'laneo; misse'laneo/ *a.* miscellaneous.

miserable /mise'raβle/ *a.* miserable, wretched.

miseria /mi'seria/ *n. f.* misery.

misericordia /miseri'korδia/ *n. f.* mercy.

misericordioso /miserikor'δioso/ *a.* merciful.

misión /mi'sion/ *n. f.* assignment; mission.

misionario /misio'nario/ **-ria, misionero -ra** *n.* missionary.

mismo /'mismo/ *a. & pron.* **1.** same; -self, -selves. —*adv.* **2.** right, exactly.

misterio /mis'terio/ *n. m.* mystery.

misterioso /miste'rioso/ *a.* mysterious, weird.

místico /'mistiko/ **-ca** *a. & n.* mystical, mystic.

mitad /mi'taδ/ *n. f.* half.

mítico /'mitiko/ *a.* mythical.

mitigar /miti'gar/ *v.* mitigate.

mitin /'mitin/ *n. m.* meeting; rally.

mito /'mito/ *n. m.* myth.

mitón /mi'ton/ *n. m.* mitten.

mitra /'mitra/ *n. f.* miter (bishop's).

mixto /'miksto/ *a.* mixed.

mixtura /miks'tura/ *n. f.* mixture.

mobiliario /moβi'liario/ *n. m.* household goods.

mocasín /moka'sin/ *n. m.* moccasin.

mocedad /moθe'δaδ; mose'δaδ/ *n. f.* youthfulness.

mochila /mo'tʃila/ *n. f.* knapsack, backpack.

mocho /'motʃo/ *a.* cropped, trimmed, shorn.

moción /mo'θion; mo'sion/ *n. f.* motion.

mocoso /mo'koso/ **-sa** *n.* brat.

moda /'moδa/ *n. f.* mode, fashion, style.

modales /mo'δales/ *n. m.pl.* manners.

moďelo /mo'δelo/ *n. m.* model, pattern.

módem /'moδem/ *n. m.* modem.

moderación /moδera'θion; moδera'sion/ *n. f.* moderation.

moderado /moδe'raδo/ *a.* moderate. —**moderar,** *v.*

modernizar /moδerni'θar; moδerni'sar/ *v.* modernize.

moderno /mo'δerno/ *a.* modern.

modestia /mo'δestia/ *n. f.* modesty.

modesto /mo'δesto/ *a.* modest.

módico /'moδiko/ *a.* reasonable, moderate.

modificación /moδifi'kaθion; moδifika'sion/ *n. f.* modification.

modificar /moδifi'kar/ *v.* modify.

modismo /mo'δismo/ *n. m. Gram.* idiom.

modista /mo'δista/ *n. f.* dressmaker; milliner.

modo /'moδo/ *n. m.* way, means.

modular /moδu'lar/ *v.* modulate.

mofarse /mo'farse/ *v.* scoff, sneer.

mofletudo /mofle'tuδo/ *a.* fat-cheeked.

mohín /mo'in/ *n. m.* grimace.

moho /'moo/ *n. m.* mold, mildew.

mohoso /mo'oso/ *a.* moldy.

mojar /mo'har/ *v.* wet.

mojón /mo'hon/ *n. m.* landmark; heap.

molde /'molde/ *n. m.* mold, form.

molécula /mo'lekula/ *n. f.* molecule.

moler /mo'ler/ *v.* grind, mill.

molestar /moles'tar/ *v.* molest, bother, disturb, annoy, trouble.

molestia /mo'lestia/ *n. f.* bother, annoyance, trouble; hassle.

molesto /mo'lesto/ *a.* bothersome; annoyed; uncomfortable.

molicie /mo'liθie; mo'lisie/ *n. f.* softness.

molinero /moli'nero/ *n. m.* miller.

molino /mo'lino/ *n. m.* mill. **m. de viento,** windmill.

mollera /mo'ʎera; mo'yera/ *n. f.* top of the head.

molusco /mo'lusko/ *n. m.* mollusk.

momentáneo /momen'taneo/ *a.* momentary.

momento /mo'mento/ *n. m.* moment.

mona /'mona/ *n. f.* female monkey.

monarca /mo'narka/ *n. m. & f.* monarch.

monarquía /monar'kia/ *n. f.* monarchy.

monarquista /monar'kista/ *n. & f.* monarchist.

monasterio /mona'sterio/ *n. m.* monastery.

mondadientes /monda'δientes/ *m.* toothpick.

moneda /mo'neδa/ *n. f.* coin; money.

monetario /mone'tario/ *a.* monetary.

monición /moni'θion; moni'sion/ *n. m.* warning.

monigote /moni'gote/ *n. m.* puppet.

monja /'monha/ *n. f.* nun.

monje /'monhe/ *n. m.* monk.

mono /'mono/ **-na** *a.* **1.** *Colloq.* cute. —*n.* **2.** *m. & f.* monkey.

monólogo /mo'nologo/ *n. m.* monologue.

monopatín /monopa'tin/ *n. m.* skateboard.

monopolio /mono'polio/ *n. m.* monopoly.

monopolizar /monopoli'θar; monopoli'sar/ *v.* monopolize.

monosílabo /mono'silaβo/ *n. m.* monosyllable.

monotonía /monoto'nia/ *n. f.* monotony.

monótono /mo'notono/ *a.* monotonous, dreary.

monstruo /'monstruo/ *n. m.* monster.

monstruosidad /monstruosi'δaδ/ *n. f.* monstrosity.

monstruoso /mon'struoso/ *a.* monstrous.

monta /'monta/ *n. f.* amount; price.

montaña /mon'taɲa/ *n. f.* mountain.

montañoso /monta'ɲoso/ *a.* mountainous.

montar /mon'tar/ *v.* mount, climb; amount; *Mech.* assemble. **m. a caballo,** ride horseback.

montaraz /monta'raθ; monta'ras/ *a.* wild, barbaric.

monte /'monte/ *n. m.* mountain; forest.

montón /mon'ton/ *n. m.* heap, pile.

montuoso /mon'tuoso/ *a.* mountainous.

montura /mon'tura/ *n. f.* mount; saddle.

monumental /monumen'tal/ *a.* monumental.

monumento /monu'mento/ *n. m.* monument.

mora /'mora/ *n. f.* blackberry.

morada /mo'raδa/ *n. f.* residence, dwelling.

morado /mo'raδo/ *a.* purple.

moral /mo'ral/ *a.* **1.** moral. —*n.* **2.** morale.

moraleja /mora'leha/ *n. f.* moral.

moralidad /morali'δaδ/ *n. f.* morality, morals.

moralista /mora'lista/ *n. m. & f.* moralist.

morar /mo'rar/ *v.* dwell, live, reside.

mórbido /'morβiδo/ *a.* morbid.

mordaz /mor'δaθ; mor'δas/ *a.* caustic, sarcastic.

mordedura /morδe'δura/ *n. f.* bite.

morder /mor'δer/ *v.* bite.

moreno /mo'reno/ **-na** *a. & n.* brown; dark-skinned; dark-haired, brunette.

morfina /mor'fina/ *n. f.* morphine.

moribundo /mori'βundo/ *a.* dying.

morir /mo'rir/ *v.* die.

morisco /mo'risko/ **-ca, moro -ra** *a. & n.* Moorish; Moor.

morriña /mo'rriɲa/ *n. f.* sadness.

morro /'morro/ *n. m.* bluff; snout.

mortaja /mor'taha/ *n. f.* shroud.

mortal /mor'tal/ *a. & n.* mortal.

mortalidad /mortali'δaδ/ *n. f.* mortality.

mortero /mor'tero/ *n. m.* mortar.

mortífero /mor'tifero/ *a.* fatal, deadly.

mortificar /mortifi'kar/ *v.* mortify.

mortuorio /mor'tuorio/ *a.* funereal.

mosaico /mo'saiko/ *a. & m.* mosaic.

mosca /'moska/ *n. f.* fly.

mosquito /mos'kito/ *n. m.* mosquito.

mostacho /mos'tatʃo/ *n. m.* mustache.

mostaza /mos'taθa; mos'tasa/ *n. f.* mustard.

mostrador /mostra'δor/ *n. m.* counter; showcase.

mostrar /mos'trar/ *v.* show, display.

mote /'mote/ *n. m.* nickname; alias.

motel /mo'tel/ *n. m.* motel.

motín /mo'tin/ *n. m.* mutiny; riot.

motivo /mo'tiβo/ *n. m.* motive, reason.

motocicleta /motoθi'kleta; motosi'kleta/ *n. f.* motorcycle.

motociclista /motoθi'klista; motosi'klista/ *n. m. & f.* motorcyclist.

motor /mo'tor/ *n. m.* motor.

motorista /moto'rista/ *n. m. & f.* motorist.

movedizo /moβe'δiθo; moβe'δiso/ *a.* movable; shaky.

mover /mo'βer/ *v.* move; stir.

movible /mo'βiβle/ *a.* movable.

móvil /'moβil/ *a.* mobile.

movilización /moβiliθa'θion; moβilisa'sion/ *n. f.* mobilization.

movilizar /moβili'θar; moβili'sar/ *v.* mobilize.

movimiento /moβi'miento/ *n. m.* movement, motion.

mozo /'moθo; 'moso/ *n. m.* boy; servant, waiter, porter.

muaré /mua're/ *n. m.* moiré.

muchacha /mu'tʃatʃa/ *n. f.* girl, youngster; maid (servant).

muchachez /mutʃa'tʃeθ; mutʃa'tʃes/ *n. m.* boyhood, girlhood.

muchacho /mu'tʃatʃo/ *n. m.* boy; youngster.

muchedumbre /mutʃe'δumbre/ *n. f.* crowd, mob.

mucho /'mutʃo/ *a.* **1.** much, many. —*adv.* **2.** much.

mucoso /mu'koso/ *a.* mucous.

muda /'muδa/ *n. f.* change.

mudanza /mu'δanθa; muδansa/ *n. f.* change; change of residence.

mudar /mu'δar/ *v.* change, shift.

mudarse /mu'δarse/ *v.* change residence, move.

mudo /'muδo/ **-da** *a. & n.* mute.

mueble /'mueβle/ *n. m.* piece of furniture; (*pl.*) furniture.

mueca /'mueka/ *n. f.* grimace.

muela /'muela/ *n. f.* (back) tooth.

muelle /'mueʎe; 'mueye/ *n. m.* pier, wharf; *Mech.* spring.

muerte /'muerte/ *n. f.* death.

muerto /'muerto/ **-ta** *a.* **1.** dead. —*n.* **2.** dead person.

muesca /'mueska/ *n. f.* notch; groove.

muestra /'muestra/ *n. f.* sample, specimen; sign.

mugido /mu'hiδo/ *n. m.* lowing; mooing.

mugir /mu'hir/ *v.* low, moo.

mugre /'mugre/ *n. f.* filth, dirt.

mugriento /mu'griento/ *a.* dirty.

mujer /mu'her/ *n. f.* woman; wife. **m. de la limpieza,** cleaning lady, charwoman.

mujeril /muhe'ril/ *a.* womanly, feminine.

mula /'mula/ *n. f.* mule.

mulato /mu'lato/ **-ta** *a. & n.* mulatto.

muleta /mu'leta/ *n. f.* crutch; prop.

mulo /'mulo/ **-la** *n.* mule.

multa /'multa/ *n. f.* fine, penalty.

multicolor /multiko'lor/ *a.* many-colored.

multinacional /multinaθio'nal; multinasio'nal/ *a.* multinational.

múltiple /'multiple/ *a.* multiple.

multiplicación /multiplika'θion; multiplika'sion/ *n. f.* multiplication.

multiplicar /multipli'kar/ *v.* multiply.

multiplicidad /multipliθi'δaδ; multiplisi'δaδ/ *n. f.* multiplicity.

multitud /multi'tuδ/ *n. f.* multitude, crowd.

mundanal /munda'nal, mun'dano/ *a.* worldly.

mundano /mun'dano/ *a.* worldly, mundane.

mundial /mun'dial/ *a.* worldwide; (of the) world.

mundo /'mundo/ *n. m.* world.

munición /muni'θion; muni'sion/ *n. f.* ammunition.

municipal /muniθi'pal; munisi'pal/ *a.* municipal.

municipio /muni'θipio; muni'sipio/ *n. m.* city hall.

muñeca /mu'ɲeka/ *n. f.* doll; wrist.

muñeco /mu'ɲeko/ *n. m.* doll; puppet.

mural /mu'ral/ *a. & m.* mural.

muralla /mu'raʎa; mu'raya/ *n. f.* wall.

murciélago /mur'θielago; mur'sielago/ *n. m.* bat.

murga /'murga/ *n. f.* musical band.

murmullo /mur'muʎo; mur'muyo/ *n. m.* murmur; rustle.

murmurar /murmu'rar/ *v.* murmur; rustle; grumble.

musa /'musa/ *n. f.* muse.

muscular /musku'lar/ *a.* muscular.

músculo /'muskulo/ *n. m.* muscle.

muselina /muse'lina/ *n. f.* muslin.

museo /mu'seo/ *n. m.* museum.

música /'musika/ *n. f.* music.

musical /musi'kal/ *a.* musical.

músico /'musiko/ **-ca** *a. & n.* musical; musician.

muslo /'muslo/ *n. m.* thigh.

mustio /'mustio/ *a.* sad.

musulmano /musul'mano/ **-na** *a. & n.* Muslim.

muta /'muta/ *n. f.* pack of hounds.

mutabilidad /mutaβili'δaδ/ *n. f.* mutability.

mutación /muta'θion; muta'sion/ *n. f.* mutation.

mutilación /mutila'θion; mutila'sion/ *n. f.* mutilation.

mutilar /muti'lar/ *v.* mutilate; mangle.

mutuo /'mutuo/ *a.* mutual.

muy /'mui/ *adv.* very.

N Ñ

nabo /'naβo/ *n. m.* turnip.

nácar /'nakar/ *n. m.* mother-of-pearl.

nacarado /naka'raδo, na'kareo/ *a.* pearly.

nacer /na'θer; na'ser/ *v.* be born.

naciente /na'θiente; na'siente/ *a.* rising; nascent.

nacimiento /naθi'miento; nasi'miento/ *n. m.* birth.

nación /na'θion; na'sion/ *n. f.* nation.

nacional /naθio'nal; nasio'nal/ *a.* national.

nacionalidad /naθionali'δaδ; nasionali'δaδ/ *n. f.* nationality.

nacionalismo /naθiona'lismo; nasiona'lismo/ *n. m.* nationalism.

nacionalista /naθiona'lista; nasiona'lista/ *n. & a.* nationalist.

nacionalización /naθionaliθa'θion; nasionalisa'sion/ *n. f.* nationalization.

nacionalizar /naθionali'θar; nasionali'sar/ *v.* nationalize.

Naciones Unidas /na'θiones u'niδas; na'siones u'niδas/ *n. f.pl.* United Nations.

nada /'naδa/ *pron.* **1.** nothing; anything. **de n.,** you're welcome. —*adv.* **2.** at all.

nadador /naδa'δor/ **-ra** *n.* swimmer.

nadar /na'δar/ *v.* swim.

nadie /'naδie/ *pron.* no one, nobody; anyone, anybody.

nafta /'nafta/ *n. f.* naphtha.

naipe /'naipe/ *n. m.* (playing) card.
naranja /na'ranha/ *n. f.* orange.
naranjada /naran'haða/ *n. f.* orangeade.
naranjo /na'ranho/ *n. m.* orange tree.
narciso /nar'θiso; nar'siso/ *n. m.* daffodil; narcissus.
narcótico /nar'kotiko/ *a.* & *m.* narcotic.
nardo /'narðo/ *n. m.* spikenard.
nariz /na'riθ; na'ris/ *n. f.* nose; (*pl.*) nostrils.
narración /narra'θion; narra'sion/ *n. f.* account.
narrador /narra'ðor/ **-ra** *n.* narrator.
narrar /na'rrar/ *v.* narrate.
narrativa /narra'tiβa/ *n. f.* narrative.
nata /'nata/ *n. f.* cream.
nata batida /'nata ba'tiða/ whipped cream.
natación /nata'θion; nata'sion/ *n. f.* swimming.
natal /na'tal/ *a.* native; natal.
natalicio /nata'liθio; nata'lisio/ *n. m.* birthday.
natalidad /natali'ðað/ *n. f.* birth rate.
natillas /na'tiʎas; na'tiyas/ *n. f.pl.* custard.
nativo /na'tiβo/ *a.* native; innate.
natural /natu'ral/ *a.* **1.** natural. —*n.* **2.** *m.* & *f.* native. **3.** *m.* nature, disposition.
naturaleza /natura'leθa; natura'lesa/ *n. f.* nature.
naturalidad /naturali'ðað/ *n. f.* naturalness; nationality.
naturalista /natura'lista/ *a.* & *n.* naturalistic; naturalist.
naturalización /naturaliθa'θion; naturalisa'sion/ *n. f.* naturalization.
naturalizar /naturali'θar; naturali'sar/ *v.* naturalize.
naufragar /naufra'gar/ *v.* be shipwrecked; fail.
naufragio /nau'frahio/ *n. m.* shipwreck; disaster.
náufrago /'naufrago/ **-ga** *a.* & *n.* shipwrecked (person).
náusea /'nausea/ *n. f.* nausea.
nausear /nause'ar/ *v.* feel nauseous.
náutico /'nautiko/ *a.* nautical.
navaja /na'βaha/ *n. f.* razor; pen knife.
naval /na'βal/ *a.* naval.
navasca /na'βaska/ *n. f.* blizzard, snowstorm.
nave /'naβe/ *n. f.* ship.
nave espacial /'naβe espa'θial; 'naβe es'pasial/ spaceship.
navegable /naβe'gaβle/ *a.* navigable.
navegación /naβega'θion; naβega'sion/ *n. f.* navigation.
navegador /naβega'ðor/ **-ra** *n.* navigator.
navegante /naβe'gante/ *n. m.* & *f.* navigator.
navegar /naβe'gar/ *v.* sail; navigate.
Navidad /naβi'ðað/ *n. f.* Christmas.
navío /na'βio/ *n. m.* ship.
neblina /ne'βlina/ *n. f.* mist, fog.
nebuloso /neβu'loso/ *a.* misty; nebulous.
necedad /neθe'ðað; nese'ðað/ *n. f.* stupidity; nonsense.
necesario /neθe'sario; nese'sario/ *a.* necessary.
necesidad /neθesi'ðað; nesesi'ðað/ *n. f.* necessity, need, want.
necesitado /neθesi'taðo; nesesi'taðo/ *a.* needy, poor.
necesitar /neθesi'tar; nesesi'tar/ *v.* need.
necio /'neθio; 'nesio/ **-cia** *a.* **1.** stupid, silly. —*n.* **2.** fool.
néctar /'nektar/ *n. m.* nectar.
nectarina /nekta'rina/ *n. f.* nectarine.
nefando /ne'fando/ *a.* nefarious.
nefasto /ne'fasto/ *a.* unlucky, ill-fated.
negable /ne'gaβle/ *a.* deniable.
negación /nega'θion; nega'sion/ *n. f.* denial, negation.
negar /ne'gar/ *v.* deny.
negarse /ne'garse/ *v.* refuse, decline.
negativa /nega'tiβa/ *n. f.* negative, refusal.
negativamente /negatiβa'mente/ *adv.* negatively.
negativo /nega'tiβo/ *a.* negative.
negligencia /negli'henθia; negli'hensia/ *n. f.* negligence, neglect.
negligente /negli'hente/ *a.* negligent.
negociación /negoθia'θion; negosia'sion/ *n. f.* negotiation, deal.
negociador /negoθia'ðor; negosia'ðor/ **-ra** *n.* negotiator.
negociante /nego'θiante; nego'siante/ **-ta** *n.* businessperson.
negociar /nego'θiar; nego'siar/ *v.* negotiate, trade.
negocio /ne'goθio; ne'gosio/ *n. m.* trade; business.
negro /'negro/ **-gra** *a.* **1.** black. —*n.* **2.** *m.* Black.
nene /'nene/ **-na** *n.* baby.
neo /'neo/ **neón** *n. m.* neon.
nervio /'nerβio/ *n. m.* nerve.
nerviosamente /nerβiosa'mente/ *adv.* nervously.
nervioso /ner'βioso/ *a.* nervous.
nesciencia /nesθien'θia; nessien'sia/ *n. f.* ignorance.
nesciente /nes'θiente; nes'siente/ *a.* ignorant.
neto /'neto/ *a.* net.
neumático /neu'matiko/ *a.* **1.** pneumatic. —*n.* **2.** *m.* (pneumatic) tire.
neumático de recambio /neu'matiko de rre'kambio/ spare tire.
neumonía /neumo'nia/ *n. f.* pneumonia.
neurótico /neu'rotiko/ *a.* neurotic.
neutral /neu'tral/ *a.* neutral.
neutralidad /neutrali'ðað/ *n. f.* neutrality.
neutro /'neutro/ *a.* neuter; neutral.
neutrón /neu'tron/ *n. m.* neutron.
nevada /ne'βaða/ *n. f.* snowfall.
nevado /ne'βaðo/ *a.* snow-white; snow-capped.
nevar /ne'βar/ *v.* snow.
nevera /ne'βera/ *n. f.* icebox.
nevoso /ne'βoso/ *a.* snowy.
ni /ni/ *conj.* **1.** nor. **ni... ni,** neither... nor. —*adv.* **2.** not even.
nicho /'nitʃo/ *n. m.* recess; niche.
nido /'niðo/ *n. m.* nest.
niebla /'nieβla/ *n. f.* fog; mist.
nieto /'nieto/ **-ta** *n.* grandchild.
nieve /'nieβe/ *n. f.* snow.
nilón /ni'lon/ *n. m.* nylon.
nimio /'nimio/ *adj.* stingy.
ninfa /'ninfa/ *n. f.* nymph.
ningún /niŋ'gun/ **-no -na** *a.* & *pron.* no, none, neither (one); any, either (one).
niñera /ni'ɲera/ *n. f.* nursemaid, nanny.
niñez /ni'ɲeθ; ni'ɲes/ *n. f.* childhood.
niño /'niɲo/ **-ña 1.** *a.* **1.** young; childish; childlike. —*n.* **2.** child.
níquel /'nikel/ *n. m.* nickel.
niquelado /nike'laðo/ *a.* nickel-plated.
nítido /'nitiðo/ *a.* neat, clean, bright.
nitrato /ni'trato/ *n. m.* nitrate.
nitro /'nitro/ *n. m.* niter.
nitrógeno /ni'troheno/ *n. m.* nitrogen.
nivel /ni'βel/ *n. m.* level; grade. —**nivelar,** *v.*
no /no/ *adv.* **1.** not. **no más,** only. —*interj.* **2.** no.
noble /'noβle/ *a.* & *m.* noble; nobleman.
nobleza /no'βleθa; no'βlesa/ *n. f.* nobility; nobleness.
noche /'notʃe/ *n. f.* night; evening.
Nochebuena /notʃe'βuena/ *n. f.* Christmas Eve.
noción /no'θion; no'sion/ *n. f.* notion, idea.
nocivo /no'θiβo; no'siβo/ *a.* harmful.
noctiluca /nokti'luka/ *n. f.* glowworm.
nocturno /nok'turno/ *a.* nocturnal.
nodriza /no'ðriθa; no'ðrisa/ *n. f.* wet nurse.
no fumador /no fuma'ðor/ **-ra** *n. m.* & *f.* nonsmoker.
nogal /no'gal/ *n. m.* walnut.
nombradía /nom'βraðia/ *n. f.* fame.
nombramiento /nombra'miento/ *n. m.* appointment, nomination.
nombrar /nom'βrar/ *v.* name, appoint, nominate; mention.
nombre /'nombre/ *n. m.* name; noun.
nombre y apellidos /'nombre i ape'ʎiðos; 'nombre i ape'yiðos/ (person's) full name.
nómina /'nomina/ *n. f.* list; payroll.
nominación /nomina'θion; nomina'sion/ *n. f.* nomination.
nominal /nomi'nal/ *a.* nominal.
nominar /nomi'nar/ *v.* nominate.
non /non/ *a.* uneven, odd.
nonada /no'naða/ *n. f.* trifle.
nordeste /nor'ðeste/ *n. m.* northeast.
nórdico /'norðiko/ *a.* Nordic; northerly.
norma /'norma/ *n. f.* norm, standard.
normal /nor'mal/ *a.* normal, standard.
normalidad /normali'ðað/ *n. f.* normality.
normalizar /normali'θar; normali'sar/ *v.* normalize; standardize.
noroeste /noro'este/ *n. m.* northwest.
norte /'norte/ *n. m.* north.
norteamericano /norteameri'kano/ **-na** *a.* & *n.* North American.
Noruega /no'ruega/ *n. f.* Norway.
noruego /no'ruego/ **-ga** *a.* & *n.* Norwegian.
nos /nos/ *pron.* us; ourselves.
nosotros /no'sotros, no'sotras/ **-as** *pron.* we, us; ourselves.
nostalgia /nos'talhia/ *n. f.* nostalgia, homesickness.
nostálgico /nos'talhiko/ *a.* nostalgic.
nota /'nota/ *n. f.* note; grade, mark.
notable /no'taβle/ *a.* notable, remarkable.
notación /nota'θion; nota'sion/ *n. f.* notation; note.
notar /no'tar/ *v.* note, notice.
notario /no'tario/ **-ria** *n.* notary.
noticia /no'tiθia; no'tisia/ *n. f.* notice; piece of news; (*pl.*) news.
noticia de última hora /no'tiθia de 'ultima 'ora; no'tisia de 'ultima 'ora/ news flash.
notificación /notifika'θion; notifika'sion/ *n. f.* notification.
notificación de reclutamiento /notifika'θion de rrekluta'miento; notifika'sion de rrekluta'miento/ draft notice.
notificar /notifi'kar/ *v.* notify.
notorio /no'torio/ *a.* well-known.
novato /no'βato/ **-ta** *n.* novice.
novecientos /noβe'θientos; noβe'sientos/ *a.* & *pron.* nine hundred.
novedad /noβe'ðað/ *n. f.* novelty; piece of news.
novel /no'βel/ *a.* new; inexperienced.
novela /no'βela/ *n. f.* novel.
novelista /noβe'lista/ *n. m.* & *f.* novelist.
novena /no'βena/ *n. f.* novena.
noveno /no'βeno/ *a.* ninth.
noventa /no'βenta/ *a.* & *pron.* ninety.
novia /'noβia/ *n. f.* bride; sweetheart; fiancée.
noviazgo /no'βiaθgo; no'βiasgo/ *n. m.* engagement.
novicio /no'βiθio; no'βisio/ **-cia** *n.* novice, beginner.
noviembre /no'βiembre/ *n. m.* November.
novilla /no'βiʎa; no'βiya/ *n. f.* heifer.
novio /'noβio/ *n. m.* bridegroom; sweetheart; fiancé.
nube /'nuβe/ *n. f.* cloud.
núbil /'nuβil/ *a.* marriageable.
nublado /nu'βlaðo/ *a.* cloudy.
nuclear /nukle'ar/ *a.* nuclear.
núcleo /'nukleo/ *n. m.* nucleus.
nudo /'nuðo/ *n. m.* knot.
nuera /'nuera/ *n. f.* daughter-in-law.
nuestro /'nuestro/ *a.* our, ours.
nueva /'nueβa/ *n. f.* news.
nueve /'nueβe/ *a.* & *pron.* nine.
nuevo /'nueβo/ *a.* new. **de n.,** again, anew.
nuez /nueθ; nues/ *n. f.* nut; walnut.
nulidad /nuli'ðað/ *n. f.* nonentity; nullity.
nulo /'nulo/ *a.* null, void.
numeración /numera'θion; numera'sion/ *n. f.* numeration.
numerar /nume'rar/ *v.* number.
numérico /nu'meriko/ *a.* numerical.
número /'numero/ *n. m.* number; size (of shoe, etc.) **n. impar,** odd number. **n. par,** even number.
numeroso /nume'roso/ *a.* numerous.
numismática /numis'matika/ *n. f.* numismatics.
nunca /'nunka/ *adv.* never; ever.
nupcial /nup'θial; nup'sial/ *a.* nuptial.
nupcias /'nupθias; 'nupsias/ *n. f.pl.* nuptials, wedding.
nutrición /nutri'θion; nutri'sion/ *n. f.* nutrition.
nutrimento /nutri'mento/ *n. m.* nourishment.
nutrir /nu'trir/ *v.* nourish.
nutritivo /nutri'tiβo/ *a.* nutritious.
nylon /'nilon/ *n. m.* nylon.
ñame /'ɲame/ *n. m.* yam.
ñapa /'ɲapa/ *n. f.* something extra.
ñoñeria /ɲoɲe'ria/ *n. f.* dotage.
ñoño /'ɲoɲo/ *a.* feeble-minded, senile.

O

o /o/ *conj.* or. **o... o,** either... or.
oasis /o'asis/ *n. m.* oasis.
obedecer /oβeðe'θer; oβeðe'ser/ *v.* obey, mind.
obediencia /oβe'ðienθia; oβe'ðiensia/ *n. f.* obedience.
obediente /oβe'ðiente/ *a.* obedient.
obelisco /oβe'lisko/ *n. m.* obelisk.
obertura /oβer'tura/ *n. f.* overture.
obeso /o'βeso/ *a.* obese.
obispo /o'βispo/ *n. m.* bishop.
obituario /oβi'tuario/ *n. m.* obituary.
objeción /oβhe'θion; oβhe'sion/ *n. f.* objection.
objetivo /oβhe'tiβo/ *a.* & *m.* objective.
objeto /oβ'heto/ *n. m.* object. —**objetar,** *v.*
objetor de conciencia /oβhe'tor de kon'θienθia; oβhe'tor de kon'siensia/ *n. m.* conscientious objector.
oblicuo /o'βlikuo/ *a.* oblique.
obligación /oβliga'θion; oβliga'sion/ *n. f.* obligation, duty.
obligar /oβli'gar/ *v.* oblige, require, compel; obligate.
obligatorio /oβliga'torio/ *a.* obligatory, compulsory.
oblongo /o'βloŋgo/ *a.* oblong.
oboe /o'βoe/ *n. m.* oboe.
obra /'oβra/ *n. f.* work. —**obrar,** *v.*
obrero /o'βrero/ **-ra** *n.* worker, laborer.
obscenidad /oβsθeni'ðað; oβsseni'ðað/ *n. f.* obscenity.
obsceno /oβs'θeno; oβs'seno/ *a.* obscene.
obscurecer /oβskure'θer; oβskure'ser/ *v.* obscure; darken.
obscuridad /oβskuri'ðað/ *n. f.* obscurity; darkness.
obscuro /oβs'kuro/ *a.* obscure; dark.
obsequiar /oβse'kiar/ *v.* court; make presents to, fete.
obsequio /oβ'sekio/ *n. m.* obsequiousness; gift; attention.
observación /oβserβa'θion; oβserβa'sion/ *n. f.* observation.
observador /oβserβa'ðor/ **-ra** *n.* observer.
observancia /oβser'βanθia; oβser'βansia/ *n. f.* observance.
observar /oβser'βar/ *v.* observe, watch.

observatorio /oβserβa'torio/ *n. m.* observatory.
obsesión /oβse'sion/ *n. f.* obsession.
obstáculo /oβs'takulo/ *n. m.* obstacle.
obstante /oβs'tante/ *adv.* **no o.,** however, yet, nevertheless.
obstar /oβs'tar/ *v.* hinder, obstruct.
obstetricia /oβste'triθia; oβste'trisia/ *n. f.* obstetrics.
obstinación /oβstina'θion; oβstina'sion/ *n. f.* obstinacy.
obstinado /oβsti'naðo/ *a.* obstinate, stubborn.
obstinarse /oβsti'narse/ *v.* persist, insist.
obstrucción /oβstruk'θion; oβstruk'sion/ *n. f.* obstruction.
obstruir /oβs'truir/ *v.* obstruct, clog, block.
obtener /oβte'ner/ *v.* obtain, get, secure.
obtuso /oβ'tuso/ *a.* obtuse.
obvio /'oββio/ *a.* obvious.
ocasión /oka'sion/ *n. f.* occasion; opportunity, chance. **de o.,** secondhand.
ocasional /okasio'nal/ *a.* occasional.
ocasionalmente /okasional'mente/ *adv.* occasionally.
ocasionar /okasio'nar/ *v.* cause, occasion.
occidental /okθiðen'tal; oksiðen'tal/ *a.* western.
occidente /okθi'ðente; oksi'ðente/ *n. m.* west.
océano /o'θeano; o'seano/ *n. m.* ocean.
Océano Atlántico /o'θeano a'tlantiko; o'seano a'tlantiko/ Atlantic Ocean.
Océano Pacífico /o'θeano pa'θifiko; o'seano pa'sifiko/ Pacific Ocean.
ocelote /oθe'lote; ose'lote/ *n. m.* ocelot.
ochenta /o'tʃenta/ *a. & pron.* eighty.
ocho /'otʃo/ *a. & pron.* eight.
ochocientos /otʃo'θientos; otʃo'sientos/ *a. & pron.* eight hundred.
ocio /'oθio; 'osio/ *n. m.* idleness, leisure.
ociosidad /oθiosi'ðað; osiosi'ðað/ *n. f.* idleness, laziness.
ocioso /o'θioso; o'sioso/ *a.* idle, lazy.
ocre /'okre/ *n. m.* ochre.
octagonal /oktago'nal/ *a.* octagonal.
octava /ok'taβa/ *n. f.* octave.
octavo /ok'taβo/ *a.* eighth.
octubre /ok'tuβre/ *n. m.* October.
oculista /oku'lista/ *n. m. & f.* oculist.
ocultación /okulta'θion; okulta'sion/ *n. f.* concealment.
ocultar /okul'tar/ *v.* hide, conceal.
oculto /o'kulto/ *a.* hidden.
ocupación /okupa'θion; okupa'sion/ *n. f.* occupation.
ocupado /oku'paðo/ *a.* occupied; busy.
ocupante /oku'pante/ *n. m. & f.* occupant.
ocupar /oku'par/ *v.* occupy.
ocuparse de /oku'parse de/ *v.* take care of, take charge of.
ocurrencia /oku'rrenθia; oku'rrensia/ *n. f.* occurrence; witticism.
ocurrente /oku'rrente/ *a.* witty.
ocurrir /oku'rrir/ *v.* occur, happen.
oda /'oða/ *n. f.* ode.
odio /'oðio/ *n. m.* hate. **—odiar,** *v.*
odiosidad /oðiosi'ðað/ *n. f.* odiousness; hatred.
odioso /o'ðioso/ *a.* obnoxious, odious.
odisea /oði'sea/ *n. f.* odyssey.
OEA, *abbr.* (**Organización de los Estados Americanos**). OAS (**Organization of American States**).
oeste /o'este/ *n. m.* west.
ofender /ofen'der/ *v.* offend, wrong.
ofenderse /ofen'derse/ *v.* be offended, take offense.
ofensa /o'fensa/ *n. f.* offense.
ofensiva /ofen'siβa/ *n. f.* offensive.
ofensivo /ofen'siβo/ *a.* offensive.
ofensor /ofen'sor/ **-ra** *n.* offender.
oferta /o'ferta/ *n. f.* offer, proposal.
ofertorio /ofer'torio/ *n. m.* offertory.
oficial /ofi'θial; ofi'sial/ *a. & m.* official; officer.
oficialmente /ofiθial'mente; ofisial'mente/ *adv.* officially.
oficiar /ofi'θiar; ofi'siar/ *v.* officiate.
oficina /ofi'θina; ofi'sina/ *n. f.* office.
oficio /o'fiθio; o'fisio/ *n. m.* office; trade; church service.
oficioso /ofi'θioso; ofi'sioso/ *a.* officious.
ofrecer /ofre'θer; ofre'ser/ *v.* offer.
ofrecimiento /ofreθi'miento; ofresi'miento/ *n. m.* offer, offering. **o. de presentación,** introductory offer.
ofrenda /o'frenda/ *n. f.* offering.
oftalmía /oftal'mia/ *n. f.* ophthalmia.
ofuscamiento /ofuska'miento/ *n. m.* obfuscation; bewilderment.
ofuscar /ofus'kar/ *v.* obfuscate; bewilder.
ogro /'ogro/ *n. m.* ogre.
oído /o'iðo/ *n. m.* ear; hearing.
oír /o'ir/ *v.* hear; listen.
ojal /o'hal/ *n. m.* buttonhole.
ojalá /oha'la/ *interj. expressing wish or hope.* **o. que...** would that...
ojeada /ohe'aða/ *n. f.* glance; peep; look.
ojear /ohe'ar/ *v.* eye, look at, glance at, stare at.
ojeriza /ohe'riθa; ohe'risa/ *n. f.* spite; grudge.
ojiva /o'hiβa/ *n. f.* pointed arch, ogive.
ojo /'oho/ *n. m.* eye. **¡Ojo!** Look out!
ola /'ola/ *n. f.* wave.
olaje /o'lahe/ *n. m.* surge of waves.
oleada /ole'aða/ *n. f.* swell.
oleo /'oleo/ *n. m.* oil; holy oil; extreme unction.
oleoducto /oleo'ðukto/ *n. m.* pipeline.
oleomargarina /oleomarga'rina/ *n. f.* oleomargarine.
oleoso /ole'oso/ *a.* oily.
oler /o'ler/ *v.* smell.
olfatear /olfate'ar/ *v.* smell.
olfato /ol'fato/ *n. m.* scent, smell.
oliva /o'liβa/ *n. f.* olive.
olivar /oli'βar/ *n. m.* olive grove.
olivo /o'liβo/ *n. m.* olive tree.
olla /'oʎa; 'oya/ *n. f.* pot, kettle. **o. podrida,** stew.
olmo /'olmo/ *n. m.* elm.
olor /o'lor/ *n. m.* odor, smell, scent.
oloroso /olo'roso/ *a.* fragrant, scented.
olvidadizo /olβiða'ðiθo; olβiða'ðiso/ *a.* forgetful.
olvidar /olβi'ðar/ *v.* forget.
olvido /ol'βiðo/ *n. m.* omission; forgetfulness.
ombligo /om'βligo/ *n. m.* navel.
ominar /omi'nar/ *v.* foretell.
ominoso /omi'noso/ *a.* ominous.
omisión /omi'sion/ *n. f.* omission.
omitir /omi'tir/ *v.* omit, leave out.
ómnibus /'omniβus/ *n. m.* bus.
omnipotencia /omnipo'tenθia; omnipo'tensia/ *n. f.* omnipotence.
omnipotente /omnipo'tente/ *a.* almighty.
omnipresencia /omnipre'senθia; omnipre'sensia/ *n. f.* omnipresence.
omnisciencia /omnis'θienθia; omnis'siensia/ *n. f.* omniscience.
omnívoro /om'niβoro/ *a.* omnivorous.
omóplato /omo'plato/ *n. m.* shoulder blade.
once /'onθe; 'onse/ *a. & pron.* eleven.
onda /'onda/ *n. f.* wave, ripple.
ondear /onde'ar/ *v.* ripple.
ondulación /ondula'θion; ondula'sion/ *n. f.* wave, undulation.
ondular /ondu'lar/ *v.* undulate, ripple.
onza /'onθa; 'onsa/ *n. f.* ounce.
opaco /o'pako/ *a.* opaque.
ópalo /'opalo/ *n. m.* opal.
opción /op'θion; op'sion/ *n. f.* option.
ópera /'opera/ *n. f.* opera.
operación /opera'θion; opera'sion/ *n. f.* operation.
operar /ope'rar/ *v.* operate; operate on.
operario /ope'rario/ **-ria** *n.* operator; (skilled) worker.
operarse /ope'rarse/ *v.* have an operation.
operativo /opera'tiβo/ *a.* operative.
opereta /ope'reta/ *n. f.* operetta.
opiato /o'piato/ *n. m.* opiate.
opinar /opi'nar/ *v.* opine.
opinión /opi'nion/ *n. f.* opinion, view.
opio /'opio/ *n. m.* opium.
oponer /opo'ner/ *v.* oppose.
Oporto /o'porto/ *n. m.* port (wine).
oportunidad /oportuni'ðað/ *n. f.* opportunity.
oportunismo /oportu'nismo/ *n. m.* opportunism.
oportunista /oportu'nista/ *n. & a.* opportunist.
oportuno /opor'tuno/ *a.* opportune, expedient.
oposición /oposi'θion; oposi'sion/ *n. f.* opposition.
opresión /opre'sion/ *n. f.* oppression.
opresivo /opre'siβo/ *a.* oppressive.
oprimir /opri'mir/ *v.* oppress.
oprobio /o'proβio/ *n. m.* infamy.
optar /op'tar/ *v.* select, choose.
óptica /'optika/ *n. f.* optics.
óptico /'optiko/ *a.* optic.
optimismo /opti'mismo/ *n. m.* optimism.
optimista /opti'mista/ *a. & n.* optimistic; optimist.
óptimo /'optimo/ *a.* best.
opuesto /o'puesto/ *a.* opposite; opposed.
opugnar /opug'nar/ *v.* attack.
opulencia /opu'lenθia; opu'lensia/ *n. f.* opulence, wealth.
opulento /opu'lento/ *a.* opulent, wealthy.
oración /ora'θion; ora'sion/ *n. f.* sentence; prayer; oration.
oráculo /o'rakulo/ *n. m.* oracle.
orador /ora'ðor/ **-ra** *n.* orator, speaker.
oral /o'ral/ *a.* oral.
orangután /oraŋgu'tan/ *n. m.* orangutan.
orar /o'rar/ *v.* pray.
oratoria /ora'toria/ *n. f.* oratory.
oratorio /ora'torio/ *a.* oratorical.
orbe /'orβe/ *n. m.* orb; globe.
órbita /'orβita/ *n. f.* orbit.
orden /'orðen/ *n. m. or f.* order.
ordenador /orðena'ðor/ *n. m.* computer; regulator.
ordenador de sobremesa /orðena'ðor de soβre'mesa/ desktop computer.
ordenador doméstico /orðena'ðor do'mestiko/ home computer.
ordenanza /orðe'nanθa; orðe'nansa/ *n. f.* ordinance.
ordenar /orðe'nar/ *v.* order; put in order; ordain.
ordeñar /orðe'ɲar/ *v.* milk.
ordinal /orði'nal/ *a. & m.* ordinal.
ordinario /orði'nario/ *a.* ordinary; common, usual.
oreja /o'reha/ *n. f.* ear.
orejera /ore'hera/ *n. f.* earmuff.
orfanato /orfa'nato/ *n. m.* orphanage.
organdí /organ'di/ *n. m.* organdy.
orgánico /or'ganiko/ *a.* organic.
organigrama /organi'grama/ *n. m.* flow chart.
organismo /orga'nismo/ *n. m.* organism.
organista /orga'nista/ *n. m. & f.* organist.
organización /organiθa'θion; organisa'sion/ *n. f.* organization.
organizar /organi'θar; organi'sar/ *v.* organize.
órgano /'organo/ *n. m.* organ.
orgía /or'hia/ *n. f.* orgy, revel.
orgullo /or'guʎo; or'guyo/ *n. m.* pride.
orgulloso /orgu'ʎoso; orgu'yoso/ *a.* proud.
orientación /orienta'θion; orienta'sion/ *n. f.* orientation.
oriental /orien'tal/ *a.* Oriental; eastern.
orientar /orien'tar/ *v.* orient.
oriente /o'riente/ *n. m.* orient, east.
orificación /orifika'θion; orifika'sion/ *n. f.* gold filling (for tooth).
origen /o'rihen/ *n. m.* origin; parentage, descent.
original /orihi'nal/ *a.* original.
originalidad /orihinali'ðað/ *n. f.* originality.
originalmente /orihinal'mente/ *adv.* originally.
originar /orihi'nar/ *v.* originate.
orilla /o'riʎa; o'riya/ *n. f.* shore; bank; edge.
orín /o'rin/ *n. m.* rust.
orina /o'rina/ *n. f.* urine.
orinar /ori'nar/ *v.* urinate.
orines /o'rines/ *n. m.pl.* urine.
oriol /o'riol/ *n. m.* oriole.
orla /'orla/ *n. f.* border; edging.
ornado /or'naðo/ *a.* ornate.
ornamentación /ornamenta'θion; ornamenta'sion/ *n. f.* ornamentation.
ornamento /orna'mento/ *n. m.* ornament. **—ornamentar,** *v.*
ornar /or'nar/ *v.* ornament, adorn.
oro /'oro/ *n. m.* gold.
oropel /oro'pel/ *n. m.* tinsel.
orquesta /or'kesta/ *n. f.* orchestra.
ortiga /or'tiga/ *n. f.* nettle.
ortodoxo /orto'ðokso/ *a.* orthodox.
ortografía /ortogra'fia/ *n. f.* orthography, spelling.
ortóptero /or'toptero/ *a.* orthopterous.
oruga /o'ruga/ *n. f.* caterpillar.
orzuelo /or'θuelo; or'suelo/ *n. m.* sty.
os /os/ *pron.* you (*pl.*); yourselves.
osadía /osa'ðia/ *n. f.* daring.
osar /o'sar/ *v.* dare.
oscilación /osθila'θion; ossila'sion/ *n. f.* oscillation.
oscilar /osθi'lar; ossi'lar/ *v.* oscillate, rock.
ósculo /'oskulo/ *n. m.* kiss.
oscurecer /oskure'θer; oskure'ser/ **oscuridad, oscuro** = obscur-.
oso /'oso/ **osa** *n.* bear.
oso de felpa /'oso de 'felpa/ teddy bear.
ostentación /ostenta'θion; ostenta'sion/ *n. f.* ostentation, showiness.
ostentar /osten'tar/ *v.* show off.
ostentoso /osten'toso/ *a.* ostentatious, flashy.
ostra /'ostra/ *n. f.* oyster.
ostracismo /ostra'θismo; ostra'sismo/ *n. m.* ostracism.
otalgia /o'talhia/ *n. f.* earache.
otero /o'tero/ *n. m.* hill, knoll.
otoño /o'toɲo/ *n. m.* autumn, fall.
otorgar /otor'gar/ *v.* grant, award.
otro /'otro/ *a. & pron.* other, another. **o. vez,** again. **el uno al o.,** one another, each other.
ovación /oβa'θion; oβa'sion/ *n. f.* ovation.
oval /o'βal/ **ovalado** *a.* oval.
óvalo /'oβalo/ *n. m.* oval.
ovario /o'βario/ *n. m.* ovary.
oveja /o'βeha/ *n. f.* sheep.
ovejero /oβe'hero/ *n. m.* sheep dog.
ovillo /o'βiʎo; o'βiyo/ *n. m.* ball of yarn.
OVNI /'oβni/ *abbr.* (objeto volador no identificado) UFO (unidentified flying object).
oxidación /oksiða'θion; oksiða'sion/ *n. f.* oxidation.
oxidar /oksi'ðar/ *v.* oxidize; rust.
óxido /'oksiðo/ *n. m.* oxide.
oxígeno /ok'siheno/ *n. m.* oxygen.
oyente /o'iente/ *n. m. & f.* hearer; (*pl.*) audience.

ozono /o'θono; o'sono/ *n. m.* ozone.

P

pabellón /paβe'ʎon; paβe'yon/ *n. m.* pavilion. **p. de deportes,** sports center.

pabilo /pa'βilo/ *n. m.* wick.

paciencia /pa'θienθia; pa'siensia/ *n. f.* patience.

paciente /pa'θiente; pa'siente/ *a.* & *n.* patient.

pacificar /paθifi'kar; pasifi'kar/ *v.* pacify.

pacífico /pa'θifiko; pa'sifiko/ *a.* pacific.

pacifismo /paθi'fismo; pasi'fismo/ *n. m.* pacifism.

pacifista /paθi'fista; pasi'fista/ *n.* & *a.* pacifist.

pacto /'pakto/ *n. m.* pact, treaty.

padecer /paðe'θer; paðe'ser/ *v.* suffer. **p. del corazón,** have heart trouble.

padrastro /pa'ðrastro/ *n. m.* stepfather.

padre /'paðre/ *n. m.* father; priest; (*pl.*) parents.

padrenuestro /paðre'nuestro/ *n. m.* paternoster, Lord's Prayer.

padrino /pa'ðrino/ *n. m.* godfather; sponsor.

paella /pa'eʎa; pa'eya/ *n. f.* dish of rice with meat or chicken.

paga /'paga/ *n. f.* pay, wages. **p. extra** bonus.

pagadero /paga'ðero/ *a.* payable.

pagador /paga'ðor/ **-ra** *n.* payer.

paganismo /paga'nismo/ *n. m.* paganism.

pagano /pa'gano/ **-na** *a.* & *n.* heathen, pagan.

pagar /pa'gar/ *v.* pay, pay for. **p. en metálico,** pay cash.

página /'pahina/ *n. f.* page.

pago /'pago/ *n. m.* pay, payment.

país /pa'is/ *n. m.* country, nation.

paisaje /pai'sahe/ *n. m.* landscape, scenery, countryside.

paisano /pai'sano/ **-na** *n.* countryman; compatriot; civilian.

paja /'paha/ *n. f.* straw.

pajar /pa'har/ *n. m.* barn.

pajarita /paha'rita/ *n. f.* bow tie.

pájaro /'paharo/ *n. m.* bird.

paje /'pahe/ *n. m.* page (person).

pala /'pala/ *n. f.* shovel, spade.

palabra /pa'laβra/ *n. f.* word.

palabrero /pala'βrero/ *a.* talkative; wordy.

palabrista /pala'βrista/ *n. m.* & *f.* talkative person.

palacio /pa'laθio; pa'lasio/ *n. m.* palace.

paladar /pala'ðar/ *n. m.* palate.

paladear /palaðe'ar/ *v.* taste; relish.

palanca /pa'lanka/ *n. f.* lever. **p. de cambio,** gearshift.

palangana /palaŋ'gana/ *n. f.* washbasin.

palco /'palko/ *n. m.* theater box.

palenque /pa'lenke/ *n. m.* palisade.

paleta /pa'leta/ *n. f.* mat, pallet.

paletilla /pale'tiʎa; pale'tiya/ *n. f.* shoulder blade.

palidecer /paliðe'θer; paliðe'ser/ *v.* turn pale.

palidez /pali'ðeθ; pali'ðes/ *n. f.* paleness.

pálido /'paliðo/ *a.* pale.

paliza /pa'liθa; pa'lisa/ *n. f.* beating.

palizada /pali'θaða; pali'saða/ *n. m.* palisade.

palma /'palma/ **palmera** *n. f.* palm (tree).

palmada /pal'maða/ *n. f.* slap, clap.

palmear /palme'ar/ *v.* applaud.

palo /'palo/ *n. m.* pole, stick; suit (in cards); *Naut.* mast.

paloma /pa'loma/ *n. f.* dove, pigeon.

palpar /pal'par/ *v.* touch, feel.

palpitación /palpita'θion; palpita'sion/ *n. f.* palpitation.

palpitar /palpi'tar/ *v.* palpitate.

paludismo /palu'ðismo/ *n. m.* malaria.

pampa /'pampa/ *n. f.* (*S.A.*) prairie, plain.

pan /pan/ *n. m.* bread; loaf. **p. de centeno,** rye bread.

pana /'pana/ *n. f.* corduroy.

panacea /pana'θea; pana'sea/ *n. f.* panacea.

panadería /panaðe'ria/ *n. f.* bakery.

panadero /pana'ðero/ **-ra** *n.* baker.

panameño /pana'meɲo/ **-ña** *a.* & *n.* Panamanian, of Panama.

panamericano /panameri'kano/ *a.* Pan-American.

páncreas /'pankreas/ *n. m.* pancreas.

pandeo /pan'deo/ *n. m.* bulge.

pandilla /pan'diʎa; pan'diya/ *n. f.* band, gang.

panecillo /pane'θiʎo; pane'siyo/ *n. m.* roll, muffin.

panegírico /pane'hiriko/ *n. m.* panegyric.

pánico /'paniko/ *n. m.* panic.

panocha /pa'notʃa/ *n. f.* ear of corn.

panorama /pano'rama/ *n. m.* panorama.

panorámico /pano'ramiko/ *a.* panoramic.

pantalla /pan'taʎa; pan'taya/ *n. f.* (movie) screen; lamp shade.

pantalones /panta'lones/ *n. m.pl.* trousers, pants.

pantano /pan'tano/ *n. m.* bog, marsh, swamp.

pantanoso /panta'noso/ *a.* swampy, marshy.

pantera /pan'tera/ *n. f.* panther.

pantomima /panto'mima/ *n. f.* pantomime.

pantorrilla /panto'rriʎa; panto'rriya/ *n. f.* calf (of body).

panza /'panθa; 'pansa/ *n. f.* belly, paunch.

pañal /pa'ɲal/ *n. m.* diaper.

paño /'paɲo/ *n. m.* piece of cloth.

pañuelo /pa'ɲuelo/ *n. m.* handkerchief.

Papa /'papa/ *n. m.* Pope.

papa /'papa/ *n. f.* potato.

papá /pa'pa/ *n. m.* papa, father.

papado /pa'paðo/ *n. m.* papacy.

papagayo /papa'gaio/ *n. m.* parrot.

papal /pa'pal/ *a.* papal.

Papá Noel /pa'pa no'el/ *n. m.* Santa Claus.

papel /pa'pel/ *n. m.* paper; role, part.

papel crespón /pa'pel kres'pon/ crepe paper.

papel de aluminio /pa'pel de alu'minio/ aluminum foil.

papel de escribir /pa'pel de es'kriβir/ writing paper.

papel de estaño /pa'pel de es'taɲo/ tin foil.

papel de lija /pa'pel de 'liha/ sandpaper.

papelera /pape'lera/ *n. f.* file cabinet; wastepaper basket.

papelería /papele'ria/ *n. f.* stationery store.

papel moneda /pa'pel mo'neða/ paper money.

paperas /pa'peras/ *n. f.pl.* mumps.

paquete /pa'kete/ *n. m.* package.

par /par/ *a.* 1. even, equal. —*n.* 2. *m.* pair; equal, peer. **abierto de p. en p.,** wide open.

para /'para/ *prep.* for; in order to. **p. que,** in order that. **estar p.,** to be about to.

parabién /para'βien/ *n. m.* congratulation.

parabrisa /para'βrisa/ *n. m.* windshield.

paracaídas /paraka'iðas/ *n. m.* parachute.

parachoques /para'tʃokes/ *n. m.* *Auto.* bumper.

parada /pa'raða/ *n. f.* stop, halt; stopover; parade.

paradero /para'ðero/ *n. m.* whereabouts; stopping place.

paradigma /para'ðigma/ *n. m.* paradigm.

paradoja /para'ðoha/ *n. f.* paradox.

parafina /para'fina/ *n. f.* paraffin.

parafrasear /parafrase'ar/ *v.* paraphrase.

paraguas /pa'raguas/ *n. m.* umbrella.

paraguayao /paragua'yao/ **-a** *n.* & *a.* Paraguayan.

paraíso /para'iso/ *n. m.* paradise.

paralelo /para'lelo/ *a.* & *m.* parallel.

parálisis /pa'ralisis/ *n. f.* paralysis.

paralizar /parali'θar; parali'sar/ *v.* paralyze.

paramédico /para'meðiko/ *n. m.* paramedic.

parámetro /pa'rametro/ *n. m.* parameter.

parapeto /para'peto/ *n. m.* parapet.

parar /pa'rar/ *v.* stop, stem, ward off; stay.

pararse /pa'rarse/ *v.* stop; stand up.

parasítico /para'sitiko/ *a.* parasitic.

parásito /pa'rasito/ *n. m.* parasite.

parcela /par'θela; par'sela/ *n. f.* plot of ground.

parcial /par'θial; par'sial/ *a.* partial.

parcialidad /parθiali'ðað; parsiali'ðað/ *n. f.* partiality; bias.

parcialmente /parθial'mente; parsial'mente/ *adv.* partially.

pardo /'parðo/ *a.* brown.

parear /pare'ar/ *v.* pair; match; mate.

parecer /pare'θer; pare'ser/ *n.* 1. *m.* opinion. —*v.* 2. seem, appear, look.

parecerse /pare'θerse; pare'serse/ *v.* look alike. **p. a,** look like.

parecido /pare'θiðo; pare'siðo/ *a.* similar.

pared /pa'reð/ *n. f.* wall.

pareja /pa'reha/ *n. f.* pair, couple; (dancing) partner.

parentela /paren'tela/ *n. f.* kinfolk.

parentesco /paren'tesko/ *n. m.* parentage, lineage; kin.

paréntesis /pa'rentesis/ *n. m.* parenthesis.

paria /'paria/ *n. m.* outcast, pariah.

paricipante /pariθi'pante; parisi'pante/ *n. m.* & *f.* participant.

paridad /pari'ðað/ *n. f.* parity.

pariente /pa'riente/ *n. m.* & *f.* relative.

parir /pa'rir/ *v.* give birth.

parisiense /pari'siense/ *n.* & *a.* Parisian.

parlamentario /parlamen'tario/ *a.* parliamentary.

parlamento /parla'mento/ *n. m.* parliament.

paro /'paro/ *n. m.* stoppage; strike. **p. forzoso,** unemployment.

parodia /pa'roðia/ *n. f.* parody.

parodista /paro'ðista/ *n. m.* & *f.* parodist.

paroxismo /parok'sismo/ *n. m.* paroxysm.

párpado /'parpaðo/ *n. m.* eyelid.

parque /'parke/ *n. m.* park.

parquímetro /par'kimetro/ *n. m.* parking meter.

parra /'parra/ *n. f.* grapevine.

párrafo /'parrafo/ *n. m.* paragraph.

parranda /pa'rranda/ *n. f.* spree.

parrandear /parrande'ar/ *v.* carouse.

parrilla /pa'rriʎa; pa'rriya/ *n. f.* grill; grillroom.

párroco /'parroko/ *n. m.* parish priest.

parroquia /pa'rrokia/ *n. f.* parish.

parroquial /parro'kial/ *a.* parochial.

parsimonia /parsi'monia/ *n. f.* economy, thrift.

parsimonioso /parsimo'nioso/ *a.* economical, thrifty.

parte /'parte/ *n. f.* part. **de p. de,** on behalf of. **alguna p.,** somewhere. **por otra p.,** on the other hand. **dar p. a,** to notify.

partera /par'tera/ *n. f.* midwife.

partición /parti'θion; parti'sion/ *n. f.* distribution.

participación /partiθipa'θion; partisipa'sion/ *n. f.* participation.

participar /partiθi'par; partisi'par/ *v.* participate; announce.

participio /parti'θipio; parti'sipio/ *n. m.* participle.

partícula /par'tikula/ *n. f.* particle.

particular /partiku'lar/ *a.* 1. particular; private. —*n.* 2. *m.* particular; detail; individual.

particularmente /partikular'mente/ *adv.* particularly.

partida /par'tiða/ *n. f.* departure; *Mil.* party; (sport) game.

partida de defunción /par'tiða de defun'θion; par'tiða de defun'sion/ death certificate.

partida de matrimonio /par'tiða de matri'monio/ marriage certificate.

partida de nacimiento /par'tiða de naθi'miento; par'tiða de nasi'miento/ birth certificate.

partidario /parti'ðario/ **-ria** *n.* partisan.

partido /par'tiðo/ *n. m.* side, party, faction; game, match.

partir /par'tir/ *v.* leave, depart; part, cleave, split.

parto /'parto/ *n. m.* delivery, childbirth.

pasa /'pasa/ *n. f.* raisin.

pasado /pa'saðo/ *a.* 1. past; last. —*n.* 2. *m.* past.

pasaje /pa'sahe/ *n. m.* passage, fare.

pasajero /pasa'hero/ **-ra** *a.* 1. passing, transient. —*n.* 2. passenger.

pasamano /pasa'mano/ *n. m.* banister.

pasaporte /pasa'porte/ *n. m.* passport.

pasar /pa'sar/ *v.* pass; happen; spend (time). **p. por alto,** overlook. **p. lista,** call the roll. **p. sin,** do without.

pasatiempo /pasa'tiempo/ *n. m.* pastime; hobby.

pascua /'paskua/ *n. f.* religious holiday; (*pl.*) Christmas (season). **P. Florida,** Easter.

pase de modelos /'pase de mo'ðelos/ *n. m.* fashion show.

paseo /pa'seo/ *n. m.* walk, stroll; drive. —**pasear,** *v.*

pasillo /pa'siʎo; pa'siyo/ *n. m.* aisle; hallway.

pasión /pa'sion/ *n. f.* passion.

pasivo /pa'siβo/ *a.* passive.

pasmar /pas'mar/ *v.* astonish, astound, stun.

pasmo /'pasmo/ *n. m.* spasm; wonder.

paso /'paso/ *a.* 1. dried (fruit). —*n.* 2. *m.* pace, step; (mountain) pass.

paso cebra /'paso 'θeβra; 'paso 'seβra/ crosswalk.

paso de ganso /'paso de 'ganso/ goose step.

paso de peatones /'paso de pea'tones/ pedestrian crossing.

pasta /'pasta/ *n. f.* paste; batter; plastic.

pasta dentífrica /'pasta den'tifrika/ toothpaste.

pastar /pas'tar/ *v.* graze.

pastel /pas'tel/ *n. m.* pastry; pie.

pastelería /pastele'ria/ *n. f.* pastry; pastry shop.

pasteurización /pasteuriθa'θion; pasteurisa'sion/ *n. f.* pasteurization.

pasteurizar /pasteuri'θar; pasteuri'sar/ *v.* pasteurize.

pastilla /pas'tiʎa; pas'tiya/ *n. f.* tablet, lozenge, coughdrop.

pasto /'pasto/ *n. m.* pasture; grass.

pastor /pas'tor/ *n. m.* pastor; shepherd.

pastorear /pastore'ar/ *v.* pasture, tend (a flock).

pastrón /pas'tron/ *n. m.* pastrami.

pastura /pas'tura/ *n. f.* pasture.

pata /'pata/ *n. f.* foot (of animal).

patada /pa'taða/ *n. f.* kick.

patán /pa'tan/ *n. m.* boor.

patanada /pata'naða/ n. f. rudeness.

patata /pa'tata/ n. f. potato. **p. asada,** baked potato.

patear /pate'ar/ v. stamp, tramp, kick.

patente /pa'tente/ a. & m. patent. —**patentar,** v.

paternal /pater'nal/ **paterno** a. paternal.

paternidad /paterni'ðað/ n. f. paternity, fatherhood.

patético /pa'tetiko/ a. pathetic.

patíbulo /pa'tiβulo/ n. m. scaffold; gallows.

patín /pa'tin/ n. m. skate. —**patinar,** v.

patín de ruedas /pa'tin de 'rrueðas/ roller skate.

patio /'patio/ n. m. yard, court, patio.

pato /'pato/ n. m. duck.

patria /'patria/ n. f. native land.

patriarca /pa'triarka/ n. m. & f. patriarch.

patrimonio /patri'monio/ n. m. inheritance.

patriota /pa'triota/ n. m. & f. patriot.

patriótico /pa'triotiko/ a. patriotic.

patriotismo /patrio'tismo/ n. m. patriotism.

patrocinar /patroθi'nar; patrosi'nar/ v. patronize, sponsor.

patrón /pa'tron/ **-ona** n. patron; boss; (dress) pattern.

patrulla /pa'truʎa; pa'truya/ n. f. patrol. —**patrullar,** v.

paulatino /paula'tino/ a. gradual.

pausa /'pausa/ n. f. pause. —**pausar,** v.

pausa para el café /'pausa 'para el ka'fe/ coffee break.

pauta /'pauta/ n. f. guideline.

pavesa /pa'βesa/ n. f. spark, cinder.

pavimentar /paβimen'tar/ v. pave.

pavimento /paβi'mento/ n. m. pavement.

pavo /'paβo/ n. m. turkey. **p. real,** peacock.

pavor /pa'βor/ n. m. terror.

payaso /pa'iaso/ **-sa** n. clown.

paz /paθ; pas/ n. f. peace.

peatón /pea'ton/ **-na** n. pedestrian.

peca /'peka/ n. f. freckle.

pecado /pe'kaðo/ n. m. sin. —**pecar,** v.

pecador /peka'ðor/ **-ra** a. & n. sinful; sinner.

pecera /pe'θera; pe'sera/ n. f. aquarium, fishbowl.

pechera /pe'tʃera/ n. f. shirt front.

pecho /'petʃo/ n. m. chest; breast; bosom.

pechuga /pe'tʃuga/ n. f. breast (of fowl).

pecoso /pe'koso/ a. freckled, freckly.

peculiar /peku'liar/ a. peculiar.

peculiaridad /pekuliari'ðað/ n. f. peculiarity.

pedagogía /peðago'hia/ n. f. pedagogy.

pedagogo /peða'gogo/ **-ga** n. pedagogue, teacher.

pedal /pe'ðal/ n. m. pedal.

pedantesco /peðan'tesko/ a. pedantic.

pedazo /pe'ðaθo; pe'ðaso/ n. m. piece.

pedernal /peðer'nal/ n. m. flint.

pedestal /peðes'tal/ n. m. pedestal.

pediatra /pe'ðiatra/ n. m. & f. pediatrician.

pediatría /peðia'tria/ n. f. pediatrics.

pedicuro /peði'kuro/ n. m. chiropodist.

pedir /pe'ðir/ v. ask, ask for, request; apply for; order.

pedo /'pedo/ n. m. fart; intoxication.

pedregoso /peðre'goso/ a. rocky.

pegajoso /pega'hoso/ a. sticky.

pegamento /pega'mento/ n. m. glue.

pegar /pe'gar/ v. beat, strike; adhere, fasten, stick.

peinado /pei'naðo/ n. m. coiffure; hairdo.

peine /'peine/ n. m. comb. —**peinar,** v.

peineta /pei'neta/ n. f. (ornamental) comb.

pelagra /pe'lagra/ n. f. pellagra.

pelar /pe'lar/ v. skin, pare, peel.

pelea /pe'lea/ n. f. fight, row. —**pelearse,** v.

pelícano /pe'likano/ n. m. pelican.

película /pe'likula/ n. f. movie, motion picture, film. **p. de terror** horror film.

peligrar /peli'grar/ v. be in danger.

peligro /pe'ligro/ n. m. peril, danger.

peligroso /peli'groso/ a. perilous, dangerous.

pelirrojo /peli'rroho/ **-ja** a. & n. redhead.

pellejo /pe'ʎeho; pe'yeho/ n. m. skin; peel (of fruit).

pellizco /pe'ʎiθko; pe'yisko/ n. m. pinch. —**pellizcar,** v.

pelo /'pelo/ n. m. hair.

pelota /pe'lota/ n. f. ball.

peltre /'peltre/ n. m. pewter.

peluca /pe'luka/ n. f. wig.

peludo /pe'luðo/ a. hairy.

peluquería /peluke'ria/ n. f. hairdresser's shop, beauty parlor.

peluquero /pelu'kero/ **-ra** n. hairdresser.

pena /'pena/ n. f. pain, grief, trouble, woe; penalty. **valer la p.,** to be worthwhile.

penacho /pe'natʃo/ n. m. plume.

penalidad /penali'ðað/ n. f. trouble; penalty.

pender /pen'der/ v. hang, dangle; be pending.

pendiente /pen'diente/ a. **1.** hanging; pending. —n. **2.** m. incline, slope; earring, pendant.

pendón /pen'don/ n. m. pennant, flag.

penetración /penetra'θion; penetra'sion/ n. f. penetration.

penetrar /pene'trar/ v. penetrate, pierce.

penicilina /peniθi'lina; penisi'lina/ n. f. penicillin.

península /pe'ninsula/ n. f. peninsula.

penitencia /peni'tenθia; peni'tensia/ n. f. penitence, penance.

penitenciaría /penitenθia'ria; penitensia'ria/ n. f. penitentiary.

penoso /pe'noso/ a. painful, troublesome, grievous, distressing.

pensador /pensa'ðor/ **-ra** n. thinker.

pensamiento /pensa'miento/ n. m. thought.

pensar /pen'sar/ v. think; intend, plan.

pensativo /pensa'tiβo/ a. pensive, thoughtful.

pensión /pen'sion/ n. f. pension; boardinghouse.

pensionista /pensio'nista/ n. m. & f. boarder.

pentagonal /pentago'nal/ a. pentagonal.

penúltimo /pe'nultimo/ a. next-to-the-last, last but one, penultimate.

penuria /pe'nuria/ n. f. penury, poverty.

peña /'peɲa/ n. f. rock.

peñascoso /peɲas'koso/ a. rocky.

peñón /pe'ɲon/ n. m. rock, crag.

Peñón de Gibraltar /pe'ɲon de hiβral'tar/ Rock of Gibraltar.

peón /pe'on/ n. m. unskilled laborer; infantryman.

peonada /peo'naða/ n. f. group of laborers.

peonía /peo'nia/ n. f. peony.

peor /pe'or/ a. worse, worst.

pepino /pe'pino/ n. m. cucumber.

pepita /pe'pita/ n. f. seed (in fruit).

pequeñez /peke'ɲeθ; peke'ɲes/ n. f. smallness; trifle.

pequeño /pe'keɲo/ **-ña** a. **1.** small, little, short, slight. —n. **2.** child.

pera /'pera/ n. f. pear.

peral /pe'ral/ n. m. pear tree.

perca /'perka/ n. f. perch (fish).

percal /per'kal/ n. m. calico, percale.

percance /per'kanθe; per'kanse/ n. m. mishap, snag, hitch.

percepción /perθep'θion; persep'sion/ n. f. perception.

perceptivo /perθep'tiβo; persep'tiβo/ a. perceptive.

percha /'pertʃa/ n. f. perch; clothes hanger, rack.

percibir /perθi'βir; persi'βir/ v. perceive, sense; collect.

perder /per'ðer/ v. lose; miss; waste. **echar a p.,** spoil. **p. el conocimiento,** lose consciousness.

perdición /perði'θion; perði'sion/ n. f. perdition, downfall.

pérdida /'perðiða/ n. f. loss.

perdiz /per'ðiθ; per'ðis/ n. f. partridge.

perdón /per'ðon/ n. m. pardon, forgiveness.

perdonar /perðo'nar/ v. forgive, pardon; spare.

perdurable /perðu'raβle/ a. enduring, everlasting.

perdurar /perðu'rar/ v. endure, last.

perecedero /pereθe'ðero; perese'ðero/ a. perishable.

perecer /pere'θer; pere'ser/ v. perish.

peregrinación /peregrina'θion; peregrina'sion/ n. f. peregrination; pilgrimage.

peregrino /pere'grino/ **-na** n. pilgrim.

perejil /pere'hil/ n. m. parsley.

perenne /pe'renne/ a. perennial.

pereza /pe'reθa; pe'resa/ n. f. laziness.

perezoso /pere'θoso; pere'soso/ a. lazy, sluggish.

perfección /perfek'θion; perfek'sion/ n. f. perfection.

perfeccionar /perfekθio'nar; perfeksio'nar/ v. perfect.

perfeccionista /perfekθio'nista; perfeksio'nista/ a. & n. perfectionist.

perfectamente /perfekta'mente/ adv. perfectly.

perfecto /per'fekto/ a. perfect.

perfidia /per'fiðia/ n. f. falseness, perfidy.

pérfido /'perfiðo/ a. perfidious.

perfil /per'fil/ n. m. profile.

perforación /perfora'θion; perfora'sion/ n. f. perforation.

perforar /perfo'rar/ v. pierce, perforate.

perfume /per'fume/ n. m. perfume, scent. —**perfumar,** v.

pergamino /perga'mino/ n. m. parchment.

pericia /pe'riθia; pe'risia/ n. f. skill, expertness.

perico /pe'riko/ n. m. parakeet.

perímetro /pe'rimetro/ n. m. perimeter.

periódico /pe'rioðiko/ a. **1.** periodic. —n. **2.** m. newspaper.

periodista /perio'ðista/ n. m. & f. journalist.

período /pe'rioðo/ n. m. period.

periscopio /peris'kopio/ n. m. periscope.

perito /pe'rito/ **-ta** a. & n. experienced; expert, connoisseur.

perjudicar /perhuði'kar/ v. damage, hurt; impair.

perjudicial /perhuði'θial; perhuði'sial/ a. harmful, injurious.

perjuicio /per'huiθio; per'huisio/ n. m. injury, damage.

perjurar /perhu'rar/ v. commit perjury.

perjurio /per'hurio/ n. m. perjury.

perla /'perla/ n. f. pearl.

permanecer /permane'θer; permane'ser/ v. remain, stay.

permanencia /perma'nenθia; perma'nensia/ n. f. permanence; stay.

permanente /perma'nente/ a. permanent.

permiso /per'miso/ n. m. permission; permit; furlough.

permitir /permi'tir/ v. permit, enable, let, allow.

permuta /per'muta/ n. f. exchange, barter.

pernicioso /perni'θioso; perni'sioso/ a. pernicious.

perno /'perno/ n. m. bolt.

pero /'pero/ conj. but.

peróxido /pe'roksiðo/ n. m. peroxide.

perpendicular /perpendiku'lar/ n. m. & a. perpendicular.

perpetración /perpetra'θion; perpetra'sion/ n. f. perpetration.

perpetrar /perpe'trar/ v. perpetrate.

perpetuar /perpe'tuar/ v. perpetuate.

perpetuidad /perpetui'ðað/ n. f. perpetuity.

perpetuo /per'petuo/ a. perpetual.

perplejo /per'pleho/ a. perplexed, puzzled.

perrito caliente /pe'rrito ka'liente/ n. m. hot dog.

perro /'perro/ **-rra** n. dog.

persecución /perseku'θion; perseku'sion/ n. f. persecution.

perseguir /perse'gir/ v. pursue; persecute.

perseverancia /perseβe'ranθia; perseβe'ransia/ n. f. perseverance.

perseverar /perseβe'rar/ v. persevere.

persiana /per'siana/ n. f. shutter, Venetian blind.

persistente /persis'tente/ a. persistent.

persistir /persis'tir/ v. persist.

persona /per'sona/ n. f. person.

personaje /perso'nahe/ n. m. personage; Theat. character.

personal /perso'nal/ a. **1.** personal. —n. **2.** m. personnel, staff.

personalidad /personali'ðað/ n. f. personality.

personalmente /personal'mente/ adv. personally.

perspectiva /perspek'tiβa/ n. f. perspective; prospect.

perspicaz /perspi'kaθ; perspi'kas/ a. perspicacious, acute.

persuadir /persua'ðir/ v. persuade.

persuasión /persua'sion/ n. f. persuasion.

persuasivo /persua'siβo/ a. persuasive.

pertenecer /pertene'θer; pertene'ser/ v. pertain; belong.

pertinencia /perti'nenθia; perti'nensia/ n. f. pertinence.

pertinente /perti'nente/ a. pertinent; relevant.

perturbar /pertur'βar/ v. perturb, disturb.

peruano /pe'ruano/ **-na** a. & n. Peruvian.

perversidad /perβersi'ðað/ n. f. perversity.

perverso /per'βerso/ a. perverse.

pesadez /pesa'ðeθ; pesa'ðes/ n. f. dullness.

pesadilla /pesa'ðiʎa; pesa'ðiya/ n. f. nightmare.

pesado /pe'saðo/ a. heavy; dull, dreary, boring.

pésame /'pesame/ n. m. condolence.

pesar /pe'sar/ n. m. sorrow; regret. **a p. de,** in spite of. v. weigh.

pesca /'peska/ n. f. fishing; catch (of fish).

pescadería /peskaðe'ria/ n. f. fish store.

pescado /pes'kaðo/ n. m. fish. —**pescar,** v.

pescador /peska'ðor/ **-ra** n. fisherman.

pesebre /pe'seβre/ n. m. stall, manger; crib.

peseta /pe'seta/ n. f. peseta (monetary unit).

pesimismo /pesi'mismo/ n. m. pessimism.

pesimista /pesi'mista/ a. & n. pessimistic; pessimist.

pésimo /'pesimo/ a. awful, terrible, very bad.

peso /'peso/ n. m. weight; load; peso (monetary unit).

pesquera /pes'kera/ n. f. fishery.

pesquisa /pes'kisa/ n. f. investigation.

pestaña /pes'taɲa/ n. f. eyelash.

pestañeo /pesta'ɲeo/ n. m. wink, blink. —**pestañear**, v.

peste /'peste/ n. f. plague.

pesticida /pesti'θiða; pesti'siða/ n. m. pesticide.

pestilencia /pesti'lenθia; pesti'lensia/ n. f. pestilence.

pétalo /'petalo/ n. m. petal.

petardo /pe'tarðo/ n. m. firecracker.

petición /peti'θion; peti'sion/ n. f. petition.

petirrojo /peti'rroho/ n. m. robin.

petrel /pe'trel/ n. m. petrel.

pétreo /'petreo/ a. rocky.

petrificar /petrifi'kar/ v. petrify.

petróleo /pe'troleo/ n. m. petroleum.

petrolero /petro'lero/ n. m. oil tanker.

petunia /pe'tunia/ n. f. petunia.

pez /peθ; pes/ n. 1. m. fish (in the water). —n. 2. f. pitch, tar.

pezuña /pe'θuɲa; pe'suɲa/ n. f. hoof.

piadoso /pia'ðoso/ a. pious; merciful.

pianista /pia'nista/ n. m. & f. pianist.

piano /'piano/ n. m. piano.

picadero /pika'ðero/ n. m. riding school.

picadura /pika'ðura/ n. f. sting, bite, prick.

picamaderos /pikama'ðeros/ n. m. woodpecker.

picante /pi'kante/ a. hot, spicy.

picaporte /pika'porte/ n. m. latch.

picar /pi'kar/ v. sting, bite, prick; itch; chop up, grind up.

pícaro /'pikaro/ -ra a. 1. knavish, mischievous. —n. 2. rogue, rascal.

picarse /pi'karse/ v. be offended, piqued.

picazón /pika'θon; pika'son/ n. f. itch.

pícea /'piθea; 'pisea/ n. f. spruce.

pichón /pi'tʃon/ n. m. pigeon, squab.

pico /'piko/ n. m. peak; pick; beak; spout; small amount.

picotazo /piko'taðo; piko'taso/ n. m. peck. —**picotear**, v.

pictórico /pik'toriko/ a. pictorial.

pie /pie/ n. m. foot. **al p. de la letra**, literally; thoroughly.

piedad /pie'ðað/ n. f. piety; pity; mercy.

piedra /'pieðra/ n. f. stone.

piel /piel/ n. f. skin, hide; fur.

pienso /'pienso/ n. m. fodder.

pierna /'pierna/ n. f. leg.

pieza /'pieθa; 'piesa/ n. f. piece; room; Theat. play.

pijama /pi'hama/ n. m. or m.pl. pajamas.

pila /'pila/ n. f. pile, stack; battery; sink.

pilar /pi'lar/ n. m. pillar, column.

píldora /'pilðora/ n. f. pill.

pillo /'piʎo; 'piyo/ -a n. thief; rascal.

piloto /pi'loto/ n. m. & f. pilot.

pimentón /pimen'ton/ n. m. paprika.

pimienta /pi'mienta/ n. f. pepper (spice).

pimiento /pi'miento/ n. m. pepper (vegetable).

pináculo /pi'nakulo/ n. m. pinnacle.

pincel /pin'θel; pin'sel/ n. m. (artist's) brush.

pinchadiscos /pintʃa'ðiskos/ m. & f. disk jockey.

pinchazo /pin'tʃaθo; pin'tʃaso/ n. m. puncture; prick. —**pinchar**, v.

pingajo /pin'gaho/ n. m. rag, tatter.

pino /'pino/ n. m. pine.

pinta /'pinta/ n. f. pint.

pintar /pin'tar/ v. paint; portray, depict.

pintor /pin'tor/ -ra n. painter.

pintoresco /pinto'resko/ a. picturesque.

pintura /pin'tura/ n. f. paint; painting.

pinzas /'pinθas; 'pinsas/ n. f.pl. pincers, tweezers; claws.

piña /'piɲa/ n. f. pineapple.

pío /'pio/ a. pious; merciful.

piojo /'pioho/ n. m. louse.

pionero /pio'nero/ -ra n. pioneer.

pipa /'pipa/ n. f. tobacco pipe.

pique /'pike/ n. m. resentment, pique. **echar a p.**, sink (ship).

pira /'pira/ n. f. pyre.

piragua /pi'ragua/ n. f. canoe.

piragüismo /pira'guismo/ n. m. canoeing.

piragüista /pira'guista/ n. m. & f. canoeist.

pirámide /pi'ramiðe/ n. f. pyramid.

pirata /pi'rata/ n. m. & f. pirate. **p. de aviones**, hijacker.

pisada /pi'saða/ n. f. tread, step. —**pisar**, v.

pisapapeles /pisapa'peles/ n. m. paperweight.

piscina /pis'θina; pis'sina/ n. f. fishpond; swimming pool.

piso /'piso/ n. m. floor.

pista /'pista/ n. f. trace, clue, track; racetrack.

pista de tenis /'pista de 'tenis/ tennis court.

pistola /pis'tola/ n. f. pistol.

pistón /pis'ton/ n. m. piston.

pitillo /pi'tiʎo; pi'tiyo/ n. m. cigarette.

pito /'pito/ n. m. whistle. —**pitar**, v.

pizarra /pi'θarra; pi'sarra/ n. f. slate; blackboard.

pizca /'piθka; 'piska/ n. f. bit, speck; pinch.

pizza /'piθθa; 'pissa/ n. f. pizza.

placentero /plaθen'tero; plasen'tero/ a. pleasant.

placer /pla'θer; pla'ser/ n. 1. m. pleasure. —v. 2. please.

plácido /'plaθiðo; 'plasiðo/ a. placid.

plaga /'plaga/ n. f. plague, scourge.

plagio /'plahio/ n. m. plagiarism; (S.A.) kidnapping.

plan /plan/ n. m. plan. —**planear**, v.

plancha /'plantʃa/ n. f. plate; slab, flatiron.

planchar /plan'tʃar/ v. iron, press.

planeta /pla'neta/ n. m. planet.

planificación /planifika'θion; planifika'sion/ n. f. planning.

planificar /planifi'kar/ v. plan.

plano /'plano/ a. 1. level, flat. —n. 2. m. plan; plane.

planta /'planta/ n. f. plant; sole (of foot).

planta baja /'planta 'baha/ n. f. ground floor.

plantación /planta'θion; planta'sion/ n. f. plantation.

plantar /plan'tar/ v. plant.

plantear /plante'ar/ v. pose, present.

plantel /plan'tel/ n. m. educational institution; Agr. nursery.

plasma /'plasma/ n. m. plasma.

plástico /'plastiko/ a. & m. plastic.

plata /'plata/ n. f. silver; Colloq. money.

plataforma /plata'forma/ n. f. platform.

plátano /'platano/ n. m. plantain; banana.

platel /pla'tel/ n. m. platter.

plática /'platika/ n. f. chat, talk. —**platicar**, v.

platillo /pla'tiʎo; pla'tiyo/ n. m. saucer.

platillo volante /pla'tiʎo bo'lante; pla'tiyo bo'lante/ flying saucer.

plato /'plato/ n. m. plate, dish.

playa /'plaia/ n. f. beach, shore.

plaza /'plaθa; 'plasa/ n. f. square. **p. de toros**, bullring.

plazo /'plaθo; 'plaso/ n. m. term, deadline; installment.

plebe /'pleβe/ n. f. common people; masses.

plebiscito /pleβis'θito; pleβis'sito/ n. m. plebiscite.

plegable /ple'gaβle/ a. foldable, folding.

plegadura /plega'ðura/ n. f. fold, pleat. —**plegar**, v.

pleito /'pleito/ n. m. lawsuit; dispute.

plenitud /pleni'tuð/ n. f. fullness; abundance.

pleno /'pleno/ a. full. **en pleno...** in the middle of...

pliego /'pliego/ n. m. sheet of paper.

pliegue /'pliege/ n. m. fold, pleat, crease.

plomería /plome'ria/ n. f. plumbing.

plomero /plo'mero/ n. m. plumber.

plomizo /plo'miθo; plo'miso/ a. leaden.

plomo /'plomo/ n. m. lead; fuse.

pluma /'pluma/ n. f. feather; (writing) pen.

pluma estiglográfica /'pluma estiglo'grafika/ fountain pen.

plumafuente /pluma'fuente/ n. f. fountain pen.

plumaje /plu'mahe/ n. m. plumage.

plumero /plu'mero/ n. m. feather duster; plume.

plumoso /plu'moso/ a. feathery.

plural /plu'ral/ a. & m. plural.

pluriempleo /pluriem'pleo/ n. m. moonlighting.

PNB, abbr. (producto nacional bruto), GNP (gross national product).

población /poβla'θion; poβla'sion/ n. f. population; town.

poblador /poβla'ðor/ -ra n. settler.

poblar /po'βlar/ v. populate; settle.

pobre /'poβre/ a. & n. poor; poor person.

pobreza /po'βreθa; po'βresa/ n. f. poverty, need.

pocilga /po'θilga; po'silga/ n. f. pigpen.

poción /po'θion; po'sion/ n. f. drink; potion.

poco /'poko/ a. & adv. 1. little, not much, (pl.) few. **por p.**, almost, nearly. —n. 2. m. **un p. (de)**, a little, a bit (of).

poder /po'ðer/ n. 1. m. power. —v. 2. be able to, can; be possible, may, might. **no p. menos de**, not be able to help.

poder adquisitivo /po'ðer aðkisi'tiβo/ purchasing power.

poderío /poðe'rio/ n. m. power, might.

poderoso /poðe'roso/ a. powerful, mighty, potent.

podrido /po'ðriðo/ a. rotten.

poema /po'ema/ n. m. poem.

poesía /poe'sia/ n. f. poetry; poem.

poeta /po'eta/ n. m. & f. poet.

poético /po'etiko/ a. poetic.

polaco /po'lako/ -ca a. & n. Polish; Pole.

polar /po'lar/ a. polar.

polaridad /polari'ðað/ n. f. polarity.

polea /po'lea/ n. f. pulley.

polen /'polen/ n. m. pollen.

policía /poli'θia; poli'sia/ n. 1. f. police. —n. 2. m. policeman.

polideportivo /polideπor'tiβo/ n. m. sports center.

poliéster /poli'ester/ n. m. polyester.

poligamia /poli'gamia/ n. f. polygamy.

polígloto /po'ligloto/ -ta n. polyglot.

polígono industrial /po'ligono indus'trial/ n. m. industrial park.

polilla /po'liʎa; po'liya/ n. f. moth.

política /po'litika/ n. f. politics; policy.

político /po'litiko/ -ca a. & n. politic; political; politician.

póliza /'poliθa; 'polisa/ n. f. (insurance) policy; permit, ticket.

polizonte /poli'θonte; poli'sonte/ n. m. policeman.

pollada /po'ʎaða; po'yaða/ n. f. brood.

pollería /poʎe'ria; poye'ria/ n. f. poultry shop.

pollino /po'ʎino; po'yino/ n. m. donkey.

pollo /'poʎo; 'poyo/ n. m. chicken.

polo /'polo/ n. m. pole; polo; popsicle.

polonés /polo'nes/ a. Polish.

Polonia /po'lonia/ n. f. Poland.

polvera /pol'βera/ n. f. powder box; powder puff.

polvo /'polβo/ n. m. powder; dust.

pólvora /'polβora/ n. f. gunpowder.

pompa /'pompa/ n. f. pomp.

pomposo /pom'poso/ a. pompous.

pómulo /'pomulo/ n. m. cheekbone.

ponche /'pontʃe/ n. m. punch (beverage).

ponchera /pon'tʃera/ n. f. punch bowl.

ponderar /ponde'rar/ v. ponder.

ponderoso /ponde'roso/ a. ponderous.

poner /po'ner/ v. put, set, lay, place.

ponerse /po'nerse/ v. put on; become, get; set (sun). **p. a**, start to.

poniente /po'niente/ n. m. west.

pontífice /pon'tifiθe; pon'tifise/ n. m. pontiff.

popa /'popa/ n. f. stern.

popular /popu'lar/ a. popular.

popularidad /populari'ðað/ n. f. popularity.

populazo /popu'laθo; popu'laso/ n. m. populace; masses.

por /por/ prep. by, through, because of; via; for. **¿p. qué?**, why?

porcelana /porθe'lana; porse'lana/ n. f. porcelain, chinaware.

porcentaje /porθen'tahe; porsen'tahe/ n. m. percentage.

porche /'portʃe/ n. m. porch; portico.

porción /por'θion; por'sion/ n. f. portion, lot.

porfiar /por'fiar/ v. persist; argue.

pormenor /porme'nor/ n. m. detail.

pornografía /pornogra'fia/ n. f. pornography.

poro /'poro/ n. m. pore.

poroso /po'roso/ a. porous.

porque /'porke/ conj. because.

porqué /por'ke/ n. m. reason, motive.

porra /'porra/ n. f. stick, club.

porrazo /po'rraθo; po'rraso/ n. m. blow.

porro /'porro/ n. m. Colloq. joint (marijuana).

portaaviones /portaa'βiones/ n. m. aircraft carrier.

portador /porta'ðor/ -ra n. bearer.

portal /por'tal/ n. m. portal.

portar /por'tar/ v. carry.

portarse /por'tarse/ v. behave, act.

portátil /por'tatil/ a. portable.

portavoz /porta'βoθ; porta'βos/ n. 1. m. megaphone. 2. m. & f. spokesperson.

porte /'porte/ n. m. bearing; behavior; postage.

portero /por'tero/ n. m. porter; janitor.

pórtico /'portiko/ n. m. porch.

portorriqueño /portorri'keɲo/ -ña n. & a. Puerto Rican.

portugués /portu'ges/ -esa a. & n. Portuguese.

posada /po'saða/ n. f. lodge, inn.

posar /po'sar/ v. pose.

posdata /pos'ðata/ n. f. postscript.

poseer /pose'er/ v. possess, own.

posesión /pose'sion/ n. f. possession.

posibilidad /posiβili'ðað/ n. f. possibility.

posible /po'siβle/ a. possible.

posiblemente /posiβle'mente/ adv. possibly.

posición /posi'θion; posi'sion/ n. f. position, stand.

positivo /posi'tiβo/ a. positive.

posponer /pospo'ner/ v. postpone.

postal /pos'tal/ a. postal; postcard.

poste /'poste/ n. m. post, pillar.

posteridad /posteri'ðað/ n. f. posterity.

posterior /poste'rior/ *a.* posterior, rear.

postizo /pos'tiθo; pos'tiso/ *a.* false, artificial.

postrado /pos'traðo/ *a.* prostrate. —**postrar,** *v.*

postre /'postre/ *n. m.* dessert.

póstumo /'postumo/ *a.* posthumous.

postura /pos'tura/ *n. f.* posture, pose; bet.

potable /po'taβle/ *a.* drinkable.

potaje /po'tahe/ *n. m.* porridge; pot stew.

potasa /po'tasa/ *n. f.* potash.

potasio /po'tasio/ *n. m.* potassium.

pote /'pote/ *n. m.* pot, jar.

potencia /po'tenθia; po'tensia/ *n. f.* potency, power.

potencial /poten'θial; poten'sial/ *a. & m.* potential.

potentado /poten'taðo/ *n. m.* potentate.

potente /po'tente/ *a.* potent, powerful.

potestad /potes'taδ/ *n. f.* power.

potro /'potro/ *n. m.* colt.

pozo /'poθo; 'poso/ *n. m.* well.

práctica /'praktika/ *n. f.* practice. —**practicar,** *v.*

práctico /'praktiko/ *a.* practical.

pradera /pra'ðera/ *n. f.* prairie, meadow.

prado /'praðo/ *n. m.* meadow; lawn.

pragmatismo /pragma'tismo/ *n. m.* pragmatism.

preámbulo /pre'ambulo/ *n. m.* preamble.

precario /pre'kario/ *a.* precarious.

precaución /prekau'θion; prekau'sion/ *n. f.* precaution.

precaverse /preka'βerse/ *v.* beware.

precavido /preka'βiðo/ *a.* cautious, guarded, wary.

precedencia /preθe'ðenθia; prese'ðensia/ *n. f.* precedence, priority.

precedente /preθe'ðente; prese'ðente/ *a. & m.* preceding; precedent.

preceder /preθe'ðer; prese'ðer/ *v.* precede.

precepto /pre'θepto; pre'septo/ *n. m.* precept.

preciar /pre'θiar; pre'siar/ *v.* value, prize.

preciarse de /pre'θiarse de; pre'siarse de/ *v.* take pride in.

precio /'preθio; 'presio/ *n. m.* price. **p. del billete de avión** air fare. **p. del cubierto** cover charge.

precioso /pre'θioso; pre'sioso/ *a.* precious; beautiful, gorgeous.

precipicio /preθi'piðio; presi'pisio/ *n. m.* precipice, cliff.

precipitación /preθipita'θion; presipita'sion/ *n. f.* precipitation.

precipitar /preθipi'tar; presipi'tar/ *v.* precipitate, rush; throw headlong.

precipitoso /preθipi'toso; presipi'toso/ *a.* precipitous; rash.

precisar /preθi'sar; presi'sar/ *v.* fix, specify; be necessary.

precisión /preθi'sion; presi'sion/ *n. f.* precision; necessity.

preciso /pre'θiso; pre'siso/ *a.* precise; necessary.

precocidad /prekoθi'ðaδ; prekosi'ðaδ/ *n. f.* precocity.

precocinado /prekoθi'naðo; prekosi'naðo/ *a.* precooked, ready-cooked.

precoz /pre'koθ; pre'kos/ *a.* precocious.

precursor /prekur'sor/ **-ra** *a.* **1.** preceding. —*n.* **2.** *m.* precursor, forerunner.

predecesor /preðeθe'sor; preðese'sor/ **-ra** *a. & n.* predecessor.

predecir /preðe'θir; preðe'sir/ *v.* predict, foretell.

predicación /preðika'θion; preðika'sion/ *n. f.* sermon.

predicador /preðika'ðor/ **-ra** *n.* preacher.

predicar /preði'kar/ *v.* preach.

predicción /preðik'θion; preðik'sion/ *n. f.* prediction.

predilecto /preði'lekto/ *a.* favorite, preferred.

predisponer /preðispo'ner/ *v.* predispose.

predisposición /preðisposi'θion; preðisposi'sion/ *n. f.* predisposition; bias.

predominante /preðomi'nante/ *a.* prevailing, prevalent, predominant.

predominar /preðomi'nar/ *v.* prevail, predominate.

predominio /preðo'minio/ *n. m.* predominance, sway.

prefacio /pre'faθio; pre'fasio/ *n. m.* preface.

preferencia /prefe'renθia; prefe'rensia/ *n. f.* preference.

preferentemente /preferente'mente/ *adv.* preferably.

preferible /prefe'riβle/ *a.* preferable.

preferir /prefe'rir/ *v.* prefer.

prefijo /pre'fiho/ *n. m.* prefix; area code, dialing code. —**prefijar,** *v.*

pregón /pre'gon/ *n. m.* proclamation; street cry.

pregonar /prego'nar/ *v.* proclaim; cry out.

pregunta /pre'gunta/ *n. f.* question, inquiry. **hacer una p.,** to ask a question.

preguntar /pregun'tar/ *v.* ask, inquire.

preguntarse /pregun'tarse/ *v.* wonder.

prehistórico /preis'toriko/ *a.* prehistoric.

prejuicio /pre'huiθio; pre'huisio/ *n. m.* prejudice.

prelacía /prela'θia; prela'sia/ *n. f.* prelacy.

preliminar /prelimi'nar/ *a. & m.* preliminary.

preludio /pre'luðio/ *n. m.* prelude.

prematuro /prema'turo/ *a.* premature.

premeditación /premeðita'θion; premeðita'sion/ *n. f.* premeditation.

premeditar /premeði'tar/ *v.* premeditate.

premiar /pre'miar/ *v.* reward; award a prize to.

premio /'premio/ *n. m.* prize, award; reward. **p. de consuelo,** consolation prize.

premisa /pre'misa/ *n. f.* premise.

premura /pre'mura/ *n. f.* pressure; urgency.

prenda /'prenda/ *n. f.* jewel; (personal) quality. **p. de vestir,** garment.

prender /pren'der/ *v.* seize, arrest, catch; pin, clip. **p. fuego a,** set fire to.

prensa /'prensa/ *n. f.* printing press; (the) press.

prensar /pren'sar/ *v.* press, compress.

preñado /pre'ɲaðo/ *a.* pregnant.

preocupación /preokupa'θion; preokupa'sion/ *n. f.* worry, preoccupation.

preocupar /preoku'par/ *v.* worry, preoccupy.

preparación /prepara'θion; prepara'sion/ *n. f.* preparation.

preparar /prepa'rar/ *v.* prepare.

preparativo /prepara'tiβo/ *n. m.* preparation.

preparatorio /prepara'torio/ *n. m.* preparatory.

preponderante /preponde'rante/ *a.* preponderant.

preposición /preposi'θion; preposi'sion/ *n. f.* preposition.

prerrogativa /prerroga'tiβa/ *n. f.* prerogative, privilege.

presa /'presa/ *n. f.* capture; (water) dam.

presagiar /presa'hiar/ *v.* presage, forebode.

presbiteriano /presβite'riano/ **-na** *n. & a.* Presbyterian.

presbítero /pres'βitero/ *n. m.* priest.

prescindir de /presθin'dir de; pressin'dir de/ *v.* dispense with; omit.

prescribir /preskri'βir/ *v.* prescribe.

prescripción /preskrip'θion; preskrip'sion/ *n. f.* prescription.

presencia /pre'senθia; pre'sensia/ *n. f.* presence.

presenciar /presen'θiar; presen'siar/ *v.* witness, be present at.

presentable /presen'taβle/ *a.* presentable.

presentación /presenta'θion; presenta'sion/ *n. f.* presentation; introduction.

presentar /presen'tar/ *v.* present; introduce.

presente /pre'sente/ *a. & m.* present.

presentimiento /presenti'miento/ *n. m.* premonition.

preservación /preserβa'θion; preserβa'sion/ *n. f.* preservation.

preservar /preser'βar/ *v.* preserve, keep.

preservativo /preserβa'tiβo/ *a. & m.* preservative; condom.

presidencia /presi'ðenθia; presi'ðensia/ *n. f.* presidency.

presidencial /presiðen'θial; presiðen'sial/ *a.* presidential.

presidente /presi'ðente/ **-ta** *n.* president.

presidiario /presi'ðiario/ **-ria** *n. m. & f.* prisoner.

presidio /pre'siðio/ *n. m.* prison; garrison.

presidir /presi'ðir/ *v.* preside.

presión /pre'sion/ *n. f.* pressure.

presión arterial /pre'sion arte'rial/ blood pressure.

preso /'preso/ **-sa** *n.* prisoner.

presta /'presta/ *n. f.* mint (plant).

prestador /presta'ðor/ **-ra** *n.* lender.

prestamista /presta'mista/ *n. m. & f.* money lender.

préstamo /'prestamo/ *n. m.* loan.

prestar /pres'tar/ *v.* lend.

presteza /pres'teθa; pres'tesa/ *n. f.* haste, promptness.

prestidigitación /prestiðihita'θion; prestiðihita'sion/ *n. f.* sleight of hand.

prestigio /pres'tihio/ *n. m.* prestige.

presto /'presto/ *a.* **1.** quick, prompt; ready. —*adv.* **2.** quickly; at once.

presumido /presu'miðo/ *a.* conceited, presumptuous.

presumir /presu'mir/ *v.* presume; boast; claim; be conceited.

presunción /presun'θion; presun'sion/ *n. f.* presumption; conceit.

presunto /pre'sunto/ *a.* presumed; prospective.

presuntuoso /presun'tuoso/ *a.* presumptuous.

presupuesto /presu'puesto/ *n. m.* premise; budget.

pretender /preten'der/ *v.* pretend; intend; aspire.

pretendiente /preten'diente/ *n. m.* suitor; pretender (to throne).

pretensión /preten'sion/ *n. f.* pretension; claim.

pretérito /pre'terito/ *a. & m.* preterit, past (tense).

pretexto /pre'teksto/ *n. m.* pretext.

prevalecer /preβale'θer; preβale'ser/ *v.* prevail.

prevención /preβen'θion; preβen'sion/ *n. f.* prevention.

prevenir /preβe'nir/ *v.* prevent; forewarn; prearrange.

preventivo /preβen'tiβo/ *a.* preventive.

prever /pre'βer/ *v.* foresee.

previamente /preβia'mente/ *adv.* previously.

previo /'preβio/ *a.* previous.

previsible /preβi'siβle/ *a.* predictable.

previsión /preβi'sion/ *n. f.* foresight. **p. social,** social security.

prieto /'prieto/ *a.* blackish, very dark.

primacía /prima'θia; prima'sia/ *n. f.* primacy.

primario /pri'mario/ *a.* primary.

primavera /prima'βera/ *n. f.* spring (season).

primero /pri'mero/ *a. & adv.* first.

primitivo /primi'tiβo/ *a.* primitive.

primo /'primo/ **-ma** *n.* cousin.

primor /pri'mor/ *n. m.* beauty; excellence; lovely thing.

primoroso /primo'roso/ *a.* exquisite, elegant; graceful.

princesa /prin'θesa; prin'sesa/ *n. f.* princess.

principal /prinθi'pal; prinsi'pal/ *a.* **1.** principal, main. —*n.* **2.** *m.* chief, head, principal.

principalmente /prinθipal'mente; prinsipal'mente/ *adv.* principally.

príncipe /'prinθipe; 'prinsipe/ *n. m.* prince.

príncipe azul /'prinθipe a'θul; 'prinsipe a'sul/ Prince Charming.

principiar /prinθi'piar; prinsi'piar/ *v.* begin, initiate.

principio /prin'θipio; prin'sipio/ *n. m.* beginning, start; principle.

pringado /priŋ'gaðo/ *n. m.* low-life, loser.

prioridad /priori'ðaδ/ *n. f.* priority.

prisa /'prisa/ *n. f.* hurry, haste. **darse p.,** hurry, hasten. **tener p.,** be in a hurry.

prisión /pri'sion/ *n. f.* prison; imprisonment.

prisionero /prisio'nero/ **-ra** *n.* captive, prisoner.

prisma /'prisma/ *n. m.* prism.

prismático /pris'matiko/ *a.* prismatic.

privación /priβa'θion; priβa'sion/ *n. f.* privation, want.

privado /pri'βaðo/ *a.* private, secret; deprived.

privar /pri'βar/ *v.* deprive.

privilegio /priβi'lehio/ *n. m.* privilege.

pro /pro/ *n. m. or f.* benefit, advantage. **en p. de,** in behalf of. **en p. y en contra,** pro and con.

proa /'proa/ *n. f.* prow, bow.

probabilidad /proβaβili'ðaδ/ *n. f.* probability.

probable /pro'βaβle/ *a.* probable, likely.

probablemente /proβaβle'mente/ *adv.* probably.

probador /proβa'ðor/ *n. m.* fitting room.

probar /pro'βar/ *v.* try, sample; taste; test; prove.

probarse /pro'βarse/ *v.* try on.

probidad /proβi'ðaδ/ *n. f.* honesty, integrity.

problema /pro'βlema/ *n. m.* problem.

probo /'proβo/ *a.* honest.

procaz /pro'kaθ; pro'kas/ *a.* impudent, saucy.

proceder /proθe'ðer; prose'ðer/ *v.* proceed.

procedimiento /proθeði'miento; proseði'miento/ *n. m.* procedure.

procesar /proθe'sar; prose'sar/ *v.* prosecute; sue; process.

procesión /proθe'sion; prose'sion/ *n. f.* procession.

proceso /pro'θeso; pro'seso/ *n. m.* process; (court) trial.

proclama /pro'klama/ **proclamación** *n. f.* proclamation.

proclamar /prokla'mar/ *v.* proclaim.

procreación /prokrea'θion; prokrea'sion/ *n. f.* procreation.

procrear /prokre'ar/ *v.* procreate.

procurar /proku'rar/ *v.* try; see to it; get, procure.

prodigalidad /proðigali'ðaδ/ *n. f.* prodigality.

prodigar /proði'gar/ *v.* lavish; squander, waste.

prodigio /pro'ðihio/ *n. m.* prodigy.

pródigo /'proðigo/ *a.* prodigal; profuse; lavish.

producción /proðuk'θion; proðuk'sion/ *n. f.* production.

producir /proðu'θir; proðu'sir/ *v.* produce.

productivo /proðuk'tiβo/ *a.* productive.

producto /pro'ðukto/ *n. m.* product.

producto nacional bruto /pro'ðukto naθio'nal 'bruto; pro'ðukto nasio'nal 'bruto/ gross national product.

proeza /pro'eθa; pro'esa/ *n. f.* prowess.

profanación /profana'θion; profana-'sion/ *n. f.* profanation.

profanar /profa'nar/ *v.* defile, desecrate.

profanidad /profani'ðað/ *n. f.* profanity.

profano /pro'fano/ *a.* profane.

profecía /profe'θia; profe'sia/ *n. f.* prophecy.

proferir /profe'rir/ *v.* utter, express.

profesar /profe'sar/ *v.* profess.

profesión /profe'sion/ *n. f.* profession.

profesional /profesio'nal/ *a.* professional.

profesor /profe'sor/ **-ra** *n.* professor, teacher.

profeta /pro'feta/ *n. m.* prophet.

profético /pro'fetiko/ *a.* prophetic.

profetizar /profeti'θar; profeti'sar/ *v.* prophesy.

proficiente /profi'θiente; profi'siente/ *a.* proficient.

profundamente /profunda'mente/ *adv.* profoundly, deeply.

profundidad /profundi'ðað/ *n. f.* profundity, depth.

profundizar /profundi'θar; profundi-'sar/ *v.* deepen.

profundo /pro'fundo/ *a.* profound, deep.

profuso /pro'fuso/ *a.* profuse.

progenie /pro'henie/ *n. f.* progeny, offspring.

programa /pro'grama/ *n. m.* program; schedule.

programador /programa'ðor/ **-ra** *n.* (computer) programmer.

progresar /progre'sar/ *v.* progress, advance.

progresión /progre'sion/ *n. f.* progression.

progresista /progre'sista/ **progresivo** *a.* progressive.

progreso /pro'greso/ *n. m.* progress.

prohibición /proiβi'θion; proiβi'sion/ *n. f.* prohibition.

prohibir /proi'βir/ *v.* prohibit, forbid.

prohibitivo /proiβi'tiβo, proiβi'torio/ *a.* prohibitive.

prole /'prole/ *n. f.* progeny.

proletariado /proleta'riaðo/ *n. m.* proletariat.

proliferación /prolifera'θion; prolifera'sion/ *n. f.* proliferation.

prolijo /pro'liho/ *a.* prolix, tedious; long-winded.

prólogo /'prologo/ *n. m.* prologue; preface.

prolongar /proloŋ'gar/ *v.* prolong.

promedio /pro'meðio/ *n. m.* average.

promesa /pro'mesa/ *n. f.* promise.

prometer /prome'ter/ *v.* promise.

prometido /prome'tiðo/ *a.* promised; engaged (to marry).

prominencia /promi'nenθia; promi-'nensia/ *n. f.* prominence.

promiscuamente /promiskua'mente/ *adv.* promiscuously.

promiscuo /pro'miskuo/ *a.* promiscuous.

promisorio /promi'sorio/ *a.* promissory.

promoción /promo'θion; promo'sion/ *n. f.* promotion.

promocionar /promoθio'nar; promosio'nar/ *v.* advertise, promote.

promover /promo'βer/ *v.* promote, further.

promulgación /promulga'θion; promulga'sion/ *n. f.* promulgation.

promulgar /promul'gar/ *v.* promulgate.

pronombre /pro'nombre/ *n. m.* pronoun.

pronosticación /pronostika'θion;

pronosticación /pronostika'sion/ *n. f.* prediction, forecast.

pronosticar /pronosti'kar/ *v.* predict, forecast.

pronóstico /pro'nostiko/ *n. m.* prediction.

prontamente /pronta'mente/ *adv.* promptly.

prontitud /pronti'tuð/ *n. f.* promptness.

pronto /'pronto/ *a.* **1.** prompt; ready. —*adv.* **2.** soon; quickly. **de p.,** abruptly.

pronunciación /pronunθia'θion; pronunsia'sion/ *n. f.* pronunciation.

pronunciar /pronun'θiar; pronun-'siar/ *v.* pronounce.

propagación /propaga'θion; propaga'sion/ *n. f.* propagation.

propaganda /propa'ganda/ *n. f.* propaganda.

propagandista /propagan'dista/ *n. m. & f.* propagandist.

propagar /propa'gar/ *v.* propagate.

propicio /pro'piθio; pro'pisio/ *a.* propitious, auspicious, favorable.

propiedad /propie'ðað/ *n. f.* property.

propietario /propie'tario/ **-ria** *n.* proprietor; owner; landlord, landlady.

propina /pro'pina/ *n. f.* gratuity, tip.

propio /'propio/ *a.* proper, suitable; typical; (one's) own; -self.

proponer /propo'ner/ *v.* propose.

proporción /propor'θion; propor-'sion/ *n. f.* proportion.

proporcionado /proporθio'naðo; proporsio'naðo/ *a.* proportionate.

proporcionar /proporθio'nar; proporsio'nar/ *v.* provide with, supply, afford.

proposición /proposi'θion; proposi'sion/ *n. f.* proposition, offer; proposal.

propósito /pro'posito/ *n. m.* purpose; plan; **a p.,** by the way, apropos; on purpose.

propuesta /pro'puesta/ *n. f.* proposal, motion.

prorrata /pro'rrata/ *n. f.* quota.

prórroga /'prorroga/ *n. f.* renewal, extension.

prorrogar /prorro'gar/ *v.* renew, extend.

prosa /'prosa/ *n. f.* prose.

prosaico /pro'saiko/ *a.* prosaic.

proscribir /proskri'βir/ *v.* prohibit, proscribe, ban.

prosecución /proseku'θion; proseku'sion/ *n. f.* prosecution.

proseguir /prose'gir/ *v.* pursue; proceed, go on.

prosélito /pro'selito/ **-ta** *n.* proselyte.

prospecto /pros'pekto/ *n. m.* prospectus.

prosperar /prospe'rar/ *v.* prosper, thrive, flourish.

prosperidad /prosperi'ðað/ *n. f.* prosperity.

próspero /'prospero/ *a.* prosperous, successful.

prosternado /proster'naðo/ *a.* prostrate.

prostitución /prostitu'θion; prostitu'sion/ *n. f.* prostitution.

prostituir /prosti'tuir/ *v.* prostitute; debase.

prostituta /prosti'tuta/ *n. f.* prostitute.

protagonista /protago'nista/ *n. m. & f.* protagonist, hero, heroine.

protección /protek'θion; protek'sion/ *n. f.* protection.

protector /protek'tor/ **-ra** *a. & n.* protective; protector.

proteger /prote'her/ *v.* protect, safeguard. **p. contra escritura,** write-protect (diskette).

protegido /prote'hiðo/ **-da** *n.* **1.** protégé. —*a.* **2.** protected. **p. contra escritura,** write-protected.

proteína /prote'ina/ *n. f.* protein.

protesta /pro'testa/ *n. f.* protest. —**protestar**, *v.*

protestante /protes'tante/ *a. & n.* Protestant.

protocolo /proto'kolo/ *n. m.* protocol.

protuberancia /protuβe'ranθia; protuβe'ransia/ *n. f.* protuberance, lump.

protuberante /protuβe'rante/ *a.* bulging.

provecho /pro'βetʃo/ *n. m.* profit, gain, benefit. **¡Buen provecho!** May you enjoy your meal!

provechoso /proβe'tʃoso/ *a.* beneficial, advantageous, profitable.

proveer /proβe'er/ *v.* provide, furnish.

provenir de /proβe'nir de/ *v.* originate in, be due to, come from.

proverbial /proβer'βial/ *a.* proverbial.

proverbio /pro'βerβio/ *n. m.* proverb.

providencia /proβi'ðenθia; proβi'ðensia/ *n. f.* providence.

providente /proβi'ðente/ *a.* provident.

provincia /pro'βinθia; pro'βinsia/ *n. f.* province.

provincial /proβin'θial; proβin'sial/ *a.* provincial.

provinciano /proβin'θiano; proβin'siano/ **-na** *a. & n.* provincial.

provisión /proβi'sion/ *n. f.* provision, supply, stock.

provisional /proβisio'nal/ *a.* provisional.

provocación /proβoka'θion; proβoka'sion/ *n. f.* provocation.

provocador /proβoka'ðor/ **-ra** *n.* provoker.

provocar /proβo'kar/ *v.* provoke, excite.

provocativo /proβoka'tiβo/ *a.* provocative.

proximidad /proksimi'ðað/ *n. f.* proximity, vicinity.

próximo /'proksimo/ *a.* next; near.

proyección /proiek'θion; proiek'sion/ *n. f.* projection.

proyectar /proiek'tar/ *v.* plan, project.

proyectil /proyek'til/ *n. m.* projectile, missile, shell.

proyecto /pro'iekto/ *n. m.* plan, project, scheme.

proyector /proiek'tor/ *n. m.* projector.

prudencia /pru'ðenθia; pru'ðensia/ *n. f.* prudence.

prudente /pru'ðente/ *a.* prudent.

prueba /'prueβa/ *n. f.* proof; trial; test.

psicoanálisis /psikoa'nalisis/ *n. m.* psychoanalysis.

psicoanalista /psikoana'lista/ *n. m. & f.* psychoanalyst.

psicodélico /psiko'ðeliko/ *a.* psychedelic.

psicología /psikolo'hia/ *n. f.* psychology.

psicológico /psiko'lohiko/ *a.* psychological.

psicólogo /psi'kologo/ **-ga** *n.* psychologist.

psiquiatra /psi'kiatra/ *n. m. & f.* psychiatrist.

psiquiatría /psikia'tria/ *n. f.* psychiatry.

publicación /puβlika'θion; puβlika-'sion/ *n. f.* publication.

publicar /puβli'kar/ *v.* publish.

publicidad /puβliθi'ðað; puβlisi'ðað/ *n. f.* publicity.

publicista /puβli'θista; puβli'sista/ *n. m. & f.* publicity agent.

público /'puβliko/ *a. & m.* public.

puchero /pu'tʃero/ *n. m.* pot.

pudiente /pu'ðiente/ *a.* powerful; wealthy.

pudín /pu'ðin/ *n. m.* pudding.

pudor /pu'ðor/ *n. m.* modesty.

pudoroso /puðo'roso/ *a.* modest.

pudrirse /pu'ðrirse/ *v.* rot.

pueblo /'pueβlo/ *n. m.* town, village; (the) people.

puente /'puente/ *n. m.* bridge.

puente para peatones /'puente para pea'tones/ *n. m.* footbridge.

puerco /'puerko/ **-ca** *n.* pig.

puericultura /puerikul'tura/ *n. f.* pediatrics.

pueril /pue'ril/ *a.* childish.

puerilidad /puerili'ðað/ *n. f.* puerility.

puerta /'puerta/ *n. f.* door; gate.

puerta giratoria /'puerta hira'toria/ revolving door.

puerta principal /'puerta prinθi'pal; 'puerta prinsi'pal/ front door.

puerto /'puerto/ *n. m.* port, harbor.

puertorriqueño /puertorri'keno/ **-ña** *a. & n.* Puerto Rican.

pues /pues/ *adv.* **1.** well... —*conj.* **2.** as, since, for.

puesto /'puesto/ *n. m.* appointment, post, job; place; stand. **p. que,** since.

pugilato /puhi'lato/ *n. m.* boxing.

pugna /'pugna/ *n. f.* conflict.

pugnacidad /pugnaθi'ðað; pugnasi'ðað/ *n. f.* pugnacity.

pugnar /pug'nar/ *v.* fight; oppose.

pulcritud /pulkri'tuð/ *n. f.* neatness; exquisitness.

pulga /'pulga/ *n. f.* flea.

pulgada /pul'gaða/ *n. f.* inch.

pulgar /pul'gar/ *n. m.* thumb.

pulir /pu'lir/ *v.* polish; beautify.

pulmón /pul'mon/ *n. m.* lung.

pulmonía /pulmo'nia/ *n. f.* pneumonia.

pulpa /'pulpa/ *n. f.* pulp.

púlpito /'pulpito/ *n. m.* pulpit.

pulque /'pulke/ *n. m.* pulque (fermented maguey juice).

pulsación /pulsa'θion; pulsa'sion/ *n. f.* pulsation, beat.

pulsar /pul'sar/ *v.* pulsate, beat.

pulsera /pul'sera/ *n. f.* wristband; bracelet.

pulso /'pulso/ *n. m.* pulse.

pulverizar /pulβeri'θar; pulβeri'sar/ *v.* pulverize.

puma /'puma/ *n. m.* puma.

pundonor /pundo'nor/ *n. m.* point of honor.

punta /'punta/ *n. f.* point, tip, end.

puntada /pun'taða/ *n. f.* stitch.

puntapié /punta'pie/ *n. m.* kick.

puntería /punte'ria/ *n. f.* (marksman's) aim.

puntiagudo /puntia'guðo/ *a.* sharp-pointed.

puntillas /pun'tiʎas; pun'tiyas/ *n. f.pl.* **de p., en p.,** on tiptoe.

punto /'punto/ *n. m.* point; period; spot, dot. **dos puntos,** *Punct.* colon. **a p. de,** about to. **al p.,** instantly.

punto de admiración /'punto de aðmira'θion; 'punto de aðmira'sion/ exclamation point.

punto de congelación /'punto de koŋgela'θion; 'punto de koŋgela'sion/ freezing point.

punto de ebullición /'punto de eβuʎi'θion; 'punto de eβuyi'sion/ boiling point.

punto de vista /'punto de 'bista/ point of view, viewpoint.

puntuación /puntua'θion; puntua-'sion/ *n. f.* punctuation.

puntual /pun'tual/ *a.* punctual, prompt.

puntuar /pun'tuar/ *v.* punctuate.

puñada /pu'naða/ *n. f.* punch.

puñado /pu'naðo/ *n. m.* handful.

puñal /pu'nal/ *n. m.* dagger.

puñalada /puna'laða/ *n. f.* stab.

puñetazo /pune'taθo; pune'taso/ *n. m.* punch, fist blow.

puño /'puno/ *n. m.* fist; cuff; handle.

pupila /pu'pila/ *n. f.* pupil (of eye).

pupitre /pu'pitre/ *n. m.* writing desk, school desk.

pureza /pu'reθa; pu'resa/ *n. f.* purity, chastity.

purgante /pur'gante/ *n. m.* laxative.

purgar /pur'gar/ *v.* purge, cleanse.

purgatorio /purga'torio/ *n. m.* purgatory.

puridad /puri'ðað/ *n. f.* secrecy.

purificación /purifika'θion; purifika-'sion/ *n. f.* purification.

purificar /purifi'kar/ *v.* purify.

purismo /pu'rismo/ *n. m.* purism.

purista /pu'rista/ *n. m. & f.* purist.

puritanismo /purita'nismo/ *n. m.* puritanism.

puro /'puro/ *a.* **1.** pure. —*n.* **2.** *m.* cigar.

púrpura /'purpura/ *n. f.* purple.

purpúreo /pur'pureo/ *a.* purple.

purulencia /puru'lenθia; puru'lensia/ *n. f.* purulence.

purulento /puru'lento/ *a.* purulent.

pus /pus/ *n. m.* pus.

pusilánime /pusi'lanime/ *a.* pusillanimous.

puta /'puta/ **-to** *n.* prostitute.

putrefacción /putrefak'θion; putrefak'sion/ *n. f.* putrefaction, rot.

putrefacto /putre'fakto/ *a.* putrid, rotten.

pútrido /'putriðo/ *a.* putrid.

puya /'puya/ *n. f.* goad.

Q

que /ke/ *rel. pron.* **1.** who, whom; that, which. —*conj.* **2.** than.

qué *a. & pron.* what. **por q., para q.,** why? *adv.* how.

quebrada /ke'βraða/ *n. f.* ravine, gully, gulch; stream.

quebradizo /keβra'ðiθo; keβra'ðiso/ *a.* fragile, brittle.

quebraley /keβra'lei/ *n. m. & f.* lawbreaker, outlaw.

quebrar /ke'βrar/ *v.* break.

queda /'keða/ *n. f.* curfew.

quedar /ke'ðar/ *v.* remain, be located; be left. **q. bien a,** be becoming to.

quedarse /ke'ðarse/ *v.* stay, remain. **q. con,** keep, hold on to; remain with.

quedo /'keðo/ *a.* quiet; gentle.

quehacer /kea'θer; kea'ser/ *n. m.* task; chore.

queja /'keha/ *n. f.* complaint.

quejarse /ke'harse/ *v.* complain, grumble.

quejido /ke'hiðo/ *n. m.* moan.

quejoso /ke'hoso/ *a.* complaining.

quema /'kema/ *n. f.* burning.

quemadura /kema'ðura/ *n. f.* burn.

quemar /ke'mar/ *v.* burn.

querella /ke'reʎa; ke'reya/ *n. f.* quarrel; complaint.

querencia /ke'renθia; ke'rensia/ *n. f.* affection, liking.

querer /ke'rer/ *v.* want, wish; will; love (a person). **q. decir,** mean. **sin q.,** without meaning to; unwillingly.

querido /ke'riðo/ *a.* dear, loved, beloved.

quesería /kese'ria/ *n. f.* dairy.

queso /'keso/ *n. m.* cheese.

queso crema /'keso 'krema/ cream cheese.

quetzal /ket'θal; ket'sal/ *n. m.* quetzal.

quiche /'kitʃe/ *n. f.* quiche.

quiebra /'kieβra/ *n. f.* break, fracture; damage; bankruptcy.

quien /kien/ *rel. pron.* who, whom.

quién *interrog. pron.* who, whom.

quienquiera /kien'kiera/ *pron.* whoever, whomever.

quietamente /kieta'mente/ *adv.* quietly.

quieto /'kieto/ *a.* quiet, still.

quietud /kie'tuð/ *n. f.* quiet, quietude.

quijada /ki'haða/ *n. f.* jaw.

quijotesco /kiho'tesko/ *a.* quixotic.

quilate /ki'late/ *n. m.* carat.

quilla /'kiʎa; 'kiya/ *n. f.* keel.

quimera /ki'mera/ *n. f.* chimera; vision; quarrel.

química /'kimika/ *n. f.* chemistry.

químico /'kimiko/ **-ca** *a. & n.* chemical; chemist.

quimoterapia /kimote'rapia/ *n. f.* chemotherapy.

quincalla /kin'kaʎa; kin'kaya/ *n. f.* (computer) hardware.

quincallería /kinkaʎe'ria; kinkaye'ria/ *n. f.* hardware store.

quince /'kinθe; 'kinse/ *a. & pron.* fifteen.

quinientos /ki'nientos/ *a. & pron.* five hundred.

quinina /ki'nina/ *n. f.* quinine.

quintana /kin'tana/ *n. f.* country home.

quinto /'kinto/ *a.* fifth.

quirúrgico /ki'rurhiko/ *a.* surgical.

quiste /'kiste/ *n. m.* cyst.

quitamanchas /kita'mantʃas/ *n. m.* stain remover.

quitanieves /kita'nieβes/ *n. m.* snowplow.

quitar /ki'tar/ *v.* take away, remove.

quitarse /ki'tarse/ *v.* take off; get rid of.

quitasol /kita'sol/ *n. m.* parasol, umbrella.

quitasueño /kita'sueɲo/ *n. m.* Colloq. nightmare; worry.

quizá /ki'θa; ki'sa/ **quizás** *adv.* perhaps, maybe.

quórum /'korum/ *n. m.* quorum.

R

rábano /'rraβano/ *n. m.* radish.

rabí /rra'βi/ **rabino** *n. m.* rabbi.

rabia /'rraβia/ *n. f.* rage; grudge; rabies.

rabiar /rra'βiar/ *v.* rage, be furious.

rabieta /rra'βieta/ *n. f.* tantrum.

rabioso /rra'βioso/ *a.* furious, rabid.

rabo /'rraβo/ *n. m.* tail.

racha /'rratʃa/ *n. f.* streak.

racimo /rra'θimo; rra'simo/ *n. m.* bunch, cluster.

ración /rra'θion; rra'sion/ *n. f.* ration. —**racionar**, *v.*

racionabilidad /rraθionaβili'ðað; rrasionaβili'ðað/ *n. f.* rationality.

racional /rraθio'nal; rrasio'nal/ *a.* rational.

racionalismo /rraθiona'lismo; rrasiona'lismo/ *n. m.* rationalism.

racionalmente /rraθional'mente; rrasional'mente/ *adv.* rationally.

radar /rra'ðar/ *n. m.* radar.

radiación /rraðia'θion; rraðia'sion/ *n. f.* radiation.

radiador /rraðia'ðor/ *n. m.* radiator.

radiante /rra'ðiante/ *a.* radiant.

radical /rraði'kal/ *a. & n.* radical.

radicalismo /rraðika'lismo/ *n. m.* radicalism.

radicoso /rraði'koso/ *a.* radical.

radio /'rraðio/ *n. m. or f.* radio.

radioactividad /rraðioaktiβi'ðað/ *n. f.* radioactivity.

radioactivo /rraðioak'tiβo/ *a.* radioactive.

radiocasete /rraðioka'sete/ *n. m.* radio cassette.

radiodifundir /rraðioðifun'dir/ *v.* broadcast.

radiodifusión /rraðioðifu'sion/ *n. f.* (radio) broadcasting.

radiografía /rraðiogra'fia/ *n. f.* X-ray.

radiografiar /rraðiogra'fiar/ *v.* X-ray.

ráfaga /'rrafaga/ *n. f.* gust (of wind).

raíz /rra'iθ; rra'is/ *n. f.* root.

raja /'rraha/ *n. f.* rip; split, crack. —**rajar**, *v.*

ralea /rra'lea/ *n. f.* stock, breed.

ralo /'rralo/ *a.* thin, scattered.

rama /'rrama/ *n. f.* branch, bough.

ramillete /rrami'ʎete; rrami'yete/ *m.* bouquet.

ramo /'rramo/ *n. m.* branch, bough; bouquet.

ramonear /rramone'ar/ *v.* browse.

rampa /'rrampa/ *n. f.* ramp.

rana /'rrana/ *n. f.* frog.

ranchero /rran'tʃero/ **-ra** *n.* small farmer.

rancho /'rrantʃo/ *n. m.* ranch.

rancidez /rranθi'ðeθ; rransi'ðes/ *n. f.* rancidity.

rancio /'rranθio; 'rransio/ *a.* rancid, rank, stale, sour.

rango /'rrango/ *n. m.* rank.

ranúnculo /rra'nunkulo/ *n. m.* ranunculus; buttercup.

ranura /rra'nura/ *n. f.* slot.

ranura de expansión /rra'nura de ekspan'sion/ expansion slot.

rapacidad /rrapaθi'ðað; rrapasi'ðað/ *n. f.* rapacity.

rapaz /rra'paθ; rra'pas/ *a.* **1.** rapacious. —*n.* **2.** *m.* young boy.

rapé /'rrape/ *n. m.* snuff.

rápidamente /rrapiða'mente/ *adv.* rapidly.

rapidez /rrapi'ðeθ; rrapi'ðes/ *n. f.* rapidity, speed.

rápido /'rrapiðo/ *a.* **1.** rapid, fast, speedy. —*n.* **2.** *m.* express (train).

rapiña /rra'piɲa/ *n. f.* robbery, plundering.

rapsodia /rrap'soðia/ *n. f.* rhapsody.

rapto /'rrapto/ *n. m.* kidnapping.

raquero /rra'kero/ **-ra** *n.* beachcomber.

raqueta /rra'keta/ *n. f.* (tennis) racket.

rareza /rra'reθa; rra'resa/ *n. f.* rarity, freak.

raridad /rrari'ðað/ *n. f.* rarity.

raro /'rraro/ *a.* rare, strange, unusual, odd, queer.

rasar /rra'sar/ *v.* skim.

rascacielos /rraska'θielos; rraska'sielos/ *n. m.* skyscraper.

rascar /rras'kar/ *v.* scrape; scratch.

rasgadura /rrasga'ðura/ *n. f.* tear, rip. —**rasgar**, *v.*

rasgo /'rrasgo/ *n. m.* trait.

rasgón /rras'gon/ *n. m.* tear.

rasguño /rras'guɲo/ *n. m.* scratch. —**rasguñar**, *v.*

raso /'rraso/ *a.* **1.** plain. **soldado r.,** *Mil.* private. —*n.* **2.** *m.* satin.

raspar /rras'par/ *v.* scrape; erase.

rastra /'rrastra/ *n. f.* trail, track. —**rastrear**, *v.*

rastrillar /rrastri'ʎar; rrastri'yar/ *v.* rake.

rastro /'rrastro/ *n. m.* track, trail, trace; rake; flea market.

rata /'rrata/ *n. f.* rat.

ratificación /rratifika'θion; rratifika'sion/ *n. f.* ratification.

ratificar /rratifi'kar/ *v.* ratify.

rato /'rrato/ *n. m.* while, spell, short time.

ratón /rra'ton/ *n. m.* mouse.

ratonera /rrato'nera/ *n. f.* mousetrap.

raya /'rraya/ *n. f.* dash, line, streak, stripe.

rayar /rra'yar/ *v.* rule, stripe; scratch; cross out.

rayo /'rrayo/ *n. m.* lightning bolt; ray; flash.

rayón /rra'yon/ *n. m.* rayon.

raza /'rraθa; 'rrasa/ *n. f.* race; breed, stock.

razón /rra'θon; rra'son/ *n. f.* reason; ratio. **a r. de,** at the rate of. **tener r.,** to be right.

razonable /rraθo'naβle; rraso'naβle/ *a.* reasonable, sensible.

razonamiento /rraθona'miento; rrasona'miento/ *n. m.* argument.

razonar /rraθo'nar; rraso'nar/ *v.* reason.

reacción /rreak'θion; rreak'sion/ *n. f.* reaction.

reaccionar /rreakθio'nar; rreaksio'nar/ *v.* react.

reaccionario /rreakθio'nario; rreaksio'nario/ **-ria** *a. & n.* reactionary.

reacondicionar /rreakondiθio'nar; rreakondisio'nar/ *v.* recondition.

reactivo /rreak'tiβo/ *a. & m.* reactive; *Chem.* reagent.

reactor /rreak'tor/ *n. m.* reactor.

real /rre'al/ *a.* royal, regal; real, actual.

realdad /rreal'dað/ *n. f.* royal authority.

realeza /rrea'leθa; rrea'lesa/ *n. f.* royalty.

realidad /rreali'ðað/ *n. f.* reality.

realidad virtual /rreali'ðað βir'tual/ virtual reality.

realista /rrea'lista/ *a. & n.* realistic; realist.

realización /rrealiθa'θion; rrealisa'sion/ *n. f.* achievement, accomplishment.

realizar /rreali'θar; rreali'sar/ *v.* accomplish; fulfill; effect; *Com.* realize.

realmente /rreal'mente/ *adv.* in reality, really.

realzar /rreal'θar; rreal'sar/ *v.* enhance.

reata /rre'ata/ *n. f.* rope; lasso, lariat.

rebaja /rre'βaha/ *n. f.* reduction.

rebajar /rreβa'har/ *v.* cheapen; reduce (in price); lower.

rebanada /rreβa'naða/ *n. f.* slice. —**rebanar**, *v.*

rebaño /rre'βaɲo/ *n. m.* flock, herd.

rebato /rre'βato/ *n. m.* alarm; sudden attack.

rebelarse /rreβe'larse/ *v.* rebel, revolt.

rebelde /rre'βelde/ *a. & n.* rebellious; rebel.

rebelión /rreβe'lion/ *n. f.* rebellion, revolt.

reborde /rre'βorðe/ *n. m.* border.

rebotar /rreβo'tar/ *v.* rebound.

rebozo /rre'βoθo; rre'βoso/ *n. m.* shawl.

rebuscar /rreβus'kar/ *v.* search thoroughly.

rebuznar /rreβuθ'nar; rreβus'nar/ *v.* bray.

recado /rre'kaðo/ *n. m.* message; errand.

recaída /rreka'iða/ *n. f.* relapse. —**recaer**, *v.*

recalcar /rrekal'kar/ *v.* stress, emphasize.

recalentar /rrekalen'tar/ *v.* reheat.

recámara /rre'kamara/ *n. f.* (Mex.) bedroom.

recapitulación /rrekapitula'θion; rrekapitula'sion/ *n. f.* recapitulation.

recapitular /rrekapitu'lar/ *v.* recapitulate.

recatado /rreka'taðo/ *n. m.* coy; prudent.

recaudador /rrekauða'ðor/ **-ra** *n.* tax collector.

recelar /rreθe'lar; rrese'lar/ *v.* fear, distrust.

receloso /rreθe'loso; rrese'loso/ *a.* distrustful.

recepción /rreθep'θion; rresep'sion/ *n. f.* reception.

recepcionista /rreθepθio'nista; rresepsio'nista/ *n. m. & f.* desk clerk.

receptáculo /rreθep'takulo; rresep'takulo/ *n. m.* receptacle.

receptividad /rreθeptiβi'ðað; rreseptiβi'ðað/ *n. f.* receptivity.

receptivo /rreθep'tiβo; rresep'tiβo/ *a.* receptive.

receptor /rreθep'tor; rresep'tor/ *n. m.* receiver.

receta /rre'θeta; rre'seta/ *n. f.* recipe; prescription.

recetar /rreθe'tar; rrese'tar/ *v.* prescribe.

rechazar /rretʃa'θar; rretʃa'sar/ *v.* reject, spurn, discard.

rechinar /rretʃi'nar/ *v.* chatter.

recibimiento /rreθiβi'miento; rresiβi'miento/ *n. m.* reception; welcome; anteroom.

recibir /rreθi'βir; rresi'βir/ *v.* receive.

recibo /rre'θiβo; rre'siβo/ *n. m.* receipt.

reciclaje /rreθi'klahe; resi'klahe/ *n. m.* recycling.

reciclar /rreθi'klar; rresi'klar/ *v.* recycle.

recidiva /rreθi'ðiβa; rresi'ðiβa/ *n. f.* relapse.

recién /rre'θien; rre'sien/ *adv.* recently, newly, just.

reciente /rre'θiente; rre'siente/ *a.* recent.

recinto /rre'θinto; rre'sinto/ *n. m.* enclosure.

recipiente /rreθi'piente; rresi'piente/ *n. m.* recipient.

reciprocación /rreθiproka'θion; rresiproka'sion/ *n. f.* reciprocation.

recíprocamente /rreθiproka'mente; rresiproka'mente/ *adv.* reciprocally.

reciprocar /rreθipro'kar; rresipro'kar/ *v.* reciprocate.

reciprocidad /rreθiproθi'ðað; rresiprosi'ðað/ *n. f.* reciprocity.

recitación /rreθita'θion; rresita'sion/ *n. f.* recitation.

recitar /rreθi'tar; rresi'tar/ *v.* recite.

reclamación /rreklama'θion; rreklama'sion/ *n. f.* claim; complaint.

reclamar /rrekla'mar/ *v.* claim; complain.

reclamo /rre'klamo/ *n. m.* claim; advertisement, advertising; decoy.

reclinar /rrekli'nar/ *v.* recline, repose, lean.

recluta /rre'kluta/ *n. m. & f.* recruit.

reclutar /rreklu'tar/ *v.* recruit, draft.

recobrar /rreko'βrar/ *v.* recover, salvage, regain.

recobro /rre'koβro/ *n. m.* recovery.

recoger /rreko'her/ *v.* gather; collect; pick up. **r. el conocimiento**, regain consciousness.

recogerse /rreko'herse/ *v.* retire (for night).

recolectar /rrekolek'tar/ *v.* gather, assemble; harvest.

recomendación /rrekomenda'θion; rrekomenda'sion/ *n. f.* recommendation; commendation.

recomendar /rrekomen'dar/ *v.* recommend; commend.

recompensa /rrekom'pensa/ *n. f.* recompense; compensation.

recompensar /rrekompen'sar/ *v.* reward; compensate.

reconciliación /rrekonθilia'θion; rrekonsilia'sion/ *n. f.* reconciliation.

reconciliar /rrekonθi'liar; rrekonsi'liar/ *v.* reconcile.

reconocer /rrekono'θer; rrekono'ser/ *v.* recognize; acknowledge; inspect, examine; *Mil.* reconnoiter.

reconocimiento /rrekonoθi'miento; rrekonosi'miento/ *n. m.* recognition; appreciation, gratitude.

reconstituir /rrekonsti'tuir/ *v.* reconstitute.

reconstruir /rrekons'truir/ *v.* reconstruct, rebuild.

record /'rrekorð/ *n. m.* (sports) record.

recordar /rrekor'ðar/ *v.* recall, recollect; remind.

recorrer /rreko'rrer/ *v.* go over; read over; cover (distance).

recorte /rre'korte/ *n. m.* clipping, cutting.

recostarse /rrekos'tarse/ *v.* recline, lean back, rest.

recreación /rrekrea'θion; rrekrea'sion/ *n. f.* recreation.

recreo /rre'kreo/ *n. m.* recreation.

recriminación /rrekrimina'θion; rrekrimina'sion/ *n. f.* recrimination.

rectangular /rrektangu'lar/ *a.* rectangular.

rectángulo /rrek'tangulo/ *n. m.* rectangle.

rectificación /rrektifika'θion; rrektifika'sion/ *n. f.* rectification.

rectificar /rrektifi'kar/ *v.* rectify.

recto /'rrekto/ *a.* straight; just, fair. **ángulo r.**, right angle.

recuento /rre'kuento/ *n. m.* recount.

recuerdo /rre'kuerðo/ *n. m.* memory; souvenir; remembrance; (*pl.*) regards.

reculada /rreku'laða/ *n. f.* recoil. **—recular,** *v.*

recuperación /rrekupera'θion; rrekupera'sion/ *n. f.* recuperation.

recuperar /rrekupe'rar/ *v.* recuperate.

recurrir /rreku'rrir/ *v.* revert; resort, have recourse.

recurso /rre'kurso/ *n. m.* resource; recourse.

red /rreð/ *n. f.* net; trap. **r. local** local area network.

redacción /rreðak'θion; rreðak'sion/ *n. f.* (editorial) staff; composition (of written material).

redactar /rreðak'tar/ *v.* draft, draw up; edit.

redactor /rreðak'tor/ **-ra** *n.* editor.

redada /rre'ðaða/ *n. f.* netful, catch, haul.

redargución /rreðargu'θion; rreðargu'sion/ *n. f.* retort. **—redargüir,** *v.*

redención /rreðen'θion; rreðen'sion/ *n. f.* redemption, salvation.

redentor /rreðen'tor/ *n. m.* redeemer.

redimir /rreði'mir/ *v.* redeem.

redoblante /rreðo'βlante/ *n. m.* snare drum; snare dummer.

redonda /rre'ðonda/ *n. f.* neighborhood, vicinity.

redondo /rre'ðondo/ *a.* round, circular.

reducción /rreðuk'θion; rreðuk'sion/ *n. f.* reduction.

reducir /rreðu'θir; rreðu'sir/ *v.* reduce.

reembolso /rreem'βolso/ *n. m.* refund. **—reembolsar,** *v.*

reemplazar /rreempla'θar; rreempla'sar/ *v.* replace, supersede.

reencarnación /rreenkarna'θion; rreenkarna'sion/ *n. f.* reincarnation.

reexaminar /rreeksami'nar/ *v.* reexamine.

reexpedir /rreekspe'ðir/ *v.* forward (mail).

referencia /rrefe'renθia; rrefe'rensia/ *n. f.* reference.

referéndum /rrefe'rendum/ *n. m.* referendum.

referir /rrefe'rir/ *v.* relate, report on.

referirse /rrefe'rirse/ *v.* refer.

refinamiento /rrefina'miento/ *n. m.* refinement.

refinar /rrefi'nar/ *v.* refine.

refinería /rrefine'ria/ *n. f.* refinery.

reflejar /rrefle'har/ *v.* reflect; think, ponder.

reflejo /rre'fleho/ *n. m.* reflection; glare.

reflexión /rreflek'sion/ *n. f.* reflection, thought.

reflexionar /rrefleksio'nar/ *v.* reflect, think.

reflujo /rre'fluho/ *n. m.* ebb; ebb tide.

reforma /rre'forma/ *n. f.* reform. **—reformar,** *v.*

reformación /rreforma'θion; rreforma'sion/ *n. f.* reformation.

reformador /rreforma'ðor/ **-ra** *n.* reformer.

reforma tributaria /rre'forma triβu'taria/ tax reform.

reforzar /rrefor'θar; rrefor'sar/ *v.* reinforce, strengthen; encourage.

refractario /rrefrak'tario/ *a.* refractory.

refrán /rre'fran/ *n. m.* proverb, saying.

refrenar /rrefre'nar/ *v.* curb, rein; restrain.

refrescar /rrefres'kar/ *v.* refresh, freshen, cool.

refresco /rre'fresko/ *n. m.* refreshment; cold drink.

refrigeración /rrefrihera'θion; rrefrihera'sion/ *n. f.* refrigeration.

refrigerador /rrefrihera'ðor/ *n. m.* refrigerator.

refrigerar /rrefrihe'rar/ *v.* refrigerate.

refuerzo /rre'fuerθo; rre'fuerso/ *n. m.* reinforcement.

refugiado /rrefu'hiaðo/ **-da** refugee.

refugiarse /rrefu'hiarse/ *v.* take refuge.

refugio /rre'fuhio/ *n. m.* refuge, asylum, shelter.

refulgencia /rreful'henθia; rreful'hensia/ *n. f.* refulgence.

refulgente /rreful'hente/ *a.* refulgent.

refulgir /rreful'hir/ *v.* shine.

refunfuñar /rrefunfu'ɲar/ *v.* mutter, grumble, growl.

refutación /rrefuta'θion; rrefuta'sion/ *n. f.* refutation; rebuttal.

refutar /rrefu'tar/ *v.* refute.

regadera /rrega'ðera/ *n. f.* watering can.

regadizo /rrega'ðiθo; rrega'ðiso/ *a.* irrigable.

regadura /rrega'ðura/ *n. f.* irrigation.

regalar /rrega'lar/ *v.* give (a gift), give away.

regaliz /rrega'liθ; rrega'lis/ *n. m.* licorice.

regalo /rre'galo/ *n. m.* gift, present, **con r.**, in luxury.

regañar /rrega'ɲar/ *v.* reprove; scold.

regaño /rre'gaɲo/ *n. m.* reprimand; scolding.

regar /rre'gar/ *v.* water, irrigate.

regatear /rregate'ar/ *v.* haggle.

regateo /rrega'teo/ *n. m.* bargaining, haggling.

regazo /rre'gaθo; rre'gaso/ *n. m.* lap.

regencia /rre'henθia; rre'hensia/ *n. f.* regency.

regeneración /rrehenera'θion; rrehenera'sion/ *n. f.* regeneration.

regenerar /rrehene'rar/ *v.* regenerate.

regente /rre'hente/ **-ta** *a. & n.* regent.

régimen /'rrehimen/ *n. m.* regime; diet.

regimentar /rrehimen'tar/ *v.* regiment.

regimiento /rrehi'miento/ *n. m.* regiment.

región /rre'hion/ *n. f.* region.

regional /rrehio'nal/ *a.* regional, sectional.

regir /rre'hir/ *v.* rule; be in effect.

registrar /rrehis'trar/ *v.* register; record; search.

registro /rre'histro/ *n. m.* register; record; search.

regla /'rregla/ *n. f.* rule, regulation. **en r.**, in order.

reglamento /rregla'mento/ *n. m.* code of regulations.

regocijarse /rregoθi'harse; rregosi'harse/ *v.* rejoice, exult.

regocijo /rrego'θiho; rrego'siho/ *n. m.* rejoicing; merriment, joy.

regordete /rregor'ðete/ *a.* chubby, plump.

regresar /rregre'sar/ *v.* go back, return.

regresión /rregre'sion/ *n. f.* regression.

regresivo /rregre'siβo/ *a.* regressive.

regreso /rre'greso/ *n. m.* return.

regulación /rregula'θion; rregula'sion/ *n. f.* regulation.

regular /rregu'lar/ *a.* **1.** regular; fair, middling. **—v. 2.** regulate.

regularidad /rregulari'ðað/ *n. f.* regularity.

regularmente /rregular'mente/ *adv.* regularly.

rehabilitación /rreaβilita'θion; rreaβilita'sion/ *n. f.* rehabilitation.

rehabilitar /rreaβili'tar/ *v.* rehabilitate.

rehén /rre'en/ *n. m.* hostage.

rehogar /rreo'gar/ *v.* brown.

rehusar /rreu'sar/ *v.* refuse; decline.

reina /'rreina/ *n. f.* queen.

reinado /rrei'naðo/ *n. m.* reign. **—reinar,** *v.*

reino /'rreino/ *n. m.* kingdom; realm; reign.

reír /rre'ir/ *v.* laugh.

reiteración /rreitera'θion; rreitera'sion/ *n. f.* reiteration.

reiterar /rreite'rar/ *v.* reiterate.

reja /'rreha/ *n. f.* grating, grillwork.

relación /rrela'θion; rrela'sion/ *n. f.* relation; account, report.

relacionar /rrelaθio'nar; rrelasio'nar/ *v.* relate, connect.

relajamiento /rrelaha'miento/ *n. m.* laxity, laxness.

relajar /rrela'har/ *v.* relax, slacken.

relámpago /rre'lampago/ *n. m.* lightning; flash (of lightning).

relatador /rrelata'ðor/ **-ra** *n.* teller.

relatar /rrela'tar/ *v.* relate, recount.

relativamente /rrelatiβa'mente/ *adv.* relatively.

relatividad /rrelatiβi'ðað/ *n. f.* relativity.

relativo /rrela'tiβo/ *a.* relative.

relato /rre'lato/ *n. m.* account, story.

relegación /rrelega'θion; rrelega'sion/ *n. f.* relegation.

relegar /rrele'gar/ *v.* relegate.

relevar /rrele'βar/ *v.* relieve.

relicario /rreli'kario/ *n. m.* reliquary; locket.

relieve /rre'lieβe/ *n. m.* (sculpture) relief.

religión /rreli'hion/ *n. f.* religion.

religiosidad /rrelihiosi'ðað/ *n. f.* religiosity.

religioso /rreli'hioso/ **-sa** *a.* **1.** religious. **—n. 2.** *m.* member of a religious order.

reliquia /rre'likia/ *n. f.* relic.

rellenar /rreʎe'nar/ *v.* refill; fill up, stuff.

relleno /rre'ʎeno/ *n. m.* filling; stuffing.

reloj /rre'loh/ *n. m.* clock; watch.

reloj de pulsera /rre'loh de pul'sera/ wrist watch.

relojería /rrelohe'ria/ *n. f.* watchmaker's shop.

relojero /rrelo'hero/ **-ra** *n.* watchmaker.

relucir /rrelu'θir; rrelu'sir/ *v.* glow, shine; excel.

relumbrar /rrelum'βrar/ *v.* glitter, sparkle.

remache /rre'matʃe/ *n. m.* rivet. **—remachar,** *v.*

remar /rre'mar/ *v.* row (a boat).

rematado /rrema'taðo/ *a.* finished; sold.

remate /rre'mate/ *n. m.* end, finish; auction. **de r.**, utterly.

remedador /rremeða'ðor/ **-ra** *n.* imitator.

remedar /rreme'ðar/ *v.* imitate.

remedio /rre'meðio/ *n. m.* remedy. **—remediar,** *v.*

remendar /rremen'dar/ *v.* mend, patch.

remesa /rre'mesa/ *n. f.* shipment; remittance.

remiendo /rre'miendo/ *n. m.* patch.

remilgado /rremil'gaðo/ *a.* prudish; affected.

reminiscencia /rreminis'θenθia; rreminis'sensia/ *n. f.* reminiscence.

remitir /rremi'tir/ *v.* remit.

remo /'rremo/ *n. m.* oar.

remolacha /rremo'latʃa/ *n. f.* beet.

remolcador /rremolka'ðor/ *n. m.* tug (boat); tow truck.

remolino /rremo'lino/ *n. m.* whirl; whirlpool; whirlwind.

remolque /rre'molke/ *n. m.* tow. **—remolcar,** *v.*

remontar /rremon'tar/ *v.* ascend, go up.

remontarse /rremon'tarse/ *v.* get excited; soar. **r. a,** date from; go back to (in time).

remordimiento /rremorði'miento/ *n. m.* remorse.

remotamente /rremota'mente/ *adv.* remotely.

remoto /rre'moto/ *a.* remote.

remover /rremo'βer/ *v.* remove; stir; shake; loosen.

rempujar /rrempu'har/ *v.* jostle.

remuneración /rremunera'θion; rremunera'sion/ *n. f.* remuneration.

remunerar /rremune'rar/ *v.* remunerate.
renacido /rrena'θiðo; rrena'siðo/ *a.* reborn, born-again.
renacimiento /rrenaθi'miento; rrenasi'miento/ *n. m.* rebirth; renaissance.
rencor /rren'kor/ *n. m.* rancor, bitterness, animosity; grudge.
rencoroso /rrenko'roso/ *a.* rancorous, bitter.
rendición /rrendi'θion; rrendi'sion/ *n. f.* surrender.
rendido /rren'diðo/ *a.* weary, worn out.
rendir /rren'dir/ *v.* yield; surrender, give up; win over.
renegado /rrene'gaðo/ **-da** *n.* renegade.
renglón /rreŋ'glon/ *n. m.* line; *Com.* item.
reno /'rreno/ *n. m.* reindeer.
renombre /rre'nombre/ *n. m.* renown.
renovación /rrenoβa'θion; rrenoβa'sion/ *f.* renovation, renewal.
renovar /rreno'βar/ *v.* renew; renovate.
renta /'rrenta/ *n. f.* income; rent.
rentar /rren'tar/ *v.* yield; rent.
renuencia /rre'nuenθia; rre'nuensia/ *n. f.* reluctance.
renuente /rre'nuente/ *a.* reluctant.
renuncia /rre'nunθia; rre'nunsia/ *n. f.* resignation; renunciation.
renunciar /rrenun'θiar; rrenun'siar/ *v.* resign; renounce, give up.
reñir /rre'ɲir/ *v.* scold, berate; quarrel, wrangle.
reo /'rreo/ *a.* & *n.* criminal; convict.
reorganizar /rreorgani'θar; rreorgani'sar/ *v.* reorganize.
reparación /rrepara'θion; rrepara'sion/ *n. f.* reparation, atonement; repair.
reparar /rrepa'rar/ *v.* repair; mend; stop, stay over. **r. en,** notice; consider.
reparo /rre'paro/ *n. m.* repair; remark; difficulty; objection.
repartición /rreparti'θion; rreparti'sion/ *n. f.*, **repartimiento, reparto,** *m.* division, distribution.
repartir /rrepar'tir/ *v.* divide, apportion, distribute; *Theat.* cast.
repaso /rre'paso/ *n. m.* review. —**repasar,** *v.*
repatriación /rrepatria'θion; rrepatria'sion/ *n. f.* repatriation.
repatriar /rrepa'triar/ *v.* repatriate.
repeler /rrepe'ler/ *v.* repel.
repente /rre'pente/ *n. m.* **de r.,** suddenly; unexpectedly.
repentinamente /rrepentina'mente/ *adv.* suddenly.
repentino /rrepen'tino/ *a.* sudden.
repercusión /rreperku'sion/ *n. f.* repercussion.
repertorio /rreper'torio/ *n. m.* repertoire.
repetición /rrepeti'θion; rrepeti'sion/ *n. f.* repetition; action replay.
repetidamente /rrepetiða'mente/ *adv.* repeatedly.
repetir /rrepe'tir/ *v.* repeat.
repisa /rre'pisa/ *n. f.* shelf.
réplica /'rreplika/ *n. f.* reply; objection; replica.
replicar /rrepli'kar/ *v.* reply; answer back.
repollo /rre'poʎo; rre'poyo/ *n. m.* cabbage.
reponer /rrepo'ner/ *v.* replace; repair.
reponerse /rrepo'nerse/ *v.* recover, get well.
reporte /rre'porte/ *n. m.* report; news.
repórter /rre'porter/ **reportero -ra** *n.* reporter.
reposado /rrepo'saðo/ *a.* tranquil, peaceful, quiet.
reposo /rre'poso/ *n. m.* repose, rest. —**reposar,** *v.*
reposte /rre'poste/ *n. f.* pantry.
represalia /rrepre'salia/ *n. f.* reprisal.
representación /rrepresenta'θion; rrepresenta'sion/ *n. f.* representation; *Theat.* performance.
representante /rrepresen'tante/ *n. m.* & *f.* representative, agent.
representar /rrepresen'tar/ *v.* represent; depict; *Theat.* perform.
representativo /rrepresenta'tiβo/ *a.* representative.
represión /rrepre'sion/ *n. f.* repression.
represivo /rrepre'siβo/ *a.* repressive.
reprimenda /rrepri'menda/ *n. f.* reprimand.
reprimir /rrepri'mir/ *v.* repress, quell.
reproche /rre'protʃe/ *n. m.* reproach. —**reprochar,** *v.*
reproducción /rreproðuk'θion; rreproðuk'sion/ *n. f.* reproduction.
reproducir /rreproðu'θir; rreproðu'sir/ *v.* reproduce.
reptil /rrep'til/ *n. m.* reptile.
república /rre'puβlika/ *n. f.* republic.
republicano /rrepuβli'kano/ **-na** *a.* & *n.* republican.
repudiación /rrepuðia'θion; rrepuðia'sion/ *n. f.* repudiation.
repudiar /rrepu'ðiar/ *v.* repudiate; disown.
repuesto /rre'puesto/ *n. m.* spare part. **de r.,** spare.
repugnancia /rrepug'nanθia; rrepug'nansia/ *n. f.* repugnance.
repugnante /rrepug'nante/ *a.* disgusting, repugnant, repulsive, revolting.
repugnar /rrepug'nar/ *v.* disgust.
repulsa /rre'pulsa/ *n. f.* refusal; repulse.
repulsivo /rrepul'siβo/ *a.* repulsive.
reputación /rreputa'θion; rreputa'sion/ *n. f.* reputation.
reputar /rrepu'tar/ *v.* repute; appreciate.
requerir /rreke'rir/ *v.* require.
requesón /rreke'son/ *n. m.* cottage cheese.
requisición /rrekisi'θion; rrekisi'sion/ *n. f.* requisition.
requisito /rreki'sito/ *n. m.* requisite, requirement.
res /rres/ *n. f.* head of cattle.
resaca /rre'saka/ *n. f.* hangover.
resbalar /rresβa'lar/ *v.* slide; slip.
resbaloso /rresβa'loso/ *a.* slippery.
rescate /rres'kate/ *n. m.* rescue; ransom. —**rescatar,** *v.*
rescindir /rresθin'dir; rressin'dir/ *v.* rescind.
resentimiento /rresenti'miento/ *n. m.* resentment.
resentirse /rresen'tirse/ *v.* resent.
reserva /rre'serβa/ *n. f.* reserve. —**reservar,** *v.*
reservación /rreserβa'θion; rreserβa'sion/ *n. f.* reservation.
resfriado /rres'friaðo/ *n. m. Med.* cold.
resfriarse /rres'friarse/ *v.* catch cold.
resguardar /rresguar'ðar/ *v.* guard, protect.
residencia /rresi'ðenθia; rresi'ðensia/ *n. f.* residence; seat, headquarters.
residente /rresi'ðente/ *a.* & *n.* resident.
residir /rresi'ðir/ *v.* reside.
residuo /rre'siðuo/ *n. m.* remainder.
resignación /rresigna'θion; rresigna'sion/ *n. f.* resignation.
resignar /rresig'nar/ *v.* resign.
resina /rre'sina/ *n. f.* resin; rosin.
resistencia /rresis'tenθia; rresis'tensia/ *n. f.* resistance.
resistir /rresis'tir/ *v.* resist; endure.
resolución /rresolu'θion; rresolu'sion/ *n. f.* resolution.
resolutivamente /rresolutiβa'mente/ *adv.* resolutely.
resolver /rresol'βer/ *v.* resolve; solve.
resonante /rreso'nante/ *a.* resonant.
resonar /rreso'nar/ *v.* resound.
resorte /rre'sorte/ *n. m. Mech.* spring.
respaldar /rrespal'dar/ *v.* endorse; back.
respaldo /rres'paldo/ *n. m.* back (of a seat).
respectivo /rrespek'tiβo/ *a.* respective.
respecto /rres'pekto/ *n. m.* relation, proportion; **r. a,** concerning, regarding.
respetabilidad /rrespetaβili'ðað/ *n. f.* respectability.
respetable /rrespe'taβle/ *a.* respectable.
respeto /rres'peto/ *n. m.* respect. —**respetar,** *v.*
respetuosamente /rrespetuosa'mente/ *adv.* respectfully.
respetuoso /rrespe'tuoso/ *a.* respectful.
respiración /rrespira'θion; rrespira'sion/ *n. f.* respiration, breath.
respirar /rrespi'rar/ *v.* breathe.
resplandeciente /rresplande'θiente; rresplande'siente/ *a.* resplendent.
resplandor /rresplan'dor/ *n. m.* brightness, glitter.
responder /rrespon'der/ *v.* respond, answer.
responsabilidad /rresponsaβili'ðað/ *n. f.* responsibility.
responsable /rrespon'saβle/ *a.* responsible.
respuesta /rres'puesta/ *n. f.* answer, response, reply.
resquicio /rres'kiθio; rres'kisio/ *n. m.* crack, slit.
resta /'rresta/ *n. f.* subtraction; remainder.
restablecer /rrestaβle'θer; rrestaβle'ser/ *v.* restore; reestablish.
restablecerse /rrestaβle'θerse; rrestaβle'serse/ *v.* recover, get well.
restar /rres'tar/ *v.* remain; subtract.
restauración /rrestaura'θion; rrestaura'sion/ *n. f.* restoration.
restaurante /rrestau'rante/ *n. m.* restaurant.
restaurar /rrestau'rar/ *v.* restore.
restitución /rrestitu'θion; rrestitu'sion/ *n. f.* restitution.
restituir /rresti'tuir/ *v.* restore, give back.
resto /'rresto/ *n. m.* remainder, rest; (*pl.*) remains.
restorán /rresto'ran/ *n. m.* restaurant.
restregar /rrestre'gar/ *v.* rub hard; scrub.
restricción /rrestrik'θion; rrestrik'sion/ *n. f.* restriction.
restrictivo /rrestrik'tiβo/ *a.* restrictive.
restringir /rrestriŋ'gir/ *v.* restrict, curtail.
resucitar /rresuθi'tar; rresusi'tar/ *v.* revive, resuscitate.
resuelto /rre'suelto/ *a.* resolute.
resultado /rresul'taðo/ *n. m.* result.
resultar /rresul'tar/ *v.* result; turn out; ensue.
resumen /rre'sumen/ *n. m.* résumé, summary, **en r.,** in brief.
resumir /rresu'mir/ *v.* sum up.
resurgir /rresur'hir/ *v.* resurge, reappear.
resurrección /rresurrek'θion; rresurrek'sion/ *n. f.* resurrection.
retaguardia /rreta'guarðia/ *n. f.* rear guard.
retal /rre'tal/ *n. m.* remnant.
retardar /rretar'ðar/ *v.* retard, slow.
retardo /rre'tarðo/ *n. m.* delay.
retención /rreten'θion; rreten'sion/ *n. f.* retention.
retener /rrete'ner/ *v.* retain, keep; withhold.
reticencia /rreti'θenθia; rreti'sensia/ *n. f.* reticence.
reticente /rreti'θente; rreti'sente/ *a.* reticent.
retirada /rreti'raða/ *n. f.* retreat, retirement.
retirar /rreti'rar/ *v.* retire, retreat, withdraw.
retiro /rre'tiro/ *n. m.* retirement.
retorcer /rretor'θer; rretor'ser/ *v.* wring.
retórica /rre'torika/ *n. f.* rhetoric.
retórico /rre'toriko/ *a.* rhetorical.
retorno /rre'torno/ *n. m.* return.
retozo /rre'toθo; rre'toso/ *n. m.* frolic, romp. —**retozar,** *v.*
retozón /rreto'θon; rreto'son/ *a.* frisky.
retracción /rretrak'θion; rretrak'sion/ *n. f.* retraction.
retractar /rretrak'tar/ *v.* retract.
retrasar /rretra'sar/ *v.* delay, set back.
retrasarse /rretra'sarse/ *v.* be slow.
retraso /rre'traso/ *n. m.* delay, lag, slowness.
retratar /rretra'tar/ *v.* portray; photograph.
retrato /rre'trato/ *n. m.* portrait; picture, photograph.
retreta /rre'treta/ *n. f. Mil.* retreat.
retrete /rre'trete/ *n. m.* toilet.
retribución /rretriβu'θion; rretriβu'sion/ *n. f.* retribution.
retroactivo /rretroak'tiβo/ *a.* retroactive.
retroalimentación /rretroalimenta'θion; rretroalimenta'sion/ *n. f.* feedback.
retroceder /rretroθe'ðer; rretrose'ðer/ *v.* recede, go back, draw back, back up.
retumbar /rretum'βar/ *v.* resound, rumble.
reumático /rreu'matiko/ *a.* rheumatic.
reumatismo /rreuma'tismo/ *n. m.* rheumatism.
reunión /rreu'nion/ *n. f.* gathering, meeting, party; reunion.
reunir /rreu'nir/ *v.* gather, collect, bring together.
reunirse /rreu'nirse/ *v.* meet, assemble, get together.
reutilizar /reutili'zar/ *v.* reuse.
revelación /rreβela'θion; rreβela'sion/ *n. f.* revelation.
revelar /rreβe'lar/ *v.* reveal; betray; *Phot.* develop.
reventa /rre'βenta/ *n. f.* resale.
reventar /rreβen'tar/ *v.* burst; split apart.
reventón /rreβen'ton/ *n. m.* blowout (of tire).
reverencia /rreβeren'θia; rreβeren'sia/ *n. f.* reverence.
reverendo /rreβe'rendo/ *a.* reverend.
reverente /rreβe'rente/ *a.* reverent.
revertir /rreβer'tir/ *v.* revert.
revés /rre'βes/ *n. m.* reverse; back, wrong side. **al r.,** just the opposite; inside out.
revisar /rreβi'sar/ *v.* revise; review.
revisión /rreβi'sion/ *n. f.* revision.
revista /rre'βista/ *n. f.* magazine, periodical; review.
revivir /rreβi'βir/ *v.* revive.
revocación /rreβoka'θion; rreβoka'sion/ *n. f.* revocation.
revocar /rreβo'kar/ *v.* revoke, reverse.
revolotear /rreβolote'ar/ *v.* hover.
revolución /rreβolu'θion; rreβolu'sion/ *n. f.* revolution.
revolucionario /rreβoluθio'nario; rreβolusio'nario/ **-ria** *a.* & *n.* revolutionary.
revolver /rreβol'βer/ *v.* revolve; stir, agitate.
revólver *n. m.* revolver, pistol.
revuelta /rre'βuelta/ *n. f.* revolt; turn.
rey /rrei/ *n. m.* king.
reyerta /rre'yerta/ *n. f.* quarrel, wrangle.
rezar /rre'θar; rre'sar/ *v.* pray.
rezongar /rreθoŋ'gar; rresoŋ'gar/ *v.* grumble; mutter.
ría /'rria/ *n. f.* estuary.
riachuelo /rria'tʃuelo/ *n. m.* creek.
riba /'rriβa/ *n. f.* embankment.
rico /'rriko/ *a.* rich, wealthy; delicious.

ridículamente /rri'ðikulamente/ *adv.* ridiculously.
ridiculizar /rriðikuli'θar; rriðikuli'sar/ *v.* ridicule.
ridículo /rri'ðikulo/ *a.* & *m.* ridiculous; ridicule.
riego /'rriego/ *n. m.* irrigation.
rienda /'rrienda/ *n. f.* rein.
riesgo /'rriesgo/ *n. m.* risk, gamble.
rifa /'rrifa/ *n. f.* raffle; lottery; scuffle.
rifle /'rrifle/ *n. m.* rifle.
rígidamente /'rrihiðamente/ *adv.* rigidly.
rigidez /rrihi'ðeθ; rrihi'ðes/ *n. f.* rigidity.
rígido /'rrihiðo/ *a.* rigid, stiff.
rigor /rri'gor/ *n. m.* rigor.
riguroso /rrigu'roso/ *a.* rigorous, strict.
rima /'rrima/ *n. f.* rhyme. **—rimar,** *v.*
rimel /rri'mel/ *n. f.* mascara.
rincón /rrin'kon/ *n. m.* corner, nook.
rinoceronte /rrinoθe'ronte; rrinose'ronte/ *n. m.* rhinoceros.
riña /'rriɲa/ *n. f.* quarrel, feud.
riñón /rri'ɲon/ *n. m.* kidney.
río /'rrio/ *n. m.* river. **r. abajo** downstream, downriver. **r. arriba,** upstream, upriver.
ripio /'rripio/ *n. m.* debris.
riqueza /rri'keθa; rri'kesa/ *n. f.* wealth.
risa /'rrisa/ *n. f.* laugh; laughter.
risco /'rrisko/ *n. m.* cliff.
risibilidad /rrisiβili'ðað/ *n. f.* risibility.
risotada /rriso'taða/ *n. f.* peal of laughter.
risueño /rri'sueɲo/ *a.* cheerful, smiling.
rítmico /'rritmiko/ *a.* rhythmical.
ritmo /'rritmo/ *n. m.* rhythm.
rito /'rrito/ *n. m.* rite.
ritual /rri'tual/ *a.* & *m.* ritual.
rivalidad /rriβali'ðað/ *n. f.* rivalry.
rivera /rri'βera/ *n. f.* brook.
rizado /rri'θaðo; rri'saðo/ *a.* curly.
rizo /'rriθo; 'rriso/ *n. m.* curl. **—rizar,** *v.*
robar /rro'βar/ *v.* rob, steal.
roble /'rroβle/ *n. m.* oak.
roblón /rro'βlon/ *n. m.* rivet. **—roblar,** *v.*
robo /'rroβo/ *n. m.* robbery, theft.
robustamente /rroβusta'mente/ *adv.* robustly.
robusto /rro'βusto/ *a.* robust.
roca /'rroka/ *n. f.* rock; cliff.
rociada /rro'θiaða; rro'siaða/ *n. f.* spray, sprinkle. **—rociar,** *v.*
rocío /'rroθio; 'rrosio/ *n. m.* dew.
rocoso /rro'koso/ *a.* rocky.
rodar /rro'ðar/ *v.* roll; roam.
rodear /rroðe'ar/ *v.* surround, encircle.
rodeo /rro'ðeo/ *n. m.* turn, winding; roundup.
rodilla /rro'ðiʎa; rro'ðiya/ *n. f.* knee.
rodillo /rro'ðiʎo; rro'ðiyo/ *n. m.* roller.
rodio /'rroðio/ *n. m.* rhodium.
rododendro /rroðo'ðendro/ *n. m.* rhododendron.
roedor /rroe'ðor/ *n. m.* rodent.
roer /rro'er/ *v.* gnaw.
rogación /rroga'θion; rroga'sion/ *n. f.* request, entreaty.
rogar /rro'gar/ *v.* beg, plead with, supplicate.
rojizo /rro'hiθo; rro'hiso/ *a.* reddish.
rojo /'rroho/ *a.* red.
rollizo /rro'ʎiθo; rro'yiso/ *a.* chubby.
rollo /'rroʎo; 'rroyo/ *n. m.* roll; coil.
romadizo /rroma'ðiθo; rroma'ðiso/ *n. m.* head cold.
romance /rro'manθe; rro'manse/ *n. m.* romance; ballad.
románico /rro'maniko/ *a.* Romance.
romano /rro'mano/ **-na** *a.* & *n.* Roman.
romántico /rro'mantiko/ *a.* romantic.
romería /rrome'ria/ *n. f.* pilgrimage; picnic.
romero /rro'mero/ **-ra** *n.* pilgrim.
rompecabezas /rrompeka'βeθas; rrompeka'βesas/ *n. m.* puzzle (pastime).
romper /rrom'per/ *v.* break, smash, shatter; sever; tear.
rompible /rrom'piβle/ *a.* breakable.
ron /rron/ *n. m.* rum.
roncar /rron'kar/ *v.* snore.
ronco /'rronko/ *a.* hoarse.
ronda /'rronda/ *n. f.* round.
rondar /rron'dar/ *v.* prowl.
ronquido /rron'kiðo/ *n. m.* snore.
ronronear /rronrone'ar/ *v.* purr.
ronzal /rron'θal; rron'sal/ *n. m.* halter.
roña /'rroɲa/ *n. f.* scab; filth.
ropa /'rropa/ *n. f.* clothes, clothing. **r. blanca,** linen. **r. interior,** underwear.
ropa de marca /'rropa de 'marka/ designer clothing.
ropero /rro'pero/ *n. m.* closet.
rosa /'rrosa/ *n. f.* rose. **r. náutica,** compass.
rosado /rro'saðo/ *a.* pink, rosy.
rosal /rro'sal/ *n. m.* rose bush.
rosario /rro'sario/ *n. m.* rosary.
rosbif /rros'βif/ *n. m.* roast beef.
rosca /'rroska/ *n. f.* thread (of screw).
róseo /'rroseo/ *a.* rosy.
rostro /'rrostro/ *n. m.* face, countenance.
rota /'rrota/ *n. f.* defeat; *Naut.* course.
rotación /rrota'θion; rrota'sion/ *n. f.* rotation.
rotatorio /rrota'torio/ *a.* rotary.
rótula /'rrotula/ *n. f.* kneecap.
rotulador /rrotula'ðor/ *n. m.* felt-tipped pen.
rótulo /'rrotulo/ *n. m.* label. **—rotular,** *v.*
rotundo /rro'tundo/ *a.* round; sonorous.
rotura /rro'tura/ *n. f.* break, fracture, rupture.
rozar /rro'θar; rro'sar/ *v.* rub against, chafe; graze.
rubí /rru'βi/ *n. m.* ruby.
rubio /'rruβio/ **-bia** *a.* & *n.* blond.
rubor /rru'βor/ *n. m.* blush; bashfulness.
rúbrica /'rruβrika/ *n. f.* caption; scroll.
rucho /'rrutʃo/ *n. m.* donkey.
rudeza /rru'ðeθa; rru'ðesa/ *n. f.* rudeness; roughness.
rudimentario /rruðimen'tario/ *a.* rudimentary.
rudimento /rruði'mento/ *n. m.* rudiment.
rudo /'rruðo/ *a.* rude, rough.
rueda /'rrueða/ *n. f.* wheel.
rueda de feria /'rrueða de 'feria/ Ferris wheel.
ruego /'rruego/ *n. m.* plea; entreaty.
rufián /rru'fian/ *n. m.* ruffian.
rufo /'rrufo/ *a.* sandy haired.
rugir /rru'hir/ *v.* bellow, roar.
rugoso /rru'goso/ *a.* wrinkled.
ruibarbo /rrui'βarβo/ *n. m.* rhubarb.
ruido /'rruiðo/ *n. m.* noise.
ruidoso /rrui'ðoso/ *a.* noisy.
ruina /'rruina/ *n. f.* ruin, wreck.
ruinar /rrui'nar/ *v.* ruin, destroy.
ruinoso /rrui'noso/ *a.* ruinous.
ruiseñor /rruise'ɲor/ *n. m.* nightingale.
ruleta /rru'leta/ *n. f.* roulette.
rumba /'rrumba/ *n. f.* rumba (dance or music).
rumbo /'rrumbo/ *n. m.* course, direction.
rumor /rru'mor/ *n. m.* rumor; murmur.
runrún /rrun'run/ *n. m.* rumor.
ruptura /rrup'tura/ *n. f.* rupture, break.
rural /rru'ral/ *a.* rural.
Rusia /'rrusia/ *n. f.* Russia.
ruso /'rruso/ **-sa** *a.* & *n.* Russian.
rústico /'rrustiko/ **-ca** *a.* & *n.* rustic. **en r.,** paperback *f.*
ruta /'rruta/ *n. f.* route.
rutina /rru'tina/ *n. f.* routine.
rutinario /rruti'nario/ *a.* routine.

S

sábado /'saβaðo/ *n. m.* Saturday.
sábalo /'saβalo/ *n. m.* shad.
sábana /sa'βana/ *n. f.* sheet.
sabañon /saβa'ɲon/ *n. m.* chilblain.
saber /sa'βer/ *n.* **1.** *m.* knowledge. **—***v.* **2.** know; learn, find out; know how to; taste. **a s.,** namely, to wit.
sabiduría /saβiðu'ria/ *n. f.* wisdom; learning.
sabio /'saβio/ **-a** *a.* **1.** wise; scholarly. **—***n.* **2.** sage; scholar.
sable /'saβle/ *n. m.* saber.
sabor /sa'βor/ *n. m.* flavor, taste, savor.
saborear /saβore'ar/ *v.* savor, relish.
sabotaje /saβo'tahe/ *n. m.* sabotage.
sabroso /sa'βroso/ *a.* savory, tasty.
sabueso /sa'βueso/ *n. m.* hound.
sacacorchos /saka'kortʃos/ *n. m.* corkscrew.
sacapuntas /saka'puntas/ *n. f.* pencil sharpener.
sacar /sa'kar/ *v.* draw out; take out; take.
sacerdocio /saθer'ðoθio; saser'ðosio/ *n. m.* priesthood.
sacerdote /saθer'ðote; saser'ðote/ *n. m.* priest.
saciar /sa'θiar; sa'siar/ *v.* satiate.
saco /'sako/ *n. m.* sack, bag, pouch; suit coat, jacket.
sacramento /sakra'mento/ *n. m.* sacrament.
sacrificio /sakri'fiθio; sakri'fisio/ *n. m.* sacrifice. **—sacrificar,** *v.*
sacrilegio /sakri'lehio/ *n. m.* sacrilege.
sacristán /sakris'tan/ *n. m.* sexton.
sacro /'sakro/ *a.* sacred, holy.
sacrosanto /sakro'santo/ *a.* sacrosanct.
sacudir /saku'ðir/ *v.* shake, jerk, jolt.
sádico /'saðiko/ *a.* sadistic.
sadismo /sa'ðismo/ *n. m.* sadism.
sagacidad /sagaθi'ðað; sagasi'ðað/ *n. f.* sagacity.
sagaz /sa'gaθ; sa'gas/ *a.* sagacious, sage.
sagrado /sa'graðo/ *a.* sacred, holy.
sal /sal/ *n. f.* salt; *Colloq.* wit.
sala /'sala/ *n. f.* room; living room, parlor; hall, auditorium.
salado /sa'laðo/ *a.* salted, salty; *Colloq.* witty.
salar /sa'lar/ *v.* salt; steep in brine.
salario /sa'lario/ *n. m.* salary, wages.
salchicha /sal'tʃitʃa/ *n. f.* sausage.
sal de la Higuera /sal de la i'gera/ Epsom salts.
saldo /'saldo/ *n. m.* remainder, balance; (bargain) sale.
saldo acreedor /'saldo akree'ðor/ credit balance.
saldo deudor /'saldo deu'ðor/ debit balance.
salero /sa'lero/ *n. m.* salt shaker.
salida /sa'liða/ *n. f.* exit, outlet; departure.
salida de urgencia /sa'liða de ur'henθia; sa'liða de ur'hensia/ emergency exit, fire exit.
salir /salir/ *v.* go out, come out; set out, leave, start; turn out, result.
salirse de /sa'lirse de/ *v.* get out of. **s. con la suya,** have one's own way.
salitre /sa'litre/ *n. m.* saltpeter.
saliva /sa'liβa/ *n. f.* saliva.
salmo /'salmo/ *n. m.* psalm.
salmón /sal'mon/ *n. m.* salmon.
salmonete /salmo'nete/ *n. m.* red mullet.
salmuera /sal'muera/ *n. f.* pickle; brine.
salobre /sa'loβre/ *a.* salty.
salón /sa'lon/ *n. m.* parlor, living room; hall. **s. de baile,** dance hall. **s. de belleza** beauty parlor.
salpicar /salpi'kar/ *v.* spatter, splash.
salpullido /salpu'ʎiðo; salpu'yiðo/ *n. m.* rash.
salsa /'salsa/ *n. f.* sauce; gravy.
saltamontes /salta'montes/ *n. m.* grasshopper.
salteador /saltea'ðor/ *n. m.* highwayman.
saltear /salte'ar/ *v.* hold up, rob; sauté.
salto /'salto/ *n. m.* jump, leap, spring. **—saltar,** *v.*
saltón /sal'ton/ *n. m.* grasshopper.
salubre /sa'luβre/ *a.* salubrious, healthful.
salubridad /saluβri'ðað/ *n. f.* health.
salud /sa'luð/ *n. f.* health.
saludable /salu'ðaβle/ *a.* healthful, wholesome.
saludar /salu'ðar/ *v.* greet; salute.
saludo /sa'luðo/ *n. m.* greeting; salutation; salute.
salutación /saluta'θion; saluta'sion/ *n. f.* salutation.
salva /'salβa/ *n. f.* salvo.
salvación /salβa'θion; salβa'sion/ *n. f.* salvation; deliverance.
salvador /salβa'ðor/ **-ra** *n.* savior; rescuer.
salvaguardia /salβa'guarðia/ *n. m.* safeguard.
salvaje /sal'βahe/ *a.* & *n.* savage, wild (person).
salvamento /salβa'mento/ *n. m.* salvation; rescue.
salvar /sal'βar/ *v.* save; salvage; rescue; jump over.
salvavidas /salβa'βiðas/ *n. m.* life preserver.
salvia /'salβia/ *n. f.* sage (plant).
salvo /'salβo/ *a.* **1.** safe. **—***prep.* **2.** except, save (for). **s. que,** unless.
San /san/ *title.* Saint.
sanar /sa'nar/ *v.* heal, cure.
sanatorio /sana'torio/ *n. m.* sanatorium.
sanción /san'θion; san'sion/ *n. f.* sanction. **—sancionar,** *v.*
sancochar /sanko'tʃar/ *v.* parboil.
sandalia /san'dalia/ *n. f.* sandal.
sandez /san'deθ; san'des/ *n. f.* stupidity.
sandía /san'dia/ *n. f.* watermelon.
saneamiento /sanea'miento/ *n. m.* sanitation.
sangrar /saŋ'grar/ *v.* bleed.
sangre /'saŋgre/ *n. f.* blood.
sangriento /saŋ'griento/ *a.* bloody.
sanguinario /saŋgi'nario/ *a.* bloodthirsty.
sanidad /sani'ðað/ *n. f.* health.
sanitario /sani'tario/ *a.* sanitary.
sano /'sano/ *a.* healthy, sound, sane; healthful, wholesome.
santidad /santi'ðað/ *n. f.* sanctity, holiness.
santificar /santifi'kar/ *v.* sanctify.
santo /'santo/ **-ta** *a.* **1.** holy, saintly. **—***n.* **2.** *m.* saint.
Santo -ta *title.* Saint.
santuario /san'tuario/ *n. m.* sanctuary, shrine.
saña /'saɲa/ *n. f.* rage, anger.
sapiente /sa'piente/ *a.* wise.
sapo /'sapo/ *n. m.* toad.
saquear /sake'ar/ *v.* sack; ransack; plunder.
sarampión /saram'pion/ *n. m.* measles.
sarape /sa'rape/ *n. m.* (Mex.) woven blanket; shawl.
sarcasmo /sar'kasmo/ *n. m.* sarcasm.
sarcástico /sar'kastiko/ *a.* sarcastic.
sardina /sar'ðina/ *n. f.* sardine.
sargento /sar'hento/ *n. m.* sergeant.
sarna /'sarna/ *n. f.* itch.
sartén /sar'ten/ *n. m.* frying pan.
sastre /'sastre/ *n. m.* tailor.
satánico /sa'taniko/ *a.* satanic.
satélite /sa'telite/ *n. m.* satellite.

sátira /'satira/ *n. f.* satire.
satírico /sa'tiriko/ *a. & m.* satirical; satirist.
satirizar /satiri'θar; satiri'sar/ *v.* satirize.
sátiro /'satiro/ *n. m.* satyr.
satisfacción /satisfak'θion; satisfak'sion/ *n. f.* satisfaction.
satisfacer /satisfa'θer; satisfa'ser/ *v.* satisfy.
satisfactorio /satisfak'torio/ *a.* satisfactory.
saturación /satura'θion; satura'sion/ *n. f.* saturation.
saturar /satu'rar/ *v.* saturate.
sauce /'sauθe; 'sause/ *n. m.* willow.
sauna /'sauna/ *n. f.* sauna.
savia /'saβia/ *n. f.* sap.
saxofón /sakso'fon/ **saxófono** *n. m.* saxophone.
saya /'saya/ *n. f.* skirt.
sazón /sa'θon; sa'son/ *n. f.* season; seasoning. **a la s.,** at that time.
sazonar /saθo'nar; saso'nar/ *v.* flavor, season.
se /se/ *pron.* -self, -selves.
seca /'seka/ *n. f.* drought.
secador /seka'ðor/ **secador de pelo** *n. m.* hair dryer.
secante /se'kante/ *a.* **papel s.,** blotting paper.
secar /se'kar/ *v.* dry.
sección /sek'θion; sek'sion/ *n. f.* section.
seco /'seko/ *a.* dry; curt.
secreción /sekre'θion; sekre'sion/ *n. f.* secretion.
secretar /sekre'tar/ *v.* secrete.
secretaría /sekreta'ria/ *n. f.* secretary's office; secretariat.
secretario /sekre'tario/ **-ra** *n.* secretary.
secreto /se'kreto/ *a. & m.* secret.
secta /'sekta/ *n. f.* denomination; sect.
secuela /se'kuela/ *n. f.* result; sequel.
secuestrar /sekues'trar/ *v.* abduct, kidnap; hijack.
secuestro /se'kuestro/ *n. m.* abduction, kidnapping.
secular /seku'lar/ *a.* secular.
secundario /sekun'dario/ *a.* secondary.
sed /seð/ *n. f.* thirst. **tener s., estar con s.,** to be thirsty.
seda /'seða/ *n. f.* silk.
sedar /se'ðar/ *v.* quiet, allay.
sedativo /seða'tiβo/ *a. & m.* sedative.
sede /'seðe/ *n. f.* seat, headquarters.
sedentario /seðen'tario/ *a.* sedentary.
sedición /seði'θion; seði'sion/ *n. f.* sedition.
sedicioso /seði'θioso; seði'sioso/ *a.* seditious.
sediento /se'ðiento/ *a.* thirsty.
sedimento /seði'mento/ *n. m.* sediment.
sedoso /se'ðoso/ *a.* silky.
seducir /seðu'θir; seðu'sir/ *v.* seduce.
seductivo /seðuk'tiβo/ *a.* seductive, alluring.
segar /se'gar/ *v.* reap, harvest; mow.
seglar /seg'lar/ *n. m. & f.* layman, laywoman.
segmento /seg'mento/ *n. m.* segment.
segregar /segre'gar/ *v.* segregate.
seguida /se'giða/ *n. f.* succession. **en s.,** right away, at once.
seguido /se'giðo/ *a.* consecutive.
seguir /se'gir/ *v.* follow; continue, keep on, go on.
según /se'gun/ *prep.* **1.** according to. —*conj.* **2.** as.
segundo /se'gundo/ *a. & m.* second. —**segundar,** *v.*
seguridad /seguri'ðað/ *n. f.* safety, security; assurance.
seguro /se'guro/ *a.* **1.** safe, secure; sure, certain. —*n.* **2.** *m.* insurance.
seis /seis/ *a. & pron.* six.
seiscientos /seis'θientos; seis'sientos/ *a. & pron.* six hundred.
selección /selek'θion; selek'sion/ *n. f.* selection, choice.
seleccionar /selekθio'nar; seleksio'nar/ *v.* select, choose.
selecto /se'lekto/ *a.* select, choice, elite.
sello /'seʎo; 'seyo/ *n. m.* seal; stamp. —**sellar,** *v.*
selva /'selβa/ *n. f.* forest; jungle.
selvoso /sel'βoso/ *a.* sylvan.
semáforo /se'maforo/ *n. m.* semaphore; traffic light.
semana /se'mana/ *n. f.* week.
semana inglesa /se'mana iŋ'glesa/ five-day work week.
semanal /sema'nal/ *a.* weekly.
semana laboral /se'mana laβo'ral/ work week.
semántica /se'mantika/ *n. f.* semantics.
semblante /sem'βlante/ *n. m.* look, expression.
sembrado /sem'βraðo/ *n. m.* sown field.
sembrar /sem'βrar/ *v.* sow, seed.
semejante /seme'hante/ *a.* **1.** like, similar; such (a). —*n.* **2.** *m.* fellow man.
semejanza /seme'hanθa; seme'hansa/ *n. f.* similarity, likeness.
semejar /seme'har/ *v.* resemble.
semilla /se'miʎa; se'miya/ *n. f.* seed.
seminario /semi'nario/ *n. m.* seminary.
sémola /'semola/ *n. f.* semolina.
senado /se'naðo/ *n. m.* senate.
senador /sena'ðor/ **-ra** *n.* senator.
sencillez /senθi'ʎeθ; sensi'yes/ *n. f.* simplicity; naturalness.
sencillo /sen'θiʎo; sen'siyo/ *a.* simple, natural; single.
senda /'senda/ *n. f.* **sendero,** *m.* path, footpath.
senectud /senek'tuð/ *n. f.* old age.
senil /se'nil/ *a.* senile.
seno /'seno/ *n. m.* breast, bosom.
sensación /sensa'θion; sensa'sion/ *n. f.* sensation.
sensacional /sensaθio'nal; sensasio'nal/ *a.* sensational.
sensato /sen'sato/ *a.* sensible, wise.
sensibilidad /sensiβili'ðað/ *n. f.* sensibility; sensitiveness.
sensible /sen'siβle/ *a.* sensitive; emotional.
sensitivo /sensi'tiβo/ *a.* sensitive.
sensual /sen'sual/ *a.* sensual.
sensualidad /sensuali'ðað/ *n. f.* sensuality.
sentar /sen'tar/ *v.* seat. **s. bien,** fit well, be becoming.
sentarse /sen'tarse/ *v.* sit, sit down.
sentencia /sen'tenθia; sen'tensia/ *n. f.* (court) sentence.
sentidamente /sentiða'mente/ *adv.* feelingly.
sentido /sen'tiðo/ *n. m.* meaning, sense; consciousness.
sentido común /sen'tiðo ko'mun/ common sense.
sentimental /sentimen'tal/ *a.* sentimental.
sentimiento /senti'miento/ *n. m.* sentiment, feeling.
sentir /sen'tir/ *v.* feel, sense; hear; regret, be sorry.
seña /'seɲa/ *n. f.* sign, indication; (*pl.*) address.
señal /se'ɲal/ *n. f.* sign, signal; mark.
señalar /seɲa'lar/ *v.* designate, point out; mark.
señal de marcar /se'ɲal de mar'kar/ dial tone.
señor /se'ɲor/ *n. m.* gentleman; lord; (title) Mr., Sir.
señora /se'ɲora/ *n. f.* lady; wife; (title) Mrs., Madam.
señora de la limpieza /se'ɲora de la lim'pieθa; se'ɲora de la lim'piesa/ cleaning woman.
señorita /seɲo'rita/ *n. f.* young lady; (title) Miss.
sépalo /'sepalo/ *n. m.* sepal.
separación /separa'θion; separa'sion/ *n. f.* separation, parting.
separadamente /separaða'mente/ *adv.* separately.
separado /sepa'raðo/ *a.* separate; separated. —**separar,** *v.*
septentrional /septentrio'nal/ *a.* northern.
septiembre /sep'tiembre/ *n. m.* September.
séptimo /'septimo/ *a.* seventh.
sepulcro /se'pulkro/ *n. m.* sepulcher.
sepultar /sepul'tar/ *v.* bury, entomb.
sepultura /sepul'tura/ *n. f.* grave.
sequedad /seke'ðað/ *n. f.* dryness.
sequía /se'kia/ *n. f.* drought.
ser /ser/ *v.* be.
serenata /sere'nata/ *n. f.* serenade.
serenidad /sereni'ðað/ *n. f.* serenity.
sereno /se'reno/ *a.* **1.** serene, calm. —*n.* **2.** *m.* dew; watchman.
ser humano /ser u'mano/ *n.* human being.
serie /'serie/ *n. f.* series, sequence.
seriedad /serie'ðað/ *n. f.* seriousness.
serio /'serio/ *a.* serious. **en s.,** seriously.
sermón /ser'mon/ *n. m.* sermon.
seroso /se'roso/ *a.* watery.
serpiente /ser'piente/ *n. f.* serpent, snake.
serpiente de cascabel /ser'piente de kaska'βel/ rattlesnake.
serrano /se'rrano/ **-na** *n.* mountaineer.
serrar /se'rrar/ *v.* saw.
serrín /se'rrin/ *n. m.* sawdust.
servicial /serβi'θial; serβi'sial/ *a.* helpful, of service.
servicio /ser'βiθio; ser'βisio/ *n. m.* service; toilet.
servidor /serβi'ðor/ **-ra** *n.* servant.
servidumbre /serβi'ðumbre/ *n. f.* bondage; staff of servants.
servil /ser'βil/ *a.* servile, menial.
servilleta /serβi'ʎeta; serβi'yeta/ *n. f.* napkin.
servir /ser'βir/ *v.* serve. **s. para,** be good for.
servirse /ser'βirse/ *v.* help oneself.
sesenta /se'senta/ *a. & pron.* sixty.
sesgo /'sesgo/ *n. m.* slant. —**sesgar,** *v.*
sesión /se'sion/ *n. f.* session; sitting.
seso /'seso/ *n. m.* brain.
seta /'seta/ *n. f.* mushroom.
setecientos /sete'θientos; sete'sientos/ *a. & pron.* seven hundred.
setenta /se'tenta/ *a. & pron.* seventy.
seto /'seto/ *n. m.* hedge.
severamente /seβera'mente/ *adv.* severely.
severidad /seβeri'ðað/ *n. f.* severity.
severo /se'βero/ *a.* severe, strict, stern.
sexismo /sek'sismo/ *n. m.* sexism.
sexista /sek'sista/ *a. & n.* sexist.
sexo /'sekso/ *n. m.* sex.
sexto /'seksto/ *a.* sixth.
sexual /sek'sual/ *a.* sexual.
si /si/ *conj.* if; whether.
sí *pron.* **1.** -self, -selves. —*interj.* **2.** yes.
sico-. See **psicoanálisis, psicología,** etc.
sicómoro /siko'moro/ *n. m.* sycamore.
SIDA /'siða/ *n. m.* AIDS.
sidra /'siðra/ *n. f.* cider.
siempre /'siempre/ *adv.* always. **para s.,** forever. **s. que,** whenever; provided that.
sierra /'sierra/ *n. f.* saw; mountain range.
siervo /'sierβo/ **-va** *n.* slave; serf.
siesta /'siesta/ *n. f.* (afternoon) nap.
siete /'siete/ *a. & pron.* seven.
sifón /si'fon/ *n. m.* siphon; siphon bottle.
siglo /'siglo/ *n. m.* century.
signatura /signa'tura/ *n. f. Mus.* signature.
significación /signifika'θion; signifika'sion/ *n. f.* significance.
significado /signifi'kaðo/ *n. m.* meaning.
significante /signifi'kante/ *a.* significant.
significar /signifi'kar/ *v.* signify, mean.
significativo /signifika'tiβo/ *a.* significant.
signo /'signo/ *n. m.* sign, symbol; mark.
siguiente /si'giente/ *a.* following, next.
sílaba /'silaβa/ *n. f.* syllable.
silbar /sil'βar/ *v.* whistle; hiss, boo.
silbato /sil'βato/ **silbido** *n. m.* whistle.
silencio /si'lenθio; si'lensio/ *n. m.* silence, stillness.
silenciosamente /silenθiosa'mente; silensiosa'mente/ *a.* silently.
silencioso /silen'θioso; silen'sioso/ *a.* silent, still.
silicato /sili'kato/ *n. m.* silicate.
silicio /si'liθio; si'lisio/ *n. m.* silicon.
silla /'siʎa; 'siya/ *n. f.* chair; saddle.
sillón /si'ʎon; si'yon/ *n. m.* armchair.
silueta /si'lueta/ *n. f.* silhouette.
silvestre /sil'βestre/ *a.* wild, uncultivated. **fauna s.,** wildlife.
sima /'sima/ *n. f.* chasm; cavern.
simbólico /sim'boliko/ *a.* symbolic.
símbolo /'simbolo/ *n. m.* symbol.
simetría /sime'tria/ *n. f.* symmetry.
simétrico /si'metriko/ *a.* symmetrical.
símil /'simil/ **similar** *a.* similar, alike.
similitud /simili'tuð/ *n. f.* similarity.
simpatía /simpa'tia/ *n. f.* congeniality; friendly feeling.
simpático /sim'patiko/ *a.* likeable, nice, congenial.
simple /'simple/ *a.* simple.
simpleza /sim'pleθa; sim'plesa/ *n. f.* silliness; trifle.
simplicidad /simpliθi'ðað; simplisi'ðað/ *n. f.* simplicity.
simplificación /simplifika'θion; simplifika'sion/ *n. f.* simplification.
simplificar /simplifi'kar/ *v.* simplify.
simular /simu'lar/ *v.* simulate.
simultáneo /simul'taneo/ *a.* simultaneous.
sin /sin/ *prep.* without. **s. sentido,** meaningless.
sinagoga /sina'goga/ *n. f.* synagogue.
sinceridad /sinθeri'ðað; sinseri'ðað/ *n. f.* sincerity.
sincero /sin'θero; sin'sero/ *a.* sincere.
sincronizar /sinkroni'θar; sinkroni'sar/ *v.* synchronize.
sindicato /sindi'kato/ *n. m.* syndicate; labor union.
síndrome /'sindrome/ *n. m.* syndrome.
sinfonía /sinfo'nia/ *n. f.* symphony.
sinfónico /sin'foniko/ *a.* symphonic.
singular /siŋgu'lar/ *a. & m.* singular.
siniestro /si'niestro/ *a.* sinister, ominous.
sino /'sino/ *conj.* but.
sinónimo /si'nonimo/ *n. m.* synonym.
sinrazón /sinra'θon; sinra'son/ *n. f.* wrong, injustice.
sinsabor /sinsa'βor/ *n. m.* displeasure, distaste, trouble.
sintaxis /sin'taksis/ *n. f.* syntax.
síntesis /'sintesis/ *n. f.* synthesis.
sintético /sin'tetiko/ *a.* synthetic.
síntoma /'sintoma/ *n. m.* symptom.
siquiera /si'kiera/ *adv.* **ni s.,** not even.
sirena /si'rena/ *n. f.* siren.
sirviente /sir'βiente/ **-ta** *n.* servant.
sistema /sis'tema/ *n. m.* system.
sistemático /siste'matiko/ *a.* systematic.
sistematizar /sistemati'θar; sistemati'sar/ *v.* systematize.
sitiar /si'tiar/ *v.* besiege.
sitio /'sitio/ *n. m.* site, location, place, spot.

situación /situa'θion; situa'sion/ *n. f.* situation; location.

situar /si'tuar/ *v.* situate; locate.

smoking /'smokiŋ/ *n. m.* tuxedo, dinner jacket.

so /so/ *prep.* under.

soba /'soβa/ *n. f.* massage. **—sobar,** *v.*

sobaco /so'βako/ *n. m.* armpit.

sobaquero /soβa'kero/ *n. f.* armhole.

soberano /soβe'rano/ **-na** *a.* & *n.* sovereign.

soberbia /so'βerβia/ *n. f.* arrogance.

soberbio /so'βerβio/ *a.* superb; arrogant.

soborno /so'βorno/ *n. m.* bribe. **—sobornar,** *v.*

sobra /'soβra/ *n. f.* excess, surplus. **de sobra,** to spare.

sobrado /so'βraðo/ *n. m.* attic.

sobrante /so'βrante/ *a.* & *m.* surplus.

sobras /'soβras/ *n. f.pl.* leftovers.

sobre /'soβre/ *prep.* **1.** about; above, over. **—***n.* **2.** *m.* envelope.

sobrecama /soβre'kama/ *n. f.* bedspread.

sobrecargo /soβre'kargo/ *n. m.* supercargo.

sobredicho /soβre'ðitʃo/ *a.* aforesaid.

sobredosis /soβre'ðosis/ *n. f.* overdose.

sobrehumano /soβreu'mano/ *a.* superhuman.

sobrenatural /soβrenatu'ral/ *a.* supernatural, weird.

sobrepasar /soβrepa'sar/ *v.* surpass.

sobresalir /soβresa'lir/ *v.* excel.

sobretodo /soβre'toðo/ *n. m.* overcoat.

sobrevivir /soβreβi'βir/ *v.* survive, outlive.

sobriedad /soβrie'ðað/ *n. f.* sobriety; moderation.

sobrina /so'βrina/ *n. f.* niece.

sobrino /so'βrino/ *n. m.* nephew.

sobrio /'soβrio/ *a.* sober, temperate.

socarrén /soka'rren/ *n. m.* eaves.

sociable /so'θiaβle; so'siaβle/ *a.* sociable.

social /so'θial; so'sial/ *a.* social.

socialismo /soθia'lismo; sosia'lismo/ *n. m.* socialism.

socialista /soθia'lista; sosia'lista/ *a.* & *n.* socialist.

sociedad /soθie'ðað; sosie'ðað/ *n. f.* society; association.

sociedad de consumo /soθie'ðað de kon'sumo; sosie'ðað de kon'sumo/ consumer society.

socio /'soθio; 'sosio/ **-cia** *n.* associate, partner; member.

sociología /soθiolo'hia; sosiolo'hia/ *n. f.* sociology.

sociológico /soθio'lohiko; sosio-'lohiko/ *a.* sociological.

sociólogo /so'θiologo; so'siologo/ **-ga** *n.* sociologist.

socorrista /soko'rrista/ *n. m.* & *f.* lifeguard.

socorro /so'korro/ *n. m.* help, aid. **—socorrer,** *v.*

soda /'soða/ *n. f.* soda.

sodio /'soðio/ *n. m.* sodium.

soez /so'eθ; so'es/ *a.* vulgar.

sofá /so'fa/ *n. m.* sofa, couch.

sofisma /so'fisma/ *n. m.* sophism.

sofista /so'fista/ *n. m.* & *f.* sophist.

sofocación /sofoka'θion; sofoka'sion/ *n. f.* suffocation.

sofocar /sofo'kar/ *v.* smother, suffocate, stifle, choke.

sofrito /so'frito/ *n. m.* sauce of sautéed tomatoes, peppers, onions, and garlic.

software /'sofθwer/ *n. m.* software.

soga /'soga/ *n. f.* rope.

soja /'soha/ *n. f.* soya.

sol /sol/ *n. m.* sun.

solada /so'laða/ *n. f.* dregs.

solanera /sola'nera/ *n. f.* sunburn.

solapa /so'lapa/ *n. f.* lapel.

solar /so'lar/ *a.* **1.** solar. **—***n.* **2.** *m.* building lot.

solaz /so'laθ; so'las/ *n. m.* solace, comfort. **—solazar,** *v.*

soldado /sol'daðo/ *n. m.* soldier.

soldar /sol'dar/ *v.* solder, weld.

soledad /sole'ðað/ *n. f.* solitude, privacy.

solemne /so'lemne/ *a.* solemn.

solemnemente /solemne'mente/ *adv.* solemnly.

solemnidad /solemni'ðað/ *n. f.* solemnity.

soler /so'ler/ *v.* be in the habit of.

solicitador /soliθita'ðor; solisita'ðor/ **-ra** *n.* applicant, petitioner.

solicitar /soliθi'tar; solisi'tar/ *v.* solicit; apply for.

solícito /so'liθito; so'lisito/ *a.* solicitous.

solicitud /soliθi'tuð; solisi'tuð/ *n. f.* solicitude; application.

sólidamente /soliða'mente/ *adv.* solidly.

solidaridad /soliðari'ðað/ *n. f.* solidarity.

solidez /soli'ðeθ; soli'ðes/ *n. f.* solidity.

solidificar /soliðifi'kar/ *v.* solidify.

sólido /'soliðo/ *a.* & *m.* solid.

soliloquio /soli'lokio/ *n. m.* soliloquy.

solitario /soli'tario/ *a.* solitary, lone.

sollozo /so'ʎoθo; so'yoso/ *n. m.* sob. **—sollozar,** *v.*

solo /'solo/ *a.* **1.** only; single; alone; lonely. **a solas,** alone. **—***n.* **2.** *m. Mus.* solo.

sólo *adv.* only, just.

solomillo /solo'miʎo; solo'miyo/ *n. m.* sirloin.

soltar /sol'tar/ *v.* release; loosen.

soltero /sol'tero/ **-ra** *a.* & *n.* single, unmarried (person).

soltura /sol'tura/ *n. f.* poise, ease, facility.

solubilidad /solußili'ðað/ *n. f.* solubility.

solución /solu'θion; solu'sion/ *n. f.* solution.

solucionar /soluθio'nar; solusio'nar/ *v.* solve, settle.

solvente /sol'βente/ *a.* solvent.

sombra /'sombra/ *n. f.* shade; shadow. **—sombrear,** *v.*

sombra de ojos /'sombra de 'ohos/ eye shadow.

sombrerera /sombre'rera/ *n. f.* hatbox.

sombrero /som'βrero/ *n. m.* hat.

sombrilla /som'βriʎa; som'βriya/ *n. f.* parasol.

sombrío /som'βrio/ *a.* somber, bleak, gloomy.

sombroso /som'βroso/ *a.* very shady.

someter /some'ter/ *v.* subject; submit.

somnífero /som'nifero/ *n. m.* sleeping pill.

somnolencia /somno'lenθia; somno'lensia/ *n. f.* drowsiness.

son /son/ *n. m.* sound. **—sonar,** *v.*

sonata /so'nata/ *n. f.* sonata.

sondar /son'dar/ *v.* sound, fathom.

sonido /so'niðo/ *n. m.* sound.

sonoridad /sonori'ðað/ *n. f.* sonority.

sonoro /so'noro/ *a.* sonorous.

sonrisa /son'risa/ *n. f.* smile. **—sonreír,** *v.*

sonrojo /son'roho/ *n. m.* flush, blush. **—sonrojarse,** *v.*

soñador /soɲa'ðor/ **-ra** *a.* & *n.* dreamy; dreamer.

soñar /so'ɲar/ *v.* dream.

soñoliento /soɲo'liento/ *a.* sleepy.

sopa /'sopa/ *n. f.* soup.

soplar /so'plar/ *v.* blow.

soplete /so'plete/ *n. m.* blowtorch.

soplo /'soplo/ *n. m.* breath; puff, gust.

soportar /sopor'tar/ *v.* abide, bear, stand.

soprano /so'prano/ *n. m.* & *f.* soprano.

sorbete /sor'βete/ *n. m.* sherbet.

sorbo /'sorβo/ *n. m.* sip. **—sorber,** *v.*

sordera /sor'ðera/ *n. f.* deafness.

sórdidamente /sorðiða'mente/ *adv.* sordidly.

sordidez /sorði'ðeθ; sorði'ðes/ *n. f.* sordidness.

sórdido /'sorðiðo/ *a.* sordid.

sordo /'sorðo/ *a.* deaf; muffled, dull.

sordomudo /sorðo'muðo/ **-da** *a.* & *n.* deaf-mute.

sorpresa /sor'presa/ *n. f.* surprise. **—sorprender,** *v.*

sorteo /sor'teo/ *n. m.* drawing lots; raffle.

sortija /sor'tiha/ *n. f.* ring.

sosa /'sosa/ *n. f. Chem.* soda.

soso /'soso/ *a.* dull, insipid, tasteless.

sospecha /sos'petʃa/ *n. f.* suspicion.

sospechar /sospe'tʃar/ *v.* suspect.

sospechoso /sospe'tʃoso/ *a.* suspicious.

sostén /sos'ten/ *n. m.* bra, brassiere; support.

sostener /soste'ner/ *v.* hold, support; maintain.

sostenimiento /sosteni'miento/ *n. m.* sustenance.

sota /'sota/ *n. f.* jack (in cards).

sótano /'sotano/ *n. m.* basement, cellar.

soto /'soto/ *n. m.* grove.

soviet /so'βiet/ *n. m.* soviet.

soya /'soya/ *n. f.* soybean.

su /su/ *a.* his, her, its, their, your.

suave /'suaβe/ *a.* smooth; gentle, soft, mild.

suavidad /suaβi'ðað/ *n. f.* smoothness; gentleness, softness, mildness.

suavizar /suaβi'θar; suaβi'sar/ *v.* soften.

subalterno /suβal'terno/ **-na** *a.* & *n.* subordinate.

subasta /su'βasta/ *n. f.* auction.

subcampeón /suβkampe'on/ **-na** *n.* runner-up.

subconsciencia /suβkons'θienθia; suβkons'siensia/ *n. f.* subconscious.

súbdito /'suβðito/ **-ta** *n.* subject.

subestimar /suβesti'mar/ *v.* underestimate.

subida /su'βiða/ *n. f.* ascent, rise.

subilla /su'βiʎa; su'βiya/ *n. f.* awl.

subir /su'βir/ *v.* rise, climb, ascend, mount. **s. a,** amount to.

súbito /'suβito/ *a.* sudden.

subjetivo /suβhe'tiβo/ *a.* subjective.

subjuntivo /suβhun'tiβo/ *a.* & *m.* subjunctive.

sublimación /suβlima'θion; suβlima-'sion/ *n. f.* sublimation.

sublimar /suβli'mar/ *v.* elevate; sublimate.

sublime /su'βlime/ *a.* sublime.

submarinismo /suβmari'nismo/ *n. m.* scuba diving.

submarino /suβma'rino/ *a.* & *m.* submarine.

subordinación /suβorðina'θion; suβorðina'sion/ *n. f.* subordination.

subordinado /suβorði'naðo/ **-da** *a.* & *n.* subordinate. **—subordinar,** *v.*

subrayar /suβra'yar/ *v.* underline.

subscri- = suscri-

subscribirse /suβskri'βirse/ *v.* subscribe; sign one's name.

subscripción /suβskrip'θion; suβskrip'sion/ *n. f.* subscription.

subsecuente /suβse'kuente/ *a.* subsequent.

subsidiario /suβsi'ðiario/ *a.* subsidiary.

subsiguiente /suβsi'giente/ *a.* subsequent.

substan- = sustan-

substi- = susti-

substraer /suβstra'er/ = subtract.

subsuelo /suβ'suelo/ *n. m.* subsoil.

subterfugio /suβter'fuhio/ *n. m.* subterfuge.

subterráneo /suβte'rraneo/ *a.* **1.** subterranean, underground. **—***n.* **2.** *m.* place underground; subway.

subtítulo /suβ'titulo/ *n. m.* subtitle.

suburbio /su'βurβio/ *n. m.* suburb.

subvención /suββen'θion; suββen-'sion/ *n. f.* subsidy, grant.

subversión /suββer'sion/ *n. f.* subversion.

subversivo /suββer'siβo/ *a.* subversive.

subvertir /suββer'tir/ *v.* subvert.

subyugación /suβyuga'θion; suβyuga'sion/ *n. f.* subjugation.

subyugar /suβyu'gar/ *v.* subjugate, quell.

succión /suk'θion; suk'sion/ *n. f.* suction.

suceder /suθe'ðer; suse'ðer/ *v.* happen, occur, befall. **s. a,** succeed, follow.

sucesión /suθe'sion; suse'sion/ *n. f.* succession.

sucesivo /suθe'siβo; suse'siβo/ *a.* successive. **en lo s.,** in the future.

suceso /su'θeso; su'seso/ *n. m.* event.

sucesor /suθe'sor; suse'sor/ **-ra** *n.* successor.

suciedad /suθie'ðað; susie'ðað/ *n. f.* filth, dirt.

sucio /'suθio; 'susio/ *a.* filthy, dirty.

suculento /suku'lento/ *a.* succulent.

sucumbir /sukum'βir/ *v.* succumb.

sud /suð/ *n. m.* south.

sudadera /suða'ðera/ *n. f.* sweatshirt.

Sudáfrica /su'ðafrika/ *n. f.* South Africa.

sudafricano /suðafri'kano/ **-na** *a.* & *n.* South African.

sudamericano /suðameri'kano/ **-na** *a.* & *n.* South American.

sudar /su'ðar/ *v.* perspire, sweat.

sudeste /su'ðeste/ *n. m.* southeast.

sudoeste /suðo'este/ *n. m.* southwest.

sudor /su'ðor/ *n. m.* perspiration, sweat.

Suecia /'sueθia; 'suesia/ *n. f.* Sweden.

sueco /'sueko/ **-ca** *a.* & *n.* Swedish; Swede.

suegra /'suegra/ *n. f.* mother-in-law.

suegro /'suegro/ *n. m.* father-in-law.

suela /'suela/ *n. f.* sole.

sueldo /'sueldo/ *n. m.* salary, wages.

suelo /'suelo/ *n. m.* soil; floor; ground.

suelto /'suelto/ *a.* **1.** loose; free; odd, separate. **—***n.* **2.** loose change.

sueño /'sueɲo/ *n. m.* sleep; sleepiness; dream. **tener s.,** to be sleepy.

suero /'suero/ *n. m.* serum.

suerte /'suerte/ *n. f.* luck; chance; lot.

suéter /'sueter/ *n. m.* sweater.

suficiente /sufi'θiente; sufi'siente/ *a.* sufficient.

sufragio /su'frahio/ *n. m.* suffrage.

sufrimiento /sufri'miento/ *n. m.* suffering, agony.

sufrir /su'frir/ *v.* suffer; undergo; endure.

sugerencia /suhe'renθia; suhe'rensia/ *n. f.* suggestion.

sugerir /suhe'rir/ *v.* suggest.

sugestión /suhes'tion/ *n. f.* suggestion.

sugestionar /suhestio'nar/ *v.* influence; hypnotize.

suicida /sui'θiða; sui'siða/ *n. m.* & *f.* suicide (person).

suicidarse /suiθi'ðarse; suisi'ðarse/ *v.* commit suicide.

suicidio /sui'θiðio; sui'siðio/ *n. m.* (act of) suicide.

Suiza /'suiθa; 'suisa/ *n. f.* Switzerland.

suizo /'suiθo; 'suiso/ **-za** *a.* & *n.* Swiss.

sujeción /suhe'θion; suhe'sion/ *n. f.* subjection.

sujetador /suheta'ðor/ *n. m.* bra, brassiere.

sujetapapeles /su'hetapa'peles/ *n. m.* paper clip.

sujetar /suhe'tar/ *v.* hold, fasten, clip.

sujeto /su'heto/ *a.* **1.** subject, liable. **—***n.* **2.** *m. Gram.* subject.

sulfato /sul'fato/ *n. m.* sulfate.

sulfuro /sul'furo/ *n. m.* sulfide.

sultán /sul'tan/ *n. m.* sultan.

suma /'suma/ *n. f.* sum, amount. **en s.,** in short. **s. global,** lump sum.

sumar /su'mar/ *v.* add up.

sumaria /su'maria/ *n. f.* indictment.

sumario /su'mario/ *a.* & *m.* summary.

sumergir /sumer'hir/ v. submerge.

sumersión /sumer'sion/ n. f. submersion.

sumisión /sumi'sion/ n. f. submission.

sumiso /su'miso/ a. submissive.

sumo /'sumo/ a. great, high, utmost.

suntuoso /sun'tuoso/ a. sumptuous.

superar /supe'rar/ v. overcome, surpass.

superficial /superfi'θial; superfi'sial/ a. superficial, shallow.

superficie /super'fiθie; super'fisie/ f. surface.

superfluo /su'perfluo/ a. superfluous.

superhombre /super'ombre/ n. m. superman.

superintendente /superinten'dente/ n. m. & f. superintendent.

superior /supe'rior/ a. **1.** superior; upper, higher. —n. **2.** m. superior.

superioridad /superiori'ðað/ n. f. superiority.

superlativo /superla'tiβo/ n. m. & a. superlative.

superstición /supersti'θion; supersti'sion/ n. f. superstition.

supersticioso /supersti'θioso; supersti'sioso/ a. superstitious.

supervisar /superβi'sar/ v. supervise.

supervivencia /superβi'βenθia; superβi'βensia/ n. f. survival.

suplantar /suplan'tar/ v. supplant.

suplementario /suplemen'tario/ a. supplementary.

suplemento /suple'mento/ n. m. supplement. —**suplementar**, v.

suplente /su'plente/ a. & n. substitute.

súplica /'suplika/ n. f. request, entreaty, plea.

suplicación /suplika'θion; suplika'sion/ n. f. supplication; request, entreaty.

suplicar /supli'kar/ v. request, entreat; implore.

suplicio /su'pliθio; su'plisio/ n. m. torture, ordeal.

suplir /su'plir/ v. supply.

suponer /supo'ner/ v. suppose, pressume, assume.

suposición /suposi'θion; suposi'sion/ n. f. supposition, assumption.

supositorio /suposi'torio/ n. m. suppository.

supremacía /suprema'θia; suprema'sia/ n. f. supremacy.

supremo /su'premo/ a. supreme.

supresión /supre'sion/ n. f. suppression.

suprimir /supri'mir/ v. suppress; abolish.

supuesto /su'puesto/ a. supposed. **por s.,** of course.

sur /sur/ n. m. south.

surco /'surko/ n. m. furrow. —**surcar,** v.

surgir /sur'hir/ v. arise; appear suddenly.

surtido /sur'tiðo/ n. m. assortment; supply, stock.

surtir /sur'tir/ v. furnish, supply.

susceptibilidad /susθeptiβili'ðað; susseptiβili'ðað/ n. f. susceptibility.

susceptible /susθep'tiβle; sussep'tiβle/ a. susceptible.

suscitar /susθi'tar; sussi'tar/ v. stir up.

suspender /suspen'der/ v. withhold; suspend; fail (in a course).

suspensión /suspen'sion/ n. f. suspension.

suspenso /sus'penso/ n. m. failing grade. **en s.,** in suspense.

suspicacia /suspi'kaθia; suspi'kasia/ n. f. suspicion, distrust.

suspicaz /suspi'kaθ; suspi'kas/ a. suspicious.

suspicazmente /suspika'θmente; suspikas'mente/ adv. suspiciously.

suspiro /sus'piro/ n. m. sigh. —**suspirar,** v.

sustancia /sus'tanθia; sus'tansia/ n. f. substance.

sustancial /sus'tanθial; sus'tansial/ a. substantial.

sustantivo /sustan'tiβo/ n. m. substantive, noun.

sustentar /susten'tar/ v. sustain, support.

sustento /sus'tento/ n. m. sustenance, support, living.

sustitución /sustitu'θion; sustitu'sion/ n. f. substitution.

sustituir /susti'tuir/ v. replace; substitute.

sustitutivo /sustitu'tiβo/ a. substitute.

sustituto /susti'tuto/ **-ta** n. substitute.

susto /'susto/ n. m. fright, scare.

susurro /su'surro/ n. m. rustle; whisper. —**susurrar,** v.

sutil /su'til/ a. subtle.

sutileza /suti'leθa, sutili'ðaθ; suti'lesa, sutili'ðað/ **sutilidad** n. f. subtlety.

sutura /su'tura/ n. f. suture.

suyo /'suyo/ a. his, hers, theirs, yours.

T

tabaco /ta'βako/ n. m. tobacco.

tábano /'taβano/ n. m. horsefly.

tabaquería /taβake'ria/ n. f. tobacco shop.

taberna /ta'βerna/ n. f. tavern, bar.

tabernáculo /taβer'nakulo/ n. m. tabernacle.

tabique /ta'βike/ n. m. dividing wall, partition.

tabla /'taβla/ n. f. board, plank; table, list. **t. de planchar,** ironing board.

tablado /ta'βlaðo/ n. m. stage, platform.

tablero /ta'βlero/ n. m. panel.

tableta /ta'βleta/ n. f. tablet.

tablilla /ta'βliʎa; ta'βliya/ n. f. bulletin board.

tabú /ta'βu/ n. m. taboo.

tabular /taβu'lar/ a. tabular.

tacaño /ta'kaɲo/ a. stingy.

tacha /'tatʃa/ n. f. fault, defect.

tachar /ta'tʃar/ v. find fault with; cross out.

tachuela /ta'tʃuela/ n. f. tack.

tácitamente /'taθitamente; 'tasitamente/ adv. tacitly.

tácito /'taθito; 'tasito/ a. tacit.

taciturno /taθi'turno; tasi'turno/ a. taciturn.

taco /'tako/ n. m. heel (of shoe); billiard cue.

tacón /ta'kon/ n. m. heel (of shoe).

táctico /'taktiko/ a. tactical.

tacto /'takto/ n. m. (sense of) touch; tact.

tafetán /tafe'tan/ n. m. taffeta.

taimado /tai'maðo/ a. sly.

tajada /ta'haða/ n. cut, slice. —**tajar,** v.

tajea /ta'hea/ n. f. channel.

tal /tal/ a. such. **con t. que.,** provided that. **t. vez,** perhaps.

taladrar /tala'ðrar/ v. drill.

taladro /ta'laðro/ n. m. Mech. drill.

talante /ta'lante/ n. m. humor, disposition.

talco /'talko/ n. m. talc.

talega /ta'lega/ n. f. bag, sack.

talento /ta'lento/ n. m. talent.

talla /'taʎa; 'taya/ n. f. engraving; stature; size (of suit).

tallador /taʎa'ðor; taya'ðor/ **-ra** n. engraver; dealer (at cards).

talle /'taʎe; 'taye/ n. m. figure; waist; fit.

taller /ta'ʎer; ta'yer/ n. m. workshop, factory.

tallo /'taʎo; 'tayo/ n. m. stem, stalk.

talón /ta'lon/ n. m. heel (of foot); (baggage) check, stub.

tamal /ta'mal/ n. m. tamale.

tamaño /ta'maɲo/ n. m. size.

tambalear /tambale'ar/ v. stagger, totter.

también /tam'bien/ adv. also, too.

tambor /tam'bor/ n. m. drum.

tamiz /ta'miθ; ta'mis/ n. m. sieve, sifter.

tampoco /tam'poko/ adv. neither, either.

tan /tan/ adv. so.

tanda /'tanda/ n. f. turn, relay.

tándem /'tandem/ n. m. tandem; pair.

tangencia /taŋ'genθia; taŋ'gensia/ n. f. tangency.

tangible /taŋ'giβle/ a. tangible.

tango /'taŋgo/ n. m. tango (dance or music).

tanque /'tanke/ n. m. tank.

tanteo /tan'teo/ n. m. estimate. —**tantear,** v.

tanto /'tanto/ a. & pron. **1.** so much, so many; as much, as many. **entre t., mientras t.,** meanwhile. **por lo t.,** therefore. **un t.,** somewhat, a bit. —n. **2.** m. point (in games) **3.** (pl.) score. **estar al t.,** to be up to date.

tañer /ta'ɲer/ v. play (an instrument); ring (bells).

tapa /'tapa/ n. f. cap, cover; snack served in a bar. —**tapar,** v.

tapadero /tapa'ðero/ n. m. stopper, lid.

tápara /'tapara/ n. f. caper.

tapete /ta'pete/ n. m. small rug, mat, cover.

tapia /'tapia/ n. f. wall.

tapicería /tapiθe'ria; tapise'ria/ n. f. tapestry.

tapioca /ta'pioka/ n. f. tapioca.

tapiz /ta'piθ; ta'pis/ n. m. tapestry; carpet.

tapizado (de pared) /tapi'θaðo de pa'reð tapi'saðo de pa'reð/ n. m. (wall) covering.

tapón /ta'pon/ n. m. plug; cork.

taquigrafía /takigra'fia/ n. f. shorthand.

taquilla /ta'kiʎa; ta'kiya/ n. f. ticket office; box office; ticket window.

tara /'tara/ n. f. hang-up.

tarántula /ta'rantula/ n. f. tarantula.

tararear /tarare'ar/ v. hum.

tardanza /tar'ðanθa; tar'ðansa/ n. f. delay; lateness.

tardar /tar'ðar/ v. delay; be late; take (of time). **a más t.,** at the latest.

tarde /'tarðe/ adv. **1.** late. —n. **2.** f. afternoon.

tardío /tar'ðio/ a. late, belated.

tarea /ta'rea/ n. f. task, assignment.

tarifa /ta'rifa/ n. f. rate; tariff; price list.

tarjeta /tar'heta/ n. f. card.

tarjeta bancaria /tar'heta ban'karia/ bank card.

tarjeta de crédito /tar'heta de 'kreðito/ credit card.

tarjeta de embarque /tar'heta de em'βarke/ boarding pass.

tarta /'tarta/ n. f. tart.

tartamudear /tartamuðe'ar/ v. stammer, falter.

tasa /'tasa/ n. f. rate.

tasación /tasa'θion; tasa'sion/ n. f. valuation.

tasar /ta'sar/ v. assess, appraise.

tasca /'taska/ n. f. bar, pub.

tasugo /ta'sugo/ n. m. badger.

tatuar /tatu'ar/ v. tattoo.

tautología /tautolo'hia/ n. f. tautology.

taxi /'taksi/ **taxímetro** n. m. taxi.

taxista /tak'sista/ n. m. & f. taxi driver.

taxonomía /taksono'mia/ n. f. taxonomy.

taza /'taθa; 'tasa/ n. f. cup.

te /te/ pron. you; yourself.

té n. m. tea.

team /tim/ n. m. team.

teátrico /te'atriko/ a. theatrical.

teatro /te'atro/ n. m. theater.

tebeo /te'βeo/ n. m. comic book.

techo /'tetʃo/ n. m. roof. —**techar,** v.

tecla /'tekla/ n. f. key (of a piano, etc.).

teclado /te'klaðo/ n. m. keyboard.

teclado numérico /te'klaðo nu'meriko/ numeric keypad.

técnica /'teknika/ n. f. technique.

técnicamente /'teknikamente/ adv. technically.

técnico /'tekniko/ a. **1.** technical; —m. **2.** repairman, technician.

tecnología /teknolo'hia/ n. f. technology.

tedio /'teðio/ n. m. tedium, boredom.

tedioso /te'ðioso/ a. tedious.

teísmo /te'ismo/ n. m. theism.

teja /'teha/ n. f. tile.

tejado /te'haðo/ n. m. roof.

tejano /te'hano/ **-na** a. & n. Texan.

tejanos /te'hanos/ n. m.pl. jeans.

tejer /te'her/ v. weave; knit.

tejido /te'hiðo/ n. m. fabric; weaving.

tejón /te'hon/ n. m. badger.

tela /'tela/ n. f. cloth, fabric, web. **t. metálica,** screen; screening. **t. vaquera,** denim.

telar /te'lar/ n. m. loom.

telaraña /tela'raɲa/ n. f. cobweb, spiderweb.

telefonista /telefo'nista/ n. m. & f. (telephone) operator.

teléfono /te'lefono/ n. m. telephone. —**telefonear,** v.

teléfono gratuito /te'lefono gra'tuito/ toll-free number.

teléfono público /te'lefono 'puβliko/ pay phone, public telephone.

teléfono rojo /te'lefono 'rroho/ hotline.

telégrafo /te'legrafo/ n. m. telegraph. —**telegrafear,** v.

telegrama /tele'grama/ n. m. telegram.

telescopio /teles'kopio/ n. m. telescope.

televisión /teleβi'sion/ n. f. television.

telón /te'lon/ n. m. Theat. curtain.

telurio /te'lurio/ n. m. tellurium.

tema /'tema/ n. m. theme, subject.

temblar /tem'blar/ v. tremble, quake; shake, shiver.

temblor /tem'blor/ n. m. tremor; shiver.

temer /te'mer/ v. fear, be afraid of, dread.

temerario /teme'rario/ a. rash.

temeridad /temeri'ðað/ n. f. temerity.

temerosamente /temerosa'mente/ adv. timorously.

temeroso /teme'roso/ a. fearful.

temor /te'mor/ n. m. fear.

témpano /'tempano/ n. m. kettledrum; iceberg.

temperamento /tempera'mento/ n. m. temperament.

temperancia /tempe'ranθia; tempe'ransia/ n. f. temperance.

temperatura /tempera'tura/ n. f. temperature.

tempestad /tempes'tað/ n. f. tempest, storm.

tempestuoso /tempes'tuoso/ a. tempestuous, stormy.

templado /tem'plaðo/ a. temperate, mild, moderate.

templanza /tem'planθa; tem'plansa/ n. f. temperance; mildness.

templar /tem'plar/ v. temper; tune (an instrument).

templo /'templo/ n. m. temple.

temporada /tempo'raða/ n. f. season, time, spell.

temporal /tempo'ral/ **temporáneo** a. temporary.

temprano /tem'prano/ a. & adv. early.

tenacidad /tenaθi'ðað; tenasi'ðað/ n. f. tenacity.

tenaz /te'naθ; te'nas/ a. tenacious, stubborn.

tenazmente /tenaθ'mente; tenas'mente/ adv. tenaciously.

tendencia /ten'denθia; tendensia/ n. f. tendency, trend.

tender /ten'der/ v. stretch, stretch out.

tendero /ten'dero/ **-ra** n. shopkeeper, storekeeper.

tendón /ten'don/ n. m. tendon, sinew.

tenebrosidad /teneβrosi'ðað/ n. f. gloom.

tenebroso /tene'βroso/ a. dark, gloomy.

tenedor /tene'ðor/ n. **1.** m. & f. keeper; holder. **2.** m. fork.

tener /te'ner/ v. have; own; hold. **t. que,** have to, must.

teniente /te'niente/ n. m. lieutenant.

tenis /'tenis/ n. m. tennis; (pl.) sneakers.

tenor /te'nor/ n. m. tenor.

tensión /ten'sion/ n. f. tension, stress, strain.

tenso /'tenso/ a. tense.

tentación /tenta'θion; tenta'sion/ n. f. temptation.

tentáculo /ten'takulo/ n. m. tentacle.

tentador /tenta'ðor/ a. alluring, tempting.

tentar /ten'tar/ v. tempt, lure; grope, probe.

tentativa /tenta'tiβa/ n. f. attempt.

tentativo /tenta'tiβo/ a. tentative.

teñir /te'ɲir/ v. tint, dye.

teología /teolo'hia/ n. f. theology.

teológico /teo'lohiko/ a. theological.

teoría /teo'ria/ n. f. theory.

teórico /te'oriko/ a. theoretical.

terapéutico /tera'peutiko/ a. therapeutic.

tercero /ter'θero; ter'sero/ a. third.

tercio /'terθio; 'tersio/ n. m. third.

terciopelo /terθio'pelo; tersio'pelo/ n. m. velvet.

terco /'terko/ a. obstinate, stubborn.

termal /ter'mal/ a. thermal.

terminación /termina'θion; termina'sion/ n. f. termination; completion.

terminal aérea /termi'nal 'airea/ n. f. air terminal.

terminar /termi'nar/ v. terminate, finish.

término /'termino/ n. m. term; end.

terminología /terminolo'hia/ n. f. terminology.

termómetro /ter'mometro/ n. m. thermometer.

termos /'termos/ n. m. thermos.

termostato /ter'mostato/ n. m. thermostat.

ternero /ter'nero/ **-ra** n. calf.

ternura /ter'nura/ n. f. tenderness.

terquedad /terke'ðað/ n. f. stubbornness.

terraza /te'rraθa; te'rrasa/ n. f. terrace.

terremoto /terre'moto/ n. m. earthquake.

terreno /te'rreno/ a. **1.** earthly, terrestrial. —n. **2.** m. ground, terrain; lot, plot.

terrible /te'rriβle/ a. terrible, awful.

terrífico /te'rrifiko/ a. terrifying.

territorio /terri'torio/ n. m. territory.

terrón /te'rron/ n. m. clod, lump; mound.

terror /te'rror/ n. m. terror.

terso /'terso/ a. smooth, glossy; terse.

tertulia /ter'tulia/ n. f. social gathering, party.

tesis /'tesis/ n. f. thesis.

tesorería /tesore'ria/ n. f. treasury.

tesorero /teso'rero/ **-ra** n. treasurer.

tesoro /te'soro/ n. m. treasure.

testamento /testa'mento/ n. m. will, testament.

testarudo /testa'ruðo/ a. stubborn.

testificar /testifi'kar/ v. testify.

testigo /tes'tigo/ n. m. & f. witness.

testimonial /testimo'nial/ a. testimonial.

testimonio /testi'monio/ n. m. testimony.

teta /'teta/ n. f. teat.

tetera /te'tera/ n. f. teapot.

tétrico /'tetriko/ a. sad; gloomy.

texto /'teksto/ n. m. text.

textura /teks'tura/ n. f. texture.

tez /teθ; tes/ n. f. complexion.

ti /ti/ pron. you; yourself.

tía /'tia/ n. f. aunt.

tibio /'tiβio/ a. lukewarm.

tiburón /tiβu'ron/ n. m. shark.

tiemblo /'tiemblo/ n. m. aspen.

tiempo /'tiempo/ n. m. time; weather; Gram. tense.

tienda /'tienda/ n. f. shop, store; tent.

tientas /'tientas/ n. f.pl. **andar a t.,** to grope (in the dark).

tierno /'tierno/ a. tender.

tierra /'tierra/ n. f. land; ground; earth, dirt, soil.

tieso /'tieso/ a. taut, stiff, hard, strong.

tiesto /'tiesto/ n. m. flower pot.

tiesura /tie'sura/ n. f. stiffness; harshness.

tifo /'tifo/ n. m. typhus.

tifoideo /tifoi'ðeo/ n. m. typhoid fever.

tigre /'tigre/ n. m. tiger.

tijeras /ti'heras/ n. f.pl. scissors.

tila /'tila/ n. f. linden.

timbre /'timbre/ n. m. seal, stamp; tone; (electric) bell.

tímidamente /'timiðamente/ adv. timidly.

timidez /timi'ðeθ; timi'ðes/ n. f. timidity.

tímido /'timiðo/ a. timid, shy.

timón /ti'mon/ n. m. rudder, helm.

tímpano /'timpano/ n. m. kettledrum; eardrum.

tina /'tina/ n. f. tub, vat.

tinaja /ti'naha/ n. f. jar.

tinta /'tinta/ n. f. ink.

tinte /'tinte/ n. m. tint, shade.

tintero /tin'tero/ n. m. inkwell.

tinto /'tinto/ a. wine-colored; red (of wine).

tintorería /tintore'ria/ n. f. dry cleaning shop.

tintorero /tinto'rero/ **-ra** n. dyer; dry cleaner.

tintura /tin'tura/ n. f. tincture; dye.

tiñoso /ti'ɲoso/ a. scabby; stingy.

tío /'tio/ n. m. uncle.

tiovivo /tio'βiβo/ n. m. merry-go-round.

típico /'tipiko/ a. typical.

tipo /'tipo/ n. m. type, sort; (interest) rate; Colloq. guy, fellow.

tipo de cambio /'tipo de 'kambio/ exchange rate.

tipo de interés /'tipo de inte'res/ interest rate.

tira /'tira/ n. f. strip.

tirabuzón /tiraβu'θon; tiraβu'son/ n. m. corkscrew.

tirada /ti'raða/ n. f. edition.

tirado /ti'raðo/ **-da** a. dirt-cheap.

tiranía /tira'nia/ n. f. tyranny.

tiránico /ti'raniko/ n. m. tyrannical.

tirano /ti'rano/ **-na** n. tyrant.

tirante /ti'rante/ a. **1.** tight, taut; tense. —n. **2.** m.pl. suspenders.

tirar /ti'rar/ v. throw; draw; pull; fire (a weapon).

tiritar /tiri'tar/ v. shiver.

tiro /'tiro/ n. m. throw; shot.

tirón /ti'ron/ n. m. pull. **de un t.,** at a stretch, at one stroke.

tísico /'tisiko/ n. & a. consumptive.

tisis /'tisis/ n. f. consumption, tuberculosis.

titanio /ti'tanio/ n. m. titanium.

títere /'titere/ n. m. puppet.

titilación /titila'θion; titila'sion/ n. f. twinkle.

titubear /tituβe'ar/ v. stagger; totter; waver.

titulado /titu'laðo/ a. entitled; so-called.

titular /titu'lar/ a. **1.** titular. —v. **2.** entitle.

título /'titulo/ n. m. title, headline.

tiza /'tiθa; 'tisa/ n. f. chalk.

tiznar /tiθ'nar; tis'nar/ v. smudge; stain.

toalla /to'aʎa; to'aya/ n. f. towel. **t. sanitaria,** sanitary napkin.

toalleta /toa'ʎeta; toa'yeta/ n. f. small towel.

tobillo /to'βiʎo; to'βiyo/ n. m. ankle.

tobogán /toβo'gan/ n. m. toboggan.

tocadiscos /toka'ðiskos/ n. m. record player.

tocadiscos compacto /toka'ðiskos kom'pakto/ **tocadiscos digital** CD player.

tocado /to'kaðo/ n. m. hairdo.

tocador /toka'ðor/ n. m. boudoir; dressing table.

tocante /to'kante/ a. touching. **t. a,** concerning, relative to.

tocar /to'kar/ v. touch; play (an instrument). **t. a uno,** be one's turn; be up to one.

tocayo /to'kayo/ **-ya** n. namesake.

tocino /to'θino; to'sino/ n. m. bacon.

tocólogo /to'kologo/ **-ga** n. obstetrician.

todavía /toða'βia/ adv. yet, still.

todo /'toðo/ a. **1.** all, whole. **todos los,** every. —pron. **2.** all, everything. **con t.,** still, however. **del t.,** wholly; at all.

todopoderoso /toðopoðe'roso/ a. almighty.

toldo /'toldo/ n. m. awning.

tolerancia /tole'ranθia; tole'ransia/ n. f. tolerance.

tolerante /tole'rante/ a. tolerant.

tolerar /tole'rar/ v. tolerate.

toma /'toma/ n. f. taking, capture, seizure.

tomaína /to'maina/ n. f. ptomaine.

tomar /to'mar/ v. take; drink. **t. el sol,** sunbathe.

tomate /to'mate/ n. m. tomato.

tomillo /to'miʎo; to'miyo/ n. m. thyme.

tomo /'tomo/ n. m. volume.

tonada /to'naða/ n. f. tune.

tonel /to'nel/ n. m. barrel, cask.

tonelada /tone'laða/ n. f. ton.

tonelaje /tone'lahe/ n. m. tonnage.

tónico /'toniko/ a. & m. tonic.

tono /'tono/ n. m. tone, pitch, shade. **darse t.,** to put on airs.

tonsila /ton'sila/ n. f. tonsil.

tonsilitis /tonsi'litis/ n. f. tonsilitis.

tontería /tonte'ria/ n. f. nonsense, foolishness.

tontifútbol /tonti'futβol/ n. m. excessively defensive strategy (in soccer).

tonto /'tonto/ **-ta** a. & n. foolish, silly; fool.

topacio /to'paθio; to'pasio/ n. m. topaz.

topar /to'par/ v. run into. **t. con,** come upon.

tópico /'topiko/ a. **1.** topical. —n. **2.** m. cliché.

topo /'topo/ n. m. mole (animal).

toque /'toke/ n. m. touch.

tórax /'toraks/ n. m. thorax.

torbellino /torβe'ʎino; torβe'yino/ n. m. whirlwind.

torcer /tor'θer; tor'ser/ v. twist; wind; distort.

toreador /torea'ðor/ **-a** n. toreador.

torero /to'rero/ **-ra** n. bullfighter.

torio /'torio/ n. m. thorium.

tormenta /tor'menta/ n. f. storm.

tormento /tor'mento/ n. m. torment.

tornado /tor'naðo/ n. m. tornado.

tornar /tor'nar/ v. return; turn.

tornarse en /tor'narse en/ v. turn into, become.

torneo /tor'neo/ n. m. tournament.

tornillo /tor'niʎo; tor'niyo/ n. m. screw.

toro /'toro/ n. m. bull.

toronja /to'ronha/ n. f. grapefruit.

torpe /'torpe/ a. awkward, clumsy; sluggish.

torpedero /torpe'ðero/ n. m. torpedo boat.

torpedo /tor'peðo/ n. m. torpedo.

torre /'torre/ n. f. tower.

torre de mando /'torre de 'mando/ control tower.

torrente /to'rrente/ n. m. torrent.

tórrido /'torriðo/ a. torrid.

torta /'torta/ n. f. cake; loaf.

tortilla /tor'tiʎa; tor'tiya/ n. f. omelet; (Mex.) tortilla, pancake.

tórtola /'tortola/ n. f. dove.

tortuga /tor'tuga/ n. f. turtle.

tortuoso /tor'tuoso/ a. tortuous.

tortura /tor'tura/ n. f. torture. **—torturar,** v.

tos /tos/ n. m. cough. **—toser,** v.

tosco /'tosko/ a. coarse, rough, uncouth.

tosquedad /toske'ðað/ n. f. coarseness, roughness.

tostador /tosta'ðor/ n. m. toaster.

tostar /'tostar/ v. toast; tan.

total /to'tal/ a. & m. total.

totalidad /totali'ðað/ n. f. totality, entirety, whole.

totalitario /totali'tario/ a. totalitarian.

totalmente /total'mente/ adv. totally; entirely.

tótem /'totem/ n. m. totem.

tóxico /'toksiko/ a. toxic.

toxicómano /toksi'komano/ **-na** n. m. & f. drug addict.

trabajador /traβaha'ðor/ **-ra** a. **1.** hardworking. —n. **2.** worker.

trabajo /tra'βaho/ n. m. work; labor. **—trabajar,** v.

trabar /tra'βar/ v. fasten, shackle; grasp; strike up.

tracción /trak'θion; trak'sion/ n. f. traction.

tracto /'trakto/ n. m. tract.

tractor /trak'tor/ n. m. tractor.

tradición /traði'θion; traði'sion/ n. f. tradition.

tradicional /traðiθio'nal; traðisio'nal/ a. traditional.

traducción /traðuk'θion; traðuk'sion/ n. f. translation.

traducir /traðu'θir; traðu'sir/ v. translate.

traductor /traðuk'tor/ **-ra** n. translator.

traer /tra'er/ v. bring; carry; wear.

tráfico /'trafiko/ n. m. traffic. **—traficar,** v.

tragaperras /traga'perras/ n. f. slot machine, one-armed bandit.

tragar /tra'gar/ v. swallow.

tragedia /tra'heðia/ n. f. tragedy.

trágicamente /'trahikamente/ adv. tragically.

trágico /'trahiko/ **-ca** a. **1.** tragic. —n. **2.** tragedian.

trago /'trago/ n. m. swallow; drink.

traición /trai'θion; trai'sion/ n. f. treason, betrayal.

traicionar /traiθio'nar; traisio'nar/ v. betray.

traidor /trai'ðor/ **-ra** a. & n. traitorous; traitor.

traje /'trahe/ n. m. suit; dress; garb, apparel.

traje de baño /'trahe de 'baɲo/ bathing suit.

trama /'trama/ v. plot (of a story).

tramador /trama'ðor/ **-ra** n. weaver; plotter.

tramar /tra'mar/ v. weave; plot, scheme.

trámite /'tramite/ n. m. (business) deal, transaction.

tramo /'tramo/ *n. m.* span, stretch, section.

trampa /'trampa/ *n. f.* trap, snare.

trampista /tram'pista/ *n. m. & f.* cheater; swindler.

trance /'tranθe/ *'transe/ n. m.* critical moment or stage. **a todo t.,** at any cost.

tranco /'tranko/ *n. m.* stride.

tranquilidad /trankili'ðað/ *n. f.* tranquility, calm, quiet.

tranquilizante /trankili'θante; trankili'sante/ *n. m.* tranquilizer.

tranquilizar /trankili'θar; trankili'sar/ *v.* quiet, calm down.

tranquilo /tran'kilo/ *a.* tranquil, calm.

transacción /transak'θion; transak'sion/ *n. f.* transaction.

transbordador /transβorða'ðor/ *n. m.* ferry.

transbordador espacial /transβorða'ðor espa'θial; transβorða'ðor espa'sial/ space, shuttle.

transcribir /transkri'βir/ *v.* transcribe.

transcripción /transkrip'θion; transkrip'sion/ *n. f.* transcription.

transcurrir /transku'rrir/ *v.* elapse.

transeúnte /tran'seunte/ *a. & n.* transient; passerby.

transexual /transek'sual/ *a.* transsexual.

transferencia /transfe'renθia; transfe'rensia/ *n. f.* transference.

transferir /transfe'rir/ *v.* transfer.

transformación /transforma'θion; transforma'sion/ *n. f.* transformation.

transformar /transfor'mar/ *v.* transform.

transfusión /transfu'sion/ *n. f.* transfusion.

transgresión /transgre'sion/ *n. f.* transgression.

transgresor /transgre'sor/ **-ra** *n.* transgressor.

transición /transi'θion; transi'sion/ *n. f.* transition.

transigir /transi'hir/ *v.* compromise, settle; agree.

transistor /transis'tor/ *n. m.* transistor.

transitivo /transi'tiβo/ *a.* transitive.

tránsito /'transito/ *n. m.* transit, passage.

transitorio /transi'torio/ *a.* transitory.

transmisión /transmi'sion/ *n. f.* transmission; broadcast.

transmisora /transmi'sora/ *n. f.* broadcasting station.

transmitir /transmi'tir/ *v.* transmit; broadcast.

transparencia /transpa'renθia; transpa'rensia/ *n. f.* transparency.

transparente /transpa'rente/ *a.* **1.** transparent. **—2.** *n. m.* (window) shade.

transportación /transporta'θion; transporta'sion/ *n. f.* transportation.

transportar /transpor'tar/ *v.* transport, convey.

transporte /trans'porte/ *n. m.* transportation; transport.

tranvía /tram'bia/ *n. m.* streetcar, trolley.

trapacero /trapa'θero; trapa'sero/ **-ra** *n.* cheat; swindler.

trapo /'trapo/ *n. m.* rag.

tráquea /'trakea/ *n. f.* trachea.

tras /tras/ *prep.* after; behind.

trasegar /trase'gar/ *v.* upset, overturn.

trasero /tra'sero/ *a.* rear, back.

traslado /tras'laðo/ *n. m.* transfer. **—trasladar,** *v.*

traslapo /tras'lapo/ *n. m.* overlap. **—traslapar,** *v.*

trasnochar /trasno'tʃar/ *v.* stay up all night.

traspalar /traspa'lar/ *v.* shovel.

traspasar /traspa'sar/ *v.* go beyond; cross; violate; pierce.

trasquilar /traski'lar/ *v.* shear; clip.

trastornar /trastor'nar/ *v.* overturn, overthrow, upset.

trastorno /tras'torno/ *m.* overthrow; upheaval.

trastorno mental /tras'torno men'tal/ mental disorder.

trasvasar /trasβa'sar/ *v.* download; download.

tratado /tra'taðo/ *n. m.* treaty; treatise.

tratamiento /trata'miento/ *n. m.* treatment.

tratar /tra'tar/ *v.* treat, handle. **t. de,** deal with; try to; call (a name).

tratarse de /tra'tarse de/ *v.* be a question of.

trato /'trato/ *n. m.* treatment; manners; *Com.* deal.

través /tra'βes/ *adv.* **a t. de,** through, across. **de t.,** sideways.

travesía /traβe'sia/ *n. f.* crossing; voyage.

travestí /traβes'ti/ *n. m.* transvestite.

travestido /traβes'tiðo/ *a.* disguised.

travesura /traβe'sura/ *n. f.* prank; mischief.

travieso /tra'βieso/ *a.* naughty, mischievous.

trayectoria /trayek'toria/ *n. f.* trajectory.

trazar /tra'θar; tra'sar/ *v.* plan, devise; trace; draw.

trazo /'traθo; 'traso/ *n.* plan, outline; line, stroke.

trébol /'treβol/ *n. m.* clover.

trece /'treθe; 'trese/ *a. & pron.* thirteen.

trecho /'tretʃo/ *n. m.* space, distance, stretch.

tregua /'tregua/ *n. f.* truce; respite; lull.

treinta /'treinta/ *a. & pron.* thirty.

tremendo /tre'mendo/ *a.* tremendous.

tremer /tre'mer/ *v.* tremble.

tren /tren/ *n. m.* train.

trenza /'trenθa; 'trensa/ *n. f.* braid. **—trenzar,** *v.*

trepar /tre'par/ *v.* climb, mount.

trepidación /trepiða'θion; trepiða'sion/ *n. f.* trepidation.

tres /tres/ *a. & pron.* three.

trescientos /tres'θientos; tres'sientos/ *a. & pron.* three hundred.

triángulo /tri'angulo/ *n. m.* triangle.

triar /triar/ *v.* sort, separate.

tribu /'triβu/ *n. f.* tribe.

tribulación /triβula'θion; triβula'sion/ *n. f.* tribulation.

tribuna /tri'βuna/ *n. f.* rostrum, stand; (*pl.*) grandstand.

tribunal /triβu'nal/ *n. m.* court, tribunal.

tributario /triβu'tario/ *a. & m.* tributary.

tributo /tri'βuto/ *n. m.* tribute.

triciclo /tri'θiklo; tri'siklo/ *n. m.* tricycle.

trigo /'trigo/ *n. m.* wheat.

trigonometría /trigonome'tria/ *n. f.* trigonometry.

trigueño /tri'geno/ *a.* swarthy, dark.

trilogía /trilo'hia/ *n. f.* trilogy.

trimestral /trimes'tral/ *a.* quarterly.

trinchar /trin'tʃar/ *v.* carve (meat).

trinchera /trin'tʃera/ *n. f.* trench, ditch.

trineo /tri'neo/ *n. m.* sled; sleigh.

trinidad /trini'ðað/ *n. f.* trinity.

tripa /'tripa/ *n. f.* tripe, entrails.

triple /'triple/ *a.* triple. **—triplicar,** *v.*

trípode /'tripoðe/ *n. m.* tripod.

tripulación /tripula'θion; tripula'sion/ *n. f.* crew.

tripulante /tripu'lante/ *m & f.* crew member.

tripular /tripu'lar/ *v.* man.

triste /'triste/ *a.* sad, sorrowful; dreary.

tristemente /triste'mente/ *adv.* sadly.

tristeza /tris'teθa; tris'tesa/ *n. f.* sadness; gloom.

triunfal /triun'fal/ *a.* triumphal.

triunfante /triun'fante/ *a.* triumphant.

triunfo /'triunfo/ *n. m.* triumph; trump. **—triunfar,** *v.*

trivial /tri'βial/ *a.* trivial, commonplace.

trivialidad /triβiali'ðað/ *n. f.* triviality.

trocar /tro'kar/ *v.* exchange, switch; barter.

trofeo /tro'feo/ *n. m.* trophy.

trombón /trom'bon/ *n. m.* trombone.

trompa /'trompa/ **trompeta** *n. f.* trumpet, horn.

tronada /tro'naða/ *n. f.* .thunderstorm.

tronar /tro'nar/ *v.* thunder.

tronco /'tronko/ *n. m.* trunk, stump.

trono /'trono/ *n. m.* throne.

tropa /'tropa/ *n. f.* troop.

tropel /tro'pel/ *n. m.* crowd, throng.

tropezar /trope'θar; trope'sar/ *v.* trip, stumble. **t. con,** come upon, run into.

trópico /'tropiko/ *a. & m.* tropical; tropics.

tropiezo /tro'pieθo; tro'pieso/ *n. m.* stumble; obstacle; slip, error.

trote /'trote/ *n. m.* trot. **—trotar,** *v.*

trovador /troβa'ðor/ *n. m.* troubadour.

trozo /'troθo; 'troso/ *n. m.* piece, portion, fragment; selection, passage.

trucha /'trutʃa/ *n. f.* trout.

trueco /'trueko/ **trueque** *n. m.* exchange, barter.

trueno /'trueno/ *n. m.* thunder.

trufa /'trufa/ *n. f.* truffle.

tu /tu/ *a.* **1.** your.

tú *pron.* **2.** you.

tuberculosis /tuβerku'losis/ *n. f.* tuberculosis.

tubo /'tuβo/ *n. m.* tube, pipe.

tubo de ensayo /'tuβo de en'sayo/ test tube.

tubo de escape /'tuβo de es'kape/ exhaust pipe.

tuerca /'tuerka/ *n. f. Mech.* nut.

tulipán /tuli'pan/ *n. m.* tulip.

tumba /'tumba/ *n. f.* tomb, grave.

tumbar /tum'bar/ *v.* knock down.

tumbarse /tum'βarse/ *v.* lie down.

tumbo /'tumbo/ *n. m.* tumble; somersault.

tumbona /tum'βona/ *n. f.* deck chair.

tumor /tu'mor/ *n. m.* tumor; growth.

tumulto /tu'multo/ *n. m.* tumult, commotion.

tumultuoso /tumul'tuoso/ *a.* tumultuous, boisterous.

tunante /tu'nante/ *n. m.* rascal, rogue.

tunda /'tunda/ *n. f.* spanking, whipping.

túnel /'tunel/ *n. m.* tunnel.

túnel del Canal de la Mancha /'tunel del ka'nal de la 'mantʃa/ Channel Tunnel, Chunnel.

tungsteno /tuŋgs'teno/ *n. m.* tungsten.

túnica /'tunika/ *n. f.* tunic, robe.

tupir /tu'pir/ *v.* pack tight, stuff; stop up.

turbación /turβa'θion; turβa'sion/ *n. f.* confusion, turmoil.

turbamulta /turβa'multa/ *n. f.* mob, disorderly crowd.

turbar /tur'βar/ *v.* disturb, upset; embarrass.

turbina /tur'βina/ *n. f.* turbine.

turbio /'turβio/ *a.* turbid; muddy.

turco /'turko/ **-ca** *a. & n.* Turkish; Turk.

turismo /tu'rismo/ *n. m.* touring, (foreign) travel, tourism.

turista /tu'rista/ *n. m. & f.* tourist.

turno /'turno/ *n. m.* turn; (work) shift.

turquesa /tur'kesa/ *n. f.* turquoise.

Turquía /tur'kia/ *n. f.* Turkey.

turrón /tu'rron/ *n. m.* nougat.

tusa /'tusa/ *n. f.* corncob; corn.

tutear /tute'ar/ *v.* use the pronoun **tú,** etc., in addressing a person.

tutela /tu'tela/ *n. f.* guardianship; aegis.

tutor /tu'tor/ **-ra** *n.* tutor; guardian.

tuyo /'tuyo/ *a.* your, yours.

U

u /u/ *conj.* or.

ubre /'uβre/ *n. f.* udder.

Ucrania /u'krania/ *n. f.* Ukraine.

ucranio /u'kranio/ **-ia** *a. & n.* Ukrainian.

ufano /u'fano/ *a.* proud, haughty.

úlcera /'ulθera; 'ulsera/ *n. f.* ulcer.

ulterior /ulte'rior/ *a.* ulterior.

último /'ultimo/ *a.* last, final; ultimate; latest. **por ú.,** finally. **ú. minuto,** last minute, eleventh hour.

ultraje /ul'trahe/ *n. m.* outrage. **—ultrajar,** *v.*

ultrasónico /ultra'soniko/ *a.* ultrasonic.

umbral /um'bral/ *n. m.* threshold.

umbroso /um'broso/ *a.* shady.

un /un/ **una** *art. & a.* a, an; one; (*pl.*) some.

unánime /u'nanime/ *a.* unanimous.

unanimidad /unanimi'ðað/ *n. f.* unanimity.

unción /un'θion; un'sion/ *n. f.* unction.

ungüento /uŋ'guento/ *n. m.* ointment, salve.

único /'uniko/ *a.* only, sole; unique.

unicornio /uni'kornio/ *n. m.* unicorn.

unidad /uni'ðað/ *n. f.* unit; unity.

unidad de cuidados intensivos /uni'ðað de kui'ðaðos inten'siβos/ **unidad de vigilancia intensiva** intensive-care unit.

unidad de disco /uni'ðað de 'disko/ disk drive.

unificar /unifi'kar/ *v.* unify.

uniforme /uni'forme/ *a. & m.* uniform.

uniformidad /uniformi'ðað/ *n. f.* uniformity.

unión /u'nion/ *n. f.* union; joining.

unir /u'nir/ *v.* unite, join.

universal /uniβer'sal/ *a.* universal.

universalidad /uniβersali'ðað/ *n. f.* universality.

universidad /uniβersi'ðað/ *n. f.* university; college.

universo /uni'βerso/ *n. m.* universe.

uno /'uno/ **una** *pron.* one; (*pl.*) some.

untar /un'tar/ *v.* spread; grease; anoint.

uña /'uɲa/ *n. f.* fingernail.

urbanidad /urβani'ðað/ *n. f.* urbanity; good breeding.

urbanismo /urβa'nismo/ *n. m.* city planning.

urbano /ur'βano/ *a.* urban; urbane; well-bred.

urbe /'urβe/ *n. f.* large city.

urgencia /ur'henθia; ur'hensia/ *n. f.* urgency.

urgente /ur'hente/ *a.* urgent, pressing. **entrega u.,** special delivery.

urgir /ur'hir/ *v.* be urgent.

urna /'urna/ *n. f.* urn; ballot box; (*pl.*) polls.

urraca /u'rraka/ *n. f.* magpie.

usanza /u'sanθa; usansa/ *n. f.* usage, custom.

usar /u'sar/ *v.* use; wear.

uso /'uso/ *n. m.* use; usage; wear.

usted /us'teð/ *pron.* you.

usual /u'sual/ *a.* usual.

usualmente /usual'mente/ *adv.* usually.

usura /u'sura/ *n. f.* usury.

usurero /usu'rero/ **-ra** *n.* usurer.

usurpación /usurpa'θion; usurpa'sion/ *n. f.* usurpation.

usurpar /usur'par/ *v.* usurp.

utensilio /uten'silio/ *n. m.* utensil.

útero /'utero/ *n. m.* uterus.

útil /'util/ *a.* useful, handy.

utilidad /utili'ðað/ *n. f.* utility, usefulness.
utilizar /utili'θar; utili'sar/ *v.* use, utilize.
útilmente /util'mente/ *adv.* usefully.
utópico /u'topiko/ *a.* utopian.
uva /'uβa/ *n. f.* grape.

V

vaca /'baka/ *n. f.* cow; beef.
vacaciones /baka'θiones; baka'siones/ *n. f.pl.* vacation, holidays.
vacancia /ba'kanθia; ba'kansia/ *n. f.* vacancy.
vacante /ba'kante/ *a.* **1.** vacant. —*n.* **2.** *f.* vacancy.
vaciar /ba'θiar; ba'siar/ *v.* empty; pour out.
vacilación /baθila'θion; basila'sion/ *n. f.* vacillation, hesitation.
vacilante /baθi'lante; basi'lante/ *a.* vacillating.
vacilar /baθi'lar; basi'lar/ *v.* falter, hesitate; waver; stagger.
vacío /ba'θio; ba'sio/ *a.* **1.** empty. —*n.* **2.** *m.* void, empty space.
vacuna /ba'kuna/ *n. f.* vaccine.
vacunación /bakuna'θion; bakuna'sion/ *n. f.* vaccination.
vacunar /baku'nar/ *v.* vaccinate.
vacuo /'bakuo/ *a.* **1.** empty, vacant. —*n.* **2.** *m.* vacuum.
vadear /baðe'ar/ *v.* wade through, ford.
vado /'baðo/ *n. m.* ford.
vagabundo /baga'βundo/ **-da** *a. & n.* vagabond.
vagar /ba'gar/ *v.* wander, rove, roam; loiter.
vago /'bago/ **-ga** *a.* **1.** vague, hazy; wandering, vagrant. —*n.* **2.** vagrant, tramp.
vagón /ba'gon/ *n. m.* railroad car.
vahído /ba'iðo/ *n. m.* dizziness.
vaina /'baina/ *n. f.* sheath; pod.
vainilla /bai'niʎa; bai'niya/ *n. f.* vanilla.
vaivén /bai'βen/ *n. m.* vibration, sway.
vajilla /ba'hiʎa; ba'hiya/ *n. f.* (dinner) dishes.
valentía /balen'tia/ *n. f.* valor, courage.
valer /ba'ler/ *n.* **1.** *m.* worth. —*v.* **2.** be worth.
valerse de /ba'lerse de/ *v.* make use of, avail oneself of.
valía /ba'lia/ *n. f.* value.
validez /bali'ðeθ; bali'ðes/ *n. f.* validity.
válido /ba'liðo/ *a.* valid.
valiente /ba'liente/ *a.* valiant, brave, courageous.
valija /ba'liha/ *n. f.* valise.
valioso /ba'lioso/ *a.* valuable.
valla /'baʎa; 'baya/ *n. f.* fence, barrier.
valle /'baʎe; 'baye/ *n. m.* valley.
valor /ba'lor/ *n. m.* value, worth; bravery, valor; (*pl., Com.*) securities.
valoración /balora'θion; balora'sion/ *n. f.* appraisal.
valorar /balo'rar/ *v.* value, appraise.
vals /bals/ *n. m.* waltz.
valsar /bal'sar/ *v.* waltz.
valuación /balua'θion; balua'sion/ *n. f.* valuation.
valuar /balu'ar/ *v.* value; rate.
válvula /'balβula/ *n. f.* valve.
válvula de seguridad /'balβula de seguri'ðað/ safety valve.
vandalismo /banda'lismo/ *n. m.* vandalism.
vándalo /'bandalo/ **-la** *n.* vandal.
vanidad /bani'ðað/ *n. f.* vanity.
vanidoso /bani'ðoso/ *a.* vain, conceited.
vano /'bano/ *a.* vain; inane.
vapor /ba'por/ *n. m.* vapor; steam; steamer, steamship.
vaquero /ba'kero/ **-ra** *n.* cowboy.
vara /'bara/ *n. f.* wand, stick, switch.
varadero /bara'ðero/ *n. m.* shipyard.
varar /ba'rar/ *v.* launch; be stranded; run aground.
variable /ba'riaβle/ *a.* variable.
variación /baria'θion; baria'sion/ *n. f.* variation.
variar /ba'riar/ *v.* vary.
varicela /bari'θela; bari'sela/ *n. f.* chicken pox.
variedad /barie'ðað/ *n. f.* variety.
varios /'barios/ *a. & pron. pl.* various; several.
variz /ba'riθ; ba'ris/ *n. f.* varicose vein.
varón /ba'ron/ *n. m.* man; male.
varonil /baro'nil/ *a.* manly, virile.
vasallo /ba'saʎo; ba'sayo/ *n. m.* vassal.
vasectomía /basekto'mia/ *n. f.* vasectomy.
vasija /ba'siha/ *n. f.* bowl, container (for liquids).
vaso /'baso/ *n. m.* water glass; vase. **v. de papel,** paper cup.
vástago /'bastago/ *n. m.* bud, shoot; twig; offspring.
vasto /'basto/ *a.* vast.
vecindad /beθin'dað; besin'dað/ *n. f.* **vecindario,** *m.* neighborhood, vicinity.
vecino /be'θino; be'sino/ **-na** *a. & n.* neighboring; neighbor.
vedar /be'ðar/ *v.* forbid; impede.
vega /'bega/ *n. f.* meadow.
vegetación /beheta'θion; beheta'sion/ *n. f.* vegetation.
vegetal /behe'tal/ *n. m.* vegetable.
vehemente /bee'mente/ *a.* vehement.
vehículo /be'ikulo/ *n. m.* vehicle; conveyance.
veinte /'beinte/ *a. & pron.* twenty.
vejez /be'heθ; be'hes/ *n. f.* old age.
vejiga /be'higa/ *n. f.* bladder.
vela /'bela/ *n. f.* vigil, watch; candle; sail.
velar /be'lar/ *v.* stay up, sit up; watch over.
vellón /be'ʎon; be'yon/ *n. m.* fleece.
velloso /be'ʎoso; be'yoso/ *a.* hairy; fuzzy.
velludo /be'ʎuðo; be'yuðo/ *a.* downy.
velo /'belo/ *n. m.* veil.
velocidad /beloθi'ðað; belosi'ðað/ *n. f.* velocity, speed; rate. **v. máxima,** speed limit.
velomotor /belomo'tor/ *n. m.* motorbike, moped.
veloz /be'loθ; be'los/ *a.* speedy, fast, swift.
vena /'bena/ *n. f.* vein.
venado /be'naðo/ *n. m.* deer.
vencedor /benθe'ðor; bense'ðor/ **-ra** *n.* victor.
vencer /ben'θer; ben'ser/ *v.* defeat, overcome, conquer; *Com.* become due, expire.
vencimiento /benθi'miento; bensi'miento/ *n. m.* defeat; expiration.
venda /'benda/ *n. f.* **vendaje,** *m.* bandage. —**vendar,** *v.*
vendedor /bende'ðor/ **-ra** *n.* seller, trader; sales clerk.
vender /ben'der/ *v.* sell.
vendimia /ben'dimia/ *n. f.* vintage; grape harvest.
Venecia /be'neθia; be'nesia/ *n. f.* Venice.
veneciano /bene'θiano; bene'siano/ **-na** *a. & n.* Venetian.
veneno /be'neno/ *n. m.* poison.
venenoso /bene'noso/ *a.* poisonous.
veneración /benera'θion; benera'sion/ *n. f.* veneration.
venerar /bene'rar/ *v.* venerate, revere.
venero /be'nero/ *n. m.* spring; origin.
véneto /'beneto/ *a.* Venetian.
venezolano /beneθo'lano; beneso'lano/ **-na** *a. & n.* Venezuelan.
vengador /beŋga'ðor/ **-ra** *n.* avenger.
venganza /beŋ'ganθa; beŋ'gansa/ *n. f.* vengeance, revenge.
vengar /beŋ'gar/ *v.* avenge.
venida /be'niða/ *n. f.* arrival, advent, coming.
venidero /beni'ðero/ *a.* future; coming.
venir /be'nir/ *v.* come.
venta /'benta/ *n. f.* sale; sales.
ventaja /ben'taha/ *n. f.* advantage; profit.
ventajoso /benta'hoso/ *a.* advantageous; profitable.
ventana /ben'tana/ *n. f.* window.
ventero /ben'tero/ **-ra** *n.* innkeeper.
ventilación /bentila'θion; bentila'sion/ *n. m.* ventilation.
ventilador /bentila'ðor/ *n. m.* ventilator, fan.
ventilar /benti'lar/ *v.* ventilate, air.
ventisquero /bentis'kero/ *n. m.* snowdrift; glacier.
ventoso /ben'toso/ *a.* windy.
ventura /ben'tura/ *n. f.* venture; happiness; luck.
ver /ber/ *v.* see. **tener que v. con,** have to do with.
vera /'bera/ *n. f.* edge.
veracidad /beraθi'ðað; berasi'ðað/ *n. f.* truthfulness, veracity.
verano /be'rano/ *n. m.* summer. —**veranear,** *v.*
veras /'beras/ *n. f.pl.* **de v.,** really, truly.
veraz /be'raθ; be'ras/ *a.* truthful.
verbigracia /berβi'graθia; berβi'grasia/ *adv.* for example.
verbo /'berβo/ *n. m.* verb.
verboso /ber'βoso/ *a.* verbose.
verdad /ber'ðað/ *n. f.* truth. **ser v.,** to be true.
verdadero /berða'ðero/ *a.* true, real.
verde /'berðe/ *a.* green; risqué, off-color.
verdor /ber'ðor/ *n. m.* greenness, verdure.
verdugo /ber'ðugo/ *n. m.* hangman.
verdura /ber'ðura/ *n. f.* verdure, vegetation; (*pl.*) vegetables.
vereda /be'reða/ *n. f.* path.
veredicto /bere'ðikto/ *n. m.* verdict.
vergonzoso /bergon'θoso; bergon'soso/ *a.* shameful, embarrassing; shy, bashful.
vergüenza /ber'guenθa; ber'guensa/ *n. f.* shame; disgrace; embarrassment.
verificar /berifi'kar/ *v.* verify, check.
verja /'berha/ *n. f.* grating, railing.
verosímil /bero'simil/ *a.* likely, plausible.
verraco /be'rrako/ *n. m.* boar.
verruga /be'rruga/ *n. f.* wart.
versátil /ber'satil/ *a.* versatile.
verse /'berse/ *v.* look, appear.
versión /ber'sion/ *n. f.* version.
verso /'berso/ *n. m.* verse, stanza; line (of poetry).
verter /ber'ter/ *v.* pour, spill; shed; empty.
vertical /berti'kal/ *a.* vertical.
vertiente /ber'tiente/ *n. f.* slope; watershed.
vertiginoso /bertihi'noso/ *a.* dizzy.
vértigo /'bertigo/ *n. m.* vertigo, dizziness.
vestíbulo /bes'tiβulo/ *n. m.* vestibule, lobby.
vestido /bes'tiðo/ *n. m.* dress; clothing.
vestigio /bes'tihio/ *n. m.* vestige, trace.
vestir /bes'tir/ *v.* dress, clothe.
veterano /bete'rano/ **-na** *a. & n.* veteran.
veterinario /beteri'nario/ **-ria** *a.* **1.** veterinary. —*n.* **2.** veterinarian.
veto /'beto/ *n. m.* veto.
vetusto /be'tusto/ *a.* ancient, very old.
vez /beθ; bes/ *n. f.* time; turn. **tal v.,** perhaps. **a la v.,** at the same time. **en v. de,** instead of. **una v.,** once. **otra v.,** again.
vía /'bia/ *n. f.* track; route, way.
viaducto /bia'ðukto/ *n. m.* viaduct.
viajante /bia'hante/ *a. & n.* traveling; traveler.
viajar /bia'har/ *v.* travel; journey; tour.
viaje /'biahe/ *n. m.* trip, journey, voyage; (*pl.*) travels.
viaje de estudios /'biahe de es'tuðios/ field trip.
viajero /bia'hero/ **-ra** *n.* traveler; passenger.
viaje todo incluido /'biahe 'toðo in'kluiðo/ package tour.
viandas /'biandas/ *n. f.pl.* victuals, food.
víbora /'biβora/ *n. f.* viper.
vibración /biβra'θion; biβra'sion/ *n. f.* vibration.
vibrar /bi'βrar/ *v.* vibrate.
vicepresidente /biθepresi'ðente; bisepresi'ðente/ **-ta** *n.* vice president.
vicio /'biθio; 'bisio/ *n. m.* vice.
vicioso /bi'θioso; bi'sioso/ *a.* vicious; licentious.
víctima /'biktima/ *n. f.* victim.
victoria /bik'toria/ *n. f.* victory.
victorioso /bikto'rioso/ *a.* victorious.
vid /bið/ *n. f.* grapevine.
vida /'biða/ *n. f.* life; living.
vídeo /bi'ðeo/ *n. m.* videotape.
videocámara /biðeo'kamara/ *n. f.* video camera.
videodisco /biðeo'ðisko/ *n. m.* videodisc.
videojuego /biðeo'huego/ *n. m.* video game.
vidrio /'biðrio/ *n. m.* glass.
viejo /'bieho/ **-ja** *a. & n.* old; old person.
viento /'biento/ *n. m.* wind. **hacer v.,** to be windy.
vientre /'bientre/ *n. m.* belly.
viernes /'biernes/ *n. m.* Friday.
viga /'biga/ *n. f.* beam, rafter.
vigente /bi'hente/ *a.* in effect (prices, etc.).
vigilante /bihi'lante/ *a. & m.* vigilant, watchful; watchman.
vigilante nocturno /bihi'lante nok'turno/ night watchman.
vigilar /bihi'lar/ *v.* guard, watch over.
vigilia /bi'hilia/ *n. f.* vigil, watchfulness; *Relig.* fast.
vigor /bi'gor/ *n. m.* vigor. **en v.,** in effect, in force.
vil /bil/ *a.* vile, low, contemptible.
vileza /bi'leθa; bi'lesa/ *n. f.* baseness; vileness.
villa /'biʎa; 'biya/ *n. f.* town; country house.
villancico /biʎan'θiko; biyan'siko/ *n. m.* Christmas carol.
villanía /biʎa'nia; biya'nia/ *n. f.* villainy.
villano /bi'ʎano; bi'yano/ *n. m.* boor.
vinagre /bi'nagre/ *n. m.* vinegar.
vinagrera /bina'grera/ *n. f.* cruet.
vínculo /'binkulo/ *n. m.* link. —**vincular,** *v.*
vindicar /bindi'kar/ *v.* vindicate.
vino /'bino/ *n. m.* wine.
viña /'biɲa/ *n. f.* vineyard.
violación /biola'θion; biola'sion/ *n. f.* violation; rape.
violador /biola'ðor/ **-ra** *n. m. & f.* rapist.
violar /bio'lar/ *v.* violate; rape.
violencia /bio'lenθia; bio'lensia/ *n. f.* violence.
violento /bio'lento/ *a.* violent; impulsive.
violeta /bio'leta/ *n. f.* violet.
violín /bio'lin/ *n. m.* violin.
violón /bio'lon/ *n. m.* bass viol.
virar /bi'rar/ *v.* veer, change course.
virgen /bir'hen/ *n. f.* virgin.
viril /bi'ril/ *a.* virile, manly.
virilidad /birili'ðað/ *n. f.* virility, manhood.
virtual /bir'tual/ *a.* virtual.
virtud /bir'tuð/ *n. f.* virtue; efficacy, power.
virtuoso /bir'tuoso/ *a.* virtuous.
viruela /bi'ruela/ *n. f.* smallpox.

viruelas locas /biˈruelas ˈlokas/ *n. f.pl.* chicken pox.
virus /ˈbirus/ *n. m.* virus.
visa /ˈbisa/ *n. f.* visa.
visaje /biˈsahe/ *n. m.* grimace.
visera /biˈsera/ *n. f.* visor.
visible /biˈsiβle/ *a.* visible.
visión /biˈsion/ *n. f.* vision.
visionario /bisioˈnario/ **-ria** *a. & n.* visionary.
visita /biˈsita/ *n. f.* visit; *m. & f.* visitor, caller. **v. con guía, v. explicada, v. programada,** guided tour.
visitación /bisitaˈθion; bisitaˈsion/ *n. f.* visitation.
visitante /bisiˈtante/ *a. & n.* visiting; visitor.
visitar /bisiˈtar/ *v.* visit; inspect, examine.
vislumbrar /bislumˈβrar/ *v.* glimpse.
vislumbre /bisˈlumbre/ *n. f.* glimpse.
viso /ˈbiso/ *n. m.* looks; outlook.
víspera /ˈbispera/ *n. f.* eve, day before.
vista /ˈbista/ *n. f.* view; scene; sight.
vista de pájaro /ˈbista de ˈpaharo/ bird's-eye view.
vistazo /bisˈtaθo; bisˈtaso/ *n. m.* glance, glimpse.
vistoso /bisˈtoso/ *a.* beautiful; showy.
visual /biˈsual/ *a.* visual.
vital /biˈtal/ *a.* vital.
vitalidad /bitaliˈðað/ *n. f.* vitality.
vitamina /bitaˈmina/ *n. f.* vitamin.
vitando /biˈtando/ *a.* hateful.
vituperar /bitupeˈrar/ *v.* vituperate; revile.
viuda /ˈbiuða/ *n. f.* widow.
viudo /ˈbiuðo/ *n. m.* widower.
vivaz /biˈβaθ; biˈβas/ *a.* vivacious, buoyant; clever.
víveres /ˈbiβeres/ *n. m.pl.* provisions.
viveza /biˈβeθa; biˈβesa/ *n. f.* animation, liveliness.
vívido /biˈβiðo/ *a.* vivid, bright.
vivienda /biˈβienda/ *n. f.* (living) quarters, dwelling.
vivificar /biβifiˈkar/ *v.* vivify, enliven.
vivir /biˈβir/ *v.* live.

vivo /ˈbiβo/ *a.* live, alive, living; vivid; animated, brisk.
vocablo /boˈkaβlo/ *n. m.* word.
vocabulario /bokaβuˈlario/ *n. m.* vocabulary.
vocación /bokaˈθion; bokaˈsion/ *n. f.* vocation, calling.
vocal /boˈkal/ *a.* **1.** vocal. —*n.* **2.** *f.* vowel.
vocear /boθeˈar; boseˈar/ *v.* vociferate.
vodca /ˈboðka/ *n. m.* vodka.
vodevil /boðeˈβil/ *n. m.* vaudeville.
volante /boˈlante/ *a.* **1.** flying. —*n.* **2.** *m.* memorandum; (steering) wheel.
volar /boˈlar/ *v.* fly; explode.
volcán /bolˈkan/ *n. m.* volcano.
volcar /bolˈkar/ *v.* upset, capsize.
voltaje /bolˈtahe/ *n. m.* voltage.
voltear /bolteˈar/ *v.* turn, whirl; overturn.
voltio /ˈboltio/ *n. m.* volt.
volumen /boˈlumen/ *n. m.* volume.
voluminoso /bolumiˈnoso/ *a.* voluminous.
voluntad /bolunˈtað/ *n. f.* will. **buena v.** goodwill.
voluntario /bolunˈtario/ **-ria** *a. & n.* voluntary; volunteer.
voluntarioso /boluntaˈrioso/ *a.* willful.
volver /bolˈβer/ *v.* turn; return, go back, come back. **v. a hacer** (etc.), do (etc.) again.
volverse /bolˈβerse/ *v.* turn around; turn, become.
vómito /ˈbomito/ *n. m.* vomit. —**vomitar,** *v.*
voracidad /boraθiˈðað; borasiˈðað/ *n. f.* voracity; greed.
voraz /boˈraθ; boˈras/ *a.* greedy, ravenous.
vórtice /ˈbortiθe; ˈbortise/ *n. m.* whirlpool.
vosotros /boˈsotros, boˈsotras/ **-as** *pron.pl.* you; yourselves.
votación /botaˈθion; botaˈsion/ *n. f.* voting; vote.
voto /ˈboto/ *n. m.* vote; vow. —**votar,** *v.*

voz /boθ; bos/ *n. f.* voice; word. **a voces,** by shouting. **en v. alta,** aloud.
vuelco /ˈbuelko/ *n. m.* upset.
vuelo /ˈbuelo/ *n. m.* flight. **v. libre,** hang gliding.
vuelo chárter /ˈbuelo ˈtʃarter/ charter flight.
vuelo regular /ˈbuelo rreguˈlar/ scheduled flight.
vuelta /ˈbuelta/ *n. f.* turn, bend; return. **a la v. de,** around. **dar una v.,** to take a walk.
vuestro /ˈbuestro/ *a.* your, yours.
vulgar /bulˈgar/ *a.* vulgar, common.
vulgaridad /bulgariˈðað/ *n. f.* vulgarity.
vulgo /ˈbulgo/ *n. m.* (the) masses, (the) common people.
vulnerable /bulneˈraβle/ *a.* vulnerable.

Y Z

y /i/ *conj.* and.
ya /ya/ *adv.* already; now; at once. **y. no,** no longer, any more. **y. que,** since.
yacer /yaˈθer; yaˈser/ *v.* lie.
yacimiento /yaθiˈmiento; yasiˈmiento/ *n. m.* deposit.
yanqui /ˈyanki/ *a. & n.* North American.
yate /ˈyate/ *n. m.* yacht.
yegua /ˈyegua/ *n. f.* mare.
yelmo /ˈyelmo/ *n. m.* helmet.
yema /ˈyema/ *n. f.* yolk (of an egg).
yerba /ˈyerβa/ *n. f.* grass; herb.
yerno /ˈyerno/ *n. m.* son-in-law.
yerro /ˈyerro/ *n. m.* error, mistake.
yeso /ˈyeso/ *n. m.* plaster.
yídish /ˈyiðis/ *n. m.* Yiddish.
yo /yo/ *pron.* I.
yodo /ˈyoðo/ *n. m.* iodine.
yoduro /joˈðuro/ *n. m.* iodide.
yonqui /ˈyonki/ *m. &amp. f. Colloq.* drug addict, junkie.
yugo /ˈyugo/ *n. m.* yoke.
yunque /ˈyunke/ *n. m.* anvil.

yunta /ˈyunta/ *n. f.* team (of animals).
zafarse /θaˈfarse; saˈfarse/ *v.* run away, escape. **z. de,** get rid of.
zafio /ˈθafio; ˈsafio/ *a.* coarse, uncivil.
zafiro /θaˈfiro; saˈfiro/ *n. m.* sapphire.
zaguán /θaˈguan; saˈguan/ *n. m.* vestibule, hall.
zalamero /θalaˈmero; salaˈmero/ **-ra** *n.* flatterer, wheedler.
zambullir /θambuˈʎir; sambuˈyir/ *v.* plunge, dive.
zampar /θamˈpar; samˈpar/ *v. Colloq.* gobble down, wolf down.
zanahoria /θanaˈoria; sanaˈoria/ *n. f.* carrot.
zanja /ˈθanha; ˈsanha/ *n. f.* ditch, trench.
zapatería /θapateˈria; sapateˈria/ *n. f.* shoe store; shoemaker's shop.
zapatero /θapaˈtero; sapaˈtero/ *n. m.* shoemaker.
zapato /θaˈpato; saˈpato/ *n. m.* shoe.
zar /θar; sar/ *n. m.* czar.
zaraza /θaˈraθa; saˈrasa/ *n. f.* calico; chintz.
zarza /ˈθarθa; ˈsarsa/ *n. f.* bramble.
zarzuela /θarˈθuela; sarˈsuela/ *n. f.* musical comedy.
zodíaco /θoˈðiako; soˈðiako/ *n. m.* zodiac.
zona /ˈθona; ˈsona/ *n. f.* zone.
zoología /θooloˈhia; sooloˈhia/ *n. f.* zoology.
zoológico /θooˈlohiko; sooˈlohiko/ *a.* zoological.
zorro /ˈθorro; ˈsorro/ **-rra** *n.* fox.
zozobra /θoˈθoβra; soˈsoβra/ *n. f.* worry, anxiety; capsizing.
zozobrar /θoθoˈβrar; sosoˈβrar/ *v.* capsize; worry.
zumba /ˈθumba; ˈsumba/ *n. f.* spanking.
zumbido /θumˈβiðo; sumˈβiðo/ *n. m.* buzz, hum. —**zumbar,** *v.*
zumo /ˈθumo; ˈsumo/ *n. m.* juice. **z. de naranja,** orange juice.
zurcir /θurˈθir; surˈsir/ *v.* darn, mend.
zurdo /ˈθurðo; ˈsurðo/ *a.* left-handed.
zurrar /θuˈrrar; suˈrrar/ *v.* flog, drub.

English–Spanish

inglés–español

A

a /ə, *when stressed* ā/ *art.* un, una.

abacus /'æbəkəs/ *n.* ábaco *m.*

abandon /ə'bændən/ *n.* **1.** desenfreno, abandono *m.* —*v.* **2.** abandonar, desamparar.

abandoned /ə'bændənd/ *a.* abandonado.

abandonment /ə'bændənmənt/ *n.* abandono, desamparo *m.*

abase /ə'beis/ *v.* degradar, humillar.

abasement /ə'beismənt/ *n.* degradación, humillación *f.*

abash /ə'bæʃ/ *v.* avergonzar.

abate /ə'beit/ *v.* menguar, moderarse.

abatement /ə'beitmənt/ *n.* disminución *f.*

abbess /'æbis/ *n.* abadesa *f.*

abbey /'æbi/ *n.* abadía *f.*

abbot /'æbət/ *n.* abad *m.*

abbreviate /ə'brivi,eit/ *v.* abreviar.

abbreviation /ə,brivi'eiʃən/ *n.* abreviatura *f.*

abdicate /'æbdɪ,keit/ *v.* abdicar.

abdication /,æbdɪ'keiʃən/ *n.* abdicación *f.*

abdomen /'æbdəmən/ *n.* abdomen *m.*

abdominal /æb'dɒmənļ/ *a.* abdominal.

abduct /æb'dʌkt/ *v.* secuestrar.

abduction /æb'dʌkʃən/ *n.* secuestración *f.*

abductor /æb'dʌktər/ *n.* secuestrador -ra.

aberrant /ə'bɛrənt, 'æbər-/ *a.* aberrante.

aberration /,æbə'reiʃən/ *n.* aberración *f.*

abet /ə'bɛt/ *v.* apoyar, favorecer.

abetment /ə'bɛtmənt/ *n.* apoyo *m.*

abettor /ə'bɛtər/ *n.* cómplice *m.* & *f.*

abeyance /ə'beiəns/ *n.* suspensión *f.*

abhor /æb'hɔr/ *v.* abominar, odiar.

abhorrence /æb'hɔrəns/ *n.* detestación *f.*; aborrecimiento *m.*

abhorrent /æb'hɔrənt/ *a.* detestable, aborrecible.

abide /ə'baid/ *v.* soportar. **to a. by,** cumplir con.

abiding /ə'baidiŋ/ *a.* perdurable.

ability /ə'bɪlɪti/ *n.* habilidad *f.*

abject /'æbdʒɛkt/ *a.* abyecto; desanimado.

abjuration /,æbdʒə'reiʃən/ *n.* renuncia *f.*

abjure /æb'dʒʊr/ *v.* renunciar.

ablative /'æblətɪv/ *a.* & *n. Gram.* ablativo *m.*

ablaze /ə'bleiz/ *a.* en llamas.

able /'eibəl/ *a.* capaz; competente. **to be a.,** poder.

able-bodied /'eibəl 'bɒdid/ *a.* robusto.

ablution /ə'bluʃən/ *n.* ablución *f.*

ably /'eibli/ *adv.* hábilmente.

abnegate /'æbnɪ,geit/ *v.* repudiar; negar.

abnegation /,æbnɪ'geiʃən/ *n.* abnegación; repudiación *f.*

abnormal /æb'nɔrməl/ *a.* anormal.

abnormality /,æbnɔr'mælɪti/ *n.* anormalidad, deformidad *f.*

abnormally /æb'nɔrməli/ *adv.* anormalmente.

aboard /ə'bɔrd/ *adv.* a bordo.

abode /ə'boud/ *n.* residencia *f.*

abolish /ə'bɒlɪʃ/ *v.* suprimir.

abolishment /ə'bɒlɪʃmənt/ *n.* abolición *f.*

abolition /,æbə'lɪʃən/ *n.* abolición *f.*

abominable /ə'bɒmənəbəl/ *a.* abominable.

abominate /ə'bɒmə,neit/ *v.* abominar, detestar.

abomination /ə,bɒmə'neiʃən/ *n.* abominación *f.*

aboriginal /,æbə'rɪdʒənļ/ *a.* & *n.* aborigen *f.*

abortion /ə'bɔrʃən/ *n.* aborto *m.*

abortive /ə'bɔrtɪv/ *a.* abortivo.

abound /ə'baund/ *v.* abundar.

about /ə'baut/ *adv.* **1.** como. **about to,** para; a punto de. —*prep.* **2.** de, sobre, acerca de.

about-face /ə'baut,feis, ə'baut'feis/ *n. Mil.* media vuelta.

above /ə'bʌv/ *adv.* **1.** arriba. —*prep.* **2.** sobre; por encima de.

aboveboard /ə'bʌv,bɔrd/ *a.* & *adv.* sincero, franco.

abrasion /ə'breiʒən/ *n.* raspadura *f.*; *Med.* abrasión *f.*

abrasive /ə'breisɪv/ *a.* raspante. *n.* abrasivo *m.*

abreast /ə'brɛst/ *adv.* de frente.

abridge /ə'brɪdʒ/ *v.* abreviar.

abridgment /ə'brɪdʒmənt/ *n.* abreviación *f.*; compendio *m.*

abroad /ə'brɔd/ *adv.* en el extranjero, al extranjero.

abrogate /'æbrə,geit/ *v.* abrogar, revocar.

abrogation /,æbrə'geiʃən/ *n.* abrogación, revocación *f.*

abrupt /ə'brʌpt/ *a.* repentino; brusco.

abruptly /ə'brʌptli/ *adv.* bruscamente, precipitadamente.

abruptness /ə'brʌptnɪs/ *n.* precipitación; brusquedad *f.*

abscess /'æbsɛs/ *n.* absceso *m.*

abscond /æb'skɒnd/ *v.* fugarse.

absence /'æbsəns/ *n.* ausencia, falta *f.*

absent /'æbsənt/ *a.* ausente.

absentee /,æbsən'ti/ *a.* & *n.* ausente *m.* & *f.*

absent-minded /'æbsənt 'maindɪd/ *a.* distraído.

absinthe /'æbsɪnθ/ *n.* absenta *f.*

absolute /'æbsə,lut/ *a.* absoluto.

absolutely /,æbsə'lutli/ *adv.* absolutamente.

absoluteness /,æbsə'lutnɪs/ *n.* absolutismo *m.*

absolution /,æbsə'luʃən/ *n.* absolución *f.*

absolutism /'æbsəlu,tɪzəm/ *n.* absolutismo, despotismo *m.*

absolve /æb'zɒlv/ *v.* absolver.

absorb /æb'sɔrb/ *v.* absorber; preocupar.

absorbed /æb'sɔrbd/ *a.* absorbido; absorto.

absorbent /æb'sɔrbənt/ *a.* absorbente.

absorbent cotton algodón hidrófilo *m.*

absorbing /æb'sɔrbiŋ/ *a.* interesante.

absorption /æb'sɔrpʃən/ *n.* absorción; preocupación *f.*

abstain /æb'stein/ *v.* abstenerse.

abstemious /æb'stimiəs/ *a.* abstemio, sobrio.

abstinence /'æbstənəns/ *n.* abstinencia *f.*

abstract /*a, v* æb'strækt, 'æbstrækt; *n* 'æbstrækt/ *a.* **1.** abstracto. —*n.* **2.** resumen *m.* —*v.* **3.** abstraer.

abstracted /æb'stræktɪd/ *a.* distraído.

abstraction /æb'strækʃən/ *n.* abstracción *f.*

abstruse /æb'strus/ *a.* abstruso.

absurd /æb'sɜrd/ *a.* absurdo, ridículo.

absurdity /æb'sɜrdɪti/ *n.* absurdo *m.*

absurdly /æb'sɜrdli/ *adv.* absurdamente.

abundance /ə'bʌndəns/ *n.* abundancia *f.*

abundant /ə'bʌndənt/ *a.* abundante.

abundantly /ə'bʌndəntli/ *adv.* abundantemente.

abuse /*n* ə'byus; *v* ə'byuz/ *n.* **1.** abuso *m.* —*v.* **2.** abusar de; maltratar.

abusive /ə'byusɪv/ *a.* abusivo.

abusively /ə'byusɪvli/ *adv.* abusivamente, ofensivamente.

abutment /ə'bʌtmənt/ *n.* (building) estribo, contrafuerte *m.*

abut (on) /ə'bʌt/ *v.* terminar (en); lindar (con).

abyss /ə'bɪs/ *n.* abismo *m.*

Abyssinian /,æbə'sɪniən/ *a.* & *n.* abisinio -nia.

acacia /ə'keiʃə/ *n.* acacia *f.*

academic /,ækə'dɛmɪk/ *a.* académico.

academy /ə'kædəmi/ *n.* academia *f.*

acanthus /ə'kænθəs/ *n. Bot.* acanto *m.*

accede /æk'sid/ *v.* acceder; consentir.

accelerate /æk'sɛlə,reit/ *v.* acelerar.

acceleration /æk,sɛlə'reiʃən/ *n.* aceleración *f.*

accelerator /æk'sɛlə,reitər/ *n. Auto.* acelerador *m.*

accent /'æksɛnt/ *n.* **1.** acento *m.* —*v.* **2.** acentuar.

accentuate /æk'sɛntʃu,eit/ *v.* acentuar.

accept /æk'sɛpt/ *v.* aceptar.

acceptability /æk,sɛptə'bɪlɪti/ *n.* aceptabilidad *f.*

acceptable /æk'sɛptəbəl/ *a.* aceptable.

acceptably /æk'sɛptəbli/ *adv.* aceptablemente.

acceptance /æk'sɛptəns/ *n.* aceptación *f.*

access /'æksɛs/ *n.* acceso *m.*, entrada *f.*

accessible /æk'sɛsəbəl/ *a.* accesible.

accessory /æk'sɛsəri/ *a.* **1.** accesorio. —*n.* **2.** cómplice *m.* & *f.*

accident /'æksɪdənt/ *n.* accidente *m.* **by a.,** por casualidad.

accidental /,æksɪ'dɛntļ/ *a.* accidental.

accidentally /,æksɪ'dɛntļi/ *adv.* accidentalmente, casualmente.

acclaim /ə'kleim/ *v.* aclamar.

acclamation /,æklə'meiʃən/ *n.* aclamación *f.*

acclimate /'æklə,meit/ *v.* aclimatar.

acclivity /ə'klɪvɪti/ *n.* subida *f.*

accolade /'ækə,leid/ *n.* acolada *f.*

accommodate /ə'kɒmə,deit/ *v.* acomodar.

accommodating /ə'kɒmə,deitiŋ/ *a.* bondadoso, complaciente.

accommodation /ə,kɒmə'deiʃən/ *n.* servicio *m.*; (pl.) alojamiento *m.*

accompaniment /ə'kʌmpənimənt/ *n.* acompañamiento *m.*

accompanist /ə'kʌmpənist/ *n.* acompañante *m.* & *f.*

accompany /ə'kʌmpəni/ *v.* acompañar.

accomplice /ə'kɒmplɪs/ *n.* cómplice *m.* & *f.*

accomplish /ə'kɒmplɪʃ/ *v.* llevar a cabo; realizar.

accomplished /ə'kɒmplɪʃt/ *a.* acabado, cumplido; culto.

accomplishment /ə'kɒmplɪʃmənt/ *n.* realización *f.*; logro *m.*

accord /ə'kɔrd/ *n.* **1.** acuerdo *m.* —*v.* **2.** otorgar.

accordance /ə'kɔrdņs/ *n.*: **in a. with,** de acuerdo con.

accordingly /ə'kɔrdɪŋli/ *adv.* en conformidad.

according to /ə'kɔrdɪŋ/ *prep.* según.

accordion /ə'kɔrdiən/ *n.* acordeón *m.*

accost /ə'kɒst/ *v.* dirigirse a.

account /ə'kaunt/ *n.* **1.** relato *m.*; *Com.* cuenta *f.* **on a. of,** a causa de. **on no a.,** de ninguna manera. —*v.* **2.** **a. for,** explicar.

accountable /ə'kauntəbəl/ *a.* responsable.

accountant /ə'kauntņt/ *n.* contador -ra.

accounting /ə'kauntiŋ/ *n.* contabilidad *f.*

accouter /ə'kutər/ *v.* equipar, ataviar.

accouterments /ə'kutərmənts/ *n.* equipo, atavío *m.*

accredit /ə'krɛdɪt/ *v.* acreditar.

accretion /ə'kriʃən/ *n.* aumento *m.*

accrual /ə'kruəl/ *n.* aumento, incremento *m.*

accrue /ə'kru/ *v.* provenir; acumularse.

accumulate /ə'kyumyə,leit/ *v.* acumular.

accumulation /ə,kyumyə'leiʃən/ *n.* acumulación *f.*

accumulative /ə'kyumyə,leitɪv/ *a.* acumulativo.

accumulator /ə'kyumyə,leitər/ *n.* acumulador *m.*

accuracy /'ækyərəsi/ *n.* exactitud, precisión *f.*

accurate /'ækyərɪt/ *a.* exacto.

accursed /ə'kɜrsɪd, ə'kɜrst/ *a.* maldito.

accusation /,ækyu'zeiʃən/ *n.* acusación *f.*, cargo *m.*

accusative /ə'kyuzətɪv/ *a.* & *n.* acusativo *m.*

accuse /ə'kyuz/ *v.* acusar.

accused /ə'kyuzd/ *a.* & *n.* acusado -da, procesado -da.

accuser /ə'kyuzər/ *n.* acusador -ra.

accustom /ə'kʌstəm/ *v.* acostumbrar.

accustomed /ə'kʌstəmd/ *a.* acostumbrado.

ace /eis/ *a.* **1.** sobresaliente. —*n.* **2.** as *m.*

acerbity /ə'sɜrbɪti/ *n.* acerbidad, amargura *f.*

acetate /'æsɪ,teit/ *n. Chem.* acetato *m.*

acetic /ə'sitɪk/ *a.* acético.

acetylene /ə'sɛtļ,in/ *a.* **1.** acetilénico. —*n.* **2.** *Chem.* acetileno *m.*

ache /eik/ *n.* **1.** dolor *m.* —*v.* **2.** doler.

achieve /ə'tʃiv/ *v.* lograr, llevar a cabo.

achievement /ə'tʃivmənt/ *n.* realización *f.*; hecho notable *m.*

acid /'æsɪd/ *a.* & *n.* ácido *m.*

acidify /ə'sɪdə,fai/ *v.* acidificar.

acidity /ə'sɪdɪti/ *n.* acidez *f.*

acidosis /,æsɪ'dousɪs/ *n. Med.* acidismo *m.*

acid rain lluvia ácida *f.*

acid test prueba decisiva.

acidulous /ə'sɪdʒələs/ *a.* agrio, acídulo.

acknowledge /æk'nɒlɪdʒ/ *v.* admitir; (receipt) acusar.

acme /'ækmi/ *n.* apogeo, colmo *m.*

acne /'ækni/ *n. Med.* acné *m.* & *f.*

acolyte /'ækə,lait/ *n.* acólito *m.*

acorn /'eikɔrn/ *n.* bellota *f.*

acoustics /ə'kustɪks/ *n.* acústica *f.*

acquaint /ə'kweint/ *v.* familiarizar. **to be acquainted with,** conocer.

acquaintance /ə'kweintņs/ *n.* conocimiento *m.*; (person known) conocido -da. **to make the a. of,** conocer.

acquiesce /,ækwi'ɛs/ *v.* consentir.

acquiescence /,ækwi'ɛsəns/ *n.* consentimiento *m.*

acquire /ə'kwaiər/ *v.* adquirir.

acquirement /ə'kwaiərmənt/ *n.* adquisición *f.*; (pl.) conocimientos *m.pl.*

acquisition /,ækwə'zɪʃən/ *n.* adquisición *f.*

acquisitive /ə'kwɪzɪtɪv/ *a.* adquisitivo.

acquit /ə'kwɪt/ *v.* exonerar, absolver.

acquittal /ə'kwɪtļ/ *n.* absolución *f.*

acre /'eikər/ *n.* acre *m.*

acreage /'eikərɪdʒ/ *n.* número de acres.

acrid /'ækrɪd/ *a.* acre, punzante.

acrimonious /,ækrə'mouniəs/ *a.* acrimonioso, mordaz.

acrimony /'ækrə,mouni/ *n.* acrimonia, aspereza *f.*

acrobat /'ækrə,bæt/ *n.* acróbata *m.* & *f.*

acrobatic /,ækrə'bætɪk/ *a.* acrobático.

across /ə'krɒs/ *adv.* **1.** a través, al otro lado. —*prep.* **2.** al otro lado de, a través de.

acrostic /ə'krɒstɪk/ *n.* acróstico *m.*

act /ækt/ *n.* **1.** acción *f.*; acto *m.* —*v.* **2.** actuar, portarse. **act as,** hacer de. **act on,** decidir sobre.

acting /'æktɪŋ/ *a.* **1.** interino. —*n.* **2.** acción *f.*; *Theat.* representación *f.*

actinism /'æktə,nɪzəm/ *n.* actinismo *m.*

actinium /æk'tɪniəm/ *n. Chem.* actinio *m.*

action /'ækʃən/ *n.* acción *f.* **take a.,** tomar medidas.

action replay /'ri,plei/ repetición *f.*

activate /'æktə,veit/ *v.* activar.

activation /ˌæktəˈveiʃən/ n. activación f.

activator /ˈæktəˌveitər/ n. Chem. activador m.

active /ˈæktɪv/ a. activo.

activity /ækˈtɪvɪti/ n. actividad f.

actor /ˈæktər/ n. actor m.

actress /ˈæktrɪs/ n. actriz f.

actual /ˈæktʃuəl/ a. real, efectivo.

actuality /ˌæktʃuˈælɪti/ n. realidad, actualidad f.

actually /ˈæktʃuəli/ adv. en realidad.

actuary /ˈæktʃuˌeri/ n. actuario m.

actuate /ˈæktʃuˌeit/ v. impulsar, mover.

acumen /əˈkyumən/ n. cacumen m., perspicacia f.

acupuncture /ˈækyuˌpʌŋktʃər/ n. acupuntura f.

acute /əˈkyut/ a. agudo; perspicaz.

acutely /əˈkyutli/ adv. agudamente.

acuteness /əˈkyutnɪs/ n. agudeza f.

adage /ˈædɪdʒ/ n. refrán, proverbio m.

adamant /ˈædəmənt/ a. firme.

Adam's apple /ˈædəmz/ nuez de la garganta.

adapt /əˈdæpt/ v. adaptar.

adaptability /əˌdæptəˈbɪlɪti/ n. adaptabilidad f.

adaptable /əˈdæptəbəl/ a. adaptable.

adaptation /ˌædəpˈteiʃən/ n. adaptación f.

adapter /əˈdæptər/ n. Elec. adaptador m.; Mech. ajustador m.

adaptive /əˈdæptɪv/ a. adaptable, acomodable.

add /æd/ v. agregar, añadir. **a. up,** sumar.

adder /ˈædər/ n. víbora; serpiente f.

addict /ˈædɪkt/ n. adicto -ta; (fan) aficionado -da.

addiction /əˈdɪʃən/ n. adición f. **in a. to,** además de.

additional /əˈdɪʃənl/ a. adicional.

addle /ˈædl/ v. confundir.

address /n əˈdrɛs, ˈædrɛs; v əˈdrɛs/ n. **1.** dirección f.; señas f.pl.; (speech) discurso. —v. **2.** dirigirse a.

addressee /ˌædrɛˈsi/ n. destinatario -ia.

adduce /əˈdus/ v. aducir.

adenoid /ˈædnˌoid/ a. adenoidea.

adept /əˈdɛpt/ a. adepto.

adeptly /əˈdɛptli/ adv. diestramente.

adeptness /əˈdɛptnɪs/ n. destreza f.

adequacy /ˈædɪkwəsi/ n. suficiencia f.

adequate /ˈædɪkwɪt/ a. adecuado.

adequately /ˈædɪkwɪtli/ adv. adecuadamente.

adhere /ædˈhɪər/ v. adherirse, pegarse.

adherence /ædˈhɪərəns/ n. adhesión f.; apego m.

adherent /ædˈhɪərənt/ n. adherente m., partidario -ria.

adhesion /ædˈhiʒən/ n. adhesión f.

adhesive /ædˈhisɪv/ a. adhesivo. **a. tape,** esparadrapo m.

adhesiveness /ædˈhisɪvnɪs/ n. adhesividad f.

adieu /əˈdu/ interj. **1.** adiós. —n. **2.** despedida f.

adjacent /əˈdʒeisənt/ a. adyacente.

adjective /ˈædʒɪktɪv/ n. adjetivo m.

adjoin /əˈdʒoin/ v. lindar (con).

adjoining /əˈdʒoinɪŋ/ a. contiguo.

adjourn /əˈdʒɜrn/ v. suspender, levantar.

adjournment /əˈdʒɜrnmənt/ n. suspensión f.; Leg. espera f.

adjunct /ˈædʒʌŋkt/ n. adjunto m.; Gram. atributo m.

adjust /əˈdʒʌst/ v. ajustar, acomodar; arreglar.

adjuster /əˈdʒʌstər/ n. ajustador m.

adjustment /əˈdʒʌstmənt/ n. ajuste, arreglo m.

adjutant /ˈædʒətənt/ n. Mil. ayudante m.

administer /ædˈmɪnəstər/ v. administrar.

administration /ædˌmɪnəˈstreiʃən/ n. administración f.; gobierno m.

administrative /ædˈmɪnəˌstreitɪv/ a. administrativo.

administrator /ædˈmɪnəˌstreitər/ n. administrador -ra.

admirable /ˈædmərəbəl/ a. admirable.

admirably /ˈædmərəbli/ adv. admirablemente.

admiral /ˈædmərəl/ n. almirante m.

admiralty /ˈædmərəlti/ n. Ministerio de Marina.

admiration /ˌædməˈreiʃən/ n. admiración f.

admire /ædˈmaiər/ v. admirar.

admirer /ædˈmaiərər/ n. admirador -ra; enamorado -da.

admiringly /ædˈmaiərɪŋli/ adv. admirativamente.

admissible /ædˈmɪsəbəl/ a. admisible, aceptable.

admission /ædˈmɪʃən/ n. admisión; entrada f.

admit /ædˈmɪt/ v. admitir.

admittance /ædˈmɪtns/ n. entrada f.

admittedly /ædˈmɪtɪdli/ adv. reconocidamente.

admixture /ædˈmɪkstʃər/ n. mezcla f.

admonish /ædˈmɒnɪʃ/ v. amonestar.

admonition /ˌædməˈnɪʃən/ n. admonición f.

adolescence /ˌædlˈɛsəns/ n. adolescencia f.

adolescent /ˌædlˈɛsənt/ n. & a. adolescente.

adopt /əˈdɒpt/ v. adoptar.

adopted child /əˈdɒptɪd/ hija adoptiva f., hijo adoptivo m.

adoption /əˈdɒpʃən/ n. adopción f.

adorable /əˈdorəbəl/ a. adorable.

adoration /ˌædəˈreiʃən/ n. adoración f.

adore /əˈdor/ v. adorar.

adorn /əˈdorn/ v. adornar.

adornment /əˈdornmənt/ n. adorno m.

adrenalin /əˈdrɛnlɪn/ n. adrenalina f.

adrift /əˈdrɪft/ adv. a la ventura.

adroit /əˈdroit/ a. diestro.

adulate /ˈædʒəˌleit/ v. adular.

adulation /ˌædʒəˈleiʃən/ n. adulación f.

adult /əˈdʌlt/ a. & n. adulto -a.

adulterant /əˈdʌltərənt/ a. & n. adulterante m.

adulterate /əˈdʌltəˌreit/ v. adulterar.

adulterer /əˈdʌltərər/ n. adúltero -ra.

adulteress /əˈdʌltərɪs/ n. adúltera f.

adultery /əˈdʌltəri/ n. adulterio m.

advance /ædˈvæns/ n. **1.** avance; adelanto m. **in a.,** de antemano, antes. —v. **2.** avanzar, adelantar.

advanced /ædˈvænst/ a. avanzado, adelantado.

advancement /ædˈvænsmənt/ n. adelantamiento m.; promoción f.

advantage /ædˈvæntɪdʒ/ n. ventaja f. **take a. of,** aprovecharse de.

advantageous /ˌædvənˈteidʒəs/ a. provechoso, ventajoso.

advantageously /ˌædvənˈteidʒəsli/ adv. ventajosamente.

advent /ˈædvɛnt/ n. venida, llegada f.

adventitious /ˌædvənˈtɪʃəs/ a. adventicio, espontáneo.

adventure /ædˈvɛntʃər/ n. aventura f.

adventurer /ædˈvɛntʃərər/ n. aventurero -ra.

adventurous /ædˈvɛntʃərəs/ a. aventurero, intrépido.

adventurously /ædˈvɛntʃərəsli/ adv. arriesgadamente.

adverb /ˈædvɜrb/ n. adverbio m.

adverbial /ædˈvɜrbiəl/ a. adverbial.

adversary /ˈædvərˌsɛri/ n. adversario -a.

adverse /ædˈvɜrs/ a. adverso.

adversely /ædˈvɜrsli/ adv. adversamente.

adversity /ædˈvɜrsɪti/ n. adversidad f.

advert /ædˈvɜrt/ v. hacer referencia a.

advertise /ˈædvərˌtaiz/ v. avisar, anunciar; (promote) promocionar.

advertisement /ˌædvərˈtaizmənt, ædˈvɜrtɪsmənt/ n. aviso, anuncio m.

advertiser /ˈædvərˌtaizər/ n. anunciante m. & f., avisador -ra.

advertising /ˈædvərˌtaizɪŋ/ n. publicidad f.

advice /ædˈvais/ n. consejos m.pl.

advisability /ædˌvaizəˈbɪlɪti/ n. prudencia, propiedad f.

advisable /ædˈvaizəbəl/ a. aconsejable, prudente.

advisably /ædˈvaizəbli/ adv. prudentemente.

advise /ædˈvaiz/ v. aconsejar. **a. against,** desaconsejar.

advisedly /ædˈvaizɪdli/ adv. avisadamente, prudentemente.

advisement /ædˈvaizmənt/ n. consideración f.; **take under a.,** someter a estudio.

adviser /ædˈvaizər/ n. consejero -ra.

advocacy /ˈædvəkəsi/ n. abogacía; defensa f.

advocate /n ˈædvəkɪt; v -ˌkeit/ n. **1.** abogado -da. —v. **2.** apoyar.

aegis /ˈidʒɪs/ n. amparo m.

aerate /ˈɛəreit/ v. airear, ventilar.

aeration /ˌɛəˈreiʃən/ n. aeración, ventilación f.

aerial /ˈɛəriəl/ a. aéreo.

aerie /ˈɛəri/ n. nido de águila.

aeronautics /ˌɛərəˈnɔtiks/ n. aeronáutica f.

aerosol bomb /ˈɛərəˌsɒl/ bomba insecticida.

afar /əˈfɑr/ adv. lejos. **from a.,** de lejos, desde lejos.

affability /ˌæfəˈbɪlɪti/ n. afabilidad, amabilidad f.

affable /ˈæfəbəl/ a. afable.

affably /ˈæfəbli/ adv. afablemente.

affair /əˈfɛər/ n. asunto m. **love a.,** aventura amorosa.

affect /əˈfɛkt/ v. afectar; (emotionally) conmover.

affectation /ˌæfɛkˈteiʃən/ n. afectación f.

affected /əˈfɛktɪd/ a. artificioso.

affecting /əˈfɛktɪŋ/ a. conmovedor.

affection /əˈfɛkʃən/ n. cariño m.

affectionate /əˈfɛkʃənɪt/ a. afectuoso, cariñoso.

affectionately /əˈfɛkʃənɪtli/ adv. afectuosamente, con cariño.

affiance /əˈfaiəns/ v. dar palabra de casamiento; **become affianced,** comprometerse.

affidavit /ˌæfɪˈdeivɪt/ n. Leg. declaración, deposición f.

affiliate /n əˈfɪliˌit; v əˈfɪliˌeit/ n. **1.** afiliado -da. —v. **2.** afiliar.

affiliation /əˌfɪliˈeiʃən/ n. afiliación f.

affinity /əˈfɪnɪti/ n. afinidad f.

affirm /əˈfɜrm/ v. afirmar.

affirmation /ˌæfərˈmeiʃən/ n. afirmación, aserción f.

affirmative /əˈfɜrmətɪv/ n. **1.** afirmativa f. —a. **2.** afirmativo.

affirmatively /əˈfɜrmətɪvli/ adv. afirmativamente, aseveradamente.

affix /n ˈæfɪks; v əˈfɪks/ n. **1.** Gram. afijo m. —v. **2.** fijar, pegar, poner.

afflict /əˈflɪkt/ v. afligir.

affliction /əˈflɪkʃən/ n. aflicción f.; mal m.

affluence /ˈæfluəns/ n. abundancia, opulencia f.

affluent /ˈæfluənt/ a. opulento, afluente.

afford /əˈford/ v. proporcionar. **be able to a.,** tener con que comprar.

affordable /əˈfordəbəl/ a. asequible.

affront /əˈfrʌnt/ n. **1.** afrenta f. —v. **2.** afrentar, insultar.

afield /əˈfild/ adv. lejos de casa; lejos del camino; lejos del asunto.

afire /əˈfaiər/ adv. ardiendo.

afloat /əˈflout/ adv. Naut. a flote.

aforementioned /əˈforˌmɛnʃənd/ a. dicho, susodicho.

afraid /əˈfreid/ a. **to be a.,** tener miedo, temer.

African /ˈæfrɪkən/ n. & a. africano -na.

aft /æft/ adv. Naut. a popa, en popa.

after /ˈæftər/ prep. **1.** después de. —conj. **2.** después que.

aftermath /ˈæftərˌmæθ/ n. resultados m.pl., consecuencias f.pl.

afternoon /ˌæftərˈnun/ n. tarde f. **good a.,** buenas tardes.

aftertaste /ˈæftərˌteist/ n. gustillo m.

afterthought /ˈæftərˌθɔt/ n. idea tardía.

afterward(s) /ˈæftərwərdz/ adv. después.

again /əˈgɛn/ adv. otra vez, de nuevo. **to do a.,** volver a hacer.

against /əˈgɛnst/ prep. contra; en contra de.

agape /əˈgeip/ adv. con la boca abierta.

agate /ˈægɪt/ n. ágata f.

age /eidʒ/ n. **1.** edad f. **of a.,** mayor de edad. **old a.,** vejez f. —v. **2.** envejecer.

aged /eidʒd; ˈeidʒɪd/ a. viejo, anciano, añejo.

ageism /ˈeidʒɪzəm/ n. discriminación contra las personas de edad.

ageless /ˈeidʒlɪs/ a. sempiterno.

agency /ˈeidʒənsi/ n. agencia f.

agenda /əˈdʒɛndə/ n. agenda f., orden m.

agent /ˈeidʒənt/ n. agente; representante m. & f.

agglutinate /əˈglutnˌeit/ v. aglutinar.

agglutination /əˌglutnˈeiʃən/ n. aglutinación f.

aggrandize /əˈgrændaiz/ v. agrandar; elevar.

aggrandizement /əˈgrændɪzmənt/ n. engrandecimiento m.

aggravate /ˈægrəˌveit/ v. agravar; irritar.

aggravation /ˌægrəˈveiʃən/ n. agravamiento; empeoramiento m.

aggregate /ˈægrɪgɪt, -ˌgeit/ a. & n. agregado m.

aggregation /ˌægrɪˈgeiʃən/ n. agregación f.

aggression /əˈgrɛʃən/ n. agresión f.

aggressive /əˈgrɛsɪv/ a. agresivo.

aggressively /əˈgrɛsɪvli/ adv. agresivamente.

aggressiveness /əˈgrɛsɪvnɪs/ n. agresividad f.

aggressor /əˈgrɛsər/ n. agresor -ra.

aghast /əˈgæst/ a. horrorizado.

agile /ˈædʒəl/ a. ágil.

agility /əˈdʒɪlɪti/ n. agilidad, ligereza, prontitud f.

agitate /ˈædʒɪˌteit/ v. agitar.

agitation /ˌædʒɪˈteiʃən/ n. agitación f.

agitator /ˈædʒɪˌteitər/ n. agitador -ra.

agnostic /ægˈnɒstɪk/ a. & n. agnóstico -ca.

ago /əˈgou/ adv. hace. **two days a.,** hace dos días.

agonized /ˈægəˌnaizd/ a. angustioso.

agony /ˈægəni/ n. sufrimiento m.; angustia f.

agrarian /əˈgrɛəriən/ a. agrario.

agree /əˈgri/ v. estar de acuerdo; convenir. **a. with one,** sentar bien.

agreeable /əˈgriəbəl/ a. agradable.

agreeably /əˈgriəbli/ adv. agradablemente.

agreement /əˈgrimənt/ n. acuerdo m.

agriculture /ˈægrɪˌkʌltʃər/ n. agricultura f.

ahead /əˈhɛd/ adv. adelante.

aid /eid/ n. **1.** ayuda f. —v. **2.** ayudar.

aide /eid/ n. ayudante -ta.

AIDS /eidz/ n. SIDA m.

ailing /ˈeilɪŋ/ adj. enfermo.

ailment /ˈeilmənt/ n. enfermedad f.

aim /eim/ n. **1.** puntería f.; (purpose) propósito m. —v. **2.** apuntar.

aimless /ˈeimlɪs/ a. sin objeto.

air /ɛər/ n. **1.** aire m. **by a.,** por avión. —v. **2.** ventilar, airear.

airbag /'ɛər,bæg/ n. (in automobiles) saco de aire m.

air-conditioned /'ɛər kən,dɪʃənd/ a. con aire acondicionado.

air-conditioning /ɛər kən,dɪʃənɪŋ/ acondicionamiento del aire.

aircraft /'ɛər,kræft/ n. avión m.

aircraft carrier portaaviones m.

airfare /'ɛər,fɛər/ n. precio del billete de avión m.

airing /'ɛərɪŋ/ n. ventilación f.

airline /'ɛər,laɪn/ n. línea aérea f.

airliner /'ɛər,laɪnər/ n. avión de pasajeros.

airmail /'ɛər,meɪl/ n. correo aéreo.

airplane /'ɛər,pleɪn/ n. avión, aeroplano m.

air pollution contaminación atmosférica, contaminación del aire.

airport /'ɛər,pɔrt/ n. aeropuerto m.

air pressure presión atmosférica.

air raid ataque aéreo.

airsick /'ɛər,sɪk/ a. mareado.

air terminal terminal aérea f.

airtight /'ɛər,taɪt/ a. hermético.

air traffic controller controlador aéreo m.

aisle /aɪl/ n. pasillo m.

ajar /ə'dʒɑr/ a. entreabierto.

akin /ə'kɪn/ a. emparentado, semejante.

alacrity /ə'lækrɪti/ n. alacridad, presteza f.

alarm /ə'lɑrm/ n. **1.** alarma f. —v. **2.** alarmar.

alarmist /ə'lɑrmɪst/ n. alarmista m. & f.

albino /æl'baɪnou/ n. albino -na.

album /'ælbəm/ n. álbum m.

alcohol /'ælkə,hɔl/ n. alcohol m.

alcoholic /,ælkə'hɔlɪk/ a. alcohólico.

alcove /'ælkouv/ n. alcoba f.

ale /eɪl/ n. cerveza inglesa f.

alert /ə'lɜrt/ n. **1.** alarma f. **on the a.,** alerta, sobre aviso. —a. **2.** listo, vivo. —v. **3.** poner sobre aviso.

alfalfa /æl'fælfə/ n. alfalfa f.

algebra /'ældʒəbrə/ n. álgebra f.

alias /'eɪliəs/ n. alias m.

alibi /'ælə,baɪ/ n. excusa f.; Leg. coartada f.

alien /'eɪliən/ a. **1.** ajeno, extranjero. —n. **2.** extranjero -ra.

alienate /'eɪliə,neɪt/ v. enajenar.

alight /ə'laɪt/ v. bajar, apearse.

align /ə'laɪn/ v. alinear.

alike /ə'laɪk/ a. **1.** semejante, igual. —adv. **2.** del mismo modo, igualmente.

alimentary canal /,ælə'mɛntəri/ n. tubo digestivo m.

alive /ə'laɪv/ a. vivo; animado.

alkali /'ælkə,laɪ/ n. Chem. álcali, cali m.

alkaline /'ælkə,laɪn/ a. alcalino.

all /ɔl/ a. & pron. todo. **not at a.,** de ninguna manera, nada.

allay /ə'leɪ/ v. aquietar.

allegation /,ælɪ'geɪʃən/ n. alegación f.

allege /ə'lɛdʒ/ v. alegar; pretender.

allegiance /ə'lidʒəns/ n. lealtad f.; (to country) homenaje m.

allegory /'ælə,gɔri/ n. alegoría f.

allergy /'ælərdʒi/ n. alergia f.

alleviate /ə'livi,eɪt/ v. aliviar.

alley /'æli/ n. callejón m. **bowling a.,** bolera f., boliche m.

alliance /ə'laɪəns/ n. alianza f.

allied /'ælaɪd/ a. aliado.

alligator /'ælɪ,geɪtər/ n. caimán m.; (Mex.) lagarto m. **a. pear,** aguacate m.

allocate /'ælə,keɪt/ v. colocar, asignar.

allot /ə'lɒt/ v. asignar.

allotment /ə'lɒtmənt/ n. lote, porción f.

allow /ə'laʊ/ v. permitir, dejar.

allowance /ə'laʊəns/ n. abono m.; dieta f. **make a. for,** tener en cuenta.

alloy /'ælɔɪ/ n. mezcla f.; (metal) aleación f.

all right está bien.

allude /ə'lud/ v. aludir.

allure /ə'lʊr/ n. **1.** atracción f. —v. **2.** atraer, tentar.

alluring /ə'lʊrɪŋ/ a. tentador, seductivo.

allusion /ə'luʒən/ n. alusión f.

ally /n 'ælaɪ, v ə'laɪ/ n. **1.** aliado -da. —v. **2.** aliar.

almanac /'ɔlmə,næk/ n. almanaque m.

almighty /ɔl'maɪti/ a. todopoderoso.

almond /'ɑmənd/ n. almendra f.

almost /'ɔlmoust/ adv. casi.

alms /ɑmz/ n. limosna f.

aloft /ə'lɔft/ adv. arriba, en alto.

alone /ə'loun/ adv. solo, a solas. **to leave a.,** dejar en paz.

along /ə'lɔŋ/ prep. por; a lo largo de. **a. with,** junto con.

alongside /ə'lɔŋ'saɪd/ adv. **1.** al lado. —prep. **2.** junto a.

aloof /ə'luf/ a. apartado.

aloud /ə'laʊd/ adv. en voz alta.

alpaca /æl'pækə/ n. alpaca f.

alphabet /'ælfə,bɛt/ n. alfabeto m.

alphabetical /,ælfə'bɛtɪkəl/ a. alfabético.

alphabetize /'ælfəbɪ,taɪz/ v. alfabetizar.

already /ɔl'rɛdi/ adv. ya.

also /'ɔlsou/ adv. también.

altar /'ɔltər/ n. altar m.

alter /'ɔltər/ v. alterar.

alteration /,ɔltə'reɪʃən/ n. alteración f.

alternate /a, n 'ɔltərnɪt; v -,neɪt/ a. **1.** alterno. —n. **2.** substituto -ta. —v. **3.** alternar.

alternative /ɔl'tɜrnətɪv/ a. **1.** alternativo. —n. **2.** alternativa f.

although /ɔl'ðou/ conj. aunque.

altitude /'æltɪ,tud/ n. altura f.

alto /'æltou/ n. contralto m.

altogether /,ɔltə'gɛðər/ adv. en junto; enteramente.

altruism /'æltru,ɪzəm/ n. altruismo m.

alum /'æləm/ n. alumbre m.

aluminum /ə'lumənəm/ n. aluminio m.

aluminum foil papel de aluminio m.

always /'ɔlweɪz/ adv. siempre.

amalgam /ə'mælgəm/ n. amalgama f.

amalgamate /ə'mælgə,meɪt/ v. amalgamar.

amass /ə'mæs/ v. amontonar.

amateur /'æmə,tʃʊr/ n. aficionado -da.

amaze /ə'meɪz/ v. asombrar; sorprender.

amazement /ə'meɪzmənt/ n. asombro m.

amazing /ə'meɪzɪŋ/ a. asombroso, pasmoso.

ambassador /æm'bæsədər/ n. embajador -ra.

amber /'æmbər/ a. **1.** ambarino. —n. **2.** ámbar m.

ambidextrous /,æmbɪ'dɛkstrəs/ a. ambidextro.

ambiguity /,æmbɪ'gyuɪti/ n. ambigüedad f.

ambiguous /æm'bɪgyuəs/ a. ambiguo.

ambition /æm'bɪʃən/ n. ambición f.

ambitious /æm'bɪʃəs/ a. ambicioso.

ambulance /'æmbyələns/ n. ambulancia f.

ambush /'æmbʊʃ/ n. **1.** emboscada f. —v. **2.** acechar.

ameliorate /ə'milyə,reɪt/ v. mejorar.

amenable /ə'minəbəl/ a. tratable, dócil.

amend /ə'mɛnd/ v. enmendar.

amendment /ə'mɛndmənt/ n. enmienda f.

amenity /ə'mɛnɪti/ n. amenidad f.

American /ə'mɛrɪkən/ a. & n. americano -na, norteamericano -na.

amethyst /'æməθɪst/ n. amatista f.

amiable /'eɪmiəbəl/ a. amable.

amicable /'æmɪkəbəl/ a. amigable.

amid /ə'mɪd/ prep. entre, en medio de.

amidships /ə'mɪd,ʃɪps/ adv. Naut. en medio del navío.

amiss /ə'mɪs/ adv. mal. **to take a.,** llevar a mal.

amity /'æmɪti/ n. amistad, armonía f.

ammonia /ə'mounyə/ n. amoníaco m.

ammunition /,æmyə'nɪʃən/ n. municiones f.pl.

amnesia /æm'niʒə/ n. amnesia f.

amnesty /'æmnəsti/ n. amnistía f., indulto m.

amniocentesis /,æmniousɛn'tisɪs/ n. amniocéntesis f.

amoeba /ə'mibə/ n. amiba f.

among /ə'mʌŋ/ prep. entre.

amoral /eɪ'mɔrəl/ a. amoral.

amorous /'æmərəs/ a. amoroso.

amorphous /ə'mɔrfəs/ a. amorfo.

amortize /'æmər,taɪz/ v. Com. amortizar.

amount /ə'maʊnt/ n. **1.** cantidad, suma f. —v. **2. a. to,** subir a.

ampere /'æmpɪər/ n. Elec. amperio m.

amphibian /æm'fɪbiən/ a. & n. anfibio m.

amphitheater /'æmfə,θiətər/ n. anfiteatro, circo m.

ample /'æmpəl/ a. amplio; suficiente.

amplify /'æmplə,faɪ/ v. amplificar.

amputate /'æmpyu,teɪt/ v. amputar.

amuse /ə'myuz/ v. entretener, divertir.

amusement /ə'myuzmənt/ n. diversión f.

an /ən, when stressed an/ art. un, una.

anachronism /ə'nækrə,nɪzəm/ n. anacronismo, m.

analogous /ə'næləgəs/ a. análogo, parecido.

analogy /ə'nælədʒi/ n. analogía f.

analysis /ə'næləsɪs/ n. análisis m.

analyst /'ænlɪst/ n. analista m. & f.

analytic /,ænl'ɪtɪk/ a. analítico.

analyze /'ænl,aɪz/ v. analizar.

anarchy /'ænərki/ n. anarquía f.

anatomy /ə'nætəmi/ n. anatomía f.

ancestor /'ænsɛstər/ n. antepasado m.

ancestral /æn'sɛstrəl/ a. de los antepasados, hereditario.

ancestry /'ænsɛstri/ n. linaje, abolengo m.

anchor /'æŋkər/ n. **1.** ancla f. **weigh a.,** levar el ancla. —v. **2.** anclar.

anchorage /'æŋkərɪdʒ/ n. Naut. ancladero, anclaje m.

anchovy /'æntʃouvi/ n. anchoa f.

ancient /'eɪnʃənt/ a. antiguo -ua.

and /ænd, ənd/ conj. y, (before i-, hi-) e.

anecdote /'ænɪk,dout/ n. anécdota f.

anemia /ə'nimiə/ n. Med. anemia f.

anesthetic /,ænəs'θɛtɪk/ n. anestesia f.

anew /ə'nu/ adv. de nuevo.

angel /'eɪndʒəl/ n. ángel m.

anger /'æŋgər/ n. **1.** ira f., enojo m. —v. **2.** enfadar, enojar.

angle /'æŋgəl/ n. ángulo m.

angry /'æŋgri/ a. enojado, enfadado.

anguish /'æŋgwɪʃ/ n. angustia f.

angular /'æŋgyələr/ a. angular.

aniline /'ænlɪn/ n. Chem. anilina f.

animal /'ænəməl/ a. & n. animal m.

animate /v 'ænə,meɪt; a -mɪt/ v. **1.** animar. —a. **2.** animado.

animated /'ænə,meɪtɪd/ a. vivo, animado.

animation /,ænə'meɪʃən/ n. animación, viveza f.

animosity /,ænə'mɒsɪti/ n. rencor m.

anise /'ænɪs/ n. anís m.

ankle /'æŋkəl/ n. tobillo m.

annals /'ænlz/ n.pl. anales m.pl.

annex /n 'ænɛks; v ə'nɛks, 'ænɛks/ n. **1.** anexo m., adición f. —v. **2.** anexar.

annexation /,ænɪk'seɪʃən/ n. anexión, adición f.

annihilate /ə'naɪə,leɪt/ v. aniquilar, destruir.

anniversary /,ænə'vɜrsəri/ n. aniversario m.

annotate /'ænə,teɪt/ v. anotar.

annotation /,ænə'teɪʃən/ n. anotación f., apunte m.

announce /ə'naʊns/ v. anunciar.

announcement /ə'naʊnsmənt/ n. anuncio, aviso m.

announcer /ə'naʊnsər/ n. anunciador -ra; (radio) locutor -ra.

annoy /ə'nɔɪ/ v. molestar.

annoyance /ə'nɔɪəns/ n. molestia, incomodidad f.

annual /'ænyuəl/ a. anual.

annuity /ə'nuɪti/ n. anualidad, pensión f.

annul /ə'nʌl/ v. anular, invalidar.

anode /'ænoud/ n. Elec. ánodo m.

anoint /ə'nɔɪnt/ v. untar; Relig. ungir.

anomalous /ə'nɒmələs/ a. anómalo, irregular.

anonymous /ə'nɒnəməs/ a. anónimo.

anorexia /,ænə'rɛksiə/ n. anorexia f.

another /ə'nʌðər/ a. & pron. otro.

answer /'ænsər, 'ɑn-/ n. **1.** contestación, respuesta f. —v. **2.** contestar, responder. **a. for,** ser responsable de.

answerable /'ænsərəbəl/ a. discutible, refutable.

answering machine /'ænsərɪŋ/ contestador automático m.

ant /ænt/ n. hormiga f.

antacid /ænt'æsɪd/ a. & n. antiácido m.

antagonism /æn'tægə,nɪzəm/ n. antagonismo m.

antagonist /æn'tægənɪst/ n. antagonista m. & f.

antagonistic /æn,tægə'nɪstɪk/ a. antagónico, hostil.

antagonize /æn'tægə,naɪz/ v. contrariar.

antarctic /ænt'ɑrktɪk/ a. & n. antártico m.

antecedent /,æntə'sidṇt/ a. & n. antecedente m.

antedate /'ænti,deɪt/ v. antedatar.

antelope /'æntḷ,oup/ n. antílope m., gacela f.

antenna /æn'tɛnə/ n. antena f.

antepenultimate /,æntipɪ'nʌltəmɪt/ a. antepenúltimo.

anterior /æn'tɪəriər/ a. anterior.

anteroom /'ænti,rum/ n. antecámara f.

anthem /'ænθəm/ n. himno m.; (religious) antífona f.

anthology /æn'θɒlədʒi/ n. antología f.

anthracite /'ænθrə,saɪt/ n. antracita f.

anthrax /'ænθræks/ n. Med. ántrax m.

anthropology /,ænθrə'pɒlədʒi/ n. antropología f.

antiaircraft /,ænti'ɛər,kræft, ,æntaɪ-/ a. antiaéreo.

antibody /'ænti,bɒdi/ n. anticuerpo m.

anticipate /æn'tɪsə,peɪt/ v. esperar, anticipar.

anticipation /æn,tɪsə'peɪʃən/ n. anticipación f.

anticlerical /,ænti'klɛrɪkəl, ,æntaɪ-/ a. anticlerical.

anticlimax /,ænti'klaɪmæks, ,æntaɪ-/ n. anticlímax m.

antidote /'ænti,dout/ n. antídoto m.

antifreeze /'ænti,friz/ n. anticongelante m.

antihistamine /,ænti'hɪstə,min, -mɪn, ,æntaɪ-/ n. antihistamínico m.

antimony /'æntə,mouni/ n. antimonio m.

antinuclear /,ænti'nukliər, æntaɪ-/ a. antinuclear.

antipathy /æn'tɪpəθi/ n. antipatía f.

antiquated /'ænti,kweitɪd/ a. anticuado.

antique /æn'tik/ a. **1.** antiguo. —n. **2.** antigüedad f.

antiquity /æn'tɪkwɪti/ n. antigüedad f.

antiseptic /,æntə'sɛptɪk/ a. & n. antiséptico m.

antisocial /,ænti'souʃəl, ,æntaɪ-/ a. antisocial.

antitoxin /ˌæntɪˈtɒksɪn/ n. Med. antitoxina f.

antler /ˈæntlər/ n. asta f.

anvil /ˈænvɪl/ n. yunque m.

anxiety /æŋˈzaɪɪti/ n. ansia, ansiedad f.

anxious /ˈæŋkʃəs, ˈæŋʃəs/ a. inquieto, ansioso.

any /ˈɛni/ a. alguno; (at all) cualquiera; (after not) ninguno.

anybody /ˈɛniˌbɒdi/ pron. alguien; (at all) cualquiera; (after not) nadie.

anyhow /ˈɛniˌhau/ adv. de todos modos; en todo caso.

anyone /ˈɛniˌwʌn/ pron. = anybody.

anything /ˈɛniˌθɪŋ/ pron. algo; (at all) cualquier cosa; (after not) nada.

anyway /ˈɛniˌwei/ adv. = anyhow.

anywhere /ˈɛniˌwɛər/ adv. en alguna parte; (at all) dondequiera; (after not) en ninguna parte.

apart /əˈpart/ adv. aparte. **to take a.,** deshacer.

apartheid /əˈparteit, -hait/ n. apartheid m.

apartment /əˈpartmənt/ n. apartamento, piso m.

apartment house casa de pisos f.

apathetic /ˌæpəˈθɛtɪk/ a. apático.

apathy /ˈæpəθi/ n. apatía f.

ape /eip/ n. **1.** mono -na. —v. **2.** imitar.

aperture /ˈæpərtʃər/ n. abertura f.

apex /ˈeipɛks/ n. ápice m.

aphorism /ˈæfəˌrɪzəm/ n. aforismo m.

apiary /ˈeipiˌɛri/ n. colmenario, abejar m.

apiece /əˈpis/ adv. por persona; cada uno.

apologetic /əˌpɒləˈdʒɛtɪk/ a. apologético.

apologist /əˈpɒlədʒɪst/ n. apologista m. & f.

apologize /əˈpɒləˌdʒaiz/ v. excusarse, disculparse.

apology /əˈpɒlədʒi/ n. excusa; apología f.

apoplectic /ˌæpəˈplɛktɪk/ a. apoplético.

apoplexy /ˈæpəˌplɛksi/ n. apoplejía f.

apostate /əˈpɒsteit/ n. apóstata m. & f.

apostle /əˈpɒsəl/ n. apóstol m.

apostolic /ˌæpəˈstɒlɪk/ a. apostólico.

appall /əˈpɔl/ v. horrorizar; consternar.

apparatus /ˌæpəˈrætəs/ n. aparato m.

apparel /əˈpærəl/ n. ropa f.

apparent /əˈpærənt/ a. aparente; claro.

apparition /ˌæpəˈrɪʃən/ n. aparición f.; fantasma m.

appeal /əˈpil/ n. **1.** súplica f.; interés m.; Leg. apelación f. —v. **2.** apelar, suplicar; interesar.

appear /əˈpɪər/ v. aparecer, asomar; (seem) parecer; Leg. comparecer.

appearance /əˈpɪərəns/ n. apariencia f., aspecto m.; aparición f.

appease /əˈpiz/ v. aplacar, apaciguar.

appeasement /əˈpizmənt/ n. apaciguamiento m.

appeaser /əˈpizər/ n. apaciguador -ra, pacificador -ra.

appellant /əˈpɛlənt/ n. apelante, demandante m. & f.

appellate /əˈpɛlɪt/ a. Leg. de apelación.

appendage /əˈpɛndɪdʒ/ n. añadidura f.

appendectomy /ˌæpənˈdɛktəmi/ n. apendectomía f.

appendicitis /əˌpɛndəˈsaitɪs/ n. apendicitis f.

appendix /əˈpɛndɪks/ n. apéndice m.

appetite /ˈæpɪˌtait/ n. apetito m.

appetizer /ˈæpɪˌtaizər/ n. aperitivo m.

appetizing /ˈæpɪˌtaizɪŋ/ a. apetitoso.

applaud /əˈplɔd/ v. aplaudir.

applause /əˈplɔz/ n. aplauso m.

apple /ˈæpəl/ n. manzana f. **a. tree,** manzano m.

applesauce /ˈæpəlˌsɔs/ n. compota de manzana.

appliance /əˈplaiəns/ n. aparato m.

applicable /ˈæplɪkəbəl/ a. aplicable.

applicant /ˈæplɪkənt/ n. suplicante m. & f.; candidato -ta.

application /ˌæplɪˈkeiʃən/ n. solicitud f., (computer) programa m.

applied /əˈplaid/ a. aplicado. **a. for,** pedido.

appliqué /ˌæplɪˈkei/ n. (sewing) aplicación f.

apply /əˈplai/ v. aplicar. **a. for,** solicitar, pedir.

appoint /əˈpɔint/ v. nombrar.

appointment /əˈpɔintmənt/ n. nombramiento m.; puesto m.

apportion /əˈpɔrʃən/ v. repartir.

apposition /ˌæpəˈzɪʃən/ n. Gram. aposición f.

appraisal /əˈpreizəl/ n. valoración f.

appraise /əˈpreiz/ v. evaluar; tasar; estimar.

appreciable /əˈpriʃiəbəl/ a. apreciable; notable.

appreciate /əˈpriʃiˌeit/ v. apreciar, estimar.

appreciation /əˌpriʃiˈeiʃən/ n. aprecio; reconocimiento m.

apprehend /ˌæprɪˈhɛnd/ v. prender, capturar.

apprehension /ˌæprɪˈhɛnʃən/ n. aprensión f.; detención f.

apprehensive /ˌæprɪˈhɛnsɪv/ a. aprensivo.

apprentice /əˈprɛntɪs/ n. aprendiz -iza.

apprenticeship /əˈprɛntɪsˌʃip/ n. aprendizaje m.

apprise /əˈpraiz/ v. informar.

approach /əˈproutʃ/ n. **1.** acceso; método m. —v. **2.** acercarse.

approachable /əˈproutʃəbəl/ a. accesible.

approbation /ˌæprəˈbeiʃən/ n. aprobación f.

appropriate /a əˈproupriit; v -ˌeit/ a. **1.** apropiado. —v. **2.** apropiar.

appropriation /əˌproupriˈeiʃən/ n. apropiación f.

approval /əˈpruvəl/ n. aprobación f.

approve /əˈpruv/ v. aprobar.

approximate /a əˈprɒksəmit; v -ˌmeit/ a. **1.** aproximado. —v. **2.** aproximar.

approximately /əˈprɒksəmitli/ adv. aproximadamente.

approximation /əˌprɒksəˈmeiʃən/ n. aproximación f.

appurtenance /əˈpɜrtnəns/ n. dependencia f.

apricot /ˈæprɪˌkɒt/ n. albaricoque, damasco m.

April /ˈeiprəl/ n. abril m.

apron /ˈeiprən/ n. delantal m.

apropos /ˌæprəˈpou/ adv. a propósito.

apt /æpt/ a. apto; capaz.

aptitude /ˈæptɪˌtud/ n. aptitud; facilidad f.

aquarium /əˈkwɛəriəm/ n. acuario m., pecera f.

aquatic /əˈkwætɪk/ a. acuático.

aqueduct /ˈækwɪˌdʌkt/ n. acueducto m.

aqueous /ˈækwiəs/ a. ácueo, acuoso, aguoso.

aquiline /ˈækwəˌlain/ a. aquilino, aguileño.

Arab /ˈærəb/ a. & n. árabe m. & f.

arable /ˈærəbəl/ a. cultivable.

arbitrary /ˈarbɪˌtrɛri/ a. arbitrario.

arbitrate /ˈarbɪˌtreit/ v. arbitrar.

arbitration /ˌarbɪˈtreiʃən/ n. arbitraje m., arbitración f.

arbitrator /ˈarbɪˌtreitər/ n. arbitrador -ra.

arbor /ˈarbər/ n. emparrado m.

arboreal /arˈbɔriəl/ a. arbóreo.

arc /ark/ n. arco m.

arch /artʃ/ n. **1.** arco m. —v. **2.** arquear, encorvar.

archaeology /ˌarkiˈɒlədʒi/ n. arqueología f.

archaic /arˈkeiɪk/ a. arcaico.

archbishop /ˈartʃˈbiʃəp/ n. arzobispo m.

archdiocese /ˌartʃˈdaiəˌsis, -sɪs/ n. archidiócesis f.

archduke /ˈartʃˈduk/ n. archiduque m.

archer /ˈartʃər/ n. arquero m.

archery /ˈartʃəri/ n. ballestería f.

archipelago /ˌarkəˈpɛləˌgou/ n. archipiélago m.

architect /ˈarkɪˌtɛkt/ n. arquitecto -ta.

architectural /ˌarkɪˈtɛktʃərəl/ a. arquitectural.

architecture /ˈarkɪˌtɛktʃər/ n. arquitectura f.

archive /ˈarkaiv/ n. archivo m.

archway /ˈartʃˌwei/ n. arcada f.

arctic /ˈarktɪk, ˈartɪk/ a. ártico.

ardent /ˈardnt/ a. ardiente.

ardor /ˈardər/ n. ardor m., pasión f.

arduous /ˈardʒuəs/ a. arduo, difícil.

area /ˈɛəriə/ n. área; extensión f.

area code prefijo m.

arena /əˈrinə/ n. arena f.

Argentine /ˈardʒəntin, -ˌtain/ a. & n. argentino -na.

argue /ˈargyu/ v. disputar; sostener.

argument /ˈargyəmənt/ n. disputa f.; razonamiento m.

argumentative /ˌargyəˈmɛntətɪv/ a. argumentoso.

aria /ˈariə/ n. aria f.

arid /ˈærɪd/ a. árido, seco.

arise /əˈraiz/ v. surgir; alzarse.

aristocracy /ˌærəˈstɒkrəsi/ n. aristocracia f.

aristocrat /əˈrɪstəˌkræt/ n. aristócrata m.

aristocratic /əˌrɪstəˈkrætɪk/ a. aristocrático.

arithmetic /əˈrɪθmətɪk/ n. aritmética f.

ark /ark/ n. arca f.

arm /arm/ n. **1.** brazo m.; (weapon) arma f. —v. **2.** armar.

armament /ˈarməmənt/ n. armamento m.

armchair /ˈarmˌtʃɛər/ n. sillón m., butaca f.

armed forces /ˈarmd ˈfɔrsɪz/ fuerzas militares.

armful /ˈarmˌful/ n. brazada f.

armhole /ˈarmˌhoul/ n. (sew.) sobaquera f.

armistice /ˈarməstɪs/ n. armisticio m.

armor /ˈarmər/ n. armadura f., blindaje m.

armored /ˈarmərd/ a. blindado.

armory /ˈarməri/ n. armería f., arsenal m.

armpit /ˈarmˌpit/ n. axila f., sobaco m.

army /ˈarmi/ n. ejército m.

arnica /ˈarnɪkə/ n. árnica f.

aroma /əˈroumə/ n. fragancia f.

aromatic /ˌærəˈmætɪk/ a. aromático.

around /əˈraund/ prep. alrededor de, a la vuelta de; cerca de. **a. here,** por aquí.

arouse /əˈrauz/ v. despertar; excitar.

arraign /əˈrein/ v. Leg. procesar criminalmente.

arrange /əˈreindʒ/ v. arreglar; concertar; Mus. adaptar.

arrangement /əˈreindʒmənt/ n. arreglo; orden m.

array /əˈrei/ n. **1.** orden; adorno m. —v. **2.** adornar.

arrears /əˈrɪrz/ n. atrasos m.pl.

arrest /əˈrɛst/ n. **1.** detención f. —v. **2.** detener, arrestar.

arrival /əˈraivəl/ n. llegada f.

arrive /əˈraiv/ v. llegar.

arrogance /ˈærəgəns/ n. arrogancia f.

arrogant /ˈærəgənt/ a. arrogante.

arrogate /ˈærəˌgeit/ v. arrogarse, usurpar.

arrow /ˈærou/ n. flecha f.

arrowhead /ˈærouˌhɛd/ n. punta de flecha f.

arsenal /ˈarsənl/ n. arsenal m.

arsenic /ˈarsənɪk/ n. arsénico m.

arson /ˈarsən/ n. incendio premeditado.

art /art/ arte m. (f. in pl.); (skill) maña f.

arterial /arˈtɪəriəl/ a. arterial.

arteriosclerosis /arˌtɪəriouskləˈrousɪs/ n. arteriosclerosis f.

artery /ˈartəri/ n. arteria f.

artesian well /arˈtiʒən/ pozo artesiano.

artful /ˈartfəl/ a. astuto.

arthritis /arˈθraitɪs/ n. artritis f.

artichoke /ˈartɪˌtʃouk/ n. alcachofa f.

article /ˈartɪkəl/ n. artículo m.

articulate /arˈtɪkyəˌleit/ v. articular.

articulation /arˌtɪkyəˈleiʃən/ n. articulación f.

artifice /ˈartəfɪs/ n. artificio m.

artificial /ˌartəˈfɪʃəl/ a. artificial.

artificially /ˌartəˈfɪʃəli/ adv. artificialmente.

artillery /arˈtɪləri/ n. artillería f.

artisan /ˈartəzən/ n. artesano -na.

artist /ˈartɪst/ n. artista m. & f.

artistic /arˈtɪstɪk/ a. artístico.

artistry /ˈartɪstri/ n. arte m. & f.

artless /ˈartlɪs/ a. natural, cándido.

as /æz/ adv. & conj. como; **as... as** tan... como.

asbestos /æsˈbɛstəs/ n. asbesto m.

ascend /əˈsɛnd/ v. ascender.

ascendancy /əˈsɛndənsi/ n. ascendiente m.

ascendant /əˈsɛndənt/ a. ascendente.

ascent /əˈsɛnt/ n. subida f., ascenso m.

ascertain /ˌæsərˈtein/ v. averiguar.

ascetic /əˈsɛtɪk/ a. **1.** ascético. —n. **2.** asceta m. & f.

ascribe /əˈskraib/ v. atribuir.

ash /æʃ/ n. ceniza f.

ashamed /əˈʃeimd/ a. avergonzado.

ashen /ˈæʃən/ a. pálido.

ashore /əˈʃɔr/ adv. a tierra. **go a.,** desembarcar.

ashtray /ˈæʃˌtrei/ n. cenicero m.

Ash Wednesday miércoles de ceniza m.

Asiatic /ˌeiʒiˈætɪk/ a. & n. asiático -ca.

aside /əˈsaid/ adv. al lado. **a. from,** aparte de.

ask /æsk/ v. preguntar; invitar; (request) pedir. **a. for,** pedir. **a. a question,** hacer una pregunta.

askance /əˈskæns/ adv. de soslayo; con recelo.

asleep /əˈslip/ a. dormido. **to fall a.,** dormirse.

asparagus /əˈspærəgəs/ n. espárrago m.

aspect /ˈæspɛkt/ n. aspecto m., apariencia f.

asperity /əˈspɛriti/ n. aspereza f.

aspersion /əˈspɜrʒən/ n. calumnia f.

asphalt /ˈæsfɔlt/ n. asfalto m.

asphyxia /æsˈfɪksiə/ n. asfixia f.

asphyxiate /æsˈfɪksiˌeit/ v. asfixiar, sofocar.

aspirant /ˈæspərənt/ a. & n. aspirante m. & f.

aspirate /ˈæspəˌreit/ v. aspirar.

aspiration /ˌæspəˈreiʃən/ n. aspiración f.

aspirator /ˈæspəˌreitər/ n. aspirador m.

aspire /əˈspaiᵊr/ v. aspirar. **a. to,** ambicionar.

aspirin /ˈæspərɪn/ n. aspirina f.

ass /æs/ n. asno, burro m.

assail /əˈseil/ v. asaltar, acometer.

assailant /əˈseilənt/ n. asaltador -ra.

assassin /əˈsæsɪn/ n. asesino m.

assassinate /əˈsæsəˌneit/ v. asesinar.

assassination /əˌsæsəˈneiʃən/ n. asesinato m.

assault /əˈsɔlt/ n. **1.** asalto m. —v. **2.** asaltar, atacar.

assay /ˈæsei/ v. examinar; ensayar.

assemblage /əˈsɛmblɪdʒ/ n. asamblea f.

assemble /əˈsɛmbəl/ v. juntar, convocar; (mechanism) montar.

assembly /ə'sɛmbli/ n. asamblea, concurrencia f.

assent /ə'sɛnt/ n. **1.** asentimiento m. —v. **2.** asentir, convenir.

assert /ə'sɜrt/ v. afirmar, aseverar. **a. oneself,** hacerse sentir.

assertion /ə'sɜrʃən/ n. aserción, aseveración f.

assertive /ə'sɜrtɪv/ a. asertivo.

assess /ə'sɛs/ v. tasar, evaluar.

assessor /ə'sɛsər/ n. asesor -ra.

asset /'æsɛt/ n. ventaja f. **assets,** Com. capital m.

asseverate /ə'sɛvə,reit/ v. aseverar, afirmar.

asseveration /ə,sɛvə'reiʃən/ n. aseveración f.

assiduous /ə'sɪdʒuəs/ a. asiduo.

assiduously /ə'sɪdʒuəsli/ adv. asiduamente.

assign /ə'sain/ v. asignar; destinar.

assignable /ə'sainəbəl/ a. asignable, transferible.

assignation /,æsɪg'neiʃən/ n. asignación f.

assignment /ə'sainmənt/ n. misión; tarea f.

assimilate /ə'sɪmə,leit/ v. asimilar.

assimilation /ə,sɪmə'leiʃən/ n. asimilación f.

assimilative /ə'sɪmələtɪv/ a. asimilativo.

assist /ə'sɪst/ v. ayudar, auxiliar.

assistance /ə'sɪstəns/ n. ayuda f., auxilio m.

assistant /ə'sɪstənt/ n. ayudante -ta, asistente -ta.

associate /n ə'souʃiit; v -si,eit/ n. **1.** socio -cia. —v. **2.** asociar.

association /ə,sousi'eiʃən/ n. asociación; sociedad f.

assonance /'æsənəns/ n. asonancia f.

assort /ə'sort/ v. surtir con variedad.

assorted /ə'sortɪd/ a. variado, surtido.

assortment /ə'sortmənt/ n. surtido m.

assuage /ə'sweidʒ/ v. mitigar, aliviar.

assume /ə'sum/ v. suponer; asumir.

assuming /ə'sumɪŋ/ a. presuntuoso. **a. that,** dado que.

assumption /ə'sʌmpʃən/ n. suposición; Relig. asunción f.

assurance /ə'ʃʊrəns/ n. seguridad; confianza f.; garantía f.

assure /ə'ʃʊr/ v. asegurar; dar confianza.

assured /ə'ʃʊrd/ a. **1.** seguro. —a. & n. **2.** Com. asegurado -da.

assuredly /ə'ʃʊrɪdli/ adv. ciertamente.

aster /'æstər/ n. aster f.

asterisk /'æstərɪsk/ n. asterisco m.

astern /ə'stɜrn/ adv. Naut. a popa.

asteroid /'æstə,rɔid/ n. asteroide m.

asthma /'æzmə/ n. Med. asma f.

astigmatism /ə'stɪgmə,tɪzəm/ n. astigmatismo m.

astir /ə'stɜr/ adv. en movimiento.

astonish /ə'stɒnɪʃ/ v. asombrar, pasmar.

astonishment /ə'stɒnɪʃmənt/ n. asombro m., sorpresa f.

astound /ə'staund/ v. pasmar, sorprender.

astral /'æstrəl/ a. astral, estelar.

astray /ə'strei/ a. desviado.

astride /ə'straid/ adv. a horcajadas.

astringent /ə'strɪndʒənt/ a. & n. astringente m.

astrology /ə'strɒlədʒi/ n. astrología f.

astronaut /'æstrə,nɔt/ n. astronauta m. & f.

astronomy /ə'strɒnəmi/ n. astronomía f.

astute /ə'stut/ a. astuto; agudo.

asunder /ə'sʌndər/ adv. en dos.

asylum /ə'sailəm/ n. asilo, refugio m.

asymmetry /ei'sɪmɪtri/ n. asimetría f.

at /æt/ prep. a, en; cerca de.

ataxia /ə'tæksiə/ n. Med. ataxia f.

atheist /'eiθiist/ n. ateo -tea.

athlete /'æθlit/ n. atleta m. & f.

athletic /æθ'lɛtɪk/ a. atlético.

athletics /æθ'lɛtɪks/ n. atletismo m., deportes m.pl.

athwart /ə'θwɔrt/ prep. a través de.

Atlantic /æt'læntɪk/ a. **1.** atlántico. —n. **2.** Atlántico m.

Atlantic Ocean Océano Atlántico m.

atlas /'ætləs/ n. atlas m.

atmosphere /'ætməs,fɪər/ n. atmósfera f.; Fig. ambiente m.

atmospheric /,ætməs'fɛrɪk/ a. atmosférico.

atoll /'ætɒl/ n. atolón m.

atom /'ætəm/ n. átomo m.

atomic /ə'tɒmɪk/ a. atómico.

atomic bomb bomba atómica f.

atomic energy energía atómica, energía nuclear f.

atomic theory teoría atómica. f.

atomic weight peso atómico m.

atonal /ei'tounl/ a. Mus. atonal.

atone /ə'toun/ v. expiar, compensar.

atonement /ə'tounmənt/ n. expiación; reparación f.

atrocious /ə'trouʃəs/ a. atroz.

atrocity /ə'trɒsɪti/ n. atrocidad f.

atrophy /'ætrəfi/ n. **1.** Med. atrofia f. —v. **2.** atrofiar.

atropine /'ætrə,pin, -pɪn/ n. atropina f.

attach /ə'tætʃ/ v. juntar; prender; (hook) enganchar; Fig. atribuir.

attaché /,ætæ'ʃei/ n. agregado -da.

attachment /ə'tætʃmənt/ n. enlace m.; accesorio m.; (emotional) afecto, cariño m.

attack /ə'tæk/ n. **1.** ataque m. —v. **2.** atacar.

attacker /ə'tækər/ n. asaltador -ra.

attain /ə'tein/ v. lograr, alcanzar.

attainable /ə'teinəbəl/ a. accesible, realizable.

attainment /ə'teinmənt/ n. logro; (pl.) dotes f.pl.

attempt /ə'tɛmpt/ n. **1.** ensayo; esfuerzo m.; tentativa f. —v. **2.** ensayar, intentar.

attend /ə'tɛnd/ v. atender; (a meeting) asistir a.

attendance /ə'tɛndəns/ n. asistencia; presencia f.

attendant /ə'tɛndənt/ a. **1.** concomitante. —n. **2.** servidor -ra.

attention /ə'tɛnʃən/ n. atención f.; obsequio m. **to pay a. to,** hacer caso a.

attentive /ə'tɛntɪv/ a. atento.

attentively /ə'tɛntɪvli/ adv. atentamente.

attenuate /ə'tɛnyu,eit/ v. atenuar, adelgazar.

attest /ə'tɛst/ v. confirmar, atestiguar.

attic /'ætɪk/ n. desván m., guardilla f.

attire /ə'taiᵊr/ n. **1.** traje m. —v. **2.** vestir.

attitude /'ætɪ,tud/ n. actitud f., ademán m.

attorney /ə'tɜrni/ n. abogado -da, apoderado -da.

attract /ə'trækt/ v. atraer. **a. attention,** llamar la atención.

attraction /ə'trækʃən/ n. atracción f., atractivo m.

attractive /ə'træktɪv/ a. atractivo; simpático.

attributable /ə'trɪbyutəbəl/ a. atribuible, imputable.

attribute /n 'ætrə,byut; v ə'trɪbyut/ n. **1.** atributo m. —v. **2.** atribuir.

attrition /ə'trɪʃən/ n. roce, desgaste m.; atrición f.

attune /ə'tun/ v. armonizar.

auction /'ɔkʃən/ n. subasta f., S.A. venduta f.

auctioneer /,ɔkʃə'nɪər/ n. subastador -ra, S.A. martillero -ra.

audacious /ɔ'deiʃəs/ a. audaz.

audacity /ɔ'dæsɪti/ n. audacia f.

audible /'ɔdəbəl/ a. audible.

audience /'ɔdiəns/ n. auditorio, público m.; entrevista f.

audiovisual /,ɔdiou'vɪʒuəl/ a. audiovisual.

audit /'ɔdɪt/ n. **1.** revisión de cuentas f. —v. **2.** revisar cuentas.

audition /ɔ'dɪʃən/ n. audición f.

auditor /'ɔdɪtər/ n. interventor -ora, revisor -ora.

auditorium /,ɔdɪ'tɔriəm/ n. sala f.; teatro m.

auditory /'ɔdɪ,tɔri/ a. & n. auditorio m.

augment /ɔg'mɛnt/ v. aumentar.

augur /'ɔgər/ v. augurar, pronosticar.

August /'ɔgəst/ n. agosto m.

aunt /ænt, ɑnt/ n. tía f.

auspice /'ɔspɪs/ n. auspicio m.

auspicious /ɔ'spɪʃəs/ a. favorable; propicio.

austere /ɔ'stɪər/ a. austero.

austerity /ɔ'stɛrɪti/ n. austeridad, severidad f.

Austrian /'ɔstriən/ a. & n. austríaco -ca.

authentic /ɔ'θɛntɪk/ a. auténtico.

authenticate /ɔ'θɛntɪ,keit/ v. autenticar.

authenticity /,ɔθɛn'tɪsɪti/ n. autenticidad f.

author /'ɔθər/ n. autor -ra, escritor -ra.

authoritarian /ə,θɔrɪ'tɛəriən/ a. & n. autoritario -ria.

authoritative /ə'θɔrɪ,teitɪv/ a. autoritativo; autorizado.

authoritatively /ə'θɔrɪ,teitɪvli/ adv. autoritativamente.

authority /ə'θɔrɪti/ n. autoridad f.

authorization /,ɔθərə'zeiʃən/ n. autorización f.

authorize /'ɔθə,raiz/ v. autorizar.

auto /'ɔtou/ n. auto, automóvil m.

autobiography /,ɔtəbai'ɒgrəfi/ n. autobiografía f.

autocracy /ɔ'tɒkrəsi/ n. autocracia f.

autocrat /'ɔtə,kræt/ n. autócrata m. & f.

autograph /'ɔtə,græf/ n. autógrafo m.

automatic /,ɔtə'mætɪk/ a. automático.

automatically /,ɔtə'mætɪkəli/ adv. automáticamente.

automobile /,ɔtəmə'bil/ n. automóvil, coche m.

automotive /,ɔtə'moutɪv/ a. automotriz.

autonomy /ɔ'tɒnəmi/ n. autonomía f.

autopsy /'ɔtɒpsi/ n. autopsia f.

autumn /'ɔtəm/ n. otoño m.

auxiliary /ɔg'zɪlyəri/ a. auxiliar.

avail /ə'veil/ n. **1. of no a.,** en vano. —v. **2. a. oneself of,** aprovecharse de.

available /ə'veiləbəl/ a. disponible.

avalanche /'ævə,læntʃ/ n. alud m.

avarice /'ævərɪs/ n. avaricia, codicia f.

avariciously /,ævə'rɪʃəsli/ adv. avaramente.

avenge /ə'vɛndʒ/ v. vengar.

avenger /ə'vɛndʒər/ n. vengador -ra.

avenue /'ævə,nu/ n. avenida f.

average /'ævərɪdʒ/ a. **1.** medio; común. —n. **2.** promedio, término medio m. —v. **3.** calcular el promedio.

averse /ə'vɜrs/ a. **to be a. to,** tener antipatía a, opuesto a.

aversion /ə'vɜrʒən/ n. aversión f.

avert /ə'vɜrt/ v. desviar; impedir.

aviary /'eivi,ɛri/ n. pajarera, avería f.

aviation /,eivi'eiʃən/ n. aviación f.

aviator /'eivi,eitər/ n. aviador -ra.

aviatrix /,eivi'eitrɪks/ n. aviatriz f.

avid /'ævɪd/ a. ávido.

avocado /,ævə'kɑdou, ,ɑvə-/ n. aguacate m.

avocation /,ævə'keiʃən/ n. pasatiempo f.

avoid /ə'vɔid/ v. evitar.

avoidable /ə'vɔidəbəl/ a. evitable.

avoidance /ə'vɔidns/ n. evitación f.; Leg. anulación f.

avow /ə'vau/ v. declarar; admitir.

avowal /ə'vauəl/ n. admisión f.

avowed /ə'vaud/ a. reconocido; admitido.

avowedly /ə'vauɪdli/ adv. reconocidamente; confesadamente.

await /ə'weit/ v. esperar, aguardar.

awake /ə'weik/ a. despierto.

awaken /ə'weikən/ v. despertar.

award /ə'wɔrd/ n. **1.** premio m. —v. **2.** otorgar.

aware /ə'wɛər/ a. enterado, consciente.

awash /ə'wɒʃ/ a. & adv. Naut. a flor de agua.

away /ə'wei/ adv. (see under verb: **go away, put away, take away,** etc.)

awe /ɔ/ n. pavor m.

awesome /'ɔsəm/ a. pavoroso; aterrador.

awful /'ɔfəl/ a. horrible, terrible, muy malo, pésimo.

awhile /ə'wail/ adv. por un rato.

awkward /'ɔkwərd/ a. torpe, desmañado; Fig. delicado, embarazoso.

awning /'ɔnɪŋ/ n. toldo m.

awry /ə'rai/ a. oblicuo, torcido.

ax /æks/ n. hacha f.

axiom /'æksiəm/ n. axioma m.

axis /'æksɪs/ n. eje m.

axle /'æksəl/ n. eje m.

ayatollah /,ayə'toulə/ n. ayatolá m.

azure /'æʒər/ a. azul.

B

babble /'bæbəl/ n. **1.** balbuceo, murmullo m. —v. **2.** balbucear.

babbler /'bæblər/ n. hablador -ra, charlador -ra.

baboon /bæ'bun/ n. mandril m.

baby /'beibi/ n. nene, bebé m.

baby carriage cochecito de niño m.

babyish /'beibiɪʃ/ a. infantil.

baby squid /skwɪd/ chipirón m.

bachelor /'bætʃələr/ n. soltero m.

bacillus /bə'sɪləs/ n. bacilo, microbio m.

back /bæk/ adv. **1.** atrás. **to be b.,** estar de vuelta. **b. of,** detrás de. —n. **2.** espalda f.; (of animal) lomo m.

backache /'bæk,eik/ n. dolor de espalda m.

backbone /'bæk,boun/ n. espinazo m.; Fig. firmeza f.

backer /'bækər/ n. sostenedor -ra.

background /'bæk,graund/ n. fondo m. antecedentes m.pl.

backing /'bækɪŋ/ n. apoyo m., garantía f.

backlash /'bæk,læʃ/ n. repercusión negativa.

backlog /'bæk,lɒg/ n. atrasos m.pl.

backpack /'bæk,pæk/ n. mochila f.

back seat asiento trasero m.

backstage /'bæk'steidʒ/ n. entre bastidores m.

backup /'bæk,ʌp/ n. copia de seguridad f.

backward /'bækwərd/ a. **1.** atrasado. —adv. **2.** hacia atrás.

backwardness /'bækwərdnɪs/ n. atraso m.

backwater /'bæk,wɔtər/ n. parte de río estancada f.

backwoods /'bæk'wʊdz/ n. región del monte apartada f.

bacon /'beikən/ n. tocino m.

bacteria /bæk'tɪəriə/ n. bacterias f.pl.

bacteriologist /,bæktɪəri'ɒlədʒɪst/ n. bacteriólogo -a.

bacteriology /,bæktɪəri'ɒlədʒi/ n. bacteriología f.

bad /bæd/ a. malo.

badge /bædʒ/ n. insignia, divisa f.

badger /'bædʒər/ n. **1.** tejón m. —v. **2.** atormentar.

badly /'bædli/ adv. mal.

badness /'bædnɪs/ n. maldad f.

bad-tempered /'bæd'tɛmpərd/ a. de mal humor.

baffle /'bæfəl/ v. desconcertar.

bafflement /'bæfəlmənt/ n. contrariedad; confusión f.

bag /bæg/ *n.* **1.** saco *m.;* bolsa *f.* **—***v.* **2.** ensacar, cazar.
baggage /ˈbægɪdʒ/ *n.* equipaje *m.* **b. check,** talón *m.*
baggage cart (airport) carrillo para llevar equipaje.
baggy /ˈbægi/ *a.* abotagado; bolsudo; hinchado.
bagpipe /ˈbægˌpaip/ *n.* gaita *f.*
bail /beil/ *n.* **1.** fianza *f.* **—***v.* **2.** desaguar.
bailiff /ˈbeilɪf/ *n.* alguacil *m.*
bait /beit/ *n.* **1.** cebo *m.* **—***v.* **2.** cebar.
bake /beik/ *v.* cocer en horno.
baked potato /beikt/ patata asada *f.*
baker /ˈbeikər/ *n.* panadero -ra, hornero -ra.
bakery /ˈbeikəri, ˈbeikri/ *n.* panadería *f.*
baking /ˈbeikɪŋ/ *n.* hornada *f.* **b. powder,** levadura *f.*
balance /ˈbæləns/ *n.* balanza *f.;* equilibrio *m.; Com.* saldo *m.*
balcony /ˈbælkəni/ *n.* balcón *m.; Theat.* galería *f.*
bald /bɔld/ *a.* calvo.
baldness /ˈbɔldnɪs/ *n.* calvicie *f.*
bale /beil/ *n.* **1.** bala *f.* **—***v.* **2.** embalar.
balk /bɔk/ *v.* frustrar; rebelarse.
Balkans /ˈbɔlkənz/ *n. pl.* Balcanes *m.pl.*
balky /ˈbɔki/ *a.* rebelón.
ball /bɔl/ *n.* bola, pelota *f.;* (dance) baile *m.*
ballad /ˈbæləd/ *n.* romance, *m.;* balada *f.*
ballast /ˈbæləst/ *n.* **1.** lastre *m.* **—***v.* **2.** lastrar.
ball bearing cojinete de bolas *m.*
ballerina /ˌbæləˈrinə/ *n.* bailarina *f.*
ballet /bæˈlei/ *n.* danza *f.;* ballet *m.*
ballistics /bəˈlɪstɪks/ *n.* balística *f.*
balloon /bəˈlun/ *n.* globo *m.* **b. tire,** neumático de balón.
ballot /ˈbælət/ *n.* **1.** balota *f.,* voto *m.* **—***v.* **2.** balotar, votar.
ballpoint pen /ˈbɔlˌpɔint/ bolígrafo *m.*
ballroom /ˈbɔlˌrum/ *n.* salón de baile *m.*
balm /bɑm/ *n.* bálsamo; ungüento *m.*
balmy /ˈbɑmi/ *a.* fragante; reparador; calmante.
balsa /ˈbɔlsə/ *n.* balsa *f.*
balsam /ˈbɔlsəm/ *n.* bálsamo *m.*
balustrade /ˈbæləˌstreid/ *n.* barandilla *f.*
bamboo /bæmˈbu/ *n.* bambú *m.,* caña *f.*
ban /bɑn/ *n.* **1.** prohibición *f.* **—***v.* **2.** prohibir; proscribir.
banal /bəˈnæl/ *a.* trivial; vulgar.
banana /bəˈnænə/ *n.* banana *f.,* cambur *m.* **b. tree,** banano, plátano *m.*
band /bænd/ *n.* **1.** banda *f.;* (of men) banda, cuadrilla, partida *f.* **—***v.* **2.** asociarse.
bandage /ˈbændɪdʒ/ *n.* **1.** vendaje *m.* **—***v.* **2.** vendar.
bandanna /bænˈdænə/ *n.* pañuelo (grande) *m.;* bandana *f.*
bandbox /ˈbændˌbɒks/ *n.* caja de cartón.
bandit /ˈbændɪt/ *n.* bandido -da.
bandmaster /ˈbændˌmæstər/ *n.* director de una banda musical *m.*
bandstand /ˈbændˌstænd/ *n.* kiosco de música.
bang /bæŋ/ *interj.* **1.** ¡pum! **—***n.* **2.** ruido de un golpe. **—***v.* **3.** golpear ruidosamente.
banish /ˈbænɪʃ/ *v.* desterrar.
banishment /ˈbænɪʃmənt/ *n.* destierro *m.*
banister /ˈbænəstər/ *n.* pasamanos *m. pl.*
bank /bæŋk/ *n.* **1.** banco *m.;* (of a river) margen *f.* **—***v.* **2.** depositar.
bank account cuenta bancaria *f.*
bankbook /ˈbæŋkˌbʊk/ *n.* libreta de depósitos *f.*
bank card tarjeta bancaria *f.*
banker /ˈbæŋkər/ *n.* banquero -ra.
banking /ˈbæŋkɪŋ/ *a.* bancaria. *n.* banca *f.*
bank note billete de banco *m.*
bankrupt /ˈbæŋkrʌpt/ *a.* insolvente.
bankruptcy /ˈbæŋkrʌptsi/ *n.* bancarrota *f.*
banner /ˈbænər/ *n.* bandera *f.;* estandarte *m.*
banquet /ˈbæŋkwɪt/ *n.* banquete *m.*
banter /ˈbæntər/ *n.* **1.** choteo *m.;* zumba; burla *f.* **—***v.* **2.** chotear; zumbar; burlarse.
baptism /ˈbæptɪzəm/ *n.* bautismo, bautizo *m.*
baptismal /bæpˈtɪzməl/ *a.* bautismal.
Baptist /ˈbæptɪst/ *n.* bautista *m. & f.*
baptize /bæpˈtaiz, ˈbæptaiz/ *v.* bautizar.
bar /bɑr/ *n.* **1.** barra *f.;* obstáculo *m.;* (tavern) taberna *f.,* bar *m.* **—***v.* **2.** barrear; prohibir, excluir.
barbarian /bɑrˈbɛəriən/ *a.* bárbaro. *n.* bárbaro -ra.
barbarism /ˈbɑrbəˌrɪzəm/ *n.* barbarismo *m.,* barbarie *f.*
barbarous /ˈbɑrbərəs/ *a.* bárbaro, cruel.
barbecue /ˈbɑrbɪˌkyu/ *n.* animal asado entero; (Mex.) barbacoa *f.*
barber /ˈbɑrbər/ *n.* barbero *m.* **b. shop,** barbería *f.*
barbiturate /bɑrˈbɪtʃərɪt/ *n.* barbitúrico *m.*
bar code código de barras *m.*
bare /bɛər/ *a.* **1.** desnudo; descubierto. **—***v.* **2.** desnudar; descubrir.
bareback /ˈbɛərˌbæk/ *adv.* sin silla.
barefoot(ed) /ˈbɛərˌfʊtɪd/ *a.* descalzo.
barely /ˈbɛərli/ *adv.* escasamente, apenas.
bareness /ˈbɛərnɪs/ *n.* desnudez *f.;* pobreza *f.*
bargain /ˈbɑrgən/ *n.* **1.** ganga *f.,* compra ventajosa *f.;* contrato *m.* **—***v.* **2.** regatear; negociar.
barge /bɑrdʒ/ *n.* lanchón *m.,* barcaza *f.*
baritone /ˈbærɪˌtoun/ *n.* barítono *m.*
barium /ˈbɛəriəm/ *n.* bario *m.*
bark /bɑrk/ *n.* **1.** corteza *f.;* (of dog) ladrido *f.* **—***v.* **2.** ladrar.
barley /ˈbɑrli/ *n.* cebada *f.*
barn /bɑrn/ *n.* granero *m.*
barnacle /ˈbɑrnəkəl/ *n.* lapa *f.*
barnyard /ˈbɑrnˌyɑrd/ *n.* corral *m.*
barometer /bəˈrɒmɪtər/ *n.* barómetro *m.*
barometric /ˌbærəˈmɛtrɪk/ *a.* barométrico.
baron /ˈbærən/ *n.* barón *m.*
baroness /ˈbærənɪs/ *n.* baronesa *f.*
baronial /bəˈrouniəl/ *a.* baronial.
baroque /bəˈrouk/ *a.* barroco.
barracks /ˈbærəks/ *n.* cuartel *m.*
barrage /bəˈrɑʒ/ *n.* cortina de fuego *f.*
barred /bɑrd/ *a.* excluído; prohibido.
barrel /ˈbærəl/ *n.* barril *m.;* (of gun) cañón *m.*
barren /ˈbærən/ *a.* estéril.
barrenness /ˈbærənˌnɪs/ *n.* esterilidad *f.*
barricade /ˈbærɪˌkeid/ *n.* barricada, barrera *f.*
barrier /ˈbæriər/ *n.* barrera *f.;* obstáculo *m.*
barroom /ˈbɑrˌrum, -ˌrʊm/ *n.* cantina *f.*
bartender /ˈbɑrˌtɛndər/ *n.* tabernero; cantinero *m.*
barter /ˈbɑrtər/ *n.* **1.** cambio, trueque *m.* **—***v.* **2.** cambiar, trocar.
base /beis/ *a.* **1.** bajo, vil. **—***n.* **2.** base *f.* **—***v.* **3.** basar.
baseball /ˈbeisˌbɔl/ *n.* béisbol *m.*
baseboard /ˈbeisˌbɔrd/ *n.* tabla de resguardo.
basement /ˈbeismənt/ *n.* sótano *m.*
baseness /ˈbeisnɪs/ *n.* bajeza, vileza *f.*
bashful /ˈbæʃfəl/ *a.* vergonzoso, tímido.
bashfully /ˈbæʃfəli/ *adv.* tímidamente; vergonzosamente.
bashfulness /ˈbæʃfəlnɪs/ *n.* vergüenza; timidez *f.*
basic /ˈbeisɪk/ *a.* fundamental, básico.
basin /ˈbeisən/ *n.* bacía *f.;* (of river) cuenca *f.*
basis /ˈbeisɪs/ *n.* base *f.*
bask /bæsk/ *v.* tomar el sol.
basket /ˈbæskɪt/ *n.* cesta, canasta *f.*
bass /bæs; beis/ *n.* (fish) lobina *f.; Mus.* bajo profundo *m.* **b. viol.** violón *m.*
bassinet /ˌbæsəˈnɛt/ *n.* bacinete *m.*
bassoon /bæˈsun/ *n.* bajón *m.*
bastard /ˈbæstərd/ *a. & n.* bastardo -da; hijo -a natural.
baste /beist/ *v.* (sew) bastear; (cooking) pringar.
bat /bæt/ *n.* **1.** (animal) murciélago *m.;* (baseball) bate *m.* **—***v.* **2.** batear.
batch /bætʃ/ *n.* cantidad de cosas.
bath /bæθ/ *n.* baño *m.*
bathe /beið/ *v.* bañar, bañarse.
bather /ˈbeiðər/ *n.* bañista *m. & f.*
bathing resort /ˈbeiðɪŋ/ balneario *m.*
bathing suit /ˈbeiðɪŋ/ traje de baño.
bathrobe /ˈbæθˌroub/ *n.* bata de baño *f.*
bathroom /ˈbæθˌrum, -ˌrʊm/ *n.* cuarto de baño.
bathtub /ˈbæθˌtʌb/ *n.* bañera *f.*
baton /bəˈtɒn/ *n.* bastón *m.; Mus.* batuta *f.*
battalion /bəˈtælyən/ *n.* batallón *m.*
batter /ˈbætər/ *n.* **1.** (cooking) batido *m.;* (baseball) voleador *m.* **—***v.* **2.** batir; derribar.
battery /ˈbætəri/ *n.* batería; *Elec.* pila *f.*
batting /ˈbætɪŋ/ *n.* agramaje, moldeaje *m.*
battle /ˈbætl̩/ *n.* **1.** batalla *f.;* combate *m.* **—***v.* **2.** batallar.
battlefield /ˈbætl̩ˌfild/ *n.* campo de batalla.
battleship /ˈbætl̩ˌʃɪp/ *n.* acorazado *m.*
bauxite /ˈbɔksait, ˈbouzait/ *n.* bauxita *f.*
bawl /bɔl/ *v.* gritar; vocear.
bay /bei/ *n.* bahía *f.* *v.* aullar.
bayonet /ˈbeiənɛt/ *n.* bayoneta *f.*
bazaar /bəˈzɑr/ *n.* bazar *m.,* feria *f.*
BC *abbr.* (**before Christ**) a.C. (antes de Cristo).
be /bi/ *v.* ser; estar. (See **hacer; hay; tener** in Sp.-Eng. section.)
beach /bitʃ/ *n.* playa *f.*
beachcomber /ˈbitʃˌkoumər/ *n.* raquero -ra *m. & f.*
beacon /ˈbikən/ *n.* faro *m.*
bead /bid/ *n.* cuenta *f.; pl. Relig.* rosario *m.*
beading /ˈbidɪŋ/ *n.* abalorio *m.*
beady /ˈbidi/ *a.* globuloso; burbujoso.
beak /bik/ *n.* pico *m.*
beaker /ˈbikər/ *n.* vaso con pico *m.*
beam /bim/ *n.* viga *f.;* (of wood) madero *m.;* (of light) rayo *m.*
beaming /ˈbimɪŋ/ *a.* radiante.
bean /bin/ *n.* haba, habichuela *f.,* frijol *m.*
bear /bɛər/ *n.* **1.** oso -sa. **—***v.* **2.** llevar; (endure) aguantar.
bearable /ˈbɛərəbəl/ *a.* sufrible; soportable.
beard /bɪərd/ *n.* barba *f.*
bearded /ˈbɪərdɪd/ *a.* barbado; barbudo.
beardless /ˈbɪərdlɪs/ *a.* lampiño; imberbe.
bearer /ˈbɛərər/ *n.* portador -ra.
bearing /ˈbɛərɪŋ/ *n.* porte, aguante *m.*
bearskin /ˈbɛərˌskɪn/ *n.* piel de oso *f.*
beast /bist/ *n.* bestia *f.;* bruto -ta.
beat /bit/ *v.* golpear; batir; pulsar; (in games) ganar, vencer.
beaten /ˈbitn̩/ *a.* vencido; batido.
beatify /biˈætəˌfai/ *v.* beatificar.
beating /ˈbitɪŋ/ *n.* paliza *f.*
beau /bou/ *n.* novio *m.*
beautiful /ˈbyutəfəl/ *a.* hermoso, bello.
beautifully /ˈbyutəfəli/ *adv.* bellamente.
beautify /ˈbyutəˌfai/ *v.* embellecer.
beauty /ˈbyuti/ *n.* hermosura, belleza *f.* **b. parlor,** salón de belleza.
beaver /ˈbivər/ *n.* castor *m.*
becalm /bɪˈkɑm/ *v.* calmar; sosegar; encalmarse.
because /bɪˈkɔz/ *conj.* porque. **b. of,** a causa de.
beckon /ˈbɛkən/ *v.* hacer señas.
become /bɪˈkʌm/ *v.* hacerse; ponerse.
becoming /bɪˈkʌmɪŋ/ *a.* propio, correcto; **be b.,** quedar bien, sentar bien.
bed /bɛd/ *n.* cama *f.;* lecho *m.;* (of river) cauce *m.*
bedbug /ˈbɛdˌbʌg/ *n.* chinche *m.*
bedclothes /ˈbɛdˌklouz, -ˌklouðz/ *n.* ropa de cama *f.*
bedding /ˈbɛdɪŋ/ *n.* colchones *m.pl.*
bedfellow /ˈbɛdˌfɛlou/ *n.* compañero -ra de cama.
bedizen /bɪˈdaizən, -ˈdɪzən/ *v.* adornar; aderezar.
bedridden /ˈbɛdˌrɪdn̩/ *a.* postrado (en cama).
bedrock /ˈbɛdˌrɒk/ *n.* (mining) lecho de roca *m.; Fig.* fundamento *m.*
bedroom /ˈbɛdˌrum/ *n.* alcoba *f.;* (Mex.) recámara *f.*
bedside /ˈbɛdˌsaid/ *n.* al lado de una cama *m.*
bedspread /ˈbɛdˌsprɛd/ *n.* cubrecama, sobrecama *f.*
bedstead /ˈbɛdˌstɛd/ *n.* armadura de cama *f.*
bedtime /ˈbɛdˌtaim/ *n.* hora de acostarse.
bee /bi/ *n.* abeja *f.*
beef /bif/ *n.* carne de vaca.
beefburger /ˈbifˌbɜrgər/ *n.* hamburguesa *f.*
beefsteak /ˈbifˌsteik/ *n.* bistec, bisté *m.*
beehive /ˈbiˌhaiv/ *n.* colmena *f.*
beer /bɪər/ *n.* cerveza *f.*
beeswax /ˈbizˌwæks/ *n.* cera de abejas.
beet /bit/ *n.* remolacha *f.;* (Mex.) betabel *m.*
beetle /ˈbitl̩/ *n.* escarabajo *m.*
befall /bɪˈfɔl/ *v.* suceder, sobrevenir.
befitting /bɪˈfɪtɪŋ/ *a.* conveniente; propio; digno.
before /bɪˈfɔr/ *adv.* antes. *prep.* antes de; (in front of) delante de. *conj.* antes que.
beforehand /bɪˈfɔrˌhænd/ *adv.* de antemano.
befriend /bɪˈfrɛnd/ *v.* amparar.
befuddle /bɪˈfʌdl̩/ *v.* confundir; aturdir.
beg /bɛg/ *v.* rogar, suplicar; (for alms) mendigar.
beget /bɪˈgɛt/ *v.* engendrar; producir.
beggar /ˈbɛgər/ *n.* mendigo -ga; *S.A.* limosnero -ra.
beggarly /ˈbɛgərli/ *a.* pobre, miserable.
begin /bɪˈgɪn/ *v.* empezar, comenzar, principiar.
beginner /bɪˈgɪnər/ *n.* principiante -ta.
beginning /bɪˈgɪnɪŋ/ *n.* principio, comienzo *m.*
begrudge /bɪˈgrʌdʒ/ *v.* envidiar.
behalf /bɪˈhæf/ *n.*: **in, on b. of,** a favor de, en pro de.
behave /bɪˈheiv/ *v.* portarse, comportarse.
behavior /bɪˈheivyər/ *n.* conducta *f.;* comportamiento *m.*
behead /bɪˈhɛd/ *v.* decapitar.
behind /bɪˈhaind/ *adv.* atrás, detrás. *prep.* detrás de.
behold /bɪˈhould/ *v.* contemplar.
beige /beiʒ/ *a.* beige.
being /ˈbiɪŋ/ *n.* existencia *f.;* (person) ser *m.*

bejewel /bɪ'dʒuəl/ v. adornar con joyas.

belated /bɪ'leitɪd/ a. atrasado, tardío.

belch /bɛltʃ/ n. **1.** eructo m. —v. **2.** vomitar; eructar.

belfry /'bɛlfrɪ/ n. campanario m.

Belgian /'bɛldʒən/ a. & n. belga m. & f.

Belgium /'bɛldʒəm/ n. Bélgica f.

belie /bɪ'lai/ v. desmentir.

belief /bɪ'lif/ n. creencia f.; parecer m.

believable /bɪ'livəbəl/ a. creíble.

believe /bɪ'liv/ v. creer.

believer /bɪ'livər/ n. creyente m. & f.

belittle /bɪ'lɪtl/ v. dar poca importancia a.

bell /bɛl/ n. campana f.; (of house) campanilla f.; (electric) timbre m.

bellboy /'bɛl,bɔi/ n. mozo, botones m.

bellicose /'bɛlɪ,kous/ a. guerrero.

belligerence /bə'lɪdʒərəns/ n. beligerancia f.

belligerent /bə'lɪdʒərənt/ a. & n. beligerante m. & f.

belligerently /bə'lɪdʒərəntli/ adv. belicosamente.

bellow /'bɛlou/ v. bramar, rugir.

bellows /'bɛlouz/ n. fuelle m.

belly /'bɛli/ n. vientre m.; panza, barriga f.

belong /bɪ'lɔŋ/ v. pertenecer.

belongings /bɪ'lɔŋɪŋz/ n. propiedad f.

beloved /bɪ'lʌvɪd/ a. querido, amado.

below /bɪ'lou/ adv. **1.** debajo, abajo. —prep. **2.** debajo de.

belt /bɛlt/ n. cinturón m.

bench /bɛntʃ/ n. banco m.

bend /bɛnd/ n. vuelta; curva f. v. encorvar, doblar.

beneath /bɪ'niθ/ adv. **1.** debajo, abajo. —prep. **2.** debajo de.

benediction /,bɛnɪ'dɪkʃən/ n. bendición f.

benefactor /'bɛnə,fæktər/ n. bienhechor -a.

benefactress /'bɛnə,fæktrɪs/ n. bienhechora f.

beneficial /,bɛnə'fɪʃəl/ a. provechoso, beneficioso.

beneficiary /,bɛnə'fɪʃɪ,ɛri/ n. beneficiario -ria, beneficiado -da.

benefit /'bɛnəfɪt/ n. **1.** provecho, beneficio m. —v. **2.** beneficiar.

benevolence /bə'nɛvələns/ n. benevolencia f.

benevolent /bə'nɛvələnt/ a. benévolo.

benevolently /bə'nɛvələntli/ adv. benignamente.

benign /bɪ'nain; bɪ'nɪgnənt/ a. benigno.

benignity /bɪ'nɪgnɪti/ n. benignidad; bondad f.

bent /bɛnt/ a. **1.** encorvado. **b. on,** resuelto a. —n. **2.** inclinación f.

benzene /'bɛnzin, bɛn'zin/ n. benceno m.

bequeath /bɪ'kwið/ v. legar.

bequest /bɪ'kwɛst/ n. legado m.

berate /bɪ'reit/ v. reñir, regañar.

bereave /bɪ'riv/ v. despojar; desolar.

bereavement /bɪ'rivmənt/ n. privación f.; despojo m.; (mourning) luto m.

berry /'bɛri/ n. baya f.

berth /bɜrθ/ n. camarote m.; Naut. litera f.; (for vessel) amarradero m.

beseech /bɪ'sitʃ/ v. suplicar; implorar.

beseechingly /bɪ'sitʃɪŋli/ adv. suplicantemente.

beset /bɪ'sɛt/ v. acosar; rodear.

beside /bɪ'said/ prep. al lado de.

besides /bɪ'saidz/ adv. además, por otra parte.

besiege /bɪ'sidʒ/ v. sitiar; asediar.

besieged /bɪ'sidʒd/ a. sitiado.

besieger /bɪ'sidʒər/ n. sitiador -ra.

besmirch /bɪ'smɜrtʃ/ v. manchar; deshonrar.

best /bɛst/ a. & adv. mejor. **at b.,** a lo más.

bestial /'bɛstʃəl/ a. bestial; brutal.

bestir /bɪ'stɜr/ v. incitar; intrigar.

best man n. padrino de boda.

bestow /bɪ'stou/ v. conferir.

bestowal /bɪ'stouəl/ n. dádiva; presentación f.

bet /bɛt/ n. **1.** apuesta f. —v. **2.** apostar.

betoken /bɪ'toukən/ v. presagiar, anunciar.

betray /bɪ'trei/ v. traicionar; revelar.

betrayal /bɪ'treiəl/ n. traición f.

betroth /bɪ'trouð/ v. contraer esponsales; prometerse.

betrothal /bɪ'trouðəl/ n. esponsales m.pl.

better /'bɛtər/ a. & adv. **1.** mejor. —v. **2.** mejorar.

between /bɪ'twin/ prep. entre, en medio de.

bevel /'bɛvəl/ n. **1.** cartabón m. —v. **2.** cortar al sesgo.

beverage /'bɛvərɪdʒ/ n. bebida f.; (cold) refresco m.

bewail /bɪ'weil/ v. llorar; lamentar.

beware /bɪ'wɛər/ v. guardarse, precaverse.

bewilder /bɪ'wɪldər/ v. aturdir.

bewildered /bɪ'wɪldərd/ a. descarriado.

bewildering /bɪ'wɪldərɪŋ/ a. aturdente.

bewilderment /bɪ'wɪldərmənt/ n. aturdimiento m.; perplejidad f.

bewitch /bɪ'wɪtʃ/ v. hechizar; embrujar.

beyond /bi'ɒnd/ prep. más allá de.

biannual /bai'ænyuəl/ a. semianual; semestral.

bias /'baiəs/ n. **1.** parcialidad f.; prejuicio m. **on the b.,** al sesgo. —v. **2.** predisponer, influir.

bib /bɪb/ n. babador m.

Bible /'baibəl/ n. Biblia f.

Biblical /'bɪblɪkəl/ a. bíblico.

bibliography /,bɪbli'ɒgrəfi/ n. bibliografía f.

bicarbonate /bai'kɑrbənɪt/ n. bicarbonato m.

bicentennial /,baisɛn'tɛniəl/ a. & n. bicentenario m.

biceps /'baisɛps/ n. bíceps m.

bicker /'bɪkər/ v. altercar.

bicycle /'baisɪkəl/ n. bicicleta f.

bicyclist /'baisɪklɪst/ n. biciclista m. & f.

bid /bɪd/ n. **1.** proposición, oferta f. —v. **2.** mandar; ofrecer.

bidder /'bɪdər/ n. postor -ra.

bide /baid/ v. aguardar; esperar.

bier /bɪər/ n. ataúd m.

bifocal /bai'foukəl/ a. bifocal.

big /bɪg/ a. grande.

bigamist /'bɪgəmɪst/ n. bígamo -ma.

bigamy /'bɪgəmi/ n. bigamia f.

bigot /'bɪgət/ n. persona intolerante.

bigotry /'bɪgətri/ n. intolerancia f.

bikini /bɪ'kini/ n. bikini m.

bilateral /bai'lætərəl/ a. bilateral.

bile /bail/ n. bilis f.

bilingual /bai'lɪŋgwəl/ a. bilingüe.

bilingualism /bai'lɪŋgwə,lɪzəm/ n. bilingüismo m.

bilious /'bɪlyəs/ a. bilioso.

bill /bɪl/ n. **1.** cuenta, factura f.; (money) billete m.; (of bird) pico m. —v. **2.** facturar.

billboard /'bɪl,bɔrd/ n. cartelera f.

billet /'bɪlɪt/ n. **1.** billete m.; Mil. boleta f. —v. **2.** aposentar.

billfold /'bɪl,fould/ n. cartera f.

billiard balls /'bɪlyərd bɔlz/ bolas de billar.

billiards /'bɪlyərdz/ n. billar m.

billion /'bɪlyən/ n. billón m.

bill of health n. certificado de sanidad.

bill of lading /'leidɪŋ/ n. conocimiento de embarque.

bill of sale n. escritura de venta.

billow /'bɪlou/ n. ola; oleada f.

bimetallic /,baimə'tælɪk/ a. bimetálico.

bimonthly /bai'mʌnθli/ a. & adv. bimestral.

bin /bɪn/ n. hucha f.; depósito m.

bind /baind/ v. atar; obligar; (book) encuadernar.

bindery /'baindəri/ n. taller de encuadernación m.

binding /'baindɪŋ/ n. encuadernación f.

bingo /'bɪŋgou/ n. bingo m.

binocular /bə'nɒkyələr/ a. binocular. n.pl. gemelos m.pl.

biochemistry /,baiou'kɛməstri/ n. bioquímica f.

biodegradable /,baioudɪ'greidəbəl/ a. biodegradable.

biofeedback /,baiou'fid,bæk/ n. biofeedback.

biographer /bai'ɒgrəfər/ n. biógrafo -fa.

biographical /,baiə'græfɪkəl/ a. biográfico.

biography /bai'ɒgrəfi/ n. biografía f.

biological /,baiə'lɒdʒɪkəl/ a. biológico.

biologically /,baiə'lɒdʒɪkəli/ adv. biológicamente.

biology /bai'ɒlədʒi/ n. biología f.

bipartisan /bai'pɑrtəzən/ a. bipartito.

biped /'baipɛd/ n. bípedo m.

bird /bɜrd/ n. pájaro m.; ave f.

birdie /'bɜrdi/ n. (golf) uno bajo par f.

bird of prey n. ave de rapiña f.

bird's-eye view /'bɜrdz,ai/ n. vista de pájaro f.

birth /bɜrθ/ n. nacimiento m. **give b. to,** dar a luz.

birth certificate partida de nacimiento f.

birth control n. contracepción f.

birthday /'bɜrθ,dei/ n. cumpleaños m.

birthmark /'bɜrθ,mɑrk/ n. marca de nacimiento f.

birthplace /'bɜrθ,pleis/ n. natalicio m.

birth rate n. natalidad f.

birthright /'bɜrθ,rait/ n. primogenitura f.

biscuit /'bɪskɪt/ n. bizcocho m.

bisect /bai'sɛkt/ v. bisecar.

bishop /'bɪʃəp/ n. obispo m.; (chess) alfil m.

bishopric /'bɪʃəprɪk/ n. obispado m.

bismuth /'bɪzməθ/ n. bismuto m.

bison /'baisən/ n. bisonte m.

bit /bɪt/ n. pedacito m.; Mech. taladro m.; (for horse) bocado m.; (computer) bit m.

bitch /bɪtʃ/ n. perra f.

bite /bait/ n. **1.** bocado m.; picada f. —v. **2.** morder; picar.

biting /'baitɪŋ/ a. penetrante; mordaz.

bitter /'bɪtər/ a. amargo.

bitterly /'bɪtərli/ adv. amargamente; agriamente.

bitterness /'bɪtərnɪs/ n. amargura f.; rencor m.

bivouac /'bɪvu,æk/ n. **1.** vivaque m. —v. **2.** vivaquear.

biweekly /bai'wikli/ a. quincenal.

black /blæk/ a. negro.

Black /blæk/ n. (person) negro -gra; persona de color.

blackberry /'blæk,bɛri/ n. mora f.

blackbird /'blæk,bɜrd/ n. mirlo m.

blackboard /'blæk,bɔrd/ n. pizarra f.

blacken /'blækən/ v. ennegrecer.

black eye n. ojo amoratado.

blackguard /'blægard/ n. tunante; pillo m.

blacklist /'blæk,lɪst/ n. lista negra f.

blackmail /'blæk,meil/ n. **1.** chantaje m. —v. **2.** amenazar con chantaje, chantajear.

black market mercado negro, estraperlo m.

black marketeer /,mɑrkɪ'tir/ estraperlista mf.

blackout /'blæk,aut/ n. oscurecimiento, apagamiento m.

blacksmith /'blæk,smɪθ/ n. herrero -ra.

bladder /'blædər/ n. vejiga f.

blade /bleid/ n. (sword) hoja f.; (oar) pala f.; (grass) brizna f.

blame /bleim/ v. culpar, echar la culpa a.

blameless /'bleimlɪs/ a. inculpable.

blanch /blæntʃ/ v. blanquear; escaldar.

bland /blænd/ a. blando.

blank /blæŋk/ a. & n. en blanco.

blanket /'blæŋkɪt/ n. manta f.; cobertor m.

blare /blɛər/ n. sonido de trompeta. v. sonar como trompeta.

blaspheme /blæs'fim/ v. blasfemar.

blasphemer /blæs'fimər/ n. blasfemo -ma, blasfemador -ra.

blasphemous /'blæsfəməs/ a. blasfemo, impío.

blasphemy /'blæsfəmi/ n. blasfemia f.

blast /blæst/ n. **1.** barreno m.; (wind) ráfaga f. —v. **2.** barrenar.

blatant /'bleitnt/ a. bramante; descarado.

blaze /bleiz/ n. **1.** llama, hoguera f. —v. **2.** encenderse en llama.

blazing /'bleizɪŋ/ a. flameante.

bleach /blitʃ/ n. **1.** lejía, blanqueador. —v. **2.** blanquear.

bleachers /'blitʃərz/ n. asientos al aire libre m.

bleak /blik/ a. frío y sombrío.

bleakness /'bliknɪs/ n. desolación f.

bleed /blid/ v. sangrar.

blemish /'blɛmɪʃ/ n. **1.** mancha f.; lunar m. —v. **2.** manchar.

blend /blɛnd/ n. **1.** mezcla f. —v. **2.** mezclar, combinar.

blended /'blɛndɪd/ a. mezclado.

blender /'blɛndər/ n. (for food) licuadora f.

bless /blɛs/ v. bendecir.

blessed /'blɛsɪd/ a. bendito.

blessing /'blɛsɪŋ/ n. bendición f.

blight /blait/ n. **1.** plaga f.; tizón m. —v. **2.** atizonar.

blind /blaind/ a. ciego.

blindfold /'blaind,fould/ v. vendar los ojos.

blinding /'blaindɪŋ/ a. deslumbrante; ofuscante.

blindly /'blaindli/ adv. ciegamente.

blindness /'blaindnɪs/ n. ceguedad, ceguera f.

blink /blɪŋk/ n. **1.** guiñada f. —v. **2.** guiñar.

bliss /blɪs/ n. felicidad f.

blissful /'blɪsfəl/ a. dichoso; bienaventurado.

blissfully /'blɪsfəli/ adv. felizmente.

blister /'blɪstər/ n. ampolla f.

blithe /blaið/ a. alegre; jovial; gozoso.

blizzard /'blɪzərd/ n. nevasca f.

bloat /blout/ v. hinchar.

bloc /blɒk/ n. grupo (político); bloc.

block /blɒk/ n. **1.** bloque m.; (street) manzana, cuadra f. —v. **2.** bloquear.

blockade /blɒ'keid/ n. **1.** bloqueo m. —v. **2.** bloquear.

blond /blɒnd/ a. & n. rubio -ia.

blood /blʌd/ n. sangre f.; parentesco, linaje m.

bloodhound /'blʌd,haund/ n. sabueso m.

bloodless /'blʌdlɪs/ a. exangüe; desangrado.

blood poisoning /'pɔizənɪŋ/ envenenamiento de sangre.

blood pressure presión arterial.

bloodshed /'blʌd,ʃɛd/ n. matanza f.

bloodthirsty /'blʌd,θɜrsti/ a. cruel, sanguinario.

bloody /'blʌdi/ a. ensangrentado, sangriento.

bloom /blum/ n. **1.** flor f. —v. **2.** florecer.

blooming /'blumɪŋ/ a. lozano; fresco; floreciente.

blossom /'blɒsəm/ n. **1.** flor f. —v. **2.** florecer.

blot /blɒt/ *n.* **1.** mancha *f.* —*v.* **2.** manchar.
blotch /blɒtʃ/ *n.* **1.** mancha, roncha *f.* —*v.* **2.** manchar.
blotter /'blɒtər/ *n.* papel secante.
blouse /blaus/ *n.* blusa *f.*
blow /blou/ *n.* **1.** golpe *m.*; *Fig.* chasco *m.* —*v.* **2.** soplar.
blowout /'blouˌaut/ *n.* reventón de neumático *m.*
blubber /'blʌbər/ *n.* grasa de ballena.
bludgeon /'blʌdʒən/ *n.* porra *f.* *v.* apalear.
blue /blu/ *a.* azul; triste, melancólico.
bluebird /'bluˌbɜrd/ *n.* azulejo *m.*
blue jeans jeans; vaqueros *m.pl.*
blueprint /'bluˌprɪnt/ *n.* heliografía *f.*
bluff /blʌf/ *n.* risco *m.* *v.* alardear; baladronar.
bluing /'bluɪŋ/ *n.* añil *m.*
blunder /'blʌndər/ *n.* **1.** desatino *m.* —*v.* **2.** desatinar.
blunderer /'blʌndərər/ *n.* desatinado -da.
blunt /blʌnt/ *a.* embotado; descortés. *v.* embotar.
bluntly /'blʌntli/ *a.* bruscamente.
bluntness /'blʌntnɪs/ *n.* grosería *f.*; brusquedad.
blur /blɜr/ *n.* **1.** trazo confuso. —*v.* **2.** hacer indistinto.
blush /blʌʃ/ *n.* **1.** rubor, sonrojo *m.* —*v.* **2.** sonrojarse.
bluster /'blʌstər/ *n.* **1.** fanfarria *f.* —*v.* **2.** fanfarrear.
boar /bɔr/ *n.* verraco *m.* **wild b.,** jabalí.
board /bɔrd/ *n.* **1.** tabla; *Govt.* consejo *m.*; junta *f.* **b. and room,** cuarto y comida, casa y comida. —*v.* **2.** (ship) abordar.
boarder /'bɔrdər/ *n.* pensionista *m.* & *f.*
boardinghouse /'bɔrdɪŋ/ *n.* pensión *f.*, casa de huéspedes.
boarding pass /'bɔrdɪŋ/ boleto de embarque *m.*, tarjeta de embarque *f.*
boast /boust/ *n.* **1.** jactancia *f.* —*v.* **2.** jactarse.
boaster /'boustər/ *n.* fanfarrón -na.
boastful /'boustfəl/ *a.* jactancioso.
boastfulness /'boustfəlnɪs/ *n.* jactancia *f.*
boat /bout/ *n.* barco, buque, bote *m.*
boathouse /'boutˌhaus/ *n.* casilla de botes *f.*
boatswain /'bousən/ *n.* contramaestre *m.*
bob /bɒb/ *v.* menear.
bobbin /'bɒbɪn/ *n.* bobina *f.*
bobby pin /'bɒbi/ *n.* gancho *m.*, horquilla.
bodice /'bɒdɪs/ *n.* corpiño *m.*
bodily /'bɒdli/ *a.* corporal.
body /'bɒdi/ *n.* cuerpo *m.*
body builder culturista *mf.*
body building culturismo *m.*
bodyguard /'bɒdiˌgɑrd/ *n.* guardaespaldas.
bog /bɒg/ *n.* pantano *m.*
bogey /'bougi/ *n.* (golf) uno sobre par *m.*
Bohemian /bou'himiən/ *a.* & *n.* bohemio -mia.
boil /bɔil/ *n.* **1.** hervor *m.*; *Med.* divieso *m.* —*v.* **2.** hervir.
boiler /'bɔilər/ *n.* marmita; caldera *f.*
boiling point /'bɔilɪŋ/ punto de ebullición *m.*
boisterous /'bɔistərəs/ *a.* tumultuoso.
boisterously /'bɔistərəsli/ *adv.* tumultuosamente.
bold /bould/ *a.* atrevido, audaz.
boldface /'bouldˌfeis/ *n.* (type) letra negra.
boldly /'bouldli/ *adv.* audazmente; descaradamente.
boldness /'bouldnɪs/ *n.* atrevimiento *m.*; osadía *f.*
Bolivian /bou'lɪviən/ *a.* & *n.* boliviano -na.
bologna /bə'louni/ *n.* salchicha *f.*, mortadela.
bolster /'boulstər/ *n.* **1.** travesero, cojín *m.* —*v.* **2.** apoyar, sostener.
bolt /boult/ *n.* perno *m.*; (of door) cerrojo *m.*; (lightning) rayo *m.* *v.* acerrojar.
bomb /bɒm/ *n.* **1.** bomba *f.* —*v.* **2.** bombardear.
bombard /bɒm'bɑrd/ *v.* bombardear.
bombardier /ˌbɒmbər'dɪər/ *n.* bombardero -ra.
bombardment /bɒm'bɑrdmənt/ *n.* bombardeo *m.*
bomber /'bɒmər/ *n.* avión de bombardeo.
bombproof /'bɒmˌpruf/ *a.* a prueba de granadas.
bombshell /'bɒmˌʃɛl/ *n.* bomba *f.*
bonbon /'bɒnˌbɒn/ *n.* dulce, bombón *m.*
bond /bɒnd/ *n.* lazo *m.*; *Com.* bono *m.*
bondage /'bɒndɪdʒ/ *n.* esclavitud, servidumbre *f.*
bonded /'bɒndɪd/ *a.* garantizado.
bone /boun/ *n.* hueso *m.*
boneless /'bounlɪs/ *a.* sin huesos.
bonfire /'bɒnˌfaiᵊr/ *n.* hoguera, fogata *f.*
bonnet /'bɒnɪt/ *n.* gorra *f.*
bonus /'bounəs/ *n.* sobrepaga *f.*
bony /'bouni/ *a.* huesudo.
boo /bu/ *v.* abuchear.
book /bʊk/ *n.* libro *m.*
bookbinder /'bʊkˌbaindər/ *n.* encuadernador -ora.
bookcase /'bʊkˌkeis/ *n.* armario para libros.
bookkeeper /'bʊkˌkipər/ *n.* tenedor -ra de libros.
bookkeeping /'bʊkˌkipɪŋ/ *n.* contabilidad *f.*
booklet /'bʊklɪt/ *n.* folleto *m.*, libreta *f.*
bookmark /'bʊkˌmɑrk/ *n.* marcapáginas *m.*
bookseller /'bʊkˌsɛlər/ *n.* librero -ra.
bookstore /'bʊkˌstɔr/ *n.* librería *f.*
boom /bum/ *n.* *Naut.* botalón *m.*; prosperidad repentina.
boon /bun/ *n.* dádiva *f.*
boor /bʊr/ *n.* patán, rústico *m.*
boorish /'bʊrɪʃ/ *a.* villano.
boost /bust/ *n.* **1.** alza; ayuda *f.* —*v.* **2.** levantar, alzar; fomentar.
booster /'bustər/ *n.* fomentador *m.*
boot /but/ *n.* bota *f.*
bootblack /'butˌblæk/ *n.* limpiabotas *m.*
booth /buθ/ *n.* cabaña; casilla *f.*
booty /'buti/ *n.* botín *m.*
border /'bɔrdər/ *n.* **1.** borde *m.*; frontera *f.* —*v.* **2.** **b. on,** lindar con.
borderline /'bɔrdərˌlain/ *a.* marginal. *n.* margen *m.*
bore /bɔr/ *n.* lata *f.*; persona pesada. *v.* aburrir, fastidiar; *Mech.* taladrar.
boredom /'bɔrdəm/ *n.* aburrimiento *m.*
boric acid /'bɔrɪk/ *n.* ácido bórico *m.*
boring /'bɔrɪŋ/ *a.* aburrido, pesado.
born /bɔrn/ *a.* nacido. **be born,** nacer.
born-again /'bɔrn ə'gɛn/ *a.* renacido.
borrow /'bɒrou/ *v.* pedir prestado.
bosom /'bʊzəm/ *n.* seno, pecho *m.*
boss /bɒs/ *n.* jefe, patrón *m.*
botany /'bɒtṇi/ *n.* botánica *f.*
both /bouθ/ *pron.* & *a.* ambos, los dos.
bother /'bɒðər/ *n.* molestia *f.* *v.* molestar, incomodar.
bothersome /'bɒðərsəm/ *a.* molesto.
bottle /'bɒtl̩/ *n.* **1.** botella *f.* —*v.* **2.** embotellar.
bottling /'bɒtl̩ɪŋ/ *n.* embotellamiento *m.*
bottom /'bɒtəm/ *n.* fondo *m.*
boudoir /'budwɑr/ *n.* tocador *m.*
bough /bau/ *n.* rama *f.*
boulder /'bouldər/ *n.* canto rodado.
boulevard /'bʊləˌvɑrd/ *n.* bulevar *m.*
bounce /bauns/ *n.* **1.** brinco *m.* —*v.* **2.** brincar; hacer saltar.
bound /baund/ *n.* **1.** salto *m.* —*v.* **2.** limitar.
boundary /'baundəri/ *n.* límite, lindero *m.*
bouquet /bou'kei, bu-/ *n.* ramillete de flores.
bourgeois /bʊr'ʒwɑ/ *a.* & *n.* burgués -esa.
bout /baut/ *n.* encuentro; combate *m.*
bow /*n* bau, bou; *v* bau/ *n.* **1.** saludo *m.*; (of ship) proa *f.*; (archery) arco *m.*; (ribbon) lazo *m.* —*v.* **2.** saludar, inclinar.
bowels /'bauəlz/ *n.* intestinos *m.pl.*; entrañas *f.pl.*
bowl /boul/ *n.* **1.** vasija *f.*; platón *m.* —*v.* **2.** jugar a los bolos. **b. over,** derribar.
bowlegged /'bouˌlɛgɪd/ *a.* perniabierto.
bowling /'boulɪŋ/ *n.* bolos *m.pl.*
bow tie /bou/ pajarita *f.*
box /bɒks/ *n.* **1.** caja *f.*; *Theat.* palco *m.* —*v.* **2.** (sports) boxear.
boxcar /'bɒksˌkɑr/ *n.* vagón *m.*
boxer /'bɒksər/ *n.* boxeador -ra, pugi'lista *m.* & *f.*
boxing /'bɒksɪŋ/ *n.* boxeo *m.*
box office *n.* taquilla *f.*
boy /bɔi/ *n.* muchacho, chico, niño *m.*
boycott /'bɔikɒt/ *n.* **1.** boicoteo *m.* —*v.* **2.** boicotear.
boyhood /'bɔihʊd/ *n.* muchachez *f.*
boyish /'bɔiɪʃ/ *a.* pueril.
boyishly /'bɔiɪʃli/ *adv.* puerilmente.
bra /brɑ/ *n.* sujetador, sostén *m.*
brace /breis/ *n.* **1.** grapón *m.*; *pl.* tirantes *m.pl.* —*v.* **2.** reforzar.
bracelet /'breislɪt/ *n.* brazalete *m.*, pulsera *f.*
bracket /'brækɪt/ *n.* ménsula *f.*
brag /bræg/ *v.* jactarse.
braggart /'brægərt/ *a.* **1.** jactancioso. —*n.* **2.** jaque *m.*
braid /breid/ *n.* **1.** trenza *f.* —*v.* **2.** trenzar.
brain /brein/ *n.* cerebro, seso *m.*
brainy /'breini/ *a.* sesudo, inteligente.
brake /breik/ *n.* **1.** freno *m.* —*v.* **2.** frenar.
bran /bræn/ *n.* salvado *m.*
branch /bræntʃ, brɑntʃ/ *n.* ramo *m.*; (of tree) rama *f.*
brand /brænd/ *n.* marca *f.*
brandish /'brændɪʃ/ *v.* blandir.
brand-new /'bræn'nu/ *a.* enteramente nuevo.
brandy /'brændi/ *n.* aguardiente, coñac *m.*
brash /bræʃ/ *a.* impetuoso.
brass /bræs/ *n.* bronce, latón *m.*
brassiere /brə'zɪər/ *n.* corpiño, sujetador, sostén *m.*
brat /bræt/ *n.* mocoso *m.*
bravado /brə'vɑdou/ *n.* bravata *f.*
brave /breiv/ *a.* valiente.
bravery /'breivəri/ *n.* valor *m.*
brawl /brɔl/ *n.* alboroto *m.* *v.* alborotar.
brawn /brɔn/ *n.* músculo *m.*
bray /brei/ *v.* rebuznar.
brazen /'breizən/ *a.* desvergonzado.
Brazil /brə'zɪl/ *n.* Brasil *m.*
Brazilian /brə'zɪlyən/ *a.* & *n.* brasileño -ña.
breach /britʃ/ *n.* rotura; infracción *f.*
breach of contract incumplimiento de contrato *m.*
bread /brɛd/ *n.* pan *m.*
breadth /brɛdθ/ *n.* anchura *f.*
break /breik/ *n.* **1.** rotura; pausa *f.* —*v.* **2.** quebrar, romper.
breakable /'breikəbəl/ *a.* rompible, frágil.
breakage /'breikɪdʒ/ *n.* rotura *f.*, destrozo *m.*
breakfast /'brɛkfəst/ *n.* **1.** desayuno, almuerzo *m.* —*v.* **2.** desayunar, almorzar.
breakneck /'breikˌnɛk/ *a.* rápido, precipitado, atropellado.
breast /brɛst/ *n.* (of human) pecho, seno *m.*; (of fowl) pechuga *f.*
breastbone /'brɛstˌboun/ *n.* esternón *m.*
breath /brɛθ/ *n.* aliento; soplo *m.*
breathe /brið/ *v.* respirar.
breathless /'brɛθlɪs/ *a.* desalentado.
breathlessly /'brɛθlɪsli/ *adv.* jadeantemente, intensamente.
bred /brɛd/ *a.* criado; educado.
breeches /'brɪtʃɪz/ *n.pl.* calzones; pantalones, *m.pl.*
breed /brid/ *n.* **1.** raza *f.* —*v.* **2.** engendrar; criar.
breeder /'bridər/ *n.* criador -ra.
breeding /'bridɪŋ/ *n.* cría *f.*
breeze /briz/ *n.* brisa *f.*
breezy /'brizi/ *a.*: **it is b.,** hace brisa.
brevity /'brɛvɪti/ *n.* brevedad *f.*
brew /bru/ *v.* fraguar; elaborar.
brewer /'bruər/ *n.* cervecero -ra.
brewery /'bruəri/ *n.* cervecería *f.*
bribe /braib/ *n.* **1.** soborno, cohecho *m.* —*v.* **2.** sobornar, cohechar.
briber /'braibər/ *n.* sobornador -ra.
bribery /'braibəri/ *n.* soborno, cohecho *m.*
brick /brɪk/ *n.* ladrillo *m.*
bricklayer /'brɪkˌleiər/ *n.* albañil *m.*
bridal /'braidl̩/ *a.* nupcial.
bride /braid/ *n.* novia *f.*
bridegroom /'braidˌgrum/ *n.* novio *m.*
bridesmaid /'braidzˌmeid/ *n.* madrina de boda.
bridge /brɪdʒ/ *n.* puente *m.*
bridged /brɪdʒd/ *a.* conectado.
bridgehead /'brɪdʒˌhɛd/ *n.* *Mil.* cabeza de puente.
bridle /'braidl̩/ *n.* brida *f.*
brief /brif/ *a.* breve.
briefcase /'brifˌkeis/ *n.* maletín *m.*
briefly /'brifli/ *adv.* brevemente.
briefness /'brifnɪs/ *n.* brevedad *f.*
brier /'braiər/ *n.* zarza *f.*
brig /brɪg/ *n.* bergantín *m.*
brigade /brɪ'geid/ *n.* brigada *f.*
bright /brait/ *a.* claro, brillante.
brighten /'braitn̩/ *v.* abrillantar; alegrar.
brightness /'braitnɪs/ *n.* resplandor *m.*
brilliance /'brɪlyəns/ *n.* brillantez *f.*
brilliant /'brɪlyənt/ *a.* brillante.
brim /brɪm/ *n.* borde *m.*; (of hat) ala *f.*
brine /brain/ *n.* escabeche, *m.* salmuera *f.*
bring /brɪŋ/ *v.* traer. **b. about,** efectuar, llevar a cabo.
brink /brɪŋk/ *n.* borde *m.*
briny /'braini/ *a.* salado.
brisk /brɪsk/ *a.* vivo; enérgico.
briskly /'brɪskli/ *adv.* vivamente.
briskness /'brɪsknɪs/ *n.* viveza *f.*
bristle /'brɪsəl/ *n.* cerda *f.*
bristly /'brɪsli/ *a.* hirsuto.
Britain /'brɪtn̩/ *n.* **Great B.,** Gran Bretaña *f.*
British /'brɪtɪʃ/ *a.* británico.
British Empire imperio británico *m.*
British Isles /ailz/ islas británicas *f.*
Briton /'brɪtn/ *n.* inglés *m.*
brittle /'brɪtl̩/ *a.* quebradizo, frágil.
broad /brɔd/ *a.* ancho.
broadcast /'brɔdˌkæst/ *n.* **1.** radiodifusión *f.* —*v.* **2.** radiodifundir.
broadcaster /'brɔdˌkæstər/ *n.* locutor -ra.
broadcloth /'brɔdˌklɔθ/ *n.* paño fino.
broaden /'brɔdn̩/ *v.* ensanchar.
broadly /'brɔdli/ *adv.* ampliamente.
broadminded /'brɔd'maindɪd/ *a.* tolerante, liberal.
brocade /brou'keid/ *n.* brocado *m.*
brocaded /brou'keidɪd/ *a.* espolinado.
broccoli /'brɒkəli/ *n.* brécol *m.*
broil /brɔil/ *v.* asar.
broiler /'brɔilər/ *n.* parrilla *f.*
broken /'broukən/ *a.* roto, quebrado.
broken-hearted /'broukən'hɑrtɪd/ *a.* angustiado.

broker /'broukər/ n. corredor -ra, bolsista m. & f.

brokerage /'broukərɪdʒ/ n. corretaje m.

bronchial /'bronkiəl/ a. bronquial.

bronchitis /broŋ'kaitis/ n. bronquitis f.

bronze /brɒnz/ n. bronce m.

brooch /broutʃ/ n. broche m.

brood /brud/ n. **1.** cría, progenie f. —v. **2.** empollar; cobijar.

brook /brʊk/ n. arroyo m., quebrada f.

broom /brum/ n. escoba f.

broomstick /'brum,stɪk/ n. palo de escoba.

broth /brɔθ/ n. caldo m.

brothel /'brɒθəl/ n. burdel m.

brother /'brʌðər/ n. hermano m.

brotherhood /'brʌðər,hʊd/ n. fraternidad f.

brother-in-law /'brʌðər ɪn ,lɔ/ n. cuñado m.

brotherly /'brʌðərli/ a. fraternal.

brow /brau/ n. ceja; frente f.

brown /braun/ a. pardo, moreno; marrón. v. rehogar.

brown sugar azúcar moreno m.

browse /brauz/ v. curiosear; ramonear.

browser /'brauzər/ n. (Internet) nagegador m., visualizador m., visor m.

bruise /bruz/ n. **1.** contusión f. —v. **2.** magullar.

brunette /bru'nɛt/ a. & n. moreno -na, trigueño -ña.

brush /brʌʃ/ n. **1.** cepillo m.; brocha f. —v. **2.** cepillar.

brushwood /'brʌʃ,wʊd/ n. matorral m.

brusque /brʌsk/ a. brusco.

brusquely /'brʌskli/ adv. bruscamente.

brutal /'brutl/ a. brutal.

brutality /bru'tælɪti/ n. brutalidad f.

brutalize /'brutl,aiz/ v. embrutecer.

brute /brut/ n. bruto -ta, bestia f.

bubble /'bʌbəl/ n. ampolla f.

bucket /'bʌkɪt/ n. cubo m.

buckle /'bʌkəl/ n. hebilla f.

buckram /'bʌkrəm/ n. bucarán m.

bucksaw /'bʌk'sɔ/ n. sierra de bastidor.

buckshot /'bʌk,ʃɒt/ n. posta f.

buckwheat /'bʌk,wit/ n. trigo sarraceno.

bud /bʌd/ n. **1.** brote m. —v. **2.** brotar.

budding /'bʌdɪŋ/ a. en capullo.

budge /bʌdʒ/ v. moverse.

budget /'bʌdʒɪt/ n. presupuesto m.

buffalo /'bʌfə,lou/ n. búfalo m.

buffer /'bʌfər/ n. parachoques m.

buffet /bə'fei/ n. bufet m.; (furniture) aparador m.

buffoon /bə'fun/ n. bufón m.

bug /bʌg/ n. insecto m.; (computer) error m.

bugle /'byugəl/ n. clarín m.; corneta f.

build /bɪld/ v. construir.

builder /'bɪldər/ n. constructor -ra.

building /'bɪldɪŋ/ n. edificio m.

bulb /bʌlb/ n. bulbo m.; (of lamp) bombilla, ampolla f.

bulge /bʌldʒ/ n. abultamiento m. v. abultar.

bulging /'bʌldʒɪŋ/ a. protuberante.

bulimia /bu'limiə/ n. bulimia f.

bulk /bʌlk/ n. masa f.; grueso m.; mayoría f.

bulkhead /'bʌlk,hɛd/ n. frontón m.

bulky /'bʌlki/ a. grueso, abultado.

bull /bʊl/ n. toro m.

bulldog /'bʊl,dɔg/ n. perro de presa.

bullet /'bʊlɪt/ n. bala f.

bulletin /'bʊlɪtɪn/ n. boletín m.

bulletproof /'bʊlɪt,pruf/ a. a prueba de bala.

bullfight /'bʊl,fait/ n. corrida de toros.

bullfighter /'bʊl,faitər/ n. torero -ra.

bullfinch /'bʊl,fɪntʃ/ n. pinzón real m.

bully /'bʊli/ n. **1.** rufián m. —v. **2.** bravear.

bulwark /'bʊlwərk/ n. baluarte m.

bum /bʌm/ n. holgazán m.

bump /bʌmp/ n. **1.** golpe, choque m. —v. **2. b. into,** chocar contra.

bumper /'bʌmpər/ n. parachoques m.

bun /bʌn/ n. bollo m.

bunch /bʌntʃ/ n. racimo; montón m.

bundle /'bʌndl/ n. **1.** bulto m. —v. **2. b. up,** abrigar.

bungalow /'bʌŋgə,lou/ n. casa de un solo piso.

bungle /'bʌŋgəl/ v. estropear.

bunion /'bʌnyən/ n. juanete m.

bunk /bʌŋk/ n. litera f.

bunny /'bʌni/ n. conejito -ta.

bunting /'bʌntɪŋ/ n. lanilla; banderas f.

buoy /'bui/ n. boya f.

buoyant /'bɔiənt/ a. boyante; vivaz.

burden /'bərdn/ n. **1.** carga f. —v. **2.** cargar.

burdensome /'bərdnsəm/ a. gravoso.

bureau /'byurou/ n. (furniture) cómoda f.; departamento m.

burglar /'bərglər/ n. ladrón -ona.

burglarize /'bərglə,raiz/ v. robar.

burglary /'bərgləri/ n. robo m.

burial /'bɛriəl/ n. entierro m.

burlap /'bərlæp/ n. arpillera f.

burly /'bərli/ a. corpulento.

burn /bərn/ v. quemar; arder.

burner /'bərnər/ n. mechero m.

burning /'bərnɪŋ/ a. ardiente.

burrow /'bərou/ v. minar; horadar.

burst /bərst/ v. reventar.

bury /'bɛri/ v. enterrar.

bus /bʌs/ n. autobús m.

bush /bʊʃ/ n. arbusto m.

bushy /'bʊʃi/ a. matoso; peludo.

business /'bɪznɪs/ n. negocios m.pl.; comercio m.

businesslike /'bɪznɪs,laik/ a. directo, práctico.

businessman /'bɪznɪs,mæn/ n. hombre de negocios, comerciante m.

businesswoman /'bɪznɪs,wʊmən/ n. mujer de negocios.

bust /bʌst/ n. busto; pecho m.

bustle /'bʌsəl/ n. bullicio m.; animación f.

busy /'bɪzi/ a. ocupado, atareado.

busybody /'bɪzi,bɒdi/ n. entremetido -da.

but /bʌt/ conj. pero; sino.

butcher /'bʊtʃər/ n. carnicero -ra.

butchery /'bʊtʃəri/ n. carnicería; matanza f.

butler /'bʌtlər/ n. mayordomo m.

butt /bʌt/ n. punta f.; cabo extremo m.

butter /'bʌtər/ n. manteca, mantequilla f.

buttercup /'bʌtər,kʌp/ n. ranúnculo m.

butterfat /'bʌtər,fæt/ n. mantequilla f.

butterfly /'bʌtər,flai/ n. mariposa f.

buttermilk /'bʌtər,mɪlk/ n. suero (de leche) m.

button /'bʌtn/ n. botón m.

buttonhole /'bʌtn,houl/ n. ojal m.

buttress /'bʌtrɪs/ n. sostén; refuerzo m.

buxom /'bʌksəm/ a. regordete.

buy /bai/ v. comprar.

buyer /'baiər/ n. comprador -ra.

buzz /bʌz/ n. **1.** zumbido m. —v. **2.** zumbar.

buzzard /'bʌzərd/ n. gallinazo m.

buzzer /'bʌzər/ n. zumbador m.; timbre m.

buzz saw n. sierra circular f.

by /bai/ prep. por; (near) cerca de, al lado de; (time) para.

by-and-by /,baiən'bai/ adv. pronto; luego.

bygone /'bai,gɒn/ a. pasado.

bylaw /'bai,lɔ/ n. estatuto, reglamento m.

bypass /'bai,pæs/ n. desvío m.

byproduct /'bai,prɒdəkt/ n. subproducto m.

bystander /'bai,stændər/ n. espectador -ra; mirón -na.

byte /bait/ n. en teoría de la información: ocho bits, byte m.

byway /'bai,wei/ n. camino desviado m.

C

cab /kæb/ n. taxi, coche de alquiler m.

cabaret /,kæbə'rei/ n. cabaret m.

cabbage /'kæbɪdʒ/ n. repollo m.

cabin /'kæbɪn/ n. cabaña f.

cabinet /'kæbənɪt/ n. gabinete; ministerio m.

cabinetmaker /'kæbənɪt,meikər/ n. ebanista m.

cable /'keibəl/ n. cable m.

cablegram /'keibəl,græm/ n. cablegrama m.

cache /kæʃ/ n. escondite m.

cackle /'kækəl/ n. charla f.; cacareo m. v. cacarear.

cacophony /kə'kɒfəni/ n. cacofonía f.

cactus /'kæktəs/ n. cacto m.

cad /kæd/ n. persona vil.

cadaver /kə'dævər/ n. cadáver m.

cadaverous /kə'dævərəs/ a. cadavérico.

caddie /'kædi/ n. (golf) ayudante m. & f.

cadence /'keidns/ n. cadencia f.

cadet /kə'dɛt/ n. cadete m.

cadmium /'kædmiəm/ n. cadmio m.

cadre /'kædri, 'kɑdrei/ n. núcleo; Mil. cuadro m.

café /kæ'fei/ n. café m., cantina f.

cafeteria /,kæfɪ'tɪəriə/ n. cafetería f.

caffeine /kæ'fin/ n. cafeína f.

cage /keidʒ/ n. jaula f. v. enjaular.

caged /keidʒd/ a. enjaulado.

caisson /'keisɒn, -sən/ n. arcón m.; Mil. furgón m.

cajole /kə'dʒoul/ v. lisonjear; adular.

cake /keik/ n. torta f.; bizcocho m.

calamitous /kə'læmɪtəs/ a. calamitoso.

calamity /kə'læmɪti/ n. calamidad f.

calcify /'kælsə,fai/ v. calcificar.

calcium /'kælsiəm/ n. calcio m.

calculable /'kælkyələbəl/ a. calculable.

calculate /'kælkyə,leit/ v. calcular.

calculating /'kælkyə,leitɪŋ/ a. interesado.

calculation /,kælkyə'leiʃən/ n. calculación f.; cálculo m.

calculus /'kælkyələs/ n. cálculo m.

caldron /'kɔldrən/ n. caldera f.

calendar /'kæləndər/ n. calendario m.

calf /kæf/ n. ternero m. (animal); pantorrilla f. (of the body).

calfskin /'kæf,skɪn/ n. piel de becerro m.

caliber /'kælɪbər/ n. calibre m.

calico /'kælɪ,kou/ n. calicó m.

caliper /'kæləpər/ n. calibrador m.

calisthenics /,kæləs'θɛnɪks/ n. calistenia, gimnasia f.

calk /kɔk/ v. calafatear; rellenar.

calker /'kɔkər/ n. calafate -ta.

call /kɔl/ n. **1.** llamada f. —v. **2.** llamar.

calligraphy /kə'lɪgrəfi/ n. caligrafía f.

calling /'kɔlɪŋ/ n. vocación f.

calling card tarjeta (de visita) f.

callously /'kæləsli/ adv. insensiblemente.

callow /'kælou/ a. sin experiencia.

callus /'kæləs/ n. callo m.

calm /kɑm/ a. **1.** tranquilo, calmado. —n. **2.** calma f. —v. **3.** calmar.

calmly /'kɑmli/ adv. serenamente.

calmness /'kɑmnɪs/ n. calma f.

caloric /kə'lɔrɪk/ a. calórico.

calorie /'kæləri/ n. caloría f.

calorimeter /,kælə'rɪmɪtər/ n. calorímetro m.

calumniate /kə'lʌmni,eit/ v. calumniar.

calumny /'kæləmni/ n. calumnia f.

Calvary /'kælvəri/ n. Calvario m.

calve /kæv/ v. parir (la vaca).

calyx /'keilɪks/ n. cáliz m.

camaraderie /,kæmə'rɑdəri/ n. compañerismo m., compadrería f.

cambric /'keimbrɪk/ n. batista f.

camcorder /'kæm,kɔrdər/ n. videocámara f.

camel /'kæməl/ n. camello -lla.

camellia /kə'milyə/ n. camelia f.

camel's hair /'kæməlz/ n. pelo de camello.

cameo /'kæmi,ou/ n. camafeo m.

camera /'kæmərə/ n. cámara f.

camouflage /'kæmə,flɑʒ/ n. camuflaje m.

camouflaging /'kæmə,flɑʒɪŋ/ n. simulacro, disfraz m.

camp /kæmp/ n. **1.** campamento m. —v. **2.** acampar.

campaign /kæm'pein/ n. campaña f.

camper /'kæmpər/ n. acampado m.

campfire /'kæmp,faiər/ n. fogata de campamento.

camphor /'kæmfər/ n. alcanfor m.

camphor ball bola de alcanfor.

campus /'kæmpəs/ n. campo de colegio (o universidad), campus m.

can /kæn/ v. (be able) poder.

can /kæn/ n. **1.** lata f. —v. **2.** conservar en latas, enlatar.

Canada /'kænədə/ n. Canadá m.

Canadian /kə'neidiən/ a. & n. canadiense.

canal /kə'næl/ n. canal m.

canalize /'kænl,aiz/ v. canalizar.

canard /kə'nɑrd/ n. embuste m.

canary /kə'nɛəri/ n. canario -ria.

cancel /'kænsəl/ v. cancelar.

cancellation /,kænsə'leiʃən/ n. cancelación f.

cancer /'kænsər/ n. cáncer m.

candelabrum /,kændl'ɑbrəm/ n. candelabro m.

candid /'kændɪd/ a. cándido, sincero.

candidacy /'kændɪdəsi/ n. candidatura f.

candidate /'kændɪ,deit/ n. candidato -ta.

candidly /'kændɪdli/ adv. cándidamente.

candidness /'kændɪdnɪs/ n. candidez; sinceridad f.

candied /'kændid/ a. garapiñado.

candle /'kændl/ n. vela f.

candlestick /'kændl,stɪk/ n. candelero m.

candor /'kændər/ n. candor m.; sinceridad f.

candy /'kændi/ n. dulces m.pl.

cane /kein/ n. caña f.; (for walking) bastón m.

canine /'keinain/ a. canino.

canister /'kænəstər/ n. frasco m.; lata f.

canker /'kæŋkər/ n. llaga; úlcera f.

cankerworm /'kæŋkər,wɜrm/ n. oruga f.

canned /kænd/ a. envasado, enlatado.

canner /'kænər/ n. envasador m.

cannery /'kænəri/ n. fábrica de conservas alimenticias f.

cannibal /'kænəbəl/ n. caníbal m. & f.

cannon /'kænən/ n. cañón m.

cannonade /,kænə'neid/ n. cañoneo m.

cannoneer /,kænə'nɪər/ n. cañonero -ra.

canny /'kæni/ a. sagaz; prudente.

canoe /kə'nu/ n. canoa, piragua f.

canoeing /kə'nuɪŋ/ n. piragüismo m.

canoeist /kə'nuɪst/ n. piragüista m. & f.

canon /'kænən/ n. canon m.; Relig. canónigo m.

canonical /kə'nɒnɪkəl/ a. canónico.

canonize /'kænə,naiz/ v. canonizar.

can opener /'oupənər/ abrelatas m.

canopy /'kænəpi/ n. dosel m.

cant /kænt/ n. hipocresía f.

cantaloupe /'kæntļ,oup/ n. melón m.

canteen /kæn'tin/ n. cantina f.

canter /'kæntər/ n. **1.** medio galope m. —v. **2.** galopar.

cantonment /kæn'tɒnmənt/ n. Mil. acuartelamiento m.

canvas /'kænvəs/ n. lona f.

canyon /'kænyən/ n. cañón, desfiladero m.

cap /kæp/ n. **1.** tapa f.; (headwear) gorro m. —v. **2.** tapar.

capability /,keipə'bɪliti/ n. capacidad f.

capable /'keipəbəl/ a. capaz.

capably /'keipəbli/ adv. hábilmente.

capacious /kə'peiʃəs/ a. espacioso.

capacity /kə'pæsiti/ n. capacidad f.

cape /keip/ n. capa f., Geog. cabo m.

caper /'keipər/ n. zapateta f.; Bot. alcaparra f.

capillary /'kæpə,lɛri/ a. capilar.

capital /'kæpitļ/ n. capital m.; Govt. capital f.

capitalism /'kæpitļ,izəm/ n. capitalismo m.

capitalist /'kæpitļist/ n. capitalista m. & f.

capitalistic /,kæpitļ'istik/ a. capitalista.

capitalization /,kæpitlə'zeiʃən/ n. capitalización f.

capitalize /'kæpitļ,aiz/ v. capitalizar.

capital letter n. mayúscula f.

capitulate /kə'pitʃə,leit/ v. capitular.

capon /'keipɒn/ n. capón m.

caprice /kə'pris/ n. capricho m.

capricious /kə'priʃəs/ a. caprichoso.

capriciously /kə'priʃəsli/ adv. caprichosamente.

capriciousness /kə'priʃəsnis/ n. capricho m.

capsize /'kæpsaiz/ v. zozobrar, volcar.

capsule /'kæpsəl/ n. cápsula f.

captain /'kæptən/ n. capitán -tana.

caption /'kæpʃən/ n. título m.; (motion pictures) subtítulo m.

captious /'kæpʃəs/ a. capcioso.

captivate /'kæptə,veit/ v. cautivar.

captivating /'kæptə,veitiŋ/ a. encantador.

captive /'kæptiv/ n. cautivo -va, prisionero -ra.

captivity /kæp'tiviti/ n. cautividad f.

captor /'kæptər/ n. apresador -ra.

capture /'kæptʃər/ n. **1.** captura f. —v. **2.** capturar.

car /kar/ n. coche, carro m.; (of train) vagón, coche m. **baggage c.,** vagón de equipajes. **parlor c.,** coche salón.

carafe /kə'ræf/ n. garrafa f.

caramel /'kærəməl/ n. caramelo m.

carat /'kærət/ n. quilate m.

caravan /'kærə,væn/ n. caravana f.

caraway /'kærə,wei/ n. alcaravea f.

carbide /'karbaid/ n. carburo m.

carbine /'karbin/ n. carabina f.

carbohydrate /,karbou'haidreit/ n. hidrato de carbono.

carbon /'karbən/ n. carbón m.

carbon dioxide /dai'ɒksaid/ anhídrido carbónico.

carbon monoxide /mɒn'ɒksaid/ monóxido de carbono.

carbon paper papel carbón m.

carbuncle /'karbʌŋkəl/ n. carbúnculo m.

carburetor /'karbə,reitər/ n. carburador m.

carcinogenic /,karsənə'dʒɛnik/ a. carcinogénico.

card /kard/ n. tarjeta f. **playing c.,** naipe m.

cardboard /'kard,bɔrd/ n. cartón m.

cardiac /'kardi,æk/ a. cardíaco.

cardigan /'kardigən/ n. chaqueta de punto.

cardinal /'kardņļ/ a. **1.** cardinal. —n. **2.** cardenal m.

cardiologist /,kardi'ɒlədʒist/ n. cardiólogo, -ga m. & f.

care /kɛər/ n. **1.** cuidado. —v. **2. c. for,** cuidar.

careen /kə'rin/ v. carenar; echarse de costado.

career /kə'riər/ n. carrera f.

carefree /'kɛər,fri/ a. descuidado.

careful /'kɛərfəl/ a. cuidadoso. **be. c.,** tener cuidado.

carefully /'kɛərfəli/ adv. cuidadosamente.

carefulness /'kɛərfəlnis/ n. esmero; cuidado m.; cautela f.

careless /'kɛərlis/ a. descuidado.

carelessly /'kɛərlisli/ adv. descuidadamente; negligentemente.

carelessness /'kɛərlisnis/ n. descuido m.

caress /kə'rɛs/ n. **1.** caricia f. —v. **2.** acariciar.

caretaker /'kɛər,teikər/ n. guardián -ana.

cargo /'kargou/ n. carga f.

caricature /'kærikətʃər/ n. caricatura f.

caricaturist /'kærikə,tʃurist/ n. caricaturista m. & f.

caries /'kɛəriz/ n. caries f.

carjacking /'kar,dʒækiŋ/ n. robo de coche m.

carload /'kar,loud/ a. furgonada, vagonada.

carnal /'karnļ/ a. carnal.

carnation /kar'neiʃən/ n. clavel m.

carnival /'karnəvəl/ n. carnaval m.

carnivorous /kar'nivərəs/ a. carnívoro.

carol /'kærəl/ n. villancico m.

carouse /kə'rauz/ v. parrandear.

carpenter /'karpəntər/ n. carpintero -ra.

carpet /'karpit/ n. alfombra f.

carpeting /'karpitiŋ/ n. alfombrado m.

car pool /'kar,pul/ uso habitual, por varias personas, de un automóvil perteneciente a una de ellas.

carriage /'kæridʒ/ n. carruaje; (bearing) porte m.

carrier /'kæriər/ n. portador -ra.

carrier pigeon paloma mensajera.

carrot /'kærət/ n. zanahoria f.

carrousel /,kærə'sɛl/ n. volantín, carrusel m.

carry /'kæri/ v. llevar, cargar. **c. out,** cumplir, llevar a cabo.

cart /kart/ n. carreta f.

cartage /'kartidʒ/ n. acarreo, carretaje m.

cartel /kar'tɛl/ n. cartel m.

cartilage /'kartilidʒ/ n. cartílago m.

carton /'kartn/ n. caja de cartón f.

cartoon /kar'tun/ n. caricatura f.

cartoonist /kar'tunist/ n. caricaturista m. & f.

cartridge /'kartridʒ/ n. cartucho m.

carve /karv/ v. esculpir; (meat) trinchar.

carver /'karvər/ n. tallador -ra; grabador -ra.

carving /'karviŋ/ n. entalladura f.; arte de trinchar. **c. knife,** trinchante m.

cascade /kæs'keid/ n. cascada f.

case /keis/ n. caso m.; (box) caja f. **in any c.,** sea como sea.

cash /kæʃ/ n. **1.** dinero contante. —v. **2.** efectuar, cambiar.

cashier /kæ'ʃiər/ n. cajero -ra.

cashmere /'kæʒmiər/ n. casimir m.

casino /kə'sinou/ n. casino m.

cask /kæsk/ n. barril m.

casket /'kæskit/ n. ataúd m.

casserole /'kæsə,roul/ n. cacerola f.

cassette /kə'sɛt/ n. cassette m., cartucho m.

cast /kæst/ n. **1.** Theat. reparto de papeles. —v. **2.** echar; Theat. repartir.

castanet /,kæstə'nɛt/ n. castañuela f.

castaway /'kæstə,wei/ n. náufrago -ga.

caste /kæst/ n. casta f.

caster /'kæstər/ n. tirador m.

castigate /'kæsti,geit/ v. castigar.

Castilian /kæ'stilyən/ a. castellano.

cast iron n. hierro colado m.

castle /'kæsəl/ n. castillo m.

castoff /'kæst,ɔf/ a. descartado.

casual /'kæʒuəl/ a. casual.

casually /'kæʒuəli/ adv. casualmente.

casualness /'kæʒuəlnis/ n. casualidad f.

casualty /'kæʒuəlti/ n. víctima f.; Mil. baja f.

cat /kæt/ n. gato -ta.

cataclysm /'kætə,klizəm/ n. cataclismo m.

catacomb /'kætə,koum/ n. catacumba f.

catalogue /'kætļ,ɔg/ n. catálogo m.

catapult /'kætə,pʌlt/ n. catapulta f.

cataract /'kætə,rækt/ n. catarata f.

catarrh /kə'tɑr/ n. catarro m.

catastrophe /kə'tæstrəfi/ n. catástrofe f.

catch /kætʃ/ v. alcanzar, atrapar, coger.

catchy /'kætʃi/ a. contagioso.

catechism /'kæti,kizəm/ n. catequismo m.

catechize /'kæti,kaiz/ v. catequizar.

categorical /,kæti'gɔrikəl/ a. categórico.

category /'kæti,gɔri/ n. categoría f.

cater /'keitər/ v. abastecer; proveer. **c. to,** complacer.

caterpillar /'kætə,pilər/ n. gusano m.

catgut /'kæt,gʌt/ n. cuerda (de tripa) f.

catharsis /kə'θarsis/ n. catarsis, purga f.

cathartic /kə'θartik/ a. **1.** catártico; purgante. —n. **2.** purgante m.

cathedral /kə'θidrəl/ n. catedral f.

cathode /'kæθoud/ n. cátodo m.

Catholic /'kæθəlik/ a. católico & n. católico -ca.

Catholicism /kə'θɒlə,sizəm/ n. catolicismo m.

catnap /'kæt,næp/ n. siesta corta.

catsup /'kætsəp, 'kɛtʃəp/ n. salsa de tomate.

cattle /'kætļ/ n. ganado m.

cattleman /'kætļmən, -,mæn/ n. ganadero m.

cauliflower /'kɔlə,flauər/ n. coliflor m.

causation /kɔ'zeiʃən/ n. causalidad f.

cause /kɔz/ n. causa f.

causeway /'kɔz,wei/ n. calzada elevada f.; terraplén m.

caustic /'kɔstik/ a. cáustico.

cauterize /'kɔtə,raiz/ v. cauterizar.

cautery /'kɔtəri/ n. cauterio m.

caution /'kɔʃən/ n. cautela f.

cautious /'kɔʃəs/ a. cauteloso.

cavalcade /,kævəl'keid/ n. cabalgata f.

cavalier /,kævə'liər/ n. caballero m.

cavalry /'kævəlri/ n. caballería f.

cave /keiv/ **cavern** n. caverna, gruta f.

cave-in /'keiv ,in/ n. hundimiento m.

caviar /'kævi,ar/ n. caviar m.

cavity /'kæviti/ n. hueco m.

cayman /'keimən/ n. caimán m.

CD player tocadiscos compacto, tocadiscos digital m.

cease /sis/ v. cesar.

ceaseless /'sislis/ a. incesante.

cedar /'sidər/ n. cedro m.

cede /sid/ v. ceder.

ceiling /'siliŋ/ n. techo; cielo m.

celebrant /'sɛləbrənt/ n. celebrante -ta.

celebrate /'sɛlə,breit/ v. celebrar.

celebration /,sɛlə'breiʃən/ n. celebración f.

celebrity /sə'lɛbriti/ n. celebridad f.

celerity /sə'lɛriti/ n. celeridad f.; prontitud f.

celery /'sɛləri/ n. apio m.

celestial /sə'lɛstʃəl/ a. celeste.

celibacy /'sɛləbəsi/ n. celibato -ta.

celibate /'sɛləbit/ a. & n. célibe m. & f.

cell /sɛl/ n. celda f.; Biol. célula f.

cellar /'sɛlər/ n. sótano m.

cellist /'tʃɛlist/ a. celista m. & f.

cello /'tʃɛlou/ n. violonchelo m.

cellophane /'sɛlə,fein/ n. celofán m.

cellular /'sɛlyələr/ a. celular.

cellular phone /foun/ teléfono móvil m.

celluloid /'sɛlyə,lɔid/ n. celuloide m.

cellulose /'sɛlyə,lous/ a. **1.** celuloso. —n. **2.** celulosa f.

Celtic /'kɛltik, 'sɛl-/ a. céltico.

cement /si'mɛnt/ n. cemento m.

cemetery /'sɛmi,tɛri/ n. cementerio m.; campo santo m.

censor /'sɛnsər/ n. censor -ra.

censorious /sɛn'sɔriəs/ a. severo; crítico.

censorship /'sɛnsər,ʃip/ n. censura f.

censure /'sɛnʃər/ n. **1.** censura f. —v. **2.** censurar.

census /'sɛnsəs/ n. censo m.

cent /sɛnt/ n. centavo, céntimo m.

centenary /sɛn'tɛnɛri/ a. & n. centenario m.

centennial /sɛn'tɛniəl/ a. & n. centenario m.

center /'sɛntər/ n. centro m.

centerfold /'sɛntər,fould/ n. página central desplegable en una revista.

centerpiece /'sɛntər,pis/ n. centro de mesa.

centigrade /'sɛnti,greid/ a. centígrado.

centigrade thermometer termómetro centígrado.

central /'sɛntrəl/ a. central.

Central American a. & n. centroamericano -na.

centralize /'sɛntrə,laiz/ v. centralizar.

century /'sɛntʃəri/ n. siglo m.

century plant maguey m.

ceramic /sə'ræmik/ a. cerámico.

ceramics /sə'ræmiks/ n. cerámica f.

cereal /'siəriəl/ n. cereal m.

cerebral /sə'ribrəl/ a. cerebral.

ceremonial /,sɛrə'mouniəl/ a. ceremonial.

ceremonious /,sɛrə'mouniəs/ a. ceremonioso.

ceremony /'sɛrə,mouni/ n. ceremonia f.

certain /'sɜrtn/ a. cierto, seguro.

certainly /'sɜrtnli/ adv. sin duda, seguramente.

certainty /'sɜrtnti/ n. certeza f.

certificate /sər'tifikit/ n. certificado m.

certification /,sɜrtəfi'keiʃən, sər,tifə-/ n. certificación f.

certified /'sɜrtə,faid/ a. certificado.

certify /'sɜrtə,fai/ v. certificar.

certitude /'sɜrti,tyud/ n. certeza f.

cessation /sɛ'seiʃən/ n. cesación, descontinuación f.

cession /'sɛʃən/ n. cesión f.

chafe /tʃeif/ v. irritar.

chafing dish /'tʃeifiŋ/ n. escalfador m.

chagrin /ʃə'grin/ n. disgusto m.

chain /tʃein/ n. **1.** cadena f. —v. **2.** encadenar.

chair /tʃɛər/ n. silla f.

chairman /'tʃɛərmən/ n. presidente -ta.

chairperson /'tʃɛər,pɜrsən/ n. presidente -ta; persona que preside.

chalk /tʃɔk/ n. tiza f.

challenge /'tʃælindʒ/ n. **1.** desafío m. —v. **2.** desafiar.

challenger /'tʃælindʒər/ n. desafiador -ra.

chamber /'tʃeimbər/ n. cámara f.

chamberlain /'tʃeimbərlin/ n. camarero m.

chambermaid /'tʃeimbər,meid/ n. camarera f.

chameleon /kə'miliən/ n. camaleón m.

chamois /'ʃæmi/ n. gamuza f.

champagne /ʃæm'pein/ n. champán m., champaña f.

champion /'tʃæmpiən/ n. **1.** campeón -na —v. **2.** defender.

championship /'tʃæmpiən,ʃip/ n. campeonato m.

chance /tʃæns/ *n.* oportunidad, ocasión *f.* **by c.,** por casualidad, por acaso. **take a c.,** aventurarse.
chancel /ˈtʃænsəl/ *n.* antealtar *m.*
chancellery /ˈtʃænsələri/ *n.* cancillería *f.*
chancellor /ˈtʃænsələr/ *n.* canciller *m.*
chandelier /ˌʃændlˈɪər/ *n.* araña de luces.
change /tʃeindʒ/ *n.* **1.** cambio; (from a bill) moneda *f.* **—***v.* **2.** cambiar.
changeability /ˌtʃeindʒəˈbɪlɪti/ *n.* mutabilidad *f.*
changeable /ˈtʃeindʒəbəl/ *a.* variable, inconstante.
changer /ˈtʃeindʒər/ *n.* cambiador -ra.
channel /ˈtʃænl̩/ *n.* **1.** canal *m.* **—***v.* **2.** encauzar.
Channel Tunnel túnel del Canal de la Mancha *m.*
chant /tʃænt/ *n.* **1.** canto llano *m.* **—***v.* **2.** cantar.
chaos /ˈkeiɒs/ *n.* caos *m.*
chaotic /keiˈɒtɪk/ *a.* caótico.
chap /tʃæp/ *n.* **1.** *Colloq.* tipo *m.* **—***v.* **2.** rajar.
chapel /ˈtʃæpəl/ *n.* capilla *f.*
chaperon /ˈʃæpəˌroun/ *n.* acompañante -ta de señorita.
chaplain /ˈtʃæplɪn/ *n.* capellán *m.*
chapter /ˈtʃæptər/ *n.* capítulo *m.*
char /tʃɑr/ *v.* carbonizar.
character /ˈkærɪktər/ *n.* carácter *m.*
characteristic /ˌkærɪktəˈrɪstɪk/ *a.* **1.** característico. **—***n.* **2.** característica *f.*
characterization /ˌkærɪktərəˈzeiʃən/ *n.* caracterización *f.*
characterize /ˈkærɪktəˌraiz/ *v.* caracterizar.
charcoal /ˈtʃɑrˌkoul/ *n.* carbón leña.
charge /tʃɑrdʒ/ *n.* **1.** acusación *f.*; ataque *m.* **—***v.* **2.** cargar; acusar; atacar.
chariot /ˈtʃæriət/ *n.* carroza *f.*
charisma /kəˈrɪzmə/ *n.* carisma *m.*
charitable /ˈtʃærɪtəbəl/ *a.* caritativo.
charitableness /ˈtʃærɪtəbəlnɪs/ *n.* caridad *f.*
charitably /ˈtʃærɪtəbli/ *adv.* caritativamente.
charity /ˈtʃærɪti/ *n.* caridad *f.*; (alms) limosna *f.*
charlatan /ˈʃɑrlətn̩/ *n.* charlatán -na.
charlatanism /ˈʃɑrlətn̩ˌɪzəm/ *n.* charlatanería *f.*
charm /tʃɑrm/ *n.* **1.** encanto *m.*; (witchcraft) hechizo *m.* **—***v.* **2.** encantar; hechizar.
charming /ˈtʃɑrmɪŋ/ *a.* encantador.
charred /tʃɑrd/ *a.* carbonizado.
chart /tʃɑrt/ *n.* tabla, esquema *f.*
charter /ˈtʃɑrtər/ *n.* **1.** carta *f.* **—***v.* **2.** alquilar.
charter flight vuelo chárter *m.*
charwoman /ˈtʃɑrˌwʊmən/ *n.* mujer de la limpieza *f.*
chase /tʃeis/ *n.* **1.** caza *f.* **—***v.* **2.** cazar; perseguir.
chaser /ˈtʃeisər/ *n.* perseguidor -ra.
chasm /ˈkæzəm/ *n.* abismo *m.*
chassis /ˈtʃæsi/ *n.* chasis *m.*
chaste /tʃeist/ *a.* casto.
chasten /ˈtʃeisən/ *v.* corregir, castigar.
chastise /tʃæsˈtaiz/ *v.* castigar.
chastisement /tʃæsˈtaizmənt/ *n.* castigo *m.*
chastity /ˈtʃæstɪti/ *n.* castidad, pureza *f.*
chat /tʃæt/ *n.* **1.** plática, charla *f.* **—***v.* **2.** platicar, charlar.
chateau /ʃæˈtou/ *n.* castillo *m.*
chattels /ˈtʃætəlz/ *n.pl.* bienes *m.*
chatter /ˈtʃætər/ *v.* **1.** cotorrear; (teeth) rechinar. **—***n.* **2.** cotorreo *m.*
chatterbox /ˈtʃætˌər bɒks/ *n.* charlador -ra.
chauffeur /ˈʃoufər/ *n.* chofer *m.*
cheap /tʃip/ *a.* barato.
cheapen /ˈtʃipən/ *v.* rebajar, menospreciar.
cheaply /ˈtʃipli/ *adv.* barato.
cheapness /ˈtʃipnɪs/ *n.* baratura *f.*
cheat /tʃit/ *v.* engañar.
cheater /ˈtʃitər/ *n.* engañador -ra.
check /tʃɛk/ *n.* **1.** verificación *f.*; (bank) cheque *m.*; (restaurant) cuenta *f.*; (chess) jaque *m.* **—***v.* **2.** verificar.
checkers /ˈtʃɛkərz/ *n.* juego de damas.
checkmate /ˈtʃɛkˌmeit/ *v.* dar mate.
checkout counter /ˈtʃɛkˌaut/ caja *f.*
cheek /tʃik/ *n.* mejilla *f.* (of face), desfachatez *f.* (gall).
cheekbone /ˈtʃikˌboun/ *n.* pómulo *m.*
cheeky /ˈtʃiki/ *a.* fresco, descarado, chulo.
cheer /tʃɪər/ *n.* **1.** alegría *f.*; aplauso *m.* **—***v.* **2.** alegrar; aplaudir.
cheerful /ˈtʃɪərfəl/ *a.* alegre.
cheerfully /ˈtʃɪərfəli/ *adv.* alegremente.
cheerfulness /ˈtʃɪərfəlnɪs/ *n.* alegría *f.*
cheerless /ˈtʃɪərlɪs/ *a.* triste.
cheery /ˈtʃɪəri/ *a.* alegre.
cheese /tʃiz/ *n.* queso *m.* **cottage c.,** requesón *m.*
chef /ʃɛf/ *n.* cocinero en jefe.
chemical /ˈkɛmɪkəl/ *a.* **1.** químico. **—***n.* **2.** reactivo *m.*
chemically /ˈkɛmɪkli/ *adv.* químicamente.
chemist /ˈkɛmɪst/ *n.* químico -ca.
chemistry /ˈkɛməstri/ *n.* química *f.*
chemotherapy /ˌkimouˈθɛrəpi/ *n.* quimioterapia *f.*
chenille /ʃəˈnil/ *n.* felpilla *f.*
cherish /ˈtʃɛrɪʃ/ *v.* apreciar.
cherry /ˈtʃɛri/ *n.* cereza *f.*
cherub /ˈtʃɛrəb/ *n.* querubín *m.*
chess /tʃɛs/ *n.* ajedrez *m.*
chest /tʃɛst/ *n.* arca *f.*; (physiology) pecho *m.*
chestnut /ˈtʃɛsˌnʌt/ *n.* castaña *f.*
chevron /ˈʃɛvrən/ *n.* sardineta *f.*
chew /tʃu/ *v.* mascar, masticar.
chewer /ˈtʃuər/ *n.* mascador -ra.
chic /ʃik/ *a.* elegante, paquete.
chicanery /ʃɪˈkeinəri/ *n.* trampería *f.*
chick /tʃɪk/ *n.* pollito -ta.
chicken /ˈtʃɪkən/ *n.* pollo *m.*, gallina *f.*
chicken-hearted /ˈtʃɪkən ˈhɑrtɪd/ *a.* cobarde.
chicken pox /pɒks/ viruelas locas, varicela *f.*
chicle /ˈtʃɪkəl/ *n.* chicle *m.*
chicory /ˈtʃɪkəri/ *n.* achicoria *f.*
chide /tʃaid/ *v.* regañar, reprender.
chief /tʃif/ *a.* **1.** principal. **—***n.* **2.** jefe -fa.
chiefly /ˈtʃifli/ *adv.* principalmente, mayormente.
chieftain /ˈtʃiftən/ *n.* caudillo *m.*; (Indian c.) cacique *m.*
chiffon /ʃɪˈfɒn/ *n.* chifón *m.*, gasa *f.*
chilblain /ˈtʃɪlblein/ *n.* sabañón *m.*
child /tʃaild/ *n.* niño -ña; hijo -ja.
childbirth /ˈtʃaildˌbɜrθ/ *n.* parto *m.*
childhood /ˈtʃaildhʊd/ *n.* niñez *f.*
childish /ˈtʃaildɪʃ/ *a.* pueril.
childishness /ˈtʃaildɪʃnɪs/ *n.* puerilidad *f.*
childless /ˈtʃaildlɪs/ *a.* sin hijos.
childlike /ˈtʃaildˌlaik/ *a.* infantil.
Chilean /ˈtʃɪliən/ *a.* & *n.* chileno -na.
chili /ˈtʃɪli/ *n.* chile, ají *m.*
chill /tʃɪl/ *n.* **1.** frío; escalofrío *m.* **—***v.* **2.** enfriar.
chilliness /ˈtʃɪlinɪs/ *n.* frialdad *f.*
chilly /ˈtʃɪli/ *a.* frío; friolento.
chimes /tʃaimz/ *n.* juego de campanas.
chimney /ˈtʃɪmni/ *n.* chimenea *f.*
chimpanzee /ˌtʃɪmpænˈzi, tʃɪmˈpænzi/ *n.* chimpancé *m.*
chin /tʃɪn/ *n.* barba *f.*
china /ˈtʃainə/ *n.* loza *f.*
chinchilla /tʃɪnˈtʃɪlə/ *n.* chinchilla *f.*
Chinese /tʃaiˈniz/ *a.* & *n.* chino -na.
chink /tʃɪŋk/ *n.* grieta *f.*
chintz /tʃɪnts/ *n.* zaraza *f.*
chip /tʃɪp/ *n.* **1.** astilla *f.* **—***v.* **2.** astillar.
chiropodist /kɪˈrɒpədɪst/ *n.* pedicuro -ra.
chiropractor /ˈkairəˌpræktər/ *n.* quiropráctico -ca.
chirp /tʃɜrp/ *n.* **1.** chirrido *m.* **—***v.* **2.** chirriar, piar.
chisel /ˈtʃɪzəl/ *n.* **1.** cincel *m.* **—***v.* **2.** cincelar, talar.
chivalrous /ˈʃɪvəlrəs/ *a.* caballeroso.
chivalry /ˈʃɪvəlri/ *n.* caballería *f.*
chive /tʃaiv/ *n.* cebollino *m.*
chloride /ˈklɔraid/ *n.* cloruro *m.*
chlorine /ˈklɔrin/ *n.* cloro *m.*
chloroform /ˈklɔrəˌfɔrm/ *n.* cloroformo *m.*
chlorophyll /ˈklɔrəfɪl/ *n.* clorofila *f.*
chock-full /ˈtʃɒkˈfʊl/ *a.* repleto, colmado.
chocolate /ˈtʃɔkəlɪt/ *n.* chocolate *m.*
choice /tʃɔis/ *a.* **1.** selecto, escogido. **—***n.* **2.** selección *f.*; escogimiento *m.*
choir /kwaiᵊr/ *n.* coro *m.*
choke /tʃouk/ *v.* sofocar, ahogar.
cholera /ˈkɒlərə/ *n.* cólera *f.*
choleric /ˈkɒlərɪk/ *a.* colérico, irascible.
cholesterol /kəˈlɛstəˌroul/ *n.* colesterol *m.*
choose /tʃuz/ *v.* elegir, escoger.
chop /tʃɒp/ *n.* **1.** chuleta, costilla *f.* **—***v.* **2.** tajar; cortar.
chopper /ˈtʃɒpər/ *n.* tajador -ra.
choppy /ˈtʃɒpi/ *a.* agitado.
choral /ˈkɔrəl/ *a.* coral.
chord /kɔrd/ *n.* cuerda *f.*; acorde *m.*
chore /tʃɔr/ *n.* tarea *f.*, quehacer *m.*
choreography /ˌkɔriˈɒgrəfi, ˌkour-/ *n.* coreografía *f.*
chorister /ˈkɔrəstər/ *n.* corista *m.*
chorus /ˈkɔrəs/ *n.* coro *m.*
christen /ˈkrɪsən/ *v.* bautizar.
Christendom /ˈkrɪsəndəm/ *n.* cristiandad *f.*
Christian /ˈkrɪsʃən/ *a.* & *n.* cristiano -na.
Christianity /ˌkrɪsʃiˈænɪti/ *n.* cristianismo *m.*
Christmas /ˈkrɪsməs/ *n.* Navidad, Pascua *f.* **Merry C.,** felices Pascuas. **C. Eve,** Nochebuena *f.*
chromatic /krouˈmætɪk/ *a.* cromático.
chromium /ˈkroumiəm/ *n.* cromo *m.*
chromosome /ˈkrouməˌsoum/ *n.* cromosoma *m.*
chronic /ˈkrɒnɪk/ *a.* crónico.
chronicle /ˈkrɒnɪkəl/ *n.* crónica *f.*
chronological /ˌkrɒnl̩ˈɒdʒɪkəl/ *a.* cronológico.
chronology /krəˈnɒlədʒi/ *n.* cronología *f.*
chrysalis /ˈkrɪsəlɪs/ *n.* crisálida *f.*
chrysanthemum /krɪˈsænθəməm/ *n.* crisantemo *m.*
chubby /ˈtʃʌbi/ *a.* regordete, rollizo.
chuck /tʃʌk/ *v.* (cluck) cloquear; (throw) echar, tirar.
chuckle /ˈtʃʌkəl/ *v.* reír entre dientes.
chum /tʃʌm/ *n.* amigo -ga; compinche *m.*
chummy /ˈtʃʌmi/ *a.* íntimo.
chunk /tʃʌŋk/ *n.* trozo *m.*
chunky /ˈtʃʌŋki/ *a.* fornido, trabado.
Chunnel /ˈtʃʌnl̩/ *n.* túnel del Canal de la Mancha *m.*
church /tʃɜrtʃ/ *n.* iglesia *f.*
churchman /ˈtʃɜrtʃmən/ *n.* eclesiástico *m.*
churchyard /ˈtʃɜrtʃˌyɑrd/ *n.* cementerio *m.*
churn /tʃɜrn/ *n.* **1.** mantequera *f.* **—***v.* **2.** agitar, revolver.
chute /ʃut/ *n.* conducto; canal *m.*
cicada /sɪˈkeidə/ *n.* cigarra, chicharra *f.*
cider /ˈsaidər/ *n.* sidra *f.*
cigar /sɪˈgɑr/ *n.* cigarro, puro *m.*
cigarette /ˌsɪgəˈrɛt/ *n.* cigarrillo, cigarro, pitillo *m.* **c. case,** cigarrillera *f.* **c. lighter,** encendedor *m.*
cinchona /sɪŋˈkounə/ *n.* cinchona *f.*
cinder /ˈsɪndər/ *n.* ceniza *f.*
cinema /ˈsɪnəmə/ *n.* cine *m.*
cinnamon /ˈsɪnəmən/ *n.* canela *f.*
cipher /ˈsaifər/ *n.* cifra *f.*
circle /ˈsɜrkəl/ *n.* círculo *m.*
circuit /ˈsɜrkɪt/ *n.* circuito *m.*
circuitous /sərˈkyuɪtəs/ *a.* tortuoso.
circuitously /sərˈkyuɪtəsli/ *adv.* tortuosamente.
circular /ˈsɜrkyələr/ *a.* circular, redondo.
circularize /ˈsɜrkyələˌraiz/ *v.* hacer circular.
circulate /ˈsɜrkyəˌleit/ *v.* circular.
circulation /ˌsɜrkyəˈleiʃən/ *n.* circulación *f.*
circulator /ˈsɜrkyəˌleitər/ *n.* diseminador -ra.
circulatory /ˈsɜrkyələˌtɔri/ *a.* circulatorio.
circumcise /ˈsɜrkəmˌsaiz/ *v.* circuncidar.
circumcision /ˌsɜrkəmˈsɪʒən/ *n.* circuncisión *f.*
circumference /sərˈkʌmfərəns/ *n.* circunferencia *f.*
circumlocution /ˌsɜrkəmlouˈkyuʃən/ *n.* circunlocución *f.*
circumscribe /ˈsɜrkəmˌskraib/ *v.* circunscribir; limitar.
circumspect /ˈsɜrkəmˌspɛkt/ *a.* discreto.
circumstance /ˈsɜrkəmˌstæns/ *n.* circunstancia *f.*
circumstantial /ˌsɜrkəmˈstænʃəl/ *a.* circunstancial, indirecto.
circumstantially /ˌsɜrkəmˈstænʃəli/ *adv.* minuciosamente.
circumvent /ˌsɜrkəmˈvɛnt/ *v.* evadir, evitar.
circumvention /ˌsɜrkəmˈvɛnʃən/ *n.* trampa *f.*
circus /ˈsɜrkəs/ *n.* circo *m.*
cirrhosis /sɪˈrousɪs/ *n.* cirrosis *f.*
cistern /ˈsɪstərn/ *n.* cisterna *f.*
citadel /ˈsɪtədl̩/ *n.* ciudadela *f.*
citation /saiˈteiʃən/ *n.* citación *f.*
cite /sait/ *v.* citar.
citizen /ˈsɪtəzən/ *n.* ciudadano -na.
citizenship /ˈsɪtəzənˌʃɪp/ *n.* ciudadanía *f.*
citric /ˈsɪtrɪk/ *a.* cítrico.
city /ˈsɪti/ *n.* ciudad *f.*
city hall ayuntamiento, municipio *m.*
city planning urbanismo *m.*
civic /ˈsɪvɪk/ *a.* cívico.
civics /ˈsɪvɪks/ *n.* ciencia del gobierno civil.
civil /ˈsɪvəl/ *a.* civil; cortés.
civilian /sɪˈvɪlyən/ *a.* & *n.* civil *m.* & *f.*
civility /sɪˈvɪlɪti/ *n.* cortesía *f.*
civilization /ˌsɪvələˈzeiʃən/ *n.* civilización *f.*
civilize /ˈsɪvəˌlaiz/ *v.* civilizar.
civil rights /raits/ derechos civiles *m. pl.*
civil service *n.* servicio civil oficial *m.*
civil war *n.* guerra civil *f.*
clabber /ˈklæbər/ *n.* **1.** cuajo *m.* **—***v.* **2.** cuajarse.
clad /klæd/ *a.* vestido.
claim /kleim/ *n.* **1.** demanda; pretensión *f.* **—***v.* **2.** demandar, reclamar.
claimant /ˈkleimənt/ *n.* reclamante -ta.
clairvoyance /klɛərˈvɔiəns/ *n.* clarividencia *f.*
clairvoyant /klɛərˈvɔiənt/ *a.* clarividente.
clam /klæm/ *n.* almeja *f.*
clamber /ˈklæmbər/ *v.* trepar.
clamor /ˈklæmər/ *n.* **1.** clamor *m.* **—***v.* **2.** clamar.
clamorous /ˈklæmərəs/ *a.* clamoroso.
clamp /klæmp/ *n.* **1.** prensa de sujeción *f.* **—***v.* **2.** asegurar, sujetar.
clan /klæn/ *n.* tribu *f.*, clan *m.*
clandestine /klænˈdɛstɪn/ *a.* clandestino.
clandestinely /klænˈdɛstɪnli/ *adv.* clandestinamente.
clangor /ˈklæŋər, ˈklæŋgər/ *n.* estruendo *m.*, estrépito *m.*

clannish /'klænɪʃ/ a. unido; exclusivista.

clap /klæp/ v. aplaudir.

clapboard /'klæbərd, 'klæp,bɔrd/ n. chilla f.

claque /klæk/ n. claque f.

claret /'klærɪt/ n. clarete m.

clarification /,klærəfə'keiʃən/ n. clarificación f.

clarify /'klærə,fai/ v. clarificar.

clarinet /,klærə'nɛt/ n. clarinete m.

clarinetist /,klærə'nɛtɪst/ n. clarinetista m. & f.

clarity /'klærɪti/ n. claridad f.

clash /klæʃ/ n. 1. choque, enfrentamiento m. —v. 2. chocar.

clasp /klæsp/ n. 1. broche m. —v. 2. abrochar.

class /klæs/ n. clase f.

classic, /'klæsɪk/ **classical** a. clásico.

classicism /'klæsə,sɪzəm/ n. clasicismo m.

classifiable /'klæsə,faiəbəl/ a. clasificable, calificable.

classification /,klæsəfɪ'keiʃən/ n. clasificación f.

classify /'klæsə,fai/ v. clasificar.

classmate /'klæs,meit/ n. compañero -ra de clase.

classroom /'klæs,rum, -,rʊm/ n. sala de clase.

clatter /'klætər/ n. 1. alboroto m. —v. 2. alborotar.

clause /klɔz/ n. cláusula f.

claustrophobia /,klɔstrə'foubiə/ n. claustrofobia f.

claw /klɔ/ n. garra f.

clay /klei/ n. arcilla f.; barro m.

clean /klin/ a. 1. limpio. —v. 2. limpiar.

cleaner /'klinər/ n. limpiador -ra.

cleaning lady, cleaning woman /'klinɪŋ/ señora de la limpieza, mujer de la limpieza f.

cleanliness /'klɛnlinɪs/ n. limpieza f.

cleanse /klɛnz/ v. limpiar, purificar.

cleanser /'klɛnzər/ n. limpiador m., purificador m.

clear /klɪər/ a. claro.

clearance /'klɪərəns/ n. espacio libre. **c. sale,** venta de liquidación.

clearing /'klɪərɪŋ/ n. despejo m.; desmonte m.

clearly /'klɪərli/ adv. claramente, evidentemente.

clearness /'klɪərnɪs/ n. claridad f.

cleavage /'klividʒ/ n. resquebradura f.

cleaver /'klivər/ n. partidor m., hacha f.

clef /klɛf/ n. clave, llave f.

clemency /'klɛmənsi/ n. clemencia f.

clench /klɛntʃ/ v. agarrar.

clergy /'klɜrdʒi/ n. clero m.

clergyman /'klɜrdʒimən/ n. clérigo m.

clerical /'klɛrɪkəl/ a. clerical. **c. work,** trabajo de oficina.

clericalism /'klɛrɪkə,lɪzəm/ n. clericalismo m.

clerk /klɜrk/ n. dependiente, escribiente m.

clerkship /'klɜrkʃɪp/ n. escribanía f., secretaría f.

clever /'klɛvər/ a. diestro, hábil.

cleverly /'klɛvərli/ adv. diestramente, hábilmente.

cleverness /'klɛvərnɪs/ n. destreza f.

cliché /kli'ʃei/ n. tópico m.

client /'klaiənt/ n. cliente -ta.

clientele /,klaiən'tɛl/ n. clientela f.

cliff /klɪf/ n. precipicio, risco m.

climate /'klaimɪt/ n. clima m.

climatic /klai'mætɪk/ a. climático.

climax /'klaimæks/ n. colmo m., culminación f.

climb /klaim/ v. escalar; subir.

climber /'klaimər/ n. trepador -ra, escalador -ra; Bot. enredadera f.

climbing plant /'klaimɪŋ/ enredadera f.

clinch /klɪntʃ/ v. afirmar.

cling /klɪŋ/ v. pegarse.

clinic /'klɪnɪk/ n. clínica f.

clinical /'klɪnɪkəl/ a. clínico.

clinically /'klɪnɪkəli/ adv. clínicamente.

clip /klɪp/ n. 1. grapa f. **paper c.,** gancho m. —v. 2. prender; (shear) trasquilar.

clipper /'klɪpər/ n. recortador m.; Aero. clíper m.

clipping /'klɪpɪŋ/ n. recorte m.

clique /klik/ n. camarilla f., compadraje m.

cloak /klouk/ n. capa f., manto m.

clock /klɒk/ n. reloj m. **alarm c.,** despertador m.

clod /klɒd/ n. terrón m.; césped m.

clog /klɒg/ v. obstruir.

cloister /'klɔistər/ n. claustro m.

clone /kloun/ n. clon m. & f. v. clonar.

close /a, adv. klous; v klouz/ a. 1. cercano. —adv. 2. cerca. **c. to,** cerca de. —v. 3. cerrar; tapar.

closely /'klousli/ adv. (near) de cerca; (tight) estrechamente; (care) cuidadosamente.

closeness /'klousnɪs/ n. contigüidad f., apretamiento m.; (airless) falta de ventilación f.

closet /'klɒzɪt/ n. gabinete m. **clothes c.,** ropero m.

clot /klɒt/ n. 1. coágulo f. —v. 2. coagularse.

cloth /klɔθ/ n. paño m.; tela f.

clothe /klouð/ v. vestir.

clothes /klouz/ n. ropa f.

clothing /'klouðɪŋ/ n. vestidos m., ropa f.

cloud /klaud/ n. nube f.

cloudburst /'klaud,bɔrst/ n. chaparrón m.

cloudiness /'klaudinɪs/ n. nebulosidad f.; obscuridad f.

cloudless /'klaudlɪs/ a. despejado, sin nubes.

cloudy /'klaudi/ a. nublado.

clove /klouv/ n. clavo m.

clover /'klouvər/ n. trébol m.

clown /klaun/ n. bufón -na, payaso -sa.

clownish /'klaunɪʃ/ a. grosero; bufonesco.

cloy /klɔi/ v. saciar, empalagar.

club /klʌb/ n. 1. porra f.; (social) círculo, club m.; (cards) basto m. —v. 2. golpear con una porra.

clubfoot /'klʌb,fʊt/ n. pateta m., pie zambo m.

clue /klu/ n. seña, pista f.

clump /klʌmp/ n. grupo m., masa f.

clumsiness /'klʌmzinɪs/ n. tosquedad f.; desmaña f.

clumsy /'klʌmzi/ a. torpe, desmañado.

cluster /'klʌstər/ n. 1. grupo m.; (fruit) racimo m. —v. 2. agrupar.

clutch /klʌtʃ/ n. 1. Auto. embrague m. —v. 2. agarrar.

clutter /'klʌtər/ n. 1. confusión f. —v. 2. poner en desorden.

coach /koutʃ/ n. 1. coche, vagón m.; coche ordinario; (sports) entrenador m. —v. 2. entrenar.

coachman /'koutʃmən/ n. cochero -ra.

coagulate /kou'ægyə,leit/ v. coagular.

coagulation /kou,ægyə'leiʃən/ n. coagulación f.

coal /koul/ n. carbón m.

coalesce /,kouə'lɛs/ v. unirse, soldarse.

coalition /,kouə'lɪʃən/ n. coalición f.

coal oil n. petróleo m.

coal tar n. alquitrán m.

coarse /kɔrs/ a. grosero, burdo; (material) tosco, grueso.

coarsen /'kɔrsən/ v. vulgarizar.

coarseness /'kɔrsnɪs/ n. grosería; tosquedad f.

coast /koust/ n. 1. costa f., litoral m. —v. 2. deslizarse.

coastal /'koustl/ a. costanero.

coast guard guardacostas m. & f.

coat /kout/ n. 1. saco m., chaqueta f.; (paint) capa f. —v. 2. cubrir.

coat of arms /ɑrmz/ n. escudo m.

coax /kouks/ v. instar.

cobalt /'koubɔlt/ n. cobalto m.

cobbler /'kɒblər/ n. zapatero -ra.

cobblestone /'kɒbəl,stoun/ n. guijarro m.

cobra /'koubrə/ n. cobra f.

cobweb /'kɒb,wɛb/ n. telaraña f.

cocaine /kou'kein/ n. cocaína f.

cock /kɒk/ n. (rooster) gallo m.; (water, etc.) llave f.; (gun) martillo m.

cockfight /'kɒk,fait/ n. riña de gallos f.

cockpit /'kɒk,pɪt/ n. gallera f.; reñidero de gallos m.; Aero. cabina f.

cockroach /'kɒk,routʃ/ n. cucaracha f.

cocktail /'kɒk,teil/ n. cóctel m.

cocky /'kɒki/ a. confiado, atrevido.

cocoa /'koukou/ n. cacao m.

coconut /'koukə,nʌt/ n. coco m.

cocoon /kə'kun/ n. capullo m.

cod /kɒd/ n. bacalao m.

code /koud/ n. código m.; clave f.

codeine /'koudin/ n. codeína f.

codfish /'kɒd,fɪʃ/ n. bacalao m.

codify /'kɒdə,fai/ v. compilar.

cod-liver oil /'kɒd 'lɪvər/ aceite de hígado de bacalao m.

coeducation /,kouɛdʒu'keiʃən/ n. coeducación f.

coequal /kou'ikwəl/ a. mutuamente igual.

coerce /kou'ɔrs/ v. forzar.

coercion /kou'ɔrʃən/ n. coerción f.

coercive /kou'ɔrsɪv/ a. coercitivo.

coexist /,kouɪg'zɪst/ v. coexistir.

coffee /'kɔfi/ n. café m. **c. plantation,** cafetal m. **c. shop,** café m.

coffee break pausa para el café f.

coffer /'kɔfər/ n. cofre m.

coffin /'kɔfin/ n. ataúd m.

cog /kɒg/ n. diente de rueda m.

cogent /'koudʒənt/ a. convincente.

cogitate /'kɒdʒɪ,teit/ v. pensar, reflexionar.

cognizance /'kɒgnəzəns/ n. conocimiento m., comprensión f.

cognizant /'kɒgnəzənt/ a. conocedor, informado.

cogwheel /'kɒg,wil/ n. rueda dentada f.

cohere /kou'hɪər/ v. pegarse.

coherent /kou'hɪərənt/ a. coherente.

cohesion /kou'hiʒən/ n. cohesión f.

cohesive /kou'hisɪv/ a. cohesivo.

cohort /'kouhɔrt/ n. cohorte f.

coiffure /kwa'fyur/ n. peinado, tocado m.

coil /kɔil/ n. 1. rollo m.; Naut. adujada f. —v. 2. enrollar.

coin /kɔin/ n. moneda f.

coinage /'kɔinidʒ/ n. sistema monetario m.

coincide /,kouɪn'said/ v. coincidir.

coincidence /kou'ɪnsidəns/ n. coincidencia; casualidad f.

coincident /kou'ɪnsidənt/ a. coincidente.

coincidental /kou,ɪnsi'dɛntl/ a. coincidental.

coincidentally /kou,ɪnsi'dɛntli/ adv. coincidentalmente, al mismo tiempo.

colander /'kɒləndər/ n. colador m.

cold /kould/ a. & n. frío m.; Med. resfriado m. **to be c.,** tener frío; (weather) hacer frío.

coldly /'kouldli/ adv. fríamente.

coldness /'kouldnɪs/ n. frialdad f.

collaborate /kə'læbə,reit/ v. colaborar.

collaboration /kə,læbə'reiʃən/ n. colaboración f.

collaborator /kə'læbə,reitər/ n. colaborador -ra.

collapse /kə'læps/ n. 1. desplome m.; Med. colapso m. —v. 2. desplomarse.

collar /'kɒlər/ n. cuello m.

collarbone /'kɒlər,boun/ n. clavícula f.

collate /kou'leit/ v. comparar.

collateral /kə'lætərəl/ a. 1. colateral. —n. 2. garantía f.

collation /kə'leiʃən/ n. comparación f.; (food) colación f., merienda f.

colleague /'kɒlig/ n. colega m. & f.

collect /kə'lɛkt/ v. cobrar; recoger; coleccionar.

collection /kə'lɛkʃən/ n. colección f.

collective /kə'lɛktɪv/ a. colectivo.

collectively /kə'lɛktɪvli/ adv. colectivamente, en masa.

collector /kə'lɛktər/ n. colector -ra; coleccionista m. & f.

college /'kɒlidʒ/ n. colegio m.; universidad f.

collegiate /kə'lidʒɪt/ n. colegiado m.

collide /kə'laid/ v. chocar.

collision /kə'lɪʒən/ n. choque m.

colloquial /kə'loukwiəl/ a. familiar.

colloquially /kə'loukwiəli/ adv. familiarmente.

colloquy /'kɒləkwi/ n. conversación f., coloquio m.

collusion /kə'luʒən/ n. colusión f., connivencia f.

Cologne /kə'loun/ n. Colonia f.

Colombian /kə'lʌmbiən/ a. & n. colombiano -na.

colon /'koulən/ n. colon m.; Punct. dos puntos m.

colonel /'kɜrnl/ n. coronel m.

colonial /kə'louniəl/ a. colonial.

colonist /'kɒlənɪst/ n. colono -na.

colonization /,kɒlənə'zeiʃən/ n. colonización f.

colonize /'kɒlə,naiz/ v. colonizar.

colony /'kɒləni/ n. colonia f.

color /'kʌlər/ n. 1. color; colorido m. —v. 2. colorar; colorir.

coloration /,kʌlə'reiʃən/ n. colorido m.

colored /'kʌlərd/ a. de color.

colorful /'kʌlərfəl/ a. vívido.

colorless /'kʌlərlɪs/ a. descolorido, sin color.

colossal /kə'lɒsəl/ a. colosal.

colt /koult/ n. potro m.

column /'kɒləm/ n. columna f.

coma /'koumə/ n. coma m.

comb /koum/ n. 1. peine m. —v. 2. peinar.

combat /n 'kɒmbæt; v kəm'bæt/ n. 1. combate m. —v. 2. combatir.

combatant /kəm'bætnt/ n. combatiente -ta.

combative /kəm'bætɪv/ a. combativo.

combination /,kɒmbə'neiʃən/ n. combinación f.

combine /kəm'bain/ v. combinar.

combustible /kəm'bʌstəbəl/ a. & n. combustible m.

combustion /kəm'bʌstʃən/ n. combustión f.

come /kʌm/ v. venir. **c. back,** volver. **c. in,** entrar. **c. out,** salir. **c. up,** subir. **c. upon,** encontrarse con.

comedian /kə'midiən/ n. cómico -ca.

comedienne /kə,midi'ɛn/ n. cómica f., actriz f.

comedy /'kɒmidi/ n. comedia f.

comet /'kɒmɪt/ n. cometa m.

comfort /'kʌmfərt/ n. 1. confort m.; solaz m. —v. 2. confortar; solazar.

comfortable /'kʌmftəbəl/ a. cómodo.

comfortably /'kʌmftəbli/ adv. cómodamente.

comforter /'kʌmfərtər/ n. colcha f.

comfortingly /'kʌmfərtɪŋli/ adv. confortantemente.

comfortless /'kɒmfərtlɪs/ a. sin consuelo; sin comodidades.

comic /'kɒmɪk/ **comical** a. cómico.

comic book n. tebeo m.

coming /'kʌmɪŋ/ n. 1. venida f., llegada f. —a. 2. próximo, que viene, entrante.

comma /'kɒmə/ n. coma f.

command /kə'mænd/ n. 1. mando m. —v. 2. mandar.

commandeer /,kɒmən'dɪər/ v. reclutir forzosamente, expropiar.

commander /kə'mændər/ *n.* comandante -ta.

commander in chief *n.* generalísimo, jefe supremo.

commandment /kə'mændmənt/ *n.* mandato; mandamiento *m.*

commemorate /kə'mɛmə,reit/ *v.* conmemorar.

commemoration /kə,mɛmə'reiʃən/ *n.* conmemoración *f.*

commemorative /kə'mɛmə,reitiv/ *a.* conmemorativo.

commence /kə'mɛns/ *v.* comenzar, principiar.

commencement /kə'mɛnsmənt/ *n.* comienzo *m.*; graduación *f.*

commend /kə'mɛnd/ *v.* encomendar; elogiar.

commendable /kə'mɛndəbəl/ *a.* recomendable.

commendably /kə'mɛndəbli/ *adv.* loablemente.

commendation /,kɒmən'deiʃən/ *n.* recomendación *f.*; elogio *m.*

commensurate /kə'mɛnsərit/ *a.* proporcionado.

comment /'kɒmɛnt/ *n.* **1.** comentario *m.* —*v.* **2.** comentar.

commentary /'kɒmən,tɛri/ *n.* comentario *m.*

commentator /'kɒmən,teitər/ *n.* comentador -ra.

commerce /'kɒmərs/ *n.* comercio *m.*

commercial /kə'mɜrʃəl/ *a.* comercial.

commercialism /kə'mɜrʃə,lizəm/ *n.* comercialismo *m.*

commercialize /kə'mɜrʃə,laiz/ *v.* mercantilizar, explotar.

commercially /kə'mɜrʃəli/ *a.* & *adv.* comercialmente.

commiserate /kə'mizə,reit/ *v.* compadecerse.

commissary /'kɒmə,sɛri/ *n.* comisario *m.*

commission /kə'miʃən/ *n.* **1.** comisión *f.* —*v.* **2.** comisionar.

commissioner /kə'miʃənər/ *n.* comisario -ria.

commit /kə'mit/ *v.* cometer.

commitment /kə'mitmənt/ *n.* compromiso *m.*

committee /kə'miti/ *n.* comité *m.*

commodious /kə'moudiəs/ *a.* cómodo.

commodity /kə'mɒditi/ *n.* mercadería *f.*

common /'kɒmən/ *a.* común; ordinario.

commonly /'kɒmənli/ *adv.* comúnmente, vulgarmente.

Common Market Mercado Común *m.*

commonplace /'kɒmən,pleis/ *a.* trivial, banal.

common sense sentido común *m.*

commonwealth /'kɒmən,wɛlθ/ *n.* estado *m.*; nación *f.*

commotion /kə'mouʃən/ *n.* tumulto *m.*

communal /kə'myunḷ/ *a.* comunal, público.

commune /'kɒmyun/ *n.* **1.** distrito municipal *m.*; comuna *f.* —*v.* **2.** conversar.

communicable /kə'myunikəbəl/ *a.* comunicable; *Med.* transmisible.

communicate /kə'myuni,keit/ *v.* comunicar.

communication /kə,myuni'keiʃən/ *n.* comunicación *f.*

communicative /kə'myuni,keitiv/ *a.* comunicativo.

communion /kə'myunyən/ *n.* comunión *f.* **take c.,** comulgar.

communiqué /kə,myuni'kei/ *n.* comunicación *f.*

communism /'kɒmyə,nizəm/ *n.* comunismo *m.*

communist /'kɒmyənist/ *n.* comunista *m.* & *f.*

communistic /,kɒmyə'nistik/ *a.* comunístico.

community /kə'myuniti/ *n.* comunidad *f.*

commutation /,kɒmyə'teiʃən/ *n.* conmutación *f.*

commuter /kə'myutər/ *n.* empleado que viaja diariamente desde su domicilio hasta la ciudad donde trabaja.

compact /*a* kəm'pækt; *n* 'kɒmpækt/ *a.* **1.** compacto. —*n.* **2.** pacto *m.*; (lady's) polvera *f.*

compact disk disco compacto *m.*

companion /kəm'pænyən/ *n.* compañero -ra.

companionable /kəm'pænyənəbəl/ *a.* sociable.

companionship /kəm'pænyən,ʃip/ *n.* compañerismo *m.*

company /'kʌmpəni/ *n.* compañía *f.*

comparable /'kɒmpərəbəl/ *a.* comparable.

comparative /kəm'pærətiv/ *a.* comparativo.

comparatively /kəm'pærətivli/ *a.* relativamente.

compare /kəm'pɛər/ *v.* comparar.

comparison /kəm'pærəsən/ *n.* comparación *f.*

compartment /kəm'pɑrtmənt/ *n.* compartimiento *m.*

compass /'kʌmpəs/ *n.* compás *m.*; *Naut.* brújula *f.*

compassion /kəm'pæʃən/ *n.* compasión *f.*

compassionate /kəm'pæʃənit/ *a.* compasivo.

compassionately /kəm'pæʃənitli/ *adv.* compasivamente.

compatible /kəm'pætəbəl/ *a.* compatible.

compatriot /kəm'peitriət/ *n.* compatriota *m.* & *f.*

compel /kəm'pɛl/ *v.* obligar.

compensate /'kɒmpən,seit/ *v.* compensar.

compensation /,kɒmpən'seiʃən/ *n.* compensación *f.*

compensatory /kəm'pɛnsə,tɔri/ *a.* compensatorio.

compete /kəm'pit/ *v.* competir.

competence /'kɒmpitəns/ *n.* competencia *f.*

competent /'kɒmpitənt/ *a.* competente, capaz.

competently /'kɒmpitəntli/ *adv.* competentemente.

competition /,kɒmpi'tiʃən/ *n.* concurrencia *f.*; concurso *m.*

competitive /kəm'pɛtitiv/ *a.* competidor.

competitor /kəm'pɛtitər/ *n.* competidor -ra.

compile /kəm'pail/ *v.* compilar.

complacency /kəm'pleisənsi/ *n.* complacencia *f.*

complacent /kəm'pleisənt/ *a.* complaciente.

complacently /kəm'pleisəntli/ *adv.* complacientemente.

complain /kəm'plein/ *v.* quejarse.

complaint /kəm'pleint/ *n.* queja *f.*

complement /'kɒmpləmənt/ *n.* complemento *m.*

complete /kəm'plit/ *a.* **1.** completo —*v.* **2.** completar.

completely /kəm'plitli/ *adv.* completamente, enteramente.

completeness /kəm'plitnis/ *n.* integridad *f.*

completion /kəm'pliʃən/ *n.* terminación *f.*

complex /kəm'plɛks/ *a.* complejo.

complexion /kəm'plɛkʃən/ *n.* tez *f.*

complexity /kəm'plɛksiti/ *n.* complejidad *f.*

compliance /kəm'plaiəns/ *n.* consentimiento *m.* **in c. with,** de acuerdo con.

compliant /kəm'plaiənt/ *a.* dócil; complaciente.

complicate /'kɒmpli,keit/ *v.* complicar.

complicated /'kɒmpli,keitid/ *a.* complicado.

complication /,kɒmpli'keiʃən/ *n.* complicación *f.*

complicity /kəm'plisiti/ *n.* complicidad *f.*

compliment /*n* 'kɒmpləmənt; *v* -,mɛnt/ *n.* **1.** elogio *m.* *Fig.* —*v.* **2.** felicitar; echar flores.

complimentary /,kɒmplə'mɛntəri/ *a.* galante, obsequioso, regaloso.

comply /kəm'plai/ *v.* cumplir.

component /kəm'pounənt/ *a.* & *n.* componente *m.*

comport /kəm'pɔrt/ *v.* portarse.

compose /kəm'pouz/ *v.* componer.

composed /kəm'pouzd/ *a.* tranquilo; (made up) compuesto.

composer /kəm'pouzər/ *n.* compositor -ra.

composite /kəm'pɒzit/ *a.* compuesto.

composition /,kɒmpə'ziʃən/ *n.* composición *f.*

composure /kəm'pouʒər/ *n.* serenidad *f.*; calma *f.*

compote /'kɒmpout/ *n.* compota *f.*

compound /'kɒmpaund/ *a.* & *n.* compuesto *m.*

comprehend /,kɒmpri'hɛnd/ *v.* comprender.

comprehensible /,kɒmpri'hɛnsəbəl/ *a.* comprensible.

comprehension /,kɒmpri'hɛnʃən/ *n.* comprensión *f.*

comprehensive /,kɒmpri'hɛnsiv/ *a.* comprensivo.

compress /*n* 'kɒmprɛs; *v* kəm'prɛs/ *n.* **1.** cabezal *m.* —*v.* **2.** comprimir.

compressed /kəm'prɛst/ *a.* comprimido.

compression /kəm'prɛʃən/ *n.* compresión *f.*

compressor /kəm'prɛsər/ *n.* compresor *m.*

comprise /kəm'praiz/ *v.* comprender; abarcar.

compromise /'kɒmprə,maiz/ *n.* **1.** compromiso *m.* —*v.* **2.** comprometer.

compromiser /'kɒmprə,maizər/ *n.* compromisario *m.*

compulsion /kəm'pʌlʃən/ *n.* compulsión *f.*

compulsive /kəm'pʌlsiv/ *a.* compulsivo.

compulsory /kəm'pʌlsəri/ *a.* obligatorio.

compunction /kəm'pʌŋkʃən/ *n.* compunción *f.*; escrúpulo *m.*

computation /,kɒmpyu'teiʃən/ *n.* computación *f.*

compute /kəm'pyut/ *v.* computar, calcular.

computer /kəm'pyutər/ *n.* computadora *f.*, ordenador *m.*

computerize /kəm'pyutə,raiz/ *v.* procesar en computadora, computerizar.

computer programmer /'prougræmər/ programador -ra de ordenadores.

computer science informática *f.*

comrade /'kɒmræd/ *n.* camarada *m.* & *f.*; compañero -ra.

comradeship /'kɒmræd,ʃip/ *n.* camaradería *f.*

concave /kɒn'keiv/ *a.* cóncavo.

conceal /kən'sil/ *v.* ocultar, esconder.

concealment /kən'silmənt/ *n.* ocultación *f.*

concede /kən'sid/ *v.* conceder.

conceit /kən'sit/ *n.* amor propio; engreimiento *m.*

conceited /kən'sitid/ *a.* engreído.

conceivable /kən'sivəbəl/ *a.* concebible.

conceive /kən'siv/ *v.* concebir.

concentrate /'kɒnsən,treit/ *v.* concentrar.

concentration /,kɒnsən'treiʃən/ *n.* concentración *f.*

concentration camp campo de concentración *m.*

concept /'kɒnsɛpt/ *n.* concepto *m.*

conception /kən'sɛpʃən/ *n.* concepción *f.*; concepto *m.*

concern /kən'sɜrn/ *n.* **1.** interés *m.*; inquietud *f.*; *Com.* negocio *m.* —*v.* **2.** concernir.

concerning /kən'sɜrniŋ/ *prep.* respecto a.

concert /'kɒnsɜrt/ *n.* concierto *m.*

concerted /kən'sɜrtid/ *a.* convenido.

concession /kən'sɛʃən/ *n.* concesión *f.*

conciliate /kən'sili,eit/ *v.* conciliar.

conciliation /kən,sili'eiʃən/ *n.* conciliación *f.*

conciliator /kən'sili,eitər/ *n.* conciliador -ra.

conciliatory /kən'siliə,tɔri/ *a.* conciliatorio.

concise /kən'sais/ *a.* conciso.

concisely /kən'saisli/ *adv.* concisamente.

conciseness /kən'saisnis/ *n.* concisión *f.*

conclave /'kɒnkleiv/ *n.* conclave *m.*

conclude /kən'klud/ *v.* concluir.

conclusion /kən'kluʒən/ *n.* conclusión *f.*

conclusive /kən'klusiv/ *a.* conclusivo, decisivo.

conclusively /kən'klusivli/ *adv.* concluyentemente.

concoct /kɒn'kɒkt/ *v.* confeccionar.

concomitant /kɒn'kɒmitənt/ *n.* & *a.* concomitante *m.*

concord /'kɒnkɔrd/ *n.* concordia *f.*

concordat /kɒn'kɔrdæt/ *n.* concordato *m.*

concourse /'kɒnkɔrs/ *n.* concurso *m.*; confluencia *f.*

concrete /'kɒnkrit/ *a.* concreto.

concretely /kɒn'kritli/ *adv.* concretamente.

concubine /'kɒŋkyə,bain/ *n.* concubina, amiga *f.*

concur /kən'kɜr/ *v.* concurrir.

concurrence /kən'kɜrəns/ *n.* concurrencia *f.*; casualidad *f.*

concurrent /kən'kɜrənt/ *a.* concurrente.

concussion /kən'kʌʃən/ *n.* concusión *f.*; (c. of the brain) conmoción cerebral *f.*

condemn /kən'dɛm/ *v.* condenar.

condemnable /kən'dɛmnəbəl/ *a.* culpable, condenable.

condemnation /,kɒndɛm'neiʃən/ *n.* condenación *f.*

condensation /,kɒndɛn'seiʃən/ *n.* condensación *f.*

condense /kən'dɛns/ *v.* condensar.

condenser /kən'dɛnsər/ *n.* condensador *m.*

condescend /,kɒndə'sɛnd/ *v.* condescender.

condescension /,kɒndə'sɛnʃən/ *n.* condescendencia *f.*

condiment /'kɒndəmənt/ *n.* condimento *m.*

condition /kən'diʃən/ *n.* **1.** condición *f.*; estado *m.* —*v.* **2.** acondicionar.

conditional /kən'diʃənḷ/ *a.* condicional.

conditionally /kən'diʃənḷi/ *adv.* condicionalmente.

condole /kən'doul/ *v.* condolerse.

condolence /kən'douləns/ *n.* pésame *m.*

condom /'kɒndəm/ *n.* forro, preservativo *m.*

condominium /,kɒndə'miniəm/ *n.* condominio *m.*

condone /kən'doun/ *v.* condonar.

conducive /kən'dusiv, -'dyu-/ *a.* conducente.

conduct /*n* 'kɒndʌkt; *v* kən'dʌkt/ *n.* **1.** conducta *f.* —*v.* **2.** conducir.

conductivity /,kɒndʌk'tiviti/ *n.* conductividad *f.*

conductor /kən'dʌktər/ *n.* conductor *m.*

conduit /'kɒnduit/ *n.* caño *m.*, canal *f.*; conducto *m.*

cone /koun/ *n.* cono *m.* **ice-cream c.,** barquillo de helado.

confection /kən'fɛkʃən/ *n.* confitura *f.*

confectioner /kən'fɛkʃənər/ *n.* confitero -ra.

confectionery /kən'fɛkʃə,nɛri/ n. dulcería f.

confederacy /kən'fɛdərəsi/ n. federación f.

confederate / kən'fɛdərɪt/ a. & n. confederado m.

confederation /kən,fɛdə'reiʃən/ n. confederación f.

confer /kən'fɜr/ v. conferenciar; conferir.

conference /'kɒnfərəns/ n. conferencia f.; congreso m.

confess /kən'fɛs/ v. confesar.

confession /kən'fɛʃən/ n. confesión f.

confessional /kən'fɛʃənl/ n. **1.** confesionario m. —a. **2.** confesional.

confessor /kən'fɛsər/ n. confesor m.

confetti /kən'fɛti/ n. confetti m.

confidant /'kɒnfɪ,dænt/ **confidante** n. confidente m. & f.

confide /kən'faid/ v. confiar.

confidence /'kɒnfɪdəns/ n. confianza f.

confident /'kɒnfɪdənt/ a. confiado; cierto.

confidential /,kɒnfɪ'dɛnʃəl/ a. confidencial.

confidentially /,kɒnfɪ'dɛnʃəli/ adv. confidencialmente, en secreto.

confidently /'kɒnfɪdəntli/ adv. confiadamente.

confine /kən'fain/ n. **1.** confín m. —v. **2.** confinar; encerrar.

confirm /kən'fɜrm/ v. confirmar.

confirmation /,kɒnfər'meiʃən/ n. confirmación f.

confiscate /'kɒnfə,skeit/ v. confiscar.

confiscation /,kɒnfə'skeiʃən/ n. confiscación f.

conflagration /,kɒnflə'greiʃən/ n. incendio m.

conflict /n 'kɒnflɪkt; v kən'flɪkt/ n. **1.** conflicto m. —v. **2.** oponerse; estar en conflicto.

conform /kən'fɔrm/ v. conformar.

conformation /,kɒnfɔr'meiʃən/ n. conformación f.

conformer /kən'fɔrmər/ n. conformista m. & f.

conformist /kən'fɔrmɪst/ n. conformista m. & f.

conformity /kən'fɔrmɪti/ n. conformidad f.

confound /kɒn'faund/ v. confundir.

confront /kən'frʌnt/ v. confrontar.

confrontation /,kɒnfrən'teiʃən/ n. enfrentamiento m.

confuse /kən'fyuz/ v. confundir.

confusion /kən'fyuʒən/ n. confusión f.

congeal /kən'dʒil/ v. congelar, helar.

congealment /kən'dʒilmənt/ n. congelación f.

congenial /kən'dʒinyəl/ a. congenial.

congenital /kən'dʒɛnɪtl/ a. congénito.

congenitally /kən'dʒɛnɪtli/ adv. congenitalmente.

congestion /kən'dʒɛstʃən/ n. congestión f.

conglomerate /v kən'glɒmə,reit; a, n kən'glɒmərɪt/ v. **1.** conglomerar. —a. & n. **2.** conglomerado.

conglomeration /kən,glɒmə'reiʃən/ n. conglomeración f.

congratulate /kən'grætʃə,leit/ v. felicitar.

congratulation /kən,grætʃə'leiʃən/ n. felicitación f.

congratulatory /kən'grætʃələ,tɔri/ a. congratulatorio.

congregate /'kɒŋgrɪ,geit/ v. congregar.

congregation /,kɒŋgrɪ'geiʃən/ n. congregación f.

congress /'kɒŋgrɪs/ n. congreso m.

conic /'kɒnɪk/ n. **1.** cónica f. —a. **2.** cónico.

conjecture /kən'dʒɛktʃər/ n. **1.** conjetura f. —v. **2.** conjeturar.

conjugal /'kɒndʒəgəl/ a. conyugal, matrimonial.

conjugate /'kɒndʒə,geit/ v. conjugar.

conjugation /,kɒndʒə'geiʃən/ n. conjugación f.

conjunction /kən'dʒʌŋkʃən/ n. conjunción f.

conjunctive /kən'dʒʌŋktɪv/ n. **1.** Gram. conjunción f. —a. **2.** conjuntivo.

conjunctivitis /kən,dʒʌŋktə'vaitɪs/ n. conjuntivitis f.

conjure /'kɒndʒər/ v. conjurar.

connect /kə'nɛkt/ v. juntar; relacionar.

connection /kə'nɛkʃən/ n. conexión f.

connivance /kə'naivəns/ n. consentimiento m.

connive /kə'naiv/ v. disimular.

connoisseur /,kɒnə'sɜr/ n. perito -ta.

connotation /,kɒnə'teiʃən/ n. connotación f.

connote /kə'nout/ v. connotar.

connubial /kə'nubiəl/ a. conyugal.

conquer /'kɒŋkər/ v. conquistar.

conquerable /'kɒŋkərəbəl/ a. conquistable, vencible.

conqueror /'kɒŋkərər/ n. conquistador -ra.

conquest /'kɒnkwɛst/ n. conquista f.

conscience /'kɒnʃəns/ n. conciencia f.

conscientious /,kɒnʃi'ɛnʃəs/ a. concienzudo.

conscientiously /,kɒnʃi'ɛnʃəsli/ adv. escrupulosamente.

conscientious objector /ɒb-'dʒɛktər/ objetor de conciencia m.

conscious /'kɒnʃəs/ a. consciente.

consciously /'kɒnʃəsli/ adv. con conocimiento.

consciousness /'kɒnʃəsnɪs/ n. conciencia f.

conscript /n 'kɒnskrɪpt; v kən'skrɪpt/ n. **1.** conscripto m., recluta m. —v. **2.** reclutar, alistar.

conscription /kən'skrɪpʃən/ n. conscripción f., alistamiento m.

consecrate /'kɒnsɪ,kreit/ v. consagrar.

consecration /,kɒnsɪ'kreiʃən/ n. consagración f.

consecutive /kən'sɛkyətɪv/ a. consecutivo, seguido.

consecutively /kən'sɛkyətɪvli/ adv. consecutivamente, de seguida.

consensus /kən'sɛnsəs/ n. consenso m., acuerdo general m.

consent /kən'sɛnt/ n. **1.** consentimiento m. —v. **2.** consentir.

consequence /'kɒnsɪ,kwɛns/ n. consecuencia f.

consequent /'kɒnsɪ,kwɛnt/ a. consiguiente.

consequential /,kɒnsɪ'kwɛnʃəl/ a. importante.

consequently /'kɒnsɪ,kwɛntli/ adv. por lo tanto, por consiguiente.

conservation /,kɒnsər'veiʃən/ n. conservación f.

conservatism /kən'sɜrvə,tɪzəm/ n. conservatismo m.

conservative /kən'sɜrvətɪv/ a. servador, conservativo.

conservatory /kən'sɜrvə,tɔri/ n. (plants) invernáculo m.; (school) conservatorio m.

conserve /kən'sɜrv/ v. conservar.

consider /kən'sɪdər/ v. considerar. **C. it done!** ¡Dalo por hecho!

considerable /kən'sɪdərəbəl/ a. considerable.

considerably /kən'sɪdərəbli/ adv. considerablemente.

considerate /kən'sɪdərɪt/ a. considerado.

considerately /kən'sɪdərɪtli/ adv. consideradamente.

consideration /kən,sɪdə'reiʃən/ n. consideración f.

considering /kən'sɪdərɪŋ/ prep. visto que, en vista de.

consign /kən'sain/ v. consignar.

consignment /kən'sainmənt/ n. consignación f., envío m.

consist /kən'sɪst/ v. consistir.

consistency /kən'sɪstənsi/ n. consistencia f.

consistent /kən'sɪstənt/ a. consistente.

consolation /,kɒnsə'leiʃən/ n. consolación f.

consolation prize premio de consuelo m.

console /'kɒnsoul/ v. consolar.

consolidate /kən'sɒlɪ,deit/ v. consolidar.

consommé /,kɒnsə'mei/ n. caldo m.

consonant /'kɒnsənənt/ n. consonante f.

consort /n 'kɒnsɔrt; v kən'sɔrt/ n. **1.** cónyuge m. & f.; socio. —v. **2.** asociarse.

conspicuous /kən'spɪkyuəs/ a. conspicuo.

conspicuously /kən'spɪkyuəsli/ adv. visiblemente, llamativamente.

conspicuousness /kən'spɪkyuəsnɪs/ n. visibilidad f.; evidencia f.; fama f.

conspiracy /kən'spɪrəsi/ n. conspiración f.; complot m.

conspirator /kən'spɪrətər/ n. conspirador -ra.

conspire /kən'spaiər/ v. conspirar.

conspirer /kən'spaiərər/ n. conspirante m. & f.

constancy /'kɒnstənsi/ n. constancia f., lealtad f.

constant /'kɒnstənt/ a. constante.

constantly /'kɒnstəntli/ adv. constantemente, de continuo.

constellation /,kɒnstə'leiʃən/ n. constelación f.

consternation /,kɒnstər'neiʃən/ n. consternación f.

constipate /'kɒnstə,peit/ v. estreñir.

constipated /'kɒnstə,peitɪd/ a. estreñido, m.

constipation /,kɒnstə'peiʃən/ n. estreñimiento, m.

constituency /kən'stɪtʃuənsi/ n. distrito electoral m.

constituent /kən'stɪtʃuənt/ a. **1.** constituyente. —n. **2.** elector m.

constitute /'kɒnstɪ,tut/ v. constituir.

constitution /,kɒnstɪ'tuʃən/ n. constitución f.

constitutional /,kɒnstɪ'tuʃənl/ a. constitucional.

constrain /kən'strein/ v. constreñir.

constraint /kən'streint/ n. constreñimiento m., compulsión f.

constrict /kən'strɪkt/ v. apretar, estrechar.

construct /kən'strʌkt/ v. construir.

construction /kən'strʌkʃən/ n. construcción f.

constructive /kən'strʌktɪv/ a. constructivo.

constructively /kən'strʌktɪvli/ adv. constructivamente; por deducción.

constructor /kən'strʌktər/ n. constructor m.

construe /kən'stru/ v. interpretar.

consul /'kɒnsəl/ n. cónsul m.

consular /'kɒnsələr/ a. consular.

consulate /'kɒnsəlɪt/ n. consulado m.

consult /kən'sʌlt/ v. consultar.

consultant /kən'sʌltənt/ n. consultor -ora.

consultation /,kɒnsəl'teiʃən/ n. consulta f.

consume /kən'sum/ v. consumir.

consumer /kən'sumər/ n. consumidor -ra.

consumer society sociedad de consumo f.

consummation /,kɒnsə'meiʃən/ n. consumación f.

consumption /kən'sʌmpʃən/ n. consumo m.; Med. tisis.

consumptive /kən'sʌmptɪv/ n. **1.** tísico m. —a. **2.** consuntivo.

contact /'kɒntækt/ n. **1.** contacto m. —v. **2.** ponerse en contacto con.

contact lens lentilla f.

contagion /kən'teidʒən/ n. contagio m.

contagious /kən'teidʒəs/ a. contagioso.

contain /kən'tein/ v. contener.

container /kən'teinər/ n. envase m.

contaminate /kən'tæmə,neit/ v. contaminar.

contemplate /'kɒntəm,pleit/ v. contemplar.

contemplation /,kɒntəm'pleiʃən/ n. contemplación f.

contemplative /kən'tɛmplətɪv/ a. contemplativo.

contemporary /kən'tɛmpə,rɛri/ n. & a. contemporáneo -nea.

contempt /kən'tɛmpt/ n. desprecio m.

contemptible /kən'tɛmptəbəl/ a. vil, despreciable.

contemptuous /kən'tɛmptʃuəs/ a. desdeñoso.

contemptuously /kən'tɛmptʃuəsli/ adv. desdeñosamente.

contend /kən'tɛnd/ v. contender; competir.

contender /kən'tɛndər/ n. competidor -ra.

content /a, v kən'tɛnt; n 'kɒntɛnt/ a. **1.** contento. —n. **2.** contenido m. —v. **3.** contentar.

contented /kən'tɛntɪd/ a. contento.

contention /kən'tɛnʃən/ n. contención f.

contentment /kən'tɛntmənt/ n. contentamiento m.

contest /n 'kɒntɛst; v kən'tɛst/ n. **1.** concurso m. —v. **2.** disputar.

contestable /kən'tɛstəbəl/ a. contestable.

context /'kɒntɛkst/ n. contexto m.

contiguous /kən'tɪgyuəs/ a. contiguo.

continence /'kɒntnəns/ n. continencia f., castidad f.

continent /'kɒntnənt/ n. continente m.

continental /,kɒntn'ɛntl/ a. continental.

contingency /kən'tɪndʒənsi/ n. eventualidad f., casualidad f.

contingent /kən'tɪndʒənt/ a. contingente.

continual /kən'tɪnyuəl/ a. continuo.

continuation /kən,tɪnyu'eiʃən/ n. continuación f.

continue /kən'tɪnyu/ v. continuar.

continuity /,kɒntn'uɪti/ n. continuidad f.

continuous /kən'tɪnyuəs/ a. continuo.

continuously /kən'tɪnyuəsli/ adv. continuamente.

contour /'kɒntur/ n. contorno m.

contraband /'kɒntrə,bænd/ n. contrabando m.

contraception /,kɒntrə'sɛpʃən/ n. contracepción f.

contraceptive /,kɒntrə'sɛptɪv/ n. & a. anticeptivo m.

contract /n 'kɒntrækt; v kən'trækt/ n. **1.** contrato m. —v. **2.** contraer.

contraction /kən'trækʃən/ n. contracción f.

contractor /'kɒntræktər/ n. contratista m. & f.

contradict /,kɒntrə'dɪkt/ v. contradecir.

contradiction /,kɒntrə'dɪkʃən/ n. contradicción f.

contradictory /,kɒntrə'dɪktəri/ a. contradictorio.

contralto /kən'træltou/ n. contralto m.

contrary /'kɒntrɛri/ a. & n. contrario -ria.

contrast /n 'kɒntræst; v kən'træst/ n. **1.** contraste m. —v. **2.** contrastar.

contribute /kən'trɪbyut/ v. contribuir.

contribution /,kɒntrə'byuʃən/ n. contribución f.

contributor /kən'trɪbyətər/ n. contribuidor -ra.

contributory /kən'trɪbyə,tɔri/ a. contribuyente.

contrite /kən'trait/ a. contrito.

contrition /kən'trɪʃən/ n. contrición f.

contrivance /kən'traivəns/ n. aparato m.; estratagema f.

contrive /kən'traiv/ v. inventar, tramar; darse maña.

control /kən'troul/ n. 1. control m. —v. 2. controlar.

controllable /kən'trouləbəl/ a. controlable, dominable.

controller /kən'troulər/ n. interventor -ra; contralor -ra.

control tower torre de mando f.

controversial /ˌkɒntrə'vɜrʃəl/ a. contencioso.

controversy /'kɒntrəˌvɜrsi/ n. controversia f.

contusion /kən'tuʒən/ n. contusión f.

convalesce /ˌkɒnvə'lɛs/ v. convalecer.

convalescence /ˌkɒnvə'lɛsəns/ n. convalecencia f.

convalescent /ˌkɒnvə'lɛsənt/ n. convaleciente m. & f.

convalescent home clínica de reposo f.

convene /kən'vin/ v. juntarse; convocar.

convenience /kən'vinyəns/ n. comodidad f.

convenient /kən'vinyənt/ a. cómodo; oportuno.

conveniently /kən'vinyəntli/ adv. cómodamente.

convent /'kɒnvɛnt/ n. convento m.

convention /kən'vɛnʃən/ n. convención f.

conventional /kən'vɛnʃənl/ a. convencional.

conventionally /kən'vɛnʃənli/ adv. convencionalmente.

converge /kən'vɜrdʒ/ v. convergir.

convergence /kən'vɜrdʒəns/ n. convergencia f.

convergent /kən'vɜrdʒənt/ a. convergente.

conversant /kən'vɜrsənt/ a. versado; entendido (de).

conversation /ˌkɒnvər'seiʃən/ n. conversación, plática f.

conversational /ˌkɒnvər'seiʃənl/ a. de conversación.

conversationalist /ˌkɒnvər'seiʃənlɪst/ n. conversador -ra.

converse /kən'vɜrs/ v. conversar.

conversely /kən'vɜrsli/ adv. a la inversa.

convert /n 'kɒnvɜrt; v kən'vɜrt/ n. 1. convertido da-. —v. 2. convertir.

converter /kən'vɜrtər/ n. convertidor m.

convertible /kən'vɜrtəbəl/ a. convertible.

convex /kɒn'vɛks/ a. convexo.

convey /kən'vei/ v. transportar; comunicar.

conveyance /kən'veiəns/ n. transporte; vehículo m.

conveyor /kən'veiər/ n. conductor m.; Mech. transportador m.

conveyor belt correa transportadora f.

convict /n 'kɒnvikt; v kən'vikt/ n. 1. reo m. —v. 2. declarar culpable.

conviction /kən'vikʃən/ n. convicción f.

convince /kən'vins/ v. convencer.

convincing /kən'vinsiŋ/ a. convincente.

convivial /kən'viviəl/ a. convival.

convocation /ˌkɒnvə'keiʃən/ n. convocación; asamblea f.

convoke /kən'vouk/ v. convocar, citar.

convoy /'kɒnvɔi/ n. convoy m.; escolta f.

convulse /kən'vʌls/ v. convulsionar; agitar violentamente.

convulsion /kən'vʌlʃən/ n. convulsión f.

convulsive /kən'vʌlsiv/ a. convulsivo.

cook /kuk/ n. 1. cocinero -ra. —v. 2. cocinar, cocer.

cookbook /'kuk,buk/ n. libro de cocina m.

cookie /'kuki/ n. galleta dulce f.

cool /kul/ a. 1. fresco. —v. 2. refrescar.

cooler /'kulər/ n. enfriadera f.

coolness /'kulnis/ n. frescura f.

coop /kup/ n. 1. jaula f. **chicken c.,** gallinero m. —v. 2. enjaular.

cooperate /kou'ɒpə,reit/ v. cooperar.

cooperation /kou,ɒpə'reiʃən/ n. cooperación f.

cooperative /kou'ɒpərətiv/ a. cooperativo.

cooperatively /kou'ɒpərətivli/ adv. cooperativamente.

coordinate /kou'ɔrdn̩,eit/ v. coordinar.

coordination /kou,ɔrdn̩'eiʃən/ n. coordinación f.

coordinator /kou'ɔrdn̩,eitər/ n. coordinador -ra.

cope /koup/ v. contender. **c. with,** superar, hacer frente a.

copier /'kɒpiər/ n. copiadora f.

copious /'koupiəs/ a. copioso, abundante.

copiously /'koupiəsli/ adv. copiosamente.

copiousness /'koupiəsnis/ n. abundancia f.

copper /'kɒpər/ n. cobre m.

copy /'kɒpi/ n. 1. copia f.; ejemplar m. —v. 2. copiar.

copyist /'kɒpiist/ n. copista m. & f.

copyright /'kɒpi,rait/ n. derechos de propiedad literaria m.pl.

coquetry /'koukitri/ n. coquetería f.

coquette /kou'kɛt/ n. coqueta f.

coral /'kɒrəl/ n. coral m.

cord /kɔrd/ n. cuerda f.

cordial /'kɔrdʒəl/ a. cordial.

cordiality /kɔr'dʒæliti/ n. cordialidad f.

cordially /'kɔrdʒəli/ adv. cordialmente.

cordon off /'kɔrdn̩/ v. acordonar.

cordovan /'kɔrdəvən/ n. cordobán m.

corduroy /'kɔrdə,rɔi/ n. pana f.

core /kɔr/ n. corazón; centro m.

cork /kɔrk/ n. corcho m.

corkscrew /'kɔrk,skru/ n. tirabuzón m.

corn /kɔrn/ n. maíz m.

cornea /'kɔrniə/ n. córnea f.

corned beef /kɔrnd/ carne acecinada f.

corner /'kɔrnər/ n. rincón m.; (of street) esquina f.

cornet /kɔr'nɛt/ n. corneta f.

cornetist /kɔr'nɛtist/ n. cornetín m.

cornice /'kɔrnis/ n. cornisa f.

cornstarch /'kɔrn,startʃ/ n. maicena f.

corollary /'kɔrə,lɛri/ n. corolario m.

coronary /'kɔrə,nɛri/ a. coronario.

coronation /ˌkɔrə'neiʃən/ n. coronación f.

corporal /'kɔrpərəl/ a. 1. corpóreo. —n. 2. cabo m.

corporate /'kɔrpərit/ a. corporativo.

corporation /ˌkɔrpə'reiʃən/ n. corporación f.

corps /kɔr/ n. cuerpo m.

corpse /kɔrps/ n. cadáver m.

corpulent /'kɔrpyələnt/ a. corpulento.

corpuscle /'kɔrpəsəl/ n. corpúsculo m.

corral /kə'ræl/ n. 1. corral m. —v. 2. acorralar.

correct /kə'rɛkt/ a. 1. correcto. —v. 2. corregir.

correction /kə'rɛkʃən/ n. corrección; enmienda f.

corrective /kə'rɛktiv/ n. & a. correctivo.

correctly /kə'rɛktli/ adv. correctamente.

correctness /kə'rɛktnis/ n. exactitud f.

correlate /'kɔrə,leit/ v. correlacionar.

correlation /ˌkɔrə'leiʃən/ n. correlación f.

correspond /ˌkɔrə'spɒnd/ v. corresponder.

correspondence /ˌkɔrə'spɒndəns/ n. correspondencia f.

correspondence course curso por correspondencia m.

correspondence school escuela por correspondencia f.

correspondent /ˌkɔrə'spɒndənt/ a. & n. correspondiente m. & f.

corresponding /ˌkɔrə'spɒndiŋ/ a. correspondiente.

corridor /'kɔridər/ n. corredor, pasillo m.

corroborate /kə'rɒbə,reit/ v. corroborar.

corroboration /kə,rɒbə'reiʃən/ n. corroboración f.

corroborative /kə'rɒbə,reitiv/ a. corroborante.

corrode /kə'roud/ v. corroer.

corrosion /kə'rouʒən/ n. corrosión f.

corrugate /'kɔrə,geit/ v. arrugar; ondular.

corrupt /kə'rʌpt/ a. 1. corrompido. —v. 2. corromper.

corruptible /kə'rʌptəbəl/ a. corruptible.

corruption /kə'rʌpʃən/ n. corrupción f.

corruptive /kə'rʌptiv/ a. corruptivo.

corset /'kɔrsit/ n. corsé m., (girdle) faja f.

cortege /kɔr'tɛʒ/ n. comitiva f., séquito m.

corvette /kɔr'vɛt/ n. corbeta f.

cosmetic /kɒz'mɛtik/ a. & n. cosmético m.

cosmic /'kɒzmik/ a. cósmico.

cosmonaut /'kɒzmə,nɔt/ n. cosmonauta m. & f.

cosmopolitan /ˌkɒzmə'pɒlitn̩/ a. & n. cosmopolita m. & f.

cosmos /'kɒzməs/ n. cosmos m.

cost /kɔst/ n. 1. coste m.; costa f. —v. 2. costar.

Costa Rican /'kɒstə'rikən/ a. & n. costarricense m. & f.

costly /'kɔstli/ a. costoso, caro.

costume /'kɒstum/ n. traje; disfraz m.

costume jewelry bisutería f., joyas de fantasía f.pl.

cot /kɒt/ n. catre m.

coterie /'koutəri/ n. camarilla f.

cotillion /kə'tilyən/ n. cotillón m.

cottage /'kɒtidʒ/ n. casita f.

cottage cheese requesón m.

cotton /'kɒtn̩/ n. algodón m.

cottonseed /'kɒtn̩,sid/ n. semilla del algodón m.

couch /kautʃ/ n. sofá m.

cougar /'kugər/ n. puma m.

cough /kɔf/ n. 1. tos f. —v. 2. toser.

council /'kaunsəl/ n. consejo, concilio m.

counsel /'kaunsəl/ n. 1. consejo; (law) abogado -da. —v. 2. aconsejar. **to keep one's c.,** no decir nada.

counselor /'kaunsələr/ n. consejero -ra; (law) abogado -da.

count /kaunt/ n. 1. cuenta f.; (title) conde m. —v. 2. contar.

countenance /'kauntn̩əns/ n. 1. aspecto m.; cara f. —v. 2. aprobar.

counter /'kauntər/ adv. 1. c. to, contra, en contra de. —n. 2. mostrador m.

counteract /ˌkauntər'ækt/ v. contrarrestar.

counteraction /ˌkauntər'ækʃən/ n. neutralización f.

counterbalance /'kauntər,bæləns/ n. 1. contrapeso m. —v. 2. contrapesar.

counterfeit /'kauntər,fit/ a. 1. falsificado. —v. 2. falsear.

countermand /ˌkauntər'mænd/ v. contramandar.

counteroffensive /ˌkauntərə'fɛnsiv/ n. contraofensiva f.

counterpart /'kauntər,part/ n. contraparte f.

counterproductive /ˌkauntərprə'dʌktiv/ a. contraproducente.

countess /'kauntis/ n. condesa f.

countless /'kauntlis/ a. innumerable.

country /'kʌntri/ n. campo m.; Pol. país m.; (homeland) patria f.

country code distintivo del país m.

countryman /'kʌntrimən/ n. paisano m. **fellow c.,** compatriota m.

countryside /'kʌntri,said/ n. campo, paisaje m.

county /'kaunti/ n. condado m.

coupé /kup/ n. cupé m.

couple /'kʌpəl/ n. 1. par m. —v. 2. unir.

coupon /'kupɒn/ n. cupón, talón m.

courage /'kɜridʒ/ n. valor m.

courageous /kə'reidʒəs/ a. valiente.

course /kɔrs/ n. curso m. **of c.,** por supuesto, desde luego.

court /kɔrt/ n. 1. corte f.; cortejo m.; (of law) tribunal m. —v. 2. cortejar.

courteous /'kɜrtiəs/ a. cortés.

courtesy /'kɜrtəsi/ n. cortesía f.

courthouse /'kɔrt,haus/ n. palacio de justicia m., tribunal m.

courtier /'kɔrtiər/ n. cortesano m.

courtly /'kɔrtli/ a. cortés, galante.

courtroom /'kɔrt,rum, -,rʊm/ n. sala de justicia f.

courtship /'kɔrtʃip/ n. cortejo m.

courtyard /'kɔrt,yard/ n. patio m.

cousin /'kʌzən/ n. primo -ma.

covenant /'kʌvənənt/ n. contrato, convenio m.

cover /'kʌvər/ n. 1. cubierta, tapa f. —v. 2. cubrir, tapar.

cover charge precio del cubierto m.

covet /'kʌvit/ v. ambicionar, suspirar por.

covetous /'kʌvitəs/ a. codicioso.

cow /kau/ n. vaca f.

coward /'kauərd/ n. cobarde m. & f.

cowardice /'kauərdis/ n. cobardía f.

cowardly /'kauərdli/ a. cobarde.

cowboy /'kau,bɔi/ n. vaquero, gaucho m.

cower /'kauər/ v. agacharse (de miedo).

cowhide /'kau,haid/ n. cuero m.

coy /kɔi/ a. recatado, modesto.

coyote /kai'outi/ n. coyote m.

cozy /'kouzi/ a. cómodo y agradable.

crab /kræb/ n. cangrejo m.

crab apple n. manzana silvestre f.

crack /kræk/ n. 1. hendedura f.; (noise) crujido m. —v. 2. hender; crujir.

cracker /'krækər/ n. galleta f.

cradle /'kreidl̩/ n. cuna f.

craft /kræft/ n. arte m.

craftsman /'kræftsmən/ n. artesano -na.

craftsmanship /'kræftsmən,ʃip/ n. artesanía f.

crafty /'kræfti/ a. ladino.

crag /kræg/ n. despeñadero m.; peña f.

cram /kræm/ v. rellenar, hartar.

cramp /kræmp/ n. calambre m.

cranberry /'kræn,bɛri/ n. arándano m.

crane /krein/ n. (bird) grulla f.; Mech. grúa f.

cranium /'kreiniəm/ n. cráneo m.

crank /kræŋk/ n. Mech. manivela f.

cranky /'kræŋki/ a. chiflado, caprichoso.

crash /kræʃ/ n. 1. choque; estallido m. —v. 2. estallar.

crate /kreit/ n. canasto m.

crater /'kreitər/ n. cráter m.

crave /kreiv/ v. desear; anhelar.

craven /'kreivən/ a. cobarde.

craving /'kreiviŋ/ n. sed m., anhelo m.

crawl /krɔl/ v. andar a gatas, arrastrarse.

crayon /'kreiɒn/ n. creyón; lápiz m.

crazy /'kreizi/ a. loco.

creak /krik/ v. crujir.
creaky /'kriki/ a. crujiente.
cream /krim/ n. crema f.
cream cheese queso crema m.
creamery /'krimɔri/ n. lechería f.
creamy /'krimi/ a. cremoso.
crease /kris/ n. **1.** pliegue m. —v. **2.** plegar.
create /kri'eit/ v. crear.
creation /kri'eiʃən/ n. creación f.
creative /kri'eitiv/ a. creativo, creador.
creator /kri'eitər/ n. creador -ra.
creature /'kritʃər/ n. criatura f.
credence /'kridns/ n. creencia f.
credentials /krɪ'dɛnʃəlz/ n. credenciales f.pl.
credibility /,kredə'bɪliti/ n. credibilidad f.
credible /'kredəbəl/ a. creíble.
credit /'kredɪt/ n. **1.** crédito m. **on c.,** al fiado. —v. **2.** Com. abonar.
creditable /'kredɪtəbəl/ a. fidedigno.
credit balance saldo acreedor.
credit card n. tarjeta de crédito f.
creditor /'kredɪtər/ n. acreedor -ra.
credit union banco cooperativo m.
credo /'kridou/ n. credo m.
credulity /krə'duliti/ n. credulidad f.
credulous /'kredʒələs/ a. crédulo.
creed /krid/ n. credo m.
creek /krik/ n. riachuelo m.
creep /krip/ v. gatear.
cremate /'krimeit/ v. incinerar.
crematory /'krimə,tɔri/ n. crematorio m.
creosote /'kriə,sout/ n. creosota f.
crepe /kreip/ n. crespón m.
crepe paper papel crespón m.
crescent /'krɛsənt/ a. & n. creciente f.
crest /krɛst/ n. cresta; cima f.; (heraldry) timbre m.
cretonne /krɪ'tɒn/ n. cretona f.
crevice /'krɛvɪs/ n. grieta f.
crew /kru/ n. tripulación f.
crew member tripulante m. & f.
crib /krɪb/ n. pesebre m.; cuna.
cricket /'krɪkɪt/ n. grillo m.
crime /kraim/ n. crimen m.
criminal /'krɪmənl/ a. & n. criminal m. & f.
criminologist /,krɪmə'nɒlədʒɪst/ n. criminólogo -ga, criminalista m. & f.
criminology /,krɪmə'nɒlədʒi/ n. criminología f.
crimson /'krɪmzən, -sən/ a. & n. carmesí m.
cringe /krɪndʒ/ v. encogerse, temblar.
cripple /'krɪpəl/ n. **1.** lisiado -da. —v. **2.** estropear, lisiar.
crisis /'kraisɪs/ n. crisis f.
crisp /krɪsp/ a. crespo, fresco.
crispness /'krɪspnɪs/ n. encrespadura f.
crisscross /'krɪs,krɔs/ a. entrelazado.
criterion /krai'tɪəriən/ n. criterio m.
critic /'krɪtɪk/ n. crítico -ca.
critical /'krɪtɪkəl/ a. crítico.
criticism /'krɪtə,sɪzəm/ n. crítica; censura f.
criticize /'krɪtə,saiz/ v. criticar; censurar.
critique /krɪ'tik/ n. crítica f.
croak /krouk/ n. **1.** graznido m. —v. **2.** graznar.
crochet /krou'ʃei/ n. **1.** crochet m. —v. **2.** hacer crochet.
crochet work ganchillo m.
crock /krɒk/ n. cazuela f.; olla de barro.
crockery /'krɒkəri/ n. loza f.
crocodile /'krɒkə,dail/ n. cocodrilo m.
crony /'krouni/ n. compinche m.
crooked /'krʊkɪd/ a. encorvado; deshonesto.
croon /krun/ v. canturrear.
crop /krɒp/ n. cosecha f.
croquet /krou'kei/ n. juego de croquet m.
croquette /krou'kɛt/ n. croqueta f.
cross /krɔs/ a. **1.** enojado, mal humorado. —n. **2.** cruz f. —v. **3.** cruzar, atravesar.
crossbreed /'krɔs,brid/ n. **1.** mestizo m. —v. **2.** cruzar (animales o plantas).
cross-examine /'krɔs ɪg,zæmɪn/ v. interrogar.
cross-eyed /'krɔs ,aid/ a. bizco.
cross-fertilization /'krɔs ,fɜrtlə-'zeiʃən/ n. alogamia f.
crossing /'krɔsɪŋ/ **crossroads** n. cruce m.
cross section corte transversal m.
crosswalk /'krɔs,wɔk/ n. paso cebra m.
crossword puzzle /'krɔs ,wɜrd/ crucigrama m.
crotch /krɒtʃ/ n. bifurcación f.; Anat. bragadura f.
crouch /krautʃ/ v. agacharse.
croup /krup/ n. Med. crup m.
croupier /'krupiər/ n. crupié m. & f.
crow /krou/ n. cuervo m.
crowd /kraud/ n. **1.** muchedumbre f.; tropel m. —v. **2.** apretar.
crowded /'kraudɪd/ a. lleno de gente.
crown /kraun/ n. **1.** corona f. —v. **2.** coronar.
crown prince príncipe heredero m.
crucial /'kruʃəl/ a. crucial.
crucible /'krusəbəl/ n. crisol m.
crucifix /'krusəfɪks/ n. crucifijo m.
crucifixion /,krusə'fɪkʃən/ n. crucifixión f.
crucify /'krusə,fai/ v. crucificar.
crude /krud/ a. crudo; (oil) bruto.
crudeness /'krudnɪs/ a. crudeza f.
cruel /'kruəl/ a. cruel.
cruelty /'kruəlti/ n. crueldad f.
cruet /'kruɪt/ n. vinagrera f.
cruise /kruz/ n. **1.** viaje por mar. —v. **2.** navegar.
cruiser /'kruzər/ n. crucero m.
crumb /krʌm/ n. miga; migaja f.
crumble /'krʌmbəl/ v. desmigajar; desmoronar.
crumple /'krʌmpəl/ v. arrugar; encogerse.
crusade /kru'seid/ n. cruzada f.
crusader /kru'seidər/ n. cruzado m.
crush /krʌʃ/ v. aplastar.
crust /krʌst/ n. costra; corteza f.
crustacean /krʌ'steiʃən/ n. crustáceo m.
crutch /krʌtʃ/ n. muleta f.
cry /krai/ n. **1.** grito m. —v. **2.** gritar; (weep) llorar.
cryosurgery /,kraiou'sɜrdʒəri/ n. criocirugía f.
crypt /krɪpt/ n. gruta f., cripta f.
cryptic /'krɪptɪk/ a. secreto.
cryptography /krɪp'tɒgrəfi/ n. criptografía f.
crystal /'krɪstl/ n. cristal m.
crystalline /'krɪstlɪn/ a. cristalino, transparente.
crystallize /'krɪstl,aiz/ v. cristalizar.
cub /kʌb/ n. cachorro m.
Cuban /'kyubən/ n. & a. cubano -na.
cube /kyub/ n. cubo m.
cubic /'kyubɪk/ a. cúbico.
cubicle /'kyubɪkəl/ n. cubículo m.
cubic measure medida de capacidad m.
cubism /'kyubɪzəm/ n. cubismo m.
cuckoo /'kuku/ n. cuco m.
cucumber /'kyukʌmbər/ n. pepino m.
cuddle /'kʌdl/ v. abrazar.
cudgel /'kʌdʒəl/ n. palo m.
cue /kyu/ n. apunte m.; (billiards) taco m.
cuff /kʌf/ n. puño de camisa. **c. links,** gemelos.
cuisine /kwɪ'zin/ n. arte culinario m.
culinary /'kyulə,neri/ a. culinario.
culminate /'kʌlmə,neit/ v. culminar.
culmination /,kʌlmə'neiʃən/ n. culminación f.
culpable /'kʌlpəbəl/ a. culpable.
culprit /'kʌlprɪt/ n. criminal; delincuente m. & f.
cult /kʌlt/ n. culto m.

cultivate /'kʌltə,veit/ v. cultivar.
cultivated /'kʌltə,veitɪd/ a. cultivado.
cultivation /,kʌltə'veiʃən/ n. cultivo m.; cultivación f.
cultivator /'kʌltə,veitər/ n. cultivador -ra.
cultural /'kʌltʃərəl/ a. cultural.
culture /'kʌltʃər/ n. cultura f.
cultured /'kʌltʃərd/ a. culto.
cumbersome /'kʌmbərsəm/ a. pesado, incómodo.
cumulative /'kyumyələtɪv/ a. acumulativo.
cunning /'kʌnɪŋ/ a. **1.** astuto. —n. **2.** astucia f.
cup /kʌp/ n. taza, jícara f.
cupboard /'kʌbərd/ n. armario, aparador m.
cupidity /kyu'pɪdɪti/ n. avaricia f.
curable /'kyurəbəl/ a. curable.
curator /kyu'reitər/ n. guardián -ana.
curb /kɜrb/ n. **1.** freno m. —v. **2.** refrenar.
curd /kɜrd/ n. cuajada f.
curdle /'kɜrdl/ v. cuajarse, coagularse.
cure /kyor/ n. **1.** remedio m. —v. **2.** curar, sanar.
curfew /'kɜrfyu/ n. toque de queda m.
curio /'kyuri,ou/ n. objeto curioso.
curiosity /,kyuri'ɒsɪti/ n. curiosidad f.
curious /'kyuriəs/ a. curioso.
curl /kɜrl/ n. **1.** rizo m. —v. **2.** rizar.
curly /'kɜrli/ a. rizado.
currant /'kɜrənt/ n. grosella f.
currency /'kɜrənsi/ n. circulación f.; dinero m.
current /'kɜrənt/ a. & n. corriente f.
current events /ɪ'vɛnts/ actualidades f.pl.
currently /'kɜrəntli/ adv. corrientemente.
curriculum /kə'rɪkyələm/ n. plan de estudio m.
curse /kɜrs/ n. **1.** maldición f. —v. **2.** maldecir.
cursor /'kɜrsər/ n. cursor m.
cursory /'kɜrsəri/ a. sumario.
curt /kɜrt/ a. brusco.
curtail /kər'teil/ v. reducir; restringir.
curtain /'kɜrtn/ n. cortina f.; Theat. telón m.
curtsy /'kɜrtsi/ n. **1.** reverencia f. —v. **2.** hacer una reverencia.
curvature /'kɜrvətʃər/ n. curvatura f.
curve /kɜrv/ n. **1.** curva f. —v. **2.** encorvar.
cushion /'kuʃən/ n. cojín m.; almohada f.
cuspidor /'kʌspɪ,dɔr/ n. escupidera f.
custard /'kʌstərd/ n. flan m.; natillas f.pl.
custodian /kʌ'stoudiən/ n. custodio m.
custody /'kʌstədi/ n. custodia f.
custom /'kʌstəm/ n. costumbre f.
customary /'kʌstə,meri/ a. acostumbrado, usual.
customer /'kʌstəmər/ n. cliente m. & f.
customhouse /'kʌstəm,haus/ **customs** n. aduana f.
customs duty /'kʌstəmz/ derechos de aduana m.pl.
customs officer /'kʌstəmz/ agente de aduana m. & f.
cut /kʌt/ n. **1.** corte m.; cortada f.; tajada f.; (printing) grabado m. —v. **2.** cortar; tajar.
cute /kyut/ a. mono, lindo.
cut glass cristal tallado m.
cuticle /'kyutɪkəl/ n. cutícula f.
cutlery /'kʌtləri/ n. cuchillería f.
cutlet /'kʌtlɪt/ n. chuleta f.
cutter /'kʌtər/ n. cortador -ra; Naut. cúter m.
cutthroat /'kʌt,θrout/ n. asesino -na.
cyberpunk /'saibər,pʌŋk/ n. ciberpunk m. & f.
cyberspace /'saibər,speis/ n. ciberespacio m.
cyclamate /'saiklə,meit, 'sɪklə-/ n. ciclamato m.

cycle /'saikəl/ n. ciclo m.
cyclist /'saiklɪst/ n. ciclista m. & f.
cyclone /'saikloun/ n. ciclón, huracán m.
cyclotron /'saiklə,trɒn, 'sɪklə-/ n. ciclotrón m.
cylinder /'sɪlɪndər/ n. cilindro m.
cylindrical /sɪ'lɪndrɪkəl/ a. cilíndrico.
cymbal /'sɪmbəl/ n. címbalo m.
cynic /'sɪnɪk/ n. cínico -ca.
cynical /'sɪnɪkəl/ a. cínico.
cynicism /'sɪnə,sɪzəm/ n. cinismo m.
cypress /'saiprəs/ n. ciprés m. **c. nut,** piñuela f.
cyst /sɪst/ n. quiste m.

D

dad /dæd/ n. papá m., papito m.
daffodil /'dæfədɪl/ n. narciso m.
dagger /'dægər/ n. puñal m.
dahlia /'dælyə/ n. dalia f.
daily /'deili/ a. diario, cotidiano.
daintiness /'deintinɪs/ n. delicadeza f.
dainty /'deinti/ a. delicado.
dairy /'dɛəri/ n. lechería, quesería f.
dais /'deiɪs/ n. tablado m.
daisy /'deizi/ n. margarita f.
dale /deil/ n. valle m.
dally /'dæli/ v. holgar; perder el tiempo.
dam /dæm/ n. presa f.; dique m.
damage /'dæmɪdʒ/ n. **1.** daño m. —v. **2.** dañar.
damask /'dæməsk/ n. damasco m.
damn /dæm/ v. condenar.
damnation /dæm'neiʃən/ n. condenación f.
damp /dæmp/ a. húmedo.
dampen /'dæmpən/ v. humedecer.
dampness /'dæmpnɪs/ n. humedad f.
damsel /'dæmzəl/ n. doncella f.
dance /dæns/ n. **1.** baile m.; danza f. —v. **2.** bailar.
dance hall salón de baile m.
dancer /'dænsər/ n. bailador -ra; (professional) bailarín -na.
dancing /'dænsɪŋ/ n. baile m.
dandelion /'dændl,aiən/ n. amargón m.
dandruff /'dændrəf/ n. caspa f.
dandy /'dændi/ n. petimetre m.
danger /'deindʒər/ n. peligro m.
dangerous /'deindʒərəs/ a. peligroso.
dangle /'dæŋgəl/ v. colgar.
Danish /'deinɪʃ/ a. & n. danés -sa; dinamarqués -sa.
dapper /'dæpər/ a. gallardo.
dare /dɛər/ v. atreverse, osar.
daredevil /'dɛər,dɛvəl/ n. atrevido m., -da f.
daring /'dɛərɪŋ/ a. **1.** atrevido. —n. **2.** osadía f.
dark /dɑrk/ a. **1.** obscuro; moreno. —n. **2.** obscuridad f.
darken /'dɑrkən/ v. obscurecer.
darkness /'dɑrknɪs/ n. obscuridad f.
darkroom /'dɑrk,rum, -,rʊm/ n. cámara obscura f.
darling /'dɑrlɪŋ/ a. & n. querido -da, amado -da.
darn /dɑrn/ v. zurcir.
darning needle /'dɑrnɪŋ/ aguja de zurcir m.
dart /dɑrt/ n. dardo m.
dartboard /'dɑrt,bɔrd/ n. diana f.
dash /dæʃ/ n. arranque m.; Punct. guión m.
data /'deitə/ n. datos m.
database /'deitə,beis/ n. base de datos m.
data processing /'prɒsɛsɪŋ/ proceso de datos m.
date /deit/ n. fecha f.; (engagement) cita f.; (fruit) dátil m.
daughter /'dɔtər/ n. hija f.
daughter-in-law /'dɔ,tər ɪn lɔ/ n. nuera f.
daunt /dɔnt, dɑnt/ v. intimidar.
dauntless /'dɔntlɪs/ a. intrépido.

davenport /'dævən,pɔrt/ *n.* sofá *m.*
dawn /dɔn/ *n.* **1.** alba, madrugada *f.* —*v.* **2.** amanecer.
day /dei/ *n.* día *m.* **good d.,** buenos días.
daybreak /'dei,breik/ *n.* alba, madrugada *f.*
daydream /'dei,drim/ *n.* fantasía *f.*
daylight /'dei,lait/ *n.* luz del día.
daze /deiz/ *v.* aturdir.
dazzle /'dæzəl/ *v.* deslumbrar.
deacon /'dikən/ *n.* diácono *m.*
dead /dɛd/ *a.* muerto.
deaden /'dɛdn/ *v.* amortecer.
dead end atolladero *m.* (impasse); callejón sin salida *m.* (street).
deadline /'dɛd,lain/ *n.* fecha límite *f.*
deadlock /'dɛd,lɒk/ *n.* paro *m.*
deadly /'dɛdli/ *a.* mortal.
deaf /dɛf/ *a.* sordo.
deafen /'dɛfən/ *v.* ensordecer.
deafening /'dɛfənɪŋ/ *a.* ensordecedor.
deaf-mute /'dɛf 'myut/ *n.* sordomudo *a.*
deafness /'dɛfnɪs/ *n.* sordera *f.*
deal /dil/ *n.* **1.** trato *m.*; negociación *f.* **a great d., a good d.,** mucho. —*v.* **2.** tratar; negociar.
dealer /'dilər/ *n.* comerciante *m.*, (at cards) tallador -ra.
dean /din/ *n.* decano -na.
dear /dɪər/ *a.* querido; caro.
dearth /dɜrθ/ *n.* escasez *f.*
death /dɛθ/ *n.* muerte *f.*
death certificate partida de defunción *f.*
deathless /'dɛθlɪs/ *a.* inmortal.
debacle /də'bɑkəl/ *n.* desastre *m.*
debase /dɪ'beis/ *v.* degradar.
debatable /dɪ'beitəbəl/ *a.* discutible.
debate /dɪ'beit/ *n.* **1.** debate *m.* —*v.* **2.** disputar, deliberar.
debauch /dɪ'bɔtʃ/ *v.* corromper.
debilitate /dɪ'bɪlɪ,teit/ *v.* debilitar.
debit /'dɛbɪt/ *n.* débito *m.*
debit balance saldo deudor *m.*
debonair /,dɛbə'nɛər/ *a.* cortés; alegre, vivo.
debris /dei'bri/ *n.* escombros *m.pl.*
debt /dɛt/ *n.* deuda *f.* **get into d.** endeudarse.
debtor /'dɛtər/ *n.* deudor -ra.
debug /di'bʌg/ *v.* depurar, limpiar.
debunk /di'bʌŋk/ *v.* desacreditar; desenmascarar.
debut /dei'byu/ *n.* debut, estreno *m.*
debutante /'dɛbyu,tɑnt/ *n.* debutante *f.*
decade /'dɛkeid/ *n.* década *f.*
decadence /'dɛkədəns/ *n.* decadencia *f.*
decadent /'dɛkədənt/ *a.* decadente.
decaffeinated /di'kæfɪ,neitɪd/ *a.* descafeinado.
decalcomania /dɪ,kælkə'meiniə/ *n.* calcomanía *f.*
decanter /dɪ'kæntər/ *n.* garrafa *f.*
decapitate /dɪ'kæpɪ,teit/ *v.* descabezar.
decay /dɪ'kei/ *n.* **1.** descaecimiento *m.*; (dental) caries *f.* —*v.* **2.** decaer; (dental) cariarse.
deceased /dɪ'sist/ *a.* muerto, difunto.
deceit /dɪ'sit/ *n.* engaño *m.*
deceitful /dɪ'sitfəl/ *a.* engañoso.
deceive /dɪ'siv/ *v.* engañar.
December /dɪ'sɛmbər/ *n.* diciembre *m.*
decency /'disənsi/ *n.* decencia *f.*; decoro *m.*
decent /'disənt/ *a.* decente.
decentralize /di'sɛntrə,laiz/ *v.* descentralizar.
deception /dɪ'sɛpʃən/ *n.* decepción *f.*
deceptive /dɪ'sɛptɪv/ *a.* deceptivo.
decibel /'dɛsə,bɛl/ *n.* decibelio *m.*
decide /dɪ'said/ *v.* decidir.
decimal /'dɛsəməl/ *a.* decimal.
decipher /dɪ'saifər/ *v.* descifrar.
decision /dɪ'sɪʒən/ *n.* decisión *f.*
decisive /dɪ'saisɪv/ *a.* decisivo.

deck /dɛk/ *n.* cubierta *f.*
deck chair tumbona *f.*
declamation /,dɛklə'meiʃən/ *n.* declamación *f.*
declaration /,dɛklə'reiʃən/ *n.* declaración *f.*
declarative /dɪ'klærətɪv/ *a.* declarativo.
declare /dɪ'klɛər/ *v.* declarar.
declension /dɪ'klɛnʃən/ *n.* declinación *f.*
decline /dɪ'klain/ *n.* **1.** decadencia *f.* —*v.* **2.** decaer; negarse; *Gram.* declinar.
decompose /,dikəm'pouz/ *v.* descomponer.
decongestant /,dikən'dʒɛstənt/ *n.* descongestionante *m.*
decorate /'dɛkə,reit/ *v.* decorar, adornar.
decoration /,dɛkə'reiʃən/ *n.* decoración *f.*
decorative /'dɛkərətɪv/ *a.* decorativo.
decorator /'dɛkə,reitər/ *n.* decorador -ra.
decorous /'dɛkərəs/ *a.* correcto.
decorum /dɪ'kɔrəm/ *n.* decoro *m.*
decrease /dɪ'kris/ *v.* disminuir.
decree /dɪ'kri/ *n.* decreto *m.*
decrepit /dɪ'krɛpɪt/ *a.* decrépito.
decry /dɪ'krai/ *v.* desacreditar.
dedicate /'dɛdɪ,keit/ *v.* dedicar; consagrar.
dedication /,dɛdɪ'keiʃən/ *n.* dedicación; dedicatoria *f.*
deduce /dɪ'dus/ *v.* deducir.
deduction /dɪ'dʌkʃən/ *n.* rebaja; deducción *f.*
deductive /dɪ'dʌktɪv/ *a.* deductivo.
deed /did/ *n.* acción; hazaña *f.*
deem /dim/ *v.* estimar.
deep /dip/ *a.* hondo, profundo.
deepen /'dipən/ *v.* profundizar, ahondar.
deep freeze congelación *f.*
deeply /'dipli/ *adv.* profundamente.
deer /dɪər/ *n.* venado, ciervo *m.*
deface /dɪ'feis/ *v.* mutilar.
defamation /,dɛfə'meiʃən/ *n.* calumnia *f.*
defame /dɪ'feim/ *v.* difamar.
default /dɪ'fɔlt/ *n.* **1.** defecto *m.* —*v.* **2.** faltar.
defeat /dɪ'fit/ *n.* **1.** derrota *f.* —*v.* **2.** derrotar.
defeatism /dɪ'fitɪzəm/ *n.* derrotismo *m.*
defect /'difɛkt, dɪ'fɛkt/ *n.* defecto *m.*
defective /dɪ'fɛktɪv/ *a.* defectivo.
defend /dɪ'fɛnd/ *v.* defender.
defendant /dɪ'fɛndənt/ *n.* acusado -da.
defender /dɪ'fɛndər/ *n.* defensor -ra.
defense /dɪ'fɛns/ *n.* defensa *f.*
defensive /dɪ'fɛnsɪv/ *a.* defensivo.
defer /dɪ'fɜr/ *v.* aplazar; deferir.
deference /'dɛfərəns/ *n.* deferencia *f.*
defiance /dɪ'faiəns/ *n.* desafío *m.*
defiant /dɪ'faiənt/ *a.* desafiador.
deficiency /dɪ'fɪʃənsi/ *n.* defecto *m.*
deficient /dɪ'fɪʃənt/ *a.* deficiente.
deficit /'dɛfəsɪt/ *n.* déficit, descubierto *m.*
defile /dɪ'fail/ *n.* **1.** desfiladero *m.* —*v.* **2.** profanar.
define /dɪ'fain/ *v.* definir.
definite /'dɛfənɪt/ *a.* exacto; definitivo.
definitely /'dɛfənɪtli/ *adv.* definitivamente.
definition /,dɛfə'nɪʃən/ *n.* definición *f.*
definitive /dɪ'fɪnɪtɪv/ *a.* definitivo.
deflation /dɪ'fleiʃən/ *n.* desinflación *f.*
deflect /dɪ'flɛkt/ *v.* desviar.
deform /dɪ'fɔrm/ *v.* deformar.
deformity /dɪ'fɔrmɪti/ *n.* deformidad *f.*
defraud /dɪ'frɔd/ *v.* defraudar.
defray /dɪ'frei/ *v.* costear.
defrost /dɪ'frɔst/ *v.* descongelar.

deft /dɛft/ *a.* diestro.
defy /dɪ'fai/ *v.* desafiar.
degenerate /a dɪ'dʒɛnərɪt; v -,reit/ *a.* **1.** degenerado. —*v.* **2.** degenerar.
degeneration /dɪ,dʒɛnə'reiʃən/ *n.* degeneración *f.*
degradation /,dɛgrɪ'deiʃən/ *n.* degradación *f.*
degrade /dɪ'greid/ *v.* degradar.
degree /dɪ'gri/ *n.* grado *m.*
deign /dein/ *v.* condescender.
deity /'diɪti/ *n.* deidad *f.*
dejected /dɪ'dʒɛktɪd/ *a.* abatido.
dejection /dɪ'dʒɛkʃən/ *n.* tristeza *f.*
delay /dɪ'lei/ *n.* **1.** retardo *m.*, demora *f.* —*v.* **2.** tardar, demorar.
delegate /n 'dɛlɪgɪt; v -,geit/ *n.* **1.** delegado -da. —*v.* **2.** delegar.
delegation /,dɛlɪ'geiʃən/ *n.* delegación *f.*
delete /dɪ'lit/ *v.* suprimir, tachar.
deliberate /a dɪ'lɪbərɪt; v -ə,reit/ *a.* **1.** premeditado. —*v.* **2.** deliberar.
deliberately /dɪ'lɪbərɪtli/ *adv.* deliberadamente.
deliberation /dɪ,lɪbə'reiʃən/ *n.* deliberación *f.*
deliberative /dɪ'lɪbərətɪv/ *a.* deliberativo.
delicacy /'dɛlɪkəsi/ *n.* delicadeza *f.*
delicate /'dɛlɪkɪt/ *a.* delicado.
delicious /dɪ'lɪʃəs/ *a.* delicioso.
delight /dɪ'lait/ *n.* deleite *m.*
delightful /dɪ'laitfəl/ *a.* deleitoso.
delinquency /dɪ'lɪŋkwənsi/ *a.* delincuencia *f.*
delinquent /dɪ'lɪŋkwənt/ *a. & n.* delincuente. *m. & f.*
delirious /dɪ'lɪəriəs/ *a.* delirante.
deliver /dɪ'lɪvər/ *v.* entregar.
deliverance /dɪ'lɪvərəns/ *n.* liberación; salvación *f.*
delivery /dɪ'lɪvəri/ *n.* entrega *f.*; *Med.* parto *m.*
delude /dɪ'lud/ *v.* engañar.
deluge /'dɛlyudʒ/ *n.* inundación *f.*
delusion /dɪ'luʒən/ *n.* decepción *f.*; engaño *m.*
delve /dɛlv/ *v.* cavar, sondear.
demagogue /'dɛmə,gɒg/ *n.* demagogo -ga.
demand /dɪ'mænd/ *n.* **1.** demanda *f.* —*v.* **2.** demandar; exigir.
demarcation /,dimɑr'keiʃən/ *n.* demarcación *f.*
demeanor /dɪ'minər/ *n.* conducta *f.*
demented /dɪ'mɛntɪd/ *a.* demente, loco.
demilitarize /di'mɪlɪtə,raiz/ *v.* desmilitarizar.
demobilize /di'moubə,laiz/ *v.* desmovilizar.
democracy /dɪ'mɒkrəsi/ *n.* democracia *f.*
democrat /'dɛmə,kræt/ *n.* demócrata *m. & f.*
democratic /,dɛmə'krætɪk/ *a.* democrático.
demolish /dɪ'mɒlɪʃ/ *v.* demoler.
demon /'dimən/ *n.* demonio *m.*
demonstrate /'dɛmən,streit/ *v.* demostrar.
demonstration /,dɛmən'streiʃən/ *n.* demostración *f.*
demonstrative /də'mɒnstrətɪv/ *a.* demostrativo.
demoralize /dɪ'mɔrə,laiz, -'mɒr-/ *v.* desmoralizar.
demure /dɪ'myʊr/ *a.* modesto, serio.
den /dɛn/ *n.* madriguera, caverna *f.*
denature /di'neitʃər/ *v.* alterar.
denial /dɪ'naiəl/ *n.* negación *f.*
denim /'dɛnəm/ *n.* dril, tela vaquera *f.*
Denmark /'dɛnmɑrk/ *n.* Dinamarca *f.*
denomination /dɪ,nɒmə'neiʃən/ *n.* denominación; secta *f.*
denote /dɪ'nout/ *v.* denotar.
denounce /dɪ'nauns/ *v.* denunciar.
dense /dɛns/ *a.* denso, espeso; estúpido.
density /'dɛnsɪti/ *n.* densidad *f.*
dent /dɛnt/ *n.* **1.** abolladura *f.* —*v.* **2.** abollar.

dental /'dɛntl/ *a.* dental.
dentist /'dɛntɪst/ *n.* dentista *m. & f.*
dentistry /'dɛntəstri/ *n.* odontología *f.*
denture /'dɛntʃər/ *n.* dentadura *f.*
denunciation /dɪ,nʌnsi'eiʃən/ *n.* denunciación *f.*
deny /dɪ'nai/ *v.* negar, rehusar.
deodorant /di'oudərənt/ *n.* desodorante *m.*
depart /dɪ'pɑrt/ *v.* partir; irse, marcharse.
department /dɪ'pɑrtmənt/ *n.* departamento *m.*
departmental /dɪ,pɑrt'mɛntl/ *a.* departamental.
department store grandes almacenes *m.pl.*
departure /dɪ'pɑrtʃər/ *n.* salida; desviación *f.*
depend /dɪ'pɛnd/ *v.* depender.
dependability /dɪ,pɛndə'bɪlɪti/ *n.* confiabilidad *f.*
dependable /dɪ'pɛndəbəl/ *a.* confiable.
dependence /dɪ'pɛndəns/ *n.* dependencia *f.*
dependent /dɪ'pɛndənt/ *a. & n.* dependiente *m. & f.*
depict /dɪ'pɪkt/ *v.* pintar; representar.
deplete /dɪ'plit/ *v.* agotar.
deplorable /dɪ'plɔrəbəl/ *a.* deplorable.
deplore /dɪ'plɔr/ *v.* deplorar.
deport /dɪ'pɔrt/ *v.* deportar.
deportation /,dipɔr'teiʃən/ *n.* deportación *f.*
deportment /dɪ'pɔrtmənt/ *n.* conducta *f.*
depose /dɪ'pouz/ *v.* deponer.
deposit /dɪ'pɒzɪt/ *n.* **1.** depósito *m.* (of money); yacimiento (of ore, etc.) *m.* —*v.* **2.** depositar.
depositor /dɪ'pɒzɪtər/ *n.* depositante *m. & f.*
depot /'dipou/ *n.* depósito *m.*; (railway) estación *f.*
depravity /dɪ'prævɪti/ *n.* depravación *f.*
deprecate /'dɛprɪ,keit/ *v.* deprecar.
depreciate /dɪ'priʃi,eit/ *v.* depreciar.
depreciation /dɪ,priʃi'eiʃən/ *n.* depreciación *f.*
depredation /,dɛprə'deiʃən/ *n.* depredación *f.*
depress /dɪ'prɛs/ *v.* deprimir; desanimar.
depression /dɪ'prɛʃən/ *n.* depresión *f.*
deprive /dɪ'praiv/ *v.* privar.
depth /dɛpθ/ *n.* profundidad, hondura *f.*
depth charge carga de profundidad *f.*
deputy /'dɛpyəti/ *n.* diputado -da.
deride /dɪ'raid/ *v.* burlar.
derision /dɪ'rɪʒən/ *n.* burla *f.*
derivation /,dɛrə'veiʃən/ *n.* derivación *f.*
derivative /dɪ'rɪvətɪv/ *a.* derivativo.
derive /dɪ'raiv/ *v.* derivar.
dermatologist /,dɜrmə'tɒlədʒɪst/ *n.* dermatólogo -ga.
derogatory /dɪ'rɒgə,tɔri/ *a.* derogatorio.
derrick /'dɛrɪk/ *n.* grúa *f.*
descend /dɪ'sɛnd/ *v.* descender, bajar.
descendant /dɪ'sɛndənt/ *n.* descendiente *m. & f.*
descent /dɪ'sɛnt/ *n.* descenso *m.*; origen *m.*
describe /dɪ'skraib/ *v.* describir.
description /dɪ'skrɪpʃən/ *n.* descripción *f.*
descriptive /dɪ'skrɪptɪv/ *a.* descriptivo.
desecrate /'dɛsɪ,kreit/ *v.* profanar.
desert /n 'dɛzərt; v dɪ'zɜrt/ *n.* **1.** desierto *m.* —*v.* **2.** abandonar.
deserter /dɪ'zɜrtər/ *n.* desertor -ra.
desertion /dɪ'zɜrʃən/ *n.* deserción *f.*
deserve /dɪ'zɜrv/ *v.* merecer.

design /dɪ'zain/ n. **1.** diseño m. —v. **2.** diseñar.

designate /'dɛzɪg,neit/ v. señalar, apuntar; designar.

designation /,dɛzɪg'neiʃən/ n. designación f.

designer /dɪ'zainər/ n. diseñador -ra; (technical) proyectista m. & f.

designer clothes, designer clothing ropa de marca f.

desirability /dɪ,zaiᵊrə'bɪliti/ n. conveniencia f.

desirable /dɪ'zaiᵊrəbəl/ a. deseable.

desire /dɪ'zaiᵊr/ n. **1.** deseo m. —v. **2.** desear.

desirous /dɪ'zaiᵊrəs/ a. deseoso.

desist /dɪ'sɪst/ v. desistir.

desk /dɛsk/ n. escritorio m.

desk clerk recepcionista m. & f.

desktop computer /'dɛsk,tɒp/ computadora de sobremesa f., ordenador de sobremesa f.

desolate /a 'dɛsəlɪt; v -,leit/ a. **1.** desolado. —v. **2.** desolar.

desolation /,dɛsə'leiʃən/ n. desolación, ruina f.

despair /dɪ'spɛər/ n. **1.** desesperación f. —v. **2.** desesperar.

despatch /dɪ'spætʃ/ **dispatch** n. **1.** despacho m.; prontitud f. —v. **2.** despachar.

desperado /,dɛspə'rɑdou/ n. bandido m.

desperate /'dɛspərɪt/ a. desesperado.

desperation /,dɛspə'reiʃən/ n. desesperación f.

despicable /'dɛspɪkəbəl/ a. vil.

despise /dɪ'spaiz/ v. despreciar.

despite /dɪ'spait/ prep. a pesar de.

despondent /dɪ'spɒndənt/ a. abatido; desanimado.

despot /'dɛspət/ n. déspota m. & f.

despotic /dɛs'pɒtɪk/ a. despótico.

dessert /dɪ'zɜrt/ n. postre m.

destination /,dɛstə'neiʃən/ n. destinación f.

destine /'dɛstɪn/ v. destinar.

destiny /'dɛstəni/ n. destino m.

destitute /'dɛstɪ,tut/ a. destituído, indigente.

destitution /,dɛstɪ'tuʃən/ n. destitución f.

destroy /dɪ'strɔi/ v. destrozar, destruir.

destroyer /dɪ'strɔiər/ n. destruidor -ra; (naval) destructor m.

destruction /dɪ'strʌkʃən/ n. destrucción f.

destructive /dɪ'strʌktɪv/ a. destructivo.

desultory /'dɛsəl,tɔri/ a. inconexo; casual.

detach /dɪ'tætʃ/ v. separar, desprender.

detachment /dɪ'tætʃmənt/ n. Mil. destacamento; desprendimiento m.

detail /dɪ'teil/ n. **1.** detalle m. —v. **2.** detallar.

detain /dɪ'tein/ v. detener.

detect /dɪ'tɛkt/ v. descubrir.

detection /dɪ'tɛkʃən/ n. detección f.

detective /dɪ'tɛktɪv/ n. detective m. & f.

détente /dei'tɑnt/ n. distensión f.; Pol. détente.

detention /dɪ'tɛnʃən/ n. detención; cautividad f.

deter /dɪ'tɜr/ v. disuadir.

detergent /dɪ'tɜrdʒənt/ n. & a. detergente m.

deteriorate /dɪ'tɪəriə,reit/ v. deteriorar.

deterioration /dɪ,tɪəriə'reiʃən/ n. deterioración f.

determination /dɪ,tɜrmə'neiʃən/ n. determinación f.

determine /dɪ'tɜrmɪn/ v. determinar.

deterrence /dɪ'tɜrəns/ n. disuasión f.

detest /dɪ'tɛst/ v. detestar.

detonate /'dɛtn,eit/ v. detonar.

detour /'ditur/ n. desvío m. v. desviar.

detract /dɪ'trækt/ v. disminuir.

detriment /'dɛtrəmənt/ n. detrimento m., daño m.

detrimental /,dɛtrə'mɛntl/ a. dañoso.

devaluate /di'vælyu,eit/ v. depreciar.

devastate /'dɛvə,steit/ v. devastar.

develop /dɪ'vɛləp/ v. desarrollar; Phot. revelar.

developing nation /dɪ'vɛləpɪŋ/ nación en desarrollo.

development /dɪ'vɛləpmənt/ n. desarrollo m.

deviate /'divi,eit/ v. desviar.

deviation /,divi'eiʃən/ n. desviación f.

device /dɪ'vais/ n. aparato; artificio m.

devil /'dɛvəl/ n. diablo, demonio m.

devious /'diviəs/ a. desviado.

devise /dɪ'vaiz/ v. inventar.

devoid /dɪ'vɔid/ a. desprovisto.

devote /dɪ'vout/ v. dedicar, consagrar.

devoted /dɪ'voutɪd/ a. devoto.

devotee /,dɛvə'ti/ n. aficionado -da.

devotion /dɪ'vouʃən/ n. devoción f.

devour /dɪ'vaur/ v. devorar.

devout /dɪ'vaut/ a. devoto.

dew /du/ n. rocío, sereno m.

dexterity /dɛk'stɛrɪti/ n. destreza f.

dexterous /'dɛkstrəs/ a. diestro.

diabetes /,daiə'bitɪs/ n. diabetes f.

diabolic /,daiə'bɒlɪk/ a. diabólico.

diadem /'daiə,dɛm/ n. diadema f.

diagnose /'daiəg,nous/ v. diagnosticar.

diagnosis /,daiəg'nousɪs/ n. diagnóstico m.

diagonal /dai'ægənl/ n. diagonal m.

diagram /'daiə,græm/ n. diagrama m.

dial /'daiəl/ n. **1.** cuadrante m., carátula f. —v. **2. dial up** marcar.

dialect /'daiə,lɛkt/ n. dialecto m.

dialing code /'daiəlɪŋ/ prefijo m.

dialogue /'daiə,lɒg/ n. diálogo m.

dial tone señal de marcar f.

diameter /dai'æmitər/ n. diámetro m.

diamond /'daimənd/ n. diamante, brillante m.

diaper /'daipər/ n. pañal m.

diarrhea /,daiə'riə/ n. diarrea f.

diary /'daiəri/ n. diario m.

diathermy /'daiə,θɜrmi/ n. diatermia f.

dice /dais/ n. dados m.pl.

dictate /'dɪkteit/ n. **1.** mandato m. —v. **2.** dictar.

dictation /dɪk'teiʃən/ n. dictado m.

dictator /'dɪkteitər/ n. dictador -ra.

dictatorship /dɪk'teitər,ʃɪp/ n. dictadura f.

diction /'dɪkʃən/ n. dicción f.

dictionary /'dɪkʃə,nɛri/ n. diccionario m.

die /dai/ n. **1.** matriz f.; (game) dado m. —v. **2.** morir.

diet /'daiɪt/ n. dieta f.

dietary /'daiɪ,tɛri/ a. dietético.

dietitian /,daiɪ'tɪʃən/ n. & a. dietético -ca.

differ /'dɪfər/ v. diferir.

difference /'dɪfərəns/ n. diferencia f. **to make no d.,** no importar.

different /'dɪfərənt/ a. diferente, distinto.

differential /,dɪfə'rɛnʃəl/ n. diferencial f.

differentiate /,dɪfə'rɛnʃi,eit/ v. diferenciar.

difficult /'dɪfɪ,kʌlt/ a. difícil.

difficulty /'dɪfɪ,kʌlti/ n. dificultad f.

diffident /'dɪfɪdənt/ a. tímido.

diffuse /dɪ'fyuz/ v. difundir.

diffusion /dɪ'fyuʒən/ n. difusión f.

dig /dɪg/ v. cavar.

digest /n 'daidʒɛst; v dɪ'dʒɛst, dai-/ n. **1.** extracto m. —v. **2.** digerir.

digestible /dɪ'dʒɛstəbəl, dai-/ a. digerible.

digestion /dɪ'dʒɛstʃən, dai-/ n. digestión f.

digestive /dɪ'dʒɛstɪv, dai-/ a. digestivo.

digital /'dɪdʒɪtl/ a. digital.

digitalis /,dɪdʒɪ'tælɪs/ n. digital f.

dignified /'dɪgnə,faid/ a. digno.

dignify /'dɪgnə,fai/ v. dignificar.

dignitary /'dɪgnɪ,tɛri/ n. dignatario -ria.

dignity /'dɪgnɪti/ n. dignidad f.

digress /dɪ'grɛs, dai-/ v. divagar.

digression /dɪ'grɛʃən, dai-/ n. digresión f.

dike /daik/ n. dique m.

dilapidated /dɪ'læpɪ,deitɪd/ a. dilapidado.

dilapidation /dɪ,læpə'deiʃən/ n. dilapidación f.

dilate /dai'leit/ v. dilatar.

dilatory /'dɪlə,tɔri/ a. dilatorio.

dilemma /dɪ'lɛmə/ n. dilema m.

dilettante /'dɪlɪ,tɑnt/ n. diletante m. & f.

diligence /'dɪlɪdʒəns/ n. diligencia f.

diligent /'dɪlɪdʒənt/ a. diligente, aplicado.

dilute /dɪ'lut, dai-/ v. diluir.

dim /dɪm/ a. **1.** oscuro. —v. **2.** oscurecer.

dimension /dɪ'mɛnʃən/ n. dimensión f.

diminish /dɪ'mɪnɪʃ/ v. disminuir.

diminution /,dɪmə'nuʃən/ n. disminución f.

diminutive /dɪ'mɪnyətɪv/ a. diminutivo.

dimness /'dɪmnɪs/ n. oscuridad f.

dimple /'dɪmpəl/ n. hoyuelo m.

din /dɪn/ n. alboroto, estrépito m.

dine /dain/ v. comer, cenar.

diner /'dainər/ n. coche comedor m.

dingy /'dɪndʒi/ a. deslucido, deslustrado.

dining room /'dainɪŋ/ comedor m.

dinner /'dɪnər/ n. comida, cena f.

dinosaur /'dainə,sɔr/ n. dinosauro m.

diocese /'daiəsɪs/ n. diócesis f.

dip /dɪp/ v. sumergir, hundir.

diphtheria /dɪf'θɪəriə/ n. difteria f.

diploma /dɪ'ploumə/ n. diploma m.

diplomacy /dɪ'plouməsi/ n. diplomacia f.

diplomat /'dɪplə,mæt/ n. diplomático -ca.

diplomatic /,dɪplə'mætɪk/ a. diplomático.

dipper /'dɪpər/ n. cucharón m.

dire /daiᵊr/ a. horrendo.

direct /dɪ'rɛkt, dai-/ a. **1.** directo. —v. **2.** dirigir.

direction /dɪ'rɛkʃən, 'dai-/ n. dirección f.

directive /dɪ'rɛktɪv, dai-/ n. directiva f.

directly /dɪ'rɛktli, dai-/ adv. directamente.

director /dɪ'rɛktər, dai-/ n. director -ra.

directory /dɪ'rɛktəri, dai-/ n. directorio m., guía f.

dirigible /'dɪrɪdʒəbəl/ n. dirigible m.

dirt /dɜrt/ n. basura f.; (earth) tierra f.

dirt-cheap /'dɜrt 'tʃip/ a. tirado.

dirty /'dɜrti/ a. sucio.

dis /dɪs/ v. Colloq. ofender, faltar al respeto.

disability /,dɪsə'bɪliti/ n. inhabilidad f.

disable /dɪs'eibəl/ v. incapacitar.

disabuse /,dɪsə'byuz/ v. desengañar.

disadvantage /,dɪsəd'væntɪdʒ/ n. desventaja f.

disagree /,dɪsə'gri/ v. desconvenir; disentir.

disagreeable /,dɪsə'griəbəl/ a. desagradable.

disagreement /,dɪsə'grimənt/ n. desacuerdo m.

disappear /,dɪsə'pɪər/ v. desaparecer.

disappearance /,dɪsə'pɪərəns/ n. desaparición f.

disappoint /,dɪsə'pɔint/ v. disgustar, desilusionar.

disappointment /,dɪsə'pɔintmənt/ n. disgusto m., desilusión f.

disapproval /,dɪsə'pruvəl/ n. desaprobación f.

disapprove /,dɪsə'pruv/ v. desaprobar.

disarm /dɪs'ɑrm/ v. desarmar.

disarmament /dɪs'ɑrməmənt/ n. desarme m.

disarrange /,dɪsə'reindʒ/ v. desordenar; desarreglar.

disaster /dɪ'zæstər/ n. desastre m.

disastrous /dɪ'zæstrəs/ a. desastroso.

disavow /,dɪsə'vau/ v. repudiar.

disavowal /,dɪsə'vauəl/ n. repudiación f.

disband /dɪs'bænd/ v. dispersarse.

disbelieve /,dɪsbɪ'liv/ v. descreer.

disburse /dɪs'bɜrs/ v. desembolsar, pagar.

discard /dɪ'skɑrd/ v. descartar.

discern /dɪ'sɜrn/ v. discernir.

discerning /dɪ'sɜrnɪŋ/ a. discernidor, perspicaz.

discernment /dɪ'sɜrnmənt/ n. discernimiento m.

discharge /dɪs'tʃɑrdʒ/ v. descargar; despedir.

disciple /dɪ'saipəl/ n. discípulo -la.

disciplinary /'dɪsəplə,nɛri/ a. disciplinario.

discipline /'dɪsəplɪn/ n. disciplina f.

disclaim /dɪs'kleim/ v. repudiar.

disclaimer /dɪs'kleimər/ n. negación f.

disclose /dɪ'sklouz/ v. revelar.

disclosure /dɪ'slouʒər/ n. revelación f.

disco /'dɪskou/ n. discoteca f.

discolor /dɪs'kʌlər/ v. descolorar.

discomfort /dɪs'kʌmfərt/ n. incomodidad f.

disconcert /,dɪskən'sɜrt/ v. desconcertar.

disconnect /,dɪskə'nɛkt/ v. desunir, desconectar.

disconnected /,dɪskə'nɛktɪd/ a. desunido.

disconsolate /dɪs'kɒnsəlɪt/ a. desconsolado.

discontent /,dɪskən'tɛnt/ n. descontento m.

discontented /,dɪskən'tɛntɪd/ a. descontento.

discontinue /,dɪskən'tɪnyu/ v. descontinuar.

discord /'dɪskɔrd/ n. discordia f.

discordant /dɪs'kɔrdənt/ a. disonante.

discotheque /'dɪskə,tɛk/ n. discoteca f.

discount /'dɪskaunt/ n. descuento m.

discourage /dɪ'skɜrɪdʒ/ v. desalentar, desanimar.

discouragement /dɪ'skɜrɪdʒmənt/ n. desaliento, desánimo m.

discourse /'dɪskɔrs/ n. discurso m.

discourteous /dɪs'kɜrtiəs/ a. descortés.

discourtesy /dɪs'kɜrtəsi/ n. descortesía f.

discover /dɪ'skʌvər/ v. descubrir.

discoverer /dɪ'skʌvərər/ n. descubridor -ra.

discovery /dɪ'skʌvəri/ n. descubrimiento m.

discreet /dɪ'skrit/ a. discreto.

discrepancy /dɪ'skrɛpənsi/ n. discrepancia f.

discretion /dɪ'skrɛʃən/ n. discreción f.

discriminate /dɪ'skrɪm,əneit/ v. distinguir. **d. against** discriminar contra.

discrimination /dɪ,skrɪmə'neiʃən/ n. discernimiento m.; discriminación f.

discuss /dɪ'skʌs/ v. discutir.

discussion /dɪ'skʌʃən/ n. discusión f.

disdain /dɪs'dein/ n. **1.** desdén m. —v. **2.** desdeñar.

disdainful /dɪs'deinfəl/ a. desdeñoso.

disease /dɪ'ziz/ n. enfermedad f., mal m.

disembark /,dɪsɛm'bɑrk/ v. desembarcar.

disentangle /ˌdɪsɛnˈtæŋgəl/ v. desenredar.

disfigure /dɪsˈfɪgyər/ v. desfigurar.

disgrace /dɪsˈgreis/ n. **1.** vergüenza; deshonra f. —v. **2.** deshonrar.

disgraceful /dɪsˈgreisfəl/ a. vergonzoso.

disguise /dɪsˈgaiz/ n. **1.** disfraz m. —v. **2.** disfrazar.

disgust /dɪsˈgʌst/ n. **1.** repugnancia. —v. **2.** fastidiar; repugnar.

dish /dɪʃ/ n. plato m.

dishearten /dɪsˈhɑrtn̩/ v. desanimar; descorazonar.

dishonest /dɪsˈɒnɪst/ a. deshonesto.

dishonesty /dɪsˈɒnəsti/ n. deshonestidad f.

dishonor /dɪsˈɒnər/ n. **1.** deshonra f. —v. **2.** deshonrar.

dishonorable /dɪsˈɒnərəbəl/ a. deshonroso.

dishwasher /ˈdɪʃˌwɒʃər/ n. lavaplatos m.

disillusion /ˌdɪsɪˈluʒən/ n. **1.** desengaño m. —v. **2.** desengañar.

disinfect /ˌdɪsɪnˈfɛkt/ v. desinfectar.

disinfectant /ˌdɪsɪnˈfɛktənt/ n. desinfectante m.

disinherit /ˌdɪsɪnˈhɛrɪt/ v. desheredar.

disintegrate /dɪsˈɪntəˌgreit/ v. desintegrar.

disinterested /dɪsˈɪntəˌrɛstɪd, -trɪstɪd/ a. desinteresado.

disk /dɪsk/ n. disco m.

disk drive disquetera f.

diskette /dɪˈskɛt/ n. disquete m.

disk jockey pinchadiscos m. & f.

dislike /dɪsˈlaik/ n. **1.** antipatía f. —v. **2.** no gustar de.

dislocate /ˈdɪsləˌkeit/ v. dislocar.

dislodge /dɪsˈlɒdʒ/ v. desalojar; desprender.

disloyal /dɪsˈlɔiəl/ a. desleal; infiel.

disloyalty /dɪsˈlɔiəlti/ n. deslealtad f.

dismal /ˈdɪzməl/ a. lúgubre.

dismantle /dɪsˈmæntl̩/ v. desmantelar, desmontar.

dismay /dɪsˈmei/ n. **1.** consternación f. —v. **2.** consternar.

dismiss /dɪsˈmɪs/ v. despedir.

dismissal /dɪsˈmɪsəl/ n. despedida f.

dismount /dɪsˈmaunt/ v. apearse, desmontarse.

disobedience /ˌdɪsəˈbidiəns/ n. desobediencia f.

disobedient /ˌdɪsəˈbidiənt/ a. desobediente.

disobey /ˌdɪsəˈbei/ v. desobedecer.

disorder /dɪsˈɔrdər/ n. desorden m.

disorderly /dɪsˈɔrdərli/ a. desarreglado, desordenado.

disown /dɪsˈoun/ v. repudiar.

dispassionate /dɪsˈpæʃənɪt/ a. desapasionado; templado.

dispatch /dɪsˈpætʃ/ n. **1.** despacho m. —v. **2.** despachar.

dispel /dɪsˈpɛl/ v. dispersar.

dispensary /dɪsˈpɛnsəri/ n. dispensario m.

dispensation /ˌdɪspənˈseiʃən/ n. dispensación f.

dispense /dɪsˈpɛns/ v. dispensar.

dispersal /dɪsˈpɜrsəl/ n. dispersión f.

disperse /dɪsˈpɜrs/ v. dispersar.

displace /dɪsˈpleis/ v. dislocar.

display /dɪsˈplei/ n. **1.** despliegue m., exhibición f. —v. **2.** desplegar, exhibir.

displease /dɪsˈpliz/ v. disgustar; ofender.

displeasure /dɪsˈplɛʒər/ n. disgusto, sinsabor m.

disposable /dɪsˈpouzəbəl/ a. disponible; desechable.

disposal /dɪsˈpouzəl/ n. disposición f.

dispose /dɪsˈpouz/ v. disponer.

disposition /ˌdɪspəˈzɪʃən/ n. disposición f.; índole f., genio m.

dispossess /ˌdɪspəˈzɛs/ v. desposeer.

disproportionate /ˌdɪsprəˈpɔrʃənɪt/ a. desproporcionado.

disprove /dɪsˈpruv/ v. confutar.

dispute /dɪˈspyut/ n. **1.** disputa f. —v. **2.** disputar.

disqualify /dɪsˈkwɒləˌfai/ v. inhabilitar.

disregard /ˌdɪsrɪˈgɑrd/ n. **1.** desatención f. —v. **2.** desatender.

disrepair /ˌdɪsrɪˈpɛər/ n. descompostura f.

disreputable /dɪsˈrɛpyətəbəl/ a. desacreditado.

disrespect /ˌdɪsrɪˈspɛkt/ n. falta de respeto, f., desacato m.

disrespectful /ˌdɪsrɪˈspɛktfəl/ a. irrespetuoso.

disrobe /dɪsˈroub/ v. desvestir.

disrupt /dɪsˈrʌpt/ v. romper; desbaratar.

dissatisfaction /ˌdɪssætɪsˈfækʃən/ n. descontento m.

dissatisfy /dɪsˈsætɪsˌfai/ v. descontentar.

dissect /dɪˈsɛkt/ v. disecar.

dissemble /dɪˈsɛmbəl/ v. disimular.

disseminate /dɪˈsɛməˌneit/ v. diseminar.

dissension /dɪˈsɛnʃən/ n. disensión f.

dissent /dɪˈsɛnt/ n. **1.** disensión f. —v. **2.** disentir.

dissertation /ˌdɪsərˈteiʃən/ n. disertación f.

dissimilar /dɪˈsɪmələr/ a. desemejante.

dissipate /ˈdɪsəˌpeit/ v. disipar.

dissipation /ˌdɪsəˈpeiʃən/ n. disipación f.; libertinaje m.

dissolute /ˈdɪsəˌlut/ a. disoluto.

dissolution /ˌdɪsəˈluʃən/ n. disolución f.

dissolve /dɪˈzɒlv/ v. disolver; derretirse.

dissonant /ˈdɪsənənt/ a. disonante.

dissuade /dɪˈsweid/ v. disuadir.

distance /ˈdɪstəns/ n. distancia f. **at a d., in the d.,** a lo lejos.

distant /ˈdɪstənt/ a. distante, lejano.

distaste /dɪsˈteist/ n. disgusto, sinsabor m.

distasteful /dɪsˈteistfəl/ a. desagradable.

distill /dɪˈstɪl/ v. destilar.

distillation /ˌdɪstl̩ˈeiʃən/ n. destilación f.

distillery /dɪˈstɪləri/ n. destilería f.

distinct /dɪˈstɪŋkt/ a. distinto.

distinction /dɪˈstɪŋkʃən/ n. distinción f.

distinctive /dɪˈstɪŋktɪv/ a. distintivo; característico.

distinctly /dɪˈstɪŋktli/ adv. distintamente.

distinguish /dɪˈstɪŋgwɪʃ/ v. distinguir.

distinguished /dɪˈstɪŋgwɪʃt/ a. distinguido.

distort /dɪˈstɔrt/ v. falsear; torcer.

distract /dɪˈstrækt/ v. distraer.

distraction /dɪˈstrækʃən/ n. distracción f.

distraught /dɪˈstrɔt/ a. aturrullado; demente.

distress /dɪˈstrɛs/ n. **1.** dolor m. —v. **2.** afligir.

distressing /dɪˈstrɛsɪŋ/ a. penoso.

distribute /dɪˈstrɪbyut/ v. distribuir.

distribution /ˌdɪstrəˈbyuʃən/ n. distribución f.; reparto m.

distributor /dɪˈstrɪbyətər/ n. distribuidor -ra.

district /ˈdɪstrɪkt/ n. distrito m.

distrust /dɪsˈtrʌst/ n. **1.** desconfianza f. —v. **2.** desconfiar.

distrustful /dɪsˈtrʌstfəl/ a. desconfiado; sospechoso.

disturb /dɪˈstɜrb/ v. incomodar; inquietar.

disturbance /dɪˈstɜrbəns/ n. disturbio m.

disturbing /dɪˈstɜrbɪŋ/ a. inquietante.

ditch /dɪtʃ/ n. zanja f.; foso m.

divan /dɪˈvæn/ n. diván m.

dive /daiv/ n. **1.** clavado m.; Colloq. leonera f. —v. **2.** echar un clavado; bucear.

diver /ˈdaivər/ n. buzo m.

diverge /dɪˈvɜrdʒ/ v. divergir.

divergence /dɪˈvɜrdʒəns/ n. divergencia f.

divergent /dɪˈvɜrdʒənt/ a. divergente.

diverse /dɪˈvɜrs/ a. diverso.

diversion /dɪˈvɜrʒən/ n. diversión f.; pasatiempo m.

diversity /dɪˈvɜrsɪti/ n. diversidad f.

divert /dɪˈvɜrt/ v. desviar; divertir.

divest /dɪˈvɛst/ v. desnudar, despojar.

divide /dɪˈvaid/ v. dividir.

dividend /ˈdɪvɪˌdɛnd/ n. dividendo m.

divine /dɪˈvain/ a. divino.

divinity /dɪˈvɪnɪti/ n. divinidad f.

division /dɪˈvɪʒən/ n. división f.

divorce /dɪˈvɔrs/ n. **1.** divorcio m. —v. **2.** divorciar.

divorcee /dɪvɔrˈsei/ n. divorciado -da.

divulge /dɪˈvʌldʒ/ v. divulgar, revelar.

dizziness /ˈdɪzinɪs/ n. vértigo, mareo m.

dizzy /ˈdɪzi/ a. mareado.

DNA abbr. (deoxyribonucleic acid) ADN (ácido deoxirribonucleico) m.

do /du/ v. hacer.

docile /ˈdɒsəl/ a. dócil.

dock /dɒk/ n. **1.** muelle m. dry d.,** astillero m. —v. **2.** entrar en muelle.

doctor /ˈdɒktər/ n. médico m.; doctor -ra.

doctorate /ˈdɒktərɪt/ n. doctorado m.

doctrine /ˈdɒktrɪn/ n. doctrina f.

document /ˈdɒkyəmənt/ n. documento m.

documentary /ˌdɒkyəˈmɛntəri/ a. documental.

documentation /ˌdɒkyəmɛnˈteiʃən/ n. documentación f.

dodge /dɒdʒ/ n. **1.** evasión f. —v. **2.** evadir.

dodgem /ˈdɒdʒɪm/ n. coche de choque m.

doe /dou/ n. gama f.

dog /dɔg/ n. perro -a.

dogma /ˈdɔgmə/ n. dogma m.

dogmatic /dɔgˈmætɪk/ a. dogmático.

dogmatism /ˈdɔgməˌtɪzəm/ n. dogmatismo m.

doily /ˈdɔili/ n. servilletita f.

doleful /ˈdoulfəl/ a. triste.

doll /dɒl/ n. muñeca -co.

dollar /ˈdɒlər/ n. dólar m.

dolorous /ˈdoulərəs/ a. lastimoso.

dolphin /ˈdɒlfɪn/ n. delfín m.

domain /douˈmein/ n. dominio m.

dome /doum/ n. domo m.

domestic /dəˈmɛstɪk/ a. doméstico.

domesticate /dəˈmɛstɪˌkeit/ v. domesticar.

domicile /ˈdɒməˌsail/ n. domicilio m.

dominance /ˈdɒmənəns/ n. dominación f.

dominant /ˈdɒmənənt/ a. dominante.

dominate /ˈdɒməˌneit/ v. dominar.

domination /ˌdɒməˈneiʃən/ n. dominación f.

domineer /ˌdɒməˈnɪər/ v. dominar.

domineering /ˌdɒməˈnɪərɪŋ/ a. tiránico, mandón.

dominion /dəˈmɪnyən/ n. dominio; territorio m.

domino /ˈdɒməˌnou/ n. dominó f.

donate /ˈdouneit/ v. donar; contribuir.

donation /douˈneiʃən/ n. donación f.

donkey /ˈdɒŋki/ n. asno, burro m.

doom /dum/ n. **1.** perdición, ruina f. —v. **2.** perder, ruinar.

door /dɔr/ n. puerta f.

doorman /ˈdɔrˌmæn, -mən/ n. portero m.

doormat /ˈdɔrˌmæt/ n. felpudo m.

doorway /ˈdɔrˌwei/ n. entrada f.

dope /doup/ n. Colloq. narcótico m.; idiota m.

dormant /ˈdɔrmənt/ a. durmiente; inactivo.

dormitory /ˈdɔrmɪˌtɔri/ n. dormitorio m.

dosage /ˈdousɪdʒ/ n. dosificación f.

dose /dous/ n. dosis f.

dot /dɒt/ n. punto m.

dotted line /ˈdɒtɪd/ línea de puntos f.

double /ˈdʌbəl/ a. **1.** doble. —v. **2.** duplicar.

double bass /beis/ contrabajo m.

double-breasted /ˈdʌbəl ˈbrɛstɪd/ a. cruzado.

double-cross /ˈdʌbəl ˈkrɔs/ v. traicionar.

doubly /ˈdʌbli/ adv. doblemente.

doubt /daut/ n. **1.** duda f. —v. **2.** dudar.

doubtful /ˈdautfəl/ a. dudoso, incierto.

doubtless /ˈdautlɪs/ a. **1.** indudable. —adv. **2.** sin duda.

dough /dou/ n. pasta, masa f.

doughnut /ˈdounət, -ˌnʌt/ n. buñuelo m.

dove /duv/ n. paloma f.

dowager /ˈdauədʒər/ n. viuda (con título) f.

down /daun/ adv. **1.** abajo. —prep. **2.** d. the street, etc. calle abajo, etc.

downcast /ˈdaunˌkæst/ a. cabizbajo.

downfall /ˈdaunˌfɔl/ n. ruina, perdición f.

downhearted /ˈdaunˈhɑrtɪd/ a. descorazonado.

download /ˈdaunˌloud/ v. bajar, descargar.

downpour /ˈdaunˌpɔr/ n. chaparrón m.

downright /ˈdaunˌrait/ a. absoluto, completo.

downriver /ˈdaunˈrɪvər/ adv. aguas abajo, río abajo.

downstairs /ˈdaunˈstɛərz/ adv. **1.** abajo. —n. **2.** primer piso.

downstream /ˈdaunˈstrim/ adv. aguas abajo, río abajo.

downtown /ˈdaunˈtaun/ adv. al centro, en el centro.

downward /ˈdaunwərd/ a. **1.** descendente. —adv. **2.** hacia abajo.

dowry /ˈdauri/ n. dote f.

doze /douz/ v. dormitar.

dozen /ˈdʌzən/ n. docena f.

draft /dræft/ n. **1.** dibujo m.; Com. giro m.; Mil. conscripción f. —v. **2.** dibujar; Mil. reclutar.

draftee /dræfˈti/ n. conscripto m.

draft notice notificación de reclutamiento f.

drag /dræg/ v. arrastrar.

dragon /ˈdrægən/ n. dragón m.

drain /drein/ n. **1.** desaguadero m. —v. **2.** desaguar.

drainage /ˈdreinɪdʒ/ n. drenaje m.

drain board escurridero m.

drama /ˈdrɑmə, ˈdræmə/ n. drama m.

dramatic /drəˈmætɪk/ a. dramático.

dramatics /drəˈmætɪks/ n. dramática f.

dramatist /ˈdræmətɪst, ˈdrɑmə-/ n. dramaturgo -ga.

dramatize /ˈdræməˌtaiz, ˈdrɑmə-/ v. dramatizar.

drape /dreip/ n. cortinas f.pl. v. vestir; adornar.

drapery /ˈdreipəri/ n. colgaduras f.pl.; ropaje m.

drastic /ˈdræstɪk/ a. drástico.

draw /drɔ/ v. dibujar; atraer. **d. up,** formular.

drawback /ˈdrɔˌbæk/ n. desventaja f.

drawer /drɔr/ n. cajón m.

drawing /ˈdrɔɪŋ/ n. dibujo m.; rifa f.

dread /drɛd/ n. **1.** terror m. —v. **2.** temer.

dreadful /ˈdrɛdfəl/ a. terrible.

dreadfully /ˈdrɛdfəli/ adv. horrendamente.

dream /drim/ n. **1.** sueño, ensueño m. —v. **2.** soñar.

dreamer /ˈdrimər/ n. soñador -ra; visionario -ia.

dreamy /ˈdrimi/ a. soñador, contemplativo.

dreary /ˈdrɪəri/ a. monótono y pesado.

dredge /drɛdʒ/ n. **1.** rastra f. —v. **2.** rastrear.

dregs /drɛgz/ n. sedimento m.

drench /drɛntʃ/ v. mojar.

dress /drɛs/ n. **1.** vestido; traje m. —v. **2.** vestir.

dresser /'drɛsər/ n. (furniture) tocador.

dressing /'drɛsɪŋ/ n. Med. curación f.; (cookery) relleno m.; salsa f.

dressing gown bata f.

dressing table tocador m.

dressmaker /'drɛs,meikər/ n. modista m. & f.

drift /drɪft/ n. **1.** tendencia f.; Naut. deriva f. —v. **2.** Naut. derivar; (snow) amontonarse.

drill /drɪl/ n. **1.** ejercicio m.; Mech. taladro m. —v. **2.** Mech. taladrar.

drink /drɪŋk/ n. **1.** bebida f. —v. **2.** beber, tomar.

drinkable /'drɪŋkəbəl/ a. potable, bebible.

drip /drɪp/ v. gotear.

drive /draiv/ n. **1.** paseo m. —v. **2.** impeler; Auto. guiar, conducir.

drive-in (movie theater) /'draiv ,ɪn/ n. autocine, autocinema m.

driver /'draivər/ n. conductor -ra; chofer m. **d.'s license,** permiso de conducir.

driveway /'draiv,wei/ n. entrada para coches.

drizzle /'drɪzəl/ n. **1.** llovizna f. —v. **2.** lloviznar.

dromedary /'drɒmɪ,dɛri/ n. dromedario m.

droop /drup/ v. inclinarse.

drop /drɒp/ n. **1.** gota f. —v. **2.** soltar; dejar caer.

dropout /'drɒp,aut/ n. joven que abandona sus estudios.

dropper /'drɒpər/ n. cuentagotas f.

dropsy /'drɒpsi/ n. hidropesía f.

drought /draut/ n. sequía f.

drove /drouv/ n. manada f.

drown /draun/ v. ahogar.

drowse /drauz/ v. adormecer.

drowsiness /'drauzɪnɪs/ n. somnolencia f.

drowsy /'drauzi/ a. soñoliento.

drudge /drʌdʒ/ n. ganapán m.

drudgery /'drʌdʒəri/ n. trabajo penoso.

drug /drʌg/ n. **1.** droga f. —v. **2.** narcotizar.

drug addict drogadicto -ta, toxicómano -na m. & f.

druggist /'drʌgɪst/ n. farmacéutico -ca, boticario -ria.

drugstore /'drʌg,stɔr/ n. farmacia, botica, droguería f.

drum /drʌm/ n. tambor m.

drummer /'drʌmər/ n. tambor m.

drumstick /'drʌm,stɪk/ n. palillo m.; Leg. pierna f.

drunk /drʌŋk/ a. & n. borracho, -a.

drunkard /'drʌŋkərd/ n. borrachón m.

drunken /'drʌŋkən/ a. borracho; ebrio.

drunkenness /'drʌŋkənnɪs/ n. embriaguez f.

dry /drai/ a. **1.** seco, árido. —v. **2.** secar.

dry cell n. pila seca f.

dry cleaner tintorero -ra.

dryness /'drainɪs/ n. sequedad f.

dual /'duəl/ a. doble.

dubious /'dubiəs/ a. dudoso.

duchess /'dʌtʃɪs/ n. duquesa f.

duck /dʌk/ n. **1.** pato m. —v. **2.** zambullir; (avoid) esquivar.

duct /dʌkt/ n. canal m.

due /du/ a. **1.** debido; Com. vencido. —n. **2.** dues cuota f.

duel /'duəl/ n. duelo m.

duelist /'duəlɪst/ n. duelista m.

duet /du'ɛt/ n. dúo m.

duke /duk/ n. duque m.

dull /dʌl/ a. apagado, desteñido; sin punta; Fig. pesado, soso.

dullness /'dʌlnɪs/ n. estupidez; pesadez f.; deslustre m.

duly /'duli/ adv. debidamente.

dumb /dʌm/ a. mudo; Colloq. estúpido.

dumbwaiter /'dʌm,weitər/ n. montaplatos m.

dumfound /dʌm'faund/ v. confundir.

dummy /'dʌmi/ n. maniquí m.

dump /dʌmp/ n. **1.** depósito m. —v. **2.** descargar.

dune /dun/ n. duna f.

dungeon /'dʌndʒən/ n. calabozo m.

dunk /dʌŋk/ v. mojar.

dupe /dup/ v. engañar.

duplicate /a, n 'duplɪkɪt; v -,keit/ a. & n. **1.** duplicado f. —v. **2.** duplicar.

duplication /,duplɪ'keiʃən/ n. duplicación f.

duplicity /du'plɪsɪti/ n. duplicidad f.

durability /,durə'bɪlɪti/ n. durabilidad f.

durable /'durəbəl/ a. durable, duradero.

duration /du'reiʃən/ n. duración f.

duress /du'rɛs/ n. compulsión f.; encierro m.

during /'durɪŋ/ prep. durante.

dusk /dʌsk/ n. crepúsculo m.

dusky /'dʌski/ a. oscuro; moreno.

dust /dʌst/ n. **1.** polvo m. —v. **2.** polvorear; despolvorear.

dusty /'dʌsti/ a. empolvado.

Dutch /dʌtʃ/ a. holandés -sa.

dutiful /'dutəfəl/ a. respetuoso.

dutifully /'dutəfəli/ adv. respetuosamente, obedientemente.

duty /'duti/ n. deber m.; Com. derechos m.pl.

duty-free /'duti 'fri/ a. libre de derechos.

dwarf /dwɔrf/ n. **1.** enano -na. —v. **2.** achicar.

dwell /dwɛl/ v. habitar, residir. **d. on,** espaciarse en.

dwelling /'dwɛlɪŋ/ n. morada, casa f.

dwindle /'dwɪndl/ v. disminuirse.

dye /dai/ n. **1.** tintura f. —v. **2.** teñir.

dyer /'daiər/ n. tintorero -ra.

dynamic /dai'næmɪk/ a. dinámico.

dynamite /'dainə,mait/ n. dinamita f.

dynamo /'dainə,mou/ n. dínamo f.

dynasty /'dainəsti/ n. dinastía f.

dysentery /'dɪsən,tɛri/ n. disentería f.

dyslexia /dɪs'lɛksiə/ n. dislexia f.

dyslexic /dɪs'lɛksɪk/ a. disléxico.

dyspepsia /dɪs'pɛpʃə/ n. dispepsia f.

E

each /itʃ/ a. **1.** cada. —pron. **2.** cada uno -na. **e. other,** el uno al otro.

eager /'igər/ a. ansioso.

eagerly /'igərli/ adv. ansiosamente.

eagerness /'igərnɪs/ n. ansia f.

eagle /'igəl/ n. águila f.

ear /ɪr/ n. oído m.; (outer) oreja f.; (of corn) mazorca f.

earache /'ɪr,eik/ n. dolor de oído m.

earl /ɜrl/ n. conde m.

early /'ɜrli/ a. & adv. temprano.

earn /ɜrn/ v. ganar.

earnest /'ɜrnɪst/ a. serio.

earnestly /'ɜrnɪstli/ adv. seriamente.

earnings /'ɜrnɪŋz/ n. ganancias f.pl.; Com. ingresos m.pl.

earphone /'ɪr,foun/ n. auricular m.

earring /'ɪr,rɪŋ/ n. pendiente, arete m.

earth /ɜrθ/ n. tierra f.

earthquake /'ɜrθ,kweik/ n. terremoto m.

ease /iz/ n. **1.** reposo m.; facilidad f. —v. **2.** aliviar.

easel /'izəl/ n. caballete m.

easily /'izəli/ adv. fácilmente.

east /ist/ n. oriente, este m.

Easter /'istər/ n. Pascua Florida.

eastern /'istərn/ a. oriental.

eastward /'istwərd/ adv. hacia el este.

easy /'izi/ a. fácil.

eat /it/ v. comer.

eau de Cologne /'ou də kə'loun/ colonia f.

eaves /ivz/ n. socarrén m.

ebb /ɛb/ n. **1.** menguante f. —v. **2.** menguar.

ebony /'ɛbəni/ n. ébano m.

eccentric /ɪk'sɛntrɪk/ a. excéntrico.

eccentricity /,ɛksən'trɪsɪti/ n. excentricidad f.

ecclesiastic /ɪ,klizi'æstɪk/ a. & n. eclesiástico.

echelon /'ɛʃə,lɒn/ n. escalón m.

echo /'ɛkou/ n. eco m.

eclipse /ɪ'klɪps/ n. **1.** eclipse m. —v. **2.** eclipsar.

ecological /,ɛkə'lɒdʒɪkəl/ a. ecológico.

ecology /ɪ'kɒlədʒi/ n. ecología f.

economic /,ɛkə'nɒmɪk, ,ikə-/ a. económico.

economical /,ɛkə'nɒmɪkəl, ,ikə-/ a. económico.

economics /,ɛkə'nɒmɪks, ,ikə-/ n. economía política.

economist /ɪ'kɒnəmɪst/ n. economista m. & f.

economize /ɪ'kɒnə,maiz/ v. economizar.

economy /ɪ'kɒnəmi/ n. economía f.

ecstasy /'ɛkstəsi/ n. éxtasis m.

Ecuadorian /,ɛkwə'dɔriən/ a. & n. ecuatoriano -na.

ecumenical /,ɛkyu'mɛnɪkəl/ a. ecuménico.

eczema /'ɛksəmə/ n. eczema f.

eddy /'ɛdi/ n. **1.** remolino f. —v. **2.** remolinar.

edge /ɛdʒ/ n. **1.** filo; borde m. —v. **2. e. one's way,** abrirse paso.

edible /'ɛdəbəl/ a. comestible.

edict /'idɪkt/ n. edicto m.

edifice /'ɛdəfɪs/ n. edificio m.

edify /'ɛdə,fai/ v. edificar.

edition /ɪ'dɪʃən/ n. edición f.

editor /'ɛdɪtər/ n. redactor -ra.

editorial /,ɛdɪ'tɔriəl/ n. editorial m. **e. board,** consejo de redacción m. **e. staff,** redacción f.

educate /'ɛdʒu,keit/ v. educar.

education /,ɛdʒu'keiʃən/ n. instrucción; enseñanza f.

educational /,ɛdʒu'keiʃənl/ a. educativo.

educator /'ɛdʒu,keitər/ n. educador -ra, pedagogo -ga.

eel /il/ n. anguila f.

efface /ɪ'feis/ v. tachar.

effect /ɪ'fɛkt/ n. **1.** efecto m. **in e.,** en vigor. —v. **2.** efectuar, realizar.

effective /ɪ'fɛktɪv/ a. eficaz; efectivo; en vigor.

effectively /ɪ'fɛktɪvli/ adv. eficazmente.

effectiveness /ɪ'fɛktɪvnɪs/ n. efectividad f.

effectual /ɪ'fɛktʃuəl/ a. eficaz.

effeminate /ɪ'fɛmənɪt/ a. afeminado.

efficacy /'ɛfɪkəsi/ n. eficacia f.

efficiency /ɪ'fɪʃənsi/ n. eficiencia f.

efficient /ɪ'fɪʃənt/ a. eficaz.

efficiently /ɪ'fɪʃəntli/ adv. eficazmente.

effigy /'ɛfɪdʒi/ n. efigie f.

effort /'ɛfərt/ n. esfuerzo m.

effrontery /ɪ'frʌntəri/ n. impudencia f.

effusive /ɪ'fyusɪv/ a. efusivo.

egg /ɛg/ n. huevo m. **fried e.,** huevo frito. **soft-boiled e.,** h. pasado por agua. **scrambled eggs,** huevos revueltos.

eggplant /'ɛg,plænt/ n. berenjena f.

egg white clara de huevo f.

egoism /'igou,ɪzəm/ n. **egotism** egoísmo m.

egoist /'igouɪst/ n. **egotist** n. egoísta m. & f.

egotism /'igə,tɪzəm/ n. egotismo m.

egotist /'igətɪst/ n. egotista m. & f.

Egypt /'idʒɪpt/ n. Egipto m.

Egyptian /ɪ'dʒɪpʃən/ a. & n. egipcio -ia.

eight /eit/ a. & pron. ocho.

eighteen /'ei'tin/ a. & pron. dieciocho.

eighth /eitθ, eiθ/ a. octavo.

eightieth /'eitiɪθ/ n. octogésimo m.

eighty /'eiti/ a. & pron. ochenta.

either /'iðər/ a. & pron. **1.** cualquiera de los dos. —adv. **2.** tampoco. —conj. **3. either... or,** o.... o.

ejaculate /ɪ'dʒækyə,leit/ v. exclamar; eyacular.

ejaculation /ɪ,dʒækyə'leiʃən/ n. eyaculación f.

eject /ɪ'dʒɛkt/ v. expeler; eyectar.

ejection /ɪ'dʒɛkʃən/ n. expulsión f.; eyección f.

elaborate /a ɪ'læbərɪt; v -ə,reit/ a. **1.** elaborado. —v. **2.** elaborar; ampliar.

elapse /ɪ'læps/ v. transcurrir; pasar.

elastic /ɪ'læstɪk/ a. & n. elástico m.

elasticity /ɪlæ'stɪsɪti/ n. elasticidad f.

elate /ɪ'leit/ v. exaltar.

elation /ɪ'leiʃən/ n. exaltación f.

elbow /'ɛlbou/ n. codo m.

elder /'ɛldər/ a. **1.** mayor. —n. **2.** anciano -na.

elderly /'ɛldərli/ a. de edad.

eldest /'ɛldɪst/ a. mayor.

elect /ɪ'lɛkt/ v. elegir.

election /ɪ'lɛkʃən/ n. elección f.

elective /ɪ'lɛktɪv/ a. electivo.

electorate /ɪ'lɛktərɪt/ n. electorado m.

electric /ɪ'lɛktrɪk/ **electrical** a. eléctrico.

electrician /ɪlɛk'trɪʃən/ n. electricista m. & f.

electricity /ɪlɛk'trɪsɪti/ n. electricidad f.

electrocardiogram /ɪ,lɛktrou'kardiə,græm/ n. electrocardiograma m.

electrocute /ɪ'lɛktrə,kyut/ v. electrocutar.

electrode /ɪ'lɛktroud/ n. electrodo m.

electrolysis /ɪlɛk'trɒləsɪs/ n. electrólisis f.

electron /ɪ'lɛktrɒn/ n. electrón m.

electronic /ɪlɛk'trɒnɪk/ a. electrónico.

electronics /ɪlɪk'trɒnɪks/ n. electrónica f.

elegance /'ɛlɪgəns/ n. elegancia f.

elegant /'ɛlɪgənt/ a. elegante.

elegy /'ɛlɪdʒi/ n. elegía f.

element /'ɛləmənt/ n. elemento m.

elemental /,ɛlə'mɛntl/ a. elemental.

elementary /,ɛlə'mɛntəri/ a. elemental.

elephant /'ɛləfənt/ n. elefante -ta.

elevate /'ɛlə,veit/ v. elevar.

elevation /,ɛlə'veiʃən/ n. elevación f.

elevator /'ɛlə,veitər/ n. ascensor m.

eleven /ɪ'lɛvən/ a. & pron. once.

eleventh /ɪ'lɛvənθ/ a. undécimo.

eleventh hour último minuto m.

elf /ɛlf/ n. duende m.

elicit /ɪ'lɪsɪt/ v. sacar; despertar.

eligibility /,ɛlɪdʒə'bɪlɪti/ n. elegibilidad f.

eligible /'ɛlɪdʒəbəl/ a. elegible.

eliminate /ɪ'lɪmə,neit/ v. eliminar.

elimination /ɪ,lɪmə'neiʃən/ n. eliminación f.

elixir /ɪ'lɪksər/ n. elixir m.

elk /ɛlk/ n. alce m., anta m.

elm /ɛlm/ n. olmo m.

elocution /,ɛlə'kyuʃən/ n. elocución f.

elongate /ɪ'lɔŋgeit/ v. alargar.

elope /ɪ'loup/ v. fugarse.

eloquence /'ɛləkwəns/ n. elocuencia f.

eloquent /'ɛləkwənt/ a. elocuente.

eloquently /'ɛləkwəntli/ adv. elocuentemente.

else /ɛls/ adv. más. **someone e.,** otra persona. **something e.,** otra cosa. **or e.,** de otro modo.

elsewhere /'ɛls,wɛər/ adv. en otra parte.

elucidate /ɪˈlusɪˌdeɪt/ v. elucidar.

elude /ɪˈlud/ v. eludir.

elusive /ɪˈlusɪv/ a. evasivo.

emaciated /ɪˈmeɪʃiˌeɪtɪd/ a. demacrado, enflaquecido.

e-mail /ˈiˌmeɪl/ n. correo electrónico m.

emanate /ˈɛməˌneɪt/ v. emanar.

emancipate /ɪˈmænsəˌpeɪt/ v. emancipar.

emancipation /ɪˌmænsəˈpeɪʃən/ n. emancipación f.

emancipator /ɪˈmænsəˌpeɪtər/ n. libertador -ra.

embalm /ɛmˈbɑm/ v. embalsamar.

embankment /ɛmˈbæŋkmənt/ n. malecón, dique m.

embargo /ɛmˈbɑrɡoʊ/ n. embargo m.

embark /ɛmˈbɑrk/ v. embarcar.

embarrass /ɛmˈbærəs/ v. avergonzar; turbar.

embarrassing /ɛmˈbærəsɪŋ/ a. penoso, vergonzoso.

embarrassment /ɛmˈbærəsmənt/ n. turbación; vergüenza f.

embassy /ˈɛmbəsi/ n. embajada f.

embellish /ɛmˈbɛlɪʃ/ v. hermosear, embellecer.

embellishment /ɛmˈbɛlɪʃmənt/ n. embellecimiento m.

embezzle /ɛmˈbɛzəl/ v. desfalcar, malversar.

emblem /ˈɛmbləm/ n. emblema m.

embody /ɛmˈbɒdi/ v. incorporar; personificar.

embrace /ɛmˈbreɪs/ n. 1. abrazo m. —v. 2. abrazar.

embroider /ɛmˈbrɔɪdər/ v. bordar.

embroidery /ɛmˈbrɔɪdəri, -dri/ n. bordado m.

embryo /ˈɛmbriˌoʊ/ n. embrión m.

embryonic /ˌɛmbriˈɒnɪk/ a. embrionario.

emerald /ˈɛmərəld/ n. esmeralda f.

emerge /ɪˈmɜrdʒ/ v. salir.

emergency /ɪˈmɜrdʒənsi/ n. emergencia f.

emergency brake freno de auxilio m.

emergency exit salida de urgencia f.

emergency landing aterrizaje forzoso m.

emergent /ɪˈmɜrdʒənt/ a. emergente.

emery /ˈɛməri/ n. esmeril m.

emetic /ɪˈmɛtɪk/ n. emético m.

emigrant /ˈɛmɪɡrənt/ a. & n. emigrante m. & f.

emigrate /ˈɛmɪˌɡreɪt/ v. emigrar.

emigration /ˌɛməˈɡreɪʃən/ n. emigración f.

eminence /ˈɛmənəns/ n. altura; eminencia f.

eminent /ˈɛmənənt/ a. eminente.

emissary /ˈɛməˌsɛri/ n. emisario m.

emission /ɪˈmɪʃən/ n. emisión f.

emit /ɪˈmɪt/ v. emitir.

emolument /ɪˈmɒlyəmənt/ n. emolumento m.

emotion /ɪˈmoʊʃən/ n. emoción f.

emotional /ɪˈmoʊʃənl/ a. emocional; sentimental.

emperor /ˈɛmpərər/ n. emperador m.

emphasis /ˈɛmfəsɪs/ n. énfasis m. or f.

emphasize /ˈɛmfəˌsaɪz/ v. acentuar, recalcar.

emphatic /ɛmˈfætɪk/ a. enfático.

empire /ˈɛmpaɪər/ n. imperio m.

empirical /ɛmˈpɪrɪkəl/ a. empírico.

employ /ɛmˈplɔɪ/ v. emplear.

employee /ɛmˈplɔɪi/ n. empleado -da.

employer /ɛmˈplɔɪər/ n. patrón -ona.

employment /ɛmˈplɔɪmənt/ n. empleo m.

employment agency agencia de colocaciones f.

empower /ɛmˈpaʊər/ v. autorizar.

emptiness /ˈɛmptɪnɪs/ n. vaciedad; futilidad f.

empty /ˈɛmpti/ a. 1. vacío. —v. 2. vaciar.

emulate /ˈɛmyəˌleɪt/ v. emular.

emulsion /ɪˈmʌlʃən/ n. emulsión f.

enable /ɛnˈeɪbəl/ v. capacitar; permitir.

enact /ɛnˈækt/ v. promulgar, decretar.

enactment /ɛnˈæktmənt/ n. ley f., estatuto m.

enamel /ɪˈnæməl/ n. 1. esmalte m. —v. 2. esmaltar.

enamored /ɪˈnæmərd/ a. enamorado.

enchant /ɛnˈtʃænt/ v. encantar.

enchantment /ɛnˈtʃæntmənt/ n. encanto m.

encircle /ɛnˈsɜrkəl/ v. circundar.

enclose /ɛnˈkloʊz/ v. encerrar. **enclosed,** (in letter) adjunto.

enclosure /ɛnˈkloʊʒər/ n. recinto m.; (in letter) incluso m.

encompass /ɛnˈkʌmpəs/ v. circundar.

encounter /ɛnˈkaʊntər/ n. 1. encuentro m. —v. 2. encontrar.

encourage /ɛnˈkɜrɪdʒ/ v. animar.

encouragement /ɛnˈkɜrɪdʒmənt/ n. estímulo m.

encroach /ɛnˈkroʊtʃ/ v. usurpar; meterse.

encryption /ɛnˈkrɪpʃən/ n. encriptación f., cifrado m.

encyclical /ɛnˈsɪklɪkəl/ n. encíclica f.

encyclopedia /ɛnˌsaɪkləˈpidiə/ n. enciclopedia f.

end /ɛnd/ n. 1. fin, término, cabo; extremo; (aim) propósito m. —v. 2. acabar; terminar.

endanger /ɛnˈdeɪndʒər/ v. poner en peligro.

endear /ɛnˈdɪər/ v. hacer querer.

endeavor /ɛnˈdɛvər/ n. 1. esfuerzo m. —v. 2. esforzarse.

ending /ˈɛndɪŋ/ n. conclusión f.

endless /ˈɛndlɪs/ a. sin fin.

endocrine gland /ˈɛndəkrɪn/ glándula endocrina f.

endorse /ɛnˈdɔrs/ v. endosar; apoyar.

endorsement /ɛnˈdɔrsmənt/ n. endoso m.

endow /ɛnˈdaʊ/ v. dotar, fundar.

endowment /ɛnˈdaʊmənt/ n. dotación f., fundación f.

endurance /ɛnˈdʊrəns/ n. resistencia f.

endure /ɛnˈdʊr/ v. soportar, resistir, aguantar.

enema /ˈɛnəmə/ n. enema; lavativa f.

enemy /ˈɛnəmi/ n. enemigo -ga.

energetic /ˌɛnərˈdʒɛtɪk/ a. enérgico.

energy /ˈɛnərdʒi/ n. energía f.

enervate /ˈɛnərˌveɪt/ v. enervar.

enervation /ˌɛnərˈveɪʃən/ n. enervación f.

enfold /ɛnˈfoʊld/ v. envolver.

enforce /ɛnˈfɔrs/ v. ejecutar.

enforcement /ɛnˈfɔrsmənt/ n. ejecución f.

engage /ɛnˈɡeɪdʒ/ v. emplear; ocupar.

engaged /ɛnˈɡeɪdʒd/ a. (to marry) prometido.

engagement /ɛnˈɡeɪdʒmənt/ n. combate; compromiso; contrato m.; cita f.

engine /ˈɛndʒɪn/ n. máquina f. (railroad) locomotora f.

engineer /ˌɛndʒəˈnɪər/ n. ingeniero -ra; maquinista m.

engineering /ˌɛndʒəˈnɪərɪŋ/ n. ingeniería f.

England /ˈɪŋɡlənd/ n. Inglaterra f.

English /ˈɪŋɡlɪʃ/ a. & n. inglés -esa.

English Channel Canal de la Mancha m.

Englishman /ˈɪŋɡlɪʃmən/ n. inglés m.

Englishwoman /ˈɪŋɡlɪʃˌwʊmən/ n. inglesa f.

engrave /ɛnˈɡreɪv/ v. grabar.

engraver /ɛnˈɡreɪvər/ n. grabador m.

engraving /ɛnˈɡreɪvɪŋ/ n. grabado m.

engross /ɛnˈɡroʊs/ v. absorber.

enhance /ɛnˈhæns/ v. aumentar en valor; realzar.

enigma /əˈnɪɡmə/ n. enigma m.

enigmatic /ˌɛnɪɡˈmætɪk/ a. enigmático.

enjoy /ɛnˈdʒɔɪ/ v. gozar de; disfrutar de. **e. oneself,** divertirse.

enjoyable /ɛnˈdʒɔɪəbəl/ a. agradable.

enjoyment /ɛnˈdʒɔɪmənt/ n. goce m.

enlarge /ɛnˈlɑrdʒ/ v. agrandar; ampliar.

enlargement /ɛnˈlɑrdʒmənt/ n. ensanchamiento m., ampliación f.

enlarger /ɛnˈlɑrdʒər/ n. amplificador m.

enlighten /ɛnˈlaɪtn/ v. informar.

enlightenment /ɛnˈlaɪtnmənt/ n. esclarecimiento m.; cultura f.

enlist /ɛnˈlɪst/ v. reclutar; alistarse.

enlistment /ɛnˈlɪstmənt/ n. alistamiento m.

enliven /ɛnˈlaɪvən/ v. avivar.

enmesh /ɛnˈmɛʃ/ v. entrampar.

enmity /ˈɛnmɪti/ n. enemistad f.

enormity /ɪˈnɔrmɪti/ v. enormidad f.

enormous /ɪˈnɔrməs/ a. enorme.

enough /ɪˈnʌf/ a. & adv. bastante. **to be e.,** bastar.

enrage /ɛnˈreɪdʒ/ v. enfurecer.

enrich /ɛnˈrɪtʃ/ v. enriquecer.

enroll /ɛnˈroʊl/ v. registrar; matricularse.

enrollment /ɛnˈroʊlmənt/ n. matriculación f.

ensign /ˈɛnsən/ n. bandera f.; (naval) subteniente m.

enslave /ɛnˈsleɪv/ v. esclavizar.

ensue /ɛnˈsu/ v. seguir, resultar.

entail /ɛnˈteɪl/ v. acarrear, ocasionar.

entangle /ɛnˈtæŋɡəl/ v. enredar.

enter /ˈɛntər/ v. entrar.

enterprise /ˈɛntərˌpraɪz/ n. empresa f.

enterprising /ˈɛntərˌpraɪzɪŋ/ a. emprendedor.

entertain /ˌɛntərˈteɪn/ v. entretener; divertir.

entertainment /ˌɛntərˈteɪnmənt/ n. entretenimiento m.; diversión f.

enthrall /ɛnˈθrɔl/ v. esclavizar; cautivar.

enthusiasm /ɛnˈθuziˌæzəm/ n. entusiasmo m.

enthusiast /ɛnˈθuziˌæst, -ɪst/ n. entusiasta m. & f.

enthusiastic /ɛnˌθuziˈæstɪk/ a. entusiasmado.

entice /ɛnˈtaɪs/ v. inducir.

entire /ɛnˈtaɪər/ a. entero.

entirely /ɛnˈtaɪərli/ adv. enteramente.

entirety /ɛnˈtaɪərti/ n. totalidad f.

entitle /ɛnˈtaɪtl/ v. autorizar; (book) titular.

entity /ˈɛntɪti/ n. entidad f.

entrails /ˈɛntreɪlz/ n. entrañas f.pl.

entrance /ˈɛntrəns/ n. entrada f.

entrance examination examen de ingreso m.

entrant /ˈɛntrənt/ n. competidor -ra.

entreat /ɛnˈtrit/ v. rogar, suplicar.

entreaty /ɛnˈtriti/ n. ruego m., súplica f.

entrench /ɛnˈtrɛntʃ/ v. atrincherar.

entrust /ɛnˈtrʌst/ v. confiar.

entry /ˈɛntri/ n. entrada f.; Com. partida f.

entry blank hoja de inscripción f.

enumerate /ɪˈnuməˌreɪt/ v. enumerar.

enumeration /ɪˌnuməˈreɪʃən/ n. enumeración f.

enunciate /ɪˈnʌnsiˌeɪt/ v. enunciar.

enunciation /ɪˌnʌnsiˈeɪʃən/ n. enunciación f.

envelop /ɛnˈvɛləp/ v. envolver.

envelope /ˈɛnvəˌloʊp/ n. sobre m.; cubierta f.

enviable /ˈɛnviəbəl/ a. envidiable.

envious /ˈɛnviəs/ a. envidioso.

environment /ɛnˈvaɪrənmənt/ n. ambiente m.

environmentalist /ɛnˌvaɪrənˈmɛntlɪst/ n. ambientalista, ecologista m. & f.

environmental protection /ɛnˌvaɪrənˈmɛntəl/ protección del ambiente.

environs /ɛnˈvaɪrənz/ n. alrededores m.

envoy /ˈɛnvɔɪ/ n. enviado m.

envy /ˈɛnvi/ n. 1. envidia f. —v. 2. envidiar.

eon /ˈiən/ n. eón m.

ephemeral /ɪˈfɛmərəl/ a. efímero.

epic /ˈɛpɪk/ a. 1. épico. —n. 2. epopeya f.

epicure /ˈɛpɪˌkyʊr/ n. epicúreo m.

epidemic /ˌɛpɪˈdɛmɪk/ a. 1. epidémico. —n. 2. epidemia f.

epidermis /ˌɛpɪˈdɜrmɪs/ n. epidermis f.

epigram /ˈɛpɪˌɡræm/ n. epigrama m.

epilepsy /ˈɛpəˌlɛpsi/ n. epilepsia f.

epilogue /ˈɛpəˌlɔɡ/ n. epílogo m.

episode /ˈɛpəˌsoʊd/ n. episodio m.

epistle /ɪˈpɪsəl/ n. epístola f.

epitaph /ˈɛpɪˌtæf/ n. epitafio m.

epithet /ˈɛpəˌθɛt/ n. epíteto m.

epitome /ɪˈpɪtəmi/ n. epítome m.

epoch /ˈɛpək/ n. época, era f.

Epsom salts /ˈɛpsəm/ n.pl. sal de la Higuera f.

equal /ˈikwəl/ a. & n. 1. igual m. —v. 2. igualar; equivaler.

equality /ɪˈkwɒlɪti/ n. igualdad f.

equalize /ˈikwəˌlaɪz/ v. igualar.

equanimity /ˌikwəˈnɪmɪti/ n. ecuanimidad f.

equate /ɪˈkweɪt/ v. igualar.

equation /ɪˈkweɪʒən/ n. ecuación f.

equator /ɪˈkweɪtər/ n. ecuador m.

equatorial /ˌikwəˈtɔriəl/ a. ecuatorial.

equestrian /ɪˈkwɛstriən/ n. 1. jinete m. —a. 2. ecuestre.

equilibrium /ˌikwəˈlɪbriəm/ n. equilibrio m.

equinox /ˈikwəˌnɒks/ n. equinoccio m.

equip /ɪˈkwɪp/ v. equipar.

equipment /ɪˈkwɪpmənt/ n. equipo m.

equitable /ˈɛkwɪtəbəl/ a. equitativo.

equity /ˈɛkwɪti/ n. equidad, justicia f.

equivalent /ɪˈkwɪvələnt/ a. & n. equivalente m.

equivocal /ɪˈkwɪvəkəl/ a. equívoco, ambiguo.

era /ˈɪərə, ˈɛrə/ n. era, época, edad f.

eradicate /ɪˈrædɪˌkeɪt/ v. extirpar.

erase /ɪˈreɪs/ v. borrar.

eraser /ɪˈreɪsər/ n. borrador m.

erasure /ɪˈreɪʃər/ n. borradura f.

erect /ɪˈrɛkt/ a. 1. derecho, erguido. —v. 2. erigir.

erection /ɪˈrɛkʃən/ **erectness** n. erección f.

ermine /ˈɜrmɪn/ n. armiño m.

erode /ɪˈroʊd/ v. corroer.

erosion /ɪˈroʊʒən/ n. erosión f.

erotic /ɪˈrɒtɪk/ a. erótico.

err /ɜr, ɛr/ v. equivocarse.

errand /ˈɛrənd/ n. encargo, recado m.

errant /ˈɛrənt/ a. errante.

erratic /ɪˈrætɪk/ a. errático.

erroneous /əˈroʊniəs/ a. erróneo.

error /ˈɛrər/ n. error m.

erudite /ˈɛryuˌdaɪt/ a. erudito.

erudition /ˌɛryuˈdɪʃən/ n. erudición f.

eruption /ɪˈrʌpʃən/ n. erupción, irrupción f.

erysipelas /ˌɛrəˈsɪpələs/ n. erisipela f.

escalate /ˈɛskəˌleɪt/ v. escalar; intensificarse.

escalator /ˈɛskəˌleɪtər/ n. escalera mecánica f.

escapade /ˈɛskəˌpeɪd/ n. escapada; correría f.

escape /ɪˈskeɪp/ n. 1. fuga, huída f. **fire e.,** escalera de salvamento. —v. 2. escapar; fugarse.

eschew /ɛsˈtʃu/ v. evadir.

escort /n. ˈɛskɔrt; v. ɪˈskɔrt/ n. 1. escolta f. —v. 2. escoltar.

escrow /ˈɛskroʊ/ n. plica f.

escutcheon /ɪˈskʌtʃən/ n. escudo de armas m.

esophagus /ɪˈsɒfəɡəs/ n. esófago m.

esoteric /ˌɛsəˈtɛrɪk/ a. esotérico.

especially /ɪˈspɛʃəli/ adv. especialmente.

espionage /ˈɛspiəˌnɑʒ/ n. espionaje m.

espresso /ɛˈsprɛsoʊ/ n. café exprés, m.

essay /ˈɛseɪ/ n. ensayo m.

essayist /'ɛseɪɪst/ n. ensayista m. & f.

essence /'ɛsəns/ n. esencia f.; perfume m.

essential /ə'sɛntʃəl/ a. esencial.

essentially /ə'sɛntʃəli/ adv. esencialmente.

establish /ɪ'stæblɪʃ/ v. establecer.

establishment /ɪ'stæblɪʃmənt/ n. establecimiento m.

estate /ɪ'steit/ n. estado m.; hacienda f.; bienes m.pl.

esteem /ɪ'stim/ n. 1. estima f. —v. 2. estimar.

estimable /'ɛstəməbəl/ a. estimable.

estimate /n 'ɛstə,mɪt/ v -,meit/ n. 1. cálculo; presupuesto m. —v. 2. estimar.

estimation /,ɛstə'meiʃən/ n. estimación f.; cálculo m.

estrange /ɪ'streindʒ/ v. extrañar; enajenar.

estuary /'ɛstʃu,ɛri/ n. estuario m.

etch /ɛtʃ/ v. grabar al agua fuerte.

etching /'ɛtʃɪŋ/ n. aguafuerte.

eternal /ɪ'tɜrnl/ a. eterno.

eternity /ɪ'tɜrniti/ n. eternidad f.

ether /'iθər/ n. éter m.

ethereal /ɪ'θɪəriəl/ a. etéreo.

ethical /'ɛθɪkəl/ a. ético.

ethics /'ɛθɪks/ n. ética f.

ethnic /'ɛθnɪk/ a. étnico.

etiquette /'ɛtɪkɛt/ n. etiqueta f.

etymology /,ɛtə'mɒlədʒi/ n. etimología f.

eucalyptus /,yukə'lɪptəs/ n. eucalipto m.

eugenic /yu'dʒɛnɪk/ a. eugenésico.

eugenics /yu'dʒɛnɪks/ n. eugenesia f.

eulogize /'yulə,dʒaiz/ v. elogiar.

eulogy /'yulədʒi/ n. elogio m.

eunuch /'yunək/ n. eunuco m.

euphonious /yu'founiəs/ a. eufónico.

Europe /'yurəp/ n. Europa f.

European /,yurə'piən/ a. & n. europeo -pea.

euthanasia /,yuθə'neiʒə, -ʒiə, -ziə/ n. eutanasia f.

evacuate /ɪ'vækyu,eit/ v. evacuar.

evade /ɪ'veid/ v. evadir.

evaluate /ɪ'vælyu,eit/ v. evaluar.

evaluation /ɪ,vælyu'eiʃən/ n. valoración f.

evangelist /ɪ'vændʒəlɪst/ n. evangelista m. & f.

evaporate /ɪ'væpə,reit/ v. evaporarse.

evaporation /ɪ,væpə'reiʃən/ n. evaporación f.

evasion /ɪ'veiʒən/ n. evasión f.

evasive /ɪ'veisɪv/ a. evasivo.

eve /iv/ n. víspera f.

even /'ivən/ a. 1. llano; igual. —adv. 2. aun; hasta. **not e.,** ni siquiera.

evening /'ivnɪŋ/ n. noche, tarde f. **good e.!** ¡buenas tardes! ¡buenas noches!

evening class clase nocturna f.

evenness /'ivənnɪs/ n. uniformidad f.

even number número par m.

event /ɪ'vɛnt/ n. acontecimiento, suceso m.

eventful /ɪ'vɛntfəl/ a. memorable.

eventual /ɪ'vɛntʃuəl/ a. eventual.

ever /'ɛvər/ adv. alguna vez; (after not) nunca. **e. since,** desde que.

everlasting /,ɛvər'læstɪŋ/ a. eterno.

every /'ɛvri/ a. cada; todos los.

everybody /'ɛvri,bɒdi, -,bʌdi/ pron. todo el mundo; cada uno.

everyday /'ɛvri,dei/ a. ordinario, de cada día.

everyone /'ɛvri,wʌn/ pron. todo el mundo; cada uno; cada cual.

everything /'ɛvri,θɪŋ/ pron. todo m.

everywhere /'ɛvri,wɛər/ adv. por todas partes, en todas partes.

evict /ɪ'vɪkt/ v. expulsar.

eviction /ɪ'vɪkʃən/ n. evicción f.

evidence /'ɛvidəns/ n. evidencia f.

evident /'ɛvidənt/ a. evidente.

evidently /'ɛvidəntli/ adv. evidentemente.

evil /'ivəl/ a. 1. malo; maligno. —n. 2. mal m.

evince /ɪ'vɪns/ v. revelar.

evoke /ɪ'vouk/ v. evocar.

evolution /,ɛvə'luʃən/ n. evolución f.

evolve /ɪ'vɒlv/ v. desenvolver; desarrollar.

ewe /yu/ v. oveja f.

exact /ɪg'zækt/ a. 1. exacto. —v. 2. exigir.

exacting /ɪg'zæktɪŋ/ a. exigente.

exactly /ɪg'zæktli/ adv. exactamente.

exaggerate /ɪg'zædʒə,reit/ v. exagerar.

exaggeration /ɪg,zædʒə'reiʃən/ n. exageración f.

exalt /ɪg'zɔlt/ v. exaltar.

exaltation /,ɛgzɔl'teiʃən/ n. exaltación f.

examination /ɪg,zæmə'neiʃən/ n. examen m.; (legal) interrogatorio m.

examine /ɪg'zæmɪn/ v. examinar.

example /ɪg'zæmpəl/ n. ejemplo m.

exasperate /ɪg'zæspə,reit/ v. exasperar.

exasperation /ɪg,zæspə'reiʃən/ n. exasperación f.

excavate /'ɛkskə,veit/ v. excavar, cavar.

exceed /ɪk'sid/ v. exceder.

exceedingly /ɪk'sidɪŋli/ adv. sumamente, extremadamente.

excel /ɪk'sɛl/ v. sobresalir.

excellence /'ɛksələns/ n. excelencia f.

Excellency /'ɛksələnsi/ n. (title) Excelencia f.

excellent /'ɛksələnt/ a. excelente.

except /ɪk'sɛpt/ prep. 1. salvo, excepto. —v. 2. exceptuar.

exception /ɪk'sɛpʃən/ n. excepción f.

exceptional /ɪk'sɛpʃənl/ a. excepcional.

excerpt /'ɛksɜrpt/ n. extracto.

excess /ɪk'sɛs, 'ɛksɛs/ n. exceso m.

excessive /ɪk'sɛsɪv/ a. excesivo.

exchange /ɪks'tʃeindʒ/ n. 1. cambio; canje m. **stock e.,** bolsa f. **telephone e.,** central telefónica. —v. 2. cambiar, canjear, intercambiar.

exchangeable /ɪks'tʃeindʒəbəl/ a. cambiable.

exchange rate tipo de cambio m.

excise /n 'ɛksaiz/ v ɪk'saiz/ n. 1. sisa f. —v. 2. extirpar.

excite /ɪk'sait/ v. agitar; provocar; emocionar.

excitement /ɪk'saitmənt/ n. agitación, conmoción f.

exciting /ɪk'saitɪŋ/ a. emocionante.

exclaim /ɪk'skleim/ v. exclamar.

exclamation /,ɛksklə'meiʃən/ n. exclamación f.

exclamation mark punto de admiración m.

exclude /ɪk'sklud/ v. excluir.

exclusion /ɪk'skluʒən/ n. exclusión f.

exclusive /ɪk'sklusɪv/ a. exclusivo.

excommunicate /,ɛkskə'myunɪ,keit/ v. excomulgar, descomulgar.

excommunication /,ɛkskə,myunɪ'keiʃən/ n. excomunión f.

excrement /'ɛkskrəmənt/ n. excremento m.

excruciating /ɪk'skruʃi,eitɪŋ/ a. penosísimo.

exculpate /'ɛkskʌl,peit/ v. exculpar.

excursion /ɪk'skɜrʒən/ n. excursión f., jira f.

excuse /n ɪk'skyus; v ɪk'skyuz/ n. 1. excusa f. —v. 2. excusar, perdonar, disculpar; dispensar.

execrable /'ɛksɪkrəbəl/ a. execrable.

execute /'ɛksɪ,kyut/ v. ejecutar.

execution /,ɛksɪ'kyuʃən/ n. ejecución f.

executioner /,ɛksɪ'kyuʃənər/ n. verdugo m.

executive /ɪg'zɛkyətɪv/ a. & n. ejecutivo -va.

executor /ɪg'zɛkyətər/ n. testamentario m.

exemplary /ɪg'zɛmpləri/ a. ejemplar.

exemplify /ɪg'zɛmplə,fai/ v. ejemplificar.

exempt /ɪg'zɛmpt/ a. 1. exento. —v. 2. exentar.

exercise /'ɛksər,saiz/ n. 1. ejercicio m. —v. 2. ejercitar.

exert /ɪg'zɜrt/ v. esforzar.

exhale /ɛks'heil/ v. exhalar.

exhaust /ɪg'zɔst/ n. 1. Auto. escape m. —v. 2. agotar.

exhaustion /ɪg'zɔstʃən/ n. agotamiento m.

exhaustive /ɪg'zɔstɪv/ a. exhaustivo.

exhaust pipe tubo de escape m.

exhibit /ɪg'zɪbɪt/ n. 1. exhibición, exposición f. —v. 2. exhibir.

exhibition /,ɛksə'bɪʃən/ n. exhibición f.

exhilarate /ɪg'zɪlə,reit/ v. alegrar; estimular.

exhort /ɪg'zɔrt/ v. exhortar.

exhortation /,ɛgzɔr'teiʃən/ n. exhortación f.

exhume /ɪg'zum/ v. exhumar.

exigency /'ɛksɪdʒənsi/ n. exigencia f., urgencia f.

exile /'ɛgzail/ n. 1. destierro m., (person) desterrado m. —v. 2. desterrar.

exist /ɪg'zɪst/ v. existir.

existence /ɪg'zɪstəns/ n. existencia f.

existent /ɪg'zɪstənt/ a. existente.

exit /'ɛgzɪt, 'ɛksɪt/ n. salida f.

exodus /'ɛksədəs/ n. éxodo m.

exonerate /ɪg'zɒnə,reit/ v. exonerar.

exorbitant /ɪg'zɔrbɪtənt/ a. exorbitante.

exorcise /'ɛksɔr,saiz/ v. exorcizar.

exotic /ɪg'zɒtɪk/ a. exótico.

expand /ɪk'spænd/ v. dilatar; ensanchar.

expanse /ɪk'spæns/ n. espacio m.; extensión f.

expansion /ɪk'spænʃən/ n. expansión f.

expansion slot ranura de expansión f.

expansive /ɪk'spænsɪv/ a. expansivo.

expatiate /ɪk'speiʃi,eit/ v. espaciarse.

expatriate /n, a ɛks'peitriɪt; v ɛks'peitri,eit/ n. & a. 1. expatriado m. —v. 2. expatriar.

expect /ɪk'spɛkt/ v. esperar; contar con.

expectancy /ɪk'spɛktənsi/ n. esperanza f.

expectation /,ɛkspɛk'teiʃən/ n. esperanza f.

expectorate /ɪk'spɛktə,reit/ v. expectorar.

expediency /ɪk'spidiənsi/ n. conveniencia f.

expedient /ɪk'spidiənt/ a. 1. oportuno. —n. 2. expediente m.

expedite /'ɛkspɪ,dait/ v. acelerar, despachar.

expedition /,ɛkspɪ'dɪʃən/ n. expedición f.

expel /ɪk'spɛl/ v. expeler; expulsar.

expend /ɪk'spɛnd/ v. desembolsar, expender.

expenditure /ɪk'spɛndɪtʃər/ n. desembolso; gasto m.

expense /ɪk'spɛns/ n. gasto m.; costa f.

expensive /ɪk'spɛnsɪv/ a. caro, costoso.

expensively /ɪk'spɛnsɪvli/ adv. costosamente.

experience /ɪk'spɪəriəns/ n. 1. experiencia f. —v. 2. experimentar.

experienced /ɪk'spɪəriənst/ a. experimentado, perito.

experiment /n ɪk'spɛrəmənt; v -,mɛnt/ n. 1. experimento m. —v. 2. experimentar.

experimental /ɪk,spɛrə'mɛntl/ a. experimental.

expert /'ɛkspɜrt/ a. & n. experto -ta.

expertise /,ɛkspər'tiz/ n. pericia f.

expiate /'ɛkspi,eit/ v. expiar.

expiration /,ɛkspə'reiʃən/ n. expiración f.

expiration date fecha de caducidad f.

expire /ɪk'spaiər/ v. expirar; Com. vencerse.

explain /ɪk'splein/ v. explicar.

explanation /,ɛksplə'neiʃən/ n. explicación f.

explanatory /ɪk'splænə,tori/ a. explicativo.

expletive /'ɛksplitɪv/ n. 1. interjección f. —a. 2. expletivo.

explicit /ɪk'splɪsɪt/ a. explícito, claro.

explode /ɪk'sploud/ v. estallar, volar; refutar.

exploit /ɪk'sploit/ n. 1. hazaña f. —v. 2. explotar.

exploitation /,ɛksploi'teiʃən/ n. explotación f.

exploration /,ɛksplə'reiʃən/ n. exploración f.

exploratory /ɪk'splorə,tori/ a. exploratorio.

explore /ɪk'splor/ v. explorar.

explorer /ɪk'splorər/ n. explorador -ra.

explosion /ɪk'splouʒən/ n. explosión f.

explosive /ɪk'splousɪv/ a. explosivo.

export /n 'ɛksport; v ɪk'sport/ n. 1. exportación f. —v. 2. exportar.

exportation /,ɛkspor'teiʃən/ n. exportación f.

expose /ɪk'spouz/ v. exponer; descubrir.

exposition /,ɛkspə'zɪʃən/ n. exposición f.

expository /ɪk'spɒzɪ,tori/ a. expositivo.

expostulate /ɪk'spɒstʃə,leit/ v. altercar.

exposure /ɪk'spouʒər/ n. exposición f.

expound /ɪk'spaund/ v. exponer, explicar.

express /ɪk'sprɛs/ a. & n. 1. expreso m. **e. company,** compañía de porteo. —v. 2. expresar.

expression /ɪk'sprɛʃən/ n. expresión f.

expressive /ɪk'sprɛsɪv/ a. expresivo.

expressly /ɪk'sprɛsli/ adv. expresamente.

expressman /ɪk'sprɛsmən, -,mæn/ n. empresario de expresos m.

expressway /ɪk'sprɛs,wei/ n. autopista f.

expropriate /ɛks'proupri,eit/ v. expropiar.

expulsion /ɪk'spʌlʃən/ n. expulsión f.

expunge /ɪk'spʌndʒ/ v. borrar, expurgar.

expurgate /'ɛkspər,geit/ v. expurgar.

exquisite /ɪk'skwɪzɪt/ a. exquisito.

extant /'ɛkstənt/ a. existente.

extemporaneous /ɪk,stɛmpə'reiniəs/ a. improvisado.

extend /ɪk'stɛnd/ v. extender.

extension /ɪk'stɛnʃən/ n. extensión f.

extensive /ɪk'stɛnsɪv/ a. extenso.

extensively /ɪk'stɛnsɪvli/ adv. extensamente.

extent /ɪk'stɛnt/ n. extensión f.; grado m. **to a certain e.,** hasta cierto punto.

extenuate /ɪk'stɛnyu,eit/ v. extenuar.

exterior /ɪk'stɪəriər/ a. & n. exterior m.

exterminate /ɪk'stɜrmə,neit/ v. exterminar.

extermination /ɪk,stɜrmə'neiʃən/ n. exterminio m.

external /ɪk'stɜrnl/ a. externo, exterior.

extinct /ɪk'stɪŋkt/ a. extinto.

extinction /ɪk'stɪŋkʃən/ n. extinción f.

extinguish /ɪk'stɪŋgwɪʃ/ v. extinguir, apagar.

extol /ɪk'stoul/ v. alabar.

extort /ɪk'stort/ v. exigir dinero sin derecho.

extortion /ɪk'stɔrʃən/ n. extorsión f.

extra /'ɛkstrə/ a. 1. extraordinario;

adicional. —*n.* **2.** (newspaper) extra *m.*
extract /*n* ˈɛkstrækt; *v* ɪkˈstrækt/ *n.* **1.** extracto *m.* —*v.* **2.** extraer.
extraction /ɪkˈstrækʃən/ *n.* extracción *f.*
extraneous /ɪkˈstreiniəs/ *a.* extraño; ajeno.
extraordinary /ɪkˈstrɔrdnˌɛri/ *a.* extraordinario.
extravagance /ɪkˈstrævəgəns/ *n.* extravagancia *f.*
extravagant /ɪkˈstrævəgənt/ *a.* extravagante.
extreme /ɪkˈstrim/ *a.* & *n.* extremo *m.*
extremity /ɪkˈstrɛmɪti/ *n.* extremidad *f.*
extricate /ˈɛkstrɪˌkeit/ *v.* desenredar.
exuberant /ɪgˈzubərənt/ *a.* exuberante.
exude /ɪgˈzud/ *v.* exudar.
exult /ɪgˈzʌlt/ *v.* regocijarse.
exultant /ɪgˈzʌltn̩t/ *a.* triunfante.
eye /ai/ *n.* **1.** ojo *m.* —*v.* **2.** ojear.
eyeball /ˈaiˌbɔl/ *n.* globo del ojo.
eyebrow /ˈaiˌbrau/ *n.* ceja *f.*
eyeglasses /ˈaiˌglæsɪz/ *n.* lentes *m.pl.*
eyelash /ˈaiˌlæʃ/ *n.* pestaña *f.*
eyelid /ˈaiˌlɪd/ *n.* párpado *m.*
eyeliner /ˈaiˌlainər/ *n.* lápiz de ojos *m.*
eye shadow *n.* sombra de ojos *f.*
eyesight /ˈaiˌsait/ *n.* vista *f.*

F

fable /ˈfeibəl/ *n.* fábula; ficción *f.*
fabric /ˈfæbrɪk/ *n.* tejido *m.*, tela *f.*
fabricate /ˈfæbrɪˌkeit/ *v.* fabricar.
fabulous /ˈfæbyələs/ *a.* fabuloso.
façade /fəˈsɑd/ *n.* fachada *f.*
face /feis/ *n.* **1.** cara *f.* **make faces,** hacer muecas. —*v.* **2.** encararse con. **f. the street,** dar a la calle.
facet /ˈfæsɪt/ *n.* faceta *f.*
facetious /fəˈsiʃəs/ *a.* chistoso.
facial /ˈfeiʃəl/ *n.* **1.** masaje facial *m.* —*a.* **2.** facial.
facile /ˈfæsɪl/ *a.* fácil.
facilitate /fəˈsɪlɪˌteit/ *v.* facilitar.
facility /fəˈsɪlɪti/ *n.* facilidad *f.*
facsimile /fækˈsɪməli/ *n.* facsímile *m.*
fact /fækt/ *n.* hecho *m.* **in f.,** en realidad.
faction /ˈfækʃən/ *n.* facción *f.*
factor /ˈfæktər/ *n.* factor *m.*
factory /ˈfæktəri/ *n.* fábrica *f.*
factual /ˈfæktʃuəl/ *a.* verdadero.
faculty /ˈfækəlti/ *n.* facultad *f.*
fad /fæd/ *n.* boga; novedad *f.*
fade /feid/ *v.* desteñirse; (flowers) marchitarse.
fail /feil/ *n.* **1. without f.,** sin falla. —*v.* **2.** fallar; fracasar. **not to f. to,** no dejar de.
failure /ˈfeilyər/ *n.* fracaso *m.*
faint /feint/ *a.* **1.** débil; vago; pálido. —*n.* **2.** desmayo *m.* —*v.* **3.** desmayarse.
faintly /ˈfeintli/ *adv.* débilmente; indistintamente.
fair /fɛər/ *a.* **1.** razonable, justo; (hair) rubio; (weather) bueno. —*n.* **2.** feria *f.*
fairly /ˈfɛərli/ *adv.* imparcialmente; regularmente; claramente; bellamente.
fairness /ˈfɛərnɪs/ *n.* justicia *f.*
fair play juego limpio *m.*
fairway /ˈfɛərˌwei/ *n.* (golf) calle *f.*
fairy /ˈfɛəri/ *n.* hada *f.*, duende *m.*
faith /feiθ/ *n.* fe; confianza *f.*
faithful /ˈfeiθfəl/ *a.* fiel.
fake /feik/ *a.* **1.** falso; postizo. —*n.* **2.** imitación; estafa *f.* —*v.* **3.** imitar; fingir.
faker /ˈfeikər/ *n.* imitador *m.*; farsante *m.*
falcon /ˈfɔlkən/ *n.* halcón *m.*
fall /fɔl/ *n.* **1.** caída; catarata *f.*; (season) otoño *m.*; (in price) baja *f.* —*v.* **2.** caer; bajar. **f. asleep,** dormirse; **f. in love,** enamorarse.
fallacious /fəˈleiʃəs/ *a.* falaz.
fallacy /ˈfæləsi/ *n.* falacia *f.*
fallible /ˈfæləbəl/ *a.* falible.
fallout /ˈfɔlˌaut/ *n.* lluvia radiactiva, polvillo radiactivo.
fallow /ˈfælou/ *a.* sin cultivar; barbecho.
false /fɔls/ *a.* falso; postizo.
falsehood /ˈfɔlshʊd/ *n.* falsedad; mentira *f.*
falseness /ˈfɔlsnɪs/ *n.* falsedad, perfidia *f.*
false teeth /tiθ/ dentadura postiza *f.*
falsetto /fɔlˈsɛtou/ *n.* falsete *m.*
falsification /ˌfɔlsəfɪˈkeiʃən/ *n.* falsificación *f.*
falsify /ˈfɔlsəfai/ *v.* falsificar.
falter /ˈfɔltər/ *v.* vacilar; (in speech) tartamudear.
fame /feim/ *n.* fama *f.*
familiar /fəˈmɪlyər/ *a.* familiar; conocido. **be f. with,** estar familiarizado con.
familiarity /fəˌmɪliˈærɪti/ *n.* familiaridad *f.*
familiarize /fəˈmɪlyəˌraiz/ *v.* familiarizar.
family /ˈfæməli/ *n.* familia; especie *f.*
family name apellido *m.*
family tree árbol genealógico *m.*
famine /ˈfæmɪn/ *n.* hambre; carestía *f.*
famished /ˈfæmɪʃt/ *a.* hambriento.
famous /ˈfeiməs/ *a.* famoso, célebre.
fan /fæn/ *n.* abanico; ventilador *m.* (sports) aficionado -da.
fanatic /fəˈnætɪk/ *a.* & *n.* fanático -ca.
fanatical /fəˈnætɪkəl/ *a.* fanático.
fanaticism /fəˈnætəˌsɪzəm/ *n.* fanatismo *m.*
fanciful /ˈfænsɪfəl/ *a.* caprichoso; fantástico.
fancy /ˈfænsi/ *a.* **1.** fino, elegante. **f. foods,** novedades *f.pl.* —*n.* **2.** fantasía *f.*; capricho *m.* —*v.* **3.** imaginar.
fanfare /ˈfænfɛər/ *n.* fanfarria *f.*
fang /fæŋ/ *n.* colmillo *m.*
fan heater estufa de aire *f.*
fantastic /fænˈtæstɪk/ *a.* fantástico.
fantasy /ˈfæntəsi/ *n.* fantasía *f.*
FAQ /fæk/ *n.* (Frequently Asked Questions) preguntas más frecuentes *f. pl.*
far /fɑr/ *a.* **1.** lejano, distante. —*adv.* **2.** lejos. **how f.,** a qué distancia. **as f. as,** hasta. **so f., thus f.,** hasta aquí.
farce /fɑrs/ *n.* farsa *f.*
fare /fɛər/ *n.* pasaje *m.*
farewell /ˌfɛərˈwɛl/ *n.* **1.** despedida *f.* **to say f.** despedirse. —*interj.* **2.** ¡adiós!
farfetched /ˈfɑrˈfɛtʃt/ *a.* forzado, inverosímil.
farm /fɑrm/ *n.* **1.** granja; hacienda *f.* —*v.* **2.** cultivar, labrar la tierra.
farmer /ˈfɑrmər/ *n.* labrador, agricultor *m.*
farmhouse /ˈfɑrmˌhaus/ *n.* hacienda, alquería *f.*
farming /ˈfɑrmɪŋ/ *n.* agricultura *f.*; cultivo *m.*
fart /fɑrt/ *n. Colloq.* pedo *m.*
fascinate /ˈfæsəˌneit/ *v.* fascinar, embelesar.
fascination /ˌfæsəˈneiʃən/ *n.* fascinación *f.*
fascism /ˈfæʃˌɪzəm/ *n.* fascismo *m.*
fashion /ˈfæʃən/ *n.* **1.** moda; costumbre; guisa *f.* **be in f.,** estilarse. —*v.* **2.** formar.
fashionable /ˈfæʃənəbəl/ *a.* de moda, en boga.
fashion show desfile de modas, pase de modelos *m.*
fast /fæst/ *a.* **1.** rápido, veloz; (watch) adelantado; (color) firme. —*adv.* **2.** ligero, de prisa. —*n.* **3.** ayuno *m.* —*v.* **4.** ayunar.
fasten /ˈfæsən/ *v.* afirmar; atar; fijar.
fastener /ˈfæsənər/ *n.* asegurador *m.*
fastidious /fæˈstɪdiəs/ *a.* melindroso.
fat /fæt/ *a.* **1.** gordo. —*n.* **2.** grasa, manteca *f.*
fatal /ˈfeitl̩/ *a.* fatal.
fatality /feiˈtælɪti/ *n.* fatalidad *f.*
fatally /ˈfeitl̩i/ *adv.* fatalmente.
fate /feit/ *n.* destino *m.*; suerte *f.*
fateful /ˈfeitfəl/ *a.* fatal; ominoso.
father /ˈfɑðər/ *n.* padre *m.*
fatherhood /ˈfɑðərˌhʊd/ *n.* paternidad *f.*
father-in-law /ˈfɑˌðər ɪn lɔ/ *n.* suegro *m.*
fatherland /ˈfɑðərˌlænd/ *n.* patria *f.*
fatherly /ˈfɑðərli/ *a.* **1.** paternal. —*adv.* **2.** paternalmente.
fathom /ˈfæðəm/ *n.* **1.** braza *f.* —*v.* **2.** sondar; *Fig.* penetrar en.
fatigue /fəˈtig/ *n.* **1.** fatiga *f.*, cansancio *m.* —*v.* **2.** fatigar, cansar.
fatten /ˈfætn̩/ *v.* engordar, cebar.
faucet /ˈfɔsɪt/ *n.* grifo *m.*, llave *f.*
fault /fɔlt/ *n.* culpa *f.*; defecto *m.* **at f.,** culpable.
faultless /ˈfɔltlɪs/ *a.* sin tacha, perfecto.
faultlessly /ˈfɔltlɪsli/ *adv.* perfectamente.
faulty /ˈfɔlti/ *a.* defectuoso, imperfecto.
fauna /ˈfɔnə/ *n.* fauna *f.*
favor /ˈfeivər/ *n.* **1.** favor *m.* —*v.* **2.** favorecer.
favorable /ˈfeivərəbəl/ *a.* favorable.
favorite /ˈfeivərɪt/ *a.* & *n.* favorito -ta.
favoritism /ˈfeivərɪˌtɪzəm/ *n.* favoritismo *m.*
fawn /fɔn/ *n.* **1.** cervato *m.* —*v.* **2.** halagar, adular.
fax /fæks/ *n.* **1.** fax *m.* —*v.* **2.** mandar un fax.
faze /feiz/ *v.* desconcertar.
fear /fɪər/ *n.* **1.** miedo, temor *m.* —*v.* **2.** temer.
fearful /ˈfɪərfəl/ *a.* temeroso, medroso.
fearless /ˈfɪərlɪs/ *a.* intrépido; sin temor.
fearlessness /ˈfɪərlɪsnɪs/ *n.* intrepidez *f.*
feasible /ˈfizəbəl/ *a.* factible.
feast /fist/ *n.* banquete *m.*; fiesta *f.*
feat /fit/ *n.* hazaña *f.*; hecho *m.*
feather /ˈfɛðər/ *n.* pluma *f.*
feature /ˈfitʃər/ *n.* **1.** facción *f.*; rasgo *m.*; (movies) película principal *f.*, largometraje *m.* —*v.* **2.** presentar como atracción especial.
February /ˈfɛbruˌɛri, ˈfɛbyu-/ *n.* febrero *m.*
federal /ˈfɛdərəl/ *a.* federal.
federation /ˌfɛdəˈreiʃən/ *n.* confederación, federación *f.*
fee /fi/ *n.* honorarios *m.pl.*
feeble /ˈfibəl/ *a.* débil.
feeble-minded /ˈfibəl ˈmaindɪd/ *a.* imbécil.
feebleness /ˈfibəlnɪs/ *a.* debilidad *f.*
feed /fid/ *n.* **1.** pasto *m.* —*v.* **2.** alimentar; dar de comer. **fed up with,** harto de.
feedback /ˈfidˌbæk/ *n.* feedback *m.*, retroalimentación *f.*
feel /fil/ *n.* **1.** sensación *f.* —*v.* **2.** sentir; palpar. **f. like,** tener ganas de.
feeling /ˈfilɪŋ/ *n.* sensación; sentimiento.
feign /fein/ *v.* fingir.
felicitate /fɪˈlɪsɪˌteit/ *v.* felicitar.
felicitous /fɪˈlɪsɪtəs/ *a.* feliz.
felicity /fɪˈlɪsɪti/ *n.* felicidad *f.*, dicha *f.*
feline /ˈfilain/ *a.* felino.
fellow /ˈfɛlou/ *n.* compañero; socio *m.*; *Colloq.* tipo *m.*
fellowship /ˈfɛlouˌʃɪp/ *n.* compañerismo; (for study) beca *f.*
felon /ˈfɛlən/ *n.* reo *m.* & *f.*, felón -ona.
felony /ˈfɛləni/ *n.* felonía *f.*
felt /fɛlt/ *n.* fieltro *m.*
felt-tipped pen /ˈfɛlt ˌtɪpt/ rotulador *m.*
female /ˈfimeil/ *a.* & *n.* hembra *f.*
feminine /ˈfɛmənɪn/ *a.* femenino.
feminist /ˈfɛmənɪst/ *a.* & *n.* feminista *m.* & *f.*
fence /fɛns/ *n.* **1.** cerca *f.* —*v.* **2.** cercar.
fender /ˈfɛndər/ *n.* guardabarros *m.pl.*
ferment /*n* ˈfɜrmɛnt; *v* fərˈmɛnt/ *n.* **1.** fermento *m.*; *Fig.* agitación *f.* —*v.* **2.** fermentar.
fermentation /ˌfɜrmɛnˈteiʃən/ *n.* fermentación *f.*
fern /fɜrn/ *n.* helecho *m.*
ferocious /fəˈrouʃəs/ *a.* feroz, fiero.
ferociously /fəˈrouʃəsli/ *adv.* ferozmente.
ferocity /fəˈrɒsɪti/ *n.* ferocidad, fiereza *f.*
Ferris wheel /ˈfɛrɪs/ rueda de feria *f.*
ferry /ˈfɛri/ *n.* transbordador *m.*, barca de transporte.
fertile /ˈfɜrtl̩/ *a.* fecundo; (land) fértil.
fertility /fərˈtɪlɪti/ *n.* fertilidad *f.*
fertilization /ˌfɜrtl̩əˈzeiʃən/ *n.* fertilización *f.*
fertilize /ˈfɜrtl̩ˌaiz/ *v.* fertilizar, abonar.
fertilizer /ˈfɜrtl̩ˌaizər/ *n.* abono *m.*
fervency /ˈfɜrvənsi/ *n.* ardor *m.*
fervent /ˈfɜrvənt/ *a.* fervoroso.
fervently /ˈfɜrvəntli/ *adv.* fervorosamente.
fervid /ˈfɜrvɪd/ *a.* férvido.
fervor /ˈfɜrvər/ *n.* fervor *m.*
fester /ˈfɛstər/ *v.* ulcerarse.
festival /ˈfɛstəvəl/ *n.* fiesta *f.*
festive /ˈfɛstɪv/ *a.* festivo.
festivity /fɛˈstɪvɪti/ *n.* festividad *f.*
festoon /fɛˈstun/ *n.* **1.** festón *m.* —*v.* **2.** festonear.
fetch /fɛtʃ/ *v.* ir por; traer.
fete /feit/ *n.* **1.** fiesta *f.* —*v.* **2.** festejar.
fetid /ˈfɛtɪd/ *a.* fétido.
fetish /ˈfɛtɪʃ/ *n.* fetiche *m.*
fetter /ˈfɛtər/ *n.* **1.** grillete *m.* —*v.* **2.** engrillar.
fetus /ˈfitəs/ *n.* feto *m.*
feud /fyud/ *n.* riña *f.*
feudal /ˈfyudl̩/ *a.* feudal.
feudalism /ˈfyudl̩ˌɪzəm/ *n.* feudalismo *m.*
fever /ˈfivər/ *n.* fiebre *f.*
feverish /ˈfivərɪʃ/ *a.* febril.
feverishly /ˈfivərɪʃli/ *adv.* febrilmente.
few /fyu/ *a.* pocos. **a. f.,** algunos, unos cuantos.
fiancé, fiancée /ˌfiɑnˈsei/ *n.* novio -via.
fiasco /fiˈæskou/ *n.* fiasco *m.*
fiat /ˈfiɑt/ *n.* fiat *m.*, orden *f.*
fib /fɪb/ *n.* **1.** mentira *f.* —*v.* **2.** mentir.
fiber /ˈfaibər/ *n.* fibra *f.*
fibrous /ˈfaibrəs/ *a.* fibroso.
fickle /ˈfɪkəl/ *a.* caprichoso.
fickleness /ˈfɪkəlnɪs/ *n.* inconstancia *f.*
fiction /ˈfɪkʃən/ *n.* ficción *f.*; (literature) novelas *f.pl.*
fictitious /fɪkˈtɪʃəs/ *a.* ficticio.
fidelity /fɪˈdɛlɪti/ *n.* fidelidad *f.*
fidget /ˈfɪdʒɪt/ *v.* inquietar.
field /fild/ *n.* campo *m.*
field trip viaje de estudios *m.*
fiend /find/ *n.* demonio *m.*
fiendish /ˈfindɪʃ/ *a.* diabólico, malvado.
fierce /fɪərs/ *a.* fiero, feroz.
fiery /ˈfaiᵊri/ *a.* ardiente.
fiesta /fiˈɛstə/ *n.* fiesta *f.*
fife /faif/ *n.* pífano *m.*
fifteen /ˈfɪfˈtin/ *a.* & *pron.* quince.
fifteenth /ˈfɪfˈtinθ/ *n.* & *a.* décimoquinto.
fifth /fɪfθ/ *a.* quinto.
fifty /ˈfɪfti/ *a.* & *pron.* cincuenta.
fig /fɪg/ *n.* higo *m.* **f. tree,** higuera *f.*
fight /fait/ *n.* **1.** lucha, pelea *f.* —*v.* **2.** luchar, pelear.
fighter /ˈfaitər/ *n.* peleador -ra, luchador -ra.

figment /ˈfɪgmənt/ n. invención f.
figurative /ˈfɪgyərətɪv/ a. metafórico.
figuratively /ˈfɪgyərətɪvli/ adv. figuradamente.
figure /ˈfɪgyər/ n. **1.** figura; cifra f. —v. **2.** figurar; calcular.
filament /ˈfɪləmənt/ n. filamento m.
file /fail/ n. **1.** archivo m.; (instrument) lima f.; (row) fila f. —v. **2.** archivar; limar.
file cabinet archivador m.
filial /ˈfɪliəl/ a. filial.
filigree /ˈfɪləˌgri/ n. filigrana f.
fill /fɪl/ v. llenar.
fillet /ˈfɪlɪt/ n. filete m.
filling /ˈfɪlɪŋ/ n. relleno m.; (dental) empastadura f. **f. station,** gasolinera f.
film /fɪlm/ n. **1.** película f., film m. —v. **2.** filmar.
filter /ˈfɪltər/ n. **1.** filtro m. —v. **2.** filtrar.
filth /fɪlθ/ n. suciedad, mugre f.
filthy /ˈfɪlθi/ a. sucio.
fin /fɪn/ n. aleta f.
final /ˈfainl/ a. final, último. —n. **2.** examen final. **finals** (sports) final f.
finalist /ˈfainlɪst/ n. finalista m. & f.
finally /ˈfainli/ adv. finalmente.
finances /ˈfainænsəz/ n. recursos, fondos m.pl.
financial /fɪˈnænʃəl/ a. financiero.
financier /ˌfɪnənˈsɪər, ˌfainən-/ n. financiero -ra.
find /faind/ n. **1.** hallazgo m. —v. **2.** hallar; encontrar. **f. out,** averiguar, enterarse, saber.
fine /fain/ a. **1.** fino; bueno. —adv. **2.** muy bien. —n. **3.** multa f. —v. **4.** multar.
fine arts /arts/ bellas artes f.pl.
finery /ˈfainəri/ n. gala f., adorno m.
finesse /fɪˈnɛs/ n. **1.** artificio m. —v. **2.** valerse de artificio.
finger /ˈfɪŋgər/ n. dedo m.
finger bowl n. enjuagatorio m.
fingernail /ˈfɪŋgərˌneil/ n. uña f.
fingerprint /ˈfɪŋgərˌprɪnt/ n. **1.** impresión digital f. —v. **2.** tomar las impresiones digitales.
finicky /ˈfɪnɪki/ a. melindroso.
finish /ˈfɪnɪʃ/ n. **1.** conclusión f. —v. **2.** acabar, terminar.
finished /ˈfɪnɪʃt/ a. acabado.
finite /ˈfainait/ a. finito.
fir /fɜr/ n. abeto m.
fire /faiᵊr/ n. **1.** fuego; incendio m. —v. **2.** disparar, tirar; Colloq. despedir.
fire alarm n. alarma de incendio f.
firearm /ˈfaiᵊrˌarm/ n. arma de fuego.
firecracker /ˈfaiᵊrˌkrækər/ n. triquitraque m., buscapiés m., petardo m.
fire engine bomba de incendios f.
fire escape escalera de incendios f.
fire exit salida de urgencia f.
fire extinguisher /ɪkˈstɪŋgwɪʃər/ matafuego m.
firefly /ˈfaiᵊrˌflai/ n. luciérnaga f.
fireman /ˈfaiᵊrmən/ n. bombero m.; (railway) fogonero m.
fireplace /ˈfaiᵊrˌpleis/ n. hogar, fogón m.
fireproof /ˈfaiᵊrˌpruf/ a. incombustible.
fireside /ˈfaiᵊrˌsaid/ n. hogar, fogón m.
fireworks /ˈfaiᵊrˌwɜrks/ n. fuegos artificiales.
firm /fɜrm/ a. **1.** firme. —n. **2.** firma, empresa f.
firmness /ˈfɜrmnɪs/ n. firmeza f.
first /fɜrst/ a. & adv. primero. **at f.,** al principio.
first aid primeros auxilios.
first-class /ˈfɜrst ˈklæs/ a. de primera clase.
fiscal /ˈfɪskəl/ a. fiscal.
fish /fɪʃ/ n. **1.** (food) pescado m.; (alive) pez m. —v. **2.** pescar.
fisherman /ˈfɪʃərmən/ n. pescador m.
fishhook /ˈfɪʃˌhʊk/ n. anzuelo m.

fishing /ˈfɪʃɪŋ/ n. pesca f. **go f.,** ir de pesca.
fishmonger /ˈfɪʃˌmʌŋgər/ n. pescadero m.
fish store pescadería f.
fission /ˈfɪʃən/ n. fisión f.
fissure /ˈfɪʃər/ n. grieta f., quebradura f.; fisura.
fist /fɪst/ n. puño m.
fit /fɪt/ a. **1.** capaz; justo. —n. **2.** corte, talle m.; Med. convulsión f. —v. **3.** caber; quedar bien, sentar bien.
fitful /ˈfɪtfəl/ a. espasmódico; caprichoso.
fitness /ˈfɪtnɪs/ n. aptitud; conveniencia f.
fitting /ˈfɪtɪŋ/ a. **1.** conveniente. **be f.,** convenir. —n. **2.** ajuste m.
fitting room probador m.
five /faiv/ a. & pron. cinco.
five-day work week /faiv ˈdei/ semana inglesa f.
fix /fɪks/ n. **1.** apuro m. —v. **2.** fijar; arreglar; componer, reparar.
fixation /fɪkˈseiʃən/ n. fijación f.; fijeza f.
fixed /fɪkst/ a. fijo.
fixture /ˈfɪkstʃər/ n. instalación; guarnición f.
flabby /ˈflæbi/ a. flojo.
flaccid /ˈflæksɪd, ˈflæsɪd/ a. flojo; flácido.
flag /flæg/ n. bandera f.
flagellant /ˈflædʒələnt/ n. & a. flagelante f.
flagon /ˈflægən/ n. frasco m.
flagrant /ˈfleigrənt/ a. flagrante.
flagrantly /ˈfleigrəntli/ adv. notoriamente.
flair /flɛər/ n. aptitud especial f.
flake /fleik/ n. **1.** escama f.; copo de nieve. —v. **2.** romperse en láminas.
flamboyant /flæmˈbɔiənt/ a. flamante, llamativo.
flame /fleim/ n. **1.** llama f. —v. **2.** llamear.
flaming /ˈfleimɪŋ/ a. llameante, flamante.
flamingo /fləˈmɪŋgou/ n. flamenco m.
flammable /ˈflæməbəl/ a. inflamable.
flank /flæŋk/ n. **1.** ijada f.; Mil. flanco m. —v. **2.** flanquear.
flannel /ˈflænl/ n. franela f.
flap /flæp/ n. **1.** cartera f. —v. **2.** aletear; sacudirse.
flare /flɛər/ n. **1.** llamarada f. —v. **2.** brillar; Fig. enojarse.
flash /flæʃ/ n. **1.** resplandor m.; (lightning) rayo, relámpago m.; Fig. instante m. —v. **2.** brillar.
flashcube /ˈflæʃˌkyub/ n. cubo de flash m.
flashlight /ˈflæʃˌlait/ n. linterna (eléctrica).
flashy /ˈflæʃi/ a. ostentoso.
flask /flæsk/ n. frasco m.
flat /flæt/ a. **1.** llano, (tire) desinflado. —n. **2.** llanura f.; apartamento m.
flatness /ˈflætnɪs/ n. llanura f.
flatten /ˈflætn/ v. aplastar, allanar; abatir.
flatter /ˈflætər/ v. adular, lisonjear.
flatterer /ˈflætərər/ n. lisonjero -ra; zalamero -ra.
flattery /ˈflætəri/ n. adulación, lisonja f.
flaunt /flɔnt/ v. ostentar.
flavor /ˈfleivər/ n. **1.** sabor m. —v. **2.** sazonar.
flavoring /ˈfleivərɪŋ/ n. condimento m.
flaw /flɔ/ n. defecto m.
flax /flæks/ n. lino m.
flay /flei/ v. despellejar; excoriar.
flea /fli/ n. pulga f.
flea market rastro m.
fleck /flɛk/ n. **1.** mancha f. —v. **2.** varetear.
flee /fli/ v. huir.
fleece /flis/ n. **1.** vellón m. —v. **2.** esquilar.

fleet /flit/ a. **1.** veloz. —n. **2.** flota f.
fleeting /ˈflitɪŋ/ a. fugaz, pasajero.
flesh /flɛʃ/ n. carne f.
fleshy /ˈflɛʃi/ a. gordo; carnoso.
flex /flɛks/ n. **1.** doblez m. —v. **2.** doblar.
flexibility /ˌflɛksəˈbɪlɪti/ n. flexibilidad f.
flexible /ˈflɛksəbəl/ a. flexible.
flier /ˈflaiər/ n. aviador -ra.
flight /flait/ n. vuelo m.; fuga f.
flight attendant n. azafata f.; ayudante de vuelo m.
flimsy /ˈflɪmzi/ a. débil.
flinch /flɪntʃ/ v. acobardarse.
fling /flɪŋ/ v. lanzar.
flint /flɪnt/ n. pedernal m.
flip /flɪp/ v. lanzar.
flippant /ˈflɪpənt/ a. impertinente.
flippantly /ˈflɪpəntli/ adv. impertinentemente.
flirt /flɜrt/ n. **1.** coqueta f. —v. **2.** coquetear, flirtear.
flirtation /flɜrˈteiʃən/ n. coqueteo m.
float /flout/ v. flotar.
flock /flɒk/ n. **1.** rebaño m. —v. **2.** congregarse.
flog /flɒg/ v. azotar.
flood /flʌd/ n. **1.** inundación f. —v. **2.** inundar.
floor /flɔr/ n. **1.** suelo, piso m. —v. **2.** derribar.
floppy disk /ˈflɒpi/ floppy, m., disquete, m.
floral /ˈflɔrəl/ a. floral.
florid /ˈflɔrɪd/ a. florido.
florist /ˈflɔrɪst/ n. florista m. & f.
flounce /flauns/ n. **1.** (sewing) volante m. —v. **2.** pernear.
flounder /ˈflaundər/ n. rodaballo m.
flour /flauᵊr/ n. harina f.
flourish /ˈflɜrɪʃ/ n. **1.** Mus. floreo m. —v. **2.** florecer; prosperar; blandir.
flow /flou/ n. **1.** flujo m. —v. **2.** fluir.
flow chart organigrama m.
flower /ˈflauər/ n. **1.** flor f. —v. **2.** florecer.
flowerpot /ˈflauərˌpɒt/ n. maceta f.
flowery /ˈflauəri/ a. florido.
fluctuate /ˈflʌktʃuˌeit/ v. fluctuar.
fluctuation /ˌflʌktʃuˈeiʃən/ n. fluctuación f.
flue /flu/ n. humero m.
fluency /ˈfluənsi/ n. fluidez f.
fluent /ˈfluənt/ a. fluido; competente.
fluffy /ˈflʌfi/ a. velloso.
fluid /ˈfluɪd/ a. & n. fluido m.
fluidity /fluˈɪdɪti/ n. fluidez f.
fluoroscope /ˈflurəˌskoup/ n. fluoroscopio m.
flurry /ˈflɜri/ n. agitación f.
flush /flʌʃ/ a. **1.** bien provisto. —n. **2.** sonrojo m. —v. **3.** limpiar con un chorro de agua; sonrojarse.
flute /flut/ n. flauta f.
flutter /ˈflʌtər/ n. **1.** agitación f. —v. **2.** agitarse.
flux /flʌks/ n. flujo m.
fly /flai/ n. **1.** mosca f. —v. **2.** volar.
flying saucer /ˈflaiɪŋ/ platillo volante m.
foam /foum/ n. **1.** espuma f. —v. **2.** espumar.
focal /ˈfoukəl/ a. focal.
focus /ˈfoukəs/ n. **1.** enfoque m. —v. **2.** enfocar.
fodder /ˈfɒdər/ n. forraje m., pienso m.
foe /fou/ n. adversario -ria, enemigo -ga.
fog /fɒg/ n. niebla f.
foggy /ˈfɒgi/ a. brumoso.
foil /fɔil/ v. frustrar.
foist /fɔist/ v. imponer.
fold /fould/ n. **1.** pliegue m. —v. **2.** doblar, plegar.
foldable /ˈfouldəbəl/ a. plegable.
folder /ˈfouldər/ n. circular m.; (for filing) carpeta f.
folding /ˈfouldɪŋ/ a. plegable.
foliage /ˈfouliɪdʒ/ n. follaje m.
folio /ˈfouliˌou/ n. infolio; folio m.

folklore /ˈfoukˌlɔr/ n. folklore m.
folks /fouks/ n. gente; familia f.
follicle /ˈfɒlɪkəl/ n. folículo m.
follow /ˈfɒlou/ v. seguir.
follower /ˈfɒlouər/ n. partidario -ria.
folly /ˈfɒli/ n. locura f.
foment /fouˈmɛnt/ v. fomentar.
fond /fɒnd/ a. cariñoso, tierno. **be f. of,** ser aficionado a.
fondle /ˈfɒndl/ v. acariciar.
fondly /ˈfɒndli/ adv. tiernamente.
fondness /ˈfɒndnɪs/ n. afición f.; cariño m.
food /fud/ n. alimento m.; comida f.
foodie /ˈfudi/ n. Colloq. gastrónomo -ma, gourmet m. & f.
food poisoning /ˈpɔizənɪŋ/ intoxicación alimenticia f.
foodstuffs /ˈfudˌstʌfs/ n.pl. comestibles, víveres m.pl.
fool /ful/ n. **1.** tonto -ta; bobo -ba; bufón -ona. —v. **2.** engañar.
foolhardy /ˈfulˌhardi/ a. temerario.
foolish /ˈfulɪʃ/ a. bobo, tonto, majadero.
foolproof /ˈfulˌpruf/ a. seguro.
foot /fut/ n. pie m.
footage /ˈfutɪdʒ/ n. longitud en pies.
football /ˈfutˌbɔl/ n. fútbol, balompié m.
footbridge /ˈfutˌbrɪdʒ/ n. puente para peatones m.
foothold /ˈfutˌhould/ n. posición establecida.
footing /ˈfutɪŋ/ n. base f., fundamento m.
footlights /ˈfutˌlaits/ n.pl. luces del proscenio.
footnote /ˈfutˌnout/ n. nota al pie de una página.
footpath /ˈfutˌpæθ/ n. sendero m.
footprint /ˈfutˌprɪnt/ n. huella f.
footstep /ˈfutˌstɛp/ n. paso m.
footstool /ˈfutˌstul/ n. escañuelo m., banqueta f.
fop /fɒp/ n. petimetre m.
for /fɔr; unstressed fər/ prep. **1.** para; por. **as f.,** en cuanto a. **what f.,** ¿para qué? —conj. **2.** porque, pues.
forage /ˈfɔrɪdʒ/ n. **1.** forraje m. —v. **2.** forrajear.
foray /ˈfɔrei/ n. correría f.
forbear /ˈfɔrˌbɛər/ v. cesar; abstenerse.
forbearance /fɔrˈbɛərəns/ n. paciencia f.
forbid /fərˈbɪd/ v. prohibir.
forbidding /fərˈbɪdɪŋ/ a. repugnante.
force /fɔrs/ n. **1.** fuerza f. —v. **2.** forzar.
forced landing /fɔrst/ aterrizaje forzoso m.
forceful /ˈfɔrsfəl/ a. fuerte; enérgico.
forcible /ˈfɔrsəbəl/ a. a la fuerza; enérgico.
ford /fɔrd/ n. **1.** vado m. —v. **2.** vadear.
fore /fɔr/ a. **1.** delantero. —n. **2.** delantera f.
fore and aft de popa a proa.
forearm /ˈfɔrˌarm/ n. antebrazo m.
forebears /ˈfɔrˌbɛərz/ n.pl. antepasados m.pl.
forebode /fɔrˈboud/ v. presagiar.
foreboding /fɔrˈboudɪŋ/ n. presentimiento m.
forecast /ˈfɔrˌkæst/ n. **1.** pronóstico m.; profecía f. —v. **2.** pronosticar.
forecastle /ˈfouksəl/ n. Naut. castillo de proa.
forefathers /ˈfɔrˌfaðərz/ n. antepasados m.pl.
forefinger /ˈfɔrˌfɪŋgər/ n. índice m.
forego /fɔrˈgou/ v. renunciar.
foregone /fɔrˈgɒn/ a. predeterminado.
foreground /ˈfɔrˌgraund/ n. primer plano.
forehead /ˈfɔrɪd/ n. frente f.
foreign /ˈfɔrɪn/ a. extranjero.
foreign aid n. ayuda exterior f.
foreigner /ˈfɔrənər/ n. extranjero -ra; forastero -ra.

foreleg /ˈfɔrˌlɛg/ *n.* pierna delantera.

foreman /ˈfɔrmən/ *n.* capataz, jefe de taller *m.*

foremost /ˈfɔrˌmoust/ *a.* **1.** primero. —*adv.* **2.** en primer lugar.

forenoon /ˈfɔrˌnun/ *n.* mañana *f.*

forensic /fəˈrɛnsɪk/ *a.* forense.

forerunner /ˈfɔrˌrʌnər/ *n.* precursor -ra.

foresee /fɔrˈsi/ *v.* prever.

foreshadow /fɔrˈʃædou/ *v.* prefigurar, anunciar.

foresight /ˈfɔrˌsait/ *n.* previsión *f.*

forest /ˈfɔrɪst/ *n.* bosque *m.*; selva *f.*

forestall /fɔrˈstɔl/ *v.* anticipar; prevenir.

forester /ˈfɔrəstər/ *n.* silvicultor -ra; guardamontes *m.pl.* & *f.pl.*

forestry /ˈfɔrəstri/ *n.* silvicultura *f.*

foretell /fɔrˈtɛl/ *v.* predecir.

forever /fɔrˈɛvər/ *adv.* por siempre, para siempre.

forevermore /fɔrˌɛvərˈmɔr/ *adv.* siempre.

forewarn /fɔrˈwɔrn/ *v.* advertir, avisar.

foreword /ˈfɔrˌwɜrd/ *n.* prefacio *m.*

forfeit /ˈfɔrfɪt/ *n.* **1.** prenda; multa *f.* —*v.* **2.** perder.

forfeiture /ˈfɔrfɪtʃər/ *n.* decomiso *m.*, multa *f.*; pérdida.

forgather /fɔrˈgæðər/ *v.* reunirse.

forge /fɔrdʒ/ *n.* **1.** fragua *f.* —*v.* **2.** forjar; falsear.

forger /ˈfɔrdʒər/ *n.* forjador -ra; falsificador -ra.

forgery /ˈfɔrdʒəri/ *n.* falsificación *f.*

forget /fərˈgɛt/ *v.* olvidar.

forgetful /fərˈgɛtfəl/ *a.* olvidadizo.

forgive /fərˈgɪv/ *v.* perdonar.

forgiveness /fərˈgɪvnɪs/ *n.* perdón *m.*

fork /fɔrk/ *n.* **1.** tenedor *m.*; bifurcación *f.* —*v.* **2.** bifurcarse.

forlorn /fɔrˈlɔrn/ *a.* triste.

form /fɔrm/ *n.* **1.** forma *f.*; (document) formulario *m.* —*v.* **2.** formar.

formal /ˈfɔrməl/ *a.* formal; ceremonioso. **f. dance,** baile de etiqueta. **f. dress,** traje de etiqueta.

formality /fɔrˈmælɪti/ *n.* formalidad *f.*

formally /ˈfɔrməli/ *adv.* formalmente.

format /ˈfɔrmæt/ *n.* formato *m.*

formation /fɔrˈmeiʃən/ *n.* formación *f.*

formative /ˈfɔrmətɪv/ *a.* formativo.

formatting /ˈfɔrmætɪŋ/ *n.* formateo *m.*

former /ˈfɔrmər/ *a.* anterior; antiguo. **the f.,** aquél.

formerly /ˈfɔrmərli/ *adv.* antiguamente.

formidable /ˈfɔrmɪdəbəl/ *a.* formidable.

formless /ˈfɔrmlɪs/ *a.* sin forma.

formula /ˈfɔrmyələ/ *n.* fórmula *f.*

formulate /ˈfɔrmyəˌleit/ *v.* formular.

formulation /ˌfɔrmyˈleiʃən/ *n.* formulación *f.*; expresión *f.*

forsake /fɔrˈseik/ *v.* abandonar.

fort /fɔrt/ *n.* fortaleza *f.*; fuerte *m.*

forte /ˈfɔrtei/ *a.* & *adv. Mus.* forte; fuerte.

forth /fɔrθ/ *adv.* adelante. **back and f.,** de aquí allá. **and so f.,** etcétera.

forthcoming /ˈfɔrθˈkʌmɪŋ/ *a.* futuro, próximo.

forthright /ˈfɔrθˌrait/ *a.* franco.

forthwith /ˌfɔrθˈwɪθ/ *adv.* inmediatamente.

fortification /ˌfɔrtəfɪˈkeiʃən/ *n.* fortificación *f.*

fortify /ˈfɔrtəˌfai/ *v.* fortificar.

fortissimo /fɔrˈtɪsəˌmou/ *a.* & *adv. Mus.* fortísimo.

fortitude /ˈfɔrtɪˌtud/ *n.* fortaleza; fortitud *f.*

fortnight /ˈfɔrtˌnait/ *n.* quincena *f.*

fortress /ˈfɔrtrɪs/ *n.* fuerte *m.*, fortaleza *f.*

fortuitous /fɔrˈtuɪtəs/ *a.* fortuito.

fortunate /ˈfɔrtʃənɪt/ *a.* afortunado.

fortune /ˈfɔrtʃən/ *n.* fortuna; suerte *f.*

fortune-teller /ˈfɔrtʃən ˌtɛlər/ *n.* sortílego -ga, adivino -na.

forty /ˈfɔrti/ *a.* & *pron.* cuarenta.

forum /ˈfɔrəm/ *n.* foro *m.*

forward /ˈfɔrwərd/ *a.* **1.** delantero; atrevido. —*adv.* **2.** adelante. —*v.* **3.** trasmitir, reexpedir.

foster /ˈfɔstər/ *n.* **1. f. child,** hijo adoptivo. —*v.* **2.** fomentar; criar.

foul /faul/ *a.* sucio; impuro.

found /faund/ *v.* fundar.

foundation /faunˈdeiʃən/ *n.* fundación *f.*; (of building) cimientos *m.pl.*

founder /ˈfaundər/ *n.* **1.** fundador -ra. —*v.* **2.** irse a pique.

foundry /ˈfaundri/ *n.* fundición *f.*

fountain /ˈfauntn̩/ *n.* fuente *f.*

fountain pen pluma estilográfica, plumafuente *f.*

four /fɔr/ *a.* & *pron.* cuatro.

fourteen /ˈfɔrˈtin/ *a.* & *pron.* catorce.

fourth /fɔrθ/ *a.* & *n.* cuarto *m.*

fowl /faul/ *n.* ave *f.*

fox /fɒks/ *n.* zorro -rra.

fox-trot /ˈfɒksˌtrɒt/ *n.* foxtrot *m.*

foxy /ˈfɒksi/ *a.* astuto.

foyer /ˈfɔiər/ *n.* salón de entrada.

fracas /ˈfreikəs, ˈfrækəs/ *n.* riña *f.*

fraction /ˈfrækʃən/ *n.* fracción *f.*

fracture /ˈfræktʃər/ *n.* **1.** fractura, rotura *f.* —*v.* **2.** fracturar, romper.

fragile /ˈfrædʒəl/ *a.* frágil.

fragment /ˈfrægmənt/ *n.* fragmento, trozo *m.*

fragmentary /ˈfrægmənˌtɛri/ *a.* fragmentario.

fragrance /ˈfreigrəns/ *n.* fragancia *f.*

fragrant /ˈfreigrənt/ *a.* fragante.

frail /freil/ *a.* débil, frágil.

frailty /ˈfreilti/ *n.* debilidad, fragilidad *f.*

frame /freim/ *n.* **1.** marco; armazón; cuadro; cuerpo *m.* —*v.* **2.** fabricar; formar; encuadrar.

frame-up /ˈfreim ˌʌp/ *n. Colloq.* conspiración *f.*

framework /ˈfreimˌwɜrk/ *n.* armazón *m.*

France /fræns/ *n.* Francia *f.*

franchise /ˈfræntʃaiz/ *n.* franquicia *f.*

frank /fræŋk/ *a.* **1.** franco. —*n.* **2.** carta franca. —*v.* **3.** franquear.

frankfurter /ˈfræŋkfərtər/ *n.* salchicha *f.*

frankly /ˈfræŋkli/ *adv.* francamente.

frankness /ˈfræŋknɪs/ *n.* franqueza *f.*

frantic /ˈfræntɪk/ *a.* frenético.

fraternal /frəˈtɜrnl̩/ *a.* fraternal.

fraternity /frəˈtɜrnɪti/ *n.* fraternidad *f.*

fraternization /ˌfrætərnəˈzeiʃən/ *n.* fraternización *f.*

fraternize /ˈfrætərˌnaiz/ *v.* confraternizar.

fratricide /ˈfrætrɪˌsaid/ *n.* fratricida *m.* & *f.*; fratricidio *m.*

fraud /frɔd/ *n.* fraude *m.*

fraudulent /ˈfrɔdʒələnt/ *a.* fraudulento.

fraudulently /ˈfrɔdʒələntli/ *adv.* fraudulentamente.

fraught /frɔt/ *a.* cargado.

freak /frik/ *n.* rareza *f.*; monstruosidad.

freckle /ˈfrɛkəl/ *n.* peca *f.*

freckled /ˈfrɛkəld/ *a.* pecoso.

free /fri/ *a.* **1.** libre; gratis. —*v.* **2.** libertar, librar.

freedom /ˈfridəm/ *n.* libertad *f.*

freeze /friz/ *v.* helar, congelar.

freezer /ˈfrizər/ *n.* heladora *f.*

freezing point /ˈfrizɪŋ/ punto de congelación *m.*

freight /freit/ *n.* **1.** carga *f.*; flete *m.* —*v.* **2.** cargar; fletar.

freighter /ˈfreitər/ *n. Naut.* fletador *m.*

French /frɛntʃ/ *a.* & *n.* francés -esa.

Frenchman /ˈfrɛntʃmən/ *n.* francés *m.*

Frenchwoman /ˈfrɛntʃˌwʊmən/ *n.* francesa *f.*

frenzied /ˈfrɛnzid/ *a.* frenético.

frenzy /ˈfrɛnzi/ *n.* frenesí *m.*

frequency /ˈfrikwənsi/ *n.* frecuencia *f.*

frequency modulation /ˌmɒdʒəˈleiʃən/ modulación de frequencia.

frequent /ˈfrikwənt/ *a.* frecuente.

frequently /ˈfrikwəntli/ *adv.* frecuentemente.

fresco /ˈfrɛskou/ *n.* fresco.

fresh /frɛʃ/ *a.* fresco. **f. water,** agua dulce.

freshen /ˈfrɛʃən/ *v.* refrescar.

freshness /ˈfrɛʃnɪs/ *n.* frescura *f.*

fret /frɛt/ *v.* quejarse, irritarse; *Mus.* traste *m.*

fretful /ˈfrɛtfəl/ *a.* irritable.

fretfully /ˈfrɛtfəli/ *adv.* de mala gana.

fretfulness /ˈfrɛtfəlnɪs/ *n.* mal humor.

friar /ˈfraiər/ *n.* fraile *m.*

fricassee /ˌfrɪkəˈsi/ *n.* fricasé *m.*

friction /ˈfrɪkʃən/ *n.* fricción *f.*

Friday /ˈfraidei/ *n.* viernes *m.* **Good F.,** Viernes Santo *m.*

fried /fraid/ *a.* frito.

friend /frɛnd/ *n.* amigo -ga.

friendless /ˈfrɛndlɪs/ *a.* sin amigos.

friendliness /ˈfrɛndlinɪs/ *n.* amistad *f.*

friendly /ˈfrɛndli/ *a.* amistoso.

friendship /ˈfrɛndʃɪp/ *n.* amistad *f.*

fright /frait/ *n.* susto *m.*

frighten /ˈfraitn̩/ *v.* asustar, espantar.

frightful /ˈfraitfəl/ *a.* espantoso.

frigid /ˈfrɪdʒɪd/ *a.* frígido; frío.

frill /frɪl/ *n.* (sewing) lechuga *f.*

fringe /frɪndʒ/ *n.* fleco; borde *m.*

frisky /ˈfrɪski/ *a.* retozón.

fritter /ˈfrɪtər/ *n.* fritura *f.*

frivolity /frɪˈvɒlɪti/ *n.* frivolidad *f.*

frivolous /ˈfrɪvələs/ *a.* frívolo.

frivolousness /ˈfrɪvələsnɪs/ *n.* frivolidad *f.*

frock /frɒk/ *n.* vestido de mujer. **f. coat,** levita *f.*

frog /frɒg/ *n.* rana *f.*

frolic /ˈfrɒlɪk/ *n.* **1.** retozo *m.* —*v.* **2.** retozar.

from /frʌm, *unstressed* frəm/ *prep.* de; desde.

front /frʌnt/ *n.* frente; (of building) fachada *f.* **in f. of,** delante de.

frontal /ˈfrʌntl̩/ *a.* frontal.

front door puerta principal *f.*

frontier /frʌnˈtɪər/ *n.* frontera *f.*

front seat asiento delantero *m.*

frost /frɔst/ *n.* helada, escarcha *f.*

frosty /ˈfrɔsti/ *a.* helado.

froth /frɔθ/ *n.* espuma *f.*

frown /fraun/ *n.* **1.** ceño *m.* —*v.* **2.** fruncir el entrecejo.

frowzy /ˈfrauzi/ *a.* desaliñado.

frozen /ˈfrouzən/ *a.* helado; congelado.

fructify /ˈfrʌktəˌfai/ *v.* fructificar.

frugal /ˈfrugəl/ *a.* frugal.

frugality /fruˈgælɪti/ *n.* frugalidad *f.*

fruit /frut/ *n.* fruta *f.*; (benefits) frutos *m.pl.* **f. tree,** árbol frutal.

fruitful /ˈfrutfəl/ *a.* productivo.

fruition /fruˈɪʃən/ *n.* fruición *f.*

fruitless /ˈfrutlɪs/ *a.* inútil, en vano.

fruit salad macedonia de frutas *f.*

fruit store frutería *f.*

frustrate /ˈfrʌstreit/ *v.* frustrar.

frustration /frʌˈstreiʃən/ *n.* frustración *f.*

fry /frai/ *v.* freír.

fuel /ˈfyuəl/ *n.* combustible *m.*

fugitive /ˈfyudʒɪtɪv/ *a.* & *n.* fugitivo -va.

fugue /fyug/ *n.* fuga *f.*

fulcrum /ˈfʊlkrəm/ *n.* fulcro *m.*

fulfill /fʊlˈfɪl/ *v.* cumplir.

fulfillment /fʊlˈfɪlmənt/ *n.* cumplimiento *m.*; realización *f.*

full /fʊl/ *a.* lleno; completo; pleno.

full name nombre y apellidos.

fullness /ˈfʊlnɪs/ *n.* plenitud *f.*

fulminate /ˈfʌlməˌneit/ *v.* volar; fulminar.

fulmination /ˌfʌlməˈneiʃən/ *n.* fulminación; detonación *f.*

fumble /ˈfʌmbəl/ *v.* chapucear.

fume /fyum/ *n.* **1.** humo *m.* —*v.* **2.** humear.

fumigate /ˈfyumɪˌgeit/ *v.* fumigar.

fumigator /ˈfyumɪˌgeitər/ *n.* fumigador *m.*

fun /fʌn/ *n.* diversión *f.* **to make f. of,** burlarse de. **to have f.,** divertirse.

function /ˈfʌŋkʃən/ *n.* **1.** función *f.* —*v.* **2.** funcionar.

functional /ˈfʌŋkʃənl̩/ *a.* funcional.

fund /fʌnd/ *n.* fondo *m.*

fundamental /ˌfʌndəˈmɛntl̩/ *a.* fundamental.

funeral /ˈfyunərəl/ *n.* funeral *m.*

funeral home, funeral parlor funeraria *f.*

fungus /ˈfʌŋgəs/ *n.* hongo *m.*

funnel /ˈfʌnl̩/ *n.* embudo *m.*; (of ship) chimenea *f.*

funny /ˈfʌni/ *a.* divertido, gracioso. **to be f.,** tener gracia.

fur /fɜr/ *n.* piel *f.*

furious /ˈfyʊriəs/ *a.* furioso.

furlough /ˈfɜrlou/ *n.* permiso *m.*

furnace /ˈfɜrnɪs/ *n.* horno *m.*

furnish /ˈfɜrnɪʃ/ *v.* surtir, proveer; (a house) amueblar.

furniture /ˈfɜrnɪtʃər/ *n.* muebles *m.pl.*

furrow /ˈfɜrou/ *n.* **1.** surco *m.* —*v.* **2.** surcar.

further /ˈfɜrðər/ *a.* & *adv.* **1.** más. —*v.* **2.** adelantar, fomentar.

furthermore /ˈfɜrðərˌmɔr/ *adv.* además.

fury /ˈfyʊri/ *n.* furor *m.*; furia *f.*

fuse /fyuz/ *n.* **1.** fusible *m.* —*v.* **2.** fundir.

fuss /fʌs/ *n.* **1.** alboroto *m.* —*v.* **2.** preocuparse por pequeñeces.

fussy /ˈfʌsi/ *a.* melindroso.

futile /ˈfyutl̩/ *a.* fútil.

future /ˈfyutʃər/ *a.* **1.** futuro. —*n.* **2.** porvenir *m.*

futurology /ˌfyutʃəˈrɒlədʒi/ *n.* futurología *f.*

fuzzy logic /ˈfʌzi/ lógica matizada *f.*

FYI *abbr.* (For Your Information) para su información.

G

gag /gæg/ *n.* chiste *m.*; mordaza *f.*

gaiety /ˈgeiɪti/ *n.* alegría *f.*

gain /gein/ *n.* **1.** ganancia *f.* —*v.* **2.** ganar.

gait /geit/ *n.* paso *m.*

gale /geil/ *n.* ventarrón *m.*

gall /gɔl/ *n.* hiel *f.*; *Fig.* amargura *f.*; descaro *m.*

gallant /ˈgælənt, gəˈlænt, -ˈlɑnt/ *a.* **1.** galante. —*n.* **2.** galán *m.*

gallery /ˈgæləri/ *n.* galería *f.*; *Theat.* paraíso *m.*

gallon /ˈgælən/ *n.* galón *m.*

gallop /ˈgæləp/ *n.* **1.** galope *m.* —*v.* **2.** galopar.

gallows /ˈgælouz/ *n.* horca *f.*

gamble /ˈgæmbəl/ *n.* **1.** riesgo *m.* —*v.* **2.** jugar, aventurar.

game /geim/ *n.* juego *m.*; (match) partida *f.*; (hunting) caza *f.*

gang /gæŋ/ *n.* cuadrilla; pandilla *f.*

gangster /ˈgæŋstər/ *n.* rufián *m.*

gap /gæp/ *n.* raja *f.*

gape /geip/ *v.* boquear.

garage /gəˈrɑʒ/ *n.* garaje *m.*

garbage /ˈgɑrbɪdʒ/ *n.* basura *f.*

garden /ˈgɑrdn̩/ *n.* jardín *m.*; (vegetable) huerta *f.*

gardener /ˈgɑrdnər/ *n.* jardinero -ra.

gargle /ˈgɑrgəl/ *n.* **1.** gárgara *f.* —*v.* **2.** gargarizar.

garland /ˈgɑrlənd/ *n.* guirnalda *f.*

garlic /ˈgɑrlɪk/ *n.* ajo *m.*

garment /ˈgɑrmənt/ *n.* prenda de vestir.

garrison /ˈgærəsən/ *n.* guarnición *f.*

garter /ˈgɑrtər/ *n.* liga *f.*; ataderas *f. pl.*
gas /gæs/ *n.* gas *m.*
gasohol /ˈgæsəˌhɔl, -ˌhɒl/ *n.* gasohol *m.*
gasoline /ˌgæsəˈlin/ *n.* gasolina *f.*
gasp /gæsp/ *n.* **1.** boqueada *f.* —*v.* **2.** boquear.
gas station gasolinera *f.*
gate /geit/ *n.* puerta; entrada; verja *f.*
gather /ˈgæðər/ *v.* recoger; inferir; reunir.
gaudy /ˈgɔdi/ *a.* brillante; llamativo.
gauge /geidʒ/ *n.* **1.** manómetro, indicador *m.* —*v.* **2.** medir; estimar.
gaunt /gɔnt/ *a.* flaco.
gauze /gɔz/ *n.* gasa *f.*
gay /gei/ *a.* **1.** alegre; homosexual. —*n.* **2.** homosexual.
gaze /geiz/ *n.* **1.** mirada *f.* —*v.* **2.** mirar con fijeza.
gear /gɪər/ *n.* engranaje *m.* **in g.,** en juego.
gearshift /ˈgɪərˌʃɪft/ *n.* palanca de cambio *f.*
gem /dʒɛm/ *n.* joya *f.*
gender /ˈdʒɛndər/ *n.* género *m.*
general /ˈdʒɛnərəl/ *a.* & *n.* general *m.*
generality /ˌdʒɛnəˈrælɪti/ *n.* generalidad *f.*
generalize /ˈdʒɛnərəˌlaiz/ *v.* generalizar.
generation /ˌdʒɛnəˈreiʃən/ *n.* generación *f.*
generator /ˈdʒɛnəˌreitər/ *n.* generador *m.*
generosity /ˌdʒɛnəˈrɒsɪti/ *n.* generosidad *f.*
generous /ˈdʒɛnərəs/ *a.* generoso.
genetic /dʒəˈnɛtɪk/ *a.* genético.
genial /ˈdʒinyəl/ *a.* genial.
genius /ˈdʒinyəs/ *n.* genio *m.*
genocide /ˈdʒɛnəˌsaid/ *n.* genocidio *m.*
gentle /ˈdʒɛntl̩/ *a.* suave; manso; benigno.
gentleman /ˈdʒɛntl̩mən/ *n.* señor; caballero *m.*
gentleness /ˈdʒɛntl̩nɪs/ *n.* suavidad *f.*
genuine /ˈdʒɛnyuɪn/ *a.* genuino.
genuineness /ˈdʒɛnyuɪnnɪs/ *n.* pureza *f.*
geographical /ˌdʒiəˈgræfɪkəl/ *a.* geográfico.
geography /dʒiˈɒgrəfi/ *n.* geografía *f.*
geometric /ˌdʒiəˈmɛtrɪk/ *a.* geométrico.
geranium /dʒəˈreiniəm/ *n.* geranio *m.*
germ /dʒɜrm/ *n.* germen; microbio *m.*
German /ˈdʒɜrmən/ *a.* & *n.* alemán -mana.
Germany /ˈdʒɜrməni/ *n.* Alemania *f.*
gesticulate /dʒɛˈstɪkyəˌleit/ *v.* gesticular.
gesture /ˈdʒɛstʃər/ *n.* **1.** gesto *m.* —*v.* **2.** gesticular, hacer gestos.
get /gɛt/ *v.* obtener; conseguir; (become) ponerse. **go and g.,** ir a buscar; **g. away,** irse; escaparse; **g. together,** reunirse; **g. on,** subirse; **g. off,** bajarse; **g. up,** levantarse; **g. there,** llegar.
ghastly /ˈgæstli/ *a.* pálido; espantoso.
ghost /goust/ *n.* espectro, fantasma *m.*
giant /ˈdʒaiənt/ *n.* gigante *m.*
gibberish /ˈdʒɪbərɪʃ/ *n.* galimatías, *m.*
gift /gɪft/ *n.* regalo, don; talento *m.*
gigabyte /ˈgɪgəˌbait, ˈdʒɪg-/ *n.* giga *m.*
gild /gɪld/ *v.* dorar.
gin /dʒɪn/ *n.* ginebra *f.*
ginger /ˈdʒɪndʒər/ *n.* jengibre *m.*
gingerbread /ˈdʒɪndʒərˌbrɛd/ *n.* pan de jengibre.
gingham /ˈgɪŋəm/ *n.* guinga *f.*
gird /gɜrd/ *v.* ceñir.
girdle /ˈgɜrdl̩/ *n.* faja *f.*
girl /gɜrl/ *n.* muchacha, niña, chica *f.*
give /gɪv/ *v.* dar; regalar. **g. back,** devolver. **g. up,** rendirse; renunciar.
giver /ˈgɪvər/ *n.* dador -ra; donador -ra.
glacier /ˈgleiʃər/ *n.* glaciar; ventisquero *m.*
glad /glæd/ *a.* alegre, contento. **be g.,** alegrarse.
gladly /ˈglædli/ *adj.* con mucho gusto.
gladness /ˈglædnɪs/ *n.* alegría *f.*; placer *m.*
glamor /ˈglæmər/ *n.* encanto *m.*; elegancia *f.*
glamorous /ˈglæmərəs/ *a.* encantador; elegante.
glamour /ˈglæmər/ *n.* encanto *m.*; elegancia *f.*
glance /glæns/ *n.* **1.** vistazo *m.*, ojeada *f.* —*v.* **2.** ojear.
gland /glænd/ *n.* glándula *f.*
glare /glɛər/ *n.* **1.** reflejo; brillo *m.* —*v.* **2.** deslumbrar; echar miradas indignadas.
glass /glæs/ *n.* vidrio; vaso *m.*; **(eyeglasses),** lentes, anteojos *m.pl.*
gleam /glim/ *n.* **1.** fulgor *m.* —*v.* **2.** fulgurar.
glee /gli/ *n.* alegría *f.*; júbilo *m.*
glide /glaid/ *v.* deslizarse.
glimpse /glɪmps/ *n.* **1.** vislumbre, vistazo *m.* —*v.* **2.** vislumbrar, ojear.
glisten /ˈglɪsən/ *n.* **1.** brillo *m.* —*v.* **2.** brillar.
glitter /ˈglɪtər/ *n.* **1.** resplandor *m.* —*v.* **2.** brillar.
globe /gloub/ *n.* globo; orbe *m.*
gloom /glum/ *n.* oscuridad; tristeza *f.*
gloomy /ˈglumi/ *a.* oscuro; sombrío, triste.
glorify /ˈglɔrəˌfai/ *v.* glorificar.
glorious /ˈglɔriəs/ *a.* glorioso.
glory /ˈglɔri/ *n.* gloria, fama *f.*
glossary /ˈglɒsəri/ *n.* glosario *m.*
glove /glʌv/ *n.* guante *m.*
glove compartment guantera *f.*
glow /glou/ *n.* **1.** fulgor *m.* —*v.* **2.** relucir; arder.
glucose /ˈglukous/ *f.* glucosa.
glue /glu/ *n.* **1.** cola *f.*, pegamento *m.* —*v.* **2.** encolar, pegar.
glum /glʌm/ *a.* de mal humor.
glutton /ˈglʌtn̩/ *n.* glotón -ona.
gnaw /nɔ/ *v.* roer.
GNP (*abbr.* **gross national product**), **PNB** (producto nacional bruto).
go /gou/ *v.* ir, irse. **g. away,** irse, marcharse. **g. back,** volver, regresar. **g. down,** bajar. **g. in,** entrar. **g. on,** seguir. **g. out,** salir. **g. up,** subir.
goal /goul/ *n.* meta *f.*; objeto *m.*
goalkeeper /ˈgoulˌkipər/ *n.* guardameta *mf.*
goat /gout/ *n.* cabra *f.*
goblet /ˈgɒblɪt/ *n.* copa *f.*
God /gɒd/ *n.* Dios *m.*
gold /gould/ *n.* oro *m.*
golden /ˈgouldən/ *a.* áureo.
gold-plated /ˈgould ˌpleitɪd/ *a.* chapado en oro.
golf /gɒlf/ *n.* golf *m.*
golf course campo de golf *m.*
golfer /ˈgɒlfər/ *n.* golfista *m.* & *f.*
good /gʊd/ *a.* **1.** bueno. —*n.* **2.** bienes *m.pl.*; *Com.* géneros *m.pl.*
good-bye /ˌgʊdˈbai/ *n.* **1.** adiós *m.* —*interj.* **2.** ¡adiós!, ¡hasta la vista!, ¡hasta luego! **say g. to,** despedirse de.
goodness /ˈgʊdnɪs/ *n.* bondad *f.*
goodwill /ˈgʊdˈwɪl/ *n.* buena voluntad. *f.*
goose /gus/ *n.* ganso *m.*
gooseberry /ˈgusˌbɛri/ *n.* uva crespa *f.*
gooseneck /ˈgusˌnɛk/ *n.* **1.** cuello de cisne *m.* —*a.* **2.** curvo.
goose step /ˈgusˌstɛp/ paso de ganso *m.*
gore /gɔr/ *n.* **1.** sangre *f.* —*v.* **2.** acornear.
gorge /gɔrdʒ/ *n.* **1.** gorja *f.* —*v.* **2.** engullir.
gorgeous /ˈgɔrdʒəs/ *a.* magnífico; precioso.
gorilla /gəˈrɪlə/ *n.* gorila *m.*
gory /ˈgɔri/ *a.* sangriento.
gosling /ˈgɒzlɪŋ/ *n.* gansarón *m.*
gospel /ˈgɒspəl/ *n.* evangelio *m.*
gossamer /ˈgɒsəmər/ *n.* **1.** telaraña *f.* —*a.* **2.** delgado.
gossip /ˈgɒsəp/ *n.* **1.** chisme *m.* —*v.* **2.** chismear.
Gothic /ˈgɒθɪk/ *a.* gótico.
gouge /gaudʒ/ *n.* **1.** gubia *f.* —*v.* **2.** escoplear.
gourd /gɔrd/ *n.* calabaza *f.*
gourmand /gʊrˈmɑnd/ *n.* glotón *m.*
gourmet /gʊrˈmei/ *a.* gastrónomo -ma.
govern /ˈgʌvərn/ *v.* gobernar.
governess /ˈgʌvərnɪs/ *n.* aya, institutriz *f.*
government /ˈgʌvərnmənt, -ərmənt/ *n.* gobierno *m.*
governmental /ˌgʌvərnˈmɛntl̩, ˌgʌvər-/ *a.* gubernamental.
governor /ˈgʌvərnər/ *n.* gobernador -ra.
governorship /ˈgʌvərnərˌʃɪp/ *n.* gobernatura *f.*
gown /gaun/ *n.* vestido *m.* **dressing g.,** bata *f.*
grab /græb/ *v.* agarrar, arrebatar.
grace /greis/ *n.* gracia; gentileza; merced *f.*
graceful /ˈgreisfəl/ *a.* agraciado.
graceless /ˈgreislɪs/ *a.* réprobo; torpe.
gracious /ˈgreiʃəs/ *a.* gentil, cortés.
grackle /ˈgrækəl/ *n.* grajo *m.*
grade /greid/ *n.* **1.** grado; nivel *m.*; pendiente; nota; calidad *f.* —*v.* **2.** graduar.
grade crossing *n.* paso a nivel *m.*
gradual /ˈgrædʒuəl/ *a.* gradual, paulatino.
gradually /ˈgrædʒuəli/ *adv.* gradualmente.
graduate /*n* ˈgrædʒuɪt; *v* -ˌeit/ *n.* **1.** graduado -da, diplomado -da. —*v.* **2.** graduar; diplomarse.
graft /græft/ *n.* **1.** injerto *m.*; soborno público. —*v.* **2.** injertar.
graham /ˈgreiəm/ *a.* centeno; acemita.
grail /greil/ *n.* grial *m.*
grain /grein/ *n.* grano; cereal *m.*
grain alcohol *n.* alcohol de madera *m.*
gram /græm/ *n.* gramo *m.*
grammar /ˈgræmər/ *n.* gramática *f.*
grammarian /grəˈmɛəriən/ *n.* gramático -ca.
grammar school *n.* escuela elemental *f.*
grammatical /grəˈmætɪkəl/ *a.* gramatical.
gramophone /ˈgræməˌfoun/ *n.* gramófono *m.*
granary /ˈgreinəri/ *n.* granero *m.*
grand /grænd/ *a.* grande, ilustre; estupendo.
grandchild /ˈgrænˌtʃaild/ *n.* nieto -ta.
granddaughter /ˈgrænˌdɔtər/ *n.* nieta *f.*
grandee /grænˈdi/ *n.* noble *m.*
grandeur /ˈgrændʒər/ *n.* grandeza *f.*
grandfather /ˈgrænˌfɑðər/ *n.* abuelo *m.*
grandiloquent /grænˈdɪləkwənt/ *a.* grandílocuo.
grandiose /ˈgrændiˌous/ *a.* grandioso.
grand jury jurado de acusación, jurado de juicio *m.*
grandly /ˈgrændli/ *adv.* grandiosamente.
grandmother /ˈgrænˌmʌðər/ *n.* abuela *f.*
grand opera ópera grande *f.*
grandparents /ˈgrændˌpɛərənts/ *n.* abuelos *m.pl.*
grandson /ˈgrænˌsʌn/ *n.* nieto *m.*
grandstand /ˈgrænˌstænd/ *n.* andanada *f.*, tribuna *f.*
grange /greindʒ/ *n.* granja *f.*
granger /ˈgreindʒər/ *n.* labriego *m.*
granite /ˈgrænɪt/ *n.* granito *m.*
granny /ˈgræni/ *n.* abuelita *f.*
grant /grænt/ *n.* **1.** concesión; subvención *f.* —*v.* **2.** otorgar; conceder; conferir. **take for granted,** tomar por cierto.
granular /ˈgrænyələr/ *a.* granular.
granulate /ˈgrænyəˌleit/ *v.* granular.
granulation /ˌgrænyəˈleiʃən/ *n.* granulación *f.*
granule /ˈgrænyul/ *n.* gránulo *m.*
grape /greip/ *n.* uva *f.*
grapefruit /ˈgreipˌfrut/ *n.* toronja *f.*
grape harvest vendimia *f.*
grapeshot /ˈgreipˌʃɒt/ *n.* metralla *f.*
grapevine /ˈgreipˌvain/ *n.* vid; parra *f.*
graph /græf/ *n.* gráfica *f.*
graphic /ˈgræfɪk/ *a.* gráfico.
graphite /ˈgræfait/ *n.* grafito *m.*
graphology /græˈfɒlədʒi/ *n.* grafología *f.*
grapple /ˈgræpəl/ *v.* agarrar.
grasp /græsp/ *n.* **1.** puño; poder; conocimiento *m.* —*v.* **2.** empuñar, agarrar; comprender.
grasping /ˈgræspɪŋ/ *a.* codicioso.
grass /græs/ *n.* hierba *f.*; (marijuana) marijuana *f.*
grasshopper /ˈgræsˌhɒpər/ *n.* saltamontes *m.*
grassy /ˈgræsi/ *a.* herboso.
grate /greit/ *n.* reja *f.*
grateful /ˈgreitfəl/ *a.* agradecido.
gratify /ˈgrætəˌfai/ *v.* satisfacer.
grating /ˈgreitɪŋ/ *n.* **1.** enrejado *m.* —*a.* **2.** discordante.
gratis /ˈgrætɪs/ *adv.* & *a.* gratis.
gratitude /ˈgrætɪˌtud/ *n.* agradecimiento *m.*
gratuitous /grəˈtuɪtəs/ *adj.* gratuito.
gratuity /grəˈtuɪti/ *n.* propina *f.*
grave /greiv/ *a.* **1.** grave. —*n.* **2.** sepultura; tumba *f.*
gravel /ˈgrævəl/ *n.* cascajo *m.*
gravely /ˈgreivli/ *adv.* gravemente.
gravestone /ˈgreivˌstoun/ *n.* lápida sepulcral *f.*
graveyard /ˈgreivˌyɑrd/ *n.* cementerio *m.*
gravitate /ˈgrævɪˌteit/ *v.* gravitar.
gravitation /ˌgrævɪˈteiʃən/ *n.* gravitación *f.*
gravity /ˈgrævɪti/ *n.* gravedad; seriedad *f.*
gravure /grəˈvyʊr/ *n.* fotograbado *m.*
gravy /ˈgreivi/ *n.* salsa *f.*
gray /grei/ *a.* gris; (hair) cano.
grayish /ˈgreiɪʃ/ *a.* pardusco.
gray matter substancia gris *f.*
graze /greiz/ *v.* rozar; (cattle) pastar.
grazing /ˈgreizɪŋ/ *a.* pastando.
grease /gris/ *n.* **1.** grasa *f.* —*v.* **2.** engrasar.
greasy /ˈgrisi/ *a.* grasiento.
great /greit/ *a.* grande, ilustre; estupendo.
Great Dane /dein/ mastín danés *m.*
great-grandfather /ˌgreit ˈgrænˌfɑðər/ *n.* bisabuelo.
great-grandmother /ˌgreit ˈgrænˌmʌðər/ *f.* bisabuela.
greatness /ˈgreitnɪs/ *n.* grandeza *f.*
Greece /gris/ *n.* Grecia *f.*
greed /grid/ **greediness** *n.* codicia, voracidad *f.*
greedy /ˈgridi/ *a.* voraz.
Greek /grik/ *a.* & *n.* griego -ga.
green /grin/ *a.* & *n.* verde *m.* **greens,** *n.* verduras *f.pl.*
greenery /ˈgrinəri/ *n.* verdor *m.*
greenhouse /ˈgrinˌhaus/ *n.* invernáculo *m.*
greenhouse effect *n.* efecto invernáculo *m.*
greet /grit/ *v.* saludar.
greeting /ˈgritɪŋ/ *n.* saludo *m.*
gregarious /grɪˈgɛəriəs/ *a.* gregario; sociable.
grenade /grɪˈneid/ *n.* granada; bomba *f.*
greyhound /ˈgreiˌhaund/ *n.* galgo *m.*
grid /grɪd/ *n.* parrilla *f.*
griddle /ˈgrɪdl̩/ *n.* tortera *f.*
griddlecake /ˈgrɪdl̩ˌkeik/ *n.* tortita de harina *f.*

gridiron /ˈgrɪdˌaiərn/ *n.* parrilla *f.;* campo de fútbol *m.*
grief /grif/ *n.* dolor *m.;* pena *f.*
grievance /ˈgrivəns/ *n.* pesar; agravio *m.*
grieve /griv/ *v.* afligir.
grievous /ˈgrivəs/ *a.* penoso.
grill /grɪl/ *n.* **1.** parrilla *f.* —*v.* **2.** asar a la parrilla.
grillroom /ˈgrɪlˌrum, -ˌrʊm/ *n.* parrilla *f.*
grim /grɪm/ *a.* ceñudo.
grimace /ˈgrɪməs/ *n.* **1.** mueca *f.* —*v.* **2.** hacer muecas.
grime /graim/ *n.* mugre *f.*
grimy /ˈgraimi/ *a.* sucio; mugroso.
grin /grɪn/ *n.* **1.** sonrisa *f.* —*v.* **2.** sonreír.
grind /graind/ *v.* moler; afilar.
grindstone /ˈgraindˌstoun/ *n.* amoladera *f.*
gringo /ˈgrɪŋgou/ *n.* gringo; yanqui *m.*
grip /grɪp/ *n.* **1.** maleta *f.* —*v.* **2.** agarrar.
gripe /graip/ *v.* **1.** agarrar. —*n.* **2.** asimiento *m.*, opresión *f.*
grippe /grɪp/ *n.* gripe *f.*
grisly /ˈgrɪzli/ *a.* espantoso.
grist /grɪst/ *n.* molienda *f.*
gristle /ˈgrɪsəl/ *n.* cartílago *m.*
grit /grɪt/ *n.* arena *f.;* entereza *f.*
grizzled /ˈgrɪzəld/ *a.* tordillo.
groan /groun/ *n.* **1.** gemido *m.* —*v.* **2.** gemir.
grocer /ˈgrousər/ *n.* abacero *m.*
grocery /ˈgrousəri/ *n.* tienda de comestibles, abacería; (Carib.) bodega *f.*
grog /grɒg/ *n.* brebaje *m.*
groggy /ˈgrɒgi/ *a.* medio borracho; vacilante.
groin /grɔin/ *n.* ingle *f.*
groom /grum/ *n.* (of horses) establero; (at wedding) novio *m.*
groove /gruv/ *n.* **1.** estría *f.* —*v.* **2.** acanalar.
grope /group/ *v.* tentar; andar a tientas.
gross /grous/ *a.* **1.** grueso; grosero. —*n.* **2.** gruesa *f.*
grossly /ˈgrousli/ *adv.* groseramente.
gross national product producto nacional bruto *m.*
grossness /ˈgrousnɪs/ *n.* grosería *f.*
grotesque /grouˈtɛsk/ *a.* grotesco.
grotto /ˈgrɒtou/ *n.* gruta *f.*
grouch /grautʃ/ *n.* gruñón; descontento *m.*
ground /graund/ *n.* tierra *f.;* terreno; suelo; campo; fundamento *m.*
ground floor planta baja *f.*
groundhog /ˈgraundˌhɔg/ *n.* marmota *f.*
groundless /ˈgraundlɪs/ *a.* infundado.
groundwork /ˈgraundˌwɜrk/ *n.* base *f.*, fundamento *m.*
group /grup/ *n.* **1.** grupo *m.* —*v.* **2.** agrupar.
groupie /ˈgrupi/ *n.* persona aficionada que acompaña a un grupo de música moderna.
grouse /graus/ *v.* quejarse
grove /grouv/ *n.* arboleda *f.*
grovel /ˈgrɒvəl/ *v.* rebajarse; envilecerse.
grow /grou/ *v.* crecer; cultivar.
growl /graul/ *n.* **1.** gruñido *m.* —*v.* **2.** gruñir.
grown /groun/ *a.* crecido; desarrollado.
grownup /ˈgrounˌʌp/ *n.* adulto -ta.
growth /grouθ/ *n.* crecimiento *m.;* vegetación *f.; Med.* tumor *m.*
grub /grʌb/ *n.* gorgojo *m.*, larva *f.*
grubby /ˈgrʌbi/ *a.* gorgojoso, mugriento.
grudge /grʌdʒ/ *n.* rencor *m.* **bear a g.,** guardar rencor.
gruel /ˈgruəl/ *n.* **1.** atole *m.* —*v.* **2.** agotar.
gruesome /ˈgrusəm/ *a.* horripilante.
gruff /grʌf/ *a.* ceñudo.
grumble /ˈgrʌmbəl/ *v.* quejarse.
grumpy /ˈgrʌmpi/ *a.* gruñón; quejoso.
grunt /grʌnt/ *v.* gruñir.
guarantee /ˌgærənˈti/ *n.* **1.** garantía *f.* —*v.* **2.** garantizar.
guarantor /ˈgærənˌtɔr/ *n.* fiador -ra.
guaranty /ˈgærənˌti/ *n.* garantía *f.*
guard /gɑrd/ *n.* **1.** guardia *m.* & *f.* —*v.* **2.** vigilar.
guarded /ˈgɑrdɪd/ *a.* cauteloso.
guardhouse /ˈgɑrdˌhaus/ *n.* prisión militar *f.*
guardian /ˈgɑrdiən/ *n.* guardián -ana.
guardianship /ˈgɑrdiənˌʃɪp/ *n.* tutela *f.*
guardsman /ˈgɑrdzmən/ *n.* centinela *m.*
guava /ˈgwɑvə/ *n.* guayaba *f.*
gubernatorial /ˌgubərnəˈtɔriəl/ *a.* gubernativo.
guerrilla /gəˈrɪlə/ *n.* guerrilla *f.;* guerrillero, -ra.
guess /gɛs/ *n.* **1.** conjetura *f.* —*v.* **2.** adivinar; *Colloq.* creer.
guesswork /ˈgɛsˌwɜrk/ *n.* conjetura *f.*
guest /gɛst/ *n.* huésped *m.* & *f.*
guest room alcoba de huéspedes *f.*, alcoba de respeto *f.*, cuarto para invitados *m.*
guffaw /gʌˈfɔ/ *n.* risotada *f.*
guidance /ˈgaidn̩s/ *n.* dirección *f.*
guide /gaid/ *n.* **1.** guía *m.* & *f.* —*v.* **2.** guiar.
guidebook /ˈgaidˌbʊk/ *n.* guía *f.*
guided tour /ˈgaidɪd/ visita explicada, visita programada, visita con guía *f.*
guideline /ˈgaidˌlain/ *n.* pauta *f.*
guidepost /ˈgaid,poust/ *n.* poste indicador *m.*
guild /gɪld/ *n.* gremio *m.*
guile /gail/ *n.* engaño *m.*
guillotine /ˈgɪləˌtin/ *n.* **1.** guillotina *f.* —*v.* **2.** guillotinar.
guilt /gɪlt/ *n.* culpa *f.*
guiltily /ˈgɪltəli/ *adv.* culpablemente.
guiltless /ˈgɪltlɪs/ *a.* inocente.
guilty /ˈgɪlti/ *a.* culpable.
guinea fowl /ˈgɪni/ gallina de Guinea *f.*
guinea pig /gɪni/ cobayo *m.*, conejillo de Indias *m.*
guise /gaiz/ *n.* modo *m.*
guitar /gɪˈtɑr/ *n.* guitarra *f.*
guitarist /gɪˈtɑrɪst/ *n.* guitarrista *m.* & *f.*
gulch /gʌltʃ/ *n.* quebrada *f.*
gulf /gʌlf/ *n.* golfo *m.*
gull /gʌl/ *n.* gaviota *f.*
gullet /ˈgʌlɪt/ *n.* esófago *m.;* zanja *f.*
gullible /ˈgʌləbəl/ *a.* crédulo.
gully /ˈgʌli/ *n.* barranca *f.*
gulp /gʌlp/ *n.* **1.** trago *m.* —*v.* **2.** tragar.
gum /gʌm/ *n.* **1.** goma *f.; Anat.* encía *f.* **chewing g.,** chicle *m.* —*v.* **2.** engomar.
gumbo /ˈgʌmbou/ *n.* quimbombó *m.*
gummy /ˈgʌmi/ *a.* gomoso.
gun /gʌn/ *n.* fusil, revólver *m.*
gunboat /ˈgʌnˌbout/ *n.* cañonero *m.*
gunman /ˈgʌnmən/ *n.* bandido *m.*
gunner /ˈgʌnər/ *n.* artillero *m.*
gun permit licencia de armas *f.*
gunpowder /ˈgʌnˌpaudər/ *n.* pólvora *f.*
gunshot /ˈgʌnˌʃɒt/ *n.* escopetazo *m.*
gunwale /ˈgʌnl̩/ *n.* borda *f.*
gurgle /ˈgɜrgəl/ *n.* **1.** gorgoteo *m.* —*v.* **2.** gorgotear.
guru /ˈgʊru, gʊˈru/ *n.* gurú *m.*
gush /gʌʃ/ *n.* **1.** chorro *m.* —*v.* **2.** brotar, chorrear.
gusher /ˈgʌʃər/ *n.* pozo de petróleo *m.*
gust /gʌst/ *n.* soplo *m.;* ráfaga *f.*
gustatory /ˈgʌstəˌtɔri/ *a.* gustativo.
gusto /ˈgʌstou/ *n.* gusto; placer *m.*
gusty /ˈgʌsti/ *a.* borrascoso.
gut /gʌt/ *n.* intestino *m.*, tripa *f.*
gutter /ˈgʌtər/ *n.* canal; zanja *f.*
guttural /ˈgʌtərəl/ *a.* gutural.
guy /gai/ *n.* tipo *m.*
guzzle /ˈgʌzəl/ *v.* engullir; tragar.
gym /dʒɪm/ *n.* gimnasio *m.*
gymnasium /dʒɪmˈnɑziəm/ *n.* gimnasio *m.*
gymnast /ˈdʒɪmnæst/ *n.* gimnasta *m.* & *f.*
gymnastic /dʒɪmˈnæstɪk/ *a.* gimnástico.
gymnastics /dʒɪmˈnæstɪks/ *n.* gimnasia *f.*
gynecologist /ˌgainɪˈkɒlədʒɪst/ *n.* ginecólogo, -ga *m.* & *f.*
gynecology /ˌgainɪˈkɒlədʒi/ *n.* ginecología *f.*
gypsum /ˈdʒɪpsəm/ *n.* yeso *m.*
Gypsy /ˈdʒɪpsi/ *a.* & *n.* gitano -na.
gyrate /ˈdʒaireit/ *v.* girar.
gyroscope /ˈdʒairəˌskoup/ *n.* giroscopio *m.*

H

habeas corpus /ˈheibiəs ˈkɔrpəs/ habeas corpus *m.*
haberdasher /ˈhæbərˌdæʃər/ *n.* camisero *m.*
haberdashery /ˈhæbərˌdæʃəri/ *n.* camisería *f.*
habiliment /həˈbɪləmənt/ *n.* vestuario *m.*
habit /ˈhæbɪt/ *n.* costumbre *f.*, hábito *m.* **be in the h. of,** estar acostumbrado a; soler.
habitable /ˈhæbɪtəbəl/ *a.* habitable.
habitat /ˈhæbɪˌtæt/ *n.* habitación *f.*, ambiente *m.*
habitation /ˌhæbɪˈteiʃən/ *n.* habitación *f.*
habitual /həˈbɪtʃuəl/ *a.* habitual.
habituate /həˈbɪtʃuˌeit/ *v.* habituar.
habitué /həˈbɪtʃuˌei/ *n.* parroquiano *m.*
hack /hæk/ *n.* **1.** coche de alquiler. —*v.* **2.** tajar.
hacker /ˈhækər/ *n.* pirata *m.* & *f.*
hackneyed /ˈhæknid/ *a.* trillado.
hacksaw /ˈhækˌsɔ/ *n.* sierra para cortar metal *f.*
haddock /ˈhædək/ *n.* merluza *f.*
haft /hæft/ *n.* mango *m.*
hag /hæg, hɑg/ *n.* bruja *f.*
haggard /ˈhægərd/ *a.* trasnochado.
haggle /ˈhægəl/ *v.* regatear.
hail /heil/ *n.* **1.** granizo; (greeting) saludo *m.* —*v.* **2.** granizar; saludar.
Hail Mary /ˈmɛəri/ Ave María *m.*
hailstone /ˈheilˌstoun/ *n.* piedra de granizo *f.*
hailstorm /ˈheilˌstɔrm/ *n.* granizada *f.*
hair /hɛər/ *n.* pelo; cabello *m.*
haircut /ˈhɛərˌkʌt/ *n.* corte de pelo.
hairdo /ˈhɛərˌdu/ *n.* peinado *m.*
hairdresser /ˈhɛərˌdrɛsər/ *n.* peluquero *m.*
hair dryer /ˈdraiər/ secador de pelo, secador *m.*
hairpin /ˈhɛərˌpɪn/ *n.* horquilla *f.;* gancho *m.*
hair's-breadth /ˈhɛərzˌbrɛdθ/ *n.* ancho de un pelo *m.*
hairspray /ˈhɛərsprei/ *n.* aerosol para cabello.
hairy /ˈhɛəri/ *a.* peludo.
halcyon /ˈhælsiən/ *n.* **1.** alcedón *m.* —*a.* **2.** tranquilo.
hale /heil/ *a.* sano.
half /hæf/ *a.* **1.** medio. —*n.* **2.** mitad *f.*
half-and-half /ˈhæf ən ˈhæf/ *a.* mitad y mitad.
half-baked /ˈhæf ˈbeikt/ *a.* medio crudo.
half-breed /ˈhæf ˌbrid/ *n.* mestizo *m.*
half brother *n.* medio hermano *m.*
half-hearted /ˈhæfˈhɑrtɪd/ *a.* sin entusiasmo.
half-mast /ˈhæf ˈmæst/ *a.* & *n.* media asta *m.*
halfpenny /ˈheipəni/ *n.* medio penique *m.*
halfway /ˈhæfˈwei/ *adv.* a medio camino.
half-wit /ˈhæf ˌwɪt/ *n.* bobo *m.*
halibut /ˈhæləbət/ *n.* hipogloso *m.*
hall /hɔl/ *n.* corredor *m.;* (for assembling) sala *f.* **city h.,** ayuntamiento *m.*
hallmark /ˈhɔlˌmɑrk/ *n.* marca del contraste *f.*
hallow /ˈhælou/ *v.* consagrar.
Halloween /ˌhæləˈwin/ *n.* víspera de Todos los Santos *f.*
hallucination /həˌlusəˈneiʃən/ *n.* alucinación *f.*
hallway /ˈhɔlˌwei/ *n.* pasadizo *m.*
halo /ˈheilou/ *n.* halo *m.;* corona *f.*
halt /hɔlt/ *a.* **1.** cojo. —*n.* **2.** parada *f.* —*v.* **3.** parar. —*interj.* **4.** ¡alto!
halter /ˈhɔltər/ *n.* cabestro *m.*
halve /hæv/ *v.* dividir en dos partes.
halyard /ˈhælyərd/ *n.* driza *f.*
ham /hæm/ *n.* jamón *m.*
hamburger /ˈhæmˌbɜrgər/ *n.* albóndiga *f.*
hamlet /ˈhæmlɪt/ *n.* aldea *f.*
hammer /ˈhæmər/ *n.* **1.** martillo *m.* —*v.* **2.** martillar.
hammock /ˈhæmək/ *n.* hamaca *f.*
hamper /ˈhæmpər/ *n.* canasta *f.*, cesto *m.*
hamstring /ˈhæmˌstrɪŋ/ *n.* **1.** tendón de la corva *m.* —*v.* **2.** desjarretar.
hand /hænd/ *n.* **1.** mano *f.* **on the other h.,** en cambio. —*v.* **2.** pasar. **h. over,** entregar.
handbag /ˈhændˌbæg/ *n.* cartera *f.*
handball /ˈhændˌbɔl/ *n.* pelota *f.*
handbook /ˈhændˌbʊk/ *n.* manual *m.*
handbrake /ˈhændbreik/ *n.* freno de mano *m.*
handcuff /ˈhændˌkʌf/ *n.* esposa *v.* esposar.
handful /ˈhændfʊl/ *n.* puñado *m.*
handicap /ˈhændiˌkæp/ *n.* desventaja *f.*
handicraft /ˈhændiˌkræft/ *n.* artífice *m.;* destreza manual.
handiwork /ˈhændiˌwɜrk/ *n.* artefacto *m.*
handkerchief /ˈhæŋkərtʃɪf/ *n.* pañuelo *m.*
handle /ˈhændl/ *n.* **1.** mango *m.* —*v.* **2.** manejar.
hand luggage equipaje de mano *m.*
handmade /ˈhændˈmeid/ *a.* hecho a mano.
handmaid /ˈhændˌmeid/ *n.* criada de mano, sirvienta *f.*
hand organ organillo *m.*
handsome /ˈhænsəm/ *a.* guapo; hermoso.
hand-to-hand /ˈhænd tə ˈhænd/ *adv.* de mano a mano.
handwriting /ˈhændˌraitɪŋ/ *n.* escritura *f.*
handy /ˈhændi/ *a.* diestro; útil; a la mano.
hang /hæŋ/ *v.* colgar; ahorcar.
hangar /ˈhæŋər/ *n.* hangar *m.*
hangdog /ˈhæŋˌdɔg/ *a.* & *n.* camastrón *m.*
hanger /ˈhæŋər/ *n.* colgador, gancho *m.*
hanger-on /ˈhæŋər ˈɒn/ *n.* dependiente; mogollón *m.*
hang glider /ˈglaidər/ aparato para vuelo libre, delta, ala delta.
hanging /ˈhæŋɪŋ/ *n.* **1.** ahorcadura *f.* —*a.* **2.** colgante.
hangman /ˈhæŋmən/ *n.* verdugo *m.*
hangnail /ˈhæŋˌneil/ *n.* padrastro *m.*
hang out *v.* enarbolar.
hangover /ˈhæŋˌouvər/ *n.* resaca *f.*
hangup /ˈhæŋʌp/ *n.* tara (psicológica) *f.*
hank /hæŋk/ *n.* madeja *f.*
hanker /ˈhæŋkər/ *v.* ansiar; apetecer.
haphazard. /hæpˈhæzərd/ *a.* casual.
happen /ˈhæpən/ *v.* acontecer, suceder, pasar.
happening /ˈhæpənɪŋ/ *n.* acontecimiento *m.*
happiness /ˈhæpinɪs/ *n.* felicidad; dicha *f.*
happy /ˈhæpi/ *a.* feliz; contento; dichoso.

happy-go-lucky /'hæpi gou 'lʌki/ *a.* & *n.* descuidado *m.*

harakiri /'harə'kiəri/ *n.* harakiri (suicidio japonés) *m.*

harangue /hə'ræŋ/ *n.* **1.** arenga *f.* —*v.* **2.** arengar.

harass /hə'ræs/ *v.* acosar; atormentar.

harbinger /'harbindʒər/ *n.* presagio *m.*

harbor /'harbər/ *n.* **1.** puerto; albergue *m.* —*v.* **2.** abrigar.

hard /hard/ *a.* **1.** duro; difícil. —*adv.* **2.** mucho.

hard coal antracita *m.*

hard disk disco duro *m.*

harden /'hardṇ/ *v.* endurecer.

hard-headed /'hard 'hedid/ *a.* terco.

hard-hearted /'hard'hartid/ *a.* empedernido.

hardiness /'hardinis/ *n.* vigor *m.*

hardly /'hardli/ *adv.* apenas.

hardness /'hardnis/ *n.* dureza; dificultad *f.*

hardship /'hardʃip/ *n.* penalidad *f.*; trabajo *m.*

hardware /'hard,wɛər/ *n.* hardware *m.*; (computer) quincalla *f.*

hardwood /'hard,wʊd/ *n.* madera dura *f.*

hardy /'hardi/ *a.* fuerte, robusto.

hare /hɛər/ *n.* liebre *f.*

harebrained /'hɛər,breind/ *a.* tolondro.

harelip /'hɛər,lip/ *n.* **1.** labio leporino *m.* —*a.* **2.** labihendido.

harem /'hɛərəm/ *n.* harén *m.*

hark /hark/ *v.* escuchar; atender.

Harlequin /'harləkwin/ *n.* arlequín *m.*

harlot /'harlət/ *n.* ramera *f.*

harm /harm/ *n.* **1.** mal, daño; perjuicio *m.* —*v.* **2.** dañar.

harmful /'harmfəl/ *a.* dañoso.

harmless /'harmlis/ *a.* inocente.

harmonic /har'mɒnik/ *a.* armónico *m.*

harmonica /har'mɒnikə/ *n.* armónica *f.*

harmonious /har'mouniəs/ *a.* armonioso.

harmonize /'harmə,naiz/ *v.* armonizar.

harmony /'harməni/ *n.* armonía *f.*

harness /'harnis/ *n.* arnés *m.*

harp /harp/ *n.* arpa *f.*

harpoon /har'pun/ *n.* arpón *m.*

harridan /'haridṇ/ *n.* vieja regañona *f.*

harrow /'hærou/ *n.* **1.** rastro *m.*; grada *f.* —*v.* **2.** gradar.

harry /'hæri/ *v.* acosar.

harsh /harʃ/ *a.* áspero.

harshness /'harʃnis/ *n.* aspereza *f.*

harvest /'harvist/ *n.* **1.** cosecha *f.* —*v.* **2.** cosechar.

hash /hæʃ/ *n.* picadillo *m.*

hashish /'hæʃiʃ/ *n.* haxis *m.*

hasn't /'hæzənt/ *v.* no tiene (neg. + tener).

hassle /'hæsəl/ *n.* lío *m.*, molestia *f.*; controversia *f.*

hassock /'hæsək/ *n.* cojín *m.*

haste /heist/ *n.* prisa *f.*

hasten /'heisən/ *v.* apresurarse, darse prisa.

hasty /'heisti/ *a.* apresurado.

hat /hæt/ *n.* sombrero *m.*

hat box /'hæt,bɒks/ sombrerera *f.*

hatch /hætʃ/ *n.* **1.** *Naut.* cuartel *m.* —*v.* **2.** incubar; *Fig.* tramar.

hatchery /'hætʃəri/ *n.* criadero *m.*

hatchet /'hætʃit/ *n.* hacha pequeña *f.*

hate /heit/ *n.* **1.** odio *m.* —*v.* **2.** odiar, detestar.

hateful /'heitfəl/ *a.* detestable.

hatred /'heitrid/ *n.* odio *m.*

haughtiness /'hɔtinis/ *n.* arrogancia *f.*

haughty /'hɔti/ *a.* altivo.

haul /hɔl/ *n.* **1.** (fishery) redada *f.* —*v.* **2.** tirar, halar.

haunch /hɔntʃ/ *n.* anca *f.*

haunt /hɔnt/ *n.* **1.** lugar frecuentado *m.* —*v.* **2.** frecuentar, andar por.

have /hæv; *unstressed* həv, əv/ *v.* tener; haber.

haven /'heivən/ *n.* puerto; asilo *m.*

haven't /'hævənt/ *v.* no tiene (neg. + tener).

havoc /'hævək/ *n.* ruina *f.*

hawk /hɔk/ *n.* halcón *m.*

hawker /'hɔkər/ *n.* buhonero *m.*

hawser /'hɔzər/ *n.* cable *m.*

hawthorn /'hɔ,θɔrn/ *n.* espino *m.*

hay /hei/ *n.* heno *m.*

hay fever *n.* fiebre del heno *f.*

hayfield /'heifild/ *n.* henar *m.*

hayloft /'hei,lɔft/ *n.* henil *m.*

haystack /'hei,stæk/ *n.* hacina de heno *f.*

hazard /'hæzərd/ *n.* **1.** azar *m.* —*v.* **2.** aventurar.

hazardous /'hæzərdəs/ *a.* peligroso.

haze /heiz/ *n.* niebla *f.*

hazel /'heizəl/ *n.* avellano *m.*

hazelnut /'heizəl,nʌt/ avellana *f.*

hazy /'heizi/ *a.* brumoso.

he /hei/ *pron.* él *m.*

head /hɛd/ *n.* **1.** cabeza *f.*; jefe *m.* —*v.* **2.** dirigir; encabezar.

headache /'hɛd,eik/ *n.* dolor de cabeza *m.*

headband /'hɛd,bænd/ *n.* venda para cabeza *f.*

headfirst /'hɛd'fərst/ *adv.* de cabeza.

headgear /'hɛd,giər/ *n.* tocado *m.*

headlight /'hɛd,lait/ *n.* linterna delantera *f.*, farol de tope *m.*

headline /'hɛd,lain/ *n.* encabezado *m.*

headlong /'hɛd,lɔŋ/ *a.* precipitoso.

head-on /'hɛd 'ɒn/ *adv.* de frente.

headphones /'hɛd,founz/ *n.pl.* auriculares *m.pl.*

headquarters /'hɛd,kwɔrtərz/ *n.* jefatura *f.*; *Mil.* cuartel general.

headstone /'hɛd,stoun/ *n.* lápida mortuoria *f.*

headstrong /'hɛd,strɔŋ/ *a.* terco.

headwaiter /'hɛd'weitər/ jefe de comedor *m.* & *f.*

headwaters /'hɛd,wɔtərz/ *n.* cabeceras *f.pl.*

headway /'hɛd,wei/ *n.* avance *m.*, progreso *m.*

headwork /'hɛd,wərk/ *n.* trabajo mental *m.*

heady /'hɛdi/ *a.* impetuoso.

heal /hil/ *v.* curar, sanar.

health /hɛlθ/ *n.* salud *f.*

healthful /'hɛlθfəl/ *a.* saludable.

healthy /'hɛlθi/ *a.* sano; salubre.

heap /hip/ *n.* montón *m.*

hear /hiər/ *v.* oír. **h. from**, tener noticias de. **h. about, h. of,** oír hablar de.

hearing /'hiəriŋ/ *n.* oído *m.*

hearing aid audífono *m.*

hearsay /'hiər,sei/ *n.* rumor *m.*

hearse /hərs/ *n.* ataúd *m.*

heart /hart/ *n.* corazón; ánimo *m.* **by h.,** de memoria. **have h. trouble** padecer del corazón.

heartache /'hart,eik/ *n.* angustia *f.*

heart attack ataque cardíaco, infarto, infarto de miocardio *m.*

heartbreak /'hart,breik/ *n.* angustia *f.*; pesar *m.*

heartbroken /'hart,broukən/ *a.* acongojado.

heartburn /'hart,bərn/ *n.* acedía *f.*, ardor de estómago *m.*

heartfelt /'hart,felt/ *a.* sentido.

hearth /harθ/ *n.* hogar *m.*, chimenea *f.*

heartless /'hartlis/ *a.* empedernido.

heartsick /'hart,sik/ *a.* desconsolado.

heart-stricken /'hart 'strikən/ *a.* afligido.

heart-to-heart /'hart tə 'hart/ *adv.* franco; sincero.

hearty /'harti/ *a.* cordial; vigoroso.

heat /hit/ *n.* **1.** calor; ardor *m.*; calefacción *f.* —*v.* **2.** calentar.

heated /'hitid/ *a.* acalorado.

heater /'hitər/ *n.* calentador *m.*

heath /hiθ/ *n.* matorral *m.*

heathen /'hiðən/ *a.* & *n.* pagano -na.

heather /'hɛðər/ *n.* brezo *m.*

heating /'hitiŋ/ *n.* calefacción *f.*

heatstroke /'hit,strouk/ *n.* insolación *f.*

heat wave onda de calor *f.*

heave /hiv/ *v.* tirar.

heaven /'hɛvən/ *n.* cielo *m.*

heavenly /'hɛvənli/ *a.* divino.

heavy /'hɛvi/ *a.* pesado; oneroso.

Hebrew /'hibru/ *a.* & *n.* hebreo -ea.

hectic /'hɛktik/ *a.* turbulento.

hedge /hɛdʒ/ *n.* seto *m.*

hedgehog /'hɛdʒ,hɒg/ *n.* erizo *m.*

hedonism /'hidṇ,izəm/ *n.* hedonismo *m.*

heed /hid/ *n.* **1.** cuidado *m.* —*v.* **2.** atender.

heedless /'hidlis/ *a.* desatento; incauto.

heel /hil/ *n.* talón *m.*; (of shoe) tacón *m.*

heifer /'hɛfər/ *n.* novilla *f.*

height /hait/ *n.* altura *f.*

heighten /'haitṇ/ *v.* elevar; exaltar.

heinous /'heinəs/ *a.* nefando.

heir /ɛər/ **heiress** *n.* heredero -ra.

helicopter /'hɛli,kɒptər/ *n.* helicóptero *m.*

heliotrope /'hiliə,troup/ *n.* heliotropo *m.*

helium /'hiliəm/ *n.* helio *m.*

hell /hɛl/ *n.* infierno *m.*

Hellenism /'hɛlə,nizəm/ *n.* helenismo *m.*

hellish /'hɛliʃ/ *a.* infernal.

hello /hɛ'lou/ *interj.* ¡hola!; (on telephone) aló; bueno.

helm /hɛlm/ *n.* timón *m.*

helmet /'hɛlmit/ *n.* yelmo, casco *m.*

helmsman /'hɛlmzmən/ *n.* limonero *m.*

help /hɛlp/ *n.* **1.** ayuda *f.* **help!** ¡socorro! —*v.* **2.** ayudar. **h. oneself,** servirse. **can't help (but),** no poder menos de.

helper /'hɛlpər/ *n.* ayudante *m.*

helpful /'hɛlpfəl/ *a.* útil; servicial.

helpfulness /'hɛlpfəlnis/ *n.* utilidad *f.*

helpless /'hɛlplis/ *a.* imposibilitado.

hem /hɛm/ *n.* **1.** ribete *m.* —*v.* **2.** ribetear.

hemisphere /'hɛmi,sfiər/ *n.* hemisferio *m.*

hemlock /'hɛm,lɒk/ *n.* abeto *m.*

hemoglobin /'himə,gloubin/ *n.* hemoglobina *f.*

hemophilia /,himə'filiə/ *n.* hemofilia *f.*

hemorrhage /'hɛməridʒ/ *n.* hemorragia *f.*

hemorrhoids /'hɛmə,rɔidz/ *n.* hemorroides *f.pl.*

hemp /hɛmp/ *n.* cáñamo *m.*

hemstitch /'hɛm,stitʃ/ *n.* **1.** vainica *f.* —*v.* **2.** hacer una vainica.

hen /hɛn/ *n.* gallina *f.*

hence /hɛns/ *adv.* por lo tanto.

henceforth /,hɛns'fɔrθ/ *adv.* de aquí en adelante.

henchman /'hɛntʃmən/ *n.* paniaguado *m.*

henna /'hɛnə/ *n.* alheña *f.*

hepatitis /,hɛpə'taitis/ *n.* hepatitis *f.*

her /hər; *unstressed* hər, ər/ *a.* **1.** su. —*pron.* **2.** ella; la; le.

herald /'hɛrəld/ *n.* heraldo *m.*

heraldic /hɛ'rældik/ *a.* heráldico.

heraldry /'hɛrəldri/ *n.* heráldica *f.*

herb /ɜrb; *esp. Brit.* hɜrb/ *n.* yerba, hierba *f.*

herbaceous /hɜr'beiʃəs, ɜr-/ *a.* herbáceo.

herbarium /hɜr'bɛəriəm, ɜr-/ *n.* herbario *m.*

herd /hɜrd/ *n.* **1.** hato, rebaño *m.* —*v.* **2.** reunir en hatos.

here /hiər/ *adv.* aquí; acá.

hereafter /hiər'æftər/ *adv.* en lo futuro.

hereby /hiər'bai/ *adv.* por éstas, por la presente.

hereditary /hə'rɛdɪ,tɛri/ *a.* hereditario.

heredity /hə'rɛditi/ *n.* herencia *f.*

herein /hiər'in/ *adv.* aquí dentro; incluso.

heresy /'hɛrəsi/ *n.* herejía *f.*

heretic /'hɛritik/ *a.* **1.** herético. —*n.* **2.** hereje *m.* & *f.*

heretical /hə'rɛtikəl/ *a.* herético.

heretofore /,hiərtə'fɔr/ *adv.* hasta ahora.

herewith /hiər'wiθ/ *adv.* con esto, adjunto.

heritage /'hɛritidʒ/ *n.* herencia *f.*

hermetic /hər'mɛtik/ *a.* hermético.

hermit /'hɜrmit/ *n.* ermitaño *m.*

hernia /'hɜrniə/ *n.* hernia *f.*

hero /'hiərou/ *n.* héroe *m.*

heroic /hi'rouik/ *a.* heroico.

heroically /hi'rouikəli/ *adv.* heroicamente.

heroin /'hɛrouin/ *n.* heroína *f.*

heroine /'hɛrouin/ *n.* heroína *f.*

heroism /'hɛrou,izəm/ *n.* heroísmo *m.*

heron /'hɛrən/ *n.* garza *f.*

herring /'hɛriŋ/ *n.* arenque *m.*

hers /hɜrz/ *pron.* suyo, de ella.

herself /hər'sɛlf/ *pron.* sí, sí misma, se. **she h.,** ella misma. **with h.,** consigo.

hertz /hɜrts/ *n.* hertzio *m.*

hesitancy /'hɛzitənsi/ *n.* hesitación *f.*

hesitant /'hɛzitənt/ *a.* indeciso.

hesitate /'hɛzi,teit/ *v.* vacilar.

hesitation /,hɛzi'teiʃən/ *n.* duda; vacilación *f.*

heterogeneous /,hɛtərə'dʒiniəs/ *a.* heterogéneo.

heterosexual /,hɛtərə'sɛkʃuəl/ *a.* heterosexual.

hexagon /'hɛksə,gɒn/ *n.* hexágono *m.*

hibernate /'haibər,neit/ *v.* invernar.

hibernation /,haibər'neiʃən/ *n.* invernada *f.*

hibiscus /hai'biskəs/ *n.* hibisco *m.*

hiccup /'hikʌp/ *n.* **1.** hipo *m.* —*v.* **2.** tener hipo.

hickory /'hikəri/ *n.* nogal americano *m.*

hidden /'hidṇ/ *a.* oculto; escondido.

hide /haid/ *n.* **1.** cuero *m.*; piel *f.* —*v.* **2.** esconder; ocultar.

hideous /'hidiəs/ *a.* horrible.

hide-out /'haid ,aut/ *n.* escondite *m.*

hiding place /'haidiŋ/ escondrijo *m.*

hierarchy /'haiə,rarki/ *n.* jerarquía *f.*

high /hai/ *a.* alto, elevado; (in price) caro.

highbrow /'hai,brau/ *n.* erudito *m.*

highfalutin /,haifə'lutṇ/ *a.* pomposo, presumido.

high fidelity de alta fidelidad.

highlighter /'hai,laitər/ *n.* marcador *m.*

highly /'haili/ *adv.* altamente; sumamente.

high school escuela secundaria *f.*

highway /'hai,wei/ *n.* carretera *f.*; camino real *m.*

hijacker /'hai,dʒækər/ *n.* secuestrador, pirata de aviones *m.*

hike /haik/ *n.* caminata *f.*

hilarious /hi'lɛəriəs/ *a.* alegre, bullicioso.

hilarity /hi'læriti/ *n.* hilaridad *f.*

hill /hil/ *n.* colina *f.*; cerro *m.*; **down h.,** cuesta abajo. **up h.,** cuesta arriba.

hilly /'hili/ *a.* accidentado.

hilt /hilt/ *n.* puño *m.* **up to the h.,** a fondo.

him /him/ *pron.* él; lo; le.

himself /him'sɛlf/ *pron.* sí, sí mismo; se. **he h.,** él mismo. **with h.,** consigo.

hinder /'hindər/ *v.* impedir.

hindmost /'haind,moust/ *a.* último.

hindquarter /'haind,kwɔrtər/ *n.* cuarto trasero *m.*

hindrance /'hindrəns/ *n.* obstáculo *m.*

hinge /hindʒ/ *n.* **1.** gozne *m.* —*v.* **2.** engoznar. **h. on,** depender de.

hint /hint/ *n.* **1.** insinuación *f.*; indicio *m.* —*v.* **2.** insinuar.

hip /hɪp/ n. cadera f.

hippopotamus /ˌhɪpə'pɒtəməs/ n. hipopótamo m.

hire /haɪər/ v. alquilar.

his /hɪz; unstressed ɪz/ a. **1.** su. —pron. **2.** suyo, de él.

Hispanic /hɪ'spænɪk/ a. hispano.

hiss /hɪs/ v. silbar, sisear.

historian /hɪ'stɔriən/ n. historiador m.

historic /hɪ'stɔrɪk/ **historical** a. histórico.

history /'hɪstəri/ n. historia f.

histrionic /ˌhɪstri'ɒnɪk/ a. histriónico.

hit /hɪt/ n. **1.** golpe m.; Colloq. éxito m.; (Internet) hit m. —v. **2.** golpear.

hitch /hɪtʃ/ v. amarrar; enganchar.

hitchhike /'hɪtʃˌhaɪk/ v. hacer autostop.

hitchhiker /'hɪtʃˌhaɪkər/ n. autostopista f.

hitchhiking /'hɪtʃˌhaɪkɪŋ/ n. autostop m.

hither /'hɪðər/ adv. acá, hacia acá.

hitherto /'hɪðərˌtu/ adv. hasta ahora.

hive /haɪv/ n. colmena f.

hives /haɪvz/ n. urticaria f.

hoard /hɔrd/ n. **1.** acumulación f. —v. **2.** acaparar; atesorar.

hoarse /hɔrs/ a. ronco.

hoax /houks/ n. **1.** engaño m. —v. **2.** engañar.

hobby /'hɒbi/ n. afición f., pasatiempo m.

hobgoblin /'hɒbˌgɒblɪn/ n. trasgo m.

hobnob /'hɒbˌnɒb/ v. tener intimidad.

hobo /'houbou/ n. vagabundo m.

hockey /'hɒki/ n. hockey m. **ice-h.,** hockey sobre hielo.

hod /hɒd/ n. esparavel m.

hodgepodge /'hɒdʒˌpɒdʒ/ n. baturrillo m.; mezcolanza f.

hoe /hou/ n. **1.** azada f. —v. **2.** cultivar con azada.

hog /hɔg/ n. cerdo, puerco m.

hoist /hɔɪst/ n. **1.** grúa f., elevador m. —v. **2.** elevar, enarbolar.

hold /hould/ n. **1.** presa f.; agarro m.; Naut. bodega f. **to get h. of,** conseguir, apoderarse de. —v. **2.** tener; detener; sujetar; celebrar.

holder /'houldər/ n. tenedor m. **cigarette h.,** boquilla f.

holdup /'hould,ʌp/ n. salteamiento m.

hole /houl/ n. agujero; hoyo; hueco m.

holiday /'hɒlɪˌdei/ n. día de fiesta.

holiness /'houlɪnɪs/ n. santidad f.

Holland /'hɒlənd/ n. Holanda f.

hollow /'hɒlou/ a. **1.** hueco. —n. **2.** cavidad f. —v. **3.** ahuecar; excavar.

holly /'hɒli/ n. acebo m.

hollyhock /'hɒli,hɒk/ n. malva real f.

holocaust /'hɒlə,kɔst/ n. holocausto m.

hologram /'hɒlə,græm/ n. holograma m.

holography /hə'lɒgrəfi/ n. holografía f.

holster /'houlstər/ n. pistolera f.

holy /'houli/ a. santo.

holy day disanto m.

Holy See Santa Sede f.

Holy Spirit Espíritu Santo m.

Holy Week Semana Santa f.

homage /'hɒmɪdʒ/ n. homenaje m.

home /houm/ n. casa, morada f.; hogar m. **at h.,** en casa. **to go h.,** ir a casa.

home appliance electrodoméstica m.

home computer ordenador doméstico m., computadora doméstica f.

homeland /'houm,lænd/ n. patria f.

homely /'houmli/ a. feo; casero.

home rule n. autonomía f.

homesick /'houm,sɪk/ a. nostálgico.

homespun /'houm,spʌn/ a. casero; tocho.

homeward /'houmwərd/ adv. hacia casa.

homework /'houm,wɜrk/ n. deberes m.pl.

homicide /'hɒmə,said/ n. homicida m. & f.

homily /'hɒməli/ n. homilía f.

homogeneous /ˌhoumə'dʒiniəs/ a. homogéneo.

homogenize /hə'mɒdʒə,naiz/ v. homogenezar.

homosexual /ˌhoumə'sɛkʃuəl/ n. & a. homosexual m.

Honduras /hɒn'dʊrəs/ n. Honduras f.

hone /houn/ n. **1.** piedra de afilar f. —v. **2.** afilar.

honest /'ɒnɪst/ a. honrado, honesto; sincero.

honestly /'ɒnɪstli/ adv. honradamente; de veras.

honesty /'ɒnəsti/ n. honradez, honestidad f.

honey /'hʌni/ n. miel f.

honeybee /'hʌni,bi/ n. abeja obrera f.

honeymoon /'hʌni,mun/ n. luna de miel.

honeysuckle /'hʌni,sʌkəl/ n. madreselva f.

honor /'ɒnər/ n. **1.** honra f.; honor m. —v. **2.** honrar.

honorable /'ɒnərəbəl/ a. honorable; ilustre.

honorary /'ɒnə,rɛri/ a. honorario.

hood /hʊd/ n. capota; capucha f.; Auto. cubierta del motor.

hoodlum /'hudləm/ n. pillo m., rufián m.

hoodwink /'hʊd,wɪŋk/ v. engañar.

hoof /hʊf/ n. pezuña f.

hook /hʊk/ n. **1.** gancho m. —v. **2.** enganchar.

hooligan /'huligən/ n. gamberro -rra.

hoop /hup/ n. cerco m.

hop /hɒp/ n. **1.** salto m. —v. **2.** saltar.

hope /houp/ n. **1.** esperanza f. —v. **2.** esperar.

hopeful /'houpfəl/ a. lleno de esperanzas.

hopeless /'houplɪs/ a. desesperado; sin remedio.

horde /hɔrd/ n. horda f.

horehound /'hɔr,haund/ n. marrubio m.

horizon /hə'raizən/ n. horizonte m.

horizontal /ˌhɔrə'zɒntl/ a. horizontal.

hormone /'hɔrmoun/ n. hormona f.

horn /hɔrn/ n. cuerno m.; (music) trompa f.; Auto. bocina f.

hornet /'hɔrnɪt/ n. avispón m.

horny /'hɔrni/ a. córneo; calloso.

horoscope /'hɔrə,skoup/ n. horóscopo m.

horrendous /hə'rɛndəs/ a. horrendo.

horrible /'hɔrəbəl/ a. horrible.

horrid /'hɔrɪd/ a. horrible.

horrify /'hɔrə,fai/ v. horrorizar.

horror /'hɔrər/ n. horror m.

horror film película de terror f.

hors d'oeuvre /ɔr 'dɜrv/ n. entremés m.

horse /hɔrs/ n. caballo m. **to ride a h.,** cabalgar.

horseback /'hɔrs,bæk/ n. **on h.,** a caballo. **to ride h.,** montar a caballo.

horseback riding equitación f.

horsefly /'hɔrs,flai/ n. tábano m.

horsehair /'hɔrs,hɛər/ n. pelo de caballo m.; tela de crin f.

horseman /'hɔrsmən/ n. jinete m.

horsemanship /'hɔrsmən,ʃɪp/ n. manejo m., equitación f.

horsepower /'hɔrs,pauər/ n. caballo de fuerza m.

horse race carrera de caballos f.

horseradish /'hɔrs,rædɪʃ/ n. rábano picante m.

horseshoe /'hɔrs,ʃu/ n. herradura f.

hortatory /'hɔrtə,tɔri/ a. exhortatorio.

horticulture /'hɔrtɪ,kʌltʃər/ n. horticultura f.

hose /houz/ n. medias f.pl; (garden) manguera f.

hosiery /'houʒəri/ n. calcetería f.

hospitable /'hɒspɪtəbəl/ a. hospitalario.

hospital /'hɒspɪtl/ n. hospital m.

hospitality /ˌhɒspɪ'tælɪti/ n. hospitalidad f.

hospitalization /ˌhɒspɪtlɪ'zeiʃən/ n. hospitalización f.

hospitalize /'hɒspɪtl,aiz/ v. hospitalizar.

host /houst/ n. anfitrión m., dueño de la casa; Relig. hostia f.

hostage /'hɒstɪdʒ/ n. rehén m.

hostel /'hɒstl/ n. hostería f.

hostelry /'hɒstlri/ n. fonda f., parador m.

hostess /'houstɪs/ n. anfitriona f., dueña de la casa.

hostile /'hɒstl/ a. hostil.

hostility /hɒ'stɪlɪti/ n. hostilidad f.

hot /hɒt/ a. caliente; (sauce) picante. **to be h.,** tener calor; (weather) hacer calor.

hotbed /'hɒt,bɛd/ n. estercolero m. Fig. foco m.

hot dog perrito caliente m.

hotel /hou'tɛl/ n. hotel m.

hotelier /ˌoutəl'yei, ,hout'ɪər/ n. hotelero -ra.

hot-headed /'hɒt 'hɛdɪd/ a. turbulento, alborotadizo.

hothouse /'hɒt,haus/ n. invernáculo m.

hot-water bottle /'hɒt 'wɔtər/ bolsa de agua caliente f.

hound /haund/ n. **1.** sabueso m. —v. **2.** perseguir; seguir la pista.

hour /auər/ n. hora f.

hourglass /'auər,glæs/ n. reloj de arena m.

hourly /'auərli/ a. **1.** por horas. —adv. **2.** a cada hora.

house /n haus; v hauz/ n. **1.** casa f.; Theat. público m. —v. **2.** alojar, albergar.

housefly /'haus,flai/ n. mosca ordinaria f.

household /'haus,hould/ n. familia; casa f.

housekeeper /'haus,kipər/ n. ama de llaves.

housemaid /'haus,meid/ n. criada f., sirvienta f.

housewife /'haus,waif/ n. ama de casa.

housework /'haus,wɜrk/ n. tareas domésticas.

hovel /'hʌvəl/ n. choza f.

hover /'hʌvər/ v. revolotear.

hovercraft /'hʌvər,kræft/ n. aerodeslizador m.

how /hau/ adv. cómo. **h. much,** cuánto. **h. many,** cuántos. **h. far,** a qué distancia.

however /hau'ɛvər/ adv. como quiera; sin embargo.

howl /haul/ n. **1.** aullido m. —v. **2.** aullar.

HTML abbr. (HyperText Markup Language) Lenguaje de Marcado de Hipertexto m.

hub /hʌb/ n. centro m.; eje m. **h. of a wheel,** cubo de la rueda.

hubbub /'hʌbʌb/ n. alboroto m., bulla f.

hue /hyu/ n. matiz; color m.

hug /hʌg/ n. **1.** abrazo m. —v. **2.** abrazar.

huge /hyudʒ/ a. enorme.

hulk /hʌlk/ n. casco de buque m.

hull /hʌl/ n. cáscara f.; (naval) casco m. —v. **2.** decascarar.

hum /hʌm/ n. **1.** zumbido m. —v. **2.** tararear; zumbar.

human /'hyumən/ a. & n. humano -na.

human being ser humano m.

humane /hyu'mein/ a. humano, humanitario.

humanism /'hyumə,nɪzəm/ n. humanidad f.; benevolencia f.

humanitarian /hyu,mænɪ'tɛəriən/ a. humanitario.

humanity /hyu'mænɪti/ n. humanidad f.

humanly /'hyumənli/ a. humanamente.

humble /'hʌmbəl/ a. humilde.

humbug /'hʌm,bʌg/ n. farsa f., embaucador m.

humdrum /'hʌm,drʌm/ a. monótono.

humid /'hyumɪd/ a. húmedo.

humidity /hyu'mɪdɪti/ n. humedad f.

humiliate /hyu'mɪli,eit/ v. humillar.

humiliation /hyu,mɪli'eiʃən/ n. mortificación f.; bochorno m.

humility /hyu'mɪlɪti/ n. humildad f.

humor /'hyumər/ n. **1.** humor; capricho m. —v. **2.** complacer.

humorist /'hyumərɪst/ n. humorista m.

humorous /'hyumərəs/ a. divertido.

hump /hʌmp/ n. joroba f.

humpback /'hʌmp,bæk/ n. jorobado m.

humus /'hyuməs/ n. humus m.

hunch /hʌntʃ/ n. giba f.; (idea) corazonada f.

hunchback /'hʌntʃ,bæk/ n. jorobado m.

hundred /'hʌndrɪd/ a. & pron. **1.** cien, ciento. 200, doscientos. 300, trescientos. 400, cuatrocientos. 500, quinientos. 600, seiscientos. 700, setecientos. 800, ochocientos. 900, novecientos. —n. **2.** centenar m.

hundredth /'hʌndrɪdθ/ n. & a. centésimo m.

Hungarian /hʌŋ'gɛəriən/ a. & n. húngaro -ra.

Hungary /'hʌŋgəri/ Hungría f.

hunger /'hʌŋgər/ n. hambre f.

hunger strike huelga de hambre f.

hungry /'hʌŋgri/ a. hambriento. **to be h.,** tener hambre.

hunt /hʌnt/ n. **1.** caza f. —v. **2.** cazar. **h. up,** buscar.

hunter /'hʌntər/ n. cazador m.

hunting /'hʌntɪŋ/ n. caza f. **to go h.,** ir de caza.

hurdle /'hɜrdl/ n. zarzo m., valla f.; dificultad f.

hurl /hɜrl/ v. arrojar.

hurricane /'hɜrɪ,kein/ n. huracán m.

hurry /'hɜri/ n. **1.** prisa f. **to be in a h.,** tener prisa. —v. **2.** apresurar; darse prisa.

hurt /hɜrt/ n. **1.** daño, perjuicio m. —v. **2.** dañar; lastimar; doler; ofender.

hurtful /'hɜrtfəl/ a. perjudicial, dañino.

hurtle /'hɜrtl/ v. lanzar.

husband /'hʌzbənd/ n. marido, esposo m.

husk /hʌsk/ n. **1.** cáscara f. —v. **2.** descascarar.

husky /'hʌski/ a. fornido.

hustle /'hʌsəl/ v. empujar.

hustle and bustle ajetreo m.

hut /hʌt/ n. choza f.

hyacinth /'haiəsɪnθ/ n. jacinto m.

hybrid /'haibrɪd/ a. híbrido.

hydrangea /hai'dreindʒə/ n. hortensia f.

hydraulic /hai'drɒlɪk/ a. hidráulico.

hydroelectric /ˌhaidrou'lɛktrɪk/ a. hidroeléctrico.

hydrogen /'haidrədʒən/ n. hidrógeno m.

hydrophobia /ˌhaidrə'foubiə/ n. hidrofobia f.

hydroplane /'haidrə,plein/ n. hidroavión m.

hydrotherapy /ˌhaidrə'θɛrəpi/ n. hidroterapia f.

hyena /hai'inə/ n. hiena f.

hygiene /'haidʒin/ n. higiene f.

hygienic /ˌhaidʒi'ɛnɪk/ a. higiénico.

hymn /hɪm/ n. himno m.

hymnal /'hɪmnl/ n. himnario m.

hype /haip/ n. Colloq. **1.** bomba publicitario f. —v. **2.** promocionar a bombo y platillo.

hypercritical /ˌhaipər'krɪtɪkəl/ a. hipercrítico.

hyperlink /'haipər,lɪŋk/ n. (Internet) hiperenlace m.

hypermarket /'haipər,mɑrkɪt/ n. hipermercado m.

hypertension /ˌhaipər'tɛnʃən/ n. hipertensión f.

hypertext /'haɪpərˌtɛkst/ *n.* (Internet) hipertexto *m.*
hyphen /'haɪfən/ *n.* guión *m.*
hyphenate /'haɪfəˌneɪt/ *v.* separar con guión.
hypnosis /hɪp'noʊsɪs/ *n.* hipnosis *f.*
hypnotic /hɪp'nɒtɪk/ *a.* hipnótico.
hypnotism /'hɪpnəˌtɪzəm/ *n.* hipnotismo *m.*
hypnotize /'hɪpnəˌtaɪz/ *v.* hipnotizar.
hypochondria /ˌhaɪpə'kɒndrɪə/ *n.* hipocondría *f.*
hypochondriac /ˌhaɪpə'kɒndrɪˌæk/ *n.* & *a.* hipocondríaco *m.*
hypocrisy /hɪ'pɒkrəsɪ/ *n.* hipocresía *f.*
hypocrite /'hɪpəkrɪt/ *n.* hipócrita *m.* & *f.*
hypocritical /ˌhɪpə'krɪtɪkəl/ *a.* hipócrita.
hypodermic /ˌhaɪpə'dɜrmɪk/ *a.* hipodérmico.
hypotenuse /haɪ'pɒtṇˌus/ *n.* hipotenusa *f.*
hypothesis /haɪ'pɒθəsɪs/ *n.* hipótesis *f.*
hypothetical /ˌhaɪpə'θɛtɪkəl/ *a.* hipotético.
hysterectomy /ˌhɪstə'rɛktəmɪ/ *n.* histerectomía *f.*
hysteria /hɪ'stɛrɪə/ **hysterics** *n.* histeria *f.*
hysterical /hɪ'stɛrɪkəl/ *a.* histérico.

I /aɪ/ *pron.* yo.
iambic /aɪ'æmbɪk/ *a.* yámbico.
ice /aɪs/ *n.* hielo *m.*
iceberg /'aɪsbɜrg/ *n.* iceberg *m.*
icebox /'aɪsˌbɒks/ *n.* refrigerador *m.*
ice cream helado, mantecado *m.*; **i.-c. cone,** barquillo de helado; **i.-c. parlor** heladería *f.*
ice cube cubito de hielo *m.*
ice skate patín de cuchilla *m.*
icon /'aɪkɒn/ *n.* icón *m.*
icy /'aɪsɪ/ *a.* helado; indiferente.
idea /aɪ'diə/ *n.* idea *f.*
ideal /aɪ'diəl/ *a.* ideal.
idealism /aɪ'diəˌlɪzəm/ *n.* idealismo *m.*
idealist /aɪ'diəlɪst/ *n.* idealista *m.* & *f.*
idealistic /aɪˌdiə'lɪstɪk/ *a.* idealista.
idealize /aɪ'diəˌlaɪz/ *v.* idealizar.
ideally /aɪ'diəlɪ/ *adv.* idealmente.
identical /aɪ'dɛntɪkəl/ *a.* idéntico.
identifiable /aɪˌdɛntɪ'faɪəbəl/ *a.* identificable.
identification /aɪˌdɛntɪfɪ'keɪʃən/ *n.* identificación *f.* **i. papers,** cédula de identidad *f.*
identify /aɪ'dɛntəˌfaɪ/ *v.* identificar.
identity /aɪ'dɛntɪtɪ/ *n.* identidad *f.*
ideology /ˌaɪdi'ɒlədʒi/ *n.* ideología *f.*
idiocy /'ɪdiəsɪ/ *n.* idiotez *f.*
idiom /'ɪdiəm/ *n.* modismo *m.*; idioma *m.*
idiot /'ɪdiət/ *n.* idiota *m.* & *f.*
idiotic /ˌɪdi'ɒtɪk/ *a.* idiota, tonto.
idle /'aɪdl/ *a.* desocupado; perezoso.
idleness /'aɪdlnɪs/ *n.* ociosidad, pereza *f.*
idol /'aɪdl/ *n.* ídolo *m.*
idolatry /aɪ'dɒlətri/ *n.* idolatría *f.*
idolize /'aɪdlˌaɪz/ *v.* idolatrar.
idyl /'aɪdl/ *n.* idilio *m.*
idyllic /aɪ'dɪlɪk/ *a.* idílico.
if /ɪf/ *conj.* si. **even if,** aunque.
ignite /ɪg'naɪt/ *v.* encender.
ignition /ɪg'nɪʃən/ *n.* ignición *f.*
ignoble /ɪg'noʊbəl/ *a.* innoble, indigno.
ignominious /ˌɪgnə'mɪniəs/ *a.* ignominioso.
ignoramus /ˌɪgnə'reɪməs/ *n.* ignorante *m.*
ignorance /'ɪgnərəns/ *n.* ignorancia *f.*
ignorant /'ɪgnərənt/ *a.* ignorante. **to be i. of,** ignorar.

ignore /ɪg'nɔr/ *v.* desconocer, pasar por alto.
ill /ɪl/ *a.* enfermo, malo.
illegal /ɪ'ligəl/ *a.* ilegal.
illegible /ɪ'lɛdʒəbəl/ *a.* ilegible.
illegibly /ɪ'lɛdʒəblɪ/ *a.* ilegiblemente.
illegitimacy /ˌɪlɪ'dʒɪtəməsɪ/ *n.* ilegitimidad *f.*
illegitimate /ˌɪlɪ'dʒɪtəmɪt/ *a.* ilegítimo; desautorizado.
illicit /ɪ'lɪsɪt/ *a.* ilícito.
illiteracy /ɪ'lɪtərəsɪ/ *n.* analfabetismo *m.*
illiterate /ɪ'lɪtərɪt/ *a.* & *n.* analfabeto -ta.
illness /'ɪlnɪs/ *n.* enfermedad, maldad *f.*
illogical /ɪ'lɒdʒɪkəl/ *a.* ilógico.
illuminate /ɪ'luməˌneɪt/ *v.* iluminar.
illumination /ɪˌlumə'neɪʃən/ *n.* iluminación *f.*
illusion /ɪ'luʒən/ *n.* ilusión *f.*; ensueño *m.*
illusive /ɪ'lusɪv/ *a.* ilusivo.
illustrate /'ɪləˌstreɪt/ *v.* ilustrar; ejemplificar.
illustration /ˌɪlə'streɪʃən/ *n.* ilustración *f.*; ejemplo; grabado *m.*
illustrative /ɪ'lʌstrətɪv/ *a.* ilustrativo.
illustrious /ɪ'lʌstriəs/ *a.* ilustre.
ill will *n.* malevolencia *f.*
image /'ɪmɪdʒ/ *n.* imagen, estatua *f.*
imagery /'ɪmɪdʒrɪ/ *n.* imaginación *f.*
imaginable /ɪ'mædʒənəbəl/ *a.* imaginable.
imaginary /ɪ'mædʒəˌnɛri/ *a.* imaginario *f.*
imagination /ɪˌmædʒə'neɪʃən/ *n.* imaginación *f.*
imaginative /ɪ'mædʒənətɪv/ *a.* imaginativo.
imagine /ɪ'mædʒɪn/ *v.* imaginarse, figurarse.
imam /ɪ'mɑm/ *n.* imán *m.*
imbecile /'ɪmbəsɪl/ *n.* & *a.* imbécil *m.*
imitate /'ɪmɪˌteɪt/ *v.* imitar.
imitation /ˌɪmɪ'teɪʃən/ *n.* imitación *f.*
imitative /'ɪmɪˌteɪtɪv/ *a.* imitativo.
immaculate /ɪ'mækyəlɪt/ *a.* inmaculado.
immanent /'ɪmənənt/ *a.* inmanente.
immaterial /ˌɪmə'tɪəriəl/ *a.* inmaterial; sin importancia.
immature /ˌɪmə'tʃʊr/ *a.* inmaduro.
immediate /ɪ'midiɪt/ *a.* inmediato.
immediately /ɪ'midiɪtlɪ/ *adv.* inmediatamente.
immense /ɪ'mɛns/ *a.* inmenso.
immerse /ɪ'mɜrs/ *v.* sumergir.
immigrant /'ɪmɪgrənt/ *n.* & *a.* inmigrante *m.* & *f.*
immigrate /'ɪmɪˌgreɪt/ *v.* inmigrar.
imminent /'ɪmənənt/ *a.* inminente.
immobile /ɪ'moʊbəl/ *a.* inmóvil.
immoderate /ɪ'mɒdərɪt/ *a.* inmoderado.
immodest /ɪ'mɒdɪst/ *a.* inmodesto; atrevido.
immoral /ɪ'mɔrəl/ *a.* inmoral.
immorality /ˌɪmə'rælɪtɪ/ *n.* inmoralidad *f.*
immortal /ɪ'mɔrtl/ *a.* inmortal.
immortality /ˌɪmɔr'tælɪtɪ/ *n.* inmortalidad *f.*
immortalize /ɪ'mɔrtlˌaɪz/ *v.* inmortalizar.
immune /ɪ'myun/ *a.* inmune.
immunity /ɪ'myunɪtɪ/ *n.* inmunidad *f.*
immunize /'ɪmyəˌnaɪz/ *v.* inmunizar.
impact /'ɪmpækt/ *n.* impacto *m.*
impair /ɪm'pɛər/ *v.* empeorar, perjudicar.
impale /ɪm'peɪl/ *v.* empalar.
impart /ɪm'pɑrt/ *v.* impartir, comunicar.
impartial /ɪm'pɑrʃəl/ *a.* imparcial.
impatience /ɪm'peɪʃəns/ *n.* impaciencia *f.*
impatient /ɪm'peɪʃənt/ *a.* impaciente.
impede /ɪm'pid/ *v.* impedir, estorbar.

impediment /ɪm'pɛdəmənt/ *n.* impedimento *m.*
impel /ɪm'pɛl/ *v.* impeler.
impenetrable /ɪm'pɛnɪtrəbəl/ *a.* impenetrable.
impenitent /ɪm'pɛnɪtənt/ *n.* & *a.* impenitente *m.*
imperative /ɪm'pɛrətɪv/ *a.* imperativo.
imperceptible /ˌɪmpər'sɛptəbəl/ *a.* imperceptible.
imperfect /ɪm'pɜrfɪkt/ *a.* imperfecto.
imperfection /ˌɪmpər'fɛkʃən/ *n.* imperfección *f.*
imperial /ɪm'pɪəriəl/ *a.* imperial.
imperialism /ɪm'pɪəriəˌlɪzəm/ *n.* imperialismo *m.*
imperious /ɪm'pɪəriəs/ *a.* imperioso.
impersonal /ɪm'pɜrsənl/ *a.* impersonal.
impersonate /ɪm'pɜrsəˌneɪt/ *v.* personificar; imitar.
impersonation /ɪmˌpɜrsə'neɪʃən/ *n.* personificación *f.*; imitación *f.*
impertinence /ɪm'pɜrtṇəns/ *n.* impertinencia *f.*
impervious /ɪm'pɜrviəs/ *a.* impermeable.
impetuous /ɪm'pɛtʃuəs/ *a.* impetuoso.
impetus /'ɪmpɪtəs/ *n.* ímpetu *m.*, impulso *m.*
impinge /ɪm'pɪndʒ/ *v.* tropezar; infringir.
implacable /ɪm'plækəbəl/ *a.* implacable.
implant /ɪm'plænt/ *v.* implantar; inculcar.
implement /'ɪmpləmənt/ *n.* herramienta *f.*
implicate /'ɪmplɪˌkeɪt/ *v.* implicar; embrollar.
implication /ˌɪmplɪ'keɪʃən/ *n.* inferencia *f.*; complicidad *f.*
implicit /ɪm'plɪsɪt/ *a.* implícito.
implied /ɪm'plaɪd/ *a.* implícito.
implore /ɪm'plɔr/ *v.* implorar.
imply /ɪm'plaɪ/ *v.* significar; dar a entender.
impolite /ˌɪmpə'laɪt/ *a.* descortés.
import /*n.* 'ɪmpɔrt; *v.* ɪm'pɔrt/ *n.* 1. importación *f.* —*v.* 2. importar.
importance /ɪm'pɔrtns/ *n.* importancia *f.*
important /ɪm'pɔrtṇt/ *a.* importante.
importation /ˌɪmpɔr'teɪʃən/ *n.* importación *f.*
importune /ˌɪmpɔr'tun/ *v.* importunar.
impose /ɪm'poʊz/ *v.* imponer.
imposition /ˌɪmpə'zɪʃən/ *n.* imposición *f.*
impossibility /ɪmˌpɒsə'bɪlɪtɪ/ *n.* imposibilidad *f.*
impossible /ɪm'pɒsəbəl/ *a.* imposible.
impotence /'ɪmpətəns/ *n.* impotencia *f.*
impotent /'ɪmpətənt/ *a.* impotente.
impregnable /ɪm'prɛgnəbəl/ *a.* impregnable.
impregnate /ɪm'prɛgneɪt/ *v.* impregnar; fecundizar.
impresario /ˌɪmprə'sɑriˌoʊ/ *n.* empresario *m.*
impress /ɪm'prɛs/ *v.* impresionar.
impression /ɪm'prɛʃən/ *n.* impresión *f.*
impressive /ɪm'prɛsɪv/ *a.* imponente.
imprison /ɪm'prɪzən/ *v.* encarcelar.
imprisonment /ɪm'prɪzənmənt/ *n.* prisión, encarcelación *f.*
improbable /ɪm'prɒbəbəl/ *a.* improbable.
impromptu /ɪm'prɒmptu/ *a.* extemporáneo.
improper /ɪm'prɒpər/ *a.* impropio.
improve /ɪm'pruv/ *v.* mejorar; progresar.
improvement /ɪm'pruvmənt/ *n.* mejoramiento; progreso *m.*
improvise /'ɪmprəˌvaɪz/ *v.* improvisar.
impudent /'ɪmpyədənt/ *a.* descarado.
impugn /ɪm'pyun/ *v.* impugnar.

impulse /'ɪmpʌls/ *n.* impulso *m.*
impulsive /ɪm'pʌlsɪv/ *a.* impulsivo.
impunity /ɪm'pyunɪtɪ/ *n.* impunidad *f.*
impure /ɪm'pyʊr/ *a.* impuro.
impurity /ɪm'pyʊrɪtɪ/ *n.* impureza *f.*; deshonestidad *f.*
impute /ɪm'pyut/ *v.* imputar.
in /ɪn/ *prep.* 1. en; dentro de. —*adv.* 2. adentro.
inadvertent /ˌɪnəd'vɜrtṇt/ *a.* inadvertido.
inalienable /ɪn'eɪlyənəbəl/ *a.* inalienable.
inane /ɪ'neɪn/ *a.* mentecato.
inaugural /ɪn'ɔgyərəl/ *a.* inaugural.
inaugurate /ɪn'ɔgyəˌreɪt/ *v.* inaugurar.
inauguration /ɪnˌɔgyə'reɪʃən/ *n.* inauguración *f.*
Inca /'ɪŋkə/ *n.* inca *m.*
incandescent /ˌɪnkən'dɛsənt/ *a.* incandescente.
incantation /ˌɪnkæn'teɪʃən/ *n.* encantación *f.*, conjuro *m.*
incapacitate /ˌɪnkə'pæsɪˌteɪt/ *v.* incapacitar.
incarcerate /ɪn'kɑrsəˌreɪt/ *v.* encarcelar.
incarnate /ɪn'kɑrnɪt/ *a.* encarnado; personificado.
incarnation /ˌɪnkɑr'neɪʃən/ *n.* encarnación *f.*
incendiary /ɪn'sɛndiˌɛri/ *a.* incendario.
incense /ɪn'sɛns/ *n.* 1. incienso *m.* —*v.* 2. indignar.
incentive /ɪn'sɛntɪv/ *n.* incentivo *m.*
inception /ɪn'sɛpʃən/ *n.* comienzo *m.*
incessant /ɪn'sɛsənt/ *a.* incesante.
incest /'ɪnsɛst/ *n.* incesto *m.*
inch /ɪntʃ/ *n.* pulgada *f.*
incidence /'ɪnsɪdəns/ *n.* incidencia *f.*
incident /'ɪnsɪdənt/ *n.* incidente *m.*
incidental /ˌɪnsɪ'dɛntl/ *a.* incidental.
incidentally /ˌɪnsɪ'dɛntlɪ/ *adv.* incidentalmente; entre paréntesis.
incinerate /ɪn'sɪnəˌreɪt/ *v.* incinerar.
incinerator /ɪn'sɪnəˌreɪtər/ *n.* incinerador *m.*
incipient /ɪn'sɪpiənt/ *a.* incipiente.
incision /ɪn'sɪʒən/ *n.* incisión *f.*; cortadura *f.*
incisive /ɪn'saɪsɪv/ *a.* incisivo; mordaz.
incisor /ɪn'saɪzər/ *n.* incisivo *m.*
incite /ɪn'saɪt/ *v.* incitar, instigar.
inclination /ˌɪnklə'neɪʃən/ *n.* inclinación *f.*; declive *m.*
incline /*n.* 'ɪnklaɪn; *v.* ɪn'klaɪn/ *n.* 1. pendiente *m.* —*v.* 2. inclinar.
inclose /ɪn'kloʊz/ *v.* incluir.
include /ɪn'klud/ *v.* incluir, englobar.
including /ɪn'kludɪŋ/ *prep.* incluso.
inclusive /ɪn'klusɪv/ *a.* inclusivo.
incognito /ˌɪnkɒg'nitoʊ/ *n.* & *adv.* incógnito *m.*
income /'ɪnkʌm/ *n.* renta *f.*; ingresos *m.pl.*
income tax impuesto sobre la renta *m.*
incomparable /ɪn'kɒmpərəbəl/ *a.* incomparable.
inconvenience /ˌɪnkən'vinyəns/ *n.* 1. incomodidad *f.* —*v.* 2. incomodar.
inconvenient /ˌɪnkən'vinyənt/ *a.* incómodo.
incorporate /ɪn'kɔrpəˌreɪt/ *v.* incorporar; dar cuerpo.
incorrigible /ɪn'kɔrɪdʒəbəl/ *a.* incorregible.
increase /ɪn'kris/ *v.* crecer; aumentar.
incredible /ɪn'krɛdəbəl/ *a.* increíble.
incredulity /ˌɪnkrɪ'dulɪtɪ/ *n.* incredulidad *f.*
incredulous /ɪn'krɛdʒələs/ *a.* incrédulo.
increment /'ɪnkrəmənt/ *n.* incremento *m.*, aumento *m.*
incriminate /ɪn'krɪməˌneɪt/ *v.* incriminar.
incrimination /ɪnˌkrɪmə'neɪʃən/ *n.* incriminación *f.*
incrust /ɪn'krʌst/ *v.* incrustar.

incubator /ˈɪnkyəˌbeitər/ *n.* incubadora *f.*
inculcate /ɪnˈkʌlkeit/ *v.* inculcar.
incumbency /ɪnˈkʌmbənsi/ *n.* incumbencia *f.*
incumbent /ɪnˈkʌmbənt/ *a.* obligatorio; colocado sobre.
incur /ɪnˈkɜr/ *v.* incurrir.
incurable /ɪnˈkyʊrəbəl/ *a.* incurable.
indebted /ɪnˈdɛtɪd/ *a.* obligado; adeudado.
indeed /ɪnˈdid/ *adv.* verdaderamente, de veras. **no i.,** de ninguna manera.
indefatigable /ˌɪndɪˈfætɪgəbəl/ *a.* incansable.
indefinite /ɪnˈdɛfənɪt/ *a.* indefinido.
indefinitely /ɪnˈdɛfənɪtli/ *adv.* indefinidamente.
indelible /ɪnˈdɛləbəl/ *a.* indeleble.
indemnify /ɪnˈdɛmnəˌfai/ *v.* indemnizar.
indemnity /ɪnˈdɛmnɪti/ *n.* indemnificación *f.*
indent /ɪnˈdɛnt/ *n.* **1.** diente *f.*, mella *f.* —*v.* **2.** indentar, mellar.
indentation /ˌɪndɛnˈteiʃən/ *n.* indentación *f.*
independence /ˌɪndɪˈpɛndəns/ *n.* independencia *f.*
independent /ˌɪndɪˈpɛndənt/ *a.* independiente.
in-depth /ˈɪn ˈdɛpθ/ *adj.* en profundidad.
index /ˈɪndɛks/ *n.* índice *m.*; (of book) tabla *f.*
index card ficha *f.*
index finger dedo índice *m.*
India /ˈɪndiə/ *n.* India *f.*
Indian /ˈɪndiən/ *a.* & *n.* indio -dia.
indicate /ˈɪndɪˌkeit/ *v.* indicar.
indication /ˌɪndɪˈkeiʃən/ *n.* indicación *f.*
indicative /ɪnˈdɪkətɪv/ *a.* & *n.* indicativo *m.*
indict /ɪnˈdait/ *v.* encausar.
indictment /ɪnˈdaitmənt/ *n.* (law) sumaria; denuncia *f.*
indifference /ɪnˈdɪfərəns/ *n.* indiferencia *f.*
indifferent /ɪnˈdɪfərənt/ *a.* indiferente.
indigenous /ɪnˈdɪdʒənəs/ *a.* indígena.
indigent /ˈɪndɪdʒənt/ *a.* indigente, pobre.
indigestion /ˌɪndɪˈdʒɛstʃən/ *n.* indigestión *f.*
indignant /ɪnˈdɪgnənt/ *a.* indignado.
indignation /ˌɪndɪgˈneiʃən/ *n.* indignación *f.*
indignity /ɪnˈdɪgnɪti/ *n.* indignidad *f.*
indirect /ˌɪndəˈrɛkt/ *a.* indirecto.
indiscreet /ˌɪndɪˈskrit/ *a.* indiscreto.
indiscretion /ˌɪndɪˈskrɛʃən/ *n.* indiscreción *f.*
indiscriminate /ˌɪndɪˈskrɪmənɪt/ *a.* promiscuo.
indispensable /ˌɪndɪˈspɛnsəbəl/ *a.* indispensable.
indisposed /ˌɪndɪˈspouzd/ *a.* indispuesto.
individual /ˌɪndəˈvɪdʒuəl/ *a.* & *n.* individuo *m.*
individuality /ˌɪndəˌvɪdʒuˈælɪti/ *n.* individualidad *f.*
individually /ˌɪndəˈvɪdʒuəli/ *adv.* individualmente.
indivisible /ˌɪndəˈvɪzəbəl/ *a.* indivisible.
indoctrinate /ɪnˈdɒktrəˌneit/ *v.* doctrinar, enseñar.
indolent /ˈɪndl̩ənt/ *a.* indolente.
indoor /ˈɪnˌdɔr/ *a.* **1.** interior. **indoors** —*adv.* **2.** en casa; bajo techo.
indorse /ɪnˈdɔrs/ *v.* endosar.
induce /ɪnˈdus/ *v.* inducir, persuadir.
induct /ɪnˈdʌkt/ *v.* instalar, iniciar.
induction /ɪnˈdʌkʃən/ *n.* introducción *f.*; instalación *f.*
inductive /ɪnˈdʌktɪv/ *a.* inductivo; introductor.
indulge /ɪnˈdʌldʒ/ *v.* favorecer. **i. in,** entregarse a.
indulgence /ɪnˈdʌldʒəns/ *n.* indulgencia *f.*
indulgent /ɪnˈdʌldʒənt/ *a.* indulgente.
industrial /ɪnˈdʌstriəl/ *a.* industrial.
industrialist /ɪnˈdʌstriəlɪst/ *n.* industrial *m.*
industrial park polígono industrial *m.*
industrious /ɪnˈdʌstriəs/ *a.* industrioso, trabajador.
industry /ˈɪndəstri/ *n.* industria *f.*
inedible /ɪnˈɛdəbəl/ *a.* incomible.
ineligible /ɪnˈɛlɪdʒəbəl/ *a.* inelegible.
inept /ɪnˈɛpt/ *a.* inepto.
inert /ɪnˈɜrt/ *a.* inerte.
inertia /ɪnˈɜrʃə/ *n.* inercia *f.*
inevitable /ɪnˈɛvɪtəbəl/ *a.* inevitable.
inexpensive /ˌɪnɪkˈspɛnsɪv/ *a.* económico.
inexplicable /ɪnˈɛksplɪkəbəl/ *a.* inexplicable.
infallible /ɪnˈfæləbəl/ *a.* infalible.
infamous /ˈɪnfəməs/ *a.* infame.
infamy /ˈɪnfəmi/ *n.* infamia *f.*
infancy /ˈɪnfənsi/ *n.* infancia *f.*
infant /ˈɪnfənt/ *n.* nene *m.*; criatura *f.*
infantile /ˈɪnfənˌtail/ *a.* infantil.
infantry /ˈɪnfəntri/ *n.* infantería *f.*
infatuated /ɪnˈfætʃuˌeitɪd/ *a.* infatuado.
infatuation /ɪnˌfætʃuˈeiʃən/ *a.* encaprichamiento *m.*
infect /ɪnˈfɛkt/ *v.* infectar.
infection /ɪnˈfɛkʃən/ *n.* infección *f.*
infectious /ɪnˈfɛkʃəs/ *a.* infeccioso.
infer /ɪnˈfɜr/ *v.* inferir.
inference /ˈɪnfərəns/ *n.* inferencia *f.*
inferior /ɪnˈfɪəriər/ *a.* inferior.
infernal /ɪnˈfɜrnl̩/ *a.* infernal.
inferno /ɪnˈfɜrnou/ *n.* infierno *m.*
infest /ɪnˈfɛst/ *v.* infestar.
infidel /ˈɪnfɪdl̩/ *n.* **1.** infiel *m.* & *f.*; pagano -na. —*a.* **2.** infiel.
infidelity /ˌɪnfɪˈdɛlɪti/ *n.* infidelidad *f.*
infiltrate /ɪnˈfɪltreit/ *v.* infiltrar.
infinite /ˈɪnfənɪt/ *a.* infinito.
infinitesimal /ˌɪnfɪnɪˈtɛsəməl/ *a.* infinitesimal.
infinitive /ɪnˈfɪnɪtɪv/ *n.* & *a.* infinitivo *m.*
infinity /ɪnˈfɪnɪti/ *n.* infinidad *f.*
infirm /ɪnˈfɜrm/ *a.* enfermizo.
infirmary /ɪnˈfɜrməri/ *n.* hospital *m.*, enfermería *f.*
infirmity /ɪnˈfɜrmɪti/ *n.* enfermedad *f.*
inflame /ɪnˈfleim/ *v.* inflamar.
inflammable /ɪnˈflæməbəl/ *a.* inflamable.
inflammation /ˌɪnfləˈmeiʃən/ *n.* inflamación *f.*
inflammatory /ɪnˈflæməˌtɔri/ *a.* inflamante; *Med.* inflamatorio.
inflate /ɪnˈfleit/ *v.* inflar.
inflation /ɪnˈfleiʃən/ *n.* inflación *f.*
inflection /ɪnˈflɛkʃən/ *n.* inflexión *f.*; (of the voice) modulación de la voz *f.*
inflict /ɪnˈflɪkt/ *v.* infligir.
infliction /ɪnˈflɪkʃən/ *n.* imposición *f.*
influence /ˈɪnfluəns/ *n.* **1.** influencia *f.* —*v.* **2.** influir en.
influential /ˌɪnfluˈɛnʃəl/ *a.* influyente.
influenza /ˌɪnfluˈɛnzə/ *n.* gripe *f.*
influx /ˈɪnˌflʌks/ *n.* afluencia *f.*
inform /ɪnˈfɔrm/ *v.* informar. **i. oneself,** enterarse.
informal /ɪnˈfɔrməl/ *a.* informal.
information /ˌɪnfərˈmeiʃən/ *n.* informaciones *f.pl.*
information technology *n.* informática *f.*
infrastructure /ˈɪnfrəˌstrʌktʃər/ *n.* infraestructura *f.*
infringe /ɪnˈfrɪndʒ/ *v.* infringir.
infuriate /ɪnˈfyʊriˌeit/ *v.* enfurecer.
ingenious /ɪnˈdʒinyəs/ *a.* ingenioso.
ingenuity /ˌɪndʒəˈnuɪti/ *n.* ingeniosidad; destreza *f.*
ingredient /ɪnˈgridiənt/ *n.* ingrediente *m.*
inhabit /ɪnˈhæbɪt/ *v.* habitar.
inhabitant /ɪnˈhæbɪtənt/ *n.* habitante *m.* & *f.*
inhale /ɪnˈheil/ *v.* inhalar.
inherent /ɪnˈhɪərənt/ *a.* inherente.
inherit /ɪnˈhɛrɪt/ *v.* heredar.
inheritance /ɪnˈhɛrɪtəns/ *n.* herencia *f.*
inhibit /ɪnˈhɪbɪt/ *v.* inhibir.
inhibition /ˌɪnɪˈbɪʃən/ *n.* inhibición *f.*
inhuman /ɪnˈhyumən/ *a.* inhumano.
inimical /ɪˈnɪmɪkəl/ *a.* hostil.
inimitable /ɪˈnɪmɪtəbəl/ *a.* inimitable.
iniquity /ɪˈnɪkwɪti/ *n.* iniquidad *f.*
initial /ɪˈnɪʃəl/ *a.* & *n.* inicial *f.*
initiate /ɪˈnɪʃiˌeit/ *v.* iniciar.
initiation /ɪˌnɪʃiˈeiʃən/ *n.* iniciación *f.*
initiative /ɪˈnɪʃiətɪv/ *n.* iniciativa *f.*
inject /ɪnˈdʒɛkt/ *v.* inyectar.
injection /ɪnˈdʒɛkʃən/ *n.* inyección *f.*
injunction /ɪnˈdʒʌŋkʃən/ *n.* mandato *m.*; (law) embargo *m.*
injure /ˈɪndʒər/ *v.* herir; lastimar; ofender.
injurious /ɪnˈdʒʊriəs/ *a.* perjudicial.
injury /ˈɪndʒəri/ *n.* herida; afrenta *f.*; perjuicio *m.*
injustice /ɪnˈdʒʌstɪs/ *n.* injusticia *f.*
ink /ɪŋk/ *n.* tinta *f.*
inland /ˈɪnlænd/ *a.* **1.** interior. —*adv.* **2.** tierra adentro.
inlet /ˈɪnlɛt/ *n.* entrada *f.*; ensenada *f.*; estuario *m.*
inmate /ˈɪnˌmeit/ *n.* residente *m.* & *f.*; (of a prison) preso -sa.
inn /ɪn/ *n.* posada *f.*; mesón *m.*
inner /ˈɪnər/ *a.* interior. **i. tube,** cámara de aire.
innocence /ˈɪnəsəns/ *n.* inocencia *f.*
innocent /ˈɪnəsənt/ *a.* inocente.
innocuous /ɪˈnɒkyuəs/ *a.* innocuo.
innovation /ˌɪnəˈveiʃən/ *n.* innovación *f.*
innuendo /ˌɪnyuˈɛndou/ *n.* insinuación *f.*
innumerable /ɪˈnumərəbəl/ *a.* innumerable.
inoculate /ɪˈnɒkyəˌleit/ *v.* inocular.
inoculation /ɪˌnɒkyəˈleiʃən/ *n.* inoculación *f.*
input /ˈɪnˌpʊt/ *n.* aducto *m.*, ingreso *m.*, entrada *f.*
inquest /ˈɪnkwɛst/ *n.* indagación *f.*
inquire /ɪnˈkwaiᵊr/ *v.* preguntar; inquirir.
inquiry /ɪnˈkwaiᵊri/ *n.* pregunta; investigación *f.*
inquisition /ˌɪnkwəˈzɪʃən/ *n.* escudriñamiento *m.*; (church) Inquisición *f.*
insane /ɪnˈsein/ *a.* loco. **to go i.,** perder la razón; volverse loco.
insanity /ɪnˈsænɪti/ *n.* locura *f.*, demencia *f.*
inscribe /ɪnˈskraib/ *v.* inscribir.
inscription /ɪnˈskrɪpʃən/ *n.* inscripción; dedicatoria *f.*
insect /ˈɪnsɛkt/ *n.* insecto *m.*
insecticide /ɪnˈsɛktəˌsaid/ *n.* & *a.* insecticida *m.*
inseparable /ɪnˈsɛpərəbəl/ *a.* inseparable.
insert /ɪnˈsɜrt/ *v.* insertar, meter.
insertion /ɪnˈsɜrʃən/ *n.* inserción *f.*
inside /ˌɪnˈsaid/ *a.* & *n.* **1.** interior *m.* —*adv.* **2.** adentro, por dentro. **i. out,** al revés. —*prep.* **3.** dentro de.
insidious /ɪnˈsɪdiəs/ *a.* insidioso.
insight /ˈɪnˌsait/ *n.* perspicacia *f.*; comprensión *f.*
insignia /ɪnˈsɪgniə/ *n.* insignias *f.pl.*
insignificance /ˌɪnsɪgˈnɪfɪkəns/ *n.* insignificancia *f.*
insignificant /ˌɪnsɪgˈnɪfɪkənt/ *a.* insignificante.
insinuate /ɪnˈsɪnyuˌeit/ *v.* insinuar.
insinuation /ɪnˌsɪnyuˈeiʃən/ *n.* insinuación *f.*
insipid /ɪnˈsɪpɪd/ *a.* insípido.
insist /ɪnˈsɪst/ *v.* insistir.
insistence /ɪnˈsɪstəns/ *n.* insistencia *f.*
insistent /ɪnˈsɪstənt/ *a.* insistente.
insolence /ˈɪnsələns/ *n.* insolencia *f.*
insolent /ˈɪnsələnt/ *a.* insolente.
insomnia /ɪnˈsɒmniə/ *n.* insomnio *m.*
inspect /ɪnˈspɛkt/ *v.* inspeccionar, examinar.
inspection /ɪnˈspɛkʃən/ *n.* inspección *f.*
inspector /ɪnˈspɛktər/ *n.* inspector -ora.
inspiration /ˌɪnspəˈreiʃən/ *n.* inspiración *f.*
inspire /ɪnˈspaiᵊr/ *v.* inspirar.
install /ɪnˈstɔl/ *v.* instalar.
installation /ˌɪnstəˈleiʃən/ *n.* instalación *f.*
installment /ɪnˈstɔlmənt/ *n.* plazo *m.*
instance /ˈɪnstəns/ *n.* ocasión *f.* **for i.,** por ejemplo.
instant /ˈɪnstənt/ *a.* & *n.* instante *m.*
instantaneous /ˌɪnstənˈteiniəs/ *a.* instantáneo.
instant coffee café soluble *m.*
instantly /ˈɪnstəntli/ *adv.* al instante.
instead /ɪnˈstɛd/ *adv.* en lugar de eso. **i. of,** en vez de, en lugar de.
instigate /ˈɪnstɪˌgeit/ *v.* instigar.
instill /ɪnˈstɪl/ *v.* instilar.
instinct /ˈɪnstɪŋkt/ *n.* instinto *m.* **by i.** por instinto.
instinctive /ɪnˈstɪŋktɪv/ *a.* instintivo.
instinctively /ɪnˈstɪŋktɪvli/ *adv.* por instinto.
institute /ˈɪnstɪˌtut/ *n.* **1.** instituto *m.* —*v.* **2.** instituir.
institution /ˌɪnstɪˈtuʃən/ *n.* institución *f.*
instruct /ɪnˈstrʌkt/ *v.* instruir.
instruction /ɪnˈstrʌkʃən/ *n.* instrucción *f.*
instructive /ɪnˈstrʌktɪv/ *a.* instructivo.
instructor /ɪnˈstrʌktər/ *n.* instructor -ora.
instrument /ˈɪnstrəmənt/ *n.* instrumento *m.*
instrumental /ˌɪnstrəˈmɛntl̩/ *a.* instrumental.
insufficient /ˌɪnsəˈfɪʃənt/ *a.* insuficiente.
insular /ˈɪnsələr/ *a.* insular; estrecho de miras.
insulate /ˈɪnsəˌleit/ *v.* aislar.
insulation /ˌɪnsəˈleiʃən/ *n.* aislamiento *m.*
insulator /ˈɪnsəˌleitər/ *n.* aislador *m.*
insulin /ˈɪnsəlɪn/ *n.* insulina *f.*
insult /*n.* ˈɪnsʌlt; *v.* ɪnˈsʌlt/ *n.* **1.** insulto *m.* —*v.* **2.** insultar.
insuperable /ɪnˈsupərəbəl/ *a.* insuperable.
insurance /ɪnˈʃʊrəns/ *n.* seguro *m.*
insure /ɪnˈʃʊr, -ˈʃɜr/ *v.* asegurar.
insurgent /ɪnˈsɜrdʒənt/ *a.* & *n.* insurgente *m.* & *f.*
insurrection /ˌɪnsəˈrɛkʃən/ *n.* insurrección *f.*
intact /ɪnˈtækt/ *a.* intacto.
intangible /ɪnˈtændʒəbəl/ *a.* intangible, impalpable.
integral /ˈɪntɪgrəl/ *a.* íntegro.
integrate /ˈɪntɪˌgreit/ *v.* integrar.
integrity /ɪnˈtɛgrɪti/ *n.* integridad *f.*
intellect /ˈɪntl̩ˌɛkt/ *n.* intelecto *m.*
intellectual /ˌɪntl̩ˈɛktʃuəl/ *a.* & *n.* intelectual *m.* & *f.*
intelligence /ɪnˈtɛlɪdʒəns/ *n.* inteligencia *f.*
intelligence quotient /ˈkwouʃənt/ coeficiente intelectual *m.*
intelligent /ɪnˈtɛlɪdʒənt/ *a.* inteligente.
intelligible /ɪnˈtɛlɪdʒəbəl/ *a.* inteligible.
intend /ɪnˈtɛnd/ *v.* pensar; intentar; destinar.
intense /ɪnˈtɛns/ *a.* intenso.
intensify /ɪnˈtɛnsəˌfai/ *v.* intensificar.
intensity /ɪnˈtɛnsɪti/ *n.* intensidad *f.*
intensive /ɪnˈtɛnsɪv/ *a.* intensivo.
intensive-care unit /ɪnˈtɛnsɪvˈkɛər/ unidad de cuidados intensivos, unidad de vigilancia intensiva *f.*
intent /ɪnˈtɛnt/ *n.* intento *m.*

intention /ɪn'tɛnʃən/ n. intención f.
intentional /ɪn'tɛnʃənḷ/ a. intencional.
intercede /ˌɪntər'sid/ v. interceder.
intercept /ˌɪntər'sɛpt/ v. interceptar; detener.
interchange /ˌɪntər'tʃɛndʒ/ v. intercambiar.
interchangeable /ˌɪntər'tʃeindʒəbəl/ a. intercambiable.
intercourse /'ɪntərˌkɔrs/ n. tráfico m.; comunicación f.; coito m.
interest /'ɪntərɪst/ n. **1.** interés m. —v. **2.** interesar.
interesting /'ɪntərəstɪŋ/ a. interesante.
interest rate n. tipo de interés m.
interface /'ɪntərˌfeis/ n. interfaz.
interfere /ˌɪntər'fɪər/ v. entremeterse, intervenir. **i. with,** estorbar.
interference /ˌɪntər'fɪərəns/ n. intervención f.; obstáculo m.
interior /ɪn'tɪəriər/ a. interior.
interject /ˌɪntər'dʒɛkt/ v. interponer; intervenir.
interjection /ˌɪntər'dʒɛkʃən/ n. interjección f.; interposición f.
interlude /'ɪntərˌlud/ n. intervalo m.; Theat. intermedio m.; (music) interludio m.
intermediary /ˌɪntər'midiˌɛri/ n. intermediario -ria.
intermediate /ˌɪntər'midiˌeit/ a. intermedio.
interment /ɪn'tɜrmənt/ n. entierro.
intermission /ˌɪntər'mɪʃən/ n. intermisión f.; Theat. entreacto m.
intermittent /ˌɪntər'mɪtṇt/ a. intermitente.
intern /ɪn'tɜrn/ n. **1.** interno -na, internado -da. —v. **2.** internar.
internal /ɪn'tɜrnḷ/ a. interno.
international /ˌɪntər'næʃənḷ/ a. internacional.
internationalism /ˌɪntər'næʃənḷˌɪzəm/ n. internacionalismo m.
Internet, the /'ɪntərˌnɛt/ n. el Internet m.
interpose /ˌɪntər'pouz/ v. interponer.
interpret /ɪn'tɜrprɪt/ v. interpretar.
interpretation /ɪnˌtɜrprɪ'teiʃən/ n. interpretación f.
interpreter /ɪn'tɜrprɪtər/ n. intérprete m. & f.
interrogate /ɪn'tɛrəˌgeit/ v. interrogar.
interrogation /ɪnˌtɛrə'geiʃən/ n. interrogación; pregunta f.
interrogative /ˌɪntə'rɒgətɪv/ a. interrogativo.
interrupt /ˌɪntə'rʌpt/ v. interrumpir.
interruption /ˌɪntə'rʌpʃən/ n. interrupción f.
intersect /ˌɪntər'sɛkt/ v. cortar.
intersection /ˌɪntər'sɛkʃən/ n. intersección f.; (street) bocacalle f.
intersperse /ˌɪntər'spɜrs/ v. entremezclar.
interval /'ɪntərvəl/ n. intervalo m.
intervene /ˌɪntər'vin/ v. intervenir.
intervention /ˌɪntər'vɛnʃən/ n. intervención f.
interview /'ɪntərˌvyu/ n. **1.** entrevista f. —v. **2.** entrevistar.
interviewer /'ɪntərˌvyuər/ n. entrevistador -ora m. & f.
intestine /ɪn'tɛstɪn/ n. intestino m.
intimacy /'ɪntəməsi/ n. intimidad; familiaridad f.
intimate /'ɪntəmɪt/ a. **1.** íntimo, familiar. —n. **2.** amigo -ga íntimo -ma. —v. **3.** insinuar.
intimidate /ɪn'tɪmɪˌdeit/ v. intimidar.
intimidation /ɪnˌtɪmɪ'deiʃən/ n. intimidación f.
into /'ɪntu; unstressed -tʊ, -tə/ prep. en, dentro de.
intonation /ˌɪntou'neiʃən/ n. entonación f.
intone /ɪn'toun/ v. entonar.
intoxicate /ɪn'tɒksɪˌkeit/ v. embriagar.
intoxication /ɪnˌtɒksɪ'keiʃən/ n. embriaguez f.
intravenous /ˌɪntrə'vinəs/ a. intravenoso.
intrepid /ɪn'trɛpɪd/ a. intrépido.
intricacy /'ɪntrɪkəsi/ n. complejidad f.; enredo m.
intricate /'ɪntrɪkɪt/ a. intrincado; complejo.
intrigue /ɪn'trig; n. also 'ɪntrig/ n. **1.** intriga f. —v. **2.** intrigar.
intrinsic /ɪn'trɪnsɪk/ a. intrínseco.
introduce /ˌɪntrə'dus/ v. introducir; (a person) presentar.
introduction /ˌɪntrə'dʌkʃən/ n. presentación; introducción f.
introductory /ˌɪntrə'dʌktəri/ a. introductor; preliminar. **i. offer,** ofrecimiento de presentación m.
introvert /'ɪntrəˌvɜrt/ n. & a. introvertido -da.
intrude /ɪn'trud/ v. entremeterse.
intruder /ɪn'trudər/ n. intruso -sa.
intuition /ˌɪntu'ɪʃən/ n. intuición f.
intuitive /ɪn'tuɪtɪv/ a. intuitivo.
inundate /'ɪnənˌdeit/ v. inundar.
invade /ɪn'veid/ v. invadir.
invader /ɪn'veidər/ n. invasor -ra.
invalid /ɪn'vælɪd/ a. & n. inválido -da.
invariable /ɪn'vɛəriəbəl/ a. invariable.
invasion /ɪn'veiʒən/ n. invasión f.
invective /ɪn'vɛktɪv/ n. **1.** invectiva f. —a. **2.** ultrajante.
inveigle /ɪn'veigəl/ v. seducir.
invent /ɪn'vɛnt/ v. inventar.
invention /ɪn'vɛnʃən/ n. invención f.
inventive /ɪn'vɛntɪv/ a. inventivo.
inventor /ɪn'vɛntər/ n. inventor -ra.
inventory /'ɪnvənˌtɔri/ n. inventario m.
invertebrate /ɪn'vɜrtəbrɪt/ n. & a. invertebrado m.
invest /ɪn'vɛst/ v. investir; Com. invertir.
investigate /ɪn'vɛstɪˌgeit/ v. investigar.
investigation /ɪnˌvɛstɪ'geiʃən/ n. investigación f.
investment /ɪn'vɛstmənt/ n. inversión f.
investor /ɪn'vɛstər/ n. inversor, -ra.
inveterate /ɪn'vɛtərɪt/ a. inveterado.
invidious /ɪn'vɪdiəs/ a. abominable, odioso, injusto.
invigorate /ɪn'vɪgəˌreit/ v. vigorizar, fortificar.
invincible /ɪn'vɪnsəbəl/ a. invencible.
invisible /ɪn'vɪzəbəl/ a. invisible.
invitation /ˌɪnvɪ'teiʃən/ n. invitación f.
invite /ɪn'vait/ v. invitar, convidar.
invocation /ˌɪnvə'keiʃən/ n. invocación f.
invoice /'ɪnvɔis/ n. factura f.
invoke /ɪn'vouk/ v. invocar.
involuntary /ɪn'vɒlənˌtɛri/ a. involuntario.
involve /ɪn'vɒlv/ v. envolver; implicar.
involved /ɪn'vɒlvd/ a. complicado.
invulnerable /ɪn'vʌlnərəbəl/ a. invulnerable.
inward /'ɪnwərd/ adv. hacia adentro.
inwardly /'ɪnwərdli/ adv. interiormente.
iodine /'aiəˌdain/ n. iodo m.
IQ abbr. CI (coeficiente intelectual) m.
irate /ai'reit/ a. encolerizado.
Ireland /'aiərlənd/ n. Irlanda f.
iris /'airɪs/ n. Anat. iris m.; (botany) flor de lis f.
Irish /'airɪʃ/ a. irlandés.
irk /ɜrk/ v. fastidiar.
iron /'aiərn/ n. **1.** hierro m.; (appliance) plancha f. —v. **2.** planchar.
ironical /ai'rɒnɪkəl/ a. irónico.
ironing board /'aiərnɪŋ/ tabla de planchar f.
irony /'airəni/ n. ironía f.
irrational /ɪ'ræʃənḷ/ a. irracional; ilógico.
irregular /ɪ'rɛgyələr/ a. irregular.
irregularity /ɪˌrɛgyə'lærɪti/ n. irregularidad f.
irrelevant /ɪ'rɛləvənt/ a. ajeno.
irresistible /ˌɪrɪ'zɪstəbəl/ a. irresistible.
irresponsible /ˌɪrɪ'spɒnsəbəl/ a. irresponsable.
irreverent /ɪ'rɛvərənt/ a. irreverente.
irrevocable /ɪ'rɛvəkəbəl/ a. irrevocable.
irrigate /'ɪrɪˌgeit/ v. regar; Med. irrigar.
irrigation /ˌɪrɪ'geiʃən/ n. riego m.
irritability /ˌɪrɪtə'bɪlɪti/ n. irritabilidad f.
irritable /'ɪrɪtəbəl/ a. irritable.
irritant /'ɪrɪtṇt/ n. & a. irritante m.
irritate /'ɪrɪˌteit/ v. irritar.
irritation /ˌɪrɪ'teiʃən/ n. irritación f.
island /'ailənd/ n. isla f.
isolate /'aisəˌleit/ v. aislar.
isolation /ˌaisə'leiʃən/ n. aislamiento m.
isosceles /ai'sɒsəˌliz/ a. isósceles.
issuance /'ɪʃuəns/ n. emisión f.; publicación f.
issue /'ɪʃu/ n. **1.** emisión; edición; progenie f.; número m.; punto en disputa. —v. **2.** emitir; publicar.
isthmus /'ɪsməs/ n. istmo m.
it /ɪt/ pron. ello; él, ella; lo, la.
Italian /ɪ'tælyən/ a. & n. italiano -na.
Italy /'ɪtḷi/ n. Italia f.
itch /ɪtʃ/ n. **1.** picazón f. —v. **2.** picar.
item /'aitəm/ n. artículo; detalle m.; inserción f.; Com. renglón m.
itemize /'aitəˌmaiz/ v. detallar.
itinerant /ai'tɪnərənt/ n. **1.** viandante m. —a. **2.** ambulante.
itinerary /ai'tɪnəˌrɛri/ n. itinerario m.
its /ɪts/ a. su.
itself /ɪt'sɛlf/ pron. sí; se.
ivory /'aivəri/ n. marfil m.
ivy /'aivi/ n. hiedra f.

J

jab /dʒæb/ n. **1.** pinchazo m. —v. **2.** pinchar.
jack /dʒæk/ n. (for lifting) gato m.; (cards) sota f.
jackal /'dʒækəl/ n. chacal m.
jackass /'dʒækˌæs/ n. asno m.
jacket /'dʒækɪt/ n. chaqueta f.; saco m.
jack-of-all-trades /'dʒæk əv 'ɔl 'treidz/ n. estuche m.
jade /dʒeid/ n. (horse) rocín m.; (woman) picarona f.; (mineral) jade m.
jaded /'dʒeidɪd/ a. rendido.
jagged /dʒægɪd/ a. mellado.
jaguar /'dʒægwɑr/ n. jaguar m.
jail /dʒeil/ n. cárcel f.
jailer /'dʒeilər/ n. carcelero m.
jam /dʒæm/ n. **1.** conserva f.; aprieto, apretón m. —v. **2.** apiñar, apretar; trabar.
janitor /'dʒænɪtər/ n. portero m.
January /'dʒænyuˌɛri/ n. enero m.
Japan /dʒə'pæn/ n. Japón m.
Japanese /ˌdʒæpə'niz/ a. & n. japonés -esa.
jar /dʒɑr/ n. **1.** jarro m. —v. **2.** chocar; agitar.
jargon /'dʒɑrgən/ n. jerga f.
jasmine /'dʒæzmɪn/ n. jazmín m.
jaundice /'dʒɔndɪs/ n. ictericia f.
jaunt /dʒɔnt/ n. paseo m.
javelin /'dʒævlɪn/ n. jabalina f.
jaw /dʒɔ/ n. quijada f.
jay /dʒei/ n. grajo m.
jazz /dʒæz/ n. jazz m.
jealous /'dʒɛləs/ a. celoso. **to be j.,** tener celos.
jealousy /'dʒɛləsi/ n. celos m.pl.
jeans /dʒinz/ n. vaqueros, tejanos m.pl.
jeer /dʒɪər/ n. **1.** burla f., mofa f. —v. **2.** burlar, mofar.
jelly /'dʒɛli/ n. jalea f.
jellyfish /'dʒɛliˌfɪʃ/ n. aguamar m.
jeopardize /'dʒɛpərˌdaiz/ v. arriesgar.
jeopardy /'dʒɛpərdi/ n. riesgo m.
jerk /dʒɜrk/ n. **1.** sacudida f. —v. **2.** sacudir.
jerky /'dʒɜrki/ a. espasmódico.
Jerusalem /dʒɪ'rusələm/ n. Jerusalén m.
jest /dʒɛst/ n. **1.** broma f. —v. **2.** bromear.
jester /'dʒɛstər/ n. bufón -ona; burlón -ona.
Jesuit /'dʒɛʒuɪt/ a. & n. jesuita m.
Jesus Christ /'dʒizəs 'kraist/ n. Jesucristo m.
jet /dʒɛt/ n. chorro m.; (gas) mechero m.
jet lag n. defase horario m., inadaptación horaria f.
jetsam /'dʒɛtsəm/ n. echazón f.
jettison /'dʒɛtəsən/ v. echar al mar.
jetty /'dʒɛti/ n. muelle m.
Jew /dʒu/ n. judío -día.
jewel /'dʒuəl/ n. joya f.
jeweler /'dʒuələr/ n. joyero -ra.
jewelry /'dʒuəlri/ n. joyas f.pl. **j. store,** joyería f.
Jewish /'dʒuɪʃ/ a. judío.
jib /dʒɪb/ n. Naut. foque m.
jiffy /'dʒɪfi/ n. instante m.
jig /dʒɪg/ n. jiga f. **j-saw,** sierra de vaivén f.
jilt /dʒɪlt/ v. dar calabazas.
jingle /'dʒɪŋgəl/ n. **1.** retintín m.; rima pueril f. —v. **2.** retiñir.
jinx /dʒɪŋks/ n. **1.** aojo m. —v. **2.** aojar.
jittery /'dʒɪtəri/ a. nervioso.
job /dʒɒb/ n. empleo m.
jobber /'dʒɒbər/ n. destajista m. & f., corredor m.
jockey /'dʒɒki/ n. jockey m.
jocular /'dʒɒkyələr/ a. jocoso.
jog /dʒɒg/ n. empujoncito m. v. empujar; estimular. **j. along,** ir a un trote corto.
join /dʒɔin/ v. juntar; unir.
joiner /'dʒɔinər/ n. ebanista m.
joint /dʒɔint/ n. juntura f.
jointly /'dʒɔintli/ adv. conjuntamente.
joke /dʒouk/ n. **1.** broma, chanza f.; chiste m. —v. **2.** bromear.
joker /'dʒoukər/ n. bromista m. & f.; comodín m.
jolly /'dʒɒli/ a. alegre, jovial.
jolt /dʒoult/ n. **1.** sacudido m. —v. **2.** sacudir.
jonquil /'dʒɒŋkwɪl/ n. junquillo m.
jostle /'dʒɒsəl/ v. empujar.
journal /'dʒɜrnḷ/ n. diario m.; revista f.
journalism /'dʒɜrnḷˌɪzəm/ n. periodismo m.
journalist /'dʒɜrnḷɪst/ n. periodista m. & f.
journey /'dʒɜrni/ n. **1.** viaje m.; jornada f. —v. **2.** viajar.
journeyman /'dʒɜrnimən/ n. jornalero m., oficial m.
jovial /'dʒouviəl/ a. jovial.
jowl /dʒaul/ n. carrillo m.
joy /dʒɔi/ n. alegría f.
joyful /'dʒɔifəl/ **joyous** a. alegre, gozoso.
jubilant /'dʒubələnt/ a. jubiloso.
jubilee /'dʒubəˌli/ n. jubileo m.
Judaism /'dʒudiˌɪzəm/ n. judaísmo m.
judge /dʒʌdʒ/ n. **1.** juez m. & f. —v. **2.** juzgar.
judgment /'dʒʌddʒmənt/ n. juicio m.
judicial /dʒu'dɪʃəl/ a. judicial.
judiciary /dʒu'dɪʃiˌɛri/ a. judiciario.
judicious /dʒu'dɪʃəs/ a. juicioso.
jug /dʒʌg/ n. jarro m.
juggle /'dʒʌgəl/ v. escamotear.
juice /dʒus/ n. jugo, zumo m.
juicy /'dʒusi/ a. jugoso.
July /dʒu'lai/ n. julio m.
jumble /'dʒʌmbəl/ n. **1.** revoltillo m. —v. **2.** arrebujar, revolver.
jump /dʒʌmp/ n. **1.** salto m. —v. **2.** saltar, brincar.

junction /'dʒʌŋkʃən/ n. confluencia f.; (railway) empalme m.
juncture /'dʒʌŋktʃər/ n. juntura f.; coyuntura f.
June /dʒun/ n. junio m.
jungle /'dʒʌŋgəl/ n. jungla, selva f.
junior /'dʒunyər/ a. menor; más joven. **Jr.,** hijo.
juniper /'dʒunəpər/ n. enebro m.
junk /dʒʌŋk/ n. basura f.
junket /'dʒʌŋkɪt/ n. **1.** leche cuajada f. —v. **2.** festejar.
junkie /'dʒʌŋki/ n. *Colloq.* yonqui m. & f., toxicómano -na.
junk mail n. porpaganda indeseada f., correo basura m.
jurisdiction /ˌdʒʊrɪs'dɪkʃən/ n. jurisdicción f.
jurisprudence /ˌdʒʊrɪs'prudns/ n. jurisprudencia f.
jurist /'dʒʊrɪst/ n. jurista m. & f.
juror /'dʒʊrər/ n. jurado -da.
jury /'dʒʊri/ n. jurado m.
just /dʒʌst/ a. **1.** justo; exacto. —adv. **2.** exactamente; (only) sólo. **j. now,** ahora mismo. **to have j.,** acabar de.
justice /'dʒʌstɪs/ n. justicia f.; (person) juez m. & f.
justifiable /'dʒʌstəˌfaiəbəl/ a. justificable.
justification /ˌdʒʌstəfɪ'keiʃən/ n. justificación f.
justify /'dʒʌstəˌfai/ v. justificar.
jut /dʒʌt/ v. sobresalir.
jute /dʒut/ n. yute m.
juvenile /'dʒuvənl/ a. juvenil.
juvenile delinquency delincuencia de menores, delincuencia juvenil f.

K

kaleidoscope /kə'laidəˌskoup/ n. calidoscopio m.
kangaroo /ˌkæŋgə'ru/ n. canguro m.
karakul /'kærəkəl/ n. caracul m.
karat /'kærət/ n. quilate m.
karate /kə'rɑti/ n. karate m.
keel /kil/ n. **1.** quilla f. —v. **2. to k. over,** volcarse.
keen /kin/ a. agudo; penetrante.
keep /kip/ v. mantener, retener; guardar; preservar. **k. on,** seguir, continuar.
keeper /'kipər/ n. guardián m.
keepsake /'kipˌseik/ n. recuerdo m.
keg /kɛg/ n. barrilito m.
kennel /'kɛnl/ n. perrera f.
kerchief /'kɜrtʃɪf/ n. pañuelo m.
kernel /'kɜrnl/ n. pepita f.; grano m.
kerosene /'kɛrəˌsin/ n. kerosén m.
ketchup /'kɛtʃəp/ n. salsa de tomate f.
kettle /'kɛtl/ n. caldera, olla f.
kettledrum /'kɛtlˌdrʌm/ n. tímpano m.
key /ki/ n. llave f.; (music) clave f.; (piano) tecla f.
keyboard /'kiˌbɔrd/ n. teclado m.
keyhole /'kiˌhoul/ n. bocallave f.
keypad /'kiˌpæd/ n. teclado m.
khaki /'kæki/ a. caqui.
kick /kɪk/ n. **1.** patada f. —v. **2.** patear; *Colloq.* quejarse.
kid /kɪd/ n. **1.** cabrito m.; *Colloq.* niño -ña, chico -ca. —v. **2.** *Colloq.* bromear.
kidnap /'kɪdnæp/ v. secuestrar.
kidnaper /'kɪdnæpər/ n. secuestrador -ora.
kidnaping /'kɪdnæpɪŋ/ n. rapto, secuestro m.
kidney /'kɪdni/ n. riñón m.
kidney bean n. frijol m.
kill /kɪl/ v. matar.
killer /'kɪlər/ n. matador -ora.
killjoy /'kɪldʒɔi/ n. aguafiestas m. & f.
kiln /kɪl/ n. horno m.
kilogram /'kɪləˌgræm/ n. kilogramo m.
kilohertz /'kɪləˌhɜrts/ n. kilohercio m.
kilometer /kɪ'lɒmɪtər/ n. kilómetro m.
kilowatt /'kɪləˌwɒt/ n. kilovatio m.
kin /kɪn/ n. parentesco m.; parientes m.pl.
kind /kaind/ a. **1.** bondadoso, amable. —n. **2.** género m.; clase f. **k. of,** algo, un poco.
kindergarten /'kɪndərˌgɑrtn/ n. kindergarten m.
kindle /'kɪndl/ v. encender.
kindling /'kɪndlɪŋ/ n. encendimiento m. **k.-wood,** leña menuda f.
kindly /'kaindli/ a. bondadoso.
kindness /'kaindnɪs/ n. bondad f.
kindred /'kɪndrɪd/ n. parentesco m.
kinetic /kɪ'nɛtɪk/ a. cinético.
king /kɪŋ/ n. rey m.
kingdom /'kɪŋdəm/ n. reino m.
king prawn langostino m.
kink /kɪŋk/ n. retorcimiento m.
kinky /'kɪŋki/ a. *Colloq.* pervertidillo; (hair) rizado.
kiosk /'kiɒsk/ n. kiosco m.
kiss /kɪs/ n. **1.** beso m. —v. **2.** besar.
kitchen /'kɪtʃən/ n. cocina f.
kite /kait/ n. cometa f.
kitten /'kɪtn/ n. gatito -ta.
kleptomania /ˌklɛptə'meiniə/ n. cleptomanía f.
kleptomaniac /ˌklɛptə'meiniæk/ n. cleptómano -na.
klutz /klʌts/ n. *Colloq.* torpe, patoso -sa.
knack /næk/ n. don m., destreza f.
knapsack /'næpˌsæk/ n. alforja f.
knead /nid/ v. amasar.
knee /ni/ n. rodilla f.
kneecap /'niˌkæp/ n. rodillera, rótula f.
kneel /nil/ v. arrodillarse.
knickers /'nɪkərz/ n. calzón corto m., pantalones m.pl.
knife /naif/ n. cuchillo m.
knight /nait/ n. caballero m.; (chess) caballo m.
knit /nɪt/ v. tejer.
knob /nɒb/ n. tirador m.
knock /nɒk/ n. **1.** golpe m.; llamada f. —v. **2.** golpear; tocar, llamar.
knot /nɒt/ n. **1.** nudo; lazo m. —v. **2.** anudar.
knotty /'nɒti/ a. nudoso.
know /nou/ v. saber; (a person) conocer.
knowledge /'nɒlɪdʒ/ n. conocimiento, saber m.
knuckle /'nʌkəl/ n. nudillo m. **k. bone,** jarrete m. **to k. under,** ceder a.
Koran /kə'rɑn/ n. Corán m.
Korea /kə'riə/ n. Corea f.
Korean /kə'riən/ a. & n. coreano.

L

label /'leibəl/ n. **1.** rótulo m. —v. **2.** rotular; designar.
labor /'leibər/ n. **1.** trabajo m.; la clase obrera. —v. **2.** trabajar.
laboratory /'læbrəˌtɔri/ n. laboratorio m.
laborer /'leibərər/ n. trabajador, obrero m.
laborious /lə'bɔriəs/ a. laborioso, difícil.
labor union gremio obrero, sindicato m.
labyrinth /'læbərɪnθ/ n. laberinto m.
lace /leis/ n. **1.** encaje m.; (of shoe) lazo m. —v. **2.** amarrar.
lacerate /'læsəˌreit/ v. lacerar, lastimar.
laceration /ˌlæsə'reiʃən/ n. laceración f., desgarro m.
lack /læk/ n. **1.** falta f. **l. of respect,** desacato m. —v. **2.** faltar, carecer.
lackadaisical /ˌlækə'deizɪkəl/ a. indiferente; soñador.
laconic /lə'kɒnɪk/ a. lacónico.
lacquer /'lækər/ n. **1.** laca f., barniz m. —v. **2.** laquear, barnizar.
lactic /'læktɪk/ a. láctico.
lactose /'læktous/ n. lactosa f.
ladder /'lædər/ n. escalera f.
ladle /'leidl/ n. **1.** cucharón m. —v. **2.** servir con cucharón.
lady /'leidi/ n. señora, dama f.
ladybug /'leidiˌbʌg/ n. mariquita f.
lag /læg/ n. **1.** retraso m. —v. **2.** quedarse atrás.
lagoon /lə'gun/ n. laguna f.
laid-back /'leid 'bæk/ a. de buen talante, ecuánime, pacífico.
laity /'leiɪti/ n. laicado m.
lake /leik/ n. lago m.
lamb /læm/ n. cordero m.
lame /leim/ a. **1.** cojo; estropeado. —v. **2.** estropear, lisiar; incapacitar.
lament /lə'mɛnt/ n. **1.** lamento m. —v. **2.** lamentar.
lamentable /lə'mɛntəbəl/ a. lamentable.
lamentation /ˌlæmən'teiʃən/ n. lamento m.; lamentación f.
laminate /'læməˌneit/ a. laminado. v. laminar.
lamp /læmp/ n. lámpara f.
lampoon /læm'pun/ n. **1.** pasquín m. —v. **2.** pasquinar.
lance /læns/ n. **1.** lanza f. —v. **2.** *Med.* abrir.
land /lænd/ n. **1.** país m.; tierra f. **native l.,** patria f. —v. **2.** desembarcar; (plane) aterrizar.
landholder /'lændˌhouldər/ n. hacendado -da.
landing /'lændɪŋ/ n. (of stairs) descanso, descansillo m.; (ship) desembarcadero m.; (airplane) aterrizaje m.
landlady /'lændˌleidi/ **landlord** n. propietario -ria.
landmark /'lændˌmɑrk/ n. mojón m., señal f.; rasgo sobresaliente m.
landscape /'lændˌskeip/ n. paisaje m.
landslide /'lændˌslaid/ n. derrumbe m.
lane /lein/ n. senda f.
language /'læŋgwɪdʒ/ n. lengua f., idioma; lenguaje m.
languid /'læŋgwɪd/ a. lánguido.
languish /'læŋgwɪʃ/ v. languidecer.
languor /'læŋgər/ n. languidez f.
lanky /'læŋki/ a. larguirucho; desgarbado.
lanolin /'lænlɪn/ n. lanolina f.
lantern /'læntərn/ n. linterna f.; farol m.
lap /læp/ n. **1.** regazo m.; falda f. —v. **2.** lamer.
lapel /lə'pɛl/ n. solapa f.
lapse /læps/ n. **1.** lapso m. —v. **2.** pasar; decaer; caer en error.
laptop computer /'læpˌtɒp/ ordenador portátil m.
larceny /'lɑrsəni/ n. ratería f.
lard /lɑrd/ n. manteca de cerdo f.
large /lɑrdʒ/ a. grande.
largely /'lɑrdʒli/ adv. ampliamente; mayormente; muy.
largo /'lɑrgou/ n. & a. *Mus.* largo m.
lariat /'læriət/ n. lazo m.
lark /lɑrk/ n. (bird) alondra f.
larva /'lɑrvə/ n. larva f.
laryngitis /ˌlærən'dʒaitɪs/ n. laringitis f.
larynx /'lærɪŋks/ n. laringe f.
lascivious /lə'sɪviəs/ a. lascivo.
laser /'leizər/ n. láser m.
lash /læʃ/ n. **1.** azote, latigazo m. —v. **2.** azotar.
lass /læs/ n. doncella f.
lassitude /'læsɪˌtud/ n. lasitud f.
lasso /'læsou/ n. **1.** lazo m. —v. **2.** enlazar.
last /læst/ a. **1.** pasado; (final) último. **at l.,** por fin. **l. but one,** penúltimo. **l. but two,** antepenútimo. —v. **2.** durar.
lasting /'læstɪŋ/ a. duradero.
latch /lætʃ/ n. aldaba f.
late /leit/ a. **1.** tardío; (deceased) difunto. **to be l.,** llegar tarde. —adv. **2.** tarde.
lately /'leitli/ adv. recientemente.
latent /'leitnt/ a. latente.
lateral /'lætərəl/ a. lateral.
lather /'læðər/ n. **1.** espuma de jabón. —v. **2.** enjabonar.
Latin /'lætn/ n. latín m.
Latin America /ə'mɛrɪkə/ Hispanoamérica, América Latina f.
Latin American hispanoamericano -na.
latitude /'lætɪˌtud/ n. latitud f.
latrine /lə'trin/ n. letrina f.
latter /'lætər/ a. posterior. **the l.,** éste.
lattice /'lætɪs/ n. celosía f.
laud /lɔd/ v. loar.
laudable /'lɔdəbəl/ a. laudable.
laudanum /'lɔdnəm/ n. láudano m.
laudatory /'lɔdəˌtɔri/ a. laudatorio.
laugh /læf/ n. **1.** risa, risotada f. —v. **2.** reír. **l. at,** reírse de.
laughable /'læfəbəl/ a. risible.
laughter /'læftər/ n. risa f.
launch /lɔntʃ/ n. **1.** *Naut.* lancha f. —v. **2.** lanzar.
launder /'lɔndər/ v. lavar y planchar la ropa.
laundry /'lɔndri/ n. lavandería f.
laundryman /'lɔndriˌmæn/ n. lavandero -ra.
laureate /'lɔriɪt/ n. & a. laureado -da.
laurel /'lɔrəl/ n. laurel m.
lava /'lɑvə/ n. lava f.
lavatory /'lævəˌtɔri/ n. lavatorio m.
lavender /'lævəndər/ n. lavándula f.
lavish /'lævɪʃ/ a. **1.** pródigo. —v. **2.** prodigar.
law /lɔ/ n. ley f.; derecho m.
lawful /'lɔfəl/ a. legal.
lawless /'lɔlɪs/ a. sin ley.
lawn /lɔn/ n. césped; prado m.
lawn mower /'mouər/ n. cortacésped m. & f.
lawsuit /'lɔˌsut/ n. pleito m.
lawyer /'lɔyər/ n. abogado m. & f.
lax /læks/ a. flojo, laxo.
laxative /'læksətɪv/ n. purgante m.
laxity /'læksɪti/ n. laxidad f.; flojedad f.
lay /lei/ a. **1.** secular. —v. **2.** poner.
layer /'leiər/ n. capa f.
layman /'leimən/ n. lego, seglar m.
lazy /'leizi/ a. perezoso.
lead /lɛd , lid/ n. **1.** plomo m.; *Theat.* papel principal. **to take the l.,** tomar la delantera. —v. **2.** conducir; dirigir.
leaden /'lɛdn/ a. plomizo; pesado; abatido.
leader /'lidər/ n. líder m. & f.; jefe m. & f.; director -ora.
leadership /'lidərˌʃɪp/ n. dirección f.
leaf /lif/ n. hoja f.
leaflet /'liflɪt/ n. *Bot.* hojilla f.; folleto m.
league /lig/ n. liga; (measure) legua f.
leak /lik/ n. **1.** escape; goteo m. —v. **2.** gotear; *Naut.* hacer agua.
leakage /'likɪdʒ/ n. goteo m., escape m., pérdida f.
leaky /'liki/ a. llovedizo, resquebrajado.
lean /lin/ a. **1.** flaco, magro. —v. **2.** apoyarse, arrimarse.
leap /lip/ n. **1.** salto m. —v. **2.** saltar.
leap year n. año bisiesto m.
learn /lɜrn/ v. aprender; saber.
learned /'lɜrnɪd/ a. erudito.
learning /'lɜrnɪŋ/ n. erudición f., instrucción f.
lease /lis/ n. **1.** arriendo m. —v. **2.** arrendar.
leash /liʃ/ n. **1.** correa f. —v. **2.** atraillar.
least /list/ a. menor; mínimo. **the l.,** lo menos. **at l.,** por lo menos.
leather /'lɛðər/ n. cuero m.
leathery /'lɛðəri/ a. coriáceo.
leave /liv/ n. **1.** licencia f. **to take l.,** despedirse. —v. **2.** dejar; (depart) salir, irse. **l. out,** omitir.
leaven /'lɛvən/ n. **1.** levadura f. —v. **2.** fermentar, imbuir.
lecherous /'lɛtʃərəs/ a. lujurioso.
lecture /'lɛktʃər/ n. conferencia f.
lecturer /'lɛktʃərər/ n. conferencista m. & f.; catedrático -ca.
ledge /lɛdʒ/ n. borde m.; capa f.
ledger /'lɛdʒer/ n. libro mayor m.

lee /li/ *n.* sotavento *m.*
leech /litʃ/ *n.* sanguijuela *f.*
leek /lik/ *n.* puerro *m.*
leer /lɪər/ *v.* mirar de soslayo.
leeward /ˈliwərd/ *a.* sotavento.
left /lɛft/ *a.* izquierdo. **the l.,** la izquierda. **to be left,** quedarse.
left-handed /ˈlɛft ˈhændɪd/ *a.* zurdo.
leftist /ˈlɛftɪst/ *n.* izquierdista *m. & f.*
leftovers /ˈlɛftˌouvərz/ *n.* sobras *f.pl.*
leg /lɛg/ *n.* pierna *f.*
legacy /ˈlɛgəsi/ *n.* legado *m.*, herencia *f.*
legal /ˈligəl/ *a.* legal.
legalize /ˈligəˌlaiz/ *v.* legalizar.
legation /lɪˈgeiʃən/ *n.* legación, embajada *f.*
legend /ˈlɛdʒənd/ *n.* leyenda *f.*
legendary /ˈlɛdʒənˌdɛri/ *a.* legendario.
legible /ˈlɛdʒəbəl/ *a.* legible.
legion /ˈlidʒən/ *n.* legión *f.*
legislate /ˈlɛdʒɪsˌleit/ *v.* legislar.
legislation /ˌlɛdʒɪsˈleiʃən/ *n.* legislación *f.*
legislator /ˈlɛdʒɪsˌleitər/ *n.* legislador -ra.
legislature /ˈlɛdʒɪsˌleitʃər/ *n.* legislatura *f.*
legitimate /lɪˈdʒɪtəmɪt/ *a.* legítimo.
legume /ˈlɛgyum/ *n.* legumbre *f.*
leisure /ˈliʒər/ *n.* desocupación *f.;* horas libres.
leisurely /ˈliʒərli/ *a.* **1.** deliberado. —*adv.* **2.** despacio.
lemon /ˈlɛmən/ *n.* limón *m.*
lemonade /ˌlɛməˈneid/ *n.* limonada *f.*
lend /lɛnd/ *v.* prestar.
length /lɛŋkθ/ *n.* largo *m.;* duración *f.*
lengthen /ˈlɛŋkθən/ *v.* alargar.
lengthwise /ˈlɛŋkθˌwaiz/ *adv.* a lo largo.
lengthy /ˈlɛŋkθi/ *a.* largo.
lenient /ˈliniənt/ *a.* indulgente.
lens /lɛnz/ *n.* lente *m. or f.*
Lent /lɛnt/ *n.* cuaresma *f.*
Lenten /ˈlɛntn̩/ *a.* cuaresmal.
lentil /ˈlɛntɪl/ *n.* lenteja *f.*
leopard /ˈlɛpərd/ *n.* leopardo *m.*
leotard /ˈliəˌtɑrd/ *n.* mallas *f.pl.*
leper /ˈlɛpər/ *n.* leproso -sa.
leprosy /ˈlɛprəsi/ *n.* lepra *f.*
lesbian /ˈlɛzbiən/ *n.* lesbiana *f.*
lesion /ˈliʒən/ *n.* lesión *f.*
less /lɛs/ *a. & adv.* menos.
lessen /ˈlɛsən/ *v.* disminuir.
lesser /ˈlɛsər/ *a.* menor; más pequeño.
lesson /ˈlɛsən/ *n.* lección *f.*
lest /lɛst/ *conj.* para que no.
let /lɛt/ *v.* dejar; permitir; arrendar.
letdown /ˈlɛtˌdaun/ *n.* decepción *f.*
lethal /ˈliθəl/ *a.* letal.
lethargic /ləˈθɑrdʒɪk/ *a.* letárgico.
lethargy /ˈlɛθərdʒi/ *n.* letargo *m.*
letter /ˈlɛtər/ *n.* carta; (of alphabet) letra *f.*
letterhead /ˈlɛtərˌhɛd/ *n.* membrete *m.*
lettuce /ˈlɛtɪs/ *n.* lechuga *f.*
leukemia /luˈkimiə/ *n.* leucemia *f.*
levee /ˈlɛvi, lɛˈvi/ *n.* recepción *f.*
level /ˈlɛvəl/ *a.* **1.** llano, nivelado. —*n.* **2.** nivel *m.;* llanura *f.* —*v.* **3.** allanar; nivelar.
lever /ˈlɛvər/ *n.* palanca *f.*
levity /ˈlɛvɪti/ *n.* levedad *f.*
levy /ˈlɛvi/ *n.* **1.** leva *f.* —*v.* **2.** imponer.
lewd /lud/ *a.* lascivo.
lexicon /ˈlɛksɪˌkɒn/ *n.* léxico *m.*
liability /ˌlaiəˈbɪlɪti/ *n.* riesgo *m.;* obligación *f.*
liable /ˈlaiəbəl/ *a.* sujeto; responsable.
liaison /liˈeizɒn/ *n.* vinculación *f.*, enlace *m.;* concubinaje *m.*
liar /ˈlaiər/ *n.* embustero -ra.
libel /ˈlaibəl/ *n.* **1.** libelo *m.* —*v.* **2.** difamar.
libelous /ˈlaibələs/ *a.* difamatorio.
liberal /ˈlɪbərəl/ *a.* liberal; generoso.
liberalism /ˈlɪbərəˌlɪzəm/ *n.* liberalismo *m.*
liberality /ˌlɪbəˈrælɪti/ *n.* liberalidad *f.*
liberate /ˈlɪbəˌreit/ *v.* libertar.
liberty /ˈlɪbərti/ *n.* libertad *f.*
libidinous /lɪˈbɪdn̩əs/ *a.* libidinoso.
librarian /laiˈbrɛəriən/ *n.* bibliotecario -ria.
library /ˈlaiˌbrɛri/ *n.* biblioteca *f.*
libretto /lɪˈbrɛtou/ *n.* libreto *m.*
license /ˈlaisəns/ *n.* licencia *f.;* permiso *m.*
licentious /laiˈsɛnʃəs/ *a.* licencioso.
lick /lɪk/ *v.* lamer.
licorice /ˈlɪkərɪʃ, ˈlɪkrɪʃ, ˈlɪkərɪs/ *n.* regaliz *m.*
lid /lɪd/ *n.* tapa *f.*
lie /lai/ *n.* **1.** mentira *f.* —*v.* **2.** mentir. **l. down,** acostarse, echarse.
lieutenant /luˈtɛnənt/ *n.* teniente *m.*
life /laif/ *n.* vida *f.*
lifeboat /ˈlaifˌbout/ *n.* bote salvavidas *m.*
life buoy boya *f.*
lifeguard /ˈlaifˌgɑrd/ socorrista *m. & f.*
life insurance seguro de vida *m.*
life jacket chaleco salvavidas *m.*
lifeless /ˈlaiflɪs/ *a.* sin vida.
life preserver /prɪˈzɜrvər/ salvavidas *m.*
lifestyle /ˈlaifstail/ *n.* modo de vida *m.*
lift /lɪft/ *v.* levantar, alzar, elevar.
ligament /ˈlɪgəmənt/ *n.* ligamento *m.*
ligature /ˈlɪgətʃər/ *n.* ligadura *f.*
light /lait/ *a.* **1.** ligero; liviano; (in color) claro. —*n.* **2.** luz; candela *f.* —*v.* **3.** encender; iluminar.
light bulb bombilla *f.*
lighten /ˈlaitn̩/ *v.* aligerar; aclarar; iluminar.
lighter /ˈlaitər/ *n.* encendedor *m.*
lighthouse /ˈlaitˌhaus/ *n.* faro *m.*
lightness /ˈlaitnɪs/ *n.* ligereza; agilidad *f.*
lightning /ˈlaitnɪŋ/ *n.* relámpago *m.*
like /laik/ *a.* **1.** semejante. —*prep.* **2.** como. —*v.* **3. I like...** me gusta, me gustan... **I should like,** quisiera.
likeable /ˈlaikəbəl/ *a.* simpático, agradable.
likelihood /ˈlaikliˌhʊd/ *n.* probabilidad *f.*
likely /ˈlaikli/ *a.* probable; verosímil.
liken /ˈlaikən/ *v.* comparar; asemejar.
likeness /ˈlaiknɪs/ *n.* semejanza *f.*
likewise /ˈlaikˌwaiz/ *adv.* igualmente.
lilac /ˈlailək/ *n.* lila *f.*
lilt /lɪlt/ *n.* **1.** cadencia alegre *f.* —*v.* **2.** cantar alegremente.
lily /ˈlɪli/ *n.* lirio *m.*
lily of the valley muguete *m.*
limb /lɪm/ *n.* rama *f.*
limber /ˈlɪmbər/ *a.* flexible. **to l. up,** ponerse flexible.
limbo /ˈlɪmbou/ *n.* limbo *m.*
lime /laim/ *n.* cal *f.;* (fruit) limoncito *m.*, lima *f.*
limestone /ˈlaimˌstoun/ *n.* piedra caliza *f.*
limewater /ˈlaimˌwɔtər/ *n.* agua de cal *f.*
limit /ˈlɪmɪt/ *n.* **1.** límite *m.* —*v.* **2.** limitar.
limitation /ˌlɪmɪˈteiʃən/ *n.* limitación *f.*
limitless /ˈlɪmɪtlɪs/ *a.* ilimitado.
limousine /ˈlɪməˌzin/ *n.* limusina *f.*
limp /lɪmp/ *n.* **1.** cojera *f.* —*a.* **2.** flojo. —*v.* **3.** cojear.
limpid /ˈlɪmpɪd/ *a.* límpido.
line /lain/ *n.* **1.** línea; fila; raya *f.;* (of print) renglón *m.* —*v.* **2.** forrar; rayar.
lineage /ˈlɪniɪdʒ/ *n.* linaje *m.*
lineal /ˈlɪniəl/ *a.* lineal.
linear /ˈlɪniər/ *a.* linear, longitudinal.
linen /ˈlɪnən/ *n.* lienzo, lino *m.;* ropa blanca.
liner /ˈlainər/ *n.* vapor *m.*
linger /ˈlɪŋgər/ *v.* demorarse.
lingerie /ˌlɑnʒəˈrei/ *n.* ropa blanca *f.*
linguist /ˈlɪŋgwɪst/ *n.* lingüista *m. & f.*
linguistic /lɪŋˈgwɪstɪk/ *a.* lingüístico.
liniment /ˈlɪnəmənt/ *n.* linimento *m.*
lining /ˈlainɪŋ/ *n.* forro *m.*
link /lɪŋk/ *n.* **1.** eslabón; vínculo *m.* —*v.* **2.** vincular.
linoleum /lɪˈnouliəm/ *n.* linóleo *m.*
linseed /ˈlɪnˌsid/ *n.* linaza *f.;* simiente de lino *f.*
lint /lɪnt/ *n.* hilacha *f.*
lion /ˈlaiən/ *n.* león *m.*
lip /lɪp/ *n.* labio *m.*
liposuction /ˈlɪpəˌsʌkʃən, ˈlaipə-/ *n.* liposucción *f.*
lipstick /ˈlɪpˌstɪk/ *n.* lápiz de labios.
liqueur /lɪˈkɜr/ *n.* licor *m.*
liquid /ˈlɪkwɪd/ *a. & n.* líquido *m.*
liquidate /ˈlɪkwɪˌdeit/ *v.* liquidar.
liquidation /ˌlɪkwɪˈdeiʃən/ *n.* liquidación *f.*
liquor /ˈlɪkər/ *n.* licor *m.*
lisp /lɪsp/ *n.* **1.** ceceo *m.* —*v.* **2.** cecear.
list /lɪst/ *n.* **1.** lista *f.* —*v.* **2.** registrar.
listen (to) /ˈlɪsən/ *v.* escuchar.
listless /ˈlɪstlɪs/ *a.* indiferente.
litany /ˈlɪtn̩i/ *n.* letanía *f.*
liter /ˈlitər/ *n.* litro *m.*
literal /ˈlɪtərəl/ *a.* literal.
literary /ˈlɪtəˌrɛri/ *a.* literario.
literate /ˈlɪtərɪt/ *a.* alfabetizado.
literature /ˈlɪtərətʃər/ *n.* literatura *f.*
litigant /ˈlɪtɪgənt/ *n. & a.* litigante *m. & f.*
litigation /ˌlɪtɪˈgeiʃən/ *n.* litigio, pleito *m.*
litter /ˈlɪtər/ *n.* **1.** litera *f.;* cama de paja. —*v.* **2.** poner en desorden.
little /ˈlɪtl̩/ *a.* pequeño; (quantity) poco.
little finger meñique *m.*
liturgical /lɪˈtɜrdʒɪkəl/ *a.* litúrgico.
liturgy /ˈlɪtərdʒi/ *n.* liturgia *f.*
live /a laiv; v lɪv/ *a.* **1.** vivo. —*v.* **2.** vivir.
livelihood /ˈlaivliˌhʊd/ *n.* subsistencia *f.*
lively /ˈlaivli/ *a.* vivo; rápido; animado.
liver /ˈlɪvər/ *n.* hígado *m.*
livery /ˈlɪvəri/ *n.* librea *f.*
livestock /ˈlaivˌstɒk/ *n.* ganadería *f.*
livid /ˈlɪvɪd/ *a.* lívido.
living /ˈlɪvɪŋ/ *a.* **1.** vivo. —*n.* **2.** sustento *m.* **to earn (make) a living,** ganarse la vida.
living room salón *m.*
lizard /ˈlɪzərd/ *n.* lagarto *m.*, lagartija *f.*
llama /ˈlɑmə/ *n.* llama *f.*
load /loud/ *n.* **1.** carga *f.* —*v.* **2.** cargar.
loaf /louf/ *n.* **1.** pan *m.* —*v.* **2.** holgazanear.
loam /loum/ *n.* marga *f.*
loan /loun/ *n.* **1.** préstamo *m.* —*v.* **2.** prestar.
loathe /louð/ *v.* aborrecer, detestar.
loathsome /ˈlouðsəm/ *a.* repugnante.
lobby /ˈlɒbi/ *n.* vestíbulo *m.*
lobe /loub/ *n.* lóbulo *m.*
lobster /ˈlɒbstər/ *n.* langosta *f.*
local /ˈloukəl/ *a.* local.
local area network red local *f.*
locale /louˈkæl/ *n.* localidad *f.*
locality /louˈkælɪti/ *n.* localidad *f.*, lugar *m.*
localize /ˈloukəˌlaiz/ *v.* localizar.
locate /ˈloukeit/ *v.* situar; hallar.
location /louˈkeiʃən/ *n.* sitio *m.;* posición *f.*
lock /lɒk/ *n.* **1.** cerradura *f.; (pl.)* cabellos *m.pl.* —*v.* **2.** cerrar con llave.
locker /ˈlɒkər/ *n.* cajón *m.;* ropero *m.*
locket /ˈlɒkɪt/ *n.* guardapelo *m.;* medallón *m.*
lockjaw /ˈlɒkˌdʒɔ/ *n.* trismo *m.*
locksmith /ˈlɒkˌsmɪθ/ *n.* cerrajero -ra.
locomotive /ˌloukəˈmoutɪv/ *n.* locomotora *f.*
locust /ˈloukəst/ *n.* cigarra *f.*, saltamontes *m.*
locution /louˈkyuʃən/ *n.* locución *f.*
lode /loud/ *n.* filón *m.*, veta *f.*
lodge /lɒdʒ/ *n.* **1.** logia; (inn) posada *f.* —*v.* **2.** fijar; alojar, morar.
lodger /ˈlɒdʒər/ *n.* inquilino *m.*
lodging /ˈlɒdʒɪŋ/ *n.* alojamiento *m.*
loft /lɔft/ *n.* desván, sobrado *m.*
lofty /ˈlɔfti/ *a.* alto; altivo.
log /lɔg/ *n.* tronco de árbol; *Naut.* barquilla *f.*
loge /louʒ/ *n.* palco *m.*
logic /ˈlɒdʒɪk/ *n.* lógica *f.*
logical /ˈlɒdʒɪkəl/ *a.* lógico.
loin /lɔin/ *n.* lomo *m.*
loincloth /ˈlɔinˌklɔθ/ *n.* taparrabos *m.*
loiter /ˈlɔitər/ *v.* haraganear.
lone /loun/ *a.* solitario.
loneliness /ˈlounlinɪs/ *n.* soledad *f.*
lonely, /ˈlounli/ **lonesome** *a.* solo y triste.
lonesome /ˈlounsəm/ *a.* solitario, aislado.
long /lɔŋ/ *a.* **1.** largo. **a l. time,** mucho tiempo. —*adv.* **2.** mucho tiempo. **how l.,** cuánto tiempo. **no longer,** ya no. —*v.* **3. l. for,** anhelar.
long-distance call /ˈlɔŋ ˈdɪstəns/ conferencia interurbana *f.*
longevity /lɒnˈdʒɛvɪti/ *n.* longevidad *f.*
long-haired /ˈlɔŋ ˈhɛərd/ *a.* melenudo.
longing /ˈlɔŋɪŋ/ *n.* anhelo *m.*
longitude /ˈlɒndʒɪˌtud/ *n.* longitud *m.*
look /lʊk/ *n.* **1.** mirada *f.;* aspecto *m.* —*v.* **2.** parecer; mirar. **l. at,** mirar. **l. for,** buscar. **l. like,** parecerse a. **l. out!,** ¡cuidado! **l. up,** buscar; ir a ver, venir a ver.
looking glass /ˈlʊkɪŋ/ espejo *m.*
loom /lum/ *n.* **1.** telar *m.* —*v.* **2.** asomar.
loop /lup/ *n.* vuelta *f.*
loophole /ˈlupˌhoul/ *n.* aspillera *f.; Fig.* callejuela, evasiva *f.*, efugio *m.*
loose /lus/ *a.* suelto; flojo.
loose change suelto *m.*
loosen /ˈlusən/ *v.* soltar; aflojar.
loot /lut/ *n.* **1.** botín *m.*, saqueo *m.* —*v.* **2.** saquear.
lopsided /ˈlɒpˈsaidɪd/ *a.* desequilibrado.
loquacious /louˈkweiʃəs/ *a.* locuaz.
lord /lɔrd/ *n.* señor *m.;* (Brit. title) lord *m.*
lordship /ˈlɔrdʃɪp/ *n.* señorío *m.*
lose /luz/ *v.* perder. **l. consciousness,** perder el concimiento.
loss /lɔs/ *n.* pérdida *f.*
lost /lɔst/ *a.* perdido.
lot /lɒt/ *n.* suerte *f.* **building l.,** solar *m.* **a lot (of), lots of,** mucho.
lotion /ˈlouʃən/ *n.* loción *f.*
lottery /ˈlɒtəri/ *n.* lotería *f.*
loud /laud/ *a.* **1.** fuerte; ruidoso. —*adv.* **2.** alto.
loudspeaker /ˈlaudˌspikər/ *n.* altavoz *m.*
lounge /laundʒ/ *n.* sofá *m.;* salón de fumar *m.*
louse /laus/ *n.* piojo *m.*
love /lʌv/ *n.* **1.** amor *m.* **in l.,** enamorado. **to fall in l.,** enamorarse. **l. at first sight,** flechazo *m.* —*v.* **2.** querer; amar; adorar.
lovely /ˈlʌvli/ *a.* hermoso.
lover /ˈlʌvər/ *n.* amante *m. & f.*
low /lou/ *a.* bajo; vil.
low-cut /ˈlou ˈkʌt/ *a.* escotado.
lower /ˈlouər/ *v.* bajar; (in price) rebajar.
lower-case letter /ˈlouər ˈkeis/ minúscula *f.*
lowly /ˈlouli/ *a.* humilde.
low neckline /ˈnɛkˌlain/ escote *m.*
loyal /ˈlɔiəl/ *a.* leal, fiel.
loyalist /ˈlɔiəlɪst/ *n.* lealista *m. & f.*
loyalty /ˈlɔiəlti/ *n.* lealtad *f.*
lozenge /ˈlɒzɪndʒ/ *n.* pastilla *f.*
lubricant /ˈlubrɪkənt/ *n.* lubricante *m.*
lubricate /ˈlubrɪˌkeit/ *v.* engrasar, lubricar.
lucid /ˈlusɪd/ *a.* claro, lúcido.

luck /lʌk/ n. suerte; fortuna f.

lucky /'lʌki/ a. afortunado. **to be l.**, tener suerte.

lucrative /'lukrətɪv/ a. lucrativo.

ludicrous /'ludɪkrəs/ a. rídiculo.

luggage /'lʌgɪdʒ/ n. equipaje m.

lukewarm /'luk'wɔrm/ a. tibio.

lull /lʌl/ n. **1.** momento de calma. —v. **2.** calmar.

lullaby /'lʌlə,bai/ n. arrullo m.

lumbago /lʌm'beigou/ n. lumbago m.

lumber /'lʌmbər/ n. madera f.

luminous /'lumənəs/ a. luminoso.

lump /lʌmp/ n. protuberancia f.; (of sugar) terrón m.

lump sum suma global f.

lunacy /'lunəsi/ n. locura f.

lunar /'lunər/ a. lunar.

lunatic /'lunətɪk/ a. & n. loco -ca.

lunch, luncheon /lʌntʃ; 'lʌntʃən/ n. **1.** merienda f., almuerzo m. —v. **2.** merendar, almorzar.

lunch box /'lʌntʃ,bɒks/ fiambrera f.

lung /lʌŋ/ n. pulmón m.

lunge /lʌndʒ/ n. **1.** estocada, arremetida f. —v. **2.** dar un estocada, arremeter.

lure /lur/ v. atraer.

lurid /'lurɪd/ a. sensacional; espeluznante.

lurk /lɜrk/ v. esconderse; espiar.

luscious /'lʌʃəs/ a. sabroso, delicioso.

lust /lʌst/ n. sensualidad; codicia f.

luster /'lʌstər/ n. lustre m.

lustful /'lʌstfəl/ a. sensual, lascivo.

lusty /'lʌsti/ a. vigoroso.

lute /lut/ n. laúd m.

Lutheran /'luθərən/ n. & a. luterano -na.

luxuriant /lʌg'ʒuriənt/ a. exuberante, frondoso.

luxurious /lʌg'ʒuriəs/ a. lujoso.

luxury /'lʌkʃəri/ n. lujo m.

lying /'laiŋ/ a. mentiroso.

lymph /lɪmf/ n. linfa f.

lynch /lɪntʃ/ v. linchar.

lyre /laiər/ n. lira f.

lyric /'lɪrɪk/ a. lírico.

lyricism /'lɪrə,sɪzəm/ n. lirismo m.

M

macabre /mə'kabrə/ a. macabro.

macaroni /,mækə'rouni/ n. macarrones m.

machine /mə'ʃin/ n. máquina f.

machine gun ametralladora f.

machinery /mə'ʃinəri/ n. maquinaria f.

machinist /mə'ʃinɪst/ n. maquinista m. & f., mecánico m.

macho /'matʃou/ a. machista.

mackerel /'mækərəl/ n. escombro m.

macro /'mækrou/ n. (computer) macro m.

mad /mæd/ a. loco; furioso.

madam /'mædəm/ n. señora f.

mafia /'mafiə/ n. mafia f.

magazine /,mægə'zin/ n. revista f.

magic /'mædʒɪk/ a. **1.** mágico. —n. **2.** magia f.

magician /mə'dʒɪʃən/ n. mágico m.

magistrate /'mædʒə,streit/ n. magistrado, -da.

magnanimous /mæg'nænəməs/ a. magnánimo.

magnate /'mægneit/ n. magnate m.

magnesium /mæg'niziəm/ n. magnesio m.

magnet /'mægnɪt/ n. imán m.

magnetic /mæg'nɛtɪk/ a. magnético.

magnificence /mæg'nɪfəsəns/ n. magnificencia f.

magnificent /mæg'nɪfəsənt/ a. magnífico.

magnify /'mægnə,fai/ v. magnificar.

magnifying glass /'mægnə,faiiŋ/ lupa f.

magnitude /'mægnɪ,tud/ n. magnitud f.

magpie /'mæg,pai/ n. hurraca f.

mahogany /mə'hɒgəni/ n. caoba f.

maid /meid/ n. criada f. **old m.**, solterona f.

maiden /'meidn/ a. soltera.

mail /meil/ n. **1.** correo m. **air m.**, correo aéreo. **by return m.**, a vuelta de correo. —v. **2.** echar al correo.

mailbox /'meil,bɒks/ n. buzón m.

mailman /'meil,mæn/ n. cartero m.

maim /meim/ v. mutilar.

main /mein/ a. principal.

mainframe /'mein,freim/ n. componente central de una computadora.

mainland /'mein,lænd/ n. continente m.

maintain /mein'tein/ v. mantener; sostener.

maintenance /'meintənəns/ n. mantenimiento; sustento m.; conservación f.

maître d' /,mei'tər di , ,meitrə, ,mɛtrə/ n. jefe de sala m. & f.

maize /meiz/ n. maíz m.

majestic /mə'dʒɛstɪk/ a. majestuoso.

majesty /'mædʒəsti/ n. majestad f.

major /'meidʒər/ a. **1.** mayor. —n. **2.** Mil. comandante m.; (study) especialidad f.

majority /mə'dʒɔriti/ n. mayoría f.

make /meik/ n. **1.** marca f. —v. **2.** hacer; fabricar; (earn) ganar.

maker /'meikər/ n. fabricante m.

makeshift /'meik,ʃift/ a. provisional.

make-up /'meik,ʌp/ n. cosméticos m. pl.

malady /'mælədi/ n. mal m., enfermedad f.

malaria /mə'lɛəriə/ n. paludismo m.

male /meil/ a. & n. macho m.

malevolent /mə'lɛvələnt/ a. malévolo.

malice /'mælɪs/ n. malicia f.

malicious /mə'lɪʃəs/ a. malicioso.

malign /mə'lain/ v. **1.** difamar. —a. **2.** maligno.

malignant /mə'lɪgnənt/ a. maligno.

malnutrition /,mælnu'trɪʃən/ n. desnutrición f.

malt /mɒlt/ n. malta f.

mammal /'mæməl/ n. mamífero m.

man /mæn/ n. hombre; varón m. v. tripular.

manage /'mænɪdʒ/ v. manejar; dirigir; administrar; arreglárselas. **m. to**, lograr.

management /'mænɪdʒmənt/ n. dirección, administración f.

manager /'mænɪdʒər/ n. director -ora.

mandate /'mændeit/ n. mandato m.

mandatory /'mændə,tɔri/ a. obligatorio.

mandolin /'mændlɪn/ n. mandolina f.

mane /mein/ n. crines f. pl.

maneuver /mə'nuvər/ n. **1.** maniobra f. —v. **2.** maniobrar.

manganese /'mæŋgə,nis, -,niz/ n. manganeso m.

manger /'meindʒər/ n. pesebre m.

mangle /'mæŋgəl/ n. **1.** rodillo, exprimidor m. —v. **2.** mutilar.

manhood /'mænhʊd/ n. virilidad f.

mania /'meiniə/ n. manía f.

maniac /'meini,æk/ a. & n. maniático -ca; maníaco -ca.

manicure /'mænɪ,kyur/ n. manicura f.

manifest /'mænə,fɛst/ a. & n. **1.** manifiesto m. —v. **2.** manifestar.

manifesto /,mænə'fɛstou/ n. manifiesto m.

manifold /'mænə,fould/ a. **1.** muchos. —n. **2.** Auto. tubo múltiple.

manipulate /mə'nɪpyə,leit/ v. manipular.

mankind /'mæn'kaind/ n. humanidad f.

manly /'mænli/ a. varonil.

manner /'mænər/ n. manera f., modo m. **manners**, modales m. pl.

mannerism /'mænə,rɪzəm/ n. manerismo m.

mansion /'mænʃən/ n. mansión f.

mantel /'mæntl/ n. manto de chimenea.

mantle /'mæntl/ n. manto m.

manual /'mænyuəl/ a. & n. manual m.

manufacture /,mænyə'fæktʃər/ v. fabricar.

manufacturer /,mænyə'fæktʃərər/ n. fabricante m.

manufacturing /,mænyə'fæktʃərɪŋ/ n. fabricación f.

manure /mə'nur/ n. abono, estiércol m.

manuscript /'mænyə,skrɪpt/ n. manuscrito m.

many /'mɛni/ a. muchos. **how m.**, cuántos. **so m.**, tantos. **too m.**, demasiados. **as m. as**, tantos como.

map /mæp/ n. mapa m.

maple /'meipəl/ n. arce m.

mar /mar/ v. estropear; desfigurar.

marble /'marbəl/ n. mármol m.

march /martʃ/ n. **1.** marcha f. —v. **2.** marchar.

March /martʃ/ n. marzo m.

mare /mɛər/ n. yegua f.

margarine /'mardʒərɪn/ n. margarina f.

margin /'mardʒɪn/ n. margen m. or f.

marijuana /,mærə'wanə/ n. marijuana f.

marine /mə'rin/ a. **1.** marino. —n. **2.** soldado de marina.

mariner /'mærənər/ n. marinero m.

marionette /,mæriə'nɛt/ n. marioneta f.

marital /'mærɪtl/ a. marital.

maritime /'mærɪ,taim/ a. marítimo.

mark /mark/ n. **1.** marca f. —v. **2.** marcar.

market /'markɪt/ n. mercado m. **meat m.**, carnicería f. **stock m.**, bolsa f., v. comercializar.

marmalade /'marmə,leid/ n. mermelada f.

maroon /mə'run/ a. & n. color rojo oscuro. v. dejar abandonado.

marquis /'markwɪs/ n. marqués m.

marriage /'mærɪdʒ/ n. matrimonio m.

marriage certificate partida de matrimonio f.

married /'mærid/ a. casado. **to get m.**, casarse.

marrow /'mærou/ n. médula f.; substancia f.

marry /'mæri/ v. casarse con; casar.

marsh /marʃ/ n. pantano m.

marshal /'marʃəl/ n. mariscal m.

marshmallow /'marʃ,mɛlou/ n. malvarisco m.; bombón de altea m.

martial /'marʃəl/ a. marcial. **m. law**, gobierno militar.

martyr /'martər/ n. mártir m. & f.

martyrdom /'martərdəm/ n. martirio m.

marvel /'marvəl/ n. **1.** maravilla f. —v. **2.** maravillarse.

marvelous /'marvələs/ a. maravilloso.

mascara /mæ'skærə/ n. rímel m.

mascot /'mæskɒt/ n. mascota f.

masculine /'mæskyəlɪn/ a. masculino.

mash /mæʃ/ v. majar. **mashed potatoes**, puré de papas m.

mask /mæsk/ n. máscara f.

mason /'meisən/ n. albañil m.

masquerade /,mæskə'reid/ n. mascarada f.

mass /mæs/ n. masa f.; Relig. misa f. **to say m.**, cantar misa. **m. production**, producción en serie.

massacre /'mæsəkər/ n. **1.** carnicería, matanza f. —v. **2.** matar atrozmente, destrozar.

massage /mə'saʒ/ n. **1.** masaje m.; soba f. —v. **2.** sobar.

masseur /mə'sɜr/ n. masajista m. & f.

massive /'mæsɪv/ a. macizo, sólido.

mast /mæst/ n. palo, árbol m.

master /'mæstər/ n. **1.** amo; maestro m. —v. **2.** domar, dominar.

masterpiece /'mæstər,pis/ n. obra maestra f.

master's degree /'mæstərz/ maestría f.

mastery /'mæstəri/ n. maestría f.

mat /mæt/ n. **1.** estera; palleta f. —v. **2.** enredar.

match /mætʃ/ n. **1.** igual m; fósforo m.; (sport) partida, contienda f.; (marriage) noviazgo; casamiento. —v. **2.** ser igual a; igualar.

matchbox /'mætʃ,bɒks/ caja de cerillas, caja de fósforos f.

mate /meit/ n. **1.** consorte m. & f.; compañero -ra. —v. **2.** igualar; casar.

material /mə'tɪəriəl/ a. & n. material m. **raw materials**, materias primas.

materialism /mə'tɪəriə,lɪzəm/ n. materialismo m.

materialize /mə'tɪəriə,laiz/ v. materializar.

maternal /mə'tɜrnl/ a. materno.

maternity /mə'tɜrniti/ n. maternidad f.

maternity hospital maternidad f.

mathematical /,mæθə'mætɪkəl/ a. matemático.

mathematics /,mæθə'mætɪks/ n. matemáticas f.pl.

matinee /,mætn'ei/ n. matiné f.

matrimony /'mætrə,mouni/ n. matrimonio m.

matron /'meitrən/ n. matrona; directora f.

matter /'mætər/ n. **1.** materia f.; asunto m. **what's the m.?**, ¿qué pasa? —v. **2.** importar.

mattress /'mætrɪs/ n. colchón m.

mature /mə'tʃur/ a. **1.** maduro. —v. **2.** madurar.

maturity /mə'tʃuriti/ n. madurez f.

maudlin /'mɔdlɪn/ a. sentimental en exceso; sensiblero.

maul /mɔl/ v. aporrear.

maxim /'mæksɪm/ n. máxima f.

maximum /'mæksəməm/ a. & n. máximo.

may /mei/ v. poder.

May /mei/ n. mayo m.

maybe /'meibi/ adv. quizá, quizás, tal vez.

mayonnaise /,meiə'neiz/ n. mayonesa f.

mayor /'meiər/ n. alcalde m. alcaldesa f.

maze /meiz/ n. laberinto m.

me /mi/ pron. mí; me. **with me**, conmigo.

meadow /'mɛdou/ n. prado m.; vega f.

meager /'migər/ a. magro; pobre.

meal /mil/ n. comida; (flour) harina f.

mean /min/ a. **1.** bajo; malo. —n. **2.** medio (see also **means**). —v. **3.** significar; querer decir.

meander /mi'ændər/ v. (river) serpentear; (person) deambular.

meaning /'minɪŋ/ n. sentido, significado m.

meaningless /'minɪŋlɪs/ a. sin sentido.

means /minz/ n.pl. medios, recursos m. **by all m.**, sin falta. **by no m.**, de ningún modo. **by m. of**, por medio de.

meanwhile /'min,wail/ adv. mientras tanto.

measles /'mizəlz/ n. sarampión m.

measure /'mɛʒər/ n. **1.** medida f.; (music) compás m. —v. **2.** medir.

measurement /'mɛʒərmənt/ n. medida, dimensión f.

meat /mit/ n. carne f.

mechanic /mə'kænɪk/ n. mecánico m. & f.

mechanical /mə'kænɪkəl/ a. mecánico.

mechanism /'mɛkə,nɪzəm/ n. mecanismo m.

mechanize /'mɛkə,naiz/ v. mecanizar.

medal /'mɛdl/ n. medalla f.

meddle /'mɛdḷ/ v. meterse, entremeterse.

mediate /'midi,eit/ v. mediar.

medical /'mɛdɪkəl/ a. médico.

medicine /'mɛdəsɪn/ n. medicina f.

medicine chest botiquín m.

medieval /,midi'ivəl/ a. medieval.

mediocre /,midi'oukər/ a. mediocre.

mediocrity /,midi'ɒkrɪti/ n. mediocridad f.

meditate /'mɛdɪ,teit/ v. meditar.

meditation /,mɛdɪ'teiʃən/ n. meditación f.

Mediterranean /,mɛdɪtə'reiniən/ n. Mediterráneo m.

medium /'midiəm/ a. **1.** mediano, medio. —n. **2.** medio m.

medley /'mɛdli/ n. mezcla f., ensalada f.

meek /mik/ a. manso; humilde.

meekness /'miknɪs/ n. modestia; humildad f.

meet /mit/ a. **1.** apropiado. —n. **2.** concurso m. —v. **3.** encontrar; reunirse; conocer.

meeting /'mitɪŋ/ n. reunión f.; mitin m.

megahertz /'mɛgə,hɜrts/ n. megahercio m.

megaphone /'mɛgə,foun/ n. megáfono m.

melancholy /'mɛlən,kɒli/ a. **1.** melancólico. —n. **2.** melancolía f.

mellow /'mɛlou/ a. suave; blando; maduro.

melodious /mə'loudiəs/ a. melodioso.

melodrama /'mɛlə,drɑmə/ n. melodrama m.

melody /'mɛlədi/ n. melodía f.

melon /'mɛlən/ n. melón m.

melt /mɛlt/ v. derretir.

meltdown /'mɛlt,daun/ n. fundición resultante de un accidente en un reactor nuclear.

member /'mɛmbər/ n. socio -ia; miembro m. **m. of the crew,** tripulante m. & f.

membership /'mɛmbər,ʃɪp/ n. número de miembros.

membrane /'mɛmbrein/ n. membrana f.

memento /mə'mɛntou/ n. recuerdo m.

memoir /'mɛmwɑr/ n. memoria f.

memorable /'mɛmərəbəl/ a. memorable.

memorandum /,mɛmə'rændəm/ n. memorándum, volante m.

memorial /mə'mɔriəl/ a. **1.** conmemorativo. —n. **2.** memorial m.

memorize /'mɛmə,raiz/ v. aprender de memoria.

memory /'mɛməri/ n. memoria f.; recuerdo m.

menace /'mɛnɪs/ n. **1.** amenaza f. —v. **2.** amenazar.

mend /mɛnd/ v. reparar, remendar.

menial /'miniəl/ a. **1.** servil. —n. **2.** sirviente -ta.

meningitis /,mɛnɪn'dʒaitɪs/ n. meningitis. f.

menopause /'mɛnə,pɔz/ n. menopausia f.

menstruation /,mɛnstru'eiʃən/ n. menstruación f.

menswear /'mɛnz,wɛər/ n. ropa de caballeros m.

mental /'mɛntḷ/ a. mental.

mental disorder trastorno mental m.

mentality /mɛn'tæliti/ n. mentalidad f.

menthol /'mɛnθɒl/ n. mentol m.

mention /'mɛnʃən/ n. **1.** mención f. —v. **2.** mencionar.

menu /'mɛnyu/ n. menú m., lista f.

mercantile /'mɜrkən,til/ a. mercantil.

mercenary /'mɜrsə,nɛri/ a. & n. mercenario -ria.

merchandise /'mɜrtʃən,daiz/ n. mercancía f.

merchant /'mɜrtʃənt/ a. **1.** mercante. —n. **2.** comerciante m.

merciful /'mɜrsɪfəl/ a. misericordioso, compasivo.

merciless /'mɜrsɪlɪs/ a. cruel, inhumano.

mercury /'mɜrkyəri/ n. mercurio m.

mercy /'mɜrsi/ n. misericordia; merced f.

mere /mɪər/ a. mero, puro.

merely /'mɪərli/ adv. solamente; simplemente.

merge /mɜrdʒ/ v. unir, combinar.

merger /'mɜrdʒər/ n. consolidación, fusión f.

meringue /mə'ræŋ/ n. merengue m.

merit /'mɛrɪt/ n. **1.** mérito m. —v. **2.** merecer.

meritorious /,mɛrɪ'tɔriəs/ a. meritorio.

mermaid /'mɜr,meid/ n. sirena f.

merriment /'mɛrɪmənt/ n. regocijo m.

merry /'mɛri/ a. alegre, festivo.

merry-go-round /'mɛri gou ,raund/ n. caballitos m. pl.; tíovivo m.

mesh /mɛʃ/ n. malla f.

mess /mɛs/ n. **1.** lío m.; confusión f.; *Mil.* salón comedor; rancho m. —v. **2. m. up,** ensuciar; enredar.

message /'mɛsɪdʒ/ n. mensaje, recado m.

messenger /'mɛsəndʒər/ n. mensajero -ra.

messy /'mɛsi/ a. confuso; desarreglado.

metabolism /mə'tæbə,lɪzəm/ n. metabolismo m.

metal /'mɛtḷ/ n. metal m.

metallic /mə'tælɪk/ a. metálico.

metaphysics /,mɛtə'fɪzɪks/ n. metafísica f.

meteor /'mitiər/ n. meteoro m.

meteorology /,mitiə'rɒlədʒi/ n. meteorología f.

meter /'mitər/ n. contador, medidor; (measure) metro m.

method /'mɛθəd/ n. método m.

meticulous /mə'tɪkyələs/ a. meticuloso.

metric /'mɛtrɪk/ a. métrico.

metropolis /mɪ'trɒpəlɪs/ n. metrópoli f.

metropolitan /,mɛtrə'pɒlɪtn̩/ a. metropolitano.

Mexican /'mɛksɪkən/ a. & n. mexicano -na.

Mexico /'mɛksɪ,kou/ n. México m.

mezzanine /'mɛzə,nin/ n. entresuelo m.

microbe /'maikroub/ n. microbio m.

microchip /'maikrou,tʃɪp/ n. microchip m.

microfiche /'maikrə,fiʃ/ n. microficha f.

microfilm /'maikrə,fɪlm/ n. microfilm m.

microform /'maikrə,fɔrm/ n. microforma f.

microphone /'maikrə,foun/ n. micrófono m.

microscope /'maikrə,skoup/ n. microscopio m.

microscopic /,maikrə'skɒpɪk/ a. microscópico.

mid /mɪd/ a. medio.

middle /'mɪdḷ/ a. & n. medio m. **in the m. of,** en medio de, a mediados de.

middle-aged /eidʒd/ a. de edad madura.

Middle East Medio Oriente m.

middle finger dedo corazón m.

midget /'mɪdʒɪt/ n. enano -na.

midnight /'mɪd,nait/ n. medianoche f.

midwife /'mɪd,waif/ n. comadrona, partera f.

might /mait/ n. poder m., fuerza f.

mighty /'maiti/ a. poderoso.

migraine /'maigrein/ n. migraña f.; jaqueca f.

migrate /'maigreit/ v. emigrar.

migration /mai'greiʃən/ n. emigración f.

migratory /'maigrə,tɔri/ a. migratorio.

mild /maild/ a. moderado, suave; templado.

mildew /'mɪl,du/ n. añublo m., moho m.

mile /mail/ n. milla f.

mileage /'mailɪdʒ/ n. kilometraje m.

militant /'mɪlɪtənt/ a. militante.

militarism /'mɪlɪtə,rɪzəm/ n. militarismo m.

military /'mɪlɪ,tɛri/ a. militar.

militia /mɪ'lɪʃə/ n. milicia f.

milk /mɪlk/ n. **1.** leche f. —v. **2.** ordeñar.

milk chocolate chocolate con leche m.

milkman /'mɪlk,mæn/ n. lechero m.

milk shake batido m.

milky /'mɪlki/ a. lácteo; lechoso.

mill /mɪl/ n. **1.** molino m.; fábrica f. —v. **2.** moler.

miller /'mɪlər/ n. molinero -ra.

millimeter /'mɪlə,mitər/ n. milímetro m.

milliner /'mɪlənər/ n. sombrerero -ra.

millinery /'mɪlə,nɛri/ n. sombrerería f.

million /'mɪlyən/ n. millón m.

millionaire /,mɪlyə'nɛər/ n. millonario -ria.

mimic /'mɪmɪk/ n. **1.** mimo -ma. —v. **2.** imitar.

mind /maind/ n. **1.** mente; opinión f. —v. **2.** obedecer. **never m.,** no se ocupe.

mindful /'maindfəl/ a. atento.

mine /main/ pron. **1.** mío. —n. **2.** mina f. —v. **3.** minar.

miner /'mainər/ n. minero m.

mineral /'mɪnərəl/ a. & n. mineral m.

mineral water agua mineral f.

mine sweeper /'main,swipər/ dragaminas f.

mingle /'mɪŋgəl/ v. mezclar.

miniature /'mɪniətʃər/ n. miniatura f.

miniaturize /'mɪniətʃə,raiz/ v. miniaturizar.

minibus /'mɪni,bʌs/ n. microbús m.

minicab /'mɪni,kæb/ n. microtaxi m.

minimize /'mɪnə,maiz/ v. menospreciar.

minimum /'mɪnəməm/ a. & n. mínimo m.

mining /'mainɪŋ/ n. minería f.

minister /'mɪnəstər/ n. **1.** ministro -tra; *Relig.* pastor m. —v. **2.** ministrar.

ministry /'mɪnəstri/ n. ministerio m.

mink /mɪŋk/ n. visón m.; (fur) piel de visón m.

minor /'mainər/ a. **1.** menor. —n. **2.** menor de edad.

minority /mɪ'nɔriti/ n. minoría f.

minstrel /'mɪnstrəl/ n. juglar m.

mint /mɪnt/ n. **1.** menta f.; casa de moneda. —v. **2.** acuñar.

minus /'mainəs/ prep. menos.

minute /mai'nut/ a. **1.** minucioso. —n. **2.** minuto, momento m.

miracle /'mɪrəkəl/ n. milagro m.

miraculous /mɪ'rækyələs/ a. milagroso.

mirage /mɪ'rɑʒ/ n. espejismo m.

mire /maiᵊr/ n. lodo m.

mirror /'mɪrər/ n. espejo m.

mirth /mɜrθ/ n. alegría; risa f.

misbehave /,mɪsbɪ'heiv/ v. portarse mal.

miscellaneous /,mɪsə'leiniəs/ a. misceláneo.

mischief /'mɪstʃɪf/ n. travesura, diablura f.

mischievous /'mɪstʃəvəs/ a. travieso, dañino.

miser /'maizər/ n. avaro -ra.

miserable /'mɪzərəbəl/ a. miserable; infeliz.

miserly /'maizərli/ a. avariento, tacaño.

misfortune /mɪs'fɔrtʃən/ n. desgracia f., infortunio, revés m.

misgiving /mɪs'gɪvɪŋ/ n. recelo m., desconfianza f.

mishap /'mɪshæp/ n. desgracia f., contratiempo m.

mislay /mɪs'lei/ v. perder.

mislead /mɪs'lid/ v. extraviar, despistar; pervertir.

misplaced /mɪs'pleist/ a. extraviado.

mispronounce /,mɪsprə'nouns/ v. pronunciar mal.

miss /mɪs/ n. **1.** señorita f. —v. **2.** perder; echar de menos, extrañar. **be missing,** faltar.

missile /'mɪsəl/ n. proyectil m.

mission /'mɪʃən/ n. misión f.

missionary /'mɪʃə,nɛri/ n. misionero -ra.

mist /mɪst/ n. niebla, bruma f.

mistake /mɪ'steik/ n. equivocación f.; error m. **to make a m.,** equivocarse.

mistaken /mɪ'steikən/ a. equivocado.

mister /'mɪstər/ n. señor m.

mistletoe /'mɪsəl,tou/ n. muérdago m.

mistreat /mɪs'trit/ v. maltratar.

mistress /'mɪstrɪs/ n. ama; señora; concubina f.

mistrust /mɪs'trʌst/ v. desconfiar; sospechar.

misty /'mɪsti/ a. nebuloso, brumoso.

misunderstand /,mɪsʌndər'stænd/ v. entender mal.

misuse /mɪs'yuz/ v. maltratar; abusar.

mite /mait/ n. pizca f., blanca f.

mitten /'mɪtn̩/ n. mitón, confortante m.

mix /mɪks/ v. mezclar. **m. up,** confundir.

mixer /'mɪksər/ (for food), n. batidora f.

mixture /'mɪkstʃər/ n. mezcla, mixtura f.

mix-up /'mɪks,ʌp/ n. confusión f.

moan /moun/ n. **1.** quejido, gemido m. —v. **2.** gemir.

mob /mɒb/ n. muchedumbre f.; gentío m.

mobilization /,moubələ'zeiʃən/ n. movilización f.

mobilize /'moubə,laiz/ v. movilizar.

mock /mɒk/ v. burlar.

mockery /'mɒkəri/ n. burla f.

mod /mɒd/ a. a la última; en boga.

mode /moud/ n. modo m.

model /'mɒdḷ/ n. **1.** modelo m. —v. **2.** modelar.

modem /'moudəm/ n. módem m.

moderate /a 'mɒdərɪt/ v. -ə,reit/ a. **1.** moderado. —v. **2.** moderar.

moderation /,mɒdə'reiʃən/ n. moderación; sobriedad f.

modern /'mɒdərn/ a. moderno.

modernize /'mɒdər,naiz/ v. modernizar.

modest /'mɒdɪst/ a. modesto.

modesty /'mɒdəsti/ n. modestia f.

modify /'mɒdə,fai/ v. modificar.

modulate /'mɒdʒə,leit/ v. modular.

moist /mɔist/ a. húmedo.

moisten /'mɔisən/ v. humedecer.

moisture /'mɔistʃər/ n. humedad f.

moisturize /'mɔistʃə,raiz/ v. hidratar.

molar /'moulər/ n. molar m.

molasses /mə'læsɪz/ n. melaza f.

mold /mould/ n. **1.** molde; moho m. —v. **2.** moldar, formar; enmohecer.

moldy /'mouldi/ a. mohoso.

mole /'moulei/ n. lunar m.; (animal) topo m.

molecule /'mɒlɪ,kyul/ n. molécula f.

molest /mə'lɛst/ v. molestar.

mollify /'mɒlə,fai/ v. molificar.

moment /'moumənt/ n. momento m.

momentary /'moumən,tɛri/ a. momentáneo.

momentous /mou'mɛntəs/ a. importante.

monarch /'mɒnərk/ n. monarca m. & f.

monarchy /'mɒnərki/ n. monarquía f.

monastery /'mɒnə,stɛri/ n. monasterio m.

Monday /'mʌndei/ n. lunes m.

monetary /'mɒnɪ,tɛri/ a. monetario.

money /'mʌni/ n. dinero m. **m. order,** giro postal.

mongrel /'mʌŋgrəl/ n. **1.** mestizo m. —a. **2.** mestizo, cruzado.

monitor /'mɒnɪtər/ n. amonestador m.; (computer) consola f., pantalla f.

monk /mʌŋk/ n. monje m.

monkey /'mʌŋki/ n. mono -na.

monocle /'mɒnəkəl/ n. monóculo m.

monologue /'mɒnə,lɔg/ n. monólogo m.

monopolize /mə'nɒpə,laiz/ v. monopolizar.

monopoly /mə'nɒpəli/ n. monopolio m.

monosyllable /'mɒnə,sɪləbəl/ n. monosílabo m.

monotone /'mɒnə,toun/ n. monotonía f.

monotonous /mə'nɒtṇəs/ a. monótono.

monotony /mə'nɒtṇi/ n. monotonía f.

monsoon /mɒn'sun/ n. monzón m.

monster /'mɒnstər/ n. monstruo m.

monstrosity /mɒn'strɒsɪti/ n. monstruosidad f.

monstrous /'mɒnstrəs/ a. monstruoso.

month /mʌnθ/ n. mes m.

monthly /'mʌnθli/ a. mensual.

monument /'mɒnyəmənt/ n. monumento m.

monumental /,mɒnyə'mɛntḷ/ a. monumental.

mood /mud/ n. humor m.; Gram. modo m.

moody /'mudi/ a. caprichoso, taciturno.

moon /mun/ n. luna f.

moonlight /'mun,lait/ n. luz de la luna.

moonlighting /'mun,laitiŋ/ n. pluriempleo m.

moor /mʊr/ n. **1.** párano m. —v. **2.** anclar.

Moor /mʊr/ n. moro -ra.

mop /mɒp/ n. **1.** fregasuelos m., fregona f., (S.A.) trapeador m. —v. **2.** fregar, (S.A.) trapear.

moped /'mou,pɛd/ n. (vehicle) velomotor m.

moral /'mɔrəl/ a. moral. —n. **2.** moraleja f. **morals,** moralidad f.

morale /mə'ræl/ n. espíritu f.

moralist /'mɔrəlɪst/ n. moralista m. & f.

morality /mə'rælɪti/ n. moralidad, ética f.

morbid /'mɔrbɪd/ a. mórbido.

more /mɔr/ a. & adv. más. **m. and m.,** cada vez más.

moreover /mɔr'ouvər/ adv. además.

morgue /mɔrg/ n. necrocomio m.

morning /'mɔrniŋ/ n. mañana f. **good m.,** buenos días.

Morocco /mə'rɒkou/ n. Marruecos m.

morose /mə'rous/ a. malhumorado.

morphine /'mɔrfin/ n. morfina f.

morsel /'mɔrsəl/ n. bocado m.

mortal /'mɔrtḷ/ a. & n. mortal m. & f.

mortality /mɔr'tælɪti/ n. mortalidad f.

mortar /'mɔrtər/ n. mortero m.

mortgage /'mɔrgɪdʒ/ n. **1.** hipoteca f. —v. **2.** hipotecar.

mortify /'mɔrtə,fai/ v. mortificar.

mosaic /mou'zeiik/ n. & a. mosaico m.

mosque /mɒsk/ n. mezquita f.

mosquito /mə'skitou/ n. mosquito m.

moss /mɔs/ n. musgo m.

most /moust/ a. **1.** más. —adv. **2.** más; sumamente. —pron. **3.** m. of, la mayor parte de.

mostly /'moustli/ adv. principalmente; en su mayor parte.

motel /mou'tɛl/ n. motel m.

moth /mɔθ/ n. polilla f.

mother /'mʌðər/ n. madre f.

mother-in-law /'mʌðər ɪn ,lɔ/ n. suegra f.

motif /mou'tif/ n. tema m.

motion /'mouʃən/ n. **1.** moción f.; movimiento m. —v. **2.** hacer señas.

motionless /'mouʃənlɪs/ a. inmóvil.

motion picture película f.

motivate /'moutə,veit/ v. motivar.

motive /'moutɪv/ n. motivo m.

motor /'moutər/ n. motor m.

motorboat /'moutər,bout/ n. lancha motora f., autobote, motorbote m., gasolinera f.

motorcycle /'moutər,saikəl/ n. motocicleta f.

motorcyclist /'moutər,saiklɪst/ n. motociclista m. & f.

motorist /'moutərɪst/ n. motorista m. & f.

motto /'mɒtou/ n. lema m.

mound /maund/ n. terrón; montón m.

mount /maunt/ n. **1.** monte m.; (horse) montura f. —v. **2.** montar; subir.

mountain /'mauntṇ/ n. montaña f.

mountaineer /,mauntṇ'ɪər/ n. montañés m.

mountainous /'mauntṇəs/ a. montañoso.

mourn /mɔrn/ v. lamentar, llorar; llevar luto.

mournful /'mɔrnfəl/ a. triste.

mourning /'mɔrniŋ/ n. luto; lamento m.

mouse /maus/ n. ratón, ratoncito m.

mouth /mauθ/ n. boca f.; (of river) desembocadura f.

mouthwash /'mauθ,wɒʃ/ n. enjuague bucal m.

movable /'muvəbəl/ a. movible, movedizo.

move /muv/ n. **1.** movimiento m.; mudanza f. —v. **2.** mover; mudarse; emocionar, conmover. **m. away,** quitar; alejarse; mudarse.

movement /'muvmənt/ n. movimiento m.

movie /'muvi/ n. película f. **m. theater, movies,** cine m.

moving /'muviŋ/ a. conmovedor; persuasivo.

mow /mou/ v. guadañar, segar.

Mr. /'mɪstər/ title. Señor (Sr.).

Mrs. /'mɪsəz/ title. Señora (Sra.).

much /mʌtʃ/ a. & adv. mucho. **how m.,** cuánto. **so m.,** tanto. **too m.,** demasiado. **as m. as,** tanto como.

mucilage /'myusəlɪdʒ/ n. mucílago m.

mucous /'myukəs/ a. mucoso.

mucous membrane n. membrana mucosa f.

mud /mʌd/ n. fango, lodo m.

muddy /'mʌdi/ a. **1.** lodoso; turbio. —v. **2.** ensuciar; enturbiar.

muff /mʌf/ n. manguito m.

muffin /'mʌfɪn/ n. panecillo m.

mug /mʌg/ n. cubilete m.

mugger /'mʌgər/ n. asaltante m. & f.

mulatto /mə'lætou/ n. mulato m.

mule /myul/ n. mula f.

mullah /'mʌlə/ n. mullah m.

multicultural /,mʌlti'kʌltʃərəl, ,mʌltai-/ a. multicultural.

multinational /,mʌlti'næʃənḷ, ,mʌltai-/ a. multinacional.

multiple /'mʌltəpəl/ a. múltiple.

multiplication /,mʌltəplɪ'keiʃən/ n. multiplicación f.

multiplicity /,mʌltə'plɪsɪti/ n. multiplicidad f.

multiply /'mʌltəpli/ v. multiplicar.

multitasking /,mʌlti'tæskɪŋ, ,mʌltai-/ n. multitarea f.

multitude /'mʌltɪ,tud/ n. multitud f.

mummy /'mʌmi/ n. momia f.

mumps /mʌmps/ n. paperas f.pl.

municipal /myu'nɪsəpəl/ a. municipal.

munificent /myu'nɪfəsənt/ a. munífico.

munitions /myu'nɪʃənz/ n. municiones m.pl.

mural /'myʊrəl/ a. & n. mural m.

murder /'mɜrdər/ n. **1.** asesinato m.; homicidio m. —v. **2.** asesinar.

murderer /'mɜrdərər/ n. asesino -na.

murmur /'mɜrmər/ n. **1.** murmullo m. —v. **2.** murmurar.

muscle /'mʌsəl/ n. músculo m.

muscular /'mʌskyələr/ a. muscular.

muse /myuz/ n. **1.** musa f. —v. **2.** meditar.

museum /myu'ziəm/ n. museo m.

mushroom /'mʌʃrum/ n. seta f., hongo m.

music /'myuzɪk/ n. música f.

musical /'myuzɪkəl/ a. musical; melodioso.

musician /myu'zɪʃən/ n. músico -ca.

Muslim /'mʌzlɪm/ a. & n. musulmano.

muslin /'mʌzlɪn/ n. muselina f.; percal m.

mussel /'mʌsəl/ n. mejillón m.

must /mʌst/ v. deber; tener que.

mustache /'mʌstæʃ/ n. bigotes m.pl.

mustard /'mʌstərd/ n. mostaza f.

muster /'mʌstər/ n. **1.** Mil. revista f. —v. **2.** reunir, juntar.

mute /myut/ a. & n. mudo -da.

mutilate /'myutḷ,eit/ v. mutilar.

mutiny /'myutṇi/ n. motín m. —v. **2.** amotinarse.

mutt /mʌt/ n. Colloq. chucho m.

mutter /'mʌtər/ v. refunfuñar, gruñir.

mutton /'mʌtṇ/ n. carnero m.

mutual /'myutʃuəl/ a. mutuo.

muzzle /'mʌzəl/ n. **1.** hocico m.; bozal m. —v. **2.** embozar.

my /mai/ a. mi.

myriad /'mɪriəd/ n. miríada f.

myrtle /'mɜrtḷ/ n. mirto m.

myself /mai'sɛlf/ pron. mí, mí mismo; me. I m., yo mismo.

mysterious /mɪ'stɪriəs/ a. misterioso.

mystery /'mɪstəri/ n. misterio m.

mystic /'mɪstɪk/ a. místico.

mystify /'mɪstə,fai/ v. confundir.

myth /mɪθ/ n. mito m.

mythical /'mɪθɪkəl/ a. mítico.

mythology /mɪ'θɒlədʒi/ n. mitología f.

N

nag /næg/ n. **1.** jaca f. —v. **2.** regañar; sermonear.

nail /neil/ n. **1.** clavo m.; (finger) uña f. **n. polish,** esmalte para las uñas. —v. **2.** clavar.

naïve /nɑ'iv/ a. ingenuo.

naked /'neikɪd/ a. desnudo.

name /neim/ n. **1.** nombre m.; reputación f. —v. **2.** nombrar, mencionar.

namely /'neimli/ adv. a saber; es decir.

namesake /'neim,seik/ n. tocayo m.

nanny /'næni/ n. niñera f.

nap /næp/ n. siesta f. **to take a n.,** echar una siesta.

naphtha /'næfθə, 'næp-/ n. nafta f.

napkin /'næpkɪn/ n. servilleta f.

narcissus /nɑr'sɪsəs/ n. narciso m.

narcotic /nɑr'kɒtɪk/ a. & n. narcótico m.

narrate /'næreit/ v. narrar.

narrative /'nærətɪv/ a. **1.** narrativo. —n. **2.** cuento, relato m.

narrow /'nærou/ a. estrecho, angosto. **n.-minded,** intolerante.

nasal /'neizəl/ a. nasal.

nasty /'næsti/ a. desagradable.

nation /'neiʃən/ n. nación f.

national /'næʃənəl/ a. nacional.

nationalism /'næʃənḷ,ɪzəm/ n. nacionalismo m.

nationality /,næʃə'nælɪti/ n. nacionalidad f.

nationalization /,næʃənḷə'zeiʃən/ n. nacionalización f.

nationalize /'næʃənḷ,aiz, 'næʃnə,laiz/ v. nacionalizar.

native /'neitɪv/ a. **1.** nativo. —n. **2.** natural; indígena m. & f.

nativity /nə'tɪvɪti/ n. natividad f.

natural /'nætʃərəl/ a. natural.

naturalist /'nætʃərəlɪst/ n. naturalista m. & f.

naturalize /'nætʃərə,laiz/ v. naturalizar.

naturalness /,nætʃərəlnɪs/ n. naturalidad f.

nature /'neitʃər/ n. naturaleza f.; índole f.; humor m.

naughty /'nɒti/ a. travieso, desobediente.

nausea /'nɔziə, -ʒə/ n. náusea f.

nauseous /'nɔʃəs/ a. nauseoso.

nautical /'nɔtɪkəl/ a. náutico.

naval /'neivəl/ a. naval.

nave /neiv/ n. nave f.

navel /'neivəl/ n. ombligo m.

navigable /'nævɪgəbəl/ a. navegable.

navigate /'nævɪ,geit/ v. navegar.

navigation /,nævɪ'geiʃən/ n. navegación f.

navigator /'nævɪ,geitər/ n. navegante m. & f.

navy /'neivi/ n. marina f.

navy blue azul marino m.

near /nɪr/ a. **1.** cercano, próximo. —adv. **2.** cerca. —prep. **3.** cerca de.

nearby /'nɪər'bai/ a. **1.** cercano. —adv. **2.** cerca.

nearly /'nɪərli/ adv. casi.

nearsighted /'nɪər,saitɪd/ a. corto de vista.

neat /nit/ a. aseado; ordenado.

neatness /'nitnɪs/ n. aseo m.

nebulous /'nɛbyələs/ a. nebuloso.

necessary /'nɛsə,sɛri/ a. necesario.

necessity /nə'sɛsɪti/ n. necesidad f.

neck /nɛk/ n. cuello m.

necklace /'nɛklɪs/ n. collar m.

necktie /'nɛk,tai/ n. corbata f.

nectar /'nɛktər/ n. néctar m.

nectarine /,nɛktə'rin/ n. nectarina f.

need /nid/ n. **1.** necesidad; (poverty) pobreza f. —v. **2.** necesitar.

needle /'nidḷ/ n. aguja f.

needless /'nidlɪs/ a. innecesario, inútil.

needy /'nidi/ a. indigente, necesitado, pobre.

nefarious /nɪ'fɛəriəs/ a. nefario.

negative /'nɛgətɪv/ a. negativo. n. negativa f.

neglect /nɪ'glɛkt/ n. **1.** negligencia f.; descuido m. —v. **2.** descuidar.

negligee /,nɛglɪ'ʒei/ n. negligé m., bata de casa f.

negligent /'nɛglɪdʒənt/ a. negligente, descuidado.

negligible /'nɛglɪdʒəbəl/ a. insignificante.

negotiate /nɪ'gouʃi,eit/ v. negociar.

negotiation /nɪ,gouʃi'eiʃən/ n. negociación f.

Negro /'nigrou/ n. negro -ra.

neighbor /'neibər/ n. vecino -na.

neighborhood /'neibər,hʊd/ n. vecindad f.

neither /'niðər, 'nai-/ a. & pron. **1.** ninguno de los dos. —adv. **2.** tampoco. —conj. **3. neither... nor,** ni... ni.

neon /'niɒn/ n. neón m. **n. light,** tubo neón m.

nephew /'nɛfyu/ n. sobrino m.

nerve /nɜrv/ n. nervio m.; Colloq. audacia f.

nervous /'nɜrvəs/ a. nervioso.

nervous breakdown /'breik,daun/ crisis nerviosa f.

nest /nɛst/ n. nido m.

net /nɛt/ n. **1.** neto. —n. **2.** red f. **hair n.,** albanega, redecilla f. v. redar; Com. ganar.

netiquette /'nɛtɪkɪt/ n. etiqueta de la red f.

netting /'nɛtɪŋ/ n. red m.; obra de malla f.

network /'nɛt,wɜrk/ n. (radio) red radiodifusora f.

neuralgia /nʊ'rældʒə/ n. neuralgia f.

neurology /nʊ'rɒlədʒi/ n. neurología f.

neurotic /nʊ'rɒtɪk/ a. neurótico.

neutral /ˈnutrəl/ *a.* neutral.
neutrality /nuˈtrælɪti/ *n.* neutralidad *f.*
neutron /ˈnutrɒn/ *n.* neutrón *m.*
neutron bomb bomba de neutrones *f.*
never /ˈnɛvər/ *adv.* nunca, jamás; **n. mind,** no importa.
nevertheless /ˌnɛvərðəˈlɛs/ *adv.* no obstante, sin embargo.
new /nu/ *a.* nuevo.
newbie /ˈnubi/ *n. Colloq.* novato -ta, inexperto -ta.
news /nuz/ *n.* noticias *f.pl.*
newsboy /ˈnuzˌbɔi/ *n.* vendedor -ra de periódicos.
news bulletin boletín informativo *m.*
news flash *n.* noticia de última hora *f.*
newsgroup /ˈnuzˌgrup/ *n.* grupo de discusion *m.*
newsletter /ˈnuzˌlɛtər/ *n.* hoja informativa *f.*
newspaper /ˈnuzˌpeipər/ *n.* periódico *m.*
New Testament Nuevo Testamento *m.*
new year *n.* año nuevo *m.*
next /nɛkst/ *a.* **1.** próximo; siguiente; contiguo. —*adv.* **2.** luego, después. **n. door,** al lado. **n. to,** al lado de.
next-to-the-last /ˈnɛkst tə ðə ˈlæst/ *a.* penúltimo.
nibble /ˈnɪbəl/ *v.* picar.
nice /nis/ *a.* simpático, agradable; amable; hermoso; exacto.
nick /nɪk/ *n.* muesca *f.,* picadura *f.* **in the n. of time,** a punto.
nickel /ˈnɪkəl/ *n.* níquel *m.*
nickname /ˈnɪkˌneim/ *n.* **1.** apodo, mote *m.* —*v.* **2.** apodar.
nicotine /ˈnɪkəˌtin/ *n.* nicotina *f.*
niece /nis/ *n.* sobrina *f.*
niggardly /ˈnɪgərdli/ *a.* mezquino.
night /nait/ *n.* noche *f.* **good n.,** buenas noches. **last n.,** anoche. **n. club,** cabaret *m.*
nightclub /ˈnaitˌklʌb/ *n.* cabaret *m.*
nightclub owner cabaretero -ra *m. & f.*
nightgown /ˈnaitˌgaun/ *n.* camisa de dormir.
nightingale /ˈnaitṇˌgeil, ˈnaitɪŋ-/ *n.* ruiseñor *m.*
nightly /ˈnaitli/ *adv.* todas las noches.
nightmare /ˈnaitˌmɛər/ *n.* pesadilla *f.*
night school escuela nocturna *f.*
night watchman vigilante nocturno *m.*
nimble /ˈnɪmbəl/ *a.* ágil.
nine /nain/ *a. & pron.* nueve.
nineteen /ˈnainˈtin/ *a. & pron.* diecinueve.
ninety /ˈnainti/ *a. & pron.* noventa.
ninth /nainθ/ *a.* noveno.
nipple /ˈnɪpəl/ *n.* teta *f.;* pezón *m.*
nitrogen /ˈnaitrədʒən/ *n.* nitrógeno *m.*
no /nou/ *a.* **1.** ninguno. **no one,** nadie. —*adv.* **2.** no.
nobility /nouˈbɪlɪti/ *n.* nobleza *f.*
noble /ˈnoubəl/ *a. & n.* noble *m.*
nobleman /ˈnoubəlmən/ *n.* noble *m.*
nobody /ˈnouˌbɒdi/ *pron.* nadie.
nocturnal /nɒkˈtɜrnḷ/ *a.* nocturno.
nocturne /ˈnɒktɜrn/ *n.* nocturno *m.*
nod /nɒd/ *n.* **1.** seña con la cabeza. —*v.* **2.** inclinar la cabeza; (doze) dormitar.
no-frills /ˈnou ˈfrɪlz/ *a.* sin extras.
noise /nɔiz/ *n.* ruido *m.*
noiseless /ˈnɔizlɪs/ *a.* silencioso.
noisy /ˈnɔizi/ *a.* ruidoso.
nominal /ˈnɒmənḷ/ *a.* nominal.
nominate /ˈnɒməˌneit/ *v.* nombrar.
nomination /ˌnɒməˈneiʃən/ *n.* nombramiento *m.,* nominación *f.*
nominee /ˌnɒməˈni/ *n.* candidato -ta.
nonaligned /ˌnɒnəˈlaind/ (in political sense), *a.* no alineado.
nonchalant /ˌnɒnʃəˈlɑnt/ *a.* indiferente.
noncombatant /ˌnɒnkəmˈbætnt/ *n.* no combatiente *m.*
noncommittal /ˌnɒnkəˈmɪtḷ/ *a.* evasivo; reservado.
nondescript /ˌnɒndɪˈskrɪpt/ *a.* difícil de describir.
none /nʌn/ *pron.* ninguno.
nonentity /nɒnˈɛntɪti/ *n.* nulidad *f.*
nonpartisan /nɒnˈpɑrtəzən/ *a.* sin afiliación.
non-proliferation /ˌnɒnprəˌlɪfəˈreiʃən/ *n.* no proliferación *m.*
nonsense /ˈnɒnsɛns/ *n.* tontería *f.*
nonsmoker /nɒnˈsmoukər/ *n.* no fumador -dora.
noodle /ˈnudḷ/ *n.* fideo *m.*
noon /nun/ *n.* mediodía *m.*
noose /nus/ *n.* lazo corredizo *m.;* dogal *m.*
nor /nɔr; *unstressed* nər/ *conj.* ni.
normal /ˈnɔrməl/ *a.* normal.
north /nɔrθ/ *n.* norte *m.*
North America /əˈmɛrɪkə/ Norte América *f.*
North American *a. & n.* norteamericano -na.
northeast /ˌnɔrθˈist; *Naut.* ˌnɔr-/ *n.* nordeste *m.*
northern /ˈnɔrðərn/ *a.* septentrional.
North Pole *n.* Polo Norte *m.*
northwest /ˌnɔrθˈwɛst; *Naut.* ˌnɔr-/ *n.* noroeste *m.*
Norway /ˈnɔrwei/ *n.* Noruega *f.*
Norwegian /nɔrˈwidʒən/ *a. & n.* noruego -ga.
nose /nouz/ *n.* nariz *f.*
nosebleed /ˈnouzˌblid/ *n.* hemorragia nasal *f.*
nostalgia /nɒˈstældʒə/ *n.* nostalgia *f.*
nostril /ˈnɒstrəl/ *n.* ventana de la nariz; (pl.) narices *f.pl.*
not /nɒt/ *adv.* no. **n. at all,** de ninguna manera. **n. even,** ni siquiera.
notable /ˈnoutəbəl/ *a.* notable.
notary /ˈnoutəri/ *n.* notario *m.*
notation /nouˈteiʃən/ *a.* notación *f.*
notch /nɒtʃ/ *n.* muesca *f.;* corte *m.*
note /nout/ *n.* **1.** nota *f.;* apunte *m.* —*v.* **2.** notar.
notebook /ˈnoutˌbʊk/ *n.* libreta *f.,* cuaderno *m.*
noted /ˈnoutɪd/ *a.* célebre.
notepaper /ˈnoutˌpeipər/ *n.* papel de notas *m.*
noteworthy /ˈnoutˌwɜrði/ *a.* notable.
nothing /ˈnʌθɪŋ/ *pron.* nada.
notice /ˈnoutɪs/ *n.* **1.** aviso *m.;* noticia *f.* —*v.* **2.** observar, fijarse en.
noticeable /ˈnoutɪsəbəl/ *a.* notable.
notification /ˌnoutəfɪˈkeiʃən/ *n.* notificación *f.*
notify /ˈnoutəˌfai/ *v.* notificar.
notion /ˈnouʃən/ *n.* noción; idea *f.;* (pl.) novedades *f.pl.*
notoriety /ˌnoutəˈraiɪti/ *n.* notoriedad *f.*
notorious /nouˈtɔriəs/ *a.* notorio.
noun /naun/ *n.* nombre, sustantivo *m.*
nourish /ˈnɜrɪʃ/ *v.* nutrir, alimentar.
nourishment /ˈnɜrɪʃmənt/ *n.* nutrimento; alimento *m.*
novel /ˈnɒvəl/ *a.* **1.** nuevo, original. —*n.* **2.** novela *f.*
novelist /ˈnɒvəlɪst/ *n.* novelista *m. & f.*
novelty /ˈnɒvəlti/ *n.* novedad *f.*
November /nouˈvɛmbər/ *n.* noviembre *m.*
novena /nouˈvinə/ *n.* novena *f.*
novice /ˈnɒvɪs/ *n.* novicio -cia, novato -ta.
novocaine /ˈnouvəˌkein/ *n.* novocaína *f.*
now /nau/ *adv.* ahora. **n. and then,** de vez en cuando. **by n.,** ya. **from n. on,** de ahora en adelante. **just n.,** ahorita. **right n.,** ahora mismo.
nowadays /ˈnauəˌdeiz/ *adv.* hoy día, hoy en día, actualmente.
nowhere /ˈnouˌwɛər/ *adv.* en ninguna parte.
nozzle /ˈnɒzəl/ *n.* boquilla *f.*
nuance /ˈnuɑns/ *n.* matiz *m.*
nuclear /ˈnukliər/ *a.* nuclear.
nuclear energy energía nuclear *f.*
nuclear warhead /ˈwɔrˌhɛd/ cabeza nuclear *f.*
nuclear waste desechos nucleares *m.pl.*
nucleus /ˈnukliəs/ *n.* núcleo *m.*
nude /nud/ *a.* desnudo.
nuisance /ˈnusəns/ *n.* molestia *f.*
nuke /nuk/ *n.* bomba atómica *f.*
nullify /ˈnʌləˌfai/ *v.* anular.
number /ˈnʌmbər/ *n.* **1.** número *m.;* cifra *f.* **license n.,** matrícula *f.* —*v.* **2.** numerar, contar.
numeric /nuˈmɛrɪk/ **numerical** *a.* numérico.
numeric keypad /nuˈmɛrɪk/ teclado numérico *m.*
numerous /ˈnumərəs/ *a.* numeroso.
nun /nʌn/ *n.* monja *f.*
nuptial /ˈnʌpʃəl/ *a.* nupcial.
nurse /nɜrs/ *n.* **1.** enfermera *f.;* (child's) ama, niñera *f.* —*v.* **2.** criar, alimentar, amamantar; cuidar.
nursery /ˈnɜrsəri/ *n.* cuarto destinado a los niños; *Agr.* plantel, criadero *m.*
nursery school jardín de infancia *m.*
nurture /ˈnɜrtʃər/ *v.* nutrir.
nut /nʌt/ *n.* nuez *f.; Mech.* tuerca *f.*
nutcracker /ˈnʌtˌkrækər/ *n.* cascanueces *m.*
nutrition /nuˈtrɪʃən/ *n.* nutrición *f.*
nutritious /nuˈtrɪʃəs/ *a.* nutritivo.
nylon /ˈnailɒn/ *n.* nilón *m.*
nymph /nɪmf/ *n.* ninfa *f.*

O

oak /ouk/ *n.* roble *m.*
oar /ɔr/ *n.* remo *m.*
OAS *abbr.* (Organization of American States) OEA (Organización de los Estados Americanos) *f.*
oasis /ouˈeisɪs/ *n.* oasis *m.*
oat /out/ *n.* avena *f.*
oath /ouθ/ *n.* juramento *m.*
oatmeal /ˈoutˌmil/ *n.* harina de avena *f.*
obedience /ouˈbidiəns/ *n.* obediencia *f.*
obedient /ouˈbidiənt/ *a.* obediente.
obese /ouˈbis/ *a.* obeso, gordo.
obey /ouˈbei/ *v.* obedecer.
obituary /ouˈbɪtʃuˌɛri/ *n.* obituario *m.*
object /*n* ˈɒbdʒɪkt; *v* əbˈdʒɛkt/ *n.* **1.** objeto *m.; Gram.* complemento *m.* —*v.* **2.** oponerse; objetar.
objection /əbˈdʒɛkʃən/ *n.* objeción *f.*
objectionable /əbˈdʒɛkʃənəbəl/ *a.* censurable.
objective /əbˈdʒɛktɪv/ *a. & n.* objetivo *m.*
obligation /ˌɒblɪˈgeiʃən/ *n.* obligación *f.*
obligatory /əˈblɪgəˌtɔri/ *a.* obligatorio.
oblige /əˈblaidʒ/ *v.* obligar; complacer.
oblique /əˈblik/ *a.* oblicuo.
obliterate /əˈblɪtəˌreit/ *v.* borrar; destruir.
oblivion /əˈblɪviən/ *n.* olvido *m.*
oblong /ˈɒbˌlɔŋ/ *a.* oblongo.
obnoxious /əbˈnɒkʃəs/ *a.* ofensivo, odioso.
obscene /əbˈsin/ *a.* obsceno, indecente.
obscure /əbˈskyʊr/ *a.* **1.** obscuro. —*v.* **2.** obscurecer.
observance /əbˈzɜrvəns/ *n.* observancia; ceremonia *f.*
observation /ˌɒbzɜrˈveiʃən/ *n.* observación *f.*
observatory /əbˈzɜrvəˌtɔri/ *n.* observatorio *m.*
observe /əbˈzɜrv/ *v.* observar; celebrar.
observer /əbˈzɜrvər/ *n.* observador -ra.
obsession /əbˈsɛʃən/ *n.* obsesión *f.*
obsolete /ˌɒbsəˈlit/ *a.* anticuado.
obstacle /ˈɒbstəkəl/ *n.* obstáculo *m.*
obstetrician /ˌɒbstɪˈtrɪʃən/ *n.* obstétrico -ca, tocólogo -ga *m. & f.*
obstinate /ˈɒbstənɪt/ *a.* obstinado, terco.
obstruct /əbˈstrʌkt/ *v.* obstruir, impedir.
obstruction /əbˈstrʌkʃən/ *n.* obstrucción *f.*
obtain /əbˈtein/ *v.* obtener, conseguir.
obtuse /əbˈtus/ *a.* obtuso.
obviate /ˈɒbviˌeit/ *v.* obviar.
obvious /ˈɒbviəs/ *a.* evidente, obvio.
occasion /əˈkeiʒən/ *n.* **1.** ocasión *f.* —*v.* **2.** ocasionar.
occasional /əˈkeiʒənḷ/ *a.* ocasional.
occult /əˈkʌlt/ *a.* oculto.
occupant /ˈɒkyəpənt/ *n.* ocupante *m. & f.;* inquilino -na.
occupation /ˌɒkyəˈpeiʃən/ *n.* ocupación *f.;* empleo *m.*
occupy /ˈɒkyəˌpai/ *v.* ocupar; emplear.
occur /əˈkɜr/ *v.* ocurrir.
occurrence /əˈkɜrəns/ *n.* ocurrencia *f.*
ocean /ˈouʃən/ *n.* océano *m.*
o'clock /əˈklɒk/ **it's one o.,** es la una. **it's two o.,** son las dos, etc. **at... o.,** a las...
octagon /ˈɒktəˌgɒn/ *n.* octágono *m.*
octave /ˈɒktɪv/ *n.* octava *f.*
October /ɒkˈtoubər/ *n.* octubre *m.*
octopus /ˈɒktəpəs/ *n.* pulpo *m.*
oculist /ˈɒkyəlɪst/ *n.* oculista *m. & f.*
odd /ɒd/ *a.* impar; suelto; raro.
odd number número impar *m.*
odious /ˈoudiəs/ *a.* odioso.
odor /ˈoudər/ *n.* olor *m.;* fragancia *f.*
of /əv/ *prep.* de.
off /ɔf/ *adv.* (see under verb: **stop off, take off,** etc.)
offend /əˈfɛnd/ *v.* ofender.
offender /əˈfɛndər/ *n.* ofensor -ra; delincuente *m. & f.*
offense /əˈfɛns/ *n.* ofensa *f.;* crimen *m.*
offensive /əˈfɛnsɪv/ *a.* **1.** ofensivo. —*n.* **2.** ofensiva *f.*
offer /ˈɔfər/ *n.* **1.** oferta *f.* —*v.* **2.** ofrecer.
offering /ˈɔfərɪŋ/ *n.* oferta *f.*
office /ˈɔfɪs/ *n.* oficina *f.;* despacho *m.;* oficio, cargo *m.*
officer /ˈɔfəsər/ *n.* oficial *m. & f.* **police o.,** agente de policía *m. & f.*
official /əˈfɪʃəl/ *a.* **1.** oficial. —*n.* **2.** oficial *m. & f.,* funcionario -ria.
officiate /əˈfɪʃiˌeit/ *v.* oficiar.
officious /əˈfɪʃəs/ *a.* oficioso.
offspring /ˈɔfˌsprɪŋ/ *n.* hijos *m.pl.;* progenie *f.*
often /ˈɔfən/ *adv.* muchas veces, a menudo. **how o.,** con qué frecuencia.
oil /ɔil/ *n.* **1.** aceite; óleo; petróleo *m.* —*v.* **2.** aceitar; engrasar.
oil refinery /rɪˈfainəri/ destilería de petróleo *f.*
oil tanker /ˈtæŋkər/ petrolero *m.*
oily /ˈɔili/ *a.* aceitoso.
ointment /ˈɔintmənt/ *n.* ungüento *m.*
okay /ˈouˈkei, ˌouˈkei/ *adv.* bien; de acuerdo.
old /ould/ *a.* viejo; antiguo. **o. man, o. woman,** viejo -ja.
old-fashioned /ˈould ˈfæʃənd/ *a.* fuera de moda, anticuado.
Old Testament Antiguo Testamento *m.*
olive /ˈɒlɪv/ *n.* aceituna, oliva *f.*
ombudsman /ˈɒmbədzmən/ *n.* ombudsman *m.*
omelet /ˈɒmlɪt/ *n.* tortilla de huevos.
omen /ˈoumən/ *n.* agüero *m.*
ominous /ˈɒmənəs/ *a.* ominoso, siniestro.
omission /ouˈmɪʃən/ *n.* omisión *f.;* olvido *m.*
omit /ouˈmɪt/ *v.* omitir.
omnibus /ˈɒmnəˌbʌs/ *n.* ómnibus *m.*
omnipotent /ɒmˈnɪpətənt/ *a.* omnipotente.
on /ɒn/ *prep.* **1.** en, sobre, encima de. —*adv.* **2.** adelante.

once /wʌns/ *adv.* una vez. **at o.,** en seguida. **o. in a while,** de vez en cuando.

one /wʌn/ *a. & pron.* uno -na.

one-armed bandit /ˈwʌn ˌɑrmd/ tragaperras *f.*

oneself /wʌnˈsɛlf/ *pron.* sí mismo -ma; se. **with o.,** consigo.

onion /ˈʌnyən/ *n.* cebolla *f.*

on-line /ˈɒn ˈlain/ *a.* conectado.

only /ˈounli/ *a.* **1.** único, solo. —*adv.* **2.** sólo, solamente.

onward /ˈɒnwərd/ *adv.* adelante.

opal /ˈoupəl/ *n.* ópalo *m.*

opaque /ouˈpeik/ *a.* opaco.

open /ˈoupən/ *a.* **1.** abierto; franco. **o. air,** aire libre. —*v.* **2.** abrir.

opening /ˈoupənɪŋ/ *n.* abertura *f.*

opera /ˈɒpərə/ *n.* ópera *f.* **o. glasses,** anteojos de ópera; gemelos *m.pl.*

operate /ˈɒpəˌreit/ *v.* operar.

operation /ˌɒpəˈreiʃən/ *n.* operación *f.* **to have an o.,** operarse, ser operado.

operative /ˈɒpərətɪv/ *a.* eficaz, operativo.

operator /ˈɒpəˌreitər/ *n.* operario -ria. **elevator o.,** ascensorista *m. & f.* **telephone o.,** telefonista *m. & f.*

operetta /ˌɒpəˈrɛtə/ *n.* opereta *f.*

ophthalmic /ɒfˈθælmɪk, ɒp-/ *a.* oftálmico.

opinion /əˈpɪnyən/ *n.* opinión *f.*

opponent /əˈpounənt/ *n.* antagonista *m. & f.*

opportunism /ˌɒpərˈtunɪzəm/ *n.* oportunismo *m.*

opportunity /ˌɒpərˈtunɪti/ *n.* ocasión, oportunidad *f.*

oppose /əˈpouz/ *v.* oponer.

opposite /ˈɒpəzɪt/ *a.* **1.** opuesto, contrario. —*prep.* **2.** al frente de. —*n.* **3.** contrario *m.*

opposition /ˌɒpəˈzɪʃən/ *n.* oposición *f.*

oppress /əˈprɛs/ *v.* oprimir.

oppression /əˈprɛʃən/ *n.* opresión *f.*

oppressive /əˈprɛsɪv/ *a.* opresivo.

optic /ˈɒptɪk/ *a.* óptico.

optical disc /ˈɒptɪkəl ˈdɪsk/ disco óptico *m.*

optical illusion /ˈɒptɪkəl/ ilusión de óptica *f.*

optician /ɒpˈtɪʃən/ *n.* óptico -ca.

optics /ˈɒptɪks/ *n.* óptica *f.*

optimism /ˈɒptəˌmɪzəm/ *n.* optimismo.

optimistic /ˌɒptəˈmɪstɪk/ *a.* optimista.

option /ˈɒpʃən/ *n.* opción, elección *f.*

optional /ˈɒpʃənl/ *a.* discrecional, facultativo.

optometry /ɒpˈtɒmɪtri/ *n.* optometría *f.*

opulent /ˈɒpyələnt/ *a.* opulento.

or /ɔr/ *conj.* o, (before *o-*, *ho-*) u.

oracle /ˈɔrəkəl/ *n.* oráculo *m.*

oral /ˈɔrəl/ *a.* oral, vocal.

orange /ˈɔrɪndʒ/ *n.* naranja *f.*

orange juice jugo de naranja, zumo de naranja *m.*

orange squeezer /ˈskwizər/ *n.* exprimidora de naranjas *f.*

oration /ɔˈreiʃən/ *n.* discurso *m.*; oración *f.*

orator /ˈɔrətər/ *n.* orador -ra.

oratory /ˈɔrəˌtɔri/ *n.* oratoria *f.*; (church) oratorio *m.*

orbit /ˈɔrbɪt/ *n.* órbita *f.*

orchard /ˈɔrtʃərd/ *n.* huerto *m.*

orchestra /ˈɔrkəstrə/ *n.* orquesta *f.* **o. seat,** butaca *f.*

orchid /ˈɔrkɪd/ *n.* orquídea *f.*

ordain /ɔrˈdein/ *v.* ordenar.

ordeal /ɔrˈdil/ *n.* prueba *f.*

order /ˈɔrdər/ *n.* orden, *m. or f.*; clase *f.*; *Com.* pedido *m.* **in o. that,** para que. *v.* ordenar; mandar; pedir.

order blank hoja de pedidos *f.*

orderly /ˈɔrdərli/ *a.* ordenado.

ordinance /ˈɔrdṇəns/ *n.* ordenanza *f.*

ordinary /ˈɔrdṇˌɛri/ *a.* ordinario.

ordination /ˌɔrdṇˈeiʃən/ *n.* ordenación *f.*

ore /ɔr/ *n.* mineral *m.*

organ /ˈɔrgən/ *n.* órgano *m.*

organdy /ˈɔrgəndi/ *n.* organdí *m.*

organic /ɔrˈgænɪk/ *a.* orgánico.

organism /ˈɔrgəˌnɪzəm/ *n.* organismo *m.*

organist /ˈɔrgənɪst/ *n.* organista *m. & f.*

organization /ˌɔrgənəˈzeiʃən/ *n.* organización *f.*

organize /ˈɔrgəˌnaiz/ *v.* organizar.

orgy /ˈɔrdʒi/ *n.* orgía *f.*

orient /ˈɔriənt/ *n.* **1.** oriente *m.* —*v.* **2.** orientar.

Orient /ˈɔriənt/ *n.* Oriente *m.*

Oriental /ˌɔriˈɛntl̩/ *a.* oriental.

orientation /ˌɔriənˈteiʃən/ *n.* orientación *f.*

origin /ˈɔrɪdʒɪn/ *n.* origen *m.*

original /əˈrɪdʒənl/ *a. & n.* original *m.*

originality /əˌrɪdʒəˈnælɪti/ *n.* originalidad *f.*

ornament /*n* ˈɔrnəmənt; *v* -ˌmɛnt/ *n.* **1.** ornamento *m.* —*v.* **2.** ornamentar.

ornamental /ˌɔrnəˈmɛntl̩/ *a.* ornamental, decorativo.

ornate /ɔrˈneit/ *a.* ornado.

ornithology /ˌɔrnəˈθɒlədʒi/ *n.* ornitología *f.*

orphan /ˈɔrfən/ *a. & n.* huérfano -na.

orphanage /ˈɔrfənɪdʒ/ *n.* orfanato *m.*

orthodox /ˈɔrθəˌdɒks/ *a.* ortodoxo.

ostentation /ˌɒstɛnˈteiʃən/ *n.* ostentación *f.*

ostentatious /ˌɒstɛnˈteiʃəs/ *a.* ostentoso.

ostrich /ˈɔstrɪtʃ/ *n.* avestruz *f.*

other /ˈʌðər/ *a. & pron.* otro. **every o. day,** un día sí otro no.

otherwise /ˈʌðərˌwaiz/ *adv.* de otra manera.

ought /ɔt/ *v.* deber.

ounce /auns/ *n.* onza *f.*

our /auᵊr; *unstressed* ɑr/ **ours** *a. & pron.* nuestro.

ourselves /ɑrˈsɛlvz/ *pron.* nosotros -as; mismos -as; nos.

oust /aust/ *v.* desalojar.

ouster /ˈaustər/ *n.* desahucio *m.*

out /aut/ *adv.* **1.** fuera, afuera. **out of,** fuera de. —*prep.* **2.** por.

outbreak /ˈautˌbreik/ *n.* erupción *f.*

outcast /ˈautˌkæst/ *n.* paria *m. & f.*

outcome /ˈautˌkʌm/ *n.* resultado *m.*

outdoors /ˌautˈdɔrz/ *adv.* fuera de casa; al aire libre.

outer /ˈautər/ *a.* exterior, externo.

outfit /ˈautˌfɪt/ *n.* **1.** equipo; traje *m.* —*v.* **2.** equipar.

outgrowth /ˈautˌgrouθ/ *n.* resultado *m.*

outing /ˈautɪŋ/ *n.* paseo *m.*

outlaw /ˈautˌlɔ/ *n.* **1.** bandido *m.* —*v.* **2.** proscribir.

outlet /ˈautlɛt/ *n.* salida *f.*

outline /ˈautˌlain/ *n.* **1.** contorno; esbozo *m.*; silueta *f.* —*v.* **2.** esbozar.

outlive /ˌautˈlɪv/ *v.* sobrevivir.

out-of-court settlement /ˈautəvˌkɔrt/ arreglo pacífico *m.*

out-of-date /ˈaut əv ˈdeit/ *a.* anticuado.

out of focus *a.* desenfocado.

outpost /ˈautˌpoust/ *n.* puesto avanzado.

output /ˈautˌpʊt/ *n.* capacidad *f.*; producción *f.*

outrage /ˈautreidʒ/ *n.* **1.** ultraje *m.*; atrocidad *f.* —*v.* **2.** ultrajar.

outrageous /autˈreidʒəs/ *a.* atroz.

outrun /ˌautˈrʌn/ *v.* exceder.

outside /*a, prep, adv* ˌautˈsaid; *n* ˈautˈsaid/ *a. & n.* **1.** exterior *m.* —*adv.* **2.** afuera, por fuera. —*prep.* **3.** fuera de.

outskirt /ˈautˌskɜrt/ *n.* borde *m.*

outward /ˈautwərd/ *adv.* hacia afuera.

outwardly /ˈautwərdli/ *adv.* exteriormente.

oval /ˈouvəl/ *a.* **1.** oval, ovalado. —*n.* **2.** óvalo *m.*

ovary /ˈouvəri/ *n.* ovario *m.*

ovation /ouˈveiʃən/ *n.* ovación *f.*

oven /ˈʌvən/ *n.* horno *m.*

over /ˈouvər/ *prep.* **1.** sobre, encima de; por. —*adv.* **2. o. here,** aquí. **o. there,** allí, por allí. **to be o.,** estar terminado.

overcoat /ˈouvərˌkout/ *n.* abrigo, sobretodo *m.*

overcome /ˌouvərˈkʌm/ *v.* superar, vencer.

overdose /ˈouvərˌdous/ *n.* sobredosis *f.*

overdue /ˌouvərˈdu/ *a.* retrasado.

overflow /*n* ˈouvərˌflou; *v* ˌouvərˈflou/ *n.* **1.** inundación *f.* —*v.* **2.** inundar.

overhaul /ˌouvərˈhɔl/ *v.* repasar.

overhead /ˈouvərˈhɛd/ *adv.* arriba, en lo alto.

overkill /ˈouvərˌkɪl/ *n.* efecto mayor que el pretendido.

overlook /ˌouvərˈlʊk/ *v.* pasar por alto.

overnight /ˈouvərˈnait/ *adv.* **to stay or stop o.,** pasar la noche.

overpower /ˌouvərˈpauər/ *v.* vencer.

overrule /ˌouvərˈrul/ *v.* predominar.

overrun /ˌouvərˈrʌn/ *v.* invadir.

oversee /ˌouvərˈsi/ *v.* superentender.

oversight /ˈouvərˌsait/ *n.* descuido *m.*

overt /ouˈvɜrt/ *a.* abierto.

overtake /ˌouvərˈteik/ *v.* alcanzar.

overthrow /*n* ˈouvərˌθrou; *v* ˌouvərˈθrou/ *n.* **1.** trastorno *m.* —*v.* **2.** trastornar.

overture /ˈouvərtʃər/ *n.* *Mus.* obertura *f.*

overturn /ˌouvərˈtɜrn/ *v.* trastornar.

overview /ˈouvərˌvyu/ *n.* visión de conjunto *f.*

overweight /ˈouvərˌweit/ *a.* demasiado pesado.

overwhelm /ˌouvərˈwɛlm/ *v.* abrumar.

overwork /ˌouvərˈwɜrk/ *v.* trabajar demasiado.

owe /ou/ *v.* deber. **owing to,** debido a.

owl /aul/ *n.* búho *m.*, lechuza *f.*

own /oun/ *a.* **1.** propio. —*v.* **2.** poseer.

owner /ˈounər/ *n.* dueño -ña.

ox /ɒks/ *n.* buey *m.*

oxygen /ˈɒksɪdʒən/ *n.* oxígeno *m.*

oxygen tent tienda de oxígeno *f.*

oyster /ˈɔistər/ *n.* ostra *f.*

P

pace /peis/ *n.* **1.** paso *m.* —*v.* **2.** pasearse. **p. off,** medir a pasos.

pacific /pəˈsɪfɪk/ *a.* pacífico.

Pacific Ocean Océano Pacífico *m.*

pacifier /ˈpæsəˌfaiər/ *n.* pacificador *m.*; (baby p.) chupete *m.*

pacifism /ˈpæsəˌfɪzəm/ *n.* pacifismo *m.*

pacifist /ˈpæsəfɪst/ *n.* pacifista *m. & f.*

pacify /ˈpæsəˌfai/ *v.* pacificar.

pack /pæk/ *n.* **1.** fardo; paquete *m.*; (animals) muta *f.* **p. of cards,** baraja *f.* —*v.* **2.** empaquetar; (baggage) empacar.

package /ˈpækɪdʒ/ *n.* paquete, bulto *m.*

package tour viaje todo incluido *m.*

pact /pækt/ *n.* pacto *m.*

pad /pæd/ *n.* **1.** colchoncillo *m.* **p. of paper,** bloc de papel. —*v.* **2.** rellenar.

paddle /ˈpædl̩/ *n.* **1.** canalete *m.* —*v.* **2.** remar.

padlock /ˈpædˌlɒk/ *n.* candado *m.*

pagan /ˈpeigən/ *a. & n.* pagano -na.

page /peidʒ/ *n.* página *f.*; (boy) paje *m.*

pageant /ˈpædʒənt/ *n.* espectáculo *m.*; procesión *f.*

pail /peil/ *n.* cubo *m.*

pain /pein/ *n.* dolor *m.* **to take pains,** esmerarse.

painful /ˈpeinfəl/ *a.* doloroso; penoso.

pain killer /ˈpeinˌkɪlər/ analgésico *m.*

paint /peint/ *n.* **1.** pintura *f.* —*v.* **2.** pintar.

painter /ˈpeintər/ *n.* pintor -ra.

painting /ˈpeintɪŋ/ *n.* pintura *f.*; cuadro *m.*

pair /pɛər/ *n.* **1.** par *m.*; pareja *f.* —*v.* **2.** parear. **p. off,** emparejarse.

pajamas /pəˈdʒɑməz, -ˈdʒæməz/ *n.* pijama *m.*

palace /ˈpælɪs/ *n.* palacio *m.*

palatable /ˈpælətəbəl/ *a.* sabroso, agradable.

palate /ˈpælɪt/ *n.* paladar *m.*

palatial /pəˈleiʃəl/ *a.* palaciego, suntuoso.

pale /peil/ *a.* pálido. **to turn pale,** palidecer.

paleness /ˈpeilnɪs/ *n.* palidez *f.*

palette /ˈpælɪt/ *n.* paleta *f.*

pallbearer /ˈpɔlˌbɛərər/ *n.* portador del féretro, portaféretro *m.*

pallid /ˈpælɪd/ *a.* pálido.

palm /pɑm/ *n.* palma *f.* **p. tree,** palmera *f.*

palpitate /ˈpælpɪˌteit/ *v.* palpitar.

paltry /ˈpɔltri/ *a.* miserable.

pamper /ˈpæmpər/ *v.* mimar.

pamphlet /ˈpæmflɪt/ *n.* folleto *m.*

pan /pæn/ *n.* cacerola *f.*

panacea /ˌpænəˈsiə/ *n.* panacea *f.*

Pan-American /ˌpænəˈmɛrɪkən/ *a.* panamericano.

pane /pein/ *n.* hoja de vidrio *f.*, cuadro *m.*

panel /ˈpænl̩/ *n.* tablero *m.*

pang /pæŋ/ *n.* dolor; remordimiento *m.*

panic /ˈpænɪk/ *n.* pánico *m.*

panorama /ˌpænəˈræmə, -ˈrɑmə/ *n.* panorama *m.*

pant /pænt/ *v.* jadear.

panther /ˈpænθər/ *n.* pantera *f.*

pantomine /ˈpæntəˌmaim/ *n.* pantomima *f.*; mímica *f.*

pantry /ˈpæntri/ *n.* despensa *f.*

pants /pænts/ *n.* pantalones, *m.pl.*

panty hose /ˈpæntiˌhouz/ *n.* pantys, pantimedias *f. pl.* (medias hasta la cintura).

papal /ˈpeipəl/ *a.* papal.

paper /ˈpeipər/ *n.* papel; periódico; artículo *m.*

paperback /ˈpeipərˌbæk/ *n.* libro en rústica *m.*

paper clip sujetapapeles *m.*

paper cup vaso de papel *m.*

paper hanger /ˈpeipərˌhæŋər/ empapelador -ra.

paper money papel moneda *m.*

paperweight /ˈpeipərˌweit/ pisapapeles *m.*

papier-mâché /ˌpeipərməˈʃei, pɑˌpyei-/ *n.* cartón piedra *m.*

paprika /pæˈprikə, pə-, pɑ-, ˈpæprɪkə/ *n.* pimentón *m.*

par /pɑr/ *n.* paridad *f.*; *Com.* par *f.*

parable /ˈpærəbəl/ *n.* parábola *f.*

parachute /ˈpærəˌʃut/ *n.* paracaídas *m.*

parade /pəˈreid/ *n.* **1.** desfile *m.*, procesión *f.* —*v.* **2.** desfilar.

paradise /ˈpærəˌdais/ *n.* paraíso *m.*

paradox /ˈpærəˌdɒks/ *n.* paradoja *f.*

paraffin /ˈpærəfɪn/ *n.* parafina *f.*

paragraph /ˈpærəˌgræf/ *n.* párrafo *m.*

parakeet /ˈpærəˌkit/ *n.* perico *m.*

parallel /ˈpærəˌlɛl/ *a.* **1.** paralelo. —*v.* **2.** correr parejas con.

paralysis /pəˈræləsɪs/ *n.* parálisis *f.*

paralyze /ˈpærəˌlaiz/ *v.* paralizar.

paramedic /ˌpærəˈmɛdɪk/ *n.* paramédico -ca.

parameter /pəˈræmɪtər/ *n.* parámetro *m.*

paramount /ˈpærəˌmaunt/ *a.* supremo.

paraphrase /ˈpærəˌfreiz/ *n.* **1.** paráfrasis *f.* —*v.* **2.** parafrasear.

paraplegic /ˌpærəˈplidʒɪk/ *n.* parapléjico -ca.

parasite /ˈpærəˌsait/ *n.* parásito *m.*

parboil /ˈpɑrˌbɔil/ v. sancochar.

parcel /ˈpɑrsəl/ n. paquete m. **p. of land**, lote de terreno.

parchment /ˈpɑrtʃmənt/ n. pergamino m.

pardon /ˈpɑrdn/ n. 1. perdón m. —v. 2. perdonar.

pare /pɛər/ v. pelar.

parentage /ˈpɛərəntɪdʒ, ˈpær-/ n. origen m.; extracción f.

parenthesis /pəˈrɛnθəsɪs/ n. paréntesis m.

parents /ˈpɛərənts/ n. padres m.pl.

parish /ˈpærɪʃ/ n. parroquia f.

Parisian /pəˈrɪʒən, -ˈriʒən, -ˈrɪziən/ a. & n. parisiense m. & f.

parity /ˈpærɪti/ n. igualdad, paridad f.

park /pɑrk/ n. 1. parque m. —v. 2. estacionar.

parking lot /ˈpɑrkɪŋ/ n. estacionamiento, aparcamiento m.

parking meter /ˈpɑrkɪŋ/ parquímetro m.

parking space /ˈpɑrkɪŋ/ estacionamiento, aparcamiento m.

parkway /ˈpɑrkˌwei/ n. bulevar m.; autopista f.

parley /ˈpɑrli/ n. conferencia f.; Mil. parlamento m.

parliament /ˈpɑrləmənt/ n. parlamento m.

parliamentary /ˌpɑrləˈmɛntəri, -tri/ sometimes ˌpɑrljə-/ a. parlamentario.

parlor /ˈpɑrlər/ n. sala f., salón m.

parochial /pəˈroukiəl/ a. parroquial.

parody /ˈpærədi/ n. 1. parodia f. —v. 2. parodiar.

parole /pəˈroul/ v. n. 1. palabra de honor f.; Mil. santo y seña. —v. 2. poner en libertad bajo palabra.

paroxysm /ˈpærəkˌsɪzəm/ n. paroxismo m.

parrot /ˈpærət/ n. loro, papagayo m.

parsimony /ˈpɑrsəˌmouni/ n. parsimonia f.

parsley /ˈpɑrsli/ n. perejil m.

parson /ˈpɑrsən/ n. párroco m.

part /pɑrt/ n. 1. parte f.; Theat. papel m. —v. 2. separarse, partirse. **p. with**, desprenderse de.

partake /pɑrˈteik/ v. tomar parte.

partial /ˈpɑrʃəl/ a. parcial.

participant /pɑrˈtɪsəpənt/ n. participante m. & f.

participate /pɑrˈtɪsəˌpeit/ v. participar.

participation /pɑrˌtɪsəˈpeiʃən/ n. participación f.

participle /ˈpɑrtəˌsɪpəl, -səpəl/ n. participio m.

particle /ˈpɑrtɪkəl/ n. partícula f.

particular /pərˈtɪkyələr/ a. & n. particular m.

parting /ˈpɑrtɪŋ/ n. despedida f.

partisan /ˈpɑrtəzən, -sən/ a. & n. partidario -ria.

partition /pɑrˈtɪʃən, pər-/ n. tabique m. v. dividir, partir.

partly /ˈpɑrtli/ adv. en parte.

partner /ˈpɑrtnər/ n. socio -cia; compañero -ra.

partridge /ˈpɑrtrɪdʒ/ n. perdiz f.

party /ˈpɑrti/ n. tertulia, fiesta f.; grupo m.; (political) partido m.

pass /pæs/ n. 1. pase; (mountain) paso m. —v. 2. pasar. **p. away**, fallecer.

passable /ˈpæsəbəl/ a. transitable; regular.

passage /ˈpæsɪdʒ/ n. pasaje; (corridor) pasillo m.

passé /pæˈsei/ a. anticuado.

passenger /ˈpæsəndʒər/ n. pasajero -ra.

passenger ship buque de pasajeros m.

passerby /ˈpæsərˌbai/ n. transeúnte m. & f.

passion /ˈpæʃən/ n. pasión f.

passionate /ˈpæʃənɪt/ a. apasionado.

passive /ˈpæsɪv/ a. pasivo.

passport /ˈpæspɔrt/ n. pasaporte m.

password /ˈpæsˌwɜrd/ n. código m., clave m., contraseña f.

past /pæst/ a. & n. 1. pasado m. —prep. 2. más allá de; después de.

paste /peist/ n. 1. pasta f. —v. 2. empastar; pegar.

pasteurize /ˈpæstʃəˌraiz/ v. pasteurizar.

pastime /ˈpæsˌtaim/ n. pasatiempo m.; diversión f.

pastor /ˈpæstər/ n. pastor m.

pastrami /pəˈstrɑmi/ n. pastrón m.

pastry /ˈpeistri/ n. pastelería f.

pasture /ˈpæstʃər/ n. 1. pasto m.; pradera f. —v. 2. pastar.

pat /pæt/ n. 1. golpecillo m. **to stand p.**, mantenerse firme. —v. 2. dar golpecillos.

patch /pætʃ/ n. 1. remiendo m. —v. 2. remendar.

patent /ˈpætnt/ a. & n. 1. patente m. —v. 2. patentar.

patent leather /ˈpætnt, ˈpætn/ charol m.

paternal /pəˈtɜrnl/ a. paterno, paternal.

paternity /pəˈtɜrnɪti/ n. paternidad f.

path /pæθ/ n. senda f.

pathetic /pəˈθɛtɪk/ a. patético.

pathology /pəˈθɒlədʒi/ n. patología f.

pathos /ˈpeiθɒs/ n. rasgo conmovedor m.

patience /ˈpeiʃəns/ n. paciencia f.

patient /ˈpeiʃənt/ a. 1. paciente. —n. 2. enfermo -ma, paciente m. & f.

patio /ˈpætiˌou/ n. patio m.

patriarch /ˈpeitriˌɑrk/ n. patriarca m.

patriot /ˈpeitriət/ n. patriota m. & f.

patriotic /ˌpeitriˈɒtɪk/ a. patriótico.

patriotism /ˈpeitriəˌtɪzəm/ n. patriotismo m.

patrol /pəˈtroul/ n. 1. patrulla f. —v. 2. patrullar.

patrolman /pəˈtroulmən/ n. vigilante m.; patrullador m.

patron /ˈpeitrən/ n. patrón m.

patronize /ˈpeitrəˌnaiz/ v. condescender; patrocinar; ser cliente de.

pattern /ˈpætərn/ n. modelo m.

pauper /ˈpɔpər/ n. indigente m. & f.

pause /pɔz/ n. 1. pausa f. —v. 2. pausar.

pave /peiv/ v. pavimentar. **p. the way**, preparar el camino.

pavement /ˈpeivmənt/ n. pavimento m.

pavilion /pəˈvɪlyən/ n. pabellón m.

paw /pɔ/ n. 1. pata f. —v. 2. patear.

pawn /pɔn/ n. 1. prenda f.; (chess) peón de ajedrez m. —v. 2. empeñar.

pay /pei/ n. 1. pago; sueldo, salario m.; —v. 2. pagar. **p. back**, pagar; vengarse de. **p. cash**, pagar en metálico.

payee /peiˈi/ n. destinatario -ria m. & f.

payment /ˈpeimənt/ n. pago m.; recompensa f.

pay phone teléfono público m.

pea /pi/ n. guisante m.

peace /pis/ n. paz f.

peaceable /ˈpisəbəl/ a. pacífico.

peaceful /ˈpisfəl/ a. tranquilo.

peach /pitʃ/ n. durazno, melocotón m.

peacock /ˈpiˌkɒk/ n. pavo real m.

peak /pik/ n. pico, cumbre; máximo m.

peal /pil/ n. repique; estruendo m. **p. of laughter**, risotada f.

peanut /ˈpiˌnʌt/ n. maní, cacahuete m.

pear /pɛər/ n. pera f.

pearl /pɜrl/ n. perla f.

peasant /ˈpɛzənt/ n. campesino -na.

pebble /ˈpɛbəl/ n. guija f.

peck /pɛk/ n. 1. picotazo m. —v. 2. picotear.

peckish /ˈpɛkɪʃ/ a. tener un poco de hambre.

peculiar /pɪˈkyulyər/ a. peculiar.

pecuniary /pɪˈkyuniˌɛri/ a. pecuniario.

pedagogue /ˈpɛdəˌgɒg/ n. pedagogo -ga.

pedagogy /ˈpɛdəˌgoudʒi, -ˌgɒdʒi/ n. pedagogía f.

pedal /ˈpɛdl/ n. pedal m.

pedant /ˈpɛdnt/ n. pedante m. & f.

peddler /ˈpɛdlər/ n. buhonero m.

pedestal /ˈpɛdəstl/ n. pedestal m.

pedestrian /pəˈdɛstriən/ n. peatón -na.

pedestrian crossing paso de peatones m.

pediatrician /ˌpidiəˈtrɪʃən/ n. pediatra m. & f.

pediatrics /ˌpidiˈætrɪks/ n. puericultura f.

pedigree /ˈpɛdɪˌgri/ n. genealogía f.

peek /pik/ n. 1. atisbo m. —v. 2. atisbar.

peel /pil/ n. 1. corteza f.; (fruit) pellejo m. —v. 2. descortezar; pelar.

peep /pip/ n. 1. ojeada f. —v. 2. mirar, atisbar.

peer /pɪər/ n. 1. par m. —v. 2. mirar fijamente.

peg /pɛg/ n. clavija; estaquilla f.; gancho m.

pelt /pɛlt/ n. 1. pellejo m. —v. 2. apedrear; (rain) caer con fuerza.

pelvis /ˈpɛlvɪs/ n. pelvis f.

pen /pɛn/ n. pluma f.; corral m. **fountain p.**, pluma fuente.

penalty /ˈpɛnlti/ n. pena; multa f.; castigo m.

penance /ˈpɛnəns/ n. penitencia f. **to do p.**, penar.

penchant /ˈpɛntʃənt;/ n. propensión f.

pencil /ˈpɛnsəl/ n. lápiz m.

pencil sharpener /ˈʃɑrpənər/ sacapuntas m.

pending /ˈpɛndɪŋ/ a. pendiente. **to be p.**, pender.

penetrate /ˈpɛnɪˌtreit/ v. penetrar.

penetration /ˌpɛnɪˈtreiʃən/ n. penetración f.

penicillin /ˌpɛnəˈsɪlɪn/ n. penicilina f.

peninsula /pəˈnɪnsələ, -ˈnɪnsyələ/ n. península f.

penitent /ˈpɛnɪtənt/ n. & a. penitente m. & f.

penknife /ˈpɛnˌnaif/ n. cortaplumas f.

penniless /ˈpɛnɪlɪs/ a. indigente.

penny /ˈpɛni/ n. penique m.

pension /ˈpɛnʃən/ n. pensión f.

pensive /ˈpɛnsɪv/ a. pensativo.

penultimate /pɪˈnʌltəmɪt/ a. penúltimo.

penury /ˈpɛnyəri/ n. penuria f.

people /ˈpipəl/ n. 1. gente f.; (of a nation) pueblo m. —v. 2. poblar.

pepper /ˈpɛpər/ n. pimienta f.; (plant) pimiento m.

per /pɜr; unstressed pər/ prep. por.

perambulator /pərˈæmbyəˌleitər/ n. cochecillo de niño m.

perceive /pərˈsiv/ v. percibir.

percent /pərˈsɛnt/ adv. por ciento.

percentage /pərˈsɛntɪdʒ/ n. porcentaje m.

perceptible /pərˈsɛptəbəl/ a. perceptible.

perception /pərˈsɛpʃən/ n. percepción f.

perch /pɜrtʃ/ n. percha f.; (fish) perca f.

perdition /pərˈdɪʃən/ n. perdición f.

peremptory /pəˈrɛmptəri/ a. perentorio, terminante.

perennial /pəˈrɛniəl/ a. perenne.

perfect /a. ˈpɜrfɪkt; v. pərˈfɛkt/ a. 1. perfecto. —v. 2. perfeccionar.

perfection /pərˈfɛkʃən/ n. perfección f.

perfectionist /pərˈfɛkʃənɪst/ a. & n. perfeccionista m. & f.

perforation /ˌpɜrfəˈreiʃən/ n. perforación f.

perform /pərˈfɔrm/ v. hacer; ejecutar; Theat. representar.

performance /pərˈfɔrməns/ n. ejecución f.; Theat. representación f.

perfume /n. ˈpɜrfyum; v. pərˈfyum/ n. 1. perfume m.; fragancia f. —v. 2. perfumar.

perfunctory /pərˈfʌŋktəri/ a. perfunctorio, superficial.

perhaps /pərˈhæps/ adv. quizá, quizás, tal vez.

peril /ˈpɛrəl/ n. peligro m.

perilous /ˈpɛrələs/ a. peligroso.

perimeter /pəˈrɪmɪtər/ n. perímetro m.

period /ˈpɪəriəd/ n. período m.; Punct. punto m.

periodic /ˌpɪəriˈɒdɪk/ a. periódico.

periodical /ˌpɪəriˈɒdɪkəl/ n. revista f.

periphery /pəˈrɪfəri/ n. periferia f.

perish /ˈpɛrɪʃ/ v. perecer.

perishable /ˈpɛrɪʃəbəl/ a. perecedero.

perjury /ˈpɜrdʒəri/ n. perjurio m.

permanent /ˈpɜrmənənt/ a. permanente. **p. wave**, ondulado permanente.

permeate /ˈpɜrmiˌeit/ v. penetrar.

permissible /pərˈmɪsəbəl/ a. permisible.

permission /pərˈmɪʃən/ n. permiso m.

permit /n. ˈpɜrmɪt; v. pərˈmɪt/ n. 1. permiso m. —v. 2. permitir.

pernicious /pərˈnɪʃəs/ a. pernicioso.

perpendicular /ˌpɜrpənˈdɪkyələr/ n. & a. perpendicular f.

perpetrate /ˈpɜrpɪˌtreit/ v. perpetrar.

perpetual /pərˈpɛtʃuəl/ a. perpetuo.

perplex /pərˈplɛks/ v. confundir.

perplexity /pərˈplɛksɪti/ n. perplejidad f.

persecute /ˈpɜrsɪˌkyut/ v. perseguir.

persecution /ˌpɜrsɪˈkyuʃən/ n. persecución f.

perseverance /ˌpɜrsəˈvɪərəns/ n. perseverancia f.

persevere /ˌpɜrsəˈvɪər/ v. perseverar.

persist /pərˈsɪst/ v. persistir.

persistent /pərˈsɪstənt/ a. persistente.

person /ˈpɜrsən/ n. persona f.

personage /ˈpɜrsənɪdʒ/ n. personaje m.

personal /ˈpɜrsənl/ a. personal.

personality /ˌpɜrsəˈnælɪti/ n. personalidad f.

personnel /ˌpɜrsəˈnɛl/ n. personal m.

perspective /pərˈspɛktɪv/ n. perspectiva f.

perspiration /ˌpɜrspəˈreiʃən/ n. sudor m.

perspire /pərˈspaiər/ v. sudar.

persuade /pərˈsweid/ v. persuadir.

persuasive /pərˈsweisɪv/ a. persuasivo.

pertain /pərˈtein/ v. pertenecer.

pertinent /ˈpɜrtnənt/ a. pertinente.

perturb /pərˈtɜrb/ v. perturbar.

peruse /pəˈruz/ v. leer con cuidado.

pervade /pərˈveid/ v. penetrar; llenar.

perverse /pərˈvɜrs/ a. perverso.

perversion /pərˈvɜrʒən/ n. perversión f.

pessimism /ˈpɛsəˌmɪzəm/ n. pesimismo m.

pester /ˈpɛstər/ v. molestar; fastidiar.

pesticide /ˈpɛstəˌsaid/ n. pesticida m.

pestilence /ˈpɛstləns/ n. pestilencia f.

pet /pɛt/ n. 1. favorito -ta; animal doméstico m. —v. 2. mimar.

petal /ˈpɛtl/ n. pétalo m.

petition /pəˈtɪʃən/ n. 1. petición, súplica f. —v. 2. pedir, suplicar.

petrify /ˈpɛtrəˌfai/ v. petrificar.

petroleum /pəˈtrouliəm/ n. petróleo m.

petticoat /ˈpɛtiˌkout/ n. enagua f.

petty /ˈpɛti/ a. mezquino, insignificante.

petulant /ˈpɛtʃələnt/ a. quisquilloso.

pew /pyu/ n. banco de iglesia m.

pewter /ˈpyutər/ n. peltre m.

phantom /ˈfæntəm/ n. espectro, fantasma m.

pharmacist /ˈfɑrməsɪst/ n. farmacéutico -ca, boticario -ria.

pharmacy /ˈfɑrməsi/ n. farmacia, botica f.

phase /feiz/ n. fase f.

pheasant /ˈfɛzənt/ n. faisán m.

phenomenal /fɪˈnɒmənl̩/ *a.* fenomenal.
phenomenon /fɪˈnɒməˌnɒn/ *n.* fenómeno *f.*
philanthropy /fɪˈlænθrəpi/ *n.* filantropía *f.*
philately /fɪˈlætl̩i/ *n.* filatelia *f.*
philosopher /fɪˈlɒsəfər/ *n.* filósofo -fa.
philosophical /ˌfɪləˈsɒfɪkəl/ *a.* filosófico.
philosophy /fɪˈlɒsəfi/ *n.* filosofía *f.*
phlegm /flɛm/ *n.* flema *f.*
phlegmatic /flɛgˈmætɪk/ *a.* flemático.
phobia /ˈfoubiə/ *n.* fobia *f.*
phone /foun/ *n.* teléfono *m.*
phonetic /fəˈnɛtɪk/ *a.* fonético.
phonograph /ˈfounəˌgræf/ *n.* fonógrafo *m.*
phosphorus /ˈfɒsfərəs/ *n.* fósforo *m.*
photocopier /ˈfoutəˌkɒpiər/ *n.* fotocopiadora *f.*
photocopy /ˈfoutəˌkɒpi/ *n.* **1.** fotocopia *f.* —*v.* **2.** fotocopiar.
photoelectric /ˌfoutouɪˈlɛktrɪk/ *a.* fotoeléctrico.
photogenic /ˌfoutəˈdʒɛnɪk/ *a.* fotogénico.
photograph /ˈfoutəˌgræf/ *n.* **1.** fotografía *f.* —*v.* **2.** fotografiar; retratar.
photography /fəˈtɒgrəfi/ *n.* fotografía *f.*
phrase /freiz/ *n.* **1.** frase *f.* —*v.* **2.** expresar.
physical /ˈfɪzɪkəl/ *a.* físico.
physician /fɪˈzɪʃən/ *n.* médico *m.* & *f.*
physics /ˈfɪzɪks/ *n.* física *f.*
physiology /ˌfɪziˈɒlədʒi/ *n.* fisiología *f.*
physiotherapy /ˌfɪziouˈθɛrəpi/ *n.* fisioterapia *f.*
physique /fɪˈzik/ *n.* físico *m.*
pianist /piˈænɪst, ˈpiənɪst/ *n.* pianista *m.* & *f.*
piano /piˈænou/ *n.* piano *m.*
picayune /ˌpɪkəˈyun/ *a.* insignificante.
piccolo /ˈpɪkəˌlou/ *n.* flautín *m.*
pick /pɪk/ *n.* **1.** pico *m.* —*v.* **2.** escoger. **p. up,** recoger.
picket /ˈpɪkɪt/ *n.* piquete *m.*
pickle /ˈpɪkəl/ *n.* **1.** salmuera *f.*; encurtido *m.* —*v.* **2.** escabechar.
pickpocket /ˈpɪkˌpɒkɪt/ *n.* cortabolsas *m.* & *f.*
picnic /ˈpɪknɪk/ *n.* picnic *m.*
picture /ˈpɪktʃər/ *n.* **1.** cuadro; retrato *m.*; fotografía *f.*; (movie) película *f.* —*v.* **2.** imaginarse.
picturesque /ˌpɪktʃəˈrɛsk/ *a.* pintoresco.
pie /pai/ *n.* pastel *m.*
piece /pis/ *n.* pedazo *m.*; pieza *f.*
pieceworker /ˈpisˌwɜrkər/ *n.* destajero -ra, destajista *m.* & *f.*
pier /pɪər/ *n.* muelle *m.*
pierce /pɪərs/ *v.* perforar; pinchar; traspasar.
piety /ˈpaiɪti/ *n.* piedad *f.*
pig /pɪg/ *n.* puerco, cerdo, lechón *m.*
pigeon /ˈpɪdʒən/ *n.* paloma *f.*
pigeonhole /ˈpɪdʒənˌhoul/ *n.* casilla *f.*
pigment /ˈpɪgmənt/ *n.* pigmento *m.*
pile /pail/ *n.* **1.** pila *f.*; montón *m.*; *Med.* hemorroides *f.pl.* —*v.* **2.** amontonar.
pilfer /ˈpɪlfər/ *v.* ratear.
pilgrim /ˈpɪlgrɪm/ *n.* peregrino -na, romero -ra.
pilgrimage /ˈpɪlgrəmɪdʒ/ *n.* romería *f.*
pill /pɪl/ *n.* píldora *f.*
pillage /ˈpɪlɪdʒ/ *n.* **1.** pillaje *m.* —*v.* **2.** pillar.
pillar /ˈpɪlər/ *n.* columna *f.*
pillow /ˈpɪlou/ *n.* almohada *f.*
pillowcase /ˈpɪlouˌkeis/ *n.* funda de almohada *f.*
pilot /ˈpailət/ *n.* **1.** piloto *m.* & *f.* —*v.* **2.** pilotar.
pimple /ˈpɪmpəl/ *n.* grano *m.*
pin /pɪn/ *n.* **1.** alfiler; broche *m.*; *Mech.* clavija *f.* —*v.* **2.** prender. **p. up,** fijar.
pinafore /ˈpɪnəˌfɔr/ *n.* delantal (de niña) *m.*
pinch /pɪntʃ/ *n.* **1.** pellizco *m.* —*v.* **2.** pellizcar.
pine /pain/ *n.* **1.** pino *m.* —*v.* **2. p. away,** languidecer. **p. for,** anhelar.
pineapple /ˈpaiˌnæpəl/ *n.* piña *f.*, ananás *m.pl.*
pink /pɪŋk/ *a.* rosado.
pinky /ˈpɪŋki/ *n.* meñique *m.*
pinnacle /ˈpɪnəkəl/ *n.* pináculo *m.*; cumbre *f.*
pint /paint/ *n.* pinta *f.*
pioneer /ˌpaiəˈnɪər/ *n.* pionero -ra.
pious /ˈpaiəs/ *a.* piadoso.
pipe /paip/ *n.* pipa *f.*; tubo; (of organ) cañón *m.*
pipeline /ˈpaipˌlain/ *n.* oleoducto *m.*
piper /ˈpaipər/ *n.* flautista *m.* & *f.*
piquant /ˈpikənt/ *a.* picante.
pirate /ˈpairət/ *n.* pirata *m.*
pistol /ˈpɪstl̩/ *n.* pistola *f.*
piston /ˈpɪstən/ *n.* émbolo, pistón *m.*
pit /pɪt/ *n.* hoyo *m.*; (fruit) hueso *m.*
pitch /pɪtʃ/ *n.* **1.** brea *f.*; grado de inclinación; (music) tono *m.*; —*v.* **2.** lanzar; (ship) cabecear.
pitchblende /ˈpɪtʃˌblɛnd/ *n.* pechblenda *f.*
pitcher /ˈpɪtʃər/ *n.* cántaro *m.*; (baseball) lanzador -ra.
pitchfork /ˈpɪtʃˌfɔrk/ *n.* horca *f.*; tridente *m.*
pitfall /ˈpɪtˌfɔl/ *n.* trampa *f.*, hoya cubierta *f.*
pitiful /ˈpɪtɪfəl/ *a.* lastimoso.
pitiless /ˈpɪtɪlɪs/ *a.* cruel.
pituitary gland /pɪˈtuɪˌtɛri/ glándula pituitaria *f.*
pity /ˈpɪti/ *n.* **1.** compasión, piedad *f.* **to be a p.,** ser lástima. —*v.* **2.** compadecer.
pivot /ˈpɪvət/ *n.* **1.** espiga *f.*, pivote *m.*; punto de partida *m.* —*v.* **2.** girar sobre un pivote.
pizza /ˈpitsə/ *n.* pizza *f.*
placard /ˈplækɑrd/ *n.* **1.** cartel *m.* —*v.* **2.** fijar carteles.
placate /ˈpleikeit/ *v.* aplacar.
place /pleis/ *n.* **1.** lugar, sitio, puesto *m.* —*v.* **2.** colocar, poner.
placid /ˈplæsɪd/ *a.* plácido.
plagiarism /ˈpleidʒəˌrɪzəm/ *n.* plagio *m.*
plague /pleig/ *n.* **1.** plaga, peste *f.* —*v.* **2.** atormentar.
plain /plein/ *a.* **1.** sencillo; puro; evidente. —*n.* **2.** llano *m.*
plaintiff /ˈpleintɪf/ *n.* demandante *m.* & *f.*
plan /plæn/ *n.* **1.** plan, propósito *m.* —*v.* **2.** planear; pensar; planificar. **p. on,** contar con.
plane /plein/ *n.* **1.** plano; (tool) cepillo *m.* —*v.* **2.** allanar; acepillar.
planet /ˈplænɪt/ *n.* planeta *m.*
planetarium /ˌplænɪˈtɛəriəm/ *n.* planetario *m.*
plank /plæŋk/ *n.* tablón *m.*
planning /ˈplænɪŋ/ *n.* planificación *f.*
plant /plænt/ *n.* **1.** mata, planta *f.* —*v.* **2.** sembrar, plantar.
plantation /plænˈteiʃən/ *n.* plantación *f.* **coffee p.,** cafetal *m.*
planter /ˈplæntər/ *n.* plantador; hacendado *m.*
plasma /ˈplæzmə/ *n.* plasma *m.*
plaster /ˈplæstər/ *n.* **1.** yeso; emplasto *m.* —*v.* **2.** enyesar; emplastar.
plastic /ˈplæstɪk/ *a.* plástico.
plate /pleit/ *n.* **1.** plato *m.*; plancha de metal. —*v.* **2.** planchear.
plateau /plæˈtou/ *n.* meseta *f.*
platform /ˈplætfɔrm/ *n.* plataforma *f.*
platinum /ˈplætn̩əm/ *n.* platino *m.*
platitude /ˈplætɪˌtud/ *n.* perogrullada *f.*
platter /ˈplætər/ *n.* fuente *f.*, platel *m.*
plaudit /ˈplɔdɪt/ *n.* aplauso *m.*
plausible /ˈplɔzəbəl/ *a.* plausible.
play /plei/ *n.* **1.** juego *m.*; *Theat.* pieza *f.* —*v.* **2.** jugar; (music) tocar; *Theat.* representar. **p. a part,** hacer un papel.
player /ˈpleiər/ *n.* jugador -ra; (music) músico -ca.; *Theat.* actor *m.*, actriz *f.*
playful /ˈpleifəl/ *a.* juguetón.
playground /ˈpleiˌgraund/ *n.* campo de deportes; patio de recreo.
playmate /ˈpleiˌmeit/. *n.* compañero -ra de juego.
playwright /ˈpleiˌrait/ *n.* dramaturgo -ga.
plea /pli/ *n.* ruego *m.*; súplica *f.*; (legal) declaración *f.*
plead /plid/ *v.* suplicar; declararse. **p. a case,** defender un pleito.
pleasant /ˈplɛzənt/ *a.* agradable.
please /pliz/ *v.* **1.** gustar, agradar. **Pleased to meet you,** Mucho gusto en conocer a Vd. —*adv.* **2.** por favor. **Please...** Haga el favor de..., Tenga la bondad de..., Sírvase...
pleasure /ˈplɛʒər/ *n.* gusto, placer *m.*
pleat /plit/ *n.* **1.** pliegue *m.* —*v.* **2.** plegar.
plebiscite /ˈplɛbəˌsait/ *n.* plebiscito *m.*
pledge /plɛdʒ/ *n.* **1.** empeño *m.* —*v.* **2.** empeñar.
plentiful /ˈplɛntɪfəl/ *a.* abundante.
plenty /ˈplɛnti/ *n.* abundancia *f.* **p. of,** bastante. **p. more,** mucho más.
pleurisy /ˈplʊrəsi/ *n.* pleuritis *f.*
pliable, pliant /ˈplaiəbəl; ˈplaiənt/ *a.* flexible.
pliers /ˈplaiərz/ *n.pl.* alicates *m.pl.*
plight /plait/ *n.* apuro, aprieto *m.*
plot /plɒt/ *n.* **1.** conspiración; (of a story) trama; (of land) parcela *f.* —*v.* **2.** conspirar; tramar.
plow /plau/ *n.* **1.** arado *m.* —*v.* **2.** arar.
pluck /plʌk/ *n.* **1.** valor *m.* —*v.* **2.** arrancar; desplumar.
plug /plʌg/ *n.* **1.** tapón; *Elec.* enchufe *m.* **spark p.,** bujía *f.* —*v.* **2.** tapar.
plum /plʌm/ *n.* ciruela *f.*
plumage /ˈplumɪdʒ/ *n.* plumaje *m.*
plumber /ˈplʌmər/ *n.* fontanero -era, plomero -era.
plume /plum/ *n.* pluma *f.*
plump /plʌmp/ *a.* regordete.
plunder /ˈplʌndər/ *n.* **1.** botín *m.*; despojos *m.pl.* —*v.* **2.** saquear.
plunge /plʌndʒ/ *v.* zambullir; precipitar.
plural /ˈplʊrəl/ *a.* & *n.* plural *m.*
plus /plʌs/ *prep.* más.
plutocrat /ˈplutəˌkræt/ *n.* plutócrata *m.* & *f.*
pneumatic /nʊˈmætɪk/ *a.* neumático.
pneumonia /nʊˈmounyə/ *n.* pulmonía *f.*
poach /poutʃ/ *v.* (eggs) escalfar; invadir; cazar en vedado.
pocket /ˈpɒkɪt/ *n.* **1.** bolsillo *m.* —*v.* **2.** embolsar.
pocketbook /ˈpɒkɪtˌbʊk/ *n.* cartera *f.*
podiatry /pəˈdaiətri/ *n.* podiatría *f.*
poem /ˈpouəm/ *n.* poema *m.*
poet /ˈpouɪt/ *n.* poeta *m.* & *f.*
poetic /pouˈɛtɪk/ *a.* poético.
poetry /ˈpouɪtri/ *n.* poesía *f.*
poignant /ˈpɔinyənt/ *a.* conmovedor.
point /pɔint/ *n.* **1.** punta *f.*; punto *m.* —*v.* **2.** apuntar. **p. out,** señalar.
pointed /ˈpɔintɪd/ *a.* puntiagudo; directo.
pointless /ˈpɔintlɪs/ *a.* inútil.
poise /pɔiz/ *n.* **1.** equilibrio *m.*; serenidad *f.* —*v.* **2.** equilibrar; estar suspendido.
poison /ˈpɔizən/ *n.* **1.** veneno *m.* —*v.* **2.** envenenar.
poisonous /ˈpɔizənəs/ *a.* venenoso.
poke /pouk/ *n.* **1.** empuje *m.*, hurgonada *f.* —*v.* **2.** picar; haronear.
Poland /ˈpoulənd/ *n.* Polonia *f.*
polar /ˈpoulər/ *a.* polar.
pole /poul/ *n.* palo; *Geog.* polo *m.*
polemical /pəˈlɛmɪkəl/ *a.* polémico.
police /pəˈlis/ *n.* policía *f.*
policeman /pəˈlismən/ *n.* policía *m.*
policy /ˈpɒləsi/ *n.* política *f.* **insurance p.,** póliza de seguro.
Polish /ˈpɒlɪʃ/ *a.* & *n.* polaco -ca.
polish /ˈpɒlɪʃ/ *n.* **1.** lustre *m.* —*v.* **2.** pulir, lustrar.
polite /pəˈlait/ *a.* cortés.
politic /ˈpɒlɪtɪk/ **political** *a.* político.
politician /ˌpɒlɪˈtɪʃən/ *n.* político -ca.
politics /ˈpɒlɪtɪks/ *n.* política *f.*
poll /poul/ *n.* encuesta *f.*; (pl.) urnas *f.pl.*
pollen /ˈpɒlən/ *n.* polen *m.*
pollute /pəˈlut/ *v.* contaminar.
pollution /pəˈluʃən/ *n.* contaminación *f.*
polo /ˈpoulou/ *n.* polo *m.*
polyester /ˌpɒliˈɛstər/ *n.* poliéster *m.*
polygamy /pəˈlɪgəmi/ *n.* poligamia *f.*
polygon /ˈpɒliˌgɒn/ *n.* polígono *m.*
pomp /pɒmp/ *n.* pompa *f.*
pompous /ˈpɒmpəs/ *a.* pomposo.
poncho /ˈpɒntʃou/ *n.* poncho *m.*
pond /pɒnd/ *n.* charca *f.*
ponder /ˈpɒndər/ *v.* ponderar, meditar.
ponderous /ˈpɒndərəs/ *a.* ponderoso, pesado.
pontiff /ˈpɒntɪf/ *n.* pontífice *m.*
pontoon /pɒnˈtun/ *n.* pontón *m.*
pony /ˈpouni/ *n.* caballito *m.*
ponytail /ˈpouniˌteil/ *n.* cola de caballo *f.*
poodle /ˈpudl/ *n.* caniche *m.*
pool /pul/ *n.* charco *m.* **swimming p.,** piscina *f.*
poor /pʊr/ *a.* pobre; (not good) malo.
pop /pɒp/ *n.* chasquido *m.*
popcorn /ˈpɒpˌkɔrn/ *n.* rosetas de maíz, palomitas de maíz *f.pl.*
pope /poup/ *n.* papa *m.*
poppy /ˈpɒpi/ *n.* amapola *f.*
popsicle /ˈpɒpsɪkəl/ *n.* polo *m.*
popular /ˈpɒpyələr/ *a.* popular.
popularity /ˌpɒpyəˈlærɪti/ *n.* popularidad *f.*
population /ˌpɒpyəˈleiʃən/ *n.* población *f.*
porcelain /ˈpɔrsəlɪn/ *n.* porcelana *f.*
porch /pɔrtʃ/ *n.* pórtico *m.*; galería *f.*
pore /pɔr/ *n.* poro *m.*
pork /pɔrk/ *n.* carne de puerco.
pornography /pɔrˈnɒgrəfi/ *n.* pornografía *f.*
porous /ˈpɔrəs/ *a.* poroso, esponjoso.
port /pɔrt/ *n.* puerto; *Naut.* babor *m.* **p. wine,** oporto *m.*
portable /ˈpɔrtəbəl/ *a.* portátil.
portal /ˈpɔrtl̩/ *n.* portal *m.*
portend /pɔrˈtɛnd/ *v.* pronosticar.
portent /ˈpɔrtɛnt/ *n.* presagio *m.*, portento *m.*
porter /ˈpɔrtər/ *n.* portero *m.*
portfolio /pɔrtˈfouliˌou/ *n.* cartera *f.*
porthole /ˈpɔrtˌhoul/ *n.* porta *f.*
portion /ˈpɔrʃən/ *n.* porción *f.*
portly /ˈpɔrtli/ *a.* corpulento.
portrait /ˈpɔrtrɪt/ *n.* retrato *m.*
portray /pɔrˈtrei/ *v.* pintar.
Portugal /ˈpɔrtʃəgəl/ *n.* Portugal *m.*
Portuguese /ˌpɔrtʃəˈgiz/ *a.* & *n.* portugués -esa.
pose /pouz/ *n.* **1.** postura; actitud *f.* —*v.* **2.** posar. **p. as,** pretender ser.
position /pəˈzɪʃən/ *n.* posición *f.*
positive /ˈpɒzɪtɪv/ *a.* positivo.
possess /pəˈzɛs/ *v.* poseer.
possession /pəˈzɛʃən/ *n.* posesión *f.*
possessive /pəˈzɛsɪv/ *a.* posesivo.
possibility /ˌpɒsəˈbɪlɪti/ *n.* posibilidad *f.*
possible /ˈpɒsəbəl/ *a.* posible.
post /poust/ *n.* **1.** poste; puesto *m.* —*v.* **2.** fijar; situar; echar al correo.
postage /ˈpoustɪdʒ/ *n.* porte de correo. **p. stamp,** sello *m.*
postal /ˈpoustl̩/ *a.* postal.
post card tarjeta postal.
poster /ˈpoustər/ *n.* cartel, letrero *m.*
posterior /pɒˈstɪəriər/ *a.* posterior.
posterity /pɒˈstɛrɪti/ *n.* posteridad *f.*
postgraduate /poustˈgrædʒuɪt/ *a.* & *n.* postgraduado -da.

postmark /'poust,mɑrk/ *n.* matasellos *m.*

post office correos *m.pl.*

postpone /poust'poun/ *v.* posponer, aplazar.

postscript /'poust,skrɪpt/ *n.* posdata *f.*

posture /'pɒstʃər/ *n.* postura *f.*

pot /pɒt/ *n.* olla, marmita; (marijuana) marijuana, hierba *f.* **flower p.,** tiesto *m.*

potassium /pə'tæsiəm/ *n.* potasio *m.*

potato /pə'teitou/ *n.* patata, papa *f.* **sweet p.,** batata *f.*

potent /'poutn̩t/ *a.* potente, poderoso.

potential /pə'tɛnʃəl/ *a. & n.* potencial *f.*

potion /'pouʃən/ *n.* poción, pócima *f.*

pottery /'pɒtəri/ *n.* alfarería *f.*

pouch /pautʃ/ *n.* saco *m.*; bolsa *f.*

poultry /'poultri/ *n.* aves de corral.

pound /paund/ *n.* **1.** libra *f.* —*v.* **2.** golpear.

pour /pɔr/ *v.* echar; verter; llover a cántaros.

poverty /'pɒvərti/ *n.* pobreza *f.*

powder /'paudər/ *n.* **1.** polvo *m.;* (gun) pólvora *f.* —*v.* **2.** empolvar; pulverizar.

power /'pauər/ *n.* poder *m.;* potencia *f.*

powerful /'pauərfəl/ *a.* poderoso, fuerte.

powerless /'pauərlɪs/ *a.* impotente.

practical /'præktɪkəl/ *a.* práctico.

practical joke inocentada *f.*

practically /'præktɪkli/ *adv.* casi; prácticamente.

practice /'præktɪs/ *n.* **1.** práctica; costumbre; clientela *f.* —*v.* **2.** practicar; ejercer.

practiced /'præktɪst/ *a.* experto.

practitioner /præk'tɪʃənər/ *n.* practicante *m. & f.*

pragmatic /præg'mætɪk/ *a.* pragmático.

prairie /'prɛəri/ *n.* llanura; *S.A.* pampa *f.*

praise /preiz/ *n.* **1.** alabanza *f.* —*v.* **2.** alabar.

prank /præŋk/ *n.* travesura *f.*

prawn /prɔn/ *n.* gamba *f.*

pray /prei/ *v.* rezar; (beg) rogar.

prayer /'preiər/ *n.* oración; súplica *f.*, ruego *m.*

preach /pritʃ/ *v.* predicar; sermonear.

preacher /'pritʃər/ *n.* predicador *m.*

preamble /'pri,æmbəl/ *n.* preámbulo *m.*

precarious /prɪ'kɛəriəs/ *a.* precario.

precaution /prɪ'kɔʃən/ *n.* precaución *f.*

precede /prɪ'sid/ *v.* preceder, anteceder.

precedent /*n.* 'prɛsɪdənt; *a.* prɪ'sidnt/ *n. & a.* precedente *m.*

precept /'prisɛpt/ *n.* precepto *m.*

precinct /'prisɪŋkt/ *n.* recinto *m.*

precious /'prɛʃəs/ *a.* precioso.

precipice /'prɛsəpɪs/ *n.* precipicio *m.*

precipitate /prɪ'sɪpɪ,teit/ *v.* precipitar.

precise /prɪ'sais/ *a.* preciso, exacto.

precision /prɪ'sɪʒən/ *n.* precisión *f.*

preclude /prɪ'klud/ *v.* evitar.

precocious /prɪ'kouʃəs/ *a.* precoz.

precooked /pri'kukt/ *a.* precocinado.

predatory /'prɛdə,tɔri/ *a.* de rapiña, rapaz.

predecessor /'prɛdə,sɛsər/ *n.* predecesor -ra, antecesor -ra.

predicament /prɪ'dɪkəmənt/ *n.* dificultad *f.;* apuro *m.*

predict /prɪ'dɪkt/ *v.* pronosticar, predecir.

predictable /prɪ'dɪktəbəl/ *a.* previsible.

predilection /,prɛdl̩'ɛkʃən/ *n.* predilección *f.*

predispose /,pridɪ'spouz/ *v.* predisponer.

predominant /prɪ'dɒmənənt/ *a.* predominante.

prefabricate /pri'fæbrɪ,keit/ *v.* fabricar de antemano.

preface /'prɛfɪs/ *n.* prefacio *m.*

prefer /prɪ'fɜr/ *v.* preferir.

preferable /'prɛfərəbəl/ *a.* preferible.

preference /'prɛfərəns/ *n.* preferencia *f.*

prefix /'prifɪks/ *n.* **1.** prefijo *m.* —*v.* **2.** prefijar.

pregnant /'prɛgnənt/ *a.* preñada.

prehistoric /,prihɪ'stɔrɪk/ *a.* prehistórico.

prejudice /'prɛdʒədɪs/ *n.* prejuicio *m.*

prejudiced /'prɛdʒədɪst/ *a.* (*S.A.*) prejuiciado.

preliminary /prɪ'lɪmə,nɛri/ *a.* preliminar.

prelude /'prɛlyud/ *n.* preludio *m.*

premature /,primə'tʃʊr/ *a.* prematuro.

premeditate /prɪ'mɛdɪ,teit/ *v.* premeditar.

premier /prɪ'mɪər/ *n.* primer ministro.

première /prɪ'mɪər/ *n.* estreno *m.*

premise /'prɛmɪs/ *n.* premisa *f.*

premium /'primiəm/ *n.* premio *m.*

premonition /,primə'nɪʃən/ *n.* presentimiento *m.*

prenatal /pri'neitl/ *a.* prenatal.

preparation /,prɛpə'reiʃən/ *n.* preparativo *m.;* preparación *f.*

preparatory /prɪ'pærə,tɔri/ *a.* preparatorio. **p. to,** antes de.

prepare /prɪ'pɛər/ *v.* preparar.

preponderant /prɪ'pɒndərənt/ *a.* preponderante.

preposition /,prɛpə'zɪʃən/ *n.* preposición *f.*

preposterous /prɪ'pɒstərəs/ *a.* prepóstero, absurdo.

prerequisite /prɪ'rɛkwəzɪt/ *n.* requisito previo.

prerogative /prɪ'rɒgətɪv/ *n.* prerrogativa *f.*

prescribe /prɪ'skraib/ *v.* prescribir; *Med.* recetar.

prescription /prɪ'skrɪpʃən/ *n.* prescripción; *Med.* receta *f.*

presence /'prɛzəns/ *n.* presencia *f.;* porte *m.*

present /*a, n* 'prɛzənt; *v* prɪ'zɛnt/ *a.* **1.** presente. **to be present at,** asistir a. —*n.* **2.** presente; (gift) regalo *m.* **at p.,** ahora, actualmente. **for the p.,** por ahora. —*v.* **3.** presentar.

presentable /prɪ'zɛntəbəl/ *a.* presentable.

presentation /,prɛzən'teiʃən/ *n.* presentación; introducción *f.; Theat.* representación *f.*

presently /'prɛzəntli/ *adv.* luego; dentro de poco.

preservative /prɪ'zɜrvətɪv/ *a. & n.* preservativo *m.*

preserve /prɪ'zɜrv/ *n.* **1.** conserva *f.;* (hunting) vedado *m.* —*v.* **2.** preservar.

preside /prɪ'zaid/ *v.* presidir.

presidency /'prɛzɪdənsi/ *n.* presidencia *f.*

president /'prɛzɪdənt/ *n.* presidente -ta.

press /prɛs/ *n.* **1.** prensa *f.* —*v.* **2.** apretar; urgir; (clothes) planchar.

pressing /'prɛsɪŋ/ *a.* urgente.

pressure /'prɛʃər/ *n.* presión *f.*

pressure cooker /'kukər/ cocina de presión *f.*

prestige /prɛ'stiʒ/ *n.* prestigio *m.*

presume /prɪ'zum/ *v.* presumir, suponer.

presumptuous /prɪ'zʌmptʃuəs/ *a.* presuntuoso.

presuppose /,prisə'pouz/ *v.* presuponer.

pretend /prɪ'tɛnd/ *v.* fingir. **p. to the throne,** aspirar al trono.

pretense /prɪ'tɛns, 'pritɛns/ *n.* pretensión *f.;* fingimiento *m.*

pretension /prɪ'tɛnʃən/ *n.* pretensión *f.*

pretentious /prɪ'tɛnʃəs/ *a.* presumido.

pretext /'pritɛkst/ *n.* pretexto *m.*

pretty /'prɪti/ *a.* **1.** bonito, lindo. —*adv.* **2.** bastante.

prevail /prɪ'veil/ *v.* prevalecer.

prevailing /prɪ'veilɪŋ/ **prevalent** *a.* predominante.

prevent /prɪ'vɛnt/ *v.* impedir; evitar.

prevention /prɪ'vɛnʃən/ *n.* prevención *f.*

preventive /prɪ'vɛntɪv/ *a.* preventivo.

preview /'pri,vyu/ *n.* vista anticipada *f.*

previous /'priviəs/ *a.* anterior, previo.

prey /prei/ *n.* presa *f.*

price /prais/ *n.* precio *m.*

priceless /'praislɪs/ *a.* sin precio.

prick /prɪk/ *n.* **1.** punzada *f.* —*v.* **2.** punzar.

pride /praid/ *n.* orgullo *m.*

priest /prist/ *n.* sacerdote, cura *m.*

prim /prɪm/ *a.* estirado, remilgado.

primary /'praimɛri/ *a.* primario, principal.

prime /praim/ *a.* **1.** primero. —*n.* **2.** flor *f.* —*v.* **3.** alistar.

prime minister primer ministro *m. & f.*

primitive /'prɪmɪtɪv/ *a.* primitivo.

prince /prɪns/ *n.* príncipe *m.*

Prince Charming Príncipe Azul *m.*

princess /'prɪnsɪs/ *n.* princesa *f.*

principal /'prɪnsəpəl/ *a.* **1.** principal. —*n.* **2.** principal *m. & f.;* director -ra.

principle /'prɪnsəpəl/ *n.* principio *m.*

print /prɪnt/ *n.* **1.** letra de molde *f.;* (art) grabado *m.* —*v.* **2.** imprimir, estampar.

printer /'prɪntər/ *n.* impresora *f.*

printing /'prɪntɪŋ/ *n.* impresión; **p. office,** imprenta *f.*

printing press prensa *f.*

printout /'prɪnt,aut/ *n.* impreso producido por una computadora, impresión *f.*

priority /prai'ɔrɪti/ *n.* prioridad, precedencia *f.*

prism /'prɪzəm/ *n.* prisma *m.*

prison /'prɪzən/ *n.* prisión, cárcel *f.*

prisoner /'prɪzənər/ *n.* presidiario -ria, prisionero -ra, preso -sa.

pristine /'prɪstin/ *a.* inmaculado.

privacy /'praivəsi/ *n.* soledad *f.*

private /'praivɪt/ *a.* **1.** particular. —*n.* **2.** soldado raso. **in p.,** en particular.

privation /prai'veiʃən/ *n.* privación *f.*

privet /'prɪvɪt/ *n.* ligustro *m.*

privilege /'prɪvəlɪdʒ/ *n.* privilegio *m.*

privy /'prɪvi/ *n.* letrina *f.*

prize /praiz/ *n.* **1.** premio *m.* —*v.* **2.** apreciar, estimar.

probability /,prɒbə'bɪlɪti/ *n.* probabilidad *f.*

probable /'prɒbəbəl/ *a.* probable.

probate /'proubeit/ *a.* testamentario.

probation /prou'beiʃən/ *n.* prueba *f.;* probación *f.;* libertad condicional *f.*

probe /proub/ *n.* **1.** indagación *f.* —*v.* **2.** indagar; tentar.

probity /'proubɪti/ *n.* probidad *f.*

problem /'prɒbləm/ *n.* problema *m.*

procedure /prə'sidʒər/ *n.* procedimiento *m.*

proceed /prə'sid/ *v.* proceder; proseguir.

process /'prɒsɛs/ *n.* proceso *m.*

procession /prə'sɛʃən/ *n.* procesión *f.*

proclaim /prou'kleim/ *v.* proclamar, anunciar.

proclamation /,prɒklə'meiʃən/ *n.* proclamación *f.;* decreto *m.*

procrastinate /prou'kræstə,neit/ *v.* dilatar.

procure /prou'kyʊr/ *v.* obtener, procurar.

prodigal /'prɒdɪgəl/ *n. & a.* pródigo -ga.

prodigy /'prɒdɪdʒi/ *n.* prodigio *m.*

produce /prə'dus/ *v.* producir.

product /'prɒdəkt/ *n.* producto *m.*

production /prə'dʌkʃən/ *n.* producción *f.*

productive /prə'dʌktɪv/ *a.* productivo.

profane /prə'fein/ *a.* **1.** profano. —*v.* **2.** profanar.

profanity /prə'fænɪti/ *n.* profanidad *f.*

profess /prə'fɛs/ *v.* profesar; declarar.

profession /prə'fɛʃən/ *n.* profesión *f.*

professional /prə'fɛʃənl/ *a. & n.* profesional *m. & f.*

professor /prə'fɛsər/ *n.* profesor -ra; catedrático -ca.

proficient /prə'fɪʃənt/ *a.* experto, proficiente.

profile /'proufail/ *n.* perfil *m.*

profit /'prɒfɪt/ *n.* **1.** provecho *m.;* ventaja *f.; Com.* ganancia *f.* —*v.* **2.** aprovechar; beneficiar.

profitable /'prɒfɪtəbəl/ *a.* provechoso, ventajoso, lucrativo.

profiteer /,prɒfɪ'tɪər/ *n.* **1.** explotador -ra. —*v.* **2.** explotar.

profound /prə'faund/ *a.* profundo, hondo.

profuse /prə'fyus/ *a.* pródigo; profuso.

prognosis /prɒg'nousɪs/ *n.* pronóstico *m.*

program /'prougræm/ *n.* programa *m.*

progress /*n.* 'prɒgrɛs; *v.* prə'grɛs/ *n.* **1.** progresos *m.pl.* **in p.,** en marcha. —*v.* **2.** progresar; marchar.

progressive /prə'grɛsɪv/ *a.* progresivo; progresista.

prohibit /prou'hɪbɪt/ *v.* prohibir.

prohibition /,prouə'bɪʃən/ *n.* prohibición *f.*

prohibitive /prou'hɪbɪtɪv/ *a.* prohibitivo.

project /*n.* 'prɒdʒɛkt; *v.* prə'dʒɛkt/ *n.* **1.** proyecto *m.* —*v.* **2.** proyectar.

projectile /prə'dʒɛktɪl/ *n.* proyectil *m.*

projection /prə'dʒɛkʃən/ *n.* proyección *f.*

projector /prə'dʒɛktər/ *n.* proyector *m.*

proliferation /prə,lɪfə'reiʃən/ *n.* proliferación *f.*

prolific /prə'lɪfɪk/ *a.* prolífico.

prologue /'proulɔg/ *n.* prólogo *m.*

prolong /prə'lɔŋ/ *v.* prolongar.

prominent /'prɒmənənt/ *a.* prominente; eminente.

promiscuous /prə'mɪskyuəs/ *a.* promiscuo.

promise /'prɒmɪs/ *n.* **1.** promesa *f.* —*v.* **2.** prometer.

promote /prə'mout/ *v.* fomentar; estimular; adelantar; promocionar.

promotion /prə'mouʃən/ *n.* promoción *f.;* adelanto *m.*

prompt /prɒmpt/ *a.* **1.** puntual. —*v.* **2.** impulsar; *Theat.* apuntar. —*adv.* **3.** pronto.

promulgate /'prɒməl,geit/ *v.* promulgar.

pronoun /'prou,naun/ *n.* pronombre *m.*

pronounce /prə'nauns/ *v.* pronunciar.

pronunciation /prə,nʌnsi'eiʃən/ *n.* pronunciación *f.*

proof /pruf/ *n.* prueba *f.*

proof of purchase certificado de compra *m.*

proofread /'pruf,rid/ *v.* corregir pruebas.

prop /prɒp/ *n.* **1.** apoyo, *m.* —*v.* **2.** sostener.

propaganda /,prɒpə'gændə/ *n.* propaganda *f.*

propagate /'prɒpə,geit/ *v.* propagar.

propel /prə'pɛl/ *v.* propulsar.

propeller /prə'pɛlər/ *n.* hélice *f.*

propensity /prə'pɛnsɪti/ *n.* tendencia *f.*

proper /'prɒpər/ *a.* propio; correcto.

property /'prɒpərti/ *n.* propiedad *f.*

prophecy /'prɒfəsi/ *n.* profecía *f.*

prophesy /'prɒfə,sai/ *v.* predecir, profetizar.

prophet /'prɒfɪt/ *n.* profeta *m.*

prophetic /prə'fɛtɪk/ *a.* profético.

propitious /prə'pɪʃəs/ *a.* propicio.

proponent /prəˈpounənt/ *n.* & *a.* proponente *m.*
proportion /prəˈpɔrʃən/ *n.* proporción *f.*
proportionate /prəˈpɔrʃənɪt/ *a.* proporcionado.
proposal /prəˈpouzəl/ *n.* propuesta; oferta *f.;* (marriage) declaración *f.*
propose /prəˈpouz/ *v.* proponer; pensar; declararse.
proposition /ˌprɒpəˈzɪʃən/ *n.* proposición *f.*
proprietor /prəˈpraiɪtər/ *n.* propietario -ria, dueño -ña.
propriety /prəˈpraiɪti/ *n.* corrección *f.*, decoro *m.*
prosaic /prouˈzeiɪk/ *a.* prosaico.
proscribe /prouˈskraib/ *v.* proscribir.
prose /prouz/ *n.* prosa *f.*
prosecute /ˈprɒsɪˌkyut/ *v.* acusar, procesar.
prospect /ˈprɒspɛkt/ *n.* perspectiva; esperanza *f.*
prospective /prəˈspɛktɪv/ *a.* anticipado, presunto.
prosper /ˈprɒspər/ *v.* prosperar.
prosperity /prɒˈspɛrɪti/ *n.* prosperidad *f.*
prosperous /ˈprɒspərəs/ *a.* próspero.
prostate gland /ˈprɒsteit/ glándula prostática *f.*
prostitute /ˈprɒstɪˌtut/ *n.* **1.** prostituta *f.* —*v.* **2.** prostituir.
prostrate /ˈprɒstreit/ *a.* **1.** postrado. —*v.* **2.** postrar.
protect /prəˈtɛkt/ *v.* proteger; amparar.
protection /prəˈtɛkʃən/ *n.* protección *f.;* amparo *m.*
protective /prəˈtɛktɪv/ *a.* protector.
protector /prəˈtɛktər/ *n.* protector -ora.
protégé /ˈproutəˌʒei/ *n.* protegido -da.
protein /ˈproutin, -tiɪn/ *n.* proteína *f.*
protest /*n.* ˈproutɛst; *v.* prəˈtɛst, ˈproutɛst/ *n.* **1.** protesta *f.* —*v.* **2.** protestar.
Protestant /ˈprɒtəstənt/ *a.* & *n.* protestante *m.* & *f.*
protocol /ˈproutəˌkɔl/ *n.* protocolo *m.*
proton /ˈproutɒn/ *n.* protón *m.*
protract /prouˈtrækt/ *v.* alargar, demorar.
protrude /prouˈtrud/ *v.* salir fuera.
protuberance /prouˈtubərəns/ *n.* protuberancia *f.*
proud /praud/ *a.* orgulloso.
prove /pruv/ *v.* comprobar.
proverb /ˈprɒvərb/ *n.* proverbio, refrán *m.*
provide /prəˈvaid/ *v.* proporcionar; proveer.
provided /prəˈvaidɪd/ *conj.* con tal que.
providence /ˈprɒvɪdəns/ *n.* providencia *f.*
province /ˈprɒvɪns/ *n.* provincia *f.*
provincial /prəˈvɪnʃəl/ *a.* **1.** provincial. —*n.* **2.** provinciano -na.
provision /prəˈvɪʒən/ *n.* **1.** provisión *f.;* (pl.) comestibles *m.pl.* —*v.* **2.** abastecer.
provocation /ˌprɒvəˈkeiʃən/ *n.* provocación *f.*
provoke /prəˈvouk/ *v.* provocar.
prowess /ˈprauɪs/ *n.* proeza *f.*
prowl /praul/ *v.* rondar.
prowler /ˈpraulər/ *n.* merodeador -dora *m.* & *f.*
proximity /prɒkˈsɪmɪti/ *n.* proximidad *f.*
proxy /ˈprɒksi/ *n.* delegado -da. **by p.,** mediante apoderado.
prudence /ˈprudn̩s/ *n.* prudencia *f.*
prudent /ˈprudn̩t/ *a.* prudente, cauteloso.
prune /prun/ *n.* ciruela pasa *f.*
pry /prai/ *v.* atisbar; curiosear; *Mech.* alzaprimar.
psalm /sɑm/ *n.* salmo *m.*
pseudonym /ˈsudn̩ɪm/ *n.* seudónimo *m.*
psychedelic /ˌsaikɪˈdɛlɪk/ *a.* psiquedélico.
psychiatrist /sɪˈkaiətrɪst, sai-/ *n.* psiquiatra *m.* & *f.*
psychiatry /sɪˈkaiətri, sai-/ *n.* psiquiatría *f.*
psychoanalysis /ˌsaikouəˈnæləsɪs/ *n.* psicoanálisis *m.*
psychoanalyst /ˌsaikouˈænl̩ɪst/ *n.* psicoanalista *m.* & *f.*
psychological /ˌsaikəˈlɒdʒɪkəl/ *a.* psicológico.
psychology /saiˈkɒlədʒi/ *n.* psicología *f.*
psychosis /saiˈkousɪs/ *n.* psicosis *f.*
ptomaine /ˈtoumein/ *n.* tomaína *f.*
pub /pʌb/ *n.* bar *m.*
public /ˈpʌblɪk/ *a.* & *n.* público *m.*
publication /ˌpʌblɪˈkeiʃən/ *n.* publicación; revista *f.*
publicity /pʌˈblɪsɪti/ *n.* publicidad *f.*
publicity agent publicista *m.* & *f.*
publish /ˈpʌblɪʃ/ *v.* publicar.
publisher /ˈpʌblɪʃər/ *n.* editor -ora.
pudding /ˈpʊdɪŋ/ *n.* pudín *m.*
puddle /ˈpʌdl/ *n.* charco, lodazal *m.*
Puerto Rican /ˈpwɛrtə ˈrikən, ˈpɔr-/ *a.* & *n.* puertorriqueño -ña.
Puerto Rico /ˈpwɛrˈtə rikou, ˈpɔrtə/ Puerto Rico *m.*
puff /pʌf/ *n.* **1.** soplo *m.;* (of smoke) bocanada *f.* **powder p.,** polvera *f.* —*v.* **2.** jadear; echar bocanadas. **p. up,** hinchar; *Fig.* engreír.
pugnacious /pʌgˈneiʃəs/ *a.* pugnaz.
puh-lease! /pʌ ˈliz/ ¡Favor!
pull /pʊl/ *n.* **1.** tirón *m.;* *Colloq.* influencia *f.* —*v.* **2.** tirar; halar.
pulley /ˈpʊli/ *n.* polea *f.*, motón *m.*
pulmonary /ˈpʌlməˌnɛri/ *a.* pulmonar.
pulp /pʌlp/ *n.* pulpa; (of fruit) carne *f.*
pulpit /ˈpʊlpɪt, ˈpʌl-/ *n.* púlpito *m.*
pulsar /ˈpʌlsɑr/ *n.* pulsar *m.*
pulsate /ˈpʌlseit/ *v.* pulsar.
pulse /pʌls/ *n.* pulso *m.*
pump /pʌmp/ *n.* **1.** bomba *f.* —*v.* **2.** bombear. **p. up,** inflar.
pumpkin /ˈpʌmpkɪn/ *n.* calabaza *f.*
pun /pʌn/ *n.* juego de palabras.
punch /pʌntʃ/ *n.* **1.** puñetazo; *Mech.* punzón; (beverage) ponche *m.* —*v.* **2.** dar puñetazos; punzar.
punch bowl ponchera *f.*
punctual /ˈpʌŋktʃuəl/ *a.* puntual.
punctuate /ˈpʌŋktʃuˌeit/ *v.* puntuar.
puncture /ˈpʌŋktʃər/ *n.* **1.** pinchazo *m.*, perforación *f.* —*v.* **2.** pinchar, perforar.
pungent /ˈpʌndʒənt/ *a.* picante, pungente.
punish /ˈpʌnɪʃ/ *v.* castigar.
punishment /ˈpʌnɪʃmənt/ *n.* castigo *m.*
punitive /ˈpyunɪtɪv/ *a.* punitivo.
puny /ˈpyuni/ *a.* encanijado.
pupil /ˈpyupəl/ *n.* alumno -na; *Anat.* pupila *f.*
puppet /ˈpʌpɪt/ *n.* muñeco *m.*
puppy /ˈpʌpi/ *n.* perrito -ta.
purchase /ˈpɜrtʃəs/ *n.* **1.** compra *f.* —*v.* **2.** comprar.
purchasing power /ˈpɜrtʃəsɪŋ/ poder adquisitivo *m.*
pure /pyʊr/ *a.* puro.
purée /pyʊˈrei/ *n.* puré *m.*
purge /pɜrdʒ/ *v.* purgar.
purify /ˈpyʊrəˌfai/ *v.* purificar.
puritanical /ˌpyʊrɪˈtænɪkəl/ *a.* puritano.
purity /ˈpyʊrɪti/ *n.* pureza *f.*
purple /ˈpɜrpəl/ *a.* **1.** purpúreo. —*n.* **2.** púrpura *f.*
purport /*n.* ˈpɜrpɔrt; *v.* pərˈpɔrt/ *n.* **1.** significación *f.* —*v.* **2.** significar.
purpose /ˈpɜrpəs/ *n.* propósito *m.* **on p.,** de propósito.
purr /pɜr/ *v.* ronronear.
purse /pɜrs/ *n.* bolsa *f.*
pursue /pərˈsu/ *v.* perseguir.
pursuit /pərˈsut/ *n.* caza; busca; ocupación *f.* **p. plane,** avión de caza *m.*
push /pʊʃ/ *n.* **1.** empuje; impulso *m.* —*v.* **2.** empujar.
put /pʊt/ *v.* poner, colocar. **p. away,** guardar. **p. in,** meter. **p. off,** dejar. **p. on,** ponerse. **p. out,** apagar. **p. up with,** aguantar.
putrid /ˈpyutrɪd/ *a.* podrido.
putt /pʌt/ *n.* (golf) golpe corto *m.*
puzzle /ˈpʌzəl/ *n.* **1.** enigma; rompecabezas *m.* —*v.* **2.** dejar perplejo. **p. out,** descifrar.
pyramid /ˈpɪrəmɪd/ *n.* pirámide *f.*
pyromania /ˌpairəˈmeiniə/ *n.* piromanía *f.*

Q

quack /kwæk/ *n.* **1.** (doctor) curandero -ra; (duck) graznido *m.* —*v.* **2.** graznar.
quadrangle /ˈkwɒdˌræŋgəl/ *n.* cuadrángulo *m.*
quadraphonic /ˌkwɒdrəˈfɒnɪk/ *a.* cuatrifónico.
quadruped /ˈkwɒdrʊˌpɛd/ *a.* & *n.* cuadrúpedo *m.*
quail /kweil/ *n.* **1.** codorniz *f.* —*v.* **2.** descorazonarse.
quaint /kweint/ *a.* curioso.
quake /kweik/ *n.* **1.** temblor *m.* —*v.* **2.** temblar.
qualification /ˌkwɒləfɪˈkeiʃən/ *n.* requisito *m.;* (pl.) preparaciones *f.pl.*
qualified /ˈkwɒləˌfaid/ *a.* calificado, competente; preparado.
qualify /ˈkwɒləˌfai/ *v.* calificar, modificar; llenar los requisitos.
quality /ˈkwɒlɪti/ *n.* calidad *f.*
quandary /ˈkwɒndəri, -dri/ *n.* incertidumbre *f.*
quantity /ˈkwɒntɪti/ *n.* cantidad *f.*
quarantine /ˈkwɔrənˌtin, ˈkwɒr-, ˌkwɔrənˈtin, ˌkwɒr-/ *n.* cuarentena *f.*
quarrel /ˈkwɔrəl, ˈkwɒr-/ *n.* **1.** riña, disputa *f.* —*v.* **2.** reñir, disputar.
quarry /ˈkwɔri, ˈkwɒri/ *n.* cantera; (hunting) presa *f.*
quarter /ˈkwɔrtər/ *n.* cuarto *m.;* (pl.) vivienda *f.*
quarterly /ˈkwɔrtərli/ *a.* **1.** trimestral. —*adv.* **2.** por cuartos.
quartet /kwɔrˈtɛt/ *n.* cuarteto *m.*
quartz /kwɔrts/ *n.* cuarzo *m.*
quasar /ˈkweizɑr/ *n.* cuasar *m.*
quaver /ˈkweivər/ *v.* temblar.
queen /kwin/ *n.* reina *f.;* (chess) dama *f.*
queer /kwɪər/ *a.* extraño, raro.
quell /kwɛl/ *v.* reprimir.
quench /kwɛntʃ/ *v.* apagar.
query /ˈkwɪəri/ *n.* **1.** pregunta *f.* —*v.* **2.** preguntar.
quest /kwɛst/ *n.* busca *f.*
question /ˈkwɛstʃən/ *n.* **1.** pregunta; cuestión *f.* **q. mark,** signo de interrogación. —*v.* **2.** preguntar; interrogar; dudar.
questionable /ˈkwɛstʃənəbəl/ *a.* dudoso.
questionnaire /ˌkwɛstʃəˈnɛər/ *n.* cuestionario *m.*
quiche /kiʃ/ *n.* quiche *f.*
quick /kwɪk/ *a.* rápido.
quicken /ˈkwɪkən/ *v.* acelerar.
quicksand /ˈkwɪkˌsænd/ *n.* arena movediza.
quiet /ˈkwaiɪt/ *a.* **1.** quieto, tranquilo; callado. **be q., keep q.,** callarse. —*n.* **2.** calma; quietud *f.* —*v.* **3.** tranquilizar. **q. down,** callarse; calmarse.
quilt /kwɪlt/ *n.* colcha *f.*
quinine /ˈkwainain/ *n.* quinina *f.*
quintet /kwɪnˈtɛt/ *n.* *Mus.* quinteto *m.*
quip /kwɪp/ *n.* **1.** pulla *f.* —*v.* **2.** echar pullas.
quit /kwɪt/ *v.* dejar; renunciar a. **q. doing** (etc.) dejar de hacer (etc.).
quite /kwait/ *adv.* bastante; completamente. **not q.,** no precisamente; no completamente.
quiver /ˈkwɪvər/ *n.* **1.** aljaba *f.;* temblor *m.* —*v.* **2.** temblar.
quixotic /kwɪkˈsɒtɪk/ *a.* quijotesco.
quorum /ˈkwɔrəm/ *n.* quórum *m.*
quota /ˈkwoutə/ *n.* cuota *f.*
quotation /kwouˈteiʃən/ *n.* citación; *Com.* cotización *f.* **q. marks,** comillas *f.pl.*
quote /kwout/ *v.* citar; *Com.* cotizar.

R

rabbi /ˈræbai/ *n.* rabí, rabino *m.*
rabbit /ˈræbɪt/ *n.* conejo *m.*
rabble /ˈræbəl/ *n.* canalla *f.*
rabid /ˈræbɪd/ *a.* rabioso.
rabies /ˈreibiz/ *n.* hidrofobia *f.*
race /reis/ *n.* **1.** raza; carrera *f.* —*v.* **2.** echar una carrera; correr de prisa.
race track /ˈreisˌtræk/ hipódromo *m.*
rack /ræk/ *n.* **1.** (cooking) pesebre *m.;* (clothing) colgador *m.* —*v.* **2.** atormentar.
racket /ˈrækɪt/ *n.* (noise) ruido *m.;* (tennis) raqueta *f.;* (graft) fraude organizado.
radar /ˈreidɑr/ *n.* radar *m.*
radiance /ˈreidiəns/ *n.* brillo *m.*
radiant /ˈreidiənt/ *a.* radiante.
radiate /ˈreidiˌeit/ *v.* irradiar.
radiation /ˌreidiˈeiʃən/ *n.* irradiación *f.*
radiator /ˈreidiˌeitər/ *n.* calorífero *m.;* *Auto.* radiador *m.*
radical /ˈrædɪkəl/ *a.* & *n.* radical *m.*
radio /ˈreidiˌou/ *n.* radio *m.* or *f.* **r. station,** estación radiodifusora *f.*
radioactive /ˌreidiouˈæktɪv/ *a.* radioactivo.
radio cassette radiocasete *m.*
radish /ˈrædɪʃ/ *n.* rábano *m.*
radium /ˈreidiəm/ *n.* radio *m.*
radius /ˈreidiəs/ *n.* radio *m.*
raffle /ˈræfəl/ *n.* **1.** rifa, lotería *f.* —*v.* **2.** rifar.
raft /ræft/ *n.* balsa *f.*
rafter /ˈræftər/ *n.* viga *f.*
rag /ræg/ *n.* trapo *m.*
ragamuffin /ˈrægəˌmʌfɪn/ *n.* galopín *m.*
rage /reidʒ/ *n.* **1.** rabia *f.* —*v.* **2.** rabiar.
ragged /ˈrægɪd/ *a.* andrajoso; desigual.
raid /reid/ *n.* *Mil.* correría *f.*
rail /reil/ *n.* baranda *f.;* carril *m.* **by r.,** por ferrocarril.
railroad /ˈreilˌroud/ *n.* ferrocarril *m.*
rain /rein/ *n.* **1.** lluvia *f.* —*v.* **2.** llover.
rainbow /ˈreinˌbou/ *n.* arco iris *m.*
raincoat /ˈreinˌkout/ *n.* impermeable *m.;* gabardina *f.*
rainfall /ˈreinˌfɔl/ *n.* precipitación *f.*
rainy /ˈreini/ *a.* lluvioso.
raise /reiz/ *n.* **1.** aumento *m.* —*v.* **2.** levantar, alzar; criar.
raisin /ˈreizɪn/ *n.* pasa *f.*
rake /reik/ *n.* **1.** rastro *m.* —*v.* **2.** rastrillar.
rally /ˈræli/ *n.* **1.** reunión *f.* —*v.* **2.** reunirse.
ram /ræm/ *n.* carnero *m.*
ramble /ˈræmbəl/ *v.* vagar.
ramp /ræmp/ *n.* rampa *f.*
rampart /ˈræmpɑrt/ *n.* terraplén *m.*
ranch /ræntʃ/ *n.* rancho *m.*
rancid /ˈrænsɪd/ *a.* rancio.
rancor /ˈræŋkər/ *n.* rencor *m.*
random /ˈrændəm/ *a.* fortuito. **at r.,** a la ventura.
range /reindʒ/ *n.* **1.** extensión *f.;* alcance *m.;* estufa; sierra *f.;* terreno de pasto. —*v.* **2.** recorrer; extenderse.
rank /ræŋk/ *a.* **1.** espeso; rancio. —*n.* **2.** fila *f.;* grado *m.* —*v.* **3.** clasificar.
ransack /ˈrænsæk/ *v.* saquear.
ransom /ˈrænsəm/ *n.* **1.** rescate *m.* —*v.* **2.** rescatar.
rap /ræp/ *n.* **1.** golpecito *m.* —*v.* **2.** golpear.
rapid /ˈræpɪd/ *a.* rápido.

rapist /ˈreipɪst/ *n.* violador -dora *m. & f.*
rapport /ræˈpɔr/ *n.* armonía *f.*
rapture /ˈræptʃər/ *n.* éxtasis *m.*
rare /rɛər/ *a.* raro; (of food) a medio cocer.
rascal /ˈræskəl/ *n.* pícaro, bribón *m.*
rash /ræʃ/ *a.* **1.** temerario. *—n.* **2.** erupción *f.*
raspberry /ˈræzˌbɛri/ *n.* frambuesa *f.*
rat /ræt/ *n.* rata *f.*
rate /reit/ *n.* **1.** velocidad; tasa *f.;* precio *m.;* (of exchange; of interest) tipo *m.* **at any r.,** de todos modos. *—v.* **2.** valuar.
rather /ˈræðər/ *adv.* bastante; más bien, mejor dicho.
ratify /ˈrætəˌfai/ *v.* ratificar.
ratio /ˈreiʃou/ *n.* razón; proporción *f.*
ration /ˈræʃən, ˈreiʃən/ *n.* **1.** ración *f.* *—v.* **2.** racionar.
rational /ˈræʃənḷ/ *a.* racional.
rattle /ˈrætḷ/ *n.* **1.** ruido *m.;* matraca *f.* **r. snake,** culebra de cascabel, serpiente de cascabel *f.* *—v.* **2.** matraquear; rechinar.
raucous /ˈrɔkəs/ *a.* ronco.
ravage /ˈrævɪdʒ/ *v.* pillar; destruir; asolar.
rave /reiv/ *v.* delirar; entusiasmarse.
ravel /ˈrævəl/ *v.* deshilar.
raven /ˈreivən/ *n.* cuervo *m.*
ravenous /ˈrævənəs/ *a.* voraz.
raw /rɔ/ *a.* crudo; verde.
ray /rei/ *n.* rayo *m.*
rayon /ˈreiɒn/ *n.* rayón *m.*
razor /ˈreizər/ *n.* navaja de afeitar. **r. blade,** hoja de afeitar.
reach /ritʃ/ *n.* **1.** alcance *m.* *—v.* **2.** alcanzar.
react /riˈækt/ *v.* reaccionar.
reaction /riˈækʃən/ *n.* reacción *f.*
reactionary /riˈækʃəˌnɛri/ *a.* **1.** reaccionario. *—n.* **2.** *Pol.* retrógrado *m.*
read /rid/ *v.* leer.
reader /ˈridər/ *n.* lector -ra; libro de lectura *m.*
readily /ˈrɛdḷi/ *adv.* fácilmente.
reading /ˈridɪŋ/ *n.* lectura *f.*
ready /ˈrɛdi/ *a.* listo, preparado; dispuesto.
ready-cooked /ˈrɛdi ˌkʊkt/ *a.* precocinado.
real /reiˈɑl/ *a.* verdadero; real.
real estate bienes inmuebles, *m.pl.*
real-estate agent /ˈriəl ɪˈsteit/ agente inmobiliario *m.*, agente inmobiliaria *f.*
realist /ˈriəlɪst/ *n.* realista *m. & f.*
realistic /ˌriəˈlɪstɪk/ *a.* realista.
reality /riˈælɪti/ *n.* realidad *f.*
realization /ˌriələˈzeiʃən/ *n.* comprensión; realización *f.*
realize /ˈriəˌlaiz/ *v.* darse cuenta de; realizar.
really /ˈriəli/ *adv.* de veras; en realidad.
realm /rɛlm/ *n.* reino; dominio *m.*
reap /rip/ *v.* segar, cosechar.
rear /rɪər/ *a.* **1.** posterior. *—n.* **2.** parte posterior. *—v.* **3.** criar; levantar.
reason /ˈrizən/ *n.* **1.** razón; causa *f.;* motivo *m.* *—v.* **2.** razonar.
reasonable /ˈrizənəbəl/ *a.* razonable.
reassure /ˌriəˈʃʊr/ *v.* calmar, tranquilizar.
rebate /ˈribeit/ *n.* rebaja *f.*
rebel /*n.* ˈrɛbəl; *v.* rɪˈbɛl/ *n.* **1.** rebelde *m. & f.* *—v.* **2.** rebelarse.
rebellion /rɪˈbɛlyən/ *n.* rebelión *f.*
rebellious /rɪˈbɛlyəs/ *a.* rebelde.
rebirth /riˈbɜrθ/ *n.* renacimiento *m.*
rebound /rɪˈbaund/ *v.* repercutir; resaltar.
rebuff /rɪˈbʌf/ *n.* **1.** repulsa *f.* *—v.* **2.** rechazar.
rebuke /rɪˈbyuk/ *n.* **1.** reprensión *f.* *—v.* **2.** reprender.
rebuttal /rɪˈbʌtḷ/ *n.* refutación *f.*
recalcitrant /rɪˈkælsɪtrənt/ *a.* recalcitrante.
recall /rɪˈkɔl/ *v.* recordar; acordarse de; hacer volver.
recapitulate /ˌrikəˈpɪtʃəˌleit/ *v.* recapitular.
recede /riˈsid/ *v.* retroceder.
receipt /rɪˈsit/ *n.* recibo *m.;* (com., pl.) ingresos *m.pl.*
receive /rɪˈsiv/ *v.* recibir.
receiver /rɪˈsivər/ *n.* receptor *m.*
recent /ˈrisənt/ *a.* reciente.
recently /ˈrisəntli/ *adv.* recién.
receptacle /rɪˈsɛptəkəl/ *n.* receptáculo *m.*
reception /rɪˈsɛpʃən/ *n.* acogida; recepción *f.*
receptionist /rɪˈsɛpʃənɪst/ *n.* recepcionista *m. & f.*
receptive /rɪˈsɛptɪv/ *a.* receptivo.
recess /rɪˈsɛs, ˈrisɛs/ *n.* nicho; retiro; recreo *m.*
recipe /ˈrɛsəpi/ *n.* receta *f.*
recipient /rɪˈsɪpiənt/ *n.* recibidor -ra, recipiente *m. & f.*
reciprocate /rɪˈsɪprəˌkeit/ *v.* corresponder; reciprocar.
recite /rɪˈsait/ *v.* recitar.
reckless /ˈrɛklɪs/ *a.* descuidado; imprudente.
reckon /ˈrɛkən/ *v.* contar; calcular.
reclaim /rɪˈkleim/ *v.* reformar; *Leg.* reclamar.
recline /rɪˈklain/ *v.* reclinar; recostar.
recognition /ˌrɛkəgˈnɪʃən/ *n.* reconocimiento *m.*
recognize /ˈrɛkəgˌnaiz/ *v.* reconocer.
recoil /*n.* ˈriˌkɔil; *v.* rɪˈkɔil/ *n.* **1.** culatada *f.* *—v.* **2.** recular.
recollect /ˌrɛkəˈlɛkt/ *v.* recordar, acordarse de.
recommend /ˌrɛkəˈmɛnd/ *v.* recomendar.
recommendation /ˌrɛkəmɛnˈdeiʃən/ *n.* recomendación *f.*
recompense /ˈrɛkəmˌpɛns/ *n.* **1.** recompensa *f.* *—v.* **2.** recompensar.
reconcile /ˈrɛkənˌsail/ *v.* reconciliar.
recondition /ˌrikənˈdɪʃən/ *v.* reacondicionar.
reconsider /ˌrikənˈsɪdər/ *v.* considerar de nuevo.
reconstruct /ˌrikənˈstrʌkt/ *v.* reconstruir.
record /*n.* ˈrɛkərd, *v.* rɪˈkɔrd/ *n.* **1.** registro; (sports) record *m.* **phonograph r.,** disco *m.* *—v.* **2.** registrar.
record player tocadiscos *m.*
recount /rɪˈkaunt/ *v.* relatar; contar.
recover /rɪˈkʌvər/ *v.* recobrar; restablecerse.
recovery /rɪˈkʌvəri/ *n.* recobro *m.;* recuperación *f.*
recruit /rɪˈkrut/ *n.* **1.** recluta *m.* *—v.* **2.** reclutar.
rectangle /ˈrɛkˌtæŋgəl/ *n.* rectángulo *m.*
rectify /ˈrɛktəˌfai/ *v.* rectificar.
recuperate /rɪˈkupəˌreit/ *v.* recuperar.
recur /rɪˈkɜr/ *v.* recurrir.
recycle /riˈsaikəl/ *v.* reciclar.
red /rɛd/ *a.* rojo, colorado.
redeem /rɪˈdim/ *v.* redimir, rescatar.
redemption /rɪˈdɛmpʃən/ *n.* redención *f.*
redhead /ˈrɛdˌhɛd/ *n.* pelirrojo -ja.
red mullet /ˈmʌlɪt/ salmonete *m.*
reduce /rɪˈdus/ *v.* reducir.
reduction /rɪˈdʌkʃən/ *n.* reducción *f.*
reed /rid/ *n.* caña *f.*, *S.A.* bejuco *m.*
reef /rif/ *n.* arrecife, escollo *m.*
reel /ril/ *n.* **1.** aspa *f.*, carrete *m.* *—v.* **2.** aspar.
refer /rɪˈfɜr/ *v.* referir.
referee /ˌrɛfəˈri/ *n.* árbitro *m. & f.*
reference /ˈrɛfərəns/ *n.* referencia *f.*
refill /*n.* ˈriˌfɪl; *v.* riˈfɪl/ *n.* **1.** relleno *m.* *—v.* **2.** rellenar.
refine /rɪˈfain/ *n.* refinar.
refinement /rɪˈfainmənt/ *n.* refinamiento *m.;* cultura *f.*
reflect /rɪˈflɛkt/ *v.* reflejar; reflexionar.
reflection /rɪˈflɛkʃən/ *n.* reflejo *m.;* reflexión *f.*
reflex /ˈriflɛks/ *a.* reflejo.
reform /rɪˈfɔrm/ *n.* **1.** reforma *f.* *—v.* **2.** reformar.
reformation /ˌrɛfərˈmeiʃən/ *n.* reformación *f.*
refractory /rɪˈfræktəri/ *a.* refractario.
refrain /rɪˈfrein/ *n.* **1.** estribillo *m.* *—v.* **2.** abstenerse.
refresh /rɪˈfrɛʃ/ *v.* refrescar.
refreshment /rɪˈfrɛʃmənt/ *n.* refresco *m.*
refrigerator /rɪˈfrɪdʒəˌreitər/ *n.* refrigerador *m.*
refuge /ˈrɛfyudʒ/ *n.* refugio *m.*
refugee /ˌrɛfyʊˈdʒi/ *n.* refugiado -da.
refund /*n* ˈrifʌnd; *v* riˈfʌnd/ *n.* **1.** reembolso *m.* *—v.* **2.** reembolsar.
refusal /rɪˈfyuzəl/ *n.* negativa *f.*
refuse /*n* ˈrɛfyus; *v* rɪˈfyuz/ *n.* **1.** basura *f.* *—v.* **2.** negarse, rehusar.
refute /rɪˈfyut/ *v.* refutar.
regain /riˈgein/ *v.* recobrar. **r. consciousness,** recobrar el conocimiento.
regal /ˈrigəl/ *a.* real.
regard /rɪˈgɑrd/ *n.* **1.** aprecio; respeto *m.* **with r. to,** con respecto a. *—v.* **2.** considerar; estimar.
regarding /rɪˈgɑrdɪŋ/ *prep.* en cuanto a, acerca de.
regardless (of) /rɪˈgɑrdlɪs/ a pesar de.
regent /ˈridʒənt/ *n.* regente *m. & f.*
regime /rəˈʒim, rei-/ *n.* régimen *m.*
regiment /*n.* ˈrɛdʒəmənt; *v.* -ˌmɛnt/ *n.* **1.** regimiento *m.* *—v.* **2.** regimentar.
region /ˈridʒən/ *n.* región *f.*
register /ˈrɛdʒəstər/ *n.* **1.** registro *m.* **cash r.,** caja registradora *f.* *—v.* **2.** registrar; matricularse; (a letter) certificar.
registration /ˌrɛdʒəˈstreiʃən/ *n.* registro *m.;* matrícula *f.*
regret /rɪˈgrɛt/ *n.* **1.** pena *f.* *—v.* **2.** sentir, lamentar.
regular /ˈrɛgyələr/ *a.* regular; ordinario.
regularity /ˌrɛgyəˈlærɪti/ *n.* regularidad *f.*
regulate /ˈrɛgyəˌleit/ *v.* regular.
regulation /ˌrɛgyəˈleiʃən/ *n.* regulación *f.*
regulator /ˈrɛgyəˌleitər/ *n.* regulador *m.*
rehabilitate /ˌrihəˈbɪlɪˌteit, ˌriə-/ *v.* rehabilitar.
rehearse /rɪˈhɜrs/ *v.* repasar; *Theat.* ensayar.
reheat /riˈhit/ *v.* recalentar.
reign /rein/ *n.* **1.** reino, reinado *m.* *—v.* **2.** reinar.
reimburse /ˌriɪmˈbɜrs/ *v.* reembolsar.
rein /rein/ *n.* **1.** rienda *f.* *—v.* **2.** refrenar.
reincarnation /ˌriɪnkɑrˈneiʃən/ *n.* reencarnación *f.*
reindeer /ˈreinˌdɪər/ *n.* reno *m.*
reinforce /ˌriɪnˈfɔrs, -ˈfours/ *v.* reforzar.
reinforcement /ˌriɪnˈfɔrsmənt, -ˈfours-/ *n.* refuerzo *m.;* armadura *f.*
reiterate /riˈɪtəˌreit/ *v.* reiterar.
reject /rɪˈdʒɛkt/ *v.* rechazar.
rejoice /rɪˈdʒɔis/ *v.* regocijarse.
rejoin /rɪˈdʒɔin/ *v.* reunirse con; replicar.
rejuvenate /rɪˈdʒuvəˌneit/ *v.* rejuvenecer.
relapse /*v.* rɪˈlæps; *n. also* ˈrilæps/ *v.* **1.** recaer. *—n.* **2.** recaída *f.*
relate /rɪˈleit/ *v.* relatar, contar; relacionar. **r. to,** llevarse bien con.
relation /rɪˈleiʃən/ *n.* relación *f.;* pariente *m. & f.*
relative /ˈrɛlətɪv/ *a.* **1.** relativo. *—n.* **2.** pariente *m. & f.*
relativity /ˌrɛləˈtɪvɪti/ *n.* relatividad *f.*
relax /rɪˈlæks/ *v.* descansar; relajar.
relay /ˈrilei; *v. also* rɪˈlei/ *n.* **1.** relevo *m.* *—v.* **2.** retransmitir.
release /rɪˈlis/ *n.* **1.** liberación *f.* *—v.* **2.** soltar.
relent /rɪˈlɛnt/ *v.* ceder.
relevant /ˈrɛləvənt/ *a.* pertinente.
reliability /rɪˌlaiəˈbɪlɪti/ *n.* veracidad *f.*
reliable /rɪˈlaiəbəl/ *a.* responsable; digno de confianza.
relic /ˈrɛlɪk/ *n.* reliquia *f.*
relief /rɪˈlif/ *n.* alivio; (sculpture) relieve *m.*
relieve /rɪˈliv/ *v.* aliviar.
religion /rɪˈlɪdʒən/ *n.* religión *f.*
religious /rɪˈlɪdʒəs/ *a.* religioso.
relinquish /rɪˈlɪŋkwɪʃ/ *v.* abandonar.
relish /ˈrɛlɪʃ/ *n.* **1.** sabor; condimento *m.* *—v.* **2.** saborear.
reluctant /rɪˈlʌktənt/ *a.* renuente.
rely /rɪˈlai/ *v.* **r. on,** confiar en; contar con; depender de.
remain /rɪˈmein/ *n.* **1.** (pl.) restos *m.pl.* *—v.* **2.** quedar, permanecer.
remainder /rɪˈmeindər/ *n.* resto *m.*
remark /rɪˈmɑrk/ *n.* **1.** observación *f.* *—v.* **2.** observar.
remarkable /rɪˈmɑrkəbəl/ *a.* notable.
remedial /rɪˈmidiəl/ *a.* reparador.
remedy /ˈrɛmɪdi/ *n.* **1.** remedio *m.* *—v.* **2.** remediar.
remember /rɪˈmɛmbər/ *v.* acordarse de, recordar.
remembrance /rɪˈmɛmbrəns/ *n.* recuerdo *m.*
remind /rɪˈmaind/ *v.* **r. of,** recordar.
reminisce /ˌrɛməˈnɪs/ *v.* pensar en o hablar de cosas pasadas.
remiss /rɪˈmɪs/ *a.* remiso; flojo.
remit /rɪˈmɪt/ *v.* remitir.
remorse /rɪˈmɔrs/ *n.* remordimiento *m.*
remote /rɪˈmout/ *a.* remoto.
remote control mando a distancia *m.*
removal /rɪˈmuvəl/ *n.* alejamiento *m.;* eliminación *f.*
remove /rɪˈmuv/ *v.* quitar; remover.
renaissance /ˌrɛnəˈsɑns/ *n.* renacimiento *m.*
rend /rɛnd/ *v.* hacer pedazos; separar.
render /ˈrɛndər/ *v.* dar; rendir; *Theat.* interpretar.
rendezvous /ˈrɑndəˌvu, -dei-/ *n.* cita *f.*
rendition /rɛnˈdɪʃən/ *n.* interpretación, rendición *f.*
renege /rɪˈnɪg, -ˈnɛg/ *v.* renunciar; faltar a su palabra, no cumplir una promesa.
renew /rɪˈnu, -ˈnyu/ *v.* renovar.
renewal /rɪˈnuəl, -ˈnyu-/ *n.* renovación; *Com.* prórroga *f.*
renounce /rɪˈnauns/ *v.* renunciar a.
renovate /ˈrɛnəˌveit/ *v.* renovar.
renown /rɪˈnaun/ *n.* renombre *m.*, fama *f.*
rent /rɛnt/ *n.* **1.** alquiler *m.* *—v.* **2.** arrendar, alquilar.
repair /rɪˈpɛər/ *n.* **1.** reparo *m.* *—v.* **2.** reparar.
repairman /rɪˈpɛərˌmæn/ *n.* técnico *m.*
repatriate /riˈpeitriˌeit/ *v.* repatriar.
repay /rɪˈpei/ *v.* pagar; devolver.
repeat /rɪˈpit/ *v.* repetir.
repel /rɪˈpɛl/ *v.* repeler, repulsar.
repent /ˈripənt, rɪˈpɛnt/ *v.* arrepentirse.
repentance /rɪˈpɛntns, -ˈpɛntəns/ *n.* arrepentimiento *m.*
repercussion /ˌripərˈkʌʃən, ˌrɛpər-/ *n.* repercusión *f.*
repertoire /ˈrɛpərˌtwɑr/ *n.* repertorio *m.*
repetition /ˌrɛpɪˈtɪʃən/ *n.* repetición *f.*
replace /rɪˈpleis/ *v.* reemplazar.
replenish /rɪˈplɛnɪʃ/ *v.* rellenar; surtir de nuevo.
reply /rɪˈplai/ *n.* **1.** respuesta *f.* *—v.* **2.** replicar; contestar.
report /rɪˈpɔrt, -ˈpourt/ *n.* **1.** informe *m.* *—v.* **2.** informar, contar; denunciar; presentarse.
reporter /rɪˈpɔrtər, -ˈpour-/ *n.* repórter *m. & f.*, reportero -ra.
repose /rɪˈpouz/ *n.* **1.** reposo *m.* *—v.* **2.** reposar; reclinar.

reprehensible /ˌrɛprɪˈhɛnsəbəl/ *a.* reprensible.

represent /ˌrɛprɪˈzɛnt/ *v.* representar.

representation /ˌrɛprɪzɛnˈteiʃən, -zən-/ *n.* representación *f.*

representative /ˌrɛprɪˈzɛntətɪv/ *a.* **1.** representativo. —*n.* **2.** representante *m. & f.*

repress /rɪˈprɛs/ *v.* reprimir.

reprimand /ˈrɛprəˌmænd, -ˌmɑnd/ *n.* **1.** regaño *m.* —*v.* **2.** regañar.

reprisal /rɪˈpraizəl/ *n.* represalia *f.*

reproach /rɪˈproutʃ/ *n.* **1.** reproche *m.* —*v.* **2.** reprochar.

reproduce /ˌriprəˈdus, -ˈdyus/ *v.* reproducir.

reproduction /ˌriprəˈdʌkʃən/ *n.* reproducción *f.*

reproof /rɪˈpruf/ *n.* censura *f.*

reprove /rɪˈpruv/ *v.* censurar, regañar.

reptile /ˈrɛptɪl, -tail/ *n.* reptil *m.*

republic /rɪˈpʌblɪk/ *n.* república *f.*

republican /rɪˈpʌblɪkən/ *a. & n.* republicano -na.

repudiate /rɪˈpyudiˌeit/ *v.* repudiar.

repulsive /rɪˈpʌlsɪv/ *a.* repulsivo, repugnante.

reputation /ˌrɛpyəˈteiʃən/ *n.* reputación; fama *f.*

repute /rɪˈpyut/ *n.* **1.** reputación *f.* —*v.* **2.** reputar.

request /rɪˈkwɛst/ *n.* **1.** súplica *f.*, ruego *m.* —*v.* **2.** pedir; rogar, suplicar.

require /rɪˈkwaiᵊr/ *v.* requerir; exigir.

requirement /rɪˈkwaiᵊrmənt/ *n.* requisito *m.*

requisite /ˈrɛkwəzɪt/ *a.* **1.** necesario. —*n.* **2.** requisito *m.*

requisition /ˌrɛkwəˈzɪʃən/ *n.* requisición *f.*

rescind /rɪˈsɪnd/ *v.* rescindir, anular.

rescue /ˈrɛskyu/ *n.* **1.** rescate *m.* —*v.* **2.** rescatar.

research /rɪˈsɜrtʃ, ˈrisɜrtʃ/ *n.* investigación *f.*

researcher /rɪˈsɜrtʃər/ *n.* investigador -dora.

resemble /rɪˈzɛmbəl/ *v.* parecerse a, asemejarse a.

resent /rɪˈzɛnt/ *v.* resentirse de.

reservation /ˌrɛzərˈveiʃən/ *n.* reservación *f.*

reserve /rɪˈzɜrv/ *n.* **1.** reserva *f.* —*v.* **2.** reservar.

reservoir /ˈrɛzərˌvwɑr, -ˌvwɔr, -ˌvɔr, ˈrɛzə-/ *n* depósito; tanque *m.*

reside /rɪˈzaid/ *v.* residir, morar.

residence /ˈrɛzɪdəns/ *n.* residencia, morada *f.*

resident /ˈrɛzɪdənt/ *n.* residente *m. & f.*

residue /ˈrɛzɪˌdu/ *n.* residuo *m.*

resign /rɪˈzain/ *v.* dimitir; resignar.

resignation /ˌrɛzɪgˈneiʃən/ *n.* dimisión; resignación *f.*

resist /rɪˈzɪst/ *v.* resistir.

resistance /rɪˈzɪstəns/ *n.* resistencia *f.*

resolute /ˈrɛzəˌlut/ *a.* resuelto.

resolution /ˌrɛzəˈluʃən/ *n.* resolución *f.*

resolve /rɪˈzɒlv/ *v.* resolver.

resonant /ˈrɛzənənt/ *a.* resonante.

resort /rɪˈzɔrt/ *n.* **1.** recurso; expediente *m.* **summer r.,** lugar de veraneo. —*v.* **2.** acudir, recurrir.

resound /rɪˈzaund/ *v.* resonar.

resource /ˈrisɔrs/ *n.* recurso *m.*

respect /rɪˈspɛkt/ *n.* **1.** respeto *m.* **with r. to,** con respecto a. —*v.* **2.** respetar.

respectable /rɪˈspɛktəbəl/ *a.* respetable.

respectful /rɪˈspɛktfəl/ *a.* respetuoso.

respective /rɪˈspɛktɪv/ *a.* respectivo.

respiration /ˌrɛspəˈreiʃən/ *n.* respiración *f.*

respite /ˈrɛspɪt/ *n.* pausa, tregua *f.*

respond /rɪˈspɒnd/ *v.* responder.

response /rɪˈspɒns/ *n.* respuesta *f.*

responsibility /rɪˌspɒnsəˈbɪlɪti/ *n.* responsabilidad *f.*

responsible /rɪˈspɒnsəbəl/ *a.* responsable.

responsive /rɪˈspɒnsɪv/ *a.* sensible a.

rest /rɛst/ *n.* **1.** descanso; reposo *m.*; (music) pausa *f.* **the r.,** el resto, lo demás; los demás. —*v.* **2.** descansar; recostar.

restaurant /ˈrɛstərənt, -təˌrɑnt, -trɑnt/ *n.* restaurante *m.*

restful /ˈrɛstfəl/ *a.* tranquilo.

restitution /ˌrɛstɪˈtuʃən, -ˈtyu-/ *n.* restitución *f.*

restless /ˈrɛstlɪs/ *a.* inquieto.

restoration /ˌrɛstəˈreiʃən/ *n.* restauración *f.*

restore /rɪˈstɔr, -ˈstour/ *v.* restaurar.

restrain /rɪˈstrein/ *v.* refrenar.

restraint /rɪˈstreint/ *n.* limitación, restricción *f.*

restrict /rɪˈstrɪkt/ *v.* restringir, limitar.

rest room aseos *m.pl.*

result /rɪˈzʌlt/ *n.* **1.** resultado *m.* —*v.* **2.** resultar.

resume /rɪˈzum/ *v.* reasumir; empezar de nuevo.

résumé /ˈrɛzʊˌmei/ *n.* resumen *m.*

resurgent /rɪˈsɜrdʒənt/ *a.* resurgente.

resurrect /ˌrɛzəˈrɛkt/ *v.* resucitar.

resuscitate /rɪˈsʌsɪˌteit/ *v.* resucitar.

retail /ˈriteil/ *n.* **at r.,** al por menor.

retain /rɪˈtein/ *v.* retener.

retaliate /rɪˈtæliˌeit/ *v.* vengarse.

retard /rɪˈtɑrd/ *v.* retardar.

retention /rɪˈtɛnʃən/ *n.* retención *f.*

reticent /ˈrɛtəsənt/ *a.* reticente.

retire /rɪˈtaiᵊr/ *v.* retirar.

retirement /rɪˈtaiᵊrmənt/ *n.* jubilación *f.*

retort /rɪˈtɔrt/ *n.* **1.** réplica; *Chem.* retorta *f.* —*v.* **2.** replicar.

retreat /rɪˈtrit/ *n.* **1.** retiro *m.*; *Mil.* retirada, retreta *f.* —*v.* **2.** retirarse.

retribution /ˌrɛtrəˈbyuʃən/ *n.* retribución *f.*

retrieve /rɪˈtriv/ *v.* recobrar.

return /rɪˈtɜrn/ *n.* **1.** vuelta *f.*, regreso; retorno *m.* **by r. mail,** a vuelta de correo. —*v.* **2.** volver, regresar; devolver.

reunion /riˈyunyən/ *n.* reunión *f.*

rev /rɛv/ *n.* **1.** revolución *f.* —*v.* **2.** (motor) acelerar.

reveal /rɪˈvil/ *v.* revelar.

revelation /ˌrɛvəˈleiʃən/ *n.* revelación *f.*

revenge /rɪˈvɛndʒ/ *n.* venganza *f.* **to get r.,** vengarse.

revenue /ˈrɛvənˌyu, -əˌnu/ *n.* renta *f.*

revere /rɪˈvɪər/ *v.* reverenciar, venerar.

reverence /ˈrɛvərəns, ˈrɛvrəns/ *n.* **1.** reverencia *f.* —*v.* **2.** reverenciar.

reverend /ˈrɛvərənd, ˈrɛvrənd/ *a.* **1.** reverendo. —*n.* **2.** pastor *m.*

reverent /ˈrɛvərənt, ˈrɛvrənt/ *a.* reverente.

reverse /rɪˈvɜrs/ *a.* **1.** inverso. —*n.* **2.** revés, inverso *m.* —*v.* **3.** invertir; revocar.

revert /rɪˈvɜrt/ *v.* revertir.

review /rɪˈvyu/ *n.* **1.** repaso *m.*; revista *f.* —*v.* **2.** repasar; *Mil.* revistar.

revise /rɪˈvaiz/ *v.* revisar.

revision /rɪˈvɪʒən/ *n.* revisión *f.*

revival /rɪˈvaivəl/ *n.* reavivamiento *m.*

revive /rɪˈvaiv/ *v.* avivar; revivir, resucitar.

revoke /rɪˈvouk/ *v.* revocar.

revolt /rɪˈvoult/ *n.* **1.** rebelión *f.* —*v.* **2.** rebelarse.

revolting /rɪˈvoultɪŋ/ *a.* repugnante.

revolution /ˌrɛvəˈluʃən/ *n.* revolución *f.*

revolutionary /ˌrɛvəˈluʃəˌnɛri/ *a. & n.* revolucionario -ria.

revolve /rɪˈvɒlv/ *v.* girar; dar vueltas.

revolver /rɪˈvɒlvər/ *n.* revólver *m.*

revolving door /rɪˈvɒlvɪŋ/ puerta giratoria *f.*

reward /rɪˈwɔrd/ *n.* **1.** pago *m.*; recompensa *f.* —*v.* **2.** recompensar.

rhetoric /ˈrɛtərɪk/ *n.* retórica *f.*

rheumatism /ˈruməˌtɪzəm/ *n.* reumatismo *m.*

rhinoceros /raiˈnɒsərəs/ *n.* rinoceronte *m.*

rhubarb /ˈrubɑrb/ *n.* ruibarbo *m.*

rhyme /raim/ *n.* **1.** rima *f.* —*v.* **2.** rimar.

rhythm /ˈrɪðəm/ *n.* ritmo *m.*

rhythmical /ˈrɪðmɪkəl/ *a.* rítmico.

rib /rɪb/ *n.* costilla *f.*

ribbon /ˈrɪbən/ *n.* cinta *f.*

rib cage caja torácica *f.*

rice /rais/ *n.* arroz *m.*

rich /rɪtʃ/ *a.* rico.

rid /rɪd/ *v.* librar. **get r. of,** deshacerse de, quitarse.

riddle /ˈrɪdl/ *n.* enigma; rompecabezas *m.*

ride /raid/ *n.* **1.** paseo (a caballo, en coche, etc.) *m.* —*v.* **2.** cabalgar; ir en coche.

ridge /rɪdʒ/ *n.* cerro *m.*; arruga *f.*; (of a roof) caballete *m.*

ridicule /ˈrɪdɪˌkyul/ *n.* **1.** ridículo *m.* —*v.* **2.** ridiculizar.

ridiculous /rɪˈdɪkyələs/ *a.* ridículo.

riding /ˈraidɪŋ/ *n.* equitación *f.*

riding school picadero *m.*

rifle /ˈraifəl/ *n.* **1.** fusil *m.* —*v.* **2.** robar.

rig /rɪg/ *n.* **1.** aparejo *m.* —*v.* **2.** aparejar.

right /rait/ *a.* **1.** derecho; correcto. **to be r.,** tener razón. —*adv.* **2.** bien, correctamente. **r. here,** etc., aquí mismo, etc. **all r.,** está bien, muy bien. —*n.* **3.** derecho *m.*; justicia *f.* **to the r.,** a la derecha. —*v.* **4.** corregir; enderezar.

righteous /ˈraitʃəs/ *a.* justo.

rigid /ˈrɪdʒɪd/ *a.* rígido.

rigor /ˈrɪgər/ *n.* rigor *m.*

rigorous /ˈrɪgərəs/ *a.* riguroso.

rim /rɪm/ *n.* margen *m. or f.*; borde *m.*

ring /rɪŋ/ *n.* **1.** anillo *m.*; sortija *f.*; círculo; campaneo *m.* —*v.* **2.** cercar; sonar; tocar.

ring finger dedo anular *m.*

rinse /rɪns/ *v.* enjuagar, lavar.

riot /ˈraiət/ *n.* motín; alboroto *m.*

rip /rɪp/ *n.* **1.** rasgadura *f.* —*v.* **2.** rasgar; descoser.

ripe /raip/ *a.* maduro.

ripen /ˈraipən/ *v.* madurar.

ripoff /ˈrɪpˌɔf/ *n.* robo, atraco *m.*

ripple /ˈrɪpəl/ *n.* **1.** onda *f.* —*v.* **2.** ondear.

rise /raiz/ *n.* **1.** subida *f.* —*v.* **2.** ascender; levantarse; (moon) salir.

risk /rɪsk/ *n.* **1.** riesgo *m.* —*v.* **2.** arriesgar.

rite /rait/ *n.* rito *m.*

ritual /ˈrɪtʃuəl/ *a. & n.* ritual *m.*

rival /ˈraivəl/ *n.* rival *m. & f.*

rivalry /ˈraivəlri/ *n.* rivalidad *f.*

river /ˈraivər/ *n.* río *m.*

rivet /ˈrɪvɪt/ *n.* **1.** remache, roblón *m.* —*v.* **2.** remachar, roblar.

road /roud/ *n.* camino *m.*; carretera *f.*

roadside /ˈroudˌsaid/ *n.* borde de la carretera *m.*

roam /roum/ *v.* vagar.

roar /rɔr, rour/ *n.* **1.** rugido, bramido *m.* —*v.* **2.** rugir, bramar.

roast /roust/ *n.* **1.** asado *m.* —*v.* **2.** asar.

rob /rɒb/ *v.* robar.

robber /ˈrɒbər/ *n.* ladrón -na.

robbery /ˈrɒbəri/ *n.* robo *m.*

robe /roub/ *n.* manto *m.*

robin /ˈrɒbɪn/ *n.* petirrojo *m.*

robust /rouˈbʌst, ˈroubʌst/ *a.* robusto.

rock /rɒk/ *n.* **1.** roca, peña *f.*; (music) rock *m.*, música (de) rock *f.* —*v.* **2.** mecer; oscilar.

rocker /ˈrɒkər/ *n.* mecedora *f.*

rocket /ˈrɒkɪt/ *n.* cohete *m.*

rocking chair /ˈrɒkɪŋ/ mecedora *f.*

Rock of Gibraltar /dʒɪˈbrɔltər/ Peñón de Gibraltar *m.*

rocky /ˈrɒki/ *a.* pedregoso.

rod /rɒd/ *n.* varilla *f.*

rodent /ˈroudnt/ *n.* roedor *m.*

rogue /roug/ *n.* bribón, pícaro *m.*

roguish /ˈrougɪʃ/ *a.* pícaro.

role /roul/ *n.* papel *m.*

roll /roul/ **1.** rollo *m.*; lista *f.*; panecillo *m.* **to call the r.,** pasar lista. —*v.* **2.** rodar. **r. up,** enrollar. **r. up one's sleeves,** arremangarse.

roller /ˈroulər/ *n.* rodillo, cilindro *m.*

roller skate patín de ruedas *m.*

Roman /ˈroumən/ *a. & n.* romano -na.

romance /rouˈmæns, ˈroumæns/ *a.* **1.** románico. —*n.* **2.** romance *m.*; amorío *m.*

romantic /rouˈmæntɪk/ *a.* romántico.

romp /rɒmp/ *v.* retozar; jugar.

roof /ruf, rʊf/ *n.* **1.** techo *m.*; —*v.* **2.** techar.

room /rum, rʊm/ *n.* **1.** cuarto *m.*, habitación *f.*; lugar *m.* —*v.* **2.** alojarse.

roommate /ˈrumˌmeit, ˈrʊm-/ *n.* compañero -ra de cuarto.

rooster /ˈrustər/ *n.* gallo *m.*

root /rut/ *n.* raíz *f.* **to take r.,** arraigar.

rootless /ˈrutlɪs/ *a.* desarraigado.

rope /roup/ *n.* cuerda, soga *f.*

rose /rouz/ *n.* rosa *f.*

rosy /ˈrouzi/ *a.* róseo, rosado.

rot /rɒt/ *n.* **1.** putrefacción *f.* —*v.* **2.** pudrirse.

rotary /ˈroutəri/ *a.* giratorio; rotativo.

rotate /ˈrouteit/ *v.* girar; alternar.

rotation /rouˈteiʃən/ *n.* rotación *f.*

rotten /ˈrɒtn/ *a.* podrido.

rouge /ruʒ/ *n.* colorete *m.*

rough /rʌf/ *a.* áspero; rudo; grosero; aproximado.

round /raund/ *a.* **1.** redondo. **r. trip,** viaje de ida y vuelta. —*n.* **2.** ronda *f.*; (boxing) asalto *m.*

rouse /rauz/ *v.* despertar.

rout /raut, rut/ *n.* **1.** derrota *f.* —*v.* **2.** derrotar.

route /rut, raut/ *n.* ruta, vía *f.*

routine /ruˈtin/ *a.* **1.** rutinario. —*n.* **2.** rutina *f.*

rove /rouv/ *v.* vagar.

rover /ˈrouvər/ *n.* vagabundo -da.

row /rou/ *n.* **1.** fila *f.* —*v.* **2.** *Naut.* remar.

rowboat /ˈrouˌbout/ *n.* bote de remos.

rowdy /ˈraudi/ *a.* alborotado.

royal /ˈrɔiəl/ *a.* real.

royalty /ˈrɔiəlti/ *n.* realeza *f.*; (pl.) regalías *f.pl.*

rub /rʌb/ *v.* frotar. **r. against,** rozar. **r. out,** borrar.

rubber /ˈrʌbər/ *n.* goma *f.*; caucho *m.*; (pl.) chanclos *m.pl.*, zapatos de goma.

rubbish /ˈrʌbɪʃ/ *n.* basura *f.*; (nonsense) tonterías *f.pl.*

ruby /ˈrubi/ *n.* rubí *m.*

rudder /ˈrʌdər/ *n.* timón *m.*

ruddy /ˈrʌdi/ *a.* colorado.

rude /rud/ *a.* rudo; grosero; descortés.

rudiment /ˈrudəmənt/ *n.* rudimento *m.*

rudimentary /ˌrudəˈmɛntəri, -tri/ *a.* rudimentario.

rue /ru/ *v.* deplorar; lamentar.

ruffian /ˈrʌfiən, ˈrʌfyən/ *n.* rufián, bandolero *m.*

ruffle /ˈrʌfəl/ *n.* **1.** volante fruncido. —*v.* **2.** fruncir; irritar.

rug /rʌg/ *n.* alfombra *f.*

rugged /ˈrʌgɪd/ *a.* áspero; robusto.

ruin /ˈruɪn/ *n.* **1.** ruina *f.* —*v.* **2.** arruinar.

ruinous /ˈruənəs/ *a.* ruinoso.

rule /rul/ *n.* **1.** regla *f.* **as a r.,** por regla general. —*v.* **2.** gobernar; mandar; rayar.

ruler /ˈrulər/ *n.* gobernante *m. & f.*; soberano -na; regla *f.*

rum /rʌm/ *n.* ron *m.*

rumble /ˈrʌmbəl/ *v.* retumbar.

rumor /ˈrumər/ *n.* rumor *m.*

rumpus /ˈrʌmpəs/ *n.* lío, jaleo, escandalo *m.*

run /rʌn/ *v.* correr; hacer correr. **r. away,** escaparse. **r. into,** chocar con.

runner /ˈrʌnər/ *n.* corredor -ra; mensajero -ra.
runner-up /ˈrʌnər ˈʌp/ *n.* subcampeón -ona.
runproof /ˈrʌnpruf/ *a.* indesmallable.
rupture /ˈrʌptʃər/ *n.* **1.** rotura; hernia *f.* —*v.* **2.** reventar.
rural /ˈrʊrəl/ *a.* rural, campestre.
rush /rʌʃ/ *n.* **1.** prisa *f.*; *Bot.* junco *m.* —*v.* **2.** ir de prisa.
rush hour hora punta *f.*
Russia /ˈrʌʃə/ *n.* Rusia *f.*
Russian /ˈrʌʃən/ *a.* & *n.* ruso -sa.
rust /rʌst/ *n.* **1.** herrumbre *f.* —*v.* **2.** aherrumbrarse.
rustic /ˈrʌstɪk/ *a.* rústico.
rustle /ˈrʌsəl/ *n.* **1.** susurro *m.* —*v.* **2.** susurrar.
rusty /ˈrʌsti/ *a.* mohoso.
rut /rʌt/ *n.* surco *m.*
ruthless /ˈruθlɪs/ *a.* cruel, inhumano.
rye /rai/ *n.* centeno *m.*
rye bread pan de centeno *m.*

S

saber /ˈseibər/ *n.* sable *m.*
sable /ˈseibəl/ *n.* cebellina *f.*
sabotage /ˈsæbəˌtɑʒ/ *n.* sabotaje *m.*
sachet /sæˈʃei/ *n.* perfumador *m.*
sack /sæk/ *n.* **1.** saco *m.* —*v.* **2.** *Mil.* saquear.
sacred /ˈseikrɪd/ *a.* sagrado, santo.
sacrifice /ˈsækrəˌfais/ *n.* **1.** sacrificio *m.* —*v.* **2.** sacrificar.
sacrilege /ˈsækrəlɪdʒ/ *n.* sacrilegio *m.*
sad /sæd/ *a.* triste.
saddle /ˈsædl̩/ *n.* **1.** silla de montar. —*v.* **2.** ensillar.
sadness /ˈsædnɪs/ *n.* tristeza *f.*
safe /seif/ *a.* **1.** seguro; salvo. —*n.* **2.** caja de caudales.
safeguard /ˈseifˌgɑrd/ *n.* **1.** salvaguardia *m.* —*v.* **2.** proteger, poner a salvo.
safety /ˈseifti/ *n.* seguridad, protección *f.*
safety belt cinturón de seguridad *m.*
safety pin imperdible *m.*
safety valve /vælv/ válvula de seguridad *f.*
sage /seidʒ/ *a.* **1.** sabio, sagaz. —*n.* **2.** sabio *m.*; *Bot.* salvia *f.*
sail /seil/ *n.* **1.** vela *f.*; paseo por mar. —*v.* **2.** navegar; embarcarse.
sailboat /ˈseilˌbout/ *n.* barco de vela.
sailor /ˈseilər/ *n.* marinero *m.*
saint /seint/ *n.* santo -ta.
sake /seik/ *n.* **for the s. of,** por; por el bien de.
salad /ˈsæləd/ *n.* ensalada *f.* **s. bowl,** ensaladera *f.*
salad dressing aliño *m.*
salary /ˈsæləri/ *n.* sueldo, salario *m.*
sale /seil/ *n.* venta *f.*
salesman /ˈseilzmən/ *n.* vendedor *m.*; viajante de comercio.
sales tax /seilz/ impuesto sobre la venta.
saliva /səˈlaivə/ *n.* saliva *f.*
salmon /ˈsæmən/ *n.* salmón *m.*
salt /sɔlt/ *a.* **1.** salado. —*n.* **2.** sal *f.* —*v.* **3.** salar.
salute /səˈlut/ *n.* **1.** saludo *m.* —*v.* **2.** saludar.
salvage /ˈsælvɪdʒ/ *v.* salvar; recobrar.
salvation /sælˈveiʃən/ *n.* salvación *f.*
salve /sælv/ *n.* emplasto, ungüento *m.*
same /seim/ *a.* & *pron.* mismo. **it's all the s.,** lo mismo da.
sample /ˈsæmpəl/ *n.* **1.** muestra *f.* —*v.* **2.** probar.
sanatorium /ˌsænəˈtɔriəm/ *n.* sanatorio *m.*
sanctify /ˈsæŋktəˌfai/ *v.* santificar.
sanction /ˈsæŋkʃən/ *n.* **1.** sanción *f.* —*v.* **2.** sancionar.
sanctity /ˈsæŋktɪti/ *n.* santidad *f.*
sanctuary /ˈsæŋktʃuˌɛri/ *n.* santuario, asilo *m.*
sand /sænd/ *n.* arena *f.*
sandal /ˈsændl̩/ *n.* sandalia *f.*
sandpaper /ˈsændˌpeipər/ *n.* papel de lija *m.*
sandwich /ˈsændwɪtʃ, ˈsæn-/ *n.* emparedado, sándwich *m.*
sandy /ˈsændi/ *a.* arenoso; (color) rufo.
sane /sein/ *a.* cuerdo; sano.
sanitary /ˈsænɪˌtɛri/ *a.* higiénico, sanitario. **s. napkin,** toalla sanitaria.
sanitation /ˌsænɪˈteiʃən/ *n.* saneamiento *m.*
sanity /ˈsænɪti/ *n.* cordura *f.*
Santa Claus /ˈsæntə klɔz/ Papá Noel *m.*
sap /sæp/ *n.* **1.** savia *f.*; *Colloq.* estúpido, bobo *m.* —*v.* **2.** agotar.
sapphire /ˈsæfaiər/ *n.* zafiro *m.*
sarcasm /ˈsɑrkæzəm/ *n.* sarcasmo *m.*
sardine /sɑrˈdin/ *n.* sardina *f.*
sash /sæʃ/ *n.* cinta *f.*
satellite /ˈsætl̩ˌait/ *n.* satélite *m.*
satellite dish antena parabólica *f.*
satin /ˈsætn̩/ *n.* raso *m.*
satire /ˈsætaiər/ *n.* sátira *f.*
satisfaction /ˌsætɪsˈfækʃən/ *n.* satisfacción; recompensa *f.*
satisfactory /ˌsætɪsˈfæktəri/ *a.* satisfactorio.
satisfy /ˈsætɪsˌfai/ *v.* satisfacer. **be satisfied that...,** estar convencido de que.
saturate /ˈsætʃəˌreit/ *v.* saturar.
Saturday /ˈsætərˌdei/ *n.* sábado *m.*
sauce /sɔs/ *n.* salsa; compota *f.*
saucer /ˈsɔsər/ *n.* platillo *m.*
saucy /ˈsɔsi/ *a.* descarado, insolente.
sauna /ˈsɔnə/ *n.* sauna *f.*
sausage /ˈsɔsɪdʒ/ *n.* salchicha *f.*
savage /ˈsævɪdʒ/ *a.* & *n.* salvaje *m.* & *f.*
save /seiv/ *v.* **1.** salvar; guardar; ahorrar, economizar. —*prep.* **2.** salvo, excepto.
savings /ˈseivɪŋz/ *n.* ahorros *m.pl.*
savings account cuenta de ahorros *m.*
savings bank caja de ahorros *f.*
savior /ˈseivyər/ *n.* salvador -ora.
savor /ˈseivər/ *n.* **1.** sabor *m.* —*v.* **2.** saborear.
savory /ˈseivəri/ *a.* sabroso.
saw /sɔ/ *n.* **1.** sierra *f.* —*v.* **2.** aserrar.
saxophone /ˈsæksəˌfoun/ *n.* saxofón, saxófono, *m.*
say /sei/ *v.* decir; recitar.
saying /ˈseiɪŋ/ *n.* dicho, refrán *m.*
scaffold /ˈskæfəld/ *n.* andamio; (gallows) patíbulo *m.*
scald /skɔld/ *v.* escaldar.
scale /skeil/ *n.* **1.** escala; (of fish) escama *f.*; (pl.) balanza *f.* —*v.* **2.** escalar; escamar.
scalp /skælp/ *n.* pericráneo *m.* *v.* escalpar.
scan /skæn/ *v.* hojear, repasar; (poetry) escandir; (computer) escanear, digitalizar.
scandal /ˈskændl̩/ *n.* escándalo *m.*
scanner /ˈskænər/ *n.* escáner *m.*
scant /skænt/ *a.* escaso.
scar /skɑr/ *n.* cicatriz *f.*
scarce /skɛərs/ *a.* escaso; raro.
scarcely /ˈskɛərsli/ *adv.* & *conj.* apenas.
scare /skɛər/ *n.* **1.** susto *m.* —*v.* **2.** asustar. **s. away,** espantar.
scarf /skɑrf/ *n.* pañueleta, bufanda *f.*
scarlet /ˈskɑrlɪt/ *n.* escarlata *f.*
scarlet fever escarlatina *f.*
scatter /ˈskætər/ *v.* esparcir; dispersar.
scavenger /ˈskævɪndʒər/ *n.* basurero *m.*
scenario /sɪˈnɛəriˌou, -ˈnɑr-/ *n.* escenario *m.*
scene /sin/ *n.* vista *f.*, paisaje *m.*; *Theat.* escena *f.* **behind the scenes,** entre bastidores.
scenery /ˈsinəri/ *n.* paisaje *m.*; *Theat.* decorado *m.*
scent /sɛnt/ *n.* **1.** olor, perfume; (sense) olfato *m.* —*v.* **2.** perfumar; *Fig.* sospechar.
schedule /ˈskɛdʒul, -ʊl, -uəl/ *n.* **1.** programa, horario *m.* —*v.* **2.** fijar la hora para.
scheme /skim/ *n.* **1.** proyecto; esquema *m.* —*v.* **2.** intrigar.
scholar /ˈskɒlər/ *n.* erudito -ta; becado -da.
scholarship /ˈskɒlərˌʃɪp/ *n.* beca; erudición *f.*
school /skul/ *n.* **1.** escuela *f.*; colegio *m.*; (of fish) banco *m.* —*v.* **2.** enseñar.
sciatica /saiˈætɪkə/ *n.* ciática *f.*
science /ˈsaiəns/ *n.* ciencia *f.*
science fiction ciencia ficción.
scientific /ˌsaiənˈtɪfɪk/ *a.* científico.
scientist /ˈsaiəntɪst/ *n.* científico -ca.
scissors /ˈsɪzərz/ *n.* tijeras *f. pl.*
scoff /skɔf, skɒf/ *v.* mofarse, burlarse.
scold /skould/ *v.* regañar.
scoop /skup/ *n.* **1.** cucharón *m.*; cucharada *f.* —*v.* **2.** **s. out,** recoger, sacar.
scope /skoup/ *n.* alcance; campo *m.*
score /skɔr/ *n.* **1.** tantos *m. pl.*; (music) partitura *f.* —*v.* **2.** marcar, hacer tantos.
scorn /skɔrn/ *n.* **1.** desprecio *m.* —*v.* **2.** despreciar.
scornful /ˈskɔrnfəl/ *a.* desdeñoso.
Scotland /ˈskɒtlənd/ *n.* Escocia *f.*
Scottish /ˈskɒtɪʃ/ *a.* escocés.
scour /skauər/ *v.* fregar, estregar.
scourge /skɜrdʒ/ *n.* azote *m.*; plaga *f.*
scout /skaut/ *n.* **1.** explorador -ra. —*v.* **2.** explorar, reconocer.
scramble /ˈskræmbəl/ *n.* **1.** rebatiña *f.* —*v.* **2.** bregar. **scrambled eggs,** huevos revueltos.
scrap /skræp/ *n.* **1.** migaja *f.*; pedacito *m.*; *Colloq.* riña *f.* **s. metal,** hierro viejo *m.* **s. paper,** papel borrador. —*v.* **2.** desechar; *Colloq.* reñir.
scrapbook /ˈskræpˌbʊk/ *n.* álbum de recortes *m.*
scrape /skreip/ *n.* **1.** lío, apuro *m.* —*v.* **2.** raspar; (feet) restregar.
scratch /skrætʃ/ *n.* **1.** rasguño *m.* —*v.* **2.** rasguñar; rayar.
scream /skrim/ *n.* **1.** grito, chillido *m.* —*v.* **2.** gritar, chillar.
screen /skrin/ *n.* biombo *m.*; (for window) tela metálica; (movie) pantalla *f.*
screw /skru/ *n.* **1.** tornillo *m.* —*v.* **2.** atornillar.
screwdriver /ˈskruˌdraivər/ *n.* destornillador *m.*
scribble /ˈskrɪbəl/ *v.* hacer garabatos.
scroll /skroul/ *n.* rúbrica *f.*; rollo de papel.
scroll bar *n.* barra de enrollar *f.*
scrub /skrʌb/ *v.* fregar, estregar.
scruple /ˈskrupəl/ *n.* escrúpulo *m.*
scrupulous /ˈskrupyələs/ *a.* escrupuloso.
scuba diving /ˈskubə ˈdaivɪŋ/ submarinismo *m.*
sculptor /ˈskʌlptər/ *n.* escultor -ra.
sculpture /ˈskʌlptʃər/ *n.* **1.** escultura *f.* —*v.* **2.** esculpir.
scythe /saið/ *n.* guadaña *f.*
sea /si/ *n.* mar *m.* or *f.*
seabed /ˈsiˌbɛd/ *n.* lecho marino *m.*
sea breeze brisa marina *f.*
seafood /ˈsiˌfud/ *n.* mariscos *m.pl.*
seal /sil/ *n.* **1.** sello *m.*; (animal) foca *f.* —*v.* **2.** sellar.
seam /sim/ *n.* costura *f.*
seamy /ˈsimi/ *a.* sórdido.
seaplane /ˈsiˌplein/ *n.* hidroavión *m.*
seaport /ˈsiˌpɔrt/ *n.* puerto de mar.
search /sɜrtʃ/ *n.* **1.** registro *m.* **in s. of,** en busca de. —*v.* **2.** registrar. **s. for,** buscar.
search engine motor de búsqueda *m.*, buscador *m.*, indexador de información *m.*
seasick /ˈsiˌsɪk/ *a.* mareado. **to get s.,** marearse.
season /ˈsizən/ *n.* **1.** estación; sazón; temporada *f.* —*v.* **2.** sazonar.
seasoning /ˈsizənɪŋ/ *n.* condimento *m.*
season ticket abono *m.*
seat /sit/ *n.* **1.** asiento *m.*; residencia, sede *f.*; *Theat.* localidad *f.* **s. belt,** cinturón de seguridad. —*v.* **2.** sentar. **be seated,** sentarse.
seaweed /ˈsiˌwid/ *n.* alga, alga marina *f.*
second /sɪˈkɒnd/ *a.* & *n.* **1.** segundo *m.* —*v.* **2.** apoyar, segundar.
secondary /ˈsɛkənˌdɛri/ *a.* secundario.
secret /ˈsikrɪt/ *a.* & *n.* secreto *m.*
secretary /ˈsɛkrɪˌtɛri/ *n.* secretario -ria; *Govt.* ministro -tra; (furniture) papelera *f.*
sect /sɛkt/ *n.* secta *f.*; partido *m.*
section /ˈsɛkʃən/ *n.* sección, parte *f.*
sectional /ˈsɛkʃənl̩/ *a.* regional, local.
secular /ˈsɛkyələr/ *a.* secular.
secure /sɪˈkyʊr/ *a.* **1.** seguro. —*v.* **2.** asegurar; obtener; *Fin.* garantizar.
security /sɪˈkyʊrɪti/ *n.* seguridad; garantía *f.*
sedative /ˈsɛdətɪv/ *a.* & *n.* sedativo *m.*
seduce /sɪˈdus/ *v.* seducir.
see /si/ *v.* ver; comprender. **s. off,** despedirse de. **s. to,** encargarse de.
seed /sid/ *n.* **1.** semilla *f.* —*v.* **2.** sembrar.
seek /sik/ *v.* buscar. **s. to,** tratar de.
seem /sim/ *v.* parecer.
seep /sip/ *v.* colarse.
segment /ˈsɛgmənt/ *n.* segmento *m.*
segregate /ˈsɛgrɪˌgeit/ *v.* segregar.
seize /siz/ *v.* agarrar; apoderarse de.
seldom /ˈsɛldəm/ *adv.* rara vez.
select /sɪˈlɛkt/ *a.* **1.** escogido, selecto. —*v.* **2.** elegir, seleccionar.
selection /sɪˈlɛkʃən/ *n.* selección *f.*
selective /sɪˈlɛktɪv/ *a.* selectivo.
selfish /ˈsɛlfɪʃ/ *a.* egoísta.
selfishness /ˈsɛlfɪʃnɪs/ *n.* egoísmo *m.*
sell /sɛl/ *v.* vender.
semester /sɪˈmɛstər/ *n.* semestre *m.*
semicircle /ˈsɛmɪˌsɜrkəl/ *n.* semicírculo *m.*
semolina /ˌsɛməˈlinə/ *n.* sémola *f.*
senate /ˈsɛnɪt/ *n.* senado *m.*
senator /ˈsɛnətər/ *n.* senador -ra.
send /sɛnd/ *v.* mandar, enviar; (a wire) poner. **s. away,** despedir. **s. back,** devolver. **s. for,** mandar buscar. **s. off,** expedir. **s. word,** mandar recado.
senile /ˈsinail/ *a.* senil.
senior /ˈsinyər/ *a.* mayor; más viejo. **Sr.,** padre.
senior citizen persona de edad avanzada.
sensation /sɛnˈseiʃən/ *n.* sensación *f.*
sensational /sɛnˈseiʃənl̩/ *a.* sensacional.
sense /sɛns/ *n.* **1.** sentido; juicio *m.* —*v.* **2.** percibir; sospechar.
sensible /ˈsɛnsəbəl/ *a.* sensato, razonable.
sensitive /ˈsɛnsɪtɪv/ *a.* sensible; sensitivo.
sensual /ˈsɛnʃuəl/ *a.* sensual.
sentence /ˈsɛntn̩s/ *n.* **1.** frase; *Gram.* oración; *Leg.* sentencia *f.* —*v.* **2.** condenar.
sentiment /ˈsɛntəmənt/ *n.* sentimiento *m.*
sentimental /ˌsɛntəˈmɛntl̩/ *a.* sentimental.
separate /*a.* ˈsɛpərɪt; *v.* -ˌreit/ *a.* **1.** separado; suelto. —*v.* **2.** separar, dividir.
separation /ˌsɛpəˈreiʃən/ *n.* separación *f.*
September /sɛpˈtɛmbər/ *n.* septiembre *m.*
sequence /ˈsikwəns/ *n.* serie *f.* **in s.,** seguidos.
serenade /ˌsɛrəˈneid/ *n.* **1.** serenata *f.* —*v.* **2.** dar serenata a.
serene /səˈrin/ *a.* sereno; tranquilo.
sergeant /ˈsɑrdʒənt/ *n.* sargento *m.*

serial /ˈsɪəriəl/ *a.* en serie, de serie.
series /ˈsɪəriz/ *n.* serie *f.*
serious /ˈsɪəriəs/ *a.* serio; grave.
sermon /ˈsɜrmən/ *n.* sermón *m.*
serpent /ˈsɜrpənt/ *n.* serpiente *f.*
servant /ˈsɜrvənt/ *n.* criado -da; servidor -ra.
serve /sɜrv/ *v.* servir.
server /ˈsɜrvər/ *n.* servidor *m.*
service /ˈsɜrvɪs/ *n.* **1.** servicio *m.* **at the s. of,** a las órdenes de. **be of s.,** servir; ser útil. —*v.* **2.** *Auto.* reparar.
service station estación de servicio *f.*
session /ˈsɛʃən/ *n.* sesión *f.*
set /sɛt/ *a.* **1.** fijo. —*n.* **2.** colección *f.*; (of a game) juego; *Mech.* aparato; *Theat.* decorado *m.* —*v.* **3.** poner, colocar; fijar; (sun) ponerse. **s. forth,** exponer. **s. off, s. out,** salir. **s. up,** instalar; establecer.
settle /ˈsɛtl/ *v.* solucionar; arreglar; establecerse.
settlement /ˈsɛtlmənt/ *n.* caserío; arreglo; acuerdo *m.*
settler /ˈsɛtlər/ *n.* poblador -ra.
seven /ˈsɛvən/ *a.* & *pron.* siete.
seventeen /ˈsɛvənˈtin/ *a.* & *pron.* diecisiete.
seventh /ˈsɛvənθ/ *a.* séptimo.
seventy /ˈsɛvənti/ *a.* & *pron.* setenta.
sever /ˈsɛvər/ *v.* desunir; romper.
several /ˈsɛvərəl/ *a.* & *pron.* varios.
severance pay /ˈsɛvərəns/ indemnización de despido.
severe /səˈvɪər/ *a.* severo; grave.
severity /səˈvɛrɪti/ *n.* severidad *f.*
sew /sou/ *v.* coser.
sewer /ˈsuər/ *n.* cloaca *f.*
sewing /ˈsouɪŋ/ *n.* costura *f.*
sewing basket costurero *m.*
sewing machine máquina de coser *f.*
sex /sɛks/ *n.* sexo *m.*
sexism /ˈsɛksɪzəm/ *n.* sexismo *m.*
sexist /ˈsɛksɪst/ *a.* & *n.* sexista *m.* & *f.*
sexton /ˈsɛkstən/ *n.* sacristán *m.*
sexual /ˈsɛkʃuəl/ *a.* sexual.
shabby /ˈʃæbi/ *a.* haraposo, desaliñado.
shade /ʃeid/ *n.* **1.** sombra *f.*; tinte *m.*; (window) transparente *m.* —*v.* **2.** sombrear.
shadow /ˈʃædou/ *n.* sombra *f.*
shady /ˈʃeidi/ *a.* sombroso; sospechoso.
shaft /ʃæft/ *n.* (columna) fuste; *Mech.* asta *f.*
shake /ʃeik/ *v.* sacudir; agitar; temblar. **s. hands with,** dar la mano a.
shallow /ˈʃælou/ *a.* poco hondo; superficial.
shame /ʃeim/ *n.* **1.** vergüenza *f.* **be a s.,** ser una lástima. —*v.* **2.** avergonzar.
shameful /ˈʃeimfəl/ *a.* vergonzoso.
shampoo /ʃæmˈpu/ *n.* champú *m.*
shape /ʃeip/ *n.* **1.** forma *f.*; estado *m.* —*v.* **2.** formar.
share /ʃɛər/ *n.* **1.** parte; (stock) acción *f.* **2** —*v.* **2.** compartir.
shareholder /ˈʃɛərˌhouldər/ *n.* accionista *m.* & *f.*
shareware /ˈʃɛərˌwɛər/ *n.* programas compartidos *m.pl.*
shark /ʃɑrk/ *n.* tiburón *m.*
sharp /ʃɑrp/ *a.* agudo; (blade) afilado.
sharpen /ˈʃɑrpən/ *v.* aguzar; afilar.
shatter /ˈʃætər/ *v.* estrellar; hacer pedazos.
shave /ʃeiv/ *n.* **1.** afeitada *f.* —*v.* **2.** afeitarse.
shawl /ʃɔl/ *n.* rebozo, chal *m.*
she /ʃi/ *pron.* ella *f.*
sheaf /ʃif/ *n.* gavilla *f.*
shear /ʃɪər/ *v.* cizallar.
shears /ʃɪərz/ *n.* cizallas *f.pl.*
sheath /ʃiθ/ *n.* vaina *f.*
shed /ʃɛd/ *n.* **1.** cobertizo *m.* —*v.* **2.** arrojar, quitarse.
sheep /ʃip/ *n.* oveja *f.*
sheet /ʃit/ *n.* sábana; (of paper) hoja *f.*
shelf /ʃɛlf/ *n.* estante, *m.*, repisa *f.*
shell /ʃɛl/ *n.* **1.** cáscara; (sea) concha *f.*; *Mil.* proyectil *m.* —*v.* **2.** desgranar; bombardear.
shellac /ʃəˈlæk/ *n.* laca *f.*
shelter /ˈʃɛltər/ *n.* **1.** albergue; refugio *m.* —*v.* **2.** albergar; amparar.
shepherd /ˈʃɛpərd/ *n.* pastor *m.*
sherry /ˈʃɛri/ *n.* jerez *m.*
shield /ʃild/ *n.* **1.** escudo *m.* —*v.* **2.** amparar.
shift /ʃɪft/ *n.* **1.** cambio; (work) turno *m.* —*v.* **2.** cambiar, mudar. **s. for oneself,** arreglárselas.
shine /ʃain/ *n.* **1.** brillo, lustre *m.* —*v.* **2.** brillar; (shoes) lustrar.
shiny /ˈʃaini/ *a.* brillante, lustroso.
ship /ʃɪp/ *n.* **1.** barco *m.*, nave *f.* —*v.* **2.** embarcar; *Com.* enviar.
shipment /ˈʃɪpmənt/ *n.* envío; embarque *m.*
shirk /ʃɜrk/ *v.* faltar al deber.
shirt /ʃɜrt/ *n.* camisa *f.*
shiver /ˈʃɪvər/ *n.* **1.** temblor *m.* —*v.* **2.** temblar.
shock /ʃɒk/ *n.* **1.** choque *m.* —*v.* **2.** chocar.
shoe /ʃu/ *n.* zapato *m.*
shoelace /ˈʃuˌleis/ *n.* lazo *m.*; cordón de zapato.
shoemaker /ˈʃuˌmeikər/ *n.* zapatero *m.*
shoot /ʃut/ *v.* tirar; (gun) disparar. **s. away, s. off,** salir disparado.
shop /ʃɒp/ *n.* tienda *f.*
shopping /ˈʃɒpɪŋ/ *n.* **to go s.,** hacer compras, ir de compras.
shop window escaparate *m.*
shore /ʃɔr/ *n.* orilla; playa *f.*
short /ʃɔrt/ *a.* corto; breve; (in stature) pequeño, bajo. **a s. time,** poco tiempo. **in s.,** en suma.
shortage /ˈʃɔrtɪdʒ/ *n.* escasez; falta *f.*
shorten /ˈʃɔrtn/ *v.* acortar, abreviar.
shortly /ˈʃɔrtli/ *adv.* en breve, dentro de poco.
shorts /ʃɔrts/ *n.* calzoncillos *m. pl.*
shot /ʃɒt/ *n.* tiro, disparo *m.*
shoulder /ˈʃouldər/ *n.* **1.** hombro *m.* —*v.* **2.** asumir; cargar con.
shoulder blade *n.* omóplato *m.*, paletilla *f.*
shout /ʃaut/ *n.* **1.** grito *m.* —*v.* **2.** gritar.
shove /ʃʌv/ *n.* **1.** empujón *m.* —*v.* **2.** empujar.
shovel /ˈʃʌvəl/ *n.* **1.** pala *f.* —*v.* **2.** traspalar.
show /ʃou/ *n.* **1.** ostentación *f.*; *Theat.* función *f.*; espectáculo *m.* —*v.* **2.** enseñar, mostrar; verse. **s. up,** destacarse; *Colloq.* asomar.
shower /ˈʃauər/ *n.* chubasco *m.*; (bath) ducha *f. v.* ducharse.
shrapnel /ˈʃræpnl/ *n.* metralla *f.*
shrewd /ʃrud/ *a.* astuto.
shriek /ʃrik/ *n.* **1.** chillido *m.* —*v.* **2.** chillar.
shrill /ʃrɪl/ *a.* chillón, agudo.
shrimp /ʃrɪmp/ *n.* camarón *m.*
shrine /ʃrain/ *n.* santuario *m.*
shrink /ʃrɪŋk/ *v.* encogerse, contraerse, **s. from,** huir de.
shroud /ʃraud/ *n.* **1.** mortaja *f.* —*v.* **2.** *Fig.* ocultar.
shrub /ʃrʌb/ *n.* arbusto *m.*
shudder /ˈʃʌdər/ *n.* **1.** estremecimiento *m.* —*v.* **2.** estremecerse.
shun /ʃʌn/ *v.* evitar, huir de.
shut /ʃʌt/ *v.* cerrar. **s. in,** encerrar. **s. up,** *Colloq.* callarse.
shutter /ˈʃʌtər/ *n.* persiana *f.*
shy /ʃai/ *a.* tímido, vergonzoso.
sick /sɪk/ *a.* enfermo. **s. of,** aburrido de, cansado de.
sickness /ˈsɪknɪs/ *n.* enfermedad *f.*
side /said/ *n.* **1.** lado; partido *m.*; parte *f.*; *Anat.* costado *m.* —*v.* **2. s. with,** ponerse del lado de.
sidewalk /ˈsaidˌwɔk/ *n.* acera, vereda *f.*
siege /sidʒ/ *n.* asedio *m.*
sieve /sɪv/ *n.* cedazo *m.*
sift /sɪft/ *v.* cerner.
sigh /sai/ *n.* **1.** suspiro *m.* —*v.* **2.** suspirar.
sight /sait/ *n.* **1.** vista *f.*; punto de interés *m.* **lose s. of,** perder de vista. —*v.* **2.** divisar.
sign /sain/ *n.* **1.** letrero; señal, seña *f.* —*v.* **2.** firmar. **s. up,** inscribirse.
signal /ˈsɪgnl/ *n.* **1.** señal *f.* —*v.* **2.** hacer señales.
signature /ˈsɪgnətʃər/ *n.* firma *f.*
significance /sɪgˈnɪfɪkəns/ *n.* significación *f.*
significant /sɪgˈnɪfɪkənt/ *a.* significativo.
significant other pareja *m.* & *f.*
signify /ˈsɪgnəˌfai/ *v.* significar.
silence /ˈsailəns/ *n.* **1.** silencio *m.* —*v.* **2.** hacer callar.
silent /ˈsailənt/ *a.* silencioso; callado.
silk /sɪlk/ *n.* seda *f.*
silken /ˈsɪlkən/ **silky** *a.* sedoso.
sill /sɪl/ *n.* umbral de puerta *m.*, solera *f.*
silly /ˈsɪli/ *a.* necio, tonto.
silo /ˈsailou/ *n.* silo *m.*
silver /ˈsɪlvər/ *n.* plata *f.*
silver-plated /ˈsɪlvər ˈpleitɪd/ *a.* chapado en plata.
silverware /ˈsɪlvərˌwɛər/ *n.* vajilla de plata *f.*
similar /ˈsɪmələr/ *a.* semejante, parecido.
similarity /ˌsɪməˈlærɪti/ *n.* semejanza *f.*
simple /ˈsɪmpəl/ *a.* sencillo, simple.
simplicity /sɪmˈplɪsɪti/ *n.* sencillez *f.*
simplify /ˈsɪmpləˌfai/ *v.* simplificar.
simulate /ˈsɪmyəˌleit/ *v.* simular.
simultaneous /ˌsaiməlˈteiniəs/ *a.* simultáneo.
sin /sɪn/ *n.* **1.** pecado *m.* —*v.* **2.** pecar.
since /sɪns/ *adv.* **1.** desde entonces. —*prep.* **2.** desde. —*conj.* **3.** desde que; puesto que.
sincere /sɪnˈsɪər/ *a.* sincero.
sincerely /sɪnˈsɪərli/ *adv.* sinceramente.
sincerity /sɪnˈsɛrɪti/ *n.* sinceridad *f.*
sinew /ˈsɪnyu/ *n.* tendón *m.*
sinful /ˈsɪnfəl/ *a.* pecador.
sing /sɪŋ/ *v.* cantar.
singe /sɪndʒ/ *v.* chamuscar.
singer /ˈsɪŋər/ *n.* cantante *m.* & *f.*
single /ˈsɪŋgəl/ *a.* solo; (room) sencillo; (unmarried) soltero. **s. room,** habitación individual.
singular /ˈsɪŋgyələr/ *a.* & *n.* singular *m.*
sinister /ˈsɪnəstər/ *a.* siniestro.
sink /sɪŋk/ *n.* **1.** fregadero *m.* —*v.* **2.** hundir; *Fig.* abatir.
sinner /ˈsɪnər/ *n.* pecador -ra.
sinuous /ˈsɪnyuəs/ *a.* sinuoso.
sinus /ˈsainəs/ *n.* seno *m.*
sip /sɪp/ *n.* **1.** sorbo *m.* —*v.* **2.** sorber.
siphon /ˈsaifən/ *n.* sifón *m.*
sir /sɜr/ *title.* señor.
siren /ˈsairən/ *n.* sirena *f.*
sirloin /ˈsɜrlɔin/ *n.* solomillo *m.*
sisal /ˈsaisəl, ˈsɪsəl/ *n.* henequén *m.*
sister /ˈsɪstər/ *n.* hermana *f.*
sister-in-law /ˈsɪstərɪnˌlɔ/ *n.* cuñada *f.*
sit /sɪt/ *v.* sentarse; posar. **be sitting,** estar sentado. **s. down,** sentarse. **s. up,** incorporarse; quedar levantado.
site /sait/ *n.* sitio, local *m.*
sitting /ˈsɪtɪŋ/ *n.* sesión *f. a.* sentado.
situate /ˈsɪtʃuˌeit/ *v.* situar.
situation /ˌsɪtʃuˈeiʃən/ *n.* situación *f.*
sit-up /ˈsɪt ˌʌp/ *n.* abdominal *m.*
six /sɪks/ *a.* & *pron.* seis.
sixteen /ˈsɪksˈtin/ *a.* & *pron.* dieciséis.
sixth /sɪksθ/ *a.* sexto.
sixty /ˈsɪksti/ *a.* & *pron.* sesenta.
size /saiz/ *n.* tamaño; (of shoe, etc.) número *m.*; talla *f.*
sizing /ˈsaizɪŋ/ *n.* upreso *m.*; sisa, cola de retazo *f.*
skate /skeit/ *n.* **1.** patín *m.* —*v.* **2.** patinar.
skateboard /ˈskeitˌbɔrd/ *n.* monopatín *m.*
skein /skein/ *n.* madeja *f.*
skeleton /ˈskɛlɪtn/ *n.* esqueleto *m.*
skeptic /ˈskɛptɪk/ *n.* escéptico -ca.
skeptical /ˈskɛptɪkəl/ *a.* escéptico.
sketch /skɛtʃ/ *n.* **1.** esbozo *m.* —*v.* **2.** esbozar.
ski /ski/ *n.* **1.** esquí *m.* —*v.* **2.** esquiar.
skid /skɪd/ *v.* **1.** resbalar. —*n.* **2.** varadera *f.*
skill /skɪl/ *n.* destreza, habilidad *f.*
skillful /ˈskɪlfəl/ *a.* diestro, hábil.
skim /skɪm/ *v.* rasar; (milk) desnatar. **s. over, s. through,** hojear.
skin /skɪn/ *n.* **1.** piel; (of fruit) corteza *f.* —*v.* **2.** desollar.
skin doctor dermatólogo -ga *m.* & *f.*
skip /skɪp/ *n.* **1.** brinco *m.* —*v.* **2.** brincar. **s. over,** pasar por alto.
skirmish /ˈskɜrmɪʃ/ *n.* escaramuza *f.*
skirt /skɜrt/ *n.* falda *f.*
skull /skʌl/ *n.* cráneo *m.*
skunk /skʌŋk/ *n.* zorrillo *m.*
sky /skai/ *n.* cielo *m.*
skylight /ˈskaiˌlait/ *n.* tragaluz *m.*
skyscraper /ˈskaiˌskreipər/ *n.* rascacielos *m.*
slab /slæb/ *n.* tabla *f.*
slack /slæk/ *a.* flojo; descuidado.
slacken /ˈslækən/ *v.* relajar.
slacks /slæks/ *n.* pantalones flojos.
slam /slæm/ *n.* **1.** portazo *m.* —*v.* **2.** cerrar de golpe. **slamming on the brakes,** frenazo *m.*
slander /ˈslændər/ *n.* **1.** calumnia *f.* —*v.* **2.** calumniar.
slang /slæŋ/ *n.* jerga *f.*
slant /slænt/ *n.* **1.** sesgo *m.* —*v.* **2.** sesgar.
slap /slæp/ *n.* **1.** bofetada, palmada *f.* —*v.* **2.** dar una bofetada.
slash /slæʃ/ *n.* **1.** cuchillada *f.* —*v.* **2.** acuchillar.
slat /slæt/ *n.* **1.** tablilla *f.* —*v.* **2.** lanzar.
slate /sleit/ *n.* **1.** pizarra *f.*; lista de candidatos. —*n.* **2.** destinar.
slaughter /ˈslɔtər/ *n.* **1.** matanza *f.* —*v.* **2.** matar.
slave /sleiv/ *n.* esclavo -va.
slavery /ˈsleivəri/ *n.* esclavitud *f.*
Slavic /ˈslɑvɪk/ *a.* eslavo.
slay /slei/ *v.* matar, asesinar.
sled /slɛd/ *n.* trineo *m.*
sleek /slik/ *a.* liso y brillante.
sleep /slip/ *n.* **1.** sueño *m.* **to get much s.,** dormir mucho. —*v.* **2.** dormir.
sleeping car /ˈslipɪŋ/ coche cama.
sleeping pill /ˈslipɪŋ/ pastilla para dormir, somnífero *m.*
sleepy /ˈslipi/ *a.* soñoliento. **to be s.,** tener sueño.
sleet /slit/ *n.* **1.** cellisca *f.* —*v.* **2.** cellisquear.
sleeve /sliv/ *n.* manga *f.*
slender /ˈslɛndər/ *a.* delgado.
slice /slais/ *n.* **1.** rebanada; (of meat) tajada *f.* —*v.* **2.** rebanar; tajar.
slide /slaid/ *v.* resbalar, deslizarse.
slide rule regla de cálculo *f.*
slight /slait/ *n.* **1.** desaire *m.* —*a.* **2.** pequeño; leve. —*v.* **3.** desairar.
slim /slɪm/ *a.* delgado.
slime /slaim/ *n.* lama *f.*
sling /slɪŋ/ *n.* **1.** honda *f.*; *Med.* cabestrillo *m.* —*v.* **2.** tirar.
slink /slɪŋk/ *v.* escabullirse.
slip /slɪp/ *n.* **1.** imprudencia; (garment) combinación *f.*; (of paper) trozo *m.*; ficha *f.* —*v.* **2.** resbalar; deslizar. **s. up,** equivocarse.
slipper /ˈslɪpər/ *n.* chinela *f.*
slippery /ˈslɪpəri/ *a.* resbaloso.
slit /slɪt/ *n.* **1.** abertura *f.* —*v.* **2.** cortar.
slogan /ˈslougən/ *n.* lema *m. f.*
slope /sloup/ *n.* **1.** declive *m.* —*v.* **2.** inclinarse.
sloppy /ˈslɒpi/ *a.* desaliñado, chapucero.
slot /slɒt/ *n.* ranura *f.*

slot machine tragaperras f.
slouch /slautʃ/ n. **1.** patán m. —v. **2.** estar gacho.
slovenly /'slʌvənli/ a. desaliñado.
slow /slou/ a. **1.** lento; (watch) atrasado. —v. **2. s. down, s. up,** retardar; ir más despacio.
slowly /'slouli/ adv. despacio.
slowness /'slounɪs/ n. lentitud f.
sluggish /'slʌgɪʃ/ a. perezoso, inactivo.
slum /slʌm/ n. barrio bajo m.
slumber /'slʌmbər/ v. dormitar.
slur /slɜr/ n. **1.** estigma m. —v. **2.** menospreciar.
slush /slʌʃ/ n. fango m.
sly /slai/ a. taimado. **on the s.** a hurtadillas.
smack /smæk/ n. **1.** manotada f. —v. **2.** manotear.
small /smɔl/ a. pequeño.
small letter minúscula f.
smallpox /'smɔl,pɒks/ n. viruela f.
smart /smart/ a. **1.** listo; elegante. —v. **2.** escocer.
smash /smæʃ/ v. aplastar; hacer pedazos.
smear /smɪər/ n. **1.** mancha; difamación f. —v. **2.** manchar; difamar.
smell /smɛl/ n. **1.** olor; (sense) olfato m. —v. **2.** oler.
smelt /smɛlt/ n. **1.** eperlano m. —v. **2.** fundir.
smile /smail/ n. **1.** sonrisa f. —v. **2.** sonreír.
smite /smait/ v. afligir; apenar.
smock /smɒk/ n. camisa de mujer f.
smoke /smouk/ n. **1.** humo m. —v. **2.** fumar; (food) ahumar.
smokestack /'smouk,stæk/ n. chimenea f.
smolder /'smouldər/ v. arder sin llama.
smooth /smuð/ a. **1.** liso; suave; tranquilo. —v. **2.** alisar.
smother /'smʌðər/ v. sofocar.
smug /smʌg/ a. presumido.
smuggle /'smʌgəl/ v. pasar de contrabando.
snack /snæk/ n. bocadillo m.
snag /snæg/ n. nudo; obstáculo m.
snail /sneil/ n. caracol m.
snake /sneik/ n. culebra, serpiente f.
snap /snæp/ n. **1.** trueno m. —v. **2.** tronar; romper.
snapshot /'snæp,ʃɒt/ n. instantánea f.
snare /snɛər/ n. trampa f.
snarl /snarl/ n. **1.** gruñido m. —v. **2.** gruñir; (hair) enredar.
snatch /snætʃ/ v. arrebatar.
sneak /snik/ v. ir, entrar, salir (etc.) a hurtadillas.
sneaker /'snikər/ n. sujeto ruín m. zapatilla de tenis.
sneer /snɪər/ n. **1.** mofa f. —v. **2.** mofarse.
sneeze /sniz/ n. **1.** estornudo m. —v. **2.** estornudar.
snicker /'snɪkər/ n. risita f.
snob /snɒb/ n. esnob m.
snore /snɔr/ n. **1.** ronquido m. —v. **2.** roncar.
snow /snou/ n. **1.** nieve f. —v. **2.** nevar.
snowball /'snou,bɔl/ n. bola de nieve f.
snowdrift /'snou,drɪft/ n. ventisquero m.
snowplow /'snou,plau/ n. quitanieves m.
snowstorm /'snou,stɔrm/ n. nevasca f.
snub /snʌb/ v. desairar.
snug /snʌg/ a. abrigado y cómodo.
so /sou/ adv. **1.** así; (also) también. **so as to,** para. **so that,** para que. **so... as,** tan... como. **so... that,** tan... que. —conj. **2.** así es que.
soak /souk/ v. empapar.
soap /soup/ n. **1.** jabón m. —v. **2.** enjabonar.
soap powder jabón en polvo m.
soar /sɔr/ v. remontarse.

sob /sɒb/ n. **1.** sollozo m. —v. **2.** sollozar.
sober /'soubər/ a. sobrio; pensativo.
sociable /'souʃəbəl/ a. sociable.
social /'souʃəl/ a. **1.** social. —n. **2.** tertulia f.
socialism /'souʃə,lɪzəm/ n. socialismo m.
socialist /'souʃəlɪst/ a. & n. socialista m. & f.
society /sə'saiiti/ n. sociedad; compañía f.
sociological /,sousiə'lɒdʒɪkəl/ a. sociológico.
sociologist /,sousi,ɒlədʒɪst/ n. sociólogo -ga m. & f.
sociology /,sousi'ɒlədʒi/ n. sociología f.
sock /sɒk/ n. **1.** calcetín; puñetazo m. —v. **2.** dar un puñetazo a.
socket /'sɒkɪt/ n. cuenca f.; Elec. enchufe m.
sod /sɒd/ n. césped m.
soda /'soudə/ n. soda; Chem. sosa f.
sodium /'soudiəm/ n. sodio m.
sofa /'soufə/ n. sofá m.
soft /sɔft/ a. blando; fino; suave.
soft drink bebida no alcohólica.
soften /'sɔfən/ v. ablandar; suavizar.
software /'sɔft,wɛər/ n. software m., programa m.
soil /sɔil/ n. **1.** suelo m. —v. **2.** ensuciar.
sojourn /'soudʒɜrn/ n. morada f., estancia f.
solace /'sɒlɪs/ n. **1.** solaz m. —v. **2.** solazar.
solar /'soulər/ a. solar.
solar system sistema solar m.
solder /'sɒdər/ v. **1.** soldar. —n. **2.** soldadura f.
soldier /'souldʒər/ n. soldado m. & f.
sole /soul/ n. **1.** suela; (of foot) planta f.; (fish) lenguado m. —a. **2.** único.
solemn /'sɒləm/ a. solemne.
solemnity /sə'lɛmnɪti/ n. solemnidad f.
solicit /sə'lɪsɪt/ v. solicitar.
solicitous /sə'lɪsɪtəs/ a. solícito.
solid /'sɒlɪd/ a. & n. sólido m.
solidify /sə'lɪdə,fai/ v. solidificar.
solidity /sə'lɪdɪti/ n. solidez f.
solitary /'sɒlɪ,tɛri/ a. solitario.
solitude /'sɒlɪ,tud/ n. soledad f.
solo /'soulou/ n. solo m.
soloist /'soulouɪst/ n. solista m. & f.
soluble /'sɒlyəbəl/ a. soluble.
solution /sə'luʃən/ n. solución f.
solve /sɒlv/ v. solucionar; resolver.
solvent /'sɒlvənt/ a. solvente.
somber /'sɒmbər/ a. sombrío.
some /sʌm, unstressed səm/ a. & pron. algo (de), un poco (de); alguno; (pl.) algunos, unos.
somebody, someone /'sʌmbɒdi; 'sʌm,wʌn/ pron. alguien.
somehow /'sʌm,hau/ adv. de algún modo.
someone /'sʌm,wʌn/ n. alguien o alguno.
somersault /'sʌmər,sɔlt/ n. salto mortal m.
something /'sʌm,θɪŋ/ pron. algo, alguna cosa.
sometime /'sʌm,taim/ adv. alguna vez.
sometimes /'sʌm,taimz/ adv. a veces, algunas veces.
somewhat /'sʌm,wʌt/ adv. algo, un poco.
somewhere /'sʌm,wɛər/ adv. en (or a) alguna parte.
son /sʌn/ n. hijo m.
song /sɔŋ/ n. canción f.
son-in-law /'sʌn ɪn ,lɔ/ n. yerno m.
soon /sun/ adv. pronto. **as s. as possible,** cuanto antes. **sooner or later,** tarde o temprano. **no sooner... than,** apenas... cuando.
soot /sʊt/ n. hollín m.
soothe /suð/ v. calmar.
soothingly /'suðɪŋli/ adv. tiernamente.

sophisticated /sə'fɪstɪ,keitɪd/ a. sofisticado.
sophomore /'sɒfə,mɔr/ n. estudiante de segundo año m.
soprano /sə'prænou/ n. soprano m. & f.
sorcery /'sɔrsəri/ n. encantamiento m.
sordid /'sɔrdɪd/ a. sórdido.
sore /sɔr/ n. **1.** llaga f. —a. **2.** lastimado; Colloq. enojado. **to be s.,** doler.
sorority /sə'rɔrɪti, -'rɒr-/ n. hermandad de mujeres f.
sorrow /'sɒrou/ n. pesar, dolor m., aflicción f.
sorrowful /'sɒrəfəl/ a. doloroso; afligido.
sorry /'sɒri/ a. **to be s.,** sentir, lamentar. **to be s. for,** compadecer.
sort /sɔrt/ n. **1.** tipo m.; clase, especie f. **s. of,** algo, un poco. —v. **2.** clasificar.
soul /soul/ n. alma f.
sound /saund/ a. **1.** sano; razonable; firme. —n. **2.** sonido m. —v. **3.** sonar; parecer.
soundproof /'saund,pruf/ a. insonorizado. v. insonorizar.
soundtrack /'saund,træk/ n. banda sonora f.
soup /sup/ n. sopa f.
sour /sauᵊr/ a. agrio; ácido; rancio.
source /sɔrs/ n. fuente; causa f.
south /sauθ/ n. sur m.
South Africa /'æfrɪkə/ Sudáfrica f.
South African a. & n. sudafricano.
South America /ə'mɛrɪkə/ Sudamérica, América del Sur.
South American a. & n. sudamericano -na.
southeast /,sauθ'ist/ Naut. ,sau-/ n. sudeste m.
southern /'sʌðərn/ a. meridional.
South Pole n. polo sur m.
southwest /,sauθ'wɛst/ Naut. ,sau-/ n. sudoeste m.
souvenir /,suvə'nɪər/ n. recuerdo m.
sovereign /'sɒvrɪn/ n. soberano -na.
sovereignty /'sɒvrɪnti/ n. soberanía f.
Soviet Russia Rusia soviética f.
sow /sau/ n. **1.** puerca f. —v. **2.** sembrar.
space /speis/ n. **1.** espacio m. —v. **2.** espaciar.
space out v. escalonar.
spaceship /'speis,ʃɪp/ n. nave espacial, astronave f.
space shuttle /'ʃʌtl/ transbordador espacial m.
spacious /'speiʃəs/ a. espacioso.
spade /speid/ n. **1.** laya; (cards) espada f. —v. **2.** layar.
spaghetti /spə'gɛti/ n. espaguetis m. pl.
Spain /spein/ n. España f.
span /spæn/ n. **1.** tramo m. —v. **2.** extenderse sobre.
Spaniard /'spænyərd/ n. español -ola.
Spanish /'spænɪʃ/ a. & n. español -ola.
spank /spæŋk/ v. pegar.
spanking /'spæŋkɪŋ/ n. tunda, zumba f.
spar /spar/ v. altercar.
spare /spɛər/ a. **1.** de repuesto. —v. **2.** perdonar; ahorrar; prestar. **have... to s.,** tener... de sobra.
spare tire neumático de recambio m.
spark /spark/ n. chispa f.
sparkle /'sparkəl/ n. **1.** destello m. —v. **2.** chispear. **sparkling wine,** vino espumoso.
spark plug /'spark,plʌg/ n. bujía f.
sparrow /'spærou/ n. gorrión m.
sparse /spars/ a. esparcido.
spasm /'spæzəm/ n. espasmo m.
spasmodic /spæz'mɒdɪk/ a. espasmódico.
spatter /'spætər/ v. salpicar; manchar.
speak /spik/ v. hablar.
speaker /'spikər/ n. conferenciante m. & f.

spear /spɪər/ n. lanza f.
spearmint /'spɪər,mɪnt/ n. menta romana f.
special /'spɛʃəl/ a. especial. **s. delivery,** entrega inmediata, entrega urgente.
specialist /'spɛʃəlɪst/ n. especialista m. & f.
specialty /'spɛʃəlti/ n. especialidad f.
species /'spiʃiz, -siz/ n. especie f.
specific /spɪ'sɪfɪk/ a. específico.
specify /'spɛsə,fai/ v. especificar.
specimen /'spɛsəmən/ n. espécimen m.; muestra f.
spectacle /'spɛktəkəl/ n. espectáculo m.; (pl.) lentes, anteojos m. pl.
spectacular /spɛk'tækyələr/ a. espectacular, aparatoso.
spectator /'spɛkteitər/ n. espectador -ra.
spectrum /'spɛktrəm/ n. espectro m.
speculate /'spɛkyə,leit/ v. especular.
speculation /,spɛkyə'leiʃən/ n. especulación f.
speech /spitʃ/ n. habla f.; lenguaje; discurso m. **part of s.,** parte de la oración.
speechless /'spitʃlɪs/ a. mudo.
speed /spid/ n. **1.** velocidad; rapidez f. —v. **2. s. up,** acelerar, apresurar.
speed limit velocidad máxima f.
speedometer /spi'dɒmɪtər/ n. velocímetro m.
speedy /'spidi/ a. veloz, rápido.
spell /spɛl/ n. **1.** hechizo; rato; Med. ataque m. —v. **2.** escribir; relevar.
spelling /'spɛlɪŋ/ n. ortografía f.
spend /spɛnd/ v. gastar; (time) pasar.
spendthrift /'spɛnd,θrɪft/ a. & n. pródigo; manirroto m.
sphere /sfɪər/ n. esfera f.
spice /spais/ n. **1.** especia f. —v. **2.** especiar.
spider /'spaidər/ n. araña f.
spider web telaraña f.
spike /spaik/ n. alcayata f.; punta f., clavo m.
spill /spɪl/ v. derramar. n. caída f., vuelco m.
spillway /'spɪl,wei/ n. vertedero m.
spin /spɪn/ v. hilar; girar.
spinach /'spɪnɪtʃ/ n. espinaca f.
spine /spain/ n. espina dorsal f.
spinet /'spɪnɪt/ n. espineta f.
spinster /'spɪnstər/ n. solterona f.
spiral /'spairəl/ a. & n. espiral f.
spire /spaiᵊr/ n. caracol m., espiral f.
spirit /'spɪrɪt/ n. espíritu; ánimo m.
spiritual /'spɪrɪtʃuəl/ a. espiritual.
spiritualism /'spɪrɪtʃuə,lɪzəm/ n. espiritismo m.
spirituality /,spɪrɪtʃu'ælɪti/ n. espiritualidad f.
spit /spɪt/ v. escupir.
spite /spait/ n. despecho m. **in s. of,** a pesar de.
splash /splæʃ/ n. **1.** salpicadura f. —v. **2.** salpicar.
splendid /'splɛndɪd/ a. espléndido.
splendor /'splɛndər/ n. esplendor m.
splice /splais/ v. **1.** empalmar. —n. **2.** empalme m.
splint /splɪnt/ n. tablilla f.
splinter /'splɪntər/ n. **1.** astilla f. —v. **2.** astillar.
split /splɪt/ n. **1.** división f. —v. **2.** dividir, romper en dos.
splurge /splɜrdʒ/ v. **1.** fachendear. —n. **2.** fachenda f.
spoil /spɔil/ n. **1.** (pl.) botín m. —v. **2.** echar a perder; (a child) mimar.
spoke /spouk/ n. rayo (de rueda) m.
spokesman /'spouksmən/ n. portavoz m. & f.
spokesperson /'spouks,pɜrsən/ n. portavoz m. & f.
sponge /spʌndʒ/ n. esponja f.
sponsor /'spɒnsər/ n. **1.** patrocinador m. —v. **2.** patrocinar; costear.
spontaneity /,spɒntə'niiti, -'nei-/ n. espontaneidad f.

spontaneous /spɒn'teiniəs/ *a.* espontáneo.
spool /spul/ *n.* carrete *m.*
spoon /spun/ *n.* cuchara *f.*
spoonful /'spunfʊl/ *n.* cucharada *f.*
sporadic /spə'rædɪk/ *a.* esporádico.
sport /spɔrt/ *n.* deporte *m.*
sport jacket chaqueta deportiva *f.*
sports center /spɔrts/ pabellón de deportes, polideportivo *m.*
sportsman /'spɔrtsmən/ *a.* **1.** deportivo. —*n.* **2.** deportista *m.* & *f.*
spot /spɒt/ *n.* **1.** mancha *f.*; lugar, punto *m.* —*v.* **2.** distinguir.
spouse /spaus/ *n.* esposo -sa.
spout /spaut/ *n.* **1.** chorro; (of teapot) pico *m.* —*v.* **2.** correr a chorro.
sprain /sprein/ *n.* **1.** torcedura *f.*, esguince *m.* —*v.* **2.** torcerse.
sprawl /sprɔl/ *v.* tenderse.
spray /sprei/ *n.* **1.** rociada *f.* —*v.* **2.** rociar.
spread /sprɛd/ *n.* **1.** propagación; extensión; (for bed) colcha *f.* —*v.* **2.** propagar; extender.
spreadsheet /'sprɛd,ʃit/ *n.* hoja de cálculo *f.*
spree /spri/ *n.* parranda *f.*
sprig /sprɪg/ *n.* ramita *f.*
sprightly /'spraitli/ *a.* garboso.
spring /sprɪŋ/ *n.* resorte, muelle *m.*; (season) primavera *f.*; (of water) manantial *m.*
springboard /'sprɪŋ,bɔrd/ *n.* trampolín *m.*
spring onion cebolleta *f.*
sprinkle /'sprɪŋkəl/ *v.* rociar; (rain) lloviznar.
sprint /sprɪnt/ *n.* carrera *f.*
sprout /spraut/ *n.* retoño *m.*
spry /sprai/ *a.* ágil.
spun /spʌn/ *a.* hilado.
spur /spɜr/ *n.* **1.** espuela *f.* **on the s. of the moment,** sin pensarlo. —*v.* **2.** espolear.
spurious /'spyʊriəs/ *a.* espurio.
spurn /spɜrn/ *v.* rechazar, despreciar.
spurt /spɜrt/ *n.* **1.** chorro *m.*; esfuerzo supremo. —*v.* **2.** salir en chorro.
spy /spai/ **1.** espía *m.* & *f.* —*v.* **2.** espiar.
squabble /'skwɒblɪŋ/ *n.* **1.** riña *f.* —*v.* **2.** reñir.
squad /skwɒd/ *n.* escuadra *f.*
squadron /'skwɒdrən/ *n.* escuadrón *m.*
squalid /'skwɒlɪd/ *a.* escuálido.
squall /skwɔl/ *n.* borrasca *f.*
squalor /'skwɒlər/ *n.* escualidez *f.*
squander /'skwɒndər/ *v.* malgastar.
square /skwɛər/ *a.* **1.** cuadrado. —*n.* **2.** cuadrado *m.*; plaza *f.*
square dance *n.* contradanza *f.*
squat /skwɒt/ *v.* agacharse.
squeak /skwik/ *n.* **1.** chirrido *m.* —*v.* **2.** chirriar.
squeamish /'skwimɪʃ/ *a.* escrupuloso.
squeeze /skwiz/ *n.* **1.** apretón *m.* —*v.* **2.** apretar; (fruit) exprimir.
squirrel /'skwɜrəl/ *n.* ardilla *f.*
squirt /skwɜrt/ *n.* **1.** chisguete *m.* —*v.* **2.** jeringar.
stab /stæb/ *n.* **1.** puñalada *f.* —*v.* **2.** apuñalar.
stability /stə'bɪlɪti/ *n.* estabilidad *f.*
stabilize /'steibə,laiz/ *v.* estabilizar.
stable /'steibəl/ *a.* **1.** estable, equilibrado. —*n.* **2.** caballeriza *f.*
stack /stæk/ *n.* **1.** pila *f.* —*v.* **2.** apilar.
stadium /'steidiəm/ *n.* estadio *m.*
staff /stæf/ *n.* personal *m.* **editorial s.,** cuerpo de redacción. **general s.,** estado mayor.
stag /stæg/ *n.* ciervo *m.*
stage /steidʒ/ *n.* **1.** etapa; *Theat.* escena *f.* —*v.* **2.** representar.
stagflation /stæg'fleiʃən/ *n.* estagflación.
stagger /'stægər/ *v.* (teeter) tambalear; (space out) escalonar.
stagnant /'stægnənt/ *a.* estancado.
stagnate /'stægneit/ *v.* estancarse.
stain /stein/ *n.* **1.** mancha *f.* —*v.* **2.** manchar.
stainless steel /'steinlɪs/ acero inoxidable *m.*
staircase /'stɛər,keis/ **stairs** *n.* escalera *f.*
stake /steik/ *n.* estaca; (bet) apuesta *f.* **at s.,** en juego; en peligro.
stale /steil/ *a.* rancio.
stalemate /'steil,meit/ *n.* estancación *f.*; tablas *f.pl.*
stalk /stɔk/ *n.* caña *f.*; (of flower) tallo *m.* *v.* acechar.
stall /stɔl/ *n.* **1.** tenderete; (for horse) pesebre *m.* —*v.* **2.** demorar; (motor) atascar.
stallion /'stælyən/ *n.* *S.A.* garañón *m.*
stalwart /'stɔlwərt/ *a.* fornido.
stamina /'stæmənə/ *n.* vigor *m.*
stammer /'stæmər/ *v.* tartamudear.
stamp /stæmp/ *n.* **1.** sello *m.*, estampilla *f.* —*v.* **2.** sellar.
stamp collecting /kə'lɛktɪŋ/ filatelia *f.*
stampede /stæm'pid/ *n.* estampida *f.*
stand /stænd/ *n.* **1.** puesto *m.*; posición; (speaker's) tribuna; (furniture) mesita *f.* —*v.* **2.** estar; estar de pie; aguantar. **s. up,** pararse, levantarse.
standard /'stændərd/ *a.* **1.** normal, corriente. —*n.* **2.** norma *f.* **s. of living,** nivel de vida.
standardize /'stændər,daiz/ *v.* uniformar.
standing /'stændɪŋ/ *a.* fijo; establecido.
standpoint /'stænd,pɔint/ *n.* punto de vista *m.*
staple /'steipəl/ *n.* materia prima *f.*; grapa *f.*
stapler /'steiplər/ *n.* grapadora *f.*
star /stɑr/ *n.* estrella *f.*
starboard /'stɑrbərd/ *n.* estribor *m.*
starch /stɑrtʃ/ *n.* **1.** almidón *m.*; (in diet) fécula *f.* —*v.* **2.** almidonar.
stare /stɛər/ *v.* mirar fijamente.
stark /stɑrk/ *a.* **1.** severo. —*adv.* **2.** completamente.
start /stɑrt/ *n.* **1.** susto; principio *m.* —*v.* **2.** comenzar, empezar; salir; poner en marcha; causar.
startle /'stɑrtl/ *v.* asustar.
starvation /stɑr'veiʃən/ *n.* hambre *f.*
starve /stɑrv/ *v.* morir de hambre.
state /steit/ *n.* **1.** estado *m.* —*v.* **2.** declarar, decir.
statement /'steitmənt/ *n.* declaración *f.*
stateroom /'steit,rum/ *n.* camarote *m.*
statesman /'steitsmən/ *n.* estadista *m.*
static /'stætɪk/ *a.* **1.** estático. —*n.* **2.** estática *f.*
station /'steiʃən/ *n.* estación *f.*
stationary /'steiʃə,nɛri/ *a.* estacionario, fijo.
stationery /'steiʃə,nɛri/ *n.* papel de escribir.
statistics /stə'tɪstɪks/ *n.* estadística *f.*
statue /'stætʃu/ *n.* estatua *f.*
stature /'stætʃər/ *n.* estatura *f.*
status /'steitəs, 'stætəs/ *n.* condición, estado *m.*
statute /'stætʃut/ *n.* ley *f.*
staunch /stɔntʃ/ *a.* fiel; constante.
stay /stei/ *n.* **1.** estancia; visita *f.* —*v.* **2.** quedar, permanecer; parar, alojarse. **s. away,** ausentarse. **s. up,** velar.
steadfast /'stɛd,fæst/ *a.* inmutable.
steady /'stɛdi/ *a.* **1.** firme; permanente; regular. —*v.* **2.** sostener.
steak /steik/ *n.* biftec, bistec *m.*
steal /stil/ *v.* robar. **s. away,** escabullirse.
stealth /stɛlθ/ *n.* cautela *f.*
steam /stim/ *n.* vapor *m.*
steamboat /'stim,bout/ **steamer, steamship** *n.* vapor *m.*
steel /stil/ *n.* **1.** acero *m.* —*v.* **2. s. oneself,** fortalecerse.
steep /stip/ *a.* escarpado, empinado.
steeple /'stipəl/ *n.* campanario *m.*
steer /stɪər/ *n.* **1.** buey *m.* —*v.* **2.** guiar, manejar.
stellar /'stɛlər/ *a.* astral.
stem /stɛm/ *n.* **1.** tallo *m.* —*v.* **2.** parar. **s. from,** emanar de.
stencil /'stɛnsəl/ *n.* **1.** estarcido. —*v.* **2.** estarcir.
stenographer /stə'nɒgrəfər/ *n.* estenógrafo -fa.
stenography /stə'nɒgrəfi/ *n.* taquigrafía *f.*
step /stɛp/ *n.* **1.** paso *m.*; medida *f.*; (stairs) escalón *m.* —*v.* **2.** pisar. **s. back,** retirarse.
stepladder /'stɛp,lædər/ *n.* escalera de mano *f.*
stereophonic /,stɛriə'fɒnɪk/ *a.* estereofónico.
stereotype /'stɛriə,taip/ *n.* **1.** estereotipo *m.* —*v.* **2.** estereotipar.
sterile /'stɛrɪl/ *a.* estéril.
sterilize /'stɛrə,laiz/ *v.* esterilizar.
sterling /'stɜrlɪŋ/ *a.* esterlina, genuino.
stern /stɜrn/ *n.* **1.** popa *f.* —*a.* **2.** duro, severo.
stethoscope /'stɛθə,skoup/ *n.* estetoscopio *m.*
stevedore /'stivɪ,dɔr/ *n.* estibador *m.*
stew /stu/ *n.* **1.** guisado *m.* —*v.* **2.** estofar.
steward /'stuərd/ *n.* camarero.
stewardess /'stuərdɪs/ *n.* azafata *f.*, aeromoza *f.*
stick /stɪk/ *n.* **1.** palo, bastón *m.* —*v.* **2.** pegar; (put) poner, meter.
sticky /'stɪki/ *a.* pegajoso.
stiff /stɪf/ *a.* tieso; duro.
stiffness /'stɪfnɪs/ *n.* tiesura *f.*
stifle /'staifəl/ *v.* sofocar; *Fig.* suprimir.
stigma /'stɪgmə/ *n.* estigma *m.*
still /stɪl/ *a.* **1.** quieto; silencioso. **to keep s.,** quedarse quieto. —*adv.* **2.** todavía, aún; no obstante. —*n.* **3.** alambique *m.*
stillborn /'stɪl,bɔrn/ *n.* & *a.* nacido -da muerto -ta.
still life *n.* naturaleza muerta *f.*
stillness /'stɪlnɪs/ *n.* silencio *m.*
stilted /'stɪltɪd/ *a.* afectado, artificial.
stimulant /'stɪmyələnt/ *a.* & *n.* estimulante *m.*
stimulate /'stɪmyə,leit/ *v.* estimular.
stimulus /'stɪmyələs/ *n.* estímulo *m.*
sting /stɪŋ/ *n.* **1.** picadura *f.* —*v.* **2.** picar.
stingy /'stɪndʒi/ *a.* tacaño.
stipulate /'stɪpyə,leit/ *v.* estipular.
stir /stɜr/ *n.* **1.** conmoción *f.* —*v.* **2.** mover. **s. up,** conmover; suscitar.
stitch /stɪtʃ/ *n.* **1.** puntada *f.* —*v.* **2.** coser.
stock /stɒk/ *n.* surtido *f.*; raza *f.*; (finance) acciones. *f.pl.* **in s.,** en existencia. **to take s. in,** tener fe en.
stock exchange bolsa *f.*
stockholder /'stɒk,houldər/ *n.* accionista *m.* & *f.*
stocking /'stɒkɪŋ/ *n.* media *f.*
stockyard /'stɒk,yɑrd/ *n.* corral de ganado *m.*
stodgy /'stɒdʒi/ *a.* pesado.
stoical /'stouɪkəl/ *a.* estoico.
stole /stoul/ *n.* estola *f.*
stolid /'stɒlɪd/ *a.* impasible.
stomach /'stʌmək/ *n.* estómago *m.*
stomachache /'stʌmək,eik/ *n.* dolor de estómago *m.*
stone /stoun/ *n.* piedra *f.*
stool /stul/ *n.* banquillo *m.*
stoop /stup/ *v.* encorvarse; *Fig.* rebajarse. espaldas encorvadas *f.pl.*
stop /stɒp/ *n.* **1.** parada *f.* **to put a s. to,** poner fin a. —*v.* **2.** parar; suspender; detener; impedir. **s. doing** (etc.), dejar de hacer (etc.).
stopgap /'stɒp,gæp/ *n.* recurso provisional *m.*
stopover /'stɒp,ouvər/ *n.* parada *f.*
stopwatch /'stɒp,wɒtʃ/ *n.* cronómetro *m.*
storage /'stɔrɪdʒ/ *n.* almacenaje *m.*
store /stɔr/ *n.* **1.** tienda; provisión *f.* **department s.,** almacén *m.* —*v.* **2.** guardar; almacenar.
store window escaparate *m.*
stork /stɔrk/ *n.* cigüeña *f.*
storm /stɔrm/ *n.* tempestad, tormenta *f.*
stormy /'stɔrmi/ *a.* tempestuoso.
story /'stɔri/ *n.* cuento; relato *m.*; historia *f.* **short s.,** cuento.
stout /staut/ *a.* corpulento.
stove /stouv/ *n.* hornilla; estufa *f.*
straight /streit/ *a.* **1.** recto; derecho. —*adv.* **2.** directamente.
straighten /'streitn/ *v.* enderezar. **s. out,** poner en orden.
straightforward /,streit'fɔrwərd/ *a.* recto, sincero.
strain /strein/ *n.* **1.** tensión *f.* —*v.* **2.** colar.
strainer /'streinər/ *n.* colador *m.*
strait /streit/ *n.* estrecho *m.*
strand /strænd/ *n.* **1.** hilo *m.* —*v.* **2. be stranded,** encallarse.
strange /streindʒ/ *a.* extraño; raro.
stranger /'streindʒər/ *n.* extranjero -ra; forastero -ra; desconocido -da.
strangle /'stræŋgəl/ *v.* estrangular.
strap /stræp/ *n.* correa *f.*
stratagem /'strætədʒəm/ *n.* estratagema *f.*
strategic /strə'tidʒɪk/ *a.* estratégico.
strategy /'strætɪdʒi/ *n.* estrategia *f.*
stratosphere /'strætə,sfɪər/ *n.* estratosfera *f.*
straw /strɔ/ *n.* paja *f.*
strawberry /'strɔ,bɛri/ *n.* fresa *f.*
stray /strei/ *a.* **1.** vagabundo. —*v.* **2.** extraviarse.
streak /strik/ *n.* **1.** racha; raya *f.*; lado *m.* —*v.* **2.** rayar.
stream /strim/ *n.* corriente *f.*; arroyo *m.*
street /strit/ *n.* calle *f.*
streetcar /'strit,kɑr/ *n.* tranvía *m.*
street lamp /'strit,læmp/ *n.* farol *m.*
strength /strɛŋkθ, strɛnθ/ *n.* fuerza *m.*
strengthen /'strɛŋkθən, 'strɛn-/ *v.* reforzar.
strenuous /'strɛnyuəs/ *a.* estrenuo.
streptococcus /,strɛptə'kɒkəs/ *n.* estreptococo *m.*
stress /strɛs/ *n.* **1.** tensión *f.*; énfasis *m.* —*v.* **2.** recalcar; acentuar.
stretch /strɛtʃ/ *n.* **1.** trecho *m.* **at one s.,** de un tirón. —*v.* **2.** tender; extender; estirarse.
stretcher /'strɛtʃər/ *n.* camilla *f.*
strew /stru/ *v.* esparcir.
stricken /'strɪkən/ *a.* agobiado.
strict /strɪkt/ *a.* estricto; severo.
stride /straid/ *n.* **1.** tranco *m.*; (fig., pl.) progresos. —*v.* **2.** andar a trancos.
strife /straif/ *n.* contienda *f.*
strike /straik/ *n.* **1.** huelga *f.* —*v.* **2.** pegar; chocar con; (clock) dar.
striker /'straikər/ *n.* huelguista *m.* & *f.*
string /strɪŋ/ *n.* cuerda *f.*; cordel *m.*
string bean *n.* habichuela *f.*
stringent /'strɪndʒənt/ *a.* estricto.
strip /strɪp/ *n.* **1.** tira *f.* —*v.* **2.** despojar; desnudarse.
stripe /straip/ *n.* raya *f.*; *Mil.* galón *m.*
strive /straiv/ *v.* esforzarse.
stroke /strouk/ *n.* golpe *m.*; (swimming) brazada *f.*; *Med.* ataque *m.* **s. of luck,** suerte *f.*
stroll /stroul/ *n.* **1.** paseo *m.* —*v.* **2.** pasearse.
stroller /'stroulər/ *n.* vagabundo *m.*; cochecito (de niño).
strong /strɔŋ/ *a.* fuerte.
stronghold /'strɔŋ,hould/ *n.* fortificación *f.*
structure /'strʌktʃər/ *n.* estructura *f.*
struggle /'strʌgəl/ *n.* **1.** lucha *f.* —*v.* **2.** luchar.
strut /strʌt/ *n.* **1.** pavonada *f.* —*v.* **2.** pavonear.
stub /stʌb/ *n.* **1.** cabo; (ticket) talón

m. —*v.* **2. s. on one's toes,** tropezar con.
stubborn /ˈstʌbərn/ *a.* testarudo.
stucco /ˈstʌkou/ *n.* **1.** estuco *m.* —*v.* **2.** estucar.
student /ˈstudnt/ *n.* alumno -na, estudiante -ta.
studio /ˈstudiˌou/ *n.* estudio *m.*
studious /ˈstudiəs/ *a.* aplicado; estudioso.
study /ˈstʌdi/ *n.* **1.** estudio *m.* —*v.* **2.** estudiar.
stuff /stʌf/ *n.* **1.** cosas *f.pl.* —*v.* **2.** llenar; rellenar.
stuffing /ˈstʌfɪŋ/ *n.* relleno *m.*
stumble /ˈstʌmbəl/ *v.* tropezar.
stump /stʌmp/ *n.* cabo; tocón; muñón *m.*
stun /stʌn/ *v.* aturdir.
stunt /stʌnt/ *n.* **1.** maniobra sensacional *f.* —*v.* **2.** impedir crecimiento.
stupendous /stuˈpɛndəs/ *a.* estupendo.
stupid /ˈstupɪd/ *a.* estúpido.
stupidity /stuˈpɪdɪti/ *n.* estupidez *f.*
stupor /ˈstupər/ *n.* estupor *m.*
sturdy /ˈstɜrdi/ *a.* robusto.
stutter /ˈstʌtər/ *v.* **1.** tartamudear. —*n.* **2.** tartamudeo *m.*
sty /stai/ *n.* pocilga *f.; Med.* orzuelo.
style /stail/ *n.* estilo *m.;* moda *f.*
stylish /ˈstailɪʃ/ *a.* elegante; a la moda.
suave /swɑv/ *a.* afable, suave.
subconscious /sʌbˈkɒnʃəs/ *a.* subconsciente.
subdue /səbˈdu/ *v.* dominar.
subject /*n.* ˈsʌbdʒɪkt; *v.* səbˈdʒɛkt/ *n.* **1.** tema *m.;* (of study) materia *f.; Pol.* súbdito -ta; *Gram.* sujeto *m.* —*v.* **2.** someter.
subjugate /ˈsʌbdʒəˌgeit/ *v.* sojuzgar, subyugar.
subjunctive /səbˈdʒʌŋktɪv/ *a.* & *n.* subjuntivo *m.*
sublimate /ˈsʌbləˌmeit/ *v.* sublimar.
sublime /səˈblaim/ *a.* sublime.
submarine /ˌsʌbməˈrin/ *a.* & *n.* submarino *m.*
submerge /səbˈmɜrdʒ/ *v.* sumergir.
submission /səbˈmɪʃən/ *n.* sumisión *f.*
submit /səbˈmɪt/ *v.* someter.
subnormal /sʌbˈnɔrməl/ *a.* subnormal.
subordinate /*a,* *n* səˈbɔrdnɪt; *v* -dnˌeit/ *a.* & *n.* **1.** subordinado -da. —*v.* **2.** subordinar.
subscribe /səbˈskraib/ *v.* aprobar; abonarse.
subscriber /səbˈskraibər/ *n.* abonado -da *m.* & *f.*
subscription /səbˈskrɪpʃən/ *n.* abono *m.*
subsequent /ˈsʌbsɪkwənt/ *a.* subsiguiente.
subservient /səbˈsɜrviənt/ *a.* servicial.
subside /səbˈsaid/ *v.* apaciguarse, menguar.
subsidy /ˈsʌbsɪdi/ *n.* subvención *f.*
subsoil /ˈsʌbˌsɔil/ *n.* subsuelo *m.*
substance /ˈsʌbstəns/ *n.* sustancia *f.*
substantial /səbˈstænʃəl/ *a.* sustancial; considerable.
substitute /ˈsʌbstɪˌtut/ *a.* **1.** sustitutivo. —*n.* **2.** sustituto -ta. —*v.* **3.** sustituir.
substitution /ˌsʌbstɪˈtuʃən/ *n.* sustitución *f.*
subterfuge /ˈsʌbtərˌfyudʒ/ *n.* subterfugio *m.*
subtitle /ˈsʌbˌtaitl̩/ *n.* subtítulo *m.*
subtle /ˈsʌtl̩/ *a.* sutil.
subtract /səbˈtrækt/ *v.* sustraer.
suburb /ˈsʌbɜrb/ *n.* suburbio *m.;* (pl.) afueras *f.pl.*
subversive /səbˈvɜrsɪv/ *a.* subversivo.
subway /ˈsʌbˌwei/ *n.* metro *m.*
succeed /səkˈsid/ *v.* lograr, tener éxito; (in office) suceder a.
success /səkˈsɛs/ *n.* éxito *m.*
successful /səkˈsɛsfəl/ *a.* próspero; afortunado.
succession /səkˈsɛʃən/ *n.* sucesión *f.*
successive /səkˈsɛsɪv/ *a.* sucesivo.
successor /səkˈsɛsər/ *n.* sucesor -ra; heredero -ra.
succor /ˈsʌkər/ *n.* **1.** socorro *m.* —*v.* **2.** socorrer.
succumb /səˈkʌm/ *v.* sucumbir.
such /sʌtʃ/ *a.* tal.
suck /sʌk/ *v.* chupar.
suction /ˈsʌkʃən/ *n.* succión *f.*
sudden /ˈsʌdn̩/ *a.* repentino, súbito. **all of a s.,** de repente.
suds /sʌdz/ *n.* jabonaduras *f. pl.*
sue /su/ *v.* demandar.
suffer /ˈsʌfər/ *v.* sufrir; padecer.
suffice /səˈfais/ *v.* bastar.
sufficient /səˈfɪʃənt/ *a.* suficiente.
suffocate /ˈsʌfəˌkeit/ *v.* sofocar.
sugar /ˈʃʊgər/ *n.* azúcar *m.*
sugar bowl azucarero *m.*
suggest /səgˈdʒɛst/ *v.* sugerir.
suggestion /səgˈdʒɛstʃən/ *n.* sugerencia *f.*
suicide /ˈsuəˌsaid/ *n.* suicidio *m.;* (person) suicida *m.* & *f.* **to commit s.,** suicidarse.
suit /sut/ *n.* **1.** traje; (cards) palo; (law) pleito *m.* —*v.* **2.** convenir a.
suitable /ˈsutəbəl/ *a.* apropiado; que conviene.
suitcase /ˈsutˌkeis/ *n.* maleta *f.*
suite /swit/ *n.* serie *f.,* séquito *m.*
suitor /ˈsutər/ *n.* pretendiente *m.*
sullen /ˈsʌlən/ *a.* hosco.
sum /sʌm/ *n.* **1.** suma *f.* —*v.* **2. s. up,** resumir.
summarize /ˈsʌməˌraiz/ *v.* resumir.
summary /ˈsʌməri/ *n.* resumen *m.*
summer /ˈsʌmər/ *n.* verano *m.*
summon /ˈsʌmən/ *v.* llamar; (law) citar.
summons /ˈsʌmənz/ *n.* citación *f.*
sumptuous /ˈsʌmptʃuəs/ *a.* suntuoso.
sun /sʌn/ *n.* **1.** sol *m.* —*v.* **2.** tomar el sol.
sunbathe /ˈsʌnˌbeið/ *v.* tomar el sol.
sunburn /ˈsʌnˌbɜrn/ *n.* quemadura de sol.
sunburned /ˈsʌnˌbɜrnd/ *a.* quemado por el sol.
Sunday /ˈsʌndei/ *n.* domingo *m.*
sunken /ˈsʌŋkən/ *a.* hundido.
sunny /ˈsʌni/ *a.* asoleado. **s. day,** día de sol. **to be s.,** (weather) hacer sol.
sunshine /ˈsʌnˌʃain/ *n.* luz del sol.
suntan /ˈsʌnˌtæn/ *n.* bronceado *m.* **s. lotion,** loción bronceadora *f.,* bronceador *m.*
superb /sʊˈpɜrb/ *a.* soberbio.
superficial /ˌsupərˈfɪʃəl/ *a.* superficial.
superfluous /sʊˈpɜrfluəs/ *a.* superfluo.
superhuman /ˌsupərˈhyumən/ *a.* sobrehumano.
superintendent /ˌsupərɪnˈtɛndənt/ *n.* superintendente *m.* & *f.;* (of building) conserje *m.;* (of school) director -ra general.
superior /səˈpɪəriər/ *a.* & *n.* superior *m.*
superiority /səˌpɪəriˈɔrɪti/ *n.* superioridad *f.*
superlative /səˈpɜrlətɪv/ *a.* superlativo.
supernatural /ˌsupərˈnætʃərəl/ *a.* sobrenatural.
supersede /ˌsupərˈsid/ *v.* reemplazar.
superstar /ˈsupərˌstɑr/ *n.* superestrella *m.* & *f.*
superstition /ˌsupərˈstɪʃən/ *n.* superstición *f.*
superstitious /ˌsupərˈstɪʃəs/ *a.* supersticioso.
supervise /ˈsupərˌvaiz/ *v.* supervisar.
supper /ˈsʌpər/ *n.* cena *f.*
supplement /ˈsʌpləmənt/ *n.* **1.** suplemento *m.* —*v.* **2.** suplementar.
supply /səˈplai/ *n.* **1.** provisión *f.; Com.* surtido *m.; Econ.* existencia *f.* —*v.* **2.** suplir; proporcionar.
support /səˈpɔrt/ *n.* **1.** sustento; apoyo *m.* —*v.* **2.** mantener; apoyar.
suppose /səˈpouz/ *v.* suponer. **be supposed to,** deber.
suppository /səˈpɒzɪˌtɔri/ *n.* supositorio *m.*
suppress /səˈprɛs/ *v.* suprimir.
suppression /səˈprɛʃən/ *n.* supresión *f.*
supreme /səˈprim/ *a.* supremo.
sure /ʃʊr, ʃɜr/ *a.* seguro, cierto. **for s.,** con seguridad. **to make s.,** asegurarse.
surety /ˈʃʊrɪti, ˈʃɜr-/ *n.* garantía *f.*
surf /sɜrf/ *n.* **1.** oleaje *m.* —*v.* **2.** (Internet) navegar; (sport) surfear.
surface /ˈsɜrfɪs/ *n.* superficie *f.*
surfboard /ˈsɜrfˌbɔrd/ *n.* tabla de surf *f.*
surfer /ˈsɜrfər/ *n.* (Internet) usuario -ria, navegante *m.* & *f.;* (sport) surfero -ra.
surge /sɜrdʒ/ *v.* surgir.
surgeon /ˈsɜrdʒən/ *n.* cirujano -na.
surgery /ˈsɜrdʒəri/ *n.* cirugía *f.*
surmise /sərˈmaiz/ *v.* suponer.
surmount /sərˈmaunt/ *v.* vencer.
surname /ˈsɜrˌneim/ *n.* apellido *m.*
surpass /sərˈpæs/ *v.* superar.
surplus /ˈsɜrplʌs/ *a.* & *n.* sobrante *m.*
surprise /sərˈpraiz, sə-/ *n.* **1.** sorpresa —*v.* **2.** sorprender. **I am surprised...,** me extraña...
surrender /səˈrɛndər/ *n.* **1.** rendición *f.* —*v.* **2.** rendir.
surround /səˈraund/ *v.* rodear, circundar.
surveillance /sərˈveiləns/ *n.* vigilancia *f.*
survey /*n.* ˈsɜrvei; *v.* sərˈvei/ *n.* **1.** examen; estudio *m.* —*v.* **2.** examinar; (land) medir.
survival /sərˈvaivəl/ *n.* supervivencia *f.*
survive /sərˈvaiv/ *v.* sobrevivir.
susceptible /səˈsɛptəbəl/ *a.* susceptible.
suspect /*v.* səˈspɛkt; *n.* ˈsʌspɛkt/ *v.* **1.** sospechar. —*n.* **2.** sospechoso -sa.
suspend /səˈspɛnd/ *v.* suspender.
suspense /səˈspɛns/ *n.* incertidumbre *f.* **in s.,** en suspenso.
suspension /səˈspɛnʃən/ *n.* suspensión *f.*
suspension bridge *n.* puente colgante *m.*
suspicion /səˈspɪʃən/ *n.* sospecha *f.*
suspicious /səˈspɪʃəs/ *a.* sospechoso.
sustain /səˈstein/ *v.* sustentar; mantener.
swallow /ˈswɒlou/ *n.* **1.** trago *m.;* (bird) golondrina *f.* —*v.* **2.** tragar.
swamp /swɒmp/ *n.* **1.** pantano *m.* —*v.* **2.** *Fig.* abrumar.
swan /swɒn/ *n.* cisne *m.*
swap /swɒp/ *n.* **1.** trueque *m.* —*v.* **2.** cambalachear.
swarm /swɔrm/ *n.* enjambre *m.*
swarthy /ˈswɔrði/ *a.* moreno.
sway /swei/ *n.* **1.** predominio *m.* —*v.* **2.** bambolearse; *Fig.* influir en.
swear /swɛər/ *v.* jurar. **s. off,** renunciar a.
sweat /swɛt/ *n.* **1.** sudor *m.* —*v.* **2.** sudar.
sweater /ˈswɛtər/ *n.* suéter *m.*
sweatshirt /ˈswɛtˌʃɜrt/ *n.* sudadera *f.*
Swede /swid/ *n.* sueco -ca.
Sweden /ˈswidn̩/ *n.* Suecia *f.*
Swedish /ˈswidɪʃ/ *a.* sueco.
sweep /swip/ *v.* barrer.
sweet /swit/ *a.* **1.** dulce; amable, simpático. —*n.* **2.** (pl.) dulces *m. pl.*
sweetheart /ˈswitˌhɑrt/ *n.* novio -via.
sweetness /ˈswitnɪs/ *n.* dulzura *f.*
sweet-toothed /ˈswit ˌtuθt/ *a.* goloso.
swell /swɛl/ *a.* **1.** *Colloq.* estupendo, excelente. —*n.* **2.** (of the sea) oleada *f.* —*v.* **3.** hincharse; aumentar.
swelter /ˈswɛltər/ *v.* sofocarse de calor.
swift /swɪft/ *a.* rápido, veloz.
swim /swɪm/ *n.* **1.** nadada *f.* —*v.* **2.** nadar.
swimming /ˈswɪmɪŋ/ *n.* natación *f.*
swimming pool alberca, piscina *f.*
swindle /ˈswɪndl̩/ *n.* **1.** estafa *f.* —*v.* **2.** estafar.
swine /swain/ *n.* puercos *m.pl.*
swing /swɪŋ/ *n.* **1.** columpio *m.* **in full s.,** en plena actividad. —*v.* **2.** mecer; balancear.
swirl /swɜrl/ *n.* **1.** remolino *m.* —*v.* **2.** arremolinar.
Swiss /swɪs/ *a.* & *n.* suizo -za.
switch /swɪtʃ/ *n.* **1.** varilla *f.; Elec.* llave *f.,* conmutador *m.;* (railway) cambiavía *m.* —*v.* **2.** cambiar; trocar.
switchboard /ˈswɪtʃˌbɔrd/ *n.* cuadro conmutador *m.,* centralita *f.*
Switzerland /ˈswɪtsərlənd/ *n.* Suiza *f.*
sword /sɔrd/ *n.* espada *f.*
syllable /ˈsɪləbəl/ *n.* sílaba *f.*
symbol /ˈsɪmbəl/ *n.* símbolo *m.*
sympathetic /ˌsɪmpəˈθɛtɪk/ *a.* compasivo. **to be s.,** tener simpatía.
sympathy /ˈsɪmpəθi/ *n.* lástima; condolencia *f.*
symphony /ˈsɪmfəni/ *n.* sinfonía *f.*
symptom /ˈsɪmptəm/ *n.* síntoma *m.*
synagogue /ˈsɪnəˌgɒg/ *n.* sinagoga *f.*
synchronize /ˈsɪŋkrəˌnaiz/ *v.* sincronizar.
syndicate / ˈsɪndɪkɪt/ *n.* sindicato *m.*
syndrome /ˈsɪndroum, -drəm/ *n.* síndrome *m.*
synonym /ˈsɪnənɪm/ *n.* sinónimo *m.*
synthetic /sɪnˈθɛtɪk/ *a.* sintético.
syringe /səˈrɪndʒ/ *n.* jeringa *f.*
syrup /ˈsɪrəp, ˈsɜr-/ *n.* almíbar; *Med.* jarabe *m.*
system /ˈsɪstəm/ *n.* sistema *m.*
systematic /ˌsɪstəˈmætɪk/ *a.* sistemático.

T

tabernacle /ˈtæbərˌnækəl/ *n.* tabernáculo *m.*
table /ˈteibəl/ *n.* mesa; (list) tabla *f.*
tablecloth /ˈteibəlˌklɔθ/ *n.* mantel *m.*
table of contents /ˈkɒntɛnts/ índice de materias *m.*
tablespoon /ˈteibəlˌspun/ *n.* cuchara *f.*
tablespoonful /ˈteibəlspunˌfʊl/ *n.* cucharada *f.*
tablet /ˈtæblɪt/ *n.* tableta; *Med.* pastilla *f.*
tack /tæk/ *n.* tachuela *f.*
tact /tækt/ *n.* tacto *m.*
tag /tæg/ *n.* etiqueta *f.,* rótulo *m.*
tail /teil/ *n.* cola *f.,* rabo *m.*
tailor /ˈteilər/ *n.* sastre *m.*
take /teik/ *v.* tomar; llevar. **t. a bath,** bañarse. **t. a shower,** ducharse. **t. away,** quitar. **t. off,** quitarse. **t. out,** sacar. **t. long,** tardar mucho.
tale /teil/ *n.* cuento *m.*
talent /ˈtælənt/ *n.* talento *m.*
talk /tɔk/ *n.* **1.** plática, habla *f.;* discurso *m.* —*v.* **2.** hablar.
talkative /ˈtɔkətɪv/ *a.* locuaz.
tall /tɔl/ *a.* alto.
tame /teim/ *a.* **1.** manso, domesticado. —*v.* **2.** domesticar.
tamper /ˈtæmpər/ *v.* **t. with,** entremeterse en.
tampon /ˈtæmpɒn/ *n.* tampón *m.*
tan /tæn/ *a.* **1.** color de arena. —*v.* **2.** curtir; tostar. *n.* bronceado.
tangerine /ˌtændʒəˈrin/ *n.* clementina *f.*
tangible /ˈtændʒəbəl/ *a.* tangible.
tangle /ˈtæŋgəl/ *n.* **1.** enredo *m.* —*v.* **2.** enredar.
tank /tæŋk/ *n.* tanque *m.*
tap /tæp/ *n.* **1.** golpe ligero. —*v.* **2.** golpear ligeramente; decentar.
tape /teip/ *n.* cinta *f.*

tape recorder /rɪˈkɔrdər/ magnetófono *m.*, grabadora *f.*
tapestry /ˈtæpəstri/ *n.* tapiz *m.*; tapicería *f.*
tar /tɑr/ *n.* **1.** brea *f.* —*v.* **2.** embrear.
target /ˈtɑrgɪt/ *n.* blanco *m.*
tarnish /ˈtɑrnɪʃ/ *n.* **1.** deslustre *m.* —*v.* **2.** deslustrar.
tarpaulin /tɑrˈpɔlɪn, ˈtɑrpəlɪn/ *n.* lona *f.*
task /tæsk/ *n.* tarea *f.*
taste /teist/ *n.* **1.** gusto; sabor *m.* —*v.* **2.** gustar; probar. **t. of,** saber a.
tasty /ˈteisti/ *a.* sabroso.
tattoo /tæˈtu/ *v.* tatuar.
taut /tɔt/ *a.* tieso.
tavern /ˈtævərn/ *n.* taberna *f.*
tax /tæks/ *n.* **1.** impuesto *m.* —*v.* **2.** imponer impuestos.
tax collector *n.* recaudador -ra *m.* & *f.*
taxi /ˈtæksi/ *n.* taxi, taxímetro *m.* **t. driver,** taxista *m.* & *f.*
taxpayer /ˈtæksˌpeiər/ *n.* contribuyente *m.* & *f.*
tax reform reforma tributaria *f.*
tax return declaración de la renta *f.*
tea /ti/ *n.* té *m.*
teach /titʃ/ *v.* enseñar.
teacher /ˈtitʃər/ *n.* maestro -tra, profesor -ra.
team /tim/ *n.* equipo *m.*; pareja *f.*
tear /tɪər/ *n.* **1.** rasgón *m.*; lágrima *f.* —*v.* **2.** rasgar, lacerar. **t. apart,** separar.
tease /tiz/ *v.* atormentar; embromar.
teaspoon /ˈtiˌspun/ *n.* cucharita *f.*
technical /ˈtɛknɪkəl/ *a.* técnico.
technician /tɛkˈnɪʃən/ *n.* técnico -ca *m.* & *f.*
technique /tɛkˈnik/ *n.* técnica *f.*
technology /tɛkˈnɒlədʒi/ *n.* tecnología *f.*
teddy bear /ˈtɛdi/ oso de felpa *m.*
tedious /ˈtidiəs/ *a.* tedioso.
telegram /ˈtɛlɪˌgræm/ *n.* telegrama *m.*
telegraph /ˈtɛlɪˌgræf/ *n.* **1.** telégrafo *m.* —*v.* **2.** telegrafiar.
telephone /ˈtɛləˌfoun/ *n.* **1.** teléfono *m.* **t. book,** directorio telefónico. —*v.* **2.** telefonear; llamar por teléfono.
telescope /ˈtɛləˌskoup/ *n.* **1.** telescopio *m.* —*v.* **2.** enchufar.
television /ˈtɛləˌvɪʒən/ *n.* televisión *f.*
tell /tɛl/ *v.* decir; contar; distinguir.
temper /ˈtɛmpər/ *n.* **1.** temperamento, genio *m.* —*v.* **2.** templar.
temperament /ˈtɛmpərəmənt, -prəmənt/ *n.* temperamento.
temperamental /ˌtɛmpərəˈmɛntl, -prəˈmɛn-/ *a.* sensitivo, emocional.
temperance /ˈtɛmpərəns/ *n.* moderación; sobriedad *f.*
temperate /ˈtɛmpərɪt/ *a.* templado.
temperature /ˈtɛmpərətʃər/ *n.* temperatura *f.*
tempest /ˈtɛmpɪst/ *n.* tempestad *f.*
tempestuous /tɛmˈpɛstʃuəs/ *a.* tempestuoso.
temple /ˈtɛmpəl/ *n.* templo *m.*
temporary /ˈtɛmpəˌrɛri/ *a.* temporal, temporario.
tempt /tɛmpt/ *v.* tentar.
temptation /tɛmpˈteiʃən/ *n.* tentación *f.*
ten /tɛn/ *a.* & *pron.* diez.
tenant /ˈtɛnənt/ *n.* inquilino -na.
tend /tɛnd/ *v.* tender. **t. to,** atender.
tendency /ˈtɛndənsi/ *n.* tendencia *f.*
tender /ˈtɛndər/ *a.* **1.** tierno. —*v.* **2.** ofrecer.
tenderness /ˈtɛndərnɪs/ *n.* ternura *f.*
tennis /ˈtɛnɪs/ *n.* tenis *m.*
tennis court cancha de tenis, pista de tenis *f.*
tenor /ˈtɛnər/ *n.* tenor *m.*
tense /tɛns/ *a.* **1.** tenso. —*n.* **2.** *Gram.* tiempo *m.*
tent /tɛnt/ *n.* tienda, carpa *f.*
tenth /tɛnθ/ *a.* décimo.
term /tɜrm/ *n.* **1.** término; plazo *m.* —*v.* **2.** llamar.
terminal /ˈtɜrmənl/ *n.* terminal *f.*
terrace /ˈtɛrəs/ *n.* terraza *f.*
terrible /ˈtɛrəbəl/ *a.* terrible, espantoso; pésimo.
territory /ˈtɛrɪˌtɔri/ *n.* territorio *m.*
terror /ˈtɛrər/ *n.* terror, espanto, pavor *m.*
test /tɛst/ *n.* **1.** prueba *f.*; examen *m.* —*v.* **2.** probar; examinar.
testament /ˈtɛstəmənt/ *n.* testamento *m.*
testify /ˈtɛstəˌfai/ *v.* atestiguar, testificar.
testimony /ˈtɛstəˌmouni/ *n.* testimonio *m.*
test tube tubo de ensayo *m.*
text /tɛkst/ *n.* texto; tema *m.*
textbook /ˈtɛkstˌbuk/ *n.* libro de texto.
textile /ˈtɛkstail/ *a.* **1.** textil. —*n.* **2.** tejido *m.*
texture /ˈtɛkstʃər/ *n.* textura *f.*; tejido *m.*
than /ðæn, ðɛn; *unstressed* ðən, ən/ *conj.* que; de.
thank /θæŋk/ *v.* agradecer, dar gracias; **thanks, th. you,** gracias.
thankful /ˈθæŋkfəl/ *a.* agradecido; grato.
that /ðæt; *unstressed* ðət/ *a.* **1.** ese, aquel. —*dem. pron.* **2.** ése, aquél; eso, aquello. —*rel. pron.* & *conj.* **3.** que.
the /*stressed* ði; *unstressed before a consonant* ðə, *unstressed before a vowel* ði/ *art.* el, la, los, las; lo.
theater /ˈθiətər/ *n.* teatro *m.*
theft /θɛft/ *n.* robo *m.*
their /ðɛər; *unstressed* ðər/ *a.* su.
theirs /ðɛərz/ *pron.* suyo, de ellos.
them /ðɛm; *unstressed* ðəm, əm/ *pron.* ellos, ellas; los, las; les.
theme /θim/ *n.* tema; *Mus.* motivo *m.*
themselves /ðəmˈsɛlvz, ˌðɛm-/ *pron.* sí, sí mismos -as. **they th.,** ellos mismos, ellas mismas. **with th.,** consigo.
then /ðɛn/ *adv.* entonces, después; pues.
thence /ðɛns/ *adv.* de allí.
theology /θiˈɒlədʒi/ *n.* teología *f.*
theory /ˈθiəri/ *n.* teoría *f.*
there /ðɛər; *unstressed* ðər/ *adv.* allí, allá, ahí. **there is, there are,** hay.
therefore /ˈðɛərˌfɔr/ *adv.* por lo tanto, por consiguiente.
thermometer /θərˈmɒmɪtər/ *n.* termómetro *m.*
thermostat /ˈθɜrməˌstæt/ *n.* termostato *m.*
they /ðei/ *pron.* ellos, ellas.
thick /θɪk/ *a.* espeso, grueso, denso; torpe.
thicken /ˈθɪkən/ *v.* espesar, condensar.
thief /θif/ *n.* ladrón -na.
thigh /θai/ *n.* muslo *m.*
thimble /ˈθɪmbəl/ *n.* dedal *m.*
thin /θɪn/ *a.* **1.** delgado; raro; claro; escaso. —*v.* **2.** enrarecer; adelgazar.
thing /θɪŋ/ *n.* cosa *f.*
thingamabob /ˈθɪŋəməˌbɒb/ *n. Colloq.* chisme *m.*
think /θɪŋk/ *v.* pensar; creer.
thinker /ˈθɪŋkər/ *n.* pensador -ra.
third /θɜrd/ *a.* tercero.
Third World Tercer Mundo *m.*
thirst /θɜrst/ *n.* sed *f.*
thirsty /ˈθɜrsti/ *a.* sediento. **to be th.,** tener sed.
thirteen /ˈθɜrˈtin/ *a.* & *pron.* trece.
thirty /ˈθɜrti/ *a.* & *pron.* treinta.
this /ðɪs/ *a.* **1.** este. —*pron.* **2.** éste; esto.
thoracic cage /θɔˈræsɪk/ *n.* caja torácica *f.*
thorn /θɔrn/ *n.* espina *f.*
thorough /ˈθɜrou/ *a.* completo; cuidadoso.
though /ðou/ *adv.* **1.** sin embargo. —*conj.* **2.** aunque. **as th.,** como si.
thought /θɔt/ *n.* pensamiento *m.*
thoughtful /ˈθɔtfəl/ *a.* pensativo; considerado.
thousand /ˈθauzənd/ *a.* & *pron.* mil.
thread /θrɛd/ *n.* hilo *m.*; (of screw) rosca *f.*
threat /θrɛt/ *n.* amenaza *f.*
threaten /ˈθrɛtn/ *v.* amenazar.
three /θri/ *a.* & *pron.* tres.
thrift /θrɪft/ *n.* economía, frugalidad *f.*
thrill /θrɪl/ *n.* **1.** emoción *f.* —*v.* **2.** emocionar.
thrive /θraiv/ *v.* prosperar.
throat /θrout/ *n.* garganta *f.*
throne /θroun/ *n.* trono *m.*
through /θru/ *prep.* **1.** por; a través de; por medio de. —*a.* **2.** continuo. **th. train,** tren directo. **to be th.,** haber terminado.
throughout /θruˈaut/ *prep.* **1.** por todo, durante todo. —*adv.* **2.** en todas partes; completamente.
throw /θrou/ *n.* **1.** tiro *m.* —*v.* **2.** tirar, lanzar. **th. away,** arrojar. **th. out,** echar.
thrust /θrʌst/ *n.* **1.** lanzada *f.* —*v.* **2.** empujar.
thumb /θʌm/ *n.* dedo pulgar, pulgar *m.*
thumbtack /ˈθʌmˌtæk/ *n.* chincheta *f.*
thunder /ˈθʌndər/ *n.* **1.** trueno *m.* —*v.* **2.** tronar.
Thursday /ˈθɜrzdei/ *n.* jueves *m.*
thus /ðʌs/ *adv.* así, de este modo.
thwart /θwɔrt/ *v.* frustrar.
ticket /ˈtɪkɪt/ *n.* billete, boleto *m.* **t. window,** taquilla *f.* **round trip t.,** billete de ida y vuelta.
tickle /ˈtɪkəl/ *n.* **1.** cosquilla *f.* —*v.* **2.** hacer cosquillas a.
ticklish /ˈtɪklɪʃ/ *a.* cosquilloso.
tide /taid/ *n.* marea *f.*
tidy /ˈtaidi/ *a.* **1.** limpio, ordenado. —*v.* **2.** poner en orden.
tie /tai/ *n.* **1.** corbata *f.*; lazo; (game) empate *m.* —*v.* **2.** atar; anudar.
tier /ˈtɪər/ *n.* hilera *f.*
tiger /ˈtaigər/ *n.* tigre *m.*
tight /tait/ *a.* apretado; tacaño.
tighten /ˈtaitn/ *v.* estrechar, apretar.
tile /tail/ *n.* teja *f.*; azulejo *m.*
till /tɪl/ *prep.* **1.** hasta. —*conj.* **2.** hasta que. —*n.* **3.** cajón *m.* —*v.* **4.** cultivar, labrar.
tilt /tɪlt/ *n.* **1.** inclinación; justa *f.* —*v.* **2.** inclinar; justar.
timber /ˈtɪmbər/ *n.* madera *f.*; (beam) madero *m.*
time /taim/ *n.* tiempo *m.*; vez *f.*; (of day) hora *f*,; *v. cronometrar.*
timetable /ˈtaimˌteibəl/ *n.* horario, itinerario *m.*
time zone huso horario *m.*
timid /ˈtɪmɪd/ *a.* tímido.
timidity /tɪˈmɪdɪti/ *n.* timidez *f.*
tin /tɪn/ *n.* estaño *m.*; hojalata *f.* **t. can,** lata *f.*
tin foil papel de estaño *m.*
tint /tɪnt/ *n.* **1.** tinte *m.* —*v.* **2.** teñir.
tiny /ˈtaini/ *a.* chiquito, pequeñito.
tip /tɪp/ *n.* **1.** punta; propina *f.* —*v.* **2.** inclinar; dar propina a.
tire /taiᵊr/ *n.* **1.** llanta, goma *f.*, neumático *m.* —*v.* **2.** cansar.
tired /taiᵊrd/ *a.* cansado.
tissue /ˈtɪʃu/ *n.* tejido *m.* **t. paper,** papel de seda.
title /ˈtaitl/ *n.* **1.** título *m.* —*v.* **2.** titular.
to /tu; *unstressed* tʊ, tə/ *prep.* a; para.
toast /toust/ *n.* **1.** tostada *f.*; (drink) brindis *m.* —*v.* **2.** tostar; brindar.
toaster /ˈtoustər/ *n.* tostador *m.*
tobacco /təˈbækou/ *n.* tabaco *m.* **t. shop,** tabaquería *f.*
toboggan /təˈbɒgən/ *n.* tobogán *m.*
today /təˈdei/ *adv.* hoy.
toe /tou/ *n.* dedo del pie.
together /təˈgɛðər/ *a.* **1.** juntos. —*adv.* **2.** juntamente.
toil /tɔil/ *n.* **1.** trabajo *m.* —*v.* **2.** afanarse.
toilet /ˈtɔilɪt/ *n.* tocado; excusado, retrete *m.* **t. paper,** papel higiénico.
token /ˈtoukən/ *n.* señal *f.*
tolerance /ˈtɒlərəns/ *n.* tolerancia *f.*
tolerate /ˈtɒləˌreit/ *v.* tolerar.
toll-free number /ˈtoul ˈfri/ teléfono gratuito *m.*
tomato /təˈmeitou/ *n.* tomate *m.*
tomb /tum/ *n.* tumba *f.*
tomorrow /təˈmɔrou/ *adv.* mañana. **day after t.,** pasado mañana.
ton /tʌn/ *n.* tonelada *f.*
tone /toun/ *n.* tono *m.*
tongue /tʌŋ/ *n.* lengua *f.*
tonic /ˈtɒnɪk/ *n.* tónico *m.*
tonight /təˈnait/ *adv.* esta noche.
tonsil /ˈtɒnsəl/ *n.* amígdala *f.*
too /tu/ *adv.* también. **t. much,** demasiado. **t. many,** demasiados.
tool /tul/ *n.* herramienta *f.*
tooth /tuθ/ *n.* diente *m.*; (back) muela *f.*
toothache /ˈtuθˌeik/ *n.* dolor de muela.
toothbrush /ˈtuθˌbrʌʃ/ *n.* cepillo de dientes.
toothpaste /ˈtuθˌpeist/ *n.* crema dentífrica, pasta dentífrica.
top /tɒp/ *n.* **1.** parte de arriba. —*v.* **2.** cubrir; sobrepasar.
topic /ˈtɒpɪk/ *n. S.A.* tópico *m.*
topical /ˈtɒpɪkəl/ *a.* tópico.
torch /tɔrtʃ/ *n.* antorcha *f.*
torment /*n.* ˈtɔrmɛnt; *v.* tɔrˈmɛnt/ *n.* **1.** tormento *m.* —*v.* **2.** atormentar.
torrent /ˈtɔrənt/ *n.* torrente *m.*
torture /ˈtɔrtʃər/ *n.* **1.** tortura *f.* —*v.* **2.** torturar.
toss /tɔs/ *v.* tirar; agitar.
total /ˈtoutl/ *a.* **1.** total, entero. —*n.* **2.** total *m.*
touch /tʌtʃ/ *n.* **1.** tacto *m.* **in t.,** en comunicación. —*v.* **2.** tocar; conmover.
tough /tʌf/ *a.* tosco; tieso; fuerte.
tour /tʊr/ *n.* **1.** viaje *m.* —*v.* **2.** viajar.
tourist /ˈtʊrɪst/ *n.* turista *m.* & *f.* *a.* turístico.
tournament /ˈtʊrnəmənt/ *n.* torneo *m.*
tow /tou/ *n.* **1.** remolque *m.* —*v.* **2.** remolcar.
toward /tɔrd, təˈwɔrd/ *prep.* hacia.
towel /ˈtauəl/ *n.* toalla *f.*
tower /ˈtauər/ *n.* torre *f.*
town /taun/ *n.* pueblo *m.*
town meeting cabildo abierto *m.*
tow truck grúa *f.*
toy /tɔi/ *n.* **1.** juguete *m.* —*v.* **2.** jugar.
trace /treis/ *n.* **1.** vestigio; rastro *m.* —*v.* **2.** trazar; rastrear; investigar.
track /træk/ *n.* **1.** huella, pista *f.* **race t.,** hipódromo *m.* —*v.* **2.** rastrear.
tract /trækt/ *n.* trecho; tracto *m.*
tractor /ˈtræktər/ *n.* tractor *m.*
trade /treid/ *n.* **1.** comercio, negocio; oficio; canje *m.* —*v.* **2.** comerciar, negociar; cambiar.
trader /ˈtreidər/ *n.* comerciante *m.*
tradition /trəˈdɪʃən/ *n.* tradición *f.*
traditional /trəˈdɪʃənl/ *a.* tradicional.
traffic /ˈtræfɪk/ *n.* **1.** tráfico *m.* —*v.* **2.** traficar.
traffic jam atasco, embotellamiento *m.*
traffic light semáforo *m.*
tragedy /ˈtrædʒɪdi/ *n.* tragedia *f.*
tragic /ˈtrædʒɪk/ *a.* trágico.
trail /treil/ *n.* **1.** sendero; rastro *m.* —*v.* **2.** rastrear; arrastrar.
train /trein/ *n.* **1.** tren *m.* —*v.* **2.** enseñar; disciplinar; (sport) entrenarse.
traitor /ˈtreitər/ *n.* traidor -ora.
tramp /træmp/ *n.* **1.** caminata *f.*; vagabundo *m.* —*v.* **2.** patear.
tranquil /ˈtræŋkwɪl/ *a.* tranquilo.
tranquilizer /ˈtræŋkwəˌlaizər/ *n.* tranquilizante *m.*
tranquillity /træŋˈkwɪlɪti/ *n.* tranquilidad *f.*
transaction /trænˈsækʃən/ *n.* transacción *f.*
transfer /*n.* ˈtrænsfər, *v.* trænsˈfɜr/ *n.* **1.** traslado *m.*; boleto de transbordo. —*v.* **2.** trasladar, transferir.
transform /trænsˈfɔrm/ *v.* transformar.

transfusion /træns'fyuʒən/ n. transfusión f.

transistor /træn'zɪstər/ n. transistor m.

transition /træn'zɪʃən/ n. transición f.

translate /træns'leit/ v. traducir.

translation /træns'leiʃən/ n. traducción f.

transmit /træns'mɪt/ v. transmitir.

transparent /træns'pɛərənt/ a. transparente.

transport /n. 'trænspərt, v. træns'pɔrt/ n. **1.** transporte m. —v. **2.** transportar.

transportation /ˌtrænspər'teiʃən/ n. transporte m.

transsexual /træns'sɛkʃuəl/ a. & n. transexual m. & f.

transvestite /træns'vɛstait/ n. travestí m. & f.

trap /træp/ n. **1.** trampa f. —v. **2.** atrapar.

trash /træʃ/ n. desecho m.; basura f.

trash can cubo de la basura m.

travel /'trævəl/ n. **1.** tráfico m.; (pl.) viajes m. pl. —v. **2.** viajar.

travel agency agencia de viajes f.

traveler /'trævələr/ n. viajero -ra.

traveler's check /'trævələrz/ cheque de viaje m.

tray /trei/ n. bandeja f.

tread /trɛd/ n. **1.** pisada f.; (of a tire) cubierta f. —v. **2.** pisar.

treason /'trizən/ n. traición f.

treasure /'trɛʒər/ n. tesoro m.

treasurer /'trɛʒərər/ n. tesorero -ra.

treasury /'trɛʒəri/ n. tesorería f.

treat /trit/ v. tratar; convidar.

treatment /'tritmənt/ n. trato, tratamiento m.

treaty /'triti/ n. tratado, pacto m.

tree /tri/ n. árbol m.

tremble /'trɛmbəl/ v. temblar.

tremendous /tri'mɛndəs/ a. tremendo.

trench /trɛntʃ/ n. foso m.; Mil. trinchera f.

trend /trɛnd/ n. **1.** tendencia f. —v. **2.** tender.

trespass /'trɛspəs, -pæs/ v. traspasar; violar.

triage /tri'ɑʒ/ n. clasificación de los heridos después del combate.

trial /'traiəl/ n. prueba f.; Leg. proceso, juicio m.

triangle /'traiˌæŋgəl/ n. triángulo m.

tribulation /ˌtribyə'leiʃən/ n. tribulación f.

tributary /'tribyəˌtɛri/ a. & n. tributario m.

tribute /'tribyut/ n. tributo m.

trick /trɪk/ n. **1.** engaño m.; maña f.; (cards) baza f. —v. **2.** engañar.

trifle /'traifəl/ n. **1.** pequeñez f. —v. **2.** juguetear.

trigger /'trɪgər/ n. gatillo m.

trim /trɪm/ a. **1.** ajustado; acicalado. —n. **2.** adorno m. —v. **3.** adornar; ajustar; cortar un poco.

trinket /'trɪŋkɪt/ n. bagatela, chuchería f.

trip /trɪp/ n. **1.** viaje m. —v. **2.** tropezar.

triple /'trɪpəl/ a. **1.** triple —v. **2.** triplicar.

tripod /'traipɒd/ n. trípode f.

trite /trait/ a. banal.

triumph /'traiəmf/ n. **1.** triunfo m. —v. **2.** triunfar.

triumphant /trai'ʌmfənt/ a. triunfante.

trivial /'triviəl/ a. trivial.

trolley /'trɒli/ n. tranvía m.

trombone /trɒm'boun/ n. trombón m.

troop /trup/ n. tropa f.

trophy /'troufi/ n. trofeo m.

tropical /'trɒpikəl/ a. tropical.

tropics /'trɒpiks/ n. trópico m.

trot /trɒt/ n. **1.** trote m. —v. **2.** trotar.

trouble /'trʌbəl/ n. **1.** apuro m.; congoja; aflicción f. —v. **2.** molestar; afligir.

troublesome /'trʌbəlsəm/ a. penoso, molesto.

trough /trɒf/ n. artesa f.

trousers /'trauzərz/ n. pantalones, calzones m.pl.

trout /traut/ n. trucha f.

truce /trus/ n. tregua f.

truck /trʌk/ n. camión m.

true /tru/ a. verdadero, cierto, verdad.

truffle /'trʌfəl/ n. trufa f.

trumpet /'trʌmpit/ n. trompeta, trompa f.

trunk /trʌŋk/ n. baúl m.; (of a tree) tronco m.

trust /trʌst/ n. **1.** confianza f. —v. **2.** confiar.

trustworthy /'trʌstˌwɜrði/ a. digno de confianza.

truth /truθ/ n. verdad f.

truthful /'truθfəl/ a. veraz.

try /trai/ n. **1.** prueba f.; ensayo m. —v. **2.** tratar; probar; ensayar; Leg. juzgar. **t. on,** probarse.

T-shirt /'tiˌʃɜrt/ n. camiseta f.

tub /tʌb/ n. tina f.

tube /tub/ n. tubo m.

tuberculosis /tuˌbɜrkyə'lousis/ n. tuberculosis f.

tuck /tʌk/ n. **1.** recogido m. —v. **2.** recoger.

Tuesday /'tuzdei/ n. martes m.

tug /tʌg/ n. **1.** tirada f.; (boat) remolcador m. —v. **2.** tirar de.

tuition /tu'ɪʃən/ n. matrícula, colegiatura f.

tumble /'tʌmbəl/ n. **1.** caída f. —v. **2.** caer, tumbar; voltear.

tumult /'tumʌlt/ n. tumulto, alboroto m.

tuna /'tʌni/ n. atún m.

tune /tun/ n. **1.** tono m.; melodía, canción f. —v. **2.** templar.

tunnel /'tʌnl/ n. túnel m.

Turkey /'tɜrki/ n. Turquía f.

Turkish /'tɜrkɪʃ/ a. turco.

turmoil /'tɜrmɔil/ n. disturbio m.

turn /tɜrn/ n. **1.** vuelta f.; giro; turno m. —v. **2.** volver, tornear, girar; **t. into,** transformar. **t. around,** volverse. **t. on,** encender; abrir. **t. off, t. out,** apagar.

turnip /'tɜrnɪp/ n. nabo m.

turret /'tɜrit/ n. torrecilla f.

turtle /'tɜrtl/ n. tortuga f.

turtleneck sweater /'tɜrtlˌnɛk/ jersey de cuello alto m.

tutor /'tutər/ n. **1.** tutor -ra. —v. **2.** enseñar.

tweezers /'twizərz/ n. pl. pinzas f. pl.

twelve /twɛlv/ a. & pron. doce.

twenty /'twɛnti/ a. & pron. veinte.

twice /twais/ adv. dos veces.

twig /twɪg/ n. varita; ramita f.; vástago m.

twilight /'twaiˌlait/ n. crepúsculo m.

twin /twɪn/ n. gemelo -la.

twine /twain/ n. **1.** guita f. —v. **2.** torcer.

twinkle /'twɪŋkəl/ v. centellear.

twist /twɪst/ v. torcer.

two /tu/ a. & pron. dos.

type /taip/ n. **1.** tipo m. —v. **2.** escribir a máquina.

typewriter /'taipˌraitər/ n. máquina de escribir.

typhoid fever /'taifɔid/ fiebre tifoidea.

typical /'tɪpikəl/ a. típico.

typist /'taipist/ n. mecanógrafo -fa.

tyranny /'tɪrəni/ n. tiranía f.

tyrant /'tairənt/ n. tirano -na.

U

udder /'ʌdər/ n. ubre f.

UFO abbr. (unidentified flying object) OVNI m. (objeto volador no identificado).

ugly /'ʌgli/ a. feo.

Ukraine /yu'krein/ n. Ucrania f.

Ukrainian /yu'kreiniən/ a. & n. ucranio.

ulcer /'ʌlsər/ n. úlcera f.

ulterior /ʌl'tɪəriər/ a. ulterior.

ultimate /'ʌltəmit/ a. último.

ultrasonic /ˌʌltrə'sɒnik/ a. ultrasónico.

umbrella /ʌm'brɛlə/ n. paraguas m. **sun u.,** quitasol m.

umpire /'ʌmpaiər/ n. árbitro m.

unable /ʌn'eibəl/ a. incapaz. **to be u.,** no poder.

unanimous /yu'nænəməs/ a. unánime.

uncertain /ʌn'sɜrtn/ a. incierto, inseguro.

uncle /'ʌŋkəl/ n. tío m.

unconscious /ʌn'kɒnʃəs/ a. inconsciente; desmayado.

uncover /ʌn'kʌvər/ v. descubrir.

undeniable /ˌʌndi'naiəbəl/ a. innegable.

under /'ʌndər/ adv. **1.** debajo, abajo. —prep. **2.** bajo, debajo de.

underestimate /ˌʌndər'ɛstəˌmeit/ v. menospreciar; subestimar.

undergo /ˌʌndər'gou/ v. sufrir.

underground /'ʌndərˌgraund/ a. subterráneo; clandestino.

underline /'ʌndərˌlain/ v. subrayar.

underneath /ˌʌndər'niθ/ adv. **1.** por debajo. —prep. **2.** debajo de.

undershirt /'ʌndərˌʃɜrt/ n. camiseta f.

understand /ˌʌndər'stænd/ v. entender, comprender.

undertake /ˌʌndər'teik/ v. emprender.

underwear /'ʌndərˌwɛər/ n. ropa interior.

undo /ʌn'du/ v. deshacer; desatar.

undress /ʌn'drɛs/ v. desnudar, desvestir.

uneasy /ʌn'izi/ a. inquieto.

uneven /ʌn'ivən/ a. desigual.

unexpected /ˌʌnik'spɛktid/ a. inesperado.

unfair /ʌn'fɛər/ a. injusto.

unfit /ʌn'fɪt/ a. incapaz; inadecuado.

unfold /ʌn'fould/ v. desplegar; revelar.

unforgettable /ˌʌnfər'gɛtəbəl/ a. inolvidable.

unfortunate /ʌn'fɔrtʃənit/ a. desafortunado, desgraciado.

unfurnished /ʌn'fɜrniʃt/ a. desamueblado.

unhappy /ʌn'hæpi/ a. infeliz.

uniform /'yunəˌfɔrm/ a. & n. uniforme m.

unify /'yunəˌfai/ v. unificar.

union /'yunyən/ n. unión f. **labor u.,** sindicato de obreros.

unique /yu'nik/ a. único.

unisex /'yunəˌsɛks/ a. unisex.

unit /'yunit/ n. unidad f.

unite /yu'nait/ v. unir.

United Nations /yu'naitid 'neiʃənz/ Naciones Unidas f. pl.

United States /yu'naitid 'steits/ Estados Unidos m. pl.

unity /'yuniti/ n. unidad f.

universal /ˌyunə'vɜrsəl/ a. universal.

universe /'yunəˌvɜrs/ n. universo m.

university /ˌyunə'vɜrsiti/ n. universidad f.

unleaded /ʌn'lɛdid/ a. sin plomo.

unless /ʌn'lɛs/ conj. a menos que, si no es que.

unlike /ʌn'laik/ a. disímil.

unload /ʌn'loud/ v. descargar.

unlock /ʌn'lɒk/ v. abrir.

unplug /ʌn'plʌg/ v. desenchufar.

unpopular /ʌn'pɒpyələr/ a. impopular.

unreasonable /ʌn'rizənəbəl/ a. desrazonable.

unscrew /ʌn'skru/ v. desatornillar.

untie /ʌn'tai/ v. desatar; soltar.

until /ʌn'tɪl/ prep. **1.** hasta. —conj. **2.** hasta que.

unusual /ʌn'yuʒuəl/ a. raro, inusitado.

up /ʌp/ adv. **1.** arriba. —prep. **2.** **u. the street,** etc. calle arriba, etc.

uphold /ʌp'hould/ v. apoyar; defender.

upholster /ʌp'houlstər, ə'poul-/ v. entapizar.

upload /'ʌpˌloud/ n. **1.** ascenso de archivos m. —v. **2.** subir, cargar.

upon /ə'pɒn/ prep. sobre, encima de.

upper /'ʌpər/ a. superior.

upper-case letter /'ʌpər 'keis/ mayúscula f.

upright /'ʌpˌrait/ a. derecho, recto.

upriver /'ʌp'rɪvər/ adv. río arriba.

uproar /'ʌpˌrɔr/ n. alboroto, tumulto m.

upset /n. 'ʌpˌsɛt; v. ʌp'sɛt/ n. **1.** trastorno m. —v. **2.** trastornar.

upsetting /ʌp'sɛtiŋ/ a. inquietante.

upstream /'ʌp'strim/ adv. aguas arriba, contra la corriente, río arriba.

uptight /'ʌp'tait/ a. (psicológicamente) tenso, tieso.

upward /'ʌpwərd/ adv. hacia arriba.

urge /ɜrdʒ/ n. **1.** deseo m. —v. **2.** instar.

urgency /'ɜrdʒənsi/ n. urgencia f.

urgent /'ɜrdʒənt/ a. urgente. **to be u.,** urgir.

us /ʌs/ pron. nosotros -as; nos.

use /n. yus; v. yuz/ n. **1.** uso m. —v. **2.** usar, emplear. **u. up,** gastar, agotar. **be used to,** estar acostumbrado a.

useful /'yusfəl/ a. útil.

useless /'yuslis/ a. inútil, inservible.

user-friendly /'yuzər 'frɛndli/ a. amigable.

username /'yuzərˌneim/ n. nombre de usuario m.

usher /'ʌʃər/ n. **1.** acomodador -ora. —v. **2.** introducir.

usual /'yuʒuəl/ a. usual.

utensil /yu'tɛnsəl/ n. utensilio m.

utmost /'ʌtˌmoust/ a. sumo, extremo.

utter /'ʌtər/ a. **1.** completo. —v. **2.** proferir; dar.

utterance /'ʌtərəns/ n. expresión f.

V

vacancy /'veikənsi/ n. vacante f.

vacant /'veikənt/ a. desocupado, libre.

vacation /vei'keiʃən/ n. vacaciones f. pl.

vaccinate /'væksəˌneit/ v. vacunar.

vacuum /'vækyum/ n. vacuo, vacío m. **v. cleaner,** aspiradora f.

vagrant /'veigrənt/ a. & n. vagabundo- da.

vague /veig/ a. vago.

vain /vein/ a. vano; vanidoso. **in v.,** en vano.

valiant /'vælyənt/ a. valiente.

valid /'vælid/ a. válido.

valley /'væli/ n. valle m.

valor /'vælər/ n. valor m., valentía f.

valuable /'vælyuəbəl/ a. valioso. **to be v.,** valer mucho.

value /'vælyu/ n. **1.** valor, importe m. —v. **2.** valorar; estimar.

van /væn/ n. furgoneta f.

vandal /'vændl/ n. vándalo m.

vandalism /'vændlˌizəm/ n. vandalismo m.

vanish /'væniʃ/ v. desaparecer.

vanity /'væniti/ n. vanidad f. **v. case,** polvera f.

vanquish /'væŋkwiʃ/ v. vencer.

vapor /'veipər/ n. vapor m.

variation /ˌvɛəri'eiʃən/ n. variación f.

varicose vein /'væriˌkous/ variz f.

variety /və'raiti/ n. variedad f.

various /'vɛəriəs/ a. varios; diversos.

varnish /'vɑrniʃ/ n. **1.** barniz m. —v. **2.** barnizar.

vary /'vɛəri/ v. variar; cambiar.

vase /veis, veiz, vɑz/ n. florero; jarrón m.

vasectomy /væ'sɛktəmi/ n. vasectomía f.

vassal /'væsəl/ n. vasallo m.

vast /væst/ a. vasto.

vat /væt/ n. tina f., tanque m.

VAT /væt/ n. IVA (impuesto sobre el valor añadido).

vault /vɔlt/ n. bóveda f.

vegetable /'vɛdʒtəbəl/ a. & n. vegetal m.; (pl.) legumbres, verduras f. pl.

vehement /'viəmənt/ a. vehemente.

vehicle /'viikəl or, sometimes, 'vihi-/ n. vehículo m.

veil /veil/ n. 1. velo m. —v. 2. velar.

vein /vein/ n. vena f.

velocity /və'lɒsiti/ n. velocidad f.

velvet /'vɛlvit/ n. terciopelo m.

Venetian /və'niʃən/ a. & n. veneciano.

vengeance /'vɛndʒəns/ n. venganza f.

Venice /'vɛnis/ n. Venecia f.

vent /vɛnt/ n. apertura f.

ventilate /'vɛntl,eit/ v. ventilar.

venture /'vɛntʃər/ n. ventura f.

verb /vɜrb/ n. verbo m.

verbose /vər'bous/ a. verboso.

verdict /'vɜrdikt/ n. veredicto, fallo m.

verge /vɜrdʒ/ n. borde m.

verify /'vɛrə,fai/ v. verificar.

versatile /'vɜrsətl/ a. versátil.

verse /vɜrs/ n. verso m.

version /'vɜrʒən/ n. versión f.

vertical /'vɜrtikəl/ a. vertical.

very /'vɛri/ a. 1. mismo. —adv. 2. muy.

vessel /'vɛsəl/ n. vasija f.; barco m.

vest /vɛst/ n. chaleco m.

veteran /'vɛtərən/ a. & n. veterano -na.

veto /'vitou/ n. veto m.

vex /vɛks/ v. molestar.

via /'vaiə, 'viə/ prep. por la vía de; por.

viaduct /'vaiə,dʌkt/ n. viaducto m.

vibrate /'vaibreit/ v. vibrar.

vibration /vai'breiʃən/ n. vibración f.

vice /vais/ n. vicio m.

vicinity /vi'siniti/ n. vecindad f.

vicious /'viʃəs/ a. vicioso.

victim /'viktəm/ n. víctima f.

victor /'viktər/ n. vencedor -ora.

victorious /vik'tɔriəs/ a. victorioso.

victory /'viktəri/ n. victoria f.

video camera /'vidi,ou/ n. videocámara f.

videoconference /'vidiou,kɒnfərəns/ videoconferencia f.

videodisc /'vidiou,disk/ n. videodisco m.

video game /'vidi,ou/ videojuego m.

videotape /'vidiou,teip/ n. vídeo m., magnetoscopio m.

view /vyu/ n. 1. vista f. —v. 2. ver.

viewpoint /'vyu,pɔint/ n. punto de vista m.

vigil /'vidʒəl/ n. vigilia, vela f.

vigilant /'vidʒələnt/ a. vigilante.

vigor /'vigər/ n. vigor m.

vile /vail/ a. vil, bajo.

village /'vilidʒ/ n. aldea f.

villain /'vilən/ n. malvado -da.

vindicate /'vindi,keit/ v. vindicar.

vine /vain/ n. parra, vid f.

vinegar /'vinigər/ n. vinagre m.

vintage /'vintidʒ/ n. vendimia f.

violate /'vaiə,leit/ v. violar.

violation /,vaiə'leiʃən/ n. violación f.

violence /'vaiələns/ n. violencia f.

violent /'vaiələnt/ a. violento.

violin /,vaiə'lin/ n. violín m.

virgin /'vɜrdʒin/ n. virgen f.

virile /'virəl/ a. viril.

virtual /'vɜrtʃuəl/ a. virtual.

virtual memory memoria virtual f.

virtual reality realidad virtual f.

virtue /'vɜrtʃu/ n. virtud f.

virtuous /'vɜrtʃuəs/ a. virtuoso.

virus /'vairəs/ n. virus m.

visa /'vizə/ n. visa f.

visible /'vizəbəl/ a. visible.

---

vision /'viʒən/ n. visión f.

visit /'vizit/ n. 1. visita f. —v. 2. visitar.

visitor /'vizitər/ n. visitante m. & f.

visual /'viʒuəl/ a. visual.

vital /vait/ a. vital.

vitality /vai'tæliti/ n. vitalidad, energía vital f.

vitamin /'vaitəmin/ n. vitamina f.

vivacious /vi'veiʃəs, vai-/ a. vivaz.

vivid /'vivid/ a. vivo; gráfico.

vocabulary /vou'kæbyə,lɛri/ n. vocabulario m.

vocal /'voukəl/ a. vocal.

vodka /'vɒdkə/ n. vodca m.

vogue /voug/ n. boga; moda f. **be in vogue** estilarse.

voice /vɔis/ n. 1. voz f. —v. 2. expresar.

voice mail correo de voz m.

voice recognition reconocimiento de voz m.

void /vɔid/ a. 1. vacío. —n. 2. vacío m. —v. 3. invalidar.

voltage /'voultidʒ/ n. voltaje m.

volume /'vɒlyum/ n. volumen; tomo m.

voluntary /'vɒlən,tɛri/ a. voluntario.

volunteer /,vɒlən'tiər/ n. 1. voluntario -ria. —v. 2. ofrecerse.

vomit /'vɒmit/ v. vomitar.

vote /vout/ n. 1. voto m. —v. 2. votar.

voter /'voutər/ n. votante m. & f.

vouch /vautʃ/ v. **v. for,** garantizar.

vow /vau/ n. 1. voto m. —v. 2. jurar.

vowel /'vauəl/ n. vocal f.

voyage /'vɔidʒ/ n. viaje m.

vulgar /'vʌlgər/ a. vulgar; común; soez.

vulnerable /'vʌlnərəbəl/ a. vulnerable.

W

wade /weid/ v. vadear.

wag /wæg/ v. menear.

wage /weidʒ/ n. 1. (pl.) sueldo, salario m. —v. 2. **w. war,** hacer guerra.

wagon /'wægən/ n. carreta f.

wail /weil/ n. 1. lamento, gemido m. —v. 2. lamentar, gemir.

waist /weist/ n. cintura f.

wait /weit/ n. 1. espera f. —v. 2. esperar. **w. for,** esperar. **w. on,** atender.

waiter /'weitər/ waitress n. camarero -ra.

waiting room /'weitiŋ/ sala de espera.

wake /weik/ v. **w. up,** despertar.

walk /wɔk/ n. 1. paseo m.; vuelta; caminata f.; modo de andar. —v. 2. andar; caminar; ir a pie.

wall /wɔl/ n. pared; muralla f.

wallcovering /'wɔl,kʌvəriŋ/ n. tapizado de pared m.

wallet /'wɒlit/ n. cartera f.

wallpaper /'wɔl,peipər/ n. 1. empapelado m. —v. 2. empapelar.

walnut /'wɔl,nʌt/ n. nuez f.

waltz /wɔlts/ n. vals m.

wander /'wɒndər/ v. vagar.

want /wɒnt/ n. 1. necesidad f. —v. 2. querer.

war /wɔr/ n. guerra f.

ward /wɔrd/ n. 1. Pol. barrio m.; (hospital) cuadra f. —v. 2. **w. off,** parar.

warehouse /'wɛər,haus/ n. almacén m.

wares /wɛərz/ n. mercancías f.pl.

warlike /'wɔr,laik/ a. belicoso.

warm /wɔrm/ a. 1. caliente; Fig. caluroso. **to be w.,** tener calor; (weather) hacer calor. —v. 2. calentar.

warmth /wɔrmθ/ n. calor m.

warn /wɔrn/ v. advertir.

warning /'wɔrniŋ/ n. aviso m.

warp /wɔrp/ v. alabear.

warrant /'wɔrənt, 'wɒr-/ v. justificar.

---

warrior /'wɔriər/ n. guerrero -ra.

warship /'wɔr,ʃip/ n. navío de guerra, buque de guerra m.

wash /wɒʃ/ v. lavar.

washing machine /'wɒʃiŋ/ máquina de lavar, lavadora f.

wasp /wɒsp/ n. avispa f.

waste /weist/ n. 1. gasto m.; desechos m.pl. —v. 2. gastar; perder.

watch /wɒtʃ/ n. 1. reloj m.; Mil. guardia f. —v. 2. observar, mirar. **w. for,** esperar. **w. out for,** tener cuidado con. **w. over,** guardar; velar por.

watchful /'wɒtʃfəl/ a. desvelado.

watchmaker /'wɒtʃ,meikər/ n. relojero -ra.

watchman /'wɒtʃmən/ n. sereno m.

water /'wɒtər/ n. 1. agua f. **w. color,** acuarela f. —v. 2. aguar.

waterbed /'wɒtər,bɛd/ n. cama de agua f.

waterfall /'wɒtər,fɔl/ n. catarata f.

watering can /'wɒtəriŋ/ regadera f.

waterproof /'wɒtər,pruf/ a. impermeable.

wave /weiv/ n. 1. onda; ola f. —v. 2. ondear; agitar; hacer señas.

waver /'weivər/ v. vacilar.

wax /wæks/ n. 1. cera f. —v. 2. encerar.

way /wei/ n. camino; modo m., manera f. **in a w.,** hasta cierto punto. **a long w.,** muy lejos. **by the w.,** a propósito. **this w.,** por aquí. **that w.,** por allí. **which w.,** por dónde.

we /wi/ pron. nosotros -as.

weak /wik/ a. débil.

weaken /'wikən/ v. debilitar.

weakness /'wiknis/ n. debilidad f.

wealth /wɛlθ/ n. riqueza f.

wealthy /'wɛlθi/ a. adinerado.

wean /win/ v. destetar.

weapon /'wɛpən/ n. arma f.

wear /wɛər/ n. 1. uso; desgaste m.; (clothes) ropa f. —v. 2. usar, llevar. **w. out,** gastar; cansar.

weary /'wiəri/ a. cansado, rendido.

weather /'wɛðər/ n. tiempo m.

weave /wiv/ v. tejer.

weaver /'wivər/ n. tejedor -ra.

web /wɛb/ n. 1. tela f.

Web /wɛb/ n. 2. (Internet) malla f., telaraña f., web m.

wedding /'wɛdiŋ/ n. boda f.

wedge /wɛdʒ/ n. cuña f.

Wednesday /'wɛnzdei/ n. miércoles m.

weed /wid/ n. maleza f.

week /wik/ n. semana f.

weekday /'wik,dei/ n. día de trabajo.

weekend /'wik,ɛnd/ n. fin de semana.

weekly /'wikli/ a. semanal.

weep /wip/ v. llorar.

weigh /wei/ v. pesar.

weight /weit/ n. peso m.

weightless /'weitlis/ v. ingrávido.

weightlessness /'weitlisnis/ n. ingravidez f.

weird /wiərd/ a. misterioso, extraño.

welcome /'wɛlkəm/ a. 1. bienvenido. **you're w.,** de nada, no hay de qué. —n. 2. acogida, bienvenida f. —v. 3. acoger, recibir bien.

welfare /'wɛl,fɛər/ n. bienestar m.

well /wɛl/ a. 1. sano, bueno. —adv. 2. bien; pues. —n. 3. pozo m.

well-done /'wɛl 'dʌn/ a. (food) bien cocido.

well-known /'wɛl 'noun/ a. bien conocido.

well-mannered /'wɛl 'mænərd/ a. educado.

west /wɛst/ n. oeste, occidente m.

western /'wɛstərn/ a. occidental.

westward /'wɛstwərd/ adv. hacia el oeste.

wet /wɛt/ a. 1. mojado. **to get w.,** mojarse. —v. 2. mojar.

whale /weil/ n. ballena f.

what /wʌt; unstressed wət/ a. 1. qué; cuál. —interrog. pron. 2. qué. —rel. pron. 3. lo que.

---

whatever /wʌt'ɛvər/ a. 1. cualquier. —pron. 2. lo que; todo lo que.

wheat /wit/ n. trigo m.

wheel /wil/ n. rueda f. **steering w.,** volante m.

when /wɛn; unstressed wən/ adv. 1. cuándo. —conj. 2. cuando.

whenever /wɛn'ɛvər/ conj. siempre que, cuando quiera que.

where /wɛər/ adv. 1. dónde, adónde. —conj. 2. donde.

wherever /wɛər'ɛvər/ conj. dondequiera que, adondequiera que.

whether /'wɛðər/ conj. si.

which /witʃ/ a. 1. qué. —interrog. pron. 2. cuál. —rel. pron. 3. que; el cual; lo cual.

whichever /witʃ'ɛvər/ a. & pron. cualquiera que.

while /wail/ conj. 1. mientras; mientras que. —n. 2. rato m.

whip /wip/ n. 1. látigo m. —v. 2. azotar.

whipped cream /wipt/ nata batida f.

whirl /wɜrl/ v. girar.

whirlpool /'wɜrl,pul/ n. vórtice m.

whirlwind /'wɜrl,wind/ n. torbellino m.

whisk broom /wisk/ escobilla f.

whisker /'wiskər/ n. bigote m.

whiskey /'wiski/ n. whisky m.

whisper /'wispər/ n. 1. cuchicheo m. —v. 2. cuchichear.

whistle /'wisəl/ n. 1. pito; silbido m. —v. 2. silbar.

white /wait/ a. 1. blanco. —n. 2. (of egg) clara f.

who /hu/ whom interrog. pron. 1. quién. —rel. pron. 2. que; quien.

whoever /hu'ɛvər/ whomever pron. quienquiera que.

whole /houl/ a. 1. entero. **the wh.,** todo el. —n. 2. totalidad f. **on the wh.,** por lo general.

wholesale /'houl,seil/ n. **at wh.,** al por mayor.

wholesaler /'houl,seilər/ n. mayorista m. & f.

wholesome /'houlsəm/ a. sano, saludable.

wholly /'houli/ adv. enteramente.

whose /huz/ interrog. adj. 1. de quién. —rel. adj. 2. cuyo.

why /wai/ adv. por qué; para qué.

wicked /'wikid/ a. malo, malvado.

wickedness /'wikidnis/ n. maldad f.

wide /waid/ a. 1. ancho; extenso. —adv. 2. **w. open,** abierto de par en par.

widen /'waidṇ/ v. ensanchar; extender.

widespread /'waid'sprɛd/ a. extenso.

widow /'widou/ n. viuda f.

widower /'widouər/ n. viudo m.

width /widθ/ n. anchura f.

wield /wild/ v. manejar, empuñar.

wife /waif/ n. esposa, señora, mujer f.

wig /wig/ n. peluca f.

wild /waild/ a. salvaje; bárbaro.

wilderness /'wildərnis/ n. desierto m.

wildlife /'waild,laif/ n. fauna silvestre f.

will /wil/ n. 1. voluntad f.; testamento m. —v. 2. querer; determinar; Leg. legar.

willful /'wilfəl/ a. voluntarioso; premeditado.

willing /'wiliŋ/ a. **to be w.,** estar dispuesto.

willingly /'wiliŋli/ adv. de buena gana.

wilt /wilt/ v. marchitar.

win /win/ v. ganar.

wind /wind/ n. 1. viento m. —v. 2. torcer; dar cuerda a.

windmill /'wind,mil/ n. molino de viento m.

window /'windou/ n. ventana; (of car) ventanilla f.; (of shop or store) escaparate m.

windshield /'wind,ʃild/ n. parabrisas m.

windy /'wɪndi/ *a.* ventoso. **to be w.,** (weather) hacer viento.

wine /wain/ *n.* vino *m.*

wing /wɪŋ/ *n.* ala *f.; Theat.* bastidor *m.*

wink /wɪŋk/ *n.* **1.** guiño *m.* —*v.* **2.** guiñar.

winner /'wɪnər/ *n.* ganador -ra.

winter /'wɪntər/ *n.* invierno *m.*

wipe /waip/ *v.* limpiar; (dry) secar. **w. out,** destruir.

wire /waiᵊr/ *n.* **1.** alambre; hilo; telegrama *m.* —*v.* **2.** telegrafiar.

wireless /'waiᵊrlɪs/ *n.* telégrafo sin hilos.

wisdom /'wɪzdəm/ *n.* juicio *m.;* sabiduría *f.*

wise /waiz/ *a.* sensato, juicioso; sabio.

wish /wɪʃ/ *n.* **1.** deseo; voto *m.* —*v.* **2.** desear; querer.

wit /wɪt/ *n.* ingenio *m.*, sal *f.*

witch /wɪtʃ/ *n.* bruja *f.*

with /wɪθ, wɪð/ *prep.* con.

withdraw /wɪð'drɔ, wɪθ-/ *v.* retirar.

wither /'wɪðər/ *v.* marchitar.

withhold /wɪθ'hould, wɪð-/ *v.* retener, suspender.

within /wɪð'ɪn, wɪθ-/ *adv.* **1.** dentro, por dentro. —*prep.* **2.** dentro de; en.

without /wɪð'aut, wɪθ-/ *adv.* **1.** fuera, por fuera. —*prep.* **2.** sin.

witness /'wɪtnɪs/ *n.* **1.** testigo; testimonio *m.* & *f.* —*v.* **2.** presenciar; atestar.

witty /'wɪti/ *a.* ingenioso, gracioso, ocurrente.

wizard /'wɪzərd/ *n.* hechicero *m.*

woe /wou/ *n.* dolor *m.;* pena *f.*

wolf /wulf/ *n.* lobo -ba.

woman /'wumən/ *n.* mujer *f.*

womb /wum/ *n.* entrañas *f.pl.*, matriz *f.*

wonder /'wʌndər/ *n.* **1.** maravilla; admiración *f.* **for a w.,** por milagro. **no w.,** no es extraño. —*v.* **2.** preguntarse; maravillarse.

wonderful /'wʌndərfəl/ *a.* maravilloso; estupendo.

woo /wu/ *v.* cortejar.

wood /wud/ *n.* madera; (for fire) leña *f.*

wooden /'wudn̩/ *a.* de madera.

wool /wul/ *n.* lana *f.*

word /wɜrd/ *n.* **1.** palabra *f.* **the words** (of a song), la letra. —*v.* **2.** expresar.

word processing /'prɒsɛsɪŋ/ procesamiento de textos *m.*

word processor /'prɒsɛsər/ procesador de textos *m.*

work /wɜrk/ *n.* **1.** trabajo *m.;* (of art) obra *f.* —*v.* **2.** trabajar; obrar; funcionar.

worker /'wɜrkər/ *n.* trabajador -ra; obrero -ra.

workman /'wɜrkmən/ *n.* obrero *m.*

work station estación de trabajo *f.*

work week /'wɜrk,wik/ semana laboral *f.*

world /wɜrld/ *n.* mundo *m.* **w. war,** guerra mundial.

worldly /'wɜrldli/ *a.* mundano.

worldwide /'wɜrld'waid/ *a.* mundial.

worm /wɜrm/ *n.* gusano *m.*

worn /wɔrn/ *a.* usado. **w. out,** gastado; cansado, rendido.

worrisome /'wɜrisəm/ *a.* inquietante.

worry /'wɜri/ *n.* **1.** preocupación *f.* —*v.* **2.** preocupar.

worrying /'wɜriɪŋ/ *a.* inquietante.

worse /wɜrs/ *a.* peor. **to get w.,** empeorar.

worship /'wɜrʃɪp/ *n.* **1.** adoración *f.* —*v.* **2.** adorar.

worst /wɜrst/ *a.* peor.

worth /wɜrθ/ *a.* **1. to be w.,** valer. —*n.* **2.** valor *m.*

worthless /'wɜrθlɪs/ *a.* sin valor.

worthy /'wɜrði/ *a.* digno.

wound /wund/ *n.* **1.** herida *f.* —*v.* **2.** herir.

wrap /ræp/ *n.* **1.** (pl.) abrigos *m. pl.* —*n.* **2.** envolver.

wrapping /'ræpɪŋ/ *n.* cubierta *f.*

wrath /ræθ/ *n.* ira, cólera *f.*

wreath /riθ/ *n.* guirnalda; corona *f.*

wreck /rɛk/ *n.* **1.** ruina *f.;* accidente *m.* —*v.* **2.** destrozar, arruinar.

wrench /rɛntʃ/ *n.* llave *f.* **monkey w.,** llave inglesa.

wrestle /'rɛsəl/ *v.* luchar.

wretched /'rɛtʃɪd/ *a.* miserable.

wring /rɪŋ/ *v.* retorcer.

wrinkle /'rɪŋkəl/ *n.* **1.** arruga *f.* —*v.* **2.** arrugar.

wrist /rɪst/ *n.* muñeca *f.* **w. watch,** reloj de pulsera.

write /rait/ *v.* escribir. **w. down,** apuntar.

writer /'raitər/ *n.* escritor -ra.

writhe /raið/ *v.* contorcerse.

writing paper /'raitɪŋ/ papel de escribir *m.*

wrong /rɒŋ/ *a.* **1.** equivocado; incorrecto. **to be w.,** equivocarse; no tener razón. —*adv.* **2.** mal, incorrectamente. —*n.* **3.** agravio *m.* **right and w.,** el bien y el mal. —*v.* **4.** agraviar, ofender.

WWW *abbr.* (World Wide Web) malla mundial *f.*

X Y Z

x-ray /'ɛks,rei/ *n.* **1.** rayo X *m.*, radiografía, *f.* —*v.* **2.** radiografiar.

xylophone /'zailə,foun/ *n.* xilófono *m.*

yacht /ypt/ *n.* yate *m.*

yard /yɑrd/ *n.* patio, corral *m.;* (measure) yarda *f.*

yarn /yɑrn/ *n.* hilo.

yawn /yɒn/ *n.* **1.** bostezo *m.* —*v.* **2.** bostezar.

year /yɪər/ *n.* año *m.*

yearly /'yɪərli/ *a.* anual.

yearn /yɜrn/ *v.* anhelar.

yell /yɛl/ *n.* **1.** grito *m.* —*v.* **2.** gritar.

yellow /'yɛlou/ *a.* amarillo.

yes /yɛs/ *adv.* sí.

yesterday /'yɛstər,dei/ *adv.* ayer.

yet /yɛt/ *adv.* todavía, aún.

Yiddish /'yɪdɪʃ/ *n.* yídish *m.*

yield /yild/ *v.* producir; ceder.

yogurt /'yougərt/ *n.* yogur *m.*

yoke /youk/ *n.* yugo *m.*

yolk /youk/ *n.* yema *f.*

you /yu; *unstressed* yu, yə/ *pron.* usted, (pl.) ustedes; lo, la, los, las; le, les; (familiar) tú, (pl.) vosotros -as; ti; te, (pl.) os. **with y.,** contigo, con usted.

young /yʌŋ/ *a.* joven.

youngster /'yʌŋstər/ *n.* muchacho -cha *m.* & *f.*

your /yur, yɔr; *unstressed* yər/ *a.* su; (familiar) tu; (pl.) vuestro.

yours /yurz, yɔrz/ *pron.* suyo; (familiar) tuyo; (pl.) vuestro.

yourself -selves /yur'sɛlf, yɔr- yər-/ *pron.* sí; se; (familiar) ti; te. **with y.,** consigo; contigo. **you y.,** usted mismo, ustedes mismos; tú mismo, vosotros mismos.

youth /yuθ/ *n.* juventud *f.;* (person) joven *m.* & *f.*

youth club club juvenil *m.*

youthful /'yuθfəl/ *a.* juvenil.

yuppie /'yʌpi/ *n.* yuppie *m.* & *f.*

zap /zæp/ *v.* desintegrar, aniquilar.

zeal /zil/ *n.* celo, fervor *m.*

zealous /'zɛləs/ *a.* celoso, fervoroso.

zero /'zɪərou/ *n.* cero *m.*

zest /zɛst/ *n.* gusto *m.*

zip code /zɪp/ número de distrito postal.

zipper /'zɪpər/ *m.* cremallera *f.*

zone /zoun/ *n.* zona *f.*

zoo /zu/ *n.* jardín zoológico.

SPANISH IRREGULAR VERBS

Infinitive	Present	Future	Preterit	Past Part.
andar	ando	andaré	anduve	andado
caber	quepo	cabré	cupe	cabido
caer	caigo	caeré	caí	caído
conducir	conduzco	conduciré	conduje	conducido
dar	doy	daré	di	dado
decir	digo	diré	dije	dicho
estar	estoy	estaré	estuve	estado
haber	he	habré	hube	habido
hacer	hago	haré	hice	hecho
ir	voy	iré	fui	ido
jugar	juego	jugaré	jugué	jugado
morir	muero	moriré	morí	muerto
oir	oigo	oiré	oí	oído
poder	puedo	podré	pude	podido
poner	pongo	pondré	puse	puesto
querer	quiero	querré	quise	querido
saber	sé	sabré	supe	sabido
salir	salgo	saldré	salí	salido
ser	soy	seré	fui	sido
tener	tengo	tendré	tuve	tenido
traer	traigo	traeré	traje	traído
valer	valgo	valdré	valí	valido
venir	vengo	vendré	vine	venido
ver	veo	veré	vi	visto

LAS FORMAS DEL VERBO INGLÉS

1. Se forma la 3ª persona singular del tiempo presente exactamente al igual que el plural de los sustantivos, añadiendo **-es** o **-s** a la forma sencilla según las mismas reglas, así:

(1)	teach	pass	wish	fix	buzz		
	teaches	passes	wishes	fixes	buzzes		
(2)	place	change	judge	please	freeze		
	places	changes	judges	pleases	freezes		
(3a)	find	sell	clean	hear	love	buy	know
	finds	sells	cleans	hears	loves	buys	knows
(3b)	think	like	laugh	stop	hope	meet	want
	thinks	likes	laughs	stops	hopes	meets	wants
(4)	cry	try	dry	carry	deny		
	cries	tries	dries	carries	denies		

Cinco verbos muy comunes tienen 3ª persona singular irregular:

| (5) | go | do | say | have | be |
| | goes | does | says | has | is |

2. Se forman el tiempo pasado y el participio de modo igual, añadiendo a la forma sencilla la terminación **-ed** o **-d** según las reglas que siguen:

(1) Si la forma sencilla termina en **-d** o **-t**, se le pone **-ed** como sílaba aparte:

| end | fold | need | load | want | feast | wait | light |
| ended | folded | needed | loaded | wanted | feasted | waited | lighted |

(2) Si la forma sencilla termina en cualquier otra consonante, se añade también **-ed** pero sin hacer sílaba aparte:

LAS FORMAS DEL VERBO INGLÉS

(2a)	bang	sail	seem	harm	earn	weigh
	banged	sailed	seemed	harmed	earned	weighed
(2b)	lunch	work	look	laugh	help	pass
	lunched	worked	looked	laughed	helped	passed

(3) Si la forma sencilla termina en **-e,** se le pone sólo **-d:**

(3a)	hate	taste	waste	guide	fade	trade
	hated	tasted	wasted	guided	faded	traded
(3b)	free	judge	rule	name	dine	scare
	freed	judged	ruled	named	dined	scared
(3c)	place	force	knife	like	hope	base
	placed	forced	knifed	liked	hoped	based

(4) Una **-y** final que sigue a cualquier consonante se cambia en **-ie** al añadir la **-d** del pasado/participio:

	cry	try	dry	carry	deny
	cried	tried	dried	carried	denied

3. Varios verbos muy comunes forman el tiempo pasado y el participio de manera irregular. Pertenecen a tres grupos.

(1) Los que tienen una sola forma irregular para el tiempo pasado y el participio, como los siguientes:

bend	bleed	bring	build	buy	catch	creep	deal
bent	bled	brought	built	bought	caught	crept	dealt
dig	feed	feel	fight	find	flee	get	hang
dug	fed	felt	fought	found	fled	got	hung
have	hear	hold	keep	lead	leave	lend	lose
had	heard	held	kept	led	left	lent	lost
make	mean	meet	say	seek	sell	send	shine
made	meant	met	said	sought	sold	sent	shone
shoot	sit	sleep	spend	stand	strike	sweep	teach
shot	sat	slept	spent	stood	struck	swept	taught

(2) Los que tienen una forma irregular para el tiempo pasado y otra forma irregular para el participio, como los siguientes:

be	beat	become	begin	bite
was	beat	became	began	bit
been	beaten	become	begun	bitten
blow	break	choose	come	do
blew	broke	chose	came	did
blown	broken	chosen	come	done
draw	drink	drive	eat	fall
drew	drank	drove	ate	fell
drawn	drunk	driven	eaten	fallen
fly	forget	freeze	give	go
flew	forgot	froze	gave	went
flown	forgotten	frozen	given	gone
grow	hide	know	ride	ring
grew	hid	knew	rode	rang
grown	hidden	known	ridden	rung
rise	run	see	shake	shrink
rose	ran	saw	shook	shrank
risen	run	seen	shaken	shrunk
sing	sink	speak	steal	swear
sang	sank	spoke	stole	swore
sung	sunk	spoken	stolen	sworn

LAS FORMAS DEL VERBO INGLÉS

swim	tear	throw	wear	write
swam	tore	threw	wore	wrote
swum	torn	thrown	worn	written

(3) Los que no varían del todo, con la forma sencilla que funciona también como pasado/participio; entre éstos son de mayor frecuencia:

bet	burst	cast	cost	cut
hit	hurt	let	put	quit
read	set	shed	shut	slit
spit	split	spread	thrust	wet

EL PLURAL DEL SUSTANTIVO INGLÉS

A la forma singular se añade la terminición **-es** o **-s** de acuerdo con las reglas siguientes.

(1) Si el singular termina en **-ch, -s, -sh, -x** o **-z**, se le pone **-es** como sílaba aparte:

| match | glass | dish | box | buzz |
| matches | glasses | dishes | boxes | buzzes |

(2) Si el singular termina en **-ce, -ge, -se,** or **-ze,** se le pone una **-s** que con la vocal precedente forma sílaba aparte:

| face | page | house | size |
| faces | pages | houses | sizes |

(3) Una **-y** final que sigue a cualquier consonante se cambia en **-ie** a ponérsele la **-s** del plural:

| sky | city | lady | ferry | penny |
| skies | cities | ladies | ferries | pennies |

(4) Los siguientes sustantivos comunes tienen plural irregular:

man	woman	child	foot	mouse	goose
men	women	children	feet	mice	geese
wife	knife	life	half	leaf	deer
wives	knives	lives	halves	leaves	deer

WEIGHTS AND MEASURES/PESOS Y MEDIDAS

1 centímetro	=	.3937 inches		1 kilolitro	=	264,18 gallons
1 metro	=	39.37 inches		1 inch	=	2,54 centímetros
1 kilómetro	=	.621 mile		1 foot	=	,305 metros
1 centigramo	=	.1543 grain		1 mile	=	1,61 kilómetros
1 gramo	=	15.432 grains		1 grain	=	,065 gramos
1 kilogramo	=	2.2046 pounds		1 pound	=	,455 kilogramos
1 tonelada	=	2.204 pounds		1 ton	=	,907 toneladas
1 centilitro	=	.338 ounces		1 ounce	=	2,96 centilitros
1 litro	=	1.0567 quart (liquid); .908 quart (dry)		1 quart	=	1,13 litros
				1 gallon	=	4,52 litros

NUMBERS/NÚMEROS

Cardinal/Cardinales

one	1	uno, una	**thirty-one**	31	treinta y uno
two	2	dos	**thirty-two**	32	treinta y dos
three	3	tres	**forty**	40	cuarenta
four	4	cuatro	**fifty**	50	cincuenta
five	5	cinco	**sixty**	60	sesenta
six	6	seis	**seventy**	70	setenta
seven	7	siete	**eighty**	80	ochenta
eight	8	ocho	**ninety**	90	noventa
nine	9	nueve	**one hundred**	100	cien
ten	10	diez	**one hundred one**	101	ciento uno
eleven	11	once	**one hundred two**	102	ciento dos
twelve	12	doce	**two hundred**	200	doscientos, -as
thirteen	13	trece	**three hundred**	300	trescientos, -as
fourteen	14	catorce	**four hundred**	400	cuatrocientos, -as
fifteen	15	quince	**five hundred**	500	quinientos, -as
sixteen	16	dieciséis	**six hundred**	600	seiscientos, -as
seventeen	17	diecisiete	**seven hundred**	700	setecientos, -as
eighteen	18	dieciocho	**eight hundred**	800	ochocientos, -as
nineteen	19	diecinueve	**nine hundred**	900	novecientos, -as
twenty	20	veinte	**one thousand**	1,000	mil
twenty-one	21	veinte y uno (*or* veintiuno)	**two thousand**	2,000	dos mil
twenty-two	22	veinte y dos (*or* veintidós)	**one hundred thousand**	100,000	cien mil
			one million	1,000,000	un millón
thirty	30	treinta	**two million**	2,000,000	dos millones

Ordinal/Ordinales

first	1st /	1°	primero
second	2nd /	2°	segundo
third	3rd /	3°	tercero
fourth	4th /	4°	cuarto
fifth	5th /	5°	quinto
sixth	6th /	6°	sexto
seventh	7th /	7°	séptimo
eighth	8th /	8°	octavo
ninth	9th /	9°	noveno
tenth	10th /	10°	décimo

DAYS OF THE WEEK/DÍAS DE LA SEMANA

Sunday	domingo
Monday	lunes
Tuesday	martes
Wednesday	miércoles
Thursday	jueves
Friday	viernes
Saturday	sábado

SIGNS/SEÑALES

By appointment	Cita previa
Caution	Precaución
Closed	Cerrado
Closed for repairs	Cerrado por refaccíon
Danger	Peligro
Do not disturb	No molesten
Down (on elevator)	Para bajar
Driveway	Vado permante/Paso de carruajes
Dumping prohibited	Se prohíbe arrojar la basura
Entrance	Entrada
Exit	Salida
For immediate occupancy	De ocupación inmediata
For sale	Se vende
Go (traffic)	Siga
Inquire within	Se dan informaciones
Keep to the left	Tome su izquierda
Keep to the right	Tome su derecha
Ladies'/Women's room	El cuarto de damas
Men	Señores, Hombres, Caballeros
Men's room	El servicio
Narrow road	Camino estrecho

No admittance	Entrada prohibida
No entry	Dirección prohibida
No thoroughfare	Prohibido el paso/ Calle cerrada
No parking	Se prohíbe estacionar
No smoking	Prohibido fumar
No tipping	No se admiten propinas
Not working	No funciona
One way	Dirección única
Open	Abierto
People working	Trabajadores
Post no bills	Se prohíbe fijar carteles
Road closed	Paso cerrado
Road repairs	Camino en reparación
Same-day service	En el día
Slow	Despacio
Slow down	Moderar su velocidad
Stop	Alto
This way to...	Dirección a...
Town ahead	Poblado próximo
Up (on elevator)	Para subir
Wet paint	Recién pintado
Women	Señoras, Mujeres, Damas

Food Terms/Alimentos

apple	manzana	lemonade	limonada
artichoke	alcachofa	lettuce	lechuga
asparagus	espárrago	liver	hígado
bacon	tocino	lobster	langosta
baked	al horno	meat	carne
banana	banana	melon	melón
bean	habichuela	milk	leche
beer	cerveza	mushroom	seta
beet	remolacha	noodle	fideo
biscuit	bizcocho	nut	nuez
boiled	hervido	omelet	tortilla de huevos
bread	pan	onion	cebolla
broccoli	bróculi	orange	naranja
broiled	a la parrilla	peach	melocotón
butter	mantequilla	pear	pera
cake	torta	pepper	pimienta
carrot	zanahoria	pie	pastel
cauliflower	coliflor	pork	carne de puerco
celery	apio	potato	patata
cheese	queso	rice	arroz
chicken	pollo	roast beef	rosbif
chocolate	chocolate	roasted	asado
coffee	café	salad	ensalada
cognac	coñac	salmon	salmón
cookie	galleta dulce	salt	sal
crab	cangrejo	sandwich	sándwich
cream	crema	sauce	salsa
cucumber	pepino	scrambled eggs	huevos revueltos
dessert	postre	shrimp	camarón
drink	bebida	soda	soda
duck	pato	sole	lenguado
egg	huevo	soup	sopa
fillet	filete	spinach	espinaca
fish	pescado	steak	biftec
fowl	ave	strawberry	fresa
fried	frito	stuffed	relleno
fruit	fruta	sugar	azúcar
goose	ganso	tea	té
grape	uva	tomato	tomate
grapefruit	toronja	trout	trucha
ham	jamón	tuna	atún
hamburger	hamburguesa	turkey	pavo
ice cream	helado	veal	ternera
jelly	jalea	vegetable	legumbre
juice	jugo	water	agua
lamb	cordero	wine	vino

Colors/Colores

Black	Negro		**Pink**	Rosa
Blue	Azul		**Purple**	Morado
Brown	Marron		**Red**	Rojo
Gold	Dorado		**Silver**	Plateado
Gray	Gris		**White**	Blanco
Green	Verde		**Yellow**	Amarillo
Orange	Anarajado			

Animals/Animales

Bear	El Oso		**Kangaroo**	El Canguro
Bird	El Pajaro		**Lion**	El Leon
Camel	El Camello		**Lizard**	La Lagartija
Cat	El Gato		**Monkey**	El Mono
Cow	La Vaca		**Owl**	El Buho
Deer	El Venado		**Peacock**	El Pavoreal
Dog	El Perro		**Pig**	El Cerdo
Donkey	El Burro		**Rabbit**	El Conejo
Duck	El Pato		**Raccoon**	El Mapache
Elephant	El Elefante		**Rhinoceros**	El Rinoceronte
Fox	El Zorro		**Rooster**	La Gallo
Giraffe	La Jirafa		**Sheep**	La Oveja
Goat	La Cabra		**Snake**	La Serpiente
Goose	El Ganso		**Tiger**	El Tigre
Gorilla	El Gorila		**Turkey**	El Pavo
Hippo	El Hipopotamo		**Wolf**	El Lobo
Horse	El Caballo		**Zebra**	La Cebra

Clothing/Vestidos

Dress	El Vestido		**Scarf**	La Bufanda
Gloves	Los Guantes		**Shirt**	La Camisa
Hat	El Sombrero		**Shoes**	Los Zapatos
Jacket	La Chaqueta		**Socks**	Los Calcetines
Jeans	Los Jeans		**Tie**	La Corbata
Pants	Los Pantalones			

WORD FIND: BODY PARTS

Instructions: The Spanish words for various body parts are listed below with their English translations. Can you find and circle all the Spanish body parts in the Word Find below?

B	C	D	O	M	E	E	H	Ñ	J	K	A	N	F	Q	G	I	A	F	I
K	B	B	A	N	G	L	M	E	J	I	L	L	A	S	Y	L	Y	J	C
A	N	R	E	I	P	N	C	I	B	C	Q	A	T	Y	L	E	E	L	G
L	O	H	A	K	M	E	F	R	O	E	S	V	D	I	H	Ñ	Q	L	H
G	E	I	K	Z	J	K	G	L	C	Ñ	I	F	B	K	P	G	O	T	Ñ
F	L	G	A	Ñ	O	E	I	M	A	V	G	R	O	D	I	L	L	A	Ñ
I	B	I	N	O	L	J	Q	T	T	D	A	Y	G	J	E	Y	P	R	A
Q	T	D	P	D	L	N	X	Ñ	A	B	D	V	A	H	T	W	D	C	D
R	B	V	I	I	E	L	Z	K	J	B	C	J	M	A	I	F	Q	S	C
J	O	S	H	S	U	Ñ	I	P	D	Q	C	G	O	V	J	I	H	K	Q
D	R	J	Y	D	C	U	R	B	W	K	I	Q	T	Q	D	U	O	M	Y
L	X	B	O	F	B	C	A	D	O	V	Ñ	V	S	Ñ	G	S	M	D	I
Z	A	E	U	S	F	A	N	V	R	T	O	Ñ	E	H	C	I	B	Y	X
X	C	Q	L	C	B	J	M	H	E	F	B	N	O	T	I	G	R	F	Q
O	T	H	I	V	L	J	K	C	J	S	E	P	F	A	E	F	O	Ñ	Ñ
O	P	E	C	H	O	F	Ñ	X	A	Q	J	E	R	X	Z	O	Z	A	H
P	K	F	S	D	A	T	B	G	S	F	R	U	E	B	U	A	N	P	E
B	Q	Q	O	A	I	U	N	B	Ñ	D	I	E	N	T	E	S	J	A	H
Ñ	A	C	E	Ñ	U	M	K	V	J	T	Q	P	T	S	T	C	L	L	M
Z	J	E	L	C	H	I	Ñ	D	G	C	A	B	E	Z	A	N	F	O	D

BODY PARTS/LAS PARTES DEL CUERPO

Barbilla	Chin	**Mejillas**	Cheeks
Boca	Mouth	**Muñeca**	Wrist
Brazo	Arm	**Nariz**	Nose
Codo	Elbow	**Ojos**	Eyes
Cuello	Neck	**Orejas**	Ears
Cabeza	Head	**Pecho**	Chest
Dientes	Teeth	**Pie**	Foot
Estomago	Stomach	**Pierna**	Leg
Frente	Forehead	**Rodilla**	Knee
Hombro	Shoulder	**Tobillo**	Ankle
Mano	Hand		

WORD FIND: MONTHS OF THE YEAR

Instructions: The Spanish words for the months of the year are listed below with their English translations. Can you find and circle all the Spanish months in the Word Find below?

```
A C K I N D J H M B L H C M I O D E I B
F I L F A M O K P N E Q D T F L S Q A K
C K E P A G O S T O S S I J V Z O H R M
N J Ñ H M O R N O F J D C R X R L T T E
O M J F T D H B S C I I I W E Ñ U O T L
V P U R L E R S A Y T C L R Y H G Z S J
I A L V A F H U J H R I B G Ñ D U R G H
E K I O W S R E M T D E B A T Z X A W Q
M S O Z J X B H J X F M K H Ñ K Ñ M Z K
B Q B U C G R E R G L B J E I Y O E A P
R O W P D D K N E M W R Ñ B D X Ñ J Y G
E V Y H T J F E I V I E P G L A W M V R
M A X B A X J R L F O L Ñ Z L L I R B A
E E R B U T C O A L C H T A Y Z P O X Q
G Q C E N Z R K Y S M G L Ñ H Ñ I Z L S
B J Q H R J M M N A Y A K T Ñ G B J J C
F A O S V E H Y V N M R C Ñ K M U F K N
D L T F L T U H L B Ñ I Ñ D Y A V H T I
H O I N U J I R Q X W Z G S Q L E S T A
C K H A L P I O A K S E P T I E M B R E
```

MONTHS OF THE YEAR/MESES DEL AÑO

Enero	January	**Julio**	July
Febrero	February	**Agosto**	August
Marzo	March	**Septiembre**	September
Abril	April	**Octubre**	October
Mayo	May	**Noviembre**	November
Junio	June	**Diciembre**	December

Body Parts/Las Partes del Cuerpo Answer Key

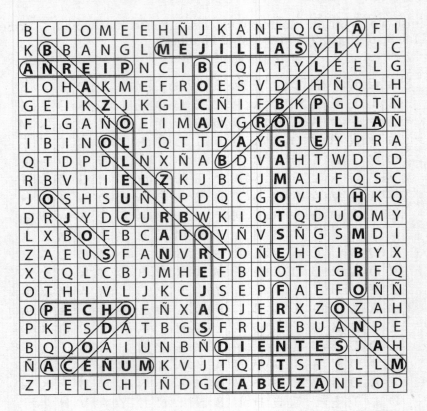

Months of the Year/Meses del Año Answer Key

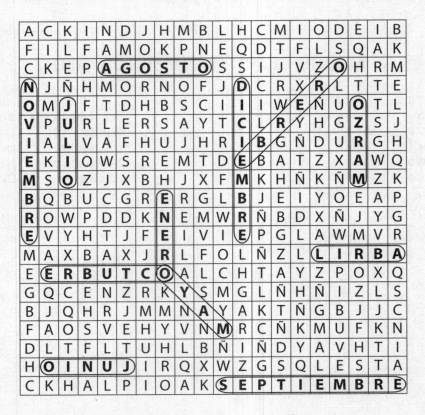

Useful Phrases/Locuciones Útiles

Good day, Good morning. Buenos días.
Good afternoon. Buenas tardes.
Good night, Good evening. Buenas noches.
Hello. ¡Hola!
Welcome! ¡Bienvenido!
See you later. Hasta luego.
Goodbye. ¡Adiós!
How are you? ¿Cómo está usted?
I'm fine, thank you. Estoy bien, gracias.
I'm pleased to meet you. Mucho gusto en conocerle.
May I introduce... Quisiera presentar...
Thank you very much. Muchas gracias.
You're welcome. De nada *or* No hay de qué.
Please. Por favor.
Excuse me. Con permiso.
Good luck. ¡Buena suerte!
To your health. ¡Salud!

Please help me. Ayúdeme, por favor.
I don't know. No sé.
I don't understand. No entiendo.
Do you understand? ¿Entiende usted?
I don't speak Spanish. No hablo español.
Do you speak English? ¿Habla usted inglés?
How do you say... in Spanish? ¿Cómo se dice... en español?
What do you call this? ¿Cómo se llama esto?
Speak slowly, please. Hable despacio, por favor.
Please repeat. Repita, por favor.
I don't like it. No me gusta.
I am lost. Ando perdido; Me he extraviado.

What is your name? ¿Cómo se llama usted?
My name is... Me llamo...
I am an American. Soy americano; Soy estadounidense.
Where are you from? ¿De dónde es usted?
I'm from... Soy de...

How is the weather? ¿Qué tiempo hace?
It's cold (hot) today. Hace frío (calor) hoy.
What time is it? ¿Qué hora es?

How much is it? ¿Cuánto es?
It is too much. Es demasiado.
What do you wish? ¿Qué desea usted?
I want to buy... Quiero comprar...
May I see something better? ¿Puedo ver algo mejor?
May I see something cheaper? ¿Puedo ver algo menos caro?
It is not exactly what I want. No es exactamente lo que quiero.

I'm hungry. Tengo hambre.
I'm thirsty. Tengo sed.
Where is there a restaurant? ¿Dónde hay un restaurante?

I have a reservation. Tengo una reservación.
I would like... Quisiera...; Me gustaría...
Please give me... Por favor, déme usted...
Please bring me... Por favor, tráigame usted...
May I see the menu? ¿Puedo ver el menú?
The bill, please. La cuenta, por favor.
Is service included in the bill? ¿El servicio está incluido en la cuenta?
Where is there a hotel? ¿Dónde hay un hotel?
Where is the post office? ¿Dónde está el correo?
Is there any mail for me? ¿Hay correo para mí?
Where can I mail this letter? ¿Dónde puedo echar esta carta al correo?

Take me to... Lléveme a...
I believe I am ill. Creo que estoy enfermo.
Please call a doctor. Por favor, llame al médico.
Please call the police. Por favor, llame a la policía.
I want to send a telegram. Quiero poner un telegrama.
As soon as possible. Cuanto antes.

Round trip. Ida y vuelta.
Please help me with my luggage. Por favor, ayúdeme con mi equipaje.
Where can I get a taxi? ¿Dónde hay taxi?
What is the fare to... ¿Cuánto es el pasaje hasta...?
Please take me to this address. Por favor, lléveme a esta dirección.
Where can I change my money? ¿Dónde puedo cambiar mi dinero?
Where is the nearest bank? ¿Dónde está el banco más cercano?
Can you accept my check? ¿Puede aceptar usted mi cheque?
Do you accept traveler's checks? ¿Aceptan cheques de viaje?
What is the postage? ¿Cuánto es el franqueo?
Where is the nearest drugstore? ¿Dónde está la farmacia más cercana?
Where is the men's (women's) room? ¿Dónde está el servicio de caballeros (de señoras)?
Please let me off at... Por favor, déjeme bajar en...

Right away. ¡Pronto!
Help. ¡Socorro!
Who is it? ¿Quién es?
Just a minute! ¡Un momento no más!
Come in. ¡Pase usted!
Pardon me. Dispense usted.
Stop. ¡Pare!
Look out. ¡Cuidado!
Hurry. ¡De prisa! *or* ¡Dése prisa!
Go on. ¡Siga!
To (on, at) the right. A la derecha.
To (on, at) the left. A la izquierda.
Straight ahead. Adelante.

Introduction to the SAT Spanish Subject Tests

What Are The Spanish Subject Tests?
There are two different Spanish Subject Tests, the traditional Spanish Subject Test and a newer test called Spanish with Listening Subject Test. Both SAT Spanish Subject Tests are hour-long, multiple-choice exams that are supposed to measure your knowledge of Spanish. In fact, the College Board claims that the subject tests "…provide a reliable measure of your academic achievement" and "can help in assessing how well prepared you are for different programs of college study." Do the SAT Spanish Subject Tests really accomplish this? Absolutely not. If you want to know how well you speak Spanish, you should try reading a Spanish newspaper, watching a Spanish television show, or speaking Spanish with a native speaker. Each of these activities will give you a better idea of how well you speak the language than will the results of the SAT Spanish Subject Tests.

Why Should You Take a Spanish Subject Test?
Other than wanting to get a higher score than one of your friends, there are only two good reasons to take an SAT Spanish Subject Test. The first of these reasons is that one of the colleges to which you are applying either requires or strongly recommends that you take several different SAT Subject Tests. If this is the case, you will want to make sure that you pick the three subjects that will best demonstrate your academic achievement. Evaluate your own strengths and weaknesses, and contact colleges to see which tests they suggest or require. The second reason you might take the SAT Spanish Subject Test is that one of the colleges to which you're applying plans to use the Spanish Subject Test as a placement exam.

When Should You Take It?
The first thing you need to decide is whether to take one of the Spanish Subject Tests. These tests are appropriate for students who have completed a minimum of two years of high school Spanish or the equivalent.

The second thing you need to decide is whether to take the Spanish Subject Test or the Spanish with Listening Subject Test. If you have a lot of experience speaking Spanish, you might want to take the Spanish with Listening Subject Test. If you learned most of your Spanish from reading a book, you should probably take the Spanish Test that does not contain a listening section.

The Spanish Subject Test is given five times each year: October, December, January, May, and June. The Spanish with Listening Subject Test is given only once each year, in November.

Structure of the Test
Both the Spanish and the Spanish with Listening Subject Tests contain 85 multiple-choice questions. You'll have one hour to complete each of the tests, but you do not necessarily need to finish either test to get a good score. The structure of each test is as follows:

Spanish Subject Test: Spanish
The Spanish Subject Test contains three sections that measure different skills. Each section is weighted equally and contains approximately the same number of questions (between 27 and 29). The three sections are:

- Part A: Vocabulary and Structure
- Part B: Paragraph Completion
- Part C: Reading Comprehension

Spanish Subject Test: Spanish with Listening
The Spanish with Listening Subject Test consists of two sections: the Listening section and the Reading section. The Listening section contains about 35 questions and must be completed in about 20 minutes. The Reading section contains about 50 questions and must be completed in 40 minutes. Each of these two sections contains questions that measure different skills. The specific format is as follows:

Listening Section
- Part A: Pictures—You will be presented with a picture and asked to select the sentence that best reflects what someone in the picture might say or what is portrayed in the picture.

- Part B: Rejoinders—You will listen to a short conversation and then select the answer choice that represents the most likely continuation of the conversation.
- Part C: Selections—You will be asked to listen to extensive selections and then choose the best possible answer.

Reading Section
- Part A: Vocabulary and Structure
- Part B: Paragraph Completion
- Part C: Reading Comprehension

Scoring

Your overall score on either the Spanish Subject Test or the Spanish with Listening Subject Test is based on the number of questions you answer correctly minus the number of questions you answer incorrectly. You get no credit and lose no points for questions you leave blank. On the Spanish Subject Test, the result of this simple calculation (# correct – of number incorrect) represents your raw score. Raw scores can range from –28 to 85. On the Spanish with Listening Subject Test, you receive several different scores: a raw score for each section, a scaled score for each section (20–80), and an overall scaled score (200–800).

Both Spanish Subject Tests are scored on a 200–800 scale. Just like with the SAT, the lowest possible score is a 200 (even if you answer every question incorrectly) and the highest possible score is an 800 (which you can get even if you miss a question or two).

Final Thoughts

Preparation is the key to success—not just on this test, but in everything you do. If you want to succeed on the Spanish Subject Test or any other test, make sure you understand the content, practice the strategies, and develop an overall plan to attain your target score. You may want to read a Spanish newspaper (looking up the words you don't know in a dictionary), listen to Spanish-language radio stations or television programs, or engage in conversations in Spanish with your classmates, friends, or family members.

Finally, RELAX. Once you've finished preparing, there's no need to stress about the tests. Just make sure you get plenty of sleep the night before the test, eat a balanced breakfast, walk into the test center with a feeling of confidence, and do your best. In the end, your score is just a number. These tests will never be able to measure the most important aspect of your academic potential: your determination.

Strategies for Cracking the Exam
Pacing

Since your earliest days in school, you were probably taught that when you take a test, finishing is important. Standardized tests, however, are a completely different ball game. The folks who write these tests are interested in how fast you can work, and they design the tests so that it's nearly impossible to finish on time. Because you're so accustomed to the idea that finishing is crucial, you may pressure yourself to answer every question. Have you ever stopped to consider how much sense this makes? It's not as if you get a special prize for finishing! In fact, in order to finish, you usually have to rush through questions, and as a result you make careless errors that could be avoided. Doesn't it make more sense to slow down a bit, answer the questions you're sure of, and leave a few blanks? Well, let's see how pacing yourself on the Spanish Subject Tests relates to actual scores:

Pacing Chart

To Get a Score of	Answer About	Leave This Many Blank
400	13	72
450	26	59
500	38	47
550	48	37
600	58	27
650	68	17
700	78	7
750 & up	85	0

Understand that the pacing chart assumes that you'll make fewer than six mistakes, and it doesn't take guesses into account. If you take your time, pick your questions carefully, and learn to guess effectively, making fewer than six errors really isn't as tough as it might sound.

You should walk into your test with a target score in mind and a pacing strategy that reflects the score you're shooting for. Remember, this is your test, and that means you can answer the questions you want, when you want, how you want, and still get an excellent score. If you want to leave most (or all) of the reading comprehension blank and concentrate on the other questions, go ahead. If you're good at the reading comprehension, but not so good on the grammar, then do more of the reading comprehension and less of the grammar sentence completions. If all the other students at your test site want to race frantically to the end of the test and make careless mistakes along the way, that's their problem. You're going to be sitting there, cool and relaxed, just taking your time, and getting a great score.

When Should You Guess?
A lot of people talk about the "guessing penalty" on the SAT and the SAT Subject Tests. What they really mean is that there's no advantage to random guessing. The truth is, there really isn't a penalty either.

Each question on the Spanish Subject Test and the Spanish with Listening Subject Test has four answer choices. If you answer a question correctly, you will receive 1 raw-score point. If you get a question wrong, you will lose 1/3 of a raw-score point. If you were to randomly guess on four questions with four answer choices each, odds are you would get one question right and three questions wrong. How would this affect your raw score?

1 question correct $=$ $+1$ point

3 questions incorrect $=$ $-1/3 \times 3 = -1$ point

Total impact on overall score $=$ 0

So should you guess? Sometimes. If you can eliminate one or more incorrect answer choices, the odds become more favorable. Imagine if you were able to eliminate two answer choices and then randomly guess on the remaining two answer choices for four different problems. In this case, you would likely get two questions right and two questions wrong. How would this affect your raw score?

2 questions correct $=$ $+2$ points

2 questions incorrect $=$ $-1/3 \times 2 = -2/3$ points

Total impact on overall score $=$ $+1\ 1/3$ points

The moral of this story is this: If you can eliminate even one answer choice, you should guess. If you can't eliminate any answer choices, there's no reason to guess. You'll just be wasting valuable time.

Three-Pass System
Because the test is written for students with varying levels of expertise in Spanish, the questions vary in difficulty. Unfortunately, they aren't arranged in any particular order of difficulty. There are questions that are much easier than others, but it's up to you to find them if you want to take advantage of them.

The Three-Pass System Says the Following:
- 1st Pass—Go through an entire section of the test from beginning to end, but only answer the easiest questions, that is, those on which you thoroughly understand all the vocabulary, etc. Skip anything that looks as if it's going to give you grief.
- 2nd Pass—Go back to the beginning of the same section and take a shot at those questions where you knew some, but not all, of the vocabulary.
- 3rd Pass—Use the Process of Elimination (which you'll learn about in a moment) on the remaining questions in that section to eliminate some answers. Then take a guess. If you can't eliminate anything, leave the question blank.

Taking a section of the test this way will keep you from getting stuck on a tough question early in the section and spending too much time on it. Your time should be spent both answering questions you're sure of and guessing intelligently, not banging your head against the wall in an attempt to crack a tough question.

Note: The Three-Pass System will not work on the Listening section of the Spanish with Listening Subject Test. During that section, you will be listening to an audiocassette and you must answer the questions in the order in which they appear (or leave them blank).

POE—Process of Elimination

The usefulness of the Process of Elimination is one of the gifts of a multiple-choice exam. The idea is simple: There are three wrong answers and only one right one; so it is easier to find answers to eliminate. If you can eliminate answers that you know are wrong, you will eventually stumble upon the right answer because it'll be the only one left. POE is going to vary a bit for the different question types, but the general idea is always the same.

Excerpted from *Cracking the SAT Subject Test Spanish, 2007–2008 Edition*, ISBN 978-0-375-76595-7, Random House, March 2007

The Princeton Review Helps You
Navigate the College Admissions Process

Find the Right School

Best 361 Colleges, 2008 Edition
978-0-375-76621-3 • $21.95/C$27.95
Previous Edition: 978-0-375-76558-2

Complete Book of Colleges, 2008 Edition
978-0-375-76620-6 • $26.95/C$34.95
Previous Edition: 978-0-375-76557-5

America's Best Value Colleges, 2008 Edition
978-0-375-76601-5 • $18.95/C$24.95

Guide to College Visits
978-0-375-76600-8 • $20.00/C$25.00

Get In

Cracking the SAT, 2008 Edition
978-0-375-76606-0 • $19.95/C$24.95

Cracking the SAT with DVD, 2008 Edition
978-0-375-76607-7 • $33.95/C$42.00

Math Workout for the NEW SAT
978-0-375-76433-2 • $16.00/C$23.00

**Reading and Writing Workout
for the NEW SAT**
978-0-375-76431-8 • $16.00/C$23.00

**11 Practice Tests for the SAT and PSAT,
2008 Edition**
978-0-375-76614-5 • $19.95/C$26.95
Previous Edition: 978-0-375-76544-5

Cracking the ACT, 2007 Edition
978-0-375-76585-8 • $19.95/C$24.95

Cracking the ACT with DVD, 2007 Edition
978-0-375-76586-5 • $31.95/C$39.95

Crash Course for the ACT, 3rd Edition
978-0-375-76587-2 • $9.95/C$12.95

Crash Course for the New SAT
978-0-375-76461-5 • $9.95/C$13.95

Get Help Paying for It

How to Save for College
978-0-375-76425-7 • $14.95/C$21.00

**Paying for College Without Going Broke,
2007 Edition**
978-0-375-76567-4 • $20.00/C$27.00

Additional Help for
Standardized Tests in Spanish

**Cracking the AP Spanish Exam,
2006–2007 Edition**
978-0-375-76530-8 • $17.00/C$24.00

**Cracking the SAT Spanish Subject Test,
2007–2008 Edition**
978-0-375-76595-7 • $18.00/C$22.00

134

Notes/Notas

NOTES/NOTAS

NOTES/NOTAS

NOTES/NOTAS

NOTES/NOTAS

NOTES/NOTAS